Ceramics

A Potter's Handbook

Holt, Rinehart and Winston, Inc.
New York   Chicago   San Francisco   Atlanta
Dallas   Montreal   Toronto   London   Sydney

Ceramics

A Potter's Handbook

third edition

Glenn C. Nelson

University of Minnesota, Duluth

Editor Dan W. Wheeler
Production editor Rita Gilbert
Picture editor Joan Curtis
Designer Marlene Rothkin Vine

Library of Congress Catalog Card Number: 70–145911
College SBN: 03–078835–8
Trade SBN: 03–086000–8
A Helvetica Press production: Printed in black-and-white and color gravure
by the Presses Centrales, Lausanne, Switzerland;
bound by Mayer & Soutter S.A., Renens, Switzerland.
First printing, 1971

Preface

Almost everyone has had some pleasurable experience feeling and forming the plasticity of moist clay, if only in the childhood acts of making mud pies or treading through rain-soaked paths, with pliant earth oozing up between the toes of bare feet. Ceramics, the art of clay and glazes, is an appealing medium, one that has attained immense popularity in our time, both as a craft to practice and as a tradition to appreciate. In its fired state clay is among the most ageless of materials. Its three-dimensional qualities, plus the effects of glaze, color, and texture, make ceramics potentially the richest of all art forms.

Commanding and irresistible, ceramics is also a fickle mistress. Not only do novice potters have many difficulties with clay, but even the experienced potter opens the kiln much as if he were coming downstairs on Christmas day—not really knowing quite what to expect. An old story has it that the ancient Chinese habitually formed a figurine to be placed in the kiln door to ward off evil spirits. While acknowledging with full respect the mystical and irreducible elements in the creative endeavor, the purpose of this handbook is to diminish the frustrations of the potter and endow him with greater control of his work, perhaps even help lead him to the artistry he seeks, by providing in systematic order the essential information about the ceramist's technology of transforming raw, wet clay into a fired and finished piece. Ceramics is the most technical of the forms artists work in, and to realize more than limited results the potter must acquire a good, basic understanding of the materials and processes of his medium. *Ceramics,* therefore, has been written in an effort to develop a reliable guide for the amateur potter as well as a reference volume for the more accomplished craftsman.

Singular as art history may seem in a handbook intended to serve the needs of working potters, the reader may well find the survey of traditional and contemporary ceramics, delineated in the first three chapters, the most rewarding part of the book. After all, the finished product—here the final potted form—is the paramount concern of most artists and conoisseurs. All technique is subservient to it, and many cultures have produced lasting works of art with a minimum of facilities. Readers familiar with previous editions of *Ceramics* will find this section considerably expanded both in coverage and in the quantity and variety of illustrations. The reproductions alone bear witness to the extraordinary vitality of the ceramist's art in our time.

Following the introductory survey chapters begins the main body of the book, a sequence of chapters dealing with the characteristics of clay, its properties and preparation; with the means of forming clay, in pots, sculpture, even architecture; with ceramic form and design; with the challenge of surface, of decoration and glazing; with the activity of the professional potter, in his studio as well as in industry; with kilns, their operation and construction; and, finally, with equipment, from wheels to the complete ceramic studio. Concluding the book is an appendix offering more technical and tabular data, sources of supplies, and a bibliography of published references. In addition, there is a glossary of ceramic terms.

Fresh to this edition are the particular attention given to the role played by the professional potter in the studio, in education, and in industry and the new ideas, materials, and equipment presented and illustrated throughout the book, especially in the chapter on kilns.

The chapters on forming, decoration, and glazing all take up problems and concepts in design, but the subtle aspects of design have been mentioned only in indirection. So elusive and individual are the qualities of form and decoration, they hardly lend themselves to verbal exposition but develop naturally in the studio as the student, the teacher, and the clay interact in an ill-defined way that is uniquely their own. There are no formulas and absolutes in design, for its secret and its truth lie in the craftsman's potential for growth and for developing diversity in his experience.

The illustrations for this edition of *Ceramics* have been selected and treated as elements fully as substantive as the text itself. Numbering over 500 in black and white and 22 reproduced in full color, they play an expressive role throughout the discussions pursued in the book. Now printed by gravure, a process especially sympathetic to the physical characteristics of textural, relief, and three-dimensional works, the illustrations suggest the immense range of forms and functions in ceramics, from the utilitarian teapot to the "one-of-a-kind" museum piece.

The acknowledgments of the many contributions made to the realization of *Ceramics* must begin with the potters already cited in the legends accompanying the illustrations. Without their photographs and the permission to reproduce their works, such a handbook as this could not have evolved. Museums and collectors have also been generous in granting rights to the materials they own. Special mention must be made of contributors outside the United States, who endured with grace and patience the difficulties of international communication. Among these are Asgar Fischer, of Bing and Grøndahl Studios, and Ivan Engle of Den Permanente, both in Copenhagen; Stig Lindberg, of the Gustavsberg Studios, and Carl-

Harry Stålhane of the Rörstrand Studios in Sweden; O. H. Gummerus, at the Finnish Society of Crafts and Design, and the Arabia Studios in Helsinki; the Norwegian Society of Arts and Crafts and Industrial Design; Murray Fieldhouse, editor of *Pottery Quarterly,* and Bill Read, both English potters; J. W. N. van Achterbergh of the Dutch Ceramic Society; Hildegard Storr-Britz of the ceramic school at Höhr-Grenzhausen, Germany; Kostas Panopoulos at the National Association of Hellenic Handicrafts in Athens; Tonito Emiliani, director of the State School of Ceramics in Faenza, Italy; the Japanese potter Hiroaki Morino of Kyoto; Wanda Garnsey of the Potter's Society of Australia; and Jack Sures, respondent for the Canadian Craftsmen's Association.

The manufacturers of ceramics and ceramic equipment have been cooperation itself, especially Syracuse China, Interpace Corporation, Pacific Stoneware, and the Bennington Potters. Peter A. Slusarski, of Kent State University, was most helpful in furnishing a series of illustrations on product design.

Ken Moran gave professional advice and practical assistance in the preparation of the process photographs. Richard Leach's color enlargements (Pls. 21–22) are both technically intriguing and beautiful in the abstract.

A large debt of gratitude must be acknowledged for the improvements and corrections made by Karl Martz, professor of ceramics at Indiana University, and Ed Traynor, member of the ceramics faculty at the University of California, Los Angeles, who read the entire manuscript and gave to the task the full range and depth of their knowledge and experience.

Thanks are also due to the staff at Holt, Rinehart and Winston for their skill in managing the monumental problems of producing a heavily illustrated art book—to Dan Wheeler, the editor of the series, to Rita Gilbert, who edited the manuscript and coordinated production, to Marlene Rothkin Vine, the creator of the book's stunning design, and to Joan Curtis, for her assistance with illustrations. To the author's wife, Edith, goes his last and warmest expression, in appreciation of her genius for deciphering an unintelligible scrawl and of her cheerful acceptance of endless changes in copy.

Duluth, Minnesota   G. C. N.
January, 1971

Ceramics
A Potter's Handbook

1 Ceramics of the Past

Prehistoric, Middle Eastern, Minoan, Mycenaean, Chinese, Greek, Etruscan and Roman, Islamic, Hispano-Moresque, and Italian Ceramics

THE PREHISTORIC WORLD

The origins of man are shrouded in mystery and subject to much speculation. It may have been as long as 500,000 years ago that an apelike creature first used a stone to break open a nut, thus beginning the critical tool-making process. By 100,000 B.C. early man was burying his dead with rudimentary stone tools and a supply of food included in the gravesite. Man's discovery of a means for making fire provided him with a vital asset. In an effort to explain and propitiate the great forces of nature and the mysteries of life and death, man slowly developed his religious beliefs and practices.

A small limestone carving with exaggerated female features (Fig. 2) discovered at Willendorf, Austria, (c. 15,000–10,000 B.C.) is one of the earliest known of the fertility fetishes that are found among the remains of all primitive cultures. The Cypriote statue in Figure 3 is also representative of this type of cult image. The animal cave paintings of France and Spain and the paintings and rock carvings of Africa (c. 15,000–8000 B.C. and perhaps earlier) reveal rare powers of observation and, certainly, an artistic ability equal to that of modern man.

As the glaciers of the last Ice Age retreated, much of Europe and Asia became heavily forested. The once plentiful mammoths, elk, and bison disappeared. Early man now found better hunting and fishing in the more temperate and fertile valleys of the Nile and the Tigris-Euphrates Rivers in the Middle East and of the Yellow River in China. The gathering of wild fruits, nuts, and wheat seeds gradually assumed a greater importance. About 8000 B.C. far-reaching changes occurred: a primitive type of wheat and barley came under cultivation, and sheep and goats and, later, cattle and pigs were domesticated.

The discovery of pottery making was crucial to this development, for primitive agriculturists needed cooking and storage containers. The prevalence of

opposite: 1. Vase, China. Sung Dynasty (960–1279). Tz'u-Chou stoneware, height 15 ½″. Victoria & Albert Museum, London. The crisp sgraffito design adds a touch of spontaneity to the bulbous form of this vase.

1

left : 2. *Venus of Willendorf.* c. 15,000–10,000 B.C. Stone, height 4 ³/₈″. Museum of Natural History, Vienna. This carving is one of the earliest known fertility fetishes.

below : 3. Female figure (fertility image?), Cyprus. c. 1500–1200 B.C. Terra cotta, height 8 ³/₈″. Metropolitan Museum of Art, New York (Cesnola Collection; purchased by subscription, 1874–76). This rather fantastic statue is typical of fertility figures found in all early cultures.

a corded basketlike design on all early ware—whether in the Middle East, China, or the Americas—has led to the theory that baskets were first coated with clay to enable them to hold small, wild grain seeds. The accidental burning of one of these baskets led to the discovery that a clay vessel baked in the hot coals of the fire would become hard and suitable for such use. It is probable that this important breakthrough occurred independently in many areas of the world.

All early pots are black in color, having been fired in a primitive kiln or bonfire. They are all round bottomed, which may reflect the use of a gourd or round stone as a partial mold. Because they were low fired and subject to constant use, none have survived to this day, except as isolated fragments. It was a universal custom to bury pottery and other artifacts with the dead. Thanks to the imperishable quality of clay, these pottery objects often constitute the only surviving record of many ancient civilizations.

In the following pages we shall trace the development of pottery form and decoration among these early cultures. Perhaps more by chance than by determination, preferences for certain shapes and decorative motifs arose in different parts of the world, and these were refined through the ages. Influences occurred as one culture reacted upon another. But such was the persistence of custom and religion—as well as the tradition of the craft as it was transmitted from father to son—that age-old preferences were often retained. Thus, we can say that certain shapes are peculiarly Chinese or Greek or that decorative styles reflect a Japanese flavor.

MIDDLE EASTERN CERAMICS

Pottery was made at an early date (c. 5000 B.C.) in Egypt, Palestine, and the Tigris-Euphrates area. Like most early ceramic ware it was black, round bottomed, and usually had an impressed, corded surface. In time it was discovered that if the clay body was burnished with a bone or a flat pebble while half dry, it would acquire a smoother surface that was harder and more impervious to water. One such burnished ware was made in Egypt (Fig. 4). Termed *red-and-black ware*, it was fired upside down on its rim. The smoke and ashes in the primitive kiln reduced this portion to a glossy black, while the balance of the pot retained the red color of the clay. In time, a proper kiln with a chamber and fire box allowed for a clear, oxidizing atmosphere and made possible the use of clay slips to cover the red earthenware body or to decorate it (Fig. 5) with slips or metallic oxides in hues of white, cream, red, brown, and black and, at a later date, in pale yellow or blue.

At first all pottery was made by the women as part of their regular household chores. But, as the early settlements grew, a market developed in which a skilled craftsman could trade his produce for grain, leather, or other items. The earliest craftsmen were the metalsmith and the potter.

The uniformity of many of the early hand-built coiled pots would suggest that a spinner was used to scrape and refine the form. Pottery with a turned foot rim dating from about 4000 B.C. has been found in northern Iran, and this may well indicate the first use of the potter's wheel. The use of the wheel spread slowly, and larger vessels continued to be hand built in a coil-and-paddle technique. It is likely that at this period pottery making had become both a predominantly masculine and a full-time occupation. By 3000 B.C. the potter's wheel was in common use in the Middle East.

above : 4. Vase, Egypt. Predynastic (4000–3200 B.C.). Red-and-black earthenware. Victoria & Albert Museum, London.

right : 5. Jar, Egypt. Predynastic (c. 4000–3500 B.C.). Earthenware with slip decoration. Brooklyn Museum. The figures depict the journey of the soul across the Nile.

6. *Ushabti of King Seti I*, Egypt, from Thebes. 1313–1292 B.C. Alkaline-silica paste, height 11 ¾″. Metropolitan Museum of Art, New York (Carnarvon Collection, gift of Edward S. Harkness, 1926). Ushabti are small, mummylike tomb figures which accompanied the dead in the afterlife.

The earliest dated glaze is on a tile fragment from the tomb of the Egyptian King Menes (c. 3000 B.C.). The initial discovery of glaze probably derives from the accidental melting of potash and sand deposits under a bonfire. All early Egyptian glazes have an alkaline flux. These early glazes were not used on pottery, however, but rather on wall tiles or for decorative furniture inlays. Glazed fig-

urines and small animal sculptures were popular, especially the turquoise Ushabti figurines (Fig. 6). The dearth of important Egyptian ceramics after a promising beginning may be explained in part by the wealth of the priesthood and the royal family. Pottery was for the poor and never developed into an art form, since the wealthy used eating vessels of gold and silver and had vases laboriously made of alabaster and even harder polished stone.

MINOAN AND MYCENAEAN CERAMICS

During the period between 3000 and 2500 B.C. a culture quite different was evolving on the island of Crete, about 600 miles northeast of Egypt. Without an oppressive priesthood and protected by the sea from invaders, the Minoans enjoyed a prosperity unique in its time. The cities and the palaces of merchant princes were unfortified, and the trading vessels of Crete were to be found in all parts of the eastern Mediterranean. The palace at Knossos (Fig. 7), home of the legendary King Minos of Homer's epic tales, was both a royal residence and a religious center, but large areas were given over to living quarters for the court, storerooms, and workshops. The principal structures rose to four and possibly five stories and were equipped with light wells and sanitary drains. The palace at Knossos and other palace buildings in Crete were undoubtedly the most advanced living quarters the world would see until the era of the Romans.

Early pottery in Crete followed the usual sequence: first a corded black ware, then a polished red and black, and finally a polished ware with simple incised cross-hatched and dotted designs. Frequent trade with Mesopotamia introduced the spouted ewer in a birdlike form characteristic of the pottery of that area. Stone vessels in the Egyptian style have also been found in Crete, as have small sculptures in Egyptian *faience* (a low-fire body high in silica and alkaline fluxes). Bronze tools, weapons, and small bronze figures were common. Delicately made gold jewelry was worn by the nobility, and gold cups and dishes were fashioned with great skill. Colorful frescoes—processions, youths with bulls, fish and bird life—covered the palace walls, and their spirit was not so much religious as athletic and exuberant.

In the Early Minoan period (c. 2800–2000 B.C.) the prevailing style of Cretan pottery was largely a decoration in white over a black slip, occasionally in a marbled imitation of stone, but also with banded and geometric motifs. The usual cups, bowls, and spouted round vases were present, but the form, like the decoration, was a bit heavy and clumsy. The following period, which is called Middle Minoan (2000–1550 B.C.), reflects the greater prosperity of the island and the increasing skill of the potter. The potter's wheel was in common use, and forms became more graceful. The favored designs were curling plant and circular motifs in white, cream, and red on a dark body. These gradually gave way to a preference for dark designs on a light tan body.

The closing years of this period and the early part of the Late Minoan era marked the high point of the island culture (1600–1500 B.C.). The flowing motifs of plant and sea life (particularly the octopus) were superbly suited to the popular oval water bottle and rounded vase forms (Fig. 8). In quality they are doubtless equal to the ceramic art of any historical period. Especially noteworthy are

above : 7. Stairwell, Palace of King Minos, Knossos, Crete. c. 1600–1500 B.C. (destroyed c. 1450 B.C.). Reconstruction.

below : 8. Jars, Crete. 1600–1500 B.C. Buff-colored earthenware with red-and-black slip. Herakleion Museum, Crete. The free decoration is characteristic of Minoan ware.

the huge palace storage jars nearly 6 feet high used for oil and wine, with numerous carrying lugs and a vigorous banded relief decoration. Also characteristic of this period, and peculiar to the region, are the so-called "snake goddesses," small faience figures with coiling snakes in their hands or around their bodies (Fig. 9). A period of decline set in after 1500 B.C. as the "palace style" vases became rather stiff with stylized floral patterns and over-elaborate with applied clay spurs.

Meanwhile, in the valleys of the Peloponnesus, the southern peninsula of the Greek mainland, a new power was growing. Shortly after 2000 B.C. a group of warlike tribes descended from the north of Greece, conquering the local inhabitants and building their fortress palaces at Mycenae and Tiryns. These were the Achaeans of Homeric legend. By 1400 B.C. the Mycenaean princes had founded most of the Greek cities we now know from Classic times (Fig. 10) and were expanding their power throughout the islands of the western Mediterranean.

above : 9. *"Snake Goddess"* (priestess ?), Crete. c. 1600 B.C. Faience, height 13 ½". Museum, Candia, Crete.

left : 10. Lion Gate, Mycenae. c. 1250 B.C.

The Minoans had early trade with the Mycenaeans, and it is likely that many craftsmen emigrated from Crete to the mainland, since much of the goldwork and pottery found in Mycenae has Minoan characteristics. But the Mycenaean ware did develop its own direction. The vase forms were higher footed and had a more rounded curve at the shoulder (Fig. 11). The foot rims and lips developed a more definite flange. High-stemmed and delicately formed cups were popular. The more dynamic floral and sea forms of the Minoans were subdued and conventionalized, and often only simple banded decoration was used (Fig. 12).

The eastern Mediterranean has a long history of intensive volcanic action, and the palace sites in Crete indicate a series of destructions and rebuildings. About 1450 B.C. a particularly violent eruption caused large portions of the island of Thera (San-

left : 11. Amphora, Greece, from Mycenae, found on Cyprus. Early 14th century B.C. Museum, Nicosia, Cyprus. The rather sketchy decoration shows the influence of Minoan ceramics.

center : 12. Amphora in sub-Minoan style, found in Cyprus. c. 1150–1000 B.C. Earthenware. Museum, Nicosia, Cyprus.

right : 13. Jar, China. Neolithic Period, c. 2000 B.C. Earthenware with double-spiral decoration in brown-black and purple slips. Victoria & Albert Museum, London.

torini) to collapse into the sea. Because it is only 70 miles from Crete, huge tidal waves swept the populous coastal towns of the Minoan island. Lesser quakes destroyed the palaces, which were built of timber and stone. Huge fires raged as stores of olive oil were ignited, and a thick layer of volcanic ash covered the fertile valleys of Crete. In the following years, the Mycenaeans gradually occupied Crete, and the island never regained its former importance.

In time the Mycenaeans had their own problems. During the thirteenth century B.C., new waves of Greek-speaking people descended from the North, a group now called the Dorians. Somewhat soft from long years of peace and prosperity and divided by local rivalries, the Mycenaeans were no match for the barbarian invaders. The Dorians lacked an art of their own and appreciated but little that of the conquered land; their coming brought about a period of dark ages in which only the crudest peasant crafts survived. But it was from this background that, Phoenixlike, Classical Greece arose.

CHINA AND THE FAR EAST

As in Europe and the Middle East, bands of hunter-fishermen inhabited the fertile valleys of China after the passing of the Ice Ages. The cultivation of wheat, the smelting of copper, and pottery making may have occurred there slightly later than in the Middle East (c. 3500 B.C.), but the dates are rather uncertain. As elsewhere, the early pottery was black, round bottomed, and had an impressed cord decoration. This gave way to a polished ware and, finally, when true kilns developed, to a pottery decorated with clay slips colored with various metallic oxides. A popular form was the oval jar with a small base, a large opening with a collar, and loops for tying down a cover. A circular double spiral design was common (Fig. 13). The cooking pot with three hollow feet was a unique form that was later taken over for ceremonial bronze vessels.

As in other cultures, most ancient Chinese pottery has been found in tombs. Very early in Chinese *above :* 14. Vase, China, from Anyang Province. Shang Dynasty (1523–1028 B.C.). Thrown earthenware with banded and incised motifs of a metallic character. Metropolitan Museum of Art, New York (Harris Brisbane Dick Fund, 1950).

below : 15. Vase, China. Han Dynasty (206 B.C.–A.D. 220). Earthenware with applied clay decoration and runny green glaze, height 14 ³/₈″. Victoria & Albert Museum, London.

history we can detect a reverence for the dead, family pride, and the beginnings of ancestor worship. Pottery, jade articles, bronze weapons, jewelry, and particularly bronze vessels intended for burial rites were common tomb objects. The bronze vessels are especially noteworthy for their excellent craftsmanship. First copied from pottery forms, they soon became quite elaborate, with numerous pictographs, fantastic stylized animals, and, finally, representational scenes. In time the pattern was reversed, and some of the pottery forms imitated the bronzes with similar impressed designs.

By the Shang Dynasty period (1523–1028 B.C.), the potter's wheel had come into common use, and a white ware was made as well as the older red ware (Fig. 14). By the Chou period (1027–256 B.C.) the ware was higher fired, perhaps an influence from bronze casters who were working in high temperatures. This pottery was generally black or gray with impressed designs similar to those on the bronze vessels. The Chou Dynasty was a period of great prosperity and enlightenment in China, and the philosophies of Confucius and Lao Tzu, written about 500 B.C., still influence Chinese thought.

In Shang and Chou times it was common for the dead ruler to be buried with his horse and servants and perhaps even his wife. By the Han Dynasty (206 B.C.–A.D. 220) this custom was felt to be too barbaric, and pottery figures were substituted. The first lead-based glazes date from early Han times and are of a green, runny character (Fig. 15). It is likely that the earlier shiny, high-fire pieces were the result of ash falling on the ware during firing. But potters were more interested in the higher-fire ware, and by late Han they were producing stoneware jars with a feldspathic glaze fluxed with lime or wood ashes. The white slips used to cover the coarser stoneware bodies have a porcelain quality, and it was only a matter of time before a true porcelain body was developed.

In the Six Dynasties period (A.D. 220–589) and the T'ang Dynasty (A.D. 618–906) a remarkable number of excellent figures were made (Fig. 16). Mythical beasts, guardian soldiers, and especially the favorite horses (Pl. 1, p. 21; Fig. 17)—as well as dancing girls and ladies in waiting (Fig. 18)—

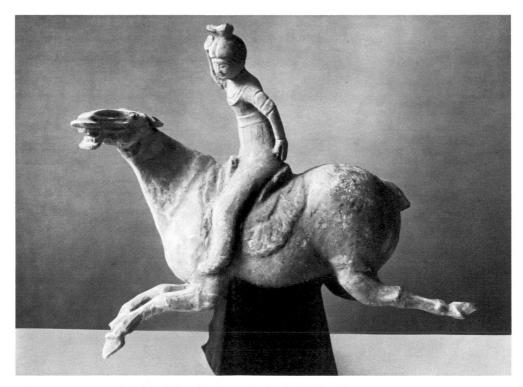

above : 16. *Horse and Rider*, China. Six Dynasties Period (220–589). Terra cotta with red, green, and blue paint. Museum of Far Eastern Antiquities, Stockholm. This horse is typical of the vigor of Chinese clay figures.

below : 17. Horse, China. T'ang Dynasty (618–906). Terra cotta with brown-black glaze. Metropolitan Museum of Art, New York (gift of Mrs. Edward S. Harkness, 1926).

right : 18. *Lady of the Court*, China. T'ang Dynasty (618–906). Painted earthenware. Victoria & Albert Museum, London.

China and the Far East   9

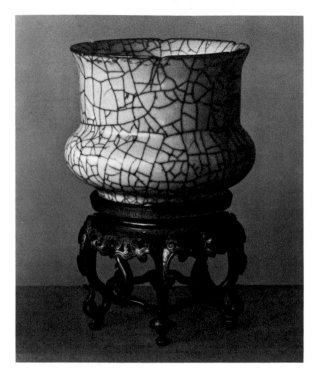

were modeled with a carefree skill and vitality seldom seen in ceramic sculpture of any age.

The T'ang period was a time of great experimentation in form and technique. Trade contacts with the Middle East were common, as is reflected in echoes of Greek and Roman vase forms, impressed decorative motifs, and marbelized clay bodies. The stoneware bodies were more refined, and it becomes a matter of opinion whether to term some pots stoneware or porcelain. Most impressive are the stoneware vases and bowls with incised lotus-leaf and dragon motifs, covered with the gray-green glaze called *celadon* (see reduction glazes, p. 213). Its similarity to jade, which was treasured by the Chinese and was thought in ancient times to possess magical properties, causes it to be universally esteemed. During the T'ang Dynasty ceramics became

a major Chinese art form, and the celadon vases took the place of honor in tomb offerings formerly accorded bronze vessels.

The Sung Dynasty period (960–1279) may be likened to the western Classical era, in that it set a standard that was emulated for the next thousand years. Sung ceramics reflect a refinement of older forms, a simplification that adds to their strength. The pieces may be heavy or thin depending upon the shape. Many earlier glazes did not fit the clay body and often crazed. The Sung potter was able to control this to produce a fine or heavy crackle or none at all (Fig. 19). The white porcelain body made possible the use of delicate blue and green glazes on which a fine crackle became a decorative element. Dark glazes, such as the *temmoku* with its pale silver-like oil spots, were popular for tea bowls. The large, *below* : 21. Bottle, China. Sung Dynasty (960–1279). Pale green celadon with silver-brown iridescent spots, height 10 ⁷/₈″. Victoria & Albert Museum, London.

bottom : 22. Pilgrim bottle, China. Ming Dynasty (1368–1644). Porcelain with dragon decoration in cobalt blue, height 14 ¹/₂″. Victoria & Albert Museum, London.

small-mouthed vase forms (T'zu-Chou) are especially attractive in a brown-black glaze, which is cut away and incised in vigorous floral patterns to expose the gray stoneware body (Fig. 20). Delicate long-necked bottle and gourd forms also originated in the Sung period (Fig. 21). Buddhism had by this time traveled from India to China, and the influence of the new religion was reflected in numerous terra cotta sculptural pieces based upon the Indian Buddha and his entourage of saints.

China has suffered during its long history from invasions by the nomadic warlike tribes to the north. Of the many invasions, that of the Mongol tribes under Genghis Khan was the most catastrophic. He invaded China in 1211, and its capital fell soon afterward. But due to conquests as far west as Persia, all of China did not fall until 1280, to his grandson and successor, Kublai Khan. The short Yuan period (1280–1368), under the Mongol conquerors, was an era of stagnation in ceramics.

The Ming Dynasty (1368–1644) brought another period of peace and prosperity. It may be likened to the Western Baroque and Rococo ages in that it was time of great technical skill, and, partly because of this, both form and decoration became rather overelaborate and fussy. Of course, many fine pieces were made in the older Sung styles and cannot be distinguished from earlier prototypes. The underglaze blue-and-white decorations on white porcelain that made such an impact on Europe were common during this period (Fig. 22). Many of these—strong, full jar forms with floral, figurative, or landscape motifs—are tastefully painted and most impressive. But these were not considered elegant enough for wealthy court tastes, and soon potters were using three- and even five-color overglaze enamel decorations in gaudy patterns. A few of the pieces have forms and decorations that are harmonious, but many are almost hideous when judged by contemporary tastes.

A more enduring technical accomplishment was the development of a rich red achieved by reducing copper with an alkaline flux (see reduction glazes, p. 213). The glaze ranged from a pale "peach bloom" to a deep purple-red, and when applied to a simple porcelain form the result could be both rich and elegant without being ostentatious. The porcelain sculpture of the Ming period also reflects the skill of the modeler, but with some loss of the vitality characteristic of the earlier T'ang pieces.

As was common in Chinese history, dissention at home and pressure from the Manchurians to the north led to the fall of the Ming Dynasty. During the subsequent long and changing Ch'ing period (1644–1912) there were several diverse trends. The technical skill evidenced in the blue-and-white ware and the multicolored enamels continued. Colors became brighter, and gold and luster were added. There is some influence of Islamic decoration, but in general the forms are those of the Sung and Ming eras except, perhaps, for a more perfect and mechanically correct execution (Fig. 23). It is possible that some cleansing influence might have taken place were it not for the increasing trade with Europe. In the midst of an industrial revolution that destroyed their own crafts, the *nouveau riche* of Europe were hardly the ones to appreciate subtleties in either form or decoration. Only the most elaborate and decadent styles were imported, and these were mass-produced in a way that was highly injurious to local Chinese traditions.

GREEK CERAMICS

After the overthrow of the Mycenaeans by the Dorians there were no longer any large Greek cities. Trade and the crafts declined, and even the rudimentary writing that the Minoans and Mycenaeans used for their record keeping was forgotten. The surviving pottery shows a crude imitation of the older forms and decoration. Perhaps the only significant change was that the focus of community life turned from the palace to the temple. Instead of the informal and even whimsical arts of the Minoans, there was a new emphasis on the monumental and the stylized art form. Beginning about 1050 B.C., ceramics in the area of Athens showed an improvement. Although the form imitated that of the Mycenaean cups, vases, and jars, it was better thrown and higher fired. The decoration—banded lines or concentric circles in a dark slip on a light red body—was executed with care and precision (Fig. 24). In

23. *Kwanyin*, China. Ch'ing Dynasty (1644–1912). Porcelain with greenish-white glaze, height 18 ½″. Art Institute of Chicago (Buckingham Collection).

time this decoration, termed Protogeometric, gave way to a more varied style.

The style that is called Geometric (c. 900 B.C.) was still a banded type, but it was enlivened with rows of triangles, zig-zags, meanders, and swastikas, with the neck and shoulder of the vase emphasized. Eventually figurative elements were introduced. First came the horse, a prestige symbol in this warrior culture, and later man and the chariot. A classic example of the style is the *Dipylon Vase* (Fig. 25), so called because it was found in the Dipylon cemetary in Athens. A funeral procession is portrayed on the *left :* 24. Protogeometric amphora, Cyprus. 1050–1000 B.C. Terra cotta, height c. 20″. Museum, Nicosia, Cyprus.

below : 25. *Dipylon Vase* (Geometric amphora), Greece, from Athens. 8th century B.C. Terra cotta, height 39″. Metropolitan Museum of Art, New York (Rogers Fund, 1914).

motifs. However, a very effective black-figure style of the human was used on a series of miniature bottle and vase forms.

During the period of the Oriental style (late eighth and seventh century B.C.) the Athenian potter continued to be interested in the human figure, but he was satisfied to paint it in an outline that was not too effective. Toward the end of the seventh century, he adopted the black-figure style with greater success. Corinthian ware was now made rather carelessly. This factor, coupled with the Persian wars, which made Eastern influences unpopular, again

shoulder and body of the vase, and the deceased and mourners are represented by stylized figures composed of circles for heads, triangles for torsos, and sticks for arms and legs. It was only a matter of time before such simple depictions would prove unsatisfactory.

As the Greek city-states grew, trade developed with the islands and finally with Asia Minor to the east. The older civilizations of the Middle East had a long tradition of fantasy in their art—winged monsters, gorgons, and sphinxes, often set against a background of imaginative floral patterns. Corinth, to the west of Athens, became the center of this new Oriental style, although Rhodes and other islands close to Syria were similarly influenced. Instead of simple zig-zags, the borders were decorative floral forms, and the central panel was enlarged to feature stylized birds and animals and finally figures from the Homeric legends. Clay slips were now carefully prepared of fine decanted red clay particles which, after burnishing and firing, assumed a smooth, black, glazelike surface (see slip glazes, p. 215). Details were added by incising, or, occasionally, by adding touches of white slip. In general the larger Corinthian pieces featured animal or bird *above :* 26. Horse and rider, Greece. 7th century B.C. Terra cotta, height c. 8″. Museum, Nicosia, Cyprus.

right : 27. EXEKIAS, Greece. *The Return of Dioscuri* (black-figure amphora). c. 540 B.C. Vatican Museum, Rome.

gave Athens the central position in the creation of Greek pottery.

In the seventh century small terra cotta figures, in human and animal forms, were made throughout the Greek islands (Fig. 26). Their forms are highly stylized, but the figures are gay and almost whimsical in character.

Due perhaps to the use of pottery in burial rites, ceramic forms had been codified into a definite series

of vase, jar, bottle, pitcher, and cup forms. The major area of the black-figure vase was given over to a figure or group representing heroes, gods (Pl. 2, p. 22), or episodes from Homeric legends, satyrs, and maenads (Fig. 27), and only later athletes and domestic scenes. It was this interest in illustration that deterred the Greeks from any attempt at a true glassy glaze, which might run and destroy their meticulous vase paintings. Perhaps their world was *right :* 28. Attic red-figure kylix, Greece. 490–480 B.C. Earthenware, height 5¹/₄″. Metropolitan Museum of Art, New York (bequest of Joseph Pulitzer, 1953).

below : 29. Interior of Fig. 28, red-figure kylix.

more isolated than we suspect today, and the Greeks might have been unaware of the Egyptian glazes made over two thousand years earlier.

The black-figure style, which portrayed the subject in profile with feet flat on the ground, proved successful in terms of harmonious ceramic design, but it offered little flexibility for the increasing skill of the vase painter. After about 520 B.C. the method changed to create a background in black which left the figure in the red body color (Figs. 28–30). Details could be added more easily with a fluid brush stroke than with the older method of incising. White was employed to highlight flesh tones, as it had been in the old black-figure style, and eventually it was used to form an allover ground on which the vase painter drew his figures. This technique appeared usually in the slender *lekythoi* (oil jugs) that served as funerary offerings, and it permitted still

Greek Ceramics 15

left : 30. *A Victorious Charioteer and the Goddess Nike* (red-figure column krater), Greece. c. 460–450 B.C. Metropolitan Museum of Art, New York (Rogers Fund, 1941).

below : 31. Figure of a woman, Italy. 3rd century B.C. Terra cotta. Metropolitan Museum of Art, New York (Rogers Fund, 1913). This figure was discovered in Tarentum, in southern Italy, but it is of a type first found at Tanagra, north of Athens, and its origin is Greek.

greater fluency in the drawing. The white ground took the role of empty space, with forms—naturalistic, foreshortened, and in three-quarter perspective—emerging from this space, thus creating an illusion of depth on the planar surface of the vessel.

In Greece, for the first time in history, pots were signed by their makers, and, as specialization grew, they were signed by both the potter and the painter. This was an uneasy partnership, which would be successful only when the painter realized the need of harmony between the pot and the decoration. It was natural, however, that as the skill of the vase painter grew, he would be tempted to make more extravagant efforts. By the fourth century B.C. Greek pottery was in the same decline that affected the sculpture of the period. The original decorative quality of the pottery was destroyed by confused overlapping, by excessive foreshorting, and, eventually, by multicolored landscape effects. The very popular Tanagra statuettes of small seated or standing figures are well known (Fig. 31). But more important were the early ceramic statues used on temple pediments. Unfortunately, constant wars among the Greek city-states resulted in their nearly complete destruction. Fragments of two large ceramic figures from Olympia (c. 470 B.C.) reveal an artistry equal to the marble sculpture of the era and indicate a long period of prior development in clay modeling (Fig. 32).

ETRUSCAN AND ROMAN CERAMICS

The Etruscans are thought to have come to the eastern area of central Italy from Syria in Asia Minor in the ninth century B.C. During the period when the Greeks were setting up colonies as far west as Sicily and southern Italy, the Etruscans were expanding their influence into the valleys of central Italy, and

32. *Zeus and Ganymede*, Greece, from Olympia. c. 470 B.C. Terra cotta, height c. 43¼". Museum, Olympia.

they finally controlled an area from near Rome to slightly beyond what is now Florence. There was considerable trade between the Greeks and the Etruscans, who were mining and exporting iron and copper. Some of the finest Greek pottery has come from Etruscan tombs, and it is likely that Greek potters also emigrated to Etruria.

The traditional Etruscan pottery is a black polished ware called *bucchero* (Figs. 33–34). An earlier ware has a red polished body, often incised with bands or cross-hatched motifs. Etruscan pottery is uneven in quality, for there were many influences: Villanovan black ware (Fig. 35), the Eastern Oriental style, the Greek, and embossed metalwork, none of which were completely assimilated into a coherent art form. Their work in bronze is perhaps more significant than their pottery.

It was in the field of ceramic sculpture that the Etruscans were most noted (Figs. 36–37). The earliest

above left : 33. Jar, Italy, from Petrina. 7th century B.C. Bucchero ware. Villa Giulia Etruscan Museum, Rome. The griffin heads indicate an Eastern influence.

left : 34. *Procession to the Sphinx,* oenochoe (wine vase), Italy. 6th century B.C. Bucchero ware with metallike carved relief. Museo dell'Opera, Orvieto.

below : 35. Cinerary urn, Italy, from Vulci. 9th–8th century B.C. Black-polished Villanovan ware. Villa Giulia Etruscan Museum, Rome.

temples of the Etruscans were not unlike those of the archaic Greeks, in that they were built of wood with colonnaded porticoes. The Etruscan temples differed, however, in the terra cotta that was used extensively in them. The roof tiles at the eaves culminated in elaborate gorgon heads. In the more ambitious temples large ceramic figures topped the roof peaks, and an entablature in high relief filled the triangular pediment of the main façade. The life-size image in Figure 38 is one such example

Etruscan and Roman Ceramics   19

above : 39. *Sarcophagus of the Spouses*, Italy, from Cerveteri. Early 6th century B.C. Terra cotta, length 6'7". Villa Giulia Etruscan Museum, Rome.

left : 40. Detail of Fig. 39, sarcophagus. The delicate modeling and forceful stylization of the *Spouses* represents a high point in Etruscan ceramic art.

arrangements, but they were essentially an exuberant and fun-loving people, qualities revealed by the colorful frescoes in the tombs. The wealthier families buried their dead in large ceramic coffins surmounted by portrait figures of the dead. Most famous are the couples, man and wife, who recline at their ease on couches, apparently in animated conversation with their friends (Figs. 39–40). It is this personal and informal quality that distinguishes the Etruscans from the Greeks, whose work was directed toward a predetermined ideal. Perhaps some of the freedom of expression is a result of working in the plastic clay, for the Greek terra cottas from Olympia display much the same vitality as the larger Etruscan pieces.

Shortly after 500 B.C. warlike Latin tribes in the vicinity of Rome began expanding north, into Etruscan territory, and south, against the Greek

from Veii, near Rome. Unfortunately, the Etruscan temples were later completely destroyed by the Romans. Well preserved, however, were the rock-cut tombs, many of which escaped the sporadic looting that has occurred over the centuries. One might suspect the Etruscans of a morbid preoccupation with death because of their elaborate burial

Plate 1. Horse, China. T'ang Dynasty (618–906). Glazed terra cotta, height
30¼″. Cleveland Museum of Art (anonymous gift). (See also Fig. 17.)

above : Plate 2. EXEKIAS, Greece. *Dionysus in a Boat* (Attic black-figure kylix). c. 540 B.C. Earthenware, diameter 12″. Staatliche Antikensammlungen, Munich.

left : Plate 3. Bowl, Persia, from Kashan. 13th century. Minai ware with opaque turquoise glaze and polychrome overglaze painting and gilding, diameter 7 ¾″. Metropolitan Museum of Art, New York (gift of Mr. and Mrs. A. Wallace Chauncey, 1957).

41. Brick wall (detail) from the Procession Street, Palace of King Nebuchadnezzar II, Babylon. 6th century B.C. Terra cotta tin-lead glazed in blue, white, and yellow. Metropolitan Museum of Art, New York (Fletcher Fund, 1931).

colonies. Neither the Etruscans, a loose confederation of twelve small kingdoms, nor the Greek colonies and their mother city-states, continually quarreling among themselves, could present a united front against the Romans. During the next two hundred years all fell before the growing power of Rome, which took over not only the eastern empire of Alexander but all the lands bordering on the western Mediterranean.

Roman art is a mixture of Etruscan and Greek elements. The Etruscan interest in portraiture became a dominant Roman characteristic, and with so many captive artisans working in Rome, it is difficult to tell where the late Greek and Etruscan art left off and the Roman began. Ornate Hellenistic ceramics were popular in luxury-loving Rome. Native Roman pottery is in the polished Etruscan bucchero tradition, but with a red oxidized body. The adopted Greek forms were usually covered with a banded pressed or applied decoration reminiscent of relief metalwork. Due to the intricate detail, the pottery pieces were often pressed in bisque molds. Although the first temple in Rome is reputed to have had terra cotta sculpture made by the craftsmen of the still-flourishing Veii, the Romans soon adopted marble as a favorite medium. Terra cotta reliefs, portraits, and small ceramic sculptured pieces continued to be made, but they lacked the nervous and sometimes crude vitality of the Etruscans.

The Roman empire fell not because of invasion from the outside but from internal decay. Futile wars, excessive sums spent on temples, and ornate public and private buildings all squandered needed resources. Captured booty gave a false sense of prosperity. Perhaps the practice of slavery, which was widespread in the ancient world, was equally at fault. As an increasingly large proportion of the populace, both in Rome and in its colonies, was unable to purchase back the products of its labor, trade stagnated, and the economy ground to a halt.

ISLAMIC CERAMICS

The earliest records of pottery making come from the area of Egypt and Mesopotamia. The Middle East saw the rise and fall of many ancient civilizations—the Sumerians, the Assyrians, the Persians, and the Egyptians—and these influences, as well as its position as a meeting place of East and West, created a complex art form. But in spite of almost perpetual conflicts and invasions, certain characteristics have remained constant. One is a preference for curved forms, like those found as early as 2500 B.C. in the stylized animals depicted on Babylonian pottery. Another interest is the use of repetative patterns and a symmetrical composition. A third is a desire for color (Fig. 41), which we find in the polychrome glazed tile reliefs (c. twelfth-

left : 42. Wall tile, Persia, from Kashan. 13th century. Tin-lead glazed earthenware with luster. Metropolitan Museum of Art, New York (bequest of Edward C. Moore, 1891).

fifth century B.C.) on the walls and palaces of the Assyrians and Babylonians.

As Rome's vast empire in the Middle East declined, numerous small states emerged, which were in constant conflict with one another. The events in the life of Mohammed (A.D. 570–632), the prophet of Islam, later generated a force that was to fill this vacuum. In the century following his death the religious and political power of Islam conquered the Middle East and spread east from Arabia toward India and west across North Africa and into Spain. With this sudden outburst of energy, there also appeared a synthesis of ancient art traditions that became characteristic of Islamic art: the flowing curve of the arabesque, intricate detail and pattern, and a love of color.

The pottery of the eighth and ninth centuries is of little interest to the contemporary craftsman. Were it not that imported Chinese pottery, particularly the porcelains, excited the ruling caliphs and their courts, it is likely that Islamic pottery would never have had its great success. Local pottery was held in low regard, but the thin and delicate porcelains were treasured by the wealthy as the equal of their vessels of gold.

Early Egyptian alkaline glazes fused satisfactorily on their sandy clay bodies, but not on the more plastic pottery clays most often used outside Egypt. By the Roman era lead-based glazes were used in the East, generally with a brown or green colorant.

In an attempt to compete with the Chinese ware, the Islamic potter first covered his earthenware body with a white slip. Incised with floral designs and decorated with a spotty, runny glaze of brown, green, and purple, it was reminiscent of the mottled T'ang lead-glazed ware in China. The next step was the addition of tin to the lead glaze to provide a white base for the painted decoration.

But even this improvement was a far cry from the desired porcelain. By about 1200, the Persian potter, after continued experiments, developed a soft paste porcelain. It was rather like that used in eighteenth-century France, but somewhat coarser and sandy in texture. Composed of a powdered silica and a glass frit held together with a small amount of white clay, it was not very plastic and was probably a factor in limiting the Islamic form to rather simple dishes, bowls, ewers, and vases.

Possibly the most unique achievement of the Islamic potter was in the use of a luster glaze (Fig. 42). A luster is essentially a thin layer of metal fused onto the glaze at a lower temperature (see p. 214). It was first used on glass during the eighth and ninth centuries to produce a goldlike effect. Early ninth-century lustered pieces exhibit a variety of metallic colors in hues of ruby red, green, brown, and yellow, applied in complicated patterns. But, perhaps due to difficulties of technique, the pale golden brown became the favorite and was used in an overall pattern in connection with polychrome decoration in blue, turquoise, manganese purple, and pale green. Intricate entwined floral designs were a favorite motif, sometimes used as a background for a stylized bird, animal, or human subject. Much has been made of the Koranic ban against the pictorial representation of man, but this pertained only to the decoration of the Mosque, which was often covered inside and out with colorful tiles, largely of *above :* 43. Jug, Persia. 13th century. Earthenware with Kufic script decoration in black slip, height 5 ¾″. Victoria & Albert Museum, London.

below left : 44. Drug jar, Syria. 13th–14th century. Earthenware with black slip decoration under turquoise glaze, height 13″. Victoria & Albert Museum, London.

below right : 45. Jar, Syria. 14th century. Earthenware with blue and black painted decoration under clear glaze, height 16″. Victoria & Albert Museum, London.

floral patterns and inscriptions from the Koran. The flowing and graceful quality of the Kufic script was a most satisfying decoration in itself (Fig. 43).

The *minai* decorations popular in Persia during the late twelfth century reveal great interest in everyday human life (Pl. 3, p. 22). Derived from manuscript illustrations (now lost), they represent in miniature scenes of horsemen, hunting, court life, and tales from the romantic legends. Quite different but equally impressive is the dark slip- and sgraffito-decorated ware of animals and floral patterns under a turquoise glaze (Fig. 44). For brief periods a pressed ware reflecting metal forms was popular, and continued Chinese imports resulted in a carved ware reminiscent of T'ang celadons.

Despite continued conflicts, the greatest period of Islamic ceramics came in the twelfth and thirteenth centuries, as power moved from Damascus, Baghdad, Samarkand, and Cairo under various ruling groups. The Mongol invasions directed by Genghis Khan and the assumption of power in Mesopotamia by his grandson, Hulaju, in 1258, began a decline in the ceramic arts. The fourteenth century was a period of renewed contacts with, and influence from, China. Brush decoration in black under turquoise or clear glaze (Fig. 45) gradually

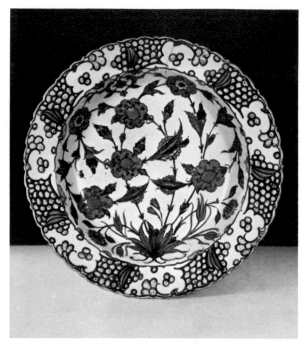

left : 46. Dish, Byzantine. 14th century. Earthenware with sgraffito decoration through white slip with yellow and green, diameter 9″. Victoria & Albert Museum, London.

right : 47. Plate, Turkey, from Isnik. 1550–60. White earthenware with polychrome floral decoration, diameter 14 ½″. Victoria & Albert Museum, London.

replaced the older luster ware and minai, and the subject matter was influenced by Chinese textiles and paintings. Stylized animal and bird forms were still popular (Fig. 46). Imports of the older Islamic pottery and cobalt ores also reached China and undoubtedly led to the development in the late Yuan (Mongol) Dynasty of the first blue-and-white decorated porcelain.

Meanwhile, the Turks were again coming to power in the Middle East. A nomadic tribe living north of Afghanistan, they moved south and west during the eleventh century, and they controlled much of the Middle East when the conquering Mongols arrived. Pushed into Asia Minor by the Mongols, the Turks renewed their expansion after the collapse of Mongol power, and by 1453 they had captured Constantinople, bringing an end to the old Byzantine-Roman empire. In 1516 Syria and Egypt fell under Turkish rule.

The fifteenth century was a confused period for the potter. Persians, imported to work on tiles for the new mosques and tombs at Bursa and Idirne (in Turkey near Constantinople), were most successful in combining Chinese and Persian floral motifs in blue and turquoise. The sixteenth and seventeenth centuries marked the high point in Turkish pottery. The initial use of blue-and-white decoration in the Chinese style gradually succumbed to the Islamic love of color. Floral decoration was still dominant, but now it took the form of distinct sprays of identifiable flowers—the tulip, the blue bell, and other garden blooms (Fig. 47). There were also attempts to imitate the carved Chinese celadons. A bright monochrome ware in blue-green and amber developed, as did a white pierced ware with the design filled in with a transparent glaze. A revival of luster ware occurred, but during the eighteenth and nineteenth centuries the decoration became increasingly rigid and mechanical. Meanwhile, to the west, Islamic pottery was taking new directions in Moslem Spain.

48. Vase, Spain, from Valencia. c. 1470. Gold and blue luster ware, height 20 ¾″. Victoria & Albert Museum, London. The overall form and wing handles on this vase are derived from the Alhambra vase style. (See Fig. 49.)

HISPANO-MORESQUE CERAMICS

Spain was invaded in 711, as the early Moslem wave of expansion spread across North Africa. In 732 the Moors were defeated at Poitiers, in the south of France, after which only the southern half of Spain remained under Moslem control. This period was one of prosperity and stimulation of the arts. Leatherwork flourished at Córdoba, metalwork at Toledo, and pottery at Málaga. The palace fortress of the Alhambra, with its pointed domes, colonnaded courts, delicate tracery in stone, and colorful tiles, remains the most distinctive architecture in Spain. Early tenth- and eleventh-century pottery of stamped or slip designs in geometric motifs or Koranic inscriptions is of little interest.

The dispersal of Persian potters following the Mongol conquests is probably the reason for the initial growth of lustered pottery. Unlike his Middle Eastern counterpart, the Spanish potter continued to use an earthenware body with a lead-tin covering glaze. The Málaga potter reflected the art of the metal engraver and textile worker in his use of a complicated overall pattern of stylized floral elements, chevrons, knotted ribbons, and Koranic inscriptions. The favorite luster was a pale gold with details in blue (Fig. 48), although occasionally a violet and a turquoise-green was also used.

In time Gothic influences from the North crept in, and a more naturalistic foliage, and even animals, birds, horsemen, and humans were used. Interested primarily in decoration, the Islamic potter, except in the Alhambra vases (Fig. 49), never developed the more graceful style of the Chinese. His forms were rather heavy—large platters with flat rims, pitchers, and drug jars with a severe vertical shape (Fig. 50).

The luster ware of Málaga and Murcia was in great demand throughout the western Mediterranean. By the early fourteenth century Moslem potters were working at Manisis, a pottery town near Valencia, which later grew in importance. Possession of large sets of luster ware became a prestige symbol for the ruling families of the many small dukedoms in northern Spain, France, and Italy (Fig. 51). The heraldic family crest surrounded by an elaborate border became the style for large platters intended primarily for display (Fig. 52).

The local rulers in the North and the leaders of the Christian Church were moved by the same spirit of gain and conquest that characterized the seventh- and eighth-century Moslems. By 1212 only the small kingdom of Granada was under Moslem rule, and that fell in 1492 to Ferdinand and Isabella. In the same year the Jews were expelled from Spain. The infamous Spanish Inquisition began, and in 1502 the remaining Moslems were forcibly converted to Christianity and, in 1609, finally expelled. The flow of gold and treasure from the looted Indians of Mexico and Peru temporarily concealed the tragedy of the expulsion of the Moors and Jews, but southern Spain never recovered its former prosperity in agriculture or in trade.

As silver and gold plate became accessible to the now-wealthy ruling families, luster ware lost its appeal. Imitative attempts to shape the raised metallic bosses and designs in a pottery form were not successful. Perhaps the association of luster with the Moors was a factor in its flagging popularity. As luster ware became increasingly scarce, the pictorial majolica of Renaissance Italy was gaining in favor. A small local market for luster remained until the seventeenth century, but its great days were past.

above : 49. Alhambra vase, Spain. Late 13th–early 14th century. Olive-green luster ware with floral and Kufic script decoration, height 5′6″. Museo Nazionale, Palermo.

left : 50. Drug jar, Spain. c. 1440. Opal and blue luster ware, height 15 ¹/₈″. Victoria & Albert Museum, London.

ITALIAN CERAMICS

Little pottery of interest was made in medieval Italy. Roman and Etruscan ware had been long forgotten. By 1400 the typical Italian functional earthenware bowls, pitchers, and jars were covered with a white slip incised with a free rendering of birds and animals with simple geometric borders (Fig. 53). The sgraffito decoration and the runny lead glaze with areas of green and yellow were not unlike the Islamic ware of the ninth and tenth centuries. It was natural that the early luster ware of Spain became highly prized in Italy. Trading vessels from Spain stopped frequently at the island of Majorca en route to Pisa and Genoa. Thus, the new tin-glazed Italian ware in the Spanish style became known as *majolica*.

By 1450 the Hispano-Moresque pottery was being extensively copied, both in form and in decoration, in Faenza, Sienna, Orvieto, Florence, and other pottery centers. But only at Deruta was luster ware made with any great success (Fig. 54). The

Italian Ceramics 29

typical majolica decoration was painted in hues of blue, purple-black, green, or yellow. More naturalistic floral motifs gradually superseded the intricate and stylized Islamic motifs. By 1500 foliage decoration became a minor interest as figurative elements took over, first portrait heads on pitchers or plates (Figs. 55–56) and, finally, whole figures and groups. This trend might be attributed to a lingering Roman influence, as well as to the greater stress on personality in the Renaissance. The major strides made by mural painters were reflected in pottery, as the decoration became increasingly crowded and illusionistic, with scenes from classical mythology, occasional biblical themes, and genre topics (Fig. 57). Like late Greek vase painting, it is hardly a successful merger of form and decoration.

In some provinces extensive use was made of architectural friezes and decorative moldings in

above left : 54. Drug pot, Italy, from Deruta. c. 1500. Majolica ware with decoration in blue, green, and yellow; height 10 ¾″. Victoria & Albert Museum, London.

above right : 55. Drug jar, Italy, from Faenza. c. 1475. Tin-lead glazed earthenware with majolica decoration featuring a portrait of a young man, height 11 ½″. Metropolitan Museum of Art, New York (Fletcher Fund, 1946).

right : 56. Plate, Italy, from Deruta. c. 1520. Blue and gold luster, diameter 15 ¾″. Victoria & Albert Museum, London.

terra cotta. As glazes were perfected, colorful tile work became more common. But perhaps the most significant ceramic contribution of the Italian Renaissance was in the field of clay sculpture. Since clay is universally used as a sketch material for sculpture, many of these were subsequently fired. A number of sculptors, including Donatello and Michelangelo, made specific works in terra cotta, but these have received little recognition beside their major works in marble.

Of the many sculptors working in glazed terra cotta, the workshop of Luca della Robbia (1400–82) is best known. The soft white glazes on his

simple, modeled madonnas were most successful
(Fig. 58). The pale blue backgrounds and unobtrusive floral borders were not in conflict with the
sculpture form, as was often the case with the
work of his followers. Glazed terra cottas were very
popular (Fig. 59) and included, besides the lunettes
and madonnas, figures in the round, baptism fonts,
and even entire altarpieces of great size. Unfortunately, by the third generation of the della Robbia
family, the same overcrowded and confused illu-
stionistic effects occurred that characterized other
later majolica pottery, and the early elegance was lost.

right : 57. *The Calydonian Boar* (decorated plate), Italy, from
Urbino. c. 1542. Polychrome majolica ware, diameter 10 ¾".
Victoria & Albert Museum, London.

below left : 58. LUCA DELLA ROBBIA, Italy. *Madonna and Child
with Scroll.* c. 1450. Glazed terra cotta, height 31 ¼".
Metropolitan Museum of Art, New York (bequest of
Benjamin Altman, 1913). This graceful madonna is modeled
in Renaissance tradition and decorated with a lead-tin glaze.

below right : 59. LEONARDO DA VINCI (?), Italy. *Ginevra
de' Benci.* c. 1500. Glazed terra cotta. Private colllection, Italy.

2 Ceramics of the Past

Later European; African;
South, Central,
and North American;
Korean;
and Japanese Ceramics

LATER EUROPEAN CERAMICS

Northern Europe lagged far behind the Middle East and the Orient in its ceramic development. It was the misfortune of this region to be overwhelmed by foreign influences before strong native traditions could emerge and take form. As a result, European ceramics, like American, are forever eclectic. Just as life quickened in thirteenth-century Italy, trade increased and small handcraft industries began in the North. During the late thirteenth and fourteenth centuries some very freely thrown and forceful pitchers, jugs, and mugs were made in England and France (Figs. 60–61), especially in the monastery workshops of the Cistercians. Incised, applied clay, and slip decoration, with a thin lead glaze in a mottled green and yellow, are typical of the style of this early period (Fig. 62). Little change took place during the fifteenth century (Fig. 63). But during the sixteenth and seventeenth centuries an interesting development occurred in slip-trailed and combed decoration (Fig. 64). The new floral, animal, and human motifs seem related to tapestry or embroiderywork, but this doubtless was due to method. The unique slip technique was snuffed out in the eighteenth century as imports increased and as industrialization accelerated.

Although high-fire stoneware was made at an early age in China, its development was very late in the West. This probably was due to the lack of high-fire and stoneware clays in the older civilizations of the Mediterranean. But during the thirteenth century (and perhaps as early as the twelfth century) a red polished pottery was being made in the Rhineland area near Cologne which had the characteristic hardness of stoneware. By the fifteenth century there were many small pottery towns near the Rhine—Höhr-Grenzhausen, Siegberg, Cologne, and Raeren in Flanders—producing a salt-glazed stoneware (see salt glaze, p. 214). This was a discovery unique to the area. The favorite shapes were the

opposite : 60. Jug, Normandy, from Rouen. Late 13th century. Thrown clay with applied clay decoration and thin yellow glaze, height 9 ½″. Guildhall Museum, London.

above left : 61. Ram's head jug, England. 14th century. Buff ware with applied clay decoration and thin yellow-green glaze, height 14″. Guildhall Museum, London.

above right : 62. Jug, England. 14th century. Red ware with yellowish green glaze, height 14″. Guildhall Museum, London.

utilitarian round jug with a small neck and a loop handle, and various vase and mug forms, including the well-known beer tankard with a pewter lid. The influence of metalwork is evident in the applied and stamped medallion decoration, which is revealed under the salt glaze. The glaze may be a near white to a chocolate brown, depending upon the body color, and it shows the pebbly surface characteristic of the salt glaze. Blue remained the major colorant applied to the raw ware before firing,

although in later periods polychrome effects appeared. Salt-glazed stoneware was made extensively during the sixteenth and seventeenth centuries (Fig. 65), and its practice spread to England.

Imported Chinese porcelain reached Northern Europe shortly after the Renaissance, and it created just as much interest with the Europeans as it had among Islamic potters many centuries earlier. Late in the fifteenth century-attempts were made in Venice to produce porcelain by adding a powdered glass and flux to white earthenware. Further efforts were made near Florence, but the ware was brittle and warped badly. During the late seventeenth century, a slightly similar but more successful soft-paste porcelain was made in France and later in Germany.

By 1715 a true high-fire porcelain, using local supplies of kaolin and feldspar, was made near *above left :* 63. Jug, Germany, from Siegberg. 15th century. White stoneware, height 10 ³/₈″. Guildhall Museum, London.

left : 64. Posset pot, England, from Staffordshire. c. 1700. Buff earthenware with white and brown slip decoration under yellow glaze, height 6″. Victoria & Albert Museum, London.

above right : 65. "Gray beard" jug, Germany, from Frechen. 17th century. Gray stoneware with mottled brown salt glaze, height 8 ⁵/₈″. Victoria & Albert Museum, London.

Meissen by Johann Böttger, a German alchemist working for the Elector of Saxony. Prior to this discovery a majolica-type earthenware (also called faience), influenced by Italian imports, had been made throughout Europe. The hard porcelain gradually supplanted this majolica ware in Germany and then in Scandinavia. After some experimentation the English developed their bone china, which *right :* 66. Jug, England, from Staffordshire. c. 1740. Salt-glazed stoneware in the form of a bear hugging a dog, height 8 ¹/₈″. Metropolitan Museum of Art, New York (gift of Carlton Macy, 1934).

below : 67. Platter, England, from Staffordshire. 18th century. Red earthenware with combed white slip decoration, length 20 ¹/₂″. Victoria & Albert Museum, London.

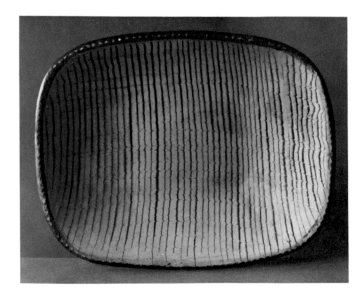

was fired at a slightly lower temperature. France clung to its early soft-paste porcelain, and the Dutch, perhaps due to their profitable import trade of Chinese porcelains, remained wedded to their popular majolica Delft ware, which was largely a low-fire imitation of the Chinese blue-and-white porcelain.

During the eighteenth century European ceramics became increasingly industrialized. A growing quantity of pottery was mechanically made by casting, pressing, or jiggering (see Chap. 10). The German stoneware and English slipware in the local tradition (Figs. 66–67) lost favor before both the imports and the production ware based on classical forms and decoration in the Chinese or Italian manner (Fig. 68). The Rococo taste, with its emphasis on elaborate detail and decoration, prevailed (Fig. 69). While eighteenth- and nineteenth-century ware is valued by the collector, it is, for the most part, of little interest to the serious student except as a history of industrial techniques. An appallingly large quantity of bad pottery was made, and its presence continues to distort public awareness of what constitutes ceramic art.

below left : 68. Vase, England, from Wedgwood. c. 1785. Green and white Jasper ware, height 10 ¾". Victoria & Albert Museum, London. The fussy decoration exemplifies the tendency to borrow inappropriate classical motifs.

below right : 69. RALPH WOOD FACTORY, England, Staffordshire. Toby jug. 1770–80. Earthenware, height 11 ½". Victoria & Albert Museum, London. This jug, with its excessive detail, lacks the strength of earlier English wares.

AFRICAN CERAMICS

Our knowledge about African pottery suffers from the same lack of historical data that, until recently, has characterized all study of ancient African cultures. Prehistoric man lived in Africa as early as did his counterpart in Europe and Asia. Skillful stone engravings and rock paintings (c. 7000 B.C. or earlier) in North, Central, and South Africa reveal a gradual change from a hunting culture to a pastoral one. It is likely that the descendents of the earliest civilizations are the Pygmies of the Congo area and the vanishing Bushmen of the South.

Prehistoric Africa was very sparsely settled. Present speculation is that a series of migrations, originating perhaps in India, began about 6000 B.C. and moved across the Straits of Aden into northeast Africa. This first group spread across North Africa, which was not as arid as it is now. Their Hamitic descendents are the Berbers of North Africa and the ancient Egyptians of the upper Nile. Next came the Bantu tribes, which presently occupy forested equatorial Africa. Finally, a third group moved into the grassland area from the Sudan to the west coast, which lies between the desert of the North and the forests of the South. In general, the movement was westward and southward.

Continual trade and at times warfare between Egypt and the ancient African kingdoms of Kush (Sudan) and Punt (Ethiopia and Somaliland) exposed Africa to all the developments in the Middle East. At Meroë, the Kush capital on the upper Nile, there was an extensive iron industry by the first century. But the technique of iron making

had earlier spread westward to Darfur and finally to northern Nigeria, where the Nok culture was working in iron as early as 300 B.C. This use of iron gave rise to many cultures in West Africa, which in material prosperity soon equaled the northern areas of Europe. Life-size terra cotta heads and figure fragments dating from about 500 B.C. of the Nok culture (900 B.C.–A.D. 200) have an impressive realism that is unique. This large and fertile area of the Niger River valley later saw the rise of many stable kingdoms: Ghana, Mali, and the Shonghay.

While trade continued between the Niger region and the Sudan and Egypt, there was also contact across the desert to the Mediterranean coast. Although this trade may have existed to a slight degree in Roman times, its greatest expansion occurred as Islam spread across North Africa. By A.D. 1000 Arab trading settlements appeared in Timbuktu and other northern Nigerian cities. The local rulers were converted, and by 1050 the first pilgrimages to Mecca had been made. This area has remained Islamic to the present.

The well-known African wood sculptures are seldom more than 150 years old, if that, but they represent an ancient tradition, and, due to their ceremonial and religious nature, they are probably similar to those made for countless years. Hundreds of seated stone figures about 2 feet high and dating between 700 and 1100 have been found near Esie in northern Nigeria. Some have bearded Mediterranean features, while others display African facial types.

Bronze casting was well established along the Niger River between 600 and 950, and from there it spread south to Ife and later (c. 1280) to Benin during the reign of the Benin Oba Oguola. A seated bronze (Fig. 70) from the village of Tada on the Niger River is unusual for its realism, yet it lacks the stiffness we associate with Egyptian or Roman sculpture. The Ife preference for realism, seen in the

left : 70. Ife figure, Nigeria, from Tada. 10th–11th century. Bronze, height 20 ½″. Department of Antiquities, Nigeria.

opposite : Plate 4. *Seated Ball Player,* Nayarit figure, Mexico. 8th–10th century. Clay with polychrome slip decoration, height 13″. Minneapolis Institute of Arts.

numerous royal portrait heads (1000–1400), gradually died out in the Benin bronzes (1400–1900), which reached a high point between 1575 and 1625. These bronzes exhibit a more emotional approach common to wood carvings, as exemplified by the exaggerated features, oversize heads, and costume detail. Since clay is a common study material for sculpture, it is not surprising that we find many terra cotta portrait heads in both the Ife and Benin styles (Figs. 71–72). They have the same plastic feeling for form and the sensitivity that characterize the bronzes made by the lost wax casting process.

As in other tribal cultures, most pottery is made by women, often by the wife of the metalsmith. However, in some cases whole villages make pottery and trade their surplus to other areas. Except in a few Moslem-influenced regions in the North, all pottery is hand built in a combination coil-and-paddle technique. The gourd so commonly used as a container has influenced many forms. Large oval vases with collar rims serve for food and water storage. Textural decorations are often applied in a basketlike weave (Fig. 73) or painted in iron oxides to produce a red or black design. Since most

above : 73. Mangbetu bottle, Congo. 19th–20th century. Paste and sand temper with stirrup handle, height 9 ³/₈″. Brooklyn Museum.

above right : 74. *Flute Player,* Ivory Coast, from Krinjabo. Before 1911. Terra cotta, height 10 ³/₈″. Museum of Primitive Art, New York. This figure reveals the same expressive modeling that is found in the gold and bronze castings of the area.

left : 75. Mangbetu portrait bottle, Congo. 19th–20th century. Terra cotta, height 11 ³/₈″. Museum of Primitive Art, New York.

right : 76. Ashanti head, Ghana. Terra cotta, height 12″. Museum of Primitive Art, New York. This stylized form, with its contrasts of smooth and textured surfaces, is not unlike the traditional wood-carved artifacts.

77. Remojades head, Mexico, from Veracruz. Classic Period (A.D. 600–900). Clay, height 7 5/8″. Museum of Primitive Art, New York. The plastic and emotional quality of Pre-Columbian ceramics is exemplified in this head.

pottery is fired in the open with straw and twigs, it is not very hard, and little early ceramic ware has survived.

In addition to the large and rather formal terra cotta sculpture of the Nok, Ife, and Benin kingdoms, many tribes made small figures (Figs. 74–75). The figurative pottery of the Mangbetu is best known. These effigy heads, like those of the Peruvian Mochica, have an elusive stylization that is quite satisfying, a form in which the late Greek portrait vases and the English Toby pots often fail. Perhaps, with our present stress on written and verbal communication, we in the Western world have forever lost the plastic inventiveness that characterizes so much of African art (Fig. 76).

CERAMICS OF THE NEW WORLD

While the Middle East was a meeting ground for the exchange of ideas among Europe, Africa, and Asia, the Americas had an entirely separate development. Though they never used iron, and rarely bronze, and had no beast of burden such as the horse or the ass, the American Indians attained a relatively high civilization. Their ceramics, made without the potter's wheel or a true glassy glaze, is of special interest (Fig. 77).

During the Ice Ages, perhaps as early as 25,000 years ago, small groups of nomadic hunters and fishermen crossed the Bering Straits and entered the North American continent. This mass migration continued intermittently for thousands of years; by 7000 B.C. the wandering hunters had traversed both continents to the tip of South America. As in the Old World, settled communities and agriculture first began in the more temperate regions. These were the fertile valleys of central Mexico, the coastal plains of Peru, and the highland plateaus of Colombia and Bolivia. Agriculture of a sort began as early as 2500 B.C. By 1000 B.C. the cultivation of maize (corn), which is thought to have begun in Mexico, had spread to Peru, and the potato was grown in many areas. Other domesticated plants were the lima and the kidney bean, squash, yams, peanuts, peppers, the chocolate bean, and fruits such as the avocado and the pineapple. Cotton was raised in both Mexico and Peru, which also had wool from the llama and the alpaca. Long before the era of the Spanish conquest gold jewelry was worn by the wealthy. Alloys of copper, gold, silver, and even platinum were not uncommon. Unfortunately, most of the jewelry, vessels, and small statues of gold, formed by either hammering or the lost wax casting process, were melted down by the Spaniards and lost forever. Although some copper was used for tools and weapons (and even bronze was used by the Mochica in Peru), stone was more universally employed for both tools and weapons. Step pyramids of adobe brick, faced with stone or polychrome stucco and surmounted by small temples, were traditional in both north and south.

right : 78. Naxca bottle, Peru. c. A.D. 500. Earthenware with burnished polychrome slip decoration, height 5 $^9/_{16}$″. Art Institute of Chicago (Buckingham Fund).

below : 79. Naxca bowl, Peru. c. A.D. 500. Earthenware with painted polychrome decoration in a tapestrylike design, height 3 $^1/_2$″. Museum of Primitive Art, New York.

44   Ceramics of the Past

below : 80. Mochica stirrup bottle, Peru. c. A.D. 500. Clay, height 8 ⁷/₈″. Museum of Primitive Art, New York. This bottle shows the Mochicas' overriding interest in form.

bottom : 81. Mochica stirrup bottle, Peru. c. A.D. 500. Earthenware with painted decoration depicting a hunting scene, height 8 ⁷/₈″. Museum of Primitive Art, New York.

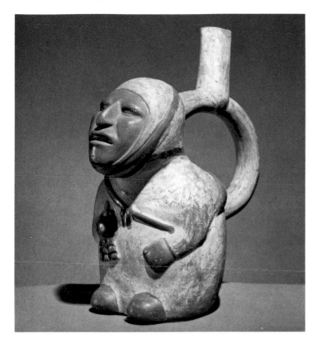

South America

The first pottery, dating from about 2500 B.C., was gray or black from the primitive firing, round bottomed, and had a corded and later a simple incised geometric design. As settlements grew in the Andean highlands and coastal areas (c. 1200–400 B.C.), a jaguar motif, evidently of religious significance, appeared on jewelry, weaving, and pottery. The pottery of this Chavín period has a burnished black surface with incised and dotted geometric and circular designs and often takes a feline form. In addition to functional bowls and jars, a unique form —the stirrup bottle, with its hollow-handled spout— developed in this era.

Gradually the ware became thinner, and better kilns permitted slip decoration. In the Experimenter Period (c. 400 B.C.–A.D. 1) the feline motif disappeared, and a red-on-white slip and a negative

clay-resist technique evolved. As the forms became more varied, sculptural additions were made, and the pots began to assume human, bird, or animal form.

The period of the Master Craftsman (c. A.D. 1–900) is best typified by the Mochica and Naxca cultures in the irrigated coastal valleys of Peru. The Naxca were highly skilled in both weaving and embroidery, and their elaborate textile designs were reflected in their slip-decorated pottery motifs. The ware was quite thin, often made in partial bisque molds, and carefully fired. Clay slips in hues of red, yellow, black, violet, and white were carefully prepared and burnished to a glossy surface. The popular Naxca bottle form has twin spouts with a connecting strap handle (Fig. 78). Bowls and tall goblets, which provided a good decorating area, were also favored (Fig. 79). In contrast to the stylized figures, animals, and plant designs favored by the Naxca, the Mochica potter to the north was interested in sculptural form. His favorite stirrup bottle might be a portrait head of a chief, a bird, a figure, or even a group of people on a mountaintop (Figs. 80–81). The portrait heads are forcefully modeled and are remarkable for their depiction

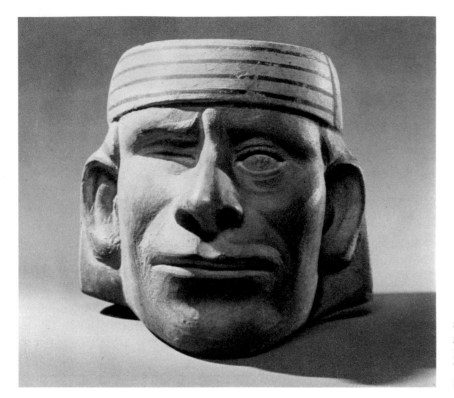

82. Mochica effigy jar, Peru. c. A.D. 500. Earthenware, height 4 5/8". Museum of Primitive Art, New York. The depiction of personality in this head is striking.

of character (Fig. 82). Also interested in figurative form were the Chancay, another coastal group (Fig. 83).

Among the numerous tribal cultures of the Expansionist Period (c. 900–1200) were the Tiahuanaco of the south Peruvian highlands, whose culture grew after the peak of the Naxca and Mochica had passed. The characteristic pottery forms of the Tiahuanaco are flaring goblets, open bowls with wide rims, and oval and modeled vessels with twin spouts and a strap handle. The slip decoration may be multicolored, but the usual decorative designs are in white on a red base color outlined in black. The puma is a favorite motif both in painted and modeled form (Fig. 84).

The Tiahuanaco culture was short-lived, and local patterns again evolved in the coastal areas, north and south, and in the divided highlands. The population increased, and towns and temple areas were enlarged. As wealth and social distinctions grew, the potter was no longer the free artisan of

earlier cultures. The dominant pottery style of the City Builder Period (c. 1200–1450) was the Chimu of the northern coastal area. Chimu ware shows the older Mochica influence in its stirrup spout bottles (Fig. 85), but the southern double spout and strap was also used. Painted decoration was rare, and the usual Chimu body was red or smoked black, reflecting the decline in craftsmanship. The use of clay bisque molds with geometric designs and bird or fish motifs also resulted in decreased individuality. Double whistling bottles with small animals modeled on the handle bases were among the most common Chimu forms.

The Incas began their expansion from the central highlands. In the period before the Spanish conquest (c. 1450–1532) they were the only unified state in the vast area of western South America. Reflecting their own origins, their pottery was quite different from that of the more subdued cultures. Their favorite form was the aryballoid jar with a pointed base, long neck, flaring collar, low side handles, and

right : 86. Inca aryballoid jar, Peru. c. 1438–1832. Earthenware with painted geometric slip decoration, height 8 ¼″. Museum of Primitive Art, New York.

below : 87. Tlatilco figure, Mexico. c. 900–300 B.C. Clay, height 4 ¼″. Museum of Primitive Art, New York.

applied small animal heads (Fig. 86). Shallow plates with bird handles, straight goblets, pedestal beakers, and pitchers with one or two handles were also common. Except for occasional bird or animal designs, the decoration was geometric with banded elements and triangular, cross-hatched, and dotted motifs in red, white, yellow, orange, and black slips. While craftsmanship was far improved over that of the Chimu, it hardly equaled the quality of the more imaginative Mochica or Naxca ware made a thousand years earlier.

Mexico and Central America

By 1500 B.C. farming communities had grown up in the fertile valleys of central Mexico. At Tlatilco, near present-day Mexico City, large quantities of small figurines, mostly female, have been found, which indicate a fertility cult of some sort (Fig. 87). Many are quite charming, lacking the grotesque and fearsome quality that characterized much of Mexico's later religious art. The Tlatilco pottery was a burnished black or red ware with simple incised designs. In addition to conventional bowl or bottle shapes, we find modeled pots in a bird or fish form. This early interest in modeled forms continued, partly because the potter's wheel, which dictates a symmetrical, rounded form, was never introduced in pre-Columbian Mexico.

The first major culture to emerge in Mexico was that of the Olmecs, who lived southeast of the Gulf of Campeche. The Olmecs (800–400 B.C.) had their major religious center on the small island of La Venta. Its stepped pyramids and large stone sculptures were repeated in most of the Mexican cultures that followed. The Olmecs were a highly sophisticated culture who used a calendar and astronomical observations to regulate sacrifices to the gods for successful crops.

left : 88. Olmec style seated figure, Mexico, from Puebla. 1200–400 B.C. Kaolin with red pigment, height 13 ³/₈″. Museum of Primitive Art, New York. This figure is typical of the rounded and fleshy form preferred by the Olmecs.

above : 89. Tripod urn, Mexico, from Teotihuacán. A.D. 200–600. Painted clay, height 9 ³/₄″. Museum of Primitive Art, New York.

Olmec sculpture is noted for its rounded, plastic forms and the fleshy, pouting, baby-faced character of its figures (Fig. 88). Its influence was wide and easy to separate from the rather stiff art of many later cultures. The large stone head of La Venta is 8 feet high, but the Olmecs made many smaller carvings and hollow pottery figures.

The extensive ruins of Teotihuacán (c. 50 B.C.–A.D. 600), near modern Mexico City, reveal that, unlike La Venta, it was both a temple area and a large city. The elaborate building complex is dominated by the famous Pyramid of the Sun. Its many sculptured reliefs of a feathered serpent, which continued in other cultures, reveal that the temple's modern name is inaccurate. Teotihuacán pottery is unlike that in other areas. The favorite shape, a straight or slightly concave low cylinder on three raised legs, is metallic in concept (Fig. 89). The body is usually brown with incised or carved areas in red. Reflecting the stucco temple and pyramid decorations are a few rare pottery pieces covered with stucco and painted in red, yellow, white, blue-green, and black with stylized depictions of the gods, chiefly the rain god, Tlaloc. Small clay figurines with elaborate headdresses were also common. Some have movable arms and legs and might be children's toys.

South of Mexico City near present-day Oaxaca rises the large mountaintop temple complex of Monte Albán, built by the Zapotec culture. The Zapotecs inhabited Mexico at a very early date, but the high point of their civilization was reached between 200 and 800. They are noted for their immense stone pyramids, temples, and ball courts, and their sculptured terra cotta pots are of equal interest. Perhaps misnamed funerary urns, the earliest examples show a head modeled on a vase form. In time a full figure evolved, usually seated, with an oversize head and a slightly open mouth. The most striking feature of the urn reproduced in

Ceramics of the New World   49

above : 90. Zapotec urn, Mexico, from Oaxaca. c. A.D. 1000. Clay, height 14 ¼″. Museum of Primitive Art, New York.

right : 91. Mixtec xantile figure, Mexico, from Puebla. 1250–1500. Clay, height 23″. Museum of Primitive Art, New York.

Figure 90 is the elaborate feathered headdress of the god or chieftain portrayed.

By the year 900 the temple site of Monte Albán was largely abandoned, and during the following century much of the Zapotec territory was taken over by the invading Mixtecs from the North who built their own temple complex at Mitla. The popular Mixtec pottery forms were a rounded vase with long tripod legs and a bowl with a flared pedestal base. The decoration (repetitive geometric designs in yellow, brown, red, blue-gray, orange, and black slips) is reminiscent of Peruvian textile designs. The Mixtecs were skillful jewelers, and it is likely that much of the gold and jadework attributed to the later Aztecs was made by captive Mixtec craftsmen.

Indicative of this interest, their stiff potlike seated figurines, unlike the more plastic work of the Zapotecs, have a wealth of detail revealed in bracelets, sandals, earrings, and tattoo markings (Fig. 91).

The Mexican culture popularly known as Tarascan—located in the western states of Michoacán, Nayarit, Colima, Jalisco, and Guerrero—is unique in many respects. There are no temple areas that required an immense and serflike labor force for construction. Nor are there the fearsome gods who demanded continual human sacrifice to ensure ample crops. The pottery figurines were made for tombs and, like Chinese figures, were intended for companionship in the hereafter. They are the products of a relaxed and fun-loving people (Fig. 92).

50   Ceramics of the Past

Although regarded as good fighters and never defeated by the fearful Aztecs, the Tarascans were as apt to depict a ball player as a warrior in their ceramic sculptures (Pl. 4, p. 39).

While small fertility figurines with elaborate hairdos were made several centuries before Christ, most of the pottery figures that survive are dated between 800 and 1300. Most depict single figures, but dancing groups are not uncommon, and the round, pot-bellied dog is a favorite motif. Pottery vessels are often shaped like a gourd or a human figure or, at the very least, have sculptured additions. The Colima figures are distinctive for their rounded, plastic style, which imparts a feeling of energy and movement (Fig. 93). Details usually are added to the polished red clay body by incising. Nayarit pottery tends to emphasize a straight torso with rather thin, flat arms. The features are animated and expressive in caricature fashion (Fig. 94). The elaborate tattooing and costume are rendered in polychrome slip, which time has weathered to an attractive speckled surface (see Pl. 4). The Jalisco style is equally interesting but hard to define, since it has characteristics of both Colima and Nayarit (Fig. 95).

Perhaps the most advanced culture of Mesoamerica was the Mayan, located in the Yucatán Peninsula, Guatemala, and Honduras. This jungle region with its poor soil was an unlikely area for the development of what was perhaps the world's greatest stone-age civilization. Even today, hitherto unknown stone temples continue to be unearthed from the growth and debris of centuries. Exhaustion of the soil, with its porous limestone base, is thought to be responsible for the abandonment of old temple pyramids and the building of new ones in other areas. Of the early Mayan era (1500 B.C.–A.D. 317) little is known. Most of the sculpture and temples date from the classic period (A.D. 317–889).

Mayan art is serene and confident, as one might expect from a peaceful culture whose temple areas and cities display no fortifications. The priests also functioned as astronomers and astrologers, which explains in part the absence of the barbarism and excessive human sacrifice practiced by many other Mexican cultures. Both their calendar and their mathematical system, which used a zero, were a thousand years in advance of Europe. The small ceramic figures of the classic period are doubtless the most plastic and well articulated of the Americas (Fig. 96); they have a repose which has caused the Mayans to be called "the Greeks of the New World." Mayan pottery was simple in form, with straight-sided bowls and footed vessels showing, perhaps, a Teotihuacán influence. Decoration consisted of incised hieroglyphs or multicolored slip patterns and ceremonial figures similar to those in the temple murals (Fig. 97).

In the late ninth century the great temples at Copán, Quirigia, and Palenque were suddenly abandoned; some Mayans moved west, while others traveled farther east in the Yucatán Peninsula. In the following century much of the Mayan territory was invaded by the Toltecs, a warlike tribe from Tula, north of Mexico City (Fig. 98). The Mayan Chichén-Itzá was transformed into a new

left : 95. Jalisco effigy vessel, Mexico. A.D. 1–600. Clay, height 17½". Museum of Primitive Art, New York. The figurative and vase forms are skillfully combined.

below : 96. Maya figure, Central America. 900–1200. Terra cotta, height 14 ½". Museum of the American Indian, New York. The fluid, plastic modeling of this figure is characteristic of Mayan art.

above : 97. Maya jar, Guatemala. 600–900. Clay with polychrome decoration, height 5 $^7/_8$″. Museum of Primitive Art, New York. The motifs are reminiscent of temple murals.

above right: 98. Toltec funerary urn, Mexico, from Hidalgo. Clay, height 12 $^1/_8$″. Museum of Primitive Art, New York. This Toltec piece is typically grotesque.

right : 99. *Girl on a Swing,* Remojadas whistle toy, Mexico, from Veracruz. c. A.D. 750. Painted clay, height 9 $^3/_4$″. Museum of Primitive Art, New York. This delightful toy evokes the lighter, more tender aspects of Indian life.

and larger Tula. After 1200 Mayapán became the center of this merged Toltec and Mayan culture. After an initial upsurge, the arts and building skills deteriorated. Relative to the Mayan era, ceramics were crudely made. The new religion demanded captives for human sacrifice. Continual strife with neighboring groups led to the sack of Mayapán in the mid-fifteenth century, and in 1541 Yucatán fell, with little difficulty, to the Spaniards.

The gulf coast area near Veracruz is the site of several ancient civilizations. Of special interest is Remojadas ceramics, with its smiling faces and swinging dolls, which displays another aspect of the Indian cultures (Fig. 99). But there is little of *above*: 100. Aztec tripod vessel, Mexico, from Mexico City. 1327–1481. Clay, height 9 ¾″. Museum of Primitive Art, New York. Teotihuacán influence is evident in this bowl.

below: 101. Water bottle, Louisiana, from Ouachita Parish. 1300–1700. Gray burnished clay with incised decoration, height 5 ¾″. Museum of the American Indian, New York.

this lighthearted character to the Aztecs (Fig. 100). Like the Incas, they were a conquering, imperialistic power. The Aztecs were the last of a succession of warlike tribes who invaded the fertile valley of Mexico from the north. In 1168 they evicted the Toltecs from Tula and forced them to move south into Mayan territory. By intrigue and constant warfare, they soon controlled most of central Mexico. Like the Romans, they were builders of roads and aqueducts, efficient administrators and tax collectors. The much admired Aztec gold, jade, and featherwork were actually the products of captured Mixtec and Zapotec craftsmen. While their capital of Tenochtitlán, on the island of Lake Texcoco, was splendid with its temples, pyramids, palaces, and marketplaces, it festered underneath with the barbarism of the priesthood, whose continual demands for human sacrifice to the Aztec gods resulted in perpetual warfare. Without the eager help of the subjected tribes, the small group of Spaniards who arrived in 1519 would have been unable to overthrow the Aztecs.

North America

European settlers arriving in North America found the area thinly populated. The natives were primarily hunters and fishermen with a limited cultivation of indigenous vegetables. Corn, dispersed from the valley of Mexico, was grown by many tribes. The Mississippi Valley area was the site of several large earthen temple and burial mounds, perhaps influenced by the Mexican pyramids. The pottery of this region was a burnished black ware with incised scrolls and geometric patterns (Fig. 101).

A more advanced culture developed in the Southwest, above the Mexican border. The high point of this Pueblo culture dates from A.D. 800 to 1100. With extensive irrigation of crops and multistoried apartment dwellings, the settled life of the Pueblo Indians allowed more leisure time to develop crafts than did the nomadic ways of the tribes to the north. The Pueblo Indians were skillful weavers whose geometric designs were often reflected in their red, brown, black, and white slip-painted pottery (Fig. 102). The pottery of the nearby Mimbres Valley in

New Mexico was unlike that of the Pueblos in that the usual stylized, decorative patterns were combined with sensitive and realistic paintings of birds and animals (Fig. 103). The Casas Grandes culture to the south, in the Mexican state of Chihuahua, shows Mimbres characteristics, as well as a more southern influence in the shape of the effigy jars (Fig. 104).

The first pottery made in Colonial America was produced by the settlers of Jamestown in about 1611. Of this early ware, mentioned in *The True Travels of Captain John Smith*, nothing remains. Essex County in Massachusetts became a pottery center in mid-century; among its resident craftsmen in 1641 were John Pride and William Vinson of Salem. The first individual potters of record in New York were Derick Claesen in 1657 and Derick Benson and William Croylas in 1698. Historical reference is also made to a pottery located in Burlington, New Jersey, in 1684. It is no wonder that nothing of this early ware has survived, since it was a low-fire, lead-glazed pottery made for kitchen use. Not surprisingly, these immigrant potters carried on the old English slipware tradition in decorating their functional platters, pitchers, and jugs. The preferred style for teapots employed a brown-black glaze colored with manganese or dark Albany slip clay. When the red clay body was covered with a cream

above : 102. Pueblo pitcher, New Mexico. 1100–1400. Earthenware with painted black decoration over a white slip, height 6 ¾". Museum of the American Indian, New York.

left : 103. Mimbres bowl, New Mexico. c. 1100. Clay with stylized fish decoration in black over white slip, diameter 10 ½". Museum of Primitive Art, New York. Mimbres bowls were "killed" by having a hole punched in the bottom before they were buried with the dead.

below : 104. Cases Grandes bird effigy jar, Mexico. 1300–1450. Yellow clay with stylized decoration in black and red, height 6 ½". Museum of the American Indian, New York.

Ceramics of the New World   55

slip, the colorless lead glaze took on a yellow hue. Pennsylvania potters, reflecting their German background, usually combined a sgraffito technique with slip decoration for their popular tulip and other floral designs (Fig. 105).

Potters in England were experimenting with stoneware and higher-fire white ware bodies, and examples of this ware were exported to the New World, where they were much prized. It was natural, then, that the Colonial potter would attempt to reproduce the technique. The first native stoneware of record is that made by General James Morgan at Madison, New Jersey, in 1775. Due to the abundant supplies of good stoneware clays in New York and New Jersey, this region took the lead as the higher-fire ware gradually supplanted red ware.

The first known pottery produced west of the Alleghenies was made in 1784 at Morgantown, West Virginia. This early red ware was cumbersome and fragile, so potters gradually moved westward in search of new clay deposits and better methods of transportation. A pottery was operating in Detroit as early as 1820; in Ripley, Illinois, in 1836; and in Sargents Bluff, Iowa, in 1838. However, it was along the Ohio River, where there were good deposits of stoneware clays and water transportation was available, that the major potteries developed. Stoneware potteries had been established in Steubenville, Zanesville, East Liverpool, and Cincinnati, which in time supplied a large part of the Middle West and the area along the Mississippi River as far south as New Orleans with its needs of crocks, jugs, dishes, and platters.

Although there were red ware potteries in the South, the plantation philosophy never encouraged them to compete with the imported ware desired by the wealthier classes. These small family-owned and isolated mountain potteries have continued to this day, producing simple lead-glazed ware for local sale, although in recent years the tourist trade has provided the major outlet.

The Colonial red ware and much of later stoneware were coarse in body and hand thrown. In an effort to compete with the imported ware, American potters gradually developed a finer body, termed *brown ware*. It was actually a cream- or buff-colored

above: 105. DAVID SPINNER, U.S.A., Bucks County, Pa. Pie plate. c. 1800. Red earthenware with sgraffito decoration. Brooklyn Museum (gift of Mrs. Huldah Cail Lorimer in memory of George Burford Lorimer).

below: 106. D. GOODALE, U.S.A., Hartford, Conn. Jug. 1818–30. Salt-glazed stoneware with incised American eagle decoration, accented with cobalt; height 15″. Brooklyn Museum (gift of Arthur W. Clement).

earthenware with a lead or alkaline glaze, higher fired than the old earthenware, but not vitrified like the stoneware. After about 1830 brown ware supplanted the earlier red ware, and stoneware, usually salt glazed, was used only for the more utilitarian jugs and crocks (Fig. 106). This development marks the transitional stage between hand-thrown pottery and that which was mechanically produced by jiggering, press molds, and, later, slip casting.

Although there were regional variations, early nineteenth-century American potters generally followed the lead of the English potters who first developed mass-production techniques. Unfortunately, not only the methods were copied, but also the form and decoration. The latter had in turn been inappropriately lifted from Baroque and Classical models. It is interesting to conjecture about the direction American pottery might have taken had it not been continually subjected to a flood of imported styles which, however technically competent, were of little esthetic merit.

Perhaps no pottery better illustrates the trend during the late eighteenth and nineteenth centuries than that of Bennington, Vermont. Founded in 1793 by Captain John Norton, a Massachusetts potter,

the Bennington pottery first produced red ware and, later, under Norton's sons, Luman and John, a yellow ware in imitation of the English "Queen's Ware" and a utilitarian stoneware. The pottery continued for three more generations until 1894. The greatest innovator in the firm was Christopher W. Fenton, brother-in-law of Julius Norton (a grandson of the founder). Fenton became a partner in 1844, then separated from the firm in 1848 and operated his own pottery in Bennington until 1858. Perhaps the best-known ware produced by Bennington was the mottled brown-glazed cream ware called Rockingham (Fig. 107). Although it originated in England, it became more popular in America and was produced everywhere, from New York through the Middle West, during the second half of the century. By employing English potters such as Daniel Greatback, and by constant experimentation, Fenton was able to duplicate most of the imported English ware. A Parian ware, copied after that of the English firms of Minton and Copeland, used a semisoft bisque porcelain for figurines, as well as for pitchers and vases with elaborately modeled figures and floral decorations (Fig. 108). Many of these pieces had a blue slip background, an

right : 107. Salamander Works, U.S.A.,Woodbridge, N. J. Hound-handled pitcher. c. 1845. Brown-glazed Rockingham cream ware. Brooklyn Museum (gift of Arthur W. Clement).

far right : 108. United States Pottery, U.S.A., Bennington, Vt. Pitcher. 1852–58. Parian porcelain in "Paul and Virginia" design (copied from Wedgwood), with Jasper technique. Brooklyn Museum (gift of Arthur W. Clement).

obvious imitation of Wedgwood jasper ware. Other innovations included the "croddle ware," made of different colored clays to give a marbled appearance, and the "Patent Flint Enamel," in which wet glaze was peppered with different coloring oxides to give a multicolored mottled effect. The Bennington styles were widely copied and, with the English imports, spread the Victorian gospel of elaborate and arbitrary decoration. For a frontier people striving for middle-class values it had a stifling influence from which American ceramics is still suffering.

The first known white ware dates from 1738 and was made in Savannah, Georgia, by the Philadelphia potter, Andrew Duché, who used local kaolin clays. Although this preceded the discovery of china clay in England, the pottery was unsuccessful, as were many early experiments conducted by other potters. The first true porcelain was made in 1826 by the short-lived Jersey Porcelain and Earthenware Company. In all these ventures American potters had difficulty competing with imported ware, which the public deemed superior (as indeed it often was). Occupying a position between the frail and somewhat heavy cream ware and expensive bone china and porcelain was a new white body, called variously ironstone, white granite, or stone china, developed early in the nineteenth century by the English Staffordshire potters. The names reflect the quality of hardness and durability of the new body, which was essentially a high-fire white earthenware with sufficient additions of Cornwall stone, feldspar, or powdered iron foundry slag to enable it to fuse into a body resembling porcelain but fired at lower temperatures. Most of the English ware was highly decorated in Chinese or Japanese motifs, often by the new engraved print transfer process. But exports to America were generally plain white or had a simple striped decoration, similar to the white granite ware commonly made in the United States after 1850. This body was the forerunner of modern "hotel china," and much American dinnerware today is of the same character. It was not until some years after the upheaval of the Civil War that commercially successful porcelain or vitrified china was made, first in Trenton, New Jersey, and soon after in Syracuse, New York, and East Liverpool,

Ohio. But such was the appeal of the imported item, even though no longer superior, that it was not until 1918 that the White House bought, from Lenox, Inc., its first domestic porcelain.

The industrialization of American potteries to meet the competition of mass-produced foreign imports was inevitable (see Chap. 10). As elsewhere in the world, it interrupted the age-old patterns of internal growth and change, since design decisions were now placed in the hands of a managerial entrepreneur, whose major interest was to produce a profit. The increasing use of plaster of paris for models and molds was not bad in itself, but it usually led to the copying of forms intended for metal, wood, or basketry. For the hand potter economical considerations had had the effect of limiting elaborate and fussy decoration. But once a model in plaster was made, the most intricate form could be reproduced by the press or slip-cast process. Fashion set the day, and the taste of the socially aspiring new bourgeoisie was for a conspicuous display of their recently acquired material wealth.

KOREAN CERAMICS

The ceramics of Korea and Japan are historically related to that of China. However, since both of these styles have had a great influence on modern potters, it is fitting that they should be considered as a prelude to our discussion of contemporary ceramics. While Korea is geographically adjacent to China, the mountainous character of the land enabled Korea to evade direct Chinese control and so develop its individuality, although Chinese influence has always been present.

After a period in which only crude, round-bottomed ware was produced, an earthenware with combed patterns and later a red burnished ware developed during the pre-Christian era. Three small kingdoms arose: Koguryo (c. 37 B.C.–A.D. 668) in the North, partially controlled by, and in continual conflict with, Han China; Paekche (c. 18 B.C.–A.D. 668) in the Southwest, which provided the contact between China and Japan; and Silla (c. 57 B.C.–A.D. 935), which was the most independent and typically Korean of the three.

Koguryo pottery shows continual Chinese influence. The ceramics of the Paekche kingdom—a red polished earthenware, a glazed earthenware, and a gray stoneware—also reflects Han influences in form, glaze, and occasionally in the pressed mat decoration. Silla gray or reddish stoneware was fired at a higher temperature and, though unglazed, developed a glazelike surface from the free ash in the kiln. A large bowl or covered jar set on a high foot with rectangular cutouts was a popular shape (Fig. 109). Incised geometric patterns were also common during this early period. The tomb mounds of the Silla Dynasty contain terra cotta sculptures, but they differ from those made in Han China. Of particular interest are the horse-and-rider figures, which have a strange archaic quality. They are too dignified to be comic, yet they have a droll air.

Buddhism was introduced to Korea in the fourth century, and by the seventh century it had become the dominant religion. Funerary customs changed from burial to cremation. The urns used for ashes were low, footed vases, with swelling shoulders, short collar rims, and low covers. The decoration was pressed rather than incised as in the earlier style. Because the vases were wheel thrown, the pressed motifs of circular and angular patterns were of a banded nature. In 668 Korea was united for the first time, when the entire area came under Silla rule. The yellow-brown and green glazes used thereafter were doubtless due to the Koguryo influence.

The porcelains and celadons of the Chinese Sung Dynasty made a tremendous impression on nearby Korea. As a result of this influence the Koryo Period (918–1392) represents the high point of Korean ceramic art. The tenth century brought a gradual change from the gray stoneware to a crude celadon. During the next century Sung forms and glazes were widely copied, but by the twelfth century unique Korean variations evolved. The blue-green hue of celadon, which is typically Korean, became common, as did an inlayed decoration called *mishima* (Fig 110). Chinese brushed decoration, often floral, was used in a white or black slip

above : 109. Covered stem cup, Korea. Early Silla Period, after A.D. 668. Stoneware with olive-green glaze, height 9 ¼″. Seattle Art Museum (Eugene Fuller Memorial Collection).

right : 110. *Sanggam* bowl, Korea. Koryo Period, 14th century. Porcelain with inlayed mishima decoration under pale celadon glaze, diameter 7 ¾″. Seattle Art Museum (Eugene Fuller Memorial Collection).

with a red iron or copper oxide under the celadon glaze. The latter, when reduced, produced a reddish or plum-colored glaze. The prunus vase, derived from the Chinese T'zu-Chou, was a popular form, which, when adapted to the fuller curve of the Korean style, took on more graceful proportions. More elaborate were the lobed vases, wine pots, and ewers derived from the melon form and the wine cups patterned after the lotus bud. Footed dishes similar to the Chinese T'ing porcelains, with their delicately incised floral patterns, were made, but in Korea mishima techniques were used.

Like China and the Middle East, Korea was upset by the Mongol invasions. The Korean capitol, Seoul, and most of Korea, was occupied from 1231 to 1260. Independence came again under the Yi Dynasty (1392–1910), which must be divided into two periods separated by the invasion (1592–98) of the Japanese warlord, Hideyoshi. Although pottery making prospered during the early Yi period, it had lost the delicate craftsmanship of the Koryo potter. The forms were heavier, and the celadon color deteriorated, because the firing of the kilns was not carefully controlled. However, the production of porcelain, which began in the late Koryo era, was widespread. Whenever possible, stamped patterns replaced hand incising in the inlayed mishima, which inevitably led to a rather mechanical style. More successful were the slip-covered wine bottles, which were incised in a vigorous floral sgraffito style.

The invasion by Hideyoshi was a great blow to the Korean ceramic industry. Many kilns were destroyed, and a number of potters were taken to Japan. Celadon production ceased after the invasion, and porcelain, decorated in Ming blue and white, became the major style. More Korean in character and more satisfying were the porcelain and stoneware bowls and vases with free brush decoration in an underglaze of iron brown and copper red. Japanese influence became stronger, and, after victorious wars against China (1894–95) and Russia (1904–05), Korea was annexed in 1910. Korea was free again in 1945, but, with rapid communications and trade, it is doubtful that Korea (or any modern nation) can ever again develop a truly unique and national character in her ceramics.

JAPANESE CERAMICS

The islands of Japan, stretching in thousand-mile arc from Korea to Siberia, were in prehistoric times joined to the mainland. The Ainu aborigines of northern Hokkaido are descendents of the original inhabitants, but the vast majority of Japanese are of ancient Korean and Chinese stock, which, over a long period, migrated from the south and by the fourth century B.C. occupied all the islands except Hokkaido.

The pottery of the early Jomon Period, which lasted until about 250 B.C., was characterized by an overall decoration of cord impressions or by incised and applied clay strips in vigorous patterns of abstract angular and circular motifs. In addition to simple cooking and storage pots, there were spouted vessels, incense burners, and effigy figures. Accompanying this ware is a group of strange, cord-marked figurines. Some are small, intended perhaps as charms (Fig. 111). Others are larger (up to 20 inches in height) and are modeled around a hollow core.

111. Head of a Dogu, Japan, probably from Kamegaoka. Jomon Period (c. 100 B.C.–A.D. 100). Clay, height 2″. Seattle Art Museum (Eugene Fuller Memorial Collection).

right : 112. *Haniwa* warrior, Japan, from Ota-Shi. Late Haniwa period. A.D. 6th century. Clay, height 4′6″. Seattle Art Museum (Eugene Fuller Memorial Collection).

Although made over a span of several thousand years, they are all of a type, with heavy, widespread legs, rudimentary arms, and flat, upturned faces with goggle eyes. Most of the pieces have been found in the northern section of Honshu. Those from the south have less of the almost frenzied detail of costume and hairdo. Perhaps reflecting outside influences they are more plastic and naturalistic in concept.

The Jomon Period was a time of stagnation and of isolation from the many cultural advances occurring on the mainland. But pressure from an expanding China encouraged migration into Japan from Korea. In the second century B.C. the tempo of life changed, as primitive Japan moved into the bronze and iron ages. A significant factor in Japan's progress was the introduction of rice growing, for food gathering and fishing had provided a rather precarious existence. The pottery of the Yayoi Period (c. 250 B.C.–A.D. 250) was, unlike the Jomon ware, simple in form, thinner, and higher fired. Much of the change was doubtless due to the introduction of the potter's wheel. The clay body had a light brown color and was occasionally painted in a red design, but shallow incised geometric bands were the more common decoration. The popular vase form—a small flared base and a full, rounded midsection which contracts and then expands into the rim— relied more upon its graceful shape than upon decoration for effect. The form reminds one somewhat of certain Han vases. These pieces are definitely not the work of a primitive people but reveal the influence of a long ceramic tradition.

The increase in population and agricultural prosperity can be seen in the appearance of huge burial mounds. That of the Emperor Nintoku (A.D. fifth century) near Osaka was 1574 feet in length and 114 feet high. Of special interest to the potter are the rows of terra cotta figures called *Haniwa*, which encircled the crest of the burial mound. The earliest Haniwa were simple clay cylinders about 2 or 3 feet in height. These were probably derived from libation urns and funeral pottery traditionally placed in or upon graves. In time they evolved into guardian figures. The fact that hundreds or even thousands of such figures might be required for a single grave led to a simplified technique. Often a round head on a cylinder, with quickly cut holes for eyes and mouth, sufficed. More elaborate were the warrior figures in padded armor and skillfully carved helmets (Fig. 112). Most of these are about 3 feet tall, but the largest are almost life size. Another favorite subject was the horse, which was a prestige symbol (Fig. 113). Costumed ladies were not neglected, nor were dogs, birds, domestic animals, and even house models. What has impressed today's sculptor is the extreme simplicity of form of the Haniwa figurines, which creates a greater impact than would a more realistic interpretation. The competition between local rulers in the construction of the huge tomb mounds was a drain on the local economy and may have been a factor in the transition to the Buddhist rites of cremation. After a short period the Haniwa figures were no longer made, and the old tomb mounds were overgrown and forgotten.

During the late Haniwa Period (c. 400–552) many Koreans migrated to Kyushu from the Paekche kingdom, perhaps because of wars with Silla. Among them were potters who began to make a gray stoneware that was much harder than the Japanese earthenware. The greater heat was achieved by using a long, single-chambered kiln built on a sloping hillside. Called an *ana-gama* kiln,

above : 113. *Haniwa* horse, Japan. Haniwa Period (A.D. 200–552). Clay, height 26 ½″. Seattle Art Museum (Eugene Fuller Memorial Collection). This horse, like most Haniwa figures, is constructed in simple, tubular form.

below : 114. Medicine jar, Japan. Nara Period, Tempyo Era (710–94). Sue ware, height 9 ¾″. Seattle Art Museum (Eugene Fuller Memorial Collection).

it was the predecessor of the multichambered climbing kiln still used in Japan today. The new ware, called *Sue*, was similar to the Korean forms of the period and used a green, runny ash glaze (Fig. 114).

Continual contacts with China led to the adoption not only of new materials and techniques but also of philosophy, religion, and the use of Chinese characters to express the Japanese language. Along with Buddhism came the influence of Indian temple and pagoda styles and Indian religious sculpture —together with their Chinese variations—which were gradually absorbed into Japanese traditions. During this period of cultural exchange, the Japanese capital was located first at Asuka (552–646) and subsequently at Nara (646–794). Due perhaps to this early stimulation, the Nara-Kyoto area remained a major artistic center through the centuries. Chinese influence continued during the following Early Heian Period (794–898), when the capital moved to Heian-kyo (modern Kyoto). T'ang-influenced pottery was made in the typical two- and three-color lead-glazed ware, as well as in the older Sue style.

At the beginning of the Late Heian Period (898–1185) contacts with China were cut off due to political turmoil in the closing years of the T'ang Dynasty. This was a period of introspection for the Japanese, during which the many Chinese influences were digested and revised to suit the Japanese temperament. It was an age of great temple building, for an accommodation was made between the older Shinto faith and Buddhism. Painting and literature prospered, but the growth of pottery making was hampered by the amazing quality and variety of the lacquer ware, which, among wealthy Japanese, inspired the same high regard that the Chinese accorded their fine porcelains and celadons.

During the Kamakura Period (1185–1333), named after the site of the new capital near modern Tokyo, contacts were renewed with China. The latter was at the height of the great Sung Dynasty, regarded as the golden age of Chinese ceramics, and the pottery that was imported into Japan had a lasting effect upon Japanese ceramic art. Seto, near the old centers of Nara and Kyoto, became and remained a major pottery center. An effort was made to reproduce the Korean and Chinese celadons, and a greater variety of forms were created than in earlier periods: vases, bottles, pitchers, tea bowls, and incense burners. Incised and impressed designs in bold floral patterns characterize the Kamakura ware.

Perhaps more important to the later philosophy of ceramics was the growing influence of Zen Buddhism and its connection with the uniquely Japanese cult of the *tea ceremony*. As originally practiced by the Zen monks, it was merely a pause in a long period of religious meditation during which a cup of tea was served. Gradually it became a standardized ritual, first among the monks and a few members of the ruling family, then among the Samurai warrior class, and finally expanding to include the wealthy merchant class. The origin of the tea ceremony is officially dated in the Muromachi Period (1392–1573), but it was formalized during the Momoyama Period (1573–1615). Eventually all Japanese claiming to be cultured participated in the tea ceremony.

The character of the tea ceremony stresses simplicity and thoughtful contemplation. It is held in a small room or in a simple structure in a garden, for no more than four or five persons are involved. The room is bare except for the tea utensils and a slight alcove, which may contain a small wall painting or a vase with perhaps a single flower. The importance of the tea ceremony to the potter lies in the fact that, apart from an iron kettle and an occasional lacquer piece, all of the tea paraphernalia is ceramic. The prescribed accouterments include, first, the tea bowls and the jar in which the powdered tea is kept, then the large water jars and bowls for washing, and finally the trays or cake dishes.

As the tea master prepares each bowl individually by beating the powdered tea into a froth with a bamboo whisk, the guests are expected to make appreciative comments upon the beauty of the pottery, the artistry of the flower arrangement, or the substance of the poem that usually accompanies the wall painting. At first rare Chinese celadon and temmoku tea bowls were used, and a cult of extravagance arose. But many tea masters preferred the simple strength and directness of the Korean ware over the sophisticated Sung porcelains. Given this philosophy, it was only a matter of time before the common pottery used by the peasant would be prized for its naturalness, the asymmetrical quality of its freely thrown form, and the uneven run of a thickly applied glaze. This predilection for an unbalanced design is an underlying characteristic of Japanese painting, prints, house and garden design, and, of course, ceramics. Japanese woodcuts had great influence on Western painters of the Impressionist school, and Japanese ceramics has had a similar effect upon Western potters in recent years.

Partly to fulfill the demands of the tea ceremony, the Seto kilns improved the quality of their traditional yellow and black glazes (Fig 115). The nearby Mino kilns produced the Shino and Oribe pottery, which was especially prized by the tea masters for its free and colorful brush decorations (Figs 116–118). Also popular was Karatsu ware, produced by immigrant Koreans in northwest Kyushu, who used their native forms but combined them with a typically Japanese brush decoration. In their search for the simple and unaffected, the tea masters discovered several isolated potteries producing a functional ware for the local trade, oblivious to the foreign celadons and porcelains. One such center

above : 115. Bowl, Japan. Momoyama Period (1573–1615). Yellow Seto ware with green decoration, diameter 6 ³/₈″. Seattle Art Museum (Eugene Fuller Memorial Collection).

below : 116. Cake plate, Japan. Momoyama Period (1573–1615). Nezumi-shino stoneware with gray glaze over mishima slip decoration in "wind-blown grasses" design, length 9″. Seattle Art Museum (gift of Mrs. John C. Atwood, Jr.).

was Bizen near Okayama, which made an unglazed pottery in the old Sue tradition. Accidental and random markings characterize this style, for the vessels were wrapped in a salt-soaked straw prior to firing. An even more primitive pottery was made on the shores of eastern Honshu at Iga and Shigaraki. The coarse clay used was suitable only for larger containers. The clay body of the Iga ware was poorly prepared, with the result that the usual green glaze is pitted and scarred from impurities and often sags out of shape. The Shigaraki also was often carelessly thrown. Its incised banded patterns and thin runny ash glaze are hardly noticed due to the pitted surface and the blotchy red and black discoloration from the kiln fire.

Many of these old Shigaraki and Iga pots, as well as the more skillfully made ware from Bizen and Tokoname, are now in museums or are highly *right :* 117. Cake plate, Japan. Momoyama Period (1573–1615). Oribe stoneware with green glaze over brown slip decoration in "half-submerged wheels" design, 7 ³/₄ × 8″. Seattle Art Museum (Eugene Fuller Memorial Collection).

treasured by individual owners. By technical standards—perfection of thrown form, quality of decoration, understanding of clay bodies, and glaze and firing skills—most old Iga and Shigaraki pots are inept and poorly made. But within the context of the philosophy of the tea ceremony they take on those qualities that we find interesting in a beach pebble or a weathered piece of driftwood, and they inspire, as it were, the respect accorded natural beauty, without the critical judgment we reserve for man-made objects. This esthetic has had considerable influence upon the contemporary potter, whether he is aware of it or not. For the most part, it has been beneficial, for it is all too easy to admire a skillful technique which might, in fact, be rather sterile. However, the influence can be destructive if nothing remains of the potter's art but the "accidental effect" so that the material itself becomes all important.

Of course, all Japanese were not satisfied with the more austere ware of the tea ceremony. As trade increased Korean Yi and Chinese Ming porcelains were greatly admired and sought after. In 1616 a Korean potter working for Lord Nabeshima discovered a kaolin clay, essential for making porcelain, near Arita in northern Kyushu. Within a few years this area, with its many Korean potters, became a center of the Japanese porcelain industry. Generally termed Imari ware, the porcelains were made first in the Korean blue-and-white style, but later the Chinese spirit prevailed, with the usual subject matter of landscapes, flowers, birds, and figures. The Westerner usually associates the term Imari with the garish multicolored enameled porcelain later exported in great quantity to Europe and related in character to the Chinese Ch'ing enamels.

Of finer quality were the Kakiemon and Nabeshima porcelains, which were each produced in a single workshop. The Kakiemon enameled ware was in the Chinese style, but the color and painting was done with more restraint and a greater feeling

118. Teapot, Japan. Momoyama Period (1573–1615). Oribe stoneware with green and transparent glazes over brown slip decoration in tortoise-shell design, height 7 ⁵/₈″. Seattle Art Museum (Eugene Fuller Memorial Collection).

Japanese Ceramics   65

of openness (Fig. 119). Nabeshima porcelains (Fig. 120) were, like the Kakiemon, more delicate than the usual Imari ware, but decorated in a more Japanese fashion with motifs from textile designs or landscapes in the Kano manner. Kutani, on the west coast of Japan near Kanazawa, was the site of another early porcelain kiln (c. 1660). Kutani ware is heavier and more vigorous than most Japanese porcelains, and the brushed decorations of birds, fruit, and landscapes are boldly executed in darker tones of green, blue, yellow, and a blackish purple, quite unlike the Imari style.

For the most part, porcelain followed the tradition of the imported wares, and, while of great commercial importance, it does not quite reflect the unique quality of Japanese artistic feeling as does the pottery. For example, there is no place of honor in the tea ceremony for the highly decorated tea bowl. Even more appropriate to the tea ceremony than the Karatsu stoneware was raku ware (see p. 216). It is thought to have been made first by an immigrant from Korea who settled in Kyoto and married a Japanese woman. Raku ware is particularly suited to the Zen philosophy, since the typical

above : 119. Plate, Japan. Edo Period (1615–1868). Kakiemon ware porcelain with floral design, diameter 7 $^3/_8$. Seattle Art Museum (Eugene Fuller Memorial Collection).

below : 120. Teapot, Japan. Edo Period, mid-18th century. Nabeshima ware porcelain with pale celadon glaze in "plum blossoms and buds" design, height 6″. Seattle Art Museum (gift of Mrs. Charles E. Stuart).

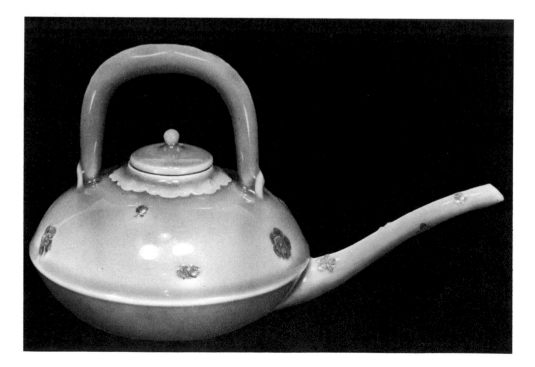

bowls are formed of a coarse clay (Fig. 121). The importance of the accidental effect, the irregularities of the rim and form, plus the runny, uneven quality of the glaze, give it a natural charm, while the insulating quality of the porous body makes it a perfect container for hot tea (see Pl. 5, p. 40).

The first raku potter's son, Chajiro (1515–92), made tea ware for the famous tea master Sen-no-Rikyu, and so began a line that lasted into the twentieth century, for the thirteenth of the line, Seinu Kaju, died in 1944. In sixteenth-century Japan, as in other cultures, pottery began to be signed by the maker. Because of the association with the tea ceremony, many cultivated Japanese began making pottery as a sort of hobby, much as the calligrapher and painter also wrote poetry. One such educated tea devotee was Honami Koetsu, who became friendly with the third raku potter, Doniu.

Best known of historical Japanese potters is Ogata Kenzan (1663–1743), who was distantly related to Koetsu and much influenced by him as well as by his older brother, Ogata Korin, a famous painter. Kenzan was not so much a potter as a painter and decorator of pottery. Trained as a calligrapher and painter, he evolved a highly personal style which was characteristically Japanese in its color and brushwork (Figs. 122–123). More than two centuries later, in 1911, the English potter, Bernard Leach, then a young painter in Tokyo, studied pottery with the sixth Kenzan. Through his work, his many students, and his writings, Leach is largely responsible for the present interest in Japanese and Korean ceramics.

top : 121. DONYU, Japan. *Tamamushi (Golden Beetle),* tea bowl. Early Edo Period, 17th century. Black raku earthenware with lead glaze, diameter 5″. Seattle Art Museum (gift of Dr. Masatoshi Okochi).

center : 122. OGATA KENZAN, Japan. *Bellflowers,* fan-shape cake tray. Edo Period, 18th century. Stoneware with enameled decoration on cream-colored glaze, length of sides 6 ⁵/₈″. Seattle Art Museum (Eugene Fuller Memorial Collection).

right : 123. OGATA KENZAN, Japan. *Camellia,* cake tray (one of a set of four). Edo Period, 18th century. Stoneware with creamy transparent glaze over brown slip, 5 ³/₄″ square. Seattle Art Museum (Eugene Fuller Memorial Collection).

3 Contemporary Ceramics

Potters in Europe,
the Far East,
and North America

For the past fifty years there has been a slow but steady growth of public interest in ceramics and in the actual craft of pottery making. Contemporary potters whose work is illustrated in this text comprise a rather mixed group, both in background and in goals. A very few grew up in pottery communities and early accepted ceramics as a natural life occupation. Most contemporary potters, however, drifted into ceramics after training in other fields. Many have attended various art and craft schools, but in most cases they studied, originally, painting or sculpture. Some art school graduates have served as apprentices in small hand potteries.

Much of the variety and strength of contemporary ceramics doubtless lies in the diverse backgrounds of these practitioners. The initial lack of skill and knowledge has proved to be a great handicap to some, for traditional workshop training teaches the beginning potter how to avoid many pitfalls. On the other hand, this very absence of systematic instruction has often led to greater vitality and experimentation.

Modern ceramics is tremendously varied. Though its diversity is, perhaps, not greater than in the past, it is remarkable in that everything is happening all at once, not over a span of milleniums. The ease of travel and the proliferation of visual materials have made the contemporary potter decidedly eclectic. We have in ceramics today an international school much like that of painting, and the great body of work that it produces is very stimulating. Variations of form and decoration are infinite, and these variations may be compared to the words in a dictionary, which, lifeless in themselves, can be combined to make a beautiful poem. It is how they are put together that matters. Not having grown up in a pottery tradition, the ceramist of today must learn both from the past and from his fellow potters in order to develop a dictionary of forms from which to select the nuances that reflect his own feelings. The student cannot help but lean

opposite : 124. ROBERT TURNER, U.S.A. Vase. 1968. Stoneware with speckled blue and cinnamon glazes, height 24″. The contemporary potter seeks the unusual form, contrasts of texture and color, and even the runny quality of a glaze.

above : 125. NORMAN SCHULMAN, U.S.A. Teapot. Red stoneware with cone-9 barium mat glaze. The pulled handle adds an individual touch to this rounded, functional teapot.

below : 126. DONALD FRITH, U.S.A. Covered jar. Stoneware with sgraffito decoration through light slip. Although this graceful jar can obviously serve as a container, its form and details would suggest a more decorative function.

upon others until the time when his own personality dictates a direction.

The explosion of communications today has made it difficult to categorize the potters of the several countries discussed in this chapter as being of specific national groups in the sense of their having distinct regional styles or similar methods of working. On the contrary, a modern ceramist may have more in common with a craftsman in another country than with the potter down the street.

Exhibitions and magazine articles to the contrary, the largest group of potters still follows what might be called the *traditional* style and produces a functional pottery (Fig. 125). Most of them cannot quite be classed with the old folk potter, since their ware is made for a rather sophisticated group. The desire to possess and to use an object bearing the imaginative touch of the human hand represents a natural reaction against the sterility of industrially produced products, and this is responsible for the recent widespread interest in all the crafts. The work of the second group of potters is what we might call *decorative* and indicates a direction that has also been with us through the ages (Fig. 126). Although derived from a functional form, often the size, decoration, or delicacy of a piece makes practical use unlikely. There is a fine line dividing the two groups, for, ideally, all functional ware should have a certain refinement of form and decoration. However, many would consider the extremely decorative ware to be decadent and not a desirable trend.

One phenomenon that is attracting much attention on the contemporary scene is what might be termed *nonpot* ceramics. Although occasionally reflecting a potlike origin, these works generally stress abstract form and the textural qualities of clay. They are as unrelated to the more traditional ceramic sculpture as the work of David Smith differs from that of Donatello. The so-called *pop-pots*, as well as the nonpots, depend not on form but on rather literary ideas or on an incongruous assembly of shapes made simply for effectiveness (Figs. 127–128). They are more closely related to a revived Dada movement than to any area of ceramics.

Many potters today hold teaching positions, and this has naturally had an effect upon their work.

There is no fast rule, but, in general, potters in crafts or ceramic schools tend to be more traditional; those in art schools often compete with their avant-garde colleagues in painting and sculpture, and, as a result, their work is usually more experimental and influenced less by pottery traditions than by new developments in painting and sculpture.

There is a much smaller group of potters oriented toward industrial design. Ideally, these designers ought to combine some of the talents and experience of the hand potters with a knowledge of production techniques. The management of industrial plants plays a key role in establishing a balance between handcraftsmanship and technology. Only in the Scandinavian countries has it been a common policy to have a design staff composed of creative potters. Since designs do not have the patent protection accorded mechanical devices, American factories have long been content to copy imported patterns and to steal designs from each other. European porcelain factories have always copied from the Chinese, so it is not really shocking to learn that the Japanese do the same with current Scandinavian designs. Unfortunately, this situation has discouraged many able potters and students from entering the industrial design field.

ENGLAND

The commercial success of industrialized ceramics in late eighteenth- and nineteenth-century England caused the demise of the English hand pottery. The few hand potteries that remained in the twentieth century survived in rural areas and specialized in making flowerpots and crocks for the local trade. The prevailing Victorian taste saw little merit in the special qualities of a hand-thrown piece when mechanically perfect ware was available in unlimited quantities and at very low cost.

The writings of John Ruskin and the efforts of William Morris and his followers to revive traditions of integrity in materials, design, and workmanship were based on a romantic idea that would ultimately fail. However, these men did bring into focus the dissatisfaction of late nineteenth-century England with the poor quality of its contemporary design. The Art Nouveau movement of the 1890s and early 1900s in England and France and the *Jugendstil* in Germany had quite different goals, but both were a reaction against the prevailing criteria of worn-out academic design. Meanwhile, isolated experiments were being carried out by potters such as Theodore Deck, Ernest Chaplet, and Auguste Delaherche in France, and the Martin brothers and William de Morgan in England, who sought to rediscover some of the lost pottery secrets of an earlier era. At first interest centered primarily on decorative techniques, such as the Islamic luster ware, and later on glazes, such as the Chinese sang-de-boeuf. The Victorian taste for the more ornate wares of the Ch'ing Dynasty slowly changed to an appreciation of classical Sung pottery, as well as that of Korea and Japan. It is ironic that while Western industrialism was undermining the ancient

Oriental manner of life, it was simultaneously beginning to adopt an Eastern esthetic philosophy.

The work and teachings of William Staite Murray (1881–1962) and Bernard Leach (1887–   ) were significant in the revival of English pottery after World War I. Although they had much in common, they held divergent views about the direction ceramics ought to take. Murray was more committed to the unique one-of-a-kind piece, whereas Leach advocated a cooperative workshop approach aimed at producing functional ware at a reasonable price, with only an occasional "show" piece. These differences of opinion are easily understandable, for while both men came from an art school background, their later experiences were quite different. Having studied at the Camberwell School of Art, Murray, after World War I, set up his own workshop, where he experimented with glazes and firing techniques. He is reputed to have built the first studio-size oil-burning kiln in England. Contacts at St. Ives with Shoji Hamada may have influenced Murray toward a looser style. His characteristic pieces are large bottles and vase forms, dynamic and freely thrown, with a vigorous decoration. Murray spent the last part of his life in Africa, but his influence has been continued by the students he taught at the Royal College of Art from 1925 to 1939. Among these were Heber Mathews, Henry Hammond, Constance Dunn, and Sam Haile.

After returning to England from Japan in 1920, accompanied by his friend Hamada, Bernard Leach established a pottery at St. Ives in Cornwall. Here he encountered the usual problems of building a kiln and becoming accustomed to the local clays and materials. Early sales in England were disappointing, but pots shipped to and sold in Japan provided an income. Sensitive as he was to all the persuasive strength of tradition of the Oriental potter, it was natural that Leach would seek his own identity as a European. Even while in Japan he had experimented with early English slipware techniques (Fig. 129). These were continued at St. Ives with

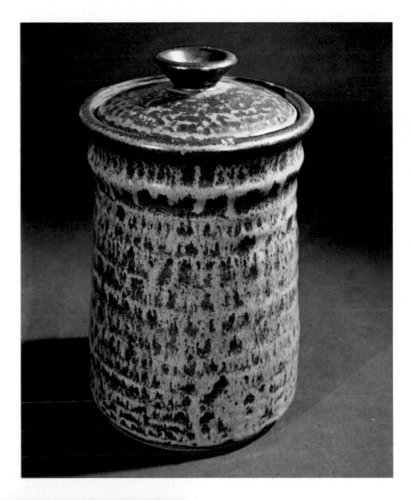

right : Plate 6. VICKI READ, England. Covered jar. Stoneware with elmwood ash glaze over red iron slip, height 9 ½″.

below : Plate 7. GEOFFREY WHITING, England. Teapot. Stoneware with carved decoration and semimat wood-ash glaze, fired in saggers in coal-burning and wood-burning kiln.

opposite : Plate 8. JOHNNY ROLF, Holland. *The Japanese Gardener.* Slab-built stoneware, partially glazed; height 15″.

above left : 130. BERNARD LEACH, England. Vase. 1931. Stoneware with brushed fish decoration in brown, height 14″. Victoria & Albert Museum, London. The influence of oriental design in Leach's work is reflected in this vase.

above center : 131. MICHAEL CARDEW, England. Covered jar. Stoneware with incised decoration.

above right : 132. HARRY DAVIS, England. Jar. Stoneware with wax resist and oxide decoration.

greater intensity, and most early work at St. Ives was in this vein. Later, medieval ware, such as the forceful Cistercian pitchers, exerted a greater influence on his work, and production was changed to stoneware (Fig. 130). To this day medieval English and Korean ware, rather than Japanese, have been the major factors in shaping his style, although they have been merged into a genre typically his own.

Leach's workshop approach—producing a quality functional ware at reasonable prices, with only an occasional unique piece—had a widening influence in the 1930s. Among early apprentices at St. Ives were Michael Cardew, Norah Braden, Katharine Pheydell-Bouverie, Dorothy Kemp, Harry Davis, and Leach's son, David, who since 1956 has had his own pottery near Bovey Tracey (Figs. 131–133). Among his former students are the

England   75

133. DAVID LEACH, England. Covered casseroles. Clay with dark temmoku glaze.

American Warren MacKenzie and Canadian John Reeve, who is now working in England (Fig. 134).

The publication of *A Potter's Book* in 1940 further spread Leach's philosophy, as did his lecture tours to the United States in 1950 and 1960. Encouraged by his old friend Soetsu Yanagi, founder of the Japanese Craft Society, Leach has returned to Japan on numerous occasions. The several publications that have followed *A Potter's Book* have continued to spread the ceramic traditions of the Orient, as well as invoking an interest in the preindustrial pottery heritage of Europe.

Although Bernard Leach has been a major influence in the rebirth of English ceramics as a creative craft, it does not follow that all potters subscribe to his functional workshop approach. With the contemporary pressure on the artist for extreme individuality, the avoidance of tradition becomes a virtue in itself. A majority of today's studio potters came from an art school background, and they are, perhaps, little inclined to make mugs or teapots. The thrown form dictates certain limitations, and its long but varied tradition makes it difficult to be strikingly different. Therefore, it is natural that the more inventive young potters would turn to coil and slab techniques to achieve greater individuality in the form of their work or a style that is wholly sculptural in nature.

above left : 134. JOHN REEVE, England. Covered jar. Stoneware with wood-ash glaze and incised decoration, height 7 ½″.

above : 135. LUCIE RIE, England. Bottle. Stoneware, sgraffito decoration. Collection J.W.N. van Achterbergh, Amsterdam. This flaring bottle is characteristic of Lucie Rie's work.

left : 136. HANS COPER, England. Bottle. Thrown and pressed form with dry mat textured glaze in off-white and brown-black. Collection J. W. N. van Achterbergh, Amsterdam.

There are many small potteries in England producing a varied and often excellent functional ware at moderate prices. Even those potters whose inclination is toward the unique piece find that some semiproduction ware is necessary in order to meet expenses, because the market for higher-priced ware is limited. For this reason many potters teach part time in art schools. Lucie Rie, originally from Austria and a former pupil of Michael Powelny of Vienna, and Hans Coper from Germany are among the best known of the potters in England who have developed a unique style (Figs. 135–136). The work of several others is shown in the text (Pls. 6–7, p. 73; Figs. 137–142).

England   77

above : 137. BRYAN NEUMAN, England. Set of matching pitchers, covered jar, soup bowl, and plate.

above right : 138. BILL READ, England. Tankard. Stoneware with cone-10 elmwood ash glaze over iron slip, height 6″.

right : 139. CHRISTOPHER CHARMAN, England. Salt jar. High-fire earthenware with lead glaze over slip, height 10 ½″.

above : 140. CHRIS HARRIS, England. Plate. Earthenware with slip-trailed decoration under lead glaze, diameter 12″.

above right : 141. IAN AULD, England. Containers. Slab-built stoneware, height of largest container 17″.

right : 142. MURRAY FIELDHOUSE, England. Bowl. Brown-ribbed body with smooth Bristol glaze on the interior surface.

below : 143. JAN VAN DER VAART, Holland. Architectural form. Stoneware with bronze-black manganese glaze.

right : 144. HANS DE JONG, Holland. *Cry Baby.* Stoneware with ash glaze, height 12″. Collection J.W.N. van Achterbergh, Amsterdam. Modern Dutch ceramics are often whimsical.

below right : 145. HELLY OESTREICHER, Holland. *Cylinders and Arcs.* 1965. Unglazed stoneware, height 19″.

80

HOLLAND

Holland has had a long history of extensive trade with the Far East, and to this day her fine museums and many antique shops have excellent collections of Oriental ceramics. The blue-and-white porcelains imported from China and Japan became immensely popular in Europe, and the Dutch were quick to capitalize on this interest. By the early eighteenth century a number of potteries were producing a majolica-type ware in the Chinese blue-and-white style, although there were elements of an Italian pictorial tradition. This ware, in a higher-fire version, has continued to be made to the present day and is popularly called Delft after the major factory.

Perhaps in reaction to the all-pervasive blue-and-white tableware, the contemporary Dutch ceramist produces little functional pottery. There is less interest in thrown form than there is in England. Most pieces are hand built, and the trend is toward architectural form, sculptural whimsy, or textural qualities of clay (Pls. 8–9, pp. 74, 91; Figs. 143–148).

left : 146. JAN DE ROODEN, Holland. *Composition in White and Black*. 1968. Stoneware with mat glaze, height 24″.

top : 147. MARIANNE FRANKEN, Holland. *The Fairy Ring*. Stoneware. Collection Kyuken-Schneider, The Hague. Even with thrown pieces, Dutch ceramists explore their preference for applied decoration and unique textural effects.

above : 148. JAN DE ROODEN, Holland. *Form in White and Black*. 1968. Stoneware with mat glaze, height 6″. The purposeful eruptions caused by internal pressure, together with the strong glaze patterns, are the dominant features of this pot.

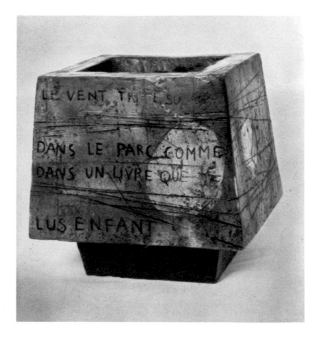

above and above right : 149–150. THEO DOBBELMANN, Holland. Ceramic forms. 1965. Height 36″, 14″. Excerpts from French poems enrich the surfaces of these constructions.

Many of the Dutch potters whose work is illustrated here have small studios in the vicinity of Amsterdam. They are, for the most part, in their early thirties and have quite varied backgrounds. A few have art school training, some have studied in England or Scandinavia, and others are largely self-taught, having had initial experience in other professions.

Some of these potters are or were members of the experimental group at the Porceleyne Fles at Delft, which was established in 1956 and patterned in part after the studio sections in many of the Scandinavian factories. The studio at Delft is under the direction of Theo Dobbelmann, a noted sculptor, glaze chemist, and a teacher at both the Art Academy and the Craft School in Amsterdam (Figs. 149–150). Perhaps because of their art school training, the Porceleyne Fles group, mostly female, has tended to emphasize a sensitive, linear, sgraffito-type decoration (Figs. 151–154). An informal workshop has developed, and often one person throws the pot while another does the decoration. Another interesting feature at the Delft factory has been the cooperation and technical help given to architectural designers in the execution of large ceramic mural projects for various schools and public buildings.

151–154. The work of several former members of the Porceleyne Fles experimental group reveals a common interest in incised decoration on a reserved, often organic, form.

above : 151. ELS BOONE, Holland. 1967. Height 6 ¾″.

right : 152. KEES VAN RENSSEN, Holland. 1966. Height 15″.

below : 153. ANNEMIEKE POST, Holland. 1966. Height 9 ³/₈″.

below right : 154. LEIS COSIJN, Holland. 1966. Height 16 ¾″.

FRANCE AND BELGIUM

Historically, Belgium has always been dominated by French styles in art and by the Delft pottery styles in ceramics. The noted painter, designer, and architect Henry Van de Velde was a leader in the Belgian Art Nouveau movement, but he was more popular and influential in France and especially in Germany. The soft-paste and porcelain factories of the eighteenth and nineteenth centuries regarded the pottery form primarily as a space for pictorial decoration in an elegant court style. In spite of the early success of Art Nouveau in France, public support for ceramics never grew to the same extent as in England or Germany. French taste prefers ornate decoration, and consequently the work of traditional French stoneware potters was regarded as having little merit. The more conven-

above : 155. PABLO PICASSO, France. *Le faune barbre.* 1952. Painted ceramic, diameter 14″. Courtesy Galerie Louise Leiris, Paris.

right : 156. PABLO PICASSO, France. *Red and White Owl.* 1953. Painted ceramic, height 13 ¾″. Private collection, New York.

tional work of French potters such as Jean-Bertrand Tessier, René-Louis Dauchy, and Francine del Pierre has received little recognition relative to the renown of the plates and sculptural pieces decorated by Joan Miró and Pablo Picasso. Picasso's ceramic works (Figs. 155–156) are not nearly as well known as his painting and sculpture, but they display the same fresh inventiveness. Made in collaboration with his potter friend Artigas, Picasso's ceramics anticipated by several decades much of the nonpot work that is being done today.

The Belgian ceramist Pierre Caille was originally a painter, but he turned to ceramics in 1937 (Figs. 157–158). Although he occasionally makes pottery, Caille's major interest is in figurative pieces and panels, often grotesque, but with a very personal style and a sociological impact that reminds one of the later paintings of his countryman James Ensor.

right : 157. PIERRE CAILLE, Belgium. Ceramic form. c. 1958. This powerful study, with its simplified form and dramatic intensity, is characteristic of the work of Pierre Caille.

below : 158. PIERRE CAILLE, Belgium. *Grinning Faces.* c. 1958. This ceramic panel has a rather medieval, macabre quality.

SPAIN

After the great period of the Hispano-Moresque luster ware of the fifteenth and sixteenth centuries, Spain slipped gradually into a ceramic doldrum. Seen against the background of the popular and rather gaudy majolica ware, the austere stoneware of Antoni Cumella comes as a surprise. Born in 1913, Cumella lives in Granolles, near Barcelona, where he has been potting since 1936, developing a severe personal style quite unlike that of his contemporaries in Spain. His typical bottle and vase forms have a stony sculptural quality (Fig. 159). Although his more recent panels have cut-out and textured surfaces (Fig. 160), Cumella's pots are unrelieved by any decoration except for the mat glazes with subtle color variations. Perhaps more in the Spanish tradition is the work of Maria Bofill, instructor at L'Scala Massana in Cataluña (Figs. 161–162).

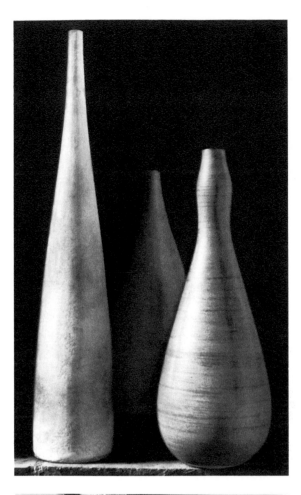

left: 159. ANTONI CUMELLA, Spain. Bottles. Stoneware with off-white mat glaze, height of tallest bottle, 19 ½".

below left: 160. ANTONI CUMELLA, Spain. Tile (detail of wall at Spanish Pavilion, New York World's Fair, 1964). Stoneware with blue, pink, and ochre glazes, 35 × 19 ½".

below: 161. MARIA BOFILL, Spain. Multispout jar. Stoneware with decoration in wax resist and iron oxides, height 7 ½".

above : 162. MARIA BOFILL, Spain. Covered jar. Stoneware with white glaze and decoration in wax resist and iron oxides, height 14 ½″. The elaborate decoration on this jar is somewhat reminiscent of old Spanish pottery styles.

below : 163. CARLO ZAULI, Italy. Sculptural form. Stoneware with white wood-ash glaze, 43 × 39″. Even in Italy, with its craft tradition, the accidental effect has assumed esthetic importance for contemporary potters.

ITALY

Indigenous crafts survived longer in Italy than in the more industrialized areas of northern Europe. Unlike glass, pottery is made in all areas of Italy, but it generally follows a low-fire majolica tradition. In keeping with the Italian temperament, the ceramic ware is colorful and exuberant, often fantastic, and sometimes sentimental. But, like any art form that feeds upon tradition, the majolica potteries have long lost their reason for being, and they find their principal audience in the tourist trade.

Italy is truly a living museum of the great periods of Etruscan, Roman, Renaissance, and Baroque art. It has been extremely difficult for the modern Italian artist and craftsman to throw off the weight of this tradition. Gio Ponti—a Milanese architect, influential designer, and founder of *Domus* the excellent magazine on architecture and decorative arts—has been a leader in bringing the craft ideas of William Morris and the functional aspects of the German Bauhaus movement to Italy. The large ceramic firm of Richard-Ginori has slowly veered toward contemporary design. The Triennale Exhibition of Decorative Arts, which was started in Milan prior to World War I, has also been a great influence in spreading new ideas, for it has become the finest international exhibition of its kind. (Unfortunately, the American contribution typically ignores crafts in favor of industrial superproducts.)

In the last few years Italian ceramics has shown a dramatic departure from the older concentration on low-fire ware to a new interest in stoneware. The many new art and crafts schools in every major city have certainly had a part in this trend. Many of the pieces shown here (Figs. 163–168) are by faculty members in these schools, chiefly from the State School of Ceramics at Faenza, which has for centuries been an Italian pottery center and where the Ceramic Museum conducts a yearly international exhibition. Architectural and sculptural ceramics follow an ancient Italian tradition, and it is not surprising that the modern Italian potter should work in this vein, but in a very contemporary manner (Figs. 169–170). Even the functional pieces are in this modern style.

top left : 164. ANGELO BIANCINI, Italy. *The Annunciation,* sculptured panel. 1963. Majolica with polychrome and luster decorative details, height 31 ½″. Vatican City.

top right : 165. LEONI ALFONSO, Italy. Ceramic assemblage. Thrown forms in deep bowl with green glaze, diameter 15″.

above : 166. GUIDO GAMBONE, Italy. Hanging wall sculpture. 1964. Manganese and white glazes, height 18″.

left : 167. FULVIO RAVAIOLI, Italy. Vases. 1964. Mat and crackle glazes, height of larger vase 13″.

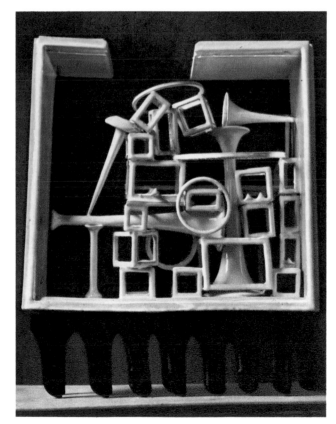

top left : 168. CARLO ZAULI, Italy. Sculptural form. Thrown and slab stoneware with wood-ash glaze, height 16″.

above : 169. GUIDO GAMBONE, Italy. Wall panel. 1967. Stoneware slab forms with white glaze, height 44 ⁷/₈″.

left : 170. LEONI ALFONSO, Italy. *Machine 11111112.* Ceramic with white and black majolica glaze, 24 × 20″.

Italy   89

GREECE

The Greek potter, even more than his Italian counterpart, is submerged under the legends and glories of an ancient past. The tourist trade, while adding immeasurably to the economy of Greece, subsidizes mainly the hotelkeeper and the souvenir shop. There are many potteries in Greece, but most are turning out copies of antique black- and red-figure ware. The imitative decoration is usualy stiff and stilted, but a few pieces have such a delicacy of line one wonders if the chipped, clay-encrusted ware offered as "classical" originals might have come from the hands of the same talented copyists.

The skill of the traditional Greek potter is evident, but the importance of the tourist trade and the conservatism of the Greek middle class have made it most difficult for the craftsmen of modern Greece to explore a contemporary direction. The situation is further complicated by the fact that kiln materials are difficult to obtain, and most glaze chemicals and colors must be imported. Greek ceramics, unlike those of Germany and Scandinavia, shows little interest in glaze effects, and this may be due to the influence of older traditions or to a more contemporary trend toward textural surfaces. In addition to study in Greece, most of the potters whose work is illustrated (Pl. 10, p. 92; Figs. 171–176) have studied at art or craft schools in France or Italy. It is encouraging to note that each seems to have developed a very personal style. There is not yet an identity of interests such as is found in many other areas, but it will undoubtedly occur as the contemporary trend continues to develop in Greece. This will depend more on public acceptance than on the interest of the individual craftsman. In this regard the Greek potter is not unlike the Italian glass blower at Murano, who continues to make Baroque forms because that is what the public expects.

top : 171. KOSTAS PANOPOULOS, Greece. Bottle. Red clay with cream glaze wiped off to expose body, height 18″.

left : 172. PANOS VALSOMAKIS, Greece. Cubistic relief panel. Terra cotta with polychrome crackle glaze, height 26″.

opposite : Plate 9. HANS DE JONG, Holland. *Two Birds.* Stoneware with oxide colorants and thin glaze.

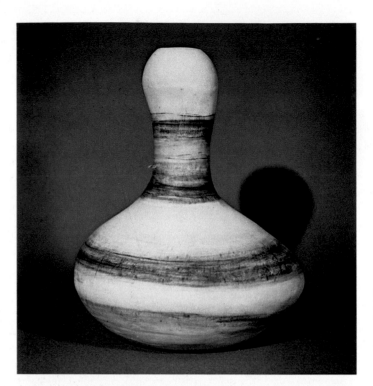

left : Plate 10. MARY HALZINICOLI, Greece. Bottle. Hand-built low-fire porcelain with brushed colorants, height 12″.

below left : Plate 11. HILDEGARD STORR-BRITZ, Germany. Wall tile. Stoneware with stamped decoration, partially glazed; height 13″.

above left : 173. MARY HATZINICOLI, Greece. Vase and bottle. Hand-formed earthenware with tracing in blue and brown on a white ground, height of vase 13″.

above right : 174. KOSTAS PANOPOULOS, Greece. Vase. Hand-formed earthenware partially glazed with blue-gray and pink, height 14″.

right : 175. ATHANASE PAPAVGERIS, Greece. Relief panel. Terra cotta with polychrome stylized design, height 33″.

far right : 176. ATHANASE PAPAVGERIS, Greece. Low-relief panel. Terra cotta with polychrome glaze decoration, height 29″. The design suggests the levels of a terraced Greek village.

GERMANY

German potters have long been interested in higher-fire ceramics, perhaps because they are influenced by the old salt-glazed stoneware tradition of the Rhine and the efforts of the early eighteenth-century potteries, which developed the first porcelain in Europe. The vast amount of porcelain produced on the Continent during this era, which might be typified by that of Meissen, grew not from a long and natural ceramic tradition but from an effort to copy Chinese form and decoration. In later years Baroque paintings in the Italian or French style became the models for decorative motifs, and by the end of the nineteenth century it was obvious to forward-looking architects and designers that this ornate and derivative ware did not fit modern needs.

Influenced by the ideals of Morris and the anti-academic philosophy of Art Nouveau, as well as by their own *Jugendstil*, German architects, artists, and designers of the pre-World War I era laid the basis for the modern design movement that culminated in the Bauhaus. The craft and trade schools which were established in the major cities, along with several magazines, exhibitions, and organizations like the Deutsche Werkbund—whose members included architects, designers, craftsmen, and manufacturers—all played a role in developing new design concepts related to the vision and function of contemporary life.

The war periods, of course, were times of retreat. The conservatism of the British prevented their accepting modern ideas of functional design in industry. In 1933 the reactionary ideals of Nazism closed the Bauhaus and drove most of its staff and its sympathizers abroad. A great many of these innovators emigrated to the United States, which, with its mass markets and large industry, was a fertile ground for the Bauhaus concept of functionalism. The principle of "form follows function" —that the design of any object must be faithful to its purpose and that integrity of materials must be respected—had been promulgated in the late nine-

top left : 177. BEATE KULN, Germany. *Spiny Creature.* 1965. White stoneware with coffee-brown mottled glaze, height 16".

top right : 178. WALTER POPP, Germany. Bottle. Stoneware with white glaze and brown and green accents, height 11".

teenth century by the American architect Louis Sullivan and subsequently refined by his disciple Frank Lloyd Wright. Interestingly, both architects employed much ceramic for the decorative details with which they embellished their buildings. Although the work of the two men was highly acclaimed, their philosophy did not, for many years, have any significant effect on American design. Wright's ideas and conceptual drawings, however, received European publication in 1910–11, and these had considerable influence on the formation of what became the "International Style," which approached its fullest expression during the 1920s in the teaching, design, and art of the faculty at the Bauhaus. It is ironic that, because of the migration of Walter Gropius, Miës van der Rohe, Josef Albers, Marcel Breuer, and László Moholy-Nagy to the United States, the Bauhaus functionalist esthetic had greater eventual impact in America, where, through the philosophy of Sullivan, it, in part, had its initial inspiration.

There are at present several fine craft and ceramic schools in the major German cities. Many train ceramic engineers and production designers as well as hand potters. A few are located in old pottery centers such as Höhr-Grenzhausen, a small Rhineland town where there are still dozens of salt-glaze potteries producing ware in a centuries-old tradition. Although some potters have had workshop training, most of those whose work is illustrated here (Figs. 177–189) attended craft schools, and many are teaching as well as maintaining their own studios.

Given the technical aptitude attributed to the Germans, it should not be surprising to find a concentration on rich glaze effects. The pieces tend to be designed and have little of the thrown feeling characteristic of English pottery. Nor is there the delight in texture that intrigues the Dutch potters. Continuing the early interest of such sculptors as Ernst Barlock (1870–1938), who illustrated the pioneering *Die Jugend* magazine, and Gerhard Marcks (1889–   ), director of the ceramics program at the Bauhaus, many contemporary potters have turned to sculpture and architectural decoration. In fact, most of the German work shown here exhibits a preference for sculptural qualities, rather than for traditional pottery forms (Pl. 11, p. 92).

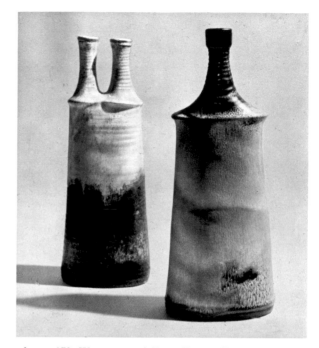

above : 179. WILHELM and ELLY KUCH, Germany. Bottles. Stoneware with beige, brown, and black glazes; height 11″.

below : 180. GÖRGE HOHLT, Germany. Columnar vases. Stoneware with intense reduction glazes in clear blue, oxblood red, and titanium blue; height of tallest vase 16 ½″.

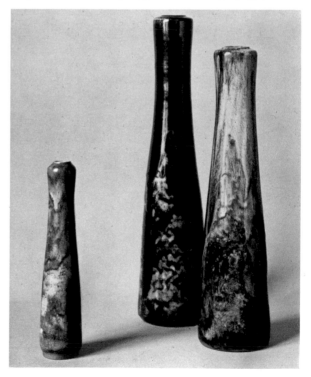

below left : 181. ULRICH GÜNTHER, Germany. Bottle. Thrown stoneware with semimat brown glazes, height 7 ½″.

below right : 182. HILDEGARD STORR-BRITZ, Germany. Vase. Stoneware with banded impressed decoration and gray-brown salt glaze, height 12 ½″.

right : 183. INGEBORG and BRUNO ASSHOFF, Germany. Bottle-shape figures. 1960. Stoneware with blue earth glaze.

bottom left : 184. WALTER POPP, Germany. Bottle. Stoneware with white and blue-black reduction glazes, height 6 ½″.

bottom right : 185. WILHELM and ELLY KUCH, Germany. Bottle. Black, brown, and blue glazes; height 22″.

above : 186. HILDEGARD STORR-BRITZ, Germany. Bottle. Stoneware with stamped and applied decoration and mottled dark gray-green salt glaze, height 10″.

right : 187. SABINE NASKE, Germany. *Tree of Life*. Stoneware with blue-green and dark brown glaze, height 21″.

below : 188. SABINE NASKE, Germany. *Garden Cock*. Groggy clay with brown-red and green glazes, height 21 ½″.

below right : 189. INGEBORG and BRUNO ASSHOFF, Germany. Double vase. Stoneware with thick ash glaze, height 30″.

SCANDINAVIA

Although the Scandinavian countries have their individual characteristics, they also have much in common. After centuries of Viking raids against the British Isles and, later, intermittent wars among themselves and with Germany and Russia, the Scandinavians long ago turned inward. Except for Sweden, the northern countries lack the mineral resources of Germany, France, and England. Until recent years their population was largely rural, and industrialization came later than elsewhere in Europe. Native crafts survived longer than in most parts of the Continent, much as they did in Italy. With the decline of the medieval guilds, craftsmanship also deteriorated, and a new system of training was needed. Architects, designers, and small manufacturers banded together in the late nineteenth century to offer design training in each of the capital cities. At first the instruction consisted of little more than drawing classes in which historical patterns were copied. Later, full-fledged craft schools emerged that were rather like those in Germany. During the eighteenth and early nineteenth centuries, Scandinavia was greatly influenced by late Rococo and Neoclassical French styles in furniture and interior decoration. Upper- and middle-class taste was influenced from abroad, while in the rural areas the more simple handcrafts prevailed.

The Morris movement, Art Nouveau, and finally the Bauhaus—each in turn had its impact upon Scandinavian designers, craftsmen, and manufacturers. However, these three successive influences, though significant, do not completely explain the sudden upsurge in design excellence and craftsmanship in furniture, silver, glass, weaving, and ceramics during the thirties and forties. Rather, it is likely that certain philosophies arising from the emergence of socialism in these countries provided the catalytic agent. Under a slogan of "beautiful ware for everyday use" designers, craftsmen, manufacturers, schools, and trade unions, with government support, were united toward a common goal of quality. Very gradually the combined efforts of these groups—through formal teaching, exhibitions, and craft societies—had an educational effect upon the public. The rights of the designer were protected, and today one finds his name listed on price tags along with that of the manufacturer. In addition to the few special retail outlets run by craft societies, all the larger cities have many shops carrying handmade items. Major department stores, such as Nordiska Kompaniet in Stockholm and Stockmans in Helsinki, have splendid displays of contemporary designed items. The large Danish craftsman's store, Den Permanente, is now world famous, and the revival of the craft workshops in the old medieval town of Fredrikstad reflects Norwegian involvement. All these elements have contributed to the wide influence of "Scandinavian modern" design.

Traditional medieval Scandinavian pottery was a dark red burnished earthenware, usually unglazed. The early pottery factories—the Royal Copenhagen (founded in 1779) and Gustavsberg in Sweden (1827)—first produced a majolica ware and later switched to porcelain and stoneware. Their products were inspired by German porcelain, Dutch majolica, and English bone china, all of which derived their decorative styles from Chinese prototypes, although the forms were often Neoclassical. Contemporary influences did not occur until the 1920s, when artists whose training was not in the traditional ceramic arts joined the staffs of several factories. The latter direction continues and is doubtless responsible for much of the success of the Scandinavian factories. The situation is not completely idyllic; conflicts do arise between the design and studio staffs and between sales and management personnel. Nevertheless, the Scandinavian design philosophy is far more progressive than that which prevails in most parts of the world. Some members of the studio staff work only on mass production, while others concentrate on one-of-a-kind pieces or on limited-production items. Their presence is bound to have a stimulating effect. Many of the early designers had painting or sculpture backgrounds, and the transition to the pottery medium proved difficult. But, as the craft schools have gradually turned to a designer-craftsman point of view, many talented people have begun to enter industry from the schools. There is a close association between the two, with many of the professional designers teaching part time.

Denmark

For years the commercial success of the traditional dinnerware patterns and figurines made by the Royal Copenhagen factory has perpetuated a conservative policy on the part of its design staff, although some contemporary patterns have been produced. Axel Salto, Royal Copenhagen's design head, has a most individual style derived from the organic bulblike growths that typify his personal work. The second large Danish porcelain factory, Bing and Grøndahls, also produces a line of conservative patterns, but in recent years it has sought a more contemporary outlook (Fig. 190). In the experimental studios at Bing and Grøndahl a group of young potters, under the direction of Asgar Fischer, are working with complete freedom in a variety of directions (Figs. 191–196). Fischer, for years the director of the craftsman's store, Den Permanente, and a brother of sculptor Adam Fischer,

below : 190. ERIK MAGNUSSEN for Bing and Grøndahl, Denmark. Thermo casserole with lid. White porcelain. The cross-section shows the ingenious heat-saving construction.

bottom : 191. STEN LYKKE MADSEN for Bing and Grøndahl, Denmark. *Fantastic Animal.* The staid functionalism of Scandinavian ceramics is increasingly enlivened by whimsical and delightful creations.

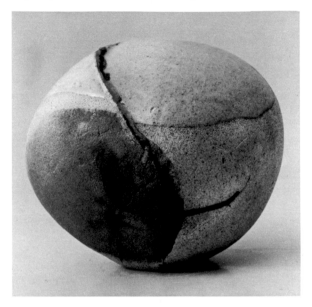

left : 192. URSULA MUNCH-PETERSEN for Bing and Grøndahl, Denmark. Vase. 1964. Stoneware with assembled thrown sections, glazed in green on the interior only; height 11 $^3/_8$″.

below : 193. BENTE HANSEN for Bing and Grøndahl, Denmark. *Fantasy*. Stoneware sphere, altered, with partial glaze and oxide decoration. This piece captures the quality of accidental charm that is often found in a beach pebble.

below : 194. ERIK MAGNUSSEN for Bing and Grøndahl, Denmark. *Abstract Sculpture*. Stoneware with lava and luster.

right : 195. STEN LYKKE MADSEN for Bing and Grøndahl, Denmark. *Fantasy Hen*. Applied and incised decoration.

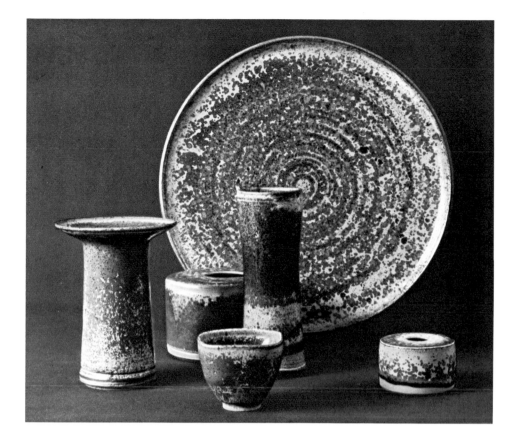

has been an enthusiastic proponent of Danish crafts since the modern movement began.

Several smaller factories and Danish workshops are also producing contemporary and distinctive patterns. In general, Danish ceramics emphasizes a sturdy, solid form with an inclination toward functionalism (Figs. 197–200). Textural effects have gradually replaced glaze perfection as the main area of concentration (Figs. 201–204), and interest in purely sculptural—even nonobjective—pieces is growing. In addition to the several larger workshops, there are many small private potteries in Denmark where apprentices may train.

top : 196. EDITH SONNE BRUUN for Bing and Grøndahl, Denmark. Vases and platter. Stoneware with crystalline glaze.

right : 197. CHRISTIAN POULSEN, Denmark. Vases and lidded jar. Stoneware with light blue, dark brown, and white glazes.

top : 198. NIELS REFOGAARD for Dansk Designs, Denmark. *Generation Mist* dinnerware. Stoneware with grayish glaze and brown decoration. (Executed by Eslau Keramik.)

above : 199. DORTHE MØLLER, Denmark. Mug and teapot. Stoneware with light gray glaze and brushed blue decoration.

left : 200. MYRE VASEGAARD, Denmark. Bowl. Stoneware with gray glaze and blue-green brushed and wiped decoration.

left : 201. Helle Allpass, Denmark. Lidded jug. Stoneware with gray-green glaze and iron red spots.

below left : 202. Gutte Eriksen, Denmark. Jar. 1962. Stoneware with off-white variegated and runny glaze.

below : 203. Hans and Birgitte Börjeson, Denmark. Tureen and bowls. Stoneware with light brown speckled glaze.

bottom : 204. Conny Walther, Denmark. Bottles. 1961. Groggy stoneware with blue-green glaze, height of each c. 5″.

Sweden

The porcelain factories of Gustavsberg and Rörstrand (founded in 1726), which recently merged
with the Upsala-Ekeby firm, dominate the Swedish
scene. Sweden has numerous small studios and
individual potters, but these three large factory
groups enjoy major contact with the public. Wilhelm
Kåge of Gustavsberg and Gunnar Nylund of
Rörstrand were most influential during the 1930s
and afterward in urging the rejection of traditional
styles based on German porcelain and English bone
china. Today Carl-Harry Stålhane and Stig Lindberg
head the large staffs at Rörstrand and Gustavsberg,
which design mass-production ware and also produce
one-of-a-kind pieces (Pl. 12, p. 125; Figs. 205–212).

The austere and streamlined designs of the
1950s are still reflected in Swedish functional ware,
but even this is becoming more colorful. As in
Denmark, the esthetic of simple form and perfect
glaze has given way to an interest in textural complexity and a more sculptural approach to form
(Figs. 213–217). Stig Lindberg heads the ceramic

above : 205. CARL-HARRY STÅLHANE for Rörstrand, Sweden.
Mural. Stoneware. Collection AB Volvo, Göteborg.

below : 206. MARIANNE WESTMAN for Rörstrand, Sweden.
Plate. Stoneware with freely brushed circular glaze decoration.

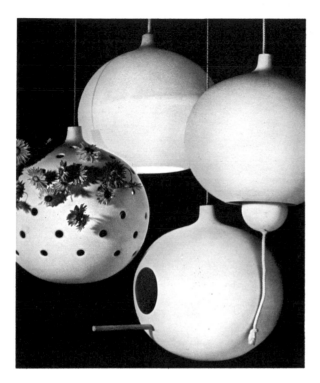

program at the Konstfackskolan in Stockholm and Carl-Harry Stålhane at the craft school in Göteborg, and for this reason there is perhaps greater cooperation in Sweden between school and industry than anywhere else in the world. While the situation might not be a true heaven on earth for the ceramic designer in Sweden, it is nevertheless remote from the distinctly earthbound conditions that prevail in the United States, where potters teach teachers how to teach and the advertising departments of some major potteries are largely content to pirate designs from their competitors at home and abroad.

left : 207. STIG LINDBERG, Sweden. *Ting* (lamp, gong, birdhouse, and flower holder). 1969. Unglazed bone china. The same globular shape is used to create four different items.

below left : 208. STIG LINDBERG, Sweden. Mural (detail) for Nacka Hospital, Gustavsberg. 1967. Cast clay, length 130'.

below : 209. CARL-HARRY STÅLHANE for Rörstrand, Sweden. Sculptural form. Stoneware with red and brown-black glaze.

top left : 210. INGER PERSSON for Rörstrand, Sweden. Vase forms. Stoneware with freely brushed glaze decoration.

top right : 211. OLLE ABERTIUS for Rörstrand, Sweden. *Forma* table service.

above : 212. SYLVIA LEUCHOVIUS for Rörstrand, Sweden. Wall plaque. Stoneware with stylized plant and polychrome flowers.

left : 213. BERTIL VALLIEN, Sweden. Sculptural form. 1969. Swedish potters have turned increasingly to fantasy.

below : 214. Britt Louise Sundell-Nemes, Sweden. Vase and plate. 1969. Stoneware with glossy crystalline glaze.

bottom : 215. Ulrica Hydman-Vallien, Sweden. *Bomb Number 6314.* 1969. Unglazed white stoneware, painted with blue, black, and brown enamels. Although the inscription suggests antiwar sentiment, the effect is of a stylized ballet.

top : 216. Bengt Berglund, Sweden. Wall plaque. 1969. The stamped technique is used here very effectively.

above : 217. Britt Ingrid Persson, Sweden. *Line Drawings.* White unglazed stoneware molded in a mushroomlike form.

Norway

Norway is a long, mountainous country, cut by numerous fjords and sparsely populated. Forestry, fishing, and shipping have for generations been major industries. Of the native crafts, weaving is perhaps the most important, as befits a cold northern country. The long dark winters have encouraged a taste for colorful patterns, and these characterize much of the weaving, the glassware, the popular majolica pottery, and the enameling on silver in which the Norwegians excell. Among early proponents of contemporary design in Norway were Thor Kielland, who later became director of the Art Industry Museum in Oslo, and Jakob Prytz, owner of the Tostrup silver firm and a teacher of silversmithing in the local craft school. In more recent years Per Tannum, whose large furniture store in Oslo has often carried craft items, has been a leading advocate of modern design. In cooperation with many others in the crafts and industry, Per Tannum

formed the Plus organization, which has developed a series of craft workshops in the old medieval town of Fredrikstad. The shops have proven to be quite a tourist attraction and are educational in an unobtrusive manner. As in the other Scandinavian capitals, there are display stores in Oslo, such as Forum, run by the various craft and design societies. The Norwegian commercial potteries have not supported studio staffs to the degree that the other Scandinavian countries have. There are, however, a number of talented individual potters. Until recent years most of them have worked in a decorated majolica pottery style, but the trend now is toward stoneware, with an emphasis on solid form and pressed or carved decoration (Figs. 218–224).

top left : 218. RICHARD DUBOURGH, Norway. Teapots. Unglazed body with rough, textured surface and cane handles.

top right : 219. ERIK PLØEN, Norway. Vase. Stoneware with pressed stamp decoration.

top : 222. DEGNY and FINN HALD, Norway. Bowl. Stoneware with cut decoration heightened by opaque glaze.

above : 223. ROLF HANSEN, Norway. Deep bowl with handles. Stoneware with stamped decoration and olive-green glaze.

below : 224. ERIK PLØEN, Norway. Square vase. 1960. Stoneware with pressed decoration and thick, viscous glaze.

top : 220. ROLF HANSEN, Norway. Bowl and vases. Thrown stoneware with brush and sgraffito glaze decoration.

above : 221. ERIK PLØEN, Norway. Vases. 1966.

Finland

The Finns migrated from central Europe to their present area before the eighth century, bringing a language distantly related to an ancient Hungarian dialect. Finland became a Duchy of Russia a hundred years before the Bolshevik revolution, but prior to that and since the twelfth century it had been a part of Sweden. Therefore, the Finns, despite

top left : 225. Annikki Hovisaari for Arabia, Finland. Covered bottle. Engraved decoration and gray glaze.

above : 226. Taisto Kaasinen for Arabia, Finland. *Virgo* (one of a series depicting the signs of the Zodiac).

left : 227. Olli Vasa for Arabia, Finland. Flasks and tumblers.

their adherence to old customs and their unique language, share many attitudes with the Swedes.

The surprising realization of excellence in contemporary Finnish design that began in the 1930s may in part be explained by the outpouring of spirit of a people suddenly freed from centuries of foreign rule, but it still remains a baffling phenomenon. Isolated from the main currents of European life, the Finns had to turn inward, perhaps to the age-old legends of the ancient national epic, the *Kalevala,* for inspiration and survival.

Eliel Saarinen, who came to the United States in 1923, and later Alvar Aalto were among the pioneering architects and designers to influence the direction of Finnish design. As in Sweden, craft societies, schools, and industry cooperated in an attempt to produce a well-designed product for common use. The Ateneum, the School of Arts and Industrial Design administered by the Society of Industrial Design in Helsinki, has played an important role in this program. Many of Finland's outstanding designers, such as Kaj Franck and Tapio Wirkkala, have studied and later taught at the Ateneum. The Finns are particularly skilled and inventive in the design and production of fabrics, glassware, laminated furniture, and ceramics.

The huge Arabia porcelain factory in Helsinki has dominated Finnish ceramics for many years. Although founded by the Swedish Rörstrand firm in 1874, it came under Finnish control in 1916. At the turn of the century A. V. Finch, a potter and painter of Belgian and English descent, had begun teaching ceramics at the Ateneum, and most of the Arabia designers were trained under him or his former pupil, Else Elenius, who succeeded him. Kurt Ekholm, who later left to head the craft school in Göteborg, was an important design leader at Arabia. Maija Grotell, known for her teaching at Detroit's Cranbrook Academy, studied under Else Elenius, as did Kyllikki Salmenhaara, an excellent potter now an instructor at the craft school.

The present Arabia design supervisor is Kaj Franck, a versatile artisan in glass and ceramics and a noted teacher, whose esthetic philosophy has great influence in Scandinavia. Most of the ceramics illustrated here (Figs. 225–230) were made by the

above : 228. RAIJA TUUMI for Arabia, Finland. Bowl. Stoneware with perforated design and mat gray glaze, diameter 18″.

below : 229. LIISA HALLAMAA for Arabia, Finland. Vase and egg cups. Stoneware.

Arabia staff, some of whom design solely for production while others create only one-of-a-kind pieces and a few work in both fields. The pieces are extremely varied and quite personal in expression, ranging from the fantasies of Birger Kaipiainen (Fig. 231) through the colorful decorations of Rut Bryk (Fig. 232), the thrown pottery of Anja Jaatinen (Fig. 233), and the textural constructions of Francesca Lindh (Pl. 13, p. 126; Fig. 234). The publicity and exibition facilities enjoyed by the Arabia potters have made it difficult for smaller potteries to compete, and, therefore, there are few unaffiliated potters (Fig. 235) such as are common in Sweden, Denmark, and the rest of Europe.

left : 230. HELJÄTUULIA LIUKKO-SUNDSTRÖM for Arabia, Finland. *Torpedo.* Stoneware with white mat glaze (metal base).

top : 231. BIRGER KAIPIAINEN for Arabia, Finland. Wall plate. Earthenware with gray-green and black decoration on gray background, beads cemented in place; diameter 18″.

above : 232. RUT BRYK for Arabia, Finland. Decorative tile. Engraved and stamped design, turquoise and other glazes on gray-white background; 9″ square.

above left : 233. ANJA JAATINEN for Arabia, Finland. *Samurai* vases. Stoneware with mat blue glaze.

above right : 234. FRANCESCA LINDH for Arabia, Finland. Vase. Slab and thrown stoneware with pressed decoration and blue glaze, height c. 19″.

left : 235. LEA HAGMAN, Finland. Vase forms (intended for lamp stands). Stoneware with gray, blue, and brown glazes.

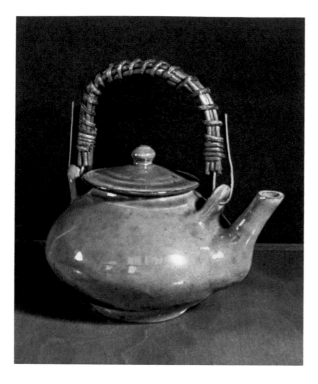

JAPAN

Ceramics has long been an integral part of Japanese culture, developing in the era of Jomon and Haniwa terra cottas and continuing through the centuries when Chinese and Korean influences were being absorbed into the Japanese tradition. The tea ceremony and the resultant high esteem for the necessary ceramic pieces are uniquely Japanese (Fig. 236). However, the changes that followed the overthrow of the Shogunate in 1868 and the subsequent restoration of the imperial house under Emperor Meiji were catastrophic for the Japanese potter. The industrialization of the old pottery centers at Seto and Arita not only destroyed the craftsmanlike manner of working but, with the introduction of new mass-produced and cheap porcelains, also doomed the many small hand potteries that were scattered throughout Japan. Only a few—the family-owned potteries with generations-old reputations and those in remote areas, such as in Onda and Koishibara in Kyushu, where potters of Korean descent continued their combined farming and potting way of life—managed to survive.

The recent revival of folk pottery is largely due to the efforts, during the 1920s and 1930s, of the late Soetsu Yanagi and his Mingei (folk art) Society, aided by the now-famous potters Shoji Hamada and Kanjiro Kawai (Fig. 237). Through constant lectures, exhibitions, and encouragement of young potters, Yanagi was able to renew interest in the native crafts, which were all but destroyed by industrialization and the disappearance of the old ways of life. Today, with craft museums, exhibitions, and sales rooms in some of the finer department stores, the traditional hand crafts are again high in public regard.

By a happy coincidence, Bernard Leach, the English potter, became acquainted with Yanagi, Hamada, Kawai, and the young architect Kenkichi Tomimoto (1886–1963) during his stay in Japan from 1909 to 1920. Hamada and Kawai were trained as engineers, but, along with Tomimoto and Leach, both were influenced by Dr. Yanagi's interest in the strength and naturalness of the neglected folk arts. Kawai in Kyoto, Hamada in Mashiko, and, later, Leach at St. Ives in England went on to gather sympathetic groups around them. Tomimoto, however, was drawn toward a more personal expression, one not within the "Mingei tradition." Applying the concept of the artist-craftsman, he explored new techniques and directions (Fig. 238). After encouraging the growth of several craft societies fostering these aims, Tomimoto established, in 1949, the first college-level ceramics program in Japan, at the Kyoto Municipal College of Fine Arts.

Japanese ceramics continues to follow diverse trends: rural potters influenced by Korean styles; the continuation of old Japanese traditions, such as Bizen; and the newer "Mingei" potters, such as those at Mashiko (Figs. 239–244). Finally, there is a younger group of potters, many of them trained as painters or sculptors, who view ceramics as a personal expression and conceive of it in sculptural terms only incidentally related to the functional use of pottery (Figs. 245–251).

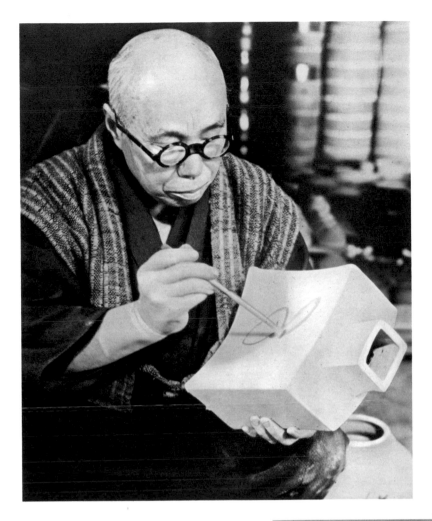

left : 237. SHOJI HAMADA in his studio at Mashiko, Japan.

below: 238. KENKICHI TOMIMOTO, Japan. Covered jar. 1958. White porcelain with clear glaze and red, gold, and silver decoration; height c. 7 ¼". The superb craftsmanship of Tomimoto is evident in this intricate design.

left : 239. MASAYUKI IMAI, Japan. Bottle vase. Stoneware with line decoration, stained with slip but unglazed.

below left : 240. YAICHI KUSUBE, Japan. Vase. Stoneware with cut-out sections and green "fern sprouts" glaze, height 10″.

below right : 241. TOSHIO KATO, Japan. *Swellfish.* Thrown stoneware, compressed and altered, oxidation fired; height 18″.

above : 242. Kako Morino, Japan. Vase. Stoneware (reduction fired with wood) with salt glaze and cobalt decoration.

above right : 243. Mutsuo Yanagihara, Japan. Vase. 1968. Stoneware with wax-resist design and umber glaze, height 8″.

right : 244. Kanzan Shinkai, Japan. *Birds in a Circle.* Applied and stamped relief decoration.

Japan   117

left : 245. HIROAKI MORINO, Japan. Slab sculpture. 1967. Textured stoneware with dark green stain, height 20″.

below : 246. HEIHACHIRO HAYASHI, Japan. Sculptural construction. Unglazed, oxidation fired; height 13″.

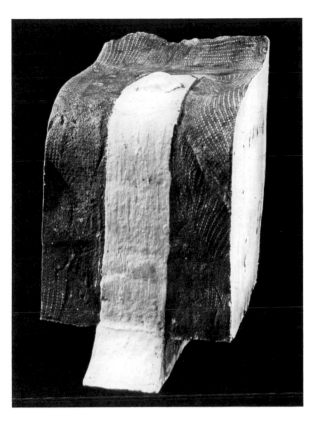

right : 247. SHIN FUJIHIRA, Japan. *A Guide Post.* Textured slab-built stoneware with contrasting light and dark areas.

below : 248. YOSHITAKA YASUHARA, Japan. Garden sculpture. Slab-built with wood-ash glaze and cut-out sections.

above left : 249. KIYOYUKI KATO, Japan. Vase. Stoneware with iron glaze.

above right : 250. HIROAKI MORINO, Japan. Vase. Thrown stoneware, compressed and joined, with mat gray slip-trailed decoration.

left : 251. SHIN HATTA, Japan. *Harmony.* Stoneware, altered, reduction fired, with blue mat glaze; height 16″. The accidental cracking becomes a decorative element.

AUSTRALIA AND NEW ZEALAND

As was the case in America, European ceramic imports dominated Australian taste during the early history of that country, especially since industrialization in England was proceeding at a rapid pace during the era of settlement. Early Australian ceramics was at first limited to the manufacture of bricks, tile, flowerpots, storage jars, simple dinnerware, and other utilitarian objects, most of which were low fired, although some salt stoneware was made.

Merric Boyd (1888–1959) was the first Australian to work in the studio art tradition. His early interest was in clay modeling in an Art Nouveau style, so it was natural that, when he turned to pottery, he preferred to use convoluted, writhing, and organic plant, animal, and human motifs to embellish his forms. His son, David, also a potter, has continued the family interest in decoration. Other ceramic pioneers were Peter Hall, Paddy Walsh, Jim Landison, and Alan Lowe.

Most early Australian work was in earthenware, but in recent years the trend has swung to stoneware (Figs. 252–254). Since World War II, there has been a tremendous increase in public interest in ceramics. Most colleges and art schools have pottery courses, exhibitions are frequent, and many small and sucessful workshops are in operation. A similar situation prevails in New Zealand. The Leach preference for the freely thrown, functional pot has been influential (Figs. 255–257), and many of the younger potters whose work is illustrated here have traveled or studied in England. Michael Cardew's work has also had an effect, and his recent extended stay in Australia and the impact of his personality and philosophy will certainly influence the course of Australian ceramics. Museum collections of Oriental ware, as well as the relative proximity to Japan, have caused the same echoes of Japanese and Korean form that are found elsewhere in the world. While a few potters are inclined toward a sculptural and decorative approach, rather than the more functional (Figs. 258–263), they have rejected the neo-Dada, avant-garde tendencies so common among American potters.

above : 252. CARL MCCONNELL, Australia. Wine jug. Stoneware with trailed decoration in black and rust red, height 12".

below : 253. MOLLIE DOUGLAS, Australia. Teapot. Stoneware with off-white glaze and rust-red accent at base, height 5".

left : 254. PETER TRAVIS, Australia. *Cathedral.* Slab and coil construction, height 18″.

above : 255. DEREK SMITH, Australia. Flanged cooking pot. Stoneware with brown and black ash glaze, diameter 16″.

left : 256. PETER RUSHFORTH, Australia. Jug with large handle. Stoneware with runny ash glaze, height 14″.

above : 257. LES BLAKEBROUGH, Australia. Flower container and small box. Mittagong blue porcelain, reduction fired, with free brush decoration in cobalt and iron oxides.

above : 258. Ian Sprague, Australia. Vase. Coiled stoneware, unglazed, with iron oxide to accentuate texture; diameter 20″.

below : 259. Margaret Tuckson, Australia. Covered casserole. Groggy clay with clear mat glaze on exterior, diameter 8″.

right : 260. Bernard Sahm, Australia. *Anthropots.* Slab and partially thrown stoneware with mat glaze, height 28″ each.

left : 261. WANDA GARNSEY, Australia. Vases. Stoneware with dolomite glaze and reduced specks, height of larger vase 8″. The applied "fins" give the vases an asymmetrical quality.

below left : 262. MAREA GAZZARD, Australia. *Dials.* High-fire coiled earthenware, unglazed, with coloring oxides; height 22″.

below : 263. IVAN ENGLUND, Australia. *Celebration.* Thrown and modeled stoneware with oxide decoration, height 19″.

opposite: Plate 12. STIG LINDBERG, Sweden. *People Bottles.* Stoneware with iron-red glaze.

CANADA

The first historical mention of pottery making in Canada dates from 1686 and relates to bricks, tile, and earthenware pottery being manufactured in Quebec. Early ware followed the French and English lead-glazed slip ware traditions. By the late eighteenth century numerous small potteries were supplying local needs. However, as the English ceramic industry grew in the early nineteenth century, the hand potters in the colonies could not compete with the inexpensive, mass-produced product, which was often technically superior, even though it lacked the unsophisticated charm of the local wares.

In North America generally the growing interest in handcrafts is in no way a continuation of colonial Old World traditions, but rather a twentieth century reaction against the sterility of industrial products. Although the idea may seem romantic, it has been suggested that modern man longs for that which displays the irregularity of the human touch as an antidote to an ordered and mechanized way of life.

Formal Canadian instruction in pottery began in 1915 at the Central Technical School in Toronto, later joined by the Ontario College of Art and the Fine Arts School in Montreal. The Canadian Guild of Potters, organized in 1936, has been, along with regional groups, an important influence in spreading interest in ceramics through its numerous exhibits and workshops. In the Maritime Provinces the Danish potters, Kjeld and Erica Deichmann, contributed to public interest from 1935 through the fifties. Among the many active potters before World War II were Molly Satterly, Bailey Leslie (Fig. 264), Bobs C. Haworth, and Gaetan Beaudin. Since the War there has been a tremendous growth in public interest in ceramics, as well as in the number of active potters and schools offering instruction. A few potters have succeeded in their own workshops, but most do some teaching in addition. The influence of Bernard Leach was great during the 1950s, especially as potters generally shifted from earthenware to stoneware (Figs. 265–266).

Present influences are quite diverse, and Oriental elements now derive more from Japanese than from Chinese styles. As elsewhere in the world, many Canadians have begun to think of clay in terms of sculptural form, free from the traditional restrictions of functional pottery (Figs. 267–272). The work illustrated gives some idea of the variety of expression found in Canadian ceramics (Figs. 273–280). It hardly represents a unified national trend, but its quality is both vigorous and experimental.

opposite : Plate 13. FRANCESCA LINDH for Arabia, Finland. Wall plaque. Stoneware with suspended clay bells and barium copper-blue glaze.

right : 264. BAILEY LESLIE, Canada. Bottles. Slab-built porcelain with wheel-thrown necks, textured with copper oxide rubbed under white mat glaze; height of largest bottle 17 ½".

above : 265. ALLAN CRIMMINS, Canada. Bottles. Stoneware with feldspathic and wood-ash glazes, height of bottle at left 8″.

right : 266. MAYTA MARKSON, Canada. Planter. Stoneware with free brush decoration and mat copper glaze, height 14″.

below : 267. MIMI CABRI, Canada. Vase. Slab-built stoneware with brushed brown engobe over white mat glaze, height 10 ¼″.

below : 268. ROBERT BOZAK, Canada, Sculptured pot. Slab-built raku ware with gray body and poured glaze, height 9".

right : 269. MARION LEWIS, Canada. Abstract sculptural form. Accented areas of glaze and color.

below : 270. JACK SURES, Canada. *Ric's Planter.* Multicolored stoneware clays with fiber glass, unglazed; 14 × 49 × 6".

left : 271. YOLANDE ROUSSEAU RIOUX, Canada. *Terre des hommes* (made for exhibit at Expo 67). 1967. Red clay.

below left : 272. DOROTHY MIDANIK, Canada. Vases. Slab-built stoneware with applied decoration glazed in white and yellow, with coloring oxides of black, brown, and ochre rubbed into unglazed body; height of largest vase 22″.

below : 273. CHARLIE SCOTT, Canada. Jar. Stoneware with reduced feldspathic glaze and zipper, height 13 ½″.

bottom : 274. MARILYN LEVINE, Canada. Vase. Stoneware, 18 × 10″. The torn rim imparts tension to a placid piece.

above : 275. JOAN BOBBS, Canada. Jar. Coiled stoneware with texture formed by joining, orange-brown glaze; height 18″.

right : 276. WILLIAM NORMAN, Canada. Cylindrical bottle. Thrown stoneware with applied clay decoration and black slip accent under a reduced clear white glaze, height 10″.

below left : 277. JULIEN CLOUTIER, Canada. Vase. Stoneware with freely poured glaze, height 20″.

below right : 278. JOHN SHAW, Canada. Bottle. Stoneware with mottled blue glaze over iron-oxide decoration, height 10″.

above : 279. MAURICE SAVOIE, Canada. Five bottles. Coiled stoneware with feldspathic glaze, height of largest bottle 16″.

below : 280. JACQUES GARNIER for Céramique de Beauce, Canada. Tea set. Earthenware with dark mat glaze.

THE UNITED STATES

As discussed in Chapter 2 (pp. 57–58), the Industrial Revolution had a devastating effect on American handcrafts. One exception to the prevailing trend of commercial production in the late nineteenth century was the Rookwood Pottery. It was founded in 1880 by Maria Longworth-Storer, a wealthy Cincinnati woman and an art school graduate, who, with several friends, had long been interested in china painting, then a popular pastime. Mrs. Storer eventually learned to throw on the wheel and, with a small factory staff, experimented with various glazes and types of decoration. Rookwood's well-known vase forms were influenced by the Chinese, their decoration by the Japanese and by Art Nouveau floral motifs. While we might question today the several international awards won by the Rookwood Pottery, the work was far superior to that of its more commercial competitors during the forty years of the company's operation (Fig. 281).

Another pioneer in ceramic design was Adelaide Robineau of Syracuse, New York, who also began as a china painter, then learned to throw and experimented with high-fire bodies and glazes. This was the era of Art Nouveau and Tiffany glass, both of which are reflected in her work (Fig. 282). In addition to her own ceramic production, Adelaide Robineau founded the Ceramic Studio magazine in about 1903, which popularized an elementary idea of craftsmanship and Art Nouveau principles among a wider audience.

More influenced by the philosophy of Morris and the reserved forms of the Chinese was the English potter, Charles Binns, who became in 1900 the first director of the New York State College of Ceramics in Alfred, New York. Through experiments in high-fire stoneware and porcelain, Binns and his many students, such as Charles Harder and

below left : 281. Rookwood Pottery, U.S.A., Cincinnati, Ohio. Mug. 1882. Earthenware with blue glaze and figurative decoration. Brooklyn Museum (gift of Arthur W. Clement).

below : 282. ADELAIDE ROBINEAU, U.S.A. Vases. Late 19th-early 20th century. Porcelain with decorative crystalline glazes in floral design. Everson Museum of Art, Syracuse, N.Y.

above : 283. Arthur Baggs, U.S.A. Cookie jar. 1938. Salt-glazed stoneware. Everson Museum of Art, Syracuse, N.Y.

above right : 284. Henry Varnum Poor, U.S.A. Bowl. 1954. Sgraffito decoration. Everson Museum of Art, Syracuse, N.Y.

right: 285. Maija Grotell, U.S.A. Vase. 1946. Stoneware with slip-trailed design. Everson Museum of Art, Syracuse, N.Y.

Arthur Baggs (Figs. 283), laid much of the technical foundation that underlies the present ceramic programs in American colleges. Also prominent during the 1930s was the California potter Glen Lukens, who developed some unusual glazes from local minerals. Henry Varnum Poor was the first well-known painter to become interested in pictorial and figurative decorations for pottery, based on the majolica tradition (Fig. 284).

Much as American architecture and design were enriched by the arrival of the Bauhaus expatriates, so also did American ceramics profit from such European potters as Marguerite and Frans Wildenhain, Gertrud and Otto Natzler, and Maija Grotell (Fig. 285), most of whom came to the United States during the 1930s.

The National Ceramic Exhibition, first organized at the Syracuse Museum of Fine Arts as a memorial to Adelaide Robineau in 1932, has played an important part in uniting potters and spreading ideas from one section of the country to another. Craft exhibitions, which were rare in the 1930s, are now common, due to the efforts of various local groups and the American Crafts Council, which maintains the Museum of Contemporary Crafts in New York, and which established the School for American Craftsmen in Rochester, N. Y. The Council also publishes the magazine, *Craft Horizons* and is affiliated with America House, a leading craft sales outlet. A recent outgrowth of the Council is a World Crafts Council, an organization formed to facilitate an exchange of ideas among craftsmen everywhere.

After the war years there was a tremendous growth in all the crafts. A new prosperity which allowed for increased leisure time, coupled with an inarticulate distaste for the impersonal products of the modern plastic genre, evoked a greater fascination for handcrafts in both the hobbyist and the professional. As college and art school programs grew, the prewar preference for earthenware and decorative techniques changed to a concentration on stoneware and higher-fire glazes. Chinese ceramics of the earlier period were studied with increasing interest. The writings and several lecture tours by Bernard Leach also had great influence.

Pots were better thrown, and glazes were more suitable and varied than ever before in American history. But the situation of the potter had also changed. Most were not producing functional pottery or even decorative ware for a local market but more often were teachers in art schools or college art departments. Under these conditions the exhibition piece assumed greater importance. If it were to stand out, it must necessarily be larger, rougher, or in some way bizarre. Thus during the 1950s there was a gradual shift toward interesting texture, asymmetrical coiled pieces, and combined slab and thrown forms. This new variety created a more exciting exhibition and provided a different challenge to the potter. Symptomatic of the change, he now preferred to be called an "artist-craftsman." This is not surprising, since in the traditional university structure the crafts were always subservient to the "fine arts," but with the trend toward mixed media, the old categories are breaking down. It is now difficult to label some works as either painting or sculpture; similarly, the distinction between pottery and ceramic sculpture is ever more nebulous.

A leader in this drastic change in the ceramic arts was the West Coast potter, Peter Voulkos. An expert craftsman, he was producing in the early 1950s a variety of thrown pieces in a more-or-less functional tradition (Fig. 286). But, possessing an exuberant and

right : 286. PETER VOULKOS, U.S.A. Covered jar. 1950s. Stoneware with sgraffito, height 17″. Museum of Contemporary Crafts, New York (gift of Mrs. Vanderbilt Webb).

left : 287. PETER VOULKOS, U.S.A. *Cross.* 1959. Stoneware with polychrome low-fire glaze, height 30 ½″. Johnson Collection of Contemporary Crafts. This piece illustrates Voulkos' complete break with traditional ceramic form.

below : 288. PETER VOULKOS, U.S.A. *Aratsa.* c. 1968. Stoneware with black mat glaze, height 26 ¼″. Johnson Collection of Contemporary Crafts. The black glaze emphasizes the stark, almost brutal explosion of form.

competitive personality, Voulkos was soon pushing the traditional forms into new directions, and by 1957 he had abandoned the functional aspect for sculptured pots and, ultimately, for large clay forms which were completely sculptural in nature (Figs. 287–288). Although in recent years Voulkos has confined his work almost exclusively to cast-bronze and metal sculpture, his radical departures from traditional pottery forms during the fifties have had a continuing influence on American ceramics.

Expressionist painting has also had its effect in developing a more vigorous decorative style totally unlike the usual glazed ceramic surface, even to the extent of replacing glaze with brilliant acrylic paints and cemented fabrics in a collage technique. Pop Art has encouraged this trend, often creating an assemblage of objects primarily for their shock value. Impressions from type faces and photographic decals have introduced literary and associative images in a neo-Dada fashion which is new to the ceramic medium. Even the recent popularity of the old Japanese raku pottery is primarily due to its firing process, which has the character of a "happening," for the patterns and colors that evolve are unpredictable and often accidental.

Contemporary ceramics is in a state of flux, and traditional values are under attack. A great deal of experimentation occurs, both in form and in materials, but the larger question is one of direction. Undoubtedly most of the present work will eventually go into the dust bin, as it has in other eras, but it is doubtful that ceramics will soon, if ever, return to anything approaching the esthetic that existed thirty years ago. There certainly is no concensus about what this direction should be, as the many illustrations of American pottery in this volume will demonstrate. If any quality can characterize this work, it is that of an iconoclastic attitude which is dynamic and vital, even if offering neither the constants nor the solutions that our confused society, at the same time pragmatic and idealistic, so desperately desires.

4 Clay and Clay Bodies

Most people confuse clay with soil, and this is quite understandable, since the two are related. Garden soil is a combination of clay, sand, and humus (partially decayed vegetable matter). Compared with other materials in the earth, this layer of soil is extremely thin, usually only a few inches—seldom over a foot—thick. There are, of course, large areas without soil, such as most desert and mountain regions. Between the soil proper and the rocky mantle of the earth there is a subsoil—composed of clay, sand, or gravelly mineral deposits in either a pure or a mixed form—that may vary from a few inches to hundreds of feet in thickness.

After a fiery genesis, the earth cooled for billions of years before water vapor and an atmosphere formed. The slow march of the seasons began. Erosion from wind and water, as well as expansions and contractions from heat and ice, gradually crumbled the rock that comprised the earth's surface. The initial composition of this rock varied from place to place. Minerals that were relatively water soluble broke down much more quickly. The evolution of plant and, later, animal life hastened this process, for organic acids contributed their decomposing action. In certain locations, the movement and melting of the ice cover during the glacial ages had considerable effect on the mixture and breakdown of minerals composing the surface rock.

Clay derives from the disintegration of granite and other feldspathic or pegmatite rocks which, as they decompose, deposit alumina and silica particles. The latter two minerals, combined with water, form pure clay, whose composition is expressed chemically as $Al_2O_3 \cdot 2\,SiO_2 \cdot 2\,H_2O$. This is an ideal formula, however, for nearly all clays contain some impurities, and it is these impurities and variations in the basic formula that account for the different characteristics of the numerous clay types.

A unique and valuable quality of clay is its plasticity; unless a clay will hold its shape while being formed, it is useless (Fig. 290). This factor depends on the fineness of particle size. In the geological forma-

opposite : 289. LYLE N. PERKINS, U.S.A. Vase. Slab-built stoneware with some glazed areas, height 26″.

290. A unique and valuable quality of clay is its plasticity.

tion of clay it is the softer, more soluble feldspar in granite rock that decomposes to leave alumina and silica particles, and for this reason clay particles are very tiny. A fine grain of sand is 1/500 inch in diameter. Even this is huge compared with a clay particle that is only 0.7 microns in diameter and 0.05 microns in thickness. (A micron is about 1/25,000 inch.) The natural structure of a clay particle is a flat, shinglelike shape, and the particles tend to slide together and give support to one another, whether in a plastic state or after a formed piece has dried. By comparison, even the finest ground minerals have large, granular crystals with no ability to adhere.

CLAY TYPES

All clays can be classified first as either *residual* or *sedimentary*. Residual clays have remained more or less at the site of the original rock formation. They are less plastic than sedimentary clays and contain many larger-size particles. Sedimentary clays are those that, by action of wind or running water, have been transported far from the site of the parent rock. This action usually affected only the clay particles of the finest size, and therefore sedimentary clays are the more plastic of the two types.

Kaolin

Kaolin is a very pure form of clay, approaching the ideal formula on page 139. Although never used alone as a body, it serves as a standard with which to compare other clays. It is white in color and can be fired to an extremely high temperature. Kaolin provides a source of alumina and silica for glazes and is an important ingredient in high-fire white ware and porcelain bodies.

The wide variety of kaolin types available is indicative of the difficulty in classifying clays. In the United States the major commercial deposits are in the Southeast. North Carolina produces a residual-type kaolin with many coarse rock particles, while the deposits in South Carolina and Georgia are of the sedimentary type. Florida deposits are even more plastic and are termed ball kaolin. No kaolin, however can truly be termed plastic in comparison with ball clay.

Ball Clay

Ball clay is chemically similar to kaolin after firing. In its unfired state, however, the color is dark gray due to the presence of organic material. Although weathered from a granite-type rock much like that which produced kaolin, the ball clay particles were deposited in swampy areas where the organic acids and gaseous compounds released from decaying vegetation served to break down the clay particles into even finer sizes than those of the sedimentary kaolins.

Ball clay imparts increased plasticity and dry strength when used as a body component. If a clay body contains 10 to 20 percent ball clay, its throwing qualities are greatly improved. Like kaolin, ball clay has a high maturing temperature. It can be used as a source of alumina and silica for glaze, as well as a binding agent. However, when they are stored for long periods, such glazes tend to form gas leading to glaze defects. In this event the glaze can be dried out and reused, or a few drops of formaldehyde can be added to discourage fermentation. Tennessee and Kentucky have the largest deposits of ball clay in the United States.

Stoneware Clays

Stoneware clays are of particular interest to the potter, because they are generally plastic and fire in a range from cone 6 to cone 10.* Depending upon the atmospheric conditions of the firing, the color will vary from buff to gray. Stoneware clays are found in scattered deposits from New York and New Jersey westward to Illinois and Missouri and also on the Pacific Coast. The clays differ in composition; in comparison with kaolin they contain impurities, such as calcium, feldspar, and iron, that lower the maturing temperatures and impart color to the clay.

It is quite unusual today for a single clay to be used as a throwing body. To the principal clay, which may be either stoneware or fireclay, portions of ball clay, flint, feldspar, and even earthenware clay are added to obtain the desired plasticity, firing temperature, color, and texture.

---

* See Appendix for temperature charts giving cone equivalents in degrees Fahrenheit and centigrade. Cones indicated in the text refer to the Orton series. Note that Seger cones have a slightly different range.

Fireclay

Fireclay is a high-firing clay commonly used for insulating brick, hard firebrick, and kiln furniture. Its physical characteristics vary; some fireclays have a fine plastic quality, while others are coarse and granular and unsuitable for throwing. Fireclays generally contain some iron as an impurity but seldom have calcium or feldspar. The more plastic varieties, like some stoneware clays, are sometimes found adjacent to coal veins. They can be high in either flint or alumina and therefore have special industrial uses. Fireclays of one type or another are found in most states, absent only from a few mountainous regions and the southeast and northeast coasts.

Earthenware Clays

Earthenware clays constitute a group of low-firing clays that mature at temperatures ranging from cone 08 to cone 02. They contain a relatively high percentage of iron oxide, which serves as a flux (a substance that lowers the maturing temperature of the clay), so that when fired they are rather fragile and quite porous. Unlike stoneware bodies, which are almost completely vitreous, the usual earthenware body, after firing, has a porosity between 5 and 15 percent. Because of the various fluxes it contains, earthenware cannot be made vitreous, for it deforms and often bloats and blisters at temperatures above 2100°F (1150°C). All of these factors limit its commercial use to building bricks and tiles.

Earthenware clays of one type or another can be found in every part of the United States, although commercial deposits are most abundant in the lower Great Lakes region. Many such clays, available commercially, are of a shale type. Shale deposits are clays laid down in prehistoric lake beds. Time, chemical reactions, and pressure from overlying material have served to cement these clay particles into shale, a hard, stratified material halfway between a clay and a rock. Shale clays are mined and ground into a powdered form similar to ordinary clay. The small lumps that remain can be troublesome if they are not screened out, for they will absorb moisture, expand, and rupture much like a piece of plaster.

Some earthenware clays are of glacial origin and therefore are quite varied in composition. They frequently contain soluble sulfates that are drawn to the surface during drying. When fired, a whitish film appears on the surface. This defect can be eliminated by the addition to the clay body of 2 percent barium carbonate.

Slip Clay

Slip clays are those clays that naturally contain sufficient fluxes to function as glaze without further additions. Although white and even blue slip clays exist, the most common are tan, brick red, or brown-black. Most slip clays fire in a range from cone 6 to cone 10. The best-known commercial slip clay is Albany, mined in small pits near Albany, New York. There are many small deposits of glacial clays scattered throughout the northern states that will make satisfactory slip glazes with little or no addition. Slip glazes are easy to apply; they usually have a long firing range and few surface defects.

Bentonite

Bentonite is an unusual clay that is used in small amounts as a plasticizer. Deposits are found in most of the western mountain states, the Dakotas, and in several Gulf states. It has the finest particle size of any clay known.

Bentonite was formed in prehistoric ages from the airborne dust of volcanic eruptions. It is composed largely of silica. A nonclay glaze may include up to 3 percent bentonite in order to assist adhesion without noticeably changing the glaze. When used in nonplastic (short) clays, one part bentonite is usually equal to five parts ball clay. It should be mixed dry, since it becomes quite gummy when mixed alone with water.

CLAY BODIES

An earthenware, stoneware, or porcelain body that is completely satisfactory in all respects seldom occurs in nature. It may not be plastic enough, nor have the right color, nor fire at the desired tempera-

ture. Even clays from the same bed will vary slightly in chemical and physical qualities. Thus it is usually necessary to mix clays in order to achieve a workable clay body.

In making up a clay body, one generally begins with a clay that is available at a reasonable price and that has no major faults, such as an excessive amount of sand or grit. No clay should be considered unless it is moderately plastic. The plasticity can be improved by additions of ball clay or bentonite. In rare cases, a clay may be so fine that it will not dry easily without cracking. In this event, a less plastic clay, a silica sand, or a fine grog (coarse, crushed, fired clay), can be added to *open up* the clay body and make it more porous so that it will dry uniformly. This treatment is often necessary to make an extremely fine or *fat clay* throw and stand up better.

Occasionally a clay will lack sufficient fluxes to fire hard enough at the desired temperature. When this occurs, inexpensive materials containing fluxes, such as feldspar, talc, dolomite, nepheline syenite, bone ash, and so on are usually added. If color is no problem, iron oxide can be used. In some cases a small amount of lower-firing clay can be added, which has the advantage of not cutting down on plasticity, as additions of any of the above materials will do. If, on the other hand, there is too large a proportion of fluxes and the clay body deforms at a relatively low temperature, the potter must either begin again with a different clay or add clays that are higher in alumina or in silica and alumina. Either a Florida kaolin or a plastic fireclay of a high maturity can be used for this purpose.

Porcelain bodies are more commonly used for commercial ware that is mechanically produced in plaster molds or by jiggering (see Chap. 10, pp. 261, 264), since the hand potter usually prefers the reduction effects and the plastic qualities of gray or reddish stoneware. Porcelain bodies are compounded principally from kaolin, feldspar, and flint. If greater plasticity is desired, some ball clay is used, resulting in increased shrinkage. For a throwing body, the ball clay may be as much as 25 percent of the body. (See Appendix, pp. 321–323, for suggested clay bodies.) Chemically, there is little difference between a stoneware and a porcelain body, except for the presence of small quantities of iron and other impurities that color the stoneware and fireclays. Bone china is similar to porcelain, with the exception that bone ash has been added to the body as a flux to increase translucency and to reduce the temperature needed for maturity to about 2275°F (1250°C). Like porcelain, bone china is very hard, white, and translucent when thin. Its greatest faults are a tendency to warp in firing and the lack of sufficient plasticity for throwing.

The term *chinaware* is used rather loosely to designate a white body usually fired between cone 4 and cone 8. Some types, such as restaurant china, are very hard and durable. However, they should not be confused with the even harder and more translucent porcelain bodies fired at cone 10 to cone 16. A white body in the cone 4 range often uses nepheline syenite, rather than feldspar, as a flux. White earthenware clay rarely occurs in nature. The low-fire white bodies often used for gift pottery contain large amounts of talc to reduce their firing temperatures to cones 08 to 04 (1750°F–1950°F, 955°C–1065°C).

TESTS FOR CLAY BODIES

Before a new clay or clay body is purchased or used, a few simple tests should be made.

Plasticity

Plasticity is essential to a throwing clay. A standard, simple test for plasticity is to loop a pencil-size roll of clay around one's finger. If the coil cracks excessively, it probably will not throw well. The ultimate test, however, is to throw several pieces. In comparring bodies, the potter should make sure that all samples have been aged for equal lengths of time. Three weeks in a plastic state usually is adequate for a clay to improve appreciably in throwing qualities. In this time the finest particles become thoroughly moist, and the slight chemical breakdown caused by the organic matter contained in all clays can occur. The increase in plasticity brought about by aging is more pronounced in acid than in alkaline clays. If

it is necessary to use an alkaline body, the addition of a small amount of vinegar to the throwing water will prove helpful.

Wedging, a process by which the clay is kneaded by hand to remove air pockets, has a considerable effect in increasing plasticity. In a coarse clay, the realignment of particles by the wedging action can also prove beneficial (see p. 147).

Water of plasticity refers to the amount of water needed to bring a dry, powdered clay into a plastic state suitable for throwing. The finer the particle size, the more plastic a clay will be and the more water it will absorb.

Porosity

The porosity of a fired clay body is directly related to the hardness and the vitrification of the clay. To make a porosity test, an unglazed fired clay sample is weighed. After an overnight soak in water, the sample is wiped clean of surface water and weighed a second time. The percentage gain in weight will be the porosity of the clay body.

Most bodies used by the hand potter can be fired with a variation of at least 50°F (10°C) from the optimum firing temperature without proving unsuitable. As a general rule, fired clay bodies fall within the following porosity ranges: earthenware, 4 to 10 percent; stoneware, 1 to 6 percent; porcelain, 0 to 3 percent (see Chap. 11, pp. 278–279). A higher firing will reduce the porosity, but normally a specific firing temperature will already have been chosen. Adjustments in the flux ratio will affect the firing temperature and, thus, the relative porosity.

Shrinkage

Shrinkage of the clay body occurs first as the clay form dries in the air and then again as the form is put through the bisque (preliminary) firing and the glaze firing. The more plastic clays will always shrink the most. The test for shrinkage is quite simple: first, a plastic clay slab is rolled out and either cut or marked to a measure; when the slab is totally dry, a second measurement is taken; a final measurement is made after firing.

Clay shrinkage rates generally range from 5 to 12 percent in the drying stage, with an additional 8 to 12 percent shrinkage during firings. Thus, the potter can expect a total shrinkage of at least 13 percent and an extreme of 24 percent, with a median of 15 to 20 percent between the wet clay state and the final glazed ware. These normal shrinkage rates apply to plastic throwing clays. Special white ware bodies using spodumene in place of feldspar and only small amounts of clay have a greatly reduced shrinkage and can even be compounded to develop a slight expansion in firing. Wollastonite as a replacement for silica and flux in a body will also decrease firing shrinkage.

Because of shrinkage strains placed upon large sculptural forms, it is often necessary to include a grog in amounts of 20 to 30 percent of the body. Since this material is already fired, little further change occurs. There is also a tendency in drying for the clay to pull away slightly from the grog and thus open air channels that facilitate the drying out of thicker portions that would otherwise crack.

QUARTZ INVERSION

A major problem in the successful compounding of ceramic bodies is quartz inversion. During the firing of a ceramic body, silica (quartz) changes its crystalline structure several times, with a rapid expansion in size. This is especially true of free silica that is not in a chemical bond with other body components. The most pronounced change occurs when the firing temperature reaches 1063°F (575°C). At this point the quartz crystals change from alpha to beta quartz, with a resultant expansion. At about 1850°F (1010°C) tough, interlocking mullite crystals composed of alumina and silica begin to form, and this chemical combination gives the fired body its strength. In the cooling process the situation is reversed; when the kiln temperature drops to 1063°F, the free silica in the body contracts. Quartz inversion is one of the reasons why a slow cycle of firing and cooling is essential. If a ceramic piece is heated or cooled too quickly, or if the distribution of heat is uneven, the piece will crack. Special precautions are required for ovenware, which must be able to withstand, with minimal thermal expansion, the heat to which it will be exposed in use.

In preparing a clay body several things can be done to control the effects of quartz inversion. A combination of pyrophyllite and talc substituted for part of the feldspar will reduce thermal expansion, as will the addition of petalite ($Li_2O \cdot Al_2O_3 \cdot 8\,SiO_2$). Spodumene ($Li_2O \cdot Al_2O_3 \cdot 4\,SiO_2$) in a clay body creates an irreversible expansion, while the inclusion of wollastonite ($CaSiO_3$) also reduces firing shrinkage and aids in developing a tougher body that is more resistant to heat shock.

Rhodesia has been a major source of petalite, but at present the political situation has made shipments uncertain. Three parts of spodumene and one part of feldspar can be substituted for four parts of petalite. The amounts needed will depend upon the alumina-silica ratio of the body and the fluxes present. A 5 to 10 percent addition of any of the suggested chemicals will often make an appreciable difference in reducing the problems of quartz inversion encountered in developing an ovenware body. The precise amounts can be determined only by testing a number of different body compositions, since the character of various stoneware and fireclay bodies, as well as the firing temperatures, precludes the setting of any arbitrary percentages.

CLAY PROSPECTING AND PREPARATION

There are few sections of the United States in which a suitable pottery clay cannot be found. Digging and preparing one's own clay is seldom an economic proposition, but it can be rewarding in other ways. If one is teaching in a summer camp, a hike can easily be turned into a prospecting trip. In commercial clay mining, the soil overburden is removed by power shovels, and the entire operation is quite mechanized. For the few hundred pounds of clay the individual wishes to obtain, he must depend upon the accidents of nature to reveal the clay bed. A river bank, a road cut, or even a building excavation will often expose a deep bed of clay that is free of surface contamination (Fig. 291). If the clay contains too much sand or gravel it may not be

291. Digging clay in the local hills at Mashiko, Japan.

worth the trouble. A few tree roots will not disqualify a clay, but any admixture of surface soil or humus will render it unusable.

On the first prospecting trip it is advisable to take samples of a few pounds of clay from several locations. These samples should be dried, pounded into a coarse powder, and then soaked in water. Passing the resultant clay slip (liquid clay) through a 30-mesh sieve is usually sufficient to remove coarse impurities. If the clay proves too sandy, one can allow the heavier particles to settle for a few minutes after stirring and then pour off the thinner slip. This slip is then poured into drying bats and tested as described earlier.

In most localities, surface clay is likely to be of an earthenware type. The samples should also be tested as possible slip glazes. It is surprising how many pockets of glacial clay work nicely as glazes, either alone or with a small amount of flux added. In some areas, the river-bank clay may be of a stoneware or fireclay type. All in all, clay prospecting can be profitable, but it is mostly fun. In this day of the super-processed item, starting out from "scratch" gives one a rare feeling of satisfaction.

5 Forming Methods

Pottery, Sculpture, and Architectural Ceramics

A ball of plastic clay and our fingers are all that we need to form a pot. The survival and continued popularity of ancient methods of hand construction (Fig. 293) are clearly a reaction to the impersonal nature of modern industrial society. Perhaps no other endeavor represents such a link with the past and reflects the continuum of human life better than ceramic art. It rejects the nineteenth-century ideal of rational progress in favor of a more natural sequence of change, forgetting, and rediscovery.

POTTERY

Early man used a natural object, such as a shell or a gourd, as a container for countless ages before he learned to fabricate a more efficient receptacle. It is probable that a gourd or round stone served as the first mold over which a layer of clay was pressed and allowed to harden, then removed to form a hollow bowl. The accidental burning of a clay-lined basket is thought to have been the means by which man learned to make pottery (see p. 2).

Preparation of Clay

Whether clay is prepared in small amounts or in large quantities in a pug mill, it should be mixed with slightly more water than is needed for forming consistency. This is because some evaporation will occur both in storage and in *wedging*. In order to achieve proper control in the forming processes, the plastic clay must be perfectly uniform in consistency and free of air bubbles. Therefore, it must be thoroughly wedged (kneaded) before any of the forming methods described in this chapter can proceed. As illustrated in Figure 294, firm pressure from the heel of the hand compresses the clay and forces air pockets to the surface. This is accomplished with a rocking motion and with a slight twist at the end of the action. The resulting spiral eventually exposes all portions of the clay mass and

opposite : 292. WARREN MacKENZIE, U.S.A. Vase. Porcelain with clear glaze, height 14″. The finger marks and slight irregularities add spontaneity to this vase, which might have been dull if it had been thrown mechanically.

147

left : 293. DON FINEGAN, U.S.A. Planter. Thrown and hand-built stoneware with glaze and polyester resin, height 18″.

294. In wedging, the plastic clay is kneaded with the fingers and the heel of the hand in a rocking spiral motion (*below, left* and *right*). A wedging table (*bottom*) can also be used.

allows the trapped air pockets to escape. Proper wedging is vital, for if any air bubbles remain in the clay after it has been wedged and formed, the finished piece may very well explode in the kiln.

Occasionally the potter will have two batches of clay that are of a slightly different composition or moisture content. The process of wedging them into a uniform body can be hastened by first cutting the clay into thin sections with a wire and then forcibly throwing the sections edgewise onto a plaster wedging table. After a few such operations, the clay can be kneaded in the usual manner.

The Pinch Pot

The pinch method is perhaps the easiest way of forming a small bowl, and it requires no apparatus whatever (Figs. 295–298). A hollow is formed with the thumb in a small ball of clay. With careful pressure between the fingers, the wall is gradually thinned, and the form is developed. If the clay is too moist, the piece will sag, while a stiff clay will crack excessively. By pressing the fissures together and smoothing with the fingers, any small cracks can be healed. It is not a good practice to use water on the surface in an attempt to seal cracks in too-dry clay. Instead, one should soak the clay, knead it into a ball, and begin again. Legs or a coiled foot can be added when the piece is leather hard (see p. 195).

296. The wall is gradually thinned, and the form develops.

297. The interior is smoothed with the thumb to heal cracks.

295. A hollow is formed with the thumb in a ball of clay.

298. A coiled foot rim is added to the completed pot.

The Hump Mold

Solid plaster of paris molds of various shapes can be used to form a vessel (Figs. 299–301). Plastic clay is pounded or rolled with a rolling pin to the desired thickness on a piece of light canvas. The resulting slab is then draped over the mold and pressed to conform to it. The excess clay is trimmed away. If a moistened paper towel is shaped smoothly over the mold, the clay form, after drying slightly, can be removed without sticking. The hump mold process, while hardly creative, is a good beginning project, especially for children, who need a bit of early success to maintain their interest. In a summer camp, rounded beach stones are a readily available source of varied and interesting forms (Fig. 302).

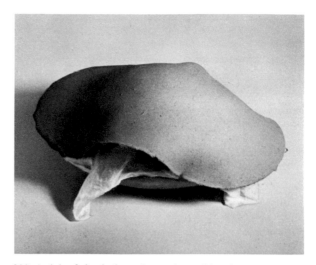

299. A slab of clay is draped over the mold and pressed down.

300. Moist paper towels separate the clay from the mold.

301. Decorative additions are applied to the drying clay.

302. Rounded beach stones can make excellent hump molds.

The Coiled Pot

The coiling method, employed for thousands of years before the invention of the potter's wheel, has continued in use by many cultures until the present. Needing no equipment except a simple turning device, it is an ideal method for beginners. Since the potter's wheel produces only a symmetrical form, many contemporary ceramists have returned to the coil method—either alone or in combination with slab and wheel-thrown forms—because of the free sculptural constructions possible. In the past very large pieces have usually been coiled and later refined on a slow-turning wheel.

The technique is simple (Figs. 303–306). A round slab of plastic clay is pounded out to the desired size and thickness to form a base and then placed on a turning wheel with a plaster bat. A lump of plastic clay is squeezed into a ropelike form and rolled with the flat of the hand on a level surface. The clay should not be so moist that it sticks to the fingers or so dry that cracks develop. Slip can

303. A rope of clay is rolled out to the desired thickness.

304. The first coil is laid upon the prepared slab base.

305. The coils are joined on the inside with a wiping motion.

306. The finished coil pot is smoothed with a metal scraper.

be used to join the coils, but it is a messy and time-consuming procedure; if the clay is of a proper consistency, no slip is needed. Not all forms are practical in the coil method. Flat, platterlike shapes can best be made from a slab on a plaster supporting mold, while small, symmetrical objects are more efficiently thrown on the wheel. However, coarse, groggy clays, which are almost impossible to throw, can be coiled.

Unless a piece is exceptionally large, it is usual to roll out a coil long enough to lay about three circles on the base. The coils are joined inside and out with a vertical wiping motion of the fingers. Squeezing or pinching should be avoided, for either will stretch and distort the form. The inside must be smoothed as the coiling proceeds, but as long as the coils are completely joined, a perfect outer surface is not needed. When the form is finished it can be refined with a flexible scraper, and applied, pressed, or carved decorations can be added.

Some shapes will sag if they are coiled too rapidly, so it may be necessary to let a portion of the work dry slightly (with the top edge protected by a damp rag) before continuing to build up the form. Interrupted work can be covered with a plastic bag to prevent its becoming too stiff, for if the clay dries beyond the leather-hard state, damp coils cannot be applied, nor can handles and other additions be made. When work is resumed on a partially dried piece, the topmost joint must be scored (roughened and slashed with a sharp tool) and slip applied to facilitate joining. The finished piece is covered with plastic or placed in a damp box to allow moisture content to equalize, for otherwise cracks will develop. If it is dried in the open air, small appendages, such as handles, should be wrapped in damp paper toweling to prevent too-rapid drying.

Thick Coil and Paddle

A variation on the coil method is the paddled pot (Figs. 307–312). In this technique the heavy coil shape should be tall and narrow, for paddling stretches the clay. A curved block of wood is held against the inside of the pot for support, while the outside is struck repeatedly with a wooden paddle to thin and shape the coils. The paddle may be textured or wrapped with cord to prevent sticking. The coils should be of a slightly stiffer clay than is used for normal coiling. It is possible to pull the form in, but not so much as on the wheel. Smaller coils can be used to complete the form, and applied or carved decoration added later.

307. Thick coils are laid upon a prepared slab base.

308. A curved piece of wood and a paddle shape the form.

309. The walls have been thinned by beating with a paddle.

310. The exterior surface of the finished pot is smoothed.

311. Small coils are added at the top to form a rim.

312. Carved and applied decorative textures are added.

The Slab Pot

In addition to the very simple mold-draped form described at the beginning of this chapter, many other forms can be made by the slab method (Pl. 14, p. 159; Figs. 313–314). The slab can be pounded with the heel of the hand or rolled to the desired thickness with a common kitchen rolling pin (Figs. 315–320). To prevent the clay from sticking, it should be rolled out on a piece of canvas, which also allows for easy transfer. A dry plaster slab or grog dusted on a table top will serve the same purpose. If the proposed form is rather flat, the clay pieces must be leather hard before assembly begins. The joints should be scored and covered with clay slip. Since flat, horizontal sections tend to sag in construction and firing, it may be advisable to insert clay partition walls. These must have cut-out openings to allow for drying.

above : 313. STEPHEN POLCHERT, U.S.A. Bottle. Slab-built stoneware with thrown additions, height 36″.

below : 314. ED TRAYNOR, U.S.A. *Slab Form.* 1969.

right : 315. A clay slab is rolled out with a rolling pin.

below right : 316. The ends are scored and joined.

154

317. The upper edge of the slab is scored with a tool.

318. A carved slab is added to form the top of the pot.

319. Spouts and legs can be thrown or pinched separately.

320. Decorative lines are incised in the finished piece.

Throwing on the Wheel

People generally think of wheel-thrown ware when they speak of pottery. For most potters, throwing is the most enjoyable aspect of the ceramic craft. Coaxed by the skillful fingers of the experienced potter, an expanding form seems to acquire a life of its own. One must learn to throw quickly and efficiently, for clay softens and sags from the water used in the throwing process. Throwing, when done by an experienced craftsman, looks deceptively easy, and the beginning potter should not be discouraged by his initial difficulties and failures, or let himself be put off by virtuoso, "show-off" demonstrations, often staged for students, in which the spinning form is made to change rapidly from one shape to another. This may make a good show at a crafts fair, but it is not useful instruction for the novice potter. To develop skill at throwing on the wheel demands much practice, even for the experts.

The first task for the student is to learn to throw the largest piece possible from the ball of clay on hand. He should have in mind a rough idea of the form he wishes to achieve, and each change in shape should be directed toward this end. Every form begins with a cylinder, but the proportions of the cylinder will depend upon the final shape desired. For example, a bowl shape requires a low cylinder with a thick lip, so that the rim can be expanded; it must be taller than the finished size that is wanted, for as the form is pulled outward, it will settle.

In throwing a tall vase or bottle the potter should not try to develop the desired form with thick walls and then attempt to make them thinner. Instead, he should throw a cylinder to the maximum height possible; neck in the top if necessary, allowing room for the hand or arm; flare out the bottom and mid-section to the desired shape and thickness; then quickly pull in the top and finish the rim. Speed is essential, for the longer one works on the neck area, the more the bottom sections will sag and settle.

In the beginning the student should confine himself to throwing simple cylinder shapes, as tall and as uniform as possible. Since the cylinder is the basis for all pottery forms, it is pointless to attempt anything else until this first step has been mastered.

As work progresses, the student should concentrate on throwing a series of similar forms, discarding the bad ones (Fig. 321). He will thus develop naturally both technique and a feeling for design. Designing forms on paper is of little use to the beginner. Only when he acquires a feeling for a clay form and a knowledge of what forms can or cannot be thrown conveniently will a meaningful design evolve.

By working with one particular form for a while the student will learn to sense subtle variations, to which earlier he was oblivious. With practice he will throw taller and thinner shapes from the same amount of clay and, eventually, will develop a dynamic quality in his throwing that comes with greater freedom and ease in handling the clay. It is a poor practice for the student to attempt to throw a different shape each time, for he thus learns nothing from previous errors and misses the most natural method of developing form and design.

Centering

Perfect centering on the wheel is essential to the success of any thrown form (Figs. 322–326). A clay ball is placed on a freshly moistened bat, and, with the wheel turning, the clay is forced down with the right hand. Bracing the elbows at the sides will increase strength and accuracy in centering. When the clay has been centered perfectly, it is opened out with the thumbs into a thick bowl shape.

321. Facility in throwing is attained by throwing a number of similar shapes and then discarding the awkward ones.

322. A ball of plastic clay is placed on a freshly moistened plaster bat.

323. While the wheel is turning, the clay is forced down.

324. With his elbows braced, the potter centers the clay.

325. When centered, the ball is opened with the thumbs.

326. The clay ball is gradually opened into a bowl shape.

327. The clay must be perfectly centered on the wheel.

328. With the hands joined, the cylinder is pulled up.

329. If the rim is uneven, it can be trimmed with a needle.

330. The walls are thickened and pulled up by necking.

right : 331. Even pressure forces the clay wall upward.

The Cylinder

As with any other form, the throwing of a cylinder begins with the clay perfectly centered on the wheel. With the hands joined for better control, the walls are gradually pulled up to form a cylinder. If the top is uneven, it can be cut off with a needle. The walls can be thickened and pulled up by necking (drawing in gently at the neck of the cylinder). Even pressure forces the wall upward (Figs. 327–331).

Plate 14. KENNETH GREEN, U.S.A. Lidded vessel. Slab-built stoneware with stamped and carved decoration, Barnard slip under a mat dolomite glaze; height 13 ½″.

Plate 15. JOHN MASON, U.S.A. *Cross*. Height 5′. The size, the stark geometric quality, and the vivid color all contribute to the excitement and impact of this piece.

332. Pressure from the inside flares out the cylinder.

333. The top of the cylinder is necked in and thickened.

334. The top is pulled up farther, and the walls are thinned.

335. Thinning continues until the desired height is reached.

right : 336. The lip is finished with a soft leather.

The Bottle Form

To create a bottle form, the potter begins with a cylinder thrown as in Figures 327 to 331. This cylinder is flared out by pressure from the inside, and the top is necked in and thickened. The top is then pulled up and thinned. This process is repeated until the desired shape or height is reached. Finally, the lip of the bottle is finished with a piece of soft leather (Figs. 332–336).

The Bowl Shape

From the basic clay form begun as in Figure 326, any number of shapes can be made. The bowl presents the fewest problems (Figs. 337–340). As always, the opened ball must be perfectly centered. The potter should throw as quickly as possible, for otherwise the clay will become too wet. The clay should not be pulled too thin where it flares up from the bat, and the concave form must be maintained as the walls are pulled up, for any flatness of the curve will cause the piece to sag. Unevenness in the outer rim is trimmed with a needle, then the rim is moistened and finished with a piece of soft leather.

337. The centered clay is opened to form a bowl shape.

338. The walls are carefully pulled up and thinned.

right : 340. The rim is finished with a soft leather.

339. Unevenness in the rim is trimmed with a needle.

341. A rib is used to thin the wall and smooth the surface.

342. The knuckle can be used to lift and shape the form.

343. Hands are interlocked, and the knuckle exerts pressure.

344. As the form rises, the knuckle and hand thin the walls.

right : 345. Pressure is exerted from inside and outside.

A slightly different technique is illustrated in Figures 341 to 345. A rib (a flat oval of hardwood) is used to thin out the wall and smooth the surface. Since the pressure is concentrated, it creates less torque and not as much water is needed as when working with the fingers alone. Use of the knuckle is common in the preliminary shaping of a form and when throwing larger pieces. The partially cut-away forms (Figs. 343, 345) illustrate how the clay is both thinned and pulled up in the forming process.

left : 346. A small piece is cut from the wheel with a wire.

below : 347. After cutting, the pot is lifted from the wheel.

Problems in Throwing

An initial error many students make is to start with a clay ball that is too soft, too stiff, or improperly wedged. It takes considerable pressure and ample water to center the ball on the wheel head. Only when the ball is perfectly centered should it be opened with the thumbs. To do otherwise will create an uneven wall thickness, which usually results in the eventual collapse of the piece.

As throwing progresses excess water will cause the clay to soften too rapidly. The slurry that forms on the hands should not be washed off but used on the pot as a lubricant. Some potters use a thin slip instead of water. The walls should be pulled up evenly without deep finger grooves, which may create a weak spot in the wall. In throwing large pieces a sponge can be used to eliminate the grooves that are caused by firm pressure on the large mass of clay.

The palms and fingers are used when centering or when necking in a large vase or bottle, but for normal throwing only the fingertips are required. They create a greater pressure with less friction and are more sensitive in revealing the action of the clay. Whenever possible one elbow is braced at the side and the thumbs are joined for better support.

It is important that the inside curve of the pot be formed when the cylinder is quite low, for it is impossible to shape it easily when the walls are higher. The clay should not flare out at the wheel head but should be pulled up as the cylinder rises. Students often leave this base section too thick.

Throwing Aids

While large bowls must be thrown on a plaster bat and trimmed later, most pieces can be thrown more conveniently on the metal wheel head, then cut off with a twisted wire (Figs. 346–347). A hinged, adjustable pointer is a handy guide for throwing sets (Fig. 348). Small pieces, such as egg cups (Figs. 349), are best thrown "off the hump" (a 50-pound ball of clay). To remove the thrown form from the mass of

348. A pointer assists in making a number of uniform pieces.

349. Small pots and cups can be thrown " off the hump. "

350. With the wheel turning, a string cuts the pot free.

351. Excess clay is trimmed from the foot of the pot.

352. The center portion of the foot rim is cut away.

clay, the potter cuts a groove at the bottom and inserts one end of a piece of string. With the wheel revolving slowly, the string cuts through the pot at its base (Fig. 350).

Trimming the Foot

Excess clay on the bottom of a thrown form can be trimmed while the pot is still on the wheel head. Small pieces are cut off with a twisted wire immediately after throwing. Larger pots are allowed to dry slightly, cut off the bat with a ground-down hacksaw blade, then trimmed as illustrated in Figures 351 and 352. A needle will serve to indicate the bottom thickness.

353–354. A large piece can be trimmed by setting the neck inside a plaster cylinder.

Small bottles can be trimmed by setting them inside a large-mouthed glass jar, which is held in position on the wheel head by a coil of clay. For larger pieces a hollow plaster form serves the same purpose (Figs. 353–354). After trimming, large bowls should be placed upside-down on a flat surface to dry evenly and to avoid warping.

The Foot and Lip

Because of the emphasis on form as a whole, the details of the foot and lip are often neglected. The most common error is to make the base area too large, thus imparting a heavy and clumsy feeling to the pot, which, instead, ought to suggest a form in space, resting lightly on its foot rim (Fig. 355).

It is quite satisfactory for a small, functional pot to have a flat base, showing the slight ridges left by the cutting wire. Generally, however, the center of the base is trimmed out with a looping tool (Fig. 352) in order to lighten this area, as well as to give a feeling of the continuing curve of the form. There are many types of foot rims—low and high, thin and broad, flat and delicate—and the kind that is used should relate to and complement the character of the pot form (Fig. 356). The foot rim may be the result of the trimming operation, or, in the case of a high foot, it may be a cylinder thrown separately and joined to the pot with slip. Because the potter's name is usually incised or stamped here, and also because it is an inconspicuous area, most pot lovers look immediately at the foot for what it reveals about the attitude and craft of the potter. Regardless of the type of foot that is used, the base of the pot should be perfectly smooth and have a slight bevel at the edges.

A small pot can have a simple, rounded rim, but a larger piece may appear weak without some accent at the lip. Apart from esthetic considerations, a slight thickening is desirable to strengthen the rim, to reduce warpage in drying, and, in the case of a very large bowl, to make lifting more convenient. Unfortunately, we can too easily become creatures of habit and, during a day's throwing, put a similar rim on all our pots. It is far better to analyze the form as it develops and plan the rim to harmonize with the total design. Occasionally just a finger depression in a flat rim or a simple impression from a roller will add distinction and emphasis.

Covers, Handles, and Spouts

Teapots and covered jars present a greater problem in design and technique, for the various parts must be thrown separately but form a unified whole when assembled (Fig. 357). This is one instance when it is desirable to make a few sketches beforehand in order to develop the form of the cover and its relationship to the body. In the case of a teapot, the type of handle and its balance with the spout should be worked out in advance.

Commercial teapots are slip cast in one piece, and the model is carved from a solid block of plaster. Students, unfortunately, tend to be influenced by such industrial products. A much more exciting and individual form will result if the character of the clay and the imprint of the finger are revealed in the joining of handles and spouts, rather than having them modeled and sponged to an impersonal smoothness.

It is imperative that the vessel and the cover be thrown at the same time and of clay with a similar moisture content. Accurate measurements should be taken with a caliper and the cover thrown to

above left: 355. HARRISON McINTOSH, U.S.A. Compote. Stoneware with blue-green and black glazes, height 6½″.

left: 356. ANGELO GARZIO, U.S.A. Oval vase. Stoneware. In this vase, as in the compote by Harrison McIntosh, the treatment of the lip and foot is in perfect accord with the form and the decoration of the entire piece.

below: 357. ANGELO GARZIO, U.S.A. Teapot. Stoneware with rust glaze. The spout and handle are sensitively balanced.

left : 358. The measurement for the lid of a pot must be perfectly accurate. A caliper is used to determine exact size.

hobby shops. It must be soaked overnight in water and then boiled for several hours. After the appropriate length is determined, half of the cane is cut away on the ends that are to fold over the clay loops. Nails driven into a board will assist in bending it to the desired curve. When dry, the cane is inserted into the loops, and the ends are whipped.

A teapot spout must be thrown at the same time as the body and cover, and the base must be broad enough and long enough to allow for loss of length in fitting it to the pot (Fig. 360). The pieces are joined as soon as the teapot is trimmed and while the spout base is damp enough to be pinched rather than cut to fit the pot. Strainer holes should be ample in size, because some filling with glaze is likely. A strainer placed low on the pot is less apt to become clogged with tea leaves. The spout should reach to the height of the teapot rim and be rather sharp in profile at the pouring edge, since a

size (Fig. 358). There can be no trimming on the rim, because drying rates are so different that a proper fit would be most unlikely.

There are many types of covers. Perhaps the easiest to make is a flat disk form with a knob thrown in place. The cover must be slightly thicker than needed, so the round rim can be formed with a soft leather. If the lid is small, it can be cut off the wheel with a twisted wire; larger lids are thrown on a plaster bat and allowed to dry slightly before removal. When a flat cover is used, the vessel must have a depressed inner flange, which can be used as a chuck (an edge support) when trimming the underside of the lid.

A domed cover is thrown like a simple dish or bowl (Fig. 359). After trimming, a knob can be thrown on top or a modeled knob can be attached with slip. A teapot lid is also thrown like a dish, with enough clay left on the rim to create a deep flange that will prevent the cover from falling out when the teapot is in use.

Teapot handles, like covers, take many forms. Pulled clay or hollow thrown handles are quite satisfactory, but the most common are made of bamboo or cane and attached to two or three clay loops on the pot. The loops must be sturdy and affixed securely to the pot, with an ample opening for the cane. Dry cane can be purchased in many

below : 359. CHARLES LAKOFSKY, U.S.A. Jar with domed cover. White porcelain with light gray to pearly blue-violet glaze, height 7″. Adding a knob to this cover would have been redundant and would detract from the form and decoration.

left : 360. A spout must be thrown at the same time as the pot, so that both pieces will dry at the same rate.

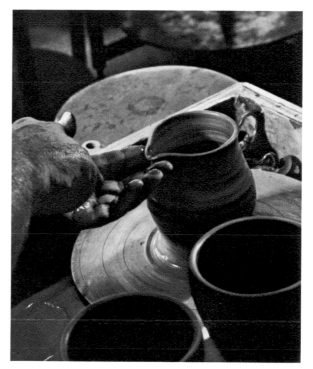

361. Pitcher spouts are formed with a wiping motion.

362. A pulled handle is made by impressing with the thumb.

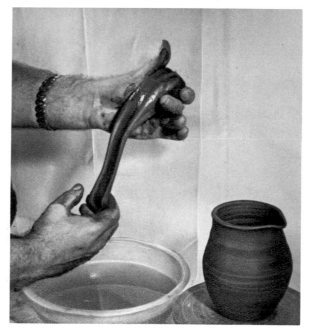

rounded edge is bound to drip. If a sharp edge on the pouring lip is not feasible, a small groove cut in it and left unglazed will also discourage dripping. A large spout is not necessary for proper pouring and may give an awkward appearance to the teapot or pitcher. Pitcher spouts are formed as in Figure 361 with a simple wiping motion of the fingers.

A properly pulled handle, revealing as it does the fluid quality of clay and the impression of the fingers, adds a note of spontaneity to any pot (Fig. 362). The clay must be very plastic but a little stiffer than that used in throwing. Starting with a thick coil of clay and ample water, the potter extends the clay with a stripping motion of the fingers and thumb, gradually thinning it to a diameter natural and comfortable to hold. The heavy upper section is pinched off, and the remaining butt end pressed firmly against a roughened area of the pot. The clay is flared around the joining for maximum support. After the proper curve is formed, the bottom of the handle is attached to the pot. The finger marks created in joining can be left if desired. Beginners invariably take too long to complete this process, and the clay handle becomes soft. If this happens, the butt end can be stuck on a shelf edge to dry slightly before joining. Smaller handles, such as those on mugs, can be attached directly to the pot and pulled in place.

New Techniques

Relatively few changes have occurred in ceramic techniques over the centuries, although attempts at refining methods and materials are made continually. For several years the Kansas potter Sheldon Carey has tried to find an acceptable substitute for water in the throwing process, one that eliminates the inevitable softening of the clay. The most successful of the many substances tried is Separan 20, a synthetic material manufactured by the Dow Chemical Company of Midland, Michigan. About 2 percent of this granular material is dissolved in hot water. The clay ball is centered with water, and throwing proceeds in the customary manner, with a small amount of Separan used as a lubricant. Since the clay does not soften, very thin walls can be thrown. This technique is especially suited to porcelain, which is much less plastic than ordinary throwing clay. It is not recommended for the beginner but could be of use to the experienced potter.

The Separan solution cannot be kneaded into the clay, for it is rather oily and will make the clay nonplastic. Hands are best cleaned with a plastic choreboy, rather than a sponge.

Another innovation by Sheldon Carey is an "upside-down" wheel (Fig. 363). The wheel is attached to a heavy shaft so that it can be raised and reversed after the basic cylinder is begun. As the illustration reveals, extremely tall cylinders and bottles can be thrown with this device. An air bubble, however, is disasterous, for the whole pot will collapse.

A further aid to the experienced potter is the inclusion of 1-inch lengths of fiber glass kneaded into the clay body. This should be done just before throwing. By increasing the strength of the clay one can throw flaring forms, such as bowls, much larger and with a thinner wall. Since the fiber is of a silica composition, it melts in firing with no apparent change in the clay body.

CERAMIC SCULPTURE

Terra cotta sculpture can be constructed in many ways (Pl. 15, p. 160; Figs. 364–365). The clay body should contain at least 20 percent grog to reduce shrinkage in firing and to allow for more rapid drying of thick sections.

If the form is relatively simple, such as a small, blocky figure or a head study, it can be modeled solid. When it has dried slightly, it is cut into two or more sections with a fine wire, and these sections are hollowed out to form walls of a uniform thickness. Then the joints are scratched and coated with slip, and the whole structure is reassembled.

Elongated forms or figures are usually constructed from hollow clay sections modeled over wooden dowels or fiber tubes. Surface additions are made after the structure has been assembled (Fig. 366). A continuous air passage must be provided to allow for uniform drying and to avoid an explosion in firing. Protruding forms will usually

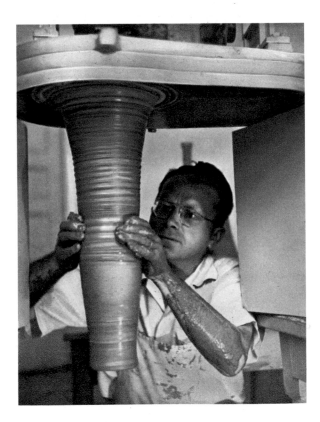

left : 363. The " upside down " wheel for throwing very tall forms was developed by SHELDON CAREY.

above left : 364. DIRK HUBERS, U.S.A. *Figure.* Medium high-fire clay (fired in several sections), height 6′.

above right : 365. JERRY ROTHMAN, U.S.A. Sculptural form. Hand-modeled clay with red and green glazes, height 30″.

right : 366. TOM SOUMALAINEN, U.S.A. *Reinvention of Tula.* Slab and modeled clay, reduction fired; height 4′2″. Collection Mr. and Mrs. Ira Julian, Winston-Salem, N.C.

below : 367. EARL HOOKS, U.S.A. *Fruit Forms*. Wheel-thrown and hand-molded clay with white mat-satin glaze, diameter 16″. Collection Fisk University, Nashville, Tenn.

right : 368. DANIEL RHODES, U.S.A. *Stoneware Form*. Stoneware and fiber glass, height 48″.

need clay supports during construction, drying, and firing (Fig. 367).

Fiber glass fabric, like that used in boat repairs, is helpful in adding strength to the clay during construction (Fig. 368). For use in slab pieces, the fiber must have an open mesh like a common window screen. The fiber glass is cut to size and placed on a rolled-out slab; then a thin layer of softer plastic clay is worked across the fabric to join it to the slab. Fiber glass gives a remarkable stiffness to the clay, allowing the construction of forms that would

369–371. Sculptor Narendra Patel has experimented with several methods of modeling over a styrofoam core.

right : 369. Clay slip is brushed onto the styrofoam surface.

center : 370. The completed sculpture is allowed to dry slowly.

bottom : 371. Vermiculite provides support for the hollow sculpture when the styrofoam is drained out through a hose.

otherwise be very difficult. If the clay is not too stiff, there is also a certain amount of "give" to the material, which permits some manipulation of the form. As mentioned earlier, fiber glass, when cut into 1-inch pieces, separated, and kneaded into the clay, will also increase the wet strength of clay used in slab, coil, and throwing techniques.

Sculptors accustomed to the usual methods of modeling clay upon a wood or metal armature are always frustrated by the need to model hollow if the form is to be dried and fired. Several new materials, if carefully used, eliminate this problem. The commercial insulating material, styrofoam, can be used as a core around which to model the clay. It is available in different shapes and sizes, which can be cemented together to create an armature. The form of the sculpture should be realized rather completely before the application of the clay. A clay slip brushed on the styrofoam surface will cause the plastic clay to adhere to the armature as the form is modeled (Fig. 369). The completed piece (Fig. 370) is allowed to dry slowly until the first crack occurs, at which time the crack is carefully filled with stiff clay. A small hole is then cut in the top of the figure, and a styrofoam solvent is poured in. If the piece is small, it can be upended when the styrofoam is completely dissolved, but for a large construction a small hole is made near the base to permit the dissolved liquid to run out. The studio must be well ventilated, because the mixture is quite volatile. When the sculptural form is such that the removal of the armature might cause the partially dried clay to deform, a hollow box can be placed around it and filled with vermiculite to furnish support (Fig. 371). A small rubber hose is used to drain off the dissolved styrofoam. The piece is then allowed to dry completely, and firing proceeds as usual.

The Wisconsin sculptor Narendra Patel has experimented with several types of combustible armatures. The method illustrated uses a styrofoam core (Fig. 372). This is covered with a layer of cellulose sponge (Fig. 373), which compresses as the modeled clay form shrinks. The sponge is coated with clay slip, and, when dry, this creates a base for modeling the form (Fig. 374). If the layer of sponge is sufficient, the completed sculpture will dry and shrink without cracking. The core material burns out in firing.

372–374. When used as a base for modeling sculpture, styrofoam can also be burned out during the firing.

left : 372. A rough styrofoam core is cemented together.

below left : 373. Cellulose sponge covers the styrofoam.

below : 374. When the piece is fired, the styrofoam burns off.

375. JOHN MASON, U.S.A. Sculptured wall mural. 1964. Black and brown stoneware, 7 × 14′. The exciting plastic and textural qualities of this mural provide a great contrast to the cast concrete of the architecture.

ARCHITECTURAL CERAMICS

When one considers the drab, factorylike atmosphere of many contemporary buildings, it would seem logical that the ceramic mural—with its possibilities of color, texture, and durability—would be relatively popular (Figs. 375–379). Its use abroad is much more common than in the United States. The customary requirement in many European countries that a certain percentage of the construction costs of public buildings be spent for art works is a factor in the widespread use of murals. A less fortunate situation prevails in America, where most buildings are financed by speculators primarily concerned with the optimum utilization of space for the maximum return of profit on their investment. There are, nevertheless, a few innovative and imaginative architects and clients who are willing to commission ceramists.

The medium-size wall panel is no problem to the potter, either in conception or in relation to studio facilities. A large decorative pot demands the same attention for a central design motif and the use of textural patterns and color accents. However, a truly large mural must be conceived on a broad scale for it may have to "carry" effectively for several hundred feet. Perhaps just as important to the potter as the design aspect are the factors of sufficient kiln space and a large and efficient work area in which to lay out and complete the project.

left : 376. RUTH DUCKWORTH, U.S.A. Sculptured reliefs. Clay, height 11′. University of Chicago.

below : 377. Detail of Fig. 376, sculptured reliefs.

right : 378. JERRY ROTHMAN, U.S.A. Sculptured triptych. Brick-red stoneware, height 8′ (figures later glazed black).

below : 379. JERRY ROTHMAN, U.S.A. Sculptured wall reliefs (detail). Clay with red, green, and blue glazes, height 8′.

6 Ceramic Form and Design

The examples of ceramics from the past illustrated in Chapters 1 and 2 are unquestionably a source of interest and inspiration for all students, reflecting as they do the efforts of countless generations of potters. There is a danger, however, in uncritically accepting them as models to emulate. When social and economic conditions change, the function of ceramics within a culture also changes. Much of the variety found in historical ceramics is the result of the different needs experienced by the cultures that produced them.

In this respect our own era is drastically unlike earlier periods. Technological advances have produced glass, metal, fiber, and plastic containers, completely eliminating the need for many of the standard forms. Never again will man make the huge earthenware oil containers of the Minoans or the stoneware storage crocks of Colonial America (Fig. 106). Nor is it likely that a modern aristocracy will collect, as status symbols, delicately decorated luster-ware plates, as did the Islamic caliphs (Fig. 47).

The Industrial Revolution, which began to change the basis of pottery making as early as 1750, severed the age-old pattern by which form and design, nurtured by a local market, evolved in the transition from father to son. With no guidance from the past, the contemporary potter is most eclectic, absorbing influences from hither and yon. Many theories have been proposed regarding ceramic design, and they serve a comforting and guiding role, much as did the older traditions. But like all theories, they can become self-defeating if applied in a didactic manner.

FORM AND FUNCTION

A generally accepted tenet of contemporary design is that the *form* of an object is largely dictated by its *function* (Fig. 381). About this there can be little debate, for if a spout on a pitcher does not pour

opposite : 380. JOHN MASON, U.S.A. Sculptural form. 1963. Brown clay with polychrome glazes, height 5′. The different glazes and varied textural areas soften only slightly the almost brutal explosion of form.

well or if the handle on a vessel is difficult to hold or is in poor balance, the value of the entire design is in question, regardless of its appearance.

The importance of this observation is somewhat obscured by the diminished need for ceramic containers in our culture. In recent years ceramic pieces have tended to fill a decorative and sculptural role (Fig. 382), which is just as valid an expression of the material as were the earlier functional wares. This transition from pottery to sculpture has produced

above : 381. ANGELO GARZIO, U.S.A. Pitcher. Stoneware with rust-red mat reduction glaze and touches of yellow, height 7″. The accents of spout and handle and the flaring rim add interest to this functional pitcher.

right : 382. CARL PAAK, U.S.A. Sculptural pot. Clay with gray and cobalt glazes, height 25″. The assembled sections in this sculpture create a compatible organic unity.

many decorative works embellished with nonfunctional spouts and handles, a device that can be incongruous if not used with taste and skill.

There is a trend among some contemporary potters deliberately to make pots that are patently useless. This Pop Art or Dada approach has had the effect of shaking us loose from conventional design stereotypes. Its greatest value is usually in the idea it presents, rather than the resulting form. The "nonpots" of a less literary nature must be evaluated from a sculptural rather than a pottery standpoint (Fig. 383). The major problem facing the ceramist who works in this idiom is his inability to free himself completely from the standard pottery forms. Once the line between a decorative pot and a fully sculptural piece has been crossed, potlike elements remaining in the work may be distracting and spoil the effectiveness of the design.

MATERIAL AND METHOD

The inherent nature of clay imposes restraint on ceramic design much as do the requirements of function. Clay in either the plastic or the fired state has unique qualities that distinguish pottery from artifacts made of wood, metal, fiber, or glass. It is logical that these characteristics be stressed in the design development (Fig. 384). While a thrown clay form and a piece of blown glass have much the same

below left : 383. PHILLIP GEARHART, U.S.A. *Untitled.* 1969. Thrown and hand-built clay with cast bronze arm, height 25″. Although the social comment in this piece is of primary importance, the form is equally arresting.

below right : 384. DANIEL RHODES, U.S.A. Sculptural form. Stoneware and fiber glass, height 12″. The plastic form emerges from a cylinder, which functions as a base.

left: 385. DAVID SHANER, U.S.A. Planter. Hand-built clay with salt glaze. A rough textural quality in this large planter becomes the major decoration.

below: 386. WARREN MACKENZIE, U.S.A. *Four Vases (for a Gynecologist's Office)*. Porcelain with celadon glaze, height of largest vase 6". The plasticity of these expanding forms has been skillfully enhanced by the pinching and distortion of the rims.

particularly satisfying medium for the designer. One is its plasticity—its ability to respond to the touch of the finger, to be stretched, impressed, incised, and added to with ease (Fig. 385). Another is its natural color and rough texture, which are often sufficient decoration, although the addition of glazes gives a new dimension of surface effect and color which may rival the attractiveness of the form itself. These two elements, form and surface decoration, must be in harmony in order for a ceramic design to the successful.

Of critical importance to the character of a ceramic piece is the forming method used. Ancient pottery was usually coil constructed, and this technique is still employed today for very large pieces, for groggy clay, or for asymmetrical forms. Not all

effect in terms of expanding volume, attempts to achieve in clay the thinness and translucency of glass would be unsuccessful. Similarly, metal has a strength that permits the construction of apparently fragile and protruding forms which would be impossible in clay. Lacking both transparency and tensile strength, clay has other qualities that make it a *above :* 387. WILLIAM DALEY, U.S.A. Planter. Stoneware, reduced and unglazed; length 24″. The slab construction is uncompromisingly revealed.

right : 388. RON GILBERT, U.S.A. Hanging weed bottle. 1969. Slab-built stoneware with thrown spouts and mat gray glaze, height 13″. The decoration stresses the plastic, textural quality of clay.

thrown pieces reveal their origin by finger-impressed throwing rings, but they have in common the tensions of expanding plastic clay and a symmetrical form (Fig. 386). Slab constructions, by their angularity, are perhaps easiest to identify (Fig. 387). It is desirable that the forming method be revealed in a clear and straightforward manner, both for the integrity of the design and for a logical economy of time and effort. It is most often pointless to laboriously coil and refine a hand-built form that might more easily be thrown on the wheel. The plastic quality of clay, which readily permits addition, encourages a combination of construction methods (Fig. 388). The contrast of expanding thrown form with angular slab can be a pleasing design element, but the potter must take care that the two elements of construction are in harmony, and not fighting each other for dominance.

ASPECTS OF CERAMIC FORM AND DESIGN

Aside from the dictates of function, and perhaps because of the unique qualities of clay, a tremendous variety of form is feasible in ceramics. The flexibility of techniques—coil, thrown, and slab or a combination of all three—permits the realization of nearly any conceivable form. A ceramic piece embodies, simultaneously, concepts of negative space and solid form. Because of the nature of the construction and firing processes, we know that every ceramic work, however heavy and solid it may appear, is hollow.

The perfect form, the sphere, when cut in half becomes a hemisphere or bowl, another esthetically pleasing form. But when we depart from these geometric absolutes, we find that some shapes are much more satisfying than others. This is because of our psychologically influenced perception. The human eye is attracted to a dominant form or color; if we are presented with two centers of interest, the effect is distracting, even psychically disturbing. A desire for order seems basic to human equilibrium.

The "stop sign" or "bull's eye" approach of advertising is useful in attracting attention, but there is little to hold the viewer after this initial and demanding contact. Pop Art, a style that began in England in the 1950s—but which, from the start, drew on such resources of American mass culture as advertising and the comic strip—had a great success in America through the 1960s and continues to

389. RUTH DUCKWORTH, U.S.A. Vase. Slab-built porcelain with crackle glaze and touch of iron oxide, height 6″.

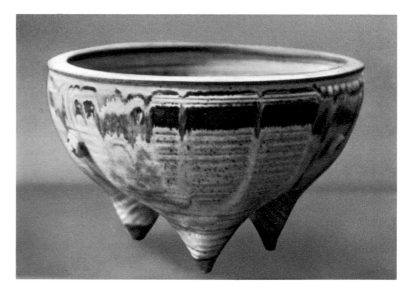

390. THEODORE RANDALL, U.S.A. Punch bowl. Stoneware, diameter 23″. The unusual tripod feet provide a sense of lightness.

be influential (Pl. 16, p. 193). By exploiting the contemporary commercial, mechanized environment, Pop assimilates images as commonplace as flags, hot dogs, beer cans, and movie posters. In this, a new humanism or a return to recognizable forms and images, after decades during which modern art seemed to move relentlessly toward greater abstraction, has been claimed for the style. Often as amusing and trenchant in its commentary on modern experience as the biting, ironic subject matter of the paintings and prints produced by Hogarth in the eighteenth century, Pop, like Hogarth's work, is significant not only for its content but for the remarkable sureness of design and composition the Pop artists imposed upon their materials—ordinary, even debased, as the sources of Pop typically have been. Still, the billboard may be an all-pervasive element in American life, but its presence in the American living room in the form of Pop Art or Pop ceramics could be an uncomfortable one.

Geometric shapes—the sphere, the cylinder, the cone, the cube—have a strength and simplicity that make them complete in themselves. When we begin to stretch and elongate these stable forms, we develop a sense of movement (Fig. 389). Interest in a form is proportionate to the length of time needed for one's eye to travel over it, sense the movement of contours, the swelling of volumes, and enjoy subtle contrasts of color and texture. To sustain our interest, the contour must maintain this flow as the volume contracts or expands. A pot with a base and top that are similar in size or one with the greatest girth in the center is generally unsuccessful, for the equal division that results creates a feeling of monotony and little sense of movement. The most satisfying design is one conceived with a definite zest and sweep. Our senses react more favorably toward forms with unhesitant conviction of roundness or straightness, with no evidence of ambiguity. This does not rule out subtlety—only indecision.

Contrasts in the character of the form heighten our enjoyment; textural areas serve the same function, as they react against smoothly defined forms or surfaces. Elaborate embellishments and colorful glaze effects are best suited to rather simple shapes, for otherwise the form and decoration compete for attention. For the same reason a brilliant color, which might be overwhelming on a large vase, will be more satisfying on a small piece.

The foot rim and the lip of a pot are details often neglected by students. The tendency is for the base to become heavy and clumsy. Unless extreme stability is a functional necessity, the foot should serve as a pedestal for the pot, to give a feeling of form suspended in space (Pl. 17, p. 194; Fig. 390). In rare cases the shape of a pot is such that no evident

391. MARC HANSEN, U.S.A. Footed bowl. Stoneware with applied clay and brown slip under salt glaze, height 10″. The plastic decoration and throwing rings are clearly visible.

lip is necessary, but normally a thickening of the lip is desirable to strengthen the rim and to reduce warpage. Just as important is its function in closing the composition—terminating the upward movement of the form—and its role as a decorative accent.

SURFACE DECORATION

Ideally, decoration should be a part of, and inseparable from, the form, such as throwing rings or stamped and applied clay accents, which reveal the plastic nature of the clay in a simple, unobtrusive manner (Fig. 391). One of the advantages of a salt glaze is that applied and incised decorations are not obscured by the glaze but retain their crispness in a pleasing contrast to the smooth glazed surfaces. The character of a form largely determines the type of decoration that would be most effective. For example, the taut outline and idealized proportions of early Greek ware seem quite suited to repetative overall geometric patterns. By contrast, the vigorously thrown Sung forms are in perfect agreement with bold brush designs and incised slip motifs.

Intricate and delicate decoration such as was used on Islamic luster ware requires a simple and reserved form for success. These curvilinear designs in overall patterns complement the typical shallow bowl forms. Spotty panel designs of a realistic nature are usually distracting on a pottery piece, for they tend to monopolize the viewer's attention and thus overpower the form.

Skill with the brush is rather rare among contemporary Western potters (Fig. 392). It is not surprising that those cultures which traditionally have used the brush as a writing medium excel in this type of ceramic decoration. Even to make a simple bold stroke of color or slip across a plate in a way that will produce the effect of careless freedom requires a certain amount of practice. The novice potter often goes overboard, with glaze patterns that look like discarded paint cans, completely devoid of any accidental charm. But in the hands of an experienced craftsman, the chance running of a heavy glaze can become a type of decoration, intriguing because it reveals the viscous nature of glazes (Fig. 393).

above : 392. PAUL SOLDNER, U.S.A. Vase. Thrown and compressed clay with lightly smoked raku glaze, brushed iron engobe and sgraffito decoration; height 10″.

right : 393. KAREN KARNES, U.S.A. Platter. Clay with runny, overlapping glazes. Reduction brings out the iron specks.

7 Decoration and Glazing

DECORATION

There can be no doubt that, in ceramics, creating a form is the most critical process, but the techniques of decoration and glazing must not be overlooked. As the final operation, the embellishment of a piece can be the deciding factor in its success or failure. Throwing must be accomplished with freedom and ease and must be expressive of the fluid, plastic quality of clay. The trimming and refining of a thrown form should not destroy this spontaneous quality. The throwing ridges left on the surface of a piece may well prove to be a more suitable decorative device than one that is laboriously contrived.

The decision about what decorating technique will be used should be made by the potter as soon as possible after the piece has been thrown, for there are certain types of decoration that must be undertaken while the clay is still plastic. The character of the thrown form will usually determine the type of decoration that is most suitable (Pls. 18–19, pp. 194, 211; Fig. 395). For example, a delicate brushwork is obviously out of place on a vigorously thrown, heavily grogged piece. It is essential that the decoration complement rather than overwhelm the form. As in all aspects of craftsmanship, practice is necessary to achieve freshness and fluency of execution.

Clay in a Plastic State

Immediately after removal from the wheel a pot can be pressed or pinched to change either its shape or its surface (Fig. 396). Figures 397 to 406 illustrate a few of the many possibilities for surface decoration of clay while it is still in the plastic state. These include scratching, incising, or cutting away with a tool. Sometimes additional clay is applied to form a raised design. Impressions can be made with various implements, with a cord or serrated roller, or with stamps fabricated from ceramic, plaster, and other materials (Fig. 407).

opposite : 394. HARRISON MCINTOSH, U.S.A. Covered jar. Clay with white mat glaze over dark engobe, height 10 ½″. The incised oval motifs echo the shape of the jar.

left : 395. Dan Schaumburg, U.S.A. Vase. Stoneware, height 12″. Pinch marks in the plastic clay, an uneven poured glaze, and reduction specks produce a spontaneous decoration.

above : 396. Dorothy Perkins, U.S.A. Vase. Thrown stoneware, altered with the fingers, with thick slip; height 10″.

below and opposite page : 397–404. Incised and stamped decoration can be made with a number of simple devices or even with the fingers.

above : 405–406. Simple stamps are used to create repeat patterns.

left : 407. RICHARD PEELER, U.S.A. Bottle. Hand-built stoneware with stamped decoration and white engobe, glazed only with falling wood ash; height 14″.

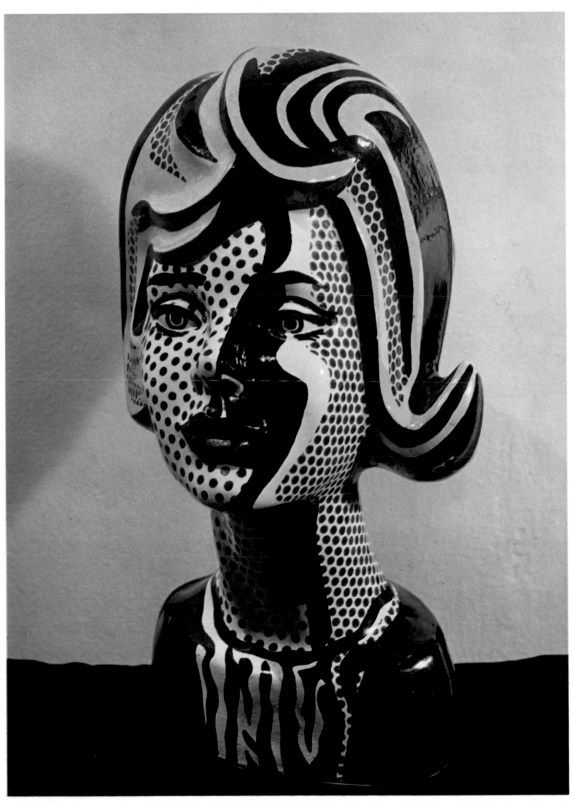

Plate 16. ROY LICHTENSTEIN, U.S.A. *Head With Black Shadow*. 1965. Glazed ceramic, height 15″. Collection Mr. and Mrs. Leo Castelli, New York.

left : Plate 17. HARRISON MCINTOSH, U.S.A. Bottle. Stoneware with swirling decoration in red and black mat glazes, height 15 ¾″. Although contemporary, this bottle has an ancient, timeless quality.

below : Plate 18. KARL MARTZ, U.S.A. Bowl. Stoneware with iron-red decoration formed by a Japanese limestone glaze over brushed oxide, diameter 4 ½″.

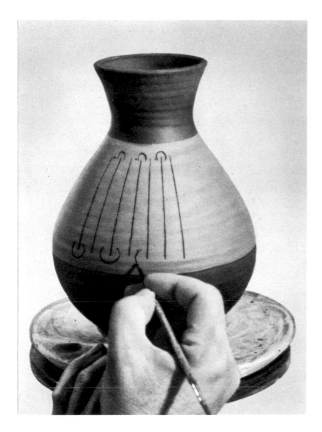

Leather-hard Clay

The term *leather hard* refers to clay that has dried enough that it can be handled without deforming or suffering other injuries, but which contains sufficient moisture to permit handles and knobs to be readily joined and clay slips applied without flaking off. Carving and incising are more conveniently done at this stage, since the clay cuts cleanly and does not stick to the tool.

Sgraffito refers to a design produced by scratching through a layer of clay slip to expose the color of the clay body underneath (Fig. 408). Care must be taken that the slip is not too dry, for otherwise it will flake off; if it is too wet, the incision will be smudged.

Mishima is a decorative technique of Korean origin (Fig. 409). An incised area or line is filled with plastic clay of a contrasting color. When partially dried, the surface is scraped flush, revealing the design underneath (Fig. 410). A slip glaze can also be used effectively.

above : 408. Sgraffito designs are scratched through slip.

below : 409. ROBERT ECKELS, U.S.A. Bowl. Clay with mishima decoration in light clay on a dark body, diameter 10″.

right : 410. Scraping reveals the mishima decoration.

Slip trailing, using a syringe in the manner of a pastry bag, must be done before the ware has dried too much. The piece should be left in a damp room for a day after the design has been applied. Raised glaze decoration can be applied in a similar fashion (Fig. 411). This technique was popular in Colonial America and earlier in England (see p. 33).

Clay in the Dry State

Decoration on a clay surface that has dried is limited to application of engobes, coloring oxides, and stains. An *engobe* is clay slip to which feldspar, flint, and a flux have been added. These reduce the shrinkage of the engobe and increase adhesion when the ware is fired (see Appendix, p. 323).

Color oxides or stains are applied to dry clay in much the same way as one would paint a watercolor. Too thick an application will flake off or cause poor glaze adhesion. A small amount of the base glaze—or feldspar and bentonite—added to the colorant is desirable.

Wax-resist decoration generally is used in conjunction with coloring oxides (Fig. 412). The wax may be a hot paraffin or beeswax; more convenient water-soluble wax emulsions that need not be heated are now available. The wax design repels the applied stain, which then serves as a background color. Incised lines through the wax will absorb stain, thus producing a linear decoration that is difficult to achieve by other methods.

Glazes can be applied to some raw clays and fired in a single operation. The glazing must be done quickly to prevent uneven moisture absorption, which will cause cracks. Glazes with a high clay content, such as the Bristol type, work best for this process. Majolica decoration can be used on the raw glazed ware in the usual manner.

Clay in the Bisque State

The possibilities of decoration become much more limited after the pottery has been bisque fired.

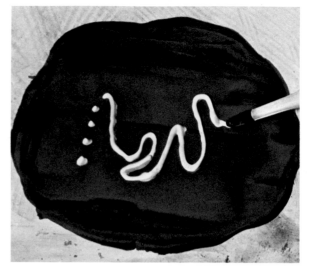

above : 411. Glaze is slip trailed onto the clay surface.

below : 412. Color oxides are applied over a wax resist.

Engobe decoration can be brushed on if the clay content is low enough to reduce shrinkage and if sufficient fluxes are present to bind the engobe to the body when it is fired. It is much more convenient to apply such decoration in the leather-hard stage.

Sgraffito decoration can be applied to this kind of engobe or to a glaze. In order to execute a linear design with precision, the glaze or slip coating must not be too heavy; if it is too dry, it will flake off and leave a ragged incision. The purpose, of course, is to reveal the contrasting color of the clay.

Color oxides or stains are sometimes used as brush decoration or as an overall colorant either on a bisque body or on a glazed surface. Designs incised into plastic clay are generally brushed with oxides prior to glazing (Fig. 413). As a rule, brush decoration with oxides is more effective over a glaze, for underglaze designs on bisque ware may be obscured by an uneven glaze or damaged during application.

Wax-resist decoration is frequently used both under and over a glaze and in combination with stain and sgraffito designs. It has a tendency, however, to ball up when used on a sprayed glaze. A binder may be necessary even in a dipped glaze to provide a stronger decorating surface.

GLAZING

Glazing in the raw-clay state was mentioned briefly in the section on decoration. This method has definite advantages. By eliminating the normal bisque fire, there are savings not only in the labor needed for the extra stacking, unloading, and operation of the kiln but also in the fuel or power needed for the extra firing. A single firing also promotes a better union between the body and the glaze. There are, however, several disadvantages to the combined firing. Because of its fragility, the dry raw-clay vessel may be broken in handling. Expansions caused by the moisture absorbed into the dry clay may cause the vessel to crack. In general, only when the body of a piece is rather thick and uniform can

glaze be poured safely. Other pieces should be sprayed, since the glaze, with its troublesome moisture content, can then be applied at a slower rate. One additional precaution must be taken in glazing raw ware: alkaline fluxes must first be fritted. These compounds have a high coefficient of thermal expansion. When they are absorbed into the outer portion of the clay, their expansion and contraction rate during firing and cooling is so great in contrast to the remainder of the body that they will cause it to crack.

Glazing in the bisque state is the most common procedure (Fig. 414). Normally bisque ware is fired to about cone 010 or 1650°F (900°C). At this stage

left : 413. Color oxides are rubbed into an incised design.

above : 414. ROBERT ECKELS, U.S.A. Bottle. Stoneware with scratched motif, height 14″. After glazing, portions of the glaze were rubbed off to reveal the decoration and the contrasts between body color and glaze.

415. In dip glazing the piece is plunged into a large pan of glaze and then quickly withdrawn.

416. Tongs are used for dip glazing small pieces or when overall coverage is desired.

the bisque is hard enough to be handled without mishap yet sufficiently porous to absorb glaze readily. Bisque ware that is fired at lower temperatures will absorb too much glaze; if fired too high, it is especially difficult to glaze, for the glaze tends to run off. An exception to the normal bisque firing is high-fire chinaware. Such pieces as thin teacups, which are fragile and likely to warp, are often placed in the kiln with supporting fireclay rings inside their lips, or they are stacked upside down and then fired to their maximum temperature. Later, these chinaware pieces are glazed and fired on their own foot rims at a lower temperature where warpage losses are much less.

How to Glaze

Glazing is a process that can be described only inadequately. Before the actual glazing operation takes place, there are a few precautions that must be taken. If bisque ware is not to be glazed immediately upon its removal from the kiln, it should be stored, if possible, where dust and soot will not settle on it. The bisque ware should not be handled

excessively, especially if the hands are oily with perspiration, for this will deter the glaze from adhering properly. All surfaces of the bisque ware should be wiped with a damp sponge or momentarily placed under a water tap to remove dust and loose particles of clay. The moisture added to the bisque ware by this procedure will prevent an excessive amount of glaze from soaking in and thus allow a little more time for glazing. Extra moisture also helps to reduce the number of air pockets and pinholes that form when the glaze dries too quickly on a very porous bisque. The amount of moisture required depends upon the absorbency of the bisque, the thickness of the piece, and the consistency of the glaze. Should the bisque-fire temperature accidentally rise much higher than cone 010, the ware should not be dampened at all. The glaze must be cleaned completely off the bottom of the pot and $\frac{1}{4}$ inch up the side as soon as it is dry enough to handle. Excess glaze will always run, so it is never advisable to allow a heavy layer of glaze to remain near the foot rim. The cleaning operation can be simplified by dipping the bottoms of bisque pots into a shallow pan of hot paraffin before glazing.

Dip glazing is probably the simplest glazing method. Its chief drawback is that a rather large amount of glaze is required. After the vessel has been cleaned and moistened with a damp sponge, it is plunged into a large pan of glaze (Fig. 415). It should be withdrawn almost immediately and shaken to remove the excess glaze. The object is then placed on a rack to dry, and any finger marks are touched up with a brush. Small-size pots can be dip glazed with metal tongs, which come in several shapes (Fig. 416). The slight blemishes in the glaze caused by the pointed tips usually heal in firing. A more uniform surface is produced if the glaze is thin enough to allow dipping two or three times within a few seconds.

Pouring requires less glaze than dipping, and the technique can be applied to a greater variety of shapes. For example, the insides of bottles and deep, vaselike forms can be glazed only in this manner.

In the case of a bottle, the glaze is poured through a funnel (Fig. 417), and then the vessel is rotated until all its surfaces are covered. The remainder is poured out, and the bottle is given a final shake to distribute the glaze evenly and to remove the excess (Fig. 418). Glazes that are poured or dipped must be a little thinner in consistency than those that are brushed on. The insides of bowls are glazed by pouring in a portion of the glaze, spreading it by rotating the bowl, and then pouring out the excess. This must be done rather quickly, or an overabundance or uneven amount of glaze will accumulate. To glaze the exterior of a bottle, the potter grasps it by either the neck or the foot rim and pours the glaze from a pitcher, allowing the extra to run off into a pan beneath. Finger marks are then touched up with a brush, and the foot rim is cleaned when dry. The outsides of bowls are glazed in the same manner, provided the foot is large enough to grasp. Otherwise the bowl can be placed

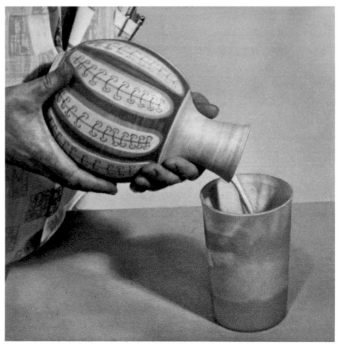

above: 417. Glaze is poured through a funnel to coat the interior of a bottle.

right: 418. The bottle is rotated to coat the entire inner surface, and extra glaze is poured off.

above : 419. Dowels support large pieces for pouring.

below : 420. A brushed glaze is best for large pieces.

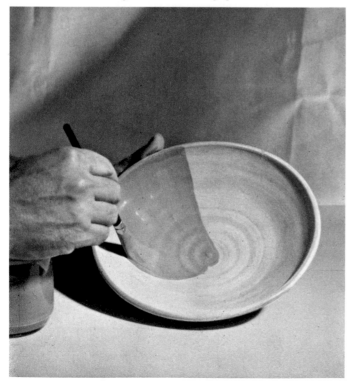

upside down on wooden dowels extending across a pan (Fig. 419). It is better to glaze the interior of a vessel first and the exterior later.

A brushed glaze (Fig. 420) is easiest for the beginner. It is also used for glazing large pieces that are difficult to pour or dip. A flat brush, at least 1 inch in width and possibly larger, is used. An oxhair bristle is preferred, for camel hair is much too soft and floppy. Unless a considerable amount of clay is in the glaze, the addition of bentonite or a gum binder is necessary for proper adhesion. The potter must work rapidly, using a full brush, and cover the piece with a second and third coat before the bottom layer is completely dry, for otherwise blisters will develop. The glaze must be neither too watery nor so thick that it will dry quickly and cause uneven laps and ridges.

Sprayed glazes permit subtle variations in color and more definite control over glaze thickness and coverage (Figs. 421–423). Actually, these advantages are more theoretical than real and apply more to the beginner than to the experienced potter. The finest Chinese glazes of the past, which we have difficulty in equaling today, were all dipped or poured. Gradations of color were achieved by blowing the color on separately through a lung-powered bamboo tube atomizer.

The spray method has two major drawbacks: large amounts of glaze are often wasted; and the glaze coating, because of its fragility, is easily damaged by handling during the process of loading the kiln. With practice smooth glazes can be poured, eliminating these disadvantages and saving time. In general, sprayed glazes are most satisfactory on flat, shallow bowls or for reglazing. Various effects can be achieved by grading one glaze into another and by toning down an underglaze with a second that may be more neutral or with a mat. When a viscous glaze covers one that tends to be runny, the underglaze may break through and run, causing a spotty decorative effect.

Because many glaze materials are toxic, glazes should be sprayed only in a booth with an adequate exhaust fan. In order to obtain an even layer, one should spray the glaze slowly, building up a coating with a soft, "woolly" surface. If the sprayed piece becomes too moist (Fig. 422), a shine may develop, blisters may form, and the glaze may run. In the latter event, the glaze will be uneven, regardless of how many more coats are applied. It may be advisable, under some conditions, to scrape off the glaze and begin again.

above : 421. Glaze is sprayed in a booth with an exhaust fan.

below : 422. Even coverage is vital in spray glazing.

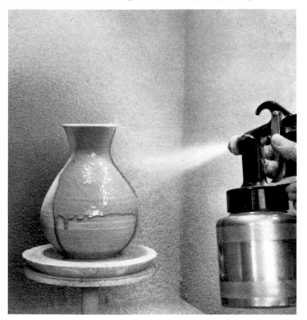

Glaze Defects

There are usually several reasons, all logical, why a particular glaze fault occurs, but trying to deduce the cause from one piece may prove quite difficult. When there are a number of pots having the same glaze from a single kiln load or when there are several glazes on a single body, the problem of deduction is much easier. The following section outlines some of the factors that can cause glaze defects. Glaze faults may result not only from the composition of the glaze but from the improper selection or preparation of the clay body, faulty kiln operation, or, as is most frequently the case, lack of skill and care in application.

Defects Caused by the Body

1. A body that is too porous because of improper wedging, kneading, blunging, or pugging may cause small bubbles, beads, and pinholes to form in the glaze as the body contracts and the gases attempt to escape.

2. Excessive water used in forming the body can result in similar conditions.

423. The finished sprayed piece is allowed to dry.

3. A large amount of manganese dioxide used as a colorant in a body or slip may cause blisters to form in both the body and the glaze.

4. Soluble sulfates are contained in some clays and come to the surface in drying, forming a whitish scum. Pinholes and bubbles develop as these sulfates react with the glaze to form gases. This condition can be eliminated by adding up to 2 percent barium carbonate to the body. A slight reduction fire at the point when the glaze begins to melt will reduce the sulfates and allow the gas to pass off before the glaze develops a glassy retaining film.

5. If the body is underfired in the bisque and therefore very porous, it may absorb too much glaze. Soluble fluxes in the glaze, because of their higher thermal expansion and contraction rates, can cause the body to crack. In any case, a glaze applied to a very absorptive body could have a coarse, or even a sandpaperlike surface.

Defects of Application

1. Blisters or pinholes may result if the bisque ware has not been moistened slightly before glazing. The glaze traps air in the surface pores of the body.

2. Dust or oil on the surface of the bisque ware may cause pinholes or a scaly surface in the glaze.

3. If the glaze is applied too heavily, it will run and obscure the decoration, perhaps causing the pot to stick to the kiln shelves.

4. In addition to flowing excessively, glazes that have been applied too thickly will usually crack in drying. When the piece is fired, these cracks will not heal but will pull farther apart and bead at the edges. If the drying contraction is great enough, the adhesion of the glaze to the body will be weak, causing portions to flake off during the initial smoking period of the firing cycle.

5. On the other hand, a glaze application that is too thin will result in a poor, dry surface. This is especially true of mat glazes, which require a slightly thicker application than do glossy glazes.

6. If a second glaze coating is applied over a completely dry first coat, blisters will form. The wetting of the lower glaze layer causes it to expand and pull away from the body.

7. If the bisque ware is considerably cooler than the glaze at the time of application, bubbles and blisters may develop later.

8. Glazes high in colemanite should be applied immediately after mixing. If they are allowed to set, they thicken from the deflocculating effect of the colemanite. The extra water necessary to restore their consistency causes the glaze to separate and crawl in drying. The addition of .5 to 1 percent soda ash will retard the tendency of colemanite to thicken.

9. Bristol glazes require perfect surface application. Because of their viscosity, thin areas will pull apart and crawl when fired.

Defects Originating in Firing

1. If freshly glazed ware is placed in the kiln and fired immediately, the hot moisture will loosen the glaze from the body, causing blisters and crawling.

2. Too-rapid firing will prevent gases from escaping normally. They will form tiny seeds and bubbles in the glaze. For some especially viscous glazes, a prolonged soaking period is necessary to remove these gas bubbles.

3. Excessive reduction will result in black and gray spots on the body and glaze and will produce a dull surface.

4. Gas-fired kilns with poor muffles employing manufactured gas are troublesome to use with lead glazes. The sulphur content in the combustion gases will dull the glaze surfaces and possibly form blisters and wrinkles.

Defects in Glaze Composition

1. Glazes that are not adjusted properly to the body are susceptible to stresses that may cause the glaze, and at times even the body, to crack. If the glaze contracts at a slower rate than the body does in cooling, it undergoes compression. This causes the glaze to crack and, in places, to buckle and separate from the body. This defect is commonly known as *shivering*.

2. Slightly similar to shivering, and also caused by unequal contraction rates in cooling, is *crazing* of

the glaze. When this happens, the glaze contracts at a greater rate than the body, causing numerous cracks to form (see p. 210).

3. Glazes that run excessively at normal firing temperatures should be adjusted by the addition of kaolin to increase the refractory quality of the glaze or, if possible, by changing the bases. Those that have a lower molecular weight will be less fluid in the glaze melt.

4. A dull surface will result if the proportion of silica to alumina or barium is too low.

5. An excessive amount of tin, rutile, or colored spinels, which are relatively insoluble in the glaze, will also cause a dull or rough-surfaced glaze.

6. Bristol and colemanite glazes not fitted properly to the body will tend to crawl or to crack. This may be due in part to an excess of zinc, which has a very high contraction rate at greater temperatures.

7. Glazes ground too finely—thus releasing soluble salts from the frits, feldspar, and so forth—will develop pinholes and bubbles.

8. Glazes that are allowed to stand too long may be affected by the decomposition of carbonates, organic matter in ball clay, or gum binders. Gases thus formed can result in pinholes and bubbles in the final glaze. In some cases, preservatives like formaldehyde will help. If washed, dried, and reground, the same glaze can be used without difficulty.

8 Glazes

Formulation and Types

SIMPLE FORMULATION

A ceramic glaze and its formulation are not as mysterious as they seem to most pottery students. Basically, a glaze is nothing more than a thin, glass-like coating that is fused to the clay surface of a pot by the heat of the kiln. While some glaze compositions are quite elaborate and use a variety of chemical compounds, a glaze need not be complex, for it contains only three necessary elements.

Silica, commonly called flint, is the essential glaze ingredient. It is also known as quartz in its pure, crystalline state. Were it not that the melting point of silica is so high—about 3100°F (1700°C)—this single material would suffice to form a glaze. However, most earthenware clays mature at about 2000°F (1093°C) and will seriously deform if fired higher, while stoneware and porcelain bodies mature between 2250°F and 2400°F (1238°C–1315°C). Thus, pure silica cannot be used on these bodies.

Flux is a term applied to those compounds that lower the melting point of a glaze. Fortunately, many chemicals with a low melting point will readily combine with silica to form a glassy crystal. Two types of materials are commonly used as fluxes in low-fire glazes: *lead oxides* (lead carbonate, red lead, galena, and litharge) and *alkaline compounds* (borax, colemanite, soda ash, boric acid, and bicarbonate of soda). Although these two categories of low-fire fluxes have comparable fluxing power, their effects on glaze colorants and many of their other qualities are different (see Chap. 9).

A refractory element helps to form a stronger glaze that will better withstand the wear of normal use. The glaze produced solely by a mixture of silica and either lead or borax compounds is soft and rather runny and therefore suitable for only low-temperature glazes. We add a third ingredient, *alumina,* to the glaze to gain this quality. Silica and

opposite : 424. SHELDON CAREY, U.S.A. Bottle. Stoneware with freely brushed color accents of iron red and cobalt blue oxides over mat glaze, height 11″.

alumina unite to form tough, needlelike mullite crystals, creating a bond more resistant to abrasion and shock.

In its final composition, then, a glaze includes its three necessary elements: silica, the *glass former*; a flux, which *lowers the fusion point* of the silica; and alumina, a refractory element that gives *added toughness* and hardness to the glaze, allows a higher maturing temperature, increases viscosity, and prevents devitrification.

It is not economically practical to use refined and pure oxides to make up glazes. The compounds used by the potter are usually those minerals that are abundant in nature in a relatively pure state. Therefore, a simple, low-fire glaze will be made from kaolin ($Al_2O_3 \cdot 2\,SiO_2 \cdot 2\,H_2O$), potash feldspar ($K_2O \cdot Al_2O_3 \cdot 6\,SiO_2$), and red lead ($Pb_3O_4$) or borax ($Na_2O \cdot 2\,B_2O_3 \cdot 10\,H_2O$) as the flux.

The silica content will be provided by both the clay (kaolin) and the feldspar. Alumina is also a constituent of both kaolin and feldspar. Feldspars are minerals that contain alumina, silica, and varying amounts of potash, sodium, and calcium. The predominant flux gives its name to the compound, such as soda feldspar. Potash feldspar, the more common type, is slightly cheaper and fires harder and higher than soda feldspar. Feldspar should be considered only incidentally as a flux in the low-fire range, since it is an important source of silica and alumina. In addition to aiding the fusion of the glaze ingredients, a flux also combines with the silica contained in the clay body of the pot to form a bond uniting the body and the glaze. This union becomes stronger as the temperature increases. Occasionally, a porous clay will absorb so much flux that the glaze will become thin and rough and require adjustments to either the glaze or the body.

Low-fire Glaze Tests

In order to gain an understanding of the qualities imparted to the glaze by silica, alumina, and the flux, the beginning student should make several tests with varying proportions of feldspar, kaolin, and lead fired to cone 04. Earthenware tiles 2 by 3 inches and ¼-inch thick make satisfactory tests. These should be bisque fired to about cone 010. The glaze samples should always be fired upright to detect a tendency in the glaze to run. The bottom quarter inch of each tile is left unglazed to catch the drips and evaluate the fluidity of the glaze.

A suggested beginning formula for an 04 glaze test is three parts red lead, three parts feldspar, and four parts kaolin. Unless the scales are extremely accurate, a total sample of 100 grams is advisable. After weighing, the ingredients are ground in a mortar, and water is added until a creamy consistency is obtained. Modern ceramic materials are finely ground, so only a brief mixing is needed for a small sample. The glaze is brushed on a clean, dust-free tile in several thin coats. Experience is the only guide to the proper thickness of application. Cracks will develop if a layer is too heavy. In succeeding tests the feldspar is left constant, the kaolin is decreased by half, and the red lead is increased by the amount necessary to replace the kaolin. The total number of parts should be kept at ten, so that valid comparisons can be made. This process is repeated until the clay content is reduced to one part. The clay also functions as a binder to hold the nonplastic ingredients together; thus, if no clay is present, methocel or another binder must be added.

The fired samples will show a gradual change from a claylike white coating to one that becomes more fluid and glassy as the increased lead combines with the silica. Finally, a point is reached at which the glaze runs excessively. This tendency can be retarded by substituting additional feldspar for some of the lead. At different firing temperatures the necessary proportions of flux, alumina, and silica will vary. When the temperature exceeds 2050°F (1230°C), the low-fire fluxes must be gradually replaced by calcium carbonate (whiting), the principal high-fire flux. At temperatures above 2100°F (1150°C), the lead and alkaline fluxes run immoderately and are used only in minute quantities. A glaze can have a different crystalline surface structure because of variations in the proportion of alumina to silica. A slight excess of alumina produces a mat instead of a glassy finish; either too much or too little silica will result in a rough surface. Silica in its pure form is easily added to glaze if necessary.

After completing successful glaze tests with these three basic ingredients, we can substitute for all or part of the feldspar other materials such as nepheline syenite, spodumene, lepidolite, or Cornwall stone. Further possibilities are cryolite, talc, and dolomite, which fire at slightly lower temperatures. Although some of these compounds contain silica and alumina, their main purpose is in varying and increasing the proportion of flux. These additions can affect the color and surface quality of the glaze. The principal advantages of having several fluxes in a glaze are the extension of the firing range and the more complete fusion of the chemicals with fewer glaze defects. (See Chap. 9, pp. 231–241, for more specific details about these materials.)

Barium carbonate additions will produce a mat glaze in cases where increasing the alumina content is not convenient. Zinc oxide can be added to the glaze in small quantities to obtain more fluxing action and reduce surface defects. It is essential that the glaze and the body cool and contract at the same rate after firing. If the body is weak and underfired, a contracting glaze may cause it to crack. Uneven contractions are also responsible for crazing. If sufficient tensions exist, the glaze will eventually craze, although this may not occur for days or even years. Expansions resulting from moisture collecting in a porous body may have a similar effect (see Chap. 7, pp. 202–203). On a decorative piece, tiny hairline cracks can add to the interest of the total design. If they are intentional, such effects are called crackle glazes to distinguish them from the unexpected and undesirable crazing.

Elimination of crazing is necessary in all functional ware to prevent seepage of moisture and to avoid odors resulting from trapped food particles. Changes can be made in the clay body to increase or reduce contraction and thereby adjust it to the glaze. The addition of silica to either the body or the glaze is one method used to prevent crazing. In the body the crystal formation developed by excess silica usually increases contraction, but in the glaze's glassy state silica is more likely to produce an expansion. Generally a potter has developed a satisfactory body with desired plasticity, vitrification, and so forth, and for this reason experimental glazes are adjusted to fit the body, rather than the other way around.

Another solution to this problem lies in the fact that mat glazes seldom if ever craze. Starting with a bright, shiny glaze that crazes badly, the potter adds increasing amounts of alumina, while holding the flux and silica constant. As the proportion of alumina rises, the glaze gradually develops a bright, uncrazed surface, then a semimat, and finally a mat finish. If this change does not occur, the silica content may be too high in proportion to the flux. Limit formulas have been worked out in great detail giving permissible ratios of silica and alumina to the flux for the production of bright or mat glazes. Because of the many variables involved, such ratios are of greater value as a means of understanding the general problem, rather than as specific guides. Among the variables are the fluxing power and contraction rates of the bases. It is often possible to make substitutions in the bases to reduce crazing. For example, boric oxide and colemanite have lower expansion rates than either borax or soda ash, and lepidolite will expand less than feldspars.

High-fire Glaze Tests

High-fire glaze tests differ from those in the low-fire range only in the substitution of calcium carbonate ($CaCO_3$), commonly called whiting, for the low-melting lead and alkaline compounds. In this experiment tiles must be made from a stoneware or porcelain body. A good starting formula for a cone 6 to 8 glaze would be four parts kaolin, four parts potash feldspar, and two parts whiting. This will produce a sample that is white and claylike in character. In succeeding tests the whiting is held constant, the amount of feldspar is gradually increased, and the proportion of the more refractory kaolin is decreased. As the kaolin is lessened, the test glazes will become smoother and glassier. Depending upon the temperature, a satisfactory glaze should be achieved at the point when the kaolin content is between 10 and 20 percent. Throughout this series of tests we have lowered the fusion point of the glaze by the addition of the active flux, potash, which is contained in the feldspar. Only at higher temperatures can feldspar be considered a flux, since it is also a major source of alumina and silica.

A successful stoneware glaze can be made using only feldspar, kaolin, and whiting. As mentioned earlier, however, it may be desirable to add small amounts of other chemicals to obtain a greater firing range, achieve a better adjustment to the body, provide a more varied color spectrum, and develop a surface free from minor defects. Flint can easily be added to supply silica if needed. The student should attempt to vary his basic glaze to produce a glossy surface, a mat surface, and one that is fairly opaque (without the use of an opacifier such as tin oxide). Substitutions of some of the feldsparlike materials with different fluxes, such as lepidolite or nepheline syenite, can be tried. Often small amounts of another flux will result in a great improvement in a glaze. Other suggested additions are zinc oxide, talc, and barium carbonate. (See Chap. 9, pp. 228–243, for more detailed information on these and other chemicals, including colorants that will be used in further tests.)

GLAZE TYPES

At the beginning of this chapter we stressed the simplicity of glaze formulation, and indeed it is so. A functional and attractive glaze can be made from only a few materials. Several glazes, however, use rather uncommon ingredients or require special firing techniques. The glaze recipes in the Appendix (pp. 313–319) will clarify the general descriptions of the glazes that follow.

Low-fire Glazes

Low-fire glazes can be grouped into two distinct categories distinguished by the major flux included in the glaze.

Lead glazes comprise the largest group, firing from cone 016 to cone 02, which is between 1450°F and 2050°F (790°C–1120°C). These glazes take their names from the fluxes used, primarily oxides of the lead compounds. The most common fluxes are lead carbonate [$2PbCO_3 \cdot Pb(OH)_2$] and red lead

(Pb_3O_4). Lead is a very active flux, melting at about 950°F (510°C), flowing uniformly, and giving a bright, glossy surface. Used alone, it may constitute 50 percent of the glaze batch; it is often combined with other fluxes. The use of more than one flux is common, since each one has slightly different qualities. In combination they tend to encourage a lower melting point and a more complex and intimate reaction than can be obtained from using a single flux.

Lead has the disadvantage of being very poisonous and requires careful handling to avoid breathing the dust or getting particles in the mouth. For this reason, lead is often converted into the nontoxic silicate form by fritting. Fritting is a procedure by which a flux and silica are melted and later ground to form a glaze addition that is both nontoxic and insoluble in water. Vessels glazed with lead should never be used to store liquids containing large percentages of acid, such as fruit juices. Lead glazes fired in gas kilns using manufactured gas will often blister unless they are fired in a muffle chamber. The blistering is caused by the sulphur contained in all manufactured gas. Natural gas and propane are free from these sulphur impurities.

Alkaline glazes have a firing range similar to the lead glazes (cones 016–02) and use an alkaline flux such as borax, colemanite, or soda ash. Alkaline fluxes encourage certain color effects, particularly the turquoise-blues that lead glazes cannot produce. Because of their extreme solubility, alkaline fluxes should never be used on raw ware. When absorbed into the clay, the expansions and contractions that alkaline compounds undergo during firing and cooling will cause the body to crack.

A very soft bisque ware also reacts poorly to an alkaline glaze, for it will absorb a portion of the flux, leaving an incomplete and usually a rough-textured glaze upon firing. Because of their solubility and their tendency to become lumpy in the glaze solution, the alkaline compounds (such as borax) are often fritted into the nonsoluble silicate form. In general, alkaline glazes have a smooth, glossy surface similar to that produced by glazes in the lead group.

High-fire Glazes

High-fire glazes are generally compounded to fire in a range from cone 6 to cone 14, or 2250°F to 2500°F (1230°C–1370°C). At these extreme temperatures, common low-fire fluxes, such as lead and borax, must be replaced with calcium carbonate, which has a higher melting point of about 1500°F (816°C). Glazes are compounded to fit the maturity of the clay body. Since earthenware can seldom be fired over 2000°F (1093°C), and stoneware usually matures above 2300°F (1260°C), there is a gap between these temperatures at which little work is fired by the average studio potter. However, numerous commercial bodies are compounded between cones 02 and 6 for use on dinnerware, gift ware, and tiles. Glazes for these temperatures must contain both high- and low-fire fluxes to adjust within these limits (see Appendix, p. 315).

Porcelain and stoneware glazes are identical, except in cases where adjustments must be made to accommodate a difference in firing shrinkage. Because feldspar is a major ingredient in such glazes, the term *feldspathic glaze* is often applied to stoneware glazes. Due to the high temperature, the union of glaze and body is quite complete. The interlocking mullite crystals prevent detection of the line of junction that is easily visible between a glassy glaze and a porous earthenware body. Feldspathic glazes are very hard (they cannot be scratched by steel), and they are resistant to most acids, the exceptions being hydrofluoric, phosphoric, and hot sulphuric acids. The surfaces may be either mat or smooth, but they never reveal the excessive gloss of low-fire glazes.

Ash Glazes

Ash glazes were probably the first glazes used by man. At present they have no commercial application, but they may be of interest to the studio potter. The ash can derive from any wood, grass, or straw. Depending upon the specific source, the chemical composition can vary considerably: it is generally very high in silica; contains some alumina and calcium; moderate amounts of fluxes, such as potash, soda, and magnesia; plus iron and small quantities of numerous other compounds. Because of the high silica content, ash can seldom be used in low-fire glazes in amounts over 15 to 20 percent. This is not sufficient to make much change in the basic glaze. A suggested starting point for a stoneware ash-glaze test would be forty parts ash, forty parts feldspar, and twenty parts whiting. Fireplace ashes should be collected in a fairly large quantity and then mixed thoroughly to ensure uniformity. The ash is first run through a coarse sieve to remove unburned particles. It can then be soaked in water that is decanted several times to remove soluble portions. However, many potters prefer to run the dry ash through a fine sieve without washing (taking care not to inhale the fine ash particles), and thus retain the soluble fluxes. The latter procedure will allow a larger percentage of ash to be used in the final glaze. Liquid glaze containing ash is quite caustic and should not be stirred with the hand.

Frit Glazes

Frit glazes may be little different chemically from the two low-fire types described earlier. Fritting is a process that renders raw-glaze materials either nontoxic or nonsoluble. Lead or alkaline fluxes (borax or soda ash) are melted in a frit kiln with silica or silica and a small amount of alumina. When the glaze becomes liquid, a plug is pulled in the bottom of the frit furnace, and the contents are discharged into a container filled with water. The fractured particles are then ground to the necessary fineness. Small amounts can be made in the studio using a crucible. One disadvantage of studio manufacture is the extremely long grinding time necessary to pulverize the frit to adequate fineness.

Many different types of frit glazes are commercially available. Frit composition is complicated, for nontoxic or nonsoluble elements must be completely absorbed within a satisfactory firing range and without creating later adjustment problems. A frit glaze is seldom a complete glaze for several reasons. Since it is usually colorless, opacifiers or colorants must be added. The frit has little ability to adhere, so a small amount of plastic clay or bentonite is usually necessary. Adjustments for the final firing ranges must also be made. Frits have extensive commercial use where large amounts of standard glaze are employed. For the studio potter, frits are of most value in eliminating the lumpy quality of borax needed in crystalline, copper reds, and similar glazes. Purchased in 100-pound lots, low-fire frits might well be used in the public schools to replace the small and expensive colored glaze packets now purchased. The addition of a few color oxides and kaolin would not raise the cost substantially.

Crackle Glazes

Crackle glazes cannot be characterized by their composition, for they are merely the result of tensions that arise when a glaze and a body expand and contract at different rates. In most glazes, except perhaps the mats, a crackle can be produced. The simplest way is to substitute similar-acting fluxes for others having a different contraction rate. The reverse is true if a noncrackling glaze is desired.

A crackle is a network of fine cracks in the glaze. It must be used on a light body to be seen

properly (Fig. 425). To strengthen the effect, a coloring oxide or strong black tea is often applied to the crackled area. The Chinese were able to achieve, by successive firings, a network of both large and fine crackles, each stained with a different coloring oxide. On certain shapes, a crackle in the glaze can have an interesting decorative quality. It is more practical on a vitreous stoneware or porcelain body, because a crackle on a porous earthenware pot will allow liquids to seep through and make it unsatisfactory for holding food.

Mat Glazes

Mat glazes generally are formed either by adding an excess of alumina or by substituting barium carbonate for some of the flux in the glaze. Therefore, they are often called *alumina mats* or *barium mats*. A mat glaze should not be confused with a thin, rough, or underfired glaze. It should be smooth to the touch, with neither gloss nor transparency. The mat effects sometimes observed on an underfired glaze are caused by incompletely dissolved particles, whereas a true mat develops a different surface

425. WARREN MACKENZIE, U.S.A. Vase. Porcelain with cloudy celadon glaze and crackle surface, height 5 ½". The cut facets add a distinct quality to the form of the vase.

left : Plate 19. TOSHIKO TAKAEZU, U.S.A. Dish. 1967. Porcelain with brush decoration. The abstract brushwork on this dish evokes the quality of a misty Oriental landscape.

below : Plate 20. RICHARD LEACH, U.S.A. Jug. Stoneware with overall salt glaze; upper part coated with Albany slip, brush decoration of china clay; titania, rutile, and cobalt glazes. (See Pls. 21–22, overleaf.)

Plates 21–22. RICHARD LEACH, U.S.A. Details of Pl. 20, jug. The base slip is 75 percent china clay, plus flint and feldspar. The light crystals are produced by 10 percent titania, the gold by rutile, the blue-green by cobalt, the orange-red by uranium oxide.

crystalline structure. An unusually long cooling time will encourage the formation of mat textures. One test for a true mat is to cool the glaze quickly to see if it will develop a shine. A mat surface caused by the incomplete fusion of particles will continue to have a mat surface, regardless of the cooling time. It is generally a bit rough to the touch and lacks the smoothness of a true mat. Mats can be calculated for all temperatures, but they are particularly attractive in the low-fire ranges, since typical lead and borax glazes are so shiny that their glare tends to obscure all decoration and form. Mat glazes are related to the crystalline group, because both depend upon the surface structure of the glaze for their effects. Therefore, mats can also be made with iron, zinc, and titanium (rutile) when properly compounded and cooled slowly.

Reduction Glazes

Reduction glazes are those that are especially compounded to develop their unique color characteristics only if fired in a kiln capable of maintaining a reduction atmosphere during certain portions of the firing cycle. The normal kiln firing is an oxidizing fire. An electric kiln always has an oxidizing fire, since there is nothing in the kiln atmosphere to consume the oxygen that is always present. To reduce the atmosphere in a gas or oil kiln, the draft is cut back to lessen the air intake, resulting in an incomplete combustion that releases carbon into the kiln interior. In a muffle kiln, some of the muffles will have to be removed to allow the combustion gases to enter the kiln chamber.

Carbon has a great affinity for oxygen when heated and will steal it from the iron and copper-coloring oxides in the glaze. It was in this manner that the Chinese produced their famous copper reds (sang-de-bœuf) and celadons. When either copper or iron oxide is deprived of its oxygen, it remains suspended in the glaze as the pure colloidal metal. Thus a normal green copper glaze becomes a beautiful ruby red with occasional blue or purple tints. The iron oxide loses its customary brownish-red tone and takes on a variety of soft gray-green hues. Because of its likeness to jade, which had religious symbolism for the ancient Chinese, celadons of remarkable quality were developed. In a small muffle kiln, a reduction can occur if pine splinters or moth balls are inserted into the peephole. The usual reduction fire starts with an oxidizing fire, and reduction does not begin until just before the melting of the first elements of the glaze. After the reduction cycle, the firing must return to oxidization in order to develop a surface free from pinholes and other defects (see Chap. 11, pp. 279–280).

A so-called local reduction can be achieved by using a small amount (about .5 percent) of silicon carbide (carborundum) in the glaze. The effects are slightly different from the standard reduction, for the color is concentrated in little spots around the silicon carbide particles. But this technique has an advantage in that it can be used in an electric kiln, since the heating elements are in no way effected. The firing range of copper-red and celadon reduction glazes is quite wide, from about cone 08 to the porcelain temperatures.

Crystalline Glazes

There are two types of crystalline glazes. One has large crystal clusters embedded in or on the surface of the glaze; the second type, called aventurine, has single crystals, often small, suspended in the glaze, which catch and reflect the light. These are interesting glazes technically, but they must be very carefully related to the pot shape. The jewellike effects seem to float off the surface of all but the most simple and reserved forms. The crystalline formation is encouraged by additions of zinc and iron or by titanium (rutile). Borax and soda can also be used, but no lead. Possible firing ranges are wide, and, as with mat formations, the rate of cooling is most important. In order to allow the crystals to develop properly, the temperature of the kiln should be permitted to drop only about 100°F (38°C) after maturity, and it must be held at this level for several hours before slow cooling. Crystalline glazes are quite runny, so a pedestal of insulating brick should be cut to the foot size and placed under the ware. If fired high, the piece can be set in a shallow bisque bowl that will collect the excess glaze.

Bristol Glazes

Bristol glazes are very similar, in most respects, to the typical porcelain glaze, except that a relatively large amount of zinc oxide is added. In most cases, this tends to lower the melting point and to add a certain opacity to the glaze. Most Bristols fall into the cones 5 to 9 range, although formulas have been successfully developed for cones 3 to 14. The most common use of the Bristol glaze is for architectural tile and bricks.

Since a large amount of clay is normally used, the ware is generally given a single firing, and there is no problem of shrinkage. However, by calcinating part of the clay, the glaze can be fitted to double firings. The commercial single fire usually takes fifty to sixty hours, not only because of the thickness of the ware being fired but also because of the extremely viscous nature of the Bristol glaze. It is this quality of the glaze that makes it valuable to the studio potter. Interesting effects can be achieved by using a Bristol glaze over a more fluid glaze that breaks through in spots. The application of the glaze must be perfect, because its viscosity prevents any cracks that may occur from healing. Moreover, in firing the edges of the cracks will pull farther apart and bead. In general, Bristol glazes are shiny, but they can be matted by increasing the amount of calcia while reducing the silica content.

Luster Glazes

Luster glazes usually consist of a thin and decorative metallic coating fired on top of a lead-tin glaze. This coating is achieved by applying a solution of pine resin, bismuth nitrate, and a metallic salt dissolved in oil of lavender over a fired glaze. The luster is fired at a low red heat, sufficiently hot to fuse the metal and burn off the resin but lower than the melting point of the original glaze. A variety of reds, yellows, browns, and silvery-white lusters, as well as nacreous and iridescent sheens, are possible. The metals normally used are lead and zinc acetates; copper, manganese, and cobalt sulfates; uranium nitrate; and silver and gold compounds. Bismuth is generally used as a flux. Until

A.D. 1529 bismuth was thought to be an impure form of silver, and therefore the silver mentioned in old records probably was a silver-bismuth compound. (See Chap. 9, pp. 243–244, for a description of the historical method of preparing lusters.)

Usually the luster is not an overall coating, but rather it is applied in the form of a design combined with colored slips or stains. This is especially true in Islamic pottery, which, because of religious edicts against representational painting, developed an intricate and interlocking decorative motif used between the ninth and the fourteenth centuries (see Fig. 42).

Salt Glazes

Salt glazes have enjoyed a revival in recent years after a long period of neglect by the studio potter (Fig. 426). From the twelfth to the mid-nineteenth century, such glazes were common in Europe and were also used in Colonial America. Commercial applications are largely limited to stoneware crocks, glazed sewer pipe, hollow building brick, and similar products.

The salt-glaze procedure is simple. The ware is fired to its body-maturing temperature, at which time common salt (sodium chloride) is thrown into the firebox or through ports entering the kiln chamber. The sodium combines with the silica in the clay to form a glassy silicate. The studio must be well ventilated, since deadly chlorine gas is also released at the moment of salting. Occasionally, silica can be added to the clay to form a better glaze coating. By reducing conditions (incomplete combustion to introduce carbon into the kiln atmosphere), buff or red clays can be glazed either brown or black. Other colors can be obtained only by using colored slips or body stains. (Pls. 20–22, pp. 211–212).

The disadvantage of the salt glaze, other than its limited color effects, is that it coats the whole interior of the kiln. This generally renders the kiln unsuitable for other types of glaze firing. The firing range of salt glazes is wide, from cones 02 to 12, but the most common firings are from cones 5 to 8. (See Chap. 11, p. 280, for more specifics on the salting technique.)

426. MARC HANSEN, U.S.A. Bowl. Stoneware with salt glaze, brown slip, and applied clay decoration; diameter 10½″. The throwing rings and applied clay decoration are revealed clearly under the pebbly salt glaze.

Slip Glazes

Slip glazes are made from raw natural clays that contain sufficient fluxes to function as glazes without further preparation beyond washing and sieving. In practice, additions are often made to enable the slip glaze to fit the body or to modify the maturing temperature, but these changes are minor. The so-called black varnish of the Greeks and the Roman terra sigillata are slip glazes formed by decanting the finer particles of a liquid slip made from red clay. Reduction produces the black color by converting the red iron oxide into black and magnetic iron oxides. A later oxidizing fire restores the iron in the more porous clay body to its red color, while leaving the black iron sealed in the denser slip. This process does not create a true glassy glaze. Rather, it is halfway between a slip and a glaze and is not completely waterproof.

Slip glazes were commonly used by early American stoneware potteries that produced such utilitarian objects as storage crocks, bowls, mugs, and pitchers. Albany slip clay is the only commercial variety that is widely used. It fires brown-black at cones 8 to 10. The addition of 2 percent cobalt to Albany slip will result in a beautiful semigloss jet black. Wrenshall slip, mined near Duluth, Minnesota, fires to a pale yellow at cones 6 to 10 with the peculiar streaked effect characteristic of rutile. There are many slip clay deposits that are not recognized as such. Frequently earthenware clays can be used as slip clays when fired high enough and with the addition of small amounts of flux. Most slip clays fire from cone 6 to cone 12. Slip-clay fluxes are generally the alkaline earth compounds, plus iron oxide in varying amounts. A high iron content serves also to produce a color ranging from tan to dark brown.

The potter must be careful in using slip clays, for they are generally mined in small pits, and their composition will vary slightly. Each new shipment of material should be tested before being used in quantity. Some Albany slip is so lacking in the usual brown colorant that the resulting glaze is a pale, semitransparent tan. Studio potters should pay more attention to this group of glazes. Slip clays are easy to apply, adhere well, and fire with few, if any, defects. The composition, chemically, is most durable, and, since additions are few, much time can be saved in glaze preparation.

Raku Glazes

Raku glazes are low-fire glazes used on bodies containing a high proportion of grog (Fig. 427). The ware is associated with the Japanese tea ceremony and with Zen Buddhism. Raku tea bowls, usually hand built and irregular, are perfectly suited

above: 427. GENE BUCKLEY, U.S.A. Bowl. Slab-built stoneware with pitted surface and a band of lustrous green and red typical of the raku technique, height 6 ½″.

to the Zen emphasis on nature and the simple, unaffected way of living.

The firing procedure is an essential part of the raku technique. The clay body used is generally a stoneware containing up to 30 percent grog. The grog and the firing process tend to limit the form and size of the ware. Simple bowl shapes are most common. Since the glaze temperature never exceeds 1750°F (955°C), the glaze may contain as much as 60 percent lead or colemanite. The ware is bisqued and then glazed.

The glaze firing is most unusual and quite dramatic. In Japan the firing is generally done outdoors, using small, charcoal-burning kilns, which often contain only a single pot. The glazed piece must be perfectly dry, and it can be placed on top of the kiln to ensure that all the moisture has evaporated. When the kiln has reached glaze temperature and the bricked-up door is opened, the pot is quickly placed in the chamber with a pair of tongs. Because of the high grog content and porous nature of the body, this sudden heat change has no effect. Firing proceeds, and in a few minutes the pot begins to glow. (Most kilns in the United States are fired with a single gas burner and have a capacity for several pieces. Insulating bricks can be easily bolted together to form a top cover.) Depending upon the character of the kiln, the glaze should begin to melt and develop a liquid shine in 10 to 15 minutes. Before running occurs, the pot is removed with tongs. The tong marks on the glazed surface are regarded as a decoration. Generally the glowing pot is placed in a covered metal container filled with sawdust, which gives a smoked and accidental quality to the glaze. After a few minutes of smoking, the ware can be immediately doused with a bucket of water. If, however, the pot has a closed form or varied thicknesses, cooling in the open air for several minutes before dousing is necessary to avoid cracking.

The raku body remains soft and porous, and the glaze is not waterproof. Nevertheless, raku has become quite popular in recent years. The glaze effects are quite varied and, while accidental, have unusual qualities. The speed of the firings, the flame, and the smoke all suggest the character of a "Happening." The oxides used in raku decoration, when reduced, tend to develop a luster with fantastic color combinations. A deep crackle often occurs, which is in keeping with the rather simple form that typifies pots made of a coarse body.

9 Glazes

Calculations and Chemicals

In Chapter 8 a trial-and-error method was suggested by which the novice potter could develop a satisfactory glaze and gain a rudimentary understanding of the properties of the common glaze materials. Despite the long history of ceramics, the scientific formulation of glazes is rather recent. The glazes and techniques evidenced in the historical pieces illustrated in Chapters 1 and 2 were the final results of centuries of such experimentation. But since ceramic techniques are no longer passed from father to son in the traditional manner, it is necessary that we find a quicker and more scientific method of glaze formulation.

CALCULATIONS

All matter composing the earth is made up of approximately one hundred chemical elements in the form of atoms. These elements do not occur in nature in a pure form but in compounds, which are groups of atoms held together by an electrical attraction or bond. The atom is much too small to be weighed, but it is possible to determine the relative weight of one type of atom to that of another. Oxygen, symbolized by the letter O, has been given the arbitrary atomic weight of 16; other atoms are attributed weights corresponding to their proportionate weights in relation to oxygen.

Silica, mentioned frequently in the chapters on clay and glazes, is a major ceramic compound and is found in every clay and glaze. The *molecular formula* for silica (or, more precisely, silicon dioxide) is SiO_2. The atomic weight table in the Appendix (p. 303) lists the weight of silicon as 28. Since two oxygen atoms weigh 32, the total molecular weight of the compound silicon dioxide is 60.

Silica can be added to a clay body or glaze in the silicon dioxide form, but it is most commonly found as part of a more complex compound, such as kaolin ($Al_2O_3 \cdot 2\,SiO_2 \cdot 2\,H_2O$), or potash feldspar ($K_2O \cdot Al_2O_3 \cdot 6\,SiO_2$).

opposite : 428. MARC HANSEN, U.S.A. Covered jar. Stoneware with nickel-green mat glaze, height 10 ½″. In this piece the calculated running of an extra layer of glaze has been used as the major decorative element.

The RO, R₂O₃, RO₂ System

There are three principal components in a glaze. One of these is silica (SiO₂), which gives the glaze its glassy, transparent quality. The second is alumina (Al₂O₃), a refractory element, which contributes toughness and abrasion resistance to the glaze. Since neither of these oxides will melt at temperatures below 3100°F, the potter must add a third ingredient, a flux, such as lead oxide or sodium, that will lower the melting point and combine with both silica and alumina to form, after firing, a hard, glassy coating on the ceramic body.

With rare exceptions, the glaze components are not single refined oxides but complex compounds that are commercially available at reasonable cost. In order to compare glazes or to understand the effects of these varied chemicals, it is necessary to separate the component oxides into the three major parts of the glaze formula. The symbol RO refers to the fluxing agents, which are chiefly metallic or alkaline elements that form their oxides by combining with one atom of oxygen, such as CaO or PbO. Similarly, alumina (Al₂O₃) can be symbolized by R₂O₃ and silica (SiO₂) by RO₂. A table will better illustrate this division of the components of a glaze.

RO	R₂O₃	RO₂
Bases	Neutrals	Acids
Li₂O*	(Amphoteric oxides)	SiO₂
Na₂O*	Al₂O₃	TiO₂
K₂O*	B₂O₃	ZrO₂
CaO	Fe₂O₃	
MgO	Sb₂O₃	Glass formers
BaO	Cr₂O₃	
ZnO	(Refractory	
FeO	elements)	
MnO		
PbO		
CdO		
Fluxing agents		

* One of the few exceptions: 2 atoms of sodium, lithium, or potassium unite with 1 of oxygen to form the oxide.

In the first column are the RO oxides that have the effect of fluxes in either a glaze or a body. They are also called the *base oxides*. Some of the *neutrals* or amphoteric oxides can function as either a base or an acid oxide. However, the major oxide in this group, alumina (Al₂O₃), always has a refractory effect in a glaze. On the other hand, red iron oxide (Fe₂O₃) is an active flux as well as a colorant. Boric oxide (B₂O₃) can react as either a base or an acid. Silica is the major oxide in the acid column. The contribution of TiO₂ and ZrO₂ to a glaze is opacity, not their glass-forming effect. With minor exceptions, the RO, R₂O₃, and RO₂ method of categorizing the main components of a glaze works very well.

The Empirical Glaze Formula

In the interests of simplifying calculations, glaze batches are usually reduced to an *empirical formula*. This is a glaze formula in which the various active ingredients are expressed in molecular proportions. By contrast, the *batch recipe* is a proportion expressed in the actual weights of the raw chemical compounds making up the glaze. Since the materials used in the average glaze batch are rather complex compounds, it is a distinct advantage to be able to define the glaze in terms of single oxides that bear the same proportional relationship to each other as when in their more complex form in the glaze batch. These oxides are grouped into RO, R₂O₃, and RO₂ units.

Before a batch recipe is converted into an empirical formula, it is first necessary to know the chemical formulas of the individual raw materials, as well as their equivalent weights. The molecular formulas and equivalent weights of the molecular compounds for all commonly used ceramic materials are listed in the Appendix (pp. 305–306). The commercial name of the raw material is in the first column, and its molecular formula is in the second. Many compounds are designated by more than one name, such as whiting and calcium carbonate.

The *molecular weight of a compound* is the sum of the atomic weights of its constituent elements. The equivalent weight will often be the same as the molecular weight of the compound, but in many cases it is smaller. This is true of potash feldspar:

Raw material	Formula	Molecular weight	Equivalent weights		
			RO	R₂O₃	RO₂
			RO	R_2O_3	RO_2
Feldspar (potash)	$K_2O \cdot Al_2O_3 \cdot 6\,SiO_2$	556.8	556.8	556.8	92.9

According to the given formula, when one molecular unit of potash feldspar is added, the glaze will have one unit of potassium oxide, one unit of alumina, and six units of silica. Since one unit each of potassium oxide and alumina form the compound, their individual equivalent weights are 556.8. And since six units of silica are necessary to form the compound, the equivalent weight of silica is 1/6 of the compound weight, or 92.9. The *equivalent weights* of the oxides of a compound are the same as its molecular weight if the oxide in question appears only once. However, if more than one unit of an oxide occurs, then its equivalent weight will be found by dividing the compound molecular weight by the number of times the oxide in question appears.

These definitions will become clearer in the actual procedure of converting the following glaze batch recipe to an empirical formula.

Glaze recipe	Raw materials	Parts by weight
A lead-borax	White lead	128
glaze maturing	Whiting	15
at cone 04	Borax	103
	Feldspar	
	(potash)	83
	Kaolin	38
	Flint	85

Before we can go into the actual calculations, we must first find the molecular formula of each of the compounds making up the glaze, plus the equivalent weights of the oxides contained in these compounds. It is convenient to put this information in table form, as illustrated (p. 222). By checking over the raw-material formulas, we can determine which of the oxides should be indicated in the spaces to the right of the table.

The batch weights of the raw materials are divided by the equivalent molecular weights of the particular oxides concerned, giving the molecular proportions in the form of single oxides. By arranging these oxides with the amounts calculated into their appropriate RO, R₂O₃, and RO₂ groups, we find that the glaze batch has the following empirical formula:

RO	R₂O₃	RO₂
.495 PbO	.295 Al₂O₃	2.599 SiO₂
.150 CaO	.540 B₂O₃	
.149 K₂O		
.270 Na₂O		

The total of the RO oxides comes to 1.064 instead of the desired unit of one, because round numbers have been used in the batch recipe. By dividing each of the above figures by 1.064 we will have the following empirical formula. The RO is now .998, a figure that is accurate enough for comparative purposes.

RO	R₂O₃	RO₂
.465 PbO	.277 Al₂O₃	2.442 SiO₂
.140 CaO	.507 B₂O₃	
.140 K₂O		
.253 Na₂O		

Considerable research has been done on the properties of ceramic materials, and some reasonable pre-

Batch to Empirical Formula

Raw material and formula	Batch weights	÷	Equivalent weights	=	PbO	CaO	Na$_2$O	B$_2$O$_3$	K$_2$O	Al$_2$O$_3$	SiO$_2$
White lead [2 PbCO$_3$ · Pb(OH)$_2$]	128	÷	(RO) 258.5	=	0.495						
Whiting (CaCO$_3$)	15	÷	(RO) 100	=		0.15					
Borax (Na$_2$O · 2 B$_2$O$_3$ · 10 H$_2$O)	103	÷	(RO) 381.04 (R$_2$O$_3$) 190.7	=			0.270	0.540			
Felspar (potash) (K$_2$O · Al$_2$O$_3$ · 6 SiO$_2$)	83	÷	(RO) 556.8 (R$_2$O$_3$) 556.8 (RO$_2$) 92.9	=					0.149	0.149	0.890
Kaolin (Al$_2$O$_3$ · 2 SiO$_2$ · 2 H$_2$O)	38	÷	(R$_2$O$_3$) 258.1 (RO$_2$) 129	=						0.146	0.294
Flint (SiO$_2$)	85	÷	(RO$_2$) 60.06	=							1.415
Totals	452				0.495	0.15	0.270	0.540	0.149	0.295	2.599

dictions can be made about the probable change that a particular chemical will cause in a known type of glaze. There are, however, many variables, such as the length of the glaze grinding time, the thickness of application, the reactions between glaze and body, the kiln atmosphere, and the rate of temperature rise and fall. Since each or all of these conditions can markedly affect a particular glaze, glaze experimentation is something less than a true science. Successful work depends largely upon the overall experience and care of the operator in controlling these factors.

The Batch Recipe

To convert an empirical formula to a batch recipe, it is necessary to reverse the procedure explained in the previous section. As before, the easiest method is to draw up a chart on which to compile the information. This type of conversion will require slightly more familiarity with raw chemical compounds, because we must select those compounds containing the proper oxides without adding any unwanted elements. The parts of compounds that pass off in the kiln as gases or water vapor are ignored. To make the process clearer, let us take the following *empirical glaze formula* and convert it into a batch recipe.

0.40 Na_2O	0.03 Al_2O_3	2.1 SiO_2
0.46 PbO	0.32 B_2O_3	
0.14 FeO		

The general procedure is as follows: First, if any alkaline fluxes are present (Na_2O or K_2O), it is best to include as much as possible in a soda or potash feldspar. This is a cheaper source of the flux, and,

Calculations from Formula to Batch Recipe

Raw material	Oxides in formula Equivalents needed	Na_2O 0.40	PbO 0.46	FeO 0.14	Al_2O_3 0.03	B_2O_3 0.32	SiO_2 2.1
Soda feldspar ($Na_2O \cdot Al_2O_3 \cdot 6\,SiO_2$) 0.03 equivalents		0.03			0.03		0.18
	remainder	0.37	0.46	0.14		0.32	1.92
Borax ($Na_2O \cdot 2\,B_2O_3 \cdot 10\,H_2O$) 0.16 equivalents		0.16				0.32	
	remainder	0.21	0.46	0.14			1.92
Soda ash (Na_2CO_3) 0.21 equivalents		0.21					
	remainder		0.46	0.14			1.92
White lead [$2\,PbCO_3 \cdot Pb(OH)_2$] 0.153 equivalents			0.46				
	remainder			0.14			1.92
Red iron oxide (Fe_2O_3) 0.07 equivalents				0.14			
	remainder						1.92
Flint (SiO_2) 1.92 equivalents							1.92

equally important, it is nonsoluble and not as likely to become lumpy in a glaze as borax will. We then fill out the other single oxides, trying to save the alumina for next to last and taking out the silica at the end. Alumina and silica are often included in other compounds, and the balance can easily be taken care of last in the form of either kaolin or silica. Since silica is always present in larger amounts than alumina and is available in a cheap, pure form, it can safely be saved for the last.

Several of the calculations on page 223 may seem incorrect at first, so perhaps we should point out a few of these seeming inconsistencies. In the first addition, when we take 0.03 equivalents of soda feldspar, we get six times as much SiO_2 as either Na_2 or Al_2O_3, because the formula for soda feldspar is $Na_2O_3 \cdot Al_2O_3 \cdot 6\ SiO_2$. Similarly, borax has twice as much B_2O_3 as Na_2O.

Now that we have the needed molecular equivalents of the chemical compounds, we can find the gram batch weights (or pounds) by multiplying each equivalent by the molecular weights of the chemical compound. Thus we have the following set of calculations:

Raw material	Equivalents		Molecular weights		Batch weights
Soda feldspar	0.03	×	524	=	15.72
Borax	0.16	×	382	=	61.12
Soda ash	0.21	×	106	=	22.26
White lead	0.153	×	775	=	118.58
Red iron oxide	0.07	×	160	=	11.20
Flint	1.91	×	60	=	114.60

Limit Formulas

In the glaze experiments described in Chapter 8 (pp. 206–208), no definite limits were mentioned regarding the ratio between the RO, R_2O_3, and RO_2 parts in a glaze. This is because the major purpose of these glaze tests was to gain familiarity with the qualities of the various glaze chemicals. The forgoing analyses have shown that there are general limits to the amounts of alumina and silica that can be used successfully in relation to a single unit of flux. The firing temperature and the type of flux are also important factors.

In the several limit formulas that follow, a number of possible fluxes are indicated; however, the total amount used must add up to a unit of one. In general, a higher proportion of alumina will result in a mat surface, provided the kiln is cooled slowly. Barium will also tend to create a mat surface. A study of these formulas indicates how the ratio of alumina and silica rises as the temperature increases.

While not intended to take the place of glaze formulas, the listing should be a helpful guide to those seeking to change the temperature range of a favorite glaze. Some glaze chemicals are quite complex, and under certain conditions an addition to a glaze will not have the desired effect. By converting the batch recipes to empirical formulas and comparing them with the suggested limits, one ought to be able to detect the direction of the error.

Variables in Glaze Formulation

Potters are frequently disturbed and disappointed when a glaze obtained from a friend or from a textbook produces quite unexpected results. Several factors may be involved in this problem. Ingredients that are more finely ground than usual will melt at a slightly lower temperature. In the same way fritted glaze additions melt more quickly than do raw compounds of a similar composition. Occasionally the thickness of application or reactions with

Limit Formulas

Cone 08–04	Lead glazes		
PbO	0.2–0.60	Al_2O_3	0.15–0.20
KNaO	0.1–0.25	B_2O_3	0.15–0.60
ZnO	0.1–0.25		
CaO	0.3–0.60	SiO_2	1.5–2.50
BaO	0 –0.15		

Cone 08–04	Alkaline glazes		
PbO	0–0.5	Al_2O_3	0.05–0.25
KNaO	.4–0.8		
CaO	0–0.3	SiO_2	1.5–2.5
ZnO	0–0.2		

Cone 2–5	Lead calcium glaze		
PbO	0.4–0.60	Al_2O_3	0.2–0.28
CaO	0.1–0.40		
ZnO	0 –0.25	SiO_2	2.0–3.0
KNaO	0.1–0.25		

Cone 2–5	Lead-borax glaze		
PbO	0.2 –0.3	Al_2O_3	0.25–0.35
KNaO	0.2 –0.3	B_2O_3	0.20–0.60
CaO	0.35–0.5		
ZnO	0 –0.1	SiO_2	2.5–3.5

Cone 2–5	Colemanite glaze		
CaO	0.2–0.50	Al_2O_3	0.2–0.28
ZnO	0.1–0.25	B_2O_3	0.3–0.6
BaO	0.1–0.25		
KNaO	0.1–0.25	SiO_2	2.0–3.0

Cone 8–12	Stoneware glaze		
KNaO	0.2–0.40	Al_2O_3	0.3–0.5
CaO	0.4–0.70	B_2O_3	0.1–0.3
MgO	0 –0.35		
ZnO	0 –0.30		
BaO	0 –0.30	SiO_2	3.0–5.0

the clay body will produce slightly different results. More distressing and troublesome is the variable nature of such major glaze ingredients as Cornwall stone and the feldspars.

In attempting to alter a glaze that has proved unsatisfactory, the potter has several simple remedies. If the glaze is too runny, he adds flint or kaolin, either of which usually raises the melting point; if it is too dry, he increases the flux to develop a more fluid glaze. Sometimes, however, the effect is quite the opposite, and in such cases the student, quite justifiably, may feel that the instructor who suggested the change doesn't know much about glaze chemistry.

The real culprit in many glaze failures is the chemical phenomenon known as a *eutectic*. A eutectic is the lowest point at which two or more chemicals will combine and melt. It is much lower than the melting point of any of the individual chemicals. For example, lead oxide has a melting point of 1616°F (880°C), and silica melts at 3119°F (1715°C).

One might expect that a 50-50 mixture of lead and silica would melt at the halfway point, 2364°F, yet the actual melting point is much lower, about 1470°F. The lowest melting point of lead and silica (the eutectic point) occurs at about 945°F (510°C), with a mixture of approximately 90 percent lead oxide and 10 percent silica. The line diagram in Figure 429 illustrates the relatively simple reaction between lead oxide and silica and the eutectic point at E.

In an actual glaze—compounded of complex minerals and containing several fluxes, alumina, and even different types of silica—the firing reaction is much more complicated. It is quite possible for there to be two and even more eutectic points.

Figure 430 shows a hypothetical reaction, with two eutectic points, between several fluxes and silica. The vertical movement represents the changing temperature of fusion as a portion of flux is replaced with a like amount of silica. Glazes that fall in areas B and C are most troublesome to *top* : 429. The eutectic fusion point of lead and silica.

above : 430. This somewhat exaggerated line demonstrates the unpredictable effects of eutectic points in a glaze.

potters, since a slight change in composition or temperature is critical. These are generally high-gloss glazes. In area B a small increase in silica will increase the gloss and raise the melting temperature, but in area C an increase in silica will lower the melting temperature and create a very runny glaze. The points E1, H, and E2 are especially critical, for a very slight temperature rise will change the character of the glaze. The most satisfactory glazes fall in the lower ranges of A and D. Because of the flattened curve in these areas a slight change in temperature or silica is not likely to cause a great variation in the fired glaze. The alumina, calcium, zinc, and dolomite mats fall in the lower area of A.

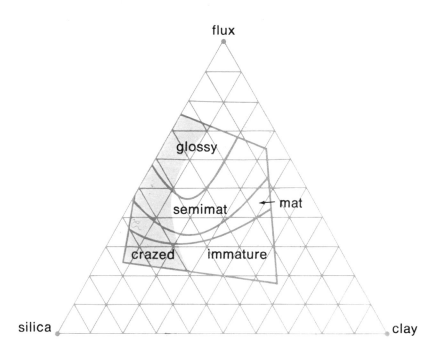

flux

glossy

semimat ← mat

crazed immature

silica clay

above : 431. This chart shows the glazes obtainable at cone 10 with various amounts of clay, silica, and fluxes.

As the silica is decreased in area A, the glazes become more mat and finally become rough and incomplete with a very low proportion of silica. Transparent and majolica glazes fall in the lower area of D; these become less glossy as the ratio of silica and the temperature are raised. Although the area D glazes can be glossy like the unpredictable glazes in B and C, they are quite stable and little affected by slight changes in silica or temperature. Ash glazes fall in all areas; those in areas B and C are runny and unpredictable.

Figure 430 is a purely theoretical attempt to visualize the reactions between the fluxes and silica. It does not represent an actual glaze, since the function of the alumina is ignored. The more usual method of diagraming a glaze is shown in Figure 431. Here we have the three major components of a glaze: fluxes, silica, and clay (alumina-silica). The small triangle at each apex contains 100 percent of the compound used. As we move along the base line of the silica-clay axis, the ratio becomes 90 percent silica to 10 percent clay (kaolin), then 80 percent

silica to 20 percent clay, and so forth. Progressing vertically, the triangles contain an increasing amount of the third glaze component, the fluxes. The roughly square section in the center covers those glaze tests which at cone 10 fuse to form a glaze. As the gradient indicates, there is a change from mat to glossy as the fluxes are increased and an area of crazed glazes where the alumina content is low. The clay content also has a decisive effect upon whether a glaze is to be glossy or mat. As indicated in both Figures 430 and 431, the mat and semimat glazes cover a much wider range of possible combinations at a given temperature. The sharp gradient of the glossy area in Figure 431 would suggest that the eutectic points for this particular glaze would fall in this range.

The use of a triaxial diagram for planning experiments has many applications in ceramics. It takes much time to complete the entire sequence, and considerable effort can be saved by concentrating on those areas in which meaningful results can be expected. This system is especially helpful in gaining knowledge about the relative fluxing power of various compounds, their effects on colorants, and the blending of colorants and opacificiers.

Calculations 227

CERAMIC CHEMICALS

The chemicals used by the potter are generally not pure single oxides but more complex compounds that are available for industrial uses in a moderately refined form at low cost. Because of differences in either the original mineral or in refining methods, the ceramic chemicals available from different dealers can vary slightly. Even items from the same supplier can change minutely from year to year. Commercial potteries constantly check new shipments of chemicals, but this is seldom done in the small studio. If a favorite glaze reacts strangely, one should consider this factor, provided, of course, there was no deviation from the normal glazing and firing procedure. The feldspars, in particular, vary in their fluxing power. It is for this reason that we have not stressed the importance of a glaze formula but rather the acquisition of an experimental knowledge of the properties of glaze ingredients. The batch glazes listed in the Appendix (pp. 313–319) are mainly for purposes of illustration, and they may have to be adjusted slightly to fit the materials available.

For the convenience of students converting an empirical glaze formula into a batch recipe, a listing follows that gives the major sources of the various oxides in the RO, R_2O_3, and RO_2 groups. A more complete chemical description will be found in the alphabetized section at the end of this chapter.

Sources of Base (RO) Oxides

Barium oxide (BaO) is a very active flux under some conditions. Its glass formation has a brilliancy second only to the lead silicates. Barium's effect on the thermal expansion of the glaze is less than that of the alkalies and calcia. The best source for barium is:

Barium carbonate ($BaCO_3$)

Calcium oxide (CaO), in comparison with the alkaline oxides, produces a glaze more resistant to abrasion, mild acids, and weathering. It also lowers the coefficient of thermal expansion, thereby increasing tensile strength. Although it is often used in

small amounts with other fluxes in low-fire glazes, calcium should not be used as the sole flux at temperatures below cone 3. It is the most common flux used at porcelain temperatures. As with alumina, an excess of calcia tends to produce mat textures. Sources of calcium are:

Calcium carbonate ($CaCO_3$)
Calcium borate ($2\,CaO \cdot 3\,B_2O_3 \cdot 5\,H_2O$), more commonly known as colemanite
Dolomite [$CaMg(CO_3)_2$]
Calcium fluoride (CaF_2), better known as the mineral fluorspar
Bone ash, refined, [$Ca_3(PO_4)_2$]
Wollastonite ($CaSiO_3$)

Lead oxide (PbO) has been mentioned frequently as one of the major low-fire fluxes. There are several reasons for its popularity. It combines readily with all other fluxes and has a lower coefficient of expansion than do the alkaline fluxes. Lead gives greater brilliancy to the glaze, although at times this can be a disadvantage. Lead glazes melt and flow well and thus tend to reduce pinholes and other defects of the more viscous type of glaze. The chief drawbacks are the poisonous nature of lead compounds (unless they are fritted) and their weakness to attack by strong fruit acids. Lead tends to blacken or develop a film if slightly reduced. The surface of a lead glaze will scratch easily unless an alkaline flux is added. There are many forms of lead, such as:

Galena (PbS)
Litharge (PbO)
Red lead (Pb_3O_4)
White lead [$2\,PbCO_3 \cdot Pb(OH_2)$]
Lead monosilicate, the fritted lead silicate composed of approximately 16 percent SiO_2 and 84 percent PbO
Lead bisilicate, another commercial lead silicate, with the approximate composition of 65 percent PbO, 33 percent SiO_2, and 2 percent Al_2O_3

Lithium oxide (Li_2O) is more commonly used by glass manufacturers, but it has several important qualities that make its occasional use in glazes valuable. Lithium (the oxide or carbonate) is expensive, because it is present in very small quantities (3–8 percent) in the producing ores. It has a much lower atomic weight than do either sodium or potassium (ratio of 1:3 and 1:5), and therefore a smaller amount of material can be used without lessening the fluxing action. This has the effect of decreasing tensions caused by thermal expansions and contractions and thus promoting a more durable glaze. Sources of lithium are:

Lepidolite ($LiF \cdot KF \cdot Al_2O_3 \cdot 3\ SiO_2$)
Spodumene ($Li_2O \cdot Al_2O_3 \cdot 4\ SiO_2$)
Lithium carbonate (Li_2CO_3)
Petalite ($Li_2O \cdot Al_2O_3 \cdot 8\ SiO_2$)
Amblygonite ($2\ LiF \cdot Al_2O_3 \cdot P_2O_5$)

Magnesium oxide (MgO) is frequently found combined with the feldspars and limestones. It lowers the thermal expansion more than do other bases, and it is as satisfactory as the alkaline fluxes in developing a durable glaze. In some combinations it will produce a slight opacity. Used with low-fire glazes, magnesium has a refractory effect; it fluxes easily at higher temperatures and becomes quite fluid. Sources of magnesium are:

Magnesium carbonate ($MgCO_3$)
Dolomite [$CaMg(CO_3)_2$]
Talc (varies from $3\ MgO \cdot 4\ SiO_2 \cdot H_2O$ to $4\ MgO \cdot 5\ SiO_2 \cdot H_2O$.) In the solid and more impure form it is also known as steatite or soapstone.
Diopside ($CaO \cdot MgO \cdot 2\ SiO_2$)

Potassium oxide (K_2O) is similar in fluxing action to sodium. It has a lower coefficient of thermal expansion, thus increasing the hardness and brilliance of a piece and lowering the fluidity of the glaze. Sources of potassium are:

Potassium carbonate (K_2CO_3), more commonly known as pearl ash
Potash feldspar ($K_2O \cdot Al_2O_3 \cdot 6\ SiO_2$)
Cornwall stone, a complex compound of variable composition, roughly similar to a feldspar and having fluxes of calcium, sodium, and potassium ($1\ RO \cdot 1.08\ Al_2O_3 \cdot 7.79\ SiO_2$)
Carolina stone, a domestic product similar to Cornwall stone

Volcanic ash, with a ceramic formula of:

0.660 K_2O	0.899 Al_2O_3	9.59 SiO_2
0.230 Na_2O	0.060 Fe_2O_3	0.05 TiO_2
0.096 CaO		
0.014 MgO		

Plastic vitrox ($1\ RO \cdot 1.69\ Al_2O_3 \cdot 14.64\ SiO_2$)

Sodium oxide (Na_2O) is one of the more common low-fire fluxes. It has the highest coefficient of expansion of all the bases and generally gives a lower tensile strength and elasticity to the silicates formed than do most other fluxes. The usual ceramic sources of sodium are:

Sodium chloride (NaCl)
Sodium carbonate (Na_2CO_3), more frequently called soda ash
Sodium bicarbonate ($NaHCO_3$)
Borax ($Na_2O \cdot 2\ B_2O_3 \cdot 10\ H_2O$)
Soda feldspar ($Na_2O \cdot Al_2O_3 \cdot 6\ SiO_2$)
Cryolite (Na_3AlF_6)
Nepheline Syenite
($K_2O \cdot 3\ Na_2O \cdot 4\ Al_2O_3 \cdot 9\ SiO_2$)

Zinc oxide (ZnO) can contribute several different qualities to a glaze. It can be used to replace some of the more soluble alkaline fluxes. Zinc is second only to magnesium in reducing the thermal expansion and to calcium in increasing the strength and resistance of a glaze. It contributes some opacity to the glaze and is helpful in reducing crazing defects. The major zinc compound used in ceramics is:

Zinc oxide (ZnO)

Sources of Neutral (R₂O₃) Oxides

Unlike the RO group, which has numerous similar compounds, the R_2O_3 group is almost limited to alumina (Al_2O_3) and a few oxides that have the same oxygen ratio. The greatest difference between a glass and a glaze is the presence of alumina in the glaze. The alumina content is a most important factor in a successful glaze. It controls the fluidity of the melting glaze and enables it to withstand the temperatures needed to mature the body. Greater amounts of alumina increase the hardness of the glaze and its resistance to abrasions and acids.

Crystalline glazes must necessarily be low in alumina, since alumina prevents the devitrification that accompanies the crystal formation.

Alumina (Al_2O_3) in a glaze can vary from 0.1 to 0.9 molecular equivalents, depending upon firing temperatures. The equivalent ratios between the alumina and the silica groups can be from 1:4 to 1:20. For glossy glazes the ratio is about 1:10. As mentioned before, an increase of alumina will tend to produce mat textures. A glossy porcelain glaze firing from cones 10 to 12 will have an alumina-silica ratio of between 1:7 and 1:8, whereas the mats will be 1:3.2 to 1:3.8. Alumina also has an effect on the colors developed. The normal blue of cobalt oxide will become a rose pink in the absence of alumina. Chromium oxide, which usually gives various green tones, will tend to become reddish in the presence of excess alumina. Sources of alumina are:

Alumina hydrate [$Al(OH)_3$]

Feldspar and Cornwall stone (see sections under RO oxides)

Kaolin (china clay) $Al_2O_3 \cdot 2\,SiO_2 \cdot 2\,H_2O$ (see sections under Clay)

Nepheline syenite
($K_2O \cdot 3\,Na_2O \cdot 4\,Al_2O_3 \cdot 9\,SiO_2$)

Plastic vitrox ($1\,RO \cdot 1.69\,Al_2O_3 \cdot 14.64\,SiO_2$)

Pyrophylite ($Al_2O_3 \cdot 4\,SiO_2 \cdot H_2O$)

Antimony oxide (Sb_2O_3) is primarily used as an opacifier and a coloring agent. It is found in:

Antimonious oxide (Sb_2O_3)

Basic antimonate of lead, [$Pb_3(SbO_4)_2$], also known as Naples yellow

Boric oxide (B_2O_3) is one of the neutral oxides (R_2O_3), which, by our previous definition, can react either as bases or acids. The refractory properties of alumina are more like those of acid silica than any of the bases. Boric oxide has a number of characteristics similar to alumina: the alumina of mat glazes can be satisfactorily replaced by boric oxide; color effects do not change by this substitution; both alumina and boric oxide harm underglaze red and green colors; and both can form mixed crystals. On the whole, however, boric oxide functions as a flux, since in comparison with silica it increases the elasticity, lowers the tensile strength, and, in limited quantities, lowers the thermal coefficient of expansion. Like lead, it increases the gloss and refractive index of the glaze. Major compounds containing boron are:

Boric acid ($B_2O_3 \cdot 2\,H_2O$)

Borax ($Na_2O \cdot 2\,B_2O_3 \cdot 10\,H_2O$)

Colemanite ($2\,CaO \cdot 3\,B_2O_3 \cdot 5\,H_2O$), technically called calcium borate

Chromic oxide (Cr_2O_3) is derived from the mineral chromite ($FeCr_2O_4$). It is used as a colorant in glazes. The fact that the mineral form is a natural spinel would indicate its use as a stain.

Red or **Ferric Iron** oxide (Fe_2O_3) is commonly used as a coloring agent to form brownish-red hues and also to modify copper and cobalt. It would have use as a flux were it not for its strong coloring action. Its presence in many compounds is regarded as an impurity, and considerable effort goes into removing iron flecks from white-ware bodies. It conforms to the R_2O_3 oxide ratio but has none of the refractory qualities that alumina has.

Sources of Acid (RO₂) Oxides

The important oxide in this group, silica, has a refractory effect on glaze, while the others function largely as opacifiers or coloring agents.

Silica (SiO_2) combines readily with the bases to form glassy silicates. It is the most common element in glaze, comprising about 50 percent of it by weight. In a glaze it has the effect of raising the melting point, decreasing fluidity, increasing resistance of the glaze to water and chemicals, increasing hardness and tensile strength, and reducing the coefficients of thermal expansion of the glaze. The amounts of silica used depend upon the flux and the maturing point of the glaze, but it is generally between 1 and 6 molecular equivalents.

Silica (SiO_2) is commonly obtained from sandstone, quartz sands, or flint pebbles. Silica is found combined with many ceramic materials that have been mentioned before. Below are listed a few of the more frequently used silica compounds.

Ball clay ($Al_2O_3 \cdot 2\ SiO_2 \cdot 2\ H_2O$)
Kaolin ($Al_2O_3 \cdot 2\ SiO_2 \cdot 2\ H_2O$)
Soda feldspar ($Na_2O \cdot Al_2O_3 \cdot 6\ SiO_2$)
Potash feldspar ($K_2O \cdot Al_2O_3 \cdot 6\ SiO_2$)
Cornwall stone ($1\ RO \cdot 1.16\ Al_2O_3 \cdot 8.95\ SiO_2$)
Wollastonite ($Ca \cdot SiO_3$)
Petalite ($Li_2O \cdot Al_2O_3 \cdot 8\ SiO_2$)

Tin oxide (SnO_2) is used primarily as an opacifier in glazes. Although rather expensive, it has continued in wide use because it has greater covering power than any other opacifier. The chief form of tin is:

Tin oxide (SnO_2), also called *stannic oxide*

Titanium oxide (TiO_2) is probably the only other oxide in the RO_2 group that has some of the refractory qualities of silicon. Its use in glazes, however, is entirely for its effect upon other colors and its action as an opacifier.

Titanium dioxide (TiO_2)
Rutile (TiO_2), an impure form containing iron and vanadium oxides

Characteristics of Ceramic Chemicals

Albany slip is a slip clay, which is a natural clay containing silica, alumina, and fluxes in the correct proportions to function as a glaze. It is mined in the vicinity of Albany, New York. Since it occurs in small pits, its composition and color will vary. Usually it fires to a glossy brown-black at temperatures between cones 8 and 12. Occasionally it may fire to a pale, nearly transparent tan. Slip clays are usually very easy to apply and fire with little, if any, defects. A typical composition and formula follow:

Composition			
	Percent		*Percent*
Silica	56.75	Magnesia	3.23
Alumina	15.47	Titania	1.00
Ferric oxide	5.73	Alkalies	3.25
Lime	5.78		

Formula		
0.195 K_2O	0.608 Al_2O_3	3.965 SiO_2
0.459 CaO	0.081 Fe_2O_3	
0.345 MgO		

Alumina hydrate [$Al(OH)_3$] is preferred to the calcined form (Al_2O_3) for some uses, since it has better adhesive qualities and remains suspended in the glaze longer. Introduction of alumina for mat effects is considered to be more effective in the hydrate form than in such compounds as clay or feldspar.

Antimonious oxide (Sb_2O_3) is poisonous and slightly soluble in water. For satisfactory effect as an opacifier, it must be used in glazes firing below cone 1. Antimony is also used to produce yellow and orange colors for glazes. The most common mixture, known as *yellow base*, has the following composition:

Red lead	15
Antimony oxide	10
Tin oxide	4

The mixture is calcined to cone 09, then ground and washed.

Barium carbonate ($BaCO_3$) is usually used in combination with other fluxes, since at lower temperatures it combines very slowly and acts as a refractory to form mat textures. At higher temperatures it reacts strongly as a flux.

Barium chromate ($BaCrO_4$) is used to produce colors in the pale yellow to light green range. It is generally used in overglaze decoration, since it is fugitive at temperatures over cone 04.

Basic antimonate of lead [$Pb_3(SbO_4)_2$], also known as *Naples yellow*, is primarily used as a paint pigment. It is a source of low-fire yellows. The presence of lead in Naples yellow is an advantage, since antimony will not produce a yellow unless combined with lead or iron.

Bentonite ($Al_2O_3 \cdot 4\ SiO_2 \cdot 9\ H_2O$) is of volcanic origin. This formula is not quite correct since bentonite contains other impurities. South Dakota bentonite has the following analysis:

	Percent		Percent
Silica	64.23	Lime	0.46
Alumina	20.74	Magnesia	2.26
Iron oxide	3.49		

It generally fires to a light cream color and fuses at about 2400°F. Its chief value is its use as a plasticizer for short clays. As such it is about five times as effective as ball clay. Purified bentonite will also make a stronger glaze covering and will help prevent settling in the glaze. An addition of about 3 percent is sufficient.

Bicarbonate of soda ($NaHCO_3$) has some use in casting slips and in forming stains with cobalt sulfate. Soda ash (Na_2CO_3) is the sodium form more commonly used as a flux.

Bismuth subnitrate ($BiONO_3 \cdot H_2O$) generally contains impurities such as arsenic, lead, and silver carbonates. It melts at a low temperature and is used primarily to produce pearly metallic lusters under reducing conditions (see luster glazes, pp. 243–244).

Bone ash in the unrefined state has a formula of $4 Ca_3(PO_4)_2 \cdot CaCO_3$ with a molecular weight of 1340. The material generally used today is the refined calcium phosphate $Ca_3(PO_4)_2$ with a molecular weight of 310. It is sometimes used as a glaze flux but more commonly as a body ingredient in bone china, chiefly in the kind produced in England. It lowers the firing temperatures required and increases translucency.

Borax ($Na_2O \cdot 2 B_2O_3 \cdot 10 H_2O$) is, next to lead, the major low-fire flux. It has a strong action on all ceramic compounds and may even be used in small amounts in the high-fire glazes that tend to be overly viscous in nature. Borax has a different effect than lead upon coloring oxides, and for this reason it is often used either alone or in combination with

lead. Borax absorbs moisture and should therefore be kept dry, or weight calculations will be inaccurate. As mentioned earlier, borax is very soluble in water and should not be used on raw ware.

Boric acid ($B_2O_3 \cdot 2 H_2O$) is a flaky material soluble in water. It is available in a fairly pure state at low price. Although boron is one of the neutral oxides (R_2O_3), it functions more as a flux, since it increases the gloss as does lead. Unlike silica, an acid, boron lowers the expansion coefficient and helps to increase elasticity.

Cadmium sulfide (CdS) is a low-fire yellow colorant. It is usually combined in a stain made of cadmium, selenium, and sulphur frits. Unfortunately it is fugitive above cone 010 and can be used only for overglaze decorations.

Calcium borate (see colemanite).

Calcium carbonate (see whiting).

Calcium fluoride (see fluorspar).

Calcium phosphate (see bone ash).

Calcium zirconium silicate is a commercially produced opacifier with the composition of ZrO_2, 51.12 percent; SiO_2, 25.41 percent; CaO, 22.23 percent. It does not have the strength of tin but is considerably cheaper. It will reduce slightly the maturing temperatures of the lower-fire glazes.

Carolina stone is similar to Cornwall stone.

China clay (see kaolin).

Chromic oxide (Cr_2O_3) and other chromium compounds are commonly used in glazes to produce green colors. Dichromates are preferred because of the greater amounts of chromium per weight. Care must be taken in the glaze composition, for, when combined with tin, a pink will result. Zinc will form a brown, and high-lead glazes may develop a yellow-lead chromate. Reducing conditions in the kiln will blacken the color. In fact, even adjacent tin-glazed and chrome-glazed pieces may affect each other in the kiln. Bright, low-temperature reds (below cone 010) can be produced by chrome oxide in a high-lead and low-alumina glaze.

Clay (see Chap. 4, pp. 139–145) is a decomposed feldspathic-type rock consisting chiefly of silicates of aluminium but often containing numerous other ingredients, such as quartz, micas, feldspars, iron oxides, carbonates of calcium and magnesium, and organic matter.

Cobalt carbonate ($CoCO_3$) is used to introduce a blue glaze color. When it is combined with manganese, iron chromate, or ochre it will produce black colorants.

Cobalt oxide (Co_2O_3) is the major blue colorant. It is extremely strong and therefore is often fritted with alumina and lime or with lead for lower-fire underglaze colors. The frit allows a lighter and more even color dispersion. Color stains made of cobalt, alumina, and zinc are uniform at all temperature ranges. Small amounts of cobalt in combination with MgO, SiO_2, and B_2O_3 will produce a variety of hues in the pink and lavender range.

Cobalt sulfate ($CoSo_4 \cdot 7 H_2O$), unlike the other cobalt compounds mentioned, is very soluble in water. It melts at a low temperature and is primarily used in decorative work or luster ware.

Colemanite ($2 CaO \cdot 3 B_2O_3 \cdot 5 H_2O$) is a natural hydrated calcium borate, which has the advantage of being only slightly soluble in water. Therefore, it does not develop the granular lumps in the glaze so characteristic of borax. Colemanite has wide use as a low-fire flux, since the boron present melts at a fairly low temperature. It tends to prevent crazing and also functions to some degree as an opacifier. Colemanite can be substituted for calcium in some glazes where calcium would harm the pink or red colors desired. Colemanite, used in both high- and low-fire glazes, tends to develop a milky blue opalescent color. It should be used immediately, since

it tends to defloccuate. Gerstley Borate, a type of colemanite, is better in this respect.

Copper carbonate ($CuCO_3$) is a major green colorant used in glazes. The carbonate form is preferred to the oxide form in the production of blue-greens or copper reds under reducing conditions.

Copper oxide is (1) cupric or black copper oxide (CuO) or (2) cuprous or red copper oxide (Cu_2O). Copper is one of the few colorants that does not change greatly under normal oxidizing conditions. Lead fluxes tend to produce a blackish green. When copper and tin are used with an alakline flux, a turquoise will result. Potash will induce a yellowish green, while zinc and copper with fluxes of sodium, potassium, and barium will develop a blue tinge.

Cornwall stone is a complex mixture derived from an English deposit of partially decomposed granite rock. It is composed of quartz (flint), feldspar, lepidolite, tourmaline, fluorspar, and small quantities of other minerals. Cornwall stone has characteristics that lie between those of kaolin and feldspar. It is a major ingredient of many English glazes and bodies and is subject to less firing strains than kaolin and feldspar. Because of the more intimate mixture of naturally occuring minerals, a smaller amount of alkali flux is necessary then would otherwise be needed. Since less bulk is required, there is less shrinkage of both the unfired and the fired glaze, thus minimizing glaze defects. Cornwall stone is roughly similar to *petuntze*, the feldspathic powered rock used for centuries by the Chinese as a major ingredient in their porcelain bodies and glazes. Like feldspars, Cornwall stone has variable composition; samples differ in the percentages of silica, potassium, sodium, and so on. If not available, a substitution of 67 parts feldspar, 22 parts flint, and 11 parts kaolin can be made for 100 units of Cornwall stone. However, as previously noted, the new glaze will not have identical characteristics.

A material similar to Cornwall stone, called Carolina stone, is mined in the United States but is not commonly available. An analysis of two samples (p. 234) shows almost identical proportions.

	Cornwall stone Percentage	Carolina stone Percentage
SiO_2	72.6	72.30
Al_2O_3	16.1	16.23
Fe_2O_3	0.23	0.07
CaO	1.4	0.62
MgO	0.1	trace
K_2O	4.56	4.42
Na_2O	3.67	4.14
CaF_2		
TiO_2	0.06	
Ignition loss	2.54	1.06

Formula for Cornwall stone sample

0.185	CaO	1.162	Al_2O_3	8.95	SiO_2
0.359	K_2O	0.0106	Fe_2O_3	0.0055	TiO_2
0.437	Na_2O		*Molecular weight 732.57*		
0.0185	MgO				

Cryolite (Na_3AlF_6) is used primarily as a flux and an opacifier for enamels and glasses. It has a limited use in glazes and bodies as a source of fluxes and alumina. In some glazes, an addition of cryolite will promote crazing.

Dolomite [$CaMg(CO_3)_2$] is a double carbonate of calcia and magnesia. It has a greater use in glass-making than in glazes. It is a cheap method of introducing calcia and magnesia into a glaze. Dolomite will promote a longer and lower firing range in clay bodies. Below cone 4, the addition of a small amount of a lower-firing alkaline flux to the dolomite will greatly increase this effect.

Epsom salts (see magnesium sulfate).

Feldspar is a crystalline rock composed of the aluminum silicates of potassium, sodium, and calcium. These silicates are never found in a pure state but in a mixture with one or the other predominating. For convenience in ceramic calculations, their formulas are usually given as follows:

Potash feldspar (microcline)
$K_2O \cdot Al_2O_3 \cdot 6\,SiO_2$
Soda feldspar (albite)
$Na_2O \cdot Al_2O_3 \cdot 6\,SiO_2$
Lime feldspar (anorthite)
$CaO \cdot Al_2O_3 \cdot 6\,SiO_2$

The feldspars are a major ingredient of porcelain and white-ware bodies and are often the only source of body flux. If the feldspar content of the body is high, the substitution of soda spar for potash feldspar will reduce the vitrification point by as much as 100°F. Feldspars are a cheap source of glaze flux and have the additional advantage of being non-soluble. Because of the presence of Al_2O_3 and SiO_2, the feldspar cannot be considered a flux at low temperature ranges, even though some flux is contributed to the glaze. The fluxing action is increased by the fineness of the particle size. Potash forms a harder glaze than does soda and decreases the thermal expansion. Thus, unless soda is desired for color purposes, potash feldspar should be preferred in the glaze composition (see Appendix, p. 308, for a comparative analysis).

Ferric chloride ($FeCl_3 \cdot 6\,H_2O$) is more commonly called *chloride of iron*. It is very soluble in water and must be stored in airtight containers. Its chief use is as a luster decoration on glass or glazes. It produces an iridescent gold-colored film under proper conditions (see luster glazes, p. 243).

Ferric oxide (see iron oxide).

Ferrous oxide (see iron oxide).

Flint (SiO_2) is also called silica or, in foreign publications, quartz. It is commonly obtained from sandstone, quartz sands, or flint pebbles. True flint is obtained from England, France, and Denmark. It is prepared by calcining and grinding flint beach pebbles. This cryptocrystalline flint has a different specific gravity (2.33) from that prepared from quartz sand or sandstone (2.65). In the United States, all silica is called *flint*. The difference between the two is slight. A "pebble" flint reacts a trifle faster in the glaze. The specific gravity is of importance only if it is used in casting slips.

When used alone, silica melts at the extremely high temperature of 3119°F and forms an unusually hard and stable crystal. It combines under heat, however, with a variety of fluxes at much lower temperatures to form a glass and with the alumina compounds to form the more refractory body structure. An increase in the silica content of a glaze has the effect of raising the maturing temperatures as well as increasing its hardness and resistance to wear. In a glaze, the addition of flint decreases its thermal expansions; in a body it increases them.

Fluorspar (CaF_2), also called *calcium fluoride*, has a limited use as a source of flux in glaze and body compositions. The particle size must be less than 100 mesh when used in the body, or pinholes are likely to form in the glaze. Fluorspar fluxes at a lower temperature than do other calcia compounds. With copper oxides, some unusual blue-green hues can be developed.

Ilmenite ($TiO_2 \cdot FeO$) is the mineral source of titanium and its compounds. Used as a coarse powder-like sand, it produces dark specks in the glaze.

Iron chromate ($FeCrO_4$) is used in combination with manganese and zinc oxide to produce underglaze brown colors or with cobalt to form a black stain. Used alone, it is fugitive above cone 04.

Iron oxides have three forms: (FeO) *ferrous oxide*, (Fe_2O_3) *ferric oxide* or hematite, and (Fe_3O_4) *ferrous-ferric oxide* or magnetite. Iron is the oxide most frequently used to produce tan or brown bodies and glazes. Were it not for its pronounced color, it would have a wide use as a flux. It is responsible for most of the low-firing characteristics and the red color of many earthenware clays. A pink stain can be made with a smaller amount of iron plus alumina, calcium, and flint. When reduced in a suitable glaze, iron will form gray-greens (see celadon, p. 213).

Kaolin ($Al_2O_3 \cdot 2 SiO_2 \cdot 2 H_2O$) is also called *china clay* or *pure clay*. Because of its composition and relative purity, kaolin is the highest-firing clay. It is an important ingredient of all white ware and china bodies, since it fires to pure white. For glazes, kaolin constitutes a major source of Al_2O_3 and SiO_2. The chief residual deposits in the United States are in North Carolina, and sedimentary deposits are found in South Carolina and Georgia. For bodies, the more plastic sedimentary types are preferred. The sedimentary kaolin deposits of Florida are even more plastic and are often termed ball kaolin (see Chap. 4, p. 140).

Lead antimonate (see basic antimonate of lead).

Lead, bisilicate (see lead silicate).

Lead, white (see lead carbonate).

Lead carbonate [$2 PbCO_3 \cdot Pb(OH)_2$] is the white powder more commonly called white lead. It is the major low-fire flux and produces a glossy glaze with relatively few faults. Its major drawback is its poisonous effects if it is inhaled in spraying. By fritting the lead in a suitable mixture with silica, a nontoxic lead silicate can be formed. A lead-glazed vessel should not be used for storing concentrated citric acid fruit juices. However, because of its ease of application and free-flowing, brilliant surface, lead carbonate continues to be the major low-fire flux. The evolution of CO_2 from the glazes is said to promote a better mixture of the glaze ingredients than that of other lead compounds. The use of lead as a flux will have a different effect on the colorants used than the alkaline compounds. The addition of calcia, silica, or alumina to a lead glaze will increase its hardness and resistance to wear.

Lead oxide as used in ceramics is of two types: (PbO) *litharge* or lead monoxide, and (Pb_3O_4) *red lead* or minium. Litharge is a yellow powder that has greater use in Europe than in the United States. Since litharge occasionally contains impurities and has larger particles than does the carbonate form, the latter is the preferred lead compound. Because of the greater amount of oxygen, the red form is often used in place of litharge. Ceramic grades of red lead are seldom pure but usually contain 75 percent red lead and about 25 percent litharge. Pound for pound, red lead contains more PbO than does the carbonate form.

Lead silicate is a frit made of lead and silica to eliminate the toxic effects of the lead compounds. The two most common types are: *lead monosilicate*, with a composition of 15 percent SiO_2 and 85 percent PbO; and *lead bisilicate*, with a formula of 65 percent PbO, 34 percent SiO_2, and 1 percent Al_2O_3.

Lead silicate, hydrous [$2\,PbSiO_2 \cdot Pb(OH_2)$] has a molecular weight of 807. This material is the basic silicate of white lead. It is used as a substitute for lead carbonate when the CO_2 released by the carbonate forms pinholes or is otherwise objectionable in the glaze.

Lead sulfide (PbS), also called *galena*, is the black powder that is the raw source of all lead compounds. It has a very limited use in glazes.

Lepidolite ($LiF \cdot KF \cdot Al_2O_3 \cdot 3\,SiO_2$), also called lithium mica, contains from 3 to 6 percent of lithia. It has some use as a body ingredient in chinaware and is a source of flux, Al_2O_3, and SiO_2 in higher-temperature glazes. It will tend to brighten most glazes, lower thermal expansions, and reduce brittleness (see lithium carbonate).

Lime (CaO), calcium oxide (see whiting).

Litharge (PbO) (see lead oxide).

Lithium carbonate (Li_2CO_3) is a common source of lithia, which is a strong flux in the higher temperature ranges. With lithia, greater amounts of Al_2O_3, SiO_2, and CaO can be used in alkaline glazes, thus producing a more durable glaze while retaining the unusual copper blues characteristic of the alkaline glazes. It can be used in place of lead in the medium temperature ranges when volitization is a problem.

Magnesium carbonate ($MgCO_3$), magnesite acts as a refractory at lower temperatures, changing to a flux at higher temperatures. It is valuable to slow down the fluid qualities of crystalline and other runny glazes. It also improves glaze adhesion.

Magnesium sulfate ($MgSO_4 \cdot 7\,H_2O$) is better known as *epsom salts*. Its primary use in glazes is to retard the settling of frits and glazes. Usually 1 percent, dissolved in hot water, will be sufficient and will have no apparent effect on the glaze.

Magnetite (see iron oxides).

Manganese dioxide (see manganese oxide).

Manganese oxide (MnO_2) is used in ceramics as a colorant. It should not be used in concentrations greater than 5 percent in either body or glaze, because blisters may develop. The usual colors produced are in the brown range. With cobalt, a black results; with the proper alkaline fluxes, purple and dark reddish hues can be produced. When fritted with alumina, a pink colorant will be formed.

Nepheline syenite ($K_2O \cdot 3\,Na_2O \cdot 4\,Al_2O_3 \cdot 9\,SiO_2$) is a material roughly similar to a feldspar and has the following composition:

	Percent
SiO_2	60.4
Al_2O_3	23.6
Fe_2O_3	0.08
CaO	0.7
MgO	0.1
Na_2O	9.8
K_2O	4.7
Ignition loss	0.7

Molecular formula			
Na_2O	0.713	Al_2O_3	1.04
K_2O	0.220		
CaO	0.056	SiO_2	4.53
MgO	0.011		

Molecular weight 447

A major use for nepheline syenite is as a substitute for potash feldspar where it lowers the firing temperatures required. It also produces a greater firing range and increased thermal expansion, which in turn will reduce crazing tendencies in the glaze. Its use in a glaze is roughly similar to potash feldspar except for the lowering of the maturing point.

Nickel oxide is used in two forms, (NiO) *green nickel oxide* or nickelous and (Ni_2O_3) *black nickel oxide* or nickelic. The function of nickel in a glaze is almost solely as a colorant. Depending upon the flux used and the ratio of alumina, a variety of colors can be produced: with zinc, a blue is obtained; with lime, a tan; with barium, a brown; and with magnesia, a green. None of these hues are particularly brilliant. In general, nickel is used to soften and alter other coloring oxides. In addition, the use of 5 to 10 percent nickel in a proper glaze results in the formation of a crystalline structure.

Ochre is a term given to clays containing varying amounts of red iron or manganese oxides. Their chief use is in paint manufacturing. However, they can be used as glaze or slip colorants to impart tan, brown, or brick-red hues.

Opax is a standard commercially produced opacifier with the following composition:

	Percent		Percent
ZrO_2	90.84	Na_2O	1.11
SiO_2	6.48	Al_2O_3	0.91

Opax does not have the power of tin oxide, but it is considerably cheaper, and for this reason it is often used to replace part of the tin oxide that would otherwise be required.

Pearl ash (see potassium carbonate).

Petalite ($Li_2O \cdot Al_2O_3 \cdot 8 SiO_2$), lithium-aluminium silicate, is chiefly used as an auxiliary body flux to reduce thermal expansions and increase shock resistance. At about cone 06 it converts into beta spodumene, which has almost no volume change when heated or cooled. It is a source of lithia and silica for medium- and high-temperature glazes.

Plastic vitrox ($1 RO \cdot 1.69 Al_2O_3 \cdot 14.64 SiO_2$) is a complex mineral mined in California that has a use in both glaze and body formulas as a source of silica, alumina, and potash. It is similar to both potash feldspar and Cornwall stone. (See Appendix, p. 307 for comparative analysis.)

Potash feldspar (see feldspar).

Potassium carbonate (K_2CO_3) is more commonly called *pearl ash*. It is used primarily to modify color effects. When pearl ash is substituted for the lead, sodium, or calcium content, the colors resulting from copper oxide can be changed from the usual green to either a yellow-green or a bright blue.

Potassium dichromate ($K_2Cr_2O_7$) is used in glazes as a green colorant. When it is calcined with tin, low-fire stains developing pink and red hues are formed (see chromic oxide).

Praseodymium oxide (Pr_6O_{11}), a black oxide, is a rare earth compound used in ceramics as a yellow colorant. It is commonly combined with zirconium oxide and silica to form a glaze stain that is stable at all normal firing temperatures.

Pyrophyllite ($Al_2O_3 \cdot 4 SiO_2 \cdot H_2O$) is used primarily in wall-tile bodies, where it decreases thermal expansions, crazing, and moisture expansions to which tile is subjected. Since it is nonplastic, it has limited use in pottery bodies.

Red lead (see lead oxide).

Rutile (TiO_2) is an impure oxide of titanium containing small amounts of iron and vanadium. It is used as a tan colorant.

Selenium (Se) is most often used as a glass colorant. It has a limited use in ceramic glazes and overglaze colors, primarily as cadmium-selenium red frits. These frits, unfortunately, are fugitive at higher temperatures.

Silica (see flint).

Silicon carbide (SiC) has many industrial uses. Its value in ceramics is as the sole or major ingredient in high-temperature kiln furniture and muffles. When added to an alkaline glaze in small amounts ($\frac{1}{2}$ of 1 percent), the carbon will reduce the copper oxides to form localized copper reds.

Sillimanite ($Al_2O_3 \cdot SiO_2$) is similar in many respects to Kyanite. Major uses are in high-temperature refractory bodies.

Silver chloride (AgCl) is the major silver compound used in luster overglaze preparations (see lusters p. 243). When silver chloride is combined with bismuth and with a resin or fat oil as a binder, an overglaze metallic luster with greenish or yellow tints will form.

Soda ash (see sodium carbonate).

Sodium aluminate ($Na_2O \cdot Al_2O_3$) is used to prevent casting slips from setting and to increase the strength of dry ware.

Sodium bicarbonate (see bicarbonate of soda).

Sodium carbonate (Na_2CO_3) is commonly called *soda ash*. It is a very active flux, but because of its solubility it is more commonly used in glazes as a frit ingredient. Small quantities of soda ash, functioning as a deflocculant, will reduce the water of plasticity required in a clay body. This increases workability and strength of the plastic body and reduces the shrinkage when it goes from the wet to the dry state.

Sodium silicate ($Na_2 \cdot XSiO_2$) is a compound that can vary from $1 Na_2O \cdot 1.6 SiO_2$ to $1 Na_2O \cdot 3.75 SiO_2$. It usually comes in liquid form and is the major deflocculant used in casting slips. Like soda ash,

it greatly reduces the water required to make the clay into a slip form. In doing so, it lessens the rate of shrinkage, the strains of drying, and breakage in the green and dry states.

Sodium uranate ($Na_2O \cdot UO_3$), more commonly called *uranium yellow*, has unfortunately not been available in the United States since World War II because of restrictions placed on uranium by the Atomic Energy Commission. Uranium yellows are still available, however, in Europe. Uranium compounds formerly were the best source of yellow colorants. When uranium compounds are combined with various fluxes or with tin and zirconium oxide, a variety of hues from bright yellow through orange to vermillion red can be developed (see also uranium oxide).

Spodumene ($Li_2O \cdot Al_2O_3 \cdot 4 SiO_2$) is an important source of lithia. The use of litha, which is an active flux, helps to develop unusual copper-blue hues. Spodumene is also added to white ware and porcelain bodies. When used to replace feldspar, it will reduce the vitrification temperature as well as the shrinkage rate. Strange as it may seem, the crystalline form of spodumene expands at about 1700°F (927°C) instead of shrinking. When a mixture of 60 percent spodumene and 40 percent lead bisilicate is used, a nonplastic, press-formed body can be made that at 1970°F (1077°C), will have zero absorption and zero shrinkage.

Steatite, a hydrous magnesium silicate, is a massive variety of talc. Most steatite is used in powdered form for electrical insulators. It has very little shrinkage, and occasionally the rocklike nuggets are turned down in a lathe for special projects. Steatite was used by the Egyptians some 5000 years ago for the creation of beads and small figurines. These were generally covered with a turquoise alkaline copper glaze (see talc).

Talc varies from $3 MgO \cdot 4 SiO_2 \cdot H_2O$ to $4 MgO \cdot 5 SiO_2 \cdot H_2O$. In the solid and more impure form, it is also known as *steatite* or *soapstone*. Talc is occasionally used in glazes, but it is more frequently employed as a major ingredient in white-ware bodies firing at moderate temperatures (cones 04–6). Like dolomite, it is used to lower the firing temperatures of kaolin, ball clays, and feldspars, which are often the other body ingredients. Talc will promote a slight opacity in glazes.

Tin oxide (SnO_2), also called *stannic oxide*, is the most effective of all opacifiers. From 5 to 7 percent will produce a completely opaque white glaze. An excess will create a dull surface. Tin also has wide use in stains, since it has considerable effect on the color qualities of most color-forming oxides. Because of its relatively high price, tin substitutes are frequently used (see opacifiers).

Titanium oxide (TiO_2), or more correctly *titanium dioxide*, is a major opacifier when used either alone or in a frit. Like rutile, which is an impure form containing iron, titanium will, if used in any quantity, encourage a semimat surface texture.

Uranium oxide, [U_3O_8 (black)], is a depleted nuclear fuel used as a yellow colorant in low-fire lead glazes. More efficient as colorants are other forms of uranium, such as sodium uranate [$Na_2O \cdot UO_2$ (orange)] and sodium diuranate (yellow). A 5-percent addition of tin oxide aids the color formation, while a reduction fire is detrimental. The tin-vanadium, zirconium-vanadium, and praseodymium yellow stains have greater flexibility and no radiation hazard. They are preferred by most potters.

Vanadium pentoxide (V_2O_5) is a rather weak yellow colorant when used alone. When fritted in the proper composition with tin, it produces a strong yellow color. This stain, known commercially as tin-vanadium stain, has largely replaced the uranium yellows, which are no longer available. It has a wide firing range (cones 06–14), is transparent, and is not affected by a reduction firing.

Volcanic ash occurs in many regions of the American West. It was formed from the dust of volcanic glass erupted in prehistoric times. Since the material often floated through the air many miles before being deposited, it is extremely fine and can be used with little preparation. Its composition is roughly similar to that of a granite-type rock (see the formula under RO oxides, p. 229). An average analysis of Kansas ash is as follows:

	Percent		*Percent*
SiO_2	72.51	MgO	0.07
Al_2O_3	11.55	K_2O	7.87
Fe_2O_3	1.21	Na_2O	1.79
TiO_2	0.54	Ignition loss	3.81
CaO	0.68		

In most glazes volcanic ash can be substituted for roughly 70 parts of feldspar and 30 parts of flint. A low-fire 04 glaze can be compounded of 60 percent ash and 40 percent borax and lead or just lead.

Whiting ($CaCO_3$) is a *calcium carbonate* produced domestically by processing marble or limestone. European whiting is generally obtained from chalk deposits, such as those at the famous cliffs of Dover. Whiting is the major high-fire flux, although it has a limited use in bodies where a small amount will lower vitrification temperatures and reduce porosity. As a flux, it produces much harder and tougher silicates than will either the lead or alkaline compounds. For this reason, small amounts are often added to the lower-fire glazes. As with other fluxes, calcium has an effect upon the coloring oxides, particularly chrome greens.

Wollastonite ($CaSiO_3$) is a natural calcium silicate. As a replacement for flint and whiting, it reduces firing shrinkage and improves heat shock. It is used in both bodies and glazes.

Zinc oxide (ZnO) is a difficult compound to classify. At high temperatures it is an active flux. When used to excess in a glaze low in alumina and cooled slowly, zinc will produce crystalline structures. Opacity will develop if zinc is used in a high-alumina low-calcium glaze, with no borosilicate fluxes, at cone 1 or higher in amounts of 0.15 equivalents. In general, zinc increases the maturing range of a glaze

Guide to Use of Colorants

Color	Oxide	Percentage	Temperature	Atmosphere
Black				
{	cobalt	1–2	any	either
	manganese	2–4		
{	cobalt	1		
	iron	8	any	either
	manganese	3		
Blue				
	cobalt	½–1	any	either
	turquoise–copper (alkaline flux)	3–5	low	oxidizing
	slate blue–nickel (with zinc)	1–3	low	oxidizing
Brown				
	rutile	5	any	reducing
	chromium (with MgO, ZnO)	2–5	low	either
	iron	3–7	any	oxidizing
	manganese	5	any	either
	nickel (with zinc)	2–4	any	either
Green				
	copper oxide	1–5	any	oxidizing
	gray-green–iron	1–4	any	reducing
	nickel-magnesia	3–5	low	oxidizing
Red				
	pink–chrome and tin (1 to 18)	5	any	oxidizing
	coral–chromium (with high PbO)	5	low	oxidizing
	purple–manganese (with KNaO)	4–6	any	oxidizing
	copper	1	any	reducing
	iron (high SiO_2, KNaO), CaO	2–5	low	oxidizing
Tan				
	iron	2	any	either
	manganese	2	any	either
	rutile	2	any	either
Yellow				
	antimony yellow stain (with high PbO)	3–5	low	either
	praseodymium yellow stain	4–6	any	either
	uranium yellow and orange (with high PbO)	5–8	low	oxidizing
	zirconium vanadium stain	5–10	any	either
	tin vanadium stain	4–6	any	either

and promotes a higher gloss, brighter colors, a reduction of expansions, and, under some conditions, an opacity.

Zirconium oxide (ZrO_2) is seldom used alone as an opacifier in ceramics but is generally combined with other oxides and fritted into a more stable silicate form. Below are listed a few commercial zirconium silicates. None have the strength of tin oxide, but they are considerably cheaper.

Calcium zirconium silicate: 51.12 percent ZrO_2, 25.41 percent SiO_2, and 22.23 percent CaO

Magnesium zirconium silicate: 53.75 percent ZrO_2, 29.92 percent SiO_2, and 18.54 percent MgO

Zinc zirconium silicate: 45.78 percent ZrO_2, 23.08 percent SiO_2, and 30.52 percent ZnO

Zirconium spinel: 39.94 percent ZrO_2, 25.25 percent SiO_2, 19.47 percent ZrO_2, and 19.41 percent Al_2O_3

Most of the above compounds are used in combination with other opacifiers, such as tin or the titanium compounds (see also opax and zircopax).

Zircopax is a standard commercially produced opacifier with the composition of 64.88 percent ZrO_2, 0.22 percent TiO_2, 34.28 percent SiO_2.

Colorants for Glazes and Decoration

Coloring Oxides

Most studio potters obtain their glaze colors from the oxides or carbonates of the more common metals, such as iron, copper, nickel, tin, zinc, and manganese. Other oxides, such as vanadium and cobalt, although rarer and more expensive, are extensively used because of a lack of cheaper substitutes. Most of these compounds have been discussed in previous sections. The list of major colorants (opposite) indicates the oxide necessary and the amount generally used to produce a particular color. However, just because an oxide is listed as producing a green does not mean that it will produce a green in every case. A study of the section on ceramic materials (pp. 231–241) will reveal that generally the particular color that develops from an oxide depends upon the type of flux used, the proportions of alumina or silica, and the firing temperature. In some cases, even the rate of cooling will have an effect upon the glaze. Therefore, the list of oxides and colors on page 240 is merely for convenience in determining color possibilities. Before using the oxide, the potter should be aware of its characteristics and the characteristics of the glaze in which it is to be used.

It is common practice to use two or more colorants in order to modify harsh colors and to obtain subtle variations or mottled color effects. Copper and nickel are often added to soften powerful cobalt hues. Opacifiers are used to brighten colors. Rutile is a frequent addition, since it contributes a runny and slightly specked quality as well as slightly matting a glaze.

Opacifiers

Opacifiers are, for the most part, a group of chemicals that are relatively insoluble in the glaze melt.

Opacifiers

Color	Oxide	Percentage	Temperature	Atmosphere
Pure white	tin	5	any	either
Weak blue white	titanium	8–12	any	either
White	zirconium	8–12	any	either
Weak yellow white	antimony	10–12	low	oxidizing
White	opax (a frit)	10	any	either
White	zircopax (a frit)	10	any	either

Tin oxide and zirconium oxide are the chief examples of this type. As such, they remain suspended in the glaze and, if dense enough, prevent light from penetrating through to the body. Most opacifiers, and of course those of the greatest value, are white. However, some give a slight yellow, pink, or bluish cast to the glaze.

Another type of opacifier is titanium (or zinc under some conditions), which tends to form minute crystalline structures within the glaze. Having a different index of refraction from the major portion of the glaze, it thus breaks up and prevents much light penetration. This is the type of crystal formation associated with mat glazes. It is the reason why all mats must be, necessarily, either wholly or partially opaque.

Spinel Stains

Under certain circumstances, the use of a raw coloring oxide may be objectionable. For example, most metallic oxides are quite soluble in the melting glaze. In the previous section, we noted that the fluxes and other elements of the glaze had considerable effect upon color quality. Overglaze and underglaze decoration with any degree of precision or control is impossible with colorants that diffuse into, or flow with, the glaze. In these cases, a special type of colorant known as a spinel is used.

A spinel stain is a colored crystal that is highly resistant to attack by fluxes in the glaze and to the effects of high temperatures. In strict chemical terms, *spinel* refers to the mineral magnesium aluminate ($MgOAl_2O_3$). However, manganese, iron, and chromium may be present by replacement. The crystal is an octahedron variety of extreme hardness. The ruby gem is a red spinel. By calcining certain oxides together, some very stable colored spinels can be formed. In general, these follow the formula $RO \cdot R_2O_3$. The RO member can be either MgO, ZnO, NiO, CaO, CdO, MnO, or FeO, and the R_2O_3 can be Cr_2O_3, Al_2O_3, or Fe_2O_3.

Preparation of a spinel stain is a long procedure, and it is not recommended unless it is necessary for advanced experimental work. There is a wide range of commercial stains, expertly prepared, available

at reasonable cost. The general idea, however, of the preparation should be understood. Detailed information can be found in the reference texts listed in the Appendix (pp. 329–331).

It is extremely necessary that the chemicals involved are mixed completely and intimately. To this end the raw chemicals should first be passed through an 80-mesh sieve. It is preferable that they be in the form of soluble salts, that is, the nitrates or sulfates of the oxides just listed. These are thoroughly mixed in a liquid solution. After the water has been evaporated, the dry mixture is placed in a crucible or a kiln and calcined. The temperature will vary with the mixture. If the mixture melts into a solid mass, it should be calcined in a pot furnace so that the crucible can be removed with tongs and the contents poured into water, thus preventing the spinel from hardening into a solid crystalline block. Afterwards, the material is broken up with an iron mortar and pestle into a coarse powder, which is then ball milled. For a uniform color without specks, the particle size of the spinel must be extremely small. This may necessitate grinding in the ball mill for well over a hundred hours. When it is sufficiently fine, the stain should be washed several times with hot water to remove any remaining soluble salts. Filters may be necessary at this point to prevent the loss of fine particles.

Other Colored Stains

Besides the spinels, a number of other chemical compounds are calcined to produce stable colorants at certain temperatures. A discussion of a few of the better-known examples will serve to illustrate some of the numerous possibilities in the preparation of colorants.

An ultramarine blue can be formed by a silicate of cobalt. It is made by calcining cobalt oxide and flint, plus a flux such as feldspar.

Green stains can be developed by calcining fluorspar and chromium oxide.

Yellow stains, such as Naples yellow and yellow base, are made from antimony, lead, and tin. Calcium and sodium uranate can also be used, when available, to form various yellow and orange colorants.

Pink and red stains are made by several methods. One of the most unusual is the precipitation of colloidal gold upon kaolin, which is then calcined and ground to form the stain. Other red stains are formed from a mixture of tin, calcium, flint, and chromium. (For further information and specific details, consult the reference texts by Parmelee and Norton and the *Literature Abstracts of Ceramic Glazes* listed in the Appendix, pp. 329–331).

Underglaze Colors

Underglaze colors were briefly mentioned before in the section on decoration (pp. 196–197). As the term indicates, they are colors used under the glaze. Since they will eventually be fired at the same temperature as the glaze, the variety of colors available is less than for overglaze colors. For example, at the hard porcelain range of cone 14, most, if not all, of the delicate hues available in overglaze colors will burn out completely. This leaves only the blues, browns, grays, gold-pinks, reduction reds, and celadon hues available for use at these higher temperatures. It is advisable to run a series of firing tests before attempting any amount of decorative work at such temperatures. The basic reason for employing underglaze rather than overglaze colors is durability. Their greatest use is in the field of dinnerware.

Underglaze colors are made up of a colorant, either a raw oxide or a spinel, a flux such as feldspar to allow the color to adhere to the body, and a diluent like silica, calcined kaolin, or ground bisque ware. The purpose of these last materials is either to lighten the color or to equalize shrinkage. It is rather important that the mixture be adjusted properly to the bisque ware and the final glaze. The glazed surface should show no change in gloss over the decoration. A preliminary firing to red heat is necessary before glazing to burn out the vehicle used to adhere the mixture, which may be either a solution of gun tragacanth or oil of lavender that has been thinned with turpentine. Failure to burn off the carbon formed by the adherent will make the glaze bubble and blister over the decoration.

Overglaze Colors

The major differences between overglaze colors and underglaze colors are the use of a lower melting flux and a wider range of colors. Since the decoration is to be applied to a previously fired glaze, the final firing need be only high enough to allow the flux to melt into the glaze and seal the color. This is usually at a temperature of cone 016, approximately 1470°F (799°C). The flux is made of varying proportions of lead, borax, and flint, depending upon the color to be used with it. The mixture is calcined lightly, ground, and washed. The colorant, and if necessary, an opacifier, is then added, and the whole mixture is ball milled to an adequate fineness. A vehicle such as gum or oil is used to help the mixture to adhere to the glazed surface. In commercial production, where decoration is standardized, printing methods are used. The colors of both types of decoration are applied by decals or silk screen.

Lusters

Since lusters are employed more as decoration than as a glaze, they are included in this section on decorative coloring materials. As was noted earlier in the discussion of glaze types (Chap. 8, p. 214), a luster is nothing more than a thin layer of metal that is deposited and fused upon the surface of the glaze. There are various methods by which this can be accomplished, some of them outlined below. Luster can give a variety of effects, depending upon the transparency or color of the composition and the type of glaze upon which it is applied. In Persian and Hispano-Moresque pieces it is very effectively combined with underglaze decoration. In fact, luster really comes into its own when it is used to enrich other types of decoration. If used alone as an overall glaze, it tends to look like a rather cheap imitation of either glass or metal. The colors available in lusters are a transparent iridescent, a nacreous silver white, and metallic hues in a variety of yellows, greens, browns, and reds.

Preparation of lusters will vary according to the method of firing employed. There are three types of preparation.

1. A mixture composed of a resin, oil of lavender, and a metallic salt is brushed on the glazed ware. The ware is then fired in an oxidizing kiln to a low temperature of between $1100°$ and $1300°F$ ($593°$–$704°C$), at which point the carbon in the resin reduces the metallic salt to its metal form. Most lusters contain bismuth nitrate, an active flux, as well as the other metal salts. This is used in combination with zinc acetate, lead acetate, and alumina to produce a clear, iridescent luster. The various metal colorants are always used in the form of a salt that decomposes at the lower temperatures needed to form the luster coating. Yellows can be made with chrome alum and bismuth nitrate. Nickel nitrate, cobalt sulphate, manganese sulphate, and iron chloride will produce a variety of browns, shading from yellowish to reddish hues. Uranium nitrate, where available, develops a greenish yellow. Gold is commonly used to produce red hues and platinum to create silvery lusters. Many combinations of these colorants are used and results will be varied, depending in part upon the basic glaze and the firing schedule. In general, the luster mixture will consist of 1 part metallic salt, 3 to 5 parts resin, and 7 to 10 parts oil of lavender. The resin, usually gum dammar, is heated; when it becomes liquid, the nitrate or chloride is added. When the nitrate dissolves, the oil is slowly poured in. The solution is then filtered or cooled and decanted. The experiments in *Literature Abstracts of Ceramic Glazes* (see Appendix, p. 330) will help in creating formulas.

2. The method previously discussed is one that is commonly used today to produce lusters. Another type is similar to that employed many centuries ago by Egyptian and Islamic potters, although it is seldom used today. The ancients developed luster and carried this decorative glaze to its highest level of artistic merit. The chief difference between their method and that described above is the use of a reduction fire to reduce the metal rather than having a reducing agent contained in the resin. The mixture, which is brushed on the glazed ware, consists of 3 parts metal, usually in a carbonate form, 7 parts red ochre, and an adhesive, such as gum tragacanth. Old recipes call for vinegar or wine, but

gum is doubtless more efficient. In the firing cycle, the atmosphere is oxidizing until a low red heat is reached, whereupon reduction is started and continued to the temperature necessary to reduce the metal, usually from $1200°$ to $1300°F$ (649–$704°C$).

3. The third method of developing a luster is also seldom used, but in rare cases it occurs by accident. The color is incorporated into the glaze, preferably in the form of a metallic salt. Various combinations can be used in proportions ranging from 0.5 to 8 percent of the total glaze. As in the resinate type of luster glaze, the use of bismuth, in addition to the other metallic salts, will aid luster development. The kiln is fired oxidizing to the maturity point of the glaze, then cooled to between $1200°$ and $1300°F$ ($649°$–$704°C$). At this point the kiln is relit and fired for about 15 minutes with a reducing atmosphere. Accurate records should be kept on reduction firings, since variations of temperature and reduction periods will produce quite different results.

Binders

Various materials can be added to either a clay body or a glaze to increase the green or dry strength of the ceramic form, to aid glaze adhesion, and to lessen injury to the fragile glaze coating during the kiln loading. The several blinders and waxes used in industrial production to increase the body strength are not really needed by the studio potter, since his plastic clay body is usually adequate in this regard.

Clay

If the glaze contains an excess of 10 percent kaolin, additional binders may not be needed. However, if the clay content is low, the inclusion of about 3 percent bentonite will increase adhesion. It should be mixed with the dry ingredients.

Gums

Traditionally, gum arabic or tragacanth have been used as glaze binders. The granular gum crystals are soaked overnight in water and stirred vigorously the following day. About one-quarter ounce will make a quart of creamlike mucilage binder. A couple of drops of carbolic acid are needed to prevent decomposition. One or two teaspoons of this solution per quart of glaze is usually adequate.

Methocel

Methocel is a synthetic methylcellulose compound that will not deteriorate as the gums will and which also serves as an agent to prevent setting. The latter is a problem to which colemanite, in particular, is susceptible. Normally 1 to 2 percent methocel by dry weight is sufficient. However, one should not attempt to add the dry powder to a liquid glaze.

Instead, he should sift the powder into hot water in a double boiler, soak the mixture overnight, and then pour the resultant jellylike mass into a larger container of hot water. When all the methocel is dissolved, it can be added to dry glaze ingredients. An electric mixer is useful for this step.

Temporary Binders

In an emergency, sugar, syrup, or wheat flour can be used as a binder. Of course, all of these will ferment, and none of them have the deflocculating action of methocel.

10 The Professional Potter

As the pottery student nears the end of his course of studies, he faces the question of what use he will make of his new knowledge. While pottery making in school can be an exciting experience, a relief from the routine of academic studies, the life of a professional potter is one of hard work and long hours, with compensation often out of proportion to the training required.

For most students the prospect is not encouraging, and ceramics fills the role of an interesting hobby, a relaxation from an industrial or professional livelihood. A few trained potters become teachers, which requires additional work at the graduate level. For the prospective teacher it is useful to have considerable background in other craft media or in sculpture, for beginning positions often include teaching assignments in more than one area. Situations vary widely in terms of facilities, class size, and administrative duties. Ideally, the college or university should provide a studio and sufficient free time to allow the potter to experiment and grow in his field. Unfortunately, many institutions hire a potter because he is creative and productive, only to overwhelm him later with oversize classes and administrative red tape.

THE STUDIO POTTER

In view of the time and energy that must necessarily be expended in teaching, it is natural that many talented students are attracted to the prospect of opening their own studios, and the general affluence of large segments of society has made the idea much more feasible now than it was in years past. The hand-made pot is today truly a luxury item—hardly a necessity.

Perhaps the most difficult task for the potter dreaming of his own studio is to develop a realistic dollars-and-cents approach. The few pots sold during student days seem to represent a great profit. Seldom does the beginner accurately calculate the time he has spent, nor does he realize that, in school,

opposite : 432. DAVID GIL for the Bennington Potters, U.S.A. Tea and coffee pots designed to match Bennington's stacking dinnerware (see Fig. 434).

247

he had the free use of a kiln worth perhaps $3000, paid nothing for the fuel, and probably purchased his chemicals and clay below cost. All these items, plus the rental of a studio, the expense of utilities, and miscellaneous expenditures such as advertising and mailing, add immeasurably to overhead once the potter is on his own.

The school environment is so unlike that of the producing studio that it would be a great advantage for the student to apprentice himself for a year or so to a professional potter or to find employment in a small pottery. If one plans to have a sales outlet in connection with a studio, location becomes very important. The expense and restrictions of a metropolitan area often make such a situation impractical. For obvious reasons, most potters prefer to live in the country. Setting up shop near a major highway is not really necessary. True pot lovers will seek out an excellent craftsman and return with their friends.

Some potters prefer to sell mainly through outside shops, but since the usual markup in these outlets is 100 percent, it is easy to price oneself out of sales, unless one can produce an attractive line that can be thrown and decorated quickly. Items placed on consignment traditionally have a 50 percent markup. Unfortunately, shops that carry consignment goods often have commercial lines as well and use the consignment pieces primarily as window dressing, without making much effort to sell them. For some years "craft fairs" have been popular in many parts of the country. A few potters have found these to be an important source of summer sales, although competition has increased in recent years. One potter operating in a rural location near a large city has had good results by holding a "kiln opening" periodically during the summer. Post cards sent to a list of interested customers ensure a good turnout over the weekend.

What to make is perhaps more important than the details of the selling procedure. It is usually a great shock for the beginning potter to realize that the public does not always have the same preferences that he does. While the craftsman may like the mottled brown-glazed bowl, it could sell twice as fast if it were blue. It is not that treasured show pieces will not sell, for indeed they will. But the new customer is more likely to buy, for example, a set of mugs. As he grows to enjoy the feel of the handle and the slight irregularity of form and glaze, he will become interested in something that is more exciting to the craftsman. Unlike the usual retail operation, a very personal relationship develops between the studio potter and his customers. They greet a kiln opening with the same degree of anticipation as does the potter. In fact, one often has the embarrassing problem of cutting short their visits in order to get on with potting.

While the ceramics teacher is to some degree subsidized so that he can make what he pleases, the professional studio potter must sell consistently. This does not mean a lowering of standards, but rather an orientation toward salable items. He is likely to find that the market for the large show piece is limited. Although the average home may have room for a few decorative vases, its capacity for mugs, sugarbowls and creamers, casseroles, pitchers, planters, and so forth, is almost unlimited, and these objects will constitute the major area of sales. To the idealistic beginner the ash-tray-and-candy-dish line may seem like the lowest form of ceramics, and most talented potters would agree. But upon opening a shop, he will discover that the customer who will pay $30 for a vase also wants a hand-made ash tray and will buy anything that could remotely serve this purpose.

In a callous and practically antiesthetic commercial world, which often seems to pander to the lowest taste, the high standards of the student potter are refreshing. However, to make what one pleases and insist that the public take it or leave it can be self-defeating. For example, it is not logical to have only one teapot on the shelf, no matter how attractive it may be. Rather, it is essential to have several styles, colors, and so forth in different price ranges. Some customers will want the most expensive, the best in the house! Others will be bargain hunters. It really makes no difference that all the teapots may represent the same amount of effort on the part of the craftsman. Just as the customer in a clothing store would be distressed to find that all the suits were brown and bore the same price, so the potential buyer of ceramics will hope to find a wide selection.

THE POTTER IN INDUSTRY

The Greek or Chinese potter of two thousand years ago, were he suddenly transported into the studio of today's hand potter, would not find the procedures unfamiliar. But the Industrial Revolution, which began in the mid-eighteenth century, changed drastically the methods in the large commercial pottery (Fig. 433). Today only the few universities that have associations with schools of ceramic engineering offer the courses necessary to an understanding of the problems of ceramic design in industry. In Europe, especially in Scandinavia, there is a much closer contact between industry and the art schools than there is in the United States. In a way it is a pity, for American industry could certainly use a little imagination.

Labor-saving devices were used by the ancients. The Etruscans worked with bisque molds as early as the fifth century B.C., and slip casting was practiced in a limited fashion in T'ang China (A.D. 618–906). But these mechanized processes were limited, and pottery remained largely a handcraft industry. During the eighteenth century the use of steam power to process clay and glaze chemicals and the new plaster of paris for molds made extreme changes in the age-old techniques. Unfortunately, while these and other technical advances made pottery and

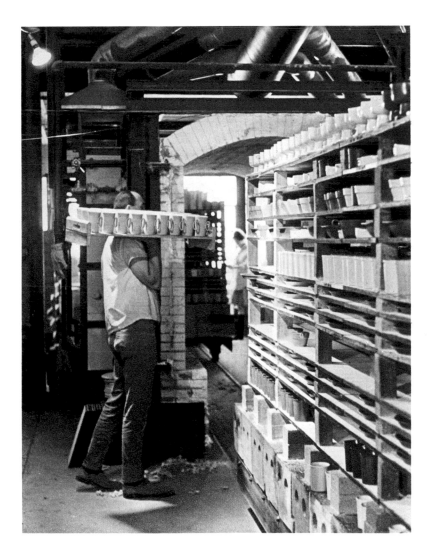

433. Loading a double-shuttle car kiln at the Bennington Potters.

above : 434. DAVID GIL for the Bennington Potters, U.S.A. Stacking dinnerware. Press-molded stoneware. (See also Fig. 432, p. 246).

soon even porcelain both cheaper and more accessible to the masses, the quality of design deteriorated rapidly. None of the small hand potteries had the capital, and often not even the business skill, necessary to manage a large commercial enterprise. Furthermore, the importation of oriental porcelains had become very profitable. Although the new porcelain factories were often not successful, they were thought to be immensely profitable, and so were either held as the property of the crown or parceled out among close retainers.

The great tragedy in the industrialization of ceramics was not so much the change in technique, but rather the fact that design decisions were no longer made by the potter, who could draw on centuries-old ceramic tradition, but were imposed by the new factory manager, an entrepreneur whose major desire was to show a profit by whatever means possible. The potter became merely a hired hand. European ceramics of the eighteenth and nineteenth centuries thus became a weird assemblage of borrowed Greek forms decorated in the Chinese or Italian fashion. The flexibility of plaster as a mold material made feasible the easy copying of forms and decoration conceived in metal, glass, and even basketry. As discussed in Chapter 2, Colonial American potters were soon overwhelmed by the mass-produced import, with the result that a native pottery tradition was never truly established in the United States.

In time American potteries became as industrialized as those abroad. With few exceptions they have continued to reflect the influence of foreign wares. (The borrowing is, of course, reciprocal, for there are European cars with Detroit styling and Japanese versions of many Scandinavian designs.)

The opportunities in contemporary dinnerware and "art gift ware" ceramics are not great. There is much competition from imports made in England, Germany, and Japan, countries that have long had important ceramics industries. The higher wages typical of American industry are also a factor, for in spite of mechanization there are still many hand operations that require training and skill. Price is not the only element in this competition, for Americans still retain to some degree a Colonial mentality that equates an import with a certain aura of superiority. Many foreign factories have larger design staffs and are more innovative than their American counterparts, which may well be another reason for the success of the import. This is largely explained by the fact that, in the United States, too many decisions are made by the advertising department, rather than by the design staff. Huge budgets are allocated to research in what will sell most profitably, so that very little time or money is left for creative projects aimed at developing a more useful and attractive product.

left: 435. JERRY ROTHMAN for Interpace Corporation, U.S.A. *Madeira* dinnerware. Earthenware.

below: 436. LONDA WEISMAN for the Bennington Potters, U.S.A. Candelabrum. Wheel-thrown clay, height 3′.

Although they represent the exception, there are several potteries with design staffs composed of producing potters and with managements that try to channel their ideas into production. Figures 434 to 436 illustrate examples of both unique pieces and production ware from two of these potteries, which have more imaginative design programs than most. The cost of design per item in mass production is extremely small. There is no doubt that most factories could do a better job in improving standards.

In all fairness it must be acknowledged that well-designed and reasonably priced objects have not always sold well. This must be attributed to the low level of taste that is prevalent in the buying public and is also characteristic of many wholesalers, store buyers, and sales clerks. It is surprising how many people are intimidated by sales personnel, especially in stores purporting to carry "quality" merchandise. Even a well-designed item is not likely to sell if poorly displayed or regarded in a deprecating manner by the sales clerk. In addition, decorator consultants often encourage the purchase of whatever industry decides will be the fashionable style of the season.

Were it not for the fact that there are numerous stores abroad and a few in the United States that consistently display an attractive line of excellently designed products, the future of the handcrafts would seem grim indeed. Unfortunately, these few shops will remain exceptions, unless American industry as a whole experiences a change of heart. The widespread availability of quality merchandise in Scandinavia is made possible by the close cooperation of the schools, the government, and industry over a period of many years.

Though few people would question the desirability of progress, one must be careful not to confuse progress with mere change. It may well be that the materialism of American industrial society rules out any improvement in public sensitivity. Typical

"art appreciation" courses in the public schools and colleges are aimed more at developing "culture" than at seeking true critical analysis. Little direction can be expected from government agencies, which tend to serve industrial rather than public needs. Only industry as a whole has the widespread resources and influence to promote a genuine improvement in design, and, with this in mind, the prospects for the future are not hopeful.

Against this rather bleak background, it is encouraging to note that there are a few large and several small potteries that are "bucking the tide" and are attempting to furnish the public with ceramics designed with originality and with a true feeling for clay (Figs. 437–439). It is fashionable among some of today's theorists to deride the relationship

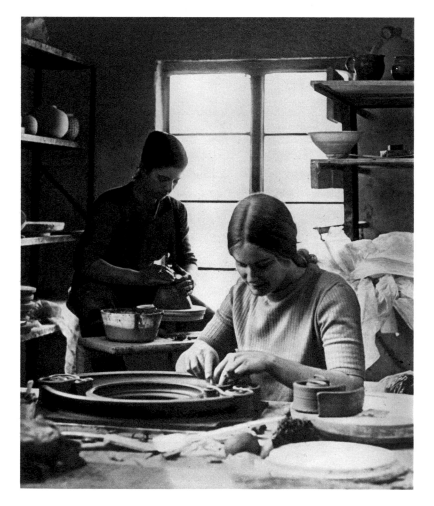

437. Studio workshop at the Bennington Potters. PAT GILMAN *(foreground)* creates a mirror frame, while LONDA WEISMAN throwns on the wheel.

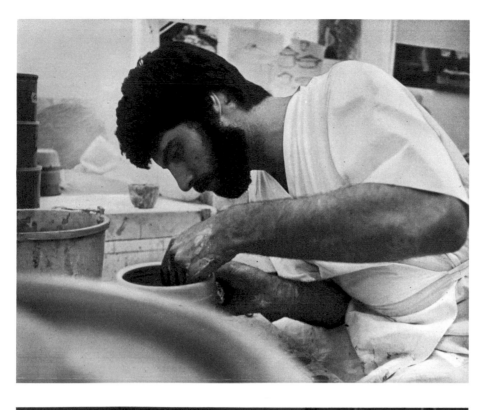

left: 438. JEFFREY TOUSSLEY throwing in the design studios of the Interpace Corporation.

below: 439. CRAIG HOLMES throwing bottles on a constant-speed, heavy-production wheel at Pacific Stoneware, Inc.

above : 440. Workshop at the Bennington Potters. Casseroles are molded on a hydraulic press using the Ram Process.

right : 441. Designer FRANCIS CHUN decorates a dish at the Interpace studios.

between material and form. This may be the direction that our plastic world is taking. But it will certainly lead to an impoverishment of our senses if the unique and authentic qualities of both material and form in the various craft media lose their identities. There is no more logic in attempting to reproduce a metal or glass form in clay than there is in making marmalade taste like mustard.

Both the Interpace Corporation and the Bennington Potters, whose work is illustrated (Figs. 432, 434–436), are noteworthy in having pottery studios attached to their factories (Figs. 440–443).

right : 442. DAVID GIL, manager of the Bennington Potters, creates a decorative tile, part of a divider screen for the Catamount Bank in Vermont.

below : 443. Design conference at the Interpace Corporation includes designers, glaze chemists, and production managers. *Clockwise from left foreground :* GEORGE TAYLOR, JEFFREY TOUSSLEY, SABERO GUZMAN, MINEO MIZUNO (standing), ELLIOTT HOUSE (director), FRANCIS CHUN, MARY J. WINANS, HENRY TAKEMOTO (standing), ROBERT CHAUSSE, AL BRUNT, OTTO LUND, and GEORGE JAMES.

Pacific Stoneware is operated by a professional potter, Bennett Welsh, who employs several trained ceramists for the creation of a production line that includes thrown ware and many hand-decorating methods (Figs. 444–445). Thus, designs can evolve from a clay prototype in a more natural and satisfying fashion, as distinguished from the usual drafting board industrial design concept.

DESIGNING FOR PRODUCTION

While the prototype for a mass-produced piece may evolve on the potter's wheel, it is essential that the ceramic designer have a working knowledge of the techniques of slip casting and jiggering. The long process that finally results in placing a pattern in production requires close cooperation between the designer, the mold maker, the glaze chemist, and the production engineer. The prototype usually is thrown on the wheel, but the mold maker most often works from a scale drawing (Fig. 446).

The designer first works up a variety of designs and then gradually eliminates those that are obviously nonfunctional, too commonplace, or too difficult to reproduce. Since the cup is the most-used item in a dinner set, it is often the starting point. When its shape has been roughly determined, other pieces are designed to relate to it. It is essential that the designer have a feeling for the clay form and a knowledge of how it can deform in firing. Heavy dinnerware is not very popular. Therefore, the foot rim and wall thickness must be of a dimension only sufficient to support the form.

After the cross sections are determined (Fig. 447), a plaster model is made. A metal template made from the profile drawing (Fig. 448) is placed

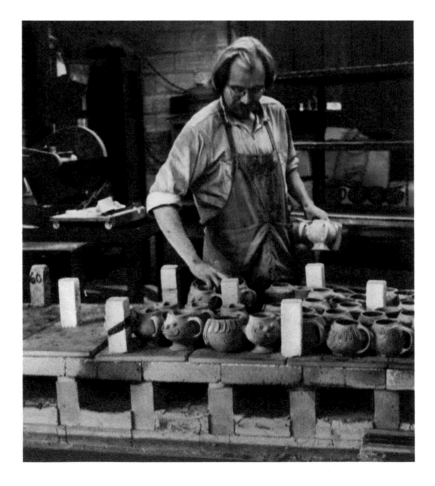

444. Don McPherson of Pacific Stoneware loading a car kiln with the daily output of decorative mugs.

above : 445. BENNETT WELSH, Director of Pacific Stoneware, correcting details in a master model of a ceramic owl-bell.

446–448. Three steps in designing for production.

top right : 446. Scale drawings are made from the thrown prototype.

above right : 447. Cross sections are used to prepare the plaster model.

right : 448. A metal template is fashioned from the profile drawing.

449–451. The plaster model is prepared for jiggering.

above : 449. Minor refinements in the form of the model are made with cutting tools.

above right : 450. The mold is trimmed to fit the wheel head of the jigger machine.

right : 451. The top and bottom sections of the case mold.

below : 452. Steel template and plaster cup mold.

on the turning rig. Plaster is poured around the pin in small amounts until the form is completed. A circular movement of the template trims off the excess and develops a solid plaster study model.

Because of shrinkage that will occur in firing, the final model is oversize. Minor refinements in form can be made with cutting tools as the final model is developed on the wheel head (Fig. 449). After the plaster cup model is complete, it is coated with a plaster separator. A retaining collar is put in place, and fresh plaster is poured over the cup model to form the original jigger mold. Figure 450 shows the trimming of the mold to fit the wheel head of the jigger machine. It is necessary to have a mold for each cup to be made in the day's production, which may be thousands. Figure 451 illustrates the top and bottom sections of the case mold used to make the jigger block mold. The ball-and-socket projections allow for an accurate positioning of the sections prior to pouring the block mold. The case molds are made of a harder and denser plaster mix than that used for the jigger cup mold, which must readily absorb water from the clay after it is jiggered.

In jiggered ware, only one surface is shaped by the plaster form. The inner cup surface is formed by the jigger template. Figure 452 shows the steel template being checked for clearance, and Figure 453 illustrates a half section of the cup handle on a plaster or marble base. After the retaining walls are in place and the surface has been shaped, a layer of plaster is poured in, forming one half of the mold. Keys are carved out of the fresh plaster, and the complete handle section is put in place. English Crown soap is commonly used as a mold separator. If the plaster mold is dry, it must be moistened before soaping and casting, for otherwise the soap would be drawn into the dry cast, causing the two sections to stick. After the cast is finished, it is a simple matter to carve pouring openings into the damp plaster (Fig. 454). Before pouring a clay handle, however, the mold sections must be dry. For the pilot design

top left : 453. Half section of a cup handle on a plaster base.

top right : 454. Two halves of a plaster mold for a cup handle.

above left : 455. A template is cut to form the bottom surface of a saucer.

above right : 456. The three sections of a plaster mold used in slip casting.

project, a single handle mold is adequate; in production, a dozen handles normally are cast at one time.

Designing a plate or saucer is a somewhat different operation from designing a cup. In this case, the plaster mold is shaped to form the inside, or upper contour, of the plate. The template is cut to form the bottom surface (Fig. 455). The mold for slip casting is not quite the same as that used in jiggering, since it usually consists of three sections (Fig. 456). However, simple, tapered tumbler shapes *above :* 457. The completed place settings.

below right : 458. Hollow, absorbent molds are filled with liquid slip clay.

can be cast in a single mold. The process from the initial sketches to the completed line (Fig. 457) is long, and several years may elapse before marketing can begin.

Mixing Plaster

There are available a variety of plasters of different hardnesses and setting rates, for use in model making, block molds, or case molds. Theoretically, 18.6 pounds of water will set up 100 pounds of plaster; in practice, at least 60 pounds of water will be needed to achieve the proper flow. The less water used, the stronger the cured plaster will be. Plaster normally sets in about twenty minutes, but it must be poured before it hardens. This time will depend upon the amount of mixing. The plaster must be sieved into the water (to avoid large lumps) until the water will absorb no more. It is then allowed to set from three to four minutes until it is thoroughly wet. Small batches can be mixed by hand or larger ones with a power mixer. After a few minutes of mixing, the plaster will begin to thicken. It must be *left :* 459. A slip-cast creamer is removed from a three-piece mold.

above : 460. Cup handles are joined to the cup with slip.

poured at this point. Once it begins to set, it is useless and must be discarded. (It cannot be poured down the sink, for it will clog the drains.) Plaster manufacturers can furnish tables giving strength and porosity for various mixtures. For production it is most important that all molds have a similar porosity.

Slip-casting Techniques

Slip casting is a method of making ceramics in which liquid clay is poured into a hollow, absorbent mold (Fig. 458). Within a few minutes after pouring, a film of firm clay appears on the inner surface of the mold. As water is absorbed, the clay becomes thicker. When the desired thickness develops, the mold is upended and the center portion, which is still liquid, is poured out. The remaining clay coating continues to harden and eventually shrinks away from the mold. Simple cup forms can be made in a single piece mold, while undercut and more complicated shapes require two, three, or occasionally more pieces in the mold (Fig. 459).

When multiple sections are used, they are keyed together with ball-and-socket projections and are held together during pouring with heavy rubber bands, such as one might cut from an automobile inner tube. As the water soaks into the plaster mold, the level of slip in the cavity falls, and a small amount must be added. To avoid frequent slip additions during casting, a collar is added to the top of the original model to serve both as a funnel for the slip and as a clay reservoir. The angle of the collar is used as a guide in trimming the top edge of the formed piece. This is done with a fettling knife when the cast piece has hardened sufficiently. At this stage the mold sections are carefully removed, and the casting seams on the piece are scraped off and sponged to create a smooth surface.

In order to avoid uneven shrinkage or air pockets, some pieces must be cast in sections and luted together with slip. This is particularly true of small handles, which are cast solid rather than drain cast (Fig. 460). Depending upon the character of the clay, this type of joining can be done at either the

461. Cup handles are cast twelve to a mold and removed and separated when they are leather hard.

leather-hard or the dry stage (Fig. 461). The procedure is quite different from that used for thrown objects, in which case sections should be joined as soon as they can be handled without distortion.

Casting Slips

Unlike a clay used in throwing, a clay body for jiggering and casting need not be very plastic. In fact, the plastic clays are often avoided, since their greater water absorption means more shrinkage, which is usually accompanied by warping. Various types of binders are used to impart greater green and dry strength to the ware. This more than compensates for the substitution of less-plastic ingredients.

Of great importance in a casting slip is the use of *deflocculants*, such as sodium silicate and soda ash. The addition of about 1 percent of either of these chemicals to the dry weight of the clay will reduce considerably the amount of water needed to make a fluid slip. A properly deflocculated casting slip is easily pourable but has a clinging, syrupy consistency that substantially retards the settling of the heavier slip particles. Georgia kaolin, which has a uniform particle size, is the major porcelain clay used in casting slips. One negative feature of the slip

body is that its bland smoothness is relatively uninteresting when compared to the color and texture of a throwing clay. Some typical casting slips for various temperatures are:

Talc body (cones 06–05)	
Plastic vitrox	16
Ball clay	35
Talc	49

Parian body (cones 3–4)	
Feldspar	60
Kaolin	30
Ball clay	10

Poreclain body (cones 8–9)	
Flint	20
Feldspar	36
Kaolin	30
Ball clay	14

A common name for sodium silicate is water glass. It is, in fact, a solution of solium silicate in water. The sodium silicate is made by fusing a mixture of soda ash and silica sand. The term is a general one, since the proportion of sodium to silica may vary greatly. N-brand solution is the trade name given to the type commonly used as a deflocculant in ceramics. Soda ash (sodium carbonate), either alone or in combination with sodium silicate, is a more effective deflocculant than sodium silicate alone in casting slips having organic matter, such as is found in ball clay. Slip should not be stored for long periods, especially in warm weather, because fermentation occurs, and this may cause pinholes in the cast ware.

A standard practice is to use about three parts N-brand sodium silicate by weight to one part soda ash. The proportions depend on the body formula.

If it includes a large amount of clay, a one-to-one mixture of soda ash and N-brand silicate solution may prove more satisfactory. After weighing, the soda ash should be dissolved in hot water and then both deflocculants added to the water. As a beginning one might take 100 pounds of slip body and slowly add it to a large crock containing 50 pounds of water, which is about six gallons (8.3 pounds to the gallon). More or less of the slip body may be needed, depending upon the ingredients and the deflocculant action. The resulting slip should have a thick, syrupy consistency. A blunger is helpful in mixing the ingredients (Fig. 462), although a large wire whisk can be used for test batches. Slip should always be screened before using, for any lumpy particles will settle and give a poor casting. Care must be taken in screening and filling the mold in order not to trap air bubbles in the slip.

462. A large blunger is used to mix the ingredients in a clay body.

It is better not to use more than 1 percent deflocculant, even less if possible, in relation to the dry ingredients' weight, since an excess will sometimes cause the slip to become pasty and nonpourable. It will also gradually seal the pores of the plaster mold with an insoluble film of calcium silicate, making it difficult to remove the casting and eventually spoiling the mold completely. Soda ash is more troublesome in this regard than silicate. Drying the molds from the outside by inverting them or covering the mouths will help to prevent this accumulation on the inner mold surface.

Jiggering Methods

As every novice potter soon learns, it is impractical to throw large, flat shapes on the potter's wheel. Countless generations of potters have used bisque molds to shape one surface of flat dishes and to support the soft clay while drying. With the use of plaster molds, the forming process is quite rapid and accurate. In addition, the plaster mold produces a smoother surface than would be possible with a bisque mold.

The composition of the clay used for jiggering is different from that of the throwing clay used by the hand potter. Since the ware is supported by the mold during the initial drying period, it need not be so plastic. In fact, since plastic clay shrinks more in drying, thus increasing the likelihood of warpage, it is used in limited amounts. To compensate for this loss in green and dry strength, various binders— such as lignin extract and methocel—are added to the clay body.

The body ingredients are weighed and mixed in a blunger as in the preparation of a casting slip. The resultant liquid is screened and pumped into a filter press, which is an accordianlike machine of metal and canvas that squeezes excess water from the slip, leaving plastic clay. The clay comes from the filter press in slabs about 1 to 1 ½ inches thick and 16 to 24 inches square. These slabs are then placed in the hopper of a pug mill, which operates much like a meat grinder. At one end is a vacuum attachment, which, combined with the compressing action of the screw blades, removes even the smallest air pockets from the clay. This feature not only eliminates possible body defects but also renders the clay more plastic. Though not as crucial as in throwing, the absence of air bubbles in clay used for jiggering is still important.

Sections of clay can be extruded from the pug mill in different diameters, depending upon the use to which they will be put (Fig. 463). The size used for the plate shown in the jigger machine (Fig. 464) would be 6 to 8 inches. A slice about 1 inch thick is cut off the pugged clay with a wire and placed over a square of canvas on the bench. The clay slice is then hit with a malletlike weight that compresses it to half this thickness. This clay bat is in turn slapped down over a plaster plate mold resting on the jigger head. The next step is to force out any air remaining between the clay and the plaster mold. This is usually done with the moistened hand as the jigger head revolves slowly. The operator then brings the steel template down toward the mold, further compressing the clay and cutting away the excess to form the bottom contours of the plate and the foot rim. The mold bat and plate are placed on a conveyor belt that carries them through a dryer. Finally, the plate is removed from the mold, and the seam that is created where the template and mold meet is trimmed away.

It is difficult to obtain a perfectly uniform thickness in slip casting. Heavy cups with attached handles are often slip cast, but thinner porcelain cups are jiggered, since even the slightest variation would be noticeable. The procedure in jiggering cups and bowls is slightly different: the mold is a hollow form, and the template is shaped to the inside surface of the piece. One method of jiggering cups is to throw a wad of clay into the mold and allow the template to force the clay downward and outward to form the walls of the cup. Another way begins with the throwing of a rough cup form on a potter's wheel (Fig. 465). This form is placed into the mold and jiggered as in the other procedure (Fig. 466). The particular method used would depend largely upon the characteristics of the clay body and to some extent upon the shape desired. The latest machines are completely automatic and produce a fantastic hourly output.

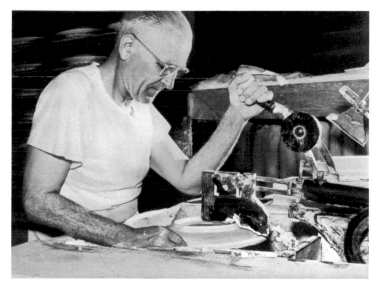

top : 463. A section of clay is cut off after extrusion from the pug mill.

above : 464. The jigger trims off the bottom profile of a dinner plate.

Press Forming

Certain forms can be duplicated very economically by the use of molds in hydraulic presses. Most electrical insulators are made in such a fashion, using a nearly dry body with wax as a forming lubricant. The process illustrated (Figs. 467–470) is more adaptable to pottery production, provided the shapes are simple and have no undercuts. Male and female dies shape the form and, under great pressure, squeeze out the excess clay. An unusual feature is that the hard but porous gypsum plaster die has a tubular grid embedded in the plaster. Compressed air flowing from the tubes into the die allows the clay form to be released immediately after pressing. Figure 467 shows a wad of stiff but plastic clay being placed into the die. The pressing operation is very rapid (Fig. 468). Compressed air released into the lower die breaks the clay suction, and the press rises (Fig. 469). The operator removes the newly formed tray on a supporting panel after the compressed air releases it from the upper die (Fig. 470).

Production Kilns

The term *commercial production* covers a wide range of activities from the manufacture of huge tonnages of building bricks to the forming of minute electrical insulators. Special kilns have been developed to fire the ever-increasing volume of commercial ware. Industrial kilns are not merely larger versions of the small pottery kiln, since a larger kiln is difficult to fire uniformly and has a long cycle of firing, cooling, and loading. Instead, part of the kiln is made movable, as in the car kiln (see p. 277). The car kiln is easy to load and unload and does not lose as much heat in the process as do standard kilns. By placing

left, top to bottom : 467–470. Four steps in press forming.

467. A wad of stiff clay is placed into the die.

468. The press is lowered, and the clay is squeezed between the two sections.

469. The suction is released, and the press rises.

470. The operator removes the finished piece.

a door at each end of the kiln, the loading cycle is speeded up even more. This type of construction is called a shuttle kiln.

As lightweight, high-temperature refractories became common, an envelope type of kiln was developed (Fig. 471). In this design, two permanent kiln beds are built, and the kiln moves back and forth over them. Its advantages are the smaller floor area required and the fact that lighter kiln furniture can be used, since there is not even the vibration of a moving kiln car. These kilns are available in many sizes, but they are primarily intended for small-size pottery or special-order production.

The huge production of the larger potteries would not be possible without the tunnel kiln, which has continuous operation, with no stoppage for cooling or loading. Figure 472 shows a loaded kiln car entering the tunnel. The chamber is approximately 5 by 9 feet and 200 feet long. The cars, fitted tightly together, move through the kiln at a slow but constant speed, taking seventy to ninety hours to heat, fire, and cool. The entering temperature is 300°F, which gradually increases to 2300°F in the center section, and then tapers off as the cars move away from the burners. The kiln cars have a heavily insulated floor. A channel iron on the car side usually projects into a sand seal on the kiln wall,

above : 471. An envelope kiln about to be rolled over a load of freshly glazed pottery.

left : 472. A car entering the kiln with a load of cups stacked lip to lip.

which protects the undercarriage from a direct flow of heat. Hot air escaping toward the end sections is piped back to preheat the burner-port air. This factor, plus the possibility of continuous operation for months on end, provides a most economical system.

As would be imagined, loading of this kiln is quite different from that of a small studio kiln. Because of the long firing cycle and the great number of duplicate shapes, a very tight load is possible. However, thin dinnerware pieces must be supported to prevent warpage. Cups are loaded in pairs, lip to lip, with a weak cement to prevent accidental slippage. Dry refractory clay is shot into openings between stacked dinner plates for support (Fig. 473). A coaster of high alumina content is placed under each stack to prevent its sticking to the shelves. It is common practice in dinnerware manufacture to fire the bisque to the maturity of the body while it is well supported.

After glazing, the ware is fired at a lower temperature, so that there is no shrinkage and less chance

right : 473. Removing bisque plates from the kiln car.

below : 474. A sagger of cups after the glaze fire.

of warping. A potter can keep a small kiln relatively clean and need not worry about dust and brick particles in an open glaze fire. However, this is not true of large kilns firing continuously for long periods. To protect the ware in the glaze fire, it is loaded into boxlike forms made of fireclay, called saggers.

Figure 474 shows a sagger load of cups after the glaze fire. A layer of bitstone (coarse silica sand), which does not adhere easily to the thin glaze on the foot rim, covers the sagger bottom. High-fire porcelains are always fired on the foot rim in the individual sagger. The foot rims will be unglazed but smoothly polished. High-fire china ware, such as the sagger load of saucers shown in Figure 475, is completely glazed. The individual pieces rest on dowels of porcelain that are inserted into the sagger wall as the pieces are loaded. This porcelain spur will cause a tiny blemish in the glaze, but it does provide a great economy in loading and firing. Figure 476 shows the loading of saggers containing glazed cups and dinner plates.

right : 475. A sagger load of saucers.

below : 476. The loading of saggers containing glazed pieces.

11 Kilns
Operation and Construction

At some remote period in time (c. 8000 B.C.) man discovered that clay, when baked in a fire, would become hard and durable. For thousands of years he fired his pottery in a shallow pit on a bed of twigs (Figure 478). Broken shards covered the heaped-up pottery to provide protection from the fuel above and to retain the heat. With a continual application of dry twigs and grass a red heat could be achieved, after which the coals were covered with soil and allowed to cool. Smothered with ash, the red-clay body was usually black from carbon. Burnished and incised surfaces were the only decoration possible. All early black ware was fired in this manner, as is the pottery of some aboriginal tribes in modern times. A pit firing is an interesting project for a summer-camp ceramics class.

In time early potters learned to dig a chamber into a hillside to provide heat insulation, a better draft, and a fire pit, with a resulting higher fire. Finally, clay bricks with a straw binder were used to construct a circular kiln chamber, a combustion area, a fire grate, and an ash pit (Fig. 479). The ware was loaded from the top, covered with shards, and basted with a clay and straw mixture leaving a few exhaust openings. Such a kiln was used to fire the slip-decorated ware made in the Middle East about 3500 B.C.

As technical proficiency increased, a kiln was developed that had a permanent dome-shape roof, a short chimney, and a door opening from the side. The Greeks, who needed controlled conditions of oxidation and reduction to achieve their red- and black-figure ware, used such a kiln. The chambers were not large—probably no more than 4 to 6 feet in diameter. This design evolved into the beehive and the taller bottle-neck updraft kiln, which, with multiple fireboxes, were used throughout Europe until the development of large commercial kilns during the Industrial Revolution.

The higher-fire stoneware and porcelain achieved early by the Chinese and Koreans was due as much to their kiln design as to their use of kaolin bodies. These early kilns were long and narrow and

opposite : 477. DOROTHY PERKINS, U.S.A. Bottle. Stoneware, squared after throwing, with sgraffito decoration; height 11".

271

built on a sloping hillside for increased draft. A large firebox was at the base, but since the kiln might be 150 feet in length, additional stoking holes were needed to increase the heat in the upper portion. The ash that fell on many of the pieces was responsible for their glazelike surface. In order to better control the heat, the long, climbing kiln was divided into chambers, first in China and later—about 1600—in Japan. Partly because of the space taken up by saggars (fireclay boxes to contain glazed ware), the Chinese kiln chambers were sometimes 15 feet high. The Japanese were smaller, usually about 6 feet high, but had as many as twenty chambers (Fig. 480). Although wood kilns are efficient at high temperatures, their use is declining because of the cost of fuel and the excess smoke they produce.

above left : 478. Primitive shallow-pit kiln.

above : 479. Early wood-burning kiln.

below: 480. Japanese wood-burning climbing kiln.

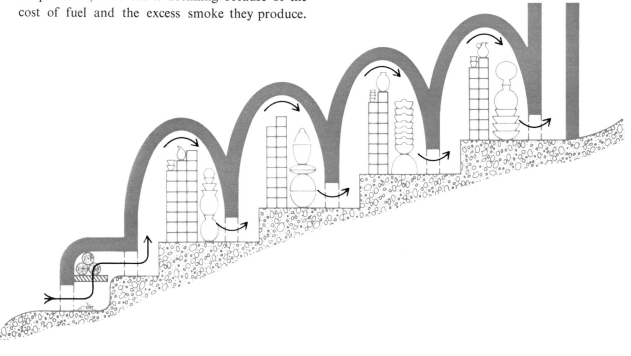

MODERN KILNS

The kiln types employed by the ancients are still in use today, but they have been modified to accommodate new fuels, new materials, and, in the case of industry, the need for expanded and efficient large-scale production. Perhaps the most drastic change in kiln design in recent times was caused by the development of a new source of power—electricity. Since the electric kiln needs no chimney or fuel lines and is comparatively portable, simple, and safe to operate, it has played a large part in the current popularity of ceramics. It is especially convenient for the potter whose studio might be relatively temporary or for the school whose original design provided for neither a chimney nor a source of fuel.

Fuel Kilns

Whether wood, coal, oil, or gas is used as a fuel, the basic kiln design is much the same. A combustion area is needed either below or to one side of the kiln chamber. Wood or coal requires a larger area equipped with a grate and an ash pit (see Figs. 479–480). Saggers, which protect the glazed ware from flying ash, take up much space. In time, small kilns were constructed with an inner muffle chamber that served the same purpose. Both fuel oil and manufactured gas contain sulphur, which is injurious to lead glazes. The updraft muffle kiln shown in Figure 481 was designed to eliminate this

481. Updraft muffle kiln.

problem. The design, however, creates extra heat in the floor area, making an even firing difficult. Placing burners closer to the side wall will alleviate the problem to some extent. Most portable gas kilns are of this type.

The downdraft kiln illustrated in Figure 482 provides a more even heat distribution and has come

482. Downdraft kiln.

front view   side view

273

to be the standard design used by most potters. This is especially true since the advent of cleaner natural gas, which has eliminated the need for a muffle. In this downdraft kiln the heat enters from multiple burners on each side, is deflected upward by the bag wall, and then is drawn down through the ware to a channel under the floor by the suction of the chimney. If the fuel supply and draft are adequate, adjustments to the bag wall height and damper can ensure a heat deviation of no more than one cone, and usually less, from top to bottom.

left: 483. Arch kiln with burners on one side.

below and opposite page: 484–487. Kilns with alternate arrangements of burners.

top view

side view

top view

side view

top view   side view

top view   side view

For a smaller-size kiln, a layout such as that illustrated in Figure 483, with the burners placed to one side, may prove equally satisfactory. Numerous other burner arrangements have been tried, despite the fact that the design sketched in Figure 482 is most efficient. Some of these alternate plans are shown in Figures 484–487. In some installations a burner or a fan at the base of the stack is desirable to induce a draft in the early stages of firing. This addition may also be needed in the case of a tall chimney, such as is found on kilns in many classroom studios.

The kiln illustrated in Figure 488 is essentially the same as the one in Figure 482, except that the

front view   side view

488. Kiln with bisque chamber in the chimney.

chimney area is enlarged to provide a separate bisque chamber. Unless the glaze temperature in the main area is unusually high, this chimney chamber will bisque at between cone 010 and cone 06. While most schools have an ample supply of both pots and kilns to ensure a full load for each firing, the individual potter may experience firing delays. The double chamber permits a more even flow of work and simultaneous bisque and glaze firings at no extra cost.

A kiln that is fired with fuel oil requires a slightly larger combustion area than does one using natural gas. The catenary arch kiln shown in Figure 489 is ideal for fuel oil, since the flare at the bottom provides the extra combustion area needed. Except for the arch construction, the design is similar to that of a gas kiln. The curve is established by suspending a chain from two points, thus forming a natural, self-supporting arch. A proportion in which the base equals the height is the most stable and provides excellent heat distribution. Because the arch is self supporting, no tie rods or steel frame are needed. Oil is a satisfactory fuel, cheaper than gas but it has some drawbacks. A separate shedlike installation is desirable, since the fumes that are

489. Catenary arch kiln.

given off, together with the noisy blowers, make an oil-burning kiln impractical for use in the studio or classroom.

Square kilns are more likely to fire evenly, and a slightly wider door width is preferable to a deep chamber for loading convenience. It is assumed that

276   Kilns

the chambers of the kilns discussed have a loading area of about 10 to 20 cubic feet. However, many schools need a larger capacity. The physical strain incurred in stretching to load the heavy shelves and ware at the far end of a 30-cubic-foot chamber is too much for many students. In such cases a car kiln (Fig. 490) may be a good solution. This, again, is essentially the Figure 482 design, but the floor section is built on steel frame and wheels, so that it can be rolled in and out of the kiln on a track. The door becomes an integral part of the car, instead of being bricked up in the usual fashion. There must be a close fit between the floor and the side walls, with a channel iron in the floor extending into a sand trough in the side wall to form a heat seal. In the car kiln the ware can be loaded from either side without undue strain.

Electric Kilns

The gas kiln, because of its cheaper operation, greater size, and ability to reduce, is preferred by most studio potters and university ceramics departments in the United States. In the Scandinavian countries, however, where electricity is cheap and gas is not common, the electric kiln is almost universally used by the studio potter. The electric kiln has many advantages for the public school. It is as simple to operate as turning on a light switch, and there are no problems of burner adjustment or draft control. The kiln, normally weighing about three hundred pounds, can be wheeled anywhere. It requires only a 220-volt electrical outlet—a minor consideration compared to the gas kiln's demand of a high-temperature chimney or large-size gas lines.

front view   490. Car kiln.   top view

Room ventilation is not a problem, provided the clay body contains no sulphur or unusual impurities.

The electric kiln comes in two basic styles—the top loader and the front loader. In either type, a kiln with less than an 18 × 18-inch interior should not be considered, for it is too small to be other than a toy. Since the heat comes from radiation produced by coiled elements recessed in the side walls, a kiln chamber bigger than 24 × 24 inches requires a large coil or strip element, which greatly increases the cost of the kiln. Because they must have a stand and a heavy frame to carry the door, plus flexible connections to the door elements, front-loading kilns are much more expensive. The top loader is not only cheaper but easier to load, and it is therefore a more logical purchase.

There are three types of electric heating elements. Suitable for a low fire (up to 2000°F) are those made of coiled nickel-nichrome wire. The Kanthol type is constructed of a different alloy and will produce temperatures up to cone 8 (2300°F), although some types will go higher. Larger and higher-firing industrial kilns use carbon compounds in the form of a rod from $\frac{1}{4}$ inch to 2 inches in diameter. Unfortunately, the special transformers needed are more expensive than the kiln itself, which places this kiln at a price disadvantage compared with the more inexpensive gas or oil kilns.

KILN LOADING AND FIRING

The final step in the potter's art—the loading and firing of the kiln—is most important, for carelessness can easily ruin one's previous efforts. It can also do permanent damage to the kiln. With the exception of salt-glazed ware and commercial high-fire porcelain (see Chap. 10, pp. 268–269), all pottery is usually fired first at a low bisque temperature. Some clay bodies can be successfully glazed in the raw state, but the fragility of unfired clay and the difficulty of glazing some shapes make a double firing desirable, especially in schools, where techniques of glazing and loading are being taught.

The bisque fire temperature is generally between cone 010 and cone 06, depending upon the clay body used.

The fired bisque ware must be hard enough to endure normal handling in the glazing operation, yet sufficiently absorbent to permit glaze adhesion. Although the stacking of a bisque kiln is quite different from that required for a glaze fire, in each case at least one inch of free space must be left between the electrical elements and the ware. In a gas kiln 2 or 3 inches is a desirable margin to allow free passage of heat and to avoid hot spots.

Raw ware must be completely dry before it is loaded in the bisque kiln. Since there is no problem of glaze sticking, kiln wash is not needed, and pieces may touch each other. It is possible to stack one piece inside or on top of others, building to a considerable height. Care must be taken to make foot rims coincide for support and to avoid placing heavy pieces on more fragile ones. Large shallow bowls, which might warp, are better fired upside down on the rim. Several smaller sizes can be placed beneath. Covers should be fired in place to prevent warping, and tall knobbed covers can be reversed to save space.

Even though apparently dry, the raw clay contains much moisture, and the firing should proceed at a low heat for several hours. Kiln doors should be left ajar or peepholes left open for an hour or so to allow this moisture to escape. Large, heavy pots or sculptural pieces must be fired at a slow speed to prevent the moisture contained in hidden air pockets from being converted into steam, which would cause the piece to explode.

Chemical changes in the body during firing are slight at first (Fig. 491). When the temperature reaches 350° to 400°F (175°–200°C), all atmospheric moisture should have left the ware, causing little or no shrinkage. Most of the chemically combined water will leave the ware at temperatures between 950° and 1300°F (510°–705°C). During this "water smoking" period considerable shrinkage occurs as both the chemically combined water and gases from organic material leave the body. The firing should not be too rapid, for the body is very weak. As the temperature approaches 1750°F (955°C) and continues to 1850°F (1010°C), needlelike crystals of alumina-silica ($3 Al_2O_3 \cdot 2 SiO_2$), called mullite, begin to form, but they are not fully developed until stoneware temperatures are reached. These give toughness to the body, and as the temperature increases, additional free silica forms a glass around these crystals. Because of impurities and varying compositions, clay bodies achieve maximum hardness at different temperatures. Earthenware clay matures at about 2000°F (1090°C), stoneware at about 2350°F (1290°C), and pure clay (kaolin) at about 3000°F (1650°C). (See also Chap. 4, pp. 139–145.)

Most potters use cones to measure the cone 06 to cone 010 bisque fire, but some judge maturity by the bright red color of the ware. A uniform bisque temperature is necessary to create the proper absorbency for glazing. When the correct temperature is reached, the electric kiln is simply turned off and allowed to cool. In the fuel-burning kiln, the chimney damper must be closed immediately to prevent a cold draft of air from being sucked into the burner ports, which might crack both the ware and the shelves. Just as the kiln must be fired slowly, so must it be allowed to cool naturally. The damper can be opened after cooling overnight, and the peephole plugs can be removed, but the door must not be opened more than a crack until the temperature is down to 400°F. An even slower cooling may be desirable for extremely large or heavy pieces. An expensive kiln, which should give at least 10 years' service before repairs are needed, may be ruined after a short time by careless firing and cooling.

The glaze fire differs in several respects from the bisque fire: the loading is different, the kiln atmosphere may be varied, and the final temperature must be carefully controlled. Since mishaps may occur from runny glazes, all kiln shelves must be coated with a *kiln wash*. This is made of equal parts of silica (flint) and kaolin in a creamy mixture. Each coat is applied before the last is completely dry. A new shelf can be sprayed with aluminum paint before the kiln wash is painted on. Additional protection can be obtained by dusting on a thin layer of coarse silica sand. The shelf edges must be cleaned to prevent this sand from sifting down on the ware below. All glazed ware should be "dry footed" —that is, all glaze cleaned off the base and about

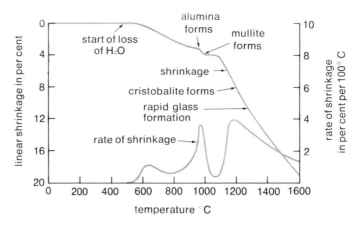

491. Linear shrinkage and rate of shrinkage for kaolin.

¼ inch up the foot rim. Glazes that are runny, such as crystalline and copper reds, can be placed on a slice of insulating brick to soak up the excess.

A uniform load without tight spots will produce an even firing. One should never try to fire a half load, since uneven temperatures are almost certain to occur. Staggering the shelves in a large kiln will create a better heat flow. In the typical electric kiln shelves should not be placed close to the bottom or the top, for a cold spot will develop in the center area. Test tiles must always be stacked in a middle position, since there is usually some temperature variation from top to bottom. A center support is desirable for larger shelves. Damp clay pads used to level uneven posts should be dusted first with dry flint to avoid sticking. If the shelves are of moderate size, three posts will eliminate leveling problems. As in the bisque fire, covers are best fired in place, but one must make certain that the contact areas are clear of glaze. Placing glazed ware too close to the upper bag wall often results in shiny spots, although gaps in the bricks may even out the heat in this area. Glazed pieces should be at least ¼ inch apart, because heat radiation can also cause shininess.

Reduction firing means that part of the firing cycle is conducted with an inadequate amount of air and oxygen to burn up all the fuel. As a result, the free carbon in the air unites with, and thus reduces, the oxygen content of the metallic oxides in both the body and the glaze, thereby altering their color. In a forced-draft burner this is accomplished by cutting down on the air, while in a natural-draft burner the flue damper is cut back slightly, so that less air is sucked into the kiln. Excessive reduction is undesirable. Not only does the temperature drop rapidly, but the body may erupt with blisters or even bloat, and the glaze becomes a dirty gray. In a natural-draft kiln a slight backing up of the flame at the burner ports will occur. This is all that is necessary for a reduction, not the belching of flame and smoke that some students seem to enjoy —until the blistered pots come out. Because of atmospheric pressure built up during reduction, one should not pull out the peep plugs with his face near the opening, for the flame will shoot out at least a foot. In a tall, bricked-up door a section of curved sheet metal under the tie rod and pressing against the top bricks is helpful, since the door bricks may lean outward.

The atmosphere should be an oxidizing one during the first part of the firing cycle, in order to ensure the most efficient heat rise. The reduction needed to produce a rich body color is most effective between cones 016 and 010. When the maximum temperature is reached, the damper can be adjusted to provide a neutral or slightly reducing fire. The usual practice is to cut back the burners slightly after the cones go over to allow a half hour or so of an oxidizing *soaking heat* in which temperature variations can stabilize and glazes become smooth.

The term *reduction fire* must not be confused with *reduction glazes*. The latter are glazes especially compounded to produce copper-red and celadon colors (see p. 213). In the firing of these glazes there is no real change in body color but rather a reduction of the coloring oxides in the glaze from an oxidic to a metallic form. Thus, copper green becomes a rich red, and the iron brown-red is transformed into a gray-green. In a reduction fire the glaze reduction begins later than the body reduction, but it must occur before the glaze begins to melt. Since the reduction causes the heat rise to diminish, there is usually an alternation of reduction and oxidation. Too much oxidation will bleach out the color. Copper-red color variations range from a mottled blue, green, and red to a deep purple-red

or a pale pink, depending upon the reduction sequence, the glaze thickness, and the body color.

A *localized reduction* can be obtained by adding $\frac{1}{2}$ of 1 percent of silicon carbide (carborundum, forty-mesh or finer) to a suitable copper alkaline glaze. The result is usually a speckled red-and-purple color. Its only real advantage is its adaptability to the electric kiln. An electric kiln can be reduced by popping a few moth balls through the peephole. The kiln should have heavy elements, which have a good oxidized coating from many previous firings. Continuous reductions will eat away the elements, but an occasional one will do little harm to the kiln.

The single-fire *salt glaze* is fired to the maturity of the body. Coarse rock salt, soaked in water and placed in small paper cups, is inserted by a wire loop into the burner ports over a two-hour interval. New kilns use more salt—about $\frac{1}{3}$ pound per cubic foot of kiln area. Clay draw rings hooked from the peephole indicate the salting progress.

Pyrometric cones provide the potter with his most accurate method of measuring the *work heat* in the kiln. The name is inaccurate, for the pyrometric "cone" is actually a tetrahedron or pyramid shape $1\frac{3}{4}$ inches high, with a base that is $\frac{1}{2}$ inch across. Cones are compounded of a material similar to a glaze. When softened by the heat they bend, and when a complete arc is formed the temperature in the kiln is that of the cone number (see Appendix, pp. 310–311). The base is beveled to indicate the proper angle at which to press them into a pad of clay. The usual practice is to use three cones, for example, 6, 8, and 9 if the firing is to reach cone 8. The bending of cone 6 warns the potter that the kiln is approaching the proper temperature, and burner or damper adjustments to stabilize the heat are made at this point. In a large kiln the cones are placed near both top and bottom, not too close to the door. As cone 8 bends, the burners can be cut back for a soaking period. A softening of cone 9 indicates an overfiring. Kilns usually fire slightly hotter at the bottom, so a dryer glaze can be used there. If the cones are difficult to see, blowing into the peephole through a tube or inserting a metal rod near the cones will reveal them more clearly.

A slower rise in temperature, and the resulting longer period of chemical reaction, will permit a glaze to mature at a lower temperature than if the heat rise is rapid. This relationship between time and temperature is called the *work heat ratio*, and it is recorded by the pyrometric cone but not by the *pyrometer*. The pyrometer consists of a pair of welded wires of dissimilar metals, called a thermocouple, which is inserted into the kiln. When the kiln is heated, a minute electrical current indicates temperature change on a millivolt meter callibrated in degrees F or C. A pyrometer is convenient to have when the potter is making adjustments to produce the most efficient heat rise, or when he wishes to determine the proper time to begin a reduction. However, unless one has an exact and unvarying firing schedule, it is not completely dependable. In time corrosion of the thermocouple tips affects the accuracy of the reading, but this can be adjusted to the proper cone by moving a tiny screw on the meter face. Thermocouples and pyrometers are available in both low- and high-fire models. The rather inexpensive ones used by potters are seldom reliable over a wide range of temperatures; that is, if the cone 8 reading is correct, the cone 04 may be inaccurate. Optical pyrometers are also available; these are quite accurate but rather expensive. Glazed draw rings, which were common before the introduction of cones, can also be used to measure the kiln temperature. Such clay rings are the only method of determining glaze buildup in a salt kiln.

KILN MATERIALS

Because of the industrial market most kiln materials are available in any large city, but prices may vary. Even in a small town a building-supply dealer can generally provide firebrick and other materials.

Firebrick is made in a number of special compositions, but the common alumina-silica *hard refractory firebrick* is satisfactory for most purposes. Different grades are produced for operating temperatures of 1600°, 2000°, 2300°, 2600°, and 2800°F (870°, 1093°, 1260°, 1427°, and 1538°C), and some can be used at temperatures as high as 3000° and 3200°F (1649° and 1742°C). The bricks used for higher operating temperatures are denser and lose much of their insulating ability. They are also more expensive. Therefore, one should not purchase a higher-grade brick than is needed. A 2600°F brick is generally used for kilns firing from cones 8 to 10. Special arch- and wedge-shape bricks can be ordered for the curve of the kiln roof. A kiln constructed entirely of hard firebrick will consume a lot of fuel, since the bricks absorb and conduct a considerable amount of heat. Fortunately, porous *insulating firebrick* is also made, which has an insulating value from three to five times as great as the hard brick. Insulating firebricks are available in a similar temperature range as hard brick, but the cost is much higher. They are most often used as a backup layer next to the hard brick, although kilns made entirely of insulating bricks are common. Although more expensive, they require less fuel, and the insulating brick can be cut easily with a coarse-tooth saw, such as an inexpensive pruning or bow-saw.

Castable refractories of varying compositions for several operating temperatures are also available. These can be mixed and poured like concrete. Although more expensive than brick, castable refractories are useful for forming odd shapes, such as burner ports or small arches. They are dense and conduct heat much as a hard brick does. A castable calcium-alumina refractory can be used as liner for a dual-purpose salt kiln, so that salt will not accumulate on the firebrick interior. With this arrangement a bisque or glaze kiln can safely be used for an occasional salt-glaze firing. Over a long period the door bricks will have to replaced several times, and the combustion area near the burner ports will require chipping out and recasting due to the salt action, but the rest of the kiln will remain unaltered.

Other insulating materials of a lower heat tolerance but of great insulating value can also be used for a backup layer. Even common soft red brick will serve this purpose. Kilns of more than 30 cubic feet are commonly built with a hard firebrick core, a middle portion of insulating firebrick, and an outer layer of red brick.

Asbestos sheets and blocks of various sizes provide a good insulation. If the outer walls rise to a height of several courses, loose granular vermiculite poured to a depth of 6 to 8 inches can be used to give further insulation to the roof crown, which in most cases tends to be rather cool. To insulate a high, curved roof, such as a catenary, vermiculite can be mixed with fireclay and water, with sodium silicate as a binder, and this mixture troweled on to a depth of several inches.

Transite, a rigid cement-asbestos sheet material, comes in several sizes and thicknesses. It is useful for the outer panels of a small kiln having an angle iron frame, for it protects and dresses up the brickwork and can serve as a retainer for loose insulation poured between the brick wall and the transite. Transite is also available in tubular form, and in this guise it makes a quite satisfactory chimney, provided sufficient air space surrounds the pipe. A thickness of ½ inch is usually sufficient; thicker sections tend to spall and flake off due to the great difference in heat to which the inner and outer surfaces are exposed.

Kiln furniture includes the shelves, posts, and other props used in the kiln. The heavy fireclay shelves that were formerly used have disappeared as better materials have replaced them. Sillmanite shelves are suitable for earthenware temperatures, but the more expensive *silicon carbide* shelves give longer service and are compounded for use at various temperatures. A ¾-inch thickness is adequate for standard loads. A center post is necessary to avoid sagging and possible breakage in spans of 24 inches or more. Since it is less subject to strain in cooling and heating, a rectangular shelf gives longer service than a square one. A slow heating and cooling cycle not only minimizes damage to the pots but will prolong the life of the kiln furniture, especially the shelves.

Posts made of fireclay are available in various sizes. They often have a center opening to promote a more even expansion. High-temperature insulating bricks can be cut to make satisfactory posts. Dipping the ends of the fireclay posts into aluminum paint will lessen their tendency to stick to the bottoms of the silicon carbide shelves. This problem does not arise with triangular slip-cast posts made of porcelainlike material. Triangular porcelain stilts having pointed contact areas and often a nickel-nichrome wire insert, can be used for some covers or for small pieces that must be glazed all over. The small contact blemishes are not noticeable. (See Chap. 10, pp. 268–269, for a description of saggers and industrial setting methods.)

KILN CONSTRUCTION

Twenty-five years ago few potters were building their own kilns, but with the burgeoning interest in ceramics and with increased knowledge, this practice is now quite commonplace. The beginner, who has little experience in the principles of kiln design, had best attempt to duplicate a proven design, rather than to experiment on his own. Not counting the value of his time, the potter may save 50 percent over the cost of a prefabricated model. Moreover, larger heavy-duty downdraft kilns are seldom available ready made.

The Electric Kiln

The electric kiln, which needs no chimney or gas lines, presents the least challenge to the novice (Fig. 492). Unless one is quite technically inclined, it is best to forgo the problems of calculating length of element wire, size, resistance, and ohms necessary to obtain the desired heat in the kiln chamber. It is easier to purchase replacement elements for a standard kiln made by a reputable manufacturer. The electrical switches might be quite difficult to locate, for the best type is not commonly available. Kiln manufacturers carry replacements.

The angle-iron frame with supporting angles can be fabricated easily, but it must be quite square and accurate. Quarter-inch-thick transite, cut a bit small to allow for heat expansion, can be used for the floor base and outer walls. The standard insulating firebrick straight (9 × 4 ½ × 2 ½ inches), laid "on the flat," is used for the side wall; the 2300°F grade is used for a cone 04 kiln, the 2300° or 2600°F for a cone 6 to 8 kiln. No cutting of the

3-way electric switch

nickel-nichrome or kanthol elements

¼″ transite panels

insulating brick

492. Construction and wiring of an electric kiln.

bricks is required for an 18 × 18-inch interior. The bricks must be staggered as the courses are built up. They can be prevented from shifting by driving long finishing nails through the bricks or by applying a thin coat of fireclay and sodium silicate after first moistening with water. No cement should be used within 1 ½ inches of the elements, in case the elements are placed in the joint.

The element recess can be cut with a coarse saw (a Swedish pruning saw, for example) and a round rasp or with a simple cutting tool in a drill press. To retard possible contamination the recesses can be coated with aluminum paint or with a thin kiln wash before inserting the elements. Low-fire nickel-nichrome replacement elements come in a coil like a screen-door spring. They can be stretched to fit the kiln by driving four nails into a section of plywood at a distance comparable to the size of the element recess and a fifth at the point where the element end enters the kiln from the control box. Most elements go twice around the kiln and need a dia-

gonal slot to complete the circle. The coils must not touch at any point, or a hot spot will develop.

Unless one has some electrical experience, it is advisable to have an electrician hook up the wiring. Bolts in the transite to hold the control panel should be inserted before the bricks are laid in place. A piece of transite can serve as the base. Brass bolts should be used as connecting posts between the elements and the insulated switch wires. The usual switch has three positions, low, medium, and high, which are hooked up on 110 volts, 210 volts in series, and 210 volts in parallel to give the needed current. After repeated firings the nickel-nichrome elements will contract, but they can be carefully stretched again and put back in place. A ventilated cover with adequate clearance must enclose the exposed connections.

The cover on a top-loading kiln presents little problem, for ¼-inch bolts—two in each brick, running through an angle iron on each side—will provide adequate support. If the angle is continued

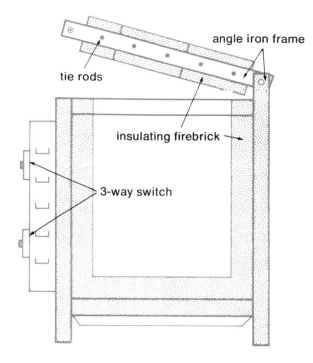

tie rods

angle iron frame

insulating firebrick

3-way switch

493. Electric kiln, lid and switches.

to the rear and the back frame angle is elevated 2 inches, a hinge can be contrived by drilling a hole and inserting a rod. Similarly, an extension in front and a rod inserted in a pipe will provide a lifting handle (see Fig. 493).

The high-fire (cone 8) electric kiln can also use bricks 4 ½ inches thick. However, in this case, an extra 1-inch backing of asbestos would be desirable. Unless a porcelain insert channel is used, greater care must be exercised in selecting firebricks. Because of the higher heat any iron impurities in the firebricks will melt and in turn will cause the element to flux and burn out. The hard Kanthol elements become brittle after use, but their tendency to contract is diminished if they are first fired to cone 8, even though subsequent firings are lower.

The Gas Kiln

Thanks to the uniformity of the insulating firebricks, one can build a small gas kiln using no cement (Fig. 494). This is particularly true of raku kilns, which are small and temporary in nature. A single

vermiculite insulation

steel corner angle iron

"U" bar to take thrust of kiln arch

tie rods

roof arch

insulating bricks, 2600 °F

insulating bricks, 2000 °F

bag wall

bottom kiln shelf

gas burner

burner port opening

draft channel   opening to chimney

concrete slab, reinforced

concrete blocks

side view

494. Construction of a gas kiln.

burner can be placed in a simple box, with the pots set on a few bricks. A flat roof with a small hole for exhaust is sufficient. Either a bolted top or a similar side section can be used, since the ware is inserted and removed from the hot kiln with tongs.

A single 4 ½-inch wall of insulating brick may be adequate for a small kiln, such as the single-bag-wall design illustrated in Figure 483. A 4- or 5-cubic-foot kiln can be fired easily with two atmospheric burners. The square kiln is most likely to have uniform heat; deep kilns are hard to load, and a tall chamber will allow a temperature variation from top to bottom. Insulating bricks are not hard to cut, but it is easier to plan a design based on the uncut unit.

After the desired size has been established (as close to a cube form as possible), a calculation should be made to determine the burner capacity needed. Manufacturers supply information on the B.t.u. (British thermal units) of their various burners. Unless the kiln is quite small, several burners are preferable to one large unit, in order to avoid a concentration of heat. Generally about 6000 or 7000 B.t.u. are required in a stoneware kiln for each cubic foot of capacity, including the combustion area. For the average Bunsen or aspirating burner, a 3-inch opening is sufficient. The chimney size should be at least equal to the area of all burner ports, even slightly larger if possible, especially if there are angles in the flue connection or if the chimney is unusually high (both of which result in friction loss).

The opening through which the depressed floor flue exhausts into the chimney should be smaller than the chimney itself to prevent a too-rapid heat loss. However, it should be constructed in such a way as to allow easy enlargment, if necessary. Unless the kiln is unusually large, a bag wall constructed of firebrick laid on edge is sufficient. Only the first few courses of bricks need be permanent. The function of the bag wall is to force the flames and heat upward in the kiln. Its height will depend upon the kiln size, the chimney draft, and other factors. Additional bricks can be laid without cement if more heat is needed in the upper kiln area. About 4 or 5 inches of combustion area between the kiln and the bag wall is sufficient in the average gas kiln. A slightly larger area is needed if oil is used for fuel.

Refractory mortar cements are available for bonding the bricks, either in dry or wet form. A cheaper and essentially similar material can be mixed from two parts fireclay and one part fine grog. An even stronger bond can be made by adding one gallon of sodium silicate to 100 pounds of the dry mix. Unless the bricks are first moistened, they will soak up too much mortar, so it is best to immerse them in water and then allow them to drain. Only the thinnest layer of mortar is needed, since the bricks are very uniform and do not require a thick layer of cement for leveling purposes. The best method is to dip the edges of the bricks in a soupy mortar and tap them into place immediately with a hammer on a wood block. Because of their porosity, the insulating bricks expand very little in heating and can be placed very close together. The dense firebricks, however, expand considerably under heat; therefore, about ¼ inch of space with no mortar should be left between every third or fourth brick, for otherwise the outside layer of cooler brick will be forced open in firing.

It is especially advisable to plan on a unit brick size when using hard bricks. They can be cut by tapping a groove on each side with a mason's hammer, then split by hitting a solid blow on a mason's chisel with a heavy hammer. No such procedure is possible with the wedge-shaped bricks needed for the kiln arch. The usual arch rises at the rate of 1 ½ inches per foot. Placing the bricks on edge for a 4 ½-inch thickness provides sufficient strength for the average-size kiln. The #1 arch brick tapers from 2 ½ to to 2 ⅛ inches. By drawing two curves 4 ½ inches apart on a large board and using a 1 ½-inch rise per foot over the desired span, the required number of #1 arch bricks can be calculated. Some straights will be needed, but they should be kept to a minimum, as should the mortar.

These calculations present no problem in an insulating brick arch, since the softer bricks can be trimmed to a wooden pattern using a coarse rasp. A sharply angled skewback brick is needed where the arch meets the side wall. The kiln will require a 2 ½-inch angle-iron support at each corner, with ½-inch take-up rods at top and bottom. While these give a slight rigidity to the kiln, their main purpose is to hold the heavy angle iron brace, which is needed on the outer wall to take up the thrust of the kiln arch.

A supporting form to hold the arch can be made easily by cutting several boards to the arch curve and covering them with a masonite sheet. It is wise to leave a bit of slack and to place wedges under the uprights so that the form can be removed easily after the steel angles and rods are in place. The catenary-arch kiln is self supporting and needs no metal bracing. Its curve can be established by suspending a chain from two nails at the desired floor width. The result will be a rather pointed curve. The structure will be most stable if the height approximates the width of the base. This design is perhaps best suited to an oil-burning kiln, since the flare at the base provides the extra combustion area needed for oil fuel.

The weight of a kiln is considerable, and it requires at least a 4-inch concrete base. In order to avoid leaning over and bumping the head in loading, it is a good idea to build the kiln on a reinforced concrete slab elevated to the necessary height with concrete blocks. Such a kiln can be moved later, if necessary, with little or no damage. In arranging the brick structure one should always plan to stagger the joints and occasionally have a tie brick to bind two courses together. The corner bricks are laid first, making certain the plan is perfectly square. A level and a guide line are essential, since the eye is not dependable. Common red bricks can be used as backup for that part of the floor area not depressed for the exhaust channel. The kind of brick to be used and the wall thickness are determined by size and general use. For the usual salt kiln and the oil-fueled kiln an inner course of 4 ½-inch hard firebrick is necessary, backed up by a 2000°F insulating firebrick. If the size approaches 30 cubic feet, an additional outer layer of common red brick would be desirable.

A properly constructed kiln will give many years of service and require few repairs. A stoneware kiln with a 15- to 25-cubic-foot capacity can be built with a 2600°F insulating brick on edge and a 2000°F brick on the flat, thus creating a 7-inch wall. Although the initial cost is high, the construction is easier and the fuel cost lower. However, insulating bricks retain little heat and cool more rapidly; therefore, a 30-cubic-foot or larger kiln should be equipped with a hard inner liner as mentioned earlier. The kiln door jambs should be built of the same brick as the inner liner, whatever the type used. Kilns that are covered by only a simple roof have been built for summer schools. To provide protection from driving rains and snow during the off season, the procedures described above are reversed, and the hard durable firebrick is placed on the outside with the insulating brick as an inner liner. The results are apparently satisfactory.

It is obvious from all these examples that there is no one way to build a kiln. The illustrations show a variety of burner placements. Most potters find the downdraft layout (Figs. 482, 489) to be the most satisfactory for the 10- to 25-cubic-foot size. A smaller kiln might use the crossdraft design shown in Figure 483. Although the updraft muffle kiln (Fig. 481) is a common design for commercial kilns, neither this nor the open-flame updraft are recommended for construction by the potter.

The Chimney

Because of the extreme temperatures involved, the kiln cannot exhaust into an ordinary household chimney. For a shedlike studio, a simple transite pipe may be sufficient to carry the exhaust. In the classroom, however, an insulated fireclay Van Packer unit may be necessary, especially for the portion within the building. The exterior section can have the usual fireclay liner and brick construction. Small kilns can exhaust into a metal hood above the kiln, thus sucking the cooler room air to the stack and eliminating some of the temperature problem.

A short, direct connection from kiln to chimney is just as important for a proper draft as is the height of the stack. If needed, overhead connections can be made with transite or a metal fireclay-lined pipe. Undue length or angles in this connection will require a much higher and larger stack size than normal. Tall stacks with unusual connections will probably need a burner or a fan in the stack base to induce an initial draft. If there are no surrounding buildings to cause a downdraft, a 15- to 20-foot chimney should be sufficient. A 6- × -6-inch flue is usually adequate for a 10-cubic-foot kiln and a 9- × -9-inch flue for a 20-cubic-foot design. However, an even larger size is recommended, especially in a taller stack which has some friction loss. A slot must be left in the draft flue at the point where it leaves the kiln for a damper. It can be made of a small or a broken kiln shelf.

Burners

There are many types of burners available, both oil and gas, and some can be improvised with simple materials. The smoke produced by the drip-type oil burner normally relegates its use to an isolated location. In some cases vacuum cleaner units can be used for added draft. The blowers needed to provide additional air and the fumes from oil fuel are disturbing factors if the kiln area is adjoining a classroom. An outdoor location in a warm climate creates no problem, but the kiln must be watched, for the burners can become clogged, and this is a fire hazard.

Although more expensive, natural gas or liquid butane are both convenient and relatively safe.

For a medium-size kiln one needs a natural-gas line at least two inches in diameter, with several pounds of pressure at the meter, even though the large regulator that is needed will reduce the pressure to about 6 ounces at the kiln. A large kiln using liquid gas requires a 500-gallon tank, which usually can be rented. There is a drop of pressure when the tank is less than half full, because of the cooling that occurs as the gas is being used rapidly. Gas pressure is also calculated in terms of the amount of pressure needed to raise a column of water in a glass tube. According to this system, 1 ounce of gas pressure equals 1.73 inches of water pressure.

For a controlled and even firing, several simple aspirating or Bunsen burners are preferable to one or two large forced-draft burners. A solenoid safety valve should be connected near the burner in case of a temporary gas interruption. All gas lines must be absolutely tight, since even the slightest leak is dangerous. In selecting a burner size one ought to allow for some excess capacity. As mentioned earlier, about 6000 or 7000 B.t.u. are required for each cubic foot of the kiln interior, including the combustion area. This figure assumes that the insulation is adequate and that the general design, draft, and so forth are efficient.

12 Studio Equipment

This chapter presents a selection of the necessary items of studio equipment available to the potter. The addresses of specific manufacturers, together with a schedule of typical prices, are listed in the Appendix (pp. 324–328).

CERAMIC KILNS

The prospective kiln buyer should first study Chapter 11 (pp. 271–287), which discusses in more detail the characteristics of various kiln designs. Since it requires neither gas lines nor a special chimney, the small electric kiln of a 3- to 5-cubic-foot size is adequate for the amateur or for the average public school (Figs. 496–497). For the college ceramics program a gas kiln is necessary (Figs. 498–501), not only for its larger size but because of the higher temperatures and the possibility of reduction firing. In an instructional situation, as opposed to a production effort, several small kilns are preferable to one large kiln. Frequent firings are needed to experiment with glazes and decorative techniques, as well as to gain experience with loading and firing procedures. Typical equipment for a university ceramics program might include two electric kilns of 3 cubic feet each and three gas kilns in the 8-, 10-, and 12-cubic-foot sizes. Dimensions refer to the shelf-loading area. In comparing kilns for purchase, care must be taken to determine the actual loading area and to exclude both the combustion area and the space needed for the flow of heat around the shelves. An excess kiln capacity is desirable to accommodate an increasing number of students. Colleges with graduate programs might well consider a car kiln for greater capacity and ease in loading (Figs. 502–503).

Although most public schools fire their ceramics to about cone 04, a higher-firing kiln is useful, for the kiln rated at only 2000°F will not stand up under continued use. The kanthal elements in a 2300°F kiln will contract from their recesses, unless the kiln is first fired to about 2300°F. After this the elements will be brittle but will remain in place.

opposite : 495. WALTER HYLECK, U.S.A. *Phoney Ringtail Cat Under Large Black Beret.* Stoneware with low-fire black and silver luster glazes, height 18″.

above : 496. Paragon top-loading electric kiln for temperatures to cone 8. Chamber $17 \times 17 \times 18''$.

right : 497. Unique front-loading electric kiln for temperatures to cones 8–10. Chamber $17 \times 17 \times 17''$, weight 600 lbs.

498. West Coast open-fire updraft gas kiln for temperatures to cones 10–12. Chamber $24 \times 24 \times 36''$.

above : 499. Alpine open-fire updraft gas kiln for temperatures to cones 8–10. Capacity 24 cubic feet.

left : 500. Denver Fire Clay updraft muffle gas kiln for temperatures to cone 6. Capacity 12 cubic feet.

left : 501. Unique heavy-duty downdraft gas kiln for temperatures to cones 8–12. Force draft with automatic cutoff controls. Capacity 30 cubic feet.

below : 502. Unique heavy-duty downdraft gas car kiln for temperatures to cone 11. Force draft with automatic shutoff controls. Capacity 30 cubic feet.

above : 503. Denver Fire Clay updraft shuttle-car gas kiln for temperatures to cone 6. Car area 24 × 60 × 25″, overall length 24′, capacity 20 cubic feet, shipping weight 7000 lbs. The double-door construction makes possible the use of an additional car for faster loading and operation.

right : 504. Unique pyrometer with insulated leads and thermocouple.

All gas kilns should be equipped with a simple automatic cutoff in case of a gas interruption. The elaborate controls and regulating pyrometer used in industrial ceramics are not only very expensive and unnecessary on a small kiln, but they often make operation more difficult. Although pyrometric cones are essential to gauge final temperatures accurately, a portable pyrometer (Fig. 504) and thermocouple are most helpful in regulating heat rise and in determining temperatures for a reduction firing.

There are several devices on the market that employ a cone and a sliding spring mechanism to turn off the power in an electric kiln, but these cannot be recommended, because all too often the metal parts become corroded, and this can lead to malfunction and possible overfiring of the kiln.

POTTER'S WHEELS

Because of their somewhat limited production, good potter's wheels are rather expensive. While an expert can throw on any wheel, a beginner will have difficulty achieving satisfactory results on poor equipment. The cheap wheels advertised in hobby magazines should be strictly avoided! It is far better to confine oneself to hand-built pottery than to settle for such an inferior wheel.

Potters usually prefer to use the kind of wheel on which they first learned to throw, and, as the illustrations reveal, there is no consensus about the perfect type. Many teachers prefer the simple kick wheel (Figs. 505–508) for beginners; when in difficulty, they forget to kick, thus slowing down the wheel at the proper time. A wheel with an integral and adjustable seat, a splash pan, and foot rests is

top left : 505. Oak Hill traditional kick wheel. Waterproof plywood frame; 31″ flywheel, iron weight 80 lbs.; 14″ aluminum wheel head; overall shipping weight 170 lbs.

center left : 506. Soldner kick wheel. Welded-pipe frame; reinforced concrete flywheel, weight 90 lbs.; 14″ aluminum wheel head; 20×38″ work table. Available with ½-horsepower 5–100 rpm motor attachment.

below left : 507. Randall kick wheel. Welded steel frame, 9″ recessed aluminum wheel head, 19″ aluminum splash pan, adjustable bucket seat; 28″ flywheel, standard weight 115 lbs. (adjustable if desired); overall shipping weight 200 lbs. Available with ½-horsepower motor attachment.

above : 508. Denton Vars side-treadle wheel designed by Bernard Leach. Hardwood frame, weighted flywheel, fiber glass pan, 13″ aluminum wheel head.

below : 511. Skutt bench-type electric wheel. One-third-horse-power variable-speed motor with adjustable belts at speeds of 35–125 or 50–165 rpm; 12″ wheel head; cast-aluminum frame.

bottom : 512. Randall special wheel. Three-quarter-horse-power 110-volt D.C. motor, variable speed 0–175 rpm, with foot control; height 19 ½″, 18 ¼″ aluminum wheel head; shipping weight 275 lbs. This wheel is designed for the production potter. It can also be used for stand-up throwing of large forms.

top : 509. Alpine heavy-duty wheel. One-half-horsepower variable-speed motor with foot controls, 0–160 rpm; platform height 16″, 13″ wheel head.

above : 510. Denver Fire Clay bench-type electric wheel. One-quarter-horsepower variable-speed motor, 48–200 rpm; 12″ wheel head.

undoubtedly the most convenient. A few of these have motorized attachments.

The choice of an electric wheel (Figs. 509–512), given the varying motor sizes available, may well depend upon the size of the pieces to be thrown. In any case, the single-speed motor should be avoided, as should motors not capable of variable and quite slow speeds. Speeds in excess of 100 rpm are not needed if the motor has adequate torque.

CLAY MIXERS

Preparing plastic clay for the classroom or active studio can require much effort. The practice of buying bagged plastic clay at high prices is not economically feasible when one uses more than 3 tons of dry clay during the school year. The blunger and filter press mixing process seems unnecessarily involved for the small studio, especially when many pounds of dry trimmings and discarded pots must be reclaimed. The three machines illustrated (Figs. 513–515) allow these clay scraps, after proper soaking, to be mixed into a plastic state. Dry powdered clay can be added if necessary. The action of the Randall and Soldner machines is not unlike that of commercial bakery dough machines. In fact, dough mixers can be used for clay, and second-hand models are occasionally available at low price. The Walker pug mill discharges clay at a container height and with a slightly stiffer consistency.

right : 513. Soldner clay mixer with reinforced concrete tub. Unit dimensions 48 × 48 × 31″, weight 450 lbs.; 2-horsepower 115/220 volt motor. Available with stainless-steel blades, improved starter, and fan-cooled motor.

below left : 514. Walker pug mill, shown with mixing and compression screw flight blades, all operating parts stainless steel. Overall dimensions 63 × 33 × 36″, hopper opening 16 × 20″, weight 270 lbs.; 3/4-horsepower 110-volt motor with 150:1 reduction gear; automatic overload switch and knee cut-off bar.

below right : 515. Randall clay mixer. Overall dimensions 56 × 36 × 34″, capacity 100 lbs. dry clay; 3-horsepower motor with heavy reduction unit, 220 or 440 volts; safety switch and overload fuse; shipping weight 600 lbs.

top : 516. Porcelain mortar and pestle. Available in 16 oz. and 32 oz. sizes.

above : 517. Craftools porcelain ball mill jars. Available in gallon, half-gallon, and quart sizes.

top : 518. Craftools ball mill. Length 20″, ¼-horsepower motor.

above : 519. Craftools brass glaze sieve. Available in 8 to 100 mesh sizes.

GLAZE-ROOM EQUIPMENT

Commercial chemicals today are so finely ground that a simple mixing with a wire whisk is usually sufficient. However, certain coarse materials, such as calcined ingredients or volcanic ash, may require the use of a mortar and pestle (Fig. 516) or, for larger amounts, a ball mill (Figs. 517–518). A portable kitchen food mixer or a paint mixer in an electric drill are quite efficient for mixing moderate quanti-

ties of glaze. A variety of brass sieves (Fig. 519) in mesh sizes of 80, 60, 30, 15, and 8 are useful. The finer sizes are for sifting glazes and the coarser for grog.

As a rule, glazes are most conveniently applied by pouring, dipping, or brushing. The sprayed glaze is very fragile and can easily be damaged in loading. Nevertheless, certain glaze and decorative effects can best be achieved by spraying (Fig. 520). Since the amount of sprayed work is likely to be small, left : 520. Craftools portable paint sprayer suitable for glazes. One-quarter-horsepower motor, gun hose, and nozzles.

right : 521. Craftools portable spray booth. Exhaust fan and fiber glass filters, inside dimensions 30×24″.

far right : 522. Craftools glaze spray booth. Exhaust fan and turntable. Available with air filter and regulator.

523. Ohaus triple-beam gram scales. Several models available from local dealers.

524. Craftools cast-iron banding wheel. Ball-bearing movement, 8″ head.

a booth with filters (Figs. 521–522) rather than a permanent exhaust system will be less expensive and usually adequate. Gram scales (Fig. 523), large pound scales, and decorating wheels (Fig. 524) are necessary in every glaze room. Dipping tongs are desirable for glazing small pieces.

SPECIAL EQUIPMENT

In view of the amount of heavy material that must be moved in the studio—bagged clay and chemicals, fire bricks, plastic clay in large cans—a shop lift on rollers is an essential item (Fig. 525). Bagged clay and chemicals should be placed on pallets upon

delivery. Large sculptural pieces are best constructed on a plywood base resting a pallet. By means of the lift, the transference into the kiln is relatively easy. Sand or small wooden rollers between the pallet and the base allow the piece to be skidded into place. The plywood base is left to burn out.

Ware racks (Fig. 526) are invaluable in loading and unloading kilns, as well as in storing and moving ware from the glazing area to the kilns. Draped with plastic they can serve as extra damp-room storage. Thrown pieces cut off the wheel can be put on 6-inch boards that fit the ware rack. Overhead racks to accommodate pots on these short boards are also common, especially in the private studio

left : 525. Big Joe hydraulic shop lift. Capacity 1000 lbs., lifting height 54″; dimensions 44 ¾ × 29″, weight 380 lbs.

above : 526. Unique welded-steel ware rack on casters. Dimensions 65 × 22 × 28″.

which is likely to have limited space. The damp room can have a similar provision to hold boards of thrown pots. A damp room is a necessity in schools because of the time lapse between classes.

A plaster bat with a hollowed center section is convenient for drying small batches of clay. One or two large bats, which may hold up to 50 pounds of slip, are also helpful for drying special mixtures. While clay slabs can be rolled out on a sanded table, large flat plaster-of-paris slabs are useful, especially if the clay is a bit moist. In the classroom it is best to have wedging tables at two different heights to accommodate both shorter and taller students. Because of their continued use a welded-steel base frame is recommended for plaster-faced wedging tables. The plaster must be scraped periodically to remove the colloidal clay particles that would otherwise seal up the surface.

THE CERAMIC STUDIO

The general layout of the studio is quite important for both the individual potter and the teacher. The various work areas should be laid out in such a way that interference and unnecessary traffic are avoided. Raw materials and clay mixing should be concentrated near the delivery entrance and this area provided with adequate ventilation. A good arrangement is a rather open studio with drop panels from the ceiling to concentrate the kiln fumes and heat, which can then be exhausted from the studio. The throwing, modeling, and decorating areas should be spacious and well lighted.

Ware racks have been mentioned before as an aid to moving thrown pots from the wheel area to the kilns. Bisque ware can also be unloaded from the kilns onto such racks for transference to the glaze area and finally back to the kilns for the glaze firing. Sinks should be conveniently located in the several work areas. Plaster work is best concentrated in a single area, and the sink used for this purpose should drain into a large open tank with several baffles to trap plaster particles, which would otherwise certainly stop up the drains.

A duplicate set of clearly labeled glaze chemicals is desirable in the glaze area. Odd lots of glaze, instead of being discarded, can be poured into a crock for use as a shop glaze for interiors. Large cans on rollers, some containing water, should be placed in the wheel area for clay trimmings and throwing water, as well as to provide a place to wash tools and hands. (This ought not be done in the sinks, for eventually the drains will become clogged.) The aged clay can be reclaimed to serve as a base for new powdered clay in the pug mill or clay mixer.

The classroom-studio is really rather like a small commercial pottery. It should be an airy, clean, and enjoyable place in which to work. Unless the studio is organized efficiently, both student and teacher can suffer many frustrations. Each student must develop the habit of cleaning up as he goes along. All students should participate in the loading of the kilns, with the firing entrusted to the advanced students, for these are skills that are as important to master as throwing. Clay preparation is a real problem in most studios, for it is laborious and time consuming regardless of the equipment. Ideally, a rotating team of students can periodically make up clay as it is needed. In practice some use more than their share, while others fail to knead clay from failed pots or thoughtlessly allow it to harden in the drying bats. As a solution many schools pay a few students to make up clay and place it in 25-pound plastic bags, which are sold at cost to the individual student. While this entails a certain amount of bookkeeping, it does help to eliminate some careless studio practices.

Appendix

Reference
Tables

Atomic Weights of Common Elements

Element	Symbol	Atomic number	Atomic weight
Aluminum	Al	13	26.97
Antimony	Sb	51	121.76
Barium	Ba	56	137.36
Bismuth	Bi	83	209.00
Boron	B	5	10.82
Cadmium	Cd	48	112.41
Calcium	Ca	20	40.08
Carbon	C	6	12.01
Chlorine	Cl	17	35.457
Chromium	Cr	24	52.01
Cobalt	Co	27	58.94
Copper	Cu	29	63.54
Fluorine	F	9	19.00
Gold	Au	79	197.20
Hydrogen	H	1	1.008

Atomic Weights of Common Elements—*continued*

Element	Symbol	Atomic number	Atomic weight
Iridium	Ir	77	193.10
Iron	Fe	26	55.84
Lead	Pb	82	207.21
Lithium	Li	3	6.94
Magnesium	Mg	12	24.32
Manganese	Mn	25	54.93
Molybdenum	Mo	42	95.98
Neon	Ne	10	20.183
Nickel	Ni	28	58.69
Nitrogen	N	7	14.008
Oxygen	O	8	16.00
Palladium	Pd	46	106.70
Phosphorus	P	15	30.98
Platinum	Pt	78	195.23
Potassium	K	19	39.096
Silicon	Si	14	28.06
Silver	Ag	47	107.88
Sodium	Na	11	22.997
Sulphur	S	16	32.066
Tin	Sn	50	118.70
Titanium	Ti	22	47.90
Uranium	U	92	238.07
Vanadium	V	23	50.95
Zinc	Zn	30	65.38
Zirconium	Zr	40	91.22

Common Ceramic Raw Materials

Material	Raw formula	Compound molecular weight	Equivalent weight	Fired formula
Aluminum hydroxide	$Al_2(OH)_6$	156	156	Al_2O_3
Antimony oxide	Sb_2O_3	292	292	Sb_2O_3
Barium carbonate	$BaCO_3$	197	197	BaO
Bone ash (calcium phosphate)	$Ca_3(PO_4)_2$	310	103	CaO
Boric acid	$B_2O_3 \cdot 3\,H_2O$	124	124	B_2O_3
Borax	$Na_2O \cdot 2\,B_2O_3 \cdot 10\,H_2O$	382	382	$Na_2O \cdot 2\,B_2O_3$
Calcium borate (colemanite)	$2\,CaO \cdot 3\,B_2O_3 \cdot 5\,H_2O$	412	206	$2\,CaO \cdot 3\,B_2O_3$
Calcium carbonate (whiting)	$CaCO_3$	100	100	CaO
Chromic oxide	Cr_2O_3	152	152	Cr_2O_3
Cobalt carbonate	$CoCO_3$	119	119	CoO
Cobalt oxide, black	Co_3O_4	241	80	CoO
Copper carbonate	$CuCO_3$	124	124	CuO
Copper oxide, green (cupric)	CuO	80	80	CuO
Copper oxide, red (cuprous)	Cu_2O	143	80	CuO
Cornwall stone[a]	$(1\,RO \cdot 1.16\,Al_2O_3 \cdot 8.95\,SiO_2)$	732	652	same
Cryolite	$Na_3 \cdot AlF_6$	210	420	$3\,Na_2O \cdot Al_2O_3$
Dolomite	$CaCO_3 \cdot MgCO_3$	184	184	$CaO \cdot MgO$
Feldspar, potash	$K_2O \cdot Al_2O_3 \cdot 6\,SiO_2$	557	557	same
Feldspar, soda	$Na_2 \cdot Al_2O_3 \cdot 6\,SiO_2$	524	524	same
Kaolin (china clay)	$Al_2O_3 \cdot 2\,SiO_2 \cdot 2\,H_2O$	258	258	$Al_2O_3 \cdot 2\,SiO_2$
Kaolin (calcined)	$Al_2O_3 \cdot 2\,SiO_2$	222	222	$Al_2O_3 \cdot 2\,SiO_2$
Iron chromate	$FeCrO_4$	172	172	$FeCrO_4$
Iron oxide, red (ferric)	Fe_2O_3	160	160	Fe_2O_3
Iron oxide, black (ferrous)	FeO	72	72	FeO
Flint (quartz, silica)	SiO_2	60	60	SiO_2
Fluorspar (calcium fluoride)	CaF_2	78	78	CaO
Lead carbonate (white lead)	$2\,PbCO_3 \cdot Pb(OH)_2$	775	258	PbO
Lead monosilicate	$3\,PbO \cdot 2\,SiO_2$	789	263	same
Lead oxide (litharge)	PbO	223	223	PbO
Lead oxide, red	Pb_3O_4	685	228	PbO

Common Ceramic Raw Materials—*continued*

Material	*Raw formula*	*Compound molecular weight*	*Equivalent weight*	*Fired formula*
Lepidolite	$LiF \cdot KF \cdot Al_2O_3 \cdot 3\ SiO_2$	356	356	same
Lithium carbonate	Li_2CO_3	74	74	Li_2O
Magnesium carbonate	$MgCO_3$	84	84	MgO
Manganese carbonate	$MnCO_3$	115	115	MnO
Manganese dioxide (black)	MnO_2	87	87	MnO
Manganese oxide (greenish)	MnO	71	71	MnO
Nepheline syenite[b]	$1\ RO \cdot 1.04\ Al_2O_3 \cdot 4.53\ SiO_2$	447	447	same
Nickel oxide, green	NiO	75	75	NiO
Nickel oxide, black	Ni_2O_3	166	83	NiO
Petalite	$Li_2O \cdot Al_2O_3 \cdot 8\ SiO_2$	197	197	same
Plastic vitrox[c]	$1\ RO \cdot 1.69Al_2O_3 \cdot 14.64\ SiO_2$	1139	1139	same
Potassium carbonate (pearl ash)	K_2CO_3	138	138	K_2O
Pyrophyllite	$Al_2O_3 \cdot 4\ SiO_2 \cdot H_2O$	360	360	$Al_2O_3 \cdot 4\ SiO_2$
Sodium bicarbonate	$NaHCO_3$	84	168	Na_2O
Sodium carbonate (soda ash)	Na_2CO_3	106	106	Na_2O
Spodumene	$Li_2O \cdot Al_2O_3 \cdot 4\ SiO_2$	372	372	same
Talc (steatite)	$3\ MgO \cdot 4\ SiO_2 \cdot H_2O$	379	126	$3\ MgO \cdot 4\ SiO_2$
Tin oxide (stannic oxide)	SnO_2	151	151	SnO_2
Titanium dioxide (rutile impure TiO_2)	TiO_2	80	80	TiO_2
Wollastonite	$Ca \cdot SiO_3$	116	116	same
Zinc oxide	ZnO	81	81	ZnO
Zirconium oxide	ZrO_2	123	123	ZrO_2

[a] Formula for Cornwall stone	K_2O	0.4453	Al_2O_3	1.0847	SiO_2	7.796
	Na_2O	0.2427	Fe_2O_3	0.0065		
	CaO	0.1873				
	MgO	0.0821		*Mol. weight 652*		
	CaF_2	0.0421				
[b] Formula for Nepheline syenite	Na_2O	0.713	Al_2O_3	1.04	SiO_3	4.53
	K_2O	0.220				
	CaO	0.056		*Mol. weight 447*		
	MgO	0.011				
[c] Formula for Plastic vitrox	CaO	0.045	Al_2O_3	1.693	SiO_2	14.634
	MgO	0.058	Fe_2O_3	0.005		
	Na_2O	0.054				
	K_2O	0.842		*Mol. weight 1139.40*		

Analysis of Common Clays and Chemicals

Material	SiO$_2$	Al$_2$O$_3$	Fe$_2$O$_3$	TiO$_2$	CaO	MgO	K$_2$O	Na$_2$O	Li$_2$O	Ignition loss
Red Dalton clay	63.2	18.3	6.3	1.3	0.3	0.5	1.6	1.2		6.4
Barnard clay	41.4	6.7	29.9	0.2	0.5	0.6	1.0	0.5		8.4
Monmouth stoneware	56.8	28.5			0.3	0.3	0.3	1.3		12.2
Jordon stoneware	69.4	17.7	1.6	1.3	0.1	0.5	1.5	1.39		6.4
Albany slip	57.6	14.6	5.2	0.4	5.8	2.7	3.2	0.8		9.5
Ball clay	51.9	31.7	0.8	1.5	0.2	0.2	0.9	0.4		12.3
Sagger clay	59.4	27.2	0.7	1.6	0.6	0.2	0.7	0.3		9.4
Fireclay	58.1	23.1	2.4	1.4	0.8	1.1	1.9	0.3		10.5
Georgia kaolin	44.9	38.9	0.4	1.3	0.1	0.1	0.2	0.2		14.21
English kaolin	47.25	37.29	0.84	0.05	0.03	0.28	1.8	0.04		12.21
Petalite	77.0	17.5					(0.5)		4.3	0.7
Pyrophyllite	73.5	20.0	0.5		0.1		1.4	1.2		3.3
Bentonite	64.32	20.7	3.47	0.11	0.46	2.26	2.9			5.15
Volcanic ash	72.51	11.55	1.21	0.54	0.68	0.07	7.87	1.79		3.81
Plastic vitrox	75.56	14.87	0.09		0.22	0.20	6.81	0.29		2.04
Feldspar, potash	68.3	17.9	0.08		0.4		10.1	3.1		0.32
Cornwall stone	72.6	16.1	0.23	0.06	1.4	0.1	4.56	3.67		2.54
Nepheline syenite	60.4	23.6	0.08		0.7	0.1	9.8	4.6		0.7
Lepidolite	55.0	25.0	0.08				9.0	1.0	4.0	0.92[a]
Spodumene	62.91	28.42	0.53		0.11	0.13	0.69	0.46	6.78	0.28

[a] plus 5 percent Fluorine.

Water of Plasticity of Various Clays

Washed kaolin	44.48–47.50
White sedimentary kaolin	28.60–56.25
Ball clays	25.00–53.30
Plastic fireclays	12.90–37.40
Flint fireclays	8.89–19.04
Sagger clays	18.40–28.56
Stoneware clays	19.16–34.80
Brick clays	13.20–40.70

$$\text{Water of plasticity} = \frac{\text{weight of plastic sample} - \text{weight of dry sample}}{\text{weight of dry sample}} \times 100$$

Analysis of Several Standard Feldspars[a]

Material	SiO_2	Al_2O_3	Fe_2O_3	CaO	MgO	K_2O	Na_2O	Ignition loss
Spruce Pine # 4	67.9	19.01	0.05	1.54	trace	4.98	6.22	0.08
Bell	68.3	17.9	0.08	0.4	trace	10.1	3.1	0.32
Eureka	69.8	17.11	0.1	trace		9.4	3.5	0.2
Kingman	66.0	18.7	0.1	0.1		12.0	2.8	0.2
Oxford	69.4	17.04	0.09	0.38		7.92	3.22	0.3
Chesterfield	70.6	16.33	0.08	0.3		8.5	3.75	0.4
Buckingham	65.58	19.54	trace	0.16	0.2	12.44	2.56	0.32

[a] The variable quality of the feldspar fluxes is a major reason why glaze recipes may need alteration unless materials are identical.

Oxide Equivalents of Selected Commercial Frits[a]

Company		K_2O	Na_2O	CaO	PbO	Al_2O_3	B_2O_3	SiO_2	Formula weight
Pemco	54		0.32	0.68			0.64	1.47	191
	67	0.12	0.19	0.69		0.37	1.16	2.17	311
	926	0.01	0.31	0.68		0.11	0.61	1.90	225
	83		0.28		0.72	0.20	0.26	2.43	276
	316				1.00	0.25		1.92	364
	349	0.09	0.09	0.58	0.24	0.19	0.36	2.80	313
Ferro	3124	0.02	0.28	0.70		0.27	0.55	2.56	279
	3134		0.32	0.68			0.63	1.47	210
	3211			1.00			1.11		133
	3223		1.00				2.00	5.00	502
	3419		0.28		0.72		0.57	0.89	276
	3386	0.02	0.08		0.90	0.13	1.77	4.42	499
	3396		0.50		0.50		1.00	2.00	332
Hommel	285	0.10	0.90			0.21	0.94	2.72	315
	267	0.13	0.31	0.56		0.29	1.24	2.05	301
	266		0.32	0.68		0.32	1.10	1.31	245
	22			0.47	0.53		0.98	2.88	385
	240		0.28		0.72		0.56	0.90	271
	13		0.30		0.70		0.39	0.41	227

[a] In most cases the above frits will constitute a complete glaze at cone 06.

Color Scale for Temperatures

Color	Degrees C	Degrees F
Lowest visible red	475	885
Lowest visible red to dark red	475–650	885–1200
Dark red to cherry red	650–750	1200–1380
Cherry red to bright cherry red	750–815	1380–1500
Bright cherry red to orange	815–900	1500–1650
Orange to yellow	900–1090	1650–2000
Yellow to light yellow	1090–1315	2000–2400
Light yellow to white	1315–1540	2400–2800
White to dazzling white	1540 and higher	2800 and higher

Average Temperatures to Which Various Ceramic Products are Fired

Products	Degrees F
Heavy clay products	
Common brick—surface clay	1600–1800
Common brick—shale	1800–2000
Face brick—fireclay	2100–2300
Enamel brick	2100–2300
Drain tile	1700–1900
Sewer pipe	2030–2320
Roofing tile	1960–2140
Terra cotta	2070–2320
Pottery	
Flower pots	1580–1850
Stoneware (chemical)	2650–2700
Stoneware (once fired)	2318–2426
Semivitreous ware	2282–2354
Pottery decalcomanias	1400–1500
Refractories	
Firebrick—clay	2300–2500
Firebrick—silica	2650–2750
Silicon carbide	3236–3992
White wares	
Electrical porcelain	2390–2500
Hotel china—bisque	2390–2436
Hotel china—glaze	2210–2282
Floor tile	2318–2498
Wall tile—bisque	1886–2354
Wall tile—glaze	1186–2246

Temperature Equivalents—Orton Standard Pyrometric Cones[a]

Cone number	Large cones		Small cones		Seger cones (used in Europe) Degrees C
	150°C[b]	270°F[b]	300°C[b]	540°F[b]	
020	635	1175	666	1231	670
019	683	1261	723	1333	690
018	717	1323	752	1386	710
017	747	1377	784	1443	730
016	792	1458	825	1517	750
015	804	1479	843	1549	790
014	838	1540			815
013	852	1566			835
012	884	1623			855
011	894	1641			880
010	894	1641	919	1686	900
09	923	1693	955	1751	920
08	955	1751	983	1801	940
07	984	1803	1008	1846	960
06	999	1830	1023	1873	980
05	1046	1915	1062	1944	1000
04	1060	1940	1098	2008	1020
03	1101	2014	1131	2068	1040
02	1120	2048	1148	2098	1060
01	1137	2079	1178	2152	1080

[a] From the Edward Orton, Jr., Ceramic Foundation, Columbus, Ohio.

[b] Temperature rise per hour.

Temperature Equivalents—Orton Standard Pyrometric Cones—*continued*

Cone number	Large cones		Small cones		Seger cones (used in Europe)
	150°C[b]	270°F[b]	300°C[b]	540°F[b]	Degrees C
1	1154	2109	1179	2154	*1100*
2	1162	2124	1179	2154	*1120*
3	1168	2134	1196	2185	*1140*
4	1186	2167	1209	2208	*1160*
5	1196	2185	1221	2230	*1180*
6	1222	2232	1255	2291	*1200*
7	1240	2264	1264	2307	*1230*
8	1263	2305	1300	2372	*1250*
9	1280	2336	1317	2403	*1280*
10	1305	2381	1330	2426	*1300*
11	1315	2399	1336	2437	*1320*
12	1326	2419	1335	2471	*1350*
13	1346	2455			*1380*
14	1366	2491			*1410*
15	1431	2608			*1430*

Conversion formula

Centigrade to Fahrenheit

example: $100°C \times \dfrac{9}{5} = 180 \quad 180 + 32 = 212°F$

Fahrenheit to Centigrade

example: $212°F - 32 = 180 \quad 180 \times \dfrac{5}{9} = 100°C$

Melting Points of Selected Compounds and Minerals

	Degrees C	Degrees F
Alumina	2050	3722
Barium carbonate	1360	2480
Bauxite	2035	3695
Borax	741	1365
Calcium oxide	2570	4658
Cobaltic oxide (O$_2$)	905	1661
Copper oxide (CuO)	1064	1947
Corundum	2035	3695
Cryolite	998	1830
Dolomite	2570–2800	4658–5072
Ferric oxide	1548	2518
Fireclay	1660–1720	3020–3128
Fluorspar	1300	2372
Kaolin	1740–1785	3164–3245
Lead oxide (litharge)	880	1616
Magnesium carbonate (dissociates)	350	662
Magnesium oxide (approx.)	2800	5072
Mullite	1810	3290
Nepheline syenite	1223	2232
Nickel oxide (O$_2$)	400	752
Orthoclase feldspar (potash)	1220	2228
Potassium oxide	red heat	
Rutile	1900	3452
Silica	1715	3119
Silicon carbide (decomposed)	2200	3992
Sillimanite	1816	3301
Sodium oxide	red heat	
Tin oxide	1130	2066
Titanium oxide	1900	3452
Whiting (dissociates)	825	1517
Zircon	2550	4622

Glaze
and
Stain Recipes

In the past ceramic glaze formulas were discussed with much secrecy. Fortunately, this attitude has changed. What is done with a glaze is much more important than how it is made. It is hoped that the reference tables in this text will allow more time to be spent on actual studio projects.

Regardless of the variety of glazes and decorative devices described, the student should not be too impressed by technique. Many of the finest potters use only a few standard glazes and stains and a minimum of decoration. Techniques are important and should be studied, but they should never overshadow the search for ideas.

The list of glazes in this section will supplement the general discussion of glaze types and the function of the various glaze chemicals (Chap. 9, pp. 231–241). For convenience, the glazes are listed in the form of batch recipes. Because of variations in local chemicals, firing procedures, and so forth, adjustments may have to be made to some of these recipes. Temperatures given are for large-size cones.

Low-fire Lead[a] and Alkaline Glazes

	Cones 05–03, Lithium blue		Cones 08–09, Chromium red
27.0	Lithium carbonate	70.04	Red lead
14.1	Kaolin	18.80	Flint
55.9	Flint	2.13	Soda ash
3.0	Bentonite	9.03	Kaolin
4.0	Copper carbonate	5.00	Potassium bichromate
	Cones 04–02, Barium mat glaze		Cones 04–02, Alumina mat
6.4	Whiting	48.0	White lead
41.6	White lead	12.0	Whiting
21.0	Potash feldspar	21.8	Potash feldspar
12.5	Barium carbonate	13.7	Calcined kaolin
6.7	Calcined kaolin	4.1	Kaolin
11.8	Flint		

[a] In substituting red for white lead, approximately 11 ½ percent less material is needed for the same PbO.

Low-fire Lead and Alkaline Glazes—*continued*

Cone 04, Lithium semiopaque (from K. Green)

18.5	Lithium carbonate
17.6	White lead
8.2	Bone ash
6.0	Soda feldspar
10.7	Kaolin
37.1	Flint
1.9	Bentonite

Cone 04, Semigloss rutile (from K. Green)

66.00	White lead
5.03	Plastic vitrox
15.68	Kaolin
13.29	Flint
5.70	Rutile

Cone 04, Semimat (very fluid)

64.0	White lead
18.3	Potash feldspar
1.4	Kaolin
2.7	Calcined kaolin
1.6	Whiting
12.0	Borax
5.0	Rutile

Cone 04, Lead-borax turquoise, fluid

12.0	Whiting
26.0	Borax
1.5	Soda ash
19.5	White lead
27.5	Potash feldspar
13.0	Flint
0.5	Kaolin
10.5	Tin oxide
2.8	Copper carbonate

Cone 04, Colemanite crackle glaze

33.5	Potash feldspar
41.5	Colemanite
14.0	Barium carbonate
11.0	Flint

Cone 04, Burnt-red glaze

48.2	White lead
7.3	Whiting
11.5	Kaolin
3.0	Zinc oxide
30.0	Flint
6.0	Tin oxide
4.0	Red iron oxide

Cone 04, Volcanic-ash mat (from A. Garzio)

22.7	Colemanite
5.8	Whiting
3.0	Barium carbonate
7.0	White lead
5.0	Borax
30.0	Volcanic ash
20.0	Kaolin
3.5	Zinc oxide
6.8	Tin oxide

Cone 04, Volcanic ash

60	Volcanic ash
20	Colemanite
10	White lead
10	Borax

Medium-fire Glazes, Cone 2

Cones 1–2, Clear glaze

52.60	White lead
15.70	Soda feldspar
3.36	Whiting
2.84	Zinc oxide
9.90	Flint
15.60	Cornwall stone
0.2	Gum tragacanth

Cone 2, Glaze

32.7	Feldspar
8.8	Whiting
26.8	Red lead
5.7	Kaolin
5.8	Ball clay
20.2	Flint

Cone 2, Plastic vitrox

29.0	White lead
16.7	Potash feldspar
44.3	Plastic vitrox
10.0	Whiting

Cone 2, Colemanite

8.20	Calcined zinc oxide
38.50	Potash feldspar
17.55	Colemanite
6.80	Barium carbonate
6.45	Steatite (talc)
22.50	Flint

Medium-fire Glazes, Cone 6

Cone 6, Barium blue

55.5	Potash feldspar
41.5	Barium carbonate
3.0	Zinc oxide
2.0	Copper carbonate
1.0	Methocel or gum

Cone 6, Ash

38	Wood ashes
20	Potash feldspar
20	Whiting
13	Talc
9	Kaolin

Cone 6, Mat

63.6	Potash feldspar
18.3	Whiting
9.1	Kaolin
4.5	Talc
4.5	Zinc oxide

Cone 6, Mat

46.15	Nepheline syenite
17.70	Kaolin
10.60	Talc
3.55	Whiting
18.45	Flint
3.55	Zinc oxide

Porcelain and Stoneware Glazes, Cone 8

Cone 8, Semimat

36.5	Potash feldspar
25.7	Kaolin
17.5	Whiting
12.0	Flint
8.2	Rutile

Cone 8, Feldspar

11.5	Soda feldspar
12.0	Whiting
7.3	Kaolin
36.2	Flint

Cone 8, Lepidolite (crackle glaze)

18.8	Lepidolite
43.4	Potash feldspar
6.3	Cryolite
6.3	Bone ash
12.6	Whiting
12.6	Colemanite

Cones 7–8, Semimat volcanic-ash glaze (from A. Garzio)

26.7	Volcanic ash
7.5	Colemanite
19.7	Nepheline syenite
6.1	Whiting
7.5	Magnesium carbonate
7.2	Kaolin
5.3	Flint

Porcelain and Stoneware Glazes, Cones 8-13

Cones 9–10, White mat (from R. Eckels)

43.0	Feldspar, potash
18.3	Whiting
11.2	Flint
22.8	Kaolin
4.7	Zinc oxide
3.0	Rutile
2.0	Tin oxide

Cones 8–11, White opaque

45.35	Feldspar (potash)
12.85	Kaolin (Florida)
17.50	Whiting
1.45	Borax
20.50	Flint
2.35	Zinc oxide
30.20	Zircopax

Cones 10–13 (from A. Garzio)

53.8	Feldspar (potash)
19.2	Whiting
19.2	Ball clay
4.6	Kaolin
3.2	Zinc oxide

Cones 10–12, Mat

40.0	Feldspar (potash)
22.3	Whiting
21.0	Kaolin
16.7	Silica
4.4	Titanium oxide

Crystalline Glazes

Cones 07–05, Aventurine

45.7	Borax
2.6	Borium carbonate
3.3	Boric acid
1.7	Kaolin
46.7	Flint
17.7	Red iron oxide

(Grind and use immediately or frit without the clay.)

Cones 03–04, Aventurine

94	Ferro frit #3304
19	Red iron oxide
6	Kaolin (Florida)

Cones 3–4, Zinc crystal

13.4	Soda ash
15.5	Boric acid
22.2	Zinc oxide
42.8	Flint
6.1	Ball clay
6.7	Rutile

(Grind and use immediately or frit without the clay.)

Cone 8, Zinc crystal (pale green)

11.6	Sodium carbonate
6.6	Whiting
18.2	Kaolin (Florida)
42.2	Silica
21.4	Zinc oxide
3.1	Copper carbonate
5.3	Titanium (rutile)

(Grind and use immediately or frit without the clay.)

Cone 11, Zinc crystal

45.5	Feldspar
15.9	Whiting
15.9	Flint
22.7	Zinc oxide

Cone 11, Titanium crystal

25	Soda ash
50	Flint
25	Zinc oxide
10	Titanium oxide

Cones 9–10, Zinc crystal (from M. Hansen)

74	Pemco frit #283	
21.5	Zinc oxide	
4.5	Flint	
1.0	Bentonite	

#1
plus MnO_2 5 percent
$CuCO_3$ 5 percent
Rutile 4 percent

#2
$CuCO_3$ 3 percent
Rutile 5 percent

#3
NiO 1 percent
$CuCO_3$ 3 percent

Reduction Glazes

Cone 04, Celadon

20.5	White lead
1.6	Whiting
52.5	Godfrey spar (soda)
25.4	Soda ash
1.5	Red iron oxide
2.5	Tin oxide

(Grind dry, use immediately if wet. Fire: reduction, cone 012–07; oxidizing, cone 07–04.)

Cone 2, Local copper-red reduction (from Harder)

34.00	Soda feldspar
28.40	Borax
0.75	Soda ash
6.60	Fluorspar
12.45	Kaolin
17.80	Flint
2.00	Tin oxide
0.50	Copper carbonate [plus .5 percent silicon carbide (180 mesh carborundum)]

Cone 6, Copper-red reduction (from Curtis)

11.8	White lead
11.8	Red lead
5.9	Whiting
2.9	Kaolin
29.4	Flint
29.4	Borax
4.4	Boric acid
4.4	Soda ash
1.7	Tin oxide
0.5	Copper oxide

Cone 04, Copper luster

66.3	White lead
24.5	Cornwall stone
9.2	Flint
1.94	Cobalt oxide
1.15	Copper oxide
9.6	Manganese oxide

(Black when thin, copper when thick. Fire: reduction cone 012–07; oxidizing cone 07–04.)

Cone 8, Copper-red reduction

27.9	Cornwall stone
32.5	Flint
4.0	Zinc oxide
9.3	Barium carbonate
4.3	Soda ash
22.0	Borax
2.0	Copper carbonate
2.0	Tin oxide

Cones 6–8, Celadon reduction

62.2	Potash feldspar
7.6	Whiting
5.0	Kaolin
25.2	Flint
1.5	Red iron oxide

Cones 8–10, Celadon

79.5	Feldspar (potash)
6.2	Whiting
14.3	Flint
2.0	Red iron oxide

Reduction Glazes—*continued*

Cone 8, Local copper reduction (from Baggs)		*Cones 9–10, Copper red*	
32.8	Soda feldspar	13.0	Ferro frit #3191
1.9	Soda ash	44.0	Feldspar (soda)
28.0	Borax	14.0	Whiting
7.3	Whiting	3.0	Kaolin (Florida)
12.3	Kaolin	25.0	Flint
17.7	Flint	1.0	Tin oxide
1.8	Tin oxide	0.2	Copper carbonate
0.3	Copper carbonate		(Add .2 silicon carbide for local reduction.)
0.65	Silicon carbide		

Ceramic Stains[a]

(For preparation, see Chap. 9)

#1 Pink stain		*#2 Pink stain*	
50	Tin oxide	50.5	Tin oxide
25	Whiting	19.0	Whiting
18	Flint	7.5	Fluorspar
4	Borax	20.5	Flint
3	Potassium dichromate	7.5	Potassium dichromate

(Calcine to cone 8; stain is lumpy and must first be broken up in iron mortar, then ground.)

(Calcine to cone 8 and grind.)

#3 Crimson stain		*#4 Ultramarine stain*	
22.9	Whiting	50	Chromium oxide
6.6	Calcium sulfate	12	Flint
4.4	Fluorspar	38	Cobalt oxide (CoO, cobaltous)
20.8	Flint		(Calcine to cone 8 and grind.)
43.7	Tin oxide		
1.6	Potassium dichromate		

(Calcine to cone 8 and grind.)

[a] These stains must be finely ground to obtain the desired color.

Ceramic Stains—*continued*

#5 Blue-green stain

41.8	Cobalt oxide (CoO)
19.3	Chromium oxide
39.0	Aluminium oxide

(Calcine to cone 8 and grind.)

#6 Orange stain

29.8	Antimony oxide
12.8	Tin oxide
14.9	Red iron oxide
42.5	Red lead

(Calcine to cone 6 and grind.)

#7 Black stain

43	Chromium oxide
43	Red iron oxide
10	Manganese dioxide
4	Cobalt oxide

(Calcine to cone 8 and grind.)

#8 Turquoise stain

56	Copper phosphate
44	Tin oxide

(Calcine to cone 6 and grind.)

#9 Red-brown stain

22	Chromium oxide
23	Red iron oxide
55	Zinc oxide

(Calcine to cone 8 and grind.)

#10 Brown stain

64.6	Zinc oxide
9.7	Chrome oxide
9.7	Red iron oxide
8.0	Red lead
8.0	Boric acid

(Calcine to cone 8 and grind.)

#11 Yellow stain

33.3	Antimony oxide
50.0	Red lead
16.7	Tin oxide

(Calcine to cone 6 and grind.)

#12 Black stain

65	Chromium oxide
35	Red iron oxide

(Calcine to cone 8 and grind.)

Clay Bodies

The clay body preferred by the studio potter is quite different from that used by a commercial pottery. For slip casting or jiggering a uniformity of texture is necessary, for obvious technical reasons. Similarly, any impurities imparting color to the body are undesirable. Therefore, bodies used in commercial production are carefully selected, ground, and refined. Plasticity is of minor importance, and, since it is associated with high shrinkage rates, it is avoided.

Local supplies of earthenware and plastic fire-clays are available in the United States, particularly in the Midwest. Since they are widely used in cement, plaster, and mortar mixtures, they are competitively priced and generally quite reasonable.

Because the volume of clay used in the school studio will normally be between one and five tons per year, both the initial cost and the shipping charges are important. Thus, clay that can be bought locally has a decided advantage, even if it needs a certain amount of sieving or small additions. Occasionally, a truckload of raw clay can be purchased reasonably from a local brick or tile works.

Earthenware bodies present no real problem of supply in the Midwest, since there are many brick and tile factories which also sell bagged clay. Shale clays with coarse particles will cause trouble unless they are run through a sieve of from 15 to 20 meshes per inch. Some earthenware clays contain soluble sulfates, which will form a whitish scum on the fired ware; however, the addition of ¼ to 2 percent barium will eliminate this fault. Many such clays will not be very plastic unless they are aged. Adding about 5 percent bentonite, which is extremely plastic, will usually render a short clay workable. Often two clays that alone are not suitable can be mixed together to form a good body. Only experimentation will indicate the necessary changes.

Occasionally, the body will lack sufficient flint to fuse with the fluxes it contains. Cream-colored clays can be rendered more plastic by the addition of ball clays. Talc has some plasticity and is often used in low-fire white ware bodies as a source of both flux and silica. Feldspar, nepheline syenite, and plastic vitrox are also added to various bodies to contribute fluxing qualities.

Stoneware and porcelain bodies are usually compounded from several ingredients. In fact, it is quite rare for a single clay to satisfy all throwing and firing requirements. There is no clay that, by itself, will make a porcelain body. Oriental porcelain is made from one or two claylike minerals which are fairly plastic. Since nothing in the Western world compares with petuntze, porcelain bodies must be compounded from clay and various minerals.

Both stoneware and porcelain will form hard, vitrified bodies at cone 10. The major difference between the two is that stoneware contains some impurities, chiefly iron, which give it a gray or tan color. Both stoneware and porcelain bodies are compounded for varying temperatures and, in the case of porcelain, for different degrees of translucency. Greater translucency is usually obtained by increasing the feldspar ratio, which has the accompanying disadvantage of an increase in warpage when the ware is fired.

Fireclay and stoneware clays differ from pure clay (kaolin) chiefly in that they contain various

Suggested Clay and Porcelain Bodies

Cone 2, Light red clay body

60	Red clay
25	Flint
15	Kaolin

Cone 2, Cream clay body

43	Ball clay
7	Kaolin
25	Soda feldspar
18	Flint
7	Red clay

Cones 2–8, Stoneware body

20	Jordan clay or Monmouth
25	Ball clay
30	Plastic fireclay
10	Nepheline syenite
5	Flint
12	Grog (fine size for wheel work)

Cones 8–10, Stoneware body

32	Jordan or Monmouth
32	Fire clay
18	Grog (fine, 60-mesh)
18	Flint

Cone 8, Stoneware body

40	Ball clay
40	Fireclay
20	Earthenware (for color and texture)

Cones 8–10, Porcelain body

45	Kaolin
25	Feldspar (potash)
16	Ball clay
14	Flint

Cones 8–12, Porcelain body

27	Ball clay
27	Kaolin
27	Feldspar (potash)
19	Flint

Cones 10–15, Porcelain body

25	Ball clay
25	Kaolin
25	Feldspar (potash)
25	Flint

fluxes and impurities which lower the fusion point and impart a gray, tan, or buff color.

The familiar crocks and old-fashioned jugs that we occasionally still see were made of stoneware clays. Since manufacturers today want completely white bodies, not many items are made of stoneware. Therefore, local sources of stoneware clays may be scarce, and transportation costs may be excessive. Fireclays, which have a more universal industrial use, can be substituted for stoneware. Some fireclays are very plastic and fine enough for throwing. They often contain some iron impurities, which give the body a flecked appearance. Depending upon the firing temperature and the effect desired, it may be necessary to blend in an earthenware or stoneware clay or ingredients such as feldspar, talc, or silica.

The table on page 322 lists several types of clay and porcelain bodies. They are included merely as suggestions, since it usually will be necessary to vary these recipes depending upon the raw materials available locally.

Engobes are essentially clay slips, with the significant difference that some engobes are intended for use on either dry or bisque ware, thus necessitating additions of flint, feldspar, and occasionally a flux to the slip in order to adjust the varying shrinkage rates. The general purpose of an engobe is to provide a smoother surface and usually a different-colored base for glaze or brushed decoration.

If the engobe is to be used on a damp piece, a sieved slip of the throwing body can be used, provided the color is not objectionable. The usual colorants can be added, except for the chrome oxides, which react unfavorably with tin. One percent of a strong oxide, such as cobalt, is sufficient, although from 5 to 7 percent of iron or vanadium may be needed. Blistering will result if over 7 percent manganese is used. Five percent of an opacifier is often needed to lighten the color.

Engobes used on leather-hard ware must be adjusted to reduce shrinkage by calcining part of the clay and by additions of flint and feldspar. On dry ware the clay content of the engobe can rarely be more than 40 percent, with the balance composed of flint and feldspar. A 5-percent addition of borax will toughen the surface and aid adhesion.

When used on bisque ware, an engobe must have a clay content of less than 25 percent, or it will shrink excessively and flake off the pot. Furthermore, it must contain sufficient fluxes to fuse with the bisque surface. Its characteristics resemble those of an underfired glaze. In view of the low clay content, a binder may be necessary.

Too thick an application of an engobe on any surface, whether leather-hard clay or bisque ware, will crack or flake off. On the other hand, a thin coating will allow the body color to show through. In addition to the usual finely ground coloring oxides, one may add coarsely ground ores, ilmenite, rust chips, chopped copper scouring pads, and other materials to the engobe. Such additions melt out into the covering glaze with interesting effects that are limited to the area of the applied engobe.

Schedule of Representative Equipment Prices *

	From	To
electric kiln, top loading, cone 8, chamber 17 × 17 × 17″	$ 300	$ 350
electric kiln, front loading, cones 8–10, chamber 17 × 17 × 17″	450	600
gas kiln, updraft, high fire, chamber 24 × 24 × 36″	1,400	1,600
gas kiln, updraft, high fire, capacity 24 cubic feet	2,500	3,000
gas kiln, updraft muffle, high fire, chamber 29 × 24 × 30″	2,000	2,500
gas kiln, downdraft, high fire, capacity 30 cubic feet	3,000	3,500
gas car kiln, capacity 20–30 cubic feet	4,000	4,500
pyrometer	35	50
kick wheel	115	350
electric wheel	250	600
clay mixer, pug mill	700	1,200
mortar and pestle	3	10
ball mill	100	150
ball mill jars	15	75
sieves	5	15
glaze sprayer	60	75
spray booth	75	85
gram scales	20	45
decorating wheels	14	25
shop lift	250	300
ware rack	75	100

* Prices of heavy equipment are F.O.B. city of manufacture.

Sources of Materials and Equipment

The cost of materials is an important factor in developing a school or college ceramics program, especially if it is to be paid out of the general budget for the course. A rough estimate of the amount per student per semester is $10 to $15, depending upon shipping costs, which may be considerable. For advanced students, who produce more pottery, the price is even higher. In addition, the firing charges, which may also be applied to the departmental budget, must be considered. Replacement of kiln shelves is another continuing expense.

A businesslike approach to the problem of purchasing materials will do much to keep the costs as low as possible. The smaller figure of $10 per student reflects the saving possible by purchasing in quantity. Supplies bought from a hobby-shop dealer will cost much more than $10 per student.

The price of clay, which seems so cheap by the pound, can be deceiving, for an enormous amount is consumed in the studio classroom. For most types of clay the shipping fees are greater than the cost of the clay itself. Of course, local clays can be dug, but the trouble and labor of processing them may make this solution undesirable. Fortunately, clay is commonly used in mortar and cement, so it is available from most building-supplies dealers in 50-pound bags, usually priced at about $1.00 per bag. These clays are generally shale earthenware, which requires sieving. Often bentonite or flint or talc must be added to render the shale clay suitable for throwing, but even so these clays represent considerable savings. Many fireclays can be procured from local dealers, who sell them for repairing furnaces or industrial ovens. With minor modifications these fireclays can be converted into satisfactory stoneware bodies.

Coloring oxides, which are used sparingly, can be purchased in small quantities. However, even a small ceramics department should buy the more common chemicals—lead, flint, borax, and the feldspars—in 100-pound lots. They may not be used up during a single semester, but the saving is so great that the larger purchase is warranted.

When ordering materials it is occasionally advisable to buy a few bulky but cheap items, so that the shipment can be sent by freight or motor truck, thus avoiding the expensive parcel-post rate.

SUPPLY DEALERS

East Coast

CLAYS

Hammill & Gillespie, Inc.
O. W. Ketcham Architectural Tile Co.
Langley Ceramic Studio
Mandl Ceramic Supply Co.
Newton Pottery Supply Co.
Pottery Arts Supply Co.
Roder Ceramic Studio
Rowantree Pottery
Stewart Clay Co.
United Clay Mines
Jack D. Wolfe, Inc.

KILNS

W. H. Fairchild (electric)
L. & L. Manufacturing Co. (electric)
Roder Ceramic Studio (electric)
Unique Kilns (gas and electric)

KILN BURNERS

Flynn Burner Corp. (gas)
Hauck Mfg. Co. (oil)
Johnson Gas Appliance Co. (gas)

MISCELLANEOUS EQUIPMENT

Craftools, Inc.
B. F. Drakenfeld, Inc.
Roder Ceramic Studio
Walker Jamar Co.

CERAMIC CHEMICALS

Ceramic Color & Chemical Mfg. Co.
B. F. Drakenfeld
Gare Ceramic Supply Co.
Ernest Hanzlicek (volcanic ash)
Langley Ceramic Studio
Newton Pottery Supply Co.
Standard Ceramic Supply Co.
Whittaker, Clark and Daniels, Inc.

POTTER'S WHEELS

Clay Art Center (electric)
Craftools, Inc. (kick and electric)
Randall Wheel (kick & electric)
Standard Ceramic Supply Co.

FRITS

Ferro Corp.
Pemco Corp.

REFRACTORY MATERIALS

Armstrong Cork Co.
Babcock and Wilcox Co.
A. P. Green Fire Brick Co.
Johns-Manville Co.
New Castle Refractories
Remey Refractories

Midwest and South

CLAYS

Cedar Heights Clay Co.
Christy Firebrick Co.
General Refractories Co.
A. P. Green Fire Brick Co.
Hammill & Gillespie, Inc.
V. R. Hood, Jr.
Kentucky-Tennessee Clay Co. (ball)
La Mo Refractory Supply Co.
Spinks Clay Co.
Trinity Ceramic Supply Co.
Western Stoneware Co. (Monmouth)
Zanesville Stoneware Co.

KILNS

Allied Engineering Corp. (gas)
American Art Clay Co. (electric)
DFC Corporation (gas and electric)
Harrop Ceramic Service Co. (electric)
Paragon Industries, Inc. (electric)

KILN BURNERS

DFC Corporation (gas)
Flynn Burner Corp. (gas)
Hauck Mfg. Co. (oil)
Johnson Gas Appliance Co. (gas)

CERAMIC CHEMICALS

Ceramic Color & Chemical Mfg. Co.
George Fetzer
General Color and Chemical Co.
Ernst Hanzlicek (volcanic ash)
Harshaw Chemical Co.
Illini Ceramic Service
Kraft Chemical Co.
Minnesota Clay Co.
Trinity Ceramic Supply Co.

FRITS

Ferro Corp.
Harshaw Chemical Co.

POTTER'S WHEELS

American Art Clay Co. (kick and electric)
H. B. Klopfenstein & Sons (kick)
Nils Lou (electric)
Oak Hill Industries Inc. (kick)
Randall Wheel (kick and electric)
Denton M. Vars (Leach wheel)

MISCELLANEOUS EQUIPMENT

American Art Clay Co.
Archie Bray Foundation (decorating wax)
Big Joe Mfg. Co.
De Vilbiss Co. (spray equipment)
Illini Ceramic Service
Minnesota Clay Co.
Tepping Ceramic Supply Co.
U.S. Stoneware Co. (ball mills)

REFRACTORY MATERIALS

A. P. Green Fire Brick Co.
Johns-Manville Corp.
La Mo Refractory Supply Co.
New Castle Refractories
Walsh Refractories Corp.

West and Pacific Coast

CLAYS

L. H. Butcher Co.
Cannon Co.
Denver Fire Clay Co.
Garden City Clay Co.
Hy-Land Mfg. & Supply Co.
Interpace Corp.
Spinks Clay Co.
Van Howe Co.
S. Paul Ward, Inc.
Western Ceramic Supply Co.
Westwood Ceramic Supply Co.

KILNS

A. D. Alpine, Inc. (gas and electric)
J. J. Cress Co. (electric)
Denver Fire Clay Co. (gas and oil)
E. W. Mendall (gas)
Nordstrom Kiln Co. (gas)
Skutt & Sons (electric)
West Coast Kiln Co. (gas)

CERAMIC CHEMICALS

Braun Corp.
L. H. Butcher Co.
Hy-Land Mfg. & Supply Co.
Leslie Ceramic Supply Co.
Van Howe Co.
S. Paul Ward, Inc.
Western Ceramic Supply Co.
Westwood Ceramic Supply Co.

POTTER'S WHEELS

A. D. Alpine, Inc. (electric)
Robert Brent (kick & electric)
Denver Fire Clay Co. (electric)
Oscar-Paul Corp. (electric)
Shimpo-West (electric)
Skutt & Sons (electric)
Paul Soldner (kick and electric)

REFRACTORY MATERIALS

B. & B. Refractories
Interpace Corp.
Pyro-Engineering

MISCELLANEOUS EQUIPMENT

L. H. Butcher Co.
Van Howe Co.
S. Paul Ward, Inc.
Westwood Ceramic Supply Co.

ADDRESSES OF LISTED DEALERS

Allied Engineering Corp. (division of Ferro Corp.), 4150 E. 56 St., Cleveland, Ohio 44105

A. D. Alpine, Inc., 353 Coral Circle, El Segundo, Calif. 90245

American Art Clay Co., 4717 W. 16 St., Indianapolis, Ind. 46222

Armstrong Cork Co., Lancaster, Pa. 17604

Babcock and Wilcox Co., 161 E. 42 St., New York, N.Y. 10017

Big Joe Mfg. Co., 7225 M. Kostner Ave., Chicago, Ill. 60646

B. & B. Refractories Corp., 11927 Rivira Rd., Santa Fe Springs, Calif. 90670

Archie Bray Foundation, P.O. Box 344, Helena, Mont. 59601

Braun Corporation, 13635 Bonnie Beach, Los Angeles, Calif. 90054

Robert Brent, 1101 Cedar St., Santa Monica, Calif. 90405

L. H. Butcher Co., 15 & Vermont Sts., San Francisco, Calif. 94107

Cannon & Co., Box 802, Sacramento, Calif. 95804

Cedar Heights Clay Co., 50 Portsmouth Rd., Oak Hill, Ohio 45656

Ceramic Color and Chemical Mfg. Co., P. O. Box 297, New Brighton, Pa. 15066

J. J. Cress Co., Inc., 1718 Floradale Ave. S., El Monte, Calif. 91733

Christy Firebrick Co., 3144 N. Broadway, St. Louis, Mo. 63147

Clay Art Center, 40 Beech St., Port Chester, N.Y. 10573

Craftools, Inc., 1 Industrial Rd., Woodridge, N.J. 07075

DFC Corporation, P. O. Box 5507, Denver, Colo. 80217

De Vilbiss Co., 300 Phillips Ave., Toledo, Ohio 43601

B. F. Drakenfeld, Inc., Washington, Pa. 15301

W. H. Fairchild, 712 Centre St., Freeland, Pa. 18224

Ferro Corp., 4150 E. 56 St., Cleveland, Ohio 44105

George Fetzer, 1205 17 Ave., Columbus, Ohio 43211

Flynn Burner Corp., 425 Fifth Ave., New Rochelle, N.Y. 10802

Garden City Clay Co., Redwood City, Calif. 94064

Gare Ceramic Supply Co., 165 Rosemont St., Haverhill, Mass. 01830

General Color and Chemical Co., P. O. Box 7, Minerva, Ohio 44657

General Refractories Co., 7640 Chicago Ave., Detroit, Mich. 48204

A. P. Green Fire Brick Co., Mexico, Mo. 65265

Hammill & Gillespie, Inc., 225 Broadway, New York, N.Y. 10007

Ernest Hanzlicek, Wilson, Kan. 67490

Harshaw Chemical Co., 1945 E. 97 St., Cleveland, Ohio 44106

Harrop Ceramic Service Co., 35 E. Gay St., Columbus, Ohio 43215

Hauck Mfg. Co., P. O. Box 26, Westchester, Ill. 60153

O. Hommel Co., P.O. Box 475, Pittsburgh, Pa. 15230

V. R. Hood, Jr., Box 1213, San Antonio, Tex. 78206

Hy-Land Mfg. & Supply Co., 4990 E. Asbury St., Denver, Colo. 80222

Illini Ceramic Service, 439 N. Wells St., Chicago, Ill. 60610

Interpace Corp., 2901 Los Feliz Blvd., Los Angeles, Calif. 90039

Johns-Manville Co., 22 E. 40 St., New York, N.Y. 10016

Johnson Gas Appliance Co., Cedar Rapids, Iowa 52405

Kentucky-Tennessee Clay Co., Mayfield, Ky. 42066

O. W. Ketcham Architectural Tile Co., 125 N. 18 St., Philadelphia, Pa. 19103

H. B. Klopfenstein & Sons, Rt. 2, Crestline, Ohio 44827

Kraft Chemical Co., 917 W. 18 St., Chicago, Ill. 60608

L & L Mfg. Co., Box 348, Twin Oaks, Pa. 19104

La Mo Refractory Supply Co., 323 Iris Ave., New Orleans, La. 70121

Langley Ceramic Studio, 413 S. 24 St., Philadelphia, Pa. 19146

Leslie Ceramic Supply Co., 1212 San Pablo Ave., Berkley, Calif. 94706

Nils Lous, 1501 Asbury Rd., St. Paul, Minn. 55108

Mandl Ceramic Supply Co., RR 1, Box 369A, Pennington, N.J. 08534

L. W. Mendall, 12330 E. Rush St., El Monte, Calif. 91733

Minnesota Clay Co., 2310 E. 38 St., Minneapolis, Minn. 55406

Newton Pottery Supply Co., Newton, Mass. 01432

Nordstrom Kiln Co., 9046 Garvey, S. San Gabriel, Calif. 91777

Oscar-Paul Corp., 522 W. 182 St., Gardena, Calif. 92247

Oak Hill Industries, RR 4, Davenport, Iowa 52804

Paragon Industries, Inc., Box 10133, Dallas, Tex. 75207

Pemco Corp., 5601 Eastern Ave., Baltimore, Md. 21224

Pottery Arts Supply Co., 2554 Greenmount Ave., Baltimore, Md. 21218

Pyro Engineering Corp., 200 S. Palm Ave., Alhambra, Calif.

Randall Wheel, Box 774, Alfred, N.Y. 14802

Remey Refractories, Hedley and Delaware Aves., Philadelphia, Pa. 19137

Roder Ceramic Studio, 500 Broadway, Clifton Heights, Pa. 19018

Rowantree Pottery, Blue Hill, Maine 04614

Shimpo-West, P.O. Box 2315, La Puente, Calif. 91746

Shutt & Sons, 2618 S.E. Steele St., Portland, Ore. 97202

Paul Soldner, Box 917, Aspen, Colo. 81611

Spinks Clay Co., Box 829, Parris, Tenn. 38242; or Box 578 Wrightwood, Calif. 92397

Standard Ceramic Supply Co., P. O. Box 4435, Pittsburgh, Pa. 15205

Stewart Clay Co., 133 Mulberry St., New York, N.Y 10013

Tepping Ceramic Supply Co., 3517 Riverside Dr., Dayton, Ohio 45405

Trinity Ceramic Supply Co., 9016 Diplomacy Row, Dallas, Tex. 75235

Unique Kilns, 530 Spruce St., Trenton, N.J. 08638

United Clay Mines Corp., Trenton, N.J. 08606

U. S. Stoneware Co., Akron, Ohio 44309

Van Howe Co., 1185 S. Cherokee Ave., Denver, Colo. 80223; and 4216 Edith N.E., Albuquerque, N.M. 87107

Denton M. Vars, 825 West Minnehaha Ave., St. Paul, Minn. 55104

Walker Jamar Co., 365 S. First Ave., E. Duluth, Minn. 55802

Walsh Refractories, 101 Ferry St., St. Louis, Mo. 63147

S. Paul Ward, Inc., 601 Mission St., South Pasadena, Calif. 91030

West Coast Kiln Co., 635 Vineland Ave., La Puente, Calif. 91746

Western Ceramic Supply Co., 1601 Howard St., San Francisco, Calif. 94103

Western Stoneware Co., Monmouth, Ill. 61462

Westwood Ceramic Supply Co., 14400 Lomitas Ave., City of Industry, Calif. 91744

Whittaker, Clark, and Daniels, Inc., 100 Church St., New York, N.Y. 10017

Jack D. Wolfe Co., Inc., 724 Meeker Ave., Brooklyn, N.Y. 11222

Zanesville Stoneware Co., Zanesville, Ohio 43701

SOURCES OF MATERIALS AND EQUIPMENT IN CANADA

CLAYS

A. P. Green Firebrick Co., Rosemount Ave., Weston, Ont.

Baroid of Canada, Ltd., 5108 Eighth Ave., S.W., Calgary, Alta.

Jean Cartier, 1029 Bleury St., Montreal, P.Q.

Clayburn Harbison, Ltd., 1690 W. Broadway, Vancouver, B.C.

Magcobac Mining Co., 510 Fifth St., S.W., Calgary, Alta.

Mercedes Ceramic Supply, 8 Wallace St., Woodbridge, Ont.

Pembena Mountain Clay, 945 Logan, Winnipeg, Man.

Pottery Supply House, 491 Wildwood Rd., P.O. Box 192, Oakville, Ont.

Saskatchewan Clay Products, P.O. Box 970, Estevan, Sask.

GLAZE MATERIALS

Barrett Co., Ltd., 1155 Dorchester Blvd., W. Montreal 2, P.Q.

Blyth Colors, Ltd., Toronto, Ont.

Greater Toronto Ceramic Center, 167 Lakeshore Rd., Toronto 14, Ont.

E. Harris & Co. of Toronto, Ltd., 73 King St., East Toronto, Ont.

Lewiscraft Supply House, 28 King St., West Toronto, Ont.

Mercedes Cermic Supply, 8 Wallace St., Woodbridge, Ont.

Pottery Supply House, 491 Wildwood Rd., P.O. Box 192, Oakville, Ont.

KILNS

Ferro Enamels, 26 Davis Rd., P.O. Box 370, Oakville, Ont.

Hurley Bennett, 1497 Pierre Ave., Windsor, Ont.

Mercedes Ceramic Supply, 8 Wallace St., Woodbridge, Ont.

Pottery Supply House, 491 Wildwood Rd., P.O. Box 192, Oakville, Ont.

POTTER'S WHEELS

Hurley Bennett, 1497 Pierre Ave., Windsor, Ont.

Mercedes Ceramic Supply, 8 Wallace St., Woodbridge, Ont.

Pottery Supply House, 491 Wildwood Rd., P.O. Box 192, Oakville, Ont.

C.W. Ride, North Hatley, P.Q.

W. H. Williams, 144 Westwood Ave., Hamilton, Ont.

SOURCES OF MATERIALS AND EQUIPMENT IN ENGLAND

CLAYS

English China Clay Ltd., 18 High Cross St., St. Austell, Cornwall

Fulham Pottery, London, S.W. 6

Pike Bros., Wareham, Dorset

Potclays, Ltd., Wharf House, Copeland St., Hanley, Stoke-on-Trent

Price Bros., Burslem, Stoke-on-Trent

Watts Blake & Bearn Ltd., Newton Abbot, Devon

GLAZE MATERIALS

Blythe Color Works, Ltd., Cresswell, Stoke-on-Trent

E. W. Good & Co., Ltd., Barker St., Longton, Stoke-on Trent

George Goodwin & Son, Ltd., Westwood Mills, Lichfield St., Hanley, Stoke-on-Trent

W. Podmore & Sons, Ltd., Caledonian Mills, Shelton, Stoke-on-Trent

Reeves & Sons, Ltd., Enfield, Middlesex

Wengers Ltd., Etruria, Stoke-on-Trent

ELECTRIC KILNS

Applied Heat Co., Ltd., Elecfurn Works, Otterspool Way, Watford-by-Pass, Watford, Herts.

British Ceramic Service Co., Ltd., Park Ave., Wolstanton, Newcastle, Staffs.

Cromartie Kilns, Dividy Road, Longton, Staffs.

Kilns & Furnaces Ltd., Keele St. Works, Tunstall, Stoke-on Trent

GAS KILNS

Dowson & Mason Gas Plant Co., Ltd., Alma Works, Levenshulme, Manchester 19

Bernard W. E. Webber Ltd., Alfred St., Fenton, Stoke-on-Trent

POTTER'S WHEELS

Corbic, Gomshall, Surrey

Judson & Hudson Ltd., Keighley, Yorks.

Potters Equipment Co., 73/77, Britannia Rd., London, S.W. 6

Alec Tiranti Ltd., 72 Charlotte St., London, W. 1

Bernard W. E. Webber Ltd., Alfred St., Fenton, Stoke-on-Trent

MISCELLANEOUS EQUIPMENT

Fulham Pottery, London, S.W. 6

Fred Nettleship, 84 New College Close, Gorliston, Norfolk (cane handles)

Oxshott Pottery, Potters Craft, Oakshade Rd., Oxshott, Surrey (plans, kilns, wheels)

References

REFERENCES FOR THE STUDENT POTTER

Leach, Bernard. *A Potter's Book.* London: Faber and Faber, 1940. Leach is perhaps the best-known independent studio potter today, and he has written an extremely readable book. From the creative point of view, it cannot be recommended too highly. Illustrated.

Norton, F. H. *Ceramics for the Artist Potter.* Reading, Mass.: Addison-Wesley, 1956. Norton covers the entire range of ceramics from the forming processes to the chemistry of glazes, with numerous illustrations.

Rhodes, Daniel. *Clay and Glazes for the Potter.* Philadelphia: Chilton, 1957. An extremely clear treatment of clays, glazes, and calculations.

————. *Kilns.* Philadelphia: Chilton, 1968. The most complete book on kilns available.

————. *Stoneware and Porcelain.* Philadelphia: Chilton, 1959. A companion book to *Clay and Glazes for the Potter.* In addition to a discussion of stoneware and porcelain, the book contains much useful studio information. Well illustrated.

Sanders, Herbert H. *The World of Japanese Ceramics.* Palo Alto, Calif: Kodansha International, 1967. A very informative and beautifully illustrated volume.

SUPPLEMENTAL TEXTS

Andrews, A. T. *Ceramic Tests and Calculations.* New York: Wiley, 1928. A standard text for ceramic glaze, clay, and frit calculations.

Billington, Dora M. *The Technique of Pottery.* London: B. T. Batsford, 1962. A very readable and complete ceramic text by an experienced English potter and teacher.

Casson, Michael. *Pottery in Britain Today.* New York: Transatlantic Press, 1967. Fine photographs, very short text.

Eley, Vincent. *A Monk at the Potter's.* Leicester, Eng.: Ward, 1952. This interesting account of a young monk who decided to start a pottery at his monastery contains some very practical information.

Green, David. *Pottery, Materials and Techniques.* New York: Praeger, 1967. This text is particularly oriented toward materials available in England, but it is of interest to all students.

Hettes, Karel, and Rada Pravoslav. *Modern Ceramics.* London: Drury House, 1965. A survey of contemporary ceramics throughout the world, with a short text and many color illustrations.

Hetherington, A. L. *Chinese Ceramic Glazes*. Los Angeles: Commonwealth Press, 1948. A small, very readable volume, dealing primarily with Sung iron and copper glazes.

Home, Ruth M. *Ceramics for the Potter*. Peoria, Ill.: Bennett, 1953. This volume contains some very useful information about clays and glazes from both the historical and the contemporary viewpoint. There is also a section on native Canadian clays.

Koenig, J. H., and W. H. Earhart. *Literature Abstracts of Ceramic Glazes*. Ellenton, Fla.: College Institute, 1951. A series of condensations—with formulas—of all important articles about glazes appearing in American trade magazines, ceramic society publications, and British, German, and other foreign journals.

Leach, Bernard. *A Potter in Japan*. London: Faber and Faber, 1960. An account of Leach's return to Japan, his visits with potter friends from his early years in that country.

Norton, F. H. *Elements of Ceramics*. Reading, Mass.: Addison Wesley, 1952. An introductory text for ceramic engineers, containing technical information about minerals, clays, and glazes, plus various commercial refining and production processes.

Parmelee, Cullen W. *Ceramic Glazes*. Chicago: Industrial Publications, 1951. A very complete and comprehensive text on ceramic glaze materials, slips, glazes, chemical reactions, and glaze calculations.

Rosenthal, Ernst. *Pottery and Ceramics*. Harmondsworth, Eng.: Pelican, 1949. A complete survey of the ceramic field, primarily from an industrial viewpoint.

Wildenhain, Marguerite. *Pottery, Form and Expression*. New York: American Craftsmen's Council, 1959. This beautifully illustrated book by one of America's foremost potters contains a moving expression of the art of living, as well as the art of ceramics.

MAGAZINES AND PROFESSIONAL JOURNALS

Ceramic Data Book, Industrial Publications, 5 S. Wabash Avenue, Chicago, Ill. 60603. Published annually, covering supplies, manufacturers, and equipment.

Ceramics Monthly, 4175 N. High Street, Columbus, Ohio 43214. Oriented toward the amateur; many useful articles.

Craft Horizons, 16 East 52 Street, New York, N.Y. 10022. Covering all craft fields, with many articles dealing with contemporary American and foreign ceramics. Well illustrated.

Design Quarterly, Walker Art Center, 1710 Lyndale Avenue S., Minneapolis, Minn. 55403. A well-illustrated periodical covering contemporary design, often ceramics.

Journal of the American Ceramic Society, Columbus, Ohio. Technical articles, usually slanted toward industrial ceramics but occasionally of interest to the studio potter.

FOREIGN PUBLICATIONS

Dansk Kunstaandvaerk, Palaegade 4, Copenhagen, Denmark. Covers the entire Danish design field; well illustrated. Many sections are in English.

Designed in Finland, Finnish Foreign Trade Association, E. Esplanaadik 18, Helsinki. Illustrated booklet on Finnish design published each year, with English text.

Domus, via Monte di Pieta 15, Milan, Italy. Covers the decorative arts fields, emphasizing architecture; beautifully illustrated.

Form, Svenska Slöjdföreningen, Nybrogatan 7, Stockholm, Sweden. This journal of the Swedish Design Society covers all design fields; well illustrated. Contains a short English section.

Kontur, Svenska Slojdforeningen, Nybrogatan 7, Stockholm, Sweden. Beautifully illustrated booklet published once a year on Swedish design and crafts. Text in English.

Kunst + Handwerk, Arnold-Heise Str. 23, Hamburg 20, Germany. Industrial design and handcrafts in Germany and Europe. Well illustrated, German text.

La Ceramica, via F. Corridoni 3, Milan, Italy. Although an industrial publication, many articles concern studio potters and sculptors. English summary very short.

Pottery Quarterly, Northfields, Tring, Herts, England. A variety of articles, both historical and contemporary, as well as critiques. Well illustrated.

Pottery in Australia, 30 Turramurra Avenue, Turramurra, N.S.W. Biannual journal of the Potters' Society, well illustrated.

Vrienden van de Nederlandse Ceramik, Paulus Potterstraat, Amsterdam—Z 1. Illustrated journal of the Dutch ceramic society. English summary.

SELECTED HISTORICAL BIBLIOGRAPHY

General Texts

Charleston, Robert J. *World Ceramics*. New York: McGraw-Hill, 1968.

Cox, Warren E. *The Book of Pottery and Porcelain.* New York: Crown, 1944.

Savage, George. *Porcelain Through the Ages.* Baltimore: Penguin, 1954.

Ancient, Mediterranean, and Classical Ceramics

Alexion, Styliaros, Nickolaos Platon, and Hanni Gunanella. *Ancient Crete.* New York: Praeger, 1968.

Arias, P. E. *Greek Vase Painting.* New York: Abrams, 1961.

Boardman, John. *Pre-Classical, from Crete to Archaic Greek.* Baltimore: Penguin, 1967.

Chamoux, François. *Greek Art.* Geenwich, Conn.: New York Graphic, 1966.

Childe, Gordon. *What Happened in History.* Baltimore: Penguin, 1962.

Demargne, Pierre. *The Birth of Greek Art.* New York: Golden Press, 1964.

Hutchinson, R. W. *Prehistoric Crete.* Baltimore: Penguin, 1962.

Martinatos, Spyridon. *Crete and Mycenae.* New York: Abrams, 1960.

Noble, Joseph Veach. *The Techniques of Painted Attic Pottery.* New York: Watson-Guptill, 1965.

Petrie, Flinders. *The Making of Egypt.* London: Sheldon Press, 1939.

Platon, Nickolaos. *Crete.* Cleveland, Ohio: World Publishing, 1966.

Raphael, Max. *Civilization in Egypt.* New York: Pantheon, 1947.

————. *Prehistoric Pottery.* New York: Pantheon, 1947.

Richardson, Emeline Hill. *The Etruscans.* Chicago: University of Chicago Press, 1964.

Swedish Institute in Rome. *Etruscan Culture.* New York: Columbia University Press, 1962.

Far Eastern Ceramics

Beurdeley, Michel. *The Chinese Collector Through the Centuries.* Rutland, Vt: Tuttle, 1966.

Griffing, Robert P. *The Art of the Korean Potter.* New York: Asia Society, 1968.

Hazashiza, Seizo, and Gakuji Hasebe. *Chinese Ceramics.* Rutland, Vt.: Tuttle, 1966.

Honey, William Bowyer. *The Ceramic Art of China.* London: Faber and Faber, 1944.

Kidder, J. Edward. *The Birth of Japanese Art.* New York: Praeger, 1964.

Kim, Chewon. *Korean Art,* Vol. II, *Ceramics.* Seoul: Ministry of Foreign Affairs, 1961.

Kim, Chewon and Won-Yong. *Treasures of Korean Art.* New York: Abrams, 1966.

Koyama, Fugio, and John Figgess. *Two Thousand Years of Oriental Ceramics.* New York: Abrams, 1960.

Leach, Bernard. *Kenzan and His Tradition.* London: Faber and Faber, 1966.

Miki, Fumio. *Haniwa.* Rutland, Vt.: Tuttle, 1960.

Munsterberg, Hugo. *The Ceramic Art of Japan.* Rutland, Vt.: Tuttle, 1964.

Prodan, Mario. *The Art of the T'ang Potter.* London: Thames and Hudson, 1960.

Islamic, Hispano-Moresque, and African Ceramics

Davidson, Basil. *The Lost Cities of Africa.* Boston: Little, Brown, 1959.

Frothingham, Alice Wilson. *Lusterware of Spain.* New York: Hispanic Society of America, 1951.

Lane, Arthur. *Early Islamic Pottery.* New York: Van Nostrand, 1948.

————. *Later Islamic Pottery.* London: Faber and Faber, 1957.

Leuzinger, Elsy. *Africa.* New York: Crown, 1960.

Meauzé, Pierre. *African Art.* Cleveland: World Publishing, 1967.

Wassing, René S. *African Art.* New York: Abrams, 1968.

Wilkinson, Charles K. *Iranian Ceramics.* New York: Abrams, 1963.

Wilson, Ralph Pinder. *Islamic Art.* New York: Macmillan, 1957.

Medieval through 19th-century European Ceramics

Honey, William B. *European Ceramic Art.* London: Faber and Faber, 1949.

Liverani, Giuseppe. *Five Centuries of Italian Majolica.* New York: McGraw-Hill, 1960.

Rackham, Bernard. *Medieval English Pottery.* New York: Van Nostrand, 1949.

Vydrova, Jirina. *Italian Majolica.* London: Spring House, 1960.

Pre-Columbian and Colonial American Ceramics

Anton, Ferdinand, and Frederick J. Dockstader. *Pre-Columbian Art.* New York: Abrams, 1968.

Bushnell, G. H. S. *Ancient Arts of the Americas.* New York: Praeger, 1965.

Disselhoff, H. D., and S. Linne. *The Art of Ancient America.* New York: Crown, 1960.

Dockstader, Frederick, J. *Indian Art in South America.* Greenwich, Conn., New York Graphic, 1967.

Haberland, Wolfgang. *The Art of North America.* New York: Crown, 1964.

Kubler, George. *The Art and Architecture of Ancient America.* Baltimore: Penguin, 1962.

Ramsay, John. *American Potters and Pottery.* New York: Tudor, 1947.

Spargo, John. *Early American Pottery and China.* New York: Century Library of American Antiques, 1926.

Willey, Gordon, R. *An Introduction to American Archaeology.* Englewood Cliffs, N. J., Prentice-Hall, 1966.

Glossary
of Ceramic
Terms

See Chapter 9
for more complete coverage of ceramic chemicals

absorbency The ability of a material (clay, plaster of paris, and so forth) to soak up water.

acid One of three types of chemicals that constitute a glaze, the other two being the bases and the intermediates or neutrals. The acid group is symbolized by the radical RO_2. The most important acid is silica (SiO_2).

Albany slip A natural clay containing sufficient fluxes to melt and function as a glaze. It develops a dark brown-black glaze at cones 8 to 10 without any additions. Since it is mined in several localities in the vicinity of Albany, N. Y., its composition may vary slightly from time to time. Similar clays, found in various sections of the United States, were much used by early American stoneware potteries.

alkali Generally, the base compounds of sodium and potassium but also the alkaline earth compounds lime and magnesia. They function as fluxes, combining easily with silica at relatively low temperatures.

alumina (Al_2O_3) A major ingredient found in all clays and glazes. It is the chief oxide in the neutral group (R_2O_3) and imparts greater strength and higher firing temperatures to the body and glaze. When added to a glaze, it will assist in the formation of mat textures, inhibit devitrification, and increase the viscosity of the glaze during firing.

ash Generally, the ashes of trees, straw, leaves, and so forth. It is commonly used in the Far East to provide from 40 to 60 percent of high-temperature glaze ingredients. Depending upon the type, it will contain from 40 to 75 percent silica, from 5 to 15 percent alumina, and smaller amounts of iron, phosphorus, lime, potash, and magnesia.

aventurine A glaze composed of a soda, lead, or boric oxide flux often with an excess of iron oxide (more than 6 percent). If it is cooled slowly, iron crystals will form, and these crystals will sparkle and glisten beneath the surface of the glaze.

bag wall A baffle wall in a kiln, separating the chamber from the combustion area.

ball clay An extremely fine-grained, plastic, sedimentary clay. Although ball clay contains much organic matter, it fires white or near white in color. It is usually added to porcelain and white-ware bodies to increase plasticity.

ball mill A porcelain jar filled with flint pebbles and rotated with either a wet or dry charge of chemicals. It is used to blend and to grind glaze and body ingredients.

333

barium carbonate ($BaCO_3$) Used in combination with other fluxes to form mats in the low-temperature range. A very small percentage (¼ to 2) added to a clay body will prevent discoloration caused by soluble sulphates, such as the whitish blotches often seen on red bricks and earthenware bodies.

basalt ware A hard, black, unglazed stoneware body developed about 1775 by the Wedgwood potteries in England in an effort to imitate classical wares.

bat A disk or slab of plaster of paris on which pottery is formed or dried. It is also used to remove excess moisture from plastic clay.

batch Raw chemicals comprising a ceramic glaze that have been weighed out in a specific proportion designed to melt at a predetermined temperature.

bentonite An extremely plastic clay, formed by decomposed volcanic ash and glass, which is used to render short clays workable and to aid glaze suspensions.

binders Various materials; gums, polyvinyl alcohol, methylcellulose used to increase glaze adherence or to impart strength to a cast or pressed clay body.

bisque or biscuit Unglazed ware.

bisque fire Preliminary firing to harden the body, usually at about cone 010, prior to glazing and subsequent glaze firing.

bistone Coarse crushed quartz used in saggers to support thin procelain in the bisque.

blowing The bursting of pots in a kiln caused by a too-rapid temperature rise. The water content of the clay turns into steam and forces the body to expand and explode.

blunger A mixing machine with revolving paddles used to prepare large quantities of clay slip or glazes.

bone china A hard, translucent china ware produced chiefly in England. The body contains a large amount of bone ash (calcium phosphate), which allows it to mature at cone 6 (2232°F). It is not very plastic and is therefore difficult to form; it also tends to warp.

calcine To heat a ceramic material or mixture to the temperature necessary to drive off the chemical water, carbon dioxide, and other volatile gases. Some fusion may occur, in which case the material must be ground. This is the process used in the production of plaster of paris, Portland cement, and ceramic stains.

casting (or slip casting) A reproductive process of forming clay objects by pouring a clay slip into a hollow plaster mold and allowing it to remain long enough for a layer of clay to thicken on the mold wall. After hardening, the clay object is removed.

chemical water Water (H_2O) chemically combined in the glaze and body compounds. At approximately 450°C (842°F) during the firing cycle this water will begin to leave the body and glaze as water vapor. Little shrinkage occurs at this point, although there is a loss in weight.

china A loosely applied term referring to white-ware bodies fired at low porcelain temperatures. They are generally vitreous, with an absorbency of less than 2 percent, and may be translucent.

china clay *See* kaolin.

clay A decomposed granite-type rock. To be classed as a clay the decomposed rock must have fine particles so that it will be plastic. Clays should be free of vegetable matter but will often contain other impurities, which affect their color and firing temperatures. They are classified into various types, such as ball clays, fireclays, and slip clays. Pure clay is expressed chemically as $Al_2O_3 \cdot 2SiO_2 \cdot 2H_2O$.

coefficient of expansion The ratio of change between the length of a material mass and the temperature.

coiling A hand method of forming pottery by building up the walls with ropelike rolls of clay and then smoothing over the joints.

combing A method of decoration developed by dragging a coarse comb or tip of a feather over two contrasting layers of wet clay slip or glaze.

Cornwall stone (also Cornish stone) A feldsparlike material found in England and widely used there for porcelain-type bodies and glazes. Compared to American feldspar, it contains more silica and a smaller amount, though a greater variety, of fluxes. It comes closest to approximating the Chinese *petuntze*, which is a major ingredient of Orient porcelain bodies and glazes.

crackle glaze. A glaze containing minute cracks in the surface. The cracks are decorative and are often accentuated by coloring matter that is rubbed in. They are caused in cooling by the different rates at which the body and the glaze contract after firing.

crawling Separation of the glaze coating during firing, which exposes areas of unglazed clay caused by too heavy application. The glaze cracks upon drying or from uneven contraction rates between glaze and body.

crazing An undesirable and excessive crackle in the glaze, which penetrates through the glaze to the clay body. It should be remedied by adjusting the glaze or body composition to obtain a more uniform contraction ratio.

crocus martis Purple red oxide of iron, used as a red-brown glaze colorant.

crystal glazes Glazes characterized by crystalline clusters of various shapes and colors embedded in a more uniform and opaque glaze. The crystals are larger than in aventurine and may on occasion cover the entire surface. The glaze ingredients generally used are iron, lime, zinc, or rutile with an alkaline flux, high silica, and low alumina ratio. A slow cooling cycle is necessary for the development of the crystals.

cupric and **cuprous oxides** Copper oxides (CuO, Cu_2O), the major green colorants. They will also produce red under reducing conditions, with an alkaline flux.

damp box A lined metal cabinet in which unfinished clay objects are stored to prevent them from drying.

deflocculant Sodium carbonate or sodium silicate used in a casting slip to reduce the amount of water necessary and to maintain a better suspension.

Delft ware A light-colored pottery body covered with a lead-tin glaze, with overglaze decoration in cobalt on the unfired glaze. Delft was first made in Holland in imitation of Chinese blue-and-white porcelain.

della Robbia ware Ceramic sculpture of glazed terra cotta, generally in relief, produced in Florence by Lucca della Robbia or his family during the fifteenth century. The glaze used was the lead-tin majolica type developed in Spain.

dipping Glazing pottery by immersing it in a large pan or vat of glaze.

dryfoot To clean the bottom of a glazed piece before firing.

dunting Cracking of fired ware in a cooling kiln, the result of opening the flues and cooling too rapidly.

earthenware Low-fire pottery (below 2000°F), usually red or tan in color with an absorbency of from 5 to 20 percent.

eggshell porcelain Translucent, thin-walled porcelain.

empirical formula A glaze formula expressed in molecular propositions.

engobe A prepared slip that is halfway between a glaze and a clay; contains clay, feldspar, flint, a flux, plus colorants. May be used on bisque ware.

equivalent weight A weight that will yield one unit of a component (RO or R_2O_3 or RO_2 in a compound). This is usually the same as the molecular weight of the chemical compound in question. In ceramic calculations, equivalent weights are also assigned to the RO, R_2O_3 and the RO_2 oxide groups that make up the compound. If one of these oxide groups contains more than one unit of the oxide, its equivalent weight would be found by dividing the compound molecular weight by this unit number. (*See* Chap. 9.)

eutectic The lowest melting point of the mixture of materials composing the glaze. This is always lower than the melting points of the individual materials.

faience Earthenware covered with a lead-tin glaze; a French term for earthenware derived from the Italian pottery center at Faenza, which, during the Renaissance, produced this ware partially in imitation of Spanish majolica. (*See* also majolica and Delft ware.)

fat clay A plastic clay such as ball clay.

ferric and **ferrous oxides** (Fe_2O_3 and FeO) Red and black iron oxide. As impurities in clay, they lower the firing temperature. They are the chief source of tan and brown ceramic colors and, under reducing conditions, the various celadon greens (*see* reduction).

fire box Combustion chamber of a gas, oil, or wood-fired kiln, usually directly below the kiln chamber.

fireclay A clay having a slightly higher percentage of fluxes than pure clay (kaolin). It fires tan or gray in color and is used in the manufacture of refractory materials, such as bricks, muffles, and so forth for industrial glass and steel furnaces. It is often quite plastic and may be used by the studio potter as an ingredient of stoneware bodies.

flues Passageways around the kiln chamber through which the heating gases pass from the firebox to the chimney.

flux Lowest-melting compound in a glaze, such as lead, borax, soda ash, or lime, and including the potash or soda contained in the feldspar. The flux combines easily with silica and thereby helps higher-melting alumina-silica compounds eventually to form a glass.

foot The ringlike base of a ceramic piece, usually heavier than the surrounding body.

frit A partial or complete glaze that is melted and then reground for the purpose of eliminating the toxic effects of lead or the solubility of borax, soda ash, and so forth.

frit china A glossy, partly translucent chinaware produced by adding a glass frit to the body.

galena Lead sulphide, used as a flux for earthenware glazes, more common in Europe than in the United States.

glaze A liquid suspension of finely ground minerals that is applied by brushing, pouring, or spraying on the surface of bisque-fired ceramic ware. After drying the ware is fired to the temperature at which the glaze ingredients will melt together to form a glassy surface coating.

glaze fire A firing cycle to the temperature at which the glaze materials will melt to form a glasslike surface coating. This is usually at the point of maximum body maturity, and it is considerably higher than the bisque fire. However, delicate porcelain, subject to warping, is often fired high in the bisque with a lower glaze fire. To prevent warping in the high bisque fire, the ware is placed upside down on its rim or with protective disks on the lips. Some pieces may be embedded in a layer of flint sand.

glost fire An older term for a glaze firing.

greenware Pottery that has not been bisque fired.

grog Hard fired clay that has been crushed or ground to various particle sizes. It is used to reduce shrinkage in such ceramic products as sculpture and architectural terra-cotta tiles, which, because of their thickness, have drying and shrinkage problems. From 20 to 40 percent grog may be used, depending upon the amount of detail desired and whether the pieces are free standing or pressed in molds.

gum arabic or **gum tragacanth** Natural gums used in glazes as binders to promote better glaze adherence to the body. Binders are necessary for fritted glazes containing little or no raw clay. They are also useful when a bisque fire accidentally goes too high, or in reglazing. The gum, of course, burns out completely during the fire.

hard paste True porcelain that is fired to cone 12 or above (2420°F); also called *hard porcelain*.

ilmenite ($TiO_2 \cdot FeO$) An important source of titanium. In the granular form it is used to give dark flecks to the glaze. It is often sprinkled upon the wet glaze without previous mixing.

iron oxide *See* ferric oxide.

jiggering, jollying An industrial method of producing pottery. A slab of soft clay is placed upon a revolving plaster mold of the object to be formed. As the wheel head turns, a metal template on a moving arm trims off the excess clay and forms the reverse side of the piece.

kanthal A special metal alloy produced in Sweden for wire or strip elements in electric kilns firing from 2000° to 2400°F.

kaolin $Al_2O_3 \cdot 2SiO_2 \cdot 2H_2O$) Pure clay, also known as china clay. It is used in glaze and porcelain bodies and fires to a pure white. Sedimentary kaolins found in Florida are more plastic than the residual types found in the Carolinas and Georgia.

kiln A furnace made of refractory clay materials for firing ceramic products.

kiln furniture Refractory shelves and posts upon which ceramic ware is placed while being fired in the kiln.

kiln wash A protective coating of refractory materials applied to the surface of the shelves and the kiln floor to prevent excess glaze from fusing the ware to the shelves. An inexpensive and effective wash can be made from equal parts of flint and kaolin.

kneading Working clay with the fingers or the heel of the hand in order to obtain a uniform consistency.

lead White lead [basic lead carbonates, $2PbCO_3 \cdot Pb(OH)_2$], red lead (Pb_3O_4), and galena (lead sulphide, PbS) are among the most common low-fire fluxes.

leather hard The condition of the raw ware when most of the moisture has left the body but when it is still soft enough to be carved or burnished easily.

limestone A major flux in the medium- and high-fire temperature ranges when it is powdered in the form of whiting (calcium cabonate). If a coarse sand is used as a grog, it should not contain limestone particles. Calcined lime will expand in the bisque and cause portions of the body to pop out.

luster A type of metallic decoration thought to have been discovered in Egypt and further developed in Persia during the ninth and fourteenth centuries. A mixture of a metallic salt, resin, and bismuth nitrate is applied to a glazed piece and then refired at a lower temperature. The temperature, however, must be sufficient to melt the metal and leave a thin layer on the decorated portions.

luting A method of joining together two pieces of dry or leather-hard clay with a slip.

majolica Earthenware covered with a soft tin-lead glaze, often with a luster decoration. The ware originally came from Spain and derived its name from the island of Majorca, which lay on the trade route to Italy. Faenza ware was greatly influenced by these Spanish imports. All Renaissance pottery of this type is now generally called majolica ware.

mat glaze A dull-surfaced glaze with no gloss but pleasant to the touch, not to be confused with an incomplete fired glaze. Mat surfaces can be developed by the addition of barium carbonate or alumina, and a slow cooling cycle.

maturity The temperature or time at which a clay or clay body develops the desirable characteristics of maximum nonporosity and hardness; or the point at which the glaze ingredients enter into complete fusion, developing a strong bond with the body, a stable structure, maximum resistance to abrasion, and a pleasant surface texture.

mold A form or box, usually made of plaster of paris, containing a hollow negative shape. The positive form is made by pouring either wet plaster or slip into this hollow. (*See* casting.)

muffle A lining, made of refractory materials, forming the kiln chamber, around which the hot gases pass from the firebox to the chimney. The purpose is to protect the ware from the direct flames of the fire and the resulting combustion impurities. Some of these panels may be removed for a redution fire.

muffle kiln A kiln with muffle features in contrast to a kiln using saggars. (*See* saggars.)

mullite Interlocking needlelike crystals of aluminum silicate ($3Al_2O_3 \cdot 2SiO_2$) which begin to form in high-temperature bodies between 1850° and 2200°F. This formation is responsible for much of the greater toughness and hardness of stoneware and porcelain, and in particular for the closer union developed between the glaze and the body.

neutral fire A fire that is neither oxidizing nor reducing. Actually this can be obtained only in practice by a slight alternation between oxidation and reduction.

opacifier A chemical whose crystals are relatively insoluble in the glaze, thereby preventing light from penetrating the glass formation. The color most sought is white, although for some purposes others may be as effective. Tin oxide is by far the best opacifier. Zirconium and titanium oxides are also used. Many other oxides are effective in certain combinations and within limited firing ranges. These are commercially available in frit forms under trade names, such as Zircopax, Opax, and Ultrox.

overglaze Decoration applied with overglaze colors on the glaze and fired ware. The third firing of the overglaze ware is at a lower temperature than the glaze fire.

overglaze colors Colors containing coloring oxides or ceramic stains, a flux, and some type of binder. The fluxes are necessary to allow the colors to melt into the harder glaze to which they are applied. The lower temperatures at which most underglazes are fired (about cone 016–013) allow the use of colorants that are unstable at higher temperatures.

oxidizing fire A fire during which the kiln chamber retains an ample supply of oxygen. This means that the combustion in the firebox must be perfectly adjusted. An electric kiln always gives an oxidizing fire.

paste The compounded bodies of European-type porcelains.

peach bloom A Chinese copper-red reduction glaze with a peachlike pink color.

peeling Separation of the glaze or slip from the body. Peeling may be caused when slip is applied to a body that is too dry, or when a glaze is applied too thickly or to a dusty surface.

peep hole A hole placed in the firebox, kiln chamber, or muffle flues of a kiln, through which one can observe the cones or the process of combustion.

petuntze A partially decomposed feldspar-type rock found in China, roughly similar in composition to Cornwall stone. With kaolin it forms the body of Oriental porcelains.

plaster of paris Hydrate of calcium sulphate, made by calcining gypsum. It hardens after being mixed with water. Because it absorbs moisture and it can be cut and shaped easily, it is used in ceramics for drying and throwing bats, as well as for molds and casting work.

plasticity The quality of clay that allows it to be manipulated and still maintain its shape without cracking or sagging.

porcelain (Chinese) A hard, nonabsorbent clay body, white or gray in color, that rings when struck.

porcelain (hard) A hard, nonabsorbent clay body that is white and translucent. In both types of hard porcelain the bisque is low fired and the glaze is very high (generally cone 14–16).

pottery Earthenware; a shop in which ceramic objects are made.

pressing Forming of clay objects by pressing soft clay between two plaster molds, such as in the production of cup handles.

pug mill A machine for mixing plastic clay.

pyrometer An instrument for measuring heat at high temperatures. It consists of a calibrated dial connected to wires made of two different alloys, the welded tips of which protrude into the kiln chamber. When heated, this welded junction sets up a minute electrical current, which registers on the indicating dial.

pyrometric cones Small triangular cones ($1^1/_8$ and $2^5/_8$ inches in height) made of ceramic materials that are compounded to bend and melt at specific temperatures, thus enabling the potter to determine when the firing is complete.

quartz Flint or silica (SiO_2).

raku A soft, lead-glazed, hand-built groggy earthenware made in Japan and associated with the tea ceremony. Raku ware is unique in that the glazed preheated bisque is placed in the red-hot kiln with long-handled tongs. The glaze matures in 15 to 30 minutes, and the ware is then withdrawn.

reducing agent Glaze or body material such as silicon carbide, which combines with oxygen to form carbon monoxide during the firing.

reduction fire A firing using insufficient oxygen; carbon monoxide thus formed unites with oxygen from the body and glaze to form carbon dioxide, producing color changes in coloring oxides.

refractory The quality of resisting the effects of high temperatures; also materials, high in alumina and silica, that are used for making kiln insulation, muffles, and kiln furniture.

rib A tool of wood, bone, or metal that is held in the hand while throwing to assist in shaping the pot or to compact the clay.

RO, R_2O_3, RO_2 The symbols or radicals for the three major groups of chemicals that make up a ceramic glaze. The RO radical refers to the base chemicals, such as the oxides of sodium, potassium, calcium, and lead which function in the glaze as fluxing agents. The R_2O_3 radical refers to the intermediate or amphoteric oxides, some of which may on occasion function either as bases or acids. The chief oxide of interest in this group is alumina (Al_2O_3), which always reacts as a refractory. The third radical RO_2 stands for the acid group, the glass formers, such as silica (SiO_2).

rouge flambé A type of Chinese copper-red reduction glaze (*sang de bœuf*) which is a mottled deep red with green and blue hues, also called a transmutation glaze.

rutile An impure form of titanium dioxide (TiO_2) containing much iron. It will give a light yellow or tan color to the glaze, with a streaked and runny effect. Used in large amounts it will raise the maturing temperature.

saggars Round boxlike containers of fireclay used in kilns lacking muffles. The glazed ware is placed in saggars to protect the glaze from the combustion gases.

salt glaze A glaze developed by throwing salt (NaCl) into a hot kiln. The salt vaporizes and combines with the silica in the body to form sodium silicate, a hard glassy glaze. A salt kiln is of a slightly different construction and is limited in use to the salt glaze.

sang de bœuf The French term for oxblood, which describes the rich, deep-red hues produced by the Chinese in their copper-red reduction glazes.

sgraffito Decoration achieved by scratching through a colored slip to show the contrasting body color beneath.

shard A broken fragment of pottery.

short A body or clay lacking in plasticity.

shrinkage Contraction of the clay in either drying or firing. In the firing cycle the major body shrinkage for stoneware clays begins at approximately 900°C (1652°F). Earthenware clays will begin to fuse and shrink at slightly lower temperatures.

siccative Agent for drying the oils used in underglaze decoration.

silica Flint (SiO_2) produced in the United States by grinding almost pure flint sand.

silicate of soda A deflocculant. A standard solution of sodium silicate (commercial N brand) has the ratio of 1 part soda to 3.3 parts silica. Specific gravity 1.395.

single fire A firing cycle in which the normal bisque and glaze firings are combined. The advantages are a great saving of fuel and labor, and development of a stronger bond between the body and the glaze. These are partially offset by the need for greater care in handling the ware, plus the danger of cracking if in glazing the raw pieces absorb too much moisture. In a salt glaze, however, these disadvantages do not occur.

sintering A firing process in which ceramic compounds fuse sufficiently to form a solid mass upon cooling but are not vitrified. An example is low-fire earthenware.

slip A clay in liquid suspension.

slip clay A clay such as Albany and Michigan containing sufficient fluxes to function as a glaze with little or no additions.

spinel Chemically, magnesium aluminate ($MgAl_2O_3$), an extremely hard crystal arranged in an octahedron atomic structure. In ceramics, a spinel is a crystal used as a colorant in place of the metallic oxides because of its greater resistance to change by either the fluxing action of the glaze or the effects of high temperatures.

spray booth A boxlike booth equipped with a ventilating fan to remove spray dust, which, whether toxic or not, is harmful.

spraying Applying glazes with a compressed-air spray machine, the chief commercial method.

sprigging Applying clay in a plastic state to form a relief decoration.

stain Sometimes a single coloring oxide, but usually a combination of oxides, plus alumina, flint, and a fluxing compound. This mixture is calcined and then finely ground and washed. The purpose is to form a stable coloring agent not likely to be altered by the action of the glaze or heat. While stains are employed as glaze colorants, their chief use is as overglaze and underglaze decorations and body colorants.

stilt A ceramic tripod upon which glazed ware is placed in the kiln. Tripods with nickel-nichrome wire points are often used to minimize blemishes to the glaze. They are never used for high-fire porcelain, which must be dry footed for greater support.

stoneware A high-fire ware (above cone 8) with slight or no absorbency. It is usually gray in color but may be tan or slightly reddish. Stoneware is similar in many respects to porcelain, the chief difference being the color, which is the result of iron and other impurities in the clay.

stoneware clays Clays more plastic than a porcelain body, firing above cone 8 to a gray color.

talc ($3MgO \cdot 4SiO_2 \cdot H_2O$) A compound used in most white-ware bodies in the low to moderate firing ranges as a source of silica and flux. It is slightly plastic and can be used to lower the firing range, if need be, of a stoneware or fireclay body.

terra cotta An earthenware body, generally red in color and containing grog. It is the common body type used for ceramic sculpture.

terra sigillata The red slip glaze of the Romans, similar to the Etruscan *bucchero* and Greek *black varnish*. It was made of fine decanted particles of red clay, and was normally oxidized to form a red body.

throwing Forming pottery of plastic clay on a potter's wheel.

tin enamel A term used incorrectly by many older historians to describe the tin-lead majolica type glaze. An enamel is a very low-fire glaze used as an over-glaze decoration. It was extensively used by the Turks and the late Ming and Ch'ing potters.

tin-vanadium stain A major yellow colorant produced by a calcined mixture of tin and vanadium oxides.

trailing A method of decorating, using a slip trailed out from a rubber syringe.

translucency The ability of a thin porcelain or white-ware body to transmit a diffused light.

turning Trimming the walls and foot of a pot on the wheel while the clay is in a leather-hard state.

underglaze Colored decoration applied on the bisque ware before the glaze is applied.

viscosity The nonrunning quality of a glaze, caused by glaze chemicals that resist the flowing action of the glaze flux.

vitreous Pertaining to the hard, glassy, and nonabsorbent quality of a body or glaze.

volatilization Action under influence of extreme heat of the kiln in which some glaze elements turn successively from a solid to a liquid, and finally into a gaseous, state.

ware Pottery or porcelain in the raw, bisque, or glazed state.

warping Distortion of a pot in drying because of uneven wall thickness or a warm draft of air, or in firing when a kiln does not heat uniformly.

water glass Another term for a liquid solution of sodium silicate that is used as a deflocculant.

water smoking The initial phase of the firing cycle up to a dull red heat (1000° to 1100°F). Depending upon the thickness of the ware, this may take from two or three hours for thin pottery, to twelve hours for sculpture. The heat rise must be gradual to allow atmospheric and chemical water to escape. In some cases there will be organic impurities which will also burn out, releasing carbon monoxide.

wax resist A method of decorating pottery by brushing on a design with a hot melted wax solution or a wax emulsion. This will prevent an applied stain or glaze from adhering to the decorated portions. The wax may be applied to either the raw or bisque ware, over or between two layers of glaze.

weathering The exposure of raw clay to the action of rain, sun, and freezing weather, which breaks down the particle size and renders the clay more plastic.

wedging Kneading plastic clay with the fingers and heel of the hands in a rocking spiral motion, which forces out trapped air pockets and develops a uniform texture.

white lead [$2PbCO_3 \cdot Pb(OH)_2$] A major low-fire flux.

white ware Pottery or china ware with a white or light cream-colored body.

whiting Calcium carbonate ($CaCO_3$), similar chemically to limestone and marble; a major high-fire flux.

yellow base A glaze stain produced by a calcined mixture of red lead, antimony, and tin oxides.

Zircopax Trade name of a commercial frit used as an opacifier. It is composed primarily of zirconium oxide and silica. It is about half as strong as tin oxide, but its price is much lower regardless of the quantity used.

Index

For ceramic terms, see Glossary, pp. 333–339;
for ceramic chemicals, see pp. 228–241.
References are to page numbers, except for
color plates and black-and-white illustrations,
which are identified by figure and plate numbers.

Swedish ceramics, 104–109, Figs. 205–217; Abertius, table service, 106, Fig. 211; Berglund, wall plaque, 107, Fig. 216; Hydman-Vallien, *Bomb Number 6314*, 107, Fig. 215; Leuchovius, wall plaque, 106, Fig. 212; Lindberg, mural, 105, Fig. 208; *People Bottles*, Pl. 12, p. 125; *Ting*, 105, Fig. 207; Persson, *Line Drawings*, 107, Fig. 217; vase forms, 106, Fig. 210; Stålhane, mural, 104, Fig. 205; sculptural form, 105, Fig. 209; Sundell-Nemes, vase and plate, 107, Fig. 214; Vallien, sculptural form, 106, Fig. 213; Westman, plate, 104, Fig. 206

Syrian ceramics, 26; drug jar, 25, Fig. 44; jar, 25, Fig. 45

talc, 238–239
Takaezu, Toshiko, dish, Pl. 19, p. 211
Takemoto, Henry, in Interpace studios, 255, Fig. 443
Tanagra, 16, Fig. 31
Tarascan ceramics, 50–51
Taylor, George, in Interpace studios, 255, Fig. 443
tea ceremony, 63–67
temmoku, 10, 76, Fig. 133
temperature color scale, 309
temperature equivalents (cones), 310–311
terra sigillata, 215
throwing on the wheel, problems in, 164; techniques of, 156–158, 161–163, Figs. 321–345
tin oxide, 24, 29, 231, 239, 241
tin vanadium stain, 239
titanium oxide, 231, 239, 241
Toltec ceramics, 52–53; urn, 53, Fig. 98
Tomimoto, Kenkichi, 114; jar, 115, Fig. 238
Toussley, Jeffrey, in Interpace studios, 253, 255, Figs. 438, 443
Travis, Peter, *Cathedral*, 122, Fig. 254
Traynor, Ed, *Slab Form*, 154, Fig. 314
trimming, 165–166, Figs. 351–354
Tuckson, Margaret, casserole, 123, Fig. 259
Turkish ceramics, 26; plate, 26, Fig. 47
Turner, Robert, vase, 68, Fig. 124
Tuumi, Raija, bowl, 111, Fig. 228
Tz'u-Chou, vase, xii, Fig. 1; vase, 10, Fig. 20

underglaze colors, 243
upside-dowl wheel, 170, Fig. 363
uranium compounds, 239
Ushabti of King Seti I, 4, Fig. 6

Vallien, Bertil, sculptural form, 106, Fig. 213

Valsomakis, Panos, relief, 90, Fig. 172
vanadium compounds, 239
van der Vaart, Jan, architectural form, 80, Fig. 143
van Renssen, Kees, sculpture, 83, Fig. 152
Vasa, Olli, flasks and tumblers, 110, Fig. 227
Vasegaard, Myre, bowl, 102, Fig. 200
Venus of Willendorf, 2, Fig. 2
Villanovan ceramics, 18, Fig. 35
vitrification of clay, 143, 278–279
volcanic ash, 239, 307
Voulkos, Peter, 135, 137; covered jar, 135, Fig. 286; *Cross*, 136, Fig. 287; *Aratsa*, 136, Fig. 288

Walther, Conny, bottles, 103, Fig. 204
water of plasticity, 143; formula for, 307
wax-resist decoration, 196, Fig. 412
weathering of clay, 139–140, 143
wedging, 143, 148, Fig. 294
Wedgwood, 58
Weisman, Londa, candelabrum, 251, Fig. 436; in Bennington studios, 252, Fig. 437
Welsh, Bennett, in Pacific Stoneware studios, 257, Fig. 445
Westman, Marianne, plate, 104, Fig. 206
wheels, historical, 3; commercial, 293–295, Figs. 505–512
white lead, 8, 24, 33, 235–236
white ware, 142–143
whiting, 239
Whiting, Geoffrey, teapot, Pl. 7, p. 89
Wildenhain, Frans, 134
Wildenhain, Marguerite, 134
Winans, Mary J., in Interpace studios, 255, Fig. 443
wollastonite, 144, 239
wood ash, 8, 59
World Crafts Council, 134

Yanagi, Soetsu, 114
Yanagihara, Mutsuo, vase, 117, Fig. 243
Yasuhara, Yoshitaka, garden sculpture, 119, Fig. 248
yellow colorants, 240, 242, 320

Zapotec ceramics, 49–50; urn, 50, Fig. 90
Zauli, Carlo, sculptural relief, 87, Fig. 163; sculptural form, 89, Fig. 168
zinc oxide, 229, 239
zirconium compounds, 241
Zircopax, 241

Photographic Sources

*References are to figure numbers
unless indicated Pl. (plate).*

Aistrup, Inga, Vedbaek, Denmark, and Den Permanente, Copenhagen, 197; Alinari–Art Reference Bureau, Ancram, N.Y., 27, 34, 36, 40, 49, 59; Bach, Larry, 387; Barrows, George, New York, 87; Beaudin, J. P., and Canadian Guild of Potters, Toronto, 279; © Beata Bergström, Stockholm, 217; Boesch, Ferdinand, New York, 286; Borchi, Florence, 164, 167; Calder, Sam, Los Angeles, 355; Canadian Guild of Potters, Toronto, 264, 266–267, 270, 272–275, 277; Den Permanente, Copenhagen, 194, 198, 200–202; Department of Technical Education, New South Wales, and *Pottery in Australia*, Turramurra, N.S.W., 263; Dutch Ceramic Society, Amsterdam, 145, 147, 149–154; Elisofon, Eliot, New York, 70; Fredericton Photo, N.B., and Canadian Guild of Potters, Toronto, 265, 276, 278; Frund, J. L., and Canadian Guild of Potters, Toronto, 280; Galerie Louise Leiris, Paris, 155; Gobbels, Bernd, 177; Hicks, Alan, Portland, Ore., 511; Hirmer Fotoarchiv, Munich, 7, 9, Pl. 2; Howard, Bob, and Canadian Guild of Potters, Toronto, 269; Industrial Photo Service, Trenton, N.J., 526; Jones, Edward C., Danville, Va., 409, 414; Jorgensen, Ole H., Naestred, Denmark, and Den Permanente, Copenhagen, 203; Karlsson, Stig T., Vauxholm, Sweden, 213; King, John, New Canaan, Conn., Pl. 5; La Nory, Armour, Montreal, and Canadian Guild of Potters, Toronto, 271; Leigh, Trenton, N.J., 497, 504; Lyttle, Douglas, Kalamazoo, Mich., 501; Maspono, Oriol, Barcelona, 159; Moore, Peter, New York, 88; Nordness, Lee, Gallery, New York, 287–288; Norwegian Society of Arts and Crafts and Industrial Design, Oslo, 218–224; Olivier Pictures, Amsterdam, and Dutch Ceramic Society, Amsterdam, 146, 148; Olsson, Jan, Göteborg, 205; Pedersen, Peer, and Den Permanente, Copenhagen, 199; *Pottery in Australia,* Turramurra, N.S.W., 252, 254–258, 260–261; *Pottery Quarterly,* Herts, England, 129, 131–133, 137, 141; Quiresi, Ezio, Cremona, 163, 168; Ram, Inc., 467–470; Robert, Sten, 215; Robinson, James, and *Pottery in Australia,* Turramurra, N.S.W., 253; Slusarski, Peter A., 446–457; Sowden, Harry, Mosman, N.S.W., and *Pottery in Australia,* Turramurra, N.S.W., 262; Storr, James, Höhr-Grenzhausen, Germany, 183, 186; Stournaras, N., Athens, 32; Strizic, Mark, Australia, and *Pottery in Australia,* Turramurra, N.S.W., 259; Strüwing, Copenhagen, and Den Permanente, Copenhagen, 204; Syracuse China Corporation, 458–466, 471–476; Uht, Charles, New York, 72, 74–77, 79–86, 89, 91–95, 97–100, 102–103, 156; Title, Robert, and Canadian Guild of Potters, Toronto, 268; van den Berg, Amsterdam, and Dutch Ceramic Society, Amsterdam, 143; van Veelen, Cees, Amsterdam, and Dutch Ceramic Society, Amsterdam, 144; Vine, David, New York, 388; Wheeler, Dan W., New York, 290.

American Art
A Cultural History

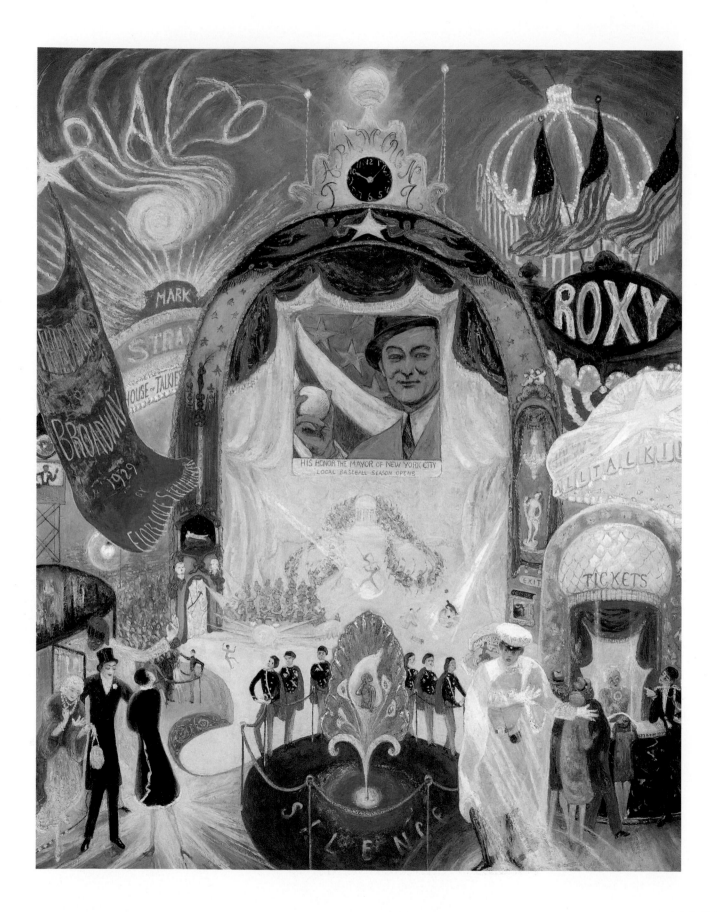

American Art
A Cultural History

Second Edition

David Bjelajac

The George Washington University

PEARSON

Prentice Hall

Prentice Hall, Inc.
Upper Saddle River, NJ 07458

Library of Congress Cataloging-in-Publication Data

Bjelajac, David.
    American art : a cultural history / David Bjelajac. -- 2nd ed.
        p. cm.
    Includes bibliographical references and index.
    ISBN 0-13-145580-X (paper) -- ISBN 0-13-145579-6 (case)
    1. Art and society--United States--History. 2. Art, American. I. Title.

N72.S6B55 2005
01'.03'0973--dc27

2004044483

Editorial Director: Charlyce Jones Owen
Editor-in-Chief: Sarah Touborg
Editorial Assistant: Sasha Anderson
Manufacturing Buyer: Sherry Lewis
Executive Marketing Manager: Sheryl Adams

Credits and acknowledgments borrowed from other sources and reproduced, with
permission, in this textbook appear on page 497.

Pearson Education LTD.
Pearson Education Australia PTY, Limited
Pearson Education Singapore, Pte. Ltd
Pearson Education North Asia Ltd

Pearson Education, Canada, Ltd
Pearson Educación de Mexico, S.A. de C.V.
Pearson Education–Japan
Pearson Education Malaysia, Pte. Ltd

This book was designed and produced by
Laurence King Publishing Ltd, London
www.laurenceking.co.uk

Senior Managing Editor: Richard Mason
Picture Researcher: Peter Kent
Design: Price Watkins Design

Front cover: John Singleton Copley, *Watson and the Shark*, 1778. Oil on canvas, 71¾ x 90½ ins
(182.2 x 229.8 cm). National Gallery of Art, Washington, D.C. Ferdinand Lammot Belin Fund.

Back cover: Simon Rodia, *Watts Towers*, Los Angeles, California, 1925–54. Photo by Julius
Schulman.

Frontispiece: Florine Stettheimer, *Cathedrals of Broadway*, 1929. Oil on canvas, 60⅛ x 50⅛ ins
(152.7 x 127.3 cm). Metropolitan Museum of Art. Gift of Ettie Stettheimer.

10 9 8 7 6 5 4 3 2 1
ISBN 0-13-145580-X

Contents

Chapter 6
Art and Commerce in the Gilded Age, 1865–1905   231

Chapter 7
Modernist Art and Politics, 1905–41   297

Chapter 8
Modernism, Postmodernism, and the Survival
of a Critical Vision, 1941–80   363

Chapter 9
Globalization and the Culture Wars, 1980–2003   437

Acknowledgments

Following publication of the first edition of this book, I received a number of
valuable comments from colleagues, students, and other thoughtful readers. I am
particularly grateful to David Cateforis for his list of corrections and constructive
suggestions for revision. I am, of course, also indebted to those reviewers of the
first edition, who took the time to write such helpful critiques, and to the
following reviewers of the present edition: Donald Harrington, University of
Arkansas; Wendy Katz, University of Nebraska, Lincoln; Christine Nelson,
Colorado State University; and Sarah K. Rich, Pennsylvania State University.
Their commentaries inspired additions for this new edition. Cynthia Mills,
Executive Editor for American Art, stimulated my thinking for the methodology
and goals of the revision, when she invited me to submit a brief article for the
journal on the process of writing an American art survey.

While writing the second edition, I received scholarly assistance from
David Morgan, Ann M. Shumard, and John Davis, and have benefited from
the work of numerous other scholars whose books and articles appear in
my revised bibliography. The editors and publishing staff at Laurence King
Publishing Ltd. have continued to provide encouragement and support. For
their contribution to the second edition, I wish to extend special thanks to
Lee Ripley Greenfield, Kara Hattersley-Smith, Richard Mason, Peter Kent, and
the designers Price Watkins.

As always, I am deeply indebted to Lou Dellaguzzo for editorial and logistical
assistance but, above all, for his sustaining friendship, patience, and enthusiasm.

David Bjelajac, March 2004

Introduction

This newly revised and expanded edition explores the diverse, conflicted history of American art and architecture within the United States from the European voyages of discovery and Colonial conquest to the first years of the new millennium. Unlike earlier surveys, my interdisciplinary narrative does not outline the stylistic evolution of American art. Drawing on socio-economic and political studies as well as histories of religion, science, literature, and popular culture, I analyze individual artworks within their specific historical contexts. I relate the visual arts of painting, sculpture, architecture, and photography to other material artifacts and cultural practices. I suggest how artists and architects, intentionally or not, composed works that visually expressed various social and political values. Similarly, it must be recognized that beholders expressed their own differing values and interests when they experienced or interpreted these same art works. In the revised chapter 8 and brand-new chapter 9, I discuss video; performance and body art; and the role of electronic, computer technology in blurring national boundaries.

Following the lead of many revisionist art historians (upon whose scholarly labors I have heavily depended), I do not explain the visual arts in terms of who influenced whom in a chain of aesthetic development that formally connects one landmark work to the next. Formalistic accounts have tended to abstractly isolate high art from the taint of politics, popular culture, and other dimensions of historical experience. Art works that once were extremely popular during the period in which they were produced, such as Hiram Powers's *The Greek Slave* (see fig. 5.65), have often been retrospectively dismissed by art historians preoccupied by the progressive advancement of American art toward more innovative, modern styles. By contrast, revisionist scholars have avoided fabricating grand stylistic schemes and patterns. They have instead preferred to analyze the popular success or failure of individual art objects by interpreting their creation and reception in historical depth from multiple cultural, political, and social viewpoints.

Readers will nonetheless encounter in this book many familiar works that have long enjoyed canonical status as masterpieces of American art. In adding images to every chapter of the revised edition, I have supplemented the material with fresh discussions of major and less familiar artworks. However, in analyzing the style and subject matter of art objects, I have not sought to endow them with supposedly transcendent aesthetic qualities beyond historical time and space. Nor do I wish to argue for the existence of a distinctively American taste for realism, neoclassicism, or some other visual style. Ever since the American Revolution, numerous artists and cultural critics have been eager to create a nationally unifying style of art. However, failed attempts to define a singular national vision demonstrate how the purported Americanness of American art and architecture has been arbitrarily constructed and reconstructed from differing aesthetic and ideological perspectives for assorted social and cultural purposes. The varied richness of visual culture in the pluralistic communities and regions of the United States has also ultimately defeated art historians' efforts to distill a characteristic national style or mode of perception from any of the arts.

The chapters that follow include generous quotations from primary sources. I wish to show how various artists and beholders from different backgrounds have interpreted specific artworks or generally talked about the cultural purposes of art. To that end, I examine contemporaneous criticism and art commentaries to demonstrate how artworks were consumed as well as produced in relation to particular political and social conditions, especially struggles over class, race, and gender.

The arrangement of chapters is both thematic and chronological. Particularly in the early chapters, there is some time overlap due to the exploration of contemporaneous cultural issues. Rather than compartmentalizing the different media in separate chapters, I have sought to thematically interrelate the arts of architecture, painting, sculpture, and photography. An integrated discussion of the visual arts makes an explanation and understanding of a number of cultural phenomena that much easier. For instance, the rural cemetery movement of the nineteenth century brought together historical-revival architecture and neoclassical sculpture, at the same time inspiring paintings and photographs of grave monuments and picturesquely landscaped grounds. Earlier in the text, the consideration of Colonial art and architecture as a means of religious expression is facilitated by an examination of different worship spaces and of media ranging from paintings and gravestones to samplers, boundary markers, and book illustrations. New material on Art Deco design and the Harlem Renaissance of the 1920s–30s demonstrates further connections between various art forms. Throughout the book, this integrated approach has been enhanced by the inclusion of numerous objects from material culture such as maps, cartoons, posters, aprons, furniture, and other visual artifacts.

The opening chapter describes the European invention and mapping of America. Space limitations have allowed only a highly selective examination of aboriginal art to demonstrate that Native Americans, prior to Christopher Columbus's 1492 voyage, had already settled significant portions of the territories that later constituted the United States. In this second edition, I also include examples of Native American art that functioned as objects of cultural exchange once European colonialism began in earnest. In their conquest, white settlers overlaid diagrammatic drawings of former Indian lands with European names. The drawings featured networks of new boundary, property, and transportation lines. Colonial maps, prints, and paintings appropriated the New World for European civilization and represented Native Americans as, at best, noble savages.

The diversity of religious expression in Colonial American art constitutes the thematic content for chapter 2. Unlike traditional art surveys, I analyze the iconography and formal qualities of religious art and architecture in relation to the spiritual beliefs and ritualistic practices of different groups. These comprise French Catholics; New Mexican Spanish Catholics; New York Dutch Protestants; Pennsylvania Quakers and Moravians; Virginia and South Carolina Anglicans; New England Puritans; African-American animists; and Newport, Rhode Island Jews. An expanded section on African-American art suggests the manner in which colonial slaves contributed to the religious landscape. By exploring visual expressions of religious faith, I wish to suggest the magical power of images for colonists who sought evidence of the spiritual within harsh, hostile environments.

Concluding the discussion of Colonial era art, chapter 3 details the eighteenth-century consumer revolution stimulated by the growth in trade between Great Britain and its North American colonies. Aspiring to emulate the English aristocracy and landed gentry, increasingly wealthy American merchants and property holders constructed large, lavishly furnished mansions. They also commissioned ennobling family portraits that expressed both their elevated social status and their cultural acquisition of refined manners and taste. Their patronage of art and architecture enabled elite Americans to fashion public self-images as pillars of civic virtue destined for political leadership. This new edition also explores how the Jewish merchant minority employed portraiture as a means of cultural assimilation. Although generally ignored by most art historians, Freemasonry and other social clubs and fraternities played an important role in the visual education of colonial Americans. For affluent consumers as well as skilled artists and craftsmen, Freemasonry's elaborate visual symbolism promoted the moral virtues of classical architecture and good design, associating aesthetic values with social and political stability and the divine harmony of God's universe.

Chapter 4 is devoted to the art and architecture of the Revolutionary era and the early national period when the United States struggled for its cultural as well as political independence. Artists and architects were now called upon to create symbols that unified the new republic and commemorated the American Revolution's heroic events, personalities, and ideals. The chapter situates revolutionary history paintings, portraits, sculptures, and public monuments within a broader visual culture of political cartoons, paper currency, government seals, and Masonic decorative arts. During this period, Freemasonry played a particularly significant role in popularizing images of fraternity and virtuous self-sacrifice for the public, national good. George Washington, the nation's first president and leading Freemason, particularly personified republican selflessness. On the other hand, as the Revolution became a more distant memory, a new generation of artists produced works that expressed anxiety over the social and cultural dangers of American democracy's empowerment of unrefined lower- and middle-class white men. Artists and elite patrons founded

museums, art academies, and other cultural institutions to educate the American public and to establish themselves as the enlightened guardians of taste and moral virtue. An expanded discussion of the Peale family of painters-entrepreneurs underscores the conflicted political climate of the early republic.

Covering the period from the opening of the Erie Canal in 1825 to the end of the Civil War in 1865, chapter 5 interprets how the visual arts developed in relation to themes of cultural democratization and the expanding urban-industrial economy. During these four decades, New York City became the art capital of the nation. New York entrepreneurs, who financed the construction of canals, railroads, and western economic development, patronized artists who produced nationalist representations of the American landscape and its people. Neoclassical public buildings and mansions in such newly settled towns as Rochester, New York, emulated those constructed in the older and larger coastal cities of the East. Their elegant designs visually manifested the national taming of the wilderness. Meanwhile, racial, feminist, and class politics, as well as ethnic and religious pluralism, also shaped the production and consumption of American art. These dissenting voices challenged the socially exclusionary nationalism of wealthy northeastern financiers and art patrons. One such voice in this new edition is that of African-American photographer, Augustus Washington.

Chapter 6, comprising America's Gilded Age from 1865 to 1905, continues many of the same themes involving the interrelationship between art and commerce. However, after the Civil War, the separation between high art and popular culture became more pronounced, as American capitalists accumulated vast fortunes through monopolistic corporations invested in railroads, oil, steel, and other commodities. During the 1870s, these wealthy men founded major museums that appealed primarily to cosmopolitan elite tastes for classical and European or Renaissance-style art. America's multimillionaires also built enormous mansions, filling them with paintings, sculptures, and decorative arts imported from Asia and Europe. As the United States became an imperial power, its artists and architects produced ambitious works that suggested America's inheritance of Europe's classical, Renaissance tradition. Painters and sculptors memorialized Civil War heroes and suggested the post-war renewal of American life. These artists produced idealized representations of families and healthy children, as well as vigorous youths—strong, intelligent men and beautiful, culturally refined women. Most dramatically, architects pronounced America's regeneration and claim to economic and cultural leadership by inventing the modern, steel-frame skyscraper. Nevertheless, as America developed a bureaucratic, corporate culture, art became a therapeutic medium for alleviating the tensions and anxieties generated by urbanization and industrialization.

Chapter 7 situates Modernist art's attack on traditional academic ideals and conventions within a broader cultural matrix of political and social rebellion, and technological, scientific innovation. Revolutionary changes in transportation and communication, and new discoveries in physics and geometry, radically altered concepts of space, time, and matter. Scientists and intellectuals cast doubts upon notions of objective truth and recast reality in more dynamic, relativistic terms. In response, artists developed experimental, subjective styles that sharply departed from Renaissance illusionism and conventional imitations of nature and the human figure. Even anti-academic painters and photographers who created realist images stressed their subjective responses to modern urban life. Following the lead of the European avant-garde, rebellious American artists attempted to ally their attack against the genteel idealism of Gilded Age art with socialist, working-class politics. Modernist painters especially jarred cultural conservatives. They produced works with abstract, fragmented forms, non-naturalistic colors, and compositions that suggested the interpenetration of space and matter or, perhaps, the juxtaposition of multiple, competing perspectives. Nevertheless, as seen in a new section on the vitalism of nature, abstract artists also sought to humanize the built environment by interpreting it in organic terms.

Although the devastating effects of World War I led some artists toward a rejection of formal beauty and reason, many painters, sculptors, and architects during the 1920s optimistically embraced a futuristic machine aesthetic. African-American painters, sculptors, and photographers participated in their own arts renaissance that overlapped with the energetic modernity of Art Deco design. Even the Great Depression of the 1930s failed to discourage artists from celebrating the virtues of industrial technology, while others more grimly represented the plight of the unemployed and homeless. Supported by federal arts programs, artists renewed their political activism, producing works that directly or indirectly promoted working-class causes and opposed the rise of European fascism.

The narrative of chapter 8, from World War II to 1980, also interweaves art, politics, and social history. During the 1940s, with the Nazi occupation of Paris, New York became the capital of Modernist art. The Abstract Expressionist movement, centered in New York, seemed to epitomize Modernism's masculine cult of spontaneity, originality, and artistic genius. A number of women challenged this masculine bias. Furthermore, already during the 1950s and 1960s, the Modernist religion of individual creativity was being questioned and satirized by artists who rejected the notion of a high art beyond popular culture, advertising, and mass media.

The imprecise term Postmodernism broadly defined the cultural break with Modernist notions of formal purity or the autonomous, self-contained art object. Postmodernism signified a new pluralism, which encompassed a diversity of hybrid styles and techniques including the following: the return of architectural ornament; Super Realism and other forms of representational painting and sculpture; assemblages of appropriated objects; performance and body art; conceptual and process works; installations, earth art and site-specific constructions; photographic appropriations of mass media imagery; and the feminist revival of traditional domestic crafts. The 1960s and 1970s were tumultuous decades during which artists increasingly rejected conservative, formalist criticism to address a range of political and social issues.

The new chapter 9 chronicles the final two decades of the twentieth century and the first few years of the twenty-first century, a period in which artists confronted a concerted conservative political attack upon artworks deemed immoral, indecent, or sacrilegious. More broadly, it has become virtually impossible to talk about American art within a limited, nationalist framework. With the end of the Cold War and the revolution in digital communications and media technology, artists and architects more than ever operate within a global arts community and marketplace dominated by multinational corporations and institutions. While American government funding for challenging, innovative art has disappeared, private corporations have increasingly sponsored traveling art exhibitions and established business partnerships with cash-starved art museums as a means of promoting their public image and association with creative ideas.

Some artists have directly criticized the corporate dominance of culture and the market policies of economic globalization. Others have employed a variety of techniques to explore issues of personal identity or spirituality in opposition to oppressive, media-driven stereotypes and consumer, materialist values. Meanwhile, a number of other artists and architects have embraced commercialization and the corporate shaping of the cultural, visual landscape.

Since the September 11, 2001 terrorist attacks on the World Trade Center in New York and the Pentagon outside Washington, D.C., questions regarding art's critical role in American public culture have become more urgent. Freedom of expression seems more vulnerable in a security-conscious, militarily aggressive nation, where the government possesses unprecedented, intrusive powers of surveillance, and a handful of corporate conglomerates monopolize the media and communications industries. More hopefully, the globalization of human rights, economic justice and environmental movements poses a challenge to a world order based upon market values and nationalist, ethnic, and religious boundaries.

While wishing the survival of a politically and critically engaged art community, I have resisted the temptation of prophesying the future direction of art during the new millennium. Instead, this revisionist history addresses major cultural and social themes in the art and architecture of America's past half-millennium.

David Bjelajac
The George Washington University
February 2004

Chapter 1

The Invention and Mapping of America
1492–1760

ON October 12, 1492, after sailing westward from Spain for over two months and covering a distance of 3,000 miles, Christopher Columbus arrived with three ships at a small island that its native inhabitants called Guanahani. However, no artist was present to record the historic event, or to document the flora and fauna of the island that Columbus renamed San Salvador in honor of Jesus Christ, the Christian Son of God. Over 500 years later, we still don't know with certainty which island in the Bahamas first received the small crew of ninety sailors, since their commander not only failed to erect a stone monument marking the site, but also neglected to make or record any navigational measurements locating the island's geographical position. Five days after exploring Guanahani and other nearby islands, Columbus mistakenly concluded that he had reached Asia or "the Indies" (cited in Sale, p. 23). The people who inhabited these islands became the first ethnic or cultural group in the Western Hemisphere to be misnamed "Indians" (cited in Sale, p. 64). In renaming these islands and their inhabitants, Columbus effectively took possession of them on behalf of his patrons, King Ferdinand and Queen Isabella of Spain. Lacking drawings or pictorial documentation, he returned to Spain with Indian captives and other specimens or visual proofs of his discovery.

Initially, Columbus had no idea that he had discovered a New World. Despite the fact that Norsemen had established short-lived settlements at sites in present-day Labrador, Newfoundland, and New England as early as the eleventh century, their explorations had gone unnoticed by European contemporaries. Before Columbus's epoch-making voyage, ships from Portugal, Bristol in England, Brittany, and elsewhere along the coast of Europe had already sighted and even landed on western islands and territories, but these relatively unpublicized events failed to make much impact on contemporary cartographers, whose maps give no hint that two major continents existed in a western hemisphere between Europe and Asia.

Upon his return, Columbus wrote a brief account of his voyage, which was first published in the Castilian language of the Spanish court and then in Latin in cities throughout western Europe. Attracting a limited readership of learned men, Columbus's travelogue was written in a fashion that caused no sudden intellectual sensation or reevaluation of traditional concepts of world geography. His text sought to underscore resemblances, not differences, between Europe and the western islands he had encountered. Columbus described Hispaniola (present-day Haiti and the Dominican Republic) in literary terms, as similar to the earthly paradises imagined in the Bible and ancient Greek and Roman literature. Nevertheless, overwhelmed by the diversity and strangeness of the flora and fauna, he found himself struggling to find words adequate to the task of description. Everything appeared "marvellous" or "beyond comparison" (cited in Myers, p. 62).

On later voyages to the Caribbean islands and the Central and South American coasts, Columbus began to conclude that he had reached a new, gold-rich continent between Asia and the shores of western Europe. Yet he continued to assimilate this dawning realization in terms of ancient texts. When he encountered the mouth of the Orinoco River along the coast of present-day Venezuela, he believed it to be one of the four biblical rivers of Paradise that would lead him inland toward the Garden of Eden, birthplace of Adam and Eve, the original parents of the human race.

Virginia Algonquian artist
Deerskin Robe: Powhatan's Mantle, 1638.
Hide and marginella shell. Ashmolean Museum, Oxford.

America was an invention of the European imagination, of both its verbal and visual representations, which mirrored European desires and fears rather than any objective reality. Thousands of years before the German geographer Martin Waldseemüller coined the name "America" in 1507 to honor the Italian explorer Amerigo Vespucci, the so-called "New World" had been inhabited by diverse peoples, numbered in millions. Primarily, this chapter explores the cultural construction of America from the point of view of white explorers and colonists. However, it is important to understand that in 1492, America was far from being a wilderness devoid of human settlements. Except for a few examples of commercial or cultural exchange between tribal groups and white settlers, this book does not survey the wide array of Native American arts and crafts, such as pottery, painted animal hides, woven fabrics, basketry, wood carvings, bead and quill work, and bone and horn sculptures. A brief discussion of rock art, monumental earthworks, and architectural practices will, however, demonstrate how the "first Americans" adapted their tribes and communities to different landscapes before the European invasion. As we shall see, aboriginal peoples created a variety of complex societies and visually rich cultures. Ultimately, their settlements, maps, and intimate knowledge of the land facilitated European invaders' adaptation to this alien environment.

Yet European explorers and settlers tended to regard native peoples as little more than primitive savages with no true culture of their own. Most associated the naked or semi-naked peoples they encountered with a long literary and pictorial tradition of fantastic stories and images depicting "wild men" (Sale, p. 134), cannibals, and subhuman beings, who lived outside civilized society in an untamed state of nature. Europeans concluded that America was less a ready-made paradise than a hostile wilderness that would have to be shaped into an ideal landscape modeled, with improvements, on the homes and towns of the Old World.

European maps and visual representations were not neutral records, but contributed to the domination of aboriginal peoples. Artistic portrayals, mostly disseminated in prints and illustrated books, encouraged and justified the conquest of exotic savages. Nonetheless, visual artists also demonstrated a strong attraction to Native American culture by sympathetically representing tribal customs. Often, dignified representations of aboriginal leaders commemorated military, political, and commercial alliances. Furthermore, during the course of the eighteenth century, colonists in British North America also came to identify themselves as "native" Americans. For many, "Indians" personified the social and political freedom of the western frontier, its moral distance from the corruptions and injustices of Old World culture.

The First Americans

The diverse American tribes and cultures that European explorers mistakenly identified as Indian actually did possess a distant Asian ancestry. Perhaps as early as 30–40,000 years ago, as the earth's atmosphere cooled and sea levels ebbed during the last ice age, nomadic hunters began populating the American continents by crossing a land bridge or vast, low-lying plain over the Bering Strait from present-day Siberia into Alaska and beyond, toward warmer, more southern latitudes. By 1492, nearly 75 million Indians were living in the Americas, with approximately 5 to 10 million inhabiting the contiguous territories that would become the United States. No pre-Columbian culture in North America attained the visual splendor and power of the Aztec, Mayan, and Incan civilizations in Central and South America, but in the colder climate of North America, hundreds of tribes speaking diverse languages developed socially complex cultures. They ranged from nomadic hunting and food-gathering economies to relatively sedentary and semi-nomadic economies based on agriculture and trade. Many tribes constructed monumental earthworks and spectacular architectural spaces.

Native American Mapping

As the original settlers of an unpopulated and untamed wilderness, North American Indians preceded Europeans as the mapmakers and architects of a New World in the Western Hemisphere. By naming and mapping their environment, they created webs of meaningful relationships with the natural world. Their maps

1.1 Map Rock
Native American petroglyph near Givens Hot Springs, Idaho, c. 1400 C.E (?) Approx. 10 x 9 x 5 ft (3 x 2.7 x 1.5 m). Idaho State Historical Society.

established regional networks of trade and communication. Few Native American maps survive today because they were part of an oral tradition that described the landscape in experiential terms, associating different sites with specific spiritual forces and gods, as well as with animal, vegetable, and mineral resources. When necessary, maps were sketched from memory in the dirt or sand or, more permanently, on other natural materials, such as animal skins, tree bark, and rocks.

At a site on the Snake River near Givens Hot Springs, Idaho, pre-Columbian Shoshone Indians covered a large basalt boulder with pictographic signs (fig. 1.1). Known as Map Rock, this petroglyph, or example of rock art with deeply etched markings, apparently represents the Shoshone's tribal territory centered on the Snake and Salmon Rivers. Situated within a field of other petroglyphs and near the architectural remains of Indian lodges that date from 4,000 years ago, Map Rock also depicts human figures and animals such as buffalo, deer, antelope, elk, and mountain sheep. These images suggest that the rock possessed pragmatic, ritualistic significance, guaranteeing successful hunts, while demonstrating spiritual harmony between the territory's human and animal realms.

Rather than attempting to conquer or set themselves above nature, Native Americans sought to find their place within the natural processes of earth, water, and sky. They did not regard land as a commodity that could be sold or traded for the exclusive use of an individual owner. Land was communally owned by members of a tribe, although its resources and use might be shared with other tribes through mutual agreement. No Indian group was entirely sedentary. Depending on the source of food, tribes generally occupied more than one home, village, or town and moved with the change of seasons between summer- and winter-living sites.

Diversity of Housing Types: The Wigwam and Algonquian Village Life

Architectural forms expressed the Indians' communal social values and their careful adaptation to diverse, often harsh, environments. Housing types varied from region to region and from one culture to another. Conically shaped tipis made from long wooden poles and tanned, stretched buffalo hides, were especially suitable for nomadic hunting tribes such as the Apaches of the western plains. However, many other tribes developed agricultural and trading economies that made possible more permanent homes and settlements. During the late sixteenth century an English artist, John White (active 1570s–93), made a detailed drawing of Secoton (fig. 1.2), an Algonquian Indian village on the Pamlico River near the coast of North Carolina. The village was governed by Powhatan, a powerful chief who reigned over nearly 200 small villages along the southeastern seaboard of what became the United States. Connected by a broad central avenue and situated next to fields of corn, oblong wigwams served Secoton villagers, not only as one- or two-family homes, but also as sacred, devotional spaces. The large wigwam at the bottom of White's watercolor represents a tomb, where former leaders were buried.

The wigwam was a common building type among the tribes and cultures of the eastern Woodlands, encompassing territory from Canada to the Carolinas and westward to the Mississippi River. Wigwams varied in shape and size, but essentially they were constructed with a frame of flexible sapling poles that were stuck into the ground and then bent and lashed together for the desired configuration. Horizontal "stringers" tied in tiers to the vertical supports strengthened the frame, which was covered with grass and reed matting or, alternatively, sheets of tree bark. As seen in a number of the wigwams depicted in White's watercolor, the grass covering could be removed from one or more of the walls for better ventilation and light. Wigwam construction was a sensible, economical means of sheltering families in this densely wooded region of North America. When English settlers first arrived in Massachusetts during the early seventeenth century, they initially built wigwams that closely resembled the homes of their Indian neighbors. In White's watercolor, groups of Indians perform ritual dances and prayers within ceremonial circles, while others tend to food preparation and hunting. In the upper left, large wigwams seem to blend in with the surrounding wilderness, thereby suggesting that Native Americans did not clear and map village spaces according to a fixed geometric grid.

Anthropologists and historians have praised this and other White watercolors for their accuracy in rendering Indian life. However, as we shall see later (see fig. 1.14), White's images should not be interpreted as disinterested, objective renderings. They expressed his particular purposes and values. Furthermore, his representations were borrowed and recirculated by writers and print-

makers, who had their own ideological agendas in clearing the eastern woodlands of forests, wildlife, and Native Americans.

Southwestern Pueblo Architecture

When, during the sixteenth century, Spaniards from Mexico City entered New Mexico, the northern frontier of New Spain, they encountered Hopi and Zuni Indian villages and towns composed of sprawling, multistory, multiroom dwellings, constructed from adobe, a sun-dried

1.2 John White
Indian Village of Secoton, c. 1585. Watercolor, 12¾ x 7¾ in (32.4 x 19.7 cm). British Museum, London.

1.3 Taos Pueblo
Taos, New Mexico.
Museum of New Mexico,
Santa Fe.

Adobe, or mud
construction, is one of the
oldest architectural
materials and techniques.
The word *adobe* has roots
in Egyptian hieroglyphs
and, later, in the Arabic
word *atob*, meaning mud
or sticky glob. The earliest
remains of adobe
structures, dating to 7100
B.C.E., have been found at
the sites of late Stone Age
farming villages in
Mesopotamia. In the
Western Hemisphere,
adobe was first used in the
Chicama Valley of Peru
around 3000 B.C.E.

mixture of mud, clay, and straw. The Spanish termed these large apartment complexes and the tribes who lived in them "*pueblos.*" Derived from the Latin word *populus*, *pueblo* literally means "people", but Spaniards also employed the word to refer to a village or communal dwelling. Taos Pueblo in the Rio Grande valley, seventy miles north of Santa Fe, New Mexico, probably had originated before 1400, over a century before Columbus's first voyage (fig. 1.3). Mimicking the sacred, mountainous terrain of the surrounding landscape, residents of the village gradually created a nest of rectangular housing blocks, rising in tiers to as high as six stories. Pueblo rooftops doubled as terraces for residents living in the upper stories of the stepped-back, irregular pyramid.

Pueblo-style architecture had spectacular origins, which date roughly from 1,000 years ago between 900 and 1150 C.E. in the rugged canyon landscape of the Four Corners area, where the state borders of Utah, Colorado, Arizona, and New Mexico now meet. Taos itself may have been built by refugees from Chaco Canyon, New Mexico, the site of monumental

"Great Houses", Pueblo complexes made with thick walls of stone, rather than adobe. At Mesa Verde in southwestern Colorado and at Canyon de Chelly in northeastern Arizona, Anasazi Indians, the so-called ancient ones, also employed dry masonry to construct multiroom cliff dwellings within shallow recesses of canyon walls. Although these sites were gradually abandoned around 1200–1300 C.E., various tribes sporadically continued to use Canyon de Chelly until the mid-eighteenth century. During the nineteenth century, after the United States had annexed this territory, artists joined government surveyors in visually documenting the ancient Pueblo ruins. The photographer Timothy O'Sullivan (1840–82) chose a distant view of the rectangular stone housing blocks at Canyon de Chelly to express the virtually seamless continuity between Native American habitation and the geology or natural history of the site (fig. 1.4). The dark, womb-like opening for the pueblo, nestling within the canyon's massive, striated walls, implies the birth of Pueblo culture from Mother Earth.

Architectural historians have concluded that

Pueblo dwellings, like other Native American building types, possess ancestral roots in the subterranean pit houses of Siberia. This architecture spatially expressed the religious belief that every home replicated the cosmos. Whether subterranean or above ground, the home's center vertically connected the "earth-navel" with a "sky door" or "sun hole" (cited in Nabokov and Easton, p. 38). Originally circular, pit houses were entered through the smoke hole or sky door opening in the roof. Below, at the center of the living space, a *sipapu* or shallow posthole magically facilitated the emergence of ancestral spirits from the earth's vitalistic core. Though they moved into above-ground dwellings, Pueblo tribes continued to employ circular subterranean structures as kivas, or ritual spaces, where religious leaders descended into the earth to communicate with sacred clan animals or ancestral spirits (fig. 1.5). The cliff dwellings at Mesa Verde comprised the Pueblo living spaces above ground and the kivas (fig. 1.6). The kiva roofs, penetrated by ladders, served above ground as communal plazas. Here, men, women, and children socialized, worked, and prepared food. But architectural historians have imagined these courtyards also as urban theaters, where the tribe's leading men would suddenly appear from below, climbing upward from the kiva's smoke

hole to reenact the gods' act of creation. On the plazas, dancers performed rituals to the rhythmic accompaniment of drums, while spectators, mostly women and children, watched from the pueblo doorways above.

Earthworks and Burial Mounds

Elsewhere, in the Mississippi and Ohio River valleys, Native American cultures expressed animistic religious beliefs through the construction of monumental earthworks or temple and burial mounds. A few miles east of St. Louis, Missouri, the pre-Columbian settlement remains of Cahokia testify to the cultural complexity of perhaps the largest Native American city north of the Rio Grande. Founded around 600 C.E., Cahokia, at its peak in 1100, possessed approximately one hundred large earth mounds and an urban core of six square miles. Although scholars have debated the size and population density of Cahokia, estimates have ranged as high as 30–40,000 people, though many may have been living in outlying areas. Before its complete abandonment around 1500, Cahokia had served as a political, trading, and religious center for a large number of villages and towns along the Mississippi, Illinois, and Missouri Rivers. Its largest mound, later named Monk's Mound by French Trappist monks, rose in terraces to create

1.4 (left)
Timothy O'Sullivan
Ancient Ruins in the Canyon de Chelly, New Mexico, 1873.
Photograph, 10⅞ x 8 in (27.6 x 20.3 cm).
Museum of Modern Art, New York. Gift of Ansel Adams in memory of Albert M. Bender.

1.5 (right) **Great Kiva** near Pueblo Bonito, Chaco Canyon, New Mexico.
Diameter approx. 63 ft (19.2 m). National Park Service.

Known as Casa Rinconada, this communal, religious structure has masonry construction partially sunken into the earth. Its interior is ringed by benches for seating during sacred ceremonies. Within the circular space is a masonry compartment for the lighting of fires during ceremonies, and rectangular vaults for the storage of foot drums made of skins or logs.

1.6 Cliff Palace
Courtyards and kivas,
Mesa Verde, Colorado,
c.1250 C.E

1.7 (left)
Monk's Mound
Cahokia, Illinois.
c. 900–1200 C.E.
Cahokia Mounds State
Historic Site.

1.8 Great Serpent Mound
near Locust Grove, Ohio.
Length approx. 1,254 ft (382 m). Ohio Historical Society, Columbus, Ohio.

Recent radiocarbon dating has suggested that the Serpent Mound may have been built around 1070 C.E., which actually postdates the Adena and Hopewell cultures. Scholars further theorize that this mound of the Mississippian Period may represent the celestial appearance of Halley's Comet in 1066.

a grand pyramid over 100 feet high, 1,000 feet long, and 700 feet wide (fig. 1.7). More than twice the size of any other mound at Cahokia, Monk's Mound was built in stages or added onto over three centuries by thousands of women and men carrying and spreading buckets of earth, amounting to nearly 22 million cubic feet. At its crest, the mammoth pyramid had a platform for a large temple or royal residence, constructed from wattle and daub, a wooden frame of young saplings, filled in with dried mud. Together with lesser mounds, Monk's Mound looked over a grand open plaza, where ritualistic games and ceremonies were performed. Archeological excavation of the mounds has demonstrated that the inhabitants of Cahokia engaged in elaborate burials and practiced human sacrifice. At the funerals of tribal leaders, close relatives were apparently sacrificed to create a royal entourage into the underworld. Human remains were accompanied by shell beads, arrowheads, gleaming mica sheets, and polished stone disks that may have been employed in a number of spear-throwing games.

Similar artifacts have been found at other North American earthworks or mound sites. In the Hopewell and Adena cultures, which once flourished in the area of present-day Ohio, burial grounds lacked rectangular platforms for temples. Instead of building pyramids, these woodland peoples frequently shaped earth mounds into effigies of birds, snakes, and other animals. Though only a few feet high, they generally ranged from forty to 500 feet long. However, the largest mound, the Great Serpent Mound near Locust Grove, Ohio, writhed for 1,254 feet over a long, rocky ridge and strangely contained no actual burials (fig. 1.8). The snake's jaws surround an egg-shaped mound, perhaps suggesting fertility and birth in the midst of death. Seeking to communicate with the gods of both the sky world and the underworld, moundbuilders may also have designed effigies in response to astronomical phenomena, such as comets, meteors, and unusually luminous supernova.

One of the most striking artifacts from an Ohio burial mound is a translucent mica image

1.9 (left) **Hand shape**
Ohio Hopewell culture,
200 B.C.E.–400 C.E.
Sheet mica, 11½ in (29
cm) high, 6⅓ in (16 cm)
wide. Ohio Historical
Society, Columbus, Ohio.

Representations of the
human hand date from the
earliest periods of art or
image-making. In 1994,
archeologists discovered
thousands of prehistoric
finger tracings in the
Cosquer cave near
Marseilles, France. Dating
from 27,000 years ago,
many of these hand images
were in inaccessible areas
of the cave, suggesting a
magical, religious purpose
or significance.

1.10 (right) **Gorget,
or neck pendant**
Spiro Site, Oklahoma,
c.1200–1350.
Shell, diameter 4½ in
(11.4 cm). Minneapolis
Institute of Arts,
Minneapolis, Minnesota.

A fairly common motif in
the ritual objects of various
Native American cultures,
the human hand, animated
by an eye, also appears in
Asian art. Buddhist divinities
are often represented with
five additional eyes on their
hands, feet, and foreheads,
as signs of spiritual
enlightenment.

of an elongated human hand (fig. 1.9). As if asserting their magical control over the forces of nature, Native Americans often painted their own hand prints onto rock surfaces at sites throughout the Americas. An incised gorget, or neck pendant, from a pre-Columbian site in Oklahoma, features a human hand decorated with an eye in the middle of the palm (fig. 1.10). Made of shell, the pendant was probably worn by a tribal priest or chief as a symbol of his creative power. Sharp, penetrating vision, coordinated with the human ability to manipulate the materials of the earth, enabled Native Americans to survive and flourish in harsh environments. However, after 1492, they encountered the highly mechanized magic of European explorers and settlers, which forced them to adapt to new technologies and the hostile invasion of an alien civilization. (Unfortunately, limited space precludes further consideration of Native American art.)

America and the European Imagination

Nearly a century after Christopher Columbus's 1492 voyage, a Flemish artist, Jan van der Straet or Johannes Stradanus (1523–1605), celebrated European exploration and conquest of the Americas in a series of engravings entitled *Nova Reperta* (*New Discoveries*) (fig. 1.11). In the title page for the series, Stradanus suggests that the discovery of America has introduced a new age of knowledge, science, military power, and commercial wealth. A gesturing, seminude woman draws our attention to a circular map of North and South America. Her youthful energy may be interpreted as a personification of the European Renaissance, the "rebirth" of learning and the arts, which supposedly had been moribund since the fall of the ancient Roman empire during the fifth century. For over a millennium, pagan antiquity's relatively optimistic faith in humanity's godlike dignity and creativeness had been supplanted by Christianity's dogmatic subordination of sinful, depraved humanity to the biblical God of the Old and New Testaments. In harmony with humanist scholars who reconciled the Christian faith with renewed interest in ancient Greek and Roman authors, fifteenth- and sixteenth-century painters and sculptors revived antiquity's reverence for the idealized human figure as an expression of divine beauty and of moral and intellectual perfection.

NOVA REPERTA.

¹ *Americe.* ² *Lapis polaris.* ³ *Ignibus Amata puluis.* ⁴ *Imprimi volumina.* ⁵ *Rotisq; uigis indita hora ferreis.* ⁶ *Hyacum.* ⁷ *Ab igne stilla.* ⁸ *Fila serica.* ⁹ *Staphaq; prisco operta cuncta saeculo.*

ALOYSIO ALAMANNIO FLOR.ᴹᴼ
I. STRAD. INVENT. DD.

1.11 Johannes Stradanus (Jan van der Straet) Title page from *Nova Reperta*, Antwerp, 1600. Engraving. Folger Shakespeare Library, Washington, D.C.

Latin inscriptions encircle the map of North and South America on the left side of the print. They identify Christopher Columbus of Genoa as the discoverer, and Amerigo Vespucci of Florence as the discloser and namesake, of the Americas. On the right side, a Latin inscription encircling the magnetic compass commemorates Flavius Amalfitanus, or Flavio Gioia d'Amalfi, a fabled Italian mariner traditionally credited with inventing or popularizing the compass.

In Stradanus's picture, both the striding nude woman and the male personification of the old world, who exits to the right, are reminiscent of the muscular figures in paintings and sculptures by the Florentine artist Michelangelo Buonarroti (1475–1564), whose career had just begun when Columbus, a native of Genoa, Italy, embarked on his epochal voyage. Though born in Spanish-controlled Flanders, Stradanus had established a successful career in Florence, where the flowering of Renaissance arts and letters had begun.

Stradanus's title page to *Nova Reperta* reads like an encyclopedic catalogue of recent inventions and accomplishments. The map of the Americas is balanced on the right side by the circular, radiating shape of a magnetic compass, an essential navigational instrument for the age of exploration. A printing press and the iron barrel of a cannon form a central axis that symmetrically divides the illustration into two halves. Both of these recent inventions were crucial for European conquest and domination of the Americas. Complementing the physical force of the military hardware, the printed dissemination of words and images representing the New World fueled the desire for conquest and the appropriation of America's wealth, particularly its gold. A saddle with stirrups in the lower-left corner of the picture alludes to the horse power that Spaniards employed to overwhelm Native American opposition. Before the European invasion, horses had been unknown in the Americas. Armored Spanish soldiers mounted on horseback initially appeared invulnerable and godlike to American Indian tribes.

Underscoring European thirst for precious American commodities, Stradanus depicts logs of dyewood in the lower-right foreground. Used for manufacturing pigments and dyes, dyewood was particularly valued by the French, who, during the mid-sixteenth century, established a South American outpost in Brazil to log the product for export to the port city of Rouen, the key marketplace for the French dye trade. Brazil itself was named after the brasel or bresel tree, a red dyewood that Europeans imported from the East Indies.

Directly above the dyewood logs, Stradanus represents an alchemical apparatus, featuring a furnace, a crucible, and glass retorts. As predecessor to the science of chemistry, the art of alchemy was largely devoted to the heating and reheating of "base" metals, such as lead, in the hope of transmuting or refining them into the higher, perfected state of gold. Significantly, each of the two human figures in Stradanus's print holds a circular, though writhing, serpent that bites its own tail. Often associated with the practice of alchemy, this strange emblem represented the cycles of nature and the alchemical transmutation of matter. Nourishing itself by eating its old skin, the serpent expressed the cyclical processes of alchemy, whereby base or primary matter underwent a repetitive, circular path of fiery dissolution and regeneration that ultimately produced the perfection of nature symbolized by incorruptible gold. For Europeans, the American wilderness constituted an alchemical base material that could be refined into an ideal, utopian state of being. Just as Stradanus's print celebrates the measurement and assimilation of vast geographical spaces, so do the metal clockworks at the left; and the human figures underscore the importance of controlling the orderly passage of time or history's progress toward higher states of civilization. While the old man of Europe's past quietly departs the scene, the vibrant, fertile-appearing woman symbolizes its future. Previously ignorant of the American continents' existence, Europe has become regenerated by the wealth and resources of this New World. The print's circular map represents an open invitation for European viewers not simply to regard the Americas as an extension of their own world, but rather to envision a paradisiacal renewal or renaissance, the creation of a New Spain or a New France.

In perhaps the most famous engraving from the *Nova Reperta* series, Stradanus represented Amerigo Vespucci awakening America, as personified by an Indian woman wearing only a belt and feather cap (fig. 1.12). Awkwardly rising from her hammock, the startled nude figure dramatically contrasts with the self-assured masculinity of the fully clothed Italian explorer. As he stands and gazes down on a vulnerable America, Vespucci authoritatively holds a Christian banner in one hand and an astrolabe in

the other. The circular navigational instrument dangles like a magical charm between the two figures. Like a magnet, its power has finally drawn European ships and technology toward America's shores. Stradanus suggests the providential necessity and justness of European conquest. Represented as indolent savages, the native peoples appear to have no culture worth preserving. Scarcely different from the exotic wild animals that live among them, Stradanus's natives are mere cannibals. In the background, they can be seen roasting human body parts over a fire. On the basis of hearsay rather than evidence, Vespucci published sensational tales of Indian cannibalism in *Mundus Novus* (*New World*), an account of his 1501 expedition to the Caribbean and South America. Translated into several languages and appearing in scores of editions, Vespucci's travelogue was far more widely read than Columbus's published letter recounting his 1492 voyage. Finally declaring the discovery of a New World, Vespucci also excited readers with provocative stories of Indian sexuality: "The women as I have said go about naked and are very libidinous; yet they have bodies which are tolerably beautiful and cleanly. . . . When they had the opportunity of copulating with Christians, urged by excessive lust, they defiled and prostituted themselves" (cited in Sale, p. 141).

Vespucci conveniently projects the desire for sex onto the strange victims of European conquest. The invading Christians apparently have no resistance to these shameless Indian women. Stradanus's engraving represents Vespucci's discovery as a sexual encounter. In contrast to the dignified explorer's rational pose, America's nudity, long, flowing hair, and placement on a hammock-bed erotically imply her character as a wanton seductress. Having been named after Amerigo Vespucci, the voluptuous America is already his possession, a feminine object willing to be dominated and exploited.

Unlike Stradanus, the Frenchman Jacques Le Moyne de Morgues (1533–88) was one of the few professional artists to observe and visually represent Native American life first hand. In 1564, Le Moyne joined an expedition under the command of René Goulaine de Laudonnière, who was seeking to reinforce an earlier expedition led by Captain Jean Ribaut. The French

1.12 Johannes Stradanus (Jan van der Straet) *Amerigo Vespucci Awakens a Sleeping America* from *Nova Reperta*, Antwerp, 1600. Engraving. Folger Shakespeare Library, Washington, D.C.

An engraving is a type of print made from an intaglio, or cutting, process. By 1600, print on paper was commonly produced by pressing the paper against a finely incised and inked metal plate, usually made of copper. Burins, or sharply pointed engraver's tools, were utilized in the metal-cutting process. The engraved incisions would eventually wear away, due to the pressure, meaning that only a limited number of prints could be pulled from an inked plate before the design lost its definition.

erected forts and commemorative monuments at the mouth of the St. John's River, near present-day Jacksonville, Florida, and further north near present-day Beaufort, South Carolina.

Laudonnière assigned Le Moyne the task of mapping the territory's important navigational features. In the process, the artist-cartographer executed a number of sketches that later, on his return to Europe, he converted into forty-two finished gouache or watercolor drawings. The pictures were subsequently engraved and published with Le Moyne's own written narrative. Only one of the gouache drawings, a scene of Indian submission and friendship, has survived (fig. 1.13). The exotic, brightly colored image should be viewed in conjunction with the artist's explanatory account:

> When the French came to Florida the second time, they were commanded by Laudonnière. Upon their arrival crowds of Indians gathered on the shore to welcome them. They assured Laudonnière that they bore no enmity against him. So he went ashore with twenty harquebusiers [musketeers] where he was met by the chief, Athore. After presents had been exchanged and promises of friendship given, the chief asked the French to go with him. This they agreed to do, though as Athore was accompanied by a great number of men, they acted with great caution.
>
> The chief took them to the island where Ribaut had set up the stone column with the arms of the King of France. When the French came closer to the column, they found Indians worshiping the stone as an idol. Athore kissed the stone with the same reverence that his subjects showed him. His men also kissed the column, and they asked us to do likewise. In front of the monument lay offerings of fruits, edible and medicinal roots, jars of perfumed oils, a bow and arrows; the stone was wreathed with flowers and boughs of the choicest trees (cited in Lorant, p. 51).

For Indian peoples who had known nothing of horses, gunpowder, cannon-bearing sailing ships, and mechanical navigational instruments, invading Europeans initially did appear to be deities or beings in possession of godlike powers. European explorers quickly learned to take advantage of Native American awe and deference. Though Le Moyne states that Chief Athore also invited his French guests to kiss the phallic column honoring the King of France, Laudonnière and his heavily armed men stand cautiously at a distance from the kneeling Timucuan natives' act of worship. Athore places an arm around Laudonnière's shoulder, but the captain shows no sign of reciprocal friendship. Instead, he holds a long, pointed spear immediately in front of Athore's body. Le Moyne describes Athore as "very handsome, wise, honorable, and strong, and at least half a foot taller than the tallest of our men" (cited in Lorant, p. 51). Yet the visual representation of Athore's seminude, painted, and bejeweled body implies cultural inferiority to the dapper, fully clothed French captain. Despite the chief's statuesque nobility, Le Moyne emphasizes Athore's primitive closeness to the animal kingdom. In addition to the feather skirt and animal-tail hat, he sharply details the chief's long, clawlike fingernails and toenails. In his narrative, he informed readers that Athore had "married his own mother and had a number of sons and daughters by her" (cited in Lorant, p. 51). Like other reports of sexual license, stories of incest served the propagandistic purpose of justifying European conquest and conversion of Native Americans to the Christian faith. Indeed, Laudonnière's expedition had intended to establish a religious refuge in the New World for French Protestants or other Christians who were dissenting from the doctrines of the dominant Catholic Church. Le Moyne's image of idol worship and submission to French power could only have encouraged Christian missionary zeal. Furthermore, the rich offerings of flower garlands, fruits, and vegetables surrounding the stone column reassured viewers that America was a garden-like paradise readily available for European settlers.

Unfortunately for Laudonnière and the French, Spanish military forces dominating the Florida peninsula were far less welcoming than Athore and his Timucuan tribesmen. Fearing the plundering of its territorial possessions and interference with shipments of American gold, Spain, by 1565, drove the French out of Florida and the Carolinas. Jealously guarding its dominant position in exploiting New World resources, it understood its possession of Florida to include all of southeastern North America, from the Panuco River on the western edge of the Gulf of Mexico to Delaware Bay on the Atlantic coast.

Nevertheless, as national rivalries intensified and the extent of American wealth became more widely appreciated and coveted, other European powers, especially France and England, challenged Spain's dominant presence in the New World. Jean Ribaut, the French captain who had erected the monument worshiped by the Timucuans, visited London in 1563. His tales of American gold, silver, and precious gems generated a "Florida fever" among English speculators and merchants. Led by John Hawkins and Sir Francis Drake, English ship captains began during the 1560s to intercept Spanish gold shipments. Subsequently, the English navy's defeat of the Spanish Armada in 1588 dramatically weakened Spain's presence in North America.

With the encouragement of Queen Elizabeth I, the English adventurers Sir Humphrey Gilbert and his half-brother Sir Walter Raleigh envisioned permanent English colonies in America. In 1584 Raleigh voyaged to a territory that he named Virginia in honor of Elizabeth, England's "Virgin Queen." The next year, he organized a second expedition to Virginia, which explored the potential for a colony on Roanoke Island, off the coast of present-day North Carolina. The artist-cartographer John White played a key role in the expedition. White's detailed watercolor drawings of the flora, fauna, and native inhabitants of Roanoke and the coastal mainland were both informational and promotional in purpose. The pictures were intended as advertisements for attracting English settlers to Virginia and Roanoke Colony. White's *Indian Village of Secoton* (see page 16) and other scenes of Native American life suggest a fruitful land, abundant with natural resources. Furthermore, according to White's associate, Thomas Hariot, whose reassuring narrative later accompanied engraved reproductions of these images:

> They [the native peoples] seem very ingenious. For although they have no such tools, nor any such crafts, sciences, and arts as we, yet in those things they do, they show excellency of wit. And by how much they upon due consideration shall find our manner of knowledges and crafts to

1.13 Jacques Le Moyne de Morgues
René Goulaine de Laudonnière and the Indian Chief Athore Visit Ribaut's Column, 27 June 1564.
Gouache and metallic inks on vellum, with traces of black chalk outlines, 7 x 10¼ in (17.8 x 26 cm). New York Public Library. Astor, Lenox, and Tilden Foundation. Bequest of James Hazen Hyde.

exceed theirs in perfection, and speed for doing or execution, by so much the more is it probable that they should desire our friendship and love, and have the greater respect for pleasing and obeying us. Whereby may be hoped, if means of good government be used, that they may in short time be brought to civility and the embracing of true religion (cited in Gunn, p. 62).

The elevated, bird's-eye view in White's *Indian Village of Secoton* implicitly expresses Hariot's condescending attitude toward Native American culture. Twentieth-century scholars have praised White for the anthropological accuracy of his representations. Yet this detached, "objective" viewpoint ideologically identified the artist as one of Hariot's superior men of science and knowledge. Though he lived among them and enjoyed their hospitality, White stood back from his Native American subjects and made them the visual objects of his investigation. Armed with these attractive, colorful images of peace and plenty, he joined with Raleigh and Hariot in planning to subject his native hosts to English authority. Certainly White's representation of a Native American sorcerer stirred Christian missionary zeal (fig. 1.14). According to Hariot's

commentary: "They have sorcerers or jugglers who use strange gestures and whose enchantments often go against the laws of nature. For they are very familiar with devils, from whom they obtain knowledge about their enemies' movements" (cited in Lorant, p. 247). In 1587, after a brief visit to London, White was appointed governor of Roanoke Island and led a small group of settlers to the colony. Virginia Dare, White's granddaughter, was the first English child born in North America. The following year, the artist returned to England so that he could resupply the fledgling settlement with necessary goods. But war with Spain delayed his return. By 1590, when White finally made it back to Roanoke, he found no trace of the colonists and spent the next several years futilely searching for them. Roanoke's "Lost Colony" may have succumbed to famine, disease, or a natural disaster. However, Native Americans also may have decided that the aggressive colonists were no longer welcome to the land and its resources.

Despite Roanoke's failure, engraved reproductions of White's pictures kept circulating. In 1590, the Flemish engraver Theodore de Bry (1528–98) published, altered, and embellished copies of the original drawings, in conjunction with a reprinting of Thomas Hariot's 1588 treatise, *A Brief and True Report of the New Found Land of Virginia*. Being "directed to the investors, farmers, and well-wishers of the project of colonizing and planting there" (cited in Lorant, p. 227), Hariot's text, with de Bry's engravings after White, were inspirational for the 1607 founding of Jamestown, Virginia, the first successful English colony in America. Established primarily for commercial reasons by a joint stock company, the Virginia Company of London, Jamestown established trade with the native Algonquian tribes and survived through the cultivation of tobacco. English entrepreneurs had learned to appreciate tobacco from the Algonquians, who valued it for religious, "medicinal," and pleasurable social reasons. In copying John White's *Indian Village of Secoton*, de Bry took the liberty of adding a large field of tobacco at the top of the engraving, thereby suggesting to white settlers the commodity's profitable cultivation.

1.14 John White
The Sorcerer, c. 1585–7. Watercolor, 7¾ in (20 cm) high. British Museum, London.

White's sorcerer wears a small bird on the side of his head. While this winged creature was a traditional, honorific emblem of a high spiritual office, Europeans may have been more inclined to interpret the adornment as a devilish symbol of pagan nature-worship.

The Jamestown colonial leader Captain John Smith (1580–1631) drew a map of Virginia reliant on White's earlier cartography and upon "information of the *Savages* . . . set downe according to their instructions" (cited in Warhus, p. 144). Furthermore, Native American figures borrowed from de Bry's reproductions of White variously decorate different editions of Smith's Virginia map. However, departing from the objectivity generated by White's relatively detached representations, English engravers of Smith's map selectively appropriated, embellished, and recombined the imagery to project a far more antagonistic attitude toward the Algonquian tribes.

Robert Vaughan's engraving of "Ould Virginia," published in John Smith's *The Generall Historie of Virginia, New-England, and the Summer Isles* (1624), surrounds a map of Virginia with historical vignettes, recounting Smith's heroic struggle against hostile Indian warriors and his 1607 imprisonment at the hands of the powerful Chief Powhatan (fig. 1.15). For the scene in the upper-left corner, Vaughan appropriated the ritualistic circle of dancers in White's *Indian Village of Secoton* to represent Smith surrounded by belligerent warriors. Vaughan also borrowed the figure of White's sorcerer for the central vignette of idol worship and heathen ritual, at the top of the engraving. Within the space at the bottom right, Vaughan represents the legend of how Smith escaped execution at the hands of the Algonquians, when Pocahontas, Powhatan's daughter, interceded upon his behalf. This imaginative composition, foregrounding a kneeling Pocahontas next to Smith's prone body, is the least dependent upon White's prototypes. Vaughan's violent, combative images complement the central map, which is inscribed as "a description of part of the adventures of Cap. Smith in Virginia." Unlike White's earlier, relatively empty map of Virginia, Smith's map is covered with signs of settlement and English place-names. In 1622, angered by escalating intrusions on their land, Powhatan warriors attacked the Jamestown colony, killing almost one quarter of the residents. Intermittent warfare between native tribes and white settlers continued for decades, yet the very title of Vaughan's "Ould Virginia" suggests historical continuity and cultural permanence. In fact, by 1677,

Virginians had confined the once-powerful Powhatans to a reservation and forced them to pay a tax for using the land they once possessed.

Sometime prior to 1638, Jamestown colonists may have acquired, as a trophy of battle, a deerskin robe that became known as "Powhatan's Mantle" (see p. 12) or "the robe of the King of Virginia" (cited in MacGregor, p. 150). Decorated with shiny, white shell beads, the prized robe entered an extensive private collection of natural and manmade curiosities owned by John Tradescant the Elder (d.1638), a British royal gardener who probably purchased it from a Virginia merchant or ship's captain trading in exotic objects. Named "The Ark" (cited in MacGregor, p. 150), Tradescant's famed collection evoked biblical associations with Noah's legendary vessel, which had preserved specimens of all God's creation from the ravages of the Flood. In addition to birds, insects, fish, minerals, coins, Egyptian and Roman antiquities, and a host of other rarities, a 1656 catalogue of the Tradescant trove listed approximately 100 Native American artifacts, many from Canada and Brazil, as well as from Virginia. For a small admis-

sion fee, the Ark enabled a significant number of visitors to experience the wonders of the world without the hardship of laborious overseas travel.

Whether or not it was actually Powhatan's robe, the deerskin's elaborate ornamentation certainly suggests that the person who wore it was gifted with shamanistic or priestly, magical powers. Within the garment's luminous field of circles, a central human figure is flanked by two totemic, sacred animals. The symmetrical design expresses a kind of cosmic harmony or desired balance, uniting humans with nature and the spirit world. However, once separated from its original ritual context, and exhibited in the Ark amidst a dizzying jumble of other objects, the robe lost its healing, religious powers. Labeled "Powhatan's Mantle," it became an ethnographic or cultural curiosity, an artifact of scholarly interest. Furthermore, within its new transatlantic exhibition space, the Native American robe paid tribute to Great Britain's imperial power.

As an agent of the colonial project, Captain John Smith ventured beyond Virginia. In 1614, he traveled north to Cape Cod and Penobscot

1.15 Robert Vaughan
"Ould Virginia" from John Smith, *The Generall Historie of Virginia, New-England, and the Summer Isles*, 1624.
Newberry Library, Chicago.

1.16 Simon van de Passe
Map of New England from John Smith, *The Generall Historie of Virginia, New-England, and the Summer Isles*, 1627.
American Antiquarian Society, Worcester, Massachusetts.

Bay, areas along the North American coast that were still devoid of successful English settlements. Even though Dutch and French explorers were making territorial claims, Smith bestowed an English character on the region when he published a map of New England (fig. 1.16). Despite the absence of actual English towns and villages, Smith's New England map is everywhere inscribed with English placenames. On the orders of Prince Charles, the future King Charles I, Captain Smith renamed Native American settlements to create an Anglicized landscape, with such familiar sites as "Oxford," "London," "Boston," and "Plimouth." The map is decorated with a royal coat of arms and a portrait of Captain Smith, who is also given the title "Admirall of New England."

Both map and portrait were engraved by Simon van de Passe (c.1595–c.1647). This Dutch artist-engraver spent much of his career in England, creating small, waist-length portraits of stiffly posed figures. His tight, linear drawing style was suitable for fine details of face, costume, and New England cartography. The same year that Smith first published his New England map, van de Passe also engraved a portrait of Pocahontas (fig. 1.17). In 1614, the Virginia colonist John Rolfe had stated his intention to marry the celebrated daughter of Chief

Powhatan, not for "the unbridled desire of carnal affection: but for the good of this plantation, for the honour of our country, for the glory of God, for my own salvation, and for converting to the true knowledge of God and Jesus Christ, an unbelieving creature, namely Pokahuntas" (cited in Middleton, p. 59). Van de Passe drew the portrait of the Indian princess after her husband had introduced her to the royal court of James I (r.1603–25).

In contrast to pictures of nude or seminude Native Americans, van de Passe completely covers Pocahontas with a thick armor of intricately embroidered English costume. As if responding to Rolfe's moral fear of carnal lust, the portraitist represents a virtually desexualized and Anglicized woman. Indeed, the portrait's Latin and English inscriptions inform viewers that the daughter of Powhatan has been renamed Rebecca. The popular biblical name associated the Indian princess with the Old Testament mother of Jacob, patriarch of the ancient Israelites. European settlers in America habitually compared themselves to the Hebrews, the "chosen people" of the Old Testament, who also had survived wilderness conditions, thanks to god's divine protection. In appropriating America, Europeans renamed both land and people. As Rebecca, the Christianized Pocahontas personified the civilizing purification of the American wilderness. However, for Pocahontas, civilization had its own dangers. While in London, she died of smallpox, one of many European diseases that had been exported to the New World, where they depopulated Native American villages and towns. From the European perspective, the diseases that ravaged aboriginal peoples were providential, since they left empty settlements that could easily be taken over by arriving settlers.

Even as epidemics of smallpox, measles, and bubonic plague were devastating Algonquian tribes along the New England coast, John Smith was peddling thousands of his maps to prospective English colonists and trading companies. Few expressed interest in colonization. Among those who did was a small group of Pilgrims, or religious dissenters from the Church of England. On September 6, 1620, approximately one hundred Pilgrims departed on the *Mayflower* from Plymouth, England. Over two months later, they

Matoaks als Rebecka daughter to the mighty Prince
Powhatan Emperour of Attanoughskomouck als virginia
converted and baptized in the Christian faith, and
wife to the wor:ᵗ Mʳ Joh: Rolff.
Si. Paſſ: ſculp: *Compton Holland excud:*

landed off the Cape Cod peninsula on the New
England coast and established Plymouth Colony
"for the glory of God, and advancement of the
Christian faith" (cited in Middleton, p. 77).
Smith's map already had supplied the name of
Plymouth as a replacement for the Algonquian
village of Patuxet. Erased by this map, Patuxet
was literally destroyed by a series of epidemics
during the three or four years prior to the
Pilgrims' landfall. Plymouth was constructed
from the ruins of the former village and survived
with the help of Native American survivors,
who taught Pilgrims how to grow corn and
acquire other useful goods. Nearly ten years
later, in 1629, the Massachusetts Bay Company
received a royal charter to establish a New
England colony north of Plymouth. The company's seal featured the lonely figure of an Indian
holding a large bow and arrow, while standing
over several small bushes or trees (fig. 1.18). A
speech bubble emerging from the figure's mouth
beseeches prospective white explorers and settlers to "come over and help us." Like the
portrait of Pocahontas, the seal represented
Native Americans as amenable, even very
eager, for the spiritual and material benefits of
European civilization.

However, neither the Pilgrims of Plymouth
nor the founders of Massachusetts Bay Colony
demonstrated much interest in helping or converting Native Americans to Christianity. As
we shall see in the next chapter, Massachusetts
became a refuge for Puritans or radical
Protestants, who were protesting the corruption
of the Roman Catholic Church and its influence on the Church of England. Rather than
carrying out missionary work among native
tribes, Puritans turned spiritually inward to
purify and protect themselves from the physical
and moral wilderness of American life. Nevertheless, they fiercely pursued their territorial and
commercial interests against hostile native
American tribes. Boston, the commercial hub of
Massachusetts, had replaced Shawmut, another
Algonquian village that had been devastated by
the epidemics of 1616–19. A smallpox epidemic
during the fall and winter of 1633–4 cleared the
New England landscape of several thousand
more Native Americans, enabling white
colonists to take over deserted settlements and
cultivated fields.

In 1637, shortly after a dissident group of
Massachusetts Puritans founded Connecticut
Colony in southern New England, officials from
both colonies purposely provoked a genocidal
war against the Pequots, a hostile tribe whose
power over other Native American groups
threatened English colonists' economic and

1.17 (left)
Simon van de Passe
Pocahontas, 1618.
Engraving, 6¾ x 4¾ in
(17.5 x 12.06 cm).
National Portrait Gallery,
Smithsonian Institution,
Washington D.C.

Pocahontas was a
nickname; her real name
was Matoaka. The Latin
inscription is translated and
expanded upon in the
English legend below the
image.

1.18 (below) **Seal of the
Massachusetts Bay
Company**
1629.
Massachusetts Historical
Society, Boston.

The Latin inscription
surrounding the image
translates as "A Seal of the
Governor and Society of
Massachusetts Bay in New
England." This early seal
was annulled once
Massachusetts became a
royal colony later in the
seventeenth century.
A new seal featured the
royal coat of arms to signify
the colony's direct rule by
the monarchy.

1.19 Indian fort
"The figure of the Indians' fort or Palisado in New England and the maner of the destroying it by Captayne Underhill and Captayne Mason" from *News from America; or a new discoverie of New England*, London, 1638. New England Historic Genealogical Society, Boston.

political interests. Under the command of Captains John Underhill and John Mason, Connecticut and Massachusetts troops chose not to engage in direct combat with Pequot warriors. Instead, they launched an early-morning attack on the Pequots' fortified coastal village at the mouth of the Mystic River. At the time, Mystic Fort was occupied by about four hundred Pequots, most of them women, children, and older men. Setting fire to the town, the Puritans killed virtually everyone who attempted to escape.

Afterward, Captain Underhill published an unapologetic narrative of the slaughter and illustrated it with a remarkable maplike drawing (fig. 1.19). From a bird's-eye perspective, the diagrammatic picture represents two concentric rings of figures surrounding the circular Pequot fort. The outer ring represents Narragansett warriors, each poised with a bow and arrow. As the unreliable allies of the Puritans, the Narragansetts actually played an uncooperative, passive role in the attack, since they refused to enter the fort and later condemned the massacre. Puritan militiamen constitute the inner ring of figures encircling the palisades of the fort. They are also pictured within the village itself, firing muskets at figures misrepresented exclusively as armed warriors. Defenseless women, children, and village elders are not represented.

Nevertheless, Underhill openly admitted in his narrative that "Many were burnt in the fort, both men, women, and children. Others [were] forced out, and came in troops to the [Narragansett] Indians, twenty and thirty at a time, which our soldiers received and entertained with the point of the sword. Down fell men, women, and children" (cited in Kibbey, p. 104). From the Puritan point of view, the killing of women and children was justified since Pequots and other Native Americans were not humans created in the image of God. Puritans regarded themselves as God's "elect." American enemies, such as the Pequots, were in league with the devil or the dark forces of evil. Puritans purposely targeted children and child-bearing women as a means of destroying the potency and fertility of the Pequot peoples.

Viewed as a whole, Underhill's pictorial representation of the massacre suggests a sexual rape. Tiny, spermlike figures penetrate openings to the village core, which strongly resembles the lips of the female genitalia. As discussed earlier in the chapter, the European imagination tended to justify conquest of the Americas by feminizing the aboriginal peoples, associating them with the dark, sinful forces of nature and sexual desire. As historian Ann Kibbey has observed, the sexual symbolism of the Puritans' genocidal act is only implicitly or subverbally expressed in Underhill's vagina-like drawing. However, in their narratives, leaders of the massacre adopted a rapist's

1.20 Cahokia Courthouse, Cahokia, Illinois
c.1737.
Photo.
Library of Congress, Washington, D.C.

Thanks to a twentieth-century reconstruction, the Cahokia Courthouse, originally the residence and shop of a French trader, still serves as an historic example of French colonial domestic architecture. Built along the Mississippi River, such structures were vulnerable to periodic floods. After the American Revolution, this spacious building functioned as a territorial courthouse from 1790 until 1814, when the perpetual threat of flooding forced judges in Illinois' St. Clair County to move to higher ground.

perspective by entirely blaming the victim for inviting the assault. Invoking the anger of a masculine, patriarchal God, Captain Mason insisted that the ungodly Pequots had brought "the mischief they plotted, and the violence they offered and exercised, upon their own heads in a moment: burning them up in the fire of His wrath, and dunging the ground with their flesh: it was the Lord's doings, and it is marvelous in our eyes!" (cited in Sanders, p. 338). New England Puritans later extended their genocidal war against other aboriginal tribes, including their former allies, the Narragansetts. Underhill's verbal and visual representation of the Pequot War apparently served as a model for the Narragansetts' defeat. In December, 1675, colonial troops surrounded the Narragansetts' village in Rhode Island and burned it to the ground, killing hundreds of people in the process.

Colonial Portraits of Native Americans and Anglo-French Rivalry

English settlers perpetually worried that their best efforts to civilize the American wilderness could be subverted by chaotic wilderness forces. Even after they had subdued or slaughtered New England's native tribes, Puritan colonists were threatened by hostile tribes beyond their borders in French Canada, or "New France." Native Americans survived and even prospered for a time by exploiting European rivalries, playing one colonial power against another. Establishing a network of alliances with Indian tribes, France during the seventeenth century claimed a North American empire stretching from the mouth of the St. Lawrence River in the north to the Mississippi delta in the south. During the course of the eighteenth century, at Cahokia, St. Louis, and on down to New Orleans, French missionaries, troops, and settlers constructed a series of forts and villages along the Mississippi River. By 1752, the French village at Cahokia, situated near an Illini Indian village and the "Monk's Mound" pre-Columbian earthworks (see fig.1.7), comprised a small, racially diverse population of white settlers, African Americans, and Native Americans. The French villagers built distinctive wooden structures, surrounded by galleries or porches, which supported the protective, shade-giving eaves of generous sloping roofs (fig.1.20). They employed *poteaux-en-terre* and *poteaux-en-sole* construction, in which closely spaced, upright timbers were either placed securely in holes in the earth or on a horizontal wooden sole plate or sill. The spaces between the posts were then filled in with a mixture of limestone plaster or mortar.

Even after the French monarchy relinquished claims to the Mississippi River Valley following the French and Indian War (1754–63), descendants of the original French settlers remained the dominant European presence in the region until early nineteenth-century waves of Anglo-American pioneers transformed the ethnic character of the population. The last of a series of Anglo-French colonial wars in North America, the French and Indian War was largely fought in French Canada and the northern British colonies.

French Canada had profited in the early eighteenth century, from the fur trade, but the colony was forced to compete with New York and New England for the precious and limited

1.21 (left) **John Simon after John Verelst**
Etow Oh Koam, King of the River Nation, 1710. Mezzotint, 15¾ x 9¹³⁄₁₆ in (40 x 25 cm). American Antiquarian Society, Worcester, Massachusetts.

Standing in a forested wilderness, Etow Oh Koam is portrayed as a proud warrior, who holds a club as a sign of his power. A small background vignette represents a figure brandishing a club against an enemy. Immediately behind the king of the River Nation, a large tortoise represents a sacred animal or clan totem. The chief's akimbo pose, with one hand on the hip and the elbow turned outward, commonly signified aristocratic or royal status in European portraiture.

1.22 (right) **John Simon after John Verelst**
Ho Nee Yeath Taw No Row, King of the Generethgarich, 1710. Mezzotint, second state, 15¾ x 9¹³⁄₁₆ in (40 x 25 cm). American Antiquarian Society, Worcester, Massachusetts.

This Mohawk Indian king also holds a formal aristocratic pose, with one hand placed akimbo while the other holds a small bow. A quiver of arrows lies in the foreground. Meanwhile, a wild, snarling wolf in the lower-right corner of the print represents the king's clan totem. In the distant background at the far right, the small figure of a hunter can be seen aiming his bow and arrow toward a wolflike creature at the far left.

supply of furs. Competition benefited Native Americans, who could charge white traders higher prices for furs, while paying less for European manufactured goods. Particularly during periods of European warfare abroad, the North American colonies also became theaters of violent conflict over territory and trade. French officials in Quebec and Montreal cultivated alliances with native tribes north of New England and New York, while also befriending refugees or vengeful remnants of those peoples conquered by Massachusetts and Connecticut colonists.

French-sponsored Indian raids on settlements in western and northern New England motivated English colonists to cultivate their own alliances with tribes hostile to the French. By the early eighteenth century, as Anglo-Americans became wealthier and more active consumers of the visual arts, they occasionally celebrated these strategic alliances by purchasing or commissioning sympathetic portraits of Native American *sachem*s or chiefs.

In Portsmouth, New Hampshire, Captain Archibald Macpheadris, a wealthy fur trader, hired an artist, possibly the New England itiner-

ant portraitist Nehemiah Partridge (1683–c. 1737), to paint the central staircase of his new mansion with a series of murals (fig. 1.23). Portraits of two oversized Mohawk *sachem*s flank a window illuminating the staircase landing. Painted with bright colors and rich brushwork, the pictures were loosely copied from a popular series of portrait prints designed in London by the painter John Verelst (1648–1734) and the engraver John Simon (1675–c.1755) (figs. 1.21–1.22). Altogether, Verelst and Simon produced images of four *sachems,* representing a confederation of Iroquois people in northern and western New York, including Mohawk, Oneida, Onondaga, Cayuga, and Seneca tribesmen. Colonial leaders from New York and elsewhere escorted the Iroquois leaders to London as a means of generating greater material support for the ongoing war against French Canadians and their Indian allies. Concerned by French intrusions on their own hunting and trading interests, the Iroquois chiefs, speaking through translators, personally petitioned Queen Anne's help, for otherwise "we must, with our Families, forsake our Country and seek other Habitations" (cited in Bond, p. 1). Several London artists painted portraits of the "Four Indian Kings" (cited in Bond, p. 67) and then printed inexpensive engravings to be marketed throughout Britain and the American colonies.

Prints of Verelst's full-length, standing portraits were displayed in private homes, as well as in colonial government buildings from New Hampshire, Connecticut, and Rhode Island southward to Pennsylvania and New Jersey. Freely adapted and simplified for Captain Macpheadris's Portsmouth mansion, the two painted copies of Verelst's portraits appear to function as exotic guardians of the rich domestic environment. Each figure holds a weapon, one a tomahawk and the other a club. Yet their gentle, somewhat feminine features and long, flowing garments suggest a ceremonial presence consistent with their placement on a staircase landing, designed for dignified processions of family members and guests.

Two decades later, Gustavus Hesselius (1682–1755), a London-trained artist from Sweden, painted two portraits of Delaware Indians for John Penn, a proprietor of the colony of Pennsylvania and son of its original founder, William Penn. Penn commissioned the portraits in 1735, shortly after he and his brother Thomas began negotiating a land dispute with the subjects of the works, Lapowinsa and Tishcohan, prominent Delaware chiefs. Within two years, Pennsylvania colonists and the Delaware tribes had signed the "Walking Purchase" treaty, which stipulated that white settlers' territory was to be expanded into Indian hunting grounds by as much of the terrain as a man could walk across in a day and a half. The Penns, however, chose athletic runners rather than walkers to claim over sixty miles of property, twice as much as the swindled Delaware chiefs had expected.

Hesselius's two portraits (figs. 1.24–1.25) have been praised for their naturalism and their

1.23 Nehemiah Partridge (?)
Mohawk Indian Kings' Mural
Macpheadris-Warner House, Portsmouth, New Hampshire, c.1716.
Warner House Association, Portsmouth.

In addition to these portraits of Indian *sachems*, three other mural scenes decorate the central staircase: a farm woman, seated at a spinning wheel, her dog and chickens menaced by an eagle; the biblical Hebrew patriarch Abraham about to sacrifice his son Isaac (Genesis 22); and the equestrian portrait of an unidentified aristocratic figure, possibly William III, the anti-Catholic, anti-French Prince of Orange, who became King of England in 1689.

1.24 (left) **Gustavus Hesselius**
Tishcohan, 1735.
Oil on canvas, 33 x 25 in
(83.8 x 63.5 cm).
Historical Society of
Pennsylvania,
Philadelphia.

1.25 (right) **Gustavus Hesselius**
Lapowinsa, 1735.
Oil on canvas, 33 x 25 in
(83.8 x 63.5 cm).
Historical Society of
Pennsylvania,
Philadelphia.

transcendence of conventional stereotypes. As Philadelphia's leading portraitist, he already had achieved a reputation for realism. James Logan, a jurist and William Penn's former secretary, wrote to his brother in 1733: "We have a Swedish painter here, no bad hand, who generally does Justice to the men, especially to their blemishes, which he never fails showing in the fullest light" (cited in McCoubrey, p. 5). A deeply religious man, Hesselius later associated himself with the Moravian community in Bethlehem, Pennsylvania (see pp. 51–53). This devout, mystical group of immigrants from Central Europe established close ties with Native American tribes, the better to convert them to Christianity.

Hesselius's *Tishcohan* represents the features of an aging man with a wrinkled brow, bulbous nose, and sunken, careworn eyes (see fig. 1.24). But the figure's firmly set jaw and piercing gaze also suggest a powerful individual, who directly engages us and demands our respect. The painting glows with light reflected from the brick-red flesh of Tishcohan's face and bared torso. Hesselius derived this red pigment from

pyrite, a locally available mineral popularly known as fool's gold because its color often deceived excited gold prospectors. Hesselius alchemically transformed lowly pyrite into a precious pigment by burning, pounding, and grinding the iron and sulphur compound into a fine powder, which he then mixed with his binding oil medium.

Thanks to the radiant color and light, Tishcohan emerges from the darkened background as a spiritual, as well as physical, presence. Hanging from his neck, a chipmunk-hide pouch holds a small, white tobacco pipe. The bowl of the pipe directs our attention toward the area of the heart, that organ of the body most often associated with an individual's spirit or soul. For John Penn, Hesselius's patron, the pipe's positioning may have signified Tishcohan's honesty and sincerity as a negotiator. Diplomatic treaties and trading agreements between white settlers and native tribes typically were sealed with the ceremonial smoking of tobacco. Many years before the portraits by Hesselius, an earlier generation of Delaware Indians had given William Penn, the colony's founding father, a belt made out of *wampum*, or beads of polished shells and glass (fig. 1.26). Like the tobacco pipe, wampum belts functioned as symbols of peaceful exchange and social, political order. According to legend, this particular belt, with its dark, silhouetted figures signifying the bond of friendship, was given to the Penn family in 1682 upon the occasion of the Shackamaxon Treaty, the first treaty in which Delaware Indians ceded land to Pennsylvania colonists. Given the history of William Penn's successful diplomacy with local tribes and the fact that his sons, John and Thomas, were attempting to gain the trust and confidence of Tishcohan and Lapowinsa, it is not surprising that Hesselius attempted to achieve dignified, sympathetic representations of the two chiefs. John Penn also may have insisted on naturalistic detail, so that he could possess an accurate visual record of the characters with whom he was negotiating. Representations of facial features and expressions typically were valued as reliable indicators of states of mind and moral worth.

Whatever John Penn's deceptive intentions in negotiating with Lapowinsa and Tishcohan, Hesselius had his own reasons for representing the chiefs with such unprecedented care and dignity. As a painter who found and prepared his own colors, he may have discussed with his sitters the best local materials for making pigments. Hesselius's *Lapowinsa* represents the Delaware chief with strange markings or signs painted across his face (see fig. 1.25). Hesselius's naturalistic but exotic and mysterious portraits expressed the fascination that white settlers felt for native peoples. Many colonists believed that aboriginal Americans possessed an ancient, secret wisdom of the land and its resources. The sphinxlike silence of Hesselius's Indian chiefs contributes to their aura as wise men and guardians of nature's hidden secrets.

White Colonists as Native Americans

Anglo-American artists soon learned how to foster their own reputations for creative genius by associating themselves with the natural wisdom of "noble savages." Benjamin West (1738–1820), representing the next generation of Philadelphia painters, claimed that during his youth in Springfield, Pennsylvania, a group of Indians had given him his first lessons in preparing pigments, particularly the reds and yellows "with which they painted their ornaments" (cited in Galt, p. 18). From these humble, primitive origins, West became an internationally famous painter and president of the Royal Academy of Art in London. According to West's official, often fanciful, biography, written at the end of his career: "a Painter who would embody the metaphor of an Artist instructed by Nature, could scarcely imagine any thing more picturesque than the real incident of the Indians instructing West to prepare the prismatic colours" (cited in Galt, p. 18).

As we shall see in chapter 4, West patriotically distinguished himself as an American artist working in London by sympathetically portraying both Native Americans and white colonists wearing Indian costume (see fig. 4.23). West became a collector of moccasins, beaded hatbands, and other Native American artifacts. Visiting Rome in 1760, the artist apparently startled the city's critics and connoisseurs by brashly comparing the *Apollo Belvedere* (see fig. 4.35), a celebrated example of ancient Greek sculpture, to "a young Mohawk warrior" (cited in Alberts, p. 34). Indeed, one of the first pictures that he painted in Rome represented the family of an American Indian chief, who strikes the

1.26 Wampum Belt
Delaware or Iroquois Indian tribes, Delaware Valley, c. 1670–82. Animal hide, glass, and shell beads. The Historical Society of Pennsylvania, Philadelphia. Gift of Granville John Penn.

During the seventeenth and eighteenth centuries, woodlands people or Indian tribes throughout the eastern part of northern America employed *wampum* as a currency or legal medium of exchange. Consisting of tubular white and purple beads, *wampum* was produced from marine shells. The beads were woven as ornaments, not only for belts but also headbands, bracelets, necklaces, and bandoleer bags. European colonists, hoping to increase their trading power with native tribes, introduced manufactured glass beads as a form of *wampum*. In this belt, the *wampum* beads are made from glass and oyster shells.

1.27 Benjamin West
The Savage Chief (The Indian Family), c. 1761. Oil on canvas, 23⅝ x 18⅞ in (60 x 48 cm). Hunterian Collection trustees, Council of Royal College of Surgeons of England.

West here alludes to ancient Greco-Roman sculpture as a means of ennobling his subjects and demonstrating his mastery of the idealized human figure. West's Indian warrior is stockier and fleshier than the youthful, androgynous *Apollo Belvedere* (see fig. 4.35). The artist establishes an ominous mood with the gloomy wilderness setting. As the worried father departs for war rather than the hunt, a child in the shadowy hut entrance at the left attempts to restrain the hunting dog from following his master.

pose of the Greek sun god Apollo (fig. 1.27). The painting was commissioned by Colonel Joseph Shippen of the Pennsylvania militia, whose encyclopedic interest in Indian costumes, ornaments, and weapons encouraged the young West's careful portrayal of Native American figures and artifacts.

Trading and negotiating with native tribes on the frontiers of British North America, many colonists chose to dress like their Indian neighbors. During the eighteenth century, startled European visitors concluded that the untamed wilderness was regressively reshaping white settlers into the image of red savages. However, for West and many other colonists, American Indians personified freedom from European corruption and decadence. By the eve of the American Revolution, colonists rebelling against British rule consciously identified themselves as "native" Americans. In appealing for military support from leaders of the Mohawk, Seneca, Delaware, and Shawnee tribes, colonial rebels in 1776 claimed a bond of brotherhood by virtue of the land they shared: "We are sprung from one common mother; we were all born in this big Island" (cited in Calloway, p. 1).

However, any notion of brotherhood quickly evaporated after the American Revolution. Native Americans lost their ability to play the middle ground between French and British imperial rivalries. They now faced a United States government aggressively determined to appropriate the entire continent. Motivated primarily by economic and political factors, land-hungry citizens also claimed that they had a mission to spread the Word of God and His providential rule all the way to the Pacific Ocean. However, already during the seventeenth and eighteenth centuries, religious art and architecture were transforming the American landscape. Colonial churches, meetinghouses, and devotional images expressed many immigrants' belief that the American continent rightly belonged to Christian peoples preparing for the millennium or the glorious thousand-year rule of Jesus Christ.

Chapter 2

Religious Rituals and the Visual Arts in Colonial America

1620–1760

I
N 1744, when Alexander Hamilton (1712–56), a Scottish-born medical doctor from Annapolis, Maryland, visited the city of Philadelphia, he wrote in his diary:

I dined at a tavern with a very mixed company of different nations and religions. There were Scots, English, Dutch, Germans, and Irish; there were Roman Catholics, Churchmen, Presbyterians, Quakers, Newlightmen, Methodists, Seventhdaymen, Moravians, Anabaptists, and one Jew. The whole company consisted of twenty-five, planted round an oblong table, in a great hall well stocked with flies (cited in Horner and Bain, p. 363).

For Dr. Hamilton, who also traveled to Boston, Massachusetts, and Albany, New York, architecture and the visual arts merely underscored this startling lack of religious unity in America. Some "genteel" congregations of the Christian faithful favored steepled, richly decorated churches (fig. 2.1). More austere religious groups such as the Quakers seemed "to shun ornament in their public edifices as well as in their apparel or dress" (cited in Horner and Bain, p. 363) (fig. 2.2). Still others, though rejecting church decorations, purchased religious paintings for their homes (see fig. 2.14). As we shall see in this chapter, Hamilton's travelogue only begins to suggest the multicultural diversity of colonial American religious life and its material expression in the visual arts.

In large measure, the religious mosaic witnessed by Hamilton was the product of the sixteenth-century Protestant Reformation in Europe, which had shattered Christianity into a host of competing denominations of churches and sects united by charismatic leaders or strict religious practices and principles. Initially led by the German monk Martin Luther, Protestant reformers had objected to the worldly and corrupt practices of the Catholic Church headed by the pope, who, from his Vatican palace in Rome, claimed to rule over all of Christendom as Christ's vicar or representative on earth. The Catholic Church not only regulated the spiritual lives of individuals from birth to death, but also exercised enormous power in the secular realm. Popes ruled like princes over the papal states of central Italy. They formed diplomatic alliances and engaged in military warfare to promote territorial, financial, and political interests. Lower in the Catholic hierarchy, other church officials also became government leaders and bureaucrats, pursuing worldly careers rather than the spiritual welfare of individual souls. Religious practice itself became corrupted by the Church's increasing need for money. The Vatican treasury benefited enormously from the systematic sale of "indulgences," or pardons, which officially remitted God's just punishment for a person's sins. The wealthy particularly had the power to purchase indulgences, "buying" their way through heaven's gates.

Cementing his political alliance with Spain, Pope Alexander VI issued a bull, or declaration, in 1493 granting the unexplored western lands discovered by Columbus to Queen Isabella and King Ferdinand. In return, the Spanish king and queen promised to convert native inhabitants of these new territories to Christianity. With the European discovery and conquest of the New World led by Catholic Spain, the Vatican could envision global missions and a truly universal Church. On the other hand, doctrinally and ethnically diverse Protestants viewed America as a *tabula rasa*, where a true Christianity could begin afresh by returning to its primitive, biblical origins antedating papal corruption.

Samuel King
Portrait of the Reverend Ezra Stiles, 1771. Oil on canvas, 33½ x 27½ in (85.1 x 69.9 cm). Yale University Art Gallery, New Haven, Connecticut. Bequest of Dr. Charles Jenkins Foote, B.A. 1883, M.D. 1890.

On a pillar to Stiles's right, King drew an emblem of the planetary system. In the background, the Hebraic name of God is encircled by flamelike spots and lines that signify the intellectual world's inclination towards the divine. The words ALL HAPPY IN GOD arch over the Hebrew letters. Christ's cross stands at the bottom of the emblematic circle, while a black spot to the left of the cross symbolizes moral evil, a space infinitely smaller than God's perfected universe.

2.1 Dr. John Kearsley
Christ Church,
Philadelphia,
Pennsylvania, 1727–54.
The Essex Institute, Salem,
Massachusetts.

This Anglican church, with
its 196-foot-tall steeple,
was designed after
classical, Renaissance-
inspired English structures
by the London architects
Sir Christopher Wren
(1632–1723) and James
Gibbs (1682–1754),
particularly Gibbs's
temple-like masterpiece,
St. Martin-in-the-Fields
(1726). At Christ Church's
east end, beneath a
triangular pediment and
heavy cornice, a large
tripartite window, styled in
the manner of the Italian
Renaissance architect
Andrea Palladio (1508–80),
pierces the wall to
illuminate the chancel,
site of the altar's
sacramental rituals.

Many Protestant denominations became established in Europe as state churches under the protection and governance of Protestant princes and monarchs. Protestant faiths displaced Catholicism primarily in northern Europe, including Scandinavia; the Netherlands; various parts of Germany; Scotland; and England. Founded as a state church by King Henry VIII, the Anglican Church, or Church of England, became officially Protestant in 1559 under Elizabeth I. Nevertheless, the Anglican Church retained many aspects of Catholic ritual and organization, including a governing structure of bishops and archbishops that enforced religious uniformity and laws against heresy and blasphemy. In America, Anglicanism became the established, tax-supported religion in England's various middle and southern colonies. Virginia was the first colony to legislate a formal establishment of the Church of England, in 1632. Others followed much later, but not without much dissension from non-Anglicans: New York (1693), Maryland (1702), North Carolina (1701), South Carolina (1706), and Georgia (1758).

European Protestant state churches generated intense opposition from more radical reform groups, further fracturing Christian unity. "Puritan" reformers became dissatisfied with the Church of England's failure to purge religious practice of Catholic, "popish" rituals. Following the teachings of the theologian John Calvin in Geneva, Switzerland, most Protestants in

2.2 Quaker Meetinghouse Stony Brook, New Jersey, 1760. New Jersey Historical Society.

England, the Netherlands, and elsewhere sought to reform the sacrament of Holy Communion, which reenacted the sacrificial death of Christ, the Son of God. During the ceremony, the officiating priest placed bread and wine upon the altar and through an act of "transubstantiation" miraculously facilitated the divine transformation of food and drink. While the bread and wine maintained their "accidental" physical appearance, they now contained the body and blood of Christ, or His "real presence." Though only priests drank the wine, members of the congregation ingested the body of Christ, spiritually nourishing themselves with His supernatural being.

The Swiss reformer Ulrich Zwingli charged that Catholics committed not only idolatry but also cannibalism when they insisted that Christ was literally present in the sacramental bread and wine. For Calvin, Christ was only spiritually present when the bread and wine were converted into a symbol of God's infinitely higher being. The Church of England generally adopted the Calvinist interpretation of Holy Communion, but retained many of Catholicism's ceremonial trappings despite the objections of Puritans. Puritans refused to kneel at the altar before the bread and wine because this worshipful gesture suggested the veneration

of idols. In their own observances, Puritans preferred to perform the sacrament as a "Last Supper," or communal meal of both the bread and the wine. This dinner ritual stressed spiritual sharing rather than the mystical authority of officiating priests.

Protestants feared the idolatrous potential of religious images in the church. They regarded these as priestly instruments for keeping worshipers, particularly the illiterate, from knowing the true Word of God as written in the Holy Bible. Puritans objected even to the Anglican clergy's Catholic practice of making the hand sign of the cross. Like the act of transubstantiation, this gesture of blessing was condemned as a form of magical trickery, because it suggested that priests possessed power to conjure forth the presence of Christ, who had suffered and died upon the cross.

During the seventeenth century, many Puritans followed dissenting Separatist groups such as the Pilgrims to America, particularly to New England, where they hoped to found a spiritual beacon of religious truth and purity for the rest of the world. New England Puritans and Pilgrims rejected the authoritarian powers of bishops by adopting a Congregationalist form of self-government, whereby each local congregation hired its own clergyman and controlled religious life within the community. However, the network of Congregationalist churches in Massachusetts, Connecticut, and New Hampshire also became an established, tax-supported religion that tended to be intolerant of dissenting views. Called upon by the Massachusetts legislative assembly, Congregationalist clergymen met at a synod in 1648 to pass the Cambridge Platform, a mission statement to guide practices of local churches.

Many dissenters from New England orthodoxy, particularly Baptists and Quakers, fled to Rhode Island, where Roger Williams (1603–83), the colony's clergyman-founder and governor, instituted religious freedom and a separation of Church and state. Elsewhere, in Pennsylvania, the Quakers, under the leadership of William Penn, had also established a colonial government that promoted religious toleration. Having suffered persecution in both England and New England, American Quakers taught pacifism and an inner-light faith of direct communication between individual souls and God without the need for clergymen to act as intermediaries. Before his arrival in Pennsylvania, Penn had published an important treatise, *The Great Case of Liberty of Conscience* (1670), which argued for the right of all individuals to be left free of coercion in matters of religious belief. Nevertheless, as we shall see, Quakers observed strict moral practices within their own communities and harbored a strong distrust of the visual arts as a form of luxury.

Colonial Alternatives to Christianity

The presence of a Jew at Alexander Hamilton's dinner table emphasizes that Christianity faced more challenges than just its own internal divisions. Non-Christian religions and secular systems of belief contributed to the cultural diversity of colonial America. In cosmopolitan Philadelphia, Hamilton discovered urbane colonists, who were happily unaffiliated with any Christian church or meetinghouse:

> I intended to have gone to church or [Quaker] meeting to edify by the Word, but was diverted from my good purpose by some polite company I fell into, who were all utter strangers to churches and meetings. But I understood that my negro Dromo very piously stepped into the Lutheran Church to be edified with a sermon preached in High Dutch, which, I believe, when dressed up in the fashion of a discourse, he understood every bit as well as English, and so might edify as much with the one as he could have done with the other (cited in Horner and Bain, p. 364).

African-Americans, Religion, and the Visual Arts

Despite Hamilton's suggestion that his black servant was instinctually drawn to virtually any Christian religious service, no matter what the particular church or language, African-Americans were not inherently attracted to Christianity. While slavery largely destroyed traditional African religions in America, many slave owners were reluctant to have their slaves instructed in the Christian faith, fearing that biblical stories such as the Jews' exodus from servitude in Egypt would only encourage rebellion.

Visual remnants of African religious practices have been discovered in colonial America. In Alexandria, Virginia, a wrought-iron figure was excavated from what was once the site of a blacksmith's shop and slave quarters (fig. 2.3). The figure's stiff, ritualistic pose and formal characteristics suggest its cultural kinship with West African iron figurines crafted by Bamana blacksmiths in Mali. The Bamana, members of the Mande peoples, constituted a significant percentage of Africans sold into American slavery. Though its precise meaning and purpose remain unknown, the Virginia wrought-iron man suggests that some American slaves sought to communicate with African spirits and gods through cult objects and ceremonies. Other excavations of slave quarters in Maryland, Virginia, and South Carolina have uncovered polished stones, crystals, beads, shells, pierced coins, and ceramic objects, which archeologists have related to bundles of magical charms. Deriving from West African religious practice, cloth- or leaf-bound bundles of objects were created as *nkisi*, or sacred medicine. Placed near hearths and doorways, the bundles protected households against disease and misfortune. Seeking to manipulate spirits inhabiting the earth, creators of bundles chose both organic and inorganic materials to divine secrets and predict the future. Colored crystals were especially prized for their prophetic and healing powers, while white buttons, stones, shells, bones, and other materials signified the vitalistic life of the underworld. Forced to submit to the humiliation of slavery, African-Americans attempted to empower themselves through occult practices that magically manipulated nature's spiritual forces.

More visibly, but still working in anonymity, African-American slaves contributed to the religious landscape of America as construction workers and skilled craftsmen. In the Gulf Coast settlement of New Orleans, Louisiana, founded by the French in 1718, African slaves from Senegal and Gambia were especially prized for their talents in building and woodcarving. Furthermore, free people of color, knowledgeable in

2.3 Anonymous
Wrought-iron figure, Alexandria, Virginia, late eighteenth century. Height 11 in (27.9 cm). Smithsonian Institution, Washington, D.C.

2.4 Ursuline convent
New Orleans, Louisiana, designed 1745, completed 1753.

the construction trades, migrated to New Orleans from the French Caribbean colonies of Haiti, St. Maarten, Martinique, and Guadeloupe. African-Americans worked with an ethnically diverse group of additional carpenters and craftsmen from French Canada and Europe, including German, Swiss, and French artisans.

The Ursuline convent in New Orleans (fig. 2.4), the only surviving example of French colonial architecture in Louisiana and, indeed, the oldest building left in the entire Mississippi Valley, was designed in 1745 by Ignace François Broutin, a French military engineer. Broutin borrowed his architectural ideas for the convent from a contemporary military engineering book published in Paris. Constructed with brick masonry and covered with stucco, the second Ursuline convent replaced an earlier wooden building and was, in fact, modeled after one of the engineering book's classical- or Renaissance-style designs for a military barracks. Claude-Joseph Villars DuBréuil, a wealthy French colonist and canal engineer, served as building contractor and directed construction of the large two-and-a-half-story structure. However, despite its imported, European-design-book style, the convent's details, from the dormer windows piercing the high-pitched roof down to the curvilinear iron hardware for door hinges and shutter fasteners, are material expressions of what has been termed "Creole" design or architecture. Creole

or "creolization" in early eighteenth-century Louisiana comprised a cultural blending of French and European values and traditions with those of Native Americans and African-Americans, whether enslaved or free.

Certainly, African-American carpenters and craftsmen contributed their talents and skills to the building and decorative detailing of the convent. The Ursuline order of nuns was, in fact, a substantial slave owner in New Orleans. In addition to its magnificent convent, the Catholic order also operated a large plantation on the lower Mississippi River. Yet, unlike Protestant slave owners in the English southern colonies, the French Ursuline sisters avidly devoted themselves to missionary work and the education of African-American and Indian women. As a means of converting Africans to Christianity, the Ursulines sought to encourage and support stable slave families through the promotion of baptism, marriage, and godparenting. On the other hand, the Ursulines punitively sold off slaves who bore children out of wedlock or were otherwise deemed guilty of immoral acts. Most importantly for the building trades and decorative arts, the Ursulines highly valued their skilled slaves, who could be rented out as artisans or craftsmen. The nuns thereby increased the income of the convent and, incidentally, helped to disseminate the African-American presence in colonial Louisiana architecture and design.

Colonial Magic and the Christian Response

Interest in magic and the occult was not confined to African slaves. Throughout the Anglo-American colonies, clergymen were forced to compete with fortune-tellers, healers, and other "wise" men and women, who practiced various forms of popular magic and folk medicine. In seventeenth-century New England, farmers sometimes erected "spirit stones" featuring crudely carved figures and magical signs that were intended to protect property and homes from evil spells and demons (fig. 2.5). Colonists also warded off unwanted spirits by decorating doorposts or entrances with horseshoes and other potent charms. Families purchased yearly almanacs filled with occult folklore and illustrated with astrological charts and signs of the zodiac, which prophetically aligned individuals and their future lives with movements of the planets and stars (fig. 2.6). While Protestant clergymen often denounced non-Christian occultism and Catholic superstitions, most colonial almanacs were actually written by ministers, who also enthralled readers with tales of God's many wonders that seemed to foretell future events and even the end of the world. Convinced that the Bible was the literal truth or inspired Word of God, colonial clergymen believed that the universe was filled with both good and evil spirits: angels; ghosts; and Satan, the prince of evil, who could magically disguise himself in almost any form. Since miraculous events and supernatural phenomena fill the pages of the Bible, colonists were inclined to give credence to contemporary wonder-inducing stories such as that of a thirty-week-old child prophesying in clear English: "It will be an hard world & you shall know it" (cited in Hall, p. 83). Laymen and clergymen alike gazed upward into the skies, interpreting comets, meteors, and violent flashes of lightning as ominous supernatural portents of things to come.

From Virginia to Massachusetts, institutional Christianity attempted to root out pagan occult practices by conducting witch-hunts and witch trials. The Bible warned of the existence of witches and the terror of Satanic or demonic possession. In Virginia from 1626 through 1705, at least nineteen people were charged with witchcraft. However, in New England, hundreds stood accused of black magic or of casting evil spells. In Salem, Massachusetts, colonial witch-hunting hysteria reached a peak in 1692, when 20 individuals were executed after inquisitorial trials that admitted as evidence forced confessions and purported eyewitness accounts of ghostly, spectral images. By a ratio of more than four to one, witch trials targeted women. Women were stereotypically defined by their bodies or sexual natures and were, therefore, regarded as more vulnerable to the temptations of demonic beings.

During the eighteenth century, the fear of witches declined among the educated elite. However, various occult practices and beliefs continued to appeal to a wide spectrum of the population. Toward the end of the century, the Reverend Ezra Stiles, president of Yale College from 1778 to 1795, was one of many intellectuals who expressed strong interest in the occult science of alchemy. An avid letter-writer, the Congregationalist clergyman was in correspondence with American alchemists who claimed to

2.5 Boundary marker
Newbury, Massachusetts, 1636–50.
Diorite, 51½ in (130.8 cm) high, 28½ in (72.4 cm) wide, 11½ in (29.2 cm) deep. Witchstone Farm, Byfield Parish, Newbury, Massachusetts. American Antiquarian Society. The D. and J. L. Farber Collection of Gravestone Photographs.

This undated boundary stone belonged to Richard Dummer (1598–1679), a farmer and mill-owner from Newbury. It relates to four stone thresholds, the earliest dated 1636, that once guarded doorways to his house. All feature mysterious signs. In the upright boundary marker, trespassers or evil spirits would have encountered the stern, glaring image of a man standing with arms akimbo in a confrontational pose.

possess a magical "philosopher's stone" that enabled them to transform base metals into gold or, alternatively, to create a universal elixir to cure all illnesses and prolong human life. Stiles even communicated with a Jewish rabbi from Poland about alchemical secrets and became interested in the Jewish mystical tradition of the Kabbala, which alchemists frequently relied upon as a source of divine wisdom and universal knowledge of God's creation. Before becoming president of Yale, the Newport, Rhode Island, clergyman had his portrait painted by Samuel King (1749–1819), a largely self-taught artist (see p. 38). Under Stiles's direction, King included in the portrait occult, Kabbalistic symbols of the cosmos centered on the mysterious tetragrammaton, or the Hebraic holy name of God. Alchemical treatises of the seventeenth and eighteenth centuries often included illustrations of the tetragrammaton, from which God's attributes and creation were held magically to flow. While Stiles reconciled alchemy and Jewish mysticism with Christianity, other eighteenth-century Americans cultivated an interest in such

esoteric subjects as a means of discovering religious truths historically antedating and superseding Christianity. Thus, the itinerant Dr. Hamilton (as we shall see in the next chapter) belonged to the secret fraternity of Freemasons, whose devotion to ancient, occult wisdom offered many colonial men a potential alternative or supplement to traditional Christianity.

Catholic Art in Spanish America

During the sixteenth century, before the English settlement of North America, Catholic Spain had established New Spain, a vast imperial territory that stretched from Peru in South America northward to the area of the Colorado River. The northern part of New Spain, which later in the nineteenth century became part of the United States, was a sparsely populated frontier. It consisted of small settlements of farmers and soldiers as well as mission churches constructed by Indian labor, mostly under the direction of

2.6 John Foster
"The Dominion of the Moon in Man's Body," from *An Almanac of Coelestial Motions for the Year of the Christian Epocha 1678*, Boston, 1678.
American Antiquarian Society, Worcester, Massachusetts.

Since the Middle Ages, almanacs, or calendars of the heavens, included the Man of Signs, who personifies the ancient belief that human health is connected with the motions of the universe. Foster's figure is encircled by the twelve names and signs of the zodiac, corresponding to twelve constellations and twelve parts of the body. Fortune-tellers and doctors warned that different organs or limbs were vulnerable to affliction, depending on lunar, stellar, and planetary movements.

2.7 San Estevan
Acoma Pueblo, New
Mexico. Photograph by
Ferenz Fedor, c. 1940.
Museum of New Mexico,
Santa Fe, New Mexico.

Franciscan friars. Founded in the thirteenth century by St. Francis of Assisi, the Franciscans were an order of Catholic brothers. They took vows of chastity and poverty and dedicated themselves to the itinerant preaching of the Christian faith. By the 1630s, dozens of mission churches had been constructed in Florida and New Mexico. While the Spanish monarchy primarily valued its American colonies for their gold and silver, missionaries hoped that the conversion of Native Americans would signify the advent of a new millennial age in the history of Christianity. During this thousand-year period, Christ's Word would spread to the four corners of the world in preparation for God's Last Judgment. During the millennium, all peoples of the earth would have the opportunity to convert to Christ, thereby escaping eternal damnation in Hell.

The Mission Church of San Estevan

No site in New Spain appeared more like one of the remote four corners of the world than the mission church of San Estevan at Acoma, New Mexico, a small Pueblo Indian village southwest of Santa Fe (figs. 2.7–2.8). Friar

Francisco Atanasio Domínguez (1740–c.1805), a Mexican-born Franciscan, observed in 1776 that the buildings of Acoma are situated high above the surrounding desert plain "on the flat top of a mesa" 350 feet high (p. 188). Resembling a cliff with "such horrible precipices that it is not possible to look over them for fear of the steep drop" (p. 189), the mesa conveyed the image of an almost impregnable fortress:

The ascent . . . is a sandy and very difficult slope (there are many footpaths leading up, which only the Indians manage with skill). It begins on the west side of the mesa, ascends almost halfway, and from there on makes a number of boxed-in turns, so difficult that in some places they have made wide steps so that the pack animals may ascend with comparative ease (p. 188).

Domínguez described Acoma as an incomparably difficult mission site, since "there is not even a brook, earth to make adobes, or a good cart road. . . . This makes what the Indians have built here of adobes with perfection, strength and grandeur, at the expense of their own backs, worthy of admiration" (p. 189).

Despite Acoma's forbidding geography, Spanish soldiers under the leadership of the explorer-conquistador Juan de Oñate successfully overcame Native American resistance and captured the mesa in 1599, killing 500 men and 300 women and children. The 580 Indian survivors, most of whom were women and children, were forced into servitude. Surviving men over the age of twenty-five also suffered mutilation, as Spaniards severed one foot from each as insurance against future rebellion.

Understandably, after this violent beginning, missionary activity was slow to bear fruit at Acoma. However, thirty years after the 1599 conquest, Friar Juan Ramírez supervised newly converted Acoma Indians in the construction of a large, two-towered church, made from fieldstones and adobe. The adobe mixture of clay, sand, and water was "puddled," or layered, by Indian women to create walls many feet thick. Since there was neither sufficient water nor loose rocks and soil on top of the mesa, most of the building materials had to be transported up the narrow trail from the valley floor below. The massive, severe church was approximately 145 feet long, 45 feet wide, and 30 feet high. Situated at a short distance from the Pueblo village, the structure loomed over the low-profile communal dwellings of the native population. Missionaries intended these monumental, fortresslike churches to awe Native Americans with the superior grandeur of the Christian God.

Borrowing from a long tradition of Catholic architecture in Europe, the building's longitudinal plan was designed to accommodate impressive ceremonial processions between the eastern entrance and the sacred, western end of the church (fig. 2.9). The long nave, consisting of a central aisle and space for worshipers, led to the sanctuary, where the clergy conducted Mass, or the sacrament of Holy Communion, over an altar decorated with Christian symbols and images. This sacramental ritual reenacting Christ's sacrificial death originally was illuminated by a hidden transverse clerestory or high window located between the roof of the nave and the somewhat higher roof of the sanctuary. Indiscernible from the nave, where the Indian congregation stood in worship, the window dramatically focused upon the altar and the sacrament of Holy Communion the light of a morning sun that metaphorically expressed Christ's ultimate Resurrection or triumph over the darkness of death. Hidden light sources were commonplace in seventeenth-century European churches and chapels. But this conventional

2.8 San Estevan
Acoma, New Mexico, 1629–42.
Museum of New Mexico, Santa Fe, New Mexico.

Though far different in its unornamented austerity, San Estevan's twin-tower façade distantly descends from the cathedrals of medieval Europe. More immediately, it originated from churches in Spain and Mexico, particularly the great cathedral in Mexico City, begun during the late sixteenth century. Minimal fenestration contributed to the mission's military defense and helped insulate the building against temperature extremes. A single small window pierces the main façade to illuminate the choir loft, while only two south windows light the nave.

association of sunlight with Christ fortuitously created a visual and religious bridge with Native American traditions of sun worship. Pueblo Indians assimilated the alien Christian faith and adapted it to their own spiritual needs by drawing upon their own religious and cultural experiences.

A Spanish colonial document dated 1664 reported that "the beautiful rock of Acoma has on its summit the church which is the most handsome, the paraphernalia of worship is abundant and unusual; [the church] has a choir and an organ" (cited in Kubler, p. 94). By 1680, the Acoma church stood in partial ruin, with its roof and clerestory window damaged or destroyed. That year, Pueblo Indians throughout New Mexico rebelled against Spanish occupation soldiers, settlers, and missionaries, killing hundreds and forcing survivors to retreat eastward to the village of El Paso in present-day Texas. The Revolt of 1680 liberated New Mexico from European domination for over a decade. According to the recorded testimony of a Pueblo Indian captured by the Spanish, Popé, the Indian rebel leader, traveled to every mission church and Pueblo village. At each location, he ordered followers to "instantly break up and burn the images of the holy Christ, the Virgin Mary and the other saints, the crosses, and everything pertaining to Christianity, and that they burn the temples, break up the bells, and separate from the wives whom God had given them in marriage and take those whom they desired" (cited in Weber, p. 136).

Native American Resistance and the Christian Reconquest

In large measure, the Revolt of 1680 was triggered by the Pueblo Indians' rejection of Christianity and its strict prohibition against native deities and customs such as polygamy. While assimilating the sun and other emblems of nature, missionaries had attempted to destroy many traditional symbols of Indian religious life. The friars particularly attacked the idolatrous *kachina* dolls and masks that Indians crafted to ensure good harvests by honoring spirits and ancestors from the underworld. Franciscans attempted to focus the attention of Indian converts exclusively upon the imagery of Jesus Christ, His holy mother the Virgin Mary,

0   25   50ft
0   5   10   15m

2.9 San Estevan
Acoma, New Mexico, 1629–42.
Plan of the church and cloister.

and a host of saintly martyrs who had died for the Christian faith. They promised Native Americans that Christian rituals, relics, and visual images surpassed the magical powers of their traditional nature gods in healing the sick, bringing rain, and guaranteeing successful harvests and hunts. Sacraments such as Baptism and Holy Communion would bring converts physical healing and prosperity as well as an eternal spiritual afterlife in heaven.

However, by 1680, most Pueblos had concluded that Christianity had not worked for them and, indeed, had become a harmful burden. Since the arrival of the Franciscan friars in New Mexico, the Pueblo population had declined by half to 17,000. In addition to war casualties inflicted by Spanish soldiers and nomadic Indian tribes, Pueblo villagers succumbed to European diseases and suffered from the forced labor demanded by missionaries and colonial officials. Despite the friars' prayers for rain, droughts were a persistent fact of nature in semiarid New Mexico. Christian magic did not surpass the efficacy of traditional religious practices in preventing crop failures or hunger.

Virtually the only Christian image to escape destruction during the Pueblo Revolt of 1680 was a small statue of the Virgin Mary, popularly known as *La Conquistadora*, or Our Lady of the Conquest (fig. 2.10). Made from painted wood and wearing a wig, colorful clothing, and jewels, the sculpture had been brought to Santa Fe from Mexico City by Friar Alonso de Benavides, who, in 1626, became chief administrator of Franciscan missions in New Mexico. In a "Memorial" that he wrote in 1630 and later revised in 1634, Benavides recalled that this image of the Virgin, which he "had placed in a chapel in the church in the villa of Santa Fe" was received with "reverence" by Indian converts, who spread word of its "great beauty" (cited in Espinosa, p. 11).

Nevertheless, by 1680, *La Conquistadora* had to be rescued from disenchanted Native American rebels. Loyal Spanish refugees built a chapel for her outside of El Paso while preparing for her triumphant return to Santa Fe. In 1693, General Diego de Vargas led the reconquest of New Mexico.

Back in Santa Fe, he executed seventy Native Americans who had refused to surrender. He also spent the better part of 1694 waging a military campaign against pockets of rebel resistance throughout the rest of New Mexico. However,

2.10 Anonymous
La Conquistadora, early seventeenth century. Museum of New Mexico, Santa Fe, New Mexico.

in 1696, another organized Indian rebellion resulted in the burning of more churches and Christian icons. Afterward, colonial officials eased demands on Indian laborers and more pragmatic Franciscan friars decided to relent in their determination to eradicate traditional Pueblo religious beliefs and rituals. By the eighteenth century, Hispanic devotion to Christ tended to coexist with Pueblo reverence for ancient nature gods.

Vargas and colonial officials in Santa Fe credited their victory and the return of peace to *La Conquistadora*. Ever since the thirteenth century, the Franciscans and other religious orders had promoted a cult of the Virgin Mary. In conquering New Spain and its northern frontier of New Mexico during the sixteenth and seventeenth centuries, Franciscan friars instituted specific practices honoring the mother of Christ, including daily recitation of the rosary, a series of devotional prayers directed toward the Virgin. Indeed, the Hispanic Catholics who venerated *La Conquistadora* also called her *Nuestra Señora del Rosario*, Our Lady of the Rosary, and recited rosary prayers in her presence.

The Virgin Mary represented the Christian faith in a more benevolent, nurturing guise. In San Antonio, Texas, where Franciscans and Indian laborers constructed several mission churches, the Marian cult received one of its most elaborate expressions in the richly decorated façade of San José y San Miguel de Aguayo (fig. 2.11). Pedro Huizar, a Mexican-trained sculptor, carved the façade's many sculptures. In addition to the Virgin's welcoming image immediately over the entrance, St. Joachim and St. Anne, the Virgin's parents, flank the portal doors. The church as a whole is dedicated to the Virgin's husband, St. Joseph, who appears atop an oval window in the façade's upper level. In visually representing Mary and Joseph, the human parents of Christ, Franciscan missionaries reassured Indian converts with comforting parental intercessors or defenders of humanity before an otherwise distant Christian God.

At the time of the Pueblo Revolt of 1680, no more than 3,000 Spaniards were living in all of New Mexico, and the number grew only modestly following the Reconquest. By the end of the eighteenth century, the town of Santa Fe, where Hispanic colonists were concentrated, had a population that numbered a mere 6,000. Nevertheless, at the beginning of that century, the Spanish residents of Santa Fe celebrated their victorious return to New Mexico by initiating an annual fiesta honoring *La Conquistadora*. They also constructed a special chapel to house the cult statue. The Rosario chapel built within La Parroquía, a Santa Fe parish church dedicated to St. Francis, was completed around 1717 to facilitate civic and religious veneration of the sculpture.

El Santo Entierro and Hispanic-Catholic Ritual

While *La Conquistadora* had been a Mexican import, by the eighteenth century the demand for sacred images was so great that local craftsmen were increasingly called on to decorate churches and supply devotional objects. The Mexican-born Franciscan friar Andrés García (active 1747–79) took up residence in various New Mexican missions, where he crafted numerous religious images, including a sculpture of *El Santo Entierro*, a conventional popular type of image representing the dead Christ lying in his sepulcher (fig. 2.12). The life-size wooden figure, which rests in the mission church of Santa Cruz, New Mexico, was carved and painted for maximum emotional effect. García liberally dripped red paint over the crucified Christ's emaciated corpse. He then placed the pitiable figure on a mattress and pillow within an open wooden casket. During Holy Week, the annual commemoration of Christ's death and Resurrection, penitents traditionally carried the sculpture in procession, seeking forgiveness for their sins. Eighteenth-century processions included flagellants, who whipped or scourged themselves as a means of physically identifying with Christ's suffering, literally mimicking the bloody corpus painted by the artist.

Such imagery had little meaning for those Indians who continued to be abused and exploited by colonial officials and wealthy Spanish landowners. In an official report written in 1750 to his religious superior within the Franciscan order, Friar Carlos Delgado blamed Spanish governors and civil authorities for impoverishing Indians with forced labor and the confiscation of crops. As a result of these abuses,

2.11 Pedro Huizar
Portal sculpture, San José y San Miguel de Aguayo, San Antonio, Texas, c. 1770–75.

The façade of this mission church seems more sculptural than architectural. The saintly figures surrounding the portal and oval window are sculpted in high relief and appear to float within a fluid, spiritually animated space of organic, sensuous ornamentation. Although Huizar's provincial style derives from medieval Gothic sculpture, the dense figural abundance of San José's portal bears close comparison with contemporaneous Catholic Baroque churches in Spain.

Delgado complained, the Indians "turn their backs to our holy mother, the Church, abandon their pueblos and missions, and flee to the heathen, there to worship the devil, and, most lamentable of all, to confirm in idolatries those who have never been illumined by the light of our holy faith, so that they will never give ear or credit to the preaching of the gospel" (cited in Gunn, p. 308). Unsurprisingly, most New Mexican artists were of Spanish rather than Indian heritage. Later in California, however, where Catholic missions were more successful, there was significant Indian participation in the decoration of churches.

2.12 Fray Andrés García
El Santo Entierro (Christ in the Holy Sepulcher), eighteenth century. Church of Santa Cruz, Santa Cruz, New Mexico.

Moravian Missions and the Depiction of the Crucified Christ

In contrast to the plethora of devotional icons in the churches of Catholic New Spain, such imagery was rarely seen in the British colonies of North America. Although Maryland was founded in 1632 as a refuge for Catholics from Protestant England, few Catholic dissenters actually settled in the colony. The anti-Catholic majority of Marylanders often resorted to vigilante violence against Catholic priests and the few Catholic churches and chapels that were constructed in the colony. The hostile atmosphere forced Maryland Catholics to worship privately and to avoid public displays of their faith.

Yet religious paintings similar to Hispano-Catholic representations of the crucified Christ did appear within the ethnically and religiously diverse culture of Pennsylvania. The Polish-born, German-trained artist John Valentine Haidt (1700–80) arrived in Bethlehem, Pennsylvania, in 1754 to support the missionary work of the Moravian Church. John Dillenberger, a theologian and historian of religion and art, has defined the Moravian Church as a "Protestant version of the Catholic tradition" (p. 35). Origi-

nating in reform movements that antedated the Lutheran Reformation of the sixteenth century, Moravian religious practice had much in common with Catholicism, including a refusal to ban biblical and devotional imagery from worship spaces. Under the leadership of the German aristocrat Count Nikolaus Zinzendorf (1700–60), settlers from Moravia in Central Europe had sought to escape religious conflict in the Old World. Establishing enduring communities in North Carolina as well as Pennsylvania, these German-speaking Moravians reacted against religious divisions within Christianity. Within Protestantism, they associated themselves with Pietism, a movement that emphasized individual piety, Bible reading, and a holy life filled with good works. Establishing missionary outposts that stretched from Greenland to South Africa and the West Indies, Moravians believed that all members of their faith had an obligation to spread Christ's message of universal salvation. More than most Protestants, they sought to convert Native Americans and African-Americans to Christianity. On the Caribbean islands and later in North Carolina, converted African-American slaves became either preachers or missionaries within their own communities. While many plantation-owners nervously suspected Moravians of secretly plotting to abolish slavery, the European missionaries themselves became slave-owners and generally remained focused on African-Americans' heavenly future rather than their present bondage.

Haidt regarded his paintings as a form of religious preaching. The pictures were intended for public display in Moravian churches and mission chapels. Like his contemporary Andrés García, Haidt represented the emotion-laden subject of Christ's suffering and death upon the cross. One of his most poignant and intimate compositions is the *Lamentation over Christ's Body*, which features the Virgin Mary, Mary Magdalene, and other mourners displaying Christ's mortal wounds for the contemplative beholder (fig. 2.13). Haidt presses Christ's torn and blood-stained corpse painfully close to the picture plane, virtually inviting viewers to reach into the picture so that they might themselves touch or

support the sacred body. Created for a place of worship, the Moravian Brethren's House in Nazareth, Pennsylvania, Haidt's painting visually complements the verbal imagery of Moravian hymns, which emphasize the sacrificial spilling of Christ's blood.

Though identifying with Protestantism, Moravians followed Catholic tradition by frequently practicing the sacrament of Holy Communion. Haidt's graphic, devotional representation of the dead Christ would have encouraged Moravians to believe that in eating and drinking the communal bread and wine they were ingesting Christ's body and blood or real presence. As in the Franciscan mission churches of New Spain, intense meditation on verbal descriptions and visual images of Christ's

2.13 John Valentine Haidt
Lamentation over Christ's Body, c. 1760.
Oil on canvas, 29 x 33 in (73.7 x 83.2 cm). The Moravian Historical Society, Nazareth, Pennsylvania.

This subject relates to the Pietà, in which the Virgin Mary mourns over Christ's body. She is here at the picture's apex, but diminished in scale. The praying Mary Magdalene, a prostitute who converted to Christ, looms as a far larger presence, lower left. Haidt's distortion of scale expresses the Moravians' missionary goal of Christian conversion.

sacrificial body led the Moravian faithful to a mystical identification with God and His visible manifestation in human flesh.

Protestant Iconoclasm and the Private Display of Biblical Art

Most Protestants attacked the idolatrous nature of Catholic religious imagery. During the sixteenth century, European Protestants became avid iconoclasts. They destroyed church icons of Christ and the Virgin Mary that decorated church façades and altars or were carried in religious processions. Reformers ridiculed Catholic priests and monks for promoting the superstitious belief that icons could facilitate miracles or magically promote health and prosperity. They feared that images within the church functioned as idols for public worship. As idols, these visual cult objects became false, material substitutes for God's infinite and essentially invisible spiritual reality.

In Boston, Massachusetts, the Puritan clergyman Samuel Willard (1640–1707) expressed strong reservations against religious images, exclaiming in one of his sermons, "How very unsuitable is it to represent the Divine Nature by any Corporeal similitude." Willard rhetorically asked: "How is it possible rightly to shadow a Spirit? Whoever was able rightly to decipher the form or shape of a being which is invisible!" He ominously warned that "It is a madness and wickedness to offer . . . any Image or Representation of God" because it is essentially "Idolatrous" (cited in McCoubrey, p. 3).

Nevertheless, Willard and other followers of Calvinist theology in Europe and America made it clear that their prohibition against religious imagery applied only to ecclesiastical spaces for public worship. When Dr. Alexander Hamilton visited Albany, New York, in 1744, he saw homes of Dutch Calvinists that were decorated with paintings of biblical subjects. Calvinist reformers permitted the civil or private display of religious images, as long as they represented the truths of the Bible and taught useful moral lessons.

Constituting the largest body of religious painting in British colonial America, nearly forty New York Dutch biblical pictures have survived from the first half of the eighteenth century. While the English had taken over the New Netherlands in 1664 (renaming it New York), Dutch colonial culture along the upper Hudson River valley survived well into the next century. The New York Dutch continued to use their own language and worshiped in the Dutch Reformed Church. This state church of the Netherlands had been established after 1609, when northern provinces of the Netherlands had declared their independence from Catholic Spain and established the Protestant Dutch Republic. Freed from foreign domination, the seafaring republic soon established a worldwide commercial empire and a flourishing industry in the visual arts.

When Dutch settlers arrived in America, they brought with them their taste for paintings, prints, and illustrated Bibles. During the seventeenth century, they imported artworks from the Netherlands. However, by the early eighteenth century, immigrant painters from England and self-taught New York Dutch artists increasingly satisfied the market for religious pictures.

In contrast to Hispano-Catholic and Moravian artists' devotional icons focusing on the miracle-working body of Christ or the cult of the Virgin Mary, colonial New York Dutch paintings represented complex, multifigure compositions based on popular biblical narratives. During their struggles with Catholic Spain and later with the English, the Dutch developed their national identity in relation to the stories of the Bible. They especially identified with the trials and tribulations of the ancient Israelites, as chronicled in the Old Testament.

Many of the surviving New York Dutch religious paintings represent Old Testament themes of God's interventions on behalf of the Jews, His "chosen people." Borrowing his composition from an imported European print, the anonymous painter of *Belshazzar's Feast* represented a scene from the fifth chapter of the book of Daniel, which prophesies the fall of Babylon, Israel's enemy and captor (fig. 2.14). Belshazzar, the Babylonian king, who sits at the far left of the composition, has been interrupted from hosting a lavish court banquet by the sudden appearance of a hand mysteriously writing a message on the far wall in the painting's upper-right corner. As later interpreted by the Jewish prophet Daniel, God's message foretells the death of Belshazzar and the abrupt collapse of his empire. With the fall of Babylon, God liberates the Jews from their captivity, enabling them to rebuild their temple in the holy city of Jerusalem. In both the Old and New Testaments, Babylon was a code name for human sin and corruption. The visual representation of God's judgment against Belshazzar would have been appreciated as a useful reminder of the moral dangers of pride and luxury. However, for the New York Dutch patron who purchased the work, this painting also may have evoked historical associations with the Netherlands' struggle for national independence from Catholic Spain. Protestant clergyman often denounced the Catholic Church as the "Whore of Babylon" (Jeffrey, p. 827). They

derived these sexual epithets from the book of Revelation, the final, visionary book of the Bible, which prophesies the Apocalypse, or the violent events leading to the end of the world and God's "Last Judgment" of humankind. Personifying the prideful, luxurious vanities of worldly evil, the Whore of Babylon appears "arrayed in purple and scarlet colour, and decked with gold and precious stones and pearls, having a golden cup in her hand full of abominations and filthiness of her fornication" (Revelation 17:4). In the Old Testament book of Daniel, on which the New Testament book of Revelation is partially based, the sinful city of Babylon stands in contrast to the holy city of Jerusalem.

The anonymous painter of *Belshazzar's Feast* expressed Protestant anxieties regarding idolatry and worldly corruption. Within the picture, a

2.14 Anonymous
Belshazzar's Feast,
c. 1742.
Oil on canvas,
31½ x 41 in
(80 x 104.1 cm).
Albany Institute of
History and Art, Albany,
New York.

golden chandelier is decorated with erotic, nude figurines. The sensuous idols hold torches to illuminate a banqueting table laden with gold and silver vessels. Having been confiscated from the Jewish temple in Jerusalem, these religious artifacts are now being misused by the Babylonians for an unholy feast at which Belshazzar's "wives and his concubines" (Daniel 5:3) were among the guests.

In displaying biblical paintings within their homes, affluent New York Dutch families attempted to establish their moral standing as a pious, godly people. During the American Revolution, Peter van Schaack (1747–1832), from New York's Hudson River valley, justified the value of religious images even within churches. Remaining loyal to the British government, van Schaack was living in temporary exile in London when, in 1779, he expressed admiration for the biblical pictures decorating the stained-glass windows of Westminster Abbey. He confessed the appropriateness of such imagery in this royal church where the monarchs of England had been crowned since the Middle Ages:

> The paintings on the window, against which we are apt to conceive a prejudice, as being a relic of popish superstition, have a very happy effect. Few can abstract their minds so totally from sensible objects, as to not require every external aid to their mental devotion. These should therefore be made auxiliary and subservient to the main purpose, and pour in virtue to the attentive eye. . . . The colors are vastly beautiful, and of an endless variety, no two of them being exactly alike; the light which is admitted through them is extremely pleasing to the sight, and the most interesting scenes from sacred history are there painted (cited in Piwonka and Blackburn, p. 17).

Though not painted with biblical narratives, the glass windows of the Dutch Reformed Church in Albany were decorated with coats of arms or heraldic emblems that symbolized the European genealogical heritage and social conservatism of New York Dutch families. As suggested by van Schaack's admiration for Westminster Abbey, the Church of England took the lead in visually transforming the landscape of the British colonies with explicitly religious forms and symbols.

Anglo-American Churches and Meetinghouses

Though most early-seventeenth-century founders of the English colonies expressly dedicated themselves to the propagation of Christianity, for decades much of colonial North America remained barren of church architecture and other symbols of Christian zeal. In New England, Puritans met in meetinghouses rather than churches. For John Winthrop, the first governor of Massachusetts Bay Colony, the term "church" referred not to a building for public assembly, but rather to a congregation or body of people who have sworn a covenant of faith with God. Puritans did not wish to idolize works of architecture by characterizing them as sacred places. Paid for by public taxes imposed on both church members and non-members, New England meetinghouses were initially designed like large homes. In fact, Winthrop's own home or parlor served for a time as a meetinghouse. Modest and crudely built, seventeenth-century meetinghouses neither appeared distinctively religious nor served exclusively religious purposes. They were regularly sites for town meetings, court trials, and other secular activities. Standing at the center of community life and its defense, meetinghouses were even used as storehouses for gunpowder.

Other denominations, such as the Baptists and Quakers in Rhode Island, Pennsylvania, and elsewhere also met in meetinghouses that purposely blended with the domestic architecture of secular life. The house form especially appealed to radical Protestant groups, who identified with the persecuted early Christians of ancient Rome and their simple worship services in private homes. The exterior of the small Quaker meetinghouse at Stony Brook, New Jersey, near Princeton, suggests nothing of its interior, religious purpose (see fig. 2.2).

Quakers particularly suffered from persecution in both England and New England. Between 1659 and 1661, Puritan authorities executed four Quakers who refused to leave the Massachusetts Bay Colony. Founded in England in 1652 by the charismatic leader George Fox, Quakerism represented an extreme form of

2.15 Elizabeth Hudson
Sampler, 1737.
Linen plain weave with
silk embroidery in satin,
15½ x 11¼ in
(39.4 x 28.6 cm).
Philadelphia Museum of
Art, Pennsylvania.
Purchased with funds
from Robert L. McNeil, Jr.,
Trusts.

The lines of Hudson's
moralistic poem alternate
with the horizontal bands of
floral motifs. The verses
were based on Genesis
28:10–12. This biblical text
narrates the story of Jacob,
the Jewish patriarch, who
rested on a stone pillow in
the wilderness and dreamt
of a ladder rising toward
heaven.

Puritanism. Not only did Quakers reject lavish art and architecture for a humble religious aesthetic of plainness but they also abolished all church sacraments and subordinated the Bible, or the written Word of God, to the notion that every individual's inner light was a sufficient guide to absolute truth. Bible-wielding Puritans feared Quakerism's egalitarianism, which dispensed with a formal clergy and extended the privilege of meetinghouse preaching to both men and women.

Within Quaker meetinghouses, there was no grand pulpit for sermons delivered by a professional clergyman. Instead, the rectangular space was defined by rows of wooden benches grouped in sections that segregated members by sex and by age or degree of spiritual prestige.

All were free to speak when moved by their inner spirit, or light; but still, all were not equal. Meetinghouse elders, overseers, and articulate lay ministers generally sat on elevated platforms at the far end of the meetinghouse facing the main body of Quakers in the central area. While Puritans and other Protestants feared the anarchic potential of Quakerism's relative egalitarianism, an individual Quaker's expression of spiritual enlightenment was carefully monitored by group approval and the collective wisdom of the meetinghouse elders. Though Quakers did not regard the meetinghouse as a sacred space, the building's unadorned interior became an emotionally charged cultural site for communally experiencing and testing statements of spiritual truth.

2.16 St. Luke's Church
Newport Parish,
Smithfield, Isle of Wight
County, Virginia,
c. 1680.
Library of Congress,
Washington, D.C.

During the eighteenth century, as the colonies became increasingly wealthy from expanded trade with Britain, Quakers did not deny themselves the pleasures of the visual arts. But they did attempt to regulate the consumption of luxuries by recalling the words of William Penn: "Are not they who sell vain and superfluous Things, exposing them at Door and Windows, Tempters of the People to the Lust of the Eye and pride of Life" (cited in Pointon, p. 407). Thus, when a young Philadelphia Quaker by the name of Elizabeth Hudson (1721–83) stitched together a silk sampler of needlework, she combined the serpentine, naturalistic pattern of leaves, buds, and flowers with a moralistic poem that warned against the vanity of "rich attire": "They in whose noble breast true vertue dwells need not so much adorn their outward shells" (fig. 2.15) (cited in Philadelphia Museum of Art, p. 44). Hudson's father was an overseer of a public school founded by Quakers. Her sampler was probably made in the school, since needlework was regarded as essential for a girl's education. While Quaker women could speak at meetings, their lives were still devoted to the domestic duties of being a good housewife and mother.

In the middle and southern colonies, where the Church of England sought to establish itself as the dominant denomination, religious conflict and spiritual lethargy left the seventeenth-century landscape largely barren of church architecture. Beginning in 1642, the English Civil War disrupted the Anglican Church's contacts with the American colonies. In 1649, Puritans and other radical Protestants forced the trial and execution of King Charles I, who had warred against the political rights of Parliament. The victorious House of Commons established a republic that officially abolished the monarchy and the Anglican Church.

The monarchy and Church of England were restored in 1660 under King Charles II. Nearly thirty years later, the Glorious Revolution of 1688–9 saw Parliament remove the Catholic sympathizer James II from the English throne in favor of two Protestants from the Netherlands, William of Orange and Mary. This more moderate revolution defended rather than attacked the Anglican Church establishment, while guaranteeing the principle of a constitutional or parliamentary monarchy.

After 1660, a revitalized Church of England began turning its attention to the American colonies. In 1650, Virginia had fewer than ten Anglican clergymen for the entire colony. By 1680, however, the number had more than tripled to thirty-five, while the number of church parishes or administrative districts

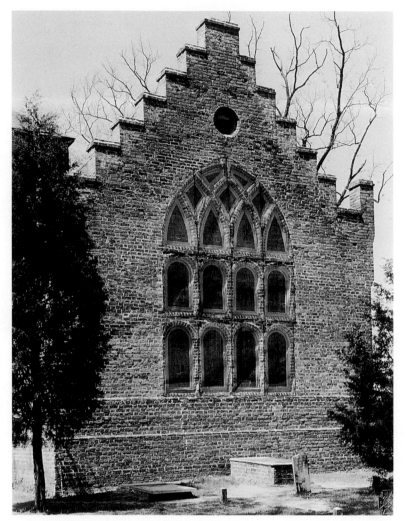

2.17 St. Luke's Church
Newport Parish,
c. 1680.
Exterior view of
southeastern end.
Library of Congress,
Washington, D.C.

St. Luke's stepped gable creates a parapet, or low wall, along the steeply pitched roof. This decorative motif was imported, via England, from Flanders and the Netherlands. The Virginia church's gabled profile closely resembles those of earlier and contemporaneous English parish churches.

mushroomed from twelve to fifty. As new parishes were established, Church of England buildings were constructed to serve the religious needs of expanding settlements and wealthier immigrant families. By 1680, approximately thirty-five Anglican churches dotted the Virginia landscape, with the number nearly doubling by 1725. Furthermore, the small wooden structures that had been built during the early decades of the seventeenth century were replaced by larger, more elegant and richly furnished churches. Aristocratic Virginians regarded houses of God as reflections of their own gentlemanly status. According to the architectural historian Dell Upton, "The Anglican Christ was an English Lord" and His residence was that "of the greatest gentleman in the neighborhood" (p. 164). The vestrymen, or wealthy parishioners who admin-

istered church affairs, conducted parish business meetings like an exclusive social club and often had their names inscribed on plaques affixed to church walls.

St. Luke's Church in Newport Parish, Isle of Wight County, is Virginia's oldest surviving church (fig. 2.16). Many have claimed that this small parish church, located in a rural setting, dates from 1632, but recent scholarship strongly suggests that it was built fifty years later. During the early seventeenth century, Virginians were economically and architecturally ill-prepared to undertake construction of brick buildings, particularly on the elaborate scale of St. Luke's with its lofty tower and ornamental tracery windows. Like the Catholic mission churches of New Spain, St. Luke's openly announced its religious purpose as a sacred space, or house of God. The

2.18 Hexangular pulpit with all-seeing eye decorating the sounding board or type. Plate CXIV from Batty Langley's *City and Country Builder's and Workman's Treasury of Designs*, 3rd edition (London, 1750). Henry Francis du Pont Winterthur Museum Library. Collection of Printed Books.

church's three-story tower was a rarity in Virginia and surely had the intended effect of inspiring reverential awe within most parishioners, who traveled from small, wooden homes to the relatively grand religious site. In deciding St. Luke's design, church vestrymen sought to establish continuity with rural England's parish churches and chapels, which were dignified by sturdy medieval towers, wall buttresses, and tracery windows. Following the religious strife of the English Civil War, St. Luke's architectural forms evoked comforting associations with the traditional piety and pre-Reformation harmony of the Middle Ages. On the other hand, a small triangular pediment over a round-arch doorway triggered even more ancient and venerable associations with classical Greek and Roman temples and with the churches of early Christian Rome. The art of ancient Rome had been revived during the Renaissance as an expression of rational geometric order and clear, simplified forms. During the eighteenth century, following the lead of London architects and builders, Virginia Anglicans would reject medieval decorative elements in favor of more austere church exteriors that had classical, pedimented doorways as their dominant feature.

St. Luke's substantial presence within the Virginia countryside reassuringly symbolized the apparently irreversible taming of the American wilderness. Almost twice as long as it is wide, St. Luke's was designed for church rituals and processions that focused on an altar at the far eastern end of the church. On the building's exterior, heavy, stepped buttresses alternate with round-arch, tracery windows to divide the side

2.19 St. James's Church
Goose Creek, South Carolina, 1708–19. Watercolor on paper by Charles Fraser, c. 1800. Gibbes Museum of Art/Carolina Art Association, Charleston, South Carolina.

Despite its small size and lack of a bell tower, St. James's Church possesses a certain monumental grandeur, thanks to the generous round-arched windows, pedimented entranceway, and the use of quoins, or large, dressed stones at the corners of the building. Charles Fraser (1782–1860) was a Charleston, South Carolina artist, who mostly painted miniature portraits in addition to architectural, topographical views such as this one.

walls into four bays, thereby emphasizing the length of the church and its ceremonial purpose. A three-tiered tracery window (fig. 2.17) illuminates the altar wall with an eastern, morning light. The intersecting Y-shaped tracery of brick flames upward to the arched top of the window, creating a pronounced visual climax for the church's exterior and interior. Above the large window, a small oculus, or circular window, floats beneath the pyramidal, "crow-stepped" gable, terminating the high-pitched roof.

Like the Franciscan mission church in Acoma, New Mexico (see fig. 2.8), St. Luke's generous illumination of the chancel, or altar area, metaphorically equated the light of the sun with the divine light of Christ. Like St. Luke's tower, the vertical thrust of both the three-tiered window and the stepped gable expresses Christianity's traditional desire for spiritual ascent beyond the dark confines of mere earthly life. Mimicking the shape of the sun or God's "all-seeing" eye, the oculus provides an additional geometric accent to suggest that the parishioners of St. Luke's are in moral harmony with Divine Providence. During the eighteenth century, partly inspired by English design books, ocular images decorated pulpits in several colonial churches and meetinghouses (fig. 2.18). The circular symbol, projecting rays of light, conveyed the sobering lesson that all of humanity is under God's constant surveillance. As we shall see in the next chapter, the all-seeing eye became especially popular among colonial Freemasons, a religious-minded fraternity that equated God with light and enlightened wisdom (see fig. 3.33).

The construction of Anglican churches accelerated in the British colonies with the foundation in 1701 of the Society for the Propagation of the Gospel in Foreign Parts (SPG). As a missionary force for the Church of England, the SPG recruited clergymen for Christian preaching and supported the construction of parish churches in new and distant settlements. With encouragement from the SPG, the small St. James's Church in Goose Creek, South Carolina, was designed and financed by wealthy plantation owners who had recently emigrated from the island of Barbados in the British West Indies (fig. 2.19). Construction of the church began shortly after 1706, when the South Carolina General Assembly declared the Church of England the established, tax-supported religion of the colony. Following instructions from the Barbados planters, craftsmen built the church with bricks, which they then covered with a smooth stucco that was originally painted brick red with white ornamental accents.

Unlike St. Luke's stylistic evocation of the Middle Ages, St. James's Church typified the English and colonial American trend toward a classical vocabulary of architectural forms. Borrowing from Greek temple architecture, the entrance to the Goose Creek Church is enframed by two pilasters (engaged columns) that support an entablature (a decorative horizontal beam) and a pediment (a triangular space for displaying sculpture). This borrowing of classical motifs from ancient temples recalled the apostolic period of early Christianity, when Christ's apostles or disciples, led by St. Paul, pioneered as Christian missionaries, preaching the message of Jesus in Greek cities and other settlements throughout the Roman Empire. For England's leading architect of the late seventeenth century, Sir Christopher Wren (1632–1723), classical architecture and its revival during the Italian Renaissance of the fifteenth and sixteenth centuries suggested a purer, more

2.20 John Potwine
Silver flagon,
c. 1720–30.
13⅜ in (34.6 cm) high,
4⁵⁄₁₆ in (11 cm) diameter.
The Gift of Mrs. Lemon to the First Church of Christ in Charlestown, Massachusetts. Yale University Art Gallery, New Haven, Connecticut.

human form of Christian practice rooted in the sermon and the spoken Word of God. Following the violent religious zealotry of the English Civil War, most Anglicans in England and America chose classical designs and motifs for their churches because they reassuringly expressed social and cultural ideals of rational harmony and emotional balance.

The "Goose Creek Men," the South Carolina plantation owners who supervised construction of their parish church, explicitly declared their allegiance to the Anglican Church and its missionary goal of civilizing America with Christian emblems and classical forms. Within the triangular pediment over the entrance door, a relief sculpture representing a pelican feeding a nest of young with its own blood greets visitors to the church. This image is a traditional symbol signifying Christ's selfless act of sacrifice for the salvation of humankind. Images of the Christlike pelican were sometimes engraved onto silver vessels carrying the wine for the sacrament of Holy Communion (fig. 2.20). More specifically, however, the SPG had appropriated the image of the self-sacrificing bird as its official emblem. The Goose Creek Church demonstrates that American Protestants could overcome their fears of idolatry by decorating their houses of worship with visual signs or mysterious emblems of the Christian faith, rather than with imagery based on Christ's human form. Craftsmen also modified the classical frieze or horizontal band immediately below the pediment to include a row of flaming hearts, which may commemorate the Christian Pentecost, when, according to the Bible, "cloven tongues" (Acts 2:3) of fire miraculously descended upon the heads of Christ's apostles, symbolizing their hearts' infusion with the Holy Spirit and their mission to preach the word of God with "other tongues" (Acts 2:4) or languages. Finally, the keystones at the top of each arched window are carved with small heads of cherubs, or angels. Compared with the elaborate façades of some Catholic mission churches in Hispanic America (see fig. 2.11), these Christian sculptural motifs do little to disrupt the cool, rational austerity of St. James's exterior design.

Having originated from within the Anglican Church, even New England Puritans were not the rigid iconoclasts caricatured in traditional

2.21 Old Ship Meetinghouse
Hingham, Massachusetts, 1681, with additions of 1731 and 1755.
Library of Congress, Washington, D.C.

accounts of American colonial history. Far from rejecting art and architecture, Puritans developed a "plain" style in the arts that shared in the taste for classical order and clarity. The Old Ship Meetinghouse in Hingham, Massachusetts, the only surviving seventeenth-century meeting-house, visually expresses Puritan strictures against Catholic rituals and religious images (figs. 2.21–2.22). But the building's plain interior was itself an image that positively symbolized the Puritans' return to early Christian first principles or the "primitive" order of worship sanctioned in the Bible. The rectangular, virtually square, plan of the Hingham meetinghouse was specifi-cally intended to discourage the idea of elaborate religious ceremonies. The main entrance is on one of the long sides of the building, while the pulpit inside is directly opposite. Thus, unlike Catholic or Anglican worship spaces, the Hingham meetinghouse has no long nave or central aisle for priestly processions. Nor did it have a fixed altar for the celebration of Holy Communion. Like domestic dining-room tables, Puritan communion tables were made of

wood and could easily be moved for the con-venience of the congregation. With a lofty ceiling shaped like an inverted ship's hull, the Hingham meetinghouse was designed primarily as an auditorium for the preaching, singing, and hearing of God's Word.

While the Hingham meetinghouse is free of paintings and sculptures, one must imagine this austere space enlivened by worshipers seated in the rows of wooden box pews. For Puritan cler-gymen, God's image was everywhere, engraved on the hearts of the Christian faithful. Members of New England's Congregationalist churches thought of themselves as living images of God. Especially during religious services, God's glory manifested itself visually through the spiritual radiance and moral bearing of God's elect, singing psalms or listening intently to sermons. As ardent Calvinists, Puritan Congregationalists believed that God had predestined or elected to save only a chosen few from eternal damnation. Membership in the congregation was restricted to those saints who could prove to church elders that they had experienced a genuine religious conversion to Christ. The conversionary experience was not an act of personal will, but was entirely the work of God, whose predestined grace made it possible for an individual sinner to become spiritually reborn. Puritan clergymen became experienced connoisseurs or critics in reading human faces and bodily gestures for visible signs of God's election.

By the early 1680s, when the Old Ship Meetinghouse was first constructed, most New England congregations had relaxed membership requirements to include individuals who had been baptized but had not yet undergone a religious conversionary experience. This new inclusiveness intensified debates over who was truly elect. Many argued that these so-called half-way members (Butler, p. 60) were not sufficiently worthy to partake in the communal sacrament of the Last Supper. Nevertheless, with the passing of the first generation of Puritan immigrants and the growing power of an affluent merchant elite, New England congregations expressed the more liberalized spirit by building larger and more visually striking meetinghouses. The Hingham structure was constructed at the

beginning of a period of economic expansion that soon blossomed during the eighteenth century with increased trade between Britain and her American colonies. As both population and wealth increased, Hingham church members expanded their meetinghouse in 1731 and again in 1755. But their first alteration was to cover over the exposed timbers of the ceiling so that the distinctive, inverted-ship design was hidden from view until an early-twentieth-century restoration.

As demonstrated by the Goose Creek plantation owners who designed St. James's Church, American colonists were developing a new taste for lighter, more refined architectural forms derived from the classical tradition. At Hingham, the heavy, unpainted wooden beams of the original ceiling must have begun to appear as crude reminders of the American wilderness, too primitive for the more sophisticated tastes of colonists who wished to display their new wealth by emulating architectural styles fashionable in England.

Hingham dwarfed most earlier New England meetinghouses. Its finely carved and polished

2.23 Parson Capen House
Topsfield, Massachusetts, 1683. Society for the Preservation of New England Antiquities, Boston, Massachusetts.

This New England parsonage derives from medieval, wood-frame building traditions. It is similar to late sixteenth-century wooden clapboard houses that still stand in Essex, England. Essex was a source of Puritan migration into Massachusetts. The medieval design is irregular, as the chimney and main door are not strictly aligned along a central axis to symmetrically divide the building. On either side of the door, brackets support the overhanging second story.

2.24 Parson Capen House
View of parlor, Topsfield, Massachusetts, 1683. Society for the Preservation of New England Antiquities, Boston, Massachusetts.

While the exterior of the Parson Capen House suggests impressively spacious living quarters, the interior feels relatively cramped. The parlor's low ceiling and heavy wooden beams weigh down the space, but also help preserve heat during the cold New England winters. In the parlor, as in the other first-floor rooms, a large brick fireplace dominates the space, providing a protective sense of security as well as necessary warmth.

2.25 Robert Twelves
Old South
Meetinghouse, Boston,
1729–30.
Society for the
Preservation of New
England Antiquities,
Boston, Massachusetts.

Above Old South's five-level, squarebrick tower rises a wooden, octagonal spire that springs from a colonnaded, eight-arched belfry. Eight pedimented dormer windows pierce the steeple, which soars 180 feet into the sky. Old South's octagonal spire was widely copied elsewhere in New England. Since early Christianity, baptismal fonts often possessed octagonal forms. In ecclesiastical architecture, the octagon symbolized purification and spiritual rebirth.

boxed pews, massive wooden pulpit, and other decorative elements expressed the affluence of its members. During the eighteenth century, the building's material richness was enhanced by a reshaped, pyramidal roof capped by a classical balustrade and a domed belfry with its spire ascending to a fine point.

In Topsfield, Massachusetts, the Parson Capen House, dating from 1683, is a further surviving sign of the social and cultural power enjoyed by the New England clergy (figs. 2.23–2.24). Distinguished by its size and central location on the town common, this wooden clapboard house was built by the community for the Reverend Joseph Capen, a Harvard-educated preacher and successful farmer, who occupied the home until his death in 1725. Although constructed according to English medieval framing methods, the

Parson Capen House included a modern parlor to the left of the entrance porch. Among the New England middle class and social elite, parlors had become fashionable domestic spaces employed primarily for the formal entertainment of guests.

By 1691, the political and religious power of the Puritan clergy was diminished when Massachusetts lost its church-dominated tradition of self-government. Under a new charter, it became a royal colony with its governor appointed by the King. Voting rights for a representative assembly were based on the possession of property rather than membership in a church congregation. Furthermore, the established churches of New England Congregationalism were now forced to compete more equally with Anglican, Baptist, and other churches.

2.26 William Burgis (attributed), *A North East View of the Great Town of Boston*, c.1723. Engraving, 13¾ in (34.9 cm) high, 9⅞ in (25.1 cm) wide. Peabody Essex Museum, Salem, Massachusetts.

Burgis, a major but relatively obscure figure in colonial printmaking, appears to have included a representation of himself in his northeastern view of Boston harbor (a companion to a southeastern view). Beneath a foreground tree at the far right, the seated, gentlemanly figure of an artist can be seen sketching the busy scene of harbor life. Burgis's artistic ambitions beyond mapping the town's skyline are evident in the atmospheric, breezy rendering of the cloudy sky.

Protestants who dissented from the established religion were granted tax relief so that they would not be forced to pay for the construction and maintenance of Congregational meetinghouses. During the eighteenth century, meetinghouses gradually lost their role as communal centers of both secular and religious life. As new public buildings or town halls displaced the meetinghouse as sites for government and community affairs, Congregationalist meetinghouses were increasingly referred to, and designed as, churches. Architects chose explicitly religious forms for edifices that were now almost exclusively dedicated to sacramental, worshipful purposes.

In Boston, the construction of Old South Meetinghouse strongly expressed this transformation of the meetinghouse form (fig. 2.25). Like the Old Ship Meetinghouse, Old South is almost square in plan and has its main entrance on the long side with a high pulpit opposite. This orientation across the width rather than the length of the meetinghouse intentionally discouraged the practice of liturgical processions or ritualistic parades. However, the architect of Old South dramatically contradicted this meetinghouse tradition by designing a lofty brick tower and wooden spire at the building's west end.

Inspired by the tower and spire of Old North, an Anglican church in Boston's North End, Old South's tower entrance unmistakably announces the religious purpose of the space, while confusingly detracting attention from the main entrance on the long south side.

With the proliferation of steepled churches and meetinghouses in Boston and other colonial towns, cartographers and painters of topographical views documented the sacralization of the American landscape. Before 1699 and the construction of the Brattle Street Meetinghouse (demolished in 1772), the Boston skyline had been devoid of towering church steeples. By 1723, before the construction of Old South, the painter William Burgis recorded seven tall church spires overlooking Boston harbor (fig. 2.26). However, these ecclesiastical vertical accents still had to compete for attention with the rigging and tall mastheads of merchant sail ships, signifying Boston's identity as a bustling commercial hub.

By contrast, a 1759 view of Quebec, the capital of New France, shows an urban skyline clearly dominated by the hierarchical institutions of the Catholic Church, in tandem with the French royal government (fig.2.27). In addition to the

2.27 Thomas Johnston
Quebec, the Capital of New-France, a Bishoprick and Seat of the Soverain Court,
1759.
Engraving, etching, and watercolor. Winterthur Museum, Wilmington, Delaware.

Cathedral of our Lady, which rises highest of all, there are substantial buildings for a seminary and for various Catholic religious orders: Jesuits, Recollects, and Ursulines. Furthermore, along the central axis of this cityscape, the "Bishop's House," really a mansion, rests comfortably in splendid isolation from the rest of the community, surrounded by land for gardens and a solid, protective fence. Thomas Johnston (c.1708–67), a native Bostonian and painter, as well as engraver, actually copied this view of Quebec from an earlier print published in Paris in 1713. The printmaker cannily timed the release of his reproduction in anticipation of the fall of Quebec to British forces in September, 1759. As shall be discussed further in chapter 4, the conquest of Quebec was interpreted in England and its American colonies as the divinely ordained triumph of Protestant principles. The citizens of colonial Boston, schooled in the relatively democratic ethos of the Puritan Congregationalist meetinghouse, probably regarded Johnston's view of Quebec's ecclesiastical wealth as evidence of Catholic worldliness and the Vatican's authoritarian corruption of religious values.

God's Word in New England Portraits

Portraiture was a means for colonial Americans to resolve difficulties in reconciling material prosperity and worldly success with spiritual purity and moral commitment. Given the Puritan notion that members of God's elect were living images of Christ, portraiture became a form of religious expression sanctioned and encouraged by the New England clergy. In 1670, the Boston printmaker John Foster (1648–81) produced the earliest known print in the British colonies (fig. 2.30). The woodcut represents the Reverend Richard Mather, who, like many other Puritans, had suffered religious persecution for refusing to conform to the religious practices of the Church of England. Having fled England for Massachusetts in 1635, Mather became a leading spokesman for New England Congregationalism. Foster's print originally may have been conceived as an illustration or frontispiece for a memorial tribute to the recently deceased minister written by his son. According

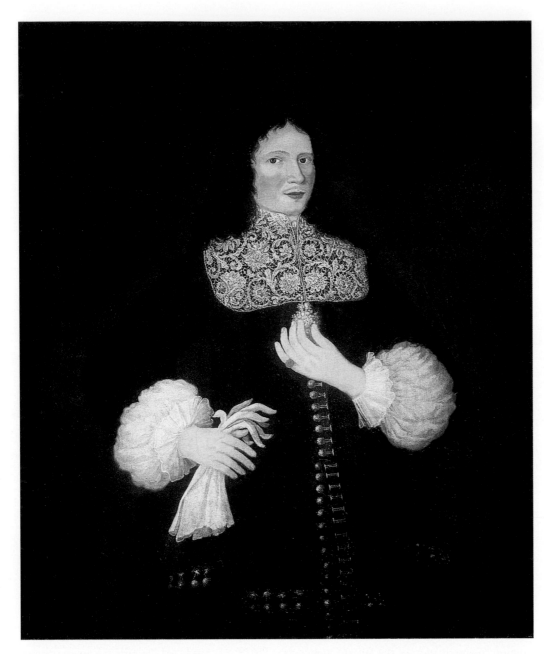

2.28 Anonymous
Portrait of John Freake,
c.1671–4.
Oil on canvas,
42½ x 36¾ in
(107.9 3 93.4 cm).
Worcester Art Museum,
Worcester, Massachusetts.
Sarah C. Garver Fund.

The unknown painter of the Freake family adopted a relatively flat, medieval style. Its linear sharpness and plainly represented forms expressed English middle-class distrust of sensuous, painterly surfaces and three-dimensional illusionism. Those qualities were associated with Catholic and courtly art. Mr. Freake's sartorial finery and shoulder-length hair distinguish him from the lower classes and Puritan extremism. But the Boston merchant also differentiated himself from England's aristocratic elite by sporting neither a wig nor curly, long lovelocks.

to Increase Mather, who also became a clergyman, Richard Mather's "way of Preaching was plain, aiming to shoot his Arrows not over his people's heads, but into their Hearts and Consciences. Whence he studiously avoided obscure phrases, Exotic Words, or an unnecessary citation of Latin Sentences, which some men addict themselves to the use of" (cited in Horner and Bain, pp. 70–71).

Emulating the clergyman's reputation for a plain, unpretentious preaching style, Foster cap- tured the massive bulk of Mather's body with flattened, simple shapes and minimal contrasts of light and shadow in the rounded hands and face. Rather than the official, ceremonial vestments of the Anglican Church, Mather wears the more austere, black costume of a scholar devoted to God's Word. Pointing with his right index finger to the open book that he holds in his left hand, Mather is also represented as a dedicated teacher, whose close interpretation of the Bible and theological texts has made him dependent on

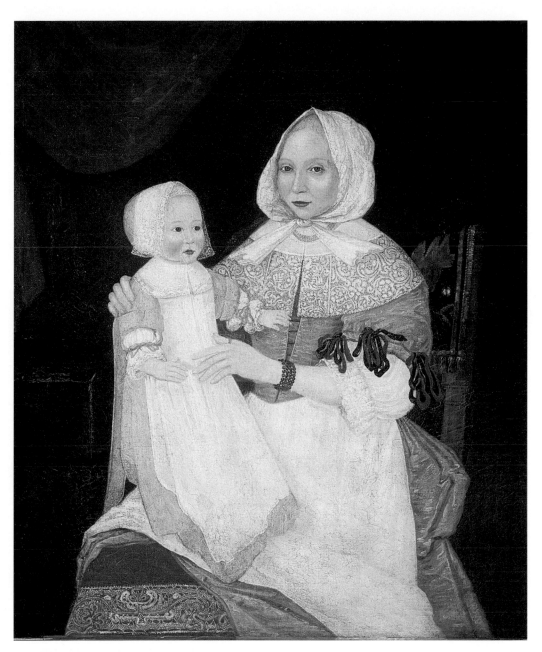

2.29 Anonymous
Elizabeth Freake and Baby Mary, c.1671–4. Oil on canvas, 42½ x 36¾ in (107.9 x 93.4 cm). Worcester Art Museum, Worcester, Massachusetts. Gift of Mr. and Mrs. Albert W. Rice.

As a marriage portrait, this picture originally represented only Elizabeth Freake, daughter of the Boston merchant Thomas Clarke. (The picture was the companion to her husband's portrait; see fig. 2.28.) However, three years later, in 1674, when their daughter Mary was born, the Freakes commissioned their portraitist to depict the baby on her mother's lap. Mrs. Freake, dressed in satin and lace, sits in an expensive but locally made chair upholstered with imported English woolen fabric called Turkey work, because it imitated exotic Middle Eastern designs.

a tiny pair of reading glasses that gleam like two beacons of light at the center of his body.

Foster's portrait of Mather reminds us of the religious importance of books and reading for Protestants in colonial America. Reformers in Europe had attacked the fact that the Catholic Mass was conducted entirely in Latin and not in the national and regional languages of everyday life. Furthermore, the Vulgate, or Roman Catholic Bible, was also written in Latin, making it inaccessible to common men and women.

Believing in the priesthood of all believers, Protestants preached God's Word in the everyday languages of ordinary people. They also undertook to translate and inexpensively publish the Bible in the vernacular so that literate members of the laity could read holy scriptures in private without the intrusive presence of a priest. Although there were earlier English translations, the publication in 1611 of the King James Bible, under the patronage of King James I, was crucially important in the dissemination of God's

2.30 John Foster
Richard Mather, c.1670.
Woodcut, 7⅛ in (18.2 cm)
high, 5⅜ in (13.7 cm)
wide. The Houghton
Library, Harvard
University, Cambridge,
Massachusetts.

Word in England and America. In 1623, Governor John Winthrop of Massachusetts received a London edition of the King James Bible as a gift from his father (fig. 2.31). Its visually complex title page is enframed by twenty-four square images, half representing the leaders of the twelve tribes of Israel, the other half portraying Christ's twelve disciples. Together they signify the complementary nature of the Bible's Old and New Testaments. However, the title page also signifies the spiritual superiority of the New Testament story of Christ over the Old Testament's history of the Jews. The central images exclusively depict Christian personalities and symbols. Around the heart in the middle of the title page are images of Saints Matthew, Mark, Luke, and John, whose Gospels narrate the life, death, and Resurrection of Christ. An emblem of Christ as the Lamb of God is situated at the base of the heart-shaped title, while the dove of the Holy Spirit flies within a cloud over the heart's crest. These animal emblems were accepted by most Protestants as purely allegorical or symbolic allusions to God.

In American portraiture, displays of literacy and of biblically educated piety became commonplace. Of the fifty or so portraits surviving from the seventeenth century, the most religiously explicit in its interplay between verbal expression and visual imagery is the *Self-Portrait* of Captain Thomas Smith (fig. 2.32). Little is known of Thomas Smith (d.1691) except that he was a sea captain who also worked as a portraitist in Boston and Cambridge, where Harvard College had been established in 1636 as America's first institution of higher learning. Within this literate atmosphere, Smith portrayed himself as a poet as well as a devout gentleman of

2.31 Title page
The Bible, printed by
Robert Barker, London,
1614–15.
Massachusetts Historical
Society, Boston,
Massachusetts.

some social standing. Dressed in black with a fancy lace jabot, or neckpiece, the aging but formidable Captain Smith sits close to the picture plane in front of an open window that reveals a naval battle in the distance.

Scholars have been unable to agree with absolute certainty if Smith's window view represents a specific sea battle in which the captain may have participated. However, the ships bear English and Dutch flags, while one of the flags flying over the monumental fortress below displays three crescents, alluding to an Islamic military force. The English and Dutch had been imperial rivals in a series of wars that led to the English takeover of the New Netherlands in 1664. But, in 1670, the two naval powers had collaborated in an attack on the Islamic Barbary States on the north coast of Africa.

Through this historical association, Smith identifies himself as a Christian soldier in the centuries-old crusade against the infidels of Islam. Opposition to Islam unites two European commercial rivals, who ought to be allies as Protestant defenders of the Christian faith. Immediately below this distant view of religious combat, Smith has placed his right hand on a

human skull that rests on the table in front of him. While he silently gazes toward us, the skull seems to speak for him like a hand puppet. The written words of a poem signed with Smith's initials flow from the skull's mouth and are clearly visible for beholders to read:

*Why why should I the World be minding
therein a World of Evils Finding.
Then Farwell World; Farwell thy Jarres
thy Joies thy Toies thy Wiles thy Warrs,
Truth Sounds Retreat: I am not sorye.
The Eternall Drawes to him my heart
By Faith (which can thy Force Subvert)
To Crowne me (after Grace) with Glory
(cited in Stein, p. 317).*

Significantly, the sheet of poetry reaches out to the viewer as it falls over the edge of the red table, virtually commanding our attention, drawing our eyes away from the relatively obscure and distant battle scene. Visually and verbally, the skull's poem diminishes the importance of the background view. In conformity with Calvinist doctrine, Smith's affirmation of Christian faith takes precedence over the good deeds of his life at sea. He dismisses the cares and woes of his past and of his present pilgrimage on earth and embraces death like a welcome friend. Apparently confident that he is one of God's elect, the beneficiary of God's grace, Smith looks forward to his future life in heaven, where there are no wars or other evils.

The verbal, religious imagery of Smith's poem regulates our interpretation of the visible world. Inspired by the Bible, Puritan sermons, and devotional themes, the poem of death leads the viewer's mind beyond the transient earthly realm accessible to the eye. Smith has drawn the skull's nose in the shape of an inverted heart that points upward and outward beyond the picture frame, visually underscoring the poetic thought that "the Eternall Drawes to him my heart." The painting is part of an emblematic tradition in literature and the visual arts that associates images or signs with implicit or explicit verbal moral messages. The human skull is a conventional emblem, a *memento mori*.

Smith's visual sermon may be compared with the earlier, more worldly portraits of John and Elizabeth Freake and their daughter (figs. 2.28–2.29). These anonymously painted pictures

2.32 Thomas Smith
Self-Portrait, c.1680–90.
Oil on canvas,
24¾ x 23¾ in
(62.9 x 60.4 cm).
Worcester Art Museum,
Worcester, Massachusetts.
Museum purchase.

Smith's self-portrait
demonstrates familiarity
with contemporary
European techniques of
pictorial composition and
three-dimensional
illusionism. The artist
created a pattern of formal
repetitions to link
foreground and background
spaces. Puffs of clouds and
white smoke from the battle
scene echo Smith's flowing
white hair and lace
neckcloth. The bell shape of
the jabot is repeated in the
red tassel dangling from the
curtain behind Smith's
head.

of a Boston merchant family are a frank display of wealth and social standing. The self-taught colonial "limner," or painter, focuses particularly on the figures' elaborate imported clothing and jewelry. Nevertheless, the artist's stiff representation of sober facial expressions suggests that these sitters, like Thomas Smith, are virtuous members of God's elect, uncorrupted by riches.

Colonial Gravestones: Emblems of Morality

Skeletons and skulls appeared most frequently on colonial gravestones, not only in New England, but also in the other colonies along the eastern seaboard. Although graveyards were usually located next to meetinghouses and churches, Protestants, unlike Catholics, regarded the funeral as a secular, civil ritual outside the power of religious authority. Clergymen encouraged grave imagery for their useful

spiritual messages directed toward the living. Stonecarvers developed their trade by copying traditional images of death and resurrection from emblem books onto the slate grave markers. Coupling engraved visual images with moralistic, explanatory texts, English emblem books circulated widely in the British colonies during the seventeenth and eighteenth centuries.

Joseph Lamson (1658–1722) of Charlestown, Massachusetts, was the founding father of four generations of stonecarvers in New England. Drawing on popular convention, he shaped his grave markers into doorways that suggested the entrance of human souls into a new heavenly home. Lamson's 1694 gravestone for Timothy Cutler features a winged skull in the curved tympanum at the top of the door-shaped stone (fig. 2.33). Immediately below, two angelic figures carry a coffin, as if they are loading it for the skull's or the soul's flight beyond the grave. Latin mottoes inscribed next to an hourglass and a pair of crossed bones remind the viewer of death and of

2.33 (above)
Joseph Lamson
(attributed), Gravestone
of Timothy Cutler, 1694.
Slate, 23 in (58.4 cm)
high, 23½ in (59.7 cm)
wide, 5 in (12.7 cm)
deep. Phipps Street Burial
Grounds, Charlestown,
Massachusetts.

2.34 John Stevens II
(attributed), Gravestone
of Rebecca Polock,
c. 1764.
Rubbing, 37 x 27 in
(94 x 68.5 cm).
Burial Ground of Touro
Synagogue. American
Antiquarian Society. From
the Daniel and Jesse Lie
Farber Collection of
Gravestone Photographs.

ther distinctively Protestant nor even Christian. In Newport, Rhode Island, the stonecarver John Stevens II (1702–28) sculpted grave markers for Jewish families that appear similar in every respect to Christian stones, except for the Hebraic inscription of the epitaph (fig. 2.34). The gravestone of Rebecca Polock is also shaped like a doorway, with floral motifs in the jambs and a winged cherub signifying the soul within the stone's arched tympanum.

Jewish-Christian Collaboration: Touro Synagogue

Polock was buried in the cemetery next to Touro Synagogue, the oldest Jewish synagogue in America (fig. 2.35). With only a thousand Jews living in all of British colonial America, it is scarcely surprising that the handful of Jewish families residing in Newport and other American cities relied heavily on Christian craftsmen, artists, and architects. Touro Synagogue was designed by the English-born architect Peter Harrison (1716–76), who had earlier designed Anglican and Congregational churches in Boston and Cambridge. For both Christian and Jewish worship spaces, Harrison employed the architectural vocabulary of classical antiquity as reinterpreted by Renaissance masters and the leading contemporary architects and designers of Great Britain.

Sir Isaac Newton and other eighteenth-century Britons regarded the ancient Jewish temple of King Solomon in Jerusalem as the original source of all architectural knowledge (see fig. 3.9). Harrison owned a copy of the *Constitutions of Freemasons* (1725), which traced the art of architecture from Solomon and the Hebrews to the Greeks and the Romans. The Romans supposedly perfected the art during the imperial reign of Augustus Caesar at the dawn of Christianity. The *Constitutions* was written by the Scottish clergyman James Anderson for members of the Masonic order, a secret social fraternity that is discussed in the following chapter. However, the book also appealed to non-Masons who were interested in the ancient lore of architecture and the building trades. Thanks, in part, to Anderson's popular treatise, classical architecture could be seen as a virtually universal language of

the flight of time. Along the door jambs on either side of the stone's epitaph, floral decorations, capped by two pudgy, childlike faces, suggest the promise of spiritual rebirth and everlasting life.

While New England colonial gravestones are often associated with the Puritan tradition, the stone carvers' vocabulary of visual motifs is nei-

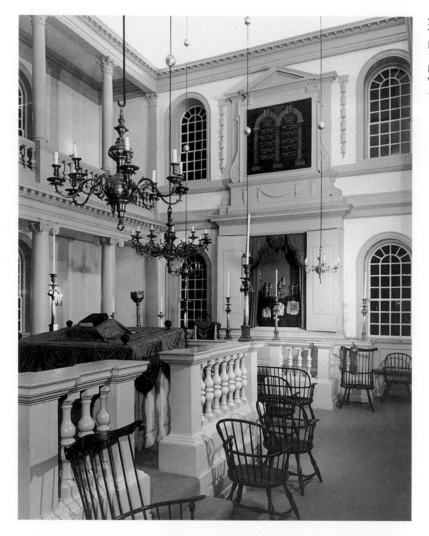

2.35 Peter Harrison
Touro Synagogue,
Newport, Rhode Island,
1759–63. Interior.
Library of Congress,
Washington, D.C.

design that was equally valid for craftsmen and builders of the eighteenth century.

Therefore, Harrison saw little contradiction in adapting Greco-Roman forms to the religious needs of Newport's Jewish community. The Anglican architect shared the tolerant, cosmopolitan spirit of his contemporary Dr. Alexander Hamilton. Stimulated by the religious and ethnic diversity of Newport, Harrison worked for free and received instruction on the layout of Sephardic, or Spanish and Portuguese Jewish, synagogues from Rabbi Isaac Touro, who had studied Judaism at the Rabbinical Academy in Amsterdam. Following Touro's liturgical requirements, Harrison designed an elevated table or reading desk, surrounded by a balustrade at the center of the worship space, where Jewish law was read and prayers were chanted. Facing toward Jerusalem, the Ark of the Covenant commands the eastern end of the synagogue. In designing this most sacred space, where the Torah, or scrolls of God's law, are stored, Harrison borrowed classical forms that he had seen in British pattern books and that he had earlier employed for King's Chapel, an Anglican church in Boston. The towering upper half of the ark displays an image of the written laws of God with classical columns and arches. The ornamental frame is capped by a small pediment, which appears cramped by a lack of wall space, being blocked by the molded cornice above. Facing toward the center and the east, men sat in pews on the other three sides of the interior space. Women sat separately in the balconies above. Twelve columns support the balcony on the first and second floors, symbolizing the twelve tribes of ancient Israel.

When Touro Synagogue was dedicated on December 2, 1763, Christians as well as Jews attended the services. On December 5, a Newport newspaper described the dedication ceremonies as a moment of profound religious and social concord:

> In the afternoon was the dedication of the new Synagogue in this town. It began by a handsome procession in which was carried the Books of the Law to be deposited in the Ark. Several Portions of Scripture, and of their Service with a prayer for the Royal Family were read and finely sung by the Priest and People. There were present many Gentlemen and Ladies. The Order and Decorum, the Harmony and Solemnity of the Music, together with a handsome assembly of People, in the Edifice the most perfect of the Temple kind in America, and splendidly illuminated, could not but raise in the Mind a faint Idea of the Majesty and Grandeur of the ancient Jewish Worship mentioned in Scripture (cited in Touro Synagogue, p. 21).

As is suggested by this sympathetic account, the Christian majority in colonial America had long cultivated an identification with ancient Israel. Like most Britons, Protestant Americans tended to regard themselves in biblical terms as the new Israelites or God's new chosen people. However, the Newport newspaper primarily chose to focus on the refined tone created by Harrison's temple architecture, the solemn religious services, and the handsome appearance of the congregation. By 1763, Americans had distanced themselves from the relatively primitive living conditions endured by the first generation of settlers in the British colonies. During the eighteenth century, wealthy colonists not only built larger and more elegant places of worship, but also constructed spacious mansions decorated with family portraits. As we shall see, American colonists began to define themselves less by their ethnic and religious differences than by their common consumption of British goods and genteel emulation of English manners and taste.

Chapter 3

Art and the Consumer Revolution in Colonial America

1700–75

DURING the first three quarters of the eighteenth century, demographic and economic expansion in the American colonies created a more liberal moral climate for consuming luxuries and patronizing art and architecture. From 1700 until the eve of the Revolution in 1775, the colonial population multiplied almost ninefold, from 250,000 to well over 2 million. Though still small by modern standards, most colonial towns doubled or even tripled in size. A village of 4,000 in 1690, Philadelphia grew into the largest metropolis, with a population of 40,000 by 1775. New York and Boston were the nearest competitors, with populations of 20,000 and 16,000 respectively by the 1770s.

From 1689 to 1760, colonial trade with Great Britain grew by 700 percent. Affluent artisans, farmers, and small shopkeepers all became eager consumers of British textiles, ceramics, glassware, tea, and other consumer goods. Per capita American expenditure on imports rose by at least fifty percent from 1720 to 1770. British exports to the American colonies doubled between 1750 and 1760, when England's Industrial Revolution was beginning to take off.

Colonial America still witnessed a marked disparity between rich and poor, with most wealth concentrated in the top one to five percent of the population. For instance, in the city of Boston, five percent of property owners possessed twenty-five percent of the city's wealth in 1687. By 1770, just one percent of Boston property owners controlled forty-four percent of the wealth. During the same period in Virginia and Maryland, approximately thirty percent of the population was poor, while wealth was concentrated in the hands of a few rich families with ties to the English aristocracy. As a sign of growing elite wealth in colonial America, the population of black slaves dramatically increased from eight percent of the population in 1690 to twenty-one percent in 1770.

Nevertheless, for most white colonists, improved living standards during the eighteenth century created opportunities for social advancement. From 1689 to 1760, per capita income in the American colonies rose half a percent per year in real terms. Over the entire period, the standard of living improved for most of the population by between fifty to 100 percent. Ordinary, middle-class Americans could begin to emulate their aristocratic superiors in purchasing luxuries that would distinguish them from the propertyless poor. Thanks to its growing prosperity and its relative tolerance of religious and cultural diversity, the British colonies of North America increasingly attracted non-English European immigrants. Prior to 1680, approximately ninety percent of European settlers in the mainland British colonies were English. By contrast, between 1680 and 1760, Scottish, Scots-Irish, French, German, and Swiss peoples accounted for seventy-five percent of the European immigrants seeking their fortunes in England's American colonies. Among these immigrants, a small but growing number of Ashkenazic Jews from Central Europe joined Iberian Sephardic Jews, such as those at Touro Synagogue (see chapter 2), to establish religious and merchant communities in seaport towns from Newport, Rhode Island, to Charleston, South Carolina.

However, despite this demographic diversification, eighteenth-century demand for British manufactures and commodities contributed to a certain "anglicization" of American culture. Colonial consumers tended to demand that American artists, craftsmen, and builders conform to British standards of fashion and taste.

Gerardus Duyckinck (attrib.) *Bilhah Abigail Levy Franks, Mrs. Jacob Franks,* c.1735. Oil on canvas, 44 x 35 in (111.7 x 88.9 cm). American Jewish Historical Society, Waltham, Massachusetts, and New York.

Her Highnefs *The Princefs Ann.*

3.1 Isaac Beckett
Princess Anne, late
seventeenth century.
Mezzotint.
Winterthur Museum,
Delaware.

Isaac Beckett
(c. 1653–c.1719), a London
printmaker, engraved this
mezzotint after a painting
by Dutch artist Willem
Wissing (1656–1687), who
worked primarily in
England. This sumptuous
portrait shows Princess
Anne, Protestant daughter
of the deposed Catholic
James II (r. 1685–88).
When she ascended the
English throne, the childless
Queen Anne (r. 1702–14)
was to become Britain's last
Stuart monarch.

Thus, when Bilhah Abigail Levy Franks, daughter of the Jewish, German-born merchant Moses Levy, sat for her portrait in New York City (see p. 76), the painter, identified by most art historians as Gerardus Duyckinck (1695–1746), posed her in the English manner, as exemplified by mezzotint prints of British aristocrats and royalty (fig. 3.1) that circulated widely in the colonies. A mid-seventeenth-century invention, mezzotint (Italian for "half-tone") prints were produced from copper plates that had been roughened, so that the entire surface would hold ink and print solid black. The final design of a print would be achieved by scraping and polishing areas, in order that they would hold less ink and print in progressively lighter tones. The result was a print that emphasized not linear effects, but fluid,

painterly qualities based on subtle tonal gradations from dark to light. Mezzotints more faithfully reproduced paintings and were, therefore, a popular learning tool for American painters who could not travel abroad to see original European masterpieces.

Gerardus Duyckinck was a third-generation member of the New York Dutch painting dynasty founded by Evert Duyckinck I (1621–1702), who had emigrated from Holland in 1638. Gerardus primarily learned the craft of picture-making from his father, Gerret (1660–1710), and from his older cousin Evert Duyckinck III (1677–1727), and has been credited with painting biblical subjects in a style similar to those found in Dutch Calvinist homes in Albany, New York (see fig. 2.14). Known for

3.2 (above)
John Greenwood
Sea Captains Carousing in Surinam, c. 1758.
Oil on bed ticking, 37¾ x 75¼ in (95.9 x 191.1 cm).
Saint Louis Art Museum, Missouri.

Greenwood spent over six years in the Dutch colony of Surinam, painting 113 portraits of local plantation owners and visiting traders. Although these individual portraits are unlocated, this tavern scene contains numerous likenesses. Just to the right of center, a Captain Ambrose Page vomits into the coat pocket of Jonas Wanton of Newport, Rhode Island. Stephen Hopkins, Rhode Island's governor and a future signatory to the Declaration of Independence, simultaneously pours a bowl of rum over the hapless, seated Wanton.

3.3 (below) **Punch bowl**
Liverpool, England, c. 1750.
Tin-glazed earthenware with design featuring Hogarth's *A Midnight Modern Conversation*.
Winterthur Museum, Delaware.

Hogarth's comedic engraving, originally published in London in 1733, represents the inebriated members of a London drinking club. Hogarth's stated intention was not to ridicule specific persons, but rather to criticize harmful vices and human weaknesses. Pirated copies of the popular print led the artist to seek passage of a copyright law protecting authorial rights. However, the law's enactment in 1735 did not prevent the English punch-bowl manufacturer from employing a crude copy of Hogarth's design.

his portraits of New York merchants and their families, Gerardus Duyckinck also painted Jacob Franks, as a companion to the likeness of his wife Abigail, and portraits of the Franks children. All of the stiffly posed, relatively plain, but dignified-looking figures are based upon fashionable prototypes readily found in the flourishing English mezzotint print trade.

Indeed, as a measure of the hegemonic or homogenizing power of English fashion, the portraits of Abigail and her family feature no motif, gesture, or symbol that specifically identify them as Jewish. This is despite the fact that Jacob and Abigail Franks devoutly educated their nine children in the traditional faith of Judaism, and of Hebrew language and culture. Undoubt-

edly wary of offending Protestant or Christian friends and business associates visiting his home, Jacob Franks ordered portraits that speak of family cohesion, continuity, and strength, but also of merchant wealth and a consumerist taste for the material values and conventions of the anglicizing social elite.

With the increase of wealth and social affluence, American clergymen warned against the moral dangers associated with immoderate consumption of luxuries. Excessive entertainments and expenditures within the middle and upper classes potentially threatened public virtue and the rule of law. During the booming decade of the 1750s, the native-born artist John Greenwood (1727–92) painted a rare

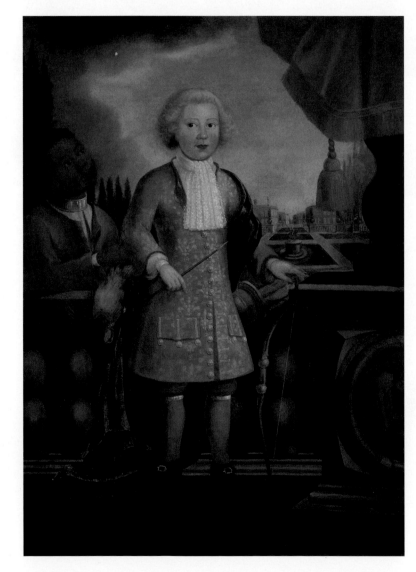

3.4 Justus Engelhardt Kühn
Henry Darnall III,
c. 1710.
Oil on canvas,
53⅞ x 44 in
(136 x 111.8 cm).
Maryland Historical
Society, Baltimore,
Maryland.

The fictive formal garden and architecture were borrowed from European prints. The garden may allude to the Roman goddess Venus's Garden of Love, a Renaissance symbolic tradition that eventually influenced English illustrated books for the moral education of youth. Within this context, Henry's bow and arrows would then identify him with Cupid, the son of Venus. Whether represented dead or alive, birds accompanying children pictorially signified the morally desirable pursuit of love and friendship.

representation of common misbehavior in *Sea Captains Carousing in Surinam* (fig. 3.2). This South American tavern scene depicts a group of mostly Rhode Island mariners, several of whom would gain important posts in colonial affairs. Greenwood's chaotic and self-critical image of overturned chairs, spilled glasses, and retching, inebriated patrons implicitly admonishes viewers about the consequences of overconsumption. In the background doorway of the picture, Greenwood represented himself vomiting from too much rum. The painting is similar to the popular print *A Midnight Modern Conversation*, by the London artist William Hogarth (1697–1764), who was famous for his pictorial satires of social morals and manners. Hogarth's engraving was widely reproduced throughout the British empire. American colonists imported ceramic punch bowls decorated with the Hogarth composition as a humorous reminder of the moral and physical dangers of consuming too much alcohol (fig. 3.3). The punch bowls taught friends and guests the virtues of moderate consumption, which contributed to social harmony and good feeling. If excess was an evil extreme, so, too, was puritanical self-denial. As we shall see, during the eighteenth-century consumer revolution, frugality was increasingly criticized as a selfish form of behavior.

Aristocratic Aspirations of Wealthy Colonists

During the early seventeenth century, British settlers were preoccupied by the problems of merely surviving the American wilderness. However, within a few decades, affluent colonists in Virginia, Maryland, and elsewhere could imagine living in the manner of the English aristocracy or landed gentry. In 1641, Sir William Berkeley, descendant of one of England's oldest noble families, arrived in Virginia as the colony's new royal governor. With a population of only 8,000, Virginia's social life suffered from a poor economy and a corrupt culture of violence, lawlessness, and heavy drinking. Over the course of Berkeley's thirty-five-year tenure, Virginia's population quintupled to 40,000. The governor attempted to create a hierarchical socioeconomic order by recruiting a powerful ruling elite from

the younger sons of wealthy English families. Like Berkeley himself, younger sons lost inheritance rights to older brothers and were compelled to leave family estates to seek their fortunes or vocations elsewhere. In 1663, Berkeley published a Virginia recruiting pamphlet, which promised Englishmen that "a small sum of money will enable a younger brother to erect a flourishing family in a new world" (cited in Fischer, p. 214). Earlier, during the 1650s, the Civil War in England had already contributed significantly to immigration to Virginia. Thousands of cavaliers, or aristocratic royalists, fled Britain following the execution of Charles I in 1649 and the subsequent establishment of a Puritan Commonwealth under the military dictator Oliver Cromwell. Though most royalist emigrés sought refuge in Europe, Governor Berkeley was able to lure many of them to Virginia. With the Restoration of the English monarchy in 1660, most of these wealthy immigrants were persuaded to remain and form Virginia's "first families" (Fischer, p. 218). While not among the original founders of the colony, the Byrds, the Washingtons, the Lees, and other families were "first" in the sense of social prestige and political influence. By 1700, fifty wealthy families, most with connections to the English aristocracy or rural gentry, dominated Virginia life. Owners of vast, slave-operated plantations, the leading men of these families served as magistrates and sat on the Virginia governor's council.

Together with Maryland to the north, Virginia was part of a larger regional society centered on the vast Chesapeake Bay and its many navigable waterways. With the encouragement of Sir William Berkeley's social recruiting policies in Virginia, Maryland also developed a hierarchical society and plantation economy dependent upon slave labor and the cultivation of tobacco as an export crop. Maryland was ruled by an aristocratic proprietor, whose right to total control of the colony originated from a 1632 land grant of 10 million acres given by King Charles I to Cecil Calvert, the second Lord Baltimore. Like Berkeley in Virginia, Lord Baltimore envisioned Maryland as an aristocratic utopia of wealthy, genteel families, who would be granted large estates of 2,000 acres or more. In reality, during most of the seventeenth century, small family farms of fifty to 100 acres typified

3.5 Robert Feke
James Bowdoin II, 1748.
Oil on canvas, 50 x 40 in
(127 x 101.6 cm).
Bowdoin College Museum
of Art, Brunswick, Maine.

Bowdoin supplemented his
mercantile career with an
avid pursuit of science. Feke
situates him next to a tall
background tree. Although
painted flatly in contrast to
Bowdoin's three-
dimensional bulk, the tree
trunk echoes his stately
body. The sweeping vertical
lines of brown velvet coat
and ivory satin waistcoat
further suggest masculine
strength. The waistcoat's
golden, foliated embroidery
expresses Bowdoin's
youthful, cultivated vigor
and appears more
animated than the leafy
background vegetation.

the Maryland economy. However, following the Restoration, Maryland also experienced an influx of wealthy "great" families, not only from England, but also from the European mainland. By the eighteenth century, large plantations of over 1,000 acres, each with a labor force of fifty or more slaves, became economically dominant in the colony. Accordingly, Maryland's slave population increased nearly tenfold between 1707 and 1755 from 4,600 to 43,000, becoming an ever-larger percentage of the total population. White indentured servants who had arrived in Maryland during the 1640s and 1650s often became small landowners once they had fulfilled the contractual terms of their servitude. However, by the end of the century, most servants remained landless even after ten years of legal freedom, and were forced to work as tenant-farmers for large plantation owners.

A portrait of young Henry Darnall III (1702–c. 88), heir to a Maryland plantation family, vividly demonstrates the aristocratic pretensions of wealthy American colonists (fig 3.4). Henry Darnall II hired a German immigrant artist, Justus Engelhardt Kühn (active c.1708–17), to portray his son as the future master of Woodyard Plantation in Calvert County (today Prince George's County), Maryland. Dressed in rich, imported clothing, Henry Darnall III stands in front of a sculpted stone balustrade overlooking a lavish formal garden and stately buildings in the far background. He holds a bow and arrow, masculine emblems of the hunt, a leisure sport associated with the British aristocracy. On the other side of the balustrade, an African-American slave holds a dead quail, while gazing upward toward his young master in loyal admiration. America's gen-

3.6 Robert Feke
*Mrs. James Bowdoin
(Elizabeth Erving)*, 1748.
Oil on canvas,
50⅛ x 40⅛ in (129 x 103
cm). Bowdoin College
Museum of Art,
Brunswick, Maine.

Elizabeth Erving Bowdoin
wears a pastel-blue satin
dress. Her elongated fingers
symbolically express her
genteel cultural refinement.
With one delicate hand, she
places a pink rose between
her breasts. With her other
hand, she cradles a basket
of blossoms in her lap.
Associated with Venus, the
goddess of love, roses were
an appropriate symbol for a
marriage portrait.

teel civilization of consumer luxuries depended upon the human barbarism of slavery. The African youth wears a shiny silver collar around his neck, an emblem of his servitude and a reminder of the iron clamps and chains used on southern plantations and American slave ships.

Benefiting from their connections to England's aristocracy and landed gentry, a number of second- and third-generation, native-born colonists accumulated sufficient capital through trade, land speculation, slave labor, family inheritance, and strategic marriages to begin to live like English aristocrats. The Darnall family was fortunate in that it had kinship ties to Charles Calvert, the third Lord Baltimore, from Maryland's founding family. Like other colonial portraits, Kühn's portrait of Henry Darnall III represented the aspirations of a social class rather than objective reality. The painting's formal gar-

dens and stone architecture are fictive, copied from imported portrait prints. But these conventional motifs expressed the colonial elite's desire to transform the American wilderness into a replica of English aristocratic culture.

As the western periphery of the British empire, the North American colonies still constituted the violent margins of European civilization. In 1737, one exasperated royal governor described North Carolina backwoodsmen living in the manner of Indian traders on the borders of the wilderness as "the lowest scum and rabble . . . [who] build themselves sorry hutts and live in a beastly sort of plenty . . . devoted to calumny, lying, and the vilest tricking and cheating; a people into whose heads no human means can beat the notion of a publick interest or persuade to live like men" (cited in Bailyn, p. 117). Throughout the colonies, travelers to frontier outposts complained of bandits and horse thieves, public drunkenness, fighting, and the complete absence of civil behavior. The British judicial system perpetuated the image and reality of American wildness and lawlessness by exporting thousands of convicts to the colonies as indentured servants. Having sold their labor for transportation to the New World, indentured servants worked years without pay, depending upon the terms of their contract, which bound them to serve a particular master. With thousands of poor immigrants arriving in coastal ports, the problem of urban disorder and crime led towns throughout the colonies to increase night patrols against robbers and burglars.

Yet among the eighteenth-century immigrants from the British Isles and the European continent, skilled artisans overshadowed the convicts. Emigration to the New World became less of a financial risk for artists and those who already had established careers in the Old World. During the eighteenth century, colonial merchants busily recruited immigrants skilled in the building trades, decorative arts, and semi-artistic crafts. The arrival of immigrant carpenters, masons, plasterers, bricklayers, joiners, gold- and silversmiths, bookbinders, engravers, musical-instrument makers, and portrait painters signified that the American colonies had crossed an economic threshold in leaving behind the wilderness environment of the seventeenth century.

Nevertheless, native-born and immigrant painters often found themselves painting houses and signs rather than easel pictures that demonstrated their mastery of art. Justus Engelhardt Kühn's modest talents as a painter of the Maryland gentry failed to provide him with sufficient income. The artist, deeply in debt, was forced to paint coats of arms for families wanting traditional signs of aristocratic social status. In mid-century, the Boston painter John Greenwood (see fig. 3.2) abandoned America altogether. After his interlude in the Dutch colony of Surinam, he headed for London and a more lucrative art career than he could have hoped for in Boston. Sometime after 1762, he opened an art dealership in the British capital.

During the first three quarters of the eighteenth century, less than one percent of the colonial American population had their portraits painted. Probably fewer than 8,000 portraits were painted, at least half of which are now lost or destroyed. Yet, with only fifty portraits surviving from the previous century, this represents a significant increase in production. As American towns grew larger, the market for portraits could sustain the careers of a small but growing number of artists. Except for the limited number of biblical paintings discussed in chapter 2, demand for pictures other than portraits remained negligible.

Mansions and the portraits that lined their walls created social and political credibility for merchants and landowners attempting to maintain or construct an aristocratic family pedigree. Wealthy colonists visually asserted their "natural" right to manage local and provincial public affairs by designing homes that rivaled the architectural grandeur of statehouses and governors' mansions. More than aesthetic objects signifying cultivated taste, portraits visually preserved for posterity the family tree and documented the transmission of family wealth from one generation to the next. Set against the constant threat of lawlessness and social violence, stable elite families became models for the sound political architecture of good government. Colonists often talked of the human body, the family, and the state in architectural terms as sacred temples or pillars of beauty and virtue. James Bowdoin II (1726–90), a member of the Boston mercantile elite, wrote a wedding poem praising the architecture of his new, seventeen-year-old wife: "Her comely neck, with symmetry and grace, / Rises majestic on its noble base, / And, like a column of superior art, / Does to the eye a fine effect impart" (cited in Sadik, p. 49). Around the same time, Bowdoin also commissioned marriage portraits that represented the couple with erect, columnar postures and relatively hard, marblelike flesh (figs. 3.5–3.6). Robert Feke (1705–51), the New York–born painter of these pictures, rendered the illusion of luxurious fabrics and expensive imported clothing, while still conveying the impression of moral sobriety in the sitters' still, dignified poses and emotionally cool expressions. In fact, the pose of Elizabeth Bowdoin is similar to that of Gerardus Duyckinck's rendering of Abigail Franks (see p. 76), suggesting that both had their origins in a common British prototype (see fig. 3.1).

3.7 Alexander Hamilton
"Mr. Neilson's Anger Restrained by Philosophy," from *The History of the Tuesday Club*, Vol. 1, pt. 1, bk. 2. John Work Garrett Library, Johns Hopkins University, Baltimore, Maryland.

Social Clubs as Vehicles for Self-Cultivation

Royal governors stood at the apex of colonial society. As surrogates for the British monarch, they set the standard for manners and taste. In Philadelphia, the provincial governor of Pennsylvania was the weekly featured guest of the Governor's Club, a gentlemen's society that met to discuss English poetry, novels, and other subjects of cultural interest.

Along with etiquette books and portrait prints imported from London, social clubs and fraternities inspired by London's cosmopolitan culture taught socially mobile Americans how to dress and conduct themselves like refined individuals. In Annapolis, Maryland, Dr. Alexander Hamilton, formerly of Edinburgh, Scotland, founded in 1745 the Tuesday Club in the hope of introducing gentlemanly conversation and

culture to this "barbarous and desolate corner of the world" (Hamilton, p. xii). The Tuesday Club attracted many prominent members of Maryland's social and political elite, including government officials, merchants, newspaper publishers, judges, lawyers, and clergymen. Club meetings consisted of entertainments in which members delivered humorous poems and speeches, conducted mock trials, performed musical compositions, and sang popular songs. Hamilton wrote a satirical history of the Tuesday Club in the manner of the English comic novel *Tom Jones* (1749) by Henry Fielding. The amateurish, cartoonlike pictures that Hamilton sketched to illustrate the club history suggest the often rowdy and bawdy nature of the evening's entertainments. However, for Hamilton, social organizations like the Tuesday Club were schools of manners that taught members how to control rather than repress their emotions. Hamilton modeled himself after Democritus, the ancient Greek philosopher, who could good-naturedly observe the world of human folly, "without Laughing Immoderately" (Hamilton, p. 295). According to the fourth earl of Chesterfield (1694–1733), whose book on manners was religiously read in Britain and America, "Frequent and loud laughter is the characteristic of folly and ill manners: it is the manner in which the mob express their silly joy, at silly things" (cited in Kasson, p. 163).

Controlling anger and violence was also an important lesson to be learned from the group dynamics of the Tuesday Club. According to Hamilton, his drawing of "Mr Neilson's Anger Restrained by Philosophy" represents a man with a "Sharp visage" and "peaked chin" who temporarily lost his temper over jokes about "the oddity of his appearance" (Hamilton, p. 28) (fig. 3.7). Just as he is about to unsheath his sword, a female personification of Philosophy pulls him away from the violent act. Philosophy, or the love of wisdom, overcomes the passions and composes even the ugliest countenance with a degree of dignity.

Society clubs and behavior manuals taught portraitists and their sitters that immoderate passions and facial expressions of any kind adversely affected personal appearance. Hamilton and other members of the Tuesday Club assumed that the arts and letters were moderating influences upon the passions. They contributed to social order and good government. However, club members also believed that the arts could flourish only within a fraternal atmosphere of political liberty. During the late seventeenth century, Maryland's Protestant majority had rallied around its legislative assembly to oppose Lord Baltimore, the colony's Catholic proprietor, whose claims to absolute political power had rested upon royalist doctrine that the King and his appointees governed by the will of God. In England and its American colonies, the authoritarian principle of "divine right" collapsed during the Glorious Revolution of 1688–9, when the Parliament in London overthrew the absolutist Catholic monarch James II in favor of the Protestant monarchs William III and Mary II. Following the Parliament's establishment of authority, the legislative assembly in Maryland asserted its rights in limiting the colony's proprietor's powers.

Freemasonry and the Visual Education of the American Public

Hamilton and other members of the Tuesday Club also joined the fraternity of Freemasons. In late-seventeenth- and early-eighteenth-century Scotland and England, Freemasonry had transformed itself from a labor guild of "operative" or professional stonemasons into a social and religious fraternity of philosophically "speculative" gentlemen (Bullock, p. 10). Influential aristocrats and, eventually, members of the British royal family became Freemasons.

Freemasonry did not fully blossom in America until after the Revolution, during the early period of the new republic from 1790 to 1826. However, already during the colonial era, the fraternity formed an important part of America's developing culture of genteel manners and refined taste. By the 1730s, London's Grand Lodge, Masonry's most important administrative body, had "warranted" or chartered provincial American lodges in Philadelphia, Boston, New York, Charleston, Savannah, and in Cape Fear, North Carolina (Bullock, p. 46). As Masons, American men could claim a fraternal bond with English aristocrats, political leaders, and even royalty. Though he did not organize a colonial lodge, the fourth Lord Baltimore, Maryland's governor from 1715 to 1751, became a Freemason in England in 1730 and, seven years later, assisted in the Masonic initiation ceremony for Frederick Louis, Prince of Wales, the son of George II and father of George III.

Along with numerous local clubs and literary and scientific societies, Freemasonry contributed to the cultural refinement of colonial society. Although colonial Masonry grew slowly and haltingly during the 1730s and 1740s, the next several decades witnessed growth with the founding of new lodges, not only in coastal towns, but also in the more remote communities of the western interior. The fraternity's exclusiveness appealed to local elites and socially aspiring members of the middle class. High initiation fees effectively barred lower-class men from membership. Within the fraternity itself, egalitarianism among the brothers was limited by the hierarchy of lodge officers and by the fraternity's hierarchical system of degrees, which began with the craft rankings of "Entered Apprentice," "Fellow Craft" (journeyman), and "Master Mason" (Bullock, pp. 16–18) and eventually, in some lodges, included higher degrees of secret knowledge with titles derived from medieval knighthood and other lofty historical sources. Far from dispensing with the notion of aristocratic superiority, Freemasons simply replaced the traditional notion of a fixed social hierarchy based upon birth or inherited wealth with a merit-based hierarchy nominally grounded upon individual achievement and virtue. Of course, wealth, whether inherited or not, automatically tended to signify virtue and achievement. Freemasonry thereby encouraged members of the colonial elite to assume that they constituted a "natural," meritorious aristocracy.

With increased travel, trade, and urban growth undermining traditional town and village life, local Masonic lodges became friendly refuges, where successful men on the move could establish social and business contacts. Masonry was particularly designed to channel the energies of restless young men seeking entrance into public life. Teaching principles of morality, politeness, learning, and aesthetics, Masonic rituals and fellowships sought to shape malleable colonial youths into stable pillars of civic virtue.

Because of the fragmentary nature of colonial lodge records, historians have had difficulty in assessing Masonry's numerical strength. However,

3.8 Wren Building
1695–8 (restored 1931 and 1968).
College of William and Mary, Williamsburg, Virginia.

in 1784, just after the American Revolution, the Reverend Ezra Stiles (see p. 38), president of Yale College and an admirer of Freemasonry, estimated that of the over 1,500 Masonic lodges then existing worldwide, 187 were in America, with each averaging around thirty members. More recently, Masonic scholars have calculated that, by the beginning of the Revolution in 1775, there were at least one hundred American lodges.

Freemasonry thus constituted only a fraction of the colonial male population. But the social and political prestige of its membership elevated the fraternity's cultural importance and public visibility. Though Masons gathered secretly in lodges, meeting primarily at taverns and inns, reports or exposés of their rituals and secrets appeared in colonial newspapers and journals. Furthermore, Freemasons organized well-publicized events at town halls, churches, and public theaters, generally involving colorful street processions for cornerstone-laying ceremonies, funerals, and celebrations honoring their biblical patrons, St. John the Baptist and St. John

the Evangelist. Inaugurating the first Masonic hall constructed in America, Philadelphia Freemasons in 1755 conducted one of the fraternity's largest parades, led by Pennsylvania's leading men, including chief justice William Allen, the current governor, Robert Hunter Morris, and the former governor, James Hamilton. In addition to the marching bands, decorated carriages, chariots, and troops of richly dressed Freemasons, lodge officers also carried models of Doric, Ionic, and Corinthian columns from classical Greek and Roman architecture, respectively symbolizing strength, wisdom, and beauty. This display of aesthetic taste encouraged Masons and non-Masonic spectators alike to associate the visual arts with virtue.

Since there was no professional school for training architects, Freemasonry became an apt vehicle for promoting good design. Numerous eighteenth-century British architects and builders were Freemasons, including James Gibbs (1682–1754) and Batty Langley (1696–1751). Both published design books that were influential for American colonial architecture. Langley's

Ancient masonry, both in the theory and practice, demonstrating the useful rules of arithmetick, geometry, and architecture, in the proportions and orders of the most eminent masters of all nations (1736) was one of many architectural treatises sold in the colonies. Masonic symbols decorated the frontispiece to Langley's *The Builder's Jewel* (1741–46).

Masonry elevated the social status of the visual arts by associating the ancient craft lore of stonemasonry and the secrets of geometry and light with the divine architecture of the universe and the revolutionary new science of Sir Isaac Newton. Opposing religious sectarianism in favor of a universal, rational religion, Freemasons searched for empirical evidence that a Supreme Architect had designed creation. They favored a classical Roman and Renaissance style in architecture because it seemed to correspond with the Newtonian model of a universe governed by predictable natural laws and mathematical principles.

Many English historians credited the ancient Romans with the unification and partial Christianization of the British Isles. Roman classical architecture constituted a British national style, which had to be "reborn" following the Middle Ages. This period in European history had begun when the Visigoths, a nomadic German tribe, sacked Rome in 410 C.E. Called "barbarians" by the Romans, the Goths, Vandals, Huns, and other Germanic peoples came to personify for British historians the Middle Ages' cultural darkness and political disunity. Protestant Britons and colonial Americans generally believed that the authoritarian, papal hierarchy of the Catholic Church had thrived on medieval ignorance and superstition stemming from the period's anarchic, barbarian origins. By contrast, Anglo-American Protestants equated the Renaissance and its revival of ancient art and learning with religious and political freedom and individual enlightenment. First flowering within Catholic Italy, Renaissance thought often conflicted with traditional Church doctrine. The ongoing struggle against Catholic France and Spain for control of North America undoubtedly contributed to Anglo-American taste for an architecture free of associations with the Middle Ages.

British and American Freemasons adopted as spiritual brothers the founding fathers of British architecture, Inigo Jones (1573–1652) and Sir Christopher Wren. Both men were credited with expunging medieval stylistic features from modern design in favor of Renaissance clarity and balance. For the advocates of classicism, the term "Gothic" had become synonymous with a barbaric lack of refinement. Wren, who was officially initiated into London Freemasonry in 1691, especially personified the Masonic equation between science and modern architecture. A professor of astronomy at Oxford and a founding member of the scientific Royal Society, he became Surveyor General of the King's Works. He was responsible for rebuilding London's St. Paul's Cathedral and designing numerous other churches and public buildings.

Wren's classical style had a major impact on the American colonies. In the new Virginia capital of Williamsburg, Wren's name became attached to the central building of the College of William and Mary (fig. 3.8). In 1722, the college's first professor of mathematics, Hugh Jones, wrote that "the building is beautiful and commodious, being first modeled by Sir Christopher Wren, adapted to the Nature of the country by the Gentlemen there" (cited in Pierson, Jr., p. 71). The Wren Building, with its central pavilion and towering cupola, may have been based on a plan submitted by the London architect. However, colonial builders modified Wren's classicism according to provincial building traditions and local craft practices. The steeply pitched slope of the pavilion pediment lacks the classical ease typical of Wren's style.

The mythology of Freemasonry made it easier for Anglo-American Protestants to dissociate classical Roman architecture from the taint of paganism. Alexander Hamilton and other Freemasons commonly traced the origins of their fraternity to the earliest builders mentioned in the Bible, particularly King Solomon, who had ordered architects and stonemasons to construct the Jewish temple in Jerusalem. In *The Chronology of Ancient Kingdoms Amended* (1728), Isaac Newton stirred the Masonic imagination by attempting to reconstruct from ancient sources what the lost temple must have looked like. The mathematician wrote that Solomon's Temple was the prototype for classical architecture. Its proportions mirrored the divine architecture of the universe and even prophesied

3.9 John Senex
A Front View of the Temple of Solomon, 1725. Hand-colored engraving on paper, 8¼ x 13½ in (20.9 x 34.3 cm). Museum of Our National Heritage, Lexington, Massachusetts.

John Senex (d.1741), a London publisher of Masonic texts, copied the façade and courtyard view from a contemporary guidebook describing a 20-foot-square model of Solomon's Temple, erected at the expense of Gerhard Schott (1641–1702), an opera patron from Hamburg, Germany. Schott had been inspired by scenery for an operatic production representing the destruction of Jerusalem. However, the wooden model temple reconstruction has been credited to a Johann Jakob Erasmus, who was inspired by the famous version of Solomon's temple by Juan Bautista Villalpando (1552–1608).

the future of humankind. Inspired by his reading of Old Testament texts, Newton drew a floor plan of the temple, believing that its dimensions and geometric ratios provided clues for biblical prophecies and timelines regarding Christ's second coming and the apocalyptic end of history, or God's final day of judgment.

This floor plan descended from a long tradition of speculation equating Solomon's Temple with the harmony of God's creation. Furthermore, during the late sixteenth century, European and English philosophers seeking to reconcile the pagan and Christian traditions were already proposing that the Greek and Roman architectural orders originated in the divine proportions of Solomon's Temple. Before Newton's floor plan, the seventeenth century witnessed a number of attempts to reconstruct the appearance of Solomon's Temple as an emblem of cosmic order and prophetic wisdom.

In 1724–5 and again in 1729–30, following the posthumous publication of Newton's treatise, competing architectural models of Solomon's Temple were exhibited in London.

The large, classically designed wooden models had been constructed during the previous century by Dutch and German designers. Their exhibition during the eighteenth century stimulated public interest in Freemasonry and the fraternity's claims to Solomonic origins. Leading English Freemasons began publishing prints of Solomon's Temple in Masonic publications (fig. 3.9). This image circulated in America and later appeared on Masonic aprons that members wore during lodge meetings, public parades, and initiation rituals. In a revolutionary-era apron from Massachusetts (fig. 3.10), the symmetrical, rectangular block representing Solomon's Temple possesses a mosaic forecourt, supported by classical pillars and ancient mythological figures: Minerva, Roman goddess of wisdom; Hercules, the Greek hero personifying strength; and Venus, Roman goddess of beauty.

Before the Revolution, few Masonic aprons were so elaborately decorated. However, colonial Freemasons already adopted mythic gods and heroes for teaching various moral and intellectual principles. When Alexander Hamilton visited the

3.10 Anonymous
Master Mason's apron,
c. 1780.
Ink and watercolor on
leather. Museum of Our
National Heritage,
Lexington, Massachusetts.

This apron, with its hand-
drawn design, belonged to
Richard Harris, Master of
Philanthropic Lodge in
Marblehead, Massachusetts
from 1778–81. Beneath
Hercules, the inscription
reads "Let Critics sport &
Fools deride / Masons
alone in strength confide."
The three sculptural figures
refer to the Master and
other supporting officers of
a Masonic lodge. Emblems
of the sun and the moon
flank Solomon's temple,
symbolizing the harmony
and divine architecture of
the universe.

Newport, Rhode Island, studio of Robert Feke, he became excited by the artist's *Judgment of Hercules*, a picture later destroyed in a fire. In this rare attempt at history painting, Feke copied a European print of the subject (fig. 3.11). Hamilton and other Freemasons identified with this popular image of Hercules because the classical hero had demonstrated moral strength in choosing the difficult mountainous path pointed to by Virtue rather than the sensual pleasures of the flesh as personified by the recumbent figure of Vice. In the Massachusetts apron, the central figure of Hercules turns toward the Roman goddess of wisdom. The inscription beneath her reads: "Wisdom fair Goddess we Persue / Virtue always have in View." Eighteenth-century Freemasons gave priority to Minerva, but they also embraced Venus as a personification of aesthetic beauty and chaste, divine love. Counteracting Vice, Venus represented the purification of nature and the senses to a higher state of spiritual being. Beneath the nude Venus, who modestly covers herself, the Masonic apron's inscription affirmed the rights of beauty "Lock'd

within our hearts." During the eighteenth and nineteenth centuries, Freemasons became leading proponents of the arts, defending the claims of beauty against puritanical moralists, who believed that art was an unnecessary luxury allied with vice. As we shall see, colonial portraits often alluded to the spiritual ideals and virtues associated with the goddesses Venus and Minerva.

Domestic Architecture as a Moral Force

During the spring and autumn of 1728, the English-educated Virginian William Byrd II (1674–1744) led a surveying expedition to establish the dividing line between North Carolina and Virginia. Byrd kept a travel journal of his experiences along the trail from the Great Dismal Swamp toward the Appalachian Mountains. He decided to publish the travelogue for the benefit of his aristocratic friends in London, many of whom were Newtonian men

3.11 Simon Gribelin
The Judgment of Hercules.
Engraving after a painting by Paolo de Matthais (1662–1728) for the frontispiece of Lord Shaftesbury's *Characteristicks of Men, Manners, Opinions, Times* (1711), vol. 3, treatise 7. Library of Congress, Washington, D.C.

of science and members of the Royal Society, Britain's leading scientific organization. Byrd himself had gained Royal Society membership in 1696 in recognition of his interest in the natural history of the American continent. By the time that he undertook his surveying expedition, he had collected over 4,000 books on science, architecture, and other subjects, the largest library in the American colonies.

The learned tobacco planter's *History of the Dividing Line* (1729) contrasted his beloved Virginia with North Carolina, which he derisively called "Lubberland" (cited in Lockridge, p. 138). While Byrd portrayed Virginia as a biblical paradise, Lubberland was a virtual wilderness, where oafish, "indolent wretches" lived in close proximity to cattle and hogs and "where there is

neither church, chapel, mosque, synagogue, or any other place of public worship of any sect or religion whatsoever" (cited in Lockridge, p. 138). In Edenton, North Carolina, Byrd observed that "a citizen here is counted extravagant if he has ambition enough to aspire to a brick chimney. Justice herself is but indifferently lodged, the courthouse having much of the air of a common tobacco house" (cited in Lockridge, p. 139).

North Carolina's dearth of public and domestic architecture signified an irreligious, lawless, and dangerously democratic society that treated governors "with all the excesses of freedom and familiarity" (cited in Lockridge, p. 139). Byrd told the story of one "bold magistrate" who ordered "a fellow to the stocks for being disorderly in his drink" only to be "carried thither himself," where he "narrowly escaped being whipped by the rabble into the bargain" (cited in Lockridge, p. 139).

Returning to Westover, his tobacco plantation on the James River just west of Williamsburg, Byrd acted to guarantee that Virginia would remain safe from the Scottish and Irish settlers of North Carolina and Pennsylvania, whom he compared to the barbarian "Goths and Vandals of old" (cited in Lockridge, p. 140). He ordered his father's old wooden manor house torn down and replaced by an elegant and spacious red-brick mansion (fig. 3.12) designed after the Renaissance-inspired style of Sir Christopher Wren's architecture. Wren's classicism, which Freemasons and Royal Society brothers promoted in concert, symbolized the modern triumph of civilization and the rational order of the Newtonian universe over barbarism.

This classical style of architecture, often named "Georgian" after the eighteenth-century German Protestant kings of Great Britain, expressed itself at Westover in the symmetrical arrangement of large sash windows that surround an elaborately decorated stone entrance on the mansion's riverfront façade (fig. 3.13). The expensive Portland stone was imported from England. A London craftsman probably carved the fluted Corinthian pilasters on the sides and the broken "swan's-neck" pediment overhead. Topping off the doorway's central axis, a pineapple finial welcomes visitors as a rich, exotic symbol of the hospitality that awaits them beyond the threshold.

The door would have reminded Byrd of the many years he had spent in London, since its design was based on a type that had been popular in the British metropolis years earlier. Built on a far smaller scale than the mansions of the English aristocracy, Westover's two-and-a-half stories nevertheless represented a significant

3.12 Westover
Riverfront façade, Charles City County, Virginia, 1730–4. Cook Collection, Valentine Museum, Richmond, Virginia.

Although Sir Christopher Wren was never known to have designed small houses, his name became stylistically associated with the simple, rectangular-block houses popular among the English middle class and country gentry during the late seventeenth and early eighteenth centuries. With its hipped roof, red brick, and white stone materials, and carefully proportioned façade, Westover bears comparison with Minster House in the city of Winchester, England, a small, detached home influenced by Wren's elegant classicism.

3.13 Westover
Riverfront door, Charles
City County, Virginia,
1730–4.
Cook Collection,
Valentine Museum,
Richmond, Virginia.

right to political power. Unlike the virtual social anarchy he witnessed in the wilds of North Carolina, the slave-owning Byrd easily envisioned himself as master of his domain at Westover and a leader of colonial Virginia:

> Like one of the patriarchs, I have my flocks and my herds, my bond-men and bond-women, and every soart of trade amongst my own servants, so that I live in a kind of independence on every one, but Providence. However tho' this soart of life is without expence yet it is attended with a great deal of trouble. I must take care to keep all my people to their duty, to set all the springs in motion, and to make every one draw his equal share to carry the machine forward. But then tis an amusement in this silent country, and a continual exercise of our patience and economy (cited in Lockridge, p. 123).

Keeping the plantation "machine" in motion meant the repeated beating of black house servants and field slaves. We know this because Byrd kept a secret, coded diary that recorded his methodical daily routine, which consistently began with readings in Greek and Hebrew and generally ended with prayers thanking God for his blessings. In response to "disobedient" or "lazy" slaves, he matter-of-factly describes whippings and other brutal punishments, such as hot-iron brandings and the use of iron boots, bits, and clamps. The harmonic, Newtonian architectural order of Westover's classical design symbolized Byrd's gentlemanly status and his membership in London's Royal Society, but the master's hospitality came at a terrible human price.

Soon southern slave owners were building houses that looked like Roman temples. On the Ashley River close to Charleston, South Carolina, John Drayton, heir to twenty plantations, constructed a two-story, redbrick mansion, elevated high above the ground by a basement floor (fig. 3.14). Two exterior staircases invited guests upward toward the two-tiered, central portico, or entrance porch. Greek Doric columns, austere symbols of masculine strength, frame the lower-story entrance. Slender-proportioned Ionic columns, expressing wisdom and refinement, ennoble the second-floor balcony, which is capped by a gently sloping pediment. The portico's elegant vertical thrust is

increase in living space for wealthy Virginians. At the time, the vast majority of Virginia's propertied elite still resided in one- and one-and-a-half-story houses, with just two rooms on the ground floor. In most areas of the colonies, small, unpainted wooden houses with very small windows continued to dominate the eighteenth-century American countryside, even as the richest citizens increasingly built larger mansions of brick or painted wood. Byrd, who coveted the office of royal governor, modeled Westover after the Governor's Palace in Williamsburg and thereby established a prestigious model for subsequent mansion architecture. In styling their private homes after the public architecture of government buildings, wealthy colonists proclaimed their inherent

3.14 Drayton Hall
Land façade, Ashley River, Charleston, South Carolina, 1738–42.

Two-story porticoes were a rarity in Great Britain, where the relatively cold, damp climate made large, airy porches impractical. Drayton Hall's temple-design portico was modeled after Andrea Palladio's Villa Pisani in Montagnana, Italy. The first English edition of Palladio's architectural designs appeared in 1715. As the earliest Palladian temple portico in the colonies, Drayton Hall helped establish the fashion for the classical villa style.

more than balanced by the horizontal breadth of the mansion and the generous square spacing between columns in both portico tiers.

The builders of Drayton Hall relied on the Renaissance villa designs of the Italian architect Andrea Palladio (1508–80), which were first promoted in seventeenth-century England by Inigo Jones and then popularized in the eighteenth century by Richard Boyle, third earl of Burlington (1694–1753), and his circle of architect friends, many of whom were Freemasons. Burlington sponsored the publication of design books, which helped spread Palladian villa architecture to the American colonies. Drayton Hall and other colonial mansions served as domestic, semi-private theaters for the display of luxuries and the performance of refined manners. Whereas single- and double-room house plans forced most colonists to combine a number of living functions—sleeping, dining, and entertaining—in a single large hall, the new multiroom mansions enabled wealthy merchants and landowners to create lavish parlors, dining rooms, and upper-story ballrooms for entertaining guests. Matching the ceremonial grandeur of Drayton Hall's exterior staircases, a dual-branched interior staircase (fig. 3.15) led visitors to a classically ornamented second-floor doorway, through which were more rooms for dancing, conversation, and card playing.

Emulating the hospitality and largesse of the English aristocracy, propertied colonists demonstrated their elite status through the expenditure of money for maintaining a convivial house open to peers, friends, relatives, and other guests. In 1744, Alexander Hamilton traveled to Albany, New York, where he found the predominantly Dutch population wanting in gentility. The doctor's appraisal is worth quoting at length, since it reveals important cultural and social attitudes regarding the role that art, architecture, and consumer luxuries played in colonial life:

The Dutch here keep their houses very neat and clean, both without and within. Their chamber floors are generally laid with rough plank, which in time, by constant rubbing and scrubbing, becomes as smooth as if it had been planed. Their chambers and rooms are large and handsome. They have their beds generally in alcoves, so that you may go thro' all the rooms of a great house and see never a bed. They affect pictures much, particularly scripture history, with which they adorn their rooms. They set out their cabinets and buffets much with china. Their kitchens are likewise very clean, and there they hang earthen

3.15 Drayton Hall
Interior staircase,
1738–42.
Charleston,
South Carolina.

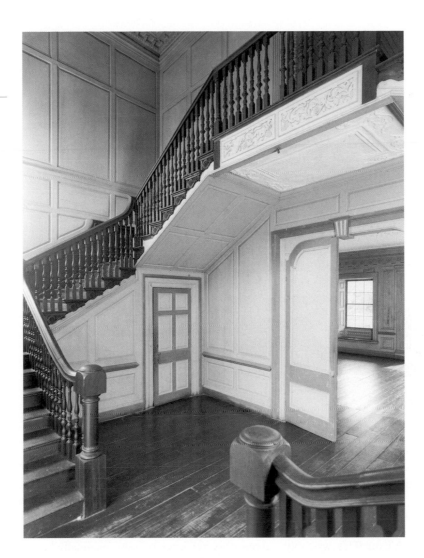

or delft plates and dishes all round the walls, in manner of pictures, having a hole drilled thro' the edge of the plate or dish and a loop of ribbon put into it to hang it by; but notwithstanding all this nicety and cleanliness in their houses, they are in their persons slovenly and dirty. They live here very frugally and plain, for the chief merit among them seems to be riches, which they spare no pains or trouble to acquire, but are a civil and hospitable people in their way, but at best rustic and unpolished . . . They live in their houses in Albany as if it were in prisons, all their doors and windows being perpetually shut. But the reason of this may be the little desire they have for conversation and society, their whole thoughts being turned upon profit and gain, which necessarily makes them live retired and frugal (cited in Horner and Bain, p. 365).

In Hamilton's view, the Albany Dutch failed to qualify for social elite status despite their considerable wealth and patronage of religious art. Their allegedly unkempt appearance and lack of personal hygiene signified not only a rustic lack of polish, but also a lack of interest in wanting to please others. Hamilton suggests that their frugality masked a selfish materialism, since they care only for "profit and gain" and little for real hospitality. The Albany Dutch retreated from conversation and social life to imprison themselves like misers and misanthropes behind shuttered windows and bolted doors. Though neat and clean, their tall, narrow town houses lacked the classical ornamentation that Hamilton elsewhere associated with gracious living and refined taste. No Dutch-American town houses have survived in Albany or New York City.

**3.16 Stadt Huys
(City Hall)**
New Amsterdam
(New York), 1679.
Lithograph by George
Hayward, 1869.
J. Clarence Davies
Collection, Museum of the
City of New York.

This nineteenth-century
lithographic representation
of New Amsterdam is based
upon a 1679 sketch by a
minor Netherlandish artist.
The cityscape recalls more
famous urban views by Jan
Vermeer (1632–75)—such
as *View of Delft*— and by
other Dutch painters. The
distinctive stepped-gable
design of colonial Dutch
architecture was adopted by
English and Anglo-
American builders of
Anglican parish churches,
as seen in St. Luke's Church
in Newport Parish, Virginia
(see fig. 2.16).

However, a nineteenth-century lithograph has preserved a view of the seventeenth-century Stadt Huys in New Amsterdam (New York) (fig. 3.16). The stepped-gable town houses surrounding the City Hall constituted a Dutch building type that continued into the eighteenth century, when Hamilton toured Albany. This was only one of many local building traditions associated with various ethnic groups that stood in contrast to the Anglophile Palladianism of colonial elite mansions.

American men of wealth imported more than London-published design books of Palladian architecture. They also imported skilled carpenters and other craftsmen, who could transform abstract plans into elegantly decorated homes. The London-trained carpenter and joiner William Buckland (1734–74) arrived at the Virginia plantation of George Mason as an indentured servant, bound to work four years without pay as a carpenter and joiner on Mason's new mansion, Gunston Hall. After working sixteen years for various Virginia patrons and establishing his own workshop of skilled craftsmen, Buckland, in 1771, began

working in Annapolis, Maryland, for Edward Lloyd, a learned gentleman who corresponded with members of London's Royal Society and had been an active participant in the Masonic culture of the Tuesday Club. Lloyd hired Buckland to finish construction of a massive, three-story brick town house, originally begun by Samuel Chase, whose debts had forced him to sell the property (fig. 3.17).

The mansion's exterior features a Palladian or Venetian-style entrance, with two narrow windows flanking the arched central door. Ionic columns and pilasters, or flattened, rectangular columns, frame the entrance windows and door, which is capped by a modest, gently sloping pediment. A far more substantial pediment adorns the middle of the roof to accentuate the projecting central block and the building's classical symmetry. The grandeur of the entrance is continued in the interior entrance hall and stairway (fig. 3.18). Dramatically framed by an Ionic columnar screen, the stately stairway leads to a half-story landing illuminated by a Palladian window motif corresponding to the exterior's three-part entrance. The ceremonial stairway

3.17 William Buckland
Samuel Chase-Edward
Lloyd House, Annapolis,
Maryland, 1769–73.
Historic Annapolis
Foundation.

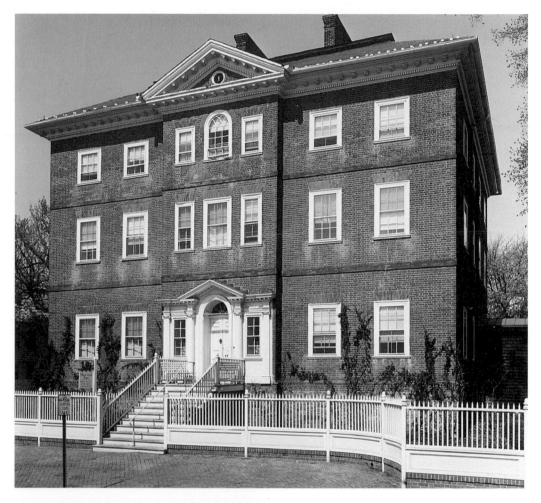

3.18 William Buckland
Interior entrance hall
and stairway, Samuel
Chase-Edward Lloyd
House, 1769–73.
Historic Annapolis
Foundation.

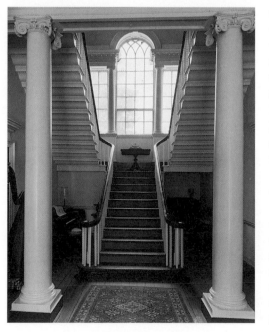

then divides into two parallel side flights that are cantilevered back over the entrance hall and upward to the second floor. Buckland supervised all the decorative wood carving to create one of the most elegant interiors in colonial America. Study of the architectural design books that Buckland was known to have had in his library has led scholars to conclude that he modeled the stairway's Palladian window after engravings in *City and Country Builder's and Workman's Treasury* (1745) by Batty Langley, English builder-designer and active promoter of Freemasonry.

By painting wooden columns, pilasters, and classical ornaments white, American builders mimicked the marble or stone architecture of ancient temples. In colonial New England, most mansions were primarily wooden constructions rather than of the red brick generally found in the South. However, for the west or garden façade of the Isaac Royall house in Medford,

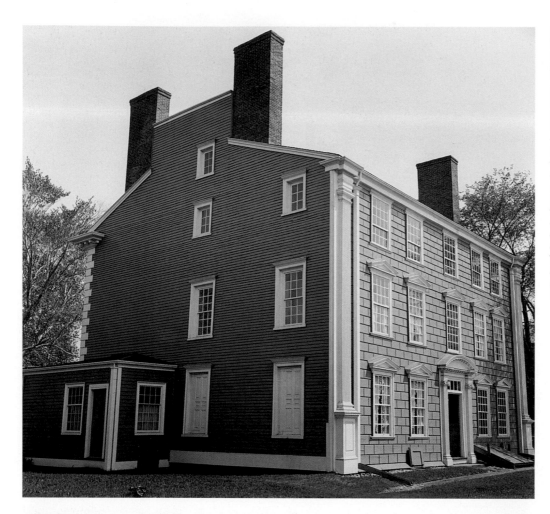

3.19 Isaac Royall House
Garden (west) façade, Medford, Massachusetts, 1733–7.
Society for the Preservation of New England Antiquities, Boston.

Palladian in design, the west façade is flanked at either end by tall wooden pilasters and features pedimented windows on the first two stories. The classically ornamented entranceway was modeled after an illustration in William Solomon's *Palladio Londinensis* (1734), a popular pattern book of Palladian designs.

3.20 Isaac Royall House
Great chamber, Medford, Massachusetts, 1733–7. Society for the Preservation of New England Antiquities, Boston.

In remodeling and expanding the original seventeenth-century farmhouse, Isaac Royall was forced to work with its low ceilings. In the second-story "great chamber," which functioned as a bedroom, the painted wooden pilasters flanking the fireplace appear relatively squat. However, the cramped feeling is eased by the room's large windows, framed by wide, rounded archways that lead into shallow alcoves.

3.21 Robert Feke
Isaac Royall and His Family, 1741.
Oil on canvas,
56³⁄₁₆ x 77¾ in
(142.7 x 197.5 cm).
Harvard Law Art
Collection, Cambridge,
Massachusetts. Gift of
Dr. George Stevens Jones.

Although intent on
capturing convincing
likenesses, Feke
demonstrated little interest
in plumbing the depths of
the individual psyche. The
family's virtually
expressionless, emotionally
cool faces reveal nothing of
interior psychological states.
Instead, the artist's
emphasis is on establishing
social class, gender, and
age distinctions. The
pictorial prominence of the
Turkish carpet was no idle
boast because a 1739
family estate inventory listed
three such carpets.

Massachusetts, builders shaped wooden boards to imitate horizontal rows of masonry stones (fig. 3.19). Royall, a merchant in the rum and slave trade, enlarged the family's original two-and-a-half-story brick house from the late seventeenth century into a much larger three-story mansion, ornamented with classical details. In addition to simulating stonemasonry on the western façade, Royall decorated his "great chamber" (Pierson, Jr., p. 94) on the second floor with wooden Corinthian pilasters, painted to imitate elegant marble (fig. 3.20). Imitative painting to create *faux* marble or stone was also practiced by the lesser gentry in England. Rather than being regarded as a deception, the technique signified Royall's refined, Anglophile taste for the ancient traditions of stonemasonry and temple architecture. Though separated by hundreds of miles, Royall was the spiritual brother of William Byrd, who believed that the classical style of Sir Christopher Wren was a cultural defense against American barbarism.

A group portrait of *Isaac Royall and His Family* by Robert Feke represents the young master of the Medford mansion standing next to his wife and baby daughter (fig. 3.21). His sister-in-law and sister sit at the far left of the painting. The stiffly posed figures appear to have been shaped by the fashionable taste for classical formality and balanced order. The English author John Evelyn, a friend of Sir Christopher Wren, had argued against the asymmetry and alleged lack of proportion in medieval or Gothic-style buildings because they contributed to irregular behavior in the people who occupied them. In Feke's group portrait, there is little evidence of emotional irregularity. The elongated necks of the expressionless women may remind us of James Bowdoin's poem dedicated to his wife (see p. 84). The rectilinear forms of the composition, from the table in the immediate foreground to the rectangular window panes in the background, suggest the Royall house-hold's dominance over nature. The geometric, symmetrical design of the Turkish carpet simultaneously signifies Isaac Royall's possession of imported luxuries and his virtuous desire for clarity and order. The painting makes a clear distinction between male and female social roles. The seated, more passive women are essentially defined by association with the baby as domestic caregivers, while the young patriarch stands with a book as a worldly man of learning and public affairs. Feke's crisply linear style and tight control of the paint surface accentuate the impression that the New England wilderness has been subdued by a civilized, moral aesthetic. As we shall soon see, Feke appropriated the composition of his ambitious group portrait from the work of John Smibert, an immigrant Scottish artist who introduced a higher level of sophistication and academic learning into American portraiture.

Political Portraiture: Colonial Governors as Pillars of State

Beginning during the late seventeenth century, portraits of royal governors were exhibited in government buildings as symbols of state authority. They usually were hung near official portraits of the King and Queen sent from London as royal gifts. To commemorate the one-hundredth anniversary of the founding of Massachusetts Bay Colony in 1730, portraits of King George II and Queen Caroline arrived in Boston to decorate the walls of the governor's council chamber. Shortly thereafter, the new governor of Massachusetts, Jonathan Belcher, commissioned a full-length portrait of himself. This son of a wealthy Boston merchant thereby accrued for himself the political benefit of basking in royalty's reflected glory.

In addition to formal state portraits, images of rulers and public notables were also disseminated through the medium of prints imported from London (see fig. 3.1). Before his formal installation as royal governor of Massachusetts in 1730, Jonathan Belcher sat for a smaller, half-length portrait painting by the Irish artist Richard Philips (1681–1741). Four years later, Belcher's son hired the London printmaker John Faber (1695–1756) to create a mezzotint reproduction of this portrait (fig. 3.22). Faber's mezzotint presents Belcher as a model of aristocratic gentility and state authority. Holding his government commission as if it were a royal scepter, Belcher commands a background view of Boston harbor, where a British naval ship fires its cannon in salute. His costume is distinguished by a long periwig with lavish curls, a velvet waistcoat with gold brocade, and a fine lace jabot. In the lower-right corner, near Belcher's family crest at the

His Excellency. JONATHAN BELCHER Esq.
Captain General & Governor in Chief of His Majesty's Provinces of
Massachuset's Bay & New Hampshire in NEW ENGLAND and
Vice Admiral of the Same

bottom of the print, the seal of King George II seems suspended from the hand holding the royal commission.

Despite his willingness to sit for portrait paintings, Belcher worried that the print would not be well received by citizens, who routinely warned against the moral dangers of pride and luxury. On August 7, 1734, he angrily chastised his son for commissioning the mezzotint without his permission:

> *I am surprised & much displeased at . . . your having my Picture done on a Copper Plate— how cou'd you presume to do such a thing without my special leave and Order—you should be wise and consider the consequences of things before you put 'em in Execution, such a*

3.22 John Faber
(after Richard Philips), *Governor Jonathan Belcher*, 1734. Mezzotint, 16 x 10⅜ in (40.6 x 26.3 cm). Special Collections, Princeton University Library, Princeton, New Jersey.

foolish affair will pull down much Envy, and give occasion to your Father's Enemies to squirt & Squib & what not—It is therefore my order, if this comes to hand timely that you destroy the plate & burn all the Impressions taken from it (cited in Saunders and Miles, p. 24).

Unlike paintings of royal governors exhibited in public buildings, inexpensive prints could be marketed like other commodities to a far larger audience that included friends and foes alike. Belcher's enemies might have been quick to point out that his portrait print masked his merchant middle-class origins. He had not been born with an aristocratic pedigree or even with a genealogical tie to the first leaders of Massachusetts. Nevertheless, Belcher imaginatively asserted descent from English nobility and prominently advertised this claim with a family coat of arms below his portrait. His son did not destroy the portrait print of his father. The governor's temper cooled to the degree that, in 1735, he requested a dozen copies of the engraving and the copper plate itself, from which he could print still more images for friends and political allies. By possessing the copper plate, Belcher could better control the print's future reproduction and distribution. Ultimately, the governor's anxiety about the symbolic power of such images was very prescient because most portraits of royalty and royal government officials would be destroyed during the American Revolution.

Portrait prints and official, state portraits of royal governors were intended as imposing images of both power and beauty. In *Government the Pillar of the Earth* (1730), a sermon celebrating Belcher's inauguration as governor, the Reverend Benjamin Colman, one of Boston's most prominent Congregationalist clergymen, employed architectural metaphors to characterize the promise of his regime:

The governments and rulers of the earth are it's [sic] pillars for ornament, to adorn it. Pillars in a fine building are made as beautiful as may be; they are plan'd and polish'd, wrought and carv'd with much art and cost, painted and gilded, for sight as well as use. As the legs are to a body comely in it's [sic] goings: Such are pillars in a stately structure for beauty to the eye . . . Solomon . . . had built the temple of God with all it's [sic]

pillars. They represented the strength of Christ and his stability, to bear the weight of government laid upon him . . . So those in power and magistracy are to be supposed, men adorn'd with superior gifts, powers and beauties of mind: Men that adorn the world wherein they live, and the offices which they sustain. And then their office adorns them also, and sets them in conspicuous places, where what is great and good in them is seen of all (cited in Sandoz, pp. 14–15).

Like a portraitist or architect, Colman transforms government authority into an aesthetic composition. Quoting the biblical Song of Solomon, the clergyman compared the wise ruler to a "beloved" husband, whose adoring wife exclaims "His Legs are as Pillars of Marble, set upon Sockets of fine Gold" (cited in Sandoz, p. 15). Colman defined effective government not in terms of coercion or the fear of punishment, but as the offspring of attractive, magnetic forces, an aesthetic love for the beautifully ordered and proportioned body politic. Colman's liberal use of architectural metaphors and repeated allusions to Solomon and Solomon's Temple implicitly acknowledged Governor Belcher's membership in Freemasonry. Belcher had joined a Masonic lodge in London in 1704 and played a prominent role in establishing the fraternity's prestige in America. Freemasonry contributed to the notion that government worked best when motivated by the positive, socially binding feelings of friendship and brotherhood.

John Smibert and the Portraitist as Man of Learning

When, in 1730, Governor Belcher ordered the official full-length standing portrait of himself to exhibit publicly next to the king and queen's, he did not have to return to London to find a qualified painter. John Smibert (1688–1751), the first fully trained professional artist to work in America, had arrived in Boston in 1729 after a brief residence in Newport, Rhode Island. A native of Edinburgh, Scotland, Smibert had begun his career humbly as an apprentice to a house painter and plasterer. But after moving to London in 1709, he attended the art academy of

3.23 John Smibert
The Bermuda Group:
Dean George Berkeley
and his Family, 1729.
Oil on canvas, 5 ft 9½ in x
7 ft 9 in (1.76 x 2.36 m).
Yale University Art Gallery,
New Haven, Connecticut.
Gift of Isaac Lothrop.

Contemporaries referred to
this intimate, informal type
of group portrait as a
conversation piece. Set
within leisurely domestic
interiors or garden, parklike
spaces, the casual
conversation piece
distinguished itself from the
formal look of official,
ceremonial group portraits.
Although it had precedents
in Renaissance painting, the
conversation piece gained
popularity in eighteenth-
century England.

the court painter Sir Godfrey Kneller (c.1646–
1723) and immersed himself in London's
Masonic culture of fraternal societies and clubs.
Smibert belonged to the Rose and the Crown, a
brotherhood of young artists and connoisseurs
who met weekly at a tavern in Covent Garden.
He also joined the London Society of Antiquaries, a learned organization that met one evening
per week "to cultivate the knowledge of antiquities of England" (Saunders, p. 53). The Society,
like Freemasonry, promoted public interest in
architecture. It sponsored publication of prints
that represented the ancient buildings and ruins
of the British Isles. The Society of Antiquaries
enabled Smibert to educate himself in the art of
architectural design.

When Smibert established his Boston painting studio in 1729, he immediately joined the
Scots Charitable Society, a brotherhood that
united Scottish-American men throughout the
colonies. The Freemason Alexander Hamilton
was also a member of the Society and became
an admirer of Smibert's paintings. Smibert
impressed studio visitors and future patrons by
exhibiting copies of old master paintings that he
had made while touring the European conti-

nent. He also displayed an ambitious group portrait, *The Bermuda Group*, representing himself in
the company of Dean George Berkeley, prominent philosopher and Anglican clergyman (fig.
3.23). Berkeley had arrived in Newport in 1729
with plans to found a university on the island of
Bermuda, pending funding from the British
Parliament. Berkeley envisioned the island as
an ideal and paradisiacal site for educating children of American plantation owners and for
training missionaries to convert Indian tribes
to Christianity. Foreseeing an important role for
the visual arts, the Irish-born churchman asked
Smibert to direct an art academy on the island,
teaching painting and the arts of design.

The Bermuda project languished and died in
Newport while Berkeley waited in vain for parliamentary funding. But Smibert's group portrait
commemorated the clergyman's leadership as a
New World educator. The painting had been
commissioned in 1728 by John Wainwright, an
English admirer of Berkeley, who remained
in London and apparently desired a visual
remembrance of the philosopher and his
entourage. Standing at the far-right side of the
painting, dressed in black clerical costume,

Berkeley dominates the composition by appearing to lecture or dictate his thoughts before other members of the group. Despite his refusal to travel with the group to Newport, John Wainwright serves as Berkeley's earnest secretary. Sitting at the far left with quill in hand, he leans forward over a large, open notebook, waiting expectantly for the words of the clergyman, who has paused from speaking and seems lost in thought.

Averting his gaze upward in apparent communion with divine ideas, Berkeley appears oblivious to the other figures in the portrait, including his wife, who sits at the table next to her husband holding their newborn son, Henry. Mrs. Berkeley's traveling companion, a Miss Handcock, sits in the middle of the painting. Standing immediately behind the two women and Wainwright are Richard Dalton and John James, "Men of Fortune" or "gentlemen of substance," who traveled to America "partly for their health & partly out of their great respect for [Berkeley] & his Design" (cited in Saunders and Miles, p. 118). Significantly, at the far left, Smibert painted a portrait of himself. He stares at us with penetrating eyes and prominently displays a sketch with one hand, visually linking himself with Berkeley, who grasps one of his sturdy philosophy books on the table in front of him. Smibert's self-portrait within *The Bermuda Group* implicitly asserts the cultural equality of the visual and verbal arts and affirms his proposed status as a professor of the design arts. As if to underscore the fact that he was more than a mere craftsman, Smibert signed his name on the end of a book resting on the table at the center of the composition.

Smibert's picture should be interpreted in relation to a poem that Berkeley composed while planning the Bermuda project. Expressing dissatisfaction with the corrupt state of European civilization, Berkeley's "Verses on the Prospect of Planting Arts and Learning in America" prophesied the westward progression of history toward a perfected fulfillment in the New World:

The Muse, disgusted at an age and clime,
Barren of every glorious theme,
In distant lands now waits a better time,
Producing subjects worthy fame:

In happy climes, where from the genial sun
And virgin earth such scenes ensue,
The force of art by nature seems outdone,
And fancied beauties by the true:

In happy climes the seat of innocence,
Where nature guides and virtue rules,
Where men shall not impose for truth and sense,
The pedantry of courts and schools:

There shall be sung another golden age,
The rise of empire and of arts,
The good and great inspiring epic rage,
The wisest heads and noblest hearts.

Not such as Europe breeds in her decay;
Such as she bred when fresh and young,
When heav'nly flame did animate her clay,
By future poets shall be sung.

Westward the course of empire takes its way;
The four first acts already past,
A fifth shall close the drama with the day;
Time's noblest offspring is the last.
(cited in Silverman, p. xix)

Berkeley's poem became one of the most widely quoted in the American colonies and inspired generations of American artists well into the nineteenth century. Smibert's *The Bermuda Group* seems to share Berkeley's conviction that the history of civilization was traveling westward with the sun toward the American continent.

At the center of the painting, Miss Handcock gestures with her left hand, drawing our attention to a New England landscape of water, rocks, evergreen trees, and a golden horizon that suggests either a sunrise or sunset. The painting's composition proposes the alchemical power of the arts and letters to transform America's "virgin earth" into Berkeley's "golden age" or final world empire. In the middle ground, three columns serve as a mediating screen between the community of learning and refinement in the foreground and the rocky Rhode Island landscape in the background. The stone pillars create a protective temple of learning in a harsh environment. They mathematically order the pictorial space and anchor the eight human pillars into three groups, dominated by the singular presence of Berkeley, who stands alone in front of the right-hand column, almost obscuring it with his height and erect posture. Within the triangular middle group of figures, Berkeley's wife and son gaze directly outward toward the beholder. Henry, who was born in Newport in 1729, appears to offer us a golden piece of fruit, an emblem of the golden age prophesied by Berkeley. Henry's hair is also golden, as is the color of his mother's dress. The color scheme links them both with the sunlit horizon, symbolizing the future and the progression of history. As the youngest and only native-born American in the group, Henry personifies the western fruition of human destiny or "Time's noblest offspring" in the New World.

Smibert never shipped *The Bermuda Group* to London, perhaps because Wainwright, the politically ambitious patron of the painting, no longer wished to be associated with Berkeley's failed Bermuda project. The portrait remained in Smibert's Boston studio, where it could be admired by potential portrait clients and emulated by younger American painters such as Robert Feke (see fig. 3.21). Even if they knew or cared little about George Berkeley and his Bermuda project, Bostonians would have found much to admire in the composition, which grandly associated the human figure with the classical columns of temple architecture. *The Bermuda Group* is the visual equivalent of Reverend Benjamin Colman's sermon on governments and rulers as earthly pillars.

The painting's spatial illusionism; luminous color harmony of reds, golden yellows, and blues; complex interweaving of figures; and convincing representation of fabrics and textures impressed Boston spectators. Certainly, Smibert's ennobling pillars must also have appealed to Governor Belcher, proclaimed the leading Massachusetts pillar of wisdom. By November of 1730, three months after the governor's inauguration and Colman's sermon, Smibert was completing Belcher's full-length standing portrait.

Smibert's portrait of Belcher has been lost, but we may gain some indication of its appearance by briefly examining another of the artist's full-length standing portraits. In his portrait of William Browne, one of New England's wealthiest landowners, Smibert posed his subject within a sharply rectilinear architectural

3.24 John Smibert
William Browne, 1734.
Oil on canvas,
92½ x 57 in
(234.9 x 144.8 cm). The
Baltimore Museum of Art.
George A. Lucas
Collection.

space, open to a rich landscape view of the Massachusetts countryside (fig. 3.24). Browne's erect posture is accentuated both by a palatial mansion wall and by a tall tree meeting the straight edge of the building. Browne's legs are carefully posed according to the recommendations of illustrated etiquette books, offering viewers both a profile and frontal view. The shapely legs, gleaming in silver-white stockings and terminating in golden-buckled shoes, recall the words from Reverend Colman's sermon: "His Legs are as Pillars of Marble, set upon Sockets of fine Gold" (cited in Sandoz, p. 15). Browne stands firmly upright, in moral harmony with the austere geometry of classical architecture and in confident possession of the land beyond his outstretched hand. The russet brown of his suit gleams with richly painted highlights, visually connecting him with the warm, glowing horizon line in the distance. While Smibert was painting the portrait, Browne was in the process of constructing a country estate in Danvers, Massachusetts. Browne Hall's most distinctive exterior feature was a porch supported by fifteen-foot-high columns in the style of the Greek Ionic order. Browne's portrait as well as a companion portrait of his wife were to hang in Browne Hall, the site of lavish social entertainments.

Altogether, Smibert painted approximately 240 portraits in America. Though his yearly income fluctuated and he supplemented his portrait fees by selling painters' pigments and engraved reproductions of art, he was able to live in the manner of a fairly successful merchant. Support from leading public figures such as Governor Belcher and Boston's Congregationalist clergymen was crucial for his success in gaining portrait commissions.

In 1734, Smibert painted a portrait of Reverend Colman, one of a series of ministerial portraits that were reproduced by Peter Pelham (c.1697–1751), a London-trained printmaker who had arrived in Boston in 1727 (fig. 3.25). Pelham became a leading Boston Freemason and not only engraved prints, but also ran a "finishing" school for teaching Boston children refined manners and various cultural attainments. The portrait prints of Boston clergymen were marketed to admiring parishioners as uplifting personifications of moral virtue. However, the richly modeled portraits also signaled New England's growing sophistication in matters of fashion and taste.

3.25 Peter Pelham
(after John Smibert),
The Reverend Benjamin Colman, 1735.
Mezzotint on laid paper,
11 x 9 in (29.8 x 23.8 cm).
Museum of Fine Arts,
Boston. Bequest of Mr.
Abram Edmands Cutter.

Reverend Colman's son-in-law, the Reverend Ebenezer Turrell, enthused that Smibert had perfectly captured Colman's likeness. Furthermore, he praised Pelham's portrait print and observed that it was on display in many Boston homes. Smibert portrayed Colman with a suitably stern expression, but he softened the moral severity of the clergyman by richly dressing him in a long, flowing wig and black satin cloak or robe. Puritan clergymen from the seventeeth century had rejected the wearing of wigs as an aristocratic, prideful affectation. By the eighteenth century, however, Congregationalist ministers were accommodating themselves to the new consumerism of the middle and upper classes. Colman's rich costume situated him within the affluent social circles of Governor Belcher and New England's merchant elite. Unlike earlier clergymen, who had warned against the moral dangers of visual images, Colman became an avid collector of pictures. He owned several Smibert paintings as well as Peter Pelham prints reproducing other Smibert portraits.

The Boston clergy functioned as supportive painting critics. In 1730, Mather Byles, who became minister for the Hollis Street Church established by Governor Belcher, published a poem in Boston newspapers welcoming Smibert's providential arrival for the hundredth anniversary of the founding of Massachusetts Bay Colony. Elevating Smibert beyond the social status of mere craftsman, Byles wrote that painting was the "Sister-Art" to poetry:

> 'Tis yours, Great Master, in just Lines to trace
> The rising Prospect, or the lovely Face,
> In the Fair Round to swell the glowing cheek,
> Give Thought to Shades, and bid the Colors speak
> (cited in McCoubrey, p. 7).

Byles attributed godlike powers to Smibert's brush. From within his canvases "Crowds of new Beings lift their dawning Heads, / In conscious Forms, and animated Shades" (cited in McCoubrey, p. 7). Smibert's figures seem to breathe and speak. His brush is like a magic wand through which life's blended colors glow with warmth. With Smibert's presence in Boston, a land that had once been "a barbarous Desert" devoid of the arts was drawing closer to a state of civilized refinement (cited in McCoubrey, p. 6).

In his portrait of Daniel, Peter, and Andrew Oliver, Smibert acted as a necromancer, who could conjure forth shades of the dead (fig. 3.26). Sons of merchant wealth and nephews of Governor Belcher, the three Oliver brothers were reunited on canvas by Smibert's magical paintbrush. Daniel, the eldest, on the left, had died six years earlier in 1726. Working from a miniature portrait of the deceased, Smibert restored him to life. Ironically, of the three, it is Daniel who seems as if he is about to speak. Gazing directly at us, he rests his left hand on the round table in front of him and seems to make a rhetorical gesture with his index finger. Opposite Daniel, Andrew is silently lost in thought. His right elbow rests upon a closed book, while his hand cradles his learned head to suggest the contemplation of intellectual truths. Meanwhile, Peter, the youngest, dressed in a cool, dark-blue suit, appears the most relaxed and informal of the three. Unlike his elder brothers, he wears no wig. He casually drapes an elegant hand over the back of his chair, while tucking the other inside his coat. Smibert's curvilinear arrangement of refined hand gestures spiritually and physically unites the brothers around the small table. Round tables became increasingly popular in colonial America because they were non-hierarchical. At a circular table, there was no head or preferred seat placement for a master or a mistress. All seats were equal in rank for informal gatherings of family and friends.

In Smibert's intimate group portrait, the circular table expresses brotherhood, an egalitarian ideal that Andrew and Peter Oliver carried into adulthood when both became Freemasons. However, the brothers' notion of fraternity and egalitarianism did not extend far beyond their own lodge. They conceived of colonial Freemasonry as a relatively exclusive order primarily for elite gentlemen. Boston's Masonic fraternity solidified the Olivers' social ties to other successful men of influence who remained loyal to British colonial rule. Nevertheless, dissident Masonic lodges formed by socially aspiring middle-class men would soon challenge the elite domination of Freemasonry.

Portraiture and Middle-Class Social Aspirations

Symptomatic of the rapid economic growth occurring during the 1750s, urban artisans and other middle-class men began to assert themselves more forcefully in colonial society and culture. In Philadelphia, where an increasing number of men were identifying themselves as gentlemen, the printer David Hall celebrated the establishment of his own printing firm by commissioning grand, full-length portraits of his three children, including his daughter, Deborah (fig. 3.27). Painted by the self-taught English-born artist William Williams (1727–91), the portrait of *Deborah Hall* represents an adolescent

3.26 John Smibert
Daniel, Peter, and Andrew Oliver, 1732. Oil on canvas, 39¼ x 56⅞ in (99.7 x 144.5 cm). Museum of Fine Arts, Boston. Emily L. Ainsley Fund.

Situated near the center of the picture, Peter Oliver's dangling left hand calls attention to itself. With his foreshortened forearm invisible and his wrist enframed by a flowerlike shirt-sleeve cuff, the delicate, elongated hand seems to float in space, pointing to the book. With simple gestures, Smibert creates a mood of refinement.

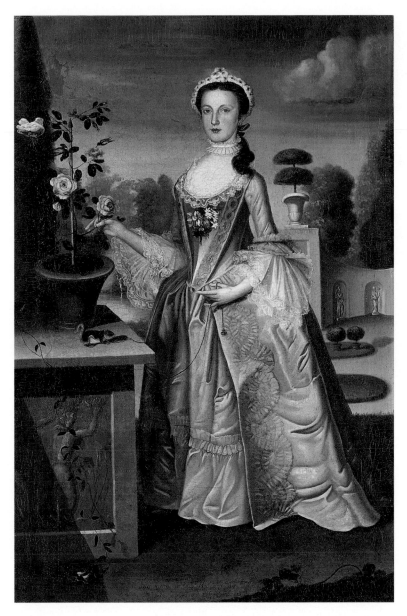

3.27 William Williams
Deborah Hall, 1766.
Oil on canvas,
71¼ x 46½ in
(180.9 x 118.1 cm).
Brooklyn Museum of Art,
New York.
Dick S. Ramsay Fund.

fancy satin gown shares the flower's luminous pink color. Standing stiffly like a living pillar of virtue, she holds with her other hand the leash of a pet squirrel, who sits quietly upon a stone plinth. The squirrel makes no effort to tug at its leash, symbolically expressing the taming of animal nature. Immediately below the squirrel, in a partial view of a relief sculpture, Williams portrays the mythological story of Apollo and Daphne, a moral tale on the virtue of chastity before marriage. The beautiful virgin Daphne is shown being transformed into a laurel tree before the god Apollo can subdue her for his sexual pleasure. A vine falls loosely over the figure of Daphne as an emblem of female dependency. According to the conventional symbolism of moralizing books and European marriage portraits, just as vines require trees to cling to permanently, so women need men and the institution of marriage to control and direct their lives.

Williams's portrait was displayed in David Hall's home as a lavish advertisement for prospective suitors seeking a beautiful, chaste wife from a socially prominent and culturally refined family. The painting's moralizing signs were especially common in colonial portraits of women and children, whose natures reputedly required greater monitoring. Women were particularly defined in terms of their sexual, animal natures. In contrast to men, they supposedly remained essentially childlike, with minds dominated more by unstable emotions and desires than by cool, objective reason.

The plethora of pictorial emblems appealed to men like David Hall, who were attuned to the secret rituals and visual symbolism of Freemasonry. Hall had been a business partner of the famous printer and man of science Benjamin Franklin, who had been active in Philadelphia Freemasonry since the early 1730s. Hall became part of a more socially inclusive movement known as "ancient Masonry" that challenged the authority of the traditional colonial elite to dominate the fraternity (Bullock, p. 97). Ancient Masons claimed a more mystical, deeper knowledge of Freemasonry's divine principles than that of so-called Modern Masons (Bullock, p. 85), whose lodges tended to exclude artisans and other men outside the inner circles of social and political power. The aristocratic ambience of

girl who is about to enter the society of marriageable women. Unlike the relatively spare portrait of the young Oliver brothers, David Hall's daughter is accompanied by a host of mysterious emblems, borrowed from various illustrated books, that define her moral and physical character. According to the art historian Roland Fleischer, Williams identifies his subject as an incarnation of Venus. The impressive enclosed garden in the background alludes to Venus's Garden of Love, while the rose that Deborah Hall delicately holds with her right hand also is an emblem of beauty and love. Hall's

3.28 Joseph Blackburn
Isaac Winslow and His Family, 1755.
Oil on canvas,
4 ft 6½ in x 6 ft 7½ in
(1.38 x 2.02 m).
Museum of Fine Arts,
Boston.
A. Shuman Collection.

Williams's portrait is a fictive space that pronounced the Hall family's genteel social status and consumerist devotion to the cult of beauty.

Colonial consumerism was not simply the expression of a profane, selfish materialism. Eighteenth-century colonists saw no necessary conflict between religious values and their acquisition of fashionable clothes, portraits, and other commodities. Consumer goods and luxuries represented the refinement and redemption of raw matter for human use and enjoyment. Assuming a sympathetic relationship between people and their material environment, colonists generally believed that luxuries or beautiful, refined objects could morally elevate individuals beyond their animalistic needs and appetites. Moderate enjoyment of the visual arts particularly signified the alchemical transmutation of the individual self to a higher state of spiritual being. Colonial families and communities prided themselves in the notion that America was becoming less of a wilderness and more of a paradisiacal garden populated by angelic, godlike beings.

In Boston during the mid-eighteenth century, the English-born painter Joseph Blackburn (c. 1730–1778) introduced a lighter, more buoyant, and sensuous style of painting that lovingly mimicked the tactile and visual pleasures of silken fabrics, ripe fruit, porcelain-smooth flesh, and feathery foliage. For his most famous portrait, *Isaac Winslow and His Family* (fig. 3.28), Blackburn reinterpreted the family group portrait popularized by John Smibert (see fig. 3.23) and, later, Robert Feke (see fig. 3.21) by emphasizing, to a greater degree than his predecessors, the propagation of the family line and the generational transmission of domestic virtues. More clearly interacting with his wife and children than either George Berkeley or Isaac Royall, the figure of Isaac Winslow, one of Boston's most successful merchants, proudly gestures and directs our attention to the other family members. We are encouraged to read from left to right, as a patriarchal index finger points to wife Lucy's lap and the most recent offspring of their marriage, baby Hannah. The parallel lines formed by the arms of Lucy and Hannah lead to an older daughter, who happily strides toward her parents and sister in order to present them with an apron full of fruit. Named after her mother, this younger Lucy Winslow is preparing herself for the duties of motherhood. Unlike William Williams, who associates Deborah Hall with the virtues of pre-marital chastity,

3.29 John Singleton Copley
Mars, Venus, and Vulcan: The Forge of Vulcan, 1754.
Oil on canvas, 30 x 24 in (76.2 x 61 cm).
Sotheby's, Inc., New York.

Copley's painting replicates a print by the French engraver Nicolas-Henry Tardieu (1675–1749), who copied *The Forge of Vulcan* by Charles-Antoine Coypel (1694–1752), former First Painter to the King of France. In the composition, Venus coats a love arrow with her chemical brew, much like a painter dipping a brush into a palette of pigments. With a cupid overhead asking for silence, Venus is like an artisan possessing powerful craft secrets.

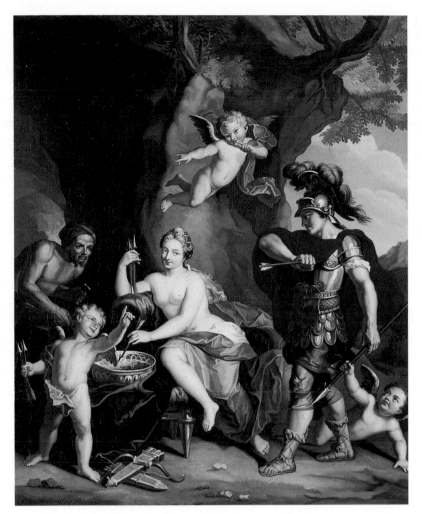

Blackburn's joyful parade of children, fruit, and subtly sexualized bodies expresses familial hopes for the fertility of present and future wives and mothers. In the background, within an idealized formal garden setting, two swans glide along a pond as symbols of the marriage union.

John Singleton Copley and the Consumer Revolution

No artist more forcefully resolved the spiritual ambivalence of the eighteenth-century consumer revolution than did the Boston painter John Singleton Copley (1738–1815). Stepson of the printmaker and Freemason Peter Pelham, Copley expressed his artistic ambition early, at the age of sixteen, when he began painting copies of mythological subjects reproduced in European engravings that may have been in Pelham's collection of prints. Copley's *The Forge of Vulcan* focused on the nude figure of Venus, whose beauty and secret love potion subdued Mars, god of war (fig. 3.29). Pelham taught his talented stepson that the beautiful art of painting was also a magical potion that could overcome violent passions and generate sociable feelings of harmony and love. Pelham would have introduced Copley to the ideas of English philosophers and Anglo-American Freemasons, who believed that the arts contributed to civic virtue and the cultivation of genteel individuals.

Learning by studying the portraits of John Smibert, Robert Feke, and other artists who worked in Boston, Copley soon began to surpass his predecessors in the degree of pictorial illusionism and individual expression. Copley's 1761 *Portrait of Mrs. Samuel Quincy* (fig. 3.30) was partly inspired by copies or imitations of a portrait by the Flemish master Peter Paul Rubens (1577– 1640). However, Copley demonstrated his own mastery by diverging considerably from the earlier prototypes. The portrait was commissioned by Samuel Quincy at the time of his marriage to Hannah Hill, daughter of a wealthy Boston distiller and landowner. Quincy was a Harvard graduate, successful lawyer, and prominent Boston Freemason, who was known for his urbane manners and refined taste. Copley's fashion-conscious portrayal of Quincy's bride strongly contrasts the sitter's radiant, European-style costume with the austere, darkened background behind her. Unlike the relatively wooden, impersonal portrayals of young women in earlier colonial portraits, Copley's portrait suggests a certain depth of individual personality. The figure's columnar stiffness is modified by the relaxed crossing of the hands, the mysterious half-smile, the large, moist eyes, and the luminous face that is sensitively shaded by the surrounding darkness to suggest an introspective woman of great intelligence. Indeed, Hannah Hill's early love for reading literature had gained her the nickname of "Sophy" or "Sophia," Greek for wisdom.

Despite Copley's more convincing naturalistic technique, Sophy still personified the abstract moral and intellectual virtues associated with philosophy and the Roman goddess Minerva (see p. 90). In her left hand, Mrs. Quincy holds a sprig of larkspur, which eighteenth-century books on the symbolic language of flowers associated with marriage vows or devotion to one's spouse. Nevertheless, the independent-minded "Sophia" eventually separated from her husband for political reasons. With the advent of the American Revolution in 1775, Samuel Quincy, a Loyalist, fled to England, leaving behind his wife, who supported the struggle for national independence.

As we shall see in the next chapter, Copley also eventually emigrated to London. But his reasons were professional as well as political. Already, in 1766, he tested his career prospects abroad by sending a portrait of his half brother, Henry Pelham (1749–1806), to the spring exhibition of the London Society of Artists. Entitled *Boy with a Squirrel* (fig. 3.31), the picture won Copley critical praise and election as a "fellow"

3.30 John Singleton Copley
Portrait of Mrs. Samuel Quincy (Hannah Hill), c.1761.
Oil on canvas, 35½ x 27⅞ in (90.2 x 70.8 cm). Museum of Fine Arts, Boston. Bequest of Miss Grace W. Treadwell.

to the Society. However, Joshua Reynolds (1723–92), one of Britain's leading portraitists, advised the young American that his painting suffered from a "Hardness in the Drawing" and "an over minuteness" in its many parts (cited in McCoubrey, p. 11). Reynolds was referring to Copley's obsessive naturalism in the careful representation of virtually every detail of the painting, including the fur and whiskers of the American flying squirrel eating a peanut on the red mahogany table in the foreground. English-school painters favored a more generalized, painterly rendering of subordinate details, so that they did not call attention to themselves and visually compete with the centrally important subject of the picture, in this case the idealized portrait of a daydreaming youth.

Rather than painting a conventional, generic squirrel borrowed from traditional emblem books, Copley attempted to impress his London audience with the representation of a species native to the eastern United States. The American flying squirrel is a nocturnal animal that can glide from tree to tree due to a thin membrane that functions like a parachute. Copley called viewers' attention to this species by shaping the bright white edge of the squirrel's gliding membrane into a shape that echoes the configuration of Henry Pelham's ear. Copley thus complicated and modified the emblematic

3.31 John Singleton Copley
Boy with a Squirrel (Henry Pelham), 1765. Oil on canvas, 30¼ x 25 in (76.8 x 63.5 cm). Museum of Fine Arts, Boston. Anonymous Gift.

More than a portrait, Copley suggests his mastery of all four of nature's elements: earth (the peanut), water (the half-filled glass), air (the flying squirrel), and fire (the gold chain). Gold was traditionally associated with light or solar fire. Taking the shape of a serpentine line composed of intersecting circular links, the gold chain as a whole suggests the alchemical cycles of nature and progress toward perfection (see p. 23).

meaning of the pet, whose delicate gold chain Pelham elegantly holds with the fingers of his right hand.

The retracted gliding membrane of a flying squirrel symbolically suggests the physical and spiritual potential for metamorphosis and the presence of a higher state of being hidden within earthly life. The squirrel's act of cracking the outer husk of a peanut to eat the nourishing food within reinforces this theme that at the core of nature's every detail there is a powerful, vitalistic force. Since this image of reverie is pervaded by a profound sense of silence, Copley's half brother appears to be listening for inner, spiritual voices or sounds. Pelham's prominently displayed ear invites the viewer inward like the opening to a mysterious cave, the site of internal membranes that vibrate with barely audible sounds and cause the human mind to soar with noble ideas and emotions. The intensely red

3.32 John Singleton Copley
Portrait of Paul Revere, 1768. Oil on canvas, 35 x 28½ in (88.9 x 72.4 cm). Museum of Fine Arts, Boston. Gift of Joseph W., William B., and Edward H.R. Revere.

This portrayal of Revere compositionally resembles a portrait print of John Theophilus Desaguliers (1683–1744) by Copley's stepfather, Peter Pelham. Desaguliers, a man of science and father of modern Freemasonry in England, was depicted seated at a table while holding a large magnifying glass. In a manner similar to Revere's gleaming silver teapot, Desaguliers' hand-held circular glass brightly reflects light as an emblem of intellectual, creative insight.

swag of curtain behind Pelham, covered with vivid, almost electric, strokes of paint, seems to take flight. The diagonal folds of the curtain appear to form flaming wings emerging from his back. More than a colorful decorative background, the ascending red cloth becomes a visual metaphor for the meditative reverie that transforms an American youth into an angelic being.

Several years later, in his *Portrait of Paul Revere*, Copley focused his attention on the transformative power of the human eye (fig. 3.32). Like Henry Pelham's ear, the Boston silversmithengraver's right eye seems to rest at the apex of a compositional triangle. The arched, penetrating eye is akin to the all-seeing, providential eye that often decorated Masonic aprons, engravings, and other artifacts. Near the time of Copley's portrait, Paul Revere (1735–1818) himself had engraved a Masonic lodge notification that featured an all-seeing eye amid a host of other mysterious signs (fig. 3.33). The all-seeing eye symbolized God's creative power as Supreme Architect. Like the sun, the Masonic eye projects life-giving rays of light outward into space.

Similarly, in Copley's portrait, Revere's right eye projects a powerful gaze toward the viewer. The silversmith, informally dressed in clean work clothes, has apparently been interrupted in his creative work by our presence. Revere holds a globular teapot with his left hand while his right hand lightly supports his head in a gesture of thoughtful contemplation. On the red mahogany table, three engraving tools point their sharp tips away from Revere and toward the silver teapot. In another moment, the craftsman will incise an elaborate design, projecting the light of his godlike eye and mind into the receptive material surface of the consumer object. Copley's painting is not simply a portrait of Revere, but a moral vindication of the visual arts and the fabrication of luxury goods. Copley's airless space, meticulous illusionism, and mysterious contrast of intense light and dark create a religious aura of silent meditation, thereby redeeming the production and appreciation of luxuries from the taint of materialism.

As expressed in Copley's portraits and in Revere's Masonic engraving, where a cherub at the left gestures for silence, moral virtue and spiritual illumination were generally associated with silence. Silent communication ensured the

3.33 Paul Revere
Masonic Lodge 169 notification, late 1760s. Engraving, 8¾ x 6⅞ in (22.2 x 17.5 cm). American Antiquarian Society, Worcester, Massachusetts.

The inscription beneath the arch invites Brother A. B. to a meeting of Lodge 169 of the Ancient York Masons. Ancient Masons identified with the English city of York because it was regarded as the site of a purer form of Freemasonry than the purportedly corrupted and modernized rituals of the London Grand Lodge. The two Corinthian columns supporting the arch and an Ionic order temple at the upper left also reaffirm the Masonic taste for ancient, classical architecture.

purity of thought or the ability to hear the inner voice of conscience connecting humanity with the divine. Copley's hyperrealism, the apparent product of *his* all-seeing eye, was a persuasive stylistic means for achieving virtuous social and cultural ends. Revere's and Copley's godlike eyes remind viewers that all are under moral surveillance, subject not only to the providential eye of God, but also to the close observation of fellow humans. Copley's seemingly magical ability to transmute raw, earthly pigments into a visual language of radiant light and reflecting surfaces spiritually generated an intimate communal bond, magnetically connecting beholders with both the portrait subject and the painter himself. Revere's Masonic engraving is dominated by a grand stone arch inscribed "Cemented with Love." Similarly, Copley conceived art in relation to Venus, the goddess of love and beauty, whose secret potion overcame the violent god of war. Venus personified the attractive forces of nature that reconciled the apparent conflict between the spiritual and material realms. In Copley's *Portrait of Paul Revere*, as well as in his other paintings of the period, physical objects gleam with a reflected light that symbolizes their harmonic relationship with the semidivine, projective powers of the human eye and mind.

This power extends as well to the artist's portraits of women, as in the formidable Elizabeth

3.34 John Singleton Copley
Portrait of Elizabeth (Mrs. Ezekiel) Goldthwait, 1770–71. Oil on canvas, 50 x 40 in (127 x 101.6 cm). Museum of Fine Arts, Boston. Bequest of John T. Bowen in memory of Eliza Bowen.

Goldthwait (fig. 3.34). Copley painted this aging but vibrant matriarch, the mother of some thirteen children, as a companion to that of her husband Ezekiel's likeness, a more soberly colored representation of a man of business and political affairs. Brilliantly illuminated against a dark background, Mrs. Goldthwait fixes us with a penetrating gaze. Her portly figure and self-assured presence suggest a woman with a booming, commanding voice. This makes her tight-lipped silence all the more palpable, as we wait for this powerful woman to speak, perhaps inviting us to join her in grasping one of the peaches or apples piled high into a pyramid, atop a shiny, mahogany dining table. As much as Revere's globular teapot seems to repeat the rounded shape of the craftsman's face, so does the fruit seem an extension of Goldthwait's fulsome self-image. More than a reference to nature and her maternal fecundity, the fruit, like Revere's teapot, must be regarded as a product of human ingenuity, skill, and aspiration toward perfected being. For wealthy Bostonians, whose livelihoods largely depended upon the risks of transatlantic commerce, the art of gardening signified an ideal transcendence of business cares and woes, particularly during a period of increased political tensions. Elizabeth

Goldthwait was renowned for her horticultural talents, exercised in extensive gardens outside the family mansion on Hanover Street, in Boston's North End. Poised now as a hostess, she offers the beholder hospitality, a domestic refuge from the troublesome anxieties of public life.

By the time that Copley had painted Revere's and Goldthwait's portraits, political conflict between rebellious Americans and the British colonial government was already well underway. Revere would play an instrumental role as a messenger for the revolutionaries during the opening battles of Lexington and Concord in 1775. Revere's Masonic engraving represented emblems for the higher, "Royal Arch" degrees invented by the more socially inclusive lodges of Ancient Masonry, founded outside the administrative control of London's Grand Lodge. The mystical degrees became popular with middle-class Americans, who were more inclined to challenge British colonial domination. Beginning during the revolutionary period, initiation rituals for the degrees dramatized the Old Testament Jews' release from captivity in Babylon and their subsequent rebuilding of Solomon's temple in Jerusalem. This biblical theme of national liberation was also pronounced from American pulpits and contributed to dreams of building an independent republic self-governed by Solomonic citizens.

Copley did not share Revere's revolutionary fervor. As we shall see in the next chapter, the artist attempted to maintain a position of neutrality. Nevertheless, his *Portrait of Paul Revere* is a significant social departure from aristocratic portraits of colonial wealth. Copley's painting represents a democratic shift toward elevating the social status of labor and of craftsmen, the producers of consumer goods. At the same time, by visually expressing the notion that the crafters of luxuries were moral, dignified individuals, Copley reassured wealthy patrons that portraits, silver teapots, and other luxury items were manifestations of virtue rather than vice. The consumer revolution of the eighteenth century helped refine and Anglicize colonial culture, but it also emboldened increasingly self-confident Americans to demand the political rights associated with British liberties.

Chapter 4

Revolutionary Icons and the Representation of Republican Virtue
1765–1825

Anonymous
Liberty, c. 1790–1800.
Bass wood, 58 in
(147.3 cm) high. Museum
of Fine Arts, Boston,
Massachusetts.
H.E. Bolles Fund.

Liberty holds a victory
wreath in one hand. Her
staff and liberty cap are
museum replacements for
lost originals. The nearly
freestanding figure was
probably intended for
attachment to a wall or
architectural support,
perhaps for a courthouse.
Borrowing ideas from the
Salem, Massachusetts,
carver Samuel McIntire
(1757–1811), *Liberty*'s
sculptor employed a
neoclassical, modular
system of measurements
and proportion, in which a
given unit of the body was
multiplied to create all the
parts of the ideal whole.

O N July 9, 1776, a mob of soldiers, artisans, and laborers in New York City tore down an equestrian sculpture of King George III. Decapitating the bullet-ridden sculpture of the British monarch, New Yorkers removed its imperial crown of laurel leaves and paraded the head to a tavern in northern Manhattan. Later, the gilt-lead sculpture was melted down into 42,088 bullets for the revolutionary army. A German printmaker, Franz Xaver Habermann (1721–96), misleadingly represented the event, attempting to inflame European opinion against the American rebels (fig. 4.1). Among the print's many inaccuracies is Habermann's imaginative recording of a non-equestrian royal statue being pulled down by seminude, dark-skinned servants, acting under the calm direction of well-dressed New York citizens.

New York's symbolic act of regicide occurred just five days after the Continental Congress, meeting in Philadelphia, approved the Declaration of Independence. Written primarily by Thomas Jefferson (1743–1826) of Virginia, the Declaration proclaimed that the American colonies were now states and "that they are absolved from all allegiance to the British crown" (cited in Fliegelman, p. 208). During the early months of the Revolutionary War, following the battles at Lexington and Concord, Massachusetts, on April 19, 1775, rumors had circulated that radical British sympathizers were plotting to overthrow George III. But the rumors proved false and the writers of the Declaration of Independence indicted not only the King and his ministers but also their "British brethren," who had become "deaf to the voice of justice and consanguinity" (cited in Fliegelman, pp. 206–207). Severing ties to the British Empire, America would become a republic, a

government "instituted among men, deriving their just powers from the consent of the governed" (cited in Fliegelman, p. 203).

Like all revolutions, the American Revolution engendered the iconoclastic destruction of traditional symbols of political authority. In 1765, a decade before the Revolutionary War, anti-British image-breaking had begun in earnest. Launching a new policy of governing the colonies directly from London, George III's ministers ordered imperial agents to enforce the revenue-raising Stamp Act. Taxing newspapers, pamphlets, almanacs, and all legal and commercial documents, the Stamp Act particularly angered colonial printers, lawyers, and merchants. Ignoring colonial assemblies, the British government enacted the tax through Parliament in London, where Americans had no direct representation.

Local colonial elites found their traditional legislative powers subordinated to the centralizing authority of British ministers. Protestors throughout America tarred and feathered Stamp Act distributors. In mock executions, they hung and burned effigies, not only of the local tax agents, but also of the British prime minister, George Grenville.

From 1754 to 1763, the French and Indian War devastated North America in an imperial struggle between Britain and France. Though Indian tribes mostly sided against them, British and American forces wrested control of Quebec, Canada, from the French royal army. After the war, Britain expected Americans to pay new taxes for defense of the northwestern frontier. At the same time, the British government sought to appease the Indians by prohibiting land-hungry colonists from settling west of the Appalachian Mountains, beyond imperial control. In this chapter, I shall discuss, among other figures, the American history painter Benjamin West

4.1 Franz Xaver Habermann
La Destruction de la Statue Royale à Nouvelle York, 1776. Hand-colored engraving, 11¼ x 16 in (28.6 x 40.6 cm). New York Historical Society, New York.

Habermann's print was one of a series that he published on the American Revolution from a perspective sympathetic to the British cause. Nevertheless, despite the print's fanciful topography, architecture, and exotic-looking characters, contemporaries with an opposing, revolutionary point of view interpreted the representation in positive terms as a symbolic repudiation of monarchical despotism. The image may have gained even greater popularity in America after the War of Independence.

(1738–1820), whose celebrated painting of the battle of Quebec underscored the competitive friction between the American colonies and the mother country (see fig. 4.23).

In 1766, Parliament repealed the Stamp Act, but simultaneously reaffirmed its sole authority to legislate colonial policies in quartering British army troops in the restive coastal cities and towns. After 1767, when Parliament passed the Townshend Acts, which levied new duties on colonial imports, Americans boycotted British goods and clashed with British soldiers. Political cartoons convey the violent, antiauthoritarian spirit of popular protests, which often were directed by colonial businessmen angered by the monopolistic privileges granted British merchants.

The polarization of colonial society into Loyalists versus revolutionary patriots deeply affected artists. While the Boston silversmith-engraver Paul Revere published a series of anti-British prints, the painter John Singleton Copley married into a Loyalist family. Nevertheless, Copley attempted to remain politically neutral, a tenuous position that he visually expressed in a complex allegory of the Revolution (see fig. 4.28).

Before the Revolution ended with the British surrender at Yorktown, Virginia, in October 1781, the thirteen American states had organized themselves under the Articles of Confederation. This loose confederation created a weak central government dominated by a single-house Congress, which lacked the vital authority to levy taxes and regulate commerce.

Once Great Britain officially recognized American independence in September 1783, American artists accelerated efforts to memorialize key events, heroes, and symbols of the Revolution. From the perspective of the propertied elite, efforts to create unifying images of nationhood became all the more urgent during the economic depression that followed the war. In 1786, indebted laborers and farmers from western Massachusetts, led by Daniel Shays, staged an insurrection against the state government, which was dominated by creditors wishing to foreclose on farm mortgages.

Shays' Rebellion called attention to the weakness of government authority under the Articles of Confederation. In 1787, delegates from every state met in Philadelphia for a Constitutional Convention. Presided over by George Washington, the fifty-five "Founding Fathers" wrote a new constitution that created a stronger federal government. Approved in 1788, the Constitution's architectural balance of state and federal powers, and of executive, legislative, and judicial branches, found symbolic expression in the urban design for the District of Columbia and its focal building, the United States Capitol.

Artists of the revolutionary generation, led by the painters Benjamin West, John Trumbull (1756–1843), Gilbert Stuart (1755–1828), and Charles Willson Peale (1741–1827), attempted to become spokesmen for the new nation. Artists and architects often competed against more professionally trained European immigrants for commissions to design government buildings and patriotic monuments. Whether native or foreign-born, painters and sculptors started to exhibit in museums, galleries, and art academies founded by civic-minded patrons and entrepreneurs.

Yet many Americans who distrusted the cosmopolitan manners of the wealthy few defined republicanism in iconoclastic opposition to the refined world of art. They insistently associated the visual arts with sensual luxuries, a self-indulgent aristocracy, and the corrupt despotism of monarchy and empire. Portraits and history paintings of contemporary subjects often drew hostile responses from politically divided audiences. Even representations of the nation's first president, George Washington, aroused popular fears that glorification of any hero invited dictatorship rather than the impersonal rule of law.

The visual commemoration of national heroes excluded or marginalized poor men and soldiers, whose lack of property barred them from voting and holding political office under most state constitutions. To an even greater degree, representations of subservient African-Americans belied the appropriateness of Liberty as a figurative symbol of American independence. Female personifications of Liberty, Wisdom, and other abstract virtues also masked the constitutional exclusion of women from electoral politics, despite contributions to the revolutionary cause from activists such as the wax sculptor Patience Wright (1725–86).

By the early nineteenth century, American artists belonging to the post-revolutionary generation composed paintings that expressed doubts regarding the legacy of the Founding Fathers. Artists such as Washington Allston (1779–1843), John Vanderlyn (1775–1852), and Rembrandt Peale (1778–1860) explored themes of moral weakness and individual ambition rather than the heroic virtues of the Revolution. Bitterly divided by political parties and conflicting socioeconomic interests, the United States struggled to maintain the republican faith in citizens' selfless devotion to the public good.

Propaganda in the Pre-Revolutionary War Era

The pre-war decade from 1765 to 1775 witnessed a proliferation of visual media to propagandize against British tyranny. Printmakers published political cartoons in newspapers, magazines, and broadsides posted in shops, taverns, and coffeehouses. The printer and almanac

4.2 Benjamin Franklin
Magna Britannia: Her Colonies Reduc'd, c. 1766.
Engraving, 4⅛ x 5⅞ in (10.2 x 14.7 cm).
Library Company of Philadelphia, Pennsylvania.

4.3 Paul Revere
The Able Doctor, or America Swallowing the Bitter Draught, 1774. Engraving, 7 x 4⅞ in (17.7 x 12.1 cm). Massachusetts Historical Society, Boston, Massachusetts.

4.3 Paul Revere
The Able Doctor, or America Swallowing the Bitter Draught, 1774. Engraving, 7 x 4⅞ in (17.7 x 12.1 cm). Massachusetts Historical Society, Boston, Massachusetts.

publisher Benjamin Franklin responded to Parliament's arbitrary taxation of the colonies by representing the British Empire as a dismembered woman (fig. 4.2). With her ships idle in the background, Britannia leans helplessly against a globe she once dominated. A spear suicidally points toward her breast. Severed arms and legs signifying the American colonies lie scattered upon the ground. Though critical of Britain's self-destructive imperial policies, Franklin's image suggests that most who initially denounced Parliament's imposition of taxes and trade duties did not envision political independence. For Franklin in 1765, the colonies were only separate limbs, entirely dependent upon the healthy body politic of the mother country.

However, as protests against trade duties and the monopolies enjoyed by London merchants intensified, political prints satirized the colonial model of dependency upon the mother country. On December 16, 1773, a group of Boston men, disguised as Mohawk Indians, secretly boarded ships of the East India Company, throwing into Boston harbor the duty-laden tea that symbolized Britain's monopolistic control of colonial trade. Following the Boston Tea Party, Paul Revere, one of the participants, personified America as a violated Indian princess (fig. 4.3). America's mother, Britannia, stands by helplessly while her daughter is sexually abused. British government officials look up her dress and force tea down her throat. After independence, print-makers, painters, and sculptors transformed the

personification of America into a Greek or Roman goddess, symbolizing Western civilization and the ideals of Liberty and Wisdom. American woodcarvers who normally crafted the figureheads of ships were now called upon to decorate courthouses and other public buildings with personifications of Liberty (see p. 114) and Wisdom (fig. 4.4). With white pine and paint, they mimicked the pristine marble of classical sculpture.

After the French and Indian War, which forced Catholic France to abandon Canada, Americans dreamed of territorial expansion far beyond the eastern seaboard, proclaiming that the course of civilization was moving westward with the sun. Magazines and newspapers quoted "Verses on the Prospect of Planting Arts and Learning in America," by George Berkeley, the philosopher-cleric celebrated in John Smibert's *The Bermuda Group* (see fig. 3.23). Berkeley contrasted a decaying Europe with America's "virgin earth," fertile for a millennial "golden age" (see p. 103).

4.4 William Rush
Wisdom, 1824. Painted pine, 8 ft (2.43 m) high. Philadelphia Museum of Art, lent by Fairmount Park Commission.

Rush carved *Wisdom* for a triumphal arch welcoming to Philadelphia the Marquis de Lafayette, French hero of the American Revolution. Alluding to the Greek goddess Athena, Wisdom holds the head of a snake, suggesting her civilizing power over nature. Standing next to a pillar stacked with books, Wisdom gazes into a mirror, which symbolizes a prudent trust in divine wisdom and self-knowledge.

4.5 Samuel Jennings
Liberty Displaying the Arts and Sciences, 1790–92.
Oil on canvas, 60¼ x 73 in (153 x 185.4 cm). Library Company of Philadelphia, Pennsylvania.

In ancient Rome, liberty caps were worn by freed slaves. Liberty's cap and staff stand triumphantly over broken chains lying on the floor. Painted for the Library Company of Philadelphia, Jennings's Quaker-inspired picture allied Liberty with learning and abolitionist politics. On the pedestal next to Liberty are books on philosophy and agriculture. Emblems of music, painting, architecture, sculpture, geometry, geography, and astronomy clutter the foreground. In the background, a group of African-Americans listen and dance to music.

Colonial clergymen echoed Berkeley. They defined the future Christian millennium as a period when the arts and letters would flourish in the New World. Political orators and pamphleteers asserted that Britain's imperial policy of taxation without representation was driving Liberty and the arts toward sanctuary in America. In a post-revolutionary painting, the Philadelphia-born artist Samuel Jennings represented Liberty as the patroness of the arts and sciences, who promises the future abolition of slavery before a grateful group of African-Americans (fig. 4.5).

Republican Motherhood: Women as Symbols

Together with African-Americans, American women continued to exist outside the active public life of electoral politics. Women's political rights were ignored in the Declaration of Independence and the U.S. Constitution. Suf-

frage qualifications were the prerogative of state and local governments, which barred women from voting, even if they held property or paid taxes apart from a husband. Women were relegated to the private domestic realm of republican motherhood to rear virtuous sons, the nation's future citizens. Protected from the world of commerce and politics, women more easily personified the bloodless, abstract ideals of Liberty and Wisdom or the cardinal virtues of Faith, Hope, and Charity.

Women's political and social influence was private, secret, and virtually invisible. Supposedly lacking their own independent wills, women were stereotyped as silent muses who motivated male heroism, chivalry, and patriotic self-sacrifice. In his *Portrait of Thomas Jefferson*, the American painter Mather Brown (1761–1831) represents the author of the Declaration of Independence seated next to a marble figurine of Liberty (fig. 4.6). Her head turned toward Jefferson's ear, she appears to inspire him without unduly calling attention to herself.

While male artists sought to address a broader public during the revolutionary era, women's art remained domestic in medium and audience. Women primarily created quilts, needlework, small watercolors, and private mourning images that memorialized loved ones and, occasionally, national heroes. John Trumbull, who eventually became known as the painter of the American Revolution, recalled in his *Autobiography* how he had first learned to draw as a young boy in Lebanon, Connecticut:

> *My two sisters, Faith and Mary, had completed their education at an excellent school in Boston, where they both had been taught embroidery; and the eldest, Faith, had acquired some knowledge of drawing, and had even painted in oil, two heads and a landscape. These wonders were hung in my mother's parlor and were among the first objects that caught my infant eye. I endeavored to imitate them, and for several*

4.6 Mather Brown
Portrait of Thomas Jefferson, 1786.
Oil on canvas,
35¾ x 28½ in (90.8 x 72.4 cm). National Portrait Gallery, Smithsonian Institution, Washington, D.C. Bequest of Charles Adams.

The original 1786 portrait, commissioned by Jefferson, is lost. This version was painted for John Adams, Jefferson's friend. Influenced by the American Gilbert Stuart and other English-school painters, the London-based Brown employed vivid brushwork and color to create a sensuous image of Jefferson's energy and charisma.

4.7 Faith Trumbull
The Death of Absalom,
c.1753.
Lyman Allyn Art Museum, New London, Connecticut.

4.8 Patience Wright
William Pitt, Earl of Chatham, 1779.
Wax effigy, life-size.
Westminster Abbey,
London.

Pitt, the first Earl of Chatham, is dressed in a parliamentary robe and wig. He is posed as an orator, holding a scroll in his right hand. Although the trunk of the body beneath the robes is made of wood, the figure's wax head and hands were carefully crafted with realistic details. Wright used pieces of hair and blue-tinted underslips to mimic veins. The commemorative sculpture was placed in Westminster Abbey a year after Pitt's death.

4.9 John Downman
Patience Wright, 1777.
Drawing, 9 x 7 in
(22.9 x 17.8 cm).
British Museum, London.

years the nicely sanded floors (for carpets were then unknown in Lebanon) were constantly scrawled with my rude attempts at drawing (Trumbull, Autobiography, *p. 5).*

Faith and Mary Trumbull had attended the

school of Elizabeth Murray (1726–85), a Scottish-born woman, who was a Boston shop-keeper and milliner, as well as an educator of girls and young women from socially prominent families. Recently attributed to Faith Trumbull (1743–75), an embroidery of *The Death of Absalom* (fig. 4.7) was apparently the product of Murray's instruction and proof of genteel, amateur accomplishment in the arts. Faith Trumbull visualized the Old Testament text of II Samuel 19:14, in which Joab slays King David's rebellious son Absalom, who hangs by the locks of his long hair from the branch of an oak tree. With its theme of youthful rebellion against a less than perfect king, this embroidered narrative probably would have acquired numerous contemporary political associations during the decade prior to the American Revolution. As some scholars have observed, Faith Trumbull's King David, enthroned in the upper-left corner of the composition, appears indifferent to the plight of his son, just as King George was viewed as oblivious to the needs and grievances of his American colonies.

Patience Wright and the Personification of Liberty

The New Jersey-born wax sculptor Patience Wright was an exceptional woman who played a major public, international role as a professional artist during the revolutionary era. The daughter of a Quaker farmer, Wright created a profitable museum of wax figures representing contemporary and historical notables dressed in period costume and placed in theatrical settings. Having exhibited in several American cities, she moved her effigies to London's fashionable West End in 1772, attracting large crowds and even the patronage of the royal court. The King, Queen, and Prince of Wales all sat for portraits. However, only Wright's memorial effigy of William Pitt the Elder, the Earl of Chatham (1708–78), parliamentary defender of America, still survives (fig. 4.8).

Wright's sitters, including Benjamin Franklin, Benjamin West, and other Americans, were attracted as much by her sexually suggestive and quasi-magical technique as by her illusionistic realism. Kneading the wax like dough, Wright manipulated portrait busts underneath her apron between her thighs, keeping the wax warm and malleable. She then dramatically gave birth to

THE HEADS OF THE NATION IN A RIGHT SITUATION.

4.10 John Williams
The "Right" Situation,
1780.
Engraving, 8⅝ x 13¾ in
(22 x 35 cm). British
Museum, London.

Patience Wright stands in
the left foreground of this
political cartoon. As she
gazes at the trio of British
officials' heads, she exclaims
that "This is a sight I have
long wish [sic] to see."

her creations. Emerging from its womb, the wax head received the finishing touches that gave it life: glass eyes, hair, color, and an appropriately clothed body.

The painter Sir Joshua Reynolds, President of the Royal Academy of Art, warned connoisseurs and aspiring artists that waxwork figures fell outside the category of true sculpture. Members of London's Royal Academy taught art students the ancient and Renaissance traditions of idealized marble and bronze sculptures. The unstable wax medium, by contrast, triggered unwanted associations with lower-class effigies crafted for festivals, parades, and popular protests. Like Wright's, these popular, anonymously produced effigies were often praised for their convincing realism.

In a portrait drawing by a young admirer, Wright visually and verbally identified herself with the personification of Liberty: "Liberty I am and Liberty is [W]Right" (fig. 4.9). During the Revolution, she worked as a spy, sending American friends secret messages hidden within wax busts. Meanwhile, other prints represented Wright with the decapitated heads of corrupt government officials (fig. 4.10).

However, for Abigail Adams, wife of the future president John Adams (1735–1826), Wright fell far short of Liberty as a model of republican motherhood. After a visit to the London wax

museum, she concluded that Wright was the "queen of sluts" (cited in Sellers, 1976, p. 210). Besides her "slattern" appearance, Wright offended Adams by crudely giving "a hearty buss" or kiss to each lady and gentleman in Adams's party (cited in Sellers, 1976, p. 209). Finally, Wright's sculptures disrupted Adams's emotional equilibrium: "There was an old clergyman sitting reading a paper in the middle of the room; and though I went prepared to see strong representations of real life, I was effectually deceived in this wax figure for ten minutes, and was finally told that it was only wax" (cited in Sellers, 1976, p. 210).

Classical Austerity and Republican Virtue: the Founding Fathers

Art that embarrassed and deceived could not win the unqualified endorsement of genteel American beholders. Adams, Jefferson, and other traveling statesmen were acutely aware that American art was now being judged by a skeptical international audience dominated by royalist and aristocratic opinion. Even those Europeans sympathetic to the Revolution tended to regard America as a degenerative wilderness, inhospitable to the arts and sciences.

Ironically, American taste tended toward the traditional classicism of Sir Joshua Reynolds, whose Royal Academy lectures in London emphasized imitation of the ancient Greeks and Romans, and study of Renaissance masters. Often praised for asserting America's cultural, as well as political, independence, Thomas Jefferson actually followed eighteenth-century British precedents when he chose to model the new Virginia State Capitol in Richmond (fig. 4.11) after the Maison Carrée, an ancient Roman temple in Nîmes, France. James Gibbs, designer of templelike churches, joined other London architects in borrowing from classical antiquity for the

purpose of creating an ennobling British national style (see pp. 87-8). Similarly, American post-revolutionary artists, critics, and patrons advocated ancient Greco-Roman forms, while defending the visual arts against traditional associations with luxury, sensuality, and moral decay. Classical austerity, severe geometric forms, or a simple, plain style best expressed the new nation's devotion to selfless republican virtue. Rather than the disorienting illusions of Patience Wright and other popular entertainments, citizens of the new republic required a visual environment that encouraged polite, rational behavior based upon deference to men of merit and virtue.

As the pageantmasters of the new republic, painters, sculptors, and architects canonized American revolutionary leaders as the "Founding Fathers," the constructors, not destroyers, of a new empire in the West. Commissioned by state and local governments, artists designed patriotic street decorations and public monuments and buildings to compete with the grandeur of classical antiquity and the European Renaissance. In 1789, the Boston architect Charles Bulfinch (1763–1844) designed a triumphal arch next to the Massachusetts State House, welcoming the nation's first president, George Washington (fig. 4.12). Over the central arch rose a twenty-foot-high canopy, crowned by an American eagle

4.13 (top left)
Anonymous
Armchair, c. 1765-85.
Mahogany with maple
and gilding, original
webbing, liner, and
horsehair cover, 50½ in
(128.2 cm) high,
25½ in (64.7 cm) wide,
19½ in (49.5 cm) deep.
Private collection.

The back of this chair
juxtaposes a number of
Masonic symbols. The
circular serpent biting its
own tail signifies the eternal
cycle of life. Within this
circle, a square block shows
Solomon's temple,
symbolized by two small
columns set in front of a
checkered pavement.
The sun and moon loom
overhead.

4.14 (top right)
Charles Bulfinch
Massachusetts State
House, Boston, 1795–8.
Massachusetts Historical
Society, Boston,
Massachusetts.

Bulfinch modeled the State
House on English sources,
particularly William
Chambers's Somerset
House (1786), then a
government building near
the Thames in London. The
templelike façade rises from
an arcaded basement to a
broad, colonnaded pavilion
with slender Corinthian
columns. Above a
pedimented upper story, the
gilded wood dome has a
light, strongly vertical
profile, accentuated by a
crowning belfry.

with its shield of thirteen stripes. An oval tablet above the central rusticated arch bears the inscription: "TO THE MAN WHO UNITED ALL HEARTS." The individual masonry stones symbolize the national union of hearts cemented by love for George Washington.

Bulfinch's inscribed arch borrows from the architectural symbolism of Freemasonry, as seen in Paul Revere's Lodge engravings (see fig. 3.33) and in Boston Masonic armchairs, the latter's arched mahogany backs mimicking fraternal masonry stones (fig. 4.13). Several years later, Bulfinch participated in the dramatic Masonic cornerstone-laying ceremony for his new, golden-domed State House on Beacon Hill (fig. 4.14). Revere presided as the grand master of the Grand Lodge of Massachusetts.

Freemasonry and Symbolism in the Early Republic

Elevated to national prominence by the august membership of George Washington, Benjamin Franklin, and other Founding Fathers, the fraternal order of Freemasonry dramatically grew in widespread popularity during the post-revolutionary era. During the early republic, Freemasons constituted a civic priesthood, presiding over cornerstone-laying rituals, not only for public buildings and monuments, but also for civic-minded engineering projects. On April

15th, 1791, the grand master of the Masonic lodge at Alexandria, Virginia, led a ceremony to lay the first milestone for the District of Columbia. Over two years later, wearing a Masonic apron, Washington himself laid the cornerstone for the United States Capitol. Deriving from Roman temple architecture, the U.S. Capitol was to be the American Pantheon, a temple to civic virtue, liberty, and national unity. Under the supervision of Thomas Jefferson, Washington's secretary of state, the French architect Pierre Charles L'Enfant (1754–1825) planned the District of Columbia as a city of grand public spaces and state-named avenues, centering upon a domed Capitol (fig. 4.15). Situated high upon a hill, the Capitol would overlook a city designed as a microcosm of the nation. A 1795 "Essay on the City of Washington" described

4.15 Pierre Charles L'Enfant
Plan of the City of
Washington, 1791.
Library of Congress,
Washington, D.C.

4.16 (left)
Thomas Jefferson
Monticello, near
Charlottesville, Virginia,
1770–82, 1796–1809.
Thomas Jefferson
Memorial Foundation, Inc.

In situating his mansion upon
a mountain, Jefferson was
attempting to replicate the
ancient Roman villa tradition,
as represented, for instance,
by Emperor Hadrian's second-
century villa near Tivoli, Italy.
The Italian name Monticello
means "little mountain." From
his lofty villa perspective,
Jefferson could gaze toward
the panorama of nature's
wildlife and the distant Blue
Ridge Mountains. Yet
Monticello was also a working
farm, symbolizing Jefferson's
ideal of an agrarian America.

4.17 (right)
John Rubens Smith
*View of the West Front of
the Capitol, c. 1828.*
Watercolor on paper,
16½ x 23¼ in
(41.9 x 59 cm).
Library of Congress,
Washington, D.C. Gift of
the Madison Council and
Mrs. Joseph Carson.

L'Enfant's plan as an allegory for the constitutional governance of the American empire:

> *Each street is also an emblem of the facility, with
> which the Capitol may be approached, in every
> respect, and at all times, by every individual, who
> shall live under the protection of the Union . . .
> The capitol [sic] and the President's house are so
> situated, that the President may have continually
> in his view, the temple where are deposited the
> laws, the execution of which is committed to him;
> and it seems, that by the multiplicity of the
> streets and their diverging direction, it was
> intended to remind him constantly of the
> importance of directing his official views to the
> most distant parts of the Empire; and this
> ingenious allegory, in its inverted sense, will call
> to his mind, at the same time, that his actions,
> are continually and unavoidably open to general
> inspection (cited in Scott, p. 47).*

The nation's survival depended upon a clarity of vision that extended to the furthest reaches of the empire and a self-conscious awareness that all government actions are visible to the all-seeing eye of the public. An experienced gentleman architect, Jefferson was simultaneously building Monticello, his own domed templelike mansion, situated high atop a mountain for maximum visibility and symbolic control over the surrounding Virginia countryside (fig. 4.16). As envisioned by Jefferson and a series of architects working under his direction, the Capitol's central domed Rotunda, joining the Senate and House wings, was designed as a great hall of the people, the architectural expression of "e pluribus unum" (one out of many) (fig. 4.17).

Charles Bulfinch designed the final appearance of the Capitol's first dome and Rotunda. Though he made some modifications, the Boston architect followed the plans of Benjamin Henry Latrobe (1764–1820), the architect responsible for restoring the Capitol after invading British troops burned the building in 1814 during the War of 1812, a "second war for independence," (Berens, p. 12) triggered by British interference with American shipping. Made of wood and sheathed in copper, the first Capitol dome was crowned by a balustrade surrounding a circular skylight twenty-four feet in diameter. The dome's viewing platform offered panoramic views of both city and countryside, expansively suggesting national unity and strength.

Illuminated from above by an oculus open to the sun, the domed Rotunda's visual and symbolic preeminence over the federal city and nation parallels the symbolism of the Great Seal of the United States (fig. 4.18). Designed by several congressional committees with the aid of both French and American artists, the Great Seal appropriated the emblem of an all-seeing eye. The eye forms a radiant, triangular apex over an Egyptian pyramid, composed of thirteen courses of dressed masonry stones inscribed with the year 1776 in Roman numerals. Solar light emblems decorated earlier congressional meeting places such as Federal Hall in New York, site of Washington's first inauguration as president. In this earlier commission, L'Enfant filled the exterior pediment with a synthesis of motifs from the Great Seal. The design depicted an American eagle set against light rays from a rising sun (fig. 4.19).

In his designs for the Capitol's interior, Latrobe attempted to connect the new Western empire with the Eastern origins of art and architecture in ancient Egypt. An English-born Freemason who had been professionally trained in Europe, Latrobe proposed designing the original Library of Congress in the Capitol's north wing with Egyptian-revival decorations such as lotus and papyrus columns. Though this plan was never realized, Latrobe successfully developed corn and tobacco orders for the capitals of columns elsewhere in the Capitol (figs. 4.20–4.21). Striking a note of cultural independence from Europe, the aesthetic elevation of

4.18 The Great Seal of the United States, 1776–82. U.S. State Department, Washington, D.C.

Along the top of the Great Seal's reverse side, the words ANNUIT COEPTIS reassured Americans that "He (God) has smiled on our undertakings." The Latin motto on the scroll beneath the pyramid, NOVUS ORDO SECLORUM, declares "A new cycle of the ages." The all-seeing eye appears on Paul Revere's Masonic lodge notification (see fig. 3.33), typifying Masonry's extensive use of the ancient symbol with its roots in Egyptian imagery and in Christian visual references to God's omnipresence.

4.19 Amos Doolittle "View of the Federal Edifice in New York," 1789, from *The Columbian Magazine* (Philadelphia), August 1789. Library of Congress, Washington, D.C.

4.20 Benjamin Henry Latrobe
Corn-capital vestibule to the Supreme Court, 1808. U.S. Capitol, Washington, D.C. Courtesy of the Architect of the Capitol.

The Supreme Court was once housed in the north wing of the U.S. Capitol, on the ground floor immediately below the Senate Chamber.

infused by solar light, corn (as well as wine and oil) was sacramentally poured during Masonic cornerstone-laying ceremonies, symbolizing the foundation stone's harmonic balance between heaven and earth. The fruits of agriculture metaphorically signify the cultivation of individuals through architecture and the fine arts. Yet, despite their patriotic associations, corn and tobacco orders did not become an architectural fashion. American respect for classical tradition mitigated against such innovative decorative motifs in buildings of the new republic.

History Painting in the Pre-Revolutionary and Revolutionary Eras

By studying European art treatises and fine-art prints, American history painters and portraitists learned to represent the human body as a sacred temple, infused by divine light. Eighteenth-century America lacked art academies and collections of original Old Master paintings and sculptures. Ambitious artists seeking to rival ancient and Renaissance art traveled abroad, touring Europe, then settled in London to study at the Royal Academy. Working within the English school of painting, Americans created a revolution in history painting: they chose modern subjects that portrayed the New World as a land of millennial promise, redemption, and brotherhood. Painters also elevated portraiture toward the moral seriousness of history painting, creating an American pantheon of virtuous patriots and notables.

native plants and crops testified to the agricultural and commercial bounty of the American continent. The corn and tobacco orders contradicted persistent European perceptions of America as a desolate wilderness. Corn was also rich in Masonic associations. As a golden grain, seemingly

4.21 Benjamin Henry Latrobe
Tobacco-leaf capital, c. 1815. Sandstone, 18 x 21 x 21 in (45.7 x 53.3 x 53.3 cm). Thomas Jefferson Foundation, Charlottesville, Virginia.

Benjamin West and the Revolution in History Painting

Before the Revolution, Benjamin West became the founder of an American school of painting. But he did so only after he left his native Pennsylvania for Europe, never to return. Born to humble innkeepers, West received basic instruction from the Philadelphia painter William Williams. More importantly, West's early interest in history painting and the academic tradition brought him to the attention of the Anglican clergyman William Smith, provost of the College of Philadelphia and a Masonic chaplain of the Grand Lodge of Pennsylvania. Smith mentored West in ancient history, but he also taught the aspiring painter that America was a sacred space, a remote refuge for Liberty and pure religion.

Financed by Smith and other prominent Philadelphians, West traveled to Italy in 1760 to study the great masterpieces of antiquity and the Renaissance. Three years later, moving to London, he helped to establish the academic tradition of grand-manner history painting in Britain. His London studio became a magnet for aspiring American artists seeking instruction in drawing and painting. West's first American pupil, Matthew Pratt (1734–1805), represented him instructing four young men in *The American School*, a painting exhibited in London in 1766 (fig. 4.22). Pratt portrays West standing at the left. He is wearing a green suit and tricorn hat, which signifies the Pennsylvanian's self-

identification with the Quaker founders of that colony. Quaker reliance upon an inner voice or spiritual light appealed to an artist who wished to assert his independence from the material luxuries of European civilization.

Moralizing subjects such as *The Departure of Regulus from Rome* won West the patronage of George III, who was renowned for his religious piety (fig. 4.24). The painting's depiction of an ancient Roman hero solemnly departing for a certain death during the Punic Wars pleased the British monarch's desire for patriotic, self-sacrificing subjects.

A year after *Regulus*, in 1770, West disturbed both his royal patron and the Royal Academy president with *The Death of General Wolfe*, a painting that radically paralleled Anglo-American agitation for political democratization (fig. 4.23). West's painting appealed to a far wider audience because he chose a celebrated modern

4.22 Matthew Pratt
The American School,
1765.
Oil on canvas,
36 x 50¼ in
(91.4 x 127.6 cm).
Metropolitan Museum of
Art, New York. Gift of
Samuel P. Avery, 1897.

Pratt represented four students whose identities are uncertain. The right-hand figure opposite the standing West has sometimes been identified as Pratt. With palette and brushes in hand, this young man sits before a virtually empty canvas that bears Pratt's signature and enframes the youth's profile. West's pupils are absorbed by the moral seriousness of the painter's craft.

4.23 Benjamin West
*The Death of General
Wolfe,* 1770.
Oil on canvas, 60 x 84½
in (152.6 3 214.5 cm).
National Gallery of
Canada, Ottawa. Gift of
the Second Duke of
Westminster.

West, through his official
biographer, claimed that
George III initially rejected
his painting for representing
noble heroes in common
breeches and coats. Yet the
painting's colorful pageantry
is formally composed
according to traditional
Renaissance and academic
conventions. General Wolfe's
body is tended to by a
pyramid of attentive figures.
Extending this pyramid, the
billowing banners overhead
evoke associations with
Christ's cross.

subject, the victory over the French at the Battle of Quebec on September 13, 1759, and dared to clothe the figures in contemporary costume. Sir Joshua Reynolds regarded West's turn toward realism as a vulgarization of high art, a descent from the universal ideals of classicism.

West's aesthetic rebellion against Reynolds and European academic tradition served the cause of American nationalism. He argued that the pivotal battle of Quebec, which decided the French and Indian War, occurred:

in a region of the world unknown to the Greeks and the Romans, and at a period of time when no such nations, nor heroes in their costumes, any longer existed. The subject I have to represent is the conquest of a great province of America by the British troops. It is a topic that history will proudly record, and the same truth that guides the pen of the historian should govern the pencil of the artist. I consider myself as undertaking to tell this great event to the eye of the world; but if, instead of the facts of the transaction, I represent classical fictions, how shall I be understood by posterity! (cited in Alberts, p. 107).

West insisted upon representing both the geographical specificity and historical uniqueness of the New World. However, far from being non-fictional, his picture imaginatively manipulated the facts. Beholders recognized the composition's religious associations with representations of Christ's disciples lamenting over his crucified body. As an immortalized type for Christ's sacrifice, Wolfe's martyred blood sanctified American soil. The battle, which West sketchily represented in the background, was fought outside Quebec's walls upon the "Plains of Abraham," evoking Old Testament associations for Anglo-Americans, who traditionally identified themselves as God's new chosen people. Over the conquered city, the dark storm

4.24 Benjamin West
The Departure of Regulus from Rome, 1769.
Oil on canvas, 88½ x 120 in (224.8 x 304.8 cm).
The Royal Collection © 1999, Her Majesty Queen Elizabeth II.

At the center of West's composition, the Roman consul Regulus stands surrounded by admirers urging him to stay in Rome. Having been taken prisoner by the Carthaginians, Regulus had been sent back to Rome by his captors on condition that he negotiate a treaty favorable to Carthaginian interests. Regulus instead advised the Roman Senate to reject it as dishonorable. He then announced his return to imprisonment and death in Carthage.

clouds and battle smoke clear for the divine light of Providence to proclaim Britain's victory.

West created a strongly competing secondary focus at the far left of the composition to underscore the specifically American nature of the victory. A seminude Iroquois Indian, wearing body paint and red feathers, gazes contemplatively upon the dying general. Romantically associating Indians with a higher, secret knowledge of nature's vitalistic powers, West identified his art with the image of the noble Indian. The muscular warrior, in a dignified and melancholic pose, personifies the ancient ideal of a spartan lifestyle. A man of Nature, West's deferential Indian universalizes the selfless moral content of Wolfe's martyrdom, while his red flesh and exotic costume insistently specify the North American locale. Hovering over the Indian, wearing a green jacket, moccasins, and beaded breeches, stands a white man, whom West explicitly identifies as William Johnson. His name and a map with the geographical names "Mohawk Valley" and "Ontario" are inscribed upon the powder horn strapped to his body, equating Johnson's personal identity with prop-

erty ceded to him by the Mohawk Indians. As a superintendent of Indian affairs, Johnson had learned Iroquois customs and language and married a Mohawk woman, more easily enabling him to convince some Native Americans to ally with Britain against France.

West's explicit inclusion of this colonial New Yorker belied the fact that Johnson, the hero of earlier battles at Lake George and Fort Niagara, was not actually present at the Battle of Quebec. Ignoring literal details of the battle, West was politically motivated to foreground the heroic American role in the war against France, lest that fact be forgotten by imperial policymakers and the British public. A painted snake that decorates the Indian's back recalls Benjamin Franklin's widely published print *Join or Die*, which equates a segmented snake with the politically divided American colonies (fig. 4.25). Only by uniting into a sinuous whole could America defend itself against French and Indian threats.

Although an English aristocrat purchased *The Death of General Wolfe* and George III later ordered a copy, West began the original painting without a commission or certain patron.

4.25 Benjamin Franklin
"Join or Die," from *Pennsylvania Gazette*, May 9, 1754. Newspaper, 2⅞ x 2 in (7.3 x 5 cm). Library of Congress, Washington, D.C.

4.26 Anonymous
Pearlware mug with print showing General Wolfe's death, c. 1800. Winterthur Museum, Delaware.

Through public exhibition and engraved prints of the composition, he reached out for a wider, international audience that included the growing middle class. The central portion of the painting even decorated English ceramic mugs and earthenware for the domestic and export market (fig. 4.26). By 1772, following upon his public acclaim, West was appointed official court history painter for George III.

John Singleton Copley: Images of Revolution and Independence

West's success intensified John Singleton Copley's desire to escape the heated environment of Boston for a career abroad (see p. 110). The Boston Massacre of 1770 had dramatically intensified the conflict, as British troops shot and killed five Boston laborers protesting the army occupation. The polarizing event made life more difficult for a painter heavily dependent upon the patronage of the colonial political establishment. Copley's half brother Henry Pelham designed an engraving of *The Bloody Massacre* that was rapidly plagiarized by Paul Revere (fig. 4.27). Unlike Pelham and Copley, Revere enthusiastically supported the colonial rebels and added the sign "Butcher's Hall" over the heads of the British troops.

The massacre divided Boston along class, ethnic, and racial lines. Even critics of imperial rule feared mob violence and supported the British version of events that soldiers had fired in self-defense at a rowdy mob. The number of poor adult males in Boston, many of them African-Americans and Irish Catholics, had doubled since 1687 to almost one-third of the adult male population. John Adams probably spoke for most of the Boston elite when he denigrated the massacre victims as "a motley rabble of saucy boys, negroes and mulattoes, Irish teagues and outlandish jack tarrs" (cited in Kaplan and Kaplan, p. 8). Defending the British troops in court, he sarcastically singled out an escaped African-American slave, Crispus Attucks, who "appears to have undertaken to be the hero of the night; and to lead this army with banners . . . and march them up to *King street* with their clubs" (cited in Kaplan and Kaplan, p. 8).

Three years later, during the Boston Tea Party, Revere and other Sons of Liberty threw into Boston harbor a shipment of tea belonging to Copley's father-in-law, Richard Clarke, a merchant for London's East India Company. Copley left America for Europe. First studying art in Italy, he then settled in London, and like West, never returned to his native land.

Copley's first major history painting in London demonstrated his commitment to modern American subject matter and contemporary costume, emulating West's *The Death of General Wolfe*. During the Revolution, Copley

4.27 Paul Revere
Bloody Massacre, 1770.
Engraving.
U.S. State Department,
Washington, D.C.

Revere produced over
seventy engravings between
c.1762 and 1780, almost
all of them copies from
cartoons and prints
imported from Britain. In
the background, Boston's
Old State House and the
steeple of the First Church
bear witness to the horror
below. The church clock
stands at 10:20 at night,
with a crescent moon
hovering at the upper left.
Shadows and a dark plume
of chimney smoke signify
the dark fate of the victims
on the left side of the
composition.

enigmatically elevated a black man to the top of
a visual pyramid in his history painting *Watson
and the Shark* (fig. 4.28). A political and religious
allegory, the picture's symbolism of white-black
or light-dark expresses the tension between
imperial order and revolutionary chaos. Painted
for Brook Watson, a wealthy London merchant
and Tory critic of the Revolution, Copley's
composition tells the story of how Watson, as a
young cabin boy, had lost his right leg to a shark
while swimming near his ship anchored in the
harbor at Havana, Cuba.

As described by London notices of the 1778
Royal Academy exhibition, Copley's painting
represents the dramatic moment when a group
of sailors in a rowboat finally rescued Watson "at
the very instant he was about to be seized the
third time," and "the shark was struck with the
boat hook, and driven from his prey" (cited in
Miles, p. 56). London newspapers emphasized
the success of the third rescue attempt, implicitly
comparing Watson's plight with Christ's
Resurrection on the third day. Further borrowing from Christian iconography, Copley
heroicized the lowly sailors, one of whom is
about to spear the shark like St. George or St.
Michael slaying the dragon. Above the dark

waters, the dawn's golden light promises salvation. The cross-shaped masts of ships on the
horizon join the crosses of Havana's cathedral
and convent towers. They suggest that Watson's
rescue symbolized his spiritual rebirth during
the Christian voyage of life.

On a political level, Brook Watson's dismembered body symbolized the damaged body
politic of the British empire, which was founded
upon the shipping and commercial wealth of
Watson and other London merchants. Watson's
lost leg evoked associations with numerous
revolutionary-era prints of a dismembered
Britannia such as Benjamin Franklin's *Magna
Britannia* (see fig. 4.2). By 1778, when *Watson and
the Shark* was exhibited, France had allied with
America, and British troops had lost the previous
year's pivotal Battle of Saratoga. Furthermore,
the French threatened British control of the
West Indies, including Caribbean ports such as
Havana, the setting for Copley's painting.

Watson and the Shark encouraged contemporary beholders to identify with Watson's fate,
knowing that this cabin boy more than survived
despite the loss of a leg. The British Empire also
would renew itself through revolutionary trial
by fire. Similarly, after the initial 1775 battles at

Lexington and Concord, Copley had prophesied from his safe haven in London that America "will finally emerge from her present Callamity and become a Mighty Empire. And it is a pleasing reflection that I shall stand amongst the first of the Artists that shall have led the country to the knowledge and cultivation of the fine Arts" (cited in Prown, 1966, II, pp. 255–256).

Copley's optimistic faith in divine providence led him to believe that both America and Britain would prosper once the revolutionary flood waters had subsided. He interpreted the American Revolution as a divinely ordained natural disaster, akin to the biblical Flood or to the drowning of a youth in shark-infested waters.

Copley's fatalistic view of the Revolution as an unavoidable act of God or Nature may explain why a black man stands at the compositional apex of the picture. London reviewers criticized the relative passivity of his black sailor: "It would not be unnatural to place a woman in the attitude of the *black*; but he, instead of being terrified, ought, in our opinion, to be busy. He has thrown a rope over to the boy. It is held, unsailorlike . . . and he makes no use of it" (cited in Miles, p. 65). For London critics, Copley's "idle Black" was like a child or a woman, too frozen by fear to take action. While not blatantly caricatured, the black sailor's passivity made him appear less a man than an abstract personification of the emotional horror associated with the shark. Both the shark and the black sailor symbolized the darkness of the underworld. Critics also referred to the African's fellow sailors as "tars," short for tarpaulin sails. But the word also punned with the visual image of the black to suggest sticky, oily tar, a dangerously combustible, yet healing black substance that was used to caulk leaking ships and cauterize amputation wounds. Copley had heard John Adams employ the term "tar" to characterize the politically volatile racial mixture that triggered the Boston massacre. Indeed, Watson's helpless nude body is strikingly similar to the figure of the dying man in the left foreground of Revere's *The Bloody Massacre*, originally composed by Copley's half brother.

4.28 John Singleton Copley
Watson and the Shark, 1778.
Oil on canvas, 71¾ x 90½ in (182.2 3 229.8 cm).
National Gallery of Art, Washington, D.C.
Ferdinand Lammot Belin Fund.

Copley appropriated biblical ideas for his painting from Peter Paul Rubens' *Jonah and the Whale* (1618-19). The Old Testament figure of Jonah survived three days inside the belly of a whale. Foreshadowing Christ's death and resurrection, Jonah provided Copley with a further parallel for Brook Watson's miraculous rescue.

4.29 Massachusetts Treasury Note
December 4, 1777. Engraving, 9 x 6 in (22.8 x 15.2 cm). American Antiquarian Society, Worcester, Massachusetts.

Headed by the African who holds a serpentine towline, the sailors form part of an elemental circle connecting them with the monstrous shark that surrounds the boat. While the shark's open jaws approach the youth, his tail in middle ground points upward toward the harpoonist and African at the top of the compositional circuit. Beholders may have associated this violent circle of fiery tars versus watery serpentine monster with the emblematic *uroboros* or circular serpent. Biting its own tail to form a perfect circle, the serpent regenerated itself, eating its old skin to signify nature's seasonal cycle or daily revolution from night to day. The circular serpent often decorated Masonic lodge certificates and furniture (see fig. 4.13), expressing Freemasons' faith that nature's cyclical laws were divinely ordained. During the Revolution, the *uroboros* appeared on the mastheads of city newspapers and government treasury notes (fig. 4.29). This image reassured citizens that a new dawn was emerging from the darkness of revolutionary violence.

In addition to the original version sold to Watson, Copley hung a replica of *Watson and the Shark* in his studio and sold engraved prints of the composition. Thanks to the success of "the Shark painting," Copley became a favorite with London merchants, painting their portraits and histories of their martyred heroes. At the same time, Copley portrayed statesmen and citizens of the new republic. Four years after *Watson and the Shark*, he painted the portrait of an entirely different Watson, a young American merchant, who wished to commemorate the dawn of a new empire (fig. 4.30). Elkanah Watson later recalled the circumstances of the portrait in his journal:

The painting was finished in most admirable style, except the background, which Copley and I designed to represent a ship, bearing to America the intelligence of the acknowledgement of independence, with a sun just rising upon the stripes of the Union, streaming from her gaff. All was complete save the flag, which Copley did not deem prudent to hoist under present circumstances, as his gallery is a constant resort of the royal family and the nobility. I dined with the artist, on the glorious 5th of December, 1782, after listening with him to the speech of the King, formally recognizing the United States of America as in the rank of nations. . . . he invited me into his studio; and there with a bold hand, a master's touch, and I believe an American heart, attached to the ship the Stars

p. 117). Yet Copley, like West, could never shed his American identity while living in London even if he had wanted to, since English critics often referred to his American origins.

Fraternal Friendship in the Work of John Trumbull

Benjamin West also exercised diplomatic caution for fear of offending wealthy British patrons. But, during the summer of 1783, he corresponded with his former student Charles Willson Peale, who had painted portraits of George Washington and other officers while serving in the revolutionary army. West wished assistance in conceiving a visual narrative of the Revolutionary War. He asked Peale for:

> The most exact knowledge of the custumes of the American Armys, [and] portraits in small (either painting or drawing) of the conspicuous charectors necessary to be introduced into such a work . . . I mean the arrangement of the subjects most expressive and most pointed, as for instance—the cause of the Quarel, the commencement of it, the carrying it on, the Battles, alliances . . . to form one work, to be given in eligent engravings—call'd the American revolution—this work I mean to do at my one expence, and to imploy the first engravers in Europe to carry them into execution, not having the least dout, as the subject has engaged all the powers of Europe all will be interested in seeing the event so portraid (cited in Prown, 1982, p. 29).

West stressed an international audience for the series, not only for the purpose of turning a profit, but also to establish the new republic's political and cultural presence within a skeptical world community dominated by despotic monarchs and princes. Even many American citizens, knowing the fates of the Greek and Roman republics, doubted the survival of a nation governed by relatively weak state and federal governments.

West began but did not finish one of the subjects for the series, a group portrait of *The American Commissioners of the Preliminary Peace Negotiations with Great Britain*, featuring his friend Benjamin Franklin seated next to the portly John Adams (fig. 4.31). Ultimately West, like Copley, preferred not to risk losing royal and

4.30 John Singleton Copley
Portrait of Elkanah Watson, 1782.
Oil on canvas.
The Art Museum,
Princeton University,
Princeton, New Jersey.

As a partner in the French-American mercantile firm of Watson and Cassoul, Elkanah Watson, a Freemason, stands proudly next to a lofty fluted column ascending beyond the picture space. His bright-red overcoat and golden, embroidered waistcoat reinforce the warmly flushed luminosity of his face. Watson's gleaming visage is bathed by the distant rising sun as he holds documents relating to his business enterprise.

and Stripes. This was, I imagine, the first American flag hoisted in Old England (cited in Neff, p. 122).

Elkanah Watson implicitly contrasts Copley's "bold hand" and "master's touch" with the artist's political timidity and unwillingness to jeopardize lucrative commissions from the British aristocracy. Copley's reputation in the United States soon suffered precisely because more radical nationalists questioned the sincerity of the artist's "American heart." Though the painting elevated his career beyond portraiture, *Watson and the Shark* became fodder for Copley's American critics, who condemned its heroic commemoration of a British Tory. William Dunlap (1766–1839), the first historian of American art, perpetuated the myth that "Copley was, when removed to England no longer an American painter in feeling" (vol. I,

4.31 Benjamin West
The American Commissioners of the Preliminary Peace Negotiations with Great Britain, 1783–4.
Oil on canvas,
28⅜ x 36⁵⁄₁₆ in
(72.1 x 92.2 cm).
Winterthur Museum, Delaware.

Behind John Adams and Benjamin Franklin stand John Jay, future Supreme Court Chief Justice, and Henry Laurens, former president of the Continental Congress. The young man seated to the right is Franklin's grandson. The right side was unfinished due to the failure of British representatives to cooperate.

aristocratic patrons. Instead, he bestowed the project upon another student, John Trumbull, son of the governor of Connecticut and a 1773 Harvard graduate, who had briefly served as an officer and cartographer in the revolutionary army. Trumbull planned to represent the key events of the American Revolution. He hoped to turn a profit by exhibiting and selling the paintings, while marketing engraved prints to a broad national and international audience.

The artist's most dramatic and politically complex painting from the series depicted a British victory. Having witnessed from a safe distance the Battle of Bunker Hill at Charlestown, Massachusetts, on June 17, 1775, Trumbull painted in West's London studio in 1785–6 *The Death of General Joseph Warren at the Battle of Bunker's Hill* (fig. 4.32). Trumbull represented a martyred general, posed as a sacrificial type for Christ. However, the picture differs from West's *The Death of General Wolfe* in its extreme violence, enhanced by more vigorous brushstrokes and fiery red pigments. Rather than resting within a quiet semicircle of admiring officers, the dying American general lies at the base of a collapsing pyramid of figures as his troops retreat before the final British onslaught. Warren dies in defeat, not victory. Only the magnanimous gesture of a British officer, Colonel John Small, prevents a grenadier from ignominiously bayoneting Warren, whose body is protectively cradled by a barefoot muscular patriot.

Nevertheless, Trumbull also suggests that this early battle represented a moral victory for the Americans, who still had not organized themselves into a regular army and yet had inflicted heavy losses upon Britain's professional force. The light-colored figures of Warren and the patriots immediately behind him are bathed in providential light. Above them, the retreating flag of Massachusetts points toward the sun and dramatically displays its emblematic pine tree against a white background. The evergreen, like the serpent that encircled it on Massachusetts Treasury notes, symbolized New England's faith in regeneration and everlasting life. Parallel to the cyclical theme of Copley's *Watson and the Shark*, Trumbull's painting prophesies that from the jaws of death the rugged Americans would live to fight another day, emerging victorious despite Britain's superior firepower.

More than the particular details of battle, Trumbull portrayed the moral characters of its participants. Trumbull later wrote in his *Autobiography* that "those eminent patriots who had given their lives for their country at Bunker Hill" and elsewhere reminded him of "the beautiful language of our Savior, in his last conversation with his disciples, as recorded by St. John, 'that greater love hath no man than this, that a man lay down his life for his friends'" (p. 287). The theme of fraternal friendship pervades Trumbull's paintings of the Revolution, even uniting opponents. Colonel Small's brotherly gesture preserves the nobility of Warren's death and acknowledges that these Americans are no longer the unruly children of the mother country. They have grown into sturdy young adults capable of governing themselves. Supplanting the parent-child metaphor of colonialism, fraternity implied the liberty and equality of national independence and republican self-government. General Warren particularly personified the fraternal ideal. A physician, he also had been grand master of the

Massachusetts Freemasons. He had led the newer, more socially inclusive network of Masonic lodges that multiplied the number of initiation rites, the better to construct a social order based upon degrees of merit rather than wealth and noble birth. These "ancient" Masons also organized military field lodges to facilitate the fraternal bond between officers and troops.

Trumbull's painting represents class differences within the anarchic violence of battle. Yet the Masonic spirit of brotherhood signifies the emergence from revolutionary chaos of a new, more egalitarian social order. Personifying the professional middle class, Dr. Warren's bleeding body joins together protective members of opposing classes and armies, as represented by a barefoot American yeoman and a British gentleman officer. At the far right, a young American lieutenant stands awestruck by this sublime scene of martyrdom and brotherhood.

But the republican brotherhood envisioned by Trumbull and other socially conservative revolutionaries excluded entire groups from political participation, including African-Americans. Trumbull marginalized the presence of African-Americans at the Battle of Bunker Hill, contrary to historical accounts that credited

4.32 John Trumbull
The Death of General Joseph Warren at the Battle of Bunker's Hill, June 17, 1775, 1786. Oil on canvas, 25 x 34 in (63.5 x 36.4 cm). Yale University Art Gallery, New Haven, Connecticut. Trumbull Collection.

two former slaves, Peter Salem and Salem Poor, for particular bravery. In Trumbull's painting, a frightened black servant stands behind his master at the far right. Another African-American face is barely visible, hidden beneath the flags at the far left of the picture. Trumbull's acknowledgment of African-American participation serves only to underscore their relative invisibility and exclusion from the pantheon of American heroes.

In 1817, over three decades after he had painted the initial sketches for the Revolutionary War series, Trumbull was commissioned by Congress to paint four large murals of that war for the U.S. Capitol Rotunda. The commission excluded violent subjects such as *The Death of General Warren*, which represented an American defeat, however noble. During the War of 1812, invading British troops had destroyed much of the Capitol and the White House. Consequently, Trumbull's theme of fraternalism between British and American officers failed to satisfy nationalist

fervor for cultural and political independence.

By contrast, Trumbull's *The Declaration of Independence* suited the temple architecture and republican meaning of the Rotunda, the American Pantheon. Originally conceived in a smaller 1787 version (fig. 4.33), the painting visualized a government of prosperous white gentlemen, aging Founding Fathers, rather than the vibrant, fraternal heroes of Bunker Hill. Enclosed within an austere neoclassical space, members of the Continental Congress stiffly stand or sit like living stones, forming the architectural foundation of the new nation. Thomas Jefferson, the author of the Declaration, acts in concert with John Adams, Benjamin Franklin, and other members of the drafting committee, submitting the document to John Hancock, president of the Congress. Trumbull soberly represents the central act of the American Revolution as a rational, legal act, undertaken by a republican aristocracy who wished to preserve rather than disrupt the "natural" social order.

4.33 John Trumbull
The Declaration of Independence 4 July 1776, 1787–1820. Oil on canvas, 21⅛ x 31⅛ in (53.7 x 79.1 cm). Yale University Art Gallery, New Haven, Connecticut. Trumbull Collection.

Probably at Thomas Jefferson's suggestion, the artist embellished the painting with flags and trophies confiscated from British troops. Yet, these symbols of American triumph were not present in the Assembly Room of the Pennsylvania State House in 1776. Trumbull also covered the windows with expensive draperies and supplied more elegant furnishings than had existed. John Hancock's gilded chair exemplifies the elevation in social stature of the Declaration's signatories.

4.34 John Trumbull
General George Washington at the Battle of Trenton, 1792.
Oil on canvas,
92½ x 63 in
(235 x 160 cm).
Yale University Art Gallery,
New Haven, Connecticut.
Gift of the Society of the
Cincinnati in Connecticut.

George Washington and Republican Citizenship

Post-revolutionary government commissions tended to favor simple, realistic portraits of American patriots. Grandly heroic, idealizing portraits held little appeal for American middle-class audiences distrustful of the propertied elite's aristocratic pretensions. Trumbull approached *The Declaration of Independence* more as a group portrait than a bravura history painting, spending years collecting accurate likenesses of the signatories and non-signatories to the Declaration. When he painted a commissioned historical portrait of *General George Washington at the Battle of Trenton*, the city of Charleston, South Carolina, voted to reject the painting, telling Trumbull that it "would be better satisfied with a more matter-of-fact likeness . . . calm, tranquil, peaceful" (cited in Cooper, p. 120) (fig. 4.34). Charlestonians desired a friendlier, approachable Washington, with whom they could identify as admiring brothers.

But Trumbull's patriarchal Washington appears to assume godlike powers beyond the constitutional rule of law. His commanding pose resembles the *Apollo Belvedere*, one of the most celebrated sculptures from classical antiquity (fig. 4.35). Washington's buff-yellow uniform and golden telescope further encourage this comparison. Like the triumphant sun god, Washington stands high above the battlefield, his omniscient gaze equivalent to the solar all-seeing eye that decorates both the Great Seal and Washington's own Masonic apron.

After Washington's death in 1799, artists and architects more frequently represented him as a god or demigod. In 1800, Benjamin Latrobe, the Anglo-American architect and Freemason, designed a grand pyramidal mausoleum for Washington's remains (fig. 4.36). Latrobe's pyramid borrowed both from the Great Seal of the United States and from the funerary architecture of the French Freemason Étienne-Louis Boullée (1728–99), whose pyramidal monuments served the new religion of hero worship. Fearing mob violence and the social radicalism of the French Revolution, American conservatives increasingly favored images of patriarchal authority rather than egalitarian brotherhood.

However, political democrats objected to the deification of any mortal. Later in the nineteenth century, the young American sculptor Horatio Greenough (1805–52) was severely criticized for his Zeus-like portrayal of a semi-nude Washington (fig. 4.37). Commissioned by Congress, Greenough's marble monument originally sat in the middle of the Capitol Rotunda, partly under the assumption that Washington's remains might be transferred from Mount Vernon to a crypt beneath the Rotunda floor. However, six years after its installation, Greenough's unpopular sculpture was transferred to the grounds outside the Capitol and now sits in relative obscurity in the basement of the National Museum of American History.

The novelist Nathaniel Hawthorne later rhetorically asked, "Did anybody ever see Washington nude? It is inconceivable. He had no nakedness, but I imagine he was born with his clothes on, and his hair powdered, and made a stately bow on his first appearance in the world. His costume, at all events, was a part of his character," including his "coat and breeches, and masonic emblems" (cited in McCoubrey, pp. 86–87).

Washington's public image was shaped by the scrutiny of fellow citizens, who believed that the nation's president was equally subject to the Constitution and the providential all-seeing eye. Debate over Washington's authority divided the artistic community. In 1795, the Philadelphia portraitist Charles Willson Peale failed to extend the existence of the Columbianum, the nation's first art academy, beyond the year of its origin. Its first and last annual exhibition of 137 works by thirty artists opened in late April for six weeks in the Pennsylvania State House. Afterward, the academy fatally split into two political factions: those who wished to solicit Washington's support as a kind of royal patron of the academy versus those who refused to tarnish Washington's republican image with the authoritarian trappings

4.35 Apollo Belvedere
Roman copy of Greek original,
c. 1st century B.C.E.
Marble, 7ft 4¼ in (2.24 m) high.
Vatican Museums, Vatican City.

4.36 Benjamin Henry Latrobe
Proposal for a Washington Mausoleum,
c. 1800.
Watercolor, 11 x 21¼ in (27.9 x 53.9 cm).
Library of Congress, Washington, D.C.

Latrobe's stepped pyramid was to have risen 100 feet high. Latrobe's imaginary view of the proposed Egyptian-revival structure unites the pyramid's apex with the sky above. Not until later in the century was Robert Mills' Washington Monument (1848–85), a towering Egyptian obelisk, constructed on the Mall in Washington, D.C.

4.37 (left)
Horatio Greenough
George Washington,
1840.
Marble, 11 ft 4 in
(3.45 m) high.
National Museum of
American History,
Smithsonian Institution,
Washington, D.C.

4.38 (right)
Charles Willson Peale
Staircase Group:
Raphaelle and Titian
Ramsay Peale, 1795.
Oil on canvas,
89½ x 39⅜ in (227.3 x
100 cm). Philadelphia
Museum of Art,
Pennsylvania. George W.
Elkins Collection.

Like Hercules choosing the
difficult path of Virtue (see
pp. 90–91), Raphaelle
Peale, the eldest son of
Charles, climbs a stairway
with paintbrushes and
palette in one hand and a
maulstick, used for
supporting and steadying
the artist's hand, in the
other. The young Titian
points coyly toward the
unseen floor above. Named
after Italian Renaissance
master painters, the sons
personify their father's
academic ambition.

4.39 Gilbert Stuart
George Washington
(Vaughan-Sinclair
portrait), 1795–6.
Oil on canvas,
29⅛ x 24⅛ in
(74.2 x 61.5 cm).
National Gallery of Art,
Washington, D.C. Andrew
W. Mellon Collection.

of royalty. Peale positioned himself firmly in the latter camp. His major contribution to the Columbianum exhibition, the *Staircase Group: Raphaelle and Titian Ramsay Peale* (fig. 4.38), acquired fame as a highly illusionistic life-size portrait of two of the artist's sons, Titian and Raphaelle. Inserted into a real doorframe and situated above a real wooden step, the deceptive painting, according to Peale family legend, was so successful that it later fooled George Washington, who bowed in greeting to the figures as he passed by. Whether true or not, the story served to underscore

Washington's status as a polite gentleman with thoroughly republican manners.

The Rhode Island native Gilbert Stuart, yet another Benjamin West student, created the most enduring images of Washington as republican citizen. Stuart's "Vaughan" portrait of Washington, named after its first owner, represents the president in his black inauguration suit (fig. 4.39). Otherwise, the portrait bust is devoid of the official trappings of power associated with the nation's chief executive. Stuart preferred to focus upon the face as the emblematic hand-writing of God or mirror of the soul. His

Society of the Cincinnati's ancient name acknowledged the danger. The ancient Roman exemplar Cincinnatus had preferred private rural retirement to the public glory of military and political power.

Artists often represented Washington as a modern Cincinnatus, who retired to the land, voluntarily subjecting himself to the public will. Even Greenough's Zeus-like sculpture represents Washington in the act of surrendering the sword of governmental authority to the viewing public. Commissioned by the state of Virginia, the French sculptor Jean-Antoine Houdon (1741–1828) designed a marble statue of Washington as a modern Cincinnatus (fig. 4.41). Mixing contemporary costume with classical allusions, he reassuringly implied the

4.40 (left)
Gilbert Stuart
*George Washington
(Lansdowne portrait)*,
1796.
Oil on canvas laid on wood, 96 x 60 in. (243.8 x 152.4 cm). Pennsylvania Academy of the Fine Arts, Philadelphia. Bequest of William Bingham.

Washington's right hand almost touches a quill rising out of a silver inkwell. These suggest a ship and its sail. Connected with the rainbow, these objects evoke the biblical Flood and Noah's Ark. Washington was regarded as a savior following the revolutionary floodwaters.

4.41 Jean-Antoine Houdon
George Washington,
1788.
Marble, lifesize.
Virginia State Capitol, Richmond, Virginia.

melting brushstrokes model a sensitive, half-smiling face, warmly radiating a spiritual energy indicated especially by the flushed cheeks and the red glow of light surrounding Washington's head.

In a full-length portrait, Stuart represented the president in the manner remembered by Hawthorne. Washington is dressed in a plain black suit with powdered wig and ceremonial sword. He politely stands with an open gesture of welcome (fig. 4.40). Behind the grand columnar architecture, a rainbow signifies God's covenant with the new nation after the revolutionary flood. Stuart placed a copy of the Constitution beneath the table and volumes of *The Federalist* and the *Journal of Congress* on it, indicating the equality of the branches of government and Washington's deference to the public will.

Most Americans feared that glorifying a singular military hero could encourage one-man dictatorship. The Society of the Cincinnati, an order of Revolutionary War officers and their eldest male descendants, generated republican fears of military despotism. Nevertheless, the

4.42 Charles Willson Peale
William Smith and his Grandson, 1788.
Oil on canvas,
51¼ x 40⅜ in
(130.2 x 102.5 cm).
Virginia Museum of Fine Arts, Richmond, Virginia.
The Cabell Foundation and the Glasgow Fund.

4.43 Charles Willson Peale
Benjamin Franklin, 1789.
Oil on canvas, 36 x 27 in (91.4 x 68.5 cm).
Historical Society of Pennsylvania, Philadelphia.

Franklin, mortally ill, was unable to pose, so Peale based his likeness on a 1785 portrait. Unfortunately, Franklin's words on the paper before him have faded over time to the point of illegibility.

general's rejection of military dictatorship for rural retirement at Mount Vernon. A plow, emblematically signifying the peaceful pursuit of agriculture, supports the back of the sculpture. Washington has taken off his sword and military riding coat, which he drapes over the *fasces*, the bound rods of discipline that symbolized Roman republican justice. He has, instead, taken up his walking stick, which he employed while supervising the cultivation of his Mount Vernon plantation. Situated within Thomas Jefferson's Roman-temple rotunda for the Virginia State Capitol (see fig. 4.41), Houdon's statue expressed conservative Americans' conviction that state and national stability depended upon the political authority of independent men of property, whose wealth was rooted in the land.

Even merchants submitted to this agrarian ideology, using their commercial wealth to purchase country estates in modest emulation of Washington's Mount Vernon or Jefferson's Monticello. In 1788, before his election to Congress, the Baltimore merchant William Smith asked Charles Willson Peale to paint him as a country gentleman attended by his grandson. In the portrait, the child holds a peach harvested from the farm orchard in the background (fig. 4.42). Peale equates agricultural cultivation with self-cultivation and the education of republican youth, heirs to the revolutionary legacy of the Founding Fathers. Temporary rural retirement also enabled men of property to pose as disinterested citizens, who did not actively run for office, but selflessly offered to serve, if the public, in its wisdom, so asked. While Peale's Smith sits in a green garden chair, the fictive classical architecture of the setting alludes to the subject's public identity as a member of the governing establishment.

Peale, Stuart, and other portraitists of the post-revolutionary era sought to represent human physiognomy as a transparent barometer of moral character and truth. Peale adopted an austere "plain style" (Fortune, p. 607), attempting to divest American portraiture of its subservient, colonial association with the English school's aristocratic flattery. His many portraits of revolutionary heroes and statesmen were both realistic and philosophical in meaning. A man of science as well as art, Peale sought to canonize lovers of wisdom, patriotic men of learning, who also belonged to the universal republic of letters. Commissioned by the American Philosophical Society in Philadelphia, he portrayed Benjamin Franklin as a man of science, the discoverer of electricity and inventor of the lightning rod (fig. 4.43). While a bolt of lightning strikes a large building in the background, Franklin calmly holds a miniature lightning rod. Another rod rests on the writing table, drawing attention to a manuscript page of Franklin's famous 1769 treatise on electricity. Peale's sedate portrait implies that the Founding Fathers acted rationally upon principles of natural law and divine providence. In words that could allude to the federal union of states, Franklin wrote in the manuscript page visible in Peale's painting that lightning rods fail to prevent explosions only "by reason of their being incompleat, disunited, too small, or not of the best materials for conducting" (cited in Sellers, 1962, p. 351).

Educating the Public and Selling Art: Problems in Public and Private Exhibitions

Beginning in 1786, Peale opened a museum in a building next to his house at Third and Lombard Street, Philadelphia. Peale had the civic-minded goal of educating the public by marrying natural history with art and private enterprise with popular entertainment. His profitable museum of art and nature attained scientific and national respectability when it moved to the American Philosophical Society's Philosophical Hall in 1794 and then, in 1802, to Independence Hall. It was at the latter hall that Jefferson, Franklin, and other signatories had declared national independence by invoking "the laws of nature and nature's god" (cited in Fliegelman, p. 203).

In 1822, when Peale's private museum became incorporated as the Philadelphia Museum, the trustees of the new public institution commissioned the eighty-one-year-old artist to paint a full length self-portrait for the museum (fig. 4.44). The

4.44 Charles Willson Peale
The Artist in his Museum, 1822.
Oil on canvas, 103¾ x 79⅞ in (263.5 x 202.9 cm). Pennsylvania Academy of the Fine Arts, Philadelphia. Gift of Mrs. Sarah Harrison (The Joseph Harrison, Jr., Collection).

In the immediate left foreground, Peale placed a dead turkey on a chest of taxidermy tools. Peale's son, Titian, had acquired the distinctively American bird for the museum on a western expedition to the state of Missouri. As suggested by the long rows of cages filled with stuffed bird specimens, the presently limp turkey will soon be reanimated by the taxidermist's craft into an artful museum display, signifying the harmony and variety of the universe.

4.45 Charles Willson Peale
The Exhumation of the Mastodon, 1806–8. Oil on canvas, 50 x 62½ in (127 x 158.7 cm). Maryland Historical Society.

Peale included portraits of eleven of his twelve children and his two successive wives, one deceased. Signifying the social subordination of manual to mental labor, Peale chose not to record the actual likenesses of the workmen in the pit. Instead, he employed anonymous Philadelphia models to pose for these laborers deemed unworthy of the portraitist's brush.

museum had been a collective effort involving contributions of natural-history specimens and anthropological curiosities from members of Peale's audience and the collaborative labor of his large family. Yet Peale portrays himself as the heroic prime mover. Receding in deep perspective, rows of gold-framed portraits crown a hierarchical exhibition of Nature's Great Chain of Being. Rivaling Noah's Ark, the museum's Long Room preserves God's creation, including extinct species. Stuffed birds in display cages line the lower walls, while various mammals appear on the right between the skeletal legs of a giant mastodon, an extinct relative of the elephant. Within the museum itself, Peale accompanied his display of the mastodon skeleton with the exhibition of an earlier painting, *The Exhumation of the Mastodon* (fig. 4.45), which represents the mental and physical labor involved in extracting the mastodon's bones from its

4.46 Thomas Jefferson
University of Virginia campus, 1826 (from an 1824 drawing). Engraving by Benjamin Tanner, 13⅛ x 26⅝ in (33.6 x 67.8 cm). From Böye, *Map of Virginia,* Jefferson Papers.

4.47 John L. Krimmel
*Fourth of July in Centre
Square*, 1810–12.
Oil on canvas,
22¾ x 29 in
(57.8 x 73.7 cm).
Pennsylvania Academy of
Fine Arts, Philadelphia.

swampy source on a farm near Newburgh, New York. In this picture, Peale more clearly personifies a latter-day Noah, as he directs work at the right edge of a rain-flooded excavation pit below a storm-darkened sky dramatically pierced by lightning. Supported by members of his family, who stand behind him, Peale holds a large anatomical drawing of a mastodon bone. Meanwhile, at the center of the painting, the artist focused upon the fruit of his intellectual, scientific knowledge: beneath the pyramidal framework of the wooden water-pumping apparatus, a bare-chested laborer holds up a recovered bone for Peale's approving gaze. In the immediate foreground, cast in shadow, John Masten, the "illiterate" German immigrant (Rigal, p. 102), farmer and owner of the site being excavated, climbs a ladder out of the pit, while deferentially looking over his shoulder to the sunlit figure of Peale, the virtuous, public-minded citizen and private entrepreneur, who is determined to preserve all the creatures of God's creation for his educational, entertaining Philadelphia museum.

Despite his intellectual pretensions, many critics argued that Peale was more of a popular showman than a man of science. In *The Artist in his Museum* (fig. 4.44), Peale teases the beholder with a theatrical curtain, partially hiding the sublime sights that paying customers may fully view. Conservatives attacked Peale's Museum for being a circuslike menagerie, the cultural expression of Jeffersonian democracy's indiscriminate social leveling. Outlasting most of his critics, Peale visually refuted claims that his museum lacked educational value. In the background, tiny figures gaze upon the exhibits: a contemplative man of learning, a father teaching his son, and a young woman awed by the mastodon bones and, perhaps, by Peale's godlike mastery of art and science.

Peale's long perspective view of a communal space for learning parallels Thomas Jefferson's contemporaneous design for the University of Virginia (fig. 4.46). At Charlottesville, Jefferson created an "academical village" (cited in Roth, p. 76), a rectangle of classically designed pavilions, classrooms, and dormitories headed by a

Pantheon-domed library that overlooked a long lawn, originally open to the landscape beyond. Like Jefferson, with whom he corresponded, Peale asserted the vitality of America's natural environment, exposing the narrow prejudices of European naturalists who argued that species degenerated in the hostile American wilderness. While Jefferson's design for the Virginia campus embraces the surrounding world, Peale's self-portrait foregrounds the American wild turkey as an emblem of New World bounty. Similarly, Peale's own mammoth stature and octogenarian longevity visually refuted European claims of American degeneracy.

European immigrants also played a role in supporting American counterclaims against foreign skeptics and detractors. The German-born artist John Lewis Krimmel (1786–1821) was lured to Philadelphia in 1809, following his brother's business success in the city. Establishing himself as a drawing instructor at a girls' school, Krimmel also painted portraits and exuberant genre scenes of Philadelphia life. These works celebrated the new republic, while also comically encouraging its inhabitants to live up to the ideals of the Founding Fathers. Krimmel's *Fourth of July in Centre Square* (fig. 4.47), represents a festive gathering of patriotic revelers commemorating Independence Day in a public square, fronting Philadelphia's new water-pumping station. Designed by Benjamin Latrobe, architect of the U.S. Capitol, this geometrically simplified building, composed of a cubical base for office space, and a cylindrical, domed encasement for a water tank, steam engine, and pump, had quickly become a source of civic pride upon its completion in 1801. Latrobe's use of Greek, Doric-order columns, symbols of Herculean strength and republican austerity, represented a novel departure from the predominately Roman-style classicism of earlier post-revolutionary architecture. Further enhancing the public space, a fountain sculpture by William Rush, a co-founder of the Columbianum and, later, the Pennsylvania Academy of the Fine Arts, represents a female personification of the Schuylkill River, the source of Philadelphia's clean drinking water.

Within this aesthetic urban park, lined with stately trees, Krimmel's socially diverse crowd seems focused upon the pleasures of drinking, socializing, and displaying their own bodies, costumed in holiday finery. Drawing upon the satirical pictorial tradition of William Hogarth (see chapter 3), Krimmel gently appears to warn viewers of the pitfalls of luxury, intemperance, and vanity. Krimmel typified the younger, post-revolutionary generation of artists in conveying doubts regarding the American capacity for self-discipline and self-governance. Though comic, Krimmel's painting seriously queries whether American citizens possess the moral will to channel political freedom and social ambition as rationally and productively as Latrobe's pumping station channels water, the life-blood of the city, to Philadelphia homes, businesses, and public buildings. The civic, technological promise of clean, flowing water provides a strong, critical counterpoint to the anarchic potential of unregulated private consumption.

John Trumbull, Charles Willson Peale, and the revolutionary war generation of American painters almost invariably chose to represent clearly virtuous subjects for their pictures. By contrast, the post-revolutionary generation of artists, including Rembrandt Peale, John Vanderlyn, and Washington Allston, turned increasingly toward subjects that expressed anxiety and ambivalence regarding the nation's political and cultural future. Wealthy patrons founded the American Academy of the Fine Arts in New York (1802) and the Pennsylvania Academy of Fine Arts in Philadelphia (1805), but the new generation of American artists suffered from American patrons' preference for European Old Master paintings. Meanwhile, to reach a broader, middle-class audience, artists continued to develop marketing strategies that mixed the fine arts with the theater and popular entertainments.

Rembrandt and Raphaelle Peale: Images of Female Sexuality and Moral Reform

Rembrandt Peale, second-oldest son of Charles Willson Peale, angered his father when he opened his own Philadelphia art gallery to exhibit *The Roman Daughter*, among other paintings (fig. 4.48). Popularized in theatrical productions, the subject focused upon female sexuality, but, at the same time, was a moral story of filial devotion and charity. The large neoclassical painting represents a loyal daughter secretly breastfeeding her starving, unjustly imprisoned father. Beholders who regarded the theater as a source of moral corruption criticized the painting's perversion of republican motherhood. According to the critic for the *Monthly Anthology and Boston Review,* "The figure of an old man, placed in the situation of an unconscious infant, is perfectly disgusting" (cited in Miller, p. 111). Charles Willson Peale warned his son against the painting's nudity and quasi-incestuous subject matter, fearing that moral and religious societies would be roused to act against the evils of art.

Rembrandt Peale learned his lesson. Years later in his Baltimore museum, he began to exhibit *The Court of Death,* a huge painting that self-consciously advocated a host of moral reforms to promote the health and well-being of American citizens (fig. 4.49). Presided over by the enthroned figure of Death, who rests his foot upon the corpse of a young man, the painting is a vast allegory, filled with personifications symbolizing the fatal evils that prematurely take the lives of the young, including War, Conflagration, Famine, Pestilence, Suicide, and Intemperance. The beseeching figures of Old Age and Faith stand as virtuous alternatives to the gloomy congregation of moral and physical diseases. Supported by the sermons of clergymen and a host of favorable newspaper reviews, the traveling painting attracted a broad, middle-class audience in cities throughout the United States.

Raphaelle Peale, Rembrandt's older brother, more poignantly addressed issues of moral propriety. Late in his career, he satirically critiqued prudish censorship of the arts with *Venus Rising from the Sea–A Deception* (fig. 4.50), a convincing example of *trompe-l'oeil* (fool-the-eye) illusionism. Raphaelle's uncannily realistic depiction of a napkin or handkerchief, pinned to hang in front of an erotic picture, contradicts its purported censorious function by, in effect, creating a titillating peep show. The improvised curtain hides a nude Venus copied from a well-known British print reproducing the Irish painter James Barry's *Venus Rising from the Sea* (1772). Unlike Barry's original representation of the idealized figure, Peale's sexually charged picture teases viewers and stimulates the voyeuristic imagina-

4.48 Rembrandt Peale
The Roman Daughter, 1811.
Oil on canvas, 84¾ x 62⅞ in (210 x 159.8 cm).
National Museum of American Art, Washington, D.C.
Gift of the James Smithson Society.

Despite misgivings over the sexual nature of the subject, Charles Willson Peale posed for the figure of the father. Having recently returned from a trip to Paris, Rembrandt Peale adopted a simplified style, inspired by the paintings of Jacques-Louis David (1748–1825) and the French school of neoclassicism.

tion by offering only a glimpse of a delicate foot and an elongated bare arm, holding locks of golden hair. The artist virtually invites frustrated beholders to pull aside the sensuous white cloth, thereby mimicking the curtain-drawing action of Raphaelle's father in the contemporaneous *The Artist in his Museum* (see fig. 4.44). Subverting the idea of censorship, the suggestive curves and folds of Raphaelle's soft white napkin emulate and call attention to the alluring body supposedly protected from intruding eyes. In rebellion against his father, who wanted his eldest son to aspire toward portraiture, if not heroic history-painting, Raphaelle transformed his representation of the ancient goddess of love and beauty into a still life of subtly modulated, silken fabric.

Throughout most of his career, Raphaelle Peale painted small, intimate pictures of fruit, desserts, and other food-and-drink offerings set upon tables, placed invitingly close to the viewer's space and touch. Traditionally, spokesmen for the European academic tradition belittled still-life painting as the mere mechanical copying of nature. Sir Joshua Reynolds, President of London's Royal Academy, insisted that still lifes

4.49 (above)
Rembrandt Peale
The Court of Death,
1820.
Oil on canvas,
11 ft 6 in x 23 ft 5 in
(3.5 x 7.1 m).
Detroit Institute of Art,
Detroit, Michigan.

4.50 (below)
Raphaelle Peale
*Venus Rising from the
Sea—A Deception (After
the Bath)*, c. 1822.
Oil on canvas,
29¼ x 24⅛ in
(74.3 x 61.3 cm). Nelson-
Atkins Museum of Art,
Kansas City, Missouri.
Purchase. Nelson Trust.

4.51 Raphaelle Peale
Blackberries, c. 1813.
Oil on wood panel,
7¼ x 10¼ in
(18.4 x 26 cm). Fine Arts
Museum of San Francisco,
California. Gift of Mr and
Mrs John D. Rockefeller III,
1993.

appealed primarily to the senses rather than to the higher mental and moral faculties. Academicians deemed pictures of fruit, flowers, or other still-life elements as suitable for amateurs and women artists, but not for those painters seriously working toward professional respectability and artistic fame. Steeped in the study of history, mythology, and literature, great painters were expected to produce inventive, edifying pictures of gods and goddesses, or of human genius, drama, and virtue.

Nevertheless, still-life paintings traditionally have triggered a host of moral associations that lead the mind beyond their intense realism. As art historian Brandon Fortune has observed, Raphaelle Peale's *Blackberries* (fig. 4.51) can evoke the idea of Christ's Passion. The juicy red berries suggest both the blood of Christ and the sacramental wine of Holy Communion, while the visible thorniness of the berries' plucked wooden stem could be interpreted as an allusion to Christ's crown of thorns. The isolation of these intensely illuminated berries against an empty, largely darkened background contributes to a mood of solitude and contemplative silence, thereby inviting a religious, possibly Christian, interpretation. On the other hand, Peale's

Blackberries could also, more heretically, encourage the eighteenth- and nineteenth-century tendency toward pantheistic nature worship. Recalling the still-life motifs of John Singleton Copley's radiant portraits, Peale's glistening berries, hovering energetically in space, imply that all of nature's elements, down to the humblest objects, are imbued with a vitalistic creative force. Similarly, as we shall see in the next chapter, nineteenth-century American painters would increasingly turn toward landscape subjects to discover evidence of a unifying, divine presence hidden within nature's colorful variety of forms.

During the early republic, Raphaelle Peale's light, relatively austere still lifes conveyed to American consumers the virtues of moderation and temperance. Though he liked to paint desserts and other tempting treats, his simple, modest dishes of food seem alien to the deadening vices of gluttony and overindulgence. Unfortunately, Raphaelle Peale himself suffered physically and mentally from excessive eating and drinking, much to the dismay of his stern father. Charles Willson Peale frequently chastised his eldest son, as in this letter from July 4, 1820:

When we reflect that in order to injoy [sic] health we ought to eat and drink only such things as our best judgment on experience have proved as most condusive [sic] to that end, also, in only such proportion as shall be in exact proportion as to quantity as will nourish the body, for a single particle more becomes a clog and a burden to the digestive powers, therefore, produces disease more or less in due proportion to the excess. When we set down at the Table (perhaps loaded with a variety of unnecessary articles, for two or three things is realy [sic] all that is needful) then think on the end! & resolve that taste shall not be superior to reason. The government of all other passions as essential to promote health, is certainly of vast import (cited in Fortune, p. 136).

In a treatise published at the beginning of the century, the Peale family patriarch had already joined other aging members of the revolutionary generation to warn that the welfare of the new American republic depended upon the moderation and self-governing powers of its citizens. Without the will to control one's own passions and appetites, there was little hope for a diverse, expanding, and youthful nation of ambitious individuals. It is hard to imagine how Raphaelle Peale's portrait of airy, glowing berries could possibly pose the danger of indigestion, much less suggest a lack of moral fiber. Raphaelle Peale never overloaded his still-life dining tables with excessive amounts of food or drink. Nevertheless, Charles Willson Peale strongly criticized his son's overindulgence in the painting of savory objects. Despite their visible signs of moderate consumption, Raphaelle's pictures of edible, potable pleasures still seemed for the father to signify an excessive, self-indulgent preoccupation with common, mere things of the material world.

Apparently validating, though not endorsing, these patriarchal fears, some art historians argue that, far from expressing the moral social values of temperance and restraint, Peale's still lifes of fruit, vegetables, meats, and desserts can be interpreted as "solipsistic", "antisocial" projections of the artist's own mortal body, and of his playful romantic imagination (Nemerov, p.26). Peale's silent, hermetic pictures embody a childlike vision that is transfixed by the "material density"

of physical objects, painted with a magical, hallucinatory intensity (Nemerov, p.53). Raphaelle Peale's small, intimate paintings invite an inward, escapist gaze, riveted by the sensuous specificity of matter. Immersed in the textures and juicy richness of natural phenomena, beholders of Raphaelle Peale's illusionistic pictures could surely be forgiven for forgetting or losing sight of nature's social utility or its conventional moral associations and traditional religious symbolism. When interpreted as affirmations of the imagination's freedom to play in private aesthetic reverie, Raphaelle Peale's still lifes signify the restless younger generation's resistance to repressive social norms and rational economic, commercial demands for unremitting industry and productivity.

John Vanderlyn and the Moral Ambiguity of Early Nineteenth-century History Painting

Seeking fame as a history painter, New York native John Vanderlyn also attempted to lure audiences with provocative subjects and the marriage of high art with popular spectacles. Having studied in revolutionary Paris during the late 1790s, Vanderlyn chose violent, anti-British subject matter that first expressed itself in *The Death of Jane McCrea*, painted in Paris in 1804 (fig. 4.52). That year Britain resumed its war with revolutionary France. Begun in 1789, the French Revolution had developed violently into a Europe-wide war by 1793, following the execution of the deposed French monarch, Louis XVI. Defending their act of regicide against the royal courts of Europe, French radicals militarily exported their revolution to other European countries. In the United States, frightened conservatives raised the spector of a foreign conspiracy to import radical French ideas from across the Atlantic. In 1798, Congress passed the Alien and Sedition Acts, making it easier to deport immigrants and to revoke freedom of speech and press for political dissidents. Following Thomas Jefferson's election as President in 1800, these repressive acts were repealed. At the same time, Jefferson's moderate social policies allayed the propertied elite's anxieties regarding a more radical social revolution. Furthermore, by 1804, after the French Revolution's collapse into military dictatorship, the self-anointed emperor, Napoleon Bonaparte, had transformed

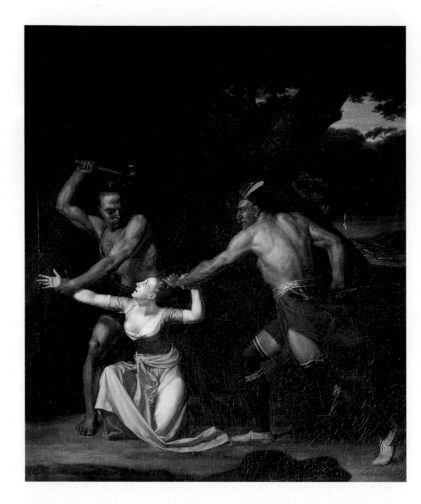

4.52 John Vanderlyn
The Death of Jane McCrea, 1804.
Oil on canvas,
32 x 26½ in
(81.2 x 67.3 cm).
Wadsworth Atheneum,
Hartford, Connecticut.

Schooled in French neoclassical art, Vanderlyn modeled his figures after Ancient Greek and Hellenistic sculptures. The foreground composition as a whole has the look of a classical frieze. However, the intense violence, strong emotions, and murky wilderness environment subvert traditional notions of classical order and calm. In the background to the right, the small figure of a soldier may be seen running toward us, but his distance precludes any possible rescue of Jane McCrea.

the revolutionary wars into a quest for imperial power, primarily on the European continent.

Many Americans who bitterly recalled British behavior during the American Revolution supported Napoleon Bonaparte's campaign to conquer the royal families of Britain and Europe. Exhibited in Paris, Vanderlyn's *The Death of Jane McCrea* attacked the moral standing of Britain. The painting represents a horrific scene from *The Columbiad*, an epic poem of the American Revolution by Joel Barlow, Thomas Jefferson's diplomatic envoy to France. Vanderlyn rejected West's romantic image of the noble savage for a caricatured representation of Indian viciousness. Selfishly motivated by the British bounty placed upon American scalps, the dark-skinned warriors murder an innocent colonial woman against the gloom of the New York wilderness.

Vanderlyn's anti-British theme expressed his political identification with the Francophile foreign policy of Jefferson. The year before he executed his painting for Barlow, Vanderlyn had carried diplomatic letters to Paris, facilitating the Louisiana Purchase from France. Acquisition of the vast Louisiana Territory meant that the United States instantly doubled in size, extending beyond the Mississippi River to the Rocky Mountains. The Louisiana Purchase dramatically increased the probability that the United States would ultimately stretch westward all the way to the Pacific Ocean. Having thrown most of their support to the British during the American Revolution, Indian tribes more than ever loomed as obstacles to national expansion. In Vanderlyn's propagandistic painting, the helpless Jane McCrea personifies the vulnerability of America or Liberty to a satanic red menace.

During the next decade, commercial warfare between Britain and Napoleonic France continued to divide Americans into opposing political factions. Responding to British interference with American shipping, the United States

4.53 John Vanderlyn
*Marius amid the Ruins of
Carthage,* 1807.
Oil on canvas,
87 x 68½ in
(220 x 173.9 cm).
Fine Arts Museums of San
Francisco, California.
Gift of M.H. de Young.

Vanderlyn appears to have
appropriated this brooding
figural type from the figure
of Brutus in Jacques-Louis
David's *The Lictors
Returning to Brutus the
Bodies of His Sons* (1789).
But unlike David's Brutus,
who heroically sacrificed
private family interests for
the good of the Roman
Republic, Vanderlyn's
Marius appears as a totally
self-absorbed, obsessive
character, whose dark,
destructive thoughts are
echoed by the gloomy ruins
of a past empire.

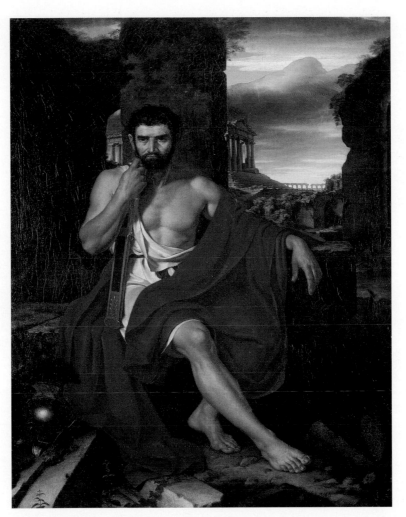

declared war against Britain in 1812. The War of 1812, America's second war for independence, would not end until 1815, the same year that Napoleon Bonaparte's fall from power brought peace to war-torn Europe.

American artists chose subjects that expressed the conspiratorial atmosphere of political paranoia pervading Europe and America during the first fifteen years of the nineteenth century. In Rome, John Vanderlyn painted *Marius amid the Ruins of Carthage*, representing a Roman general who was the moral opposite of Cincinnatus and George Washington (fig. 4.53). According to the ancient Roman biographer Plutarch, Marius had been a power-hungry military leader, banished to the ruined North African city of Carthage. Vanderlyn later stated that he intended to represent "the instability of human grandeur—a city in ruins and a fallen general. I endeavoured to

express in the countenance of Marius the bitterness of disappointed ambitions, mixed with the meditation of revenge" (cited in Simpson, Mills, and Saville, p. 56).

Vanderlyn probably intended *Marius* as a melancholic political allegory of his former patron, Aaron Burr, Jefferson's vice-president. Burr's political ambitions had collapsed in 1804, when he killed Treasury secretary Alexander Hamilton in a duel. Burr fled in an unsuccessful attempt to establish his own political empire in the American Southwest. Tried for treason, he managed an acquittal, but decided to live in European exile like a brooding Marius. In Paris, Burr again met Vanderlyn, whose *Marius* had won a gold medal from the French government at the Salon of 1808. The painting's reception may have been aided by Napoleon's admiration for the ancient Roman general, who had been the first to create a professional, citizens' army, composed primarily of proletarians, or men without property.

In 1815, following the fall of Napoleon Bonaparte and the collapse of the French Empire, Vanderlyn returned to New York with *Marius* and several other history paintings in hand, including a classical nude subject, *Ariadne Asleep on the Island of Naxos* (fig. 4.54). But his career foundered as American critics questioned the moral content of his paintings. *Marius* failed to find an American buyer until 1834. The painting's grim anti-hero, draped in red, tensely clutching his sword, represented an unappealing, violent character, the antithesis of civic-minded republicanism. Meanwhile, Vanderlyn's voluptuous *Ariadne* aroused the opposition of moralists, not simply because it represented a

female nude, but also because it clearly represented the mythic Greek princess in a state of postcoital pleasure. Vanderlyn reduced Theseus, whom Ariadne had saved from the Cretan labyrinth, to a tiny figure in the background. Having seduced Ariadne, he secretly boards a ship for the return to Athens. Ariadne's curvaceous body represented another labyrinth that the Athenian hero ultimately had to escape for the sake of Western civilization. Vanderlyn's sensual representation of Ariadne's pink, glowing flesh boldly foregrounds the private temptation of sexual pleasure at the expense of the hero's public duty to the Athenian city-state. When he began *Ariadne* in 1805, Vanderlyn wrote to a friend: "The subject may not be chaste enough for the more chaste and modest Americans, at least to be displayed in the house of any private

4.54 John Vanderlyn
Ariadne Asleep on the Island of Naxos,
1809–14.
Oil on canvas,
68½ x 87 in
(173.9 x 220.9 cm).
Pennsylvania Academy of the Fine Arts, Philadelphia. Gift of Mrs. Sarah Harrison (The Joseph Harrison, Jr., Collection).

individual, to either the company of the parlor or drawing room, but on that account it may attract a greater crowd if exhibited publickly" (cited in Lubin, p. 12).

Yet *Ariadne* failed to produce the scandalous publicity that may have drawn large crowds, since Vanderlyn also intended to educate the American public in the Renaissance ideals of high art. His painting was partially purified through art-historical associations with sixteenth-century Venetian nudes by Giorgione and Titian. Realizing that *Ariadne* and *Marius* would fail to attract a sufficient audience, Vanderlyn painted large panoramas that imaginatively transported viewers to European cities and tourist sites such as Versailles Palace. But after a decade, Vanderlyn's New York rotunda of circular panoramas and ideal history paintings went bankrupt, forcing the artist to salvage his career through portraiture.

Washington Allston and Biblical Painting

Washington Allston, the scion of a wealthy South Carolina plantation family, traveled with Vanderlyn to Paris and then Rome, where he painted an evocative *Self-Portrait* (fig. 4.55) asserting his claim to artistic genius. A Harvard College graduate (class of 1800), Allston studied painting in London under Benjamin West, prior to his grand tour of the European continent. His androgynous, mysterious *Self-Portrait* garnered considerable positive critical attention among the international community of artists, critics, and connoisseurs residing in Rome.

The aristocratic, politically conservative South Carolinian appears emotionally distant, coolly detached as he ambiguously sits or stands in a gloomy space, defined by crumbling, moldering walls. The enigmatic mood and reclusive ambience of the painting was inspired by Leonardo

4.55 Washington Allston
Self-Portrait, 1805. Oil on canvas, 31½ x 26½ in (80 x 67.31 cm). Museum of Fine Arts, Boston. Bequest of Miss Alice Hooper.

Allston's representation of creative genius caught the attention of the English Romantic poet, critic, and philosopher Samuel Taylor Coleridge, who also briefly resided in Rome. Becoming Allston's close friend and intellectual mentor, Coleridge wrote a favorable commentary on his imaginative spiritual paintings, and he helped the American artist find an English audience for his later religious pictures.

da Vinci's portrait of *Mona Lisa* (c.1503–13), with which the young American artist had fallen in love while visiting the Louvre in Paris. Like the half-smiling Mona Lisa, Allston's distance is enhanced by the mystery of a shadowy, moist environment. In fact, the irregular pattern of the ruined background walls alludes to a passage from Leonardo's *Treatise on Painting*, in which the Renaissance master challenged young art students to discover new forms by looking at the accidental shapes and discolorations of moldering walls. During the late eighteenth and early nineteenth centuries, Romantic artists and critics, advocating the creative powers of the imagination, cited Leonardo's practical advice as a means for eliciting individual genius. True genius was not to be defined by the slavish imitation of external nature. By projecting the internal light of the mind outward, the godlike artist-genius could distill aesthetic meaning and coherent design from the apparently chaotic, random patterns of billowing clouds, marbled stones, or dying embers.

Allston's soft, melting, pale-pink and bluish-white flesh tones illuminate the subterranean darkness. His head, nestled comfortably in a pure-white collar, wrapped in a golden cravat, glows with the light of genius. Cloudlike, organic stains of mold on the walls echo the tousled waves and curling wisps of hair cascading over Allston's forehead, drawing attention to the artist's dreamy, meditative eyes. Meanwhile, at the bottom of the painting, a gleaming Phi Beta Kappa key, emblematic of his Harvard education, hangs at the artist's waist like a golden seed, promising future success. Founded in 1776, the year of American Independence, the Phi Beta Kappa Society established itself on American college campuses as a quasi-Masonic secret student society, devoted to philosophy or the love of wisdom.

4.56 Washington Allston
Belshazzar's Feast,
1817–43.
Oil on canvas, 12 ft ½ in x
16 ft ⅛ in (3.67 x 4.88 m).
Detroit Institute of Arts,
Detroit, Michigan.
Gift of the Allston Trust.

In the distant background, tiny figures run along two flights of steps leading to a pagan idol. Allston identified these figures as Jews, who celebrate both the overthrow of idolatry and their prospective return to Jerusalem. The fiery chandelier illuminating the idol represents a competing light source to the foreground's divine light. The enthroned idol echoes the pose of the evil king Belshazzar, whose recoiling body draws him closer to a Satanic serpent, coiled around the post of his throne.

Allston's Phi Beta Kappa key expressed his conservative vision for the development of American culture under the guidance of an intellectual, college-educated elite. Responding to the reality that they had lost control of the American government to the more democratic, populist Jeffersonian Republicans, members of the conservative Federalist Party, such as Allston and his wealthy New England patrons, turned their attention to the cultural battlefield. The *Self-Portrait*'s Phi Beta Kappa key prudently signifies that an artist's imagination should be firmly regulated by learning and the rational love of divine wisdom.

During lengthy residences abroad, Allston started painting large-scale biblical pictures that encouraged audiences to turn their imaginations toward traditional Christian truths and values. But when he returned from Europe to Boston in 1818, he, too, complained of a lack of patronage and the vulgarity of American materialism. After 1815, with the arrival of peace, an entrepreneurial market economy increasingly challenged traditional republican values of civic-minded virtue. As an antidote to the capitalist political economy of private self-interest, Allston returned to the Old Testament imagery of America's colonial past (see fig. 2.14). In 1817, in London, he began his most famous biblical painting, *Belshazzar's Feast* (fig. 4.56). Allston depicted the Jewish prophet Daniel interpreting God's handwritten message, which foretold the doom of the pagan King Belshazzar and his Babylonian empire. According to Allston, Daniel stands in the middle of the picture, "like an animated pillar . . . breathing forth the oracular destruction of the empire!" (cited in Bjelajac, 1988, p. 101).

Over a quarter-century later, when he died in 1843, Allston was still working on this large masterpiece representing the book of Daniel's prophetic tale of divine retribution. The artist had labored upon the painting during the 1820s, only to abandon it in frustration for most of the 1830s. Yet, during the last four years of his life, he sacrificed other commissions to perfect this single painting.

Allston conceived the painting as a visual sermon. Originally inspired by the fall of Napoleon Bonaparte, *Belshazzar* warned Americans against the French Revolution's prideful cult of human reason. The painting expressed the religious fervor of the Second Great Awakening, when evangelical clergymen and laymen's missionary societies called upon Americans to renew their covenant with the Old Testament Jehovah. More than a painting of divine judgment, *Belshazzar* represented the Jews' liberation from their Babylonian captivity, promising their restoration to Jerusalem and their rebuilding of Solomon's Temple. Allston's golden, supernatural light calls attention to the gleaming vessels from the Jewish temple and to a group of grateful Jews, led by reverent women, who bow before Daniel.

Allied with the clergy, women played a crucial role in America's religious revival, not only as organizers of reform societies, but also as exemplars of moral virtue. Stereotypically, women seemed innately drawn toward a religion of the heart. Born-again, conversionary experiences represented Americans' liberation from a spiritual Babylon of material luxury and imperial hubris. Protestants interpreted the restoration of the Jews as a prophetic type for the Christian millennium, when a spiritual Jerusalem would be built in the new American Israel.

Unlike West or Trumbull, Allston refused to memorialize an event in America's national history. Only by turning to the prophetic stories of the Old Testament could he allegorically suggest America's central role in the fulfillment of providential history. *Belshazzar* was collectively funded by a group of Boston merchants who also sponsored such patriotic projects as the Bunker Hill Monument (see p. 162). Allston was on the design committee that chose an Egyptian obelisk to honor the martyred heroes of Bunker Hill. The artist had planned to finish *Belshazzar* in 1825 for the fiftieth anniversary of the battle and for the monument's Masonic cornerstone-laying ceremony, led by the Marquis de Lafayette, the aging French hero of the American Revolution. Allston's representation of Jewish liberation from Babylon fortuitously appealed to Freemasons' legendary ties to the building and rebuilding of Solomon's Temple. But, by continually repainting, Allston failed to finish *Belshazzar*. Gilbert Stuart accurately prophesied to a friend that Allston would never finish it: "Mr. Allston's mind grows by, and beyond his work. What he does in one month, becomes imperfect to the next, by the very growth of his mind" (cited in Bjelajac, 1988, p. 2).

4.57 Washington Allston
Elijah in the Desert, 1817–18.
Oil on canvas, 48¾ x 72½ in (123.8 x 184.1 cm).
Museum of Fine Arts, Boston, Massachusetts. Gift of Mrs. Samuel Hooper and Miss Alice Hooper.

Frustrating his wealthy Boston patrons, Allston increasingly lost faith in the efficacy of biblical symbolism. In one of his many poems, he mused that "Things blank and imageless in human speech / Have oft a truth imperative in might" (cited in Bjelajac, 1988, p. 16). Deeply religious, Allston may have seen a positive moral value in perpetually reworking but never finishing *Belshazzar*. After the artist's death, the Unitarian clergyman C. A. Bartol wrote a sermon based upon Allston's *Belshazzar* asking how is it possible to "turn the Words of the rapt prophet into colors?" (cited in Bjelajac, 1988, p. 16). Arguing against a theology of human perfectionism, Bartol cited the unfinished masterpiece: "The idea is, not that we should grasp perfection as an immediate result, but make it our aim" (cited in Bjelajac, 1988, p. 16). Remarkably, Allston's patrons posthumously exhibited *Belshazzar* in its unfinished state as Christian testament to the artist's spiritual striving.

Far from generating national consensus, biblical pictures aroused contentious debate and traditional Protestant fears of idolatrous image worship. Allston acknowledged this fear in representing a grotesque pagan idol in the background of Belshazzar's Babylonian court. Furthermore, he conceived the picture's divine message in the non-visual terms of a formless handwriting or immaterial light, orally interpreted by the voice of a prophet.

Allston may have halted work upon *Belshazzar* during the late 1820s and 1830s because anti-Masonic and anti-Catholic Protestants were attacking alleged abuses of biblical imagery. Former president John Quincy Adams criticized Masonic initiation ceremonies for theatrically dramatizing Holy Scripture, blaspheming against the pure, incorporeal essence of the Word. Harboring anti-Catholic prejudices, Allston's former student Samuel F. B. Morse (1791–1872), president of New York's National Academy of Design, refused to paint biblical subjects. Morse published a series of letters that accused the papacy of conspiring to subvert the United States by encouraging the emigration of paupers from Catholic Europe. A flood of Catholic icons threatened to undermine Protestants' vision of America as a nation of God's elect.

Meanwhile, a congressional majority opposed the New England clergy's attempts to formally ally the federal government with the Protestant establishment. Shortly after Protestant evangelicals' Sabbatarian movement had failed to halt Sunday mail service, Allston unsuccessfully proposed the three Marys at Christ's tomb for one of the four remaining murals in the U.S. Capitol Rotunda. Admitting his proposal was "a forlorn hope" (cited in Bjelajac, 1988, p. 161), he sought to recast the subject of Christ's Resurrection in the more abstract terms of color and chiaroscuro:

> The . . . preternatural brightness [of the angel] . . . the streak of distant daybreak, lighting the city of Jerusalem out of the darkness, and the deep-toned spell of the chiaroscuro mingling as it were the night with the day, I see now before me; I wish I could see them on the walls at Washington (cited in Bjelajac, 1988, p. 160).

Illuminated by the oculus of the Capitol's dome, Allston's representation of daylight breaking over the skyline of Jerusalem would have symbolized America as the new Jerusalem, bringing the world to the dawn of the millennial age.

Besides *Belshazzar*, Allston painted other Old Testament subjects, but more emphatically subordinated biblical narrative to the suggestive power of paint. In *Elijah in the Desert*, Allston experimented with skim milk as a medium for his pigments, while puzzling his Boston audience by diminishing the size of the hermit-prophet relative to a wilderness landscape (fig. 4.57). According to the clergyman-critic William Ware, the title of the painting raised "false expectations" and "disappointment. . . . when looking upon the picture, no Elijah was to be seen; at least you had to search for him as among the subordinate objects" (cited in Bjelajac, 1992, p. 123).

However, for Allston, the drama of God's Word was embedded in the dense milky brushstrokes overlaid with thin, transparent oil glazes. He employed a system of painting based upon the three primary colors and the combination of all three into tertiary colors—olive, citrine, and russet—to suggest the corresponding harmony of the universe, ruled by a Christian God defined as three persons, Father, Son, and Holy Ghost, in

one Holy Trinity. In *Elijah*, the russet browns and olive greens of the desert wilderness are reflected in the dark clouds above. The milky pigments and golden-yellow highlights in the foreground and middle ground lead the eye in a diagonal zigzag toward the cream-yellow horizon, a blurred margin that unites heaven and earth. Allston's additional mixture of skim milk in this unique painting symbolically evoked St. Peter's admonition in the New Testament: "As newborn babes, desire the sincere milk of the word, that ye may grow thereby" (cited in Bjelajac, 1997, p. 121). Men of learning like Allston associated the Bible's spiritual milk with Sophia or "Sapientia," the female personification of wisdom or of God's luminous Word.

Samuel Morse: The Symbolism of Color and Light

Having been an apprentice in Allston's London studio, Samuel F. B. Morse turned from dramatic narrative paintings toward the philosophical symbolism of color and light. Though he rejected biblical subjects, he insisted with Allston that the mixture of the three primary colors could bear the weight of political and religious truth, proving both the theological doctrine of the Holy Trinity and the providential nature of America's harmonically balanced government.

Inspired by Trumbull's *The Declaration of Independence*, Morse traveled to Washington, D.C., to paint a large exhibition picture, *The Old House of Representatives* (fig. 4.58). Both paintings are group portraits of American legislators and statesmen; but Morse represented the informal scene of a congressional recess rather than the official public actions of a legislative body.

Morse typified the skepticism of conservatives toward the actual practice of American democracy. The artist implicitly contrasted the harmonic architecture of America's tripartite system of government with the dissonant reality of democratic debate and partisan politics. Morse's painting focuses upon the architecture and luminous space of the Capitol as emblematic of America's balance of legislative, executive, and judicial branches of government. Morse had planned two further pictures of the Senate and executive branch. Meanwhile, his nighttime scene of the House illuminates portraits of six Supreme Court justices as well as sixty-eight legislators.

Representing recent diplomatic achievements of the executive branch, Morse also portrayed on the House floor the negotiator of the 1819 treaty with Spain that ceded Florida to the United States. At the far right of Morse's painting, sitting in the visitors' gallery, Petalesharo, chief of the Pawnee Indians, gazes quietly upon the scene below as a guest of President James Monroe, with whom he had signed a peace treaty. By including these two figures, Morse optimistically suggests that an expanding American empire might be peacefully accepted by awed, Christianized Indians. In 1820, the year before Morse undertook *The House of Representatives*, Congress had passed the Missouri Compromise, which allowed Missouri to enter the union as a slave state, counterbalancing Maine's entrance as a free state. Morse's painting represented an apparent moment of political harmony. The contentious issue of slavery dividing the North from the slave states in the South temporarily receded from congressional debate. Within the

happy spirit of a national recess from bitter sectional conflict, the central action of Morse's painting is not the passage of legislation, but the lighting of the chandelier that casts a golden glow over the House interior, as if it were the heavenly temple of Jerusalem descended to earth. Colossal, multicolored columns support this semicircular, Solomonic space. The architect of the House's chamber, Benjamin Latrobe, had chosen a native outcropping of breccia, a polychromatic conglomerate stone, for the column shafts. Quarried from the banks of the Potomac River, the geological conglomeration of differently colored rocks and stones embodied the national motto of "e pluribus unum" (one out of many), the animating theme for the federal union of states and for the design of the U.S. Capitol as a whole (see p. 126). Like Allston, Morse would have recalled Leonardo da Vinci's advice to young painters in finding order and unity from nature's random patterns and colors. The commingled colors of the veined breccia columns reflect the golden

4.58 Samuel F. B. Morse
The Old House of Representatives, 1822. Oil on canvas, 86½ x 130¾ in (219.7 x 332.1 cm). The Corcoran Gallery of Art, Washington, D.C.

Morse's painting celebrates the restoration of the United States Capitol after its burning by the British during the War of 1812. The old House of Representatives chamber, now serving as Statuary Hall, was rebuilt by Charles Bulfinch according to the original design of Benjamin Latrobe. Morse carefully painted the half-domed space supported by tall Corinthian columns. The powerful sweeping lines of the chamber's cornice contribute to the pictorial unity and grandeur of the composition.

light from the central chandelier and serve as the symbolic, Herculean pillars of the Union.

Despite his hopes for profitable exhibition in various American cities, Morse's emblematic painting failed to excite the public. In contrast to the popular sensationalism of Rembrandt Peale's *The Court of Death* (see fig. 4.49), *The House of Representatives* silently mirrored the American elite's ideal world of polite sociability. Only by representing a recess in congressional debate could Morse represent a unified body politic. Members of opposing parties and different regions harmoniously mix together in private conversation. Morse's grand architectural salon suggests that national unity is dependent upon the private cultivation of genteel manners. In his universe, the age of revolution and heroic self-sacrifice has been superseded by the polite arts of cultural domestication.

During the early nineteenth century, as a new professional class of politicians rose to displace the traditional aristocracy from public office, American artists also attempted to establish their own professional independence from both patrons and the people. Despite his failure as a history painter, Morse led American artists in establishing the National Academy of Design in 1825. Intended to educate both future artists and the public at large, the academy's founding virtually coincided with the opening of the Erie Canal. The canal immediately elevated New York to its position of economic and cultural power, connecting the city to the commercial wealth of westward expansion. Aided by art academies that claimed to be national and American, New York artists, critics, and patrons successfully promoted a nationalist art that masked northeastern entrepreneurs' economic interest in western development. As we shall see in the next chapter, artists optimistically represented the expanding American landscape, its pioneers, and diverse inhabitants in the millennialist terms of an undivided nation that surmounted narrow self-interest.

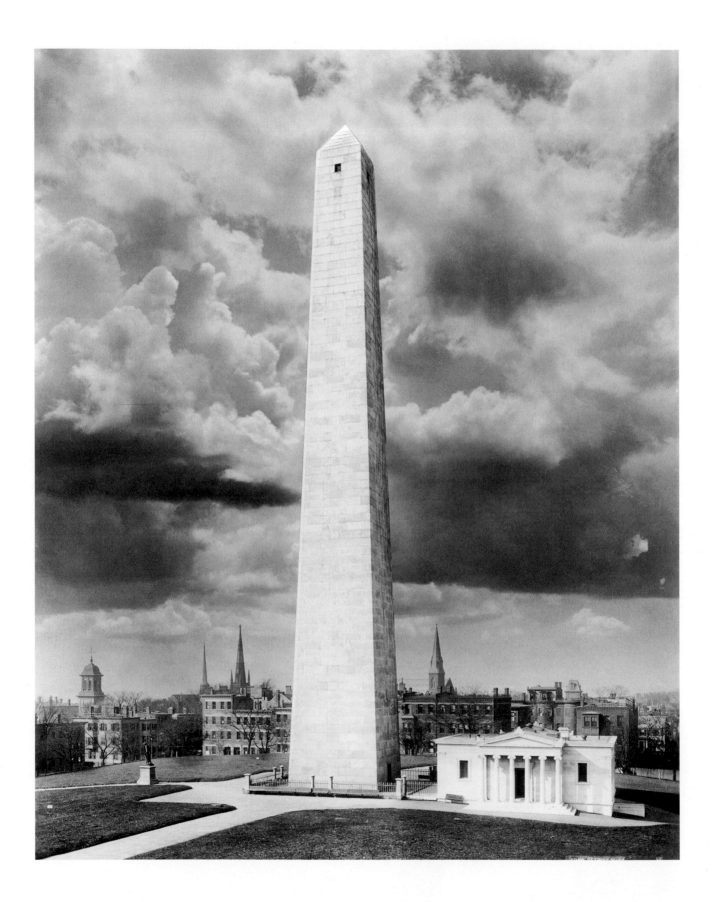

Chapter 5

National Identity and Private Interests in Antebellum America
1825–65

Bunker Hill Monument
Charlestown, Massachusetts, 1825–43.
Library of Congress.

Horatio Greenough originally conceived the Egyptian obelisk form for this Revolutionary War monument. The young sculptor later wrote that the ancient form probably had originated for some astronomical purpose, although he also readily conceded the obelisk's phallic associations as a symbol for patriarchal power. In building the monument, planners took into account the structure's relationship to the earth's rotation around the sun and how it would be seen from great distances in the Boston area.

A NEW era in the American visual arts began in 1825 as painters, sculptors, and architects searched for a national style distinguished from European tradition. That year, Americans commemorated the fiftieth anniversary of the opening battles of the American Revolution, but, more importantly, they celebrated the opening of the Erie Canal, which facilitated the nation's expansion westward. The devastation of the Civil War from 1861 to 1865 marked the era's terminal point, when the new invention of photography brutally recorded the war's battlefields and a nation divided between North and South. In retrospect, antebellum, or pre-Civil War, American art scarcely masked the growing chasm between Northern and Southern states.

During this four-decade period, American expansion toward the Pacific Ocean motivated artists' quest for national forms of expression, while politically dividing North and South further over the spread of slavery to new western territories and states. Expansionist ideology was sustained by venture capitalists and evangelical Christians, who assumed that the private pursuit of wealth and the conquest of the West would translate into national happiness, as long as America remained a Protestant nation governed by white Anglo-Saxon men.

Art patrons who grew wealthy from canal and railroad construction, textile factories, and the commercialization of agriculture promoted paintings and sculptures replete with moral messages. Decorating private homes and public spaces, these works reminded beholders that domestic prosperity still depended upon individual virtue and a national covenant with God. Sculptors and painters expressed faith in American exceptionalism, which taught that Americans were God's new chosen people,

succeeding the ancient Israelites of the Old Testament.

In addition to the popular national analogies with Old Testament Israel, historical-revival architecture—whether Greek-Revival, Gothic-Revival, or some other revival style— conservatively situated antebellum Americans within a settled New World landscape that symbolized the fulfillment of Western civilization. State capitols, banks, and even textile towns were designed to evoke reassuring associations with classical Greece, Rome, and Renaissance Italy. With the nation's population nearly quadrupling between 1814 and 1860 to over 31 million, cities grew denser with foreign immigrants. During this period, 5 million people arrived in the United States, approximately half from England and four-fifths of the remainder from Ireland. The tide of immigrants rose during the 1830s and 1840s, cresting in 1854, when nearly 428,000 arrived. The Irish potato famine of 1845–8 contributed to a flood of impoverished people seeking new lives in American towns. The first American suburbs were built by middle- and upper-class families seeking a semirural refuge from the urban poor and working classes. The American suburb originated in the genteel taste for country estates, rural cemeteries, and architecture that appeared rooted in nature and the pre-industrial past.

Even before the completion of the Erie Canal in 1825, New York City, with a population exceeding 125,000, had surpassed Philadelphia as the nation's largest metropolis. Aided by its strategic location for shipping and transportation, New York had become the commercial and financial capital of the United States, fueling its imperial aspirations. A magnet for immigrants and entrepreneurs, New York, or the "Empire City" as it became known, experienced a nearly seven-fold population increase during the next three-and-a-half decades. On the eve of the Civil War, well over 800,000 were living in New York City, as Manhattan became subject to an expanding grid of city streets and avenues.

While Americans industrialized and expanded westward, artists organized themselves professionally and socially. By establishing art academies and exhibition spaces, they assumed leadership roles in American culture. To distinguish themselves from mere craftsmen and manual laborers, many artists claimed the magical, godlike powers of genius. Writing to his sister from Rome, the New York sculptor Thomas Crawford (1813–57) described in 1839 his ideal sculpture, representing Orpheus rushing through the gates of hell (fig. 5.1):

5.1 Thomas Crawford
Orpheus, 1839–43.
Marble, 67½ in
(171.4 cm) high.
Museum of Fine Arts,
Boston, Massachusetts,
on loan from the Boston
Athenaeum.

> *I am writing in the midst of a terrible thunder storm, and can scarcely proceed, for the incessant flashes of lightning which dart every moment into the window of my studio: my statue of Orpheus is before me, and when I look upon it in the midst of this thick darkness, which is brightened occasionally by a glare of rapid red light, it is difficult to persuade myself, that this inanimate creation of mine is not starting from its pedestal, and actually rushing into the realms of Pluto. The thunder is getting really awful, and I must stop to compose myself. I have been thinking of the story about Phidias and his wonderful statue of Jove. You know that upon finishing it, he requested some sign from the god, to know if he were pleased with the representation; it seems the nod was given, for at that moment the statue was circled by lightning, which came and passed off with such a noise as could only be produced by heaven's artillery. Were we living in that age, or were ours the religion of the ancient Greeks, I too might interpret the sign in my favor (cited in Dimmick, pp. 54–56).*

Crawford's dramatic account sounds a note of envy for the ancient Greek sculptor's confident ability to represent and communicate with the most powerful god. In antebellum America, Crawford and other artists were forced to contend with an even more demanding critic, a fractious public schooled in Protestant and republican fears of art's sensual, immoral effects. Crawford's *Orpheus* was a commission for the Boston Athenaeum, a private library and art gallery for the city's wealthiest patrons and most sophisticated connoisseurs. Yet Crawford felt compelled to accommodate American prudishness by providing a fig leaf to cover Orpheus's genitals. Furthermore, like many other American artists, he still looked to Europe for his art education and inspiration. Lacking adequate teaching academies and museums in the United States, aspiring sculptors established studios in Florence and Rome to create an expatriate school of American marble sculpture.

In searching for an independent American style and subject matter, some artists chose not to travel abroad. For instance, early in his career, Thomas Crawford had been apprenticed to the New York sculptor John Frazee (1790–1852), who never voyaged to Europe. Frazee later criticized fellow sculptors who decided to reside abroad. Expressing, perhaps, his own professional jealousy, he claimed that these expatriates, such as his arch rival Horatio Greenough, were in danger of losing their American identities, becoming virtually indistinguishable from the many foreign artists also competing for major government commissions in the United States. Born to a working-class family and himself the father of some twenty children, Frazee's responsibilities and limited funds militated against an expensive, time-consuming transatlantic course of study. He progressed from working in the building and decorative stonecarving trades to becoming a fine-arts sculptor, specializing in marble, neoclassical portraits of leading American businessmen, statesmen, and men of learning. Regarding himself as an American pioneer in the art of sculpture, Frazee was, in 1825, the sole sculptor among the cadre of artists founding New York City's National Academy of Design, the nation's only art academy operated by, and for the benefit of, American artists rather than art collectors. Two years later, at the academy's second annual exhibition, he displayed a plaster *Self-Portrait* (fig. 5.3), inspired by a copy of an ancient Greek portrait bust representing Alexander the Great. Frazee thus compared his own working-class genius with the famed world conqueror of antiquity. Furthermore, at the base of the *Self-Portrait*,

he inscribed his name and lines in Latin that translate as "He himself made it in the fifty-second year of American Liberty" (Voorsanger and Howat, p.138). The inscription identified its creator with the nation's Founding Fathers and celebrated the anniversary of the American Revolution as a declaration of cultural independence from Great Britain and Europe.

For some American artists, the nation's very soil seemed to hold the key to cultural independence and individual creative genius. The Long Island, New York, painter William Sidney Mount (1807–68) not only resisted travel abroad, he also avoided as much as possible the use of foreign, imported pigments for his pictures of Long Island scenery and daily life. Beginning during the 1830s, after becoming a full member of the National Academy of Design, Mount persistently experimented with indigenous Long Island pigments. He apparently believed that native materials, extracted from the island's sandstones and beach dunes, would better enable him to capture the local color, light, and atmosphere of his home environment. From 1825 until the advent of the Civil War,

5.2 William Sidney Mount
Eel Spearing at Setauket, 1845.
Oil on canvas,
28½ x 36 in
(72.39 x 91.44 cm).
Fenimore Art Museum.
New York State Historical Association, Cooperstown, New York.

Mount's active, armed slave contrasts with the relatively passive African sailor in Copley's *Watson and the Shark* (see fig. 4.28). Both paintings suggestively express the revolutions or cycles of nature, as signified by dark, hidden, serpentine creatures contrasting with luminous horizons.

American nationalism expressed itself in terms of a diverse unity of specific locales and regional cultures, interconnected by new systems of transportation and communication. However, Mount's sunlit pictures of Long Island's rural life were also purposeful political statements that expressed the fatal disharmony within this national union of local cultures.

One of the artist's most famous pictures, *Eel Spearing at Setauket* (fig. 5.2), was painted for George Washington Strong (1783–1855), a wealthy New York lawyer, who wanted a nostalgic picture that represented his boyhood on the north shore of eastern Long Island. St. George's Manor, the Strong family estate, appears on the horizon. In the foreground, a family slave stands in a rowboat offshore, accompanied by the young George and his pet dog. Mount represented the aging female slave in the traditional pose of St. George, the dragonslayer of medieval legend, as she prepares to slay an eel, a modern, Long Island substitute for the mythic dragon. The artist intended a humorous visual pun, as the African-American woman merely foreshadows the bright future of little "St. George," her young master, who intently gazes toward the impending thrust of the spear, thereby preparing himself to become lord of St. George's Manor.

Mount's Long Island family also possessed slaves, and *Eel Spearing at Setauket* evoked the artist's own personal boyhood memories of how an old slave once taught him to spear eels. Since eels tend to hide and camouflage themselves at the bottom of sandy, gravelly water beds, spear fishing educated Mount's eye in distinguishing the subtle variety of nature's colors, better preparing him for his later professional excavations of native pigments, buried within Long Island's sandy shores. One can assume that *Eel Spearing at Setauket* was painted with at least some native pigments, so that the artist was not simply re-presenting a scene of Long Island life. The painting literally *is* Long Island, being composed of its actual soil or material elements.

Surprisingly, given Mount's general popular success as a painter, *Eel Spearing at Setauket* received a mixed reception from contemporary New Yorkers. Even the patron's son disliked the painting, perhaps because he was embarrassed by his distinguished father's youthful apprenticeship to an old slave. In placing an armed black slave at

5.3 John Frazee
Self-Portrait, 1727. Plaster, 23 in (58.4 cm), high. National Portrait Gallery, Smithsonian Institution, Washington D.C.

the apex of the composition, Mount's picture violated the popular consensus of a divinely ordained social hierarchy. Indeed, the painting's smooth, crystalline surface and stable, compositional geometry seems to freeze this violation into a permanent state. Despite his humorous intent, Mount aroused fears as well as smiles and nervous laughter. In the racially charged atmosphere of antebellum America, even an elderly African-American woman wielding a fishing spear could spark discordant notes and call into question the stability and authenticity of the nation's self-identification as God's chosen people.

American artists were not godlike geniuses who could expect universal critical assent to their art. Individual creativity negotiated its claims for recognition with an expanding audience, whose conflicting tastes represented the development of an increasingly pluralistic society. Rather than grandiose mythological or historical subjects, Mount chose to paint luminous scenes from everyday life, which he could more easily market to a broad audience seeking expressions of regional and national harmony. However, despite the optimistic, consensual rhetoric of mainstream American culture, dissenting voices resisted easy assimilation into nationalist ideology. Religious nonconformists, feminists, abolitionists, and other reformers and radicals challenged the exclusionary limits of the nation's fragile union.

Historical Styles and Functional Architecture

During the spring and summer months of 1825, Americans celebrated the fiftieth anniversary of the American Revolution, as the aging Marquis de Lafayette toured the nation's cities and towns. Lafayette had first endeared himself to American patriots in 1777 by leaving France and volunteering for service in the revolutionary army. He had sacrificed his comfortable life as a wealthy aristocrat to fight for liberty under the command of George Washington, who became a kind of father figure to the young Frenchman. After the war, Lafayette expressed his continuing friendship with Washington by giving the American general a Masonic apron. Now, five decades after the battles of Lexington, Concord, and Bunker Hill, the French general had returned to receive the accolades of grateful United States citizens. In city after city, he led parades and cornerstone-laying ceremonies for numerous public buildings and patriotic memorials such as the Bunker Hill Monument overlooking Boston Harbor (see p. 162).

Made of granite from a local quarry in Quincy, Massachusetts, the Bunker Hill obelisk was constructed as a patriotic synthesis of ancient wisdom and modern Yankee ingenuity. As in the Great Seal of the United States (see fig. 4.18), an Egyptian pyramidal form tapers upward toward a central point, drawing downward the enlightening rays of God's providential eye. At the same time, the monument was made possible by modern processes of industrialization. Solomon Willard (1783–1861), elected the monument's architect in 1825, operated the Quincy granite quarry as a modern, mechanized system of stonecutting and handling that helped to revolutionize the building trades. The monument in turn inspired construction of the first railroad in the United States, linking the granite quarries of Quincy with the commercial shipping wharves of Massachusetts Bay.

Stone construction could create a more monumental effect for public buildings than wood or red brick. Alexander Parris (1789–1852), who prepared the cornerstone for the Bunker Hill Monument, employed large blocks of Quincy granite for Boston's new Faneuil Hall Market, popularly known as Quincy Market, in

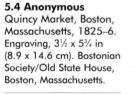

5.4 Anonymous
Quincy Market, Boston, Massachusetts, 1825–6. Engraving, 3½ x 5¾ in (8.9 x 14.6 cm). Bostonian Society/Old State House, Boston, Massachusetts.

the harbor district (fig. 5.4). The market's central building was designed with Greek-Revival façades at both ends of its long, rectangular plan. Extending beyond the façade, the market's main shopping arcade was defined by a granite skeleton of massive piers and lintels, framing two stories of windows. The functional plan was divided by a central block, capped by a low, circular dome. Two-story Doric columns support triangular pediments to create the image of a sanctified temple for commerce. Boston merchants habitually defined their investments and private interests in terms of civic virtue or the public good.

Ever since the eighteenth century, Americans had learned to associate the ancient Greek city-states with the origins of republican government and of Western civilization and the arts. The clarity, simplicity, and symmetry of classical Greek architecture symbolized those personal qualities of strength, wisdom, self-discipline, and eloquence, regarded as necessary for citizens to govern themselves. The fashion for Greek rather than Roman classicism was more immediately stimulated by the struggle of modern Greece for political independence from the Turks. The conflict, which lasted over a decade from 1821 until 1833, captured the European and American imaginations. While touring the United States in 1824–5, the Marquis de Lafayette repeatedly toasted contemporary Greek heroes as genuine descendants of ancient Spartan warriors and praised Greece itself as the birthplace of the arts and sciences.

By 1825, Boston was no longer a town where the wealthy and learned few could assume paternalistic leadership roles in town meetings at Faneuil Hall, the eighteenth-century building adjacent to Quincy Market. Serving a growing city of 50,000, Quincy Market was named for Boston's mayor, Josiah Quincy (1772–1864), who attained office by appealing to the "Middling Interest" (Cayton, pp. 143–167) of shopkeepers and artisans. The austere geometry of Quincy Market's spare Doric order, the oldest order of Greek temple architecture, spoke to middle-class Americans' taste for republican simplicity and rational order.

In 1824, Quincy sat for a portrait by the elderly Gilbert Stuart, who represented the energetic mayor next to a view of the proposed

market (fig. 5.5). In his hands, Quincy holds a drawing for the plan and elevation of the new building. Like his uncle Samuel Quincy, who had commissioned portraits from the hand of John Singleton Copley (see fig. 3.30), Mayor Quincy was a Freemason, having joined St. John's Lodge of Boston in 1795. For Masons in particular, classical stone architecture expressed enlightened thought, refined taste, and high moral values. Complementing the geometric clarity of the market's design, Stuart painted a fluid, brilliantly illuminated portrait, with Quincy's ruddy face reflecting sunlight against a bright-blue sky. Because the market would be constituted from Quincy granite, the building façade in the background also functioned as a highly personal emblem. In 1792, the nearby town of Quincy, Massachusetts, had been named after Josiah Quincy's wealthy and distinguished family. The

5.5 Gilbert Stuart
Portrait of Josiah Quincy,
1824.
Oil on canvas,
36⅛ x 28⅛ in
(91.4 x 71.1 cm).
Museum of Fine Arts,
Boston, Massachusetts.
Gift of Miss Eliza Susan
Quincy.

During the time he painted this portrait of Boston's newly elected mayor, the ageing Stuart suffered a severe stroke, which resulted in his left arm being partially paralyzed. Nevertheless, he completed the picture, one of the last before his death in 1828.

mayor's ancestors had been among the early-seventeenth-century settlers of Massachusetts Bay Colony, and his father, also named Josiah Quincy (1744–75), had been a celebrated American patriot during the years leading up to the Revolutionary War. Seated next to a stone column dramatically entwined with a rose-colored drapery, Mayor Quincy is posed as a wise and strong pillar of city government, representing a family that helped build Massachusetts and the new nation.

The popularity of austere geometric forms for commercial enterprises, government offices, and private homes contributed to a modern, functionalist aesthetic in architecture. The sculptor Horatio Greenough (1805–52) became a leading spokesman for a national architecture, which taught that form should follow naturally from a building's function. Casting his argument in seafaring terms that practical American merchants could readily grasp, Greenough urged his readers in an 1843 journal article to:

> Observe a ship at sea! Mark the majestic form of her hull as she rushes through the water, observe the graceful bend of her body, the gentle transition from round to flat, the grasp of her keel, the leap of her bows, the symmetry and rich tracery of her spars and rigging, and those grand wind muscles, her sails. Behold an organization second only to that of an animal, obedient as the horse, swift as the stag, and bearing the burden of a thousand camels from pole to pole! What academy of design, what research of connoisseurship, what imitation of the Greeks produced this marvel of construction? Here is the result of the study of man upon the great deep, where Nature spake of the laws of building, not in the feather and in the flower, but in winds and waves, and he bent all his mind to hear and to obey. Could we carry into our civil architecture the responsibilities that weigh upon our shipbuilding, we should ere long have edifices as superior to the Parthenon, for the purposes that we require. . . . Instead of forcing the functions of every sort of building into one general form, adopting an outward shape for the sake of the eye or of association, without reference to the inner distribution, let us begin from the heart as the nucleus, and work outward (cited in Greenough, pp. 60–62).

Greenough conceived buildings in terms of nature rather than historical styles and associations. The study of Greek, Roman, or any other period architecture was valuable only insofar as it revealed the functional, organic principles of construction, which Greenough termed "the law of adaptation . . . the fundamental law of nature in all structure" (cited in Greenough, p. 58). In truth, Greenough's aesthetic was indebted to British architectural theory, yet the emphasis upon nature and utility struck a particularly resonant chord among American builders.

Responding to the growing social needs of an urbanizing mass society, American architects were already developing a functional aesthetic during the 1820s and 1830s, even if building exteriors were ornamented with historical motifs. In Philadelphia, the English-born architect John Haviland (1792–1852) designed the Eastern State Penitentiary in the guise of a medieval castle with octagonal turrets, battlemented towers, and massive black ashlar walls (fig. 5.6).

Haviland's imposing castle-prison anticipated Greenough's organic principle that the architect should work outward from the heart or nucleus. Haviland devised a radial plan stemming from a central rotunda or guards' tower. Like spokes from the hub of a wheel, seven elongated blocks, containing a series of eight-by-ten-foot cells, radiated outward toward the prison walls. Under surveillance from the central watchtower, prisoners were expected to communicate only with their consciences, which were instructed by a Bible left in each isolated cell.

Creating an institution that controlled the movements of inmates through time and space, prison officials in Philadelphia, Boston, and other cities were in the vanguard, promoting a "moral architecture" (Rothman, p. 84) for modifying human behavior. During the early years of the republic, the Founding Fathers expressed concern that democratic federal and state governments would be unable to restrain the anarchic tendencies of a geographically dispersed mass society. The managerial aspiration to control the living environment through the fine and useful arts preoccupied American educators. According to the Philadelphia man of letters Benjamin Rush (1746–1813), education made it "possible to convert men into republican

BIRDS EYE VIEW OF THE NEW STATE PENITENTIARY, NOW ERECTING NEAR PHILADELPHIA

5.6 John Haviland
Eastern State Penitentiary, 1821–37.
Engraving by C. G. Childs.
Historical Society of Pennsylvania, Philadelphia.

machines. This must be done," he said, "if we expect them to perform their parts properly, in the great machine of the government of the state" (cited in Cremin, p. 118).

Between 1825 and 1865, new technology forced the fine arts to compete with the mechanical or useful arts for public admiration. In struggling for professional recognition from practical-minded Americans, artists attempted, often vainly, to distinguish themselves from engineers, mechanics, and inventors, who magically transformed American life before the Civil War.

Economic Modernization and the Arts

By the autumn of 1825, national commemoration of the opening battles of the American Revolution gave way to the grand opening of the Erie Canal, which marked a revolution in transportation and facilitated new settlements in the West. Public discourse shifted from retrospection over the revolutionary Founding Fathers to prophecies of the nation's future westward expansion.

In Albany, New York, on the cold and blustery morning of November 2, 1825, a flotilla of boats arrived at the last lock of the newly completed Erie Canal. A week earlier, the flotilla had departed from Buffalo, New York, on Lake Erie, the canal's western point of origin. Throughout the inaugural procession of canal boats, cities and towns celebrated with parades, speeches, and festive street decorations. In Albany, Governor DeWitt Clinton, the canal's principal advocate, was among the thousands of spectators who witnessed a Masonic ceremony marking the completion of a commemorative canal monument. Afterward, the boats glided through the last canal lock and into the Hudson River. Two days later, on November 4, the journey ended in New York City with a climactic street parade to greet the flotilla. Every tradesmen's association marched together next to gigantic floats, decorated with emblematic murals and symbols. Demonstrating the public's keen familiarity with the visual language of classical antiquity, boys attending the Printers' Society float wore the winged costume of Mercury, Roman god of transportation, commerce, and the arts and sciences.

In *The Erie Canal Celebration, New York, 1825* (fig. 5.7), Anthony Imbert (1794–1834), a French-born artist, represented the conclusion of the festivities, when an American fleet of ships and boats saluted the arrival of two British naval ships. Imbert's painting was actually purchased by one of the British ship captains. In cultural, social and economic terms, Great Britain's ties to the United States remained a dominating force, as more than half of all immigrants arriving in the United States during the 1820s were from the British Isles. British commercial and manufacturing interests also undoubtedly regarded the Erie Canal as a golden opportunity for expanding trade with an American nation, whose population was still primarily agrarian and whose vast territories were largely undeveloped beyond the eastern seaboard.

In addition to this painting, Imbert supplied some thirty-seven illustrations of *The Erie Canal Celebration* for an official New York City *Memoir* of the festivities, written by Cadwallader Colden, a former mayor. For this project, Imbert employed the revolutionary new technique of lithography, first invented in Germany during the late 1790s. Imbert was instrumental in helping to popularize this radically simplified printing medium in the United States. Unlike other print processes, which require more labor and training, lithography enabled artists to draw quickly on a flat stone surface, using only a greasy pen or crayon. Once the image is fixed by a coating of gum Arabic and nitric acid, the stone is dampened with water. Based upon the principle that oil and water do not mix, when printer's ink is rolled over this wetted stone, the oily, greasy ink will adhere only to the greasy drawing, not to the stone's unmarked, wet surface. The inked stone is finally covered with paper and passed through a press to print a mirror copy of the drawn image.

While Imbert generally only produced a small edition of fifty to one hundred prints per drawn image, potentially thousands of high-quality prints could be reproduced from the durable, planar surface of the lithographic stone. By contrast, copper plates for engravings and mezzotints were especially prone to wear, so that earlier printed impressions were distinctly superior in definition to later ones. Anticipating the mass reproductive power of photography, lithography promised a revolution in visual communications. Indeed, Archibald Robertson, a New York City drawing teacher who collaborated with Imbert in the new medium, claimed that lithography's importance and utility was comparable to the invention of the steamboat, two decades earlier, by the American artist

and engineer Robert Fulton (1765–1815).

Coincidentally, a hand-colored lithograph of a catastrophic steamboat disaster in Long Island Sound helped bolster the fame of Nathaniel Currier (1813–88), whose later partnership with James Ives (1824–95) in 1857 transformed lithographic practice into a veritable factory-like industry of assembly-line designing, printing, and handcoloring, coupled with a national marketing system of direct mail-ordering, branch showrooms, and salesmen. The Currier and Ives firm lasted fifty years and mass produced lithographs representing thousands of different popular subjects. As evident by the success of Currier's *Awful Conflagration of the Steamboat "Lexington"* (fig. 5.8), topical disaster pictures sold particularly well and were imaginatively composed for maximum dramatic effect and marketability. Currier's intense contrast of orange-red flames and smoke with the silvery blue of moonlit sky and water is emotionally evocative and far from mere reportage. Unlike the celebratory Imbert painting, Currier's lithograph is a sober moral warning against overweening American pride in the power of technology and human progress. A couple of male figures floating upon makeshift rafts or debris in the foreground are still neatly wearing their expensive suits and top hats, thereby signifying their upper-class status and heightening the notion of a sudden reversal of fortune.

In general, however, sensational disaster pictures did little to shake Americans' faith in technology and the mechanical arts. With many beginning their careers as artisans or craftsmen, American artists prior to the Civil War often found themselves working to commemorate popular inventions or useful improvements to city and country life. Contemporaneous with the Erie Canal festivities, in Philadelphia, William Rush (1756–1833), one of the founders of the Pennsylvania Academy of Fine Arts, also celebrated the harnessing of water power. Rush carved two sculptures from Spanish cedar for the Fairmount Waterworks in 1825. He painted both of them white to simulate marble or stone. *The Schuylkill Enchained* (fig. 5.9) represents a bearded river god, who is chained to his bed of rocks by the uncontrolled rapids of the Schuylkill River. *The Schuylkill Freed* represents a seated woman, dressed in classical clothing, who

5.7 Anthony Imbert
The Erie Canal Celebration, New York, 1825, 1825–6.
Oil on canvas, 24 x 45 in (60.9 x 114.3 cm).
Museum of the City of New York. Anonymous Gift.

personifies the waterworks, or the taming of the river, through modern technology (fig. 5.10). She serenely tends a waterwheel and conduit that allow the water to run "freely" for human needs. Behind her, the water flows into a classical urn, symbolizing the Fairmount reservoir. Rush's sculptures expressed the entrepreneurial conviction that nature must not lie dormant or undeveloped. Only through civilization may Mother Nature realize her true potential. For urban developers and advocates of cultural refinement, she was freest when she served humanity, God's highest form of being in the visible hierarchy of creation.

Industrialization and a growing national transportation network of canals and railroads forced formerly self-sufficient yeoman farmers into growing cash crops for sale in distant mar-

5.8 Nathaniel Currier
Awful Conflagration of the Steamboat "Lexington", 1840.
Lithograph with hand coloring. American Anitquarian Society, Worcester, Massachusetts.

5.9 William Rush
The Schuylkill Enchained,
1825.
White-painted Spanish cedar, 39⅜ x 87¼ x 26⁷⁄₁₆ in (100 x 221.6 x 67 cm).
Philadelphia Museum of Art, Philadelphia.
Commissioners of Fairmount Park, Philadelphia.

The pained expression and uncomfortable pose of the aged male figure suggests the ancient Schuylkill River's unproductive, wild character. By contrast, the old man is accompanied by a vibrant American eagle. Undoubtedly inspired by the imagery of the Great Seal of the United States the eagle, with outspread wings, promises national progress and the river's liberation from uncontrolled nature.

kets. Unlucky farmers who became indebted to city bankers often failed to survive the volatility of the market. Many entered factories or workshops as wage laborers, while others decided to move further west, where land was cheaper and more plentiful. In New England, Boston industrialists purposely chose rural sites for textile factories, better enabling them to recruit the daughters of financially strapped farm families to operate mill machinery.

Thomas Doughty (1793–1856), one of the earliest artists to specialize in landscape painting,

depicted the new mill town of Lowell, Massachusetts, as a quiet, pastoral utopia of factory buildings and obelisk-like smokestacks surrounded by trees and placid waterways (fig. 5.11). With factory labor well hidden from view, the standing boatman in the foreground seems reminiscent of a gondolier navigating a Venetian canal. Seeking to create industrial communities that evaded Britain's history of labor strife and overcrowded manufacturing cities, Boston capitalists financed company towns that amazed British and European tourists. Compared with

5.10 William Rush
The Schuylkill Freed,
1825.
White-painted Spanish cedar, 39⅜ x 87¼ x 26⁷⁄₁₆ in (100 x 221.6 x 67 cm).
Philadelphia Museum of Art, Philadelphia.
Commissioners of Fairmount Park, Philadelphia.

The woman's youth and grace suggest that the Schuylkill River has been channeled and elevated into a higher plane of being. Striking a relaxed pose, the figure's horizontally extended arm seems in turn to mirror and calm the river below. Her hand appears to bless the waterwheel. Like a cornucopia of plenty, the diagonally tilted water main behind her promises a bountiful supply of water for productive human purposes.

5.11 Thomas Doughty
*Mill Pond and Mills,
Lowell, Massachusetts,*
c. 1833.
Oil on canvas,
26 x 35½ in
(66 x 90.2 cm).
Harvard Business School,
Cambridge,
Massachusetts.

Doughty's atmospheric view of this early factory town's terrain contains no suggestion of industrially polluted air or water. The water's mirrorlike reflections of trees and buildings reinforce the impression of order and balance between man and nature.

Britain's polluted industrial cities, pastoral Lowell during the 1820s and 1830s appeared to be a workers' paradise brightly lit by what one tourist described as soot-free "Italian skies" (cited in Josephson, p. 183). Most astonishing for European eyes, young women operated the textile mill machinery. Boston industrialists assumed that unmarried daughters of New England farmers constituted a more manageable and cheaper labor force than male workers. Nevertheless, young women took advantage of factory work to free themselves from the restrictions of family life. In 1848, the year that the first women's rights convention was held in Seneca Falls, New York, the Vermont-born mill operative Margaret Foley (c.1827–77) left Lowell's textile factories for Boston and a career as a sculptor. Yet she maintained contact with the Lowell community and received a portrait commission from a local Lowell hospital. Moving to Rome in 1860, Foley joined other American women artists in producing neoclassical marble sculptures. Foley's austere portrait bust *Cleopatra* represents the ancient, Greek-born queen of Egypt (fig. 5.12). Exhibited in Philadelphia at the 1876 centennial celebration of American independence, *Cleopatra* metaphorically expressed the former Lowell operative's assertion of feminine power and independence. Foley's career path suggests that the northeast's capitalist economy was generating a more mobile labor force and new professional opportunities in its major cities. Benefiting from the economic boom generated by canal-building and then railroads, an increasing number of private academies and schools for girls and women in the United States taught drawing and painting as genteel, refined accomplishments. Most often, watercolor was the preferred painting medium for young women, since it was associated with the middle- and upper-class world of amateur, leisure-time pursuits. Watercolor was also devoted primarily to small-scale pictures, suitable for humble or private, sentimental subjects. Students of female academies learned to draw and paint by copying popular prints. Beyond these girls' academies, women were not generally encouraged to develop their artistic talents professionally with more formal training, though New York's National Academy of Design did begin to admit women into classes by 1846.

In upstate New York, Fanny A. Coney (1814–38), the product of a private female academy, based her watercolor *A View of Skeneatless Village* (fig. 5.13) upon an illustration from an 1830 issue of *Ariel Magazine*, published in Philadelphia. Situated on one of the Finger Lakes, in Onandaga County, New York, this village was just one of the many towns that blossomed in the Great Lakes region, thanks to the opening of the Erie Canal. Views of the new towns and villages, accompanied by local histories, were widely published in documenting or promoting the Canal's impact upon national expansion and prosperity. The daughter of a New England family that had moved westward, Fanny Coney may have been alluding to her impending marriage when she altered the scene by adding a well-dressed couple, standing arm in arm in the left foreground. Yet, more broadly, the couple's fashionable presence also reassuringly suggests the cultural refinement of newly settled boom towns and villages.

Complicating New England manufacturers' search for an adequate labor force, the Erie Canal lured restless New England farm families to western New York and the Great Lakes, where land was cheaper, more abundant, and more productive. However, farmers were also lured by supernatural tales and folk legends to search for

buried treasure in the territory opened up by the canal. In 1831 a Palmyra, New York, newspaper reported that "money-digging" had become a "mania" (cited in Taylor, pp. 8–9). The following year, John Quidor (1801–81), a New York painter who specialized in scenes of Hudson River folk legends, produced a Gothic-comic picture entitled *Money Diggers* (fig. 5.14). Basing the painting upon a short story by the New York author Washington Irving (1783–1859), Quidor represents a nocturnal hunt in Long Island for a pirate's buried treasure. The hunt has been comically interrupted by the pirate's ghost in the upper-right corner, frightening the three money diggers. At the upper rim of the picture's central black hole, a divining rod and a book of magical incantations have fallen to the ground. While Quidor caricatures the figures for maximum comic effect, his painterly representation of moonlit earth, rocks, and trees suggests a shared belief in the animistic, spiritual powers hidden within Nature. Economically marginal farmers who failed to adapt to the modernization of agriculture were especially prone to seek quick fixes for their mortgaged farms. Treasure hunting was a byproduct of the economic booms and busts that jarred traditional folk ways and farming methods, especially in western New York and northern New England.

From a very early age, John Quidor would have been attuned to myths and folk legends of buried treasure, since he had spent his early boyhood living on a farm in western New York. After a fire destroyed his studio on Canal Street in 1835, Quidor moved to Adams County in western Illinois, where he farmed and continued to paint fantastic pictures of the occult and supernatural. Quidor's failure as an Illinois farmer led him in 1850 to return to his marginally successful painting career in New York City. However, in 1863, while living on West 43rd Street, Quidor was listed as a farmer in the city directory. Like other New York City residents, he periodically moved further and further away from the congestion and noise of Lower Manhattan in search of suburban or semirural spaces uptown. Quidor's paintings of rural folk tales and his continued professional identification with agriculture suggest strong cultural and social resistance to economic modernization in antebellum America. Almost twenty-five years

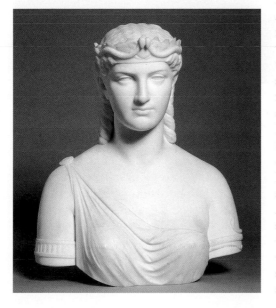

5.12 Margaret Foley
Cleopatra, 1876.
Marble, 23¾ in (60.3 cm) high, 19⅝ in (49.8 cm) wide, 11⅞ in (30.2 cm) deep. National Museum of American Art, Washington, D.C.

5.13 Fanny A. Coney
A View of Skeneatless Village, 1832.
Watercolor on paper,
14⅛ x 17¼ in
(35.8 x 43.8 cm).
American Folk Art
Museum, New York.

5.14 (below)
John Quidor
Money Diggers, 1832.
Oil on canvas,
16⅝ x 21½ in
(42.2 x 54.6 cm).
Brooklyn Museum of Art,
New York. Gift of
Mr. and Mrs. Alastair
Bradley Martin.

The figure awkwardly
climbing out of the black
hole is an African-
American, Black Fisherman
Sam. African-Americans
were stereotypically
identified with fish, reptiles,
and other dark creatures of
the underworld (see fig.
5.2). Significantly, a frog or
toad has perched itself
prominently in the
immediate foreground, at
the opposite edge of the
hole, and directs its
gaze toward Black
Fisherman Sam.

after his 1832 version of *Money Diggers*, Quidor painted a second, larger picture of the subject with even more mysterious, irrational light effects.

Rochester, New York, as a Boom Town

In western New York, the city of Rochester vividly exemplified the new market economy's ability to generate commercial and industrial wealth during the "canal boom" of the 1820s. Rochester capitalists purchased wheat from the rich farms of the Genesee River valley and grew wealthy by operating flour mills that processed wheat for export to New York City, the nation's largest metropolis and commercial banking center. Within a decade or so, Rochester's population had ballooned from a few hundred to over 20,000. During the late 1820s, the painter and future art historian William Dunlap (1766–1839), a student of Benjamin West, exhibited large-scale religious pictures in cities along the Hudson River and Erie Canal. In his diary, and later in his two-volume *A History of the Rise*

5.15 Campbell-Whittlesey House
Rochester, New York, 1835–6.
The Landmark Society of Western New York.

and Progress of the Arts of Design in the United States (1834), Dunlap claimed that other cities within this freshly tamed wilderness "sink into insignificance in comparison with Rochester. . . . In 1815 it was unknown: now the canal, bridges, court house, hotels, all upon a great scale, excite my astonishment anew at the wonders of the west" (Dunlap, Vol. I, p. 299).

Expressing their new-found social status, Rochester's merchant-industrial elite patronized the arts, choosing historical-revival designs for both public buildings and their own private residences. Benjamin Campbell, a Rochester flour-mill owner, ordered his mansion constructed in the guise of a Greek temple (fig. 5.15). In western New York, where there were few professional architects, pattern or design

books provided masons and carpenters with engraved illustrations of floor plans, elevations, and decorative ornaments. Campbell's home was modeled from a design book published by a carpenter and self-trained architect from upstate New York, Minard Lafever (1798–1854).

Greek-Revival Architecture and the Southern Plantation Economy

For nearly three decades, from 1829 to 1855, multiple editions of Lafever's pattern books helped to popularize local variations upon the Greek-Revival style throughout the Northeast; westward into the Great Lakes territories of Ohio, Michigan, and Wisconsin; and southward to the Gulf Coast states of Mississippi and Alabama. During the 1820s and 1830s, Greek-Revival architecture attained national popularity. The ancient classical style symbolized republican values of moral rectitude and self-discipline and alluded to the origins of democracy in the Greek city-states. In Demopolis, Alabama, a town named to honor the democratic principles of the Greek city-state, a slave-owner, planter, and amateur architect, Nathan Bryan Whitfield, borrowed ideas from Lafever's pattern books to construct a Greek-Revival mansion for Gaineswood, his cotton plantation (fig. 5.16). With a multiroom, irregular floor plan and many-columned porticoes on every side, Whitfield's plantation house dwarfs Benjamin Campbell's smaller and far simpler Rochester home. Southern plantation owners growing

5.16 Gaineswood
Demopolis, Alabama, 1843–59.
Courtesy Alabama Historical Commission.

wealthy through the exportation of cotton, tobacco, and other cash crops cultivated aristocratic lifestyles that emulated the English and European nobility. Since the Greek city-states also had depended upon slave labor, white Southerners could argue that their plantation slaves possessed no rights to the political inheritance of Greek democracy. Nevertheless, African-Americans worked as skilled craftsmen in the building and decoration of Greek-Revival plantation houses. At Gaineswood, most of the interior ornamental plasterwork was executed by an African-American slave named Sandy.

In the South, art and architecture increasingly represented sectional pride in opposition to the economic, political, and cultural dominance of the North. Stylistically, public and domestic architecture differed little between North and South. However, as the art historian Jessie Poesch has observed, grand, white-pillared mansions, located both in towns and on virtually self-sufficient country plantations, came to symbolize the leisurely, aristocratic lifestyle and power

of wealthy slave-owners. Greek-revival and other revival-style mansions prominently decorated rivers and roads in the deep South, casting into cultural shadow the far more modest homes of the majority of white Southerners who owned no or few slaves. In 1850, there were 8,000 landowners who possessed fifty or more slaves, and this socioeconomic elite set the South's sectionalist political agenda. Rejecting the sanctity of American nationalism in favor of every individual state's right to nullify objectionable federal laws and to secede from the Union, Southerners admired the decentralized nature of Greek democracy: the fierce independence of Athens, Sparta, and other city-states.

Northern industrial superiority over the agricultural South translated into the North's cultural dominance. Southern plantation owners had less liquid capital than Northern capitalists. Except for the border cities of Baltimore and Washington, D.C., the nation's capital, southeastern cities offered few opportunities for painters and sculptors beyond the limited market for

5.17 Alexander Jackson Davis
Edward W. Nicholls House, Llewellyn Park, Orange, New Jersey, 1858–9.
Courtesy Newark Public Library, Newark, New Jersey.

Instead of horizontal clapboards, vertical board and batten siding contributes to the building's ornamental mixture of aspiring Gothic forms. The roof's three clustered chimney pots are elongated for decorative effect, while the narrow, pointed lancet windows, featuring diamond-shaped panes, echo the look of Gothic-style parish churches.

portraiture. In the decades leading to the Civil War, the city of Charleston, South Carolina, which had been a vital seaport before 1812, declined in economic power and failed to support the visual arts. In 1848, a writer for the *Southern Literary Gazette* complained "that we not only derived our Paintings and Statuary from the North and from Europe, but even form our conceptions of excellence in these departments by the standard of others" (cited in L. Miller, pp. 229–230).

Architecture and Suburban Space

New canals, railroads, and roads gave more farms, villages, and towns access to commercial metropolitan hubs. The growing transportation network caused artists and architects in New York, Boston, and Philadelphia to envision a burgeoning national market for their work that extended to new western cities such as Cincinnati, Pittsburgh, Detroit, New Orleans, and St. Louis. However, cultural critics were concerned that national mobility and social restlessness adversely affected the stability of American home life. The New England landscape architect Andrew Jackson Downing (1815–52) published several design books, which sought to foster Americans' "love of

home." He asserted in *The Architecture of Country Houses* (1850) that the home was a "powerful means of civilization," for "so long as men are forced to dwell in log huts and follow a hunter's life, we must not be surprised by lynch law and the use of the bowie knife. But, when smiling lawns and tasteful cottages begin to embellish a country, we know that order and culture are established" (cited in Schuyler, p. 135).

Downing's treatises on landscape gardening, country cottages, and villas spoke to middle- and upper-class families, who moved outward from urban centers to the greener periphery of a suburban environment. Improved transportation facilitated the creation of suburbs. Outside of Boston, during the 1830s and 1840s, wealthy inhabitants of Cambridgeport and the old village of Cambridge pioneered the American tradition of commuting between private, suburban residences and urban places of business. Meanwhile, with the New York City metropolitan area's population surpassing 1 million by 1860, affluent families moved further northward beyond the older areas of downtown Manhattan and westward across the Hudson River to new communities in New Jersey.

The New York architect Alexander Jackson Davis (1803–92) supplied many of the house designs that illustrated Downing's popular pattern books. Davis's Gothic-Revival cottage for the

5.18 Plan of Llewellyn Park
Orange, New Jersey, 1852–69.
New Jersey Historical Society.

landscape painter Edward W. Nicholls typifies the models illustrated in Downing's books and copied with variations by builders throughout the nation (fig. 5.17). Located in the suburban community of Llewellyn Park, Orange, New Jersey, within commuting distance from New York City, the spacious English Gothic cottage, with steeply pitched roofs and gables, arched lancet windows, and ornamented porches, strongly contrasts with the geometric regularity and simplicity of Greek-Revival homes. The picturesque irregularity of Davis's cottage suggests a living organism in harmony with the varied nature of the surrounding lawn and gardens. Llewellyn Haskell, a chemical manufacturer and real-estate developer, financed Llewellyn Park (fig. 5.18) as a picturesque escape from New York City's congested streets. The planned community consisted of a fifty-acre central park called the Ramble and about fifty houses situated within unfenced, spacious lots, connected by winding streets. According to the real-estate prospectus, the communally owned Ramble allowed a "family occupying a small place in the country, costing only a few thousand dollars, to enjoy all the advantages of an extensive country seat, without the expense or trouble attending the latter" (cited in Schuyler, p. 209). Davis designed all of the original buildings for Llewellyn Park, including his own home and various rustic buildings for the park such as a gatehouse that seems to mushroom naturally from within the shaded garden environment (fig. 5.19).

5.19 (below, left)
Alexander Jackson Davis
Gatehouse, Llewellyn Park, Orange, New Jersey, 1853.
Courtesy Newark Public Library, Newark, New Jersey.

5.20 (above, right)
Asa Ames
Phrenological Head, 1847–50.
Polychromed pine. Museum of American Folk Art, New York, New York. Bequest of Jeanette Virgin.

The woodcarver painted the skull of this girl with a multicolored pattern of forms to demonstrate how different parts of the brain are governed by particular mental qualities and character traits. Ames marked each of the colored areas with identifying inscriptions, including (among other human tendencies) conscientiousness, caution, and secretiveness.

Phrenology and the Octagon

The conception of a building as a living natural organism, advocated by Horatio Greenough and other writers, also undergirded the popularity of the octagon as an architectural form during the 1850s. With expansion westward and the suburbanization of the American landscape, octagonal buildings appeared to address the ecological problem of the growing scarcity of trees and lumber for constructing wooden houses. Advocates of the octagon argued that it was a particularly suitable building type for the new era of urban and suburban growth because it lent itself to inexpensive gravel and cement construction.

Taking advantage of public thirst for advice books on designing new homes, the American phrenologist Orson S. Fowler (1809–87) published *The Octagon House: A Home for All*, which

5.21 John Richards
Watertown, Wisconsin,
1854–6.
Watertown Historical
Society, Watertown,
Wisconsin.

When first built by John
Richards, this octagon was
claimed as the largest
single-family home in the
state of Wisconsin. At the
center of the interior, a
cantilevered, spiral staircase
leads to a small,
balustraded lookout over
the roof. The substantial
brick building is
generously illuminated on
its two main stories with
tall, shuttered windows,
thereby contributing to
the octagonal ideal of
airy openness.

went through new editions every year between
1848 and 1857. Phrenology measured the shape
and size of the human skull, mapping its protu-
berances as a means for deciphering personality
traits and intelligence (fig. 5.20). Many American
artists were drawn to phrenological theory and
practice, so that they could produce more
"objective," accurate renderings of both the
external appearance and internal character of the
human figure. John Quidor attempted to establish

5.22 Hiram Powers
Daniel Webster,
1836–41.
Marble. Height 23 in
(58.6 cm), width 16¾ in
(42.5 cm), depth 10⅛ in
(25.7 cm). Boston
Athenaeum, Boston,
Massachusetts.

a phrenological society in Columbus, Illinois.
Working in Washington, D.C., during the mid-
1830s, the Vermont-born sculptor Hiram
Powers (1805–73) created portrait busts of
American statesmen, based on phrenological
principles. His sculpture of Daniel Webster
accentuated the Massachusetts senator's massive
forehead (fig. 5.22). For Powers, the fiery orator's
sizable cranium signified Webster's genius and
superior intellectual faculties.

Hoping to reform American society by
encouraging the proper exercise and development of the brain, Fowler saw architecture as a
moral science that could stimulate desirable
brain "organs" and character traits. Though
Fowler had no previous experience as an architect, he insisted that "Phrenology points out an
organ of Inhabitiveness, or love of Home, as well
as of Constructiveness, so that building cheap
houses, and telling the Poor—for it also points
out an organ of Benevolence—how to build
themselves cheap and good houses, comes properly within its sphere" (p. 86).

Fowler criticized confining, boxlike houses in
favor of a freer, more spacious octagon plan suitable for suburban villas and cottages. He praised
the near-spherical form of the octagon as being
closer to nature's "fruits, eggs, tubers, nuts, grains,
seeds, trees, etc." (p. 82). Fowler associated the
circular nature of the octagon with the social
values of family harmony, friendship, and
sociability:

> The nearer we can approach the circular *form
> the better. To gather around a spherical or
> elliptical table, occasions more harmony and
> agreeable sensations than around a square one. To
> have a truly agreeable chit-chat, we require to
> form into a* circle. *Why our universal use of "the
> family circle," "circle around the fireside," and the
> like, but that this circular arrangement of the
> parties facilitates that magnetic flux and reflux of
> emotion which creates these delights? As in
> magnetic and electrical experiments we must
> complete a* circle, *so, that several* minds *may act
> in concert, it is requisite that they form around
> and face a common center (p. 151).*

Benefiting from the fame he enjoyed as a leading
phrenologist, Fowler's architectural advice created a national building craze for the octagonal
form, from Watertown, Wisconsin, in the North

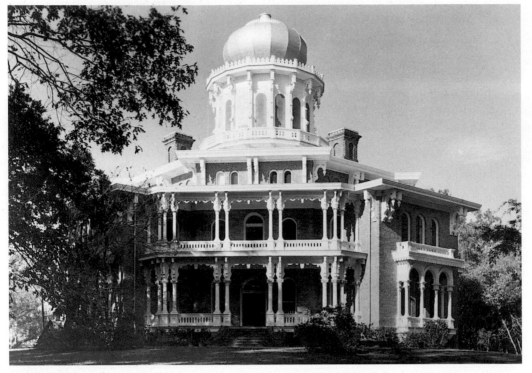

5.23 Samuel Sloan
Longwood, Natchez,
Mississippi, begun 1860.
Historic New Orleans
Collection, New Orleans,
Louisiana. Kemper and
Leila Williams Foundation.

(fig. 5.21) to Natchez, Mississippi, in the South (fig. 5.23). Designed by the Philadelphia architect Samuel Sloan (1815–84), the "Longwood" octagon at Natchez rose three stories before being capped by a central tower and an oriental, onion-style dome. Fowler's own octagonal home in Fishkill, New York, also helped to popularize an inexpensive concrete mixture of gravel, broken slate, sand, and lime for supporting walls. Thanks to Fowler's advocacy, concrete soon became an important modern material, especially for building foundations.

The Rural Cemetery Movement and the Arts

The suburban search for green space transformed the American way of death as well as life. Beginning in 1825, a small group of wealthy Bostonians explored the practicality of establishing a major cemetery outside city limits. They had concluded that the old city graveyards next to churches were seriously overcrowded and ill-suited for properly respectful monuments to the dead. By 1831, under the auspices of the Massachusetts Horticultural Society, Bostonians finally established Mount Auburn Cemetery in Cambridge as burial grounds that doubled as a

park with gardens and romantic, pastoral walking trails (fig. 5.24). Dr. Jacob Bigelow, a Harvard medical school professor and primary founder of Mount Auburn, designed the Egyptian-Revival gateway (fig. 5.25). The ancient Egyptians were regarded as experts in the funerary arts and in the building of monumental architecture for the dead.

Attracted by Mount Auburn's spacious, park-like atmosphere, upper-class families eagerly purchased burial plots where they could erect ennobling sculptures and monuments for deceased loved ones. Many of the earliest memorials were small-scale replicas of the Bunker Hill obelisk. Ultimately, however, Mount Auburn and other rural cemeteries in New York, Philadelphia, and elsewhere helped create a new market for marble sculptures. For a grave in Greenmount Cemetery in Baltimore, the Maryland sculptor William Henry Rinehart (1825–74) commemorated the deaths of two children born to Hugh and Sarah Sisson (fig. 5.26). Like Crawford, Rinehart also worked in Rome, where he made at least twenty-five replicas of *Sleeping Children* for other bereaved clients. The recumbent, pure-white sculpture portrays death as a deep, restful sleep. Partially covered by a shroud-blanket, the

5.24 Thomas Chambers
Mount Auburn Cemetery, c. 1850.
Oil on canvas,
14 x 18⅛ in
(35.6 x 46 cm).
National Gallery of Art, Washington, D.C.
Gift of Edgar William and Bernice Chrysler Garbisch.

Thomas Chambers (1808–after 1866), an English-born painter, copied this scene of Mount Auburn from a published engraving. Similar in shape to a figure eight, the pond at the center of the picture establishes the serpentine character of the walking paths that wind around the cemetery's hilly, verdant grounds.

5.25 Jacob Bigelow
Gateway, Mount Auburn Cemetery, 1831.
Courtesy Mount Auburn Cemetery, Cambridge, Massachusetts.

Bigelow's Egyptian-style gateway was originally built out of painted wood made to look like stone. However, responding to new demands for truth in the use of materials, Mount Auburn officials authorised the rebuilding of the gateway with Quincy granite by 1843.

pudgy, Cupid-like infants rest comfortably upon pillows and a mattress, enabling grieving parents to imagine their imminent reawakening. Rural cemeteries became tourist sites and virtual galleries of art and architecture, attracting painters and, later, photographers, who recorded memorials and landscape views (fig. 5.27). Mount Auburn and other idyllic cemeteries became suburban escapes from the cares and woes of contemporary urban life. Within their shaded spaces, mourners and visitors learned to appreciate the beauty of art as a means of spiritual communication.

The National Academy of Design and the Art Market

Thanks to western development and the wealth generated by the transportation revolution, New York City became the nation's financial capital and most lucrative art market. In 1825, New York artists capitalized upon public euphoria over the Erie Canal and the fiftieth anniversary

5.26 William Henry Rinehart
Sleeping Children, 1869. Marble. National Museum of American Art, Washington, D.C.

As was customary for American sculptors working in Rome and Florence, Rinehart conceived the design of the marble group, but the actual cutting and polishing of the stone was carried out by hired Italian craftsmen. The sleeping figures are reminiscent of *amors*, winged children that decorated ancient Roman funerary sculptures. Amors symbolized the soul's transcendence of earthly desire.

of the American Revolution to found the National Academy of Design, the nation's only art academy managed exclusively by and for artists. Over two decades earlier, in 1802, the American Academy of the Fine Arts had been founded in New York by wealthy art patrons, whose private tastes and collections tended toward the European Old Masters more than contemporary American art. The American Academy's aristocratic indifference to the professional needs of American artists motivated the founders of the National Academy of Design, who established an artistic brotherhood devoted to the instruction of young artists and the exhibition of original works by living American artists. The academy's "Antique School" taught "the universal language" of the human body. Students learned to copy expressive gestures and figural poses from plaster casts of famous ancient sculptures.

With the growth of illustrated periodicals and the rise of the penny press, art-academy exhibi-

5.27 Albert S. Southworth and Josiah J. Hawes
Mount Auburn Cemetery, c. 1850. Whole-plate daguerrotype. George Eastman House, International Museum of Photography, Rochester, New York.

5.28 Richard Caton Woodville
War News from Mexico,
1848.
Oil on canvas, 27 x 24¾
in (68.6 x 62.9 cm).
National Gallery of Art,
Washington, D.C. Loan,
Manoogian Foundation,
New York.

Below the small post-office
sign, affixed to the wooden
post to the left, a small
printed broadside, or
leaflet, summons volunteers
for the war against Mexico.
The picture's explosive news
is barely contained by the
rickety but classically
designed porch that already
suggests American
expansion into cruder, less-
settled western territories.
The pyramidal arrangement
of figures is repeated by
the rustic wooden
pediment, decorated with
the hotel sign and its
American eagle.

War generation, sits at the right edge of the porch. Thoughtful, rather than excited, the old man may be privately questioning whether America's imperial expansion into California and the Hispanic Southwest measures up to the moral standards of the American Revolution. The distraught, mature woman, peering through an open window, may also express concerns of the feminine, domestic sphere over the damage to families incurred by the casualties of war.

Woodville's painting was exhibited in New York at the gallery of the American Art-Union (AAU). Founded in 1839 by the portraitist and prominent Freemason James Herring (1794–1867), the Art-Union had dramatically expanded the audience for contemporary American art through innovative marketing strategies. With the support of a group of wealthy New York businessmen, including newspaper editors, as well as merchants, lawyers, and bankers, the American Art-Union cast itself in patriotic terms as an organization designed to assist American artists and support the production of specifically American subject matter. For a $5 membership fee, subscribers to the Art-Union were given an engraved reproduction of a contemporary American painting. Additionally, members automatically received a lottery ticket for the chance to win an original oil painting or other artworks at festive public drawings held during the Christmas season. At its height, when Woodville exhibited his picture in 1849, the Art-Union had a national membership of 18,960 and its lottery, in that year alone, distributed 460 paintings, 400 medals, 20 bronze statuettes, and 100 sets of engravings reproducing sketches by the late Washington Allston. In just over a decade, from 1839 to 1851, the organization purchased over 2,000 paintings from American artists. Furthermore, it publicized its activities and the works of its artists through publication of an annual report, and a monthly *Bulletin*, which promoted Woodville's work as "perfectly AMERICAN in its character" (April 1851 *Bulletin*, cited in Hills, p. 329).

The Art-Union, however, was not a uniquely American idea, nor did it remain unique nationally. James Herring and his entrepreneurial supporters had appropriated its organizational structure from prior art unions operating in Britain, Germany, Italy, and Switzerland. By the

tions generated an unprecedented level of publicity for American artists. The encouraging words of sympathetic editors and critics soon reached a mass audience. By the 1840s, a publishing industry, dominated by a corporate, market-oriented elite, had displaced local aristocrats or community leaders as the primary molders of public opinion. American genre painters such as the Baltimore native Richard Caton Woodville (1825–55) often represented newspapers as the magnetic core of pictorial compositions. Woodville's *War News from Mexico* represents an excited group, drawn to the words of an open-mouthed young man, reading aloud from a newspaper that carries the banner heading "EXTRA" (fig. 5.28). Overhead, a sign decorated with an American eagle reads: "American Hotel." The newspaper creates a national community from a diverse group of individual white men, while excluding the politically powerless African-Americans and the elderly white woman at the picture's right margin. Among the white males, an elderly, top-hatted man, personifying the Revolutionary late 1840s, additional art unions were founded in Boston; Philadelphia; Newark, New Jersey; and Cincinnati, Ohio. Due, in part, to this competition and the growth of commercial art dealerships, American Art-Union membership began to decline.

Furthermore, the New York organization came under attack from James Bennett, a newspaperman and pro-Southern sympathizer, who sensationally charged that the AAU was being operated by an anti-slavery, abolitionist clique, led by a rival newspaperman and New York politician, Henry Jarvis Raymond, founder of the *New York Times*. Bennett brought a successful law suit against the Art-Union, claiming that its lottery was an illegal form of gambling. As the United States expanded westward, AAU managers, many of them heavily invested in the transportation and shipping industries, had hoped that the dissemination of American art would serve to create a national consensus, despite the far-flung geography and sectional divisions of the republic. But, by 1852, the AAU was forced to disband, victim of the divisive debate over slavery, more than the legal or moral arguments over lotteries.

The very marginalized and forlorn African-American figures in Woodville's painting already called into question the AAU's optimistic vision. The red, white, and blue colors of their tattered clothing ironically create a visual link between this couple and the red, white, and blue shield of the American eagle, patriotically decorating the hotel sign overhead. The disconsolate father-daughter pair implicitly raise the controversial issue of slavery's extension into the new territories. They pose a sobering reminder of the fragility of the national union, even in the exuberant aftermath of imperial victory over Mexico.

American artists recognized the expanding art market as a function of the socio-economic expansion westward. After his biblical paintings had toured the boomtowns along the Erie Canal and Great Lakes, William Dunlap, the oldest founding member of the National Academy, insisted in his history of American art that, in contrast to aristocratic Europe, an artist's true audience was the anonymous public as a whole, constituted as a body of free and equal citizens:

5.29 Charles Bird King
The Anatomy of Art Appreciation, 'The Vanity of the Artist's Dream,' 1830.
Oil on canvas, 35 x 29½ in (89.2 x 74.9 cm).
Fogg Art Museum, Harvard University, Cambridge, Massachusetts. Gift of Grenville L. Winthrop.

The laws are here the only protectors. Industry, virtue, and talents, the only patrons. The ignorant, the afflicted, the weak, the unfortunate may want aid, instruction, protection, from the strong, and the rich, and the wise; but the artist—the man who possesses the genius, skill, and knowledge which entitles him to that name—will look to be honoured and esteemed by his fellow-citizens; not seeking protection, from them; or acknowledging superiority, except in superior worth.

. . . The artist who feels the necessity of patronage, must do one of two things—abandon his high and responsible character, bow to the golden calf that he may partake of the bread and wine set before the idol, or abandon his profession—grasp the axe and the plough, instead of the crayon and pencil. The agriculturist, the mechanic, the sailor, the cartman, the sawyer, the chimney-sweeper, need no protectors. When they are wanted they are sought for—so should it be with the artist; at least let him be as independent as the last (Dunlap, Vol. I, pp. 16–17).

Dunlap embraced capitalist laws of supply and demand as a liberation from personal servility to rich connoisseurs. Rejecting their protection as a sign of weakness, he optimistically assumed that industry, virtue, and talent would guarantee artists sufficient buyers for their labor. Yet Dunlap was not naively unaware that market demand often went flat, even for the best of artists. He therefore granted them an escape clause denied to mechanics and chimney-sweeps: "The man who is blessed with taste and benevolence, and with riches to gratify both, cheerfully assists struggling genius through the impediments poverty throws in his way, and enjoys in conscious rectitude the reward which the good deed assuredly brings, but he never boasts or assumes the title of patron" (II, p. 109).

Claiming the mantle of genius, American artists sought to displace wealthy collectors as the arbiters of taste without challenging the social hierarchies of class, race, and gender. Together, professional artists and their philanthropic benefactors intended to educate the untutored masses in the morally edifying principles of high art. However, American artists often found themselves railing vainly against newspapers and magazines that pandered to the low-brow tastes of consumers who preferred more sensational entertainments to the morally refining atmosphere of art exhibitions. In his *The Anatomy of Art Appreciation*, 'The Vanity of the Artist's Dream,' the Washington, D.C., painter Charles Bird King (1785–1862) represented the forlorn head of the *Apollo Belvedere*, crammed into a cupboard filled with tattered books, stale bread, and other signs of an artist's failed ambitions (fig. 5.29). King's confused jumble of objects purposely expressed the emotionally distraught state of an impoverished artist. Illusionistically tacked to the cupboard's wooden frame, the foreclosure announcement of a "Sheriff's Sale" lists the artist's few assets for auction and payment of debts. Though King himself was a relatively affluent artist, he was a friend of Washington Allston (see chapter 4) and other artists who repeatedly complained of indebtedness.

Catholic Icons and Hispanic Resistance to U.S. Culture

Samuel F. B. Morse, the first president of the National Academy of Design, became one of the nation's leading missionaries for the moral value of high art, which he contrasted with vulgar, lower-class entertainments and with the rituals and idolatrous imagery of the

Catholic Church. When he toured Italy in 1830 and visited Milan Cathedral, he condemned its paintings and sculpture for creating a theatrical effect as a substitute for God's Word:

I am sometimes even constrained to doubt the lawfulness of my own art when I perceive its prostitution, were I not fully persuaded that the art itself, when used for its legitimate purposes, is one of the greatest correctors of grossness and promoters of refinement. I have been led, since I have been in Italy, to think much of the propriety of introducing pictures into churches in aid of devotion. I have certainly every inducement to decide in favor of the practice did I consult alone the seeming interest of art. That pictures may and do have the effect upon some rightly to raise the affections, I have no doubt, and, abstractly considered, the practice would not merely be harmless but useful; but, knowing that man is led astray by his imagination more than by any other of his other faculties, I consider it so dangerous to his best interests that I had rather sacrifice the interests of the arts, if there is any collision, than run the risk of endangering those compared with which all others are not for a moment to be considered (cited in Mabee, pp. 131–132).

More than the educated elite, the lower classes were deemed especially vulnerable to the enchantments of visual images. Back in America, Morse associated Catholic veneration of cult images and relics with illiterate foreign immigrants from Ireland and southern Europe, whose dependence upon an autocratic priesthood and loyalty to the Roman papacy seemed to threaten America's republican institutions. In New York, Boston, and other cities, "nativist" violence often erupted against Irish and other Catholic immigrants.

After 1846, when the United States began to occupy the territories of California and New Mexico, Anglo-American Protestant culture clashed with the indigenous Hispanic Catholic population. Led by the Brotherhood of Our Father Jesus Nazarene, a Catholic lay fraternity, Hispanic artists resisted assimilation into U.S. culture. They continued to produce *santos*, or religious icons that concentrated upon the poignant suffering and crucifixion of Christ and offered comforting images of the Virgin Mary.

In the Santa Cruz Valley of New Mexico, José Rafael Aragón (c.1795–1862) decorated numerous mountain village chapels and churches with colorful wooden sculptures and *retablos*, or panel paintings. Aragón's charming, brightly painted picture of *The Flight into Egypt* (fig. 5.30) focuses on the maternal figure of the Virgin Mary, who cradles a sleeping baby Jesus in her arms while she rides upon a donkey being led by a guardian angel. According to the Bible (Matthew 2:13–14), an angel of God had appeared to Joseph, Mary's husband, to warn the holy family that the jealous King Herod was seeking to destroy the newborn child, fearing he would become King of the Jews. In Aragón's symmetrically balanced picture, Joseph appears on the left, deferentially walking behind the Virgin and Christ child, and he protectively raises his hand toward Mary's back.

In this cartoonlike, spatially flattened image, the artist appears less concerned with the literal details of the biblical narrative than with the visionary splendor of the holy figures and accompanying decorative elements. Red polka-dot curtains with blue and red fringe and red tassels frame the painting's upper register, while plumes of vivid blue and red fill a crest at the top of the picture frame. The red-and-blue color harmony continues in the costume of the Virgin Mary, who appears crowned as the Queen of Heaven, despite her ride upon a humble donkey. Immediately above Mary's crown and halo, or spiritual light rays, the descending dove of the Holy Ghost signifies the supernatural character of Mary as the mother of Jesus Christ, the Son of God. In the lower register of the painting, a lush garden implicitly prophesies the heavenly paradisiacal future awaiting faithful believers in Christ's divinity. Colorfully painted *santos* were devotional objects that visually bridged the moral and spiritual distance between heaven and earth. Worshipers often attributed miraculous powers to such sacred imagery, believing that it manifested the presence of the holy person being portrayed. By contrast, Protestant, Anglo-American settlers generally ridiculed these crude-appearing images as relics of superstition and unenlightened craftsmanship.

5.30 José Rafael Aragón
The Flight into Egypt, c. 1850.
Tempera and gesso on wood, 20½ x 8⅞ in (52 x 22.6 cm). Museum of International Folk Art, Santa Fe, New Mexico.

Artists and Domestic Virtue

The mysterious power of religious icons motivated a number of Anglo-American artists to represent not only biblical subjects, but also images of Catholic piety. Samuel Morse painted the *Chapel of the Virgin at Subiaco*, while on his tour of Italy (fig. 5.31). Though the picture is primarily a landscape, it emphasizes a roadside shrine dedicated to the Virgin Mary. In the golden-yellow background, obscured by the morning haze, a Catholic monastery in Subiaco forms a towering, mountainous peak. A pious woman, kneeling in front of the small shrine,

5.31 Samuel Morse
Chapel of the Virgin at Subiaco, 1830.
Oil on canvas,
29⅞ x 37 in
(76 x 94 cm). Worcester
Art Museum,
Massachusetts. Bequest of
Stephen Salisbury III.

This pilgrimage shrine near the village of Subiaco, about 45 miles east of Rome, was popular with visiting artists who, according to Morse, admired its rustic, picturesque character. The shrine's dark masonry structure appears to grow out of the red earth of a cliff. Behind the kneeling woman, a well-dressed young man also pays homage to the shrine by doffing his hat.

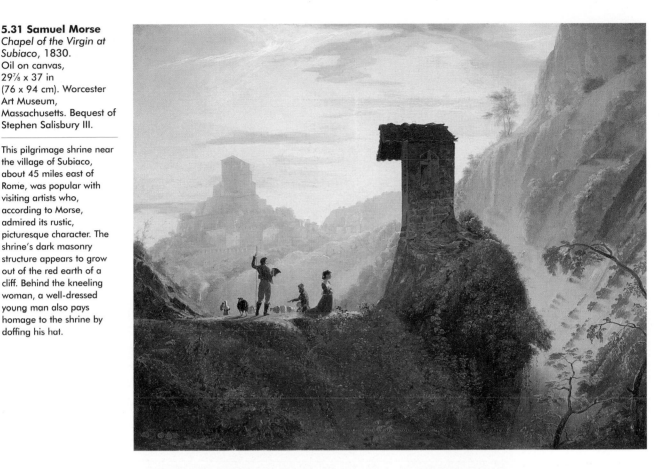

serves as the painting's central figure. Rather than featuring a view of the shrine's cult statue, Morse hid the image from the eyes of his primarily Protestant American audience. In so doing, the National Academy president expressed the iconoclastic values of Puritan, Calvinist tradition and questioned the secretive, suspect rituals of Catholic image worship.

As self-proclaimed guardians of national virtue, painters and sculptors in New York and other cities socially elevated themselves above the ranks of mere craftsmen. Artists joined clergymen, lawyers, and other college-educated men of learning as members of the professional classes responsible for the republic's moral direction. When the National Academy was first organized in 1825, America was already in the midst of a Protestant religious revival that found its most profound expression in Rochester, New York, and other boom towns along the Erie Canal. Made anxious by the rapidity of modernization, Americans in northwestern New York and elsewhere turned for reassurance not only to

a religion of the heart, but also to virtuous and idealizing themes in literature and the visual arts.

Encouraged by clergymen and moral reformers, artists and architects attempted to foster the love of home life as a counterweight to the destabilizing forces of social and economic change. Jeremiah Pearson Hardy (1800–88), a former student of Samuel Morse in New York, took his academic training to Bangor, Maine, where he painted a luminous portrait of his wife and daughter seated comfortably upon a parlor couch (fig. 5.32). Silhouetted against the radiant view of the Penobscot River, the relatively homely figures seem transfigured by the light. The Hardy home has become a temple or sanctuary for private reveries, stimulated by the spiritual beauties of Nature and the arts. Growing up within this aesthetic environment and encouraged by her father, the daughter in Hardy's portrait, Anne Eliza Hardy (1839–1934), became a painter of fruit and flower still lifes. As discussed earlier in relation to the paintings of Raphaelle Peale, such humble subjects were widely regarded as suitable

5.32 Jeremiah Pearson Hardy
Catherine Wheeler Hardy and Her Daughter, 1842.
Oil on canvas, 29¼ x 36⅛ in (74.3 x 91.8 cm). Museum of Fine Arts, Boston, Massachusetts. Gift of Maxim Karolik for the Mr. and Mrs. Karolik Collection of American Paintings, 1815–65.

5.33 Henry F. Darby
Portrait of Reverend John Atwood and His Family, 1845.
Oil on canvas, 72 x 96¼ in (182.8 x 244.4 cm). Museum of Fine Arts, Boston, Massachusetts. Gift of Maxim Karolik for the Mr. and Mrs. Karolik Collection of American Paintings, 1815–65.

The moral sobriety of this New England clergyman's family is expressed, in part, by the relatively austere, rectilinear, boxlike space of the parlor. The small, framed religious images are widely separated and call attention to the largely empty wall space, against which they float.

for women artists. Fruit and flower arrangements were domestic displays for dining rooms and parlors, social spaces normally associated with the feminine sphere.

Nevertheless, women's cultural influence in the home was challenged by the tradition of patriarchal authority. The large *Portrait of Reverend John Atwood and His Family* by self-taught Massachusetts artist Henry F. Darby (1829–97) represents a New Hampshire Baptist minister and his family, seated around a parlor table with Bibles open for private devotions (fig.

5.33). While paintings and sculptures were still discouraged in most Protestant churches, two pictures hanging prominently behind the Atwoods signify the importance of the visual arts in supplementing their reading of God's Word. On the right, a mourning picture of a funerary memorial for a deceased son reminds us of the role rural cemeteries had in popularizing art as a form of spiritual expression. More surprisingly, on the left hangs a colored mezzotint print of an Old Testament subject, *Samson Carrying off the Gates of Gaza,* by an English

5.34 Lilly Martin Spencer
Shake Hands?, 1854.
Oil on canvas with arched top, 30⅛ x 25⅛ in (76.8 x 64.1 cm).
Ohio Historical Society, Columbus, Ohio.

artist-engraver. The violent biblical story of the Hebrew strongman contributes a disturbing counterpoint to the pious quiet of the domestic space. As agent of God's revenge against the Philistines, Samson reinforces the stern image of patriarchal authority personified by Reverend Atwood, who also served as chaplain of the state prison in Concord, New Hampshire.

The painter Lilly Martin Spencer (1822–1902) addressed female audiences by rejecting such images of patriarchal dominance. Spencer, who began her career in Cincinnati before moving to New York in 1849, also dissented from the morally restrictive tendency in art to represent women as idealized domestic saints. While Jeremiah Hardy hermetically isolated his wife and daughter from real life, Spencer frankly represented women as working housewives or cooks who prepare meals in kitchens cluttered with ingredients and utensils. In *Shake Hands?*, a smiling woman boldly greets beholders as real visitors (fig. 5.34). Her flour-covered hand reaches out to us from the picture space. Spencer does not liberate her subject from

the domestic sphere, but *Shake Hands?* humorously asserts a limited social equality. Genteel American critics found Spencer's "grinning housemaids" vulgar and offensive (cited in Lubin, p. 173). A critic for *The Crayon*, an artists' journal, asked, "Is there in her woman's soul no serene grave thought, no quiet happiness, no tearful aspiration, to the expression of which she may give her pencil?" (cited in Lubin, p. 173). Far from being self-effacing personifications of religious feeling, Spencer's assertive women dare to speak with a physical directness that shocked moralists and art connoisseurs alike. *Shake Hands?* and similar Spencer paintings of domestic life found a receptive audience among many middle-class viewers. The Cosmopolitan Art Association, successor to the American Art-Union, commissioned an inexpensive engraving of *Shake Hands?* and distributed it to subscribers. The organization advertised the painting in the *Cosmopolitan Art Journal* for a readership composed primarily of women.

Though her French-born parents were social radicals supporting feminist and abolitionist causes, Spencer was not a political activist. Writing to her mother, she claimed that she was too preoccupied by her painting career to attend women's rights meetings. Nevertheless, her paintings challenged patriarchal control over family life, and her career within a male-dominated profession unconventionally supported a husband, who performed domestic chores and helped care for their numerous children.

Landscape Painting and National Identity

During the second third of the nineteenth century, landscape paintings of American scenery also reached a wide middle-class audience. The American Art-Union urged its middle-class membership to purchase landscape paintings as a therapeutic antidote to urbanization. For city residents confined by congested streets and a relatively polluted, noisy environment, parlors decorated with serene landscape views would soothe tense nerves and uplift depressed spirits. Pictures of country life were deemed a vicarious healthful substitute for actually owning a country home. Furthermore, landscapes encouraged the nationalist love of America's diverse beauties and scenic views.

Since the late eighteenth century, periodicals in New York, Philadelphia, and Boston had begun publishing engravings of America's unique natural beauty. Pictures of aristocratic country seats, new roads or waterways, and striking tourist sites were intended to instill in Americans a cultural pride of place. In 1822, a new map of North America featured a landscape vignette that combined views of two tourist attractions in the United States: the Natural Bridge of Virginia, in the Southern Shenandoah Valley, and Niagara Falls, on the border between New York and Canada (fig. 5.35). The tactful synthesis of Southern and Northern natural wonders was undoubtedly intended to bolster the Missouri Compromise of 1820 (see p. 161)

and to minimize sectional divisions, following the admission of Missouri and Maine as slave and free states respectively. A Pennsylvania Quaker by the name of Edward Hicks (1789–1849) borrowed motifs from this map for a series of paintings inspired by the Old Testament prophecy of Isaiah: "The wolf also shall dwell with the lamb, and the leopard shall lie down with the kid; and the calf and the young lion and the fatling together; and a little child shall lead them"(11:6). In early versions of "The Peaceable Kingdom" series, the itinerant artist represented Isaiah's comforting vision of reconciled animal foes in conjunction with the Natural Bridge, a popular symbol of God's benevolent regard for the American republic (fig. 5.37). Beneath the bridge, another figural group represents William Penn, accompanied by other colonial Quakers,

5.37 Edward Hicks
The Peaceable Kingdom of the Branch, 1822–5. Oil on wood, 37 x 44 in (93.9 x 111.7 cm). Yale University Art Gallery, New Haven, Connecticut. Gift of Robert W. Carle.

By the end of his life, Hicks, a Quaker minister, had painted over sixty *"Peaceable Kingdom"* pictures with many variations for friends and relatives in the faith. The original frame bears the inscription of Isaiah's hopeful prophecy in gold letters. The text's Christian meaning is expressed by the little boy's grasping a branch of grape clusters and leaves, signifying Christ's blood and redemptive sacrifice for the sins of humankind.

making peace with Native Americans, supposed enemies transformed into friends and brothers.

During the first half of the nineteenth century, painters interpreted the American landscape in metaphorical terms as a reliable moral, religious compass for mapping the nation's material and spiritual destiny. No site seemed to signify more the notion of America as God's Promised Land than Niagara Falls. In 1808, the history painter John Trumbull finished two panoramic views of Niagara Falls. Thanks to Trumbull and many other painters, Niagara Falls would become a sacred icon of American nationalism. Measuring fourteen feet long, Trumbull's *View of the Falls of Niagara From Under Table Rock* (fig. 5.36) was a preparatory study for a never-finished circular panorama.

First developed as a popular form of entertainment in eighteenth-century London, panoramas were enormous paintings that anticipated the illusionism of modern cinema. They were usually exhibited in the round within circular spaces or specially built rotundas. Dramatic lighting and elevated viewing platforms visually transported spectators to imagine that they commanded an "all-seeing," 360-degree view of the actual site. Kept at a distance from the paint surface, beholders could not see individual brushstrokes or other signs of the painter's artifice. Though Trumbull never transformed his study into a theatrically scaled work, panoramas

became popular entertainments in antebellum America. In 1829, the Boston artist Robert Salmon (1775–c.1848) exhibited a large, semicircular battle painting in the rotunda of Alexander Parris's Quincy Market (see fig. 5.4). By the 1830s and 1840s, American panoramas were increasingly representing scenes of the national landscape. Their popularity coincided with the development in America of a loosely organized school of landscape painting. After the Civil War, critics retrospectively designated this group of landscapists, who painted primarily in New York and New England, as the Hudson River School.

Thomas Cole

The birth of the Hudson River School may be traced to the 1825 Erie Canal celebration, when John Trumbull, President of the American Academy of the Fine Arts, visited the artists' supply shop of a New York art dealer. There he saw three pictures of the Hudson River and Catskill Mountains region by Thomas Cole (1801–48), a young painter who had just arrived in New York from Philadelphia. Cole and the shop owner, William Colman, had timed this exhibition of upstate New York landscapes to coincide with the state's celebration, from October 26 to November 4, of the opening of the Erie Canal.

William Dunlap, who joined Trumbull in purchasing one of Cole's paintings, reported in the November 22 issue of the *New-York Evening Post*: "These pictures will now be seen with delight by those who visit our Academy, and they will be astonished when they compare them with the works of the first European masters, in the Gallery, to find that an American boy, comparatively speaking, for such truly is a man of twenty-two, has equalled those works which have been the boast of Europe and the admiration of ages." Dunlap's article mythologized Cole as an "untutored" American genius, quoting Trumbull's deferential judgment that "this youth has done at once, and without instruction, what I cannot do after 50 years' practice" (cited in Parry, p. 26).

In fact, Cole was neither an American nor an untutored prodigy. He had been born in Lancashire, England, and had begun his career in the industrial arts, learning to engrave designs for a calico printworks in Liverpool, England. In 1818, Cole and his family emigrated to the United States, but not until 1834 did he actually become an American citizen. Dunlap's insistence

that the immigrant Cole was an "American boy" expressed both the United States' persistent familial identification with "Mother England" and the national desire to discover an American art distinct from European models. For Trumbull and Dunlap, Cole's landscapes of American scenery could be used to wean wealthy Anglophile patrons away from collecting European Old Masters in favor of collecting contemporary American art.

A replica of the lost Cole painting that Trumbull purchased in 1825 represents a view of Kaaterskill Falls in the Catskill Mountains from under a cavern (fig. 5.38). Although the picture represents a wilderness untainted by signs of tourism or European settlement, the cavern's natural pointed arch enframes an awe-inspiring view of God's handiwork that surpasses in grandeur the Gothic architecture of European cathedrals. While demonstrating for connoisseurs a proper reverence for European tradition, Cole simultaneously appealed to Americans' national pride in a wilderness that

5.38 Thomas Cole
Kaaterskill Falls, 1826.
Oil on canvas,
25¼ x 36³⁄₁₆ in
(64.2 x 91.9 cm).
Wadsworth Atheneum,
Hartford, Connecticut.
Bequest of Daniel
Wadsworth.

Kaaterskill Falls was one of the primary attractions for tourists staying at the Catskill Mountain House, a resort hotel located on a lofty palisade overlooking the Hudson River near Catskill, New York. Opened in 1824, the Mountain House, expanded from an earlier dormitory, soon became a great attraction for New York's social elite and the city's growing band of landscape painters.

was rapidly disappearing through economic development. He later asserted by way of contrast that in "civilized Europe" the morally elevating remnants of God's original creation "have long since been destroyed or modified" (cited in McCoubrey, p. 102).

The British-born fraternity of Freemasonry facilitated Cole's assimilation into American society and its art circles. Working as an itinerant portraitist in Ohio during the early 1820s, Cole had joined a Masonic lodge in Zanesville. As was the case for eighteenth-century portraitists in England and America (see chapter 3), early-nineteenth-century Masonic lodges continued to assist artists with loans, commissions for emblematic engravings, costumes, and decorations, and introductions to affluent, potential clients. In antebellum America, many itinerant painters such as the young Cole and the aging Dunlap could rely on Freemasonry as a very useful patronage and communications network.

Cole's paintings evoke associations with Freemasonry's mythology and symbolism. The arched, cathedral-like view of *Kaaterskill Falls* with its sunlit horizon recalls the architectural and light symbolism of Masonic lodge certificates such as the late-eighteenth-century example by Paul Revere (see fig. 3.33). In 1826, Cole celebrated a patron saint of Freemasonry, St. John the Baptist, whose baptismal initiation rituals created the first Christian brotherhood.

Inspired by the scenery of upstate New York and New England, Cole's imaginative landscape composition *St. John in the Wilderness* (fig. 5.39) visualizes the words of St. Matthew's Gospel: "In those days came John the Baptist, preaching in the wilderness of Judea, and saying 'Repent for the kingdom of heaven is at hand'" (Matt. 3:1–2). Cole was a devout Protestant as well as a Freemason. His representation of St. John

5.39 Thomas Cole
St. John in the Wilderness, 1827.
Oil on canvas,
36 x 28^{15}/$_{16}$ in
(91.4 x 73.4 cm).
Wadsworth Atheneum,
Hartford, Connecticut.
Bequest of Daniel
Wadsworth.

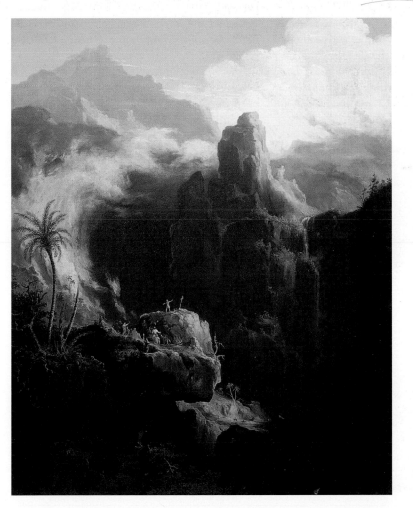

preaching in the wilderness to a group of emotionally wrought sinners bears thematic comparison to contemporaneous pictures of outdoor revivalist camp meetings. Listeners excitedly respond to the heated words and gestures of St. John, who stands aloft upon an overhanging rock pulpit. Cole roughly shaped this natural stone pulpit into the craggy profile of a face, staring downward into the valley below. The human-appearing face draws our attention to minute but brightly illuminated figures, reminiscent of Christ's holy family on the road to Bethlehem.

Throughout Cole's career, landscape forms expressed the spiritual content of spoken and written words. In the architectural, craft symbolism of Freemasonry, rough ashlar stones symbolized humankind in its imperfect, natural state after the expulsion of Adam and Eve from the Garden of Eden. Masonic brothers referred to themselves as living stones, who aspired to shape themselves into the perfected masonry stones of monumental temple and cathedral architecture. High above the dark abyss against which St. John preaches, Cole painted a large natural column of rock, rising into the clouds. Further back, a pyramidal mountain reaches heavenward into the blue sky.

During the nineteenth century, Americans identified their natural topography with the biblical landscape of the Holy Land. Local communities adopted the names of Bethlehem, Canaan, and Goshen to identify their towns with the sacred history of the Old and New Testaments. Evangelical Protestants harbored the belief that Americans, the new chosen people, would begin the thousand-year reign of Christ by converting the Jews to Christianity.

Cole rejected the idea of American chosenness, but believed that the wilderness constituted a moral environment for meditating on the Hebraic origins of literature and the visual arts. In a lecture he later wrote for the National Academy of Design, the painter described the roots of all languages in relation to the Hebrew letters of the Old Testament, because each Hebraic letter "was the representation of some object, or animal, whose spoken name commenced with it" (Cole, p. 105). The study of Hebrew demonstrated that all human languages derived from the imitation of nature or the arts of design.

In his panoramic *View from Mount Holyoke, Northampton, Massachusetts, after a Thunderstorm (The Oxbow)*, Cole inscribed Hebrew letters into the gently rising hillside above the oxbow loop

5.40 Thomas Cole
View from Mount Holyoke, Northampton, Massachusetts, after a Thunderstorm (The Oxbow), 1836.
Oil on canvas,
51½ x 76 in
(131 x 193 cm).
Metropolitan Museum of Art, New York. Gift of Mrs. Russell Sage, 1908.

Rustic overnight accommodations were already appearing atop Mount Holyoke in 1821. But in 1825 a group of Northampton citizens began to build a larger, more comfortable Mountain House, thereby luring an elite clientele of landscape tourists. Except for his own self-representation as an enterprising landscapist at Mount Holyoke, Cole here repressed signs of its commercial development.

5.41 Thomas Cole
*The Course of Empire:
The Savage State*, 1834.
Oil on canvas,
39¼ x 63¼ in
(99.7 x 160.6 cm).
The New York Historical
Society, New York.

Symbolizing the beginnings of civilization, this first painting in *The Course of Empire* cycle is set at dawn during early springtime. With the swirling, dark storm clouds and rugged, uncultivated appearance of nature, human life precariously depends on the fortunes of the hunt, as personified by the running figure at the far left. The huntsman's prey, a frightened deer, leaps over a rocky stream in the central foreground. The clearing dawn sky promises the hope of future human progress.

of the meandering Connecticut River (fig. 5.40). Right side up, the letters roughly spell the name "Noah," the Old Testament hero who survived the Flood described in the book of Genesis. Upside down, the same Hebraic letters spell the name "Shaddai," meaning the Almighty. Since the 1820s, Mount Holyoke had become a popular tourist site; its commanding view of the Connecticut River valley was celebrated by travel writers in typically biblical terms, suggesting, like Cole's Hebraic inscriptions, that the American landscape was a holy text revealing God's Word.

Situating a tiny representation of himself and his sketching equipment toward the lower right of the picture, Cole visually confirmed his direct experience of Mount Holyoke's moral effects. The dramatic composition diagonally divides the rich, placid farmland of the Connecticut River valley from the storm-drenched, rugged mountain peak. Cole purposefully ignored the fact that Mount Holyoke itself had become relatively tamed by the steady stream of tourists. He thereby created a stark contrast between the violent wilderness and the valley's pastoral calm. While his patrons regarded the pastoral balance of man and nature as the ideal state of human civilization, Cole's calm presence on the wilderness side of the canvas visually expressed his belief that "the most distinctive . . . most impres-

sive characteristic of American scenery is its wildness" (cited in McCoubrey, p. 102). He worried in an essay on American scenery, written the year before he painted *View from Mount Holyoke*, that the advance of civilization westward would obliterate what made the wilderness morally distinctive:

> There are those who regret that with the improvements of cultivation the sublimity of the wilderness should pass away: for those scenes of solitude from which the hand of nature has never been lifted, affect the mind with a more deep toned emotion than aught which the hand of man has touched. Amid them the consequent associations are of God the creator—they are his undefiled works, and the mind is cast into the contemplation of eternal things (cited in McCoubrey, p. 102).

Comfortably at home in an American wilderness that had virtually disappeared in the East, the politically conservative Cole feared the dangers of a rootless urban-industrial society. Writing in 1836 to one of his most important patrons, a wholesale grocery merchant named Luman Reed, the artist especially condemned the railroad's intrusion into the Catskill Mountains, where he spent his summers and early autumns sketching. He referred to the owners of the Catskill and Canajoharie Railroad

5.42 Thomas Cole
The Course of Empire: The Consummation of Empire, 1835–6. Oil on canvas, 51¼ x 76 in (130.2 x 193 cm). The New York Historical Society, New York.

Although Cole's series seems to represent the pagan Roman Empire, contemporaries also interpreted the imagery with reference to Jerusalem and other biblical cities that fell victim to pride and decadence. The picture's architecture bears some resemblance to John Nash's *Cumberland Terrace* (1826) in Regent's Park, London, which Cole would have seen in 1829.

as "the copper-hearted barbarians" who "are cutting all the trees down in the beautiful valley on which I have looked so often with a loving eye" (cited in Wallach, p. 73). That same year, Cole completed for Reed a pessimistic series of five large historical landscapes collectively entitled *The Course of Empire*. Inspired in large measure by his 1829–32 trip to England and the European continent, the series traces the cyclical birth and death of an ancient civilization through five stages: *The Savage State* (fig. 5.41), *The Pastoral or Arcadian State, The Consummation of Empire* (fig. 5.42), *Destruction, and Desolation*. The last three panels expressed Cole's conservative opinion that human pride and greed were poison seeds for civilization's self-destruction. He arranged the series according to the seasons of the year and the times of the day. *The Consummation of Empire*, the central panel, represents the high noon of an overheated summer's day. Nature's presence has been marginalized by lavish, non-functional architecture. Evoking associations with the last days of the Roman Empire, Cole tightly paints an orgy of tiny human figures celebrating the military conquests of an emperor, whose procession through a gaudy triumphal arch can be seen in the lower-left foreground.

According to the art historians Angela Miller and Alan Wallach, Cole probably intended his imperial conqueror as a veiled reference to President Andrew Jackson. First elected president in 1828, Jackson incurred the fears and wrath of political conservatives. While rhetorically appealing to the common man, Jackson largely ignored the nation's aristocratic elite in making appointments to political office. Instead of genteel society's elite, he rewarded Democratic Party loyalists and social upstarts with the spoils of office. Jackson's administration angered orthodox Protestants by refusing to halt the Sunday mail service and insisting upon the constitutional separation of church and state. On the other hand, the President's aggressive campaign to extend American power westward disturbed supporters of the Supreme Court. Defying the constitutional rule of law, Jackson openly encouraged the state of Georgia to ignore a decision written by Supreme Court Justice John Marshall, which would have prevented the expulsion of Cherokee Indians from native lands. By 1838, Jackson's cruel policy had removed 70,000 Native Americans into territories west of the Mississippi, causing thousands of deaths during the forced march.

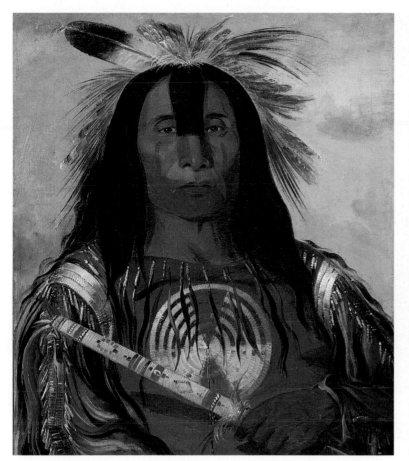

5.43 George Catlin
*Buffalo Bull's Back Fat,
Head Chief, Blood Tribe
(Blackfoot)*, 1832.
Oil on canvas, 29 x 24 in
(73.7 x 60.9 cm).
National Museum of
American Art,
Washington, D.C.

Possessing a powerful
square jaw and thick neck,
the chief stares directly at
the beholder. His red-
painted face, head feathers,
and colorfully ornamented
costume and pipe are
sketched with free, often
wispy brushstrokes. Set
against a contrasting,
cloudy blue sky, the
warrior's portrait possesses
almost visionary intensity.

Artists and Imperial Expansion

Cole's *The Course of Empire: The Savage State* (see fig. 5.41) does not explicitly represent Native American huntsmen, but the first painting in the series does prophesy the inevitable extinction of primitive, nomadic tribesmen. Within the middle ground of the imaginative wilderness, a circle of tiny teepees alludes to Indian rituals and domestic life, which will soon disappear with the more settled civilization of the *Pastoral State*. Other painters took a more anthropological approach to the plight of Native Americans. Artists rushed to meet the public's demand for a visual record of Indian rituals, customs, and costumes. Most famously, the Pennsylvania-born artist George Catlin (1796–1872) claimed that in his pictures of "the noble races of red men" he had "flown to their rescue—not of their lives or of their race (for

they are "*doomed*" and must perish), but to the rescue of their looks and their modes" (cited in McCoubrey, pp. 94–95). Catlin was saving the memory of Indians, though doomed in the real world, for his white patrons: "Phoenix-like, they may rise from the 'stain on a painter's palette' and live again upon canvas, and stand forth for centuries yet to come, the living monuments of a noble race" (cited in McCoubrey, p. 95). In travels to the western frontier, Catlin painted several hundred portraits of subjects belonging to approximately fifty different tribes (fig. 5.43). The exhibition of his "Indian Gallery" throughout America and Europe began in 1837. In London, at the Egyptian Hall in Piccadilly, Catlin's pictures were accompanied by a living group of Iowa Indians. The Egyptian-revival building implicitly suggested the belief held by many of Catlin's contemporaries that Native Americans were descendants of the ancient Egyptians or were, perhaps, one of the lost tribes of Israel.

Cole viewed American imperial expansion with a jaundiced eye, for it posed a threat to traditional values of civic virtue and self-sacrifice. The land rush westward and the commercialization of American life signified the danger that material selfishness and consumer luxuries would dissipate public morals. For Cole, the decadent architectural wilderness of *The Course of Empire: The Consummation of Empire* (see fig. 5.42) was far more worrisome than the vibrant energy of the *Savage State*. In his earlier painting of *Kaaterskill Falls* (see fig. 5.38), he nostalgically included a tiny Native American standing upon a precipice in the center of the picture.

Anxiety regarding private and public morality in an expanding empire led Cole to paint an additional series of imaginative landscapes. Commissioned originally by Samuel Ward, a wealthy, deeply pious New York banker, *The Voyage of Life* is composed of four panels, representing the ages of man from birth to death: *Childhood, Youth* (fig 5.44), *Manhood,* and *Old Age*. If *The Course of Empire* was an allegorical warning for the nation at large, *The Voyage of Life* narrowed its focus to the fate of an individual soul and its stages of development metaphorically expressed by dramatic changes in the times of the day, seasons of the year, weather conditions, and landscape configurations.

5.44 Thomas Cole
*The Voyage of Life:
Youth*, 1840.
Oil on canvas,
52 x 78 in
(133 x 199 cm).
Munson-Williams-Proctor
Arts Institute, Utica,
New York.

Throughout the quartet, the voyager travels in a boat, decorated with golden angels, and is accompanied initially by a guardian angel. In *Youth*, the happy baby of *Childhood* has become an adventurous young man, who has impetuously declared his independence, leaving the guardian angel standing upon a river bank. Now sole commander of the boat, the excited boy, dressed in bright red, gazes upward toward an immense cloud in the shape of an exotic, Oriental-style castle. Cole was, perhaps, recalling his own Masonic youth, since apprentice Freemasons were admonished against fanciful "castle building" or pie-in-the-sky schemes, and were urged, instead, to pursue "useful knowledge" (cited in Bjelajac, 2001, p.183). Indeed, the fabulous architecture projected by the imagination of the inexperienced, impressionable youth recalls the dangers of the wildly exuberant, overbuilt urban environment earlier represented in *The Course of Empire: The Consummation of Empire.* Beyond the lush, paradisiacal foreground, the river makes a sudden, sharp turn to the right

and, in the background behind the guardian angel, viewers can see what the youth entirely fails to notice: rough, craggy cliffs looming ominously along a river that is becoming treacherous rapids. Cole's *Manhood* then represents an older, wiser voyager, praying for God's assistance as he fearfully descends through a stormy, cavernous landscape toward the distant sunset of life. *The Voyage of Life* became Cole's most popular work, in part, because it ended more hopefully than did *The Course of Empire.* Possessing more faith in the destiny of the human soul than in the earthly glory of empire, Cole represented *Old Age* as a period of spiritual revelation, when the aging Christian voyager, at rest and reunited with his guardian angel, gratefully looks forward to a heavenly future.

Cole eventually painted two, virtually identical, versions of *The Voyage of Life* for public exhibition, and the series was widely reproduced in engraved editions. Following the artist's unexpected death in 1848, a memorial retrospective exhibition of his paintings at the American Art

Union attracted some 500,000 visitors. The original version of *The Voyage of Life* was then purchased by the Art-Union as a prize for its annual lottery. In 1849, the organization distributed some 20,000 engraved reproductions of *Youth* to its members, making the panel of fallible enthusiasm and hope the best-known picture in the series.

Cole died after seeing the United States triumph in a war against Mexico that he adamantly opposed. One might imagine that he regarded this military action as an unwise adventure and exercise in castle-building, engendered by the republic's overheated, youthful imagination. Under the terms of the Treaty of Guadalupe-Hidalgo, signed in February 1848, the war had ended after two years of bloodshed and the United States had become a continental power, acquiring all of California, as well as New Mexico. Annexation of Texas, which had contributed to the outbreak of hostilities, was reconfirmed by Mexico's recognition of the Rio Grande as the southern border of the United States.

In the wake of the United States' victory over Mexico and its new identity as a Pacific power, Congress voted in 1850 to expand the Capitol building in Washington to accommodate the growing number of senators and representatives from the new states. The Philadelphia architect Thomas Ustick Walter (1804–87) offered a plan for two additional north and south wings that would blend with the neoclassical appearance of the old building (fig. 5.45). Walter also proposed to replace the old dome with a much higher and more elaborately decorated cast-iron dome, similar in profile to St. Peter's basilica in the Vatican or to St. Paul's Cathedral in London.

Construction of the Capitol expansion necessitated new paintings and sculptures to decorate the building's interior and exterior. During the 1830s and 1840s, painters already were working on murals for the remaining panels of the Rotunda, finishing the job that John Trumbull had begun in 1817. Unlike Trumbull's relatively secular subjects of Revolutionary War scenes (see chapter 4), the artists Robert W. Weir (1803–89) and John Gadsby Chapman (1808–89) represented the colonial founders of Massachusetts and Virginia in explicitly religious terms (figs. 5.46–5.47). Weir's New England Pilgrims kneel in prayer to form a covenant with God. Chapman's Virginians piously convert the Indian princess Pocahontas to Christianity.

5.45 Thomas U. Walter
United States Capitol, Senate, and House Wings, Washington, D.C., 1855–65. Architect of the Capitol, Washington, D.C.

5.46 Robert W. Weir
Embarkation of the Pilgrims at Delft Haven, Holland, 22 July 1620, 1836–43.
Oil on canvas, 12 x 18 ft (3.65 x 5.48 m).
Architect of the Capitol, Washington, D.C.

Representing the Old World, a group of Pilgrims is seen departing from Delft Haven in the Netherlands toward religious asylum in America. Kneeling on the deck of the Speedwell, the Pilgrims are led in prayer by the Reverend John Robinson, who gazes upward and, with open hands, asks God's blessing. The Dutch town is visible at the right, while a rainbow at the left beckons toward the American future.

5.47 (right)
John Chapman
Baptism of Pocahontas at Jamestown, Virginia, 1613, 1836–40.
Oil on canvas, 12 x 18 ft (3.65 x 5.48 m).
Architect of the Capitol, Washington, D.C.

Dressed in white, the Indian princess Pocahontas kneels before the Reverend Alexander Whiteaker, who dips one hand into an octagonal baptismal font, preparing to administer the sacrament of purification. The maiden's betrothed, John Rolfe, stands behind her, while a group of five unconverted Indians at the right represents family from her former tribal life.

Both these pictures contributed to the mid-nineteenth-century ideology of the Manifest Destiny, a term employed by politicians, clergymen, and newspaper editors to justify the war against Mexico and the confiscation of Indian territories as a holy mission to bring the western wilderness under enlightened Christian rule.

Thomas Crawford's pedimental sculpture for the east façade of the new Senate wing, *The Progress of Civilization*, represents an Indian family defeated by white settlers and the superiority of Western civilization (fig. 5.48). In Crawford's words, an Indian boy is returning from a hunting trip: "His looks are directed to the pioneer,

● **5.48** (above)
Thomas Crawford
Progress of Civilization
(detail), 1855–63.
Architect of the Capitol,
Washington, D.C.

●**5.49** (below)
Horatio Greenough
Rescue, 1837–53.
Marble, 11 ft 9 in x
10 ft 2 in (3.5 x 3 m).
Architect of the Capitol,
Washington, D.C.

In contrast to the menacing
Indians in John Vanderlyn's
The Death of Jane McCrea
(see fig. 4.52), here the
Native American warrior is
overpowered by a
formidable white settler. The
conquering rescuer of the
white woman and child is
dressed in academic,
Renaissance-style costume
to symbolize the triumph of
enlightened Anglo-Saxon
values. The figure's flat hat
and robe resemble those
worn by humanists at the
court of Henry VIII, as
depicted in the portraits of
Hans Holbein
(1497/8–1543).

whose advance he regards with surprise" (cited in Fryd, pp. 114–115). The Indian boy's father personifies fatalistic resignation. A critic for the journal *The Crayon* wrote of the Indian: "His Tribe has disappeared, he is left alone, the solitary offshoot of a mighty race; like the tree stump beside him he is old and withered, already the ax of the backwoodsman disturbs his last hours; civilization and Art, and agriculture... have desecrated his home" (cited in Fryd, p. 119). Crawford's portrayal seems relatively sympathetic, compared with Horatio Greenough's contemporaneous (now dismantled) sculptural group for the east façade of the Capitol (fig. 5.49), representing a gigantic pioneer rescuing a white woman and her baby from a bloodthirsty Indian.

George Caleb Bingham

Many admirers of Greenough's *Rescue* interpreted the conquering pioneer as a representation of the Indian fighter Daniel Boone, who, in 1775 at the beginning of the American Revolution, had led one group of frontiersmen westward into Kentucky through the Allegheny Mountains. While Greenough was

finishing his sculpture, the Missouri painter George Caleb Bingham (1811–79) unsuccessfully proposed a mural for the U.S. Capitol commemorating Boone's daring accomplishment. Bingham had painted a very widely reproduced painting, *Daniel Boone Escorting Settlers through the Cumberland Gap*, which represents Boone and his wife as if they were Mary and Joseph, Christ's holy family (fig. 5.50). Like Cole, whom he deeply admired, Bingham represented a wilderness redeemed by religious symbolism. The pyramidal group of settlers also evokes associations with the children of Israel's forty years of wandering in the wilderness before they entered the Promised Land. As Boone leads his wife's white horse forward into the light, they are flanked on either side by rough emblems of Christ's cross in the intersecting dead tree branches at the left and in a horizontal root and vertical branch in the painting's lower right.

A native of Virginia, Bingham had moved with his parents to Franklin, Missouri, where his father ran the Square and the Compass, an inn that probably doubled as a Masonic lodge. Bingham's career began when he became a stu-

5.50 George Caleb Bingham
Daniel Boone Escorting Settlers Through the Cumberland Gap, 1851–2.
Oil on canvas, 36½ x 50¼ in (92.7 x 127.6 cm). Washington University Gallery of Art, St. Louis, Missouri. Gift of Nathaniel Phillips, 1890.

5.51 George Caleb ● Bingham
Jolly Flatboatmen, 1846.
Oil on canvas,
38⅛ x 48½ in
(96.9 x 123.2 cm).
National Gallery of Art,
Washington D.C. Loan,
Manoogian Foundation,
New York.

Bingham's pyramid of sculpturesque workmen may be compared to the Egyptian pyramid decorating the Great Seal of the United States (see fig. 4.18). The implied apex of Bingham's triangular composition is the radiant solar light, against which the dancing flatboatman is silhouetted. Often the sun was interpreted as a symbol of the all-seeing eye of God.

dio assistant to the itinerant portraitist Chester Harding (1792–1866). Harding gained fame by painting portraits of the aging Boone, who lived sixty miles south of Franklin on the Missouri River. Initially following Harding as a portraitist, Bingham turned toward genre paintings of Missouri and Mississippi river life. A trip to New York had convinced him that there was a substantial market in the East for such pictures. Bingham produced his major paintings primarily for the American Art-Union, which encouraged pictures with nationalist themes.

One of Bingham's most famous paintings of river life capitalized upon the popularity of John Banvard's (1815–91) *Panorama of the Mississippi River*, a moving panorama that was advertised as "three miles of canvas" exhibiting 1200 miles of countryside "from the mouth of the Missouri River to the City of New Orleans" (cited in Oettermann, p. 328). Banvard's moving panorama was exhibited over a period of hours on a stage displaying changing scenery to narrative commentary and musical accompaniment. Experiencing the

mammoth work was akin to a steamboat river tour. When the panorama first opened in Louisville, Kentucky, Banvard gave away free tickets to riverboatmen, who testified to the accuracy of the panorama's scenery.

An 1847 review of Banvard's "Great Picture" was illustrated by an engraved reproduction of Bingham's *Jolly Flatboatmen*. Painted for the American Art-Union, Bingham's painting reassuringly represented eight muscular, working-class riverboatmen as a happy group listening and dancing to music (fig. 5.51). The artist's stable, pyramidal composition orders the play of workers, whose reputation for rowdy, immoral behavior ordinarily generated middle- and upper-class fears of social violence. Illuminated by the rising morning sun, the bright pyramid of figures denies the reality of hard labor. Despite realistic, still-life details in the foreground cabin of the flatboat, Bingham's dreamlike picture is a nostalgic memory of pre-industrial harmony. By the late 1840s, steamboats largely had displaced the manual labor of flatboatmen in transporting cargoes for markets downstream.

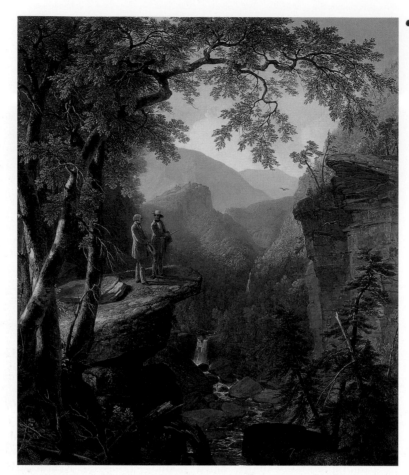

● **5.52 Asher B. Durand**
Kindred Spirits, 1849.
Oil on canvas,
44 x 36 in
(111.8 x 91.4 cm).
New York Public Library,
New York. Astor, Lenox,
Tilden Foundation.

Visions of Millennial Progress and Religious Conflict

Unlike Cole, other American painters mostly celebrated America's imperial expansion and prosperity. Yet they, too, expressed doubts or ambivalence about national progress. Five years older than Cole, Asher B. Durand (1796–1886) was one of Cole's principal disciples and lived twice as long as his mentor to become a president of the National Academy of Design. Differing from Cole's preference for dramatic, historical landscapes, Durand generally devoted most of his career as a landscapist to themes of pastoral harmony or of quiet, contemplative solitude in coolly shaded wilderness settings. The artist's most famous painting, *Kindred Spirits* (fig. 5.52), a visual eulogy to Cole, represents the recently deceased painter, sketchbook in hand, standing upon a pulpit-like outcropping of rock, in the company of his friend, the New York poet and journalist William Cullen Bryant. Out of reverence for Cole and the sublimity of nature, Bryant has removed his hat and appears to be in a state of solemn reverie. Author of "Thanatopsis," a highly praised poem on death and the healing, moral virtues of nature, Bryant had delivered Cole's funeral oration at the National Academy of Design, the year prior to Durand's painting.

Despite the rocky grandeur of the picture's Catskill wilderness setting, *Kindred Spirits* invites emotional, spiritual comparison with the pastoral mix of lofty trees and stone monuments characterizing rural cemeteries, such as Mount Auburn (see pp. 182–4). The rock outcropping upon which the two friends stand resembles a rough-hewn sarcophagus or overturned, door-shaped tombstone. Durand's reassuring picture progresses serenely from a shaded foreground of overturned trees and fallen branches, emblems of death, upward to the distant Kaaterskill Falls, and beyond to softened mountain peaks, gently bathed in sunlight and atmospheric haze. Durand seems to have shared the optimism expressed in rural cemetery landscapes: death was not to be feared, but welcomed as a natural, seamless progression toward a blissful, heavenly afterlife, symbolized in *Kindred Spirits* by soft, pillow-like white clouds and a luminous powder-blue sky. This pictorial remembrance of Cole had been commissioned as a gift to Bryant by one of Durand's principal patrons, Jonathan Sturges, a New York merchant and financier, who shared Durand's vision that the friendship of Bryant and Cole signified the elevation of painting from mere mechanical craft to high poetic art. Like poetry, the sister art of painting could lead the mind's eye toward transcendent truths or reveal God's Word through the careful

rendering of the Creator's handiwork.

Three years after *Kindred Spirits*, with its reassuring imagery of peaceful meditation and natural ascent heavenward, Durand startled the expectations of critics when he exhibited *God's Judgment upon Gog* at the National Academy in 1852 (fig. 5.53). Based on the Old Testament text from Ezekiel, chapter 39, this unusually violent picture of divine retribution was painted for Sturges, an admirer of Thomas Cole's cataclysmic *The Course of Empire*. However, unlike that pessimistic series for Sturges's former business partner, Luman Reed, Durand's biblical subject expressed nationalists' faith that America had succeeded ancient Israel as God's chosen nation. Gog, the pagan ruler of the land of Magog, had invited God's violent punishment because of his aggression against the Hebrews. As once described by Daniel Huntington, a fellow academician, Durand's biblical painting:

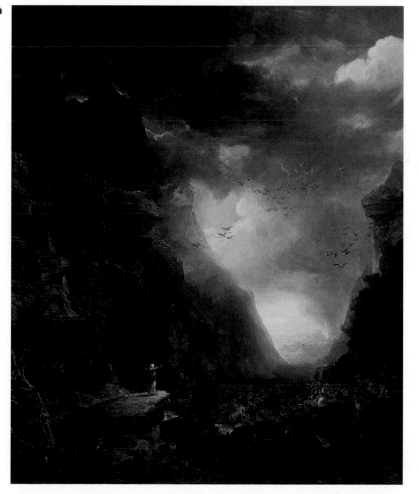

5.53 Asher B. Durand
God's Judgment upon Gog, c 1852.
Oil on canvas,
60¾ x 50½ in
(154.3 x 128.3 cm).
Chrysler Museum of Art,
Norfolk, Virginia. Gift of
Walter P. Chrysler, Jr.

represents a scene of darkness and desolation in the valley of graves. The hosts of Gog are scattered and falling in terror, while the blackened air is horrid with the ominous flight of birds of prey snuffing the blood of the slain oppressors of Israel. Out of a cavernous gap in the mountains rush forth hordes of wild beasts—tigers and leopards, swift and stealthy, thirsting for blood. There is something of an awful and demoniac spirit about this scene, the widest departure from Durand's favourite themes (cited in J Durand, pp. 174–175).

The art historian Gail Husch has found that while most contemporary reviews of Durand's painting were positive, others lamented the violent character of the picture. One reviewer argued that the cruelty of God's punishment unfortunately made one sympathetic to Gog and the enemies of Israel. The artist painted the sensational subject with unusually vigorous brushwork, which reduced the forces of Gog in the middle ground to virtual illegibility. Within the cavernous abyss, human figures and animals

5.54 Sunstone Capital from the Nauvoo, Illinois, Mormon temple
National Museum of American History, Smithsonian Institution, Washinton, D.C.

swirl about in a chaotic frenzy of destruction. Meanwhile, Ezekiel stands upon a rock pulpit similar in shape to the outcropping in *Kindred Spirits* (see fig. 5.52). Like a powerful magician, hands raised and cloak blowing in the wind, the prophet appears to orchestrate nature's destructive powers. The bright red of his cloak visually links him with the lightning and the fiery, volcanic explosion overhead.

5.55 Hannah Cohoon
Gift Drawing: The Tree of Light or Blazing Tree, 1845.
Ink, pencil, and gouache on paper, 16 x 20⅞ in (40.6 x 53 cm). Museum of American Folk Art, New York.

The inscription below the image reads: "The bright silver coulered [sic] light streaming from the edges of each green leaf resembles so/ many torches . . . I saw the whole tree as the angel held it before me as distinctly as I ever/ saw a natural tree, I felt very cautious about taking hold of the tree lest the blaze should/ touch my hand." Reflecting the feminine origins of Shakerism, most of those who produced gift drawings were women. According to an inscription on the back, Cohoon intended this work for a "Sister" Shaker.

Sturges, the patron, orginally suggested the Old Testament subject to Durand. A deeply religious man, Sturges was not an abolitionist. Like other members of the social elite, he feared abolutionist politics as a disruptive threat to national unity and stability. At the same time, however, the pious Sturges apparently regarded slavery as an immoral, evil institution. In 1850, just before Durand's painting, Congress had passed the Fugitive Slave Act, which made it easier for Southern slave owners to recapture former and runaway slaves who had fled to the North. Fiery abolitionist clergymen promised that an angry Old Testament Jehovah would punish the United States with "an earthquake voice through the land" (cited in Zinn, p. 181). Many of those who saw the painting at the 1852 academy exhibition may have interpreted *God's Judgment upon Gog* in relation to the angry rhetoric of anti-slavery.

However, far from being an entirely violent, gloomy painting, Durand's picture draws the viewer inward toward a distant background of blue sky, white clouds, and sunbathed fields of green. The artist appears to promise an era of peace and prosperity once the cataclysmic storms of the present have passed. Many antebellum Protestants believed in a future millennium—the thousand-year reign of Christian harmony before God's final judgment of humankind.

Whether Durand intended it or not, *God's Judgment upon Gog* could arouse associations with more extreme forms of political radicalism and religious zealotry. Durand affiliated himself with the Unitarian Church, a liberal Protestant denomination, whose clergy criticized revivalist camp meetings by comparing them to natural catastrophes that overwhelmed audiences. Inundated by a flood of emotion, individual souls lost their free will. They became "machines," manipulated by artful demagogues or tyrants. During the 1840s, the Baptist preacher William Miller (1782–1849) had created a wave of national hysteria by forecasting the Second Coming of Christ. Throughout the country, thousands of people were motivated by Miller and fellow revivalists to abandon their homes and possessions, dress in white robes, and meet on hilltops for this supernatural, millennial event. Christ's failure to appear as prophesied resulted in the collapse of the Millerite movement in 1844.

Millennial dreams of Christ's return or of a heavenly "New Jerusalem" literally descending to earth continued to generate and sustain new religious sects, contributing to national conflict rather than peaceful harmony. In 1846, the Mormons, or members of the Church of Jesus Christ of Latter-Day Saints, completed construction of a temple that towered over their quasi-independent city-state Nauvoo, Illinois, on the banks of the Mississippi River. The Mormon religion originated from the visions of Joseph Smith (1805–44) from western upstate New York, where myriad religious sects arose in response to social dislocations caused by capitalist development. Steeped in the occult search for buried treasures and the Masonic delight in secret rituals, Smith announced that he had dug up a set of golden tablets, inscribed with "reformed Egyptian" hieroglyphics. Translating the mysterious text with a magical set of "seer stones," he claimed to reveal the history of ancient American Indian tribes, who had migrated from Egypt and the Holy Land. Smith's *Book of Mormon* prophesied the establishment of God's heavenly kingdom in the American West. Incurring charges of blasphemy and sexual immorality, Mormon "saints" practiced polygamy, conducted secret rituals in their temples, and chose to live communally apart from the American mainstream. At Nauvoo, they established a virtually autonomous theocracy, a divinely guided government or city-state, administered by the church fathers. However, on June 27, 1844, a mob of Illinois state militiamen, motivated by religious bigotry and fears of political separatism, lynched Smith, leaving plans for a Mormon empire in the Far West to his successor, Brigham Young. Only remnants of the original Nauvoo temple have survived. Among the remains is a capital that once looked down from atop one of the building's exterior pilasters (fig. 5.54). As a substitute for traditional Doric, Ionic, or Corinthian capitals, the Mormon "sunstones" symbolized the celestial sphere, the highest glory of God, to which all Latter-Day Saints aspire. Above the radiant sun's visage, with its deep-set eyes, large nose, and puckered lips, are two disembodied hands, holding trumpets to announce the apocalyptic advent of the heavenly kingdom. Although the Mormon sunstones can be compared to New England gravestone motifs (see fig. 2.34), scholars have also related them to the emblematic sun and moon faces decorating Masonic aprons and lodge certificates (see figs. 3.10 and 3.33).

Originating in eighteenth-century England, the Shakers, or The United Society of Believers in Christ's Second Appearing, also employed the visual arts to draw together the heavenly and earthly spheres. So named because of their highly emotional, ecstatic worship services, Shakers were followers of Ann Lee (1736–84), "Mother Ann," a charismatic prophetess or spiritual seer from Manchester, England, who eventually led her small sect of believers to America. Practicing celibacy and avoiding the world at large, Shakers organized themselves into small, isolated villages, based upon the communal ownership of property.

Following her death, Mother Ann's disciples established Shaker communities in New England, New York, Ohio, Kentucky, and Indiana. Many Shaker villages did not survive long and were in decline after the mid-nineteenth century. However, as they gradually disappeared, these farming communities became admired aesthetically for the functional simplicity of their buildings, domestic interiors, and furniture.

Traditionally, Shakers, like other radical Protestant sects, rejected visual images as idolatrous. Yet, by the late 1830s, in a climate of religious revivalism, Shakers began producing "gift drawings" that purported to communicate spiritual "gifts" or revelations from Mother Ann and other ancestors of the faith, who had passed over into the spirit world. Gift drawings kept alive and made visible the millennial vision of Ann Lee, whose life and teachings were said to mark the advent of the Second Coming of Christ. Deified following her earthly death, Ann Lee was resurrected as a female incarnation of Christ. In the Shaker community of Hancock, Massachusetts, Hannah Cohoon (1788–1864) carefully composed her *Gift Drawing: The Tree of Light or Blazing Tree* (fig. 5.55) as the record of a personal visionary experience. Symmetrically balanced around the central axis of the firmly rooted tree trunk, the sharply pointed leaves glow with radiating, squiggly lines. The five-pointed leaf clusters along the outer edges of the tree particularly suggest celestial stars, symbolizing the millennial reunification of earthly and heavenly spheres.

Liberal Protestants did not believe in the imminent return of Christ to earth. Rather, they put their faith in the notion of human per-

●**5.56 Asher B. Durand**
Progress (The Advance of Civilization), 1853.
Oil on canvas, 4 x 6 ft (1.22 x 1.83 m). Warner Collection of Gulf States Paper Corporation, Tuscaloosa, Alabama.

**5.57 Jasper Francis ●
Cropsey**
*Starrucca Viaduct,
Pennsylvania*, 1865.
Oil on canvas,
22⅜ x 36⅜ in
(56.9 x 92.5 cm).
Toledo Museum of Art,
Toledo, Ohio.

Even more than Thomas
Cole and other artists of the
Hudson River School,
Cropsey liked to paint
autumnal landscapes for
their rich contrasts of
colorful foliage. Painted
toward the end of the Civil
War, this panoramic view of
bounty and progress
celebrates the benefits of
peaceful pursuits.

fectibility. Unitarians rejected the divinity of
Christ. Durand admired the Boston Unitarian
clergyman William Ellery Channing, who
argued that Jesus Christ represented a human
ideal toward which all humankind must strive.
Unitarians and other liberal Protestants assumed
that the Christian millennium was achievable
through human agency. Human progress toward
Christ's perfection was especially promising in
America. For Channing, the cyclical rise and fall
of empires would be broken in the free and open
society of the New World.

In Boston, Sunday-school teachers at
Channing's Federal Street Church voted not to
teach children the Old Testament. They believed
that the Hebraic stories of human depravity and
God's angry judgment were too demoralizing
and frightening for the very young. Certainly
Durand's painting of *God's Judgment upon Gog*
may have been thought unsuitable for innocent
young eyes or for individuals with sensitive tem-
peraments. However, Durand's next major
painting more clearly expressed a millennial
optimism in the nation's future.

Commissioned by Charles Gould, a financier
for the Ohio and Mississippi Railroad, Durand's

Progress (The Advance of Civilization) celebrates
the transformative power of American industry
and technology ●(fig. 5.56). Durand visually
rejects Cole's pessimistic *The Course of Empire*,
with its central image of human depravity in *The
Consummation of Empire* (see fig. 5.42). By combining the stages of civilization into a single
painting, Durand marginalized a group of
diminutive Indians to a remnant of wilderness
located far left on the canvas. From their shaded
space, the Native Americans gaze in apparent
wonder at the luminous vision of civilization
in the valley below. The shade trees in the
wilderness are tinged by the golden light of
the rising sun, symbolizing the new millennial
age of Christian striving toward perfection.
The tree that rises highest into the light blue
sky bends toward the sun in deference to its
divine potency.

From the picture's lower-right corner, telegraph wires lead the eye past the pastoral space of
cattle and a horse-drawn wagon toward a canal
and river, transportation arteries for a commercial, industrialized civilization. The telegraph
poles would have triggered contemporary associations with Durand's fellow painter Samuel F.

B. Morse, the inventor of the telegraph. During the 1830s and 1840s, experimentation with electromagnetism had reportedly, according to a friend, led Morse, the president of the National Academy of Design, to believe that:

> God had created the great forces of Nature not only as manifestations of his own infinite power, but as expressions of good-will to man, to do him good, and that every one of God's great forces could yet be utilized for man's welfare; that modern science was constantly evolving from the hitherto hidden secrets of Nature some new development promotive of human welfare, and . . . that analogically magnetism would do in the advancement of human welfare what the Spirit of God would do in the moral renovation of man's nature; that it would educate and enlarge the forces of the world (cited in Prime, p. 305).

For both Morse and Durand, scientific and technological progress went hand in hand with moral and spiritual enlightenment. In antebellum America, the Christian God of the Bible was being reconceived as a deity defined by nature's energy forces, which were being harnessed for the welfare of humankind. Unlike Cole's stultifying, overdeveloped empire in *Consummation*, Durand's optimistic vision of America's technological progress is providentially blessed by the elemental flux of air, water, and radiant sunlight bathing and softening gently rolling hills. The artist represents factories, steamboats, and a railroad train puffing a thin trail of white steam that emulates in miniature the golden grandeur of nature's clouds. In contrast to Cole's critique of railroad magnates' destruction of the wilderness, Durand's inoffensive train is scarcely visible, constituting no threat to the divine beauty of the panoramic landscape. Durand's painting served the ideological purposes of Charles Gould, who financially supported train excursions by painters into the wilderness. Seeking to unify the nation through transportation and communication technology, railroad entrepreneurs wished to alleviate environmental concerns and encourage tourist travel by commissioning inspiring landscapes that harmonized nature with industry.

Other Cole disciples emulated Durand's more optimistic view of railroads as engines of progress. In *Starrucca Viaduct, Pennsylvania*, Jasper Francis Cropsey (1823–1900) represented the distant view of a newly constructed railroad bridge that itself had become a tourist attraction (fig. 5.57). The stone viaduct was regarded as an engineering miracle, rising over one hundred feet high to cross over more than one thousand feet of the Starrucca creek and Starrucca valley near Lanesboro, Pennsylvania. Cropsey chose this scenic viewpoint because it recorded a popular tourist train stop along the Erie Railroad. A contemporary newspaper described the site in terms parallel to Cropsey's panoramic composition:

> From the summit of the hill, just before you descend to Lanesboro, as perfect a picture lies before you as the eye ever longed for. The landscape is skirted by thickly-wooded hills—the mirror-like Susquehanna sleeps through the midst of green meadows. Over it you see an old rural bridge, contrasting, pleasingly, with the elegant Tressel Bridge near by. . . . The solid masonry of the Starrucca Viaduct, with its regular arches, is seen in the distance, blending with the scenery, the grandeur, and dignity of art, like the effect of a piece of colossal statuary in a green park (cited in Howat, p. 211).

Both the newspaper account and Cropsey's painting encouraged beholders to identify technology and engineering projects with the fine arts of painting and sculpture. Displacing Durand's Native Americans in *Progress*, Cropsey's internal beholders are tourists, whose relaxed presence reinforces the composition's easy, sweeping continuity between foreground wilderness and the background's artful, industrialized garden. Cropsey's distant, atmospheric view of the viaduct allows it to blend seamlessly with the surrounding topography.

Transcendentalism, Spiritualism, and American Art

Economic depressions periodically shook confidence in national progress. From 1837 until 1843, the United States experienced its first major economic depression. Bankruptcies and high unemployment led many to question the magic of free markets, the growing disparity of wealth between rich and poor, and America's very identity as a Christian nation. In Boston, the former Unitarian clergyman Ralph Waldo Emerson challenged the nation's social and religious establishment by abandoning the Christian faith and its fragmentation into separate denominations and sects. He urged a new Transcendentalist philosophy, which rejected established institutions and traditional authority figures in favor of self-reliant, individuals, communing with the natural, vitalistic energies of God's universe.

Transcendentalist philosophers and their followers looked for commonalities rather than differences among religious faiths, including Buddhism and other non-Christian religions. They hoped to "transcend" human conflict through social as well as religious reforms. While Emerson emphasized individual self-reliance, other Transcendentalists founded socialist communes as experimental alternatives to capitalist greed and competition. Participants in the Brook Farm commune, established in 1841 at West Roxbury, Massachusetts, later founded the American or Religious Union of Associationists. Also known as the First Church of Humanity, this Boston organization advocated socialist principles and a union of diverse faiths under a broad theological umbrella.

The services of the Religious Union of Associationists centered upon an empty chair "symbolizing the Invisible Presence" (cited in Ellis, p. 89). On the nearby altar, a candelabrum with three candles signified members' tripartite unity with God, nature, and humanity. During meetings, Associationists discussed a range of issues from labor abuses and communist political theory to phrenology and Spiritualist séances. Several members of the group were Spiritualist mediums.

Joining Transcendentalism in opposition to the social and religious establishment, the Spiritualist movement developed during the late 1840s as a radical alternative to the denominational sectarianism of Christian churches. In 1848, two young sisters, Margaret and Kate Fox, from upstate New York, gained national attention for their reputed ability to communicate with the dead. Spiritualist mediums and their supporters argued in quasi-scientific terms that just as the recently invented telegraph could transmit messages across vast distances, so could spirits from a higher life beyond the grave communicate through encoded rappings analogous to the Morse code.

By the early 1860s, the notion of a "Spiritual Telegraph" had gripped the national imagination, while attracting approximately 1 million followers. The Poughkeepsie, New York, seer Andrew Jackson Davis helped to legitimize Spiritualist rappings and séances by framing them within a "Harmonial Philosophy." Dispensing entirely with the existence of Hell, Davis interpreted the earth as a lower sphere of Heaven. After death, individual souls would continue to develop in spiritual harmony, beauty, and wisdom.

Many artists and writers were attracted by the Transcendentalist and Spiritualist movements. The Gloucester, Massachusetts, painter Fitz Hugh Lane (1804–65) was a member of the Religious Union of Associationists as were other Boston-area artists who attempted to synthesize Spiritualist and socialist principles to create a heaven upon earth. Lane's early topographical views represented and promoted Gloucester's development as a fishing and tourist community north of Boston on the Atlantic coast. However, later pictures that he painted in Boston and Maine as well as Gloucester are luminous and geometric distillations of real life, suggesting a spiritual transcendence of materialist, economic interests. *Boston Harbor at Sunset* nostalgically celebrates Boston's seafaring history, while relegating the presence of a modern steamboat to the distant background (fig. 5.58). Recalling Horatio Greenough's admiration for the organic, functional beauty of American sailing ships, Lane carefully depicts the sleek, linear architecture of masts, rigging, and hulls against multicolored sky and mirrorlike water. Receding into the colorful distance from a darkened foreground, his great ships appear as silent, ghostly witnesses to the sun's slow descent into the underworld. With darkened white sails ascending like church spires or towers into the glowing twilight, they inevitably evoked moral associations with life's spiritual voyage and quest for perfection. The crystallized stillness of the picture contrasts with Durand's animated painting of *Progress*. Lane's sunset view seems to have more in common with the spiritual atmosphere of Mount Auburn Cemetery than with the activist ideology of westward expansionism and industrial modernization.

●**5.58 Fitz Hugh Lane**
Boston Harbor at Sunset,
1850–55.
Oil on canvas,
26¼ x 42 in
(66.8 x 106.6 cm).
Museum of Fine Arts,
Boston, Massachusetts.
Gift of Maxim Karolik for
the Mr. and Mrs. Karolik
Collection of American
Paintings, 1815–65.

The yellow light of sunset
forms a great arc across the
horizon, contrasting with
the cool blue of the
evening sky above. The
strong color note of a red-
shirted oarsman calls
attention to the small
central boat that draws us
toward the water's reflected
glory of golden light.

Lane worked in relative isolation from Hudson River School artists, but a number of New York–based landscapists also tended toward a more quiet, "luminist" style that depicted simplified scenes of the Atlantic coast. By the end of 1858, the widely traveled Pennsylvania-born painter Martin Johnson Heade (1819–1904) had settled into the new Studio Building on Tenth Street (see fig. 6.10), which also contained the studios of Frederic Church and numerous other American artists. Spending summers on the Rhode Island coast, Heade began to paint a series of mysteriously evocative seascapes that focused primarily upon the dramatic effects of light. Heade's first in the series, *Approaching Thunder Storm* (fig. 5.59), adopts a strongly

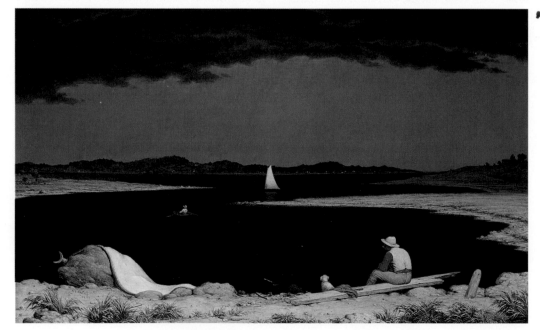

●**5.59 Martin Johnson
Heade**
*Approaching Thunder
Storm*, 1859.
Oil on canvas,
28 x 44 in
(71.1 x 111.8 cm).
Metropolitan Museum,
New York City. Gift of
Erving Wolfe Foundation
and Mr and Mrs Erving
Wolfe, 1975.

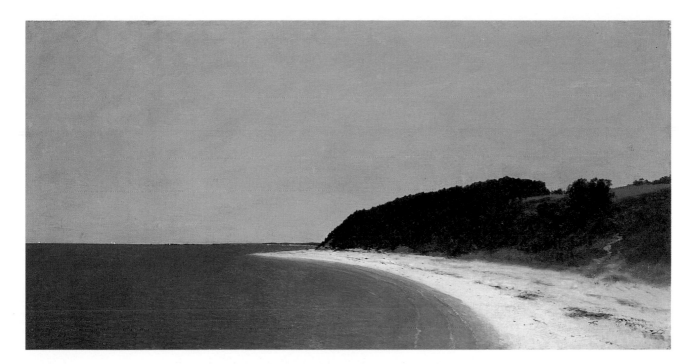

horizontal, panoramic shape, and yet the painting possesses the meditative intimacy of a moment frozen in time, transforming ordinary life into an extraordinary, revelatory experience. Heade seems to have learned more than the rudimentary craft techniques of painting from his early apprenticeship with the Quaker artist-preacher Edward Hicks, during the 1830s (see fig.5.37). Quaker and radical Protestant emphasis upon an inner spiritual light or "still small voice" (I Kings 19:12) undoubtedly influenced Heade. Yet this pacific, mystical strain of Protestantism bears comparison with the self-reliant

individualism of Transcendentalist thought and its notion of introspective communion with a universal divine presence.

In Heade's painting, small details do, indeed, seem to speak in moral, religious tones. A young man, brightly dressed in red and yellow clothes, sits on a broken, weathered wooden plank and, together with a white dog, quietly looks out over a portion of Narragansett Bay, Rhode Island. In contrast with the placid water, blackened by dark storm clouds overhead, the middle and foreground ellipse of sand and lime-green shore appears eerily illuminated by partial breaks in the sky. Heade deployed a small, ghostly white sailboat at the center of this ominous scene. Left of center and closer in, another man rows a boat to shore. He serves as a further visual link in the circular chain that connects the central sailboat with the youth, his dog, and the white, shroudlike sail, which is suggestive of a burial garment and is draped over a heart-shaped rock in the left foreground. Void of grandiose rhetoric, Heade's picture reinterprets the voyage-of-life theme that Thomas Cole had explored two decades earlier. In minimizing dramatic narrative in favor of mundane, naturalistic details and quietly intense, transfiguring light effects, Heade created a pictorial meditation upon the human, natural cycles of life and death upon the eve of the Civil War. In fact, the artist continued to paint pictures of thunderstorms during the 1860s. These works were particularly popular with Protestant clergymen, who employed storm imagery in sermons as moral warnings of life's trials and tribulations.

Heade was a great admirer of the New York artist John Frederick Kensett (1816–72), who had a particularly successful career highlighted by a series of austerely elemental, light-filled seascapes of Newport, Rhode Island, and Long Island (fig. 5.60). Kensett's friend, the Reverend Samuel Osgood, characterized the artist's paintings of Long Island Sound by comparing them to the stark, funereal landscape of ancient Egypt: "Under his touch we see the marvel of the Egyptian sands reappearing in the shore of our great Sound, and that stone looks upon you with the face of the Sphinx. That rock whispers to you the secret of earth, and sea, and sky" (cited in Roque, pp. 148–149). Unlike Cole's dramatic, often violent landscapes and Durand's and Cropsey's tributes to national progress, Kensett's abstractly minimal views of air, water, light, and earth are virtually silent, sphinxlike meditations on nature's hidden truths. Even Protestant clergymen such as Osgood were turning away from denominational dogmatism and biblical revelation toward the individual soul's direct communications with divine mysteries. No longer able to agree upon specific theological doctrines, many Protestants joined Transcendentalists and Spiritualists in banking their faith on signs for the orderly design of the universe.

Frederic Church: Natural History and the Protestant Imagination

Frederic Edwin Church (1826–1900) emerged from a traditional Protestant background to become a painter who catalogued nature's cosmic wonders from infinitesimal details to grand panoramic views. Following his teacher, Thomas Cole, Church, during the late 1840s and early 1850s, painted biblical landscapes and American historical landscapes that strongly expressed nationalist identification with Old Testament Israel.

Church's most famous work, *Niagara Falls*, may also be interpreted as a painting that stirred nationalist feeling for America's Manifest Destiny (fig. 5.61). Yet the picture was also designed to generate a degree of fear and anxiety, testing viewers' faith in God's orderly, benign universe. *Niagara Falls* thrillingly transported beholders to the dangerous edge of Niagara's Horseshoe Falls, forcing them to confront its sheer, physical power. At the lower left a dead tree branch or snag, awash with the flow of white-capped waves, points toward the fatal abyss. Commentators praised the elongated composition, which daringly eliminated a safe foreground:

> *The spectator stands looking directly upon the troubled waters, flowing at the very base line of the canvas, . . . the eye naturally travels with the current until it reaches the brink of the invisible abyss into which the water tumbles. . . (cited in Kelly, p. 51).*

When the painting was exhibited at a private New York art gallery during the spring of 1857, thousands of spectators rushed to see the work before it left for a tour through England and Scotland.

Ever since John Trumbull and other artists had begun painting views of Niagara Falls (see fig. 5.36), the sublime site had become an icon of national pride. The nearly perpetual rainbow that appeared through the prismatic mist over the Falls conjured forth the rainbow that followed the Flood in the Old Testament book of Genesis. For American tourists, the Niagara Falls' rainbow signified the nation's special identity as a chosen land and people. Church's sweeping, panoramic painting interlinks the powerful arch of the Falls with the relatively tenuous, broken arch of a rainbow. The fractured rainbow descends from

The lofty Andes Mountains are powerful presences in the background, but their rounded, softened peaks do not aspire beyond the picture frame and the strongly horizontal format of Church's panorama. Despite his imaginative juxtaposition of contrasting weather conditions and types of terrain, Church emphasized the seamless harmony of nature, expressed by the foaming, misty waterfall at the right, bearing the water of melted snow from the higher elevations.

left to right through a wall of white mist before disappearing beyond the edge of the Falls.

Church's desire to accurately record physical phenomena competed with his opposing inclination to incorporate biblical symbols into landscapes. Church admired the German natural historian Alexander von Humboldt's (1769–1859) treatise *Cosmos: A Sketch of a Physical Description of the Universe*, published in four volumes beginning during the 1840s. Having traveled extensively throughout North and South America, Humboldt sought to summarize his life's work in an encyclopedic "portrait" of the entire universe. Of particular interest to Church and other artists, Humboldt advocated the art of landscape painting and geological panoramic drawings as a means for exploring and mapping the earth.

In *Niagara Falls*, Church visually replicates Humboldt's cosmic ambition by combining into a single picture views of both the near and far sides of Horseshoe Falls. This panoramic, "all-seeing" perspective expanded the normal power and range of the human eye. Furthermore, by slightly curving the long horizon line, Church suggested the curvature of the earth, the spherical shape of the planet. Moving from the macroscopic to the microscopic, he obsessively studied and sketched the movement of water in preparation for his careful, detailed rendering of its cascading, swirling flow and its misting upward into the atmosphere.

Like Humboldt, Church traveled widely throughout the western hemisphere, recording nature as if he were the original Adam naming the flora and fauna in the Garden of Eden. In 1859, Church exhibited one of his largest and most celebrated paintings, *The Heart of the Andes*, which he had finished after a second trip to Ecuador (fig. 5.62). He imaginatively harmonized into one panoramic canvas a variety of geographical regions and meteorological phenomena. ranging from snow-capped mountain peaks to a tropical forest and waterfall in the foreground.

Church ordered a specially built wooden frame for *The Heart of the Andes* that appeared to transform the picture into an upper-story palatial window overlooking a paradisiacal space. The gallery exhibition space was darkened except for the brightly lit and theatrically draped picture window. Visitors were supplied opera glasses for viewing the landscape's myriad details, which were itemized in gallery guides that read like travelogues. Perhaps the most prominent detail is a small cross in the left foreground, which attracts pious pilgrims.

For Church and his traveling companion Cyrus Field, who financed the transatlantic telegraph cable, South America seemed a natural extension of the United States, an untapped area of the New World ripe for economic development and aesthetic appropriation. Church was not the only artist from the United States to explore South America's natural resources or to be captivated by its popular association with the biblical Garden of Eden. The Indian painter George Catlin and the landscape painter Martin Johnson Heade were among those who also toured South America.

Abolitionist and Feminist Art

Though he did not travel to South America, the African-American artist Robert S. Duncanson (1821–72) deeply admired Church's *The Heart of the Andes* when it was exhibited in Cincinnati, Ohio. Duncanson's *The Land of the Lotus Eaters* (1861) emulated Church's tropical landscape. However, the Cincinnati artist already had been painting Edenic pastoral landscapes before witnessing Church's South American masterpiece.

A light-skinned mulatto who was the son of a free African-American carpenter-house painter, Duncanson was born in upstate New York, but began his career in Cincinnati as a largely self-taught landscapist working in the Hudson River School style. Located on the Ohio River, across

from the slave state of Kentucky, Cincinnati was divided over the issue of slavery. A sizable community of free blacks and white abolitionists confronted the institutional racism of the city's discriminatory "Black Laws" as well as anti-abolitionist mob violence that frequently targeted the black neighborhood of Bucktown.

Duncanson's racially mixed ancestry and lighter skin color facilitated his career, since white patrons tended to regard mulattoes as intellectually and emotionally superior to the dark-skinned African-Americans. Ambiguously situated between black and white, Duncanson angrily rejected accusations that he sometimes attempted to pass as white. He contributed to activities sponsored by the abolitionist movement and painted the portraits of Cincinnati's leading abolitionists. Yet, for the most part, he avoided explicit anti-slavery themes in his paintings, undoubtedly fearing that he might alienate his white clientele with overt, politically volatile subject matter.

Duncanson's *Uncle Tom and Little Eva* is the singular exception to the artist's avoidance of the controversy over slaves (fig. 5.63). An Episcopalian clergyman and abolitionist, Rev. James Francis Conover, commissioned the

5.63 Robert Duncanson
Uncle Tom and Little Eva, 1853.
Oil on canvas, 27¼ x 38¼ in (69.2 x 97.1 cm). Detroit Institute of Art. Gift of Mrs. Jefferson Butler and Miss Grace R. Conover.

painting and probably worked with Duncanson in conceiving the subject. The picture represents a scene from chapter twenty-two of the celebrated anti-slavery novel *Uncle Tom's Cabin* (1852) by Harriet Beecher Stowe, daughter of Lyman Beecher, a renowned Calvinist theologian. Depicting an Edenic, tropical landscape, Duncanson focuses upon the Christlike, otherworldly figure of Little Eva, the dying daughter of a Louisiana plantation owner, and of Uncle Tom, an aging, loyal slave for Eva's ungrateful father. Gesturing toward a colorful sunset over Lake Pontchartrain, near New Orleans, Duncanson's angelic Eva, dressed in white, links arms with the seated Tom, who listens intently to her vision of the heavenly afterlife, where all souls are free and equal. The painting suggests that the reconciliation of black and white and the liberation from slave labor may have to wait for another world spiritually superior to the imperfect present. The painting's gardenlike setting and statuesque little girl bear resemblance to the pastoral environments of rural cemeteries with their white marble sculptures,

promising the continued spiritual presence of the deceased. Duncanson was a follower of the Spiritualist movement, as were many abolitionists. They, like the artist, harshly judged the institution of slavery against the higher moral standards of the spirit world. Later in his career, Duncanson reportedly told friends that a spirit was assisting him in paintings of paradisiacal landscapes. Such claims were not unique to Duncanson, nor were they necessarily signs of mental derangement. As we shall see, other Spiritualist artists also were inspired by visions of spirits.

Though few other artists dared to paint scenes from Stowe's controversial novel, the impact of the book was clearly evident in art criticism on the eve of the Civil War. In 1859, a critic for the *New York Daily Tribune*, reviewing the spring exhibition at the National Academy of Design, referred to the show's most admired painting, *Negro Life at the South* (fig. 5.64), by Maine-born artist Eastman Johnson (1824–1906), as "a sort of 'Uncle Tom's Cabin' of pictures" or "a stirring speech from the Antislavery platform" (cited in John Davis, p.83). Johnson, his Northern, Yankee family transplanted to the nation's capital, was representing a scene of urban slave life in Washington, D.C. More specifically, he focused upon a ramshackle slaves' quarters and enclosed backyard that happened to be situated next to his father's substantial, three-story brick home (visible at the far right), near the corner of F and 13th Streets, a neighborhood otherwise dominated by ardent Southern proponents of slavery.

Johnson studied painting in Düsseldorf, Germany, acquiring a meticulous, realist style. In *Negro Life at the South* he carefully renders the crumbling architecture and domestic details of a decaying, urban space, within which a group of African-American figures engage in various leisure activities. A banjo-playing man just to the right of center sets the relaxed mood of private sociability. Children in close proximity to the musician listen or dance, while a young man and woman at the left, perhaps inspired by the harmonic tones, engage in the rituals of courtship. A woman with a baby leans out of an upper-story window to share in these simple pleasures, amidst the general squalor of a run-down, wood-frame building anchored, in part, by a red-brick chimney. Meanwhile, at the far right, the secluded atmosphere of this scene has been interrupted by the intrusion of a fashionably dressed white woman, the slaves' apparent mistress, who peers around an entrance doorway in the high wall that seals off the slaves' space from the world outside. The mistress's spying gaze is met with the apparent consternation and dismay of two children, especially a small, black girl in a dark-blue dress, who confronts the intruder. Her smaller frame seems to mirror the pose of the peaking, policing mistress.

While abolitionist critics interpreted Johnson's painting as an image of impoverished living conditions and slavery's moral bankruptcy, their proslavery opponents chose to see the picture as a representation of slavery's benign effects. They ignored its urban setting and associated the painting's message not with *Uncle Tom's Cabin*, but rather "My Old Kentucky Home" (1853), a minstrel song written by Stephen Foster. The song was often performed by minstrel groups of white men wearing blackface, the nostalgic lyrics romantically idealizing the supposedly idyllic, trouble-free lives of plantation slaves.

Though the artist's father was affiliated with the Democratic Party, which supported slaveholders' rights in the interests of national unity, he owned no slaves, but did employ two live-in, free black servants. Art historian John Davis suggests that *Negro Life at the South* anticipated Eastman Johnson's pro-Union stance during the Civil War. The picture was a politically engaged portrayal of a "secret city" (John Davis, p.67) of African-American slaves, confined in dilapidated housing and backyard enclosures, all existing in the shadows of official Washington, its government buildings and monuments ostensibly dedicated to liberty. Northern abolitionists bitterly denounced the presence of slavery in the nation's capital, while Southern politicians in Congress and the city's dominant Southern families sought to silence all debate upon the subject. By discounting or ignoring the geographic specificity of the painting's Washington, D.C., locale, most critics, with a few abolitionist exceptions, mitigated or softened the picture's political edge, defusing it into a generic representation of African-American stereotypes, going so far as to rename it *Old Kentucky Home*.

Prior to the popular but politically mixed reception of Johnson's topical masterpiece, another major work seemed to invite debate over the institution of slavery. Having earlier worked in Washington, D.C., Hiram Powers, a sculptor of phrenologically inspired portraits (see fig. 5.2), had become an expatriate artist in Florence, Italy, where he created his most celebrated, controversial sculpture, *The Greek Slave* (fig. 5.65). Powers had begun his career in Cincinnati and shared abolitionist sympathies with Robert Duncanson, who later visited him in Florence. Belonging to the Swedenborgian Church, named after the Swedish mystic Emanuel Swedenborg (1688–1772), Powers transformed his Florentine home into a meeting place for Spiritualist séances. Possibly Powers encouraged Duncanson's inclination toward communication with the souls of the spirit world.

In his general avoidance of overt references to African-American slavery, Duncanson took a lesson from Powers, whose *The Greek Slave* symbolized the early-nineteenth-century Greek struggle for independence against the Muslim Turks of the Ottoman Empire. In hope of gaining greater sympathy for slavery's abolition in the United States, American abolitionists publicized horrific stories of Turkish "infidels" enslaving white-skinned Caucasians. The Scottish artist Sir William Allan's painting *Sale of Circassian Captives in a Turkish Bashaw* (1818) was favorably reviewed by the abolitionist press. Although Allan's picture may have influenced Powers's decision to sculpt the *The Greek Slave*, Powers apparently feared that abolitionist zeal would destroy the national union.

Powers attributed the origins of this erotic nude sculpture not to political concerns over slavery, but to a recurrent boyhood dream. In 1851, he wrote his cousin:

> *I used to see in my sleep, when a child, a white female figure across the . . . . river. . . . It stood upon a pillar, or pedestal, was naked and to my eyes very beautiful. But the water was between me and it, too deep to ford. I had a strong desire to see it nearer, but was always prevented by the river, which was always high. This dream ceased years after, when I began to model. Altogether, one may conclude that the dream was not entirely a phantom. At that time I had no wakeful thought of sculpture, nor had I ever seen anything likely to excite such a dream (cited in Wunder, I. p. 181).*

The Greek Slave was just one of many female nudes that materialized Powers's libidinal desire to cross the river into manhood. But the manacled figure is particularly charged with sadomasochistic overtones. Anticipating hostile reviews from prudish critics, Powers attempted to "clothe" his idealized nude with morality and chastity. When the sculpture was exhibited to enthusiastic crowds in London in 1845 and then American cities beginning in 1847, visitors were given catalogues with Powers's narrative, explaining the reason and meaning of the figure's nudity. With a crucifix dangling at her side, the victimized woman attempts to deflect the corrupt, sexual gaze of her Turkish captors. She stares at them with dignified defiance, while modestly covering her pubic region with one hand.

So popular was *The Greek Slave*'s synthesis of eroticism and Christian moralism that

Powers finished six versions of the figure. Choosing to ignore possible, if unintended, allusions to African-American slavery, Southerners also flocked to see the controversial, world-famous sculpture. As a personification of female virtue and Protestant opposition to paganism, the statue won over numerous clergymen, although some insisted upon separate viewing hours for women and children. Ironically, however, in Cincinnati, where Powers began his career, *The Greek Slave* received a barrage of negative criticism from religious journals. The *Western Christian Advocate* implicitly equated the sculpture and other nude statuary with prostitutes "traveling from city to city, and from town to town, exhibiting themselves for money; and strange to say, they draw large audiences even among the ladies!" (cited in Wunder, I. p. 233).

To counter the danger of sexual voyeurism in the appreciation of sculptures, art advocates recommended that beholders stand at a distance from the work. Close-up views were discouraged because they emphasized the marble or the

●**5.65 Hiram Powers**
The Greek Slave, 1843.
Marble, 65 in
(165.1 cm) high.
Yale University Art Gallery,
New Haven, Connecticut.
Olive L. Dann Fund.

●**5.66 Harriet Hosmer**
Zenobia, 1857–9.
Marble, 88 in (223.5 cm)
high. Wadsworth
Atheneum, Hartford,
Connecticut.

Hosmer may have been
inspired by the English
author Anna
Jameson's popular
*Memoirs of
Celebrated Female
Sovereigns* (1831).

material representation of flesh. The superior distant view, by contrast, was "poetic" because it invited viewers to meditate upon the spiritual whole and moral meaning of the piece rather than its seductive, physical parts. From this poetic point of view, *The Greek Slave*'s message of victimization and chaste defiance appealed to American women, who clothed the figure with their own narratives. Feminist and abolitionist associations coalesced in the minds of some women. One woman writer imagined the white slave's "capture, her exposure in the market place; the freezing of every drop of her young blood beneath the libidinous gaze of shameless traffickers in beauty" (cited in Kasson, p. 63).

As the art historian Charles Colbert has demonstrated, Powers's sculpture also seemed to express the concerns of middle-class women involved in health and clothing reform. Groups such as the Ladies' Physiological Institute, founded in Boston in 1848, studied ways to improve the well-being and development of the female body within an increasingly urbanized environment. Resisting the male-dictated fashion industry's promotion of corsets, girdles, and other articles of tight-fitting clothing that constricted the natural contours and movements of the female body, reform-minded women could admire the beauty of *The Greek Slave* as a healthful and liberated image of ideal womanhood.

The financial success of *The Greek Slave* encouraged other sculptors to emulate or compete with the celebrated statue. In Rome, the Massachusetts-born sculptor Harriet Hosmer (1830–1908) responded to Powers's image of female powerlessness with her fully clothed historical figure of *Zenobia* (fig. 5.66). Zenobia, Queen of Palmyra in Syria during the third century C.E., had defied Roman domination of the Middle East but was captured by the Emperor Aurelian, who paraded her in chains through the streets of Rome.

While perpetuating the stereotypical image of female captivity, Hosmer's *Zenobia*, like Margaret Foley's *Cleopatra* (see fig. 5.12), commemorated a woman who had wielded governmental authority against powerful men and military forces. Hosmer was not active in the struggle for women's suffrage until the end of the century, but her dignified sculpture expressed feminists' resistance to political power-

● **5.67 Anonymous**
Harriet Hosmer at Work on her Statue of Senator Benton, c. 1861. Albumen print. Schlesinger Library, Radcliffe College, Cambridge, Massachusetts.

lessness. In an 1859 letter to the *Cosmopolitan Art Journal*, Hosmer characterized her *Zenobia* as an unsentimental personification of strength: "I have tried to make her too proud to exhibit passion or emotion of any kind; not subdued, though a prisoner; but calm, grand, and strong within herself" (cited in Kasson, p. 155).

Hosmer's later political portrait of the United States Senator Thomas Hart Benton was clothed and posed in a manner closely resembling the *Zenobia*. Hosmer had herself photographed standing next to the clay model of the colossal statue (fig. 5.67), which had been commissioned by the state of Missouri. Cloaking Benton in a Roman togalike costume that hangs like the Palmyran queen's, Hosmer wore masculine "Zouave trousers" beneath her skirt rather than petticoats, which enabled her to move more freely on the scaffolding surrounding the sculpture. When the final bronze sculpture was unveiled in St. Louis in 1868, her detractors criticized the cloak for being in conflict with Senator Benton's ruggedly masculine character.

Hosmer's sculptures implicitly suggested the fluidity or interchangeability of gender roles. Her own unconventional life as an unmarried woman who dressed and behaved in masculine ways also challenged stereotypes. In addition to pursuing a professional career overwhelmingly dominated by men, Hosmer identified herself as a Spiritualist medium. As an artist, she confronted the common male prejudice that women could not create original works of art. Perhaps for this reason, Hosmer openly discussed her experiences as a Spiritualist medium and, early in her career, chose to represent sprites or playful spirit-children, who had appeared to her in personal visions.

More powerfully, photography also served Hosmer's purpose in proving herself an accomplished artist. The photograph of Hosmer touching the Benton statue with one hand while holding a sculpting instrument with the other documented her creativity, refuting charges that her statues were conceived by Italian male assistants. Nevertheless, later in the century, the American novelist Henry James dismissively referred to Hosmer and other American women sculptors in Rome as the "white marmorean flock" (cited in Kasson, p. 11). The phrase derided the group's collective preference for the traditional, non-classical medium of marble rather than bronze, the malleable material favored by more naturalistic sculptors after the Civil War.

Photography and the Democratization of Art

Unlike the idealizing medium of white marble, the photographic process appeared inherently realistic and objective when introduced to the American public in 1839. Literally translated as "writing with light," photography seemed to exclude the fallible hand of an artist. Piercing through a camera's lens, sunlight "drew" nature's image upon a chemically sensitized plate or film. Nature, a New York critic claimed, "shall paint herself . . . by virtue of the sun's patent, all nature, animate and inanimate, shall be henceforth its own painter, engraver, printer, and publisher" (cited in Foresta and Wood, p. 224). Yet the photographer seemed to possess magical, occult powers in recording phenomena that the human eye misses or overlooks. In *The House of Seven Gables* (1851) the New England novelist Nathaniel Hawthorne (1804–64) featured a "daguerreotypist," or photographer, who enigmatically states: "There

is a wonderful insight in heaven's broad and simple sunshine. While we give it credit only for depicting the merest surface, it actually brings out the secret character with a truth that no painter would ever venture upon, even could he detect it" (p. 68).

Samuel F. B. Morse led American artists in embracing the optical and chemical process that could "fix the image of the *camera obscura*" (cited in Kloss, p. 143). Ever since the Renaissance, artists had known of this "darkened chamber" or box, which could project exterior images onto a surface interior. But, until the nineteenth century, artists could preserve the naturalistic image only by tracing over it manually. Morse recalled that during his youth, while a student at Yale University, he had experimented with camera images, attempting to make them permanent through use of paper that had been made light-sensitive by being "dipped into a solution of nitrate of silver" (cited in Kloss, p. 146). But he discovered to his frustration that the tonal areas were reversed in the final result: "light produced dark, and dark light" (cited in Kloss, p. 146). Morse had produced a negative image but did not yet know that negative film could be used to make positive photographic prints.

Later in his career, after he had become President of the National Academy of Design, Morse met the Parisian artist-inventor Louis Jacques Mandé Daguerre (1787–1851), whose daguerreotype process employed polished, light-sensitized metal plates for producing positive images that did not invert light and dark areas. Using the vapors given off by heated mercury, Daguerre developed the film plate to "bring out" the latent image, fixed it by washing away the remaining photosensitive salts, and then toned the plate with gold chloride to heighten the light-dark contrast and the image's durability. Because of its fragility and the tendency of the silver plate to tarnish, the daguerreotype had to be protected further by a glass covering. Nevertheless, Daguerre had created clear, detailed pictures that amazed Morse.

When Morse returned from his visit to Paris in 1839, he experimented with the daguerreotype photographic process and publicized it as an important advance in the worldwide democratization of art. He announced to his former painting teacher, Washington Allston:

Art is to be wonderfully enriched by this discovery. How narrow and foolish the idea which some express that it will be the ruin of art, or rather artists, for every one will be his own painter. One effect, I think, will undoubtedly be to banish the sketchy, slovenly daubs that pass for spirited and learned: those works which possess mere general effect without detail, because, forsooth, detail destroys general effect. Nature in the results of Daguerre's process, has taken the pencil into her own hands, and she shows that the minutest detail disturbs not the general repose. Artists will learn how to paint, and amateurs, or rather connoisseurs, how to criticise, how to look at Nature, and, therefore, how to estimate the value of true art. Our studies will now be enriched with sketches from nature which we can store up during the summer, as the bee gathers her sweets for winter, and we shall thus have rich materials for composition and an exhaustless store for the imagination to feed upon (cited in Kloss, p. 146).

For Morse, photography was a teaching tool that could visually educate the public, enabling every American to become an artist or informed art critic. Following his advice, many American painters minimized sketchlike brushwork to produce detailed, quasi-photographic pictures. Engraved reproductions of daguerreotypes began appearing in popular magazines, competing with illustrations of artists' paintings. Since there was no negative, the daguerreotype print was a unique image that could be reproduced only by taking another picture of it with a camera or by manual printing methods. The daguerreotype was also laterally reversed like a mirror image. The reversal was particularly noticeable in city views, where store signs read backward. By attaching a mirror to the camera lens, daguerreotypists later rectified the error. Engraved reproductions or rephotographing the original daguerreotype also corrected the mirror reversal although copies inevitably lacked the original's clarity.

Lengthy exposure times made it impossible to record figures in motion and initially made portraits an uncomfortable ordeal for sitters, who had to remain motionless, held in place by iron headrests for long minutes while being blinded by lights from windows and mirrors. However, by the 1840s American daguerreotypists had made technical improvements that

●5.68 Augustus Washington
John Brown.
Daguerreotype.
National Portrait Gallery,
Smithsonian Institution,
New York, 1847.

reduced exposure times to a few minutes and finally to less than half a minute. Throughout America, daguerreotypists, some of them former painters, established photographic studios and galleries that displayed rows of framed portraits.

Yet daguerreotypists mostly emerged from outside the usual art-world circles and professions. Photography was introduced into the United States during a period of severe economic depression that had begun in 1837 and extended into the early 1840s. In an article entitled "Daguerreotypists and Beggars Are Moneymakers in New York," one journalist for the *Daily National Intelligencer* sarcastically reported in late February, 1843, that "Daguerreotyping, which is now done for a dollar and a half, is [after begging] the next most profitable vocation.... A Frenchman has opened a shop in Fulton street for the sale of apparatuses for daguerreotyping, so that any pedler can take up the trade" (cited in Shumard, p. 2).

Certainly it was economic hardship rather than prior formal training in the arts that led Augustus Washington (c.1820–1875), the sole African-American then attending Dartmouth College in Hanover, New Hampshire, to undertake a daguerreotype business, as a means of extricating himself from school-related debts. An educated, free black, Washington had been unable to find satisfactory teaching positions. Despite criticism from Dartmouth's president, Washington began his new career photographing faculty and other members of the college community. By 1844, he had moved to Hartford, Connecticut, a larger, more active commercial hub that was also a center for antislavery activities. After teaching at Hartford's North African School, sponsored by the Reverend James W.C. Pennington, one of New England's leading abolitionists, Washington finally established a "Daguerrean Gallery," which he widely advertised in broadsides and abolitionist newspapers. Advertisements for the gallery mixed business pitches with democratic political rhetoric and the cause of freedom: "Why should not the Daguerreotype be within the reach of every body? Why may not every man delight to 'view his shadow,' traced by the sun and descant on his own perfections? While others are advocating every man a house, free soil, and free speech, it remains for WASHINGTON to advocate and furnish free Daguerreotypes, for the next 60 days" (1851 broadside, reproduced in Shumard, p.7).

Antebellum American photographers, whether itinerant peddlers or operators of a fixed establishment, often appealed to new groups of customers, including the working poor and socially marginal, who otherwise were barred from the far more expensive market for original paintings and sculptures, produced by academically trained artists. Furthermore, unlike paintings and sculptures, which were commonly associated with the affectations and pretensions of the social elite, daguerreotype portraits, "traced by the sun," seemed to represent the unvarnished truth of individual character.

One of Augustus Washington's earliest surviving daguerreotypes starkly portrays John Brown (fig. 5.68), a stern, abolitionist activist from neighboring Springfield, Massachusetts. Later executed in 1859 for attempting to lead a slave revolt at Harpers Ferry, West Virginia, Brown is here represented as if swearing an oath for the antislavery cause. With one hand raised, the other grasps a standard or flag, perhaps for the "Subterranean Pass Way," a militant organization seeking to insure safe passage for fugitive slaves in their escape from the South through the Allegheny Mountains (Shumard, p. 4). For relatives, friends, and admirers, the veracity and sincerity of Brown's oath was certainly only reinforced by the mantle of transparent truth claimed by Washington and other nineteenth-century daguerreotypists.

Augustus Washington soon despaired of the abolitionist cause, following congressional passage of the Compromise of 1850, which legally strengthened the position of southern plantation owners in recovering fugitive slaves. By 1853, Washington and his family left the United States for Liberia, an independent republic in western Africa that had been founded and formerly controlled by the white-dominated American Colonization Society (ACS). Attempting to evade the issue of abolition, the ACS advocated the immigration of free American blacks and freed slaves to Liberia. Hoping to live more freely and to educate the indigenous peoples of Africa, Washington transplanted his daguerreotype practice to Monrovia, Liberia, named after President James Monroe. There, he photographed other immigrants who, perhaps, wished to send portraits of themselves to friends and relatives left behind in the United States. Washington's Liberian portraits of government leaders and prominent citizens (fig. 5.69) implicitly countered racist pro-slavery arguments that blacks were incapable of republican self-governance.

5.69 Augustus Washington
Portrait of Urias A. McGill, 1854. Daguerreotype. American Colorization Society Records, Library of Congress, Washington, D.C.

●**5.70 Mathew B. Brady**
*On the Antietam
Battlefield*, 1862.
Library of Congress,
Washington, D.C.

Though photographs were deemed more truthful and honest than paintings, daguerreotypists often attempted to appeal to a genteel, refined clientele by mimicking the aesthetic effects of the more traditional fine-art medium. In Cincinnati, Ohio, where there were thirty-seven daguerreotype studios by 1851, James Presley Ball (1825–1904), another African-American daguerreotypist, displayed the landscape paintings of Robert Duncanson above his photographic portraits of the city's leading citizens. Ball also asked Duncanson to hand-color photographs to make them look more like paintings.

However, even in their black-and-white state, daguerreotypes often mimicked painterly qualities. In Boston, the photographic team of Albert Sands Southworth (1811–94) and Josiah Johnson Hawes (1808–1901) excelled in capturing subtle tonal patterns of sunlight and shade. The series of photographs that Southworth and Hawes made of Mount Auburn Cemetery contrasts ghostly white tombstones and mausoleums with the surrounding darkness of trees and landscape (see fig. 5.27). Art historians have compared the tonal qualities of these photographs to the luminist paintings of Fitz Hugh Lane (see fig. 5.58).

On the eve of the Civil War, the popularity of the daguerreotype had declined in favor of a negative-positive process first invented by the English photographer William Henry Fox Talbot (1800–77). During the late 1830s, Talbot had demonstrated that a negative image on paper film could be transferred to another surface, creating a positive paper print with both light and dark areas and lateral directions corresponding to the appearance of the subject. Owing to the granular quality of the chemically treated paper film, Talbot's photographs lacked the crisp clarity of the daguerreotype's metal-plate images. However, after 1851, the collodion process displaced paper with grainless glass negatives, enabling the reproduction of finely detailed photographic prints.

Technical improvements in the negative-positive process facilitated the mobility of documentary photographers. Once Confederate forces began firing on Union troops at Fort Sumter, South Carolina, on April 12, 1861, photographers took to the field with wagons filled with equipment and chemicals to record history in the making. Hampered by their cumbersome equipment and technical difficulties in recording figures in motion, the 1,500 photographers who produced tens of thousands of images documenting the war and its participants could not capture actual battle scenes. Nor could photographers travel to many battlefields distant from urban centers. Because of a Union naval blockade of the South, few photographers had the necessary supplies to record Confederate military life.

Despite its limitations, the modern mechanical process of photography provided an unprecedented

5.71 Emanuel Leutze
Westward the Course of Empire Takes Its Way,
1861–2.
Fresco, 20 x 30 ft
(6 x 9.1 m).
Architect of the Capitol,
Washington, D.C.

At the apex of Leutze's pyramidal composition, the small figure of a young man celebrates the pioneers' crossing of the Rocky Mountains by triumphantly waving one arm and reaching for an American flag with the other. Closer to the foreground, a frontiersman, protecting a praying Madonna-like mother, gestures toward the distant, golden horizon. In the crowd below, a free African-American leads the donkey of an Irishwoman, thereby suggesting the racial-ethnic openness of the Promised Land.

visual record of warfare's increasingly mechanized, devastating effects. During four years, nearly 10,500 military actions occurring over eighteen states and territories took a toll of over 1 million casualties and at least 623,000 deaths of Union and Confederate troops. Virtually every family in both the North and the South was affected by the loss of relatives and friends. For the United States president, Abraham Lincoln, the primary goal was not to abolish slavery, but to preserve the Union and defeat the Confederacy as a separate nation.

Photographers brought Civil War battlefields into American consciousness in a manner that seemed to surpass the communicative power of history painting. Civil War photographs of corpses on the battlefield transfixed beholders (fig. 5.70). Civilians in the North flocked to the New York gallery of Mathew Brady (1823–96). Brady employed a team of photographers to follow Union troops. On October 20, 1862, the *New York Times* reviewed an exhibition at Brady's gallery, following the Union victory at the Battle of Antietam:

5.72 Albert Bierstadt
*The Rocky Mountains,
Lander's Peak*, 1863.
Oil on canvas,
73½ x 120¾ in
(186.7 x 306.7 cm).
Metropolitan Museum of
Art, Washington D.C.
Rogers Fund, 1907.

5.73 Alexander Gardner and Timothy O'Sullivan
A Harvest of Death, Gettysburg, Pennsylvania, 1863, from *Gardner's Photographic Sketchbook of the War* by A. Gardner, 1865. Wet plate, albumen. New York Public Library, New York.

Mr. Brady has done something to bring home to us the terrible reality and earnestness of war. If he has not brought bodies and laid them in our dooryards and long the streets, he has done something very like it. At the door of his gallery hangs a little placard, "The Dead of Antietam." Crowds of people are constantly going up the stairs; follow them and you find them bending over photographic views of that fearful battle-field, taken immediately after the action. Of all objects of horror one would think the battlefield should stand pre-eminent, that it should bear away the palm of repulsiveness. But, on the contrary, there is a terrible fascination about it that draws one near these pictures, and makes him loth [sic] to leave them. You will see hushed, reverend groups standing around these weird copies of carnage, bending down to look in the pale faces of the dead, chained by the strange spell that dwells in dead men's eyes …

The ground whereon they lie is torn by shot and shell, the grass is trampled down by the tread of hot, hurrying feet, and little rivulets that can scarcely be of water are trickling along the earth like tears over a mother's face. It is a bleak, barren plain and above it bends an ashen, sullen sky … .

These pictures have a terrible distinctness. By the aid of the magnifying glass, the very features of the slain may be distinguished (cited in Keith F. Davis, pp. 150–152).

Contradicting the poetic, distant gaze recommended for marble sculptures, photographs invited close, magnified viewing of details that the unaided eye could not hope to notice. The photograph's optical realism created an uncanny, hallucinatory effect that forced viewers to make verbal sense of the blank, mute faces of the dead. As if to comfort visitors to Brady's exhibit, the *Times* critic poetically buries the dead within the tearful, blood-stained embrace of Mother Earth. "Hushed, reverend" beholders add to the impression that Brady's gallery has been transformed into a funeral parlor or wake for the dead.

Battlefield photographs not only laid soldiers' corpses in dooryards and city streets, but they brought them into the parlors of private homes. One of Brady's best photographers, Alexander Gardner (1821–82), established his own studio by 1863 with the intention of publishing a photographic album of the war. Juxtaposing word and image, he attempted to give poetic, nationalist meaning to the fratricidal conflict. His most famous photograph, *A Harvest of Death, Gettysburg, Pennsylvania,* 1863, metaphorically transforms the specific horror of the Battle of Gettysburg into an allegory of the cycles of life (fig. 5.73). The seeds of discord sown in previous decades are now being harvested by Death. Receding from the foreground toward the misty horizon, Gardner's corpses become less corporeal, more ethereal, as if their souls are being drawn heavenward by the sun's light.

Through poetic titles and moralizing commentary, *Gardner's Photographic Sketchbook of the*

Civil War created ideological, aesthetic distance from the war's carnage. Verbally framed by the themes of sacrifice and renewal, Gardner's corpses become living sculptures anticipating the restoration of the Union and its memorialization in marble and bronze. However, photography's relative realism dealt a powerful blow to the cultural prestige of history painting, which traditionally represented important heroes performing virtuous or ennobling deeds, as exemplified by John Trumbull's Revolutionary War paintings (see fig. 4.32) or Benjamin West's *The Death of General Wolfe* (see fig. 4.23). The seemingly matter-of-fact photographs of Civil War battlefields seriously deflated the dramatic and grandiose visual rhetoric normally employed for representing history subjects.

Civil War and the Imperial Eye

The most heroic and patriotic grand-scale paintings produced during the Civil War focused not upon the battlefield, but rather upon American imperial expansion. For instance, not long after the Southern states had seceded from the Union, the German-born artist Emanuel Gottlieb Leutze (1816–68) painted a mural for the U.S. Capitol in Washington, D.C., that optimistically expressed biblical faith in America's divinely ordained civilizing mission. *Westward The Course of Empire Takes Its Way* (fig. 5.71) harkens backward to John Smibert's *Bermuda Group* (see fig. 3.23) and borrows its title from the eighteenth-century poem by the Anglican clergyman-philosopher George Berkeley, who prophesied that history, continually moving westward, would have its perfected fulfillment in the New World. In the spirit of Berkeley's verses, Leutze represented excited American pioneers as if they were the children of Israel about to enter the Promised Land. In the mural's decorative frame, a scene of "Moses leading the Israelites through the desert" (cited in Fryd, p. 211) foreshadows settlement of the West.

In New York City, during April, 1864, a "Metropolitan Fair" benefiting the Union war effort featured an art exhibition, dominated by panoramic landscapes. In addition to Frederic Church's *Heart of the Andes* (see fig. 5.62), Albert Bierstadt (1830–1902) exhibited his popular painting of *The Rocky Mountains, Lander's Peak* (fig. 5.72). Born in Germany, Bierstadt was Church's rival in composing theatrical pictures of sublime scenery in nationalist, imperial terms. Unlike Church, who never traveled to America's western territories, Bierstadt became known for his awe-inspiring depictions of lofty mountain ranges in the American West. This view of the Wyoming Rockies is a pictorial amalgamation derived from various sketches and is not a topographically accurate representation of an actual, peak. Composed in the Tenth Street Studio Building in New York (see fig. 6.10), *The Rocky Mountains, Lander's Peak* is an imaginative commemoration of a Civil War hero, Colonel Frederic W. Lander, who died from battle wounds in February, 1862. Earlier, in 1859, Bierstadt had accompanied Lander on a surveying expedition, intended to improve travel through the Rockies to the Pacific coast.

Bierstadt made sketches of this journey and also employed a double-lens camera to produce stereographic images, or side-by-side photographs, of the same subject on a single mount. When viewed through an optical device or stereoscope, stereographs appeared to replicate the three-dimensional, binocular nature of human vision. Contemporary critics praised the stereograph and stereoscope for enhancing the naturalistic illusionism of photography. In *The Rocky Mountains, Lander's Peak*, the foreground scene of a Shoshone Indian encampment was based upon stereographic images. Bierstadt's synthesis of macrocosmic grandeur and microcosmic detail empowered beholders with an almost godlike, omniscient sense of vision, expressing the imperial reach of the nation, even during the terrible years of fratricidal warfare.

However, during the decades that followed the war between the states, many artists responded to the accelerated pace of urbanization and modernization by turning inward toward more private and spiritual forms of aesthetic communication. Supported by a growing number of critics, art dealers, and patrons, American artists also functioned as canny entrepreneurs in marketing their work and promoting themselves as the arbiters of fashion. In the chapter that follows, we shall examine how post–Civil War artists attempted to reconstruct national unity through the healing, therapeutic powers of art.

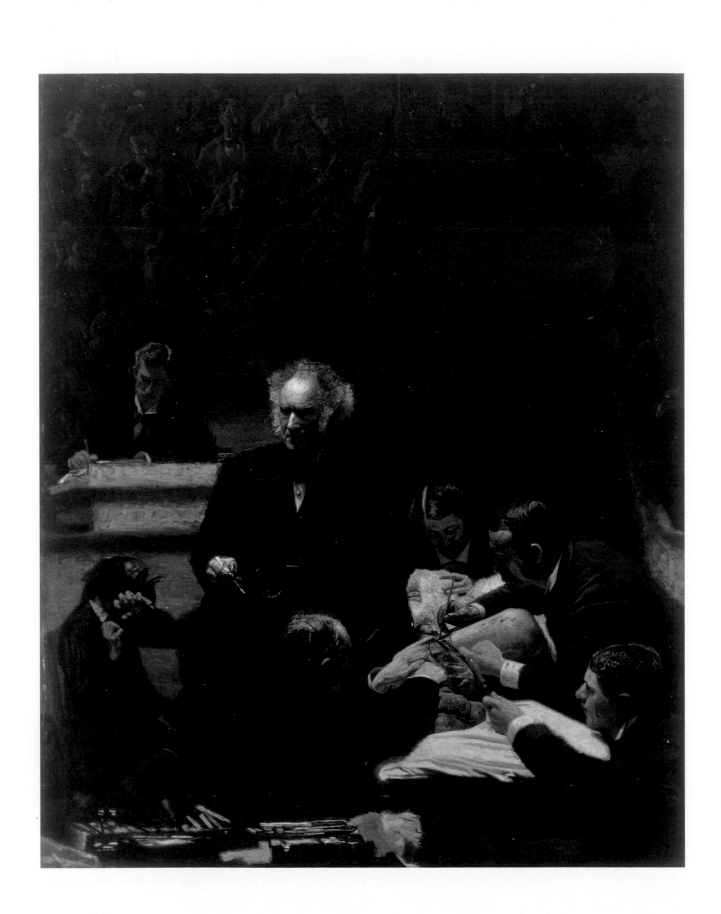

Chapter 6

Art and Commerce in the Gilded Age
1865–1905

THE four decades from 1865 to 1905 comprise America's Gilded Age, in which the nation resurrected itself from the ashes of the Civil War and became the world's leading industrial power. The country's most prominent industrialists and financiers, including Andrew Carnegie in steel manufacturing, John D. Rockefeller in oil, and Cornelius Vanderbilt in railroads, became multimillionaires. Unencumbered by personal income taxes, they ostentatiously spent their wealth by living like European aristocrats. Commissioning American architects and artists to build and decorate palatial mansions, they also collected European Old Master paintings and sculptures as well as Japanese and other Oriental decorative arts. Interest in non-Western art was abetted by American foreign policy. During the early 1850s, Commodore Matthew C. Perry had led U.S. diplomatic expeditions to persuade Japanese officials to permit the business ventures of American merchants. By the time that World War I began in Europe in 1914, the United States had become an imperial power in Asia and Latin America.

In 1867, just two years after the end of the Civil War, Secretary of State William H. Seward successfully negotiated the purchase of Alaska from Russia for just over $7 million in gold. Approved by Congress the following year, the acquisition of the new territory of Alaska, twice the size of Texas, pushed Americans further westward toward the coast of Siberia and the continent of Asia. In 1893, as Americans continued to celebrate the four-hundredth anniversary of Christopher Columbus's 1492 voyage of discovery, the Hawaiian Islands in the Pacific Ocean became a U.S. protectorate. A few years earlier, an invading force of United States Marines had installed a new Hawaiian govern-ment friendly to American commercial investments in the sugar industry. In 1898, the United States declared war against Spain and asserted authority over Latin America by expelling Spanish colonial forces from Cuba and acquiring the colony of Puerto Rico. The Spanish-American War also extended to the Pacific Ocean as the United States pushed further westward to take possession of the Philippine Islands and Samoa. Finally, during the early twentieth century, the United States forcibly appropriated a ten-mile-wide strip of land from Panama in Central America to build a canal that would facilitate naval and commercial ship traffic between the Atlantic and Pacific Oceans. Begun in 1906, the Panama Canal was completed in August of 1914 just as World War I was beginning in Europe.

America's Gilded Age visually manifested the country's economic and imperial power with spectacular social and cultural displays. Believing that the United States could not surpass Europe unless it appropriated cultural capital or masterpieces and symbols of high art, American men of wealth, beginning during the 1870s, founded major city art museums such as the Museum of Fine Arts in Boston, the Metropolitan Museum of Art in New York, the Art Institute of Chicago, and the Philadelphia Museum of Art. Members of the corporate elite dominated museum boards of trustees. They envisioned the building of art museums, libraries, and other cultural institutions as a means of competing with European nations in claiming the legacy of Western civilization as descended from Greco-Roman antiquity and the Italian Renaissance. In Boston, the socially exclusive, newly constructed Back Bay neighborhood featured Art Square, site of the first Museum of Fine Arts Building and the monumental Trinity Church, decorated by a team of

Thomas Eakins ●
The Gross Clinic, 1875. Oil on canvas, 96 x 78 in (243.8 x 198.1 cm). Jefferson Medical College of Thomas Jefferson University, Philadelphia.

Eakins's heroic portrait of Dr. Samuel Gross has often been compared to Rembrandt van Rijn's *The Anatomy Lesson of Dr. Nicolaas Tulp* (1632). However, the Dutch painter's graphic painting represents the dissection of a cadaver rather than a surgical act of healing. Eakins depicts the modern advancement of medical practice for the direct benefit of patients. Dr. Gross's removal of a dead bone for the treatment of osteomyelitis, a bone disease, superseded the past practice of amputating entire limbs.

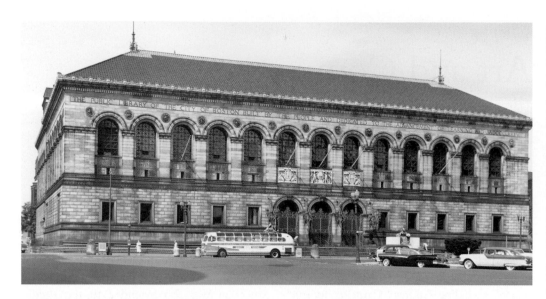

6.1 McKim, Mead, & White ●
Boston Public Library, Exterior view, 1888.

This building exemplifies American Renaissance style architecture. Though historical-revival styles evoked nostalgia for pre-industrial social and cultural values, they also expressed America's modern corporate power. During the Gilded Age, American Renaissance artists and architects borrowed from the Italian Renaissance to demonstrate the triumphant westward shift of high culture to the United States and its expanding western empire.

artists (see fig. 6.58). In 1883, the city renamed the square in honor of John Singleton Copley, the famed portraitist of New England's colonial elite (see chapter 3). A few years later, the New York architectural firm of McKim, Mead, & White designed the Boston Public Library on the west end of Copley Square, in the manner of an Italian Renaissance palazzo (fig. 6.1). The architects worked with sculptors and painters to embellish the building with noble statues and inspiring murals, including John Singer Sargent's *Triumph of Religion* on the library's third floor, which celebrated the evolutionary progress of Western civilization toward Christianity and liberal, humanistic values (fig. 6.2). Christened "a palace for the people" by its wealthy trustees (cited in Roth, p. 292), the Boston Public Library epitomized the American Renaissance style in its classical, Italianate grandeur and collaborative orchestration of architecture and the visual arts. Through such buildings and other civic monuments and urban beautification plans, the United States identified itself as the enlightened inheritor of western culture, descended from the European Renaissance's age of discovery and exploration.

During the colonial period, European explorers had busied themselves collecting American curiosities and artifacts. But by the Gilded Age of the late nineteenth century, an increasingly wealthy, class-conscious American elite systematically began to colonize or raid the art treasures of Europe. Multimillionaires such as the banker J. Pierpont Morgan and the coal and steel magnate

Henry Clay Frick filled newly built New York mansions with vast collections of European art objects, manuscripts, and rare books.

Descendants of the railroad magnate Cornelius Vanderbilt were particularly prolific in building and furnishing lavish new mansions. More than any other family, the Vanderbilts emulated the famous Medici banking family of the Italian Renaissance in their extensive art patronage. From 1876 to 1917, Vanderbilt family members constructed and furnished seventeen large mansions, significantly contributing to an American Renaissance of art and architecture. The Vanderbilt family's favorite architect, Richard Morris Hunt (1827–95), designed their most spectacular estate, "Biltmore," near Asheville, North Carolina (fig. 6.3). Intended as the principal residence for George Washington Vanderbilt, grandson of Cornelius, the 255-room mansion on 125,000 acres of forest and landscaped woodland cost $5 million and was designed in the aristocratic style of a French château. The largest private home in the United States, Biltmore housed a vast collection of European art objects and a large library of rare books. George W. Vanderbilt's father, William H. Vanderbilt, owned a Fifth Avenue, New York City, mansion that became the subject of a ten-volume description of its art collection and interior decoration. An American decorator, Christian Herter (1840–83), was responsible for designing and supervising work on all the ornamental details, creating an eclectic mélange of

6.2 McKim, Mead, & White
Boston Public Library, 1887–95.
Special Collections Hall, looking north toward John Singer Sargent's *Israelites Oppressed* (north wall lunette, installed 1895) and *Frieze of the Prophets* (north wall, below lunette, installed 1895). The Trustees of the Public Library of the City of Boston, Massachusetts.

This photograph of the third-floor Special Collections Hall focuses on the north wall of Sargent's religious history cycle. The wall's large lunette painting, *Israelites Oppressed*, represented the Jews' persecution at the hands of an Egyptian pharaoh and an Assyrian king. Sargent appropriated the flattened, hieratic styles of ancient Egyptian and Assyrian art to represent the picture's dominant figures.

Japanese, Italian Renaissance, and other cultural styles (fig. 6.4). Having been removed from their original sites or historical contexts, the art objects collected by American industrialists lost their traditional symbolic, moral, or religious meanings. Judged by supposedly universal standards of aesthetic quality, decontextualized objects of Western and non-Western art became interchangeable and more precisely measurable in monetary terms as marketable commodities and precious investments.

Bolstering America's international standing, a series of spectacular world's fairs, held at home and abroad, celebrated the latest advances in science and modern technology such as the telephone, the electric light bulb, and the latest industrial machinery. They also attracted crowds with extensive cultural exhibitions that showcased participating nations' contributions to architecture and the decorative and fine arts. Visited by many affluent, cosmopolitan Americans, the Exposition Universelle held in Paris in 1867 created a fashion for French art in the United States, leading many younger artists to abandon provincial or uniquely American subject matter in favor of more generalized, non-narrative themes and more personal, sketchlike techniques. In 1876, nearly ten years later, Philadelphia's Centennial Exposition, celebrat-

ing the one-hundredth anniversary of the Declaration of Independence, nostalgically revived interest in the arts and crafts of colonial America. At the same time, however, the Japanese pavilion became one of the most widely praised exhibitions at the fair, with its rich display of porcelain vases, bronze objects, painted silks, embroidered fabrics, and lacquered ware. Inspired by the Centennial Exposition, the architects Charles Follen McKim (1847–1909), William Rutherford Mead (1846–1928), and Stanford White (1853–1906) designed a casino, or entertainment pavilion, in the fashionable ocean resort community of Newport, Rhode Island, that featured a Japanese-style interior of continuous open spaces interwoven with skeletal, light wooden screens and moldings (fig. 6.5).

The 1876 Centennial Exposition stimulated the Aesthetic movement in the United States, as middle- and upper-class Americans, concerned over the quality of mass-produced industrial goods, applied aesthetic principles to a wide array of household and consumer goods, including furniture, textiles, wallpaper, ceramics, metalwork, glassware, and books. Beginning with the Great Exhibition of 1851, held in London's Crystal Palace, which made evident the poor design of most manufactured objects, British reformers established industrial training programs, design schools, and, in 1857, the South Kensington Museum (today the Victoria and Albert Museum), a national museum of design.

These developments were widely praised by American art critics. Just before the end of the Civil War, James Jackson Jarves (1818–88), an art collector and son of a glass manufacturer, published *The Art-Idea* (1864), in which he called upon American industrialists to surpass their British rivals:

England preserves her preeminence by schooling her artisans in matters of refined taste and perfect workmanship. Under similar advantages, there is no reason why our people, with more cosmopolitan brains, acuter sensibilities, readier impressibility, and quicker inventive faculties, should not excel her in these respects, as we do already in some of the industrial arts. We have a continent of fast-multiplying millions to supply with all the fabrics into which aesthetic enjoyment may enter, as well as with absolute

6.3 Richard Morris Hunt ●
Biltmore, Asheville, North Carolina, 1895. Biltmore Estate, Asheville, North Carolina.

Conceived in an early French Renaissance style, the three-story limestone mansion features two lateral projecting wings, balanced on either side of an entrance pavilion. Recessed courts connect the wings to the central pavilion, from which a grand staircase projects on the left side. The essentially symmetrical arrangement of the building masses is picturesquely complicated by a wealth of decorative detail. The ornamented dormer windows piercing the steeply pitched roof contribute Gothic, vertical accents to the building façade.

works of art. And what utensil is there with which we may not, as did the Greeks, connect beauty of form and color, and which we may not make suggestive of hidden meaning, pointing a moral or narrating a tale? (p. 266).

During the next four decades, American artists and architects directly and indirectly addressed public anxieties over the effects of industrialization and urbanization. Most were influenced by the Aesthetic movement's emphasis on the decorative arts and by the development of an Arts and Crafts movement, which promoted the handmade, nonmechanized products of artisans and their small workshops over factory labor. Even architects of steel-framed skyscrapers conceived their designs in terms of natural, organic growth and ornamented the buildings with historical and vegetal motifs (see fig. 6.14). In response to the new, corporate age of assembly-line production, advertising, and illustrated magazines and newspapers, artists and critics increasingly placed a high value on originality and irreproducible signs of artistic creativity. With its voluntary societies, professional design firms, magazines, and educational classes, the Arts and Crafts movement extended the Aesthetic movement's campaign to beautify the home into the 1890s and early twentieth century. While there was a considerable overlap between the two movements, with each drawing upon medieval and Oriental stylistic sources, and the talents of numerous women as well as men, Arts and Crafts reformers more readily espoused a democratic, progressive ideology devoted to the improvement of life.

Though she was not a radical feminist or political reformer, the career of Candace Wheeler (1827-1923) demonstrates how middle-class women were mobilized by the Arts and Crafts, and Aesthetic movements. A pioneer in establishing the profession of interior decoration, Wheeler learned the textile arts of weaving, sewing, and embroidery by attending a private co-educational academy, while growing up on a dairy farm in central New York. Born Candace Thurber, she married Thomas Wheeler, a New York City bookkeeper and then independent business owner, who encouraged her inclination toward the arts. Together, the couple established friendships with leading New York artists, including Frederic Church, Albert Bierstadt, and other landscape painters. During the 1860s, Candace Wheeler took lessons in still-life painting from George Henry Hall (1825–1913), an American disciple of the English art theorist and critic John Ruskin (1819–1900), who advocated "truthful" art works based upon the careful observation of nature. In later years, Wheeler exhibited flower paintings at the National Academy of Design.

However, Philadelphia's Centennial Exhibition dramatically changed Wheeler's life. Inspired by its display of British textiles from the Royal School of Art Needlework in South Kensington, she began to produce her own embroideries (fig. 6.6) that echoed the floral designs of the English Arts and Crafts reformer William Morris (1836–96). In its handcrafted simplicity of form, Wheeler's *Madonna-lily Pillow Cover* affirmed Morris's idealization of pre-industrial, artisan labor.

More importantly, in 1877, Wheeler attempted to emulate British design practices by founding the Society of Decorative Art (SDA) of New York City. Supported by the wives of New York's social elite, Wheeler intended the organi-zation to be a means for employing "educated" women, who otherwise found themselves in economically distressed or "untoward circum-stances" (cited in Peck and Irish, p.24). With an eye for quality design, the SDA would sell needlework, embroideries, and other articles manufactured by women. Christian Herter, Louis Comfort Tiffany (1848–1933), and other New York decorators placed orders and submit-ted designs for women who crafted objects in the SDA's New York workrooms. Wheeler also helped to found similar societies in other American cities. Objects produced by women from throughout the country were shipped to the organization's salesrooms in New York.

Despite the SDA's success, Wheeler found herself at odds with the rich, Fifth Avenue socie-ty women who dominated its governing board. For the middle-class artist/organizer, these afflu-

6.4 The Japanese Room
from a plate in Edward Strahan (Earl Shinn), *Mr. Vanderbilt's House and Collection* (New York, 1883–4). Morris Library, University of Delaware, Newark, Delaware.

Bearing comparison with James Abbott McNeill Whistler's earlier Peacock Room for Frederick Leyland (see fig. 6.65), Herter's Japanese Parlor had its gold-brocaded walls lined with lacquered shelves and cabinets to hold Vanderbilt's collection of Japanese-imported art objects. The upper walls and ceiling were lined with bamboo to accentuate the oriental character of this jewelbox-like space.

6.5 McKim, Mead, & White
Casino, Newport, Rhode Island (1879–80). Paper print. Newport Historical Society, Newport, Rhode Island.

This sprawling, picturesque resort housed a ballroom, theater, restaurant, tennis courts, piazzas, and rooms for parties and receptions. James Gordon Bennett, son of a New York newspaper publisher, spent $100,000 on the Casino's construction, a sizeable sum for the period. During the 1880s, the Casino was a popular rendezvous for Newport society.

ent women seemed more interested in collecting art as a means of displaying their refined taste than in philanthropy and the moral power of art to improve public and family life. Wheeler thus founded the more socially inclusive Woman's Exchange, which modeled itself after the SDA, but accepted for sale a broader range of art objects and utilitarian goods, produced by respectable women in economic need. The Women's Exchange was more clearly a philanthropic response to the demographic, economic devastation of the Civil War, which had left thousands of wives widowed and many, previously middle-class, families without regular income. Economic downturns, such as the depression of 1873, only exacerbated the problem. While lower-class women found work in factories and domestic service, women from the middle of the social spectrum resisted such labor as too demeaning. Wheeler's Women's Exchange offered these women the opportunity of self-help through the production and sale of traditional homemakers' arts and crafts, from needlework and embroidery to baked goods.

For disloyally founding a competing organization, the SDA board forced Wheeler's resignation. But shortly afterward, Wheeler joined the interior decorating firm of Louis C. Tiffany. The son of Charles Louis Tiffany (1812–1902), a renowned jeweler and silversmith, Louis Comfort Tiffany had abandoned painting for a more lucrative career in the deco-

rative arts. A proponent of the Aesthetic movement's credo of "art for art's sake," Tiffany recognized that the construction boom in mansions and public buildings would require the services of energetic decorators, who could organize teams of artists specializing in a variety of different media.

Wheeler's collaboration with Tiffany included one of the most ambitious commissions his firm ever undertook, the 1,600 square-foot Veterans' Room of the Seventh Regiment Armory on New York's fashionable Park Avenue (fig. 6.7). After conceiving the overall decorative scheme of the room, an eclectic mélange of Celtic, Islamic, Greek, Egyptian, Persian, and Japanese styles, Tiffany assigned the architect Stanford White, of McKim, Mead, & White, to supervise the design and installation of architectural details. The landscape painter Samuel Colman (1832–1920) devised the room's color harmonies, ornamental detailing, and decorative stenciling. Meanwhile two other painters, Frank Millet (1846–1912) and George Henry Yewell (1830–1923) composed a high wall frieze, representing military shields alternating with historical pictures of warfare. Tiffany himself designed the room's five stained-glass windows and the turquoise-blue glass tiles surrounding the fireplace, the dominant focal point of this opulent room for the well-heeled volunteer members of the Seventh "Silk Stocking" Regiment. Wheeler was assigned the task of embroidering window draperies and portieres, or doorway curtains (all now lost), decorated with square, velvet appliqués, representing scenes of medieval knighthood and warfare. Such martial motifs were probably not Wheeler's idea, given her preference for simple floral designs, but she deferred to Tiffany's taste and the masculine, military tenor of the commission. During her four years with Tiffany, Wheeler was primarily responsible for supervising the workshop of some twenty women, who produced the company's embroidered textiles. In keeping with her philanthropic, self-help goals, Wheeler regarded the women not as workers, but as students of design, who already had prior art education and were now preparing themselves to become independent decorators.

Wheeler followed the path of independence when she left Tiffany in 1883 to establish her own textile design firm, Associated Artists. She was assisted in the enterprise by several close associates, including her second daughter Dora (1856–1940), who had studied painting under William Merritt Chase (1849–1916), one of the leading artists of the Gilded Age (see pp.292-3). As a principal designer for Associated Artists, Dora Wheeler won widespread praise for her needlewoven tapestries representing famous female characters from literature and the arts. Based upon an award-winning pastel drawing she had completed in Paris, Dora created a silk embroidered tapestry representing *Penelope Unraveling Her Work at Night* (fig. 6.8) for the drawing room of the New York City mansion of Cornelius Vanderbilt II, son of William H. Vanderbilt. Wheeler's embroidery stitches were woven into a silk ground or canvas, manufactured by Cheney Brothers silk mills in South Manchester, Connecticut. As the only known surviving needlewoven tapestry from Associated Artists, *Penelope Unraveling* has faded considerably over the years and is itself unraveling or materially disintegrating. Yet one can still appreciate something of the subtle tonalities Dora Wheeler achieved in her fulsome, statuesque figure of Penelope, a virtuous personification of the weaving textile arts, as described in the ancient Greek poem, the *Odyssey*.

Associated Artists stayed in business until 1907 by establishing a relationship with Cheney Brothers to produce distinctively American-designed textiles, decorated with patterns of American flora and fauna. In addition to luxurious, needlewoven tapestries, Associated Artists developed less expensive fabrics for more modest homes and middle-class family budgets. Yet in advocating the home manufactures of rural and urban American women, Candace Wheeler, and, indeed, the Arts and Crafts movement in general, had nothing to offer industrial factory workers and the poor European immigrants streaming into America.

As the national population more than doubled between 1860 and 1900, from 31 million to approximately 76 million, some 15 million immigrants crowded into the nation's rapidly growing cities. Initially, most of these immigrants came from Britain, Ireland, Germany, and Scandinavia. However, after 1890, immigrants from eastern and southern Europe—Poles, Russian Jews, Ukrainians, Italians, Greeks, Slovaks, Hungarians, and others—outnumbered those from northwestern Europe. Thousands of Chinese immigrants joined Irish laborers and Civil War veterans in completing, by 1869, the transcontinental railway for the Union Pacific and Central Pacific railroads. Expressing the prejudices of many white, Anglo-Saxon Protestant Americans, popular magazines and newspapers routinely published cartoons filled with demeaning racial caricatures or ethnic stereotypes, warning that the tide of poor immigrants threatened American liberties and institutions.

Even national trade unions such as the American Federation of Labor (founded in 1886) excluded from membership Asian and Eastern European immigrants as well as African-Americans and women. Unions largely refrained from organizing unskilled workers in iron and steel manufacturing and other industries. Though the American workforce grew with cheap immigrant labor, manufacturing actually became more dependent upon heavy investments in machinery and new technologies. Money invested in low-wage workers paled in comparison, as mechanized, assembly-line factories grew ever larger. To keep labor costs low, capitalist entrepreneurs hired teams of managers to monitor workers' efficiency. Industrialists such as Andrew Carnegie and Henry Clay Frick, who became renowned for their philanthropy and art

6.6 Candace Wheeler
Madonna-lily Pillow Cover, c.1876–7. Wool twill, embroidered with wool and silk thread; silk-velvet border, 22 x 22½ in (55.9 x 57.2 cm). Metropolitan Museum of Art, New York. Collection of Candace Pullman Wheeler.

With a long history of Christian associations signifying purity and innocence, the lily became one of the most popular floral motifs in the Aesthetic, and Arts and Crafts movements. Oscar Wilde, English playwright and leading proponent of the Aesthetic movement, chose the lily as a personal favorite, thereby contributing to its cult status as a symbol of beauty.

6.7 Louis C. Tiffany & Co., Associated Artists
Veterans Room of the Seventh Regiment Armory, New York, 1881.

6.8 Dora Wheeler ●
Penelope Unraveling Her Work at Night, 1886. Silk embroidered with silk thread, 45 x 68 in (114.3 x 172.7 cm). Metropolitan Museum of Art, New York.

According to the ancient Homeric epic, Penelope refused to believe that her husband Odysseus, the Trojan War hero, had died, despite his failure to return home during years of wandering the world. She avoided remarriage by promising to choose a new spouse only after having completed the weaving of a burial shroud for her father-in-law. But, at night, she secretly unraveled each day's work.

collecting, readily employed strikebreakers and private, armed security forces to destroy unions and drive down workers' wages. Furthermore, to protect themselves against competition and the unpredictable fluctuations of market supply and demand, bureaucratic corporations combined to form large trusts or monopolies in the production and distribution of agricultural and manufactured goods.

At the beginning of this period, James Jackson Jarves agreed with the English art critic John Ruskin that the beautification of even the humblest utensil could point toward an uplifting moral value. However, by the end of the Gilded Age, a number of artists and writers were criticizing the artificiality and aesthetic illusions created by the leisured classes. In her novel *The House of Mirth* (1905), the New York author Edith Wharton (1862–1937) created the tragic heroine Lily Bart, who uses her physical beauty to enter New York City's elite social circles. One evening, Lily triumphantly participates in a lavish high-

society entertainment, *tableaux vivants,* or Old Master paintings that are brought to life in staged performances. Following several other *tableaux vivants,* Lily impresses her audience with a living representation of a portrait by the eighteenth-century English painter Sir Joshua Reynolds:

. . . the unanimous 'Oh!' of the spectators was a tribute, not to the brushwork of Reynolds's "Mrs. Lloyd" but to the flesh and blood loveliness of Lily Bart. She had shown her artistic intelligence in selecting a type so like her own that she could embody the person represented without ceasing to be herself. It was as though she had stepped, not out of, but into, Reynolds's canvas, banishing the phantom of his dead beauty by the beams of her living grace. The impulse to show herself in a splendid setting—she had thought for a moment of representing Tiepolo's Cleopatra—had yielded to the truer instinct of trusting to her unassisted beauty, and she had purposely chosen a picture without distracting accessories of dress or

surroundings. Her pale draperies, and the background of foliage against which she stood, served only to relieve the long dryad-like curves that swept upward from her poised foot to her lifted arm (p. 106).

To the novel's aesthete Lawrence Seldon, this was "the real Lily Bart, divested of the trivialities of her little world, and catching for a moment a note of that eternal harmony of which her beauty was a part." Transfixed by Lily as an aesthetic object, Selden later stands idly by while she falls into debt and is forced into a working-class existence before ultimately committing suicide. During the Gilded Age, art more than ever became immersed in an amoral economy of conspicuous consumption and elite entertainments.

In her portrait of Mrs. Larz Anderson (fig. 6.9), the Philadelphia-born painter Cecilia Beaux (1855-1942) visually expressed something of the social ambience described in Wharton's novel, although the sitter was not a New Yorker, but a wealthy Boston heiress. In 1893, Isabel Weld Perkins married Larz Anderson, an American foreign-service officer and member of the Society of the Cincinnati, the elite fraternity composed of descendents of Revolutionary War officers. Together, the couple built an $800,000 mansion on Massachusetts Avenue in Washington, D.C. Beaux's portrait was destined to hang in the dining room. Nicknamed "The Hostess," the portrait of Mrs. Anderson assumes an audience of invited guests, who are encouraged to admire her as an aesthetic beauty, situated in the midst of a richly decorated space, filled with other *objets d'art*. Schooled in Paris in the painterly techniques of the French Impressionists, Beaux rendered Mrs. Anderson's diaphanous dress with a fluidity that unites its creamy, vegetal patterns with the curvilinear forms of the mirror frame, fireplace, and wall design. Avid collectors of art and antiques, the Andersons also decorated their mansion with architectural motifs and emblems of the Society of the Cincinnati, later bequeathing the entire building as the society's permanent headquarters. By such means, private wealth and consumption assumed a patriotic sheen, and another Gilded Age mansion became a public museum and tourist attraction.

6.9 Cecilia Beaux
Portrait of Mrs. Larz Anderson, 1900–01. Oil on canvas, 82 x 40 in (208.3 x 101.6 cm). Society of the Cincinnati, Anderson House, Washington, D.C.

Commercialization and the Uninterrupted Progress of Art

Already at the beginning of this period, critics were acutely conscious that the spiritual and moral content of American art was threatened by art's inescapable status as a marketable commodity. In 1867, two years after the end of the Civil War, the New York art historian and critic Henry Tuckerman (1813–71) published *Book of the Artists: American Artist Life*, a survey of American art. He concluded that the Civil War had done little or no damage to the production and dissemination of the visual arts in the

United States, even in the defeated South. He observed that exhibitions of American art were now held frequently throughout the country from Chicago, Illinois, and Buffalo, New York, southward to Baltimore, Maryland, and Charleston, South Carolina. It seemed that Americans everywhere were, at the very least, commissioning portraits from hundreds of artists. Particularly in New York, the nation's financial and cultural capital, new galleries, art dealerships, and other art organizations appeared to be flourishing:

> *In fact, the entire relation of Art to the public has changed within the last ten years: its products are a more familiar commodity; studio-buildings, artist-receptions, auction sales of special productions, the influence of the press, constant exhibitions, and the popularity of certain foreign and native painters, to say nothing of the multiplication of copies, the brisk trade in 'old masters', the increase of travel securing a vast interchange of artistic products—these and many other circumstances have greatly increased the mercantile and social importance of Art (p. 22).*

New York's Tenth Street Studio Building (fig. 6.10) had become one of the centers of the city's artistic life. Designed in 1857 by Richard Morris Hunt, it was intended specifically for the use of artists and architects, providing studios, living quarters, and gallery space all under one roof. During the post-Civil War era, painters' studios became art markets for middle- and upper-class patrons. Tuckerman was already worried that American art was being aesthetically victimized by its own popularity. It was "too dependent on the market" and artists' eagerness for financial success. In Tuckerman's view, art that was produced for purely materialistic reasons lacked the necessary imprint of individual and national character, which could only be expressed apart from selfish, commercial interests. The critic bemoaned the fact that, in order to make a comfortable living, American artists simply repeated popular motifs and conventions. Under these circumstances, art became monotonous, superficial, and mechanical. While Tuckerman praised America's "atmosphere of Freedom" and prosperity for animating the "manly artist" (p. 28), he also expressed admiration for the more traditional, refined atmosphere of Europe, where beauty and art

6.10 Richard Morris Hunt
Studio Building, 15 West Tenth Street, New York City, 1857.
City of New York Museum.

Trained at the École des Beaux-Arts in Paris, Hunt designed his first major project in terms of the French rationalist style of Pierre-François-Henri Labrouste (1801–75). Constructed from red brick with brown sandstone trim, the Studio Building's symmetrically balanced façade featured large recessed windows. The generous fenestration and a skylight over the building's interior courtyard provided artists' studios and exhibition spaces with ample illumination.

intended for use of artists & architects all together.

6.11 Peter B. Wight
National Academy of Design, New York City, 1862–5.
National Academy of Design.

Modeled after the Doge's Palace (1345–1438) in Venice, Wight's building was constructed with bands of gray and white marble, bluestone trim, and red Vermont marble columns. The upper story featured a diamond pattern made from buff and red brick. Approached by a two-winged staircase, the entranceway reached the ornamental frieze, providing a vertical contrast to the building's horizontal bands and stringcourses. Windows are repeated, on a smaller scale, in the entranceway's arch.

Venentian Gothic

appeared rooted in an idealized Renaissance past that seemed to transcend the crass world of commerce. Conceiving the artist in masculine terms, Tuckerman warned that pandering to the whims of the marketplace risked an artist's creative potency or manhood. When, on the other hand, "a painter really expresses what is in him, and not what the public *fiat* approves," he is no longer a passive imitator but finally may generate the life-giving "spark of artistic genius" (p. 27). Contrarily, as the art historian Sarah Burns has demonstrated, artists' and critics' emphasis on godlike powers of genius was itself a marketing strategy for promoting public interest in specific personalities and their incomparable works.

By the end of the Civil War, New York artists could celebrate the opening of a spacious new building for the National Academy of Design, one of the nation's leading art academies (fig. 6.11). Tuckerman praised this new "Temple of Art," designed after "the famed Ducal palace at Venice," as "one of the finest buildings in the city" (p. 19). Standing on the corner of 23rd Street and 4th Avenue, the handsome building consisted of three stories and cost $200,000. Tuckerman dutifully noted that most of this money had been "contributed by our wealthy citizens, lovers of art" (p. 19). The architect, Peter B. Wight (1838–1925), chose an historical-revival, Venetian Gothic style. The richly ornamented façade features a pointed-arch entrance and polychromatic masonry with alter-

nating courses of light and dark stones for the main story's pillars and arched openings. Wight's selection of Venetian Gothic was undoubtedly influenced by the English critic John Ruskin, whose books *The Seven Lamps of Architecture* (1849) and *The Stones of Venice* (1851–3) nostalgically associated medieval art and architecture with truth and nature. Contradicting earlier associations of Gothic architecture with primitive barbarism (see p. 88), Ruskin valued the organic variety and ornamental richness of the medieval style. Unlike the more austere classical tradition, Gothic decorativeness permitted designers and craftsmen a greater freedom for creative expression. For Ruskin, the handiwork of individual stonemasons and craftsmen was, by definition, honest and natural in contrast to the shoddy, machine-made products of the industrial age.

However, American architects saw no necessary contradiction in employing medieval or other historical-revival styles for modern commercial buildings or engineering projects. In 1870–71, Wight published a translation of the lectures of Eugène-Emanuel Viollet-le-Duc (1814–79), who taught at the prestigious École des Beaux-Arts in Paris. The French scholar compared the structural skeleton of a Gothic cathedral to the iron skeletons of contemporary nineteenth-century buildings. He argued that Gothic construction methods were a rational foundation for modern principles of design.

Economic Modernization and the Appropriation of European Architecture

No monument more dramatically symbolized the new age of modern technology than the Brooklyn Bridge (fig. 6.12), and yet its designer, John Augustus Roebling (1806–69), also looked backward toward an ennobling Gothic-Revival style. Alleviating ferry traffic on the East River, the bridge connected Manhattan to Brooklyn and ultimately inspired the 1898 consolidation of the five boroughs—Manhattan, Brooklyn, Queens, the Bronx, and Staten Island—into the greater city of New York. Begun in 1869, the engineering project was completed in 1883 by Roebling's son, Washington Augustus Roebling (1837–1926). Through the use of twisted steel wires suspended from monumental masonry towers, the Roeblings were able to support a high, 1600-foot span of roadway without intermediate supports from below. River traffic could continue to flow freely beneath the bridge deck, while streetcars shuttled back and forth through pointed-arch tower openings designed to resemble the windows of a Gothic cathedral. Called the "eighth wonder of the world" and "the 19th Century Wonder" (cited in McNamara, pp. 140–41) when it was publicly dedicated on May 24, 1883, the Brooklyn Bridge became a symbol of American ambition and ingenuity.

Skyscrapers, the building type most closely associated with corporate power, also were designed in terms of traditional, historical styles. While the new bridge was under construction, improvements in metal framing, foundation work, fireproofing, power equipment, elevator service, and other technologies allowed architects to plan office buildings that rose far higher than four or five stories. In 1873, Richard Morris Hunt, the architect of the Studio Building (see fig. 6.10), designed one of the nation's first skyscrapers—a description accurate at least regarding its great height, if not its new materials or means of construction (fig. 6.13). New York's eight-story Tribune Building, housing the offices and printing presses of the *Tribune* newspaper, had a two-story attic and rose 260 feet from the

6.12 John A. Roebling ●
Brooklyn Bridge, New York City, 1869–83.
© Collection of The New York Historical Society.

The bridge's sweeping roadway suspended from a web of steel cables essentially marked the beginning in America of modern architectural ideas regarding the construction of continuous, grand-scale urban spaces. The horizontal vault across the river contrasts with the vertical, Gothic towers, which foreshadowed the triumph of the modern skyscraper.

sidewalk level to the top of its clock tower. Supported by massive brick piers and thick masonry walls, the blocklike heaviness of the building evokes traditional associations with Italian Renaissance architecture. Nevertheless, Hunt's office spaces were generously illuminated by natural light, as the architect designed every room with at least one window to the outside. When the building opened in 1875, people in the upper stories marveled over the superior quality of light and air high above the noise and dust of street-level traffic.

As a writer for *Building News* concluded in 1883, building vertically made practical, economic sense:

> *The present . . . is likely to be known in the history of New York as the High-Building Epoch. Seven or eight years ago, after struggling in vain to pack the lower or business end of the city more closely with buildings, in order to supply the insatiable demand for office room, real estate capitalists suddenly discovered that there was plenty of room in the air, and that by doubling the height of its buildings the same result would be reached as if the island had been stretched to twice its present width (cited in Landau and Condit, p. 111).*

By the 1880s, architects were beginning to use steel-skeleton frames to support floors and exterior walls. Earlier, a number of high-rise buildings had been constructed with iron frames; but iron, unlike steel, proved unreliable in fires, wilting rapidly when the temperature increased. Louis Sullivan (1856–1924), a partner in the Chicago firm of Adler & Sullivan, designed the Wainwright Building, a speculative office building in St. Louis, as a nine-story, steel-framed skyscraper sheathed in brick masonry and terra-cotta panels (fig. 6.14). Sullivan conceived the building in organic terms, believing that its aesthetic form should express its internal functions and social purposes. Although Sullivan adapted and incorporated historical references into his architecture, he did not believe that historical styles should be reproduced unmodified without regard to the contemporary socioeconomic environment. More than any other material, steel symbolized for Sullivan the progress and efficiency of a new entrepreneurial, industrial culture. Therefore, it seemed contra-

6.13 Richard Morris Hunt
Tribune Building, New York City, 1875.
© Collection of The New York Historical Society, New York.

dictory to the organic evolution of architecture to design banks like Greek temples or business buildings like Gothic cathedrals, as other architects would do on into the twentieth century (see fig. 7.24).

The Wainwright Building is divided functionally and visually into three parts. The two-story base, with its large display windows at ground level, housed spacious shops and their offices. The next seven stories of smaller office units rise dramatically upward to form the main body of the building. Narrow windows and terra-cotta panels are set back from the narrow brick piers, so that there is a strong, uninterrupted vertical thrust. As Sullivan wrote, the repetitious grid of windows transparently reveals the interior arrangement of individual office cells and they "look all alike because they are all alike" (cited in Upton, p. 212). Sullivan actually doubled the number of thin vertical piers between the windows, since only every other one sheathes a steel structural column. The multiplication of piers not only expressed the interior division of office cells, but also accentuated the essentially vertical character of skyscraper design.

Nevertheless, the building's attic floor with crowning cornice provides a strong horizontal cap to the whole structure's upward movement. Housing essential mechanical services for plumbing and heating, the corniced attic is covered by terra-cotta panels decorated with organic, foliate forms expressing the presence of the building's internal organs and arteries. The

Wainwright Building thus rises like a tree from its foundational roots, through its main trunk, to terminate in a leafy canopy. However, its tripartite division also subtly mimics the elements of a classical column—base, shaft, and foliated capital. Sullivan was still drawing on classical Greco-Roman and Renaissance traditions. More immediately, he was influenced by Henry Hobson Richardson's (1838–86) dynamic Marshall Field Wholesale Store (fig. 6.15). Designed for the men working in the Marshall Field Wholesale division, Richardson chose a distinctively masculine style. The store was constructed entirely in ashlar masonry like a modern-day Renaissance palazzo with high arches that encompass several stories of windows.

6.14 Louis Sullivan
Wainwright Building, St. Louis, Missouri, 1890–91.
Art Institute of Chicago, Chicago, Illinois.

6.15 Henry Hobson Richardson
Marshall Field Wholesale Store, Chicago, Illinois, 1885–7.
Chicago Historical Society.

Built around a central court, this massive, seven-story building had minimal decorative detail. Variations in fenestration and the size and arrangement of the masonry stones constituted the primary ornamentation for the boxlike store's otherwise flat, planar surfaces. As they decreased in size, the number of windows doubled and quadrupled in the upper stories. The building's corners were defined by broad, powerful piers, while narrower but still substantial piers vertically divided the windows into a regular sequence of bays.

Meanwhile, the building's generously fenestrated exterior seems horizontally stretched to express its continuous interior space. Adapted to modern commercial needs, European historical styles lent an aura of cultural dignity to the American urban environment. Symbolizing the New World energy of ambitious, restless Americans, skyscrapers simultaneously looked backward and forward, evoking associations with the historical monuments of the Old World, while implicitly challenging Europe's economic and cultural domination.

Led by Daniel Hudson Burnham (1846–1912), a group of architects planned the 1893 World's Columbian Exposition in Chicago as a modern urban utopia. Commemorating the four-hundredth anniversary of Christopher Columbus's 1492 voyage of discovery, the architects' temporary "White City" featured spectacular exhibition buildings with classical, Roman-style façades, symmetrically arranged around Venetian-style lagoons or waterways (fig. 6.16). The White City's ancient Roman and Renaissance-Revival architecture was criticized by Louis Sullivan for its apparent lack of modernity. Yet the participating architects agreed that neoclassicism, based on a modular system of design, was suitable for modern American architecture and urban planning. The overall uniformity and rationality of the White City expressed the values of American business interests, the corporate desire for social harmony and political consensus. Anticipating Disneyland and the elaborate theme parks of the twentieth century (see fig. 9.25), this controlled environment on the shores of Lake Michigan seemed entirely free of the cacophony, congestion, and social problems of Chicago's nearby downtown. Employing the latest technology in sewage and water-filtration systems, the White City hired street cleaners for the daily removal of litter. Professionally trained guards or policemen kept the social order, while acting in a polite, solicitous manner. One commentator, writing for *Cosmopolitan* magazine, marveled that out of a crowd of more than 300,000 fair-goers, he was unable to find "one ill-tempered face, one drunken man" (cited in Lovell, p. 47, n. 23). At night, the White City became a fantasyland of colored lights, illuminated fountains, and shimmering waterways bearing passengers in elegant Venetian gondolas (fig. 6.18).

The architect of several major skyscrapers, Burnham had helped Chicago rebuild after a disastrous 1871 fire that destroyed over 1,600 acres of downtown property. He now intended the White City as a model for the city's future urban development. Burnham was a member of

6.16 The Great Basin
World's Columbian
Exposition, 1893.
Chicago, Illinois.

6.17 (below)
Daniel H. Burnham
City Center Plan,
Chicago, 1909.
Chicago Historical Society,
Chicago, Illinois.

the Swedenborgian Church, which was founded on the visionary writings of the eighteenth-century Swedish mystic Emanuel Swedenborg. Burnham equated the White City with Swedenborg's detailed personal visions of the heavenly New Jerusalem, which he described in his book *Heaven and its Wonders, and Hell from Things Heard and Seen* (1758). Claiming to have visited the heavenly city on numerous occasions, Swedenborg outlined an urban paradise that Burnham and his late Chicago partner, John Wellborn Root (1850–91), had found inspirational. Swedenborg's celestial citizens walk through spacious avenues, public squares, and landscaped parks. They enjoy impressive civic, commercial, and cultural buildings, including colleges, museums, libraries, and auditoriums. Influenced, in part, by Swedenborg's dynamic urban vision, Burnham's Chicago City Center Plan (fig. 6.17) features a central civic core as a point of gravitational convergence and radiating energy. A symmetrical system of ten arterial avenues or boulevards fans out through the city from a domed city hall, which Burnham apparently intended as a civic cathedral, the worldly manifestation of a heavenly prototype.

Burnham's plan was a major contribution to the City Beautiful movement, in which late-nineteenth- and early-twentieth-century

6.18 Charles C. Curran
Machinery Hall, Administration Building, and MacMonnies Fountain: World's Columbian Exposition of 1893, 1893.
Oil on canvas, 18⅛ x 22½ in (46 x 57.1 cm).
Chicago Historical Society, Chicago, Illinois.

Curran's representation of the White City at night focuses on Richard Morris Hunt's domed Administration Building, located at one end of the Fair's Court of Honor that overlooked the Grand Basin, a lagoon designed by the landscape architect Frederic Law Olmsted.

architects and urban planners attempted to control the rapid growth of American cities by designing public parks, amenities, and ennobling civic buildings. Chicago adopted many of the ideas in Burnham's proposal, including the expansion of parks along the lakefront and formation of the Cook County Forest Preserve beyond the city's center. Though a domed city hall was never constructed, the city's major cultural institutions, including the Art Institute of Chicago and the Field Museum of Natural History, formed an urban core around Grant Park on Lake Michigan.

Meanwhile, the Wisconsin-born architect Frank Lloyd Wright (1869–1959) was also in Chicago and its suburbs, working to revolutionize the modern home. Influenced by the domestic architecture of H. H. Richardson and sharing many of the views of Louis Sullivan, for whom he initially worked, Wright viewed architecture more in organic than historical terms. Rejecting the arbitrary reproduction of historical-revival styles, he equated buildings with the natural growth of a plant, with every form functionally necessary to the life of the entire organism. Working within the American Midwest's characteristic geography of flat plains and prairies, Wright developed what he called the Prairie style of domestic architecture. As seen

in the Ward Willitts House (fig. 6.19), Wright's Prairie homes were defined by overlapping, low-pitched, or horizontal roofs and porches, which clustered around the building's chimney core or central hearth (heart). The house seems to hug the land by repeating the flattened ground plane. The overhanging horizontal planes protect or shade long ribbons of windows, which illuminate and open the interior space to the outside world. Wright rejected the idea that rooms and houses were enclosed boxes with fixed walls, favoring instead movable panels and screens. Though he avoided copying traditional historical styles, he was strongly influenced by Japanese domestic architecture, which he was able to study at the official Japanese pavilion for the 1893 Columbian Exposition. An admirer of John Ruskin, Wright identified with the anti-industrial aesthetic of the Arts and Crafts movement. The architect was also an interior decorator and designer of furniture and household objects. Like other exponents of the Arts and Crafts aesthetic, Wright believed in the power of art to transform and vitalize family life during an increasingly mechanized age. Nevertheless, though Wright's Prairie houses were far more modestly scaled than Richard Morris Hunt's mansions for the Vanderbilts and other elite clients, working-class families, who suffered

6.19 Frank Lloyd Wright
Ward W. Willitts House, Highland Park, Illinois, 1900–2.

During the period in which he was working on this home, Wright published a drawing of the prototypical Prairie-style house in the February 1901 issue of the *Ladies Home Journal*. Wright's advertisement for the virtues of his expansive, horizontal structures demonstrates his desire to reach a relatively wide, middle-class clientele.

the most from factory machinery, certainly could not afford Wright's services or most Arts and Crafts home furnishings.

Contemporaneous with Wright's practice in the Midwest, the Pasadena, California, architects Henry M. Greene (1870–1954) and Charles S. Greene (1868–1957) were similarly influenced by Japanese architecture and the aesthetic ideals of the Arts and Crafts movement. Together, the two brothers developed a suburban, bungalow style of domestic architecture. Popularized in numerous architectural and mass-market design magazines, the bungalow building type had originated in India and derived from the Hindu word for a low, one-story dwelling with surrounding porches or galleries. In its American context, the bungalow was identified as a small, detached house, built simply with wood-shingled or clapboarded walls, a low but generous overhanging roof, and minimal architectural ornament. Ideal for the warm, California climate, bungalows with porches, verandas or patios were meant to incorporate the health-giving benefits of outdoor life. They were also intended to be affordable for a broad, middle-class public.

During the early years of their practice, Greene and Greene were particularly successful in pioneering inexpensive bungalow housing in Southern California. But the quality of their designs soon attracted wealthy clients, such as David Gamble, second-generation magnate of

6.20 Henry M. Greene and Charles S. Greene
David B. Gamble House, Pasadena, California, 1907–9.

the Procter and Gamble Company, manufacturers of Ivory Soap and other household products (see fig. 6.41). Having left business for retirement in Pasadena, Gamble commissioned Greene and Greene to design a spacious, rambling wooden structure, adapted to the natural rolling contours of the site (fig. 6.20). As in Wright's prairie houses, the low, overhanging eaves shade ribbons of windows and establish a strong, horizontal profile. Light, airy sleeping porches and shaded terraces extend the living space well beyond the wood-paneled interior rooms, randomly clustered around a broad, central hall. Like Wright, Greene and Greene also sought to create a total aesthetic environment by designing all the interior details, including furniture, hardware, carpets, and stained-glass windows. The glass was carefully chosen from Tiffany Studios in New York. Technologically up to date, Greene and Greene installed electrical lighting and, again, turned to Tiffany for glass lightshades. The Gamble house expanded the bungalow aesthetic to the scale of a lavish, resort-like estate.

Images of Renewal and the Family in the Aftermath of War

In the aftermath of the Civil War, painters and sculptors addressed the problems of modern family life and the need to heal the racial and geopolitical divisions within American society. John Rogers (1829–1904), a New York sculptor, specialized in small, inexpensive plaster figural groups that represented genre subjects, or scenes of ordinary daily life. During the Civil War, Rogers's sculptures of common Union soldiers and victims of war and slavery garnered considerable public attention. Day after day, crowds of people reportedly gathered in front of the storefront windows of Rogers's art dealer on Broadway to admire the latest statuettes from the artist's studio. After the war, Rogers continued to represent his sentimental war themes. In *The Fugitive's Story* (fig. 6.21), an African-American woman, holding a child in her arms, stands before three white abolitionists and social reformers: the poet John Greenleaf Whittier, the Protestant clergyman Henry Ward Beecher, and the leading anti-slavery spokesman, William Lloyd Garrison.

As the editor of the abolitionist journal *The Liberator*, Garrison possesses the greatest air of authority. He sits at his writing desk while gazing at the young woman as she relates the story of how she became a fugitive from slavery. The small, makeshift sack of earthly possessions resting at her feet poignantly expresses the woman's plight and her dependence on the protection of these sympathetic, well-dressed men, who clearly are represented as her social superiors. Apparently, Rogers's rejection of the austere neoclassicism of Hiram Powers's *The Greek Slave* (see fig. 5.65) in favor of a detailed sculptural realism appeared original to the critic Henry Tuckerman's eyes. Nevertheless, Rogers's studio virtually became an assembly-line factory. Over the course of his career, he produced approximately 80,000 replicas, representing around eighty figural groups.

6.21 John Rogers ●
The Fugitive's Story,
1869.
Plaster, 22 in (55.8 cm)
high. New York Historical
Society, New York.

6.22 Edmonia Lewis ●
Forever Free, 1867.
Howard University Art
Gallery, Washington, D.C.

Lewis originally named this
sculptural group *The
Morning of Liberty*, but she
changed the title and
inscribed the words
"Forever Free" from
Lincoln's Emancipation
Proclamation on the
sculpture's base. The male
figure's physique was
carefully softened by Lewis
into smooth, gentle planes
of marble flesh. She
thereby made the grateful
figures a non-threatening
presence for white
audiences, who feared
violent, black male anger
and revenge as the legacy
of American slavery.

Reaching a broad middle-class audience, Rogers's $10–15 plaster statuettes were displayed in thousands of home parlors during the second half of the nineteenth century.

Anti-slavery and Civil War themes became popular during the twelve-year Reconstruction period (1865–77) that followed the Civil War. Once the war had ended, the victorious North struggled to formulate a policy for reconstructing the South, or readmitting the Southern states back into the Union. After the assassination of President Abraham Lincoln in 1865, President Andrew Johnson adopted a more lenient attitude toward the defeated South. Johnson's administration initially enabled the unrepentant white plantation elite to return to political power.

Southern state legislatures agreed to the abolition of slavery, but they soon passed "Black Codes," which forced African-Americans to sign yearly labor contracts. The codes declared jobless and landless blacks vagrants, who could be arrested and hired out as laborers to plantation owners. In 1867, however, the United States Congress, dominated by Radical Republicans from the North, passed a strict set of Reconstruction policies, which divided the South into military districts and forced southern states to recognize the civil and political rights of black citizens. Aided by numerous "carpetbaggers," or newly arriving teachers, businessmen, and retired Union soldiers from the North, former African-American slaves finally were able to vote in elections, initiating a liberalization of the South's political life. During the next ten years, sixteen African-Americans from the South served in the United States Congress, while hundreds more were elected to state legislatures and to local offices. By 1870, the Fifteenth Amendment to the U.S. Constitution prohibited states from discriminating against voters because of their race or previous state of servitude. However, this amendment did not apply to African-American women, since women in general were not given the right to vote until after World War I. Furthermore, after Reconstruction ended in 1877, the United States government withdrew oversight of Southern states' political affairs, thereby allowing the return of a racist legal system and giving free rein to white terrorist organizations such as the Ku Klux Klan.

The tenuous expansion of civil and political rights for African-Americans inspired some artists to celebrate their new constitutional status. In contrast to John Rogers with his realistic, small-scale plaster figures, other sculptors represented the demise of slavery in more idealized terms, evoking traditional associations with ancient Greco-Roman art. Working in Rome, Edmonia Lewis (1845–?), daughter of an African-American father and a Chippewa Indian mother, commemorated President Abraham Lincoln's famous 1863 Emancipation Proclamation, which declared slaves "forever free." Her marble sculptural group *Forever Free* features an African-American couple celebrating the proclamation (fig. 6.22). With one foot resting on a broken ball and chain, the powerful male figure raises an arm in triumph. The ineffectual manacle still on his wrist now becomes an emblem of the victory over slavery. With his other arm, the man places a protective hand on the kneeling woman, whose hands are clasped in a prayer of thanks. Conceived as a unified, married pair, rather than two separate figures, *Forever Free* symbolically expressed the restoration of the black family. With the abolition of slavery, African-American families could remain intact. Husbands could now protect their wives from physical abuse and sexual exploitation, allowing them to live as virtuous mothers of children born into freedom.

Although Lewis herself lived an unconventional life as a single woman working in a male-dominated profession, *Forever Free* expressed the conventional attitude of most Americans regarding inequality between men and women. Lewis's white, middle-class patrons were primarily abolitionists, not feminists. On October 18, 1869, the sculpture was dedicated at Tremont Temple, a Baptist church in Boston, in a public ceremony attended by numerous abolitionists, including William Lloyd Garrison (see fig. 6.21) and the Reverend Leonard A. Grimes, who formally accepted the marble group. Writing for a religious journal, the *Christian Register*, the Boston critic Elizabeth Palmer Peabody described the abolitionist audience's "profound emotion" in viewing *Forever Free*. Asserting that the sculpture was "poetry" in stone, she imagined hearing its two figures sing "Praise de Lord" (cited in Buick, p. 194).

By using the definite article "de" instead of "the," Peabody, a schoolteacher as well as critic, condescendingly attributed to the African-American figures an illiterate black dialect. Curiously, however, Edmonia Lewis's representation of the kneeling woman is free of ethnic attributes. In contrast to the clearly African character of the husband, the wife's hair and facial features appear more white or European than African. The art historian Kirsten P. Buick has speculated that Lewis avoided representing the female figure with strong, African features because she didn't wish her white audience to interpret the work in autobiographical terms. In their reviews of Lewis's sculptures, critics tended to focus more on the novelty of a part-African,

6.23 Thomas Satterwhite Noble
The Price of Blood, 1868.
Oil on canvas, 39¼ x 49½ in (99.6 x 125.7 cm).
Morris Museum of Art, Augusta, Georgia.

6.24 Winslow Homer
The Veteran in a New Field, 1865.
Oil on canvas,
24⅛ x 38⅛ in
(61.3 x 96.8 cm).
The Metropolitan Museum
of Art, New York. Bequest
of Adelaide Milton de
Groot, 1967.

Soon after the Civil War,
tour books guided
American readers through
Northern and Southern
battlefields. Authors
meditated over the soil
sanctified by the blood of so
many young men, who
were compared to
harvested sheaves reaped
by the scythe-wielding
figure of Death. Homer's
solitary veteran similarly
evokes associations with
Death and somberly recalls
the lost lives of countless
fellow soldiers.

part-Indian woman artist rather than the actual art work. Henry Tuckerman, in his *Book of Artists*, quoted at length a letter from a correspondent in Rome, who wrote that Lewis herself was the object of that city's curiosity. The correspondent proceeded to describe the physical appearance of this "little American girl," which clearly confirmed her "Indian and negro parentage" (cited in Tuckerman, p. 603). By expunging signs of African ethnicity in the kneeling wife, Lewis sought to shift the critical focus from herself to her creative work. The white marble medium, neoclassical style, and ethnic "whitening" of the female figure enabled Lewis to claim the aesthetic objectivity and professional credibility that most of her fellow artists could take for granted.

The cool, neoclassical style, with its austere reduction of realistic detail, was particularly associated with the life of the mind or noble feelings and universal ideas. By choosing to work in this traditional Greco-Roman manner, Lewis could more convincingly establish her artistic legitimacy before a primarily white audience. Indeed,

when the Museum of Fine Arts in Boston and other major city museums first opened their doors during the 1870s, curators initially filled the galleries with plaster copies or reproductions of Greek and Roman antiquities.

The familial meaning of Lewis's sculpture appears in greater relief when contrasted with a virtually contemporaneous painting by the Kentucky artist Thomas Satterwhite Noble (1835–1907). Though personally opposed to slavery, Noble had been a supporter of Southern states' right to secede from the Union and had served in the Confederate army. After the Civil War, however, he painted a series of pictures with anti-slavery themes. In *The Price of Blood*, he represented a heartless plantation owner who sells his own slave-son to a slave dealer (fig. 6.23). Examining the bill of sale, the dealer stands in the middle of the picture, physically and symbolically dividing it into two halves, separating the seated father from the barefoot, defiant son at the left side of the painting. The youth's only slightly dark complexion identifies him as mulatto, or part African. His African mother, also the father's slave, is absent from this cruel scene, but she is implicitly present, as viewers are left to imagine the coercive and illegitimate sexual relationship between master and slave. Noble's bifurcated composition strongly suggests that slavery tore at the moral fabric of white as well as black family life.

The Boston-born painter Winslow Homer (1836–1910) first gained fame with his simplified and unsentimental pictures of the Civil War. During the war, Homer worked as an artist-illustrator for *Harper's Weekly*, a New York magazine. Competing with the army of Civil War photographers, Homer sketched unheroic, matter-of-fact scenes of military life, which were then reproduced as wood engravings for the popular periodical. Homer continued to paint Civil War themes after the Union's victory. Perhaps the most poignant of his post-Civil War paintings is *The Veteran in a New Field* (fig. 6.24), which was finished just a few months after the South's surrender and Lincoln's assassination at the hands of a Southern sympathizer. In this starkly simple and sketchily painted composition, the artist represented a former Union soldier returning to the peaceful pursuit of agriculture after years of military service. As seen in the picture's lower-right corner, the soldier's military jacket and canteen have been set aside. Harvested stalks of wheat, represented by slashing strokes of paint, are beginning to shroud the well-worn emblems of war. The critic for the *New York Weekly Tribune* suggested that Homer's painting recalled the ancient story of Cincinnatus, the Roman general who preferred a life of farming to military and political power. Similarly, George Washington, the American Cincinnatus, had abandoned his military command for rural retirement at his Mount Vernon plantation, following the Revolutionary War (see fig. 4.41). For the New York critic, Homer's *The Veteran in a New Field* expressed the post-war necessity for productive, economic renewal: "we must now take our soldiers from the camp and make them farmers" (cited in Cikovsky, Jr., and Kelly, p. 25). Couching the need for national regeneration in religious terms, the sympathetic critic also alluded to the well-known Old Testament passage, which metaphorically expressed in agricultural terms the transition from war to peace: "They shall beat their swords into plowshares and their spears into pruning hooks" (Isaiah 2:4).

However, Homer's painting also has a darker symbolism that compares with Alexander Gardner's battlefield photograph *A Harvest of Death* (see fig. 5.71). In wielding his scythe, the anonymous Union soldier evokes associations with Death or the Grim Reaper, harvester of souls. As the art historian Nikolai Cikovsky, Jr., has observed, sheaves of wheat were funerary symbols and often were placed on coffins before burial. Despite its vigorous brushwork and bright, sun-drenched colors, Homer's quiet painting somberly mourns the martyrdom of the nation's soldiers and its assassinated president, Abraham Lincoln.

For this and other pictures during the 1860s and 1870s, Homer was often criticized for his sketchlike technique. Critics who were used to smoothly finished painting surfaces claimed that Homer's compositions were mere blotches or smears of paint applied in a relatively slapdash manner. Contemporaneously in Paris, art critics also ridiculed a number of French painters for exhibiting pictures that appeared unfinished or sloppily executed. Homer visited Paris toward the end of 1866, staying almost a year, and may have seen the brilliantly colored, sketchlike paintings of Édouard Manet (1832–83), the most important precursor of the Impressionist movement, which formally organized itself into an independently exhibiting group of artists during the next decade. Often painting outdoors, young French painters such as Claude Monet (1840–1926) and also Pierre Auguste Renoir (1841–1919) sought to record the effects of natural light and their own fleeting impressions of nature and modern life.

However, Homer was already sketching outdoors and painting in a loose, sunlit style before his Paris trip. His war experience as an artist-illustrator contributed to his preference for working up compositions quickly in the open air. As Homer continued to paint scenes of American life, including nostalgic pictures of rural New England schoolchildren (fig. 6.26), critics soon began praising his relatively crude painting technique for its distinctively American, nationalist character. Awkwardness and roughness in paint application became a virtue for many, as Homer's pictures seemed to emerge organically from American soil, free from the

6.25 Eastman ◗ Johnson
The Brown Family,
1869.
Oil on canvas,
38½ x 32⅜ in
(97.7 x 82.3 cm).
Fine Arts Museums of
San Francisco,
San Francisco, California.
Gift of Mr. and Mrs. John
D. Rockefeller 3rd.

Johnson's painting is as
much a portrait of a room
as it is of a family.
Contemporary critics
denounced the picture for
its portrayal of the parlor's
old-fashioned, Renaissance-
Revival style, designed by a
French interior decorator
during the 1840s. Clarence
Cook, propagandist for
simpler, Asian-influenced
designs, particularly
ridiculed the Browns'
ornately carved woodwork
and furnishings, and he
compared the chandelier's
crystals to the tears of the
artist forced to paint such
tasteless ornamentation.

taint of foreign influence. For an American public in mourning for its Civil War dead, his representation of healthy, apple-cheeked boys at play in *Snap the Whip* expressed hope and confidence in the nation's future. The boys in the foreground seem to form a tenuous unit as they hold hands and run barefoot through the flowering field outside the wooden red schoolhouse. One might imagine that a number of these boys, born during the Civil War, had lost fathers, older brothers, or uncles in battle. The line of boys mimics the wartime struggle to hang together. However, just as the war has ended and soldiers have returned home to productive employment, so must the playful solidarity of boyhood ultimately give way to the manly responsibilities of adulthood.

In the middle distance, two boys, who can no longer hang on to the others, fall to the ground in the direction of two girls and a waving husband–wife couple among other figures in the background. Homer's dynamic composition thus pulls the viewer inward, away from an isolated brotherhood of young boys toward a marriage of the sexes and a renewal of family life designed to replenish post-Civil War America.

Images of family life were especially popular during the years immediately following the war. Group portraits of children with their parents and grandparents reassuringly expressed generational continuity after the violent disruption of the Civil War and during an age when medical science still had no defense against many deadly diseases. Beginning in 1865, Eastman Johnson painted several detailed group portraits of wealthy New York families. One of the most intimate was *The Brown Family* (fig. 6.25), which focuses on young William Brown, grandson and future heir of banker James Brown, who sits with his second wife, Eliza, in the lavishly decorated parlor of their mansion at Park Avenue and 37th

Street. Although the middle generation between grandson and grandfather is not visibly represented, Johnson's picture was commissioned and owned by William's father and James's son, John Crosby Brown, who was taking over management of the family's extensive banking business. In strongly gripping his grandfather's arm and crossing his legs in the same manner as James Brown, little William seems to demonstrate that one day he, too, will manage the family business. By 1869, James Brown had already lost six children and nine grandchildren in premature or unexpected deaths. Another grandchild, Eliza Coe Brown, William's sister, was still alive. However, the granddaughter is absent from the group portrait, probably because, as a girl, she was deemed inessential to preservation of the family business. Certainly, Johnson expressed this gender bias more explicitly by marginalizing William's grandmother. As she sits in a corner performing a domestic task, she is virtually ignored by grandfather and grandson, who seem to communicate secretly with each other behind the screen of James's open newspaper, itself an emblem of the male-dominated world of finance.

Science, Capitalism, and Masculine Identity

American capitalists often spoke of business in martial terms. According to the English naturalist Charles Darwin (1809–92), whose scientific treatise *On the Origin of Species* (1859) haunted late-nineteenth-century American thought, the evolution of all earthly life was itself a deadly struggle of "natural selection," whereby only the fittest species survive, while the weak disappear into extinction. By the 1880s, Winslow Homer began to specialize in painting powerful seascapes and hunting pictures that represented the harshness of nature and suggested the Darwinian struggle for survival. In 1881, Homer spent several months living near Tynemouth, northeast England, a small fishing village on the North Sea, where he painted the statuesque wives of fishermen waiting patiently on storm-tossed shores for the safe return of the fishing boats. After 1883, when his well-to-do family built a house and made real-estate investments at Prout's Neck on the coast of Maine, Homer

•6.26 Winslow Homer
Snap the Whip, 1872.
Oil on canvas, 22 x 36 in
(55.9 x 91.4 cm).
The Butler Institute of
American Art,
Youngstown, Ohio.

6.27 Harriet Powers •
Pictorial quilt, 1895–8.
Pieced, appliquéd,
embroidered, and
quilted cotton.
Museum of Fine Arts,
Boston. Bequest of
Maxim Karolik.

A representation of the story
of Jonah and the whale
appears in the far-left,
second-row panel of a
fifteen-paneled quilt by
Harriet Powers (1837–1911),
a former Georgia slave,
whose handiwork gained
the attention of art
collectors. This quilt was
purchased by the faculty
ladies of Atlantic University,
an African-American
institution of higher learning,
founded at the end of the
Civil War. The quilt narrates
not only biblical scenes, but
also more recent wondrous
events, such as an 1833
meteor storm that Powers
heard about as a child.

continued to depict seascapes with heroic figures contending with the powerful forces of nature. Apparently inspired by a trip with a fishing fleet to the Grand Banks off the coast of Nova Scotia, *The Fog Warning* (fig. 6.29) was painted at Prout's Neck. A local fisherman agreed to pose for Homer, who had set up a dory, a flat-bottomed rowboat, on a large sand dune outside his studio. After initially naming the painting *Halibut Fishing*, Homer changed the title before exhibiting it at a private Boston gallery in 1886. The new title called attention to the danger that Homer's lone fisherman was facing from an approaching bank of fog that could prevent him from finding his way back to the sailing ship on the distant horizon. The ocean-swells and the weight of the large fish appear to work against the fisherman, who pauses to look over his shoulder while calculating the great distance he must row before the obscuring fog rolls in. Homer's broad masses of pigment in both water and sky convey nature's raw physical power, while the more tightly painted architecture of the dory suggests human ingenuity in overcoming nature and navigating the perils of life. Significantly, Homer failed to sell *The Fog Warning* until years later. The art historian Sarah Burns suggests that American businessmen were not inclined to buy the work

and similar pictures because it reminded them all too well of the financial risks and uncertainties they confronted as the American economy unpredictably ebbed and flowed, frequently hitting periods of depression.

Toward the end of his career, following a visit to Florida and the Bahamas in 1898–9, Homer painted an even grimmer painting to unnerve wary critics and clients. Unlike the heroic fisherman in *The Fog Warning*, the single, Caribbean black sailor in *The Gulf Stream* (fig. 6.28) appears helplessly adrift. Lying on the deck of his mastless, storm-damaged vessel, the man directs his gaze not toward the ghostly outline of a potential rescue ship on the horizon, but, instead, toward a dangerously close waterspout.

Meanwhile, opportunistic sharks menacingly swim next to the Key West boat, which displays the name "Annie" on a rear plaque. Homer's picture has been compared to John Singleton Copley's allegory of the American Revolution, *Watson and the Shark* (see fig. 4.28), which also prominently features a black sailor within shark-infested waters. Both pictures allude to the history of the slave trade, since dead or ailing African captives were routinely thrown overboard to sharks and other predators, during arduous transatlantic voyages to American

6.28 Winslow Homer
The Gulf Stream, 1899.
Oil on canvas,
28⅛ x 49⅛ in
(71.4 x 124.8 cm).
Metropolitan Museum of
Art. Catharine Lorillard
Wolfe Fund, 1906.

6.29 Winslow Homer
The Fog Warning, 1885.
Oil on canvas,
30¼ x 48½ in
(76.8 x 123.2 cm).
Museum of Fine Arts,
Boston, Massachusetts.
Otis Norcross Fund.

Homer represents only a single fisherman in a dory, looking over his shoulder toward a sailing vessel. However, in fishing for halibut in the deep waters of the Grand Banks, schooners usually transported a fleet of small rowboats, each manned by a pair of fishermen, who set and tended trawl lines. Homer's focus on a lonely, isolated figure intensifies the dramatic impact of the picture and its allegorical implications about the human struggle against nature's chaotic forces.

slave markets and sugar plantations. In African-American literature and visual arts, biblical references to Jonah and the whale and nautical metaphors of ships in storm-tossed seas were commonplace (fig. 6.27).

The conspicuous presence of sugar cane on the deck of Homer's Annie certainly suggests that this harsh, predatory seascape, splattered with passages of blood-red paint, serves as a metaphorical commentary on plantation slavery and its post-Reconstruction afterlife in anti-black vigilante violence, segregationist laws, and impoverished living conditions. Following the Spanish-American War, the United States acquired the sugar-producing territories of Cuba, Puerto Rico, Hawaii, and the Philippines. Their plantations were also worked by people of color, who would find no solace or rescue

6.30 William Michael Harnett
After the Hunt, 1885.
Oil on canvas,
71½ x 48½ in
(181.6 x 123.2 cm).
Fine Arts Museums of San Francisco, San Francisco, California. Mildred Anna Williams Collection.

Thomas Eakins's Circle and the Human Figure

Like Homer and Harnett, the Philadelphia artist Thomas Eakins (1844–1916) painted numerous pictures with pronounced masculine themes. Undoubtedly influenced by his father, who taught penmanship, Eakins was a careful draftsman and, in 1876, became a drawing instructor at the Pennsylvania Academy of the Fine Arts after several years of art study in Paris (1866–9) and classes in human anatomy at Philadelphia's Jefferson Medical College. That same year, the members of the Pennsylvania Academy, the nation's oldest existing art academy (founded in 1805), dedicated their new building on the corner of Broad and Cherry Streets (fig. 6.31). The primary architect, Frank Furness (1839–1912), designed an eclectic mixture of historical styles, drawing ornamental details from both the classical and medieval traditions. However, despite the decorative richness of the façade, with its polychromatic brickwork and Gothic rose window, the building's symmetrical longitudinal plan borrowed from the contemporary commercial architecture of shopping arcades.

The opening of the new Pennsylvania Academy was timed for the celebration of the nation's 1876 Centennial. The building's dedication mixed art, religion, and nationalism as the architect's father, the Reverend William H. Furness, announced the dawn of a new day for the arts and the moral refinement of American society. After the clergyman's inspirational address, officials unveiled two marble statues representing biblical subjects. G. B. Lombardi's sculpture of *Deborah* depicted an Old Testament woman prophet and songstress of ancient Israel's victories, while *Jerusalem* (fig. 6.32) by William Wetmore Story (1819–95) ideally personified the Hebrews' holy city. Both sculptures patriotically reaffirmed the nation's traditional identification with the ancient Jews, as white, Anglo-Saxon Protestant Americans continued to think of themselves as God's new chosen people.

The relatively realistic modern paintings of Thomas Eakins fit uneasily within this moral atmosphere of genteel refinement. While he assumed his new post as a drawing instructor at the Pennsylvania Academy, his most famous painting, *The Gross Clinic* (see p. 230), was

from the policies of an imperial regime burdened by the legacy of slavery and from the unpredictable cyclical waves of a capitalist market economy.

More popular with American capitalists than images of turmoil were the *trompe-l'oeil* (fool-the-eye) still-life paintings of William Michael Harnett (1848–92). Illusionistic pictures such as his *After the Hunt* (fig. 6.30) appealed to New York City businessmen, many of whom fished and hunted at expensive resorts and lodges in upstate New York and parts of New England. Harnett's images of dead game and hunting paraphernalia, rendered life size and with uncanny attention to textures and material surfaces, represented the literal and pictorial conquest of nature. Harnett could have expected affluent patrons to draw parallels between his trophy pictures and the predatory practices of capitalism, notably the competition with arch-rivals in the pursuit of new markets and clients. For many years, *After the Hunt* contributed to the masculine atmosphere of Stewart saloon on Warren Street in Lower Manhattan, a well-known bar patronized by successful New York businessmen.

6.31 Frank Furness and George W. Hewitt
Pennsylvania Academy of the Fine Arts, Philadelphia, 1871–6.

A student of Richard Morris Hunt, Furness shared his teacher's interest in the contemporary French neoclassical style known as "Neo-Grec." Furness lined the academy's façade on the upper story with square panels of relief sculptures, stacked above grooved triglyph blocks, like the frieze of a Greek temple. However, like Wight's National Academy of Design (see fig. 6.11), Furness's polychromatic building with its pointed-arch windows was also indebted to the Gothic revivalism of Ruskin and English architecture.

rejected by a jury for exhibition in the art galleries at the Philadelphia Centennial Exposition. Modeled after a series of European world's fairs, beginning with London's Great Exhibition of 1851, the 1876 Centennial Exposition was designed to celebrate American economic and cultural progress within the competitive context of an international display of art and industry. Eakins's painting represents a contemporary historical portrait of Dr. Samuel David Gross (1805–84), professor and surgeon at Philadelphia's Jefferson Medical College, where Eakins attended anatomy classes as a young student in 1864–5 and later, again, in 1873–4.

Through the course of his long career, Dr. Gross had published important treatises on anatomy, surgery, and the treatment of various diseases. In this portrait, the doctor stands in a crowded amphitheater performing a lecture-demonstration on the subject of the bone disease osteomyelitis. Following procedures that he had published in his *Elements of Surgery* (1859), Dr. Gross is operating to remove a dead bone from the thigh of a young boy. The youth lies on the surgeon's table at the right and is only partially visible. By representing this figure in strict perspective sharply receding backward into space, Eakins forced viewers' attention on the boy's lower body: his feet, thigh, and buttocks. A team of surgeons directs our gaze to the open surgical wound, while an anesthesiologist hovers over the patient's hidden face, waiting to apply more chloroform if the boy should start to awaken. Blood-soaked gauze and more sharp surgical instruments in the immediate foreground form the base of a compositional pyramid that has its apex in the gleaming forehead of Gross. Eakins signifies through geometry and light the pre-eminence of the professor's great intellect. Surrounding Gross's luminous head, a halo of gray hair appears almost electric with mental energy. The aging doctor has temporarily turned away from the operation and seems lost in profound thought, his eyes furrowed and darkened to suggest introspection and the powers of reason. At the same time, the heroic surgeon is a man of action. His right hand glistens with bright red blood as he holds a scalpel, also tinged with red.

6.32 William Wetmore Story
Jerusalem, 1876.
Marble,
71 x 40 x 44 in (180.3 x 101.6 x 111.8 cm).
Pennsylvania Academy of the Fine Arts.
Gift of Arthur Klein.

This brooding personification of Jerusalem was inspired by the Old Testament's Lamentations of Jeremiah, in which the biblical prophet mourns over the Babylonians' destruction of the Jewish holy city: "How doth the city sit solitary, that was full of people! how is she become a widow! she that was great among the nations, and princess among the provinces. . . . She weepeth sore in the night, and her tears are on her cheeks. . . ."
(Lamentations I: 1-2).

rational males and irrational female accentuates its controlled violence, as the dark-suited surgeons earnestly strive to cure the maladies of the body or the imperfections of nature. Beholders have responded to *The Gross Clinic* with the same kind of polarized views expressed by the male-female figures represented in the amphitheater. One critic later compared the boy to a blackboard and suggested that Gross was merely a classroom lecturer, who was inscribing the day's lesson on the board with a piece of chalk. Similarly, Gross has often been compared to a painter who holds a brush dripping with red paint. The boy's thigh then becomes a canvas for the expression of the doctor's creative genius. Such interpretations have tended to sanitize the painting, defusing the violent impact of the bloody incision, the picture's compositional focus and vagina-like symbol of nature's torturous penetration by masculine science and realist art.

However, the more common response when the painting was first exhibited was revulsion over the gory, frank subject matter. Though the art jury for the Centennial Exposition refused to exhibit the picture, Gross apparently intervened on Eakins's behalf so that the portrait did appear in the U.S. Army Post Hospital, displayed with the latest developments in medical technology. The medical setting undoubtedly intensified the public impression that *The Gross Clinic* was a relatively crude and unpleasant slice of real life rather than an ennobling work of high art in the tradition of Rembrandt and other Old Masters.

Throughout his career, Eakins offended the genteel sensibilities of Philadelphia's social elite. Despite his reputation for realism, the artist possessed an almost mystical faith in the physical beauty and purity of the human body. As drawing instructor at the Pennsylvania Academy, Eakins urged students to move quickly beyond copying antique sculptures or plaster casts. He insisted that all students, both male and female, participate in life-drawing classes, using both female and male nude models. Furthermore, he petitioned the academy's board of directors to hire amateurs or respectable society women rather than "professional models," a euphemism for prostitutes, to work as models. For Eakins, the traditional practice of employing prostitutes unjustly tainted academic art classes with an atmosphere of sexual immorality.

Eakins juxtaposed the bloody hand next to the only female figure in the painting. In contrast to the man of reason and his skillful handling of a scalpel, the woman, probably the patient's mother, displays ineffectual, contorted hands that screen her eyes from the operation. While the male student body intently observes the operation and a male secretary coolly records Gross's lecture, the woman sits below in an apparent fit of hysteria, unable to control her body and emotions. So complete is the woman's painful identification with the patient that she, too, seems in need of the doctor's care.

The painting's stereotypical division between

6.33 Thomas Eakins
William Rush Carving his Allegorical Figure of the Schuylkill River, 1876–7. Oil on canvas on masonite, 20⅛ x 26⅛ in (51.4 x 67.1 cm). Philadelphia Museum of Art. Gift of Mrs. Thomas Eakins and Miss Mary Adeline Williams.

Toward the end of his career, Eakins returned to the subject of William Rush and the use of a nude model for carving his famous personification of the Schuylkill River. However, in an austere, simplified painting entitled *William Rush and His Model* (1908), Eakins essentially represented himself as Rush gallantly assisting the nude model as she steps down from her wooden posing stand.

The controversy over *The Gross Clinic* had scarcely passed when Eakins completed another contentious picture, *William Rush Carving His Allegorical Figure of the Schuylkill River* (fig. 6.33), which forcefully addressed the issue of nude female models. The painting pays homage to William Rush (see pp. 171-3), an original founder of the Pennsylvania Academy and a sculptor of idealized wooden figures. However, the primary subject is not Rush, but the fleshy, strongly illuminated nude model who stands on a tree-stump platform in the foreground. In a written statement, Eakins identified Rush's model as Louisa Vanuxem, daughter of James Vanuxem, a prominent merchant who had served on a city committee responsible for providing Philadelphians with pure drinking water.

In the shadowy background, Rush, who also served on the water committee, hammers away with mallet and chisel to sculpt his most famous work, *Water Nymph and Bittern* (1809), a female personification of the Schuylkill River intended for a fountain outside the city's new water-pumping station (see fig. 4.47). Contradicting any suggestion of sexual immorality, Eakins represents

Rush as the epitome of civic pride, artistic professionalism, and moral respectability. Though working in a studio littered with wood chips and sawdust, Rush wears his Sunday-best clothing. He does not leer at the model, but looks down in absorption at the task of perfecting the wooden sculpture. Meanwhile, seated in the right foreground, an older woman serves as a chaperone for the model. This matronly woman apparently has little cause for moral anxiety as she looks down at her knitting rather than keeping a watchful eye on the propriety of Rush's behavior. The only figure who gazes at the nude model is Rush's lifelike sculpture of George Washington standing amid the shadows in the right background. Eakins's witty inclusion of this figure suggests that the "Father" of the nation was also expressing his approval of this particular artistic practice.

There is no historical evidence that Louisa Vanuxem posed nude in 1809 or that William Rush ever worked from a nude model. In fact, it was not until the 1850s that life-drawing classes with nude models became the norm at both the National Academy of Design and the Pennsylvania Academy. As the art historian

Elizabeth Johns has argued, Eakins's deliberate historical fiction was inspired by his own belief that respectable women from good Philadelphia families had little to fear in posing for professional artists and aspiring art students. Eakins represents the artist's studio as a cluttered workplace ill-suited for sexual liaisons. The model herself is working hard as she rests a heavy book on her right shoulder and holds the desired pose for long and boring periods of time. Nevertheless, Eakins titillated the sexual imagination of beholders by draping the model's discarded clothing over a chair in the immediate foreground. These richly painted objects are so brightly highlighted and are pushed so close to the picture plane that they seem to invite viewers to reach into the fictive space. The fine lace

6.34 Frederick MacMonnies
Bacchante and Infant Faun, 1893. Bronze, 83 in (210.8 cm) high. Metropolitan Museum of Art. Gift of Charles F. McKim, 1897.

and ruffled articles of clothing identify the model's elevated social status. They also evoke the image of the model's act of disrobing before the male artist. Rather than representing an ideal nude figure who seems to exist outside of any specific time and place, Eakins represents a nineteenth-century woman who has just removed her clothing and displays her less-than-perfect naked body as a symbol of sincerity and truth to nature.

Eakins rejected middle-class American prudery, strongly arguing that no shame or embarrassment should be felt in admiring the physical sensuality of the nude form. Eakins shared many of the views of the National Liberal League, founded in Philadelphia in 1876 to oppose a growing right-wing movement against free speech, women's equality, and sexual freedom. After the Civil War, organizations like the New England Society for the Suppression of Vice and the Young Men's Christian Association (YMCA) supported moral purity campaigns for the eradication of "obscene" books, pictures, and contraceptive devices. In Boston, the Women's Christian Temperance Union, Citizens' Law and Order League, and Anti-Saloon League, aided by Harvard educators, successfully campaigned in 1896–7 to banish the American sculptor Frederick MacMonnies' *Bacchante and Infant Faun* (fig. 6.34) from the courtyard of the Boston Public Library. For temperance advocates, the female figure's unabashed nudity was less problematic then her high, exuberant grasp of a bunch of grapes, identifying her as a devotee of Bacchus, the Roman god of wine. Meanwhile, in Philadelphia during the Centennial celebration, moral reformers attacked lewd entertainments such as can-can dancing in variety halls. Later, during the 1880s, a Philadelphia clergyman, the Reverend J. Gray Bolton, founded a group known as the Moral Committee of One Hundred, while another leading moralist, Josiah W. Leeds, questioned the moral wisdom of representing nudes in art. In 1886, Eakins resigned from his teaching post at the Pennsylvania Academy, apparently because members of the board of directors had criticized his use of nude male models in a class that mixed both male and female students.

In fact, Eakins had become preoccupied with study of the nude figure, and he took up photography as a useful technology for examining the human body in motion. His famous painting *The Swimming Hole* (fig. 6.36) was composed from photographic studies of the artist and his male students (fig. 6.35). In 1882 or 1883, they had made an outing together to Dove Lake on Mill Creek, immediately outside Philadelphia. The group was chaperoned by an older man, who remained fully clothed, while Eakins and his students swam and posed for the camera. In the photograph, Eakins can be seen at the right climbing out of the water and onto the rocky ledge. In the painting, he is further isolated from the group as he swims toward the others from the lower-right corner of the picture. As is evident from both the photographs and the painting, the outing became a self-conscious attempt to re-create the ancient Greek ideal of male beauty and camaraderie. As much as the painting, the photograph appears artfully composed. The young men display their bodies as if they were modern re-creations of classical sculptures. As the United States became increasingly urbanized and industrialized, Eakins and other American artists produced works that expressed a yearning for simpler, less complicated modes of living, closer to the regenerative energies of nature. In the painting, Eakins set the figures further back into space, more clearly integrating them with the lush, surrounding landscape. Furthermore, he arranged the composition to suggest an energetic circle of figures moving into and out of the cool, revivifying water.

Originally titled *Swimming* or *The Swimmers*, this open-air portrait of Eakins's studio was commissioned by Edward Coates, chair of the instruction committee at the Pennsylvania Academy. However, Coates finally rejected the work, probably fearing that its homoerotic celebration of the male figure would raise unwanted questions regarding the employment of students as nude models. Coates instead purchased a safer Eakins painting, *The Pathetic Song* (1881), one of a series of portraits featuring musicians and musical performances. The series culminated in *The Concert Singer* (fig. 6.37), a performance portrait of Weda Cook, a singer of oratorios and sacred songs, who appeared frequently on the concert stage, as represented here, and as a choir soloist in churches. Here, too, Eakins represents a figure in a momentary, transient state. Head slightly tilted, the open-mouthed Cook sings under the direction of her teacher, whose presence is suggested only by a baton-holding hand emerging from below stage. At the left edge of the painting, the sharp pointed fronds of a potted palm extend themselves toward Cook, as if they are resonating in harmony with Cook's contralto voice. Meanwhile, a bouquet of flowers thrown onto the stage, matching the pink color of her dress, further suggests the enthusiastic approval of an otherwise unseen audience. Eakins thus created a speaking, singing picture. He even invited beholders to aurally/orally participate in Cook's specific performance by carving into the picture's frame the opening words from her rendition of "O Rest in the Lord," a spiritually reassuring aria from the popular biblical oratorio *Elijah* by the German Romantic composer Felix Mendelssohn. Like Washington Allston's Old Testament history paintings (see figs. 4.56-4.57) and William Wetmore Story's *Jerusalem* (see fig. 6.32), Eakins's portrait drew upon Americans' nationalistic identification with the ancient Hebrews, God's chosen people.

Eakins's interest in recording physically active bodies was further stimulated by the English-born photographer Eadweard Muybridge (1830–1904), who, while living in California, had become a pioneer in the development of motion photography. By using banks of cameras closely placed together, Muybridge was able to make a rapid succession of photographs that captured the split-second movements of animals and humans as they moved through space (fig. 6.38). After meeting Muybridge in 1884 at the University of Pennsylvania and assisting him in his photographic experiments, Eakins began to shoot his own motion photographs. But instead of following Muybridge's technique, he adopted the methods of the Frenchman Étienne-Jules Marey (1830–1904), who was able to record motion on a single photographic negative. By spinning a disc before an open camera lens, admitting light through a single point, Eakins could make quick, successive exposures, thereby recording on one plate the transit of the body as it ran, walked, or jumped (fig. 6.39).

Eakins taught many younger artists to focus on the human body as a site of truth. One of his

Art and Commerce in the Gilded Age

6.35 Circle of Eakins
Thomas Eakins and Students Swimming Nude, c. 1883.
Platinum print,
8$\frac{15}{16}$ x 11$\frac{1}{16}$ in
(22.6 x 28.1 cm).
Pennsylvania Academy of the Fine Arts. Charles Bregler's Thomas Eakins Collection.

students, Thomas Pollock Anshutz (1851–1912), painted a rare industrial subject, *The Ironworkers' Noontime* (fig. 6.40), which represents a group of working-class men washing up, relaxing, and posing outside an iron factory during the heat of the day. Anshutz came from a family that had owned and operated iron mills earlier in the century, and he had grown up in Wheeling, West Virginia, where iron mills lined the banks of the Ohio River. As an adult, Anshutz frequently visited relatives in Wheeling, and, in 1880, he began to sketch its workers and iron factories. Most artists avoided such subjects because American factory laborers were commonly represented in the popular media as animalistic or primitive beings. Unlike the romanticized artisans of the pre-industrial past, modern wage-laborers were viewed as human cogs within the vast and ingenious machinery of factory production. The fact that many workers were foreign immigrants,

African-Americans, and union members (and some were political radicals), made them even less desirable as subjects for high art. Certainly, few capitalists or businessmen wished to be reminded of their exploited workers while relaxing in their homes and private clubs.

Understandably enough, Thomas Anshutz had difficulty selling *The Ironworkers' Noontime*. Though the painting is not explicitly political and does not necessarily foreshadow the artist's later conversion to socialism, the picture represents strong and independent-looking workers. Temporarily freed from the factory machinery, they are not a unified group, but are relaxing as individuals—many standing, walking, or sitting alone, some lost in thought. While the figure closest to the picture plane self-consciously poses for the artist, others seem to express a certain class antagonism or distrust toward the affluent producers and consumers of fine arts as they suspiciously stare outward, looking directly at us, the viewers/outsiders. Unlike Eakins's later *The Swimming Hole*, Anshutz's unsentimental painting lacks any romantic nostalgia for an ideal world of pastoral harmony. The younger artist's hot and dusty realism may not be overtly political, but for many contemporaries it must have appeared unusually frank and confrontational. On the other hand, much to Anshutz's embarrassment, his composition was copied or pirated by corporate America soon after the painting's exhibition. Inspired by the picture's group of figures who wash and clean themselves at a water pump, the Procter & Gamble Company transformed the image into an advertisement for Ivory Soap (fig. 6.41). With the growth of American advertising and the simultaneous expansion of the art market, this type of commercial appropriation became increasingly commonplace and also eventually

worked in reverse, as artists began to borrow images from advertisers.

The masculine visions of Homer, Eakins, and Anshutz implicitly expressed the notion, argued by many artists and art critics, that the art profession should be the preserve of men. Though he taught many young women at the Pennsylvania Academy, Eakins wrote to a friend in 1886 that he did not believe a woman could ever produce art works that were truly great. According to the art historian Randall C. Griffin, Anshutz's *The Ironworkers' Noontime* and Eakins's many paintings of athletic young men masked contemporary anxieties that modern culture was becoming feminized and even emasculated, not only by the proliferation of ladies' magazines and the genteel decorative arts, but also by the increased demand for mental rather than physical labor among the middle and upper classes. Cultural critics informed men who worked in business offices or

6.36 Thomas Eakins
The Swimming Hole,
c. 1885.
Oil on canvas,
27⅜ x 36⅜ in
(69.6 x 92.5 cm).
Amon Carter Museum,
Fort Worth, Texas.

Ironically, despite the picture's nostalgic aura, Eakins and his students are enjoying the pleasures of a man-made lake or resevoir, which also satisfied the industrial needs of a nearby copper rolling mill. The stone pier represents the remains of an earlier mill building. Eakins's painting suggests the possible harmony between industry and nature.

6.37 Thomas Eakins
The Concert Singer,
1890–2.
Oil on canvas,
75⅛ x 54¼ in
(191 x 137.79 cm).
Philadelphia Museum of
Art, Pennsylvania.

6.38 (below)
Eadweard Muybridge
Twisting Summersault,
from *The Attitudes of
Animals in Motion*,
1881, plate 106.
Albumen print. Addison
Gallery of American Art,
Phillips Academy,
Andover, Massachusetts.
Partial gift of the Beinecke
Foundation, Inc.

Muybridge had gained fame
during the 1870s, when his
photographic technique
captured a racehorse in
motion. The sequential
photographs demonstrated
the inaccuracy of painters'
traditional flying
"hobbyhorse" convention for
depicting a speeding horse,
whereby the horse's front
legs were extended entirely
forward off the ground and
the hind legs entirely
backward off the ground.
Muybridge advanced the
reputation of photography
as a scientific instrument.

6.39 Thomas Eakins
Motion Study: George Reynolds nude, pole-vaulting, 1885.
Dry-plate negative,
3⅞ x 4⅝ in
(9.6 x 12.4 cm).
Pennsylvania Academy
of the Fine Arts.
Charles Bregler's
Thomas Eakins Collection.

had intellectual careers that they were especially in danger of losing their manly will. Remedies for this dissipation of male energy included strenuous recreational activities and the development of organized sports. Furthermore, membership in private men's clubs and ritualistic fraternal orders such as Freemasonry mushroomed during the post-Civil War era. For many years, Daniel Burnham's twenty-two-story Masonic Temple in Chicago was the tallest building in the world (fig. 6.42). Not to be outdone, the Odd Fellows, an organizational spin-off from Freemasonry, commissioned Louis Sullivan to design an even higher, thirty-six-story Fraternity Temple Building, although the project never left the planning stage.

6.40 Thomas Pollock Anshutz
The Ironworkers' Noontime, 1880.
Oil on canvas, 17 x 23⅞ in (43.2 x 60.7 cm). Fine Arts Museums of San Francisco, San Francisco, California. Gift of Mr. and Mrs. John D. Rockefeller 3rd.

The dark factory building behind the workers and the overlapping lines of wheel ruts beginning in the foreground create a strong diagonal movement. The shadowed factory and the gritty, gray ground dust contrast with the freshly washed white flesh of the workers. Polluting smoke belches from chimneys. Ironically, this painting was purchased by descendants of oil baron John D. Rockefeller, the personification of Gilded Age capitalism's anti-labor practices.

6.41 (above)
Procter & Gamble
c. 1883.
Lithograph on paper,
8 ft 4 in x 13 ft 4 in
(2.5 x 4 m).

The Procter & Gamble
advertisement represents
Anshutz's workers washing
themselves, while supplying
them with washcloths, clean
towels, and large tubs of
water. Even the background
factory appears neater and
cleaner than in Anshutz's
original work.

6.42 (below)
Daniel H. Burnham
Masonic Temple,
Chicago, 1890–92.
Chicago Historical Society,
Chicago, Illinois.

Together with his partner
John Wellborn Root,
Burnham created one of
Chicago's most
distinguished skyscrapers.
Located downtown at the
corner of State and
Randolph streets, this grand
steel-frame structure, faced
with brick and terra-cotta,
was demolished in 1939.
Between its sturdy, arcaded
base and its lofty, steeply
gabled roof, the building's
main shaft featured narrow
continuous piers that
accentuated the skyscraper's
vertical character.

War Memorials and the Heroic White Male

While photographers had undercut the traditional masculine heroism of history painting, American sculptors answered the post-Civil War demand for public memorials of military officers, soldiers, and statesmen. The 1876 Centennial celebration also inspired commissions that nostalgically glorified America's colonial settlers and revolutionary Founding Fathers. In 1872, in anticipation of the nation's one-hundredth birthday, the town of Concord, Massachusetts, commissioned a young local sculptor, Daniel Chester French (1850–1931), to create a Revolutionary War sculpture commemorating the April 19, 1775, battle of Concord, one of the war's opening skirmishes. Working in his Boston studio, French designed plaster and clay models for the *Minute Man*, a seven-foot statue that was then cast into bronze at a nearby foundry (fig. 6.43). French's anonymous noble figure represents an eighteenth-century farmer, who, at a moment's notice, voluntarily joins his fellow citizens to form a militia against the British in defense of political freedom. Though the sculptor clothed the figure in realistic, revolutionary-period costume, its striding pose led contemporaries to recognize the young artist's debt to ancient Greece and the ever-popular *Apollo Belvedere* (see fig. 4.35). Furthermore, as in Homer's painting *The Veteran in a New Field* (see fig. 6.24), French's inclusion of a plow next to the militiaman evoked associations with the ancient Roman general Cincinnatus and his American counterpart, George Washington (see fig. 4.41). Significantly, in casting the bronze sculpture, the Ames Foundry in Chicopee, Massachusetts, melted down discarded Civil War cannons donated by the United States government. Thus, the *Minute Man* symbolically celebrated the end of the Civil War and the return of American unity, while idealizing the masculine strength and valor of the nation's founders.

Shortly after the nation's Centennial, a committee of eminent New York City businessmen and state leaders commissioned another young sculptor, Augustus Saint-Gaudens (1848–1907), to create a memorial for Admiral David Glasgow Farragut, a naval hero during the Civil War (fig. 6.44). The bronze statue, over eight feet high, stands in New York's Madison Square Park on a Hudson River bluestone pedestal designed by Saint-Gaudens's collaborator, the architect Stanford White. Favoring bronze over white marble for its greater malleability and potential for realistic detail, Saint-Gaudens endowed Farragut with a naturalistic aura of masculine vigor and resolute will as he seems to stand on the deck of his ship, his coat flapping open in the ocean breeze. By contrast, Saint-Gaudens created two rather bloodless female personifications of Loyalty and Courage, carved in low relief, for the semicircular sandstone base. These idealized yet relatively listless, funereal women blend with nature and the stylized waves of the sea. The placid, horizontal arrangement of their elongated arms and legs provides a counterpoint to the vertical Farragut, who stands straight as an arrow, ready for action. In memorializing the admiral, Saint-Gaudens implicitly reinforced the stereotypical notion that women could not be active creators or conquerors of nature because they themselves were immersed like mermaids within nature's watery ebb and flow.

However, for Saint-Gaudens, who shared the elitist views of his wealthy patrons, not all men were created equal. In 1884, the sculptor received a commission for another Civil War memorial, this one from a group of Boston citizens who wished to honor Captain Robert G. Shaw (1837–63). The only son of a genteel Boston family, Shaw had commanded the Massachusetts 54th Regiment, composed

6.43 Daniel Chester French
Minute Man, 1873–5, Concord, Massachusetts. Bronze and stone, height 84 in (213.3 cm).

6.44 Augustus Saint-Gaudens
The Admiral David Farragut Memorial, New York City, 1881 (base designed by Stanford White).
Bronze and stone.
Collection of the City of New York, Madison Square, Manhattan, New York.

Below the figure of Farragut, Saint-Gaudens sculpted the admiral's long sword in low relief on the central pedestal block. The sword's strong vertical line, symbolizing masculine strength, continues that of the bronze scabbard hanging from the naval hero's waist. Later, Saint-Gaudens created for New York's Central Park the more grandiose Civil War memorial (1892–1903) dedicated to General William Tecumseh Sherman.

primarily of African-American volunteers. Shaw and most members of the regiment were killed during a suicidal attack on the Confederate Army at Fort Wagner, South Carolina, on July 16, 1863.

Taking almost fourteen years to complete the monumental bronze sculpture, Saint-Gaudens again contrasted male and female figures (fig. 6.45). Set within a stone framework designed by the architect Charles Follen McKim, an ethereal female figure sculpted in low relief floats over the parade of men. Like an angel of death, she holds poppies and an olive branch, traditional symbols of eternal sleep and peace or victory, respectively. By contrast, the naturalistically rendered regiment of men below stands out in high relief. While most scholars have praised Saint-Gaudens for his sympathetic portrayal of African-American foot soldiers, the art historian Albert Boime argues that the Shaw Memorial implicitly expressed a racist dichoto-

my between white and black. Saint-Gaudens's sculpture reinforced the conventional military wisdom that no African-American could be relied on to command an all-black regiment. While Shaw, the noble white officer, sits erect astride a powerful horse, his black troops appear more tired and bedraggled than heroic. Far from being energized by the prospect of fighting for their own freedom, they appear weighed down by the heavy burden of warfare.

One can certainly attribute the black soldiers' appearance to the influence of non-heroic photographic journalism and Saint-Gaudens's desire for objective truth. However, the sculptor clearly represented Shaw upon a higher, ideal plane, as the equestrian figure was designed to evoke associations with ancient Roman and Italian Renaissance prototypes. The image of African-American men carrying rifles in heroic fashion would have been too disturbing and threatening for a white audience. Saint-Gaudens employed

6.45 Augustus Saint-Gaudens
The Robert Gould Shaw Memorial, Boston, Massachusetts, 1884–97. Massachusetts Historical Society, Boston, Massachusetts.

Saint-Gaudens's Civil War memorial directly faces Charles Bulfinch's Massachusetts State House on Boston's Beacon Hill (see fig. 4.14). At the far right, the sculpture's bronze surface bears the Latin inscription *Omnia Relinquit Servare Republicam* ("He forsook all to preserve the public weal"). These words are the motto of the Society of the Cincinnati, to which Shaw belonged as the descendant of a Revolutionary War officer. The Shaw Memorial thus establishes a link with the nation's Founding Fathers.

African-American models to create individualized black soldiers, but none stands out from the group and a number are obscured by Shaw's monumental horse. Indeed, the legs of the troops blend with those of the horse, the symbol of Shaw's strict control over animal nature. Saint-Gaudens's correspondence amply demonstrates his belief that African-Americans, or "darkeys" as he repeatedly called them, were inherently slavish beings in need of strong discipline. In his *American Masters of Sculpture* (1913), critic Charles Caffin applauded the sculpture's racial distinctions:

> He [Saint-Gaudens] portrays the humble soldiers with varying characteristics of pathetic devotion, and from the halting uniformity of their movement, even from the uncouthness of their ill-fitting uniforms, from such details as the water-bottles and rifles, secures an impressiveness of decorative composition, distinguished by virile contrasts and repetitions of line and by vigorous handsomeness of light and shade. Mingled with our enjoyment of these qualities is the emotion aroused by the intent and steadfast onward movement of the troops, whose doglike trustfulness is contrasted with the serene elevation of their white leader (cited in Boime, p. 209).

By 1898, when Saint-Gaudens had completed the Shaw Memorial, the United States Supreme Court had ruled in the case of *Plessy v. Ferguson* (1896) that "if one race be inferior to the other socially, the Constitution of the United States cannot put them upon the same plane" (cited in Boime, p. 39). The decision officially authorized the segregationist doctrine of "separate but equal accommodations" for whites and blacks. However, equality could hardly have been the court's goal given the justices' presumption of black inferiority. The landmark ruling essentially nullified the political and civil rights that African-Americans had gained during Reconstruction.

Henry Ossawa Tanner and the Expression of African-American Creativity

Many white Americans borrowed from Charles Darwin's evolutionary theory that only the fittest species survive to insist that the inherently inferior black race was destined, like the American Indian, for ultimate extinction. Contrary to Edmonia Lewis's affirmation of African-American creativity and dignity (see fig 6.22.), influential white American artists and critics continued to argue well into the twentieth century that women and blacks were incapable of producing significant art. Just before his death, the printmaker Joseph Pennell (1857–1926) wrote a memoir that implicitly scorned the painting career of the black artist Henry Ossawa Tanner (1859–1937), who had been Pennell's fellow student at the Pennsylvania Academy during the early 1880s. Though Thomas Eakins welcomed Tanner into his drawing class and later painted a sympathetic portrait of his former student, he apparently was unaware that Pennell and other students were victimizing Tanner with an intense campaign of racial harassment. In his account entitled "The Advent of the Nigger," Pennell recalled that "One night his [Tanner's] easel was carried out in the middle of Broad Street and, though not painfully crucified, he was firmly tied to it and left there" (cited in Bearden and Henderson, p. 82). While not identifying Tanner by name, Pennell concluded with the assertion that "There has never been a great Negro or a great Jew artist" (cited in Bearden and Henderson, p. 82).

Despite these hateful remarks, Tanner achieved artistic fame by leaving the racially hostile environment of Post-Reconstruction America for the more tolerant atmosphere of Paris. The son of a bishop in the African Methodist Episcopal Church, Tanner ultimately specialized in painting biblical subjects bathed in atmospheric tones of color (fig. 6.46). Earlier, however, he painted scenes of African-American life. One of his best-known works, *The Banjo Lesson* (fig. 6.47), seems to represent a conventional subject in its portrayal of an old African-American man teaching a barefoot boy, probably his grandson, how to play a musical instrument. However, Tanner's picture, with its theme of education, contradicted the racial stereotype that blacks were inherently musical. Tanner celebrates the image of African-American self-cultivation and creative development as transmitted from one generation to the next. Like Eakins, he worked from a photograph in composing the picture and he gave his figures

6.46 Henry Ossawa Tanner
Christ Appearing to Nicodemus, 1899.
Oil on canvas,
33¹¹⁄₁₆ x 39½ in
(86.1 x 100.3 cm).
Pennsylvania Academy of the Fine Arts, Philadelphia, Pennsylvania.
Joseph E. Temple Fund.

This picture was painted in Jerusalem during Tanner's second visit to the Middle East. The painting represents Jesus in his teaching role, as described in the Gospel of John (3:1–21). The mysterious, nocturnal ambience of the rooftop encounter between Nicodemus the aging Pharisee and a visionary-appearing Christ was based upon a series of sketches that also provided a topographical sense of place. Through such pictures, Tanner gained fame as the "poet-painter of Palestine" (cited in Edwards, p.146).

a sculptural solidity and weight reminiscent of his former teacher's painterly realism. However, *The Banjo Lesson* possesses a blurring atmospheric haze that suggests a more spiritualized strand of American painting.

Cosmopolitanism and the Lure of French Art

Before the Civil War, Rome had been the most popular destination on the European continent for Americans studying the arts. Rome, the "eternal city," was like an art-historical museum of ruins and artifacts from antiquity through the Renaissance. After the war, however, cosmopolitan American artists who wished to break with tradition flocked to Paris, where they found a number of artists representing modern subjects in fresh, innovative ways. Unlike Homer and Eakins, who studied in Paris for relatively brief periods of time, other Americans became long-term residents in this foreign capital of contemporary art. The French sculptor Frédéric-Auguste Bartholdi's (1834–1904) monumental *Statue of Liberty* (fig. 6.48) was erected in New York harbor in 1886 as a symbol of the close historic and economic ties between France and the United States. Richard Morris Hunt, who had trained at the École des Beaux-Arts prior to the Civil War, designed the neoclassical pedestal for this gift from the French republic. It has been estimated that over 1,800 American artists studied in Paris during the later nineteenth century. As the novelist Henry James observed in the 1880s, "When we look for 'American art' we find it mainly in Paris. When we find it out of Paris, we at least find a great deal of Paris in it" (cited in Pollock, p. 76).

The daughter of an investment broker and merchant from Allegheny City, Pennsylvania, Mary Cassatt (1844–1926) first studied painting at the Pennsylvania Academy from 1861 to 1865 before traveling extensively in Europe and then settling in Paris by the 1870s. Unable to study at the École des Beaux-Arts because of her sex, Cassatt drifted away from traditional academic styles and joined the circle of French Impressionists, who were the leading avant-garde painters in Paris. Originally a military term for an advanced guard that precedes the

6.47 Henry Ossawa Tanner
The Banjo Lesson, 1893. Oil on canvas, 49 x 35½ in (124.4 x 90.2 cm). Hampton University Museum, Hampton, Virginia.

Tanner shared Thomas Eakins's admiration for the painterly, golden tonalities of Rembrandt van Rijn's compositions. However, the evocative blue and blue-green colors of Tanner's painting differ from both Eakins's and Rembrandt's palettes and suggest the influence of French Post-Impressionist art.

main force of troops, during the nineteenth century the "avant-garde" in art came to refer to modern, forward-looking artists who broke with past, conventional styles and challenged the perceptual habits of the public with innovative means of expression. The Impressionists, led by Monet, Renoir, and Edgar Degas (1834–1917), had generally stopped sending works to the Paris Salon, the annual state-supported exhibition juried by conservative French academic artists. Instead, in 1874, they began exhibiting independently as a group, startling the public with their sketchily painted, spontaneous impressions of modern Paris and its surrounding suburbs.

Invited by Degas, Cassatt joined the Impressionists in 1877 and exhibited with them

6.48 Frédéric-Auguste Bartholdi
Statue of Liberty, New York City, 1886. Library of Congress, Washington, D.C.

6.49 Mary Cassatt
At the Opera (In the Loge), 1879. Oil on canvas, 32 x 26 in (81.3 x 66 cm). Museum of Fine Arts, Boston, Massachusetts. The Hayden Collection.

This picture began a series of theater paintings by Cassatt that focused on young women variously situated alone or in pairs in balcony spaces. Appropriating the Impressionist techniques of Edgar Degas, Cassatt experimented with different angles of vision and the cropping of images to draw viewers' attention dynamically away from the compositional center toward the periphery and the spaces beyond the picture frame. Cassatt thus expressed the Impressionist tendency to merge art with modern life.

from 1879 to 1886, when the group broke up. As a single woman, Cassatt was unable to frequent many of the café and entertainment sites that her male counterparts depicted in their paintings. Cassatt's *At the Opera* (fig. 6.49) represents a strong feminist point of view, as it depicts a lone woman attending a theatrical event. The young woman is turned away from us, while our gaze is mirrored in the background by a sketchily painted man with opera glasses, who also intently directs his attention toward the attractive foreground figure. Cassatt's woman is not a beautiful seductress or passive object of voyeuristic pleasure. She has her own independence as she, too, actively looks beyond the picture frame with a small pair of opera glasses. Emulating other Impressionists, Cassatt composed the picture as a kind of photographic snapshot, or slice of life, but she employed the Impressionist emphasis on the act of seeing to assert the principle of sexual

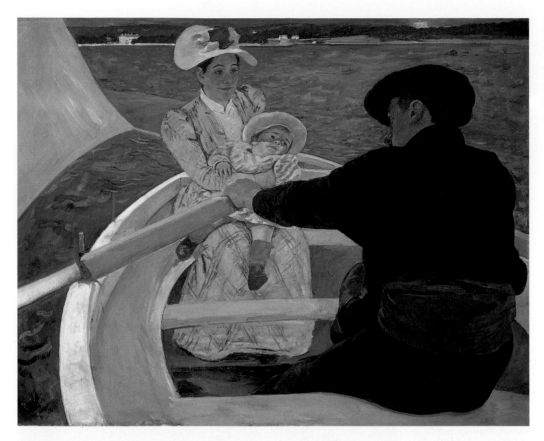

6.50 Mary Cassatt
The Boating Party,
1893–4.
Oil on canvas,
35⁷⁄₁₆ x 46⅛ in
(90.9 x 117.3 cm).
National Gallery of Art,
Washington D.C.
Chester Dale Collection.

equality with men. The painter primarily produced images of mothers and their children but, in general, without the cloying sentimentality normally associated with the theme of motherhood. For instance, in *The Boating Party* (fig. 6.50), Cassatt transformed what appears to be a holiday outing into an ambiguous, somewhat unnerving, exchange of gazes between an unidentified oarsman and a woman and infant child. Only the baby's innocent presence seems to neutralize or defuse a sexually charged arrangement of directional forces, as the man's probing eyes are reinforced by his extended arm and oar, held by a clenched fist directly in front of the laps of both opposing figures.

Significantly, Cassatt's portrait of her own mother represents the visiting parent as she reads a Paris newspaper (fig. 6.51). Traditionally in American and European art, reading women were absorbed in novels or romances, works of fiction rather than newspapers. As we saw with Eastman Johnson's portrait of *The Brown Family* (see fig. 6.25) and Richard Caton Woodville's *War News from Mexico* (see fig. 5.28), newspapers were conventionally read by men, since the news was dominated by the masculine realm of politics and business. Once again, the older woman is absorbed by her own intellectual activity and ignores our obtrusive gaze. A mirror next to the mother might have allowed us to see the news story that she is reading, but Cassatt's liquid brushstrokes render illegible such niggling narrative details, thereby preserving her mother's privacy.

John Singer Sargent (1856–1925), another American in Paris, also created pictures that explored the psychic, social tensions of gazing, gazed-upon figures. Born in Florence, Italy, to wealthy parents, Sargent was educated abroad and spent most of his career traveling and living in Europe, especially in Paris and London. Sargent's group portrait, *The Daughters of Edward Boit* (fig. 6.52) was painted for Edward Darley Boit, a fellow-expatriate American artist. Inspired by the work of the seventeenth-century Spanish artist Diego Velázquez (1599–1660), Sargent activated the space of the beholder and suggested the invisible presence of Edward Boit himself.

6.51 Mary Cassatt
Reading "Le Figaro,"
1877–8.
Oil on canvas,
39¾ x 32 in
(101 x 81.2 cm).
Private Collection,
Washington, D.C.

Mirrors traditionally served
as metaphors for painted
pictures. But in obscuring or
minimizing the mirror's
reflective power or
precision, Cassatt suggests
that her painting is not an
objective reflection or mere
imitation of external
reality. Impressionist
brushwork stressed the
creative, subjective nature
of artistic vision.

**6.52 John Singer
Sargent**
*The Daughters of
Edward Darley Boit,*
1882–3.
Oil on canvas,
7 ft 3 in x 7 ft 3 in
(2.21 x 2.21 m).
Museum of Fine Arts,
Boston, Massachusetts.
Gift of Mary Louisa Boit,
Julia Overing Boit, and
Florence D. Boit in
memory of their father,
Edward Darley Boit.

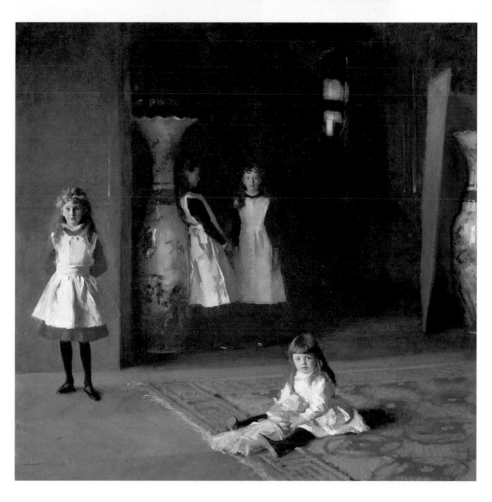

Beginning with the youngest girl, who plays with a doll on a plush carpet, three of the four daughters stare outward toward us. Their attentive, obedient poses suggest that they are returning the monitoring gaze of their father, who stands opposite them in our space. The very title of the painting suggests the possessive power of the father. The daughters are identified by his name, while their subordinate status as children is underscored by the size of the enormous oriental vase at the left, which dwarfs even the two older daughters standing at a distance in a second darkened room.

Yet Sargent adumbrates an incipient rebellion in the poses of these two young women. The eldest daughter has defiantly turned away from our/the father's surveillance, as she leans her back against the giant womb-like vase. Meanwhile, her younger sister stands with a mouth slightly opened, as if she is about to speak or find her own, independent voice. The notion of an adolescent, sexual awakening is further broached by the bright-red, phallic-shaped edge of a screen, coupled on the painting's right edge with a second oriental vessel, a symbol of womanhood. In turning away from her father, the eldest daughter gazes toward the razor-sharp screen enclosing the gently curvilinear, blue-and-white porcelain. In the process, she moves psychically away from her childhood home, from daughter to future wife and marriage, traditionally another domestic, box-like space of female dependence and subordination.

As David Lubin has observed, the eldest daughter's rebellious aversion of her face became the basis for another Sargent painting, the scandalous *Madame X* (fig. 6.53), representing Virginie Gautreau, the artist's cousin and American-born wife of a wealthy French businessman. Influenced by Édouard Manet's sexually charged pictures of the female nude, Sargent collaborated with Virginie Gautreau to create a frank and icily sexual image of a "professional beauty". Contemporary critics employed the term to refer to women who used their beauty, personal manners, and skills to advance themselves into elite social circles. Unlike the young woman in Cassatt's *At the Opera*, Gautreau is fully aware of our presence and presents herself as a beautifully composed body or visual object. Her provocative, deeply cut gown reveals unblemished, porcelain-white flesh

6.53 John Singer Sargent
Madame X, 1883–4. Oil on canvas, 82¼ x 43¼ in (208.6 x 109.9 cm). The Metropolitan Museum of Art, New York. Arthur Hoppock Hearn Fund, 1916.

and a fashion-plate figure with swelling breasts and slim waist. Sargent originally painted Gautreau with a shoulder strap slipped down along her arm, but he later reworked the picture and returned the strap to its proper position. In her classical-Greek-style hair, Gautreau wears a diamond crescent, symbol of the moon goddess Diana, patroness of the hunt. Like a modern-day goddess, the celebrated beauty proudly turns away from the beholder. Her sharp, linear profile contributes to the impression of a tightly coiled sexual energy that can be admired safely only from a distance. Though the painting was exhibited at the Paris Salon of 1884 with an anonymous title, critics immediately recognized the identity of the sitter and denounced both Sargent and Gautreau for collaborating in a sexually suggestive, immoral painting.

6.54 Albert Bierstadt
The Last of the Buffalo,
1889.
Oil on canvas,
71¼ x 119¼ in
(180.9 x 302.9 cm).
The Corcoran Gallery of
Art, Washington, D.C.

As a sign of changing
aesthetic tastes, the
selection committee for the
American galleries at the
1889 Exposition Universelle
in Paris rejected this work
as unrepresentative of
contemporary trends in
American Art. The painting
fictively attributes the
decimation of American
buffalo herds entirely to
avaricious, warring Indians.
In fact, the United States
government itself
significantly contributed to
the declining buffalo
population by strategically
encouraging their
slaughter so as to deprive
rebellious Native tribes of
their food supply.

Sargent soon escaped the scandal by moving to London in 1886, followed by a brief working visit to America in 1887–8, which established his reputation as the leading, most fashionable portraitist of the American social elite. Controversy over *Madame X* had served to publicize the artist's fame and aesthetic daring. Sargent's success as a portraitist led in 1890 to a major mural commission for Boston's new public library designed by the New York architects Charles Follen McKim and Stanford White (see figs. 6.1, 6.2). For the next three decades, much of Sargent's career was occupied by the task of decorating the large, third-floor vaulted gallery at the top of the library's main staircase. Eager to demonstrate that he was intellectually and artistically capable of Renaissance-style history paintings, Sargent chose to represent the evolutionary progress of Western civilization as manifested in the history of religion. Although his *Triumph of Religion* was never entirely completed, the artist, beginning in 1895, made four major installments of panels representing some sixteen subjects that traced the development of religion from the ancient pagan gods to the advent of Christianity.

The West as Myth

Meanwhile Frederic Church, Albert Bierstadt and other painters continued to produce panoramic landscapes of the fast-disappearing American wilderness and western frontier (fig. 6.54). Indeed, a younger generation of artists, led by Yale-educated Frederic Remington (1861–1909) helped to invent the popular mythology of the western cowboy. In paintings such as *The Flight (A Sage-Brush Pioneer)* (fig. 6.55), Remington's singularly self-confident, fearless cowboy, horse galloping, poses for this snapshot view. He blithely ignores the distant Indian warriors giving him chase to oblige us with this show of bravado. In fact, Remington's pictures appealed to a mass American audience that enjoyed the open-air Wild West Shows of William F. "Buffalo Bill" Cody (1846–1917), a former western scout turned theatrical orchestrator of cowboy and Indian shootouts, stagecoach robberies, and other reenactments. Critical of impoverished immigrants from southern and eastern Europe arriving in the United States, Remington self consciously identified himself as an English American. Implicitly in *The Flight*, the diminutive, ineffectual

6.55 Frederick Remington
The Flight (A Sage-Brush Pioneer), 1895.
Oil on canvas,
23 x 33³⁄₁₆ in
(58.4 x 84.3 cm).
Museum of Fine Arts,
Houston, Texas.
Hogg Brothers Collection.
Gift of Miss Ima Hogg.

Native American horsemen also suggest their inferiority to the independent, Anglo-Saxon cowboy of the West. In addition to his paintings, Remington produced and marketed small-scale bronze sculptures representing energetic cowboys on rearing, leaping steeds (fig. 6.56). Propelled upward and outward into space, their air-borne vitality symbolized American imperial power.

During this period, a growing number of artists and critics dissented from the popular illusionism of Church and Bierstadt, and the entertaining theatricality of Remington and other artists of the West. For instance, Ralph Albert Blakelock (1847–1919), a New York-born painter who traveled West in 1869–72 and lived among different Native American tribes, refused to narrate dramatic action or detailed naturalistic landscapes. Instead, Blakelock's *Moonlight and Indian Encampment* (fig. 6.57) expresses his visionary subordination of narrative subject matter to a painterly, abstract style, emphasizing tonal values, or chiaroscuro, to create introspective moods. In Blakelock's paintings, the quiet presence of Native Americans, whom he clearly admired, merges with a religious, cosmic feeling of spiritual transcendence, symbolized by the pale glowing light of the moon.

6.56 Frederick Remington
The Bronco Buster, 1895
(cast 1906).
Bronze, green over brown patina, lost wax cast,
22⁵⁄₈ x 22³⁄₄ x 15¼ in
(57.6 x 57.7 x 38.7 cm).
Museum of Fine Arts,
Houston, Texas.

While Blakelock was not successful in marketing his own paintings for health and other personal reasons, his tonal style was shared by a number of American landscapists, who were rejecting the Hudson River School's provincial celebration of national tourist sites.

The Society of American Artists: Art as Religion

With the accelerated pace of urbanization and economic modernization threatening to overwhelm American culture in a sea of mass-produced goods and popular entertainments, elite critics sought out artists who expressed higher, more poetic truths than the unimaginative imitation of nature. Post-Civil War painters increasingly turned toward subjects and techniques that expressed spiritual and introspective moods in contrast to the naturalism or photographic details of Hudson River School paintings. In 1878, the newly founded Society of American Artists challenged the National Academy of Design by offering New Yorkers a rival exhibition of contemporary art devoted to the expression of inner feelings. Led by the painter Helena de Kay Gilder (1848–1916), most

artists who joined the Society came from patrician, socially connected New York and Massachusetts families. Many of the artists had just returned from extensive study abroad and had become dissatisfied with what they perceived as the provincial, narrow-minded nature of National Academy exhibitions. In 1874, the academy jury had rejected all of the submissions offered by the painter John La Farge (1835–1910), who was also an art theorist and a lecturer on aesthetics at Harvard University. Born in New York to a French émigré family, La Farge developed an international, cosmopolitan perspective, which led him to an interest in Japanese as well as European art. La Farge was one of the first American artists to intensively study Japanese prints, admiring their flexible distortions of form and illusionistic space as well as their sensuous, expressive use of color. Drawing on his wide knowledge of Western and non-Western art, La Farge concluded that the visual arts, the formal properties of color, line, and perspective, were governed by divinely inspired, universal laws. Rejecting the need for narrative subject matter, La Farge, like his friend Candace Wheeler, painted a number of flower pictures during the 1860s

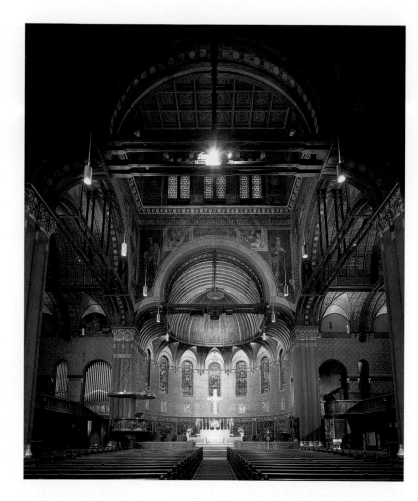

6.58 Henry Hobson Richardson with John La Farge Trinity Church, Boston, c. 1875. Interior view toward the chancel.

John La Farge's aesthetic of color and light was indebted to the Venetian Renaissance as exemplified by the luminous paintings of Titian (c.1485/90–1576). During the nineteenth century, the French Romantic painter Eugène Delacroix (1789-1863), an accomplished muralist, most famously continued this colorful, painterly tradition in Paris, strongly influencing the work of La Farge.

and 1870s which synthesized naturalistic observation with jewel-like colors and stylized compositions influenced by Japanese as well as English and French art.

Though La Farge was a member of the National Academy, his paintings appeared too foreign or unconventional for the Academy jury. Martyred by the Academy, La Farge came to personify the new, more individual and stylistically innovative art advocated by the Society of American Artists. Though he had difficulty in selling his paintings and was often in financial straits, he helped to launch the American Renaissance movement when, in 1876, he received a commission to decorate the interior of Henry Hobson Richardson's Trinity Church in Boston's Copley Square (fig. 6.58). Richardson, who supported the decorative aesthetic principles of the Arts and Crafts movement, chose a monumental Romanesque, rather than a Gothic, style for this episcopal church. Unlike Gothic cathedral architecture, the earlier medieval Romanesque style allowed for greater, uninterrupted wall space that could more easily be decorated with murals and mosaics. Indeed, a rich coloristic effect for the worship space was essential to Richardson's conception of the church. Therefore, he plastered over the granite piers and arches to create continuity between these structural elements and the plastered wall surfaces. The architect provided a clear field for La Farge, who, with a number of assistants, including Augustus Saint-Gaudens, created a golden, jewel-like interior glowing with colorful murals, stained-glass windows, and mosaics of sparkling colored glass.

The decoration of Trinity Church exemplified the American Renaissance collaboration of architects and artists and expressed the late nineteenth-century tendency to view art or aesthetic beauty as a virtual religion, or spiritual end in itself. Throughout his career, La Farge received commissions to decorate Protestant churches with painted murals, stained-glass windows, and other media. Even Congregationalists and Presbyterians, theologically descended from the iconoclastic, Puritan tradition, now sought solace in art. During a scientific age, when Darwinian theories of evolution were undermining the Christian story of creation and the literal truth of biblical history, many American Protestants from the northeastern elite found it more reasonable to interpret the Bible in poetic terms and to view the experience of art as a spiritual substitute for traditional religious doctrines. In arranging Trinity Church's Old and New Testament scenes, La Farge was not guided by any particular theological or doctrinal program. The artist based his decorative scheme on aesthetic principles, or the compositional harmonization of colors and formal patterns. Inspired by an 1890–91 trip to the South Sea Islands, La Farge's *The Entrance to the Tautira River, Tahiti: Fisherman Spearing a Fish* (fig. 6.59) was

painted with strong colors, violating traditional naturalistic hues. Contemporaries compared the artist's polychromatic richness with the luminous effects of stained glass. Despite the lushness of the landscape, the painter suggests flat, empty stillness and action frozen in time by aesthetic, introspective contemplation. The result is very different from Frederic Church's exuberant revel in the material details of the South American landscape (see fig. 5.62).

For La Farge and the genteel members of the Society of American Artists, art functioned as a guide for ascending toward a higher state of civilization and spiritual refinement. Another artist affiliated with the Society was the landscapist George Inness (1825–94), who began his career before the Civil War by emulating the Hudson River School style of Thomas Cole and Asher B. Durand (see chapter 5). However, by the 1860s, Inness was seeking to evoke inward religious feelings inspired by the visionary writings

6.59 John La Farge
The Entrance to the Tautira River, Tahiti: Fisherman Spearing a Fish, c. 1895.
Oil on canvas,
5⅓ x 6 in
(13.6 x 15.2 cm).
National Gallery of Art, Washington D.C. Adolph Caspar Miller Fund.

of Swedenborg. To that end, he adopted a less detailed, more atmospheric, and more tonal style borrowed from a group of mid-nineteenth-century French landscapists known collectively as the Barbizon School. Named after a French village and art colony in the Forest of Fontainebleau near Paris, this group of artists also influenced the art of La Farge and many other American painters.

Inness's painting of *Sunset in the Woods* exemplifies his mature style (fig. 6.60). He blurs details and mutes the light with misty and smoky veils of paint. Inness's dissolution of sharp lines and forms stills movement to create a quiet space for spiritual reverie. Though he appropriated a style of painting derived from French landscapists such as Jean Baptiste Camille Corot (1796–1875) and Théodore Rousseau (1812–67), his continued choice of primarily American subjects, in this case a secluded woods near Hastings,

6.60 George Innes
Sunset in the Woods,
1891.
Oil on canvas, 48 x 70 in (121.9 x 177.8 cm). Corcoran Gallery of Art, Washington D.C. Purchase.

6.61 Albert Pinkham Ryder
The Dead Bird (The Dead Canary), c. late 1870s.
Oil on wood, 4¼ x 9⅞ in (10.7 x 25.1 cm). The Phillips Collection, Washington, D.C.

6.62 Albert Pinkham Ryder
Jonah, c. 1885.
Canvas mounted on
fiberboard, 27¼ x 34⅜ in
(69.2 x 87.3 cm).
National Museum of
American Art,
Smithsonian Institution,
Washington, D.C. Gift of
John Gellatly.

Although painted in an
entirely different style and
historical context, Ryder's
painting thematically recalls
the death and resurrection
imagery of John Singleton
Copley's *Watson and the
Shark* (see fig. 4.28). Ryder
was a great admirer of the
elemental seascapes of
J.M.W. Turner (1775–1851).
The English painter's *Slavers
Throwing Overboard the
Dead and Dying – Typhoon
Coming On* (1840),
exhibited in the United
States and purchased by the
Boston Museum of Fine
Arts, was an inspiration for
Ryder's biblical sea disaster.

Westchester County, New York, enabled friendly critics to couple him with Winslow Homer as a self-reliant painter of national themes and values.

Following in the footsteps of La Farge and Inness, Albert Pinkham Ryder (1847–1917) found a more sympathetic audience for his sketchily painted canvases when he left the National Academy of Design and began exhibiting with the Society of American Artists in 1878. Early in his career, Ryder had abandoned the realistic imitation of nature. Rather than painting detailed, illusionistic deceptions, he chose to paint his private visions and dreams. While admirers often noted the awkwardness of Ryder's drawing technique and the naive, almost childlike simplicity of his forms, they interpreted these oddities as signs of individual sincerity, or the artist's struggle to express his soul.

Ryder's small painting *The Dead Bird* (fig. 6.61) strongly contrasts with the *trompe-l'oeil* still lifes of William Michael Harnett (see fig. 6.30), whose pictures of dead game were hung in saloons and hunting lodges. Far from expressing masculine bravado, Ryder's modest image of a pale-yellow canary represents a poignant meditation on death. Thinly painted on wood panel, the songbird's frail form is surrounded by a ghostly shroud. The artist used the butt-end of

his brush to scratch in lines for the bird's feathers, while building up paint to accentuate its contorted, skeletal legs. As the art historian Elizabeth Broun observes, the canary's half-opened beak underscores the tragic stilling of its voice. Within the harsh Darwinian struggle for survival, Ryder clearly sympathizes with life's vulnerable creatures. Born to a poor, working-class family from New Bedford, Massachusetts, he tended to identify with society's outsiders and eccentrics.

Inspired in part by New Bedford's history as a whaling and fishing community, Ryder painted numerous seascapes that symbolically suggested the individual's perilous voyage through life. But more than Winslow Homer with his relatively realistic paintings of man against the sea (see fig. 6.28-6.29), Ryder tended to subordinate narrative almost entirely to the drama of paint. In his painting of *Jonah* (fig. 6.62), the Old Testament story is overwhelmed by his gestural brushwork and visionary representation of oceanic fury. Tossed overboard by fellow mariners for incurring God's wrath, Jonah is virtually immersed within the sea of swirling paint. He cries out and raises his arms in the air in front of a flimsy boat crowded with barely legible, huddled human figures. From the far right, an enormous whale emerges from the vortex of ocean waves, its open mouth preparing to swallow poor Jonah alive. Meanwhile, overhead, a bearded God floats between two elongated, winglike clouds. Holding a globe in one hand, the Christian Deity gives a sign of blessing with the other. The symmetrical arrangement of the heavenly sphere promises the triumph of order over chaos and Jonah's ultimate Christlike resurrection from entombment in the whale's stomach.

Fiercely independent, Ryder did not adhere to any particular religious doctrine or faith. But, like his mentor La Farge, the younger painter identified art with spirituality. In some reminiscences that he published in New York's *Broadway Magazine* in 1905, Ryder described the discovery of his painting method as if it had been a religious conversionary experience. After futilely attempting to imitate nature's range of colors, he suddenly began to see nature as a framed picture, subordinate to his own art and to his own godlike creative powers:

The old scene presented itself one day before my eyes framed in an opening between two trees. It stood out like a painted canvas—the deep blue of a midday sky—a solitary tree, brilliant with the green of early summer, a foundation of brown earth and gnarled roots. There was no detail to vex the eye. Three solid masses of form and color—sky, foliage and earth—the whole bathed in an atmosphere of golden luminosity. I threw my brushes aside; they were too small for the work in hand. I squeezed out big chunks of pure, moist color and taking my palette knife, I laid on blue, green, white and brown in great sweeping strokes. As I worked I saw that it was good and clean and strong. I saw nature springing into life upon my dead canvas. It was better than nature, for it was vibrating with the thrill of a new creation. Exultantly I painted until the sun sank below the horizon, then I raced around the fields like a colt let loose, and literally bellowed for joy (cited in McCoubrey, pp. 187–188).

More than other artists, Ryder developed a reputation for being a hermitlike loner, who cared little for the practical necessities of selling his art. In fact, Ryder had appreciative patrons, but he tended to return to or hang on to many of his paintings, adding layer after layer of color glazing until the thick surfaces were as glowing as Japanese lacquerwork. Ryder painted *Jonah* around 1885 and reworked it at some point before 1895, even though the picture's first owner, a New York stockbroker, had lent it to the New York Athletic Club for an 1890 exhibition. Because Ryder did not allow earlier layers of paint to dry properly before adding new glazes, his paint surfaces have tended to crack and slip over time. Continually experimenting with painting materials, the artist also employed bituminous varnishes that have caused his colors to fade into powerful light-dark contrasts.

Whistler and the Triumph of Aestheticism

Ryder's anti-commercial attitude was inspired, in part, by the cosmopolitan painter James Abbott McNeill Whistler (1834–1903), a Lowell, Massachusetts, native who spent most of his career abroad in Paris and London after dropping out of the U.S. Military Academy at West Point. In Paris, Whistler quickly rejected tradi-

tional academic art and soon associated himself with stylistically innovative artists such as Manet and Gustave Courbet (1819–77), who were challenging the traditional academic rule that the highest art must possess a high degree of finish and illusionistic detail at the same time as conveying moral narratives or ennobling ideas. Whistler readily adopted the controversial credo of the French poet and art critic Théophile Gautier (1811–72), who had argued already during the 1830s that art was an end in itself and, therefore, had no need to tell an uplifting story or serve any particular moral purpose. In London, Whistler allied himself with the classical scholar and art historian Walter Pater (1839–94) and the playwright and poet Oscar Wilde (1854–1900) in becoming a leading spokesman for the Aesthetic movement, which rejected the distinction between the fine and decorative arts. As Wilde argued during a well-publicized lecture tour of the United States in 1882–3, an easel painting was no more spiritual than a well-crafted painted vase or a decorative tile from Damascus. Each "is a beautifully-coloured surface, nothing more, and affects us by no suggestion stolen from philosophy, no pathos pilfered from literature, no feeling filched from a poet, but by its own incommunicable artistic essence" (cited in Stein, pp. 25–26).

Similarly, Whistler regarded his paintings as decoratively arranged surfaces. Though his portrait of his mother, Anne Matilda McNeill Whistler, has become a popular symbol of American motherhood appropriated by mass-media advertising and entertainment, the artist's title for the painting, *Arrangement in Gray and Black (Portrait of the Artist's Mother)* (fig. 6.63), subordinates the maternal figure, with all of its moral and psychological associations, to the purely aesthetic or formal arrangement of tones. Unlike Thomas Eakins, whose portraits were intense studies of human character and emotion (see p. 230), Whistler chose a strict profile view to minimize beholders' inclination to decipher an internal state of mind from facial features and expression. Whistler's flatly painted mother also contrasts with the more lively, flesh-and-blood naturalism of Mary Cassatt's mother (see fig. 6.51).

Nevertheless, despite Whistler's stated belief that the public could not have much interest in the personal identity of his mother, the picture's formal arrangement does suggest her sober New England moral character. Forming a relatively strict right angle, the seated figure adheres to the rectilinear geometry of the shallow pictorial space. The floor and background wall create a decorative grid of rectangular and oblong shapes painted with thin washes of mostly colorless gray and black oil pigments, with only touches of yellow and pink.

Despite his loyalty to the Aesthetic movement, which divorced art from overt moral themes, Whistler, in a 1867 letter to the French painter Henri Fantin-Latour (1836–1904) characterized the formal means of expression in strongly moral terms:

> *Color—color is the vice. Certainly it can be and has the right to be one of the finest virtues. Grasped with a strong hand, controlled by her master, drawing, color then is a splendid girl with a husband worthy of her—her lover, but her master too—the most magnificent mistress in the world, and the result is to be seen in all the lovely things produced from their union. But coupled with indecision, with a weak, timid, vicious drawing, easily satisfied, color becomes a filthy whore. . . (cited in Pyne, pp. 110–111).*

Whistler's attitude toward the painter's technique derives from a long tradition of academic criticism which cast the dichotomy between color and drawing in terms of gender. Because of its fluid sensuosity and rich visual appearance, color was a feminine quality in need of formal discipline from the austere, manly rigor of drawing. Whistler favored arrangements of light and dark tones and muted atmospheric canvases because they evoked associations with the immaterial tonal harmonies of music. The feminine beauty of color was thereby spiritualized or elevated beyond vulgar physical desire.

6.64 James Abbott McNeill Whistler
Nocturne in Black and Gold (The Falling Rocket), c.1875. Oil on oak panel, 23⅝ x 18½ in (60 x 47 cm). Detroit Institute of Art. Dexter M. Ferry Jr. Fund.

Whistler employed a minimal amount of black in this picture. His night sky was formed through thin veils of dark blue-green pigments. In the left background, he depicted the twin-towered fireworks platform encircled by lights. Overhead, a variety of hues create the shower of lights from exploding rockets: salmon pink, beige, lemon yellow, and blue-green. Down below, where spectral figures watch the fireworks, traces of red create a warm counterpoint to the painting's cool, dark-blue tones.

In his controversial painting *Nocturne in Black and Gold (The Falling Rocket)* (fig. 6.64), Whistler abandoned rational geometric rigor. The highly abstract picture of a fireworks display over London's Cremorne Gardens was one of a series of atmospheric "nocturnes," the pictorial equivalent of piano nocturnes with their contemplative musical tones. When Whistler exhibited his nocturnes at a London gallery in 1877, the English art critic John Ruskin accused the artist of "flinging a pot of paint in the public's face" (cited in McCoubrey, p. 181). For Ruskin, who thought paintings should provide some edifying moral message or legible narrative content, *Nocturne in Black and Gold (The Falling Rocket)* was simply an unreadable, sloppily executed painting with no redeeming social value. In retaliation, Whistler sued Ruskin for libel and during the highly publicized trial argued that the value of art did not reside in the imitation of nature or in the representation of any particular story or subject. Under cross-examination, the painter denied that his representation of the fireworks was an actual view of Cremorne Gardens: "If it were called a view of Cremorne, it would certainly bring about nothing but disappointment on the part of the beholders. . . . It is an artistic arrangement" (cited in McCoubrey, p. 182). The formal arrangement of tones and colors defined painting's autonomy from external reality. Though Whistler won the lawsuit, he was awarded only one farthing in damages and was forced into bankruptcy over the court costs.

Nevertheless, Whistler used the trial's publicity to establish his European and American reputation as a self-proclaimed "preacher" for the new religion of art. In a May 22, 1878, article for *The World*, a London newspaper, Whistler asserted that "Art should be independent of all claptrap—should stand alone, and appeal to the artistic sense of eye or ear, without confounding this with emotions entirely foreign to it, as devotion, pity, love, patriotism, and the like" (cited in Bendix, p. 33). The artist later argued in biblical terms that true art was intended only for the initiated or elect few, who could rise above the middle-class materialism of the majority to experience a higher, spiritual consciousness. Whistler's aestheticism merged with his interest in Spiritualist séances. As a Spiritualist medium, the artist claimed the ability to communicate beyond the grave with the more refined realm of spiritual beings. Similarly, the reveries produced by beauty and art could elevate individuals toward an ethereal, transcendent state. More than a religion of art, Whistler pursued a religion of life whereby, ideally, the entire human environment would become transformed into aestheticized spaces conducive to higher forms of spiritual communication. *Thus, Nocturne in Black and Gold (The Falling Rocket)* and the other London nocturnes can be interpreted as Whistler's attempt to reimagine the city according to the harmonic principles of art and beauty.

Whistler's nocturnes and arrangements were informed by his love of the decorative arts, particularly the arts and crafts of Japan and the Orient. Just before his libel suit against Ruskin, the artist decorated the dining room of a London house owned by Frederick R. Leyland, a shipowner from Liverpool, England (fig. 6.65). Originally inspired by a desire to have the room's decor harmonize with his Orientalist painting *The Princess from the Land of Porcelain*, which hung over the fireplace, Whistler produced an aestheticized environment that was also intended to showcase Leyland's valuable collection of blue-and-white Chinese porcelain. Ironically, the painter's *Harmony in Blue and Gold: The Peacock Room* features a frankly discordant mural of fighting peacocks, which he bitterly referred to as "Art and Money; or The Story of The Room." The battling peacocks represented an assaulted Whistler and an angry Leyland, who had refused to pay Whistler's asking price of 2,000 guineas for an interior decoration that exceeded his original order and expectations. Silver coins lie at the feet of the aggressive, right-hand peacock. The coins signified Whistler's opinion that Leyland had a miserly personality. Elsewhere in the room, Whistler painted three pairs of window shutters with four additional peacocks and further deco-

6.65 James Abbott McNeill Whistler
Harmony in Blue and Gold: The Peacock Room, 1876–7.
Oil on leather and wood,
13 ft 11⅞ in x 33 ft 2 in x 19 ft 11½ in
(4.26 x 10.11 x 6.08 m).
Freer Gallery of Art, Smithsonian Institution, Washington, D.C.

rated the walls and ceiling with overlapping peacock feathers. Leyland's collection of Oriental
vases, placed on gilded shelves along the walls,
was overwhelmed by Whistler's lavish decoration. Painted in the patron's absence, the Peacock
Room, with its contentious, insulting mural, nevertheless remained intact. Over a decade after
Leyland's death in 1892, the room was purchased
by an American industrialist, Charles Lang Freer,
who had it reinstalled in his Detroit, Michigan,
home and later bequeathed it to a new
Washington, D.C., museum that would house
his collection of Asian and American art.

Freer, a manufacturer of railroad cars and
investor in pharmaceuticals, gradually retired
from the cares of business to pursue the aesthetic cult of beauty. In addition to collecting
Oriental art and works by Whistler, Freer com-

missioned paintings from Dwight William
Tryon (1849–1925) and Thomas Wilmer
Dewing (1851–1938), both of whom had fallen
under the spell of the Aesthetic movement and
the tonalist technique of Whistler. Dewing's
After Sunset (Summer Evening) (fig. 6.66) represents two richly gowned women in an
amorphous landscape of thinly painted blue-
green tones. This quiet, non-narrative painting
evokes the environment of Cornish, New
Hampshire, where Dewing and his artist-
wife Maria Oakey Dewing (1845–1927) were
part of an artists' colony far from the social
problems of modern urban life. Rather than
imitating the natural landscape of Cornish,
Dewing sought to express its restorative cosmic
energy as an antidote for the overwrought
nerves of wealthy businessmen and art patrons

6.66 Thomas Dewing
After Sunset (Summer Evening), 1892.
Oil on canvas,
42⅛ x 54⅛ in
(107 x 137.4 cm).
Freer Gallery of Art,
Smithsonian Institution,
Washington, D.C.

This painting was partially
inspired by the English
painter and poet Dante
Gabriel Rossetti (1828–82),
whose sonnet "The One
Hope" from *The House of
Life*, a cycle of sonnets,
asked the question of what
awaited the individual soul
after death. Rossetti's poem
searches for answers to the
unknown terrain of life
beyond the grave.

6.67 William Merritt Chase
James A. M. Whistler,
1885.
Oil on canvas,
74⅛ x 36¼ in
(188.9 x 92 cm).
Metropolitan Museum of
Art, New York. Bequest of
William H. Walker, 1918.

like Freer. Frequently engaging in theatrical performances and ritualized costume parties, the Dewings and other artists of the Cornish colony attempted to extend Whistler's aestheticism into the fabric of their daily lives. Most famously, in 1905, at the Cornish residence of the sculptor Augustus Saint-Gaudens, the Boston Symphony Orchestra joined a cast of 200 in the performance of an outdoor theatrical ritual entitled *Masque of the Ours, the Gods and the Golden Bowl*. Before a small Greek temple and altar, seventy of the players impersonated Greek gods and goddesses to present Saint-Gaudens with an honorific golden bowl.

Concentrating much of their wrath on the figure of Oscar Wilde, many American critics denounced the hedonistic amorality of the Aesthetic movement. In caricatures that were published in both England and America during the 1880s and 1890s, Wilde and male aesthetes in general were represented as effeminate dandies, who appeared primarily in the company of

admiring society women. Aestheticism thus seemed to threaten American manhood by promoting the feminization of culture and the worship of sensuous beauty divorced from moral truth. Whistler managed to avoid most of the venom directed against Wilde, partly because he stressed the spiritual dimension of his art, but also because he did not share Wilde's socialist politics and displayed an intimidating, masculine aggressiveness in attacking his critics and enemies. In 1885, the New York artist William Merritt Chase (1849–1916) portrayed Whistler in relatively caricatured terms as a hyper-refined aesthete (fig. 6.67). Whistler publicly denounced the painting as a mocking lampoon and accused Chase of an act of betrayal. However, as the admiring Chase recalled, Whistler was an immaculately dressed and groomed man, a dandy who had virtually transformed himself into a work of art. Whistler's trademark lock of white hair appears like a spiritual flame of inspiration atop his head. Whistler, too, had included

6.68 William Merritt Chase
In the Studio, c. 1880. Oil on canvas, 28⅛ x 40⅟₁₆ in (71.8 x 101.6 cm). Brooklyn Museum of Art, New York. Gift of Mrs. Carl H. De Silver.

Chase's representation of his studio's opulent furnishings seems a manifesto for aestheticism. A customer leafs through a heavy book resting on an expensive Turkish rug. Oriental fabrics, Japanese fans, musical instruments, and gold-framed paintings line the walls. An elaborately carved Renaissance chest displays vases, sculptures, and other objects, including a model ship. A reproduction of Frans Hals's *Malle Babbe* (c.1650) suggests Chase's indebtedness to the Dutch painter.

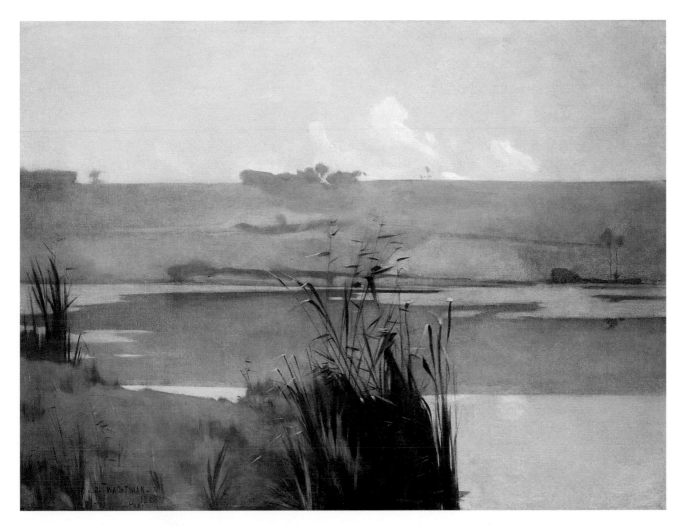

6.69 John Twachtman
Arques-la-Bataille, 1885.
Oil on canvas, 60 x 78⅞
in (152.4 x 200.3 cm).
Metropolitan Museum of
Art, New York. Morris K.
Jesup Fund, 1968.

For Twachtman, art was to
provide a quiet,
contemplative refuge from
the tensions of modern
urban-industrial life.
Emphasizing relaxation, the
artist's broad horizontal
bands of tone and delicate
feathery brushwork were
influenced by Japanese
prints, Whistler's tonalism,
and French Impressionist
paintings. Twachtman
regarded Japanese art as
a tasteful antidote to the
crass vulgarity of American
mass culture.

this characteristic tuft of white hair to identify himself as one of the battling peacocks in Leyland's Peacock Room.

Chase adopted the art-for-art's-sake credo of the Aesthetic movement. Unlike Whistler and Dewing, however, he cultivated an aesthetic that was more earthbound, less abstract, and oriented toward a more colorful palette under the influence of French Impressionism. Before meeting Whistler, he represented his own studio, located in Richard Morris Hunt's Studio Building (see fig. 6.10), as an elegantly furnished space filled with his own collection of beautiful, rare, and exotic art objects (fig. 6.68). In marked contrast to Thomas Eakins's portrayal of William Rush's studio (see fig. 6.33), Chase's lavishly decorated chamber appears as a place for the consumption of art rather than its messy production. As the art historian Sarah Burns has observed, Chase's stu-

dio with its fashionably dressed female customer compares closely with contemporary department-store displays. By the 1880s, newly established large-scale stores such as Wanamaker's in Philadelphia and Macy's in New York were selling paintings as well as expensive, exotic art objects, in addition to the usual underwear, socks, and other dry goods. If the Aesthetic movement had transformed art into a substitute religion, it also served to commercialize art objects, transforming them into expensive commodities for an anonymous art market. In other pictures of his studio rooms, Chase offered glimpses of female students painting. Dora Wheeler was only one of many women who benefited from his instruction (see fig. 6.8).

Chase, who painted Impressionist seascapes at his summer studio at Shinnecock, Long Island, later joined Thomas Dewing in exhibitions of

6.70 Childe Hassam
Washington Arch,
Spring, 1890.
Oil on canvas,
27⅛ x 22½ in
(68.9 x 57.1 cm).
The Phillips Collection,
Washington, D.C.

The Ten or Ten American Painters, a group of New York and Boston artists who resigned from the Society of American Artists to exhibit as a small group without the intrusion of exhibition juries or Society officers. The group formed in 1898 and was active until 1919, but Chase did not join until 1902, when he replaced John Henry Twachtman (1853–1902), who died that year. Though most members of the group were influenced by French Impressionism, they tended to work in a more poetic style that suggested dissatis-faction with the materialism or naturalism of the Impressionistic aesthetic. When, for instance, the Cincinnati-born Twachtman studied in Paris from 1883 to 1885, he adopted a contemplative, tonal style that was far closer in mood and technique to Whistler's nocturnes than to the bright colors of French Impressionism (fig. 6.69).

When, in 1886, the first major American exhibition of French Impressionist paintings took place in New York, a number of critics attacked the ugly, vulgar subject matter and

6.71 Jacob Riis
Street Arabs, Mulberry Street, 1898.
Photograph. Museum of the City of New York.

The term "Street Arabs" did not define the ethnicity of these children. The term was used to refer to the nomadic lives of these young social outcasts. Yet the phrase also suggests the ethnic, religious prejudices that actual Arab immigrants and other non-Western peoples, confronted upon arriving in America.

associated the bright, clashing colors of the Impressionist palette with revolutionary politics or the red flag of Communism. That same year, in fact, labor strikes and protests had culminated in the infamous Haymarket Square bombing and riots in Chicago, which left a number of workers and policemen dead and injured.

One of The Ten, (Frederick) Childe Hassam (1859–1935), worked in an Impressionist style, but, like other members of the group, he carefully avoided views of overcrowded urban environments and lower-class subjects. Hassam's pictures of New York depicted the spacious and light-filled ambience of Fifth Avenue, the city's most aesthetic and architecturally fashionable thoroughfare. In his painting of *Washington Arch, Spring* (fig. 6.70), Hassam represents the monumental arch that marks the terminus of the avenue in Greenwich Village. The brightly lit, sketchily painted scene is inhabited not only by horse-drawn carriages and well-dressed society women, but also by a street cleaner clothed in white, who dutifully keeps this urban paradise free from debris. The painting seems to anticipate Daniel Burnham's immaculate and utopian White City for the 1893 Columbian Exposition

(see fig. 6.16). Indeed, Hassam later painted a small sketch of the White City in a more detailed, less Impressionist rendering of the classical architecture and pristine Venetian waterways.

During the Gilded Age, art tended to appeal to the genteel taste for beauty, harmony, and refined subject matter. By the early twentieth century, however, socialist and progressive reformers were forcefully challenging the monopolistic and anti-labor practices of American capitalists. Documentary photographers such as the Danish immigrant Jacob A. Riis (1849–1914) used new flashlight camera technology to record crime-infested, dilapidated tenements and so-called "street Arabs" or homeless children, who slept in alleyways or the hidden, back corners of city buildings (fig. 6.71). Riis's bleak pictures contrasted sharply with the sunny urbanscapes of Hassam and other Impressionists. As we shall see, many American artists began to view themselves as avant-garde challengers of the cultural and political status quo. This new generation of artists sought to move beyond Aestheticism by arguing that art's purpose was not simply to beautify but to radically transform or revolutionize life.

Chapter 7

Modernist Art and Politics
1905–41

FROM 1905 until America's entrance into World War II in 1941, culturally and politically radical new subjects, forms, media, and experimental concepts challenged academic styles. During this period, many American artists and architects continued to work in a conservative, historicist manner. Particularly in Washington, D.C., ancient, classical styles remained revered symbols of national prestige and political stability, as architects designed Greek and Roman temple fronts for government buildings and memorials (fig. 7.1). The muralist Kenyon Cox (1856–1919) defended Italian Renaissance masters as the academic ideal in painting and insisted on the existence of immutable commandments for art, equivalent to the laws of physics (fig. 7.2). But, by the early twentieth century, economic modernization and scientific and intellectual developments were helping to displace the moral certitudes and conventional assumptions of the Gilded Age with a Modernist culture that reshaped reality in more fluid, relativistic, and dynamic terms. In addition to the automobile, other inventions such as the airplane, telephone, radio, motion picture, and photo magazine dramatically shrank spatial and temporal distances between both places and people. Using cinematic editing, film directors could represent an action or scene from different perspectives, thereby demonstrating the relativism of vision. Meanwhile, from high airplane altitudes, earth's landscapes could be quickly reduced into flattened geometric patterns and grids.

Scientists and mathematicians complicated the mapping of the universe, which had been explained by the predictable, mechanistic physics of Sir Isaac Newton and the ancient geometric axioms of the Greek philosopher Euclid. The French mathematician Henri Poincaré argued in 1902 that Euclid's geometry and all other competing geometries were arbitrarily grounded on convention or convenience rather than objective truth. Scientific "truths" were now acknowledged as relative rather than absolute, being dependent on the position of the observing scientist in relation to the observed object of investigation. In studying both the macrocosmic and microcosmic universes, twentieth-century scientists learned the fallacy of drawing firm distinctions between space and time or energy and matter. Atomic physicists proved that matter was far from solid as its orbiting particles could be transformed into radioactive energy. Meanwhile, in expounding his theory of relativity, Albert Einstein employed non-Euclidean geometry to prove that space and time are not separate categories, as previously assumed, but coexist as a dynamic continuum shaped and slowed by the presence of matter. The discoveries or new hypotheses of geometers and physicists fueled the speculations of visionary thinkers and artists that there existed a fourth dimension beyond the perceptible three-dimensional spaces and forms of everyday experience. For twentieth-century painters, the traditional, three-dimensional illusionism of landscapes, still lifes, and portraits seemed increasingly arbitrary and old-fashioned. Many artists distorted or fragmented objects and figures to suggest new physics theories of space, time, and matter.

Following upon the evolutionary theories of Charles Darwin, which came to public attention during the 1860s and 1870s, anthropologists and philosophers increasingly questioned the traditional, pre-modern thinking that elevated humans to a special, ideal realm beyond the animal kingdom. While clergymen and educators since the Colonial period had constructed strict moral codes of behavior based on sharp distinctions between man and animal or civilization

Mark Tobey
Broadway, 1935–6.
Tempera on composition board, 26 x 19⁹⁄₁₆ in (66 x 48.7 cm).
Metropolitan Museum of Art. Arthur Hoppock Hearn Fund, 1942.

297

7.1 Henry Bacon
Lincoln Memorial,
1911–22,
Washington, D.C.
Exterior view.

The Greek temple design by
Henry Bacon (1866–1924)
houses a colossal sculpture
of an enthroned Abraham
Lincoln by Daniel Chester
French. In a concession to
modernity, the marble
temple rests upon a
foundation of steel and
concrete. President
Theodore Roosevelt
regarded the memorial as
an emblem of the
Republican Party and his
own progressive policies.

and savagery, the American philosopher William James (1842–1910) argued that humans existed on an evolutionary continuum with other animals. For James, the human brain, as a biological organ, made the so-called "higher" intellectual faculty dependent on the body's raw sensory experiences and passions. Believing that intellectual constructs were at a further remove from truth than an active pursuit of new experiences and discoveries, James played a key role in shaping America's Modernist culture of perpetual experimentation and innovation.

Modernist art may be defined by its self-conscious interest in experimentation with the materials and creative processes of each individual medium. Freed from the obligation of representing "objective" reality, Modernist artists have tended to stress the subjective uniqueness of their own particular visions. They willfully manipulated subjects, colors, shapes, and forms in new,

7.2 Kenyon Cox
Tradition, 1916.
Oil on canvas
41¾ x 65⅛ in
(106 x165.5cm).
Cleveland Museum of Art,
Cleveland, Ohio,
Gift of J.D. Cox.

Cox's allegory represents
Greek-inspired
personifications of the past,
who pass the lamp of
knowledge or tradition to
personifications of Art and
Literature dressed in
Renaissance costumes. The
neoclassical clarity of Cox's
style was an implicit
renunciation of
Modernism's flagrant
violation of traditional
academic idealizations
of the human figure.

expressive ways and thereby called attention to the relativity of vision and the contradictions, ambiguities, and uncertainties of modern urban life. From rebellious European painters and sculptors, American Modernists learned to identify themselves as an avant-garde of forward-looking individuals. As such, they sought to create works that not only redefined the conventions and institutions of art, but also critically challenged repressive political and social conditions.

If nineteenth-century artists had appealed primarily to genteel upper- and middle-class tastes, those who now gained prominence in the art world shocked the American public with works that were intentionally unrefined or in rebellion against academic standards and conventional ideals. Doubting the primacy of abstract reason, Modernist artists dissented from the traditional moral wisdom of repressing sexual desires and sensual pleasures. For many, the creative act of self-expression became a powerful metaphor for political freedom and social regeneration. To varying degrees, avant-garde artists tended to empathize with the plight of immigrants and the struggles of workers, political reformers, and social radicals against capitalist, corporate power. Conservative critics frequently

likened experimental Modernist artists' defiance of Renaissance traditions and academic rules to the acts of bomb-throwing anarchists and political revolutionaries. On the other hand, American corporations eventually learned to value the dynamic visual forms and rhythms of Modern art for advertising, public relations, industrial design, and functional, sleek commercial architecture. Furthermore, though Modernist critics frequently ridiculed corporate-sponsored mass culture, the artists of Modernism borrowed extensively from popular media such as the cinema and illustrated newspapers and magazines.

Modernization and Architecture

The original Pennsylvania Station in New York was the world's largest railroad station when it was built in 1905–10 (fig. 7.3). In its synthesis of modern urban functionalism and ancient, classical grandeur, the station bears comparison with the Roman and Renaissance-Revival architecture of the White City for the 1893 World's Columbian Exposition in Chicago (see fig. 6.16).

7.3 Mckim, Mead, & White
Pennsylvania Station, New York City, 1906–10 (demolished).
New York Historical Society, New York.

Pennsylvania Station's Seventh Avenue façade expressed its monumentality with unfluted Doric-order columns, austere symbols of masculine strength. The massive columns supported an almost continuous cornice, interrupted only for the slightly projecting central entrance and two pedimented bays at the 31st and 33rd Street ends of the façade. From a distance, the exterior of the station's huge waiting room, with its semicircular thermal windows, could be seen projecting upward behind the façade.

7.4 McKim, Mead, & White
Pennsylvania Station, New York City, 1906–10, original view of concourse (demolished). Avery Architectural and Fine Arts Library, Columbia University, New York.

Designed by the architectural firm of McKim, Mead, & White, the vast, templelike building boasted an impressive façade colonnade: a row of thirty-two freestanding columns, each towering sixty-eight feet high. However, while the interior waiting room recalled the ancient Roman Baths of Caracalla, the architects also employed every modern technological convenience to move people efficiently in and out of the station. The terminal was fed by a system of river and land tunnels and a maze of electrified rail lines that arrived well below ground. Passenger luggage and freight were guided through a multilevel network of ramps and overpasses. For the concourse leading from the waiting room to the trains, a steel skeleton of columns and arches supported intersecting glass vaults, illuminating a free flow of open space (fig. 7.4).

The building of Pennsylvania Station had necessitated the demolition of approximately 400 homes and stores, bordered by 31st and 33rd Streets, and Seventh and Ninth Avenues. Newspapers and magazines carried photographs and drawings representing the excavation site dramatically emptied by blasting and wrecking machinery, while headlines and articles compared the engineering feat to the contemporaneous, U.S. government-sponsored construction of the Panama Canal in Central America. Despite its classical, historical-revival style, Pennsylvania Station signified the progress of economic modernization. Indeed, the architects argued that only by building in the style of the ancient Roman empire could they express the new imperial ambitions of a United States taking its place as a dominant force in the world economy.

New York Realists and Modern Urban Life

From 1907 to 1909, the young Ohio-born artist George Bellows (1882–1925) painted a series of pictures representing the gaping excavation and construction site for Pennsylvania Station. Unlike the genteel urban views of Childe Hassam (see fig. 6.70) and other Gilded Age Impressionists, Bellows's *Pennsylvania Excavation* (fig. 7.5) represents a dirty, wintry scene with sketchily painted workers and steam-driven digging machinery within a vast urban canyon. The dense cluster of tall buildings on the far horizon accentuates the subterranean depths that dominate the picture. While Hassam painted his upper-class urban scenes with light, pastel hues and feathery brushwork, Bellows emphasized the working-class, industrial nature of his subject with thick brushstrokes and a somber palette of grays, browns, and off-whites, contrasting with a blue and gold sky.

7.5 George Bellows
Pennsylvania Excavation,
c. 1907–09.
Oil on canvas,
31¼ x 38¼ in
(104 x 121.3 cm).
Brooklyn Museum of Art,
New York. A. Augustus
Healy Fund.

Bellows arrived in New York in 1904 from Columbus, where he had attended Ohio State University, and fell under the influence of Robert Henri (1865–1929), who taught painting at the New York School of Art. An admirer of Thomas Eakins and a former student of Thomas Anshutz at the Pennsylvania Academy of the Fine Arts, Henri was the leader of a group of New York realist painters who were rebelling against the conventional, elevated styles of the National Academy of Design and the refined, art-for-art's-sake aestheticism of artists such as Whistler and Thomas Dewing. Promoting the credo of an art for life's sake, Henri had inspired a small band of painters, who had once worked as illustrators or artist-reporters for various Philadelphia newspapers. The group included George B. Luks (1866–1933), John Sloan (1871–1951), Everett Shinn (1876–1953), and William Glackens (1870–1938). By the turn of the century, when a screen halftone, or photomechanical, process was invented for reproducing photographs on the printed page, these newspaper artists lost their jobs and moved to New York to pursue painting careers. Having been trained as journalists to sketch subjects quickly outside the controlled studio environment, these Philadelphia émigrés drew inspiration from Henri, who insisted that artists must search for subjects like perpetual hunters:

The sketch hunter has delightful days of drifting about among people, in and out of the city, going anywhere, everywhere, stopping as long as he likes—no need to reach any point, moving in any direction following the call of interests. He moves through life as he finds it, not passing negligently the things he loves, but stopping to know them, and to note them down in the shorthand of his sketchbook. . . . Like any hunter he hits or misses. He is looking for what he loves, he tries to capture it. It's found anywhere, everywhere. Those who are not hunters do not see these things. The hunter is learning to see and to understand—to enjoy (p. 17).

7.6 Robert Henri
Eva Green, 1907.
Oil on canvas,
24 x 20⅛ in
(60.9 x 51.4 cm).
Wichita Art Museum,
Wichita, Kansas. Roland P.
Murdock Collection.

Fancily dressed with a large
black hat, Eva Green smiles
warmly as she gazes
directly toward us. Her
chocolate-brown face is
luminous against the inky
background and contrasts
with her broadly painted
dark costume. The energetic
sparkle in her eyes and face
is echoed by a small ivory-
colored hat pin and a
bright-red hair ribbon.
Henri's vivid likeness recalls
the painterly style of the
seventeenth-century Dutch
artist Frans Hals
(c. 1580–1666).

In its emphasis upon the artist-hunter's intense love for subjects, Henri's modern realist aesthetic was emotionally expressive and individualistic. Henri and his protégés were less social reformers than enthusiastic sportsmen seeking novel, exotic experiences from the noisy, crowded spectacle of lower-class urban life. In 1907, while Bellows was working on *Pennsylvania Excavation*, his teacher encountered a young African-American girl named Eva Green from one of New York's poorer neighborhoods. Employing quick, broad brushstrokes, Henri painted an energetic portrait that expresses a magnetic bond with the smiling girl (fig. 7.6). Henri and his circle of artist-disciples painted numerous pictures of poor or immigrant children, whose youthful exuberance seemed to typify the new century's urban diversity and dynamism. In George Luks's *The Spielers* (fig. 7.7), two immigrant girls dance closely together in a manner known as "spieling." This German type of dancing, also called "pivoting,"

was popular among the working class around the turn of the century. In contrast to the upper-class waltz, which involved elegant, graceful movements, spieling brought couples into close physical contact as they swirled wildly across the dance floor. Cultural moralists were critical of spieling for its potential to stimulate sexual desire. In his painting, Luks defused this concern by depicting innocent, fun-loving girls rather than adults. Situated within an ambiguous, relatively bare gray space, the girls' motion is suggested by a sketchlike blurring of their bodies. The right-hand figure's wispy blonde hair particularly creates the breezy illusion of twirling in space.

More controversial were Luks's and Bellows's representations of brutal wrestling and boxing matches. Though public prizefights were then illegal, private clubs were formed to stage fights exclusively for their members. Appealing initially to a lower-class male underworld, these

7.7 George Benjamin Luks
The Spielers, 1905. Oil on canvas, 36 x 26 in (91.4 x 66 cm). Addison Gallery of American Art, Phillips Academy, Andover, Massachusetts. Gift of anonymous donor.

private athletic clubs soon attracted an increasing number of middle- and upper-class men, whose patronage helped to transform successful fighters from social outcasts into popular, newsworthy celebrities. In contrast to Thomas Eakins's ideal male nudes in *The Swimming Hole* (see fig. 6.36) or Thomas Anshutz's relatively sedate, seminude figures in *The Ironworkers' Noontime* (see fig. 6.40), Bellows's *Both Members of This Club* (fig. 7.8) startled audiences with the raw, animal brutality of its muscular figures. The artist places us at ringside amid a demonic, bloodthirsty group of fans, transfixed by the bloodied head and torso of a white boxer, recoiling from the powerful onslaught of a lunging black fighter. After originally titling the picture *A Nigger and a White Man*, Bellows soon renamed it *Both Members of This Club*. The new title alluded to the popular strategy for circumventing the law against public prizefighting. Saloon owners frequently staged backroom fights by transforming their bars into private athletic clubs, which offered one-night memberships to ticket-buyers and to black and white fighters alike. In representing the powerful black fighter as the dominant force, Bellows implicitly expressed the anxiety of America's white majority over its presumed racial superiority. Though *Both Members of This Club* represents anonymous fighters, it indirectly referred to the African-American heavyweight

7.8 George Bellows
Both Members of This Club, 1909. Oil on canvas, 45¼ x 63⅛ in (114.9 x 160 cm). National Gallery of Art, Washington, D.C. Chester Dale Collection.

Although New York realists prided themselves on the direct observation of modern urban life, they appropriated visual ideas from a number of past European masters. Bellows's boxing pictures, with their grotesque array of spectators, seem particularly indebted to prints and paintings by the Spanish artist Francisco Goya (1746–1828). Goya's many images of bull-fighting scenes especially may have been a source of inspiration for Bellows.

boxing champion Jack Johnson, who first won the championship title in 1908. Bellows's unflattering representation of the boxing audience suggests that he shared middle-class moralists' objections to prizefighting. Yet he was also a member of Sharkey's athletic club, where he could freely observe and sketch virtually nude males under non-studio, "real-life" conditions. Amid the blood and gore, Bellows implicitly conveys the inherent homoerotic and sadistic content of the sport, as the all-male audience leers in delight at the tortured physiques of the combatants. Having led a sheltered life in the Midwest, the artist also thrilled to the exotic spectacles of New York's underworld.

The New York realists challenged traditional notions of beauty by choosing subjects that were considered vulgar and ugly by genteel, Gilded Age standards. In his book *The Story of American Art* (1907), the influential critic Charles Caffin especially credited John Sloan for expanding the conventional repertoire of images to include the congested, transient life of street traffic, working-class or immigrant tenements, and popular entertainments. In June of 1907, while walking to Henri's studio, Sloan directed his journalistic eye toward the second-story window of a shabby commercial building, where, according to his diary, a hairdresser was bleaching the hair of a customer. What made the scene humorous and aesthetically compelling was that a group of spectators was standing about gazing at the public display of private grooming. Shortly afterward, Sloan reproduced this piece of street theater in a colorful picture filled with gawking onlookers and a hairdresser's window surrounded by shop and restaurant signs (fig. 7.9). The scene through the window also serves as a sign advertising the skills of the hairdresser. Undoubtedly hoping to attract yet more business, the matronly woman purposefully exhibits her client's lush, red hair, flowing over the back of a chair. Meanwhile, two female mannequin heads visible in the display window below apparently

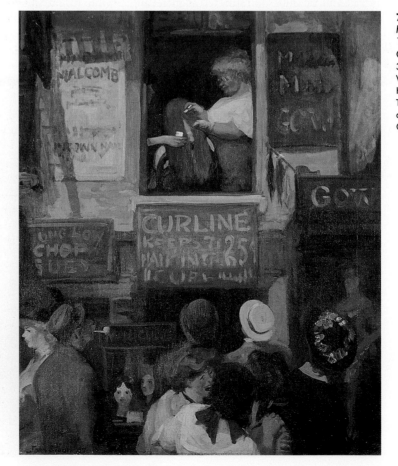

7.9 John Sloan
Hairdresser's Window, 1907.
Oil on canvas, 31⅞ x 26 in (81 x 66 cm).
Wadsworth Atheneum, Hartford, Connecticut.
The Ella Gallup Sumner and Mary Catlin Sumner Collection.

JUNE, 1914   10 CENTS

The MASSES

IN THIS ISSUE
CLASS WAR IN COLORADO—Max Eastman
WHAT ABOUT MEXICO?—John Reed

7.10 John Sloan
Class War in Colorado,
cover for *The Masses*,
June 1914.
Delaware Art Museum,
Wilmington, Delaware.
Gift of Helen Farr Sloan.

Against a bright wall of fiery
orange flames, Sloan
represented a lone Ludlow,
Colorado mineworker
holding the limp body of a
child in one hand. With the
other he fires a gun at an
unseen National Guardsman
or security agent for the
Rockefellers, the capitalist
mine owners. Sloan
sympathetically portrays the
worker as a family man who
avenges the apparent
massacre of his wife and
children. Lying beneath the
striking miner are the bodies
of a mother and child.

demonstrate the beautiful results of the hairstyl-ist's art, even in this lower-class environment. Sloan painted numerous pictures of women cleaning, laundering, and self-grooming. For him, these simple, daily cleansing rituals suggest-ed the hopeful theme of social renewal and regeneration amid the filthy squalor of urban slums.

More than most New York realists, Sloan actively involved himself in radical, working-class political causes. In 1909, he published several prints of New York City life for *The Craftsman*. The editor of this Arts and Crafts journal, the furniture designer Gustav Stickley (1848–1942), had argued in a 1907 issue that:

Social unrest is, without question, the
distinguishing characteristic of this age. Especially
is this true in America, where greed and
arrogance on the one hand and class hatred and

jealousy on the other seem to have arrayed the
people into two great factions, represented by the
terms Capital and Labor. The prevailing feeling
is that a relatively small class has possessed itself
of the land and its treasures: that a few great
corporations of the same men, control the main
arteries of the nation's industry and commerce
(cited in Hills, p. 313).

Historians have estimated that in 1900, approx-imately 40 percent of all Americans were living in poverty. President Theodore Roosevelt's antitrust lawsuits against banking and corporate monopolies and the passage of such progressive reforms as the graduated income tax helped to stabilize the nation's economy, but they did not halt labor unrest nor lower-class demands for higher wages and better working and living conditions.

During the summer of 1905, a "Continental Congress of the Working Class," comprising 200 delegates from thirty-four different American labor organizations, met in Chicago to form a single large union or "union of unions" called the Industrial Workers of the World (IWW). In its constitution the IWW explicitly dedicated itself to the radical principle of class struggle and the workers' overthrow of the capitalist elite's ownership of the means of production. Unlike the older, exclusionary American Federation of Labor (AFL), the "Wobblies," or IWW members, included unskilled workers, immi-grants from all ethnic backgrounds, African-Americans, and women.

John Sloan became an active member of the Socialist Party in 1909. In political cartoons published in left-wing journals, the artist expressed sympathy for the IWW and its dedication to the uncompromising pursuit of class warfare. His cover illustration for the June 1914 issue of *The Masses*, entitled *Class War in Colorado* (fig. 7.10), dramatically imagines a scene from the "Ludlow Massacre" of April 1914, in which striking miners in Ludlow, Colorado, defended themselves against National Guard troops and the strikebreaking agents of the Rockefellers, the wealthy New York family who owned the powerful Colorado Fuel & Iron Corporation.

Sloan sharply distinguished his political car-toons from his paintings, which remained free of overt socialist or anti-capitalist messages. Robert Henri, who favored the anarchistic position of a libertarian, stateless society, encouraged Sloan's inclination to employ the painting medium for the non-doctrinaire expression of individual feeling. Nevertheless, many contemporary friends and critics associated the New York realists' preference for lower-class subjects with socialism and radical political ideas. In organizing, in 1908, an independent exhibition of eight painters at New York's Macbeth Gallery at 450 Fifth Avenue, Henri was consciously rebelling against established cultural authority as symbolized by the conservative National Academy of Design. The exhibition of "The Eight" included Henri, Luks, Sloan, Glackens, and Shinn, the five original members of the Philadelphia realist circle, but not the younger Bellows, who was just beginning his career. These six painters later became known as the "Ashcan School," a term that referred to the group's gritty urban subjects, general preference for a dark palette, and roughly sketched painting style. Ashcan realists rebelled against feminine prettiness and academic correctness to express a masculine, virile energy, primarily symbolized by the teeming humanity of an increasingly urbanized America.

The Modernist Turn from Realism

The Eight included three other artists, whose works diverged from the Ashcan School's realist aesthetic: the Impressionist Ernest Lawson (1873–1939), the symbolist figure painter Arthur B. Davies (1862–1928), and Maurice Prendergast (1859–1924), an innovative painter of highly decorative, non-narrative pictures of parks and beach resorts. Influenced by the French artists Paul Cézanne (1839–1906), Henri Matisse (1869–1954), and others who went beyond Impressionism toward more abstract and non-naturalistic styles, Prendergast painted colorful pictures that differed significantly from the relatively conservative, illustrational painting techniques of the New York realists (fig. 7.11). In words that also could apply to later pictures of

7.11 Maurice Prendergast
Central Park, c. 1914. Oil on canvas, 20¾ x 27 in (52.7 x 68.6 cm). Metropolitan Museum of Art. George A. Hearn Fund, New York, 1950.

Prendergast admired the French painters Pierre Bonnard (1867–1947) and Edouard Vuillard (1867–1940), artists who integrated the human figure into an overall pattern of decorative colors. Similarly, Prendergast seems to weave a tapestry of dry-color patches, merging figures into flattened bands of space.

Central Park and other leisure sites, Arthur Hoeber, a hostile critic for the *New York Globe*, wrote in 1908 that the artist had sent to the Macbeth Gallery:

> *nearly a score of modest sized canvases, full of spots of color, with many people mainly on the beach at the French St. Malo, obviously a place where the sun shines in a curious manner, where color is made wonderfully manifest, where the people are careless about their drawing and construction, and where everything is a jumble of riotous pigment, such as one does not see elsewhere. Hung in a group, these canvases of Mr. Prendergast look for all the world like an explosion in a color factory (cited in Wattenmaker, p. 95).*

On the other hand, James Huneker, a critic who was more familiar with Modernist art in Paris, declared that, on the whole, the exhibition of the Eight at the Macbeth Gallery was "decidedly reactionary," "provincial," and "far from revolutionary" (cited in Wattenmaker, p. 96) when compared with the works of such avant-garde Europeans as Cézanne, Paul Gauguin (1848–1903), and Vincent van Gogh (1853–90). Yet Huneker's comparison was itself out of date, since all three of these Post-Impressionist painters had died and were being superseded by a new, even more stylistically radical generation of European artists working in Paris, Munich, and elsewhere.

Alfred Stieglitz, Photography, and the 291 Gallery

Even as The Eight's exhibition was creating a sensation with extensive newspaper publicity and crowds of visitors at the Macbeth Gallery, the photographer Alfred Stieglitz (1864–1946) was quietly operating a small gallery further downtown at 291 Fifth Avenue. Originally opened in 1905 as an exhibition space for fine-arts photographers, by 1907, Stieglitz's Little Galleries of the Photo-Secession, which came to be known as the 291 Gallery, was exhibiting the art of European and American painters and sculptors who had adopted various non-realist, individually expressive styles. Pamela Colman Smith (1877?–c. 1950), an American painter of decorative, visionary pictures symbolically representing mystical states of mind (fig. 7.12), was the first non-photographer to have a show at the gallery. Employing evocative analogies with the invisible tones and harmonies of music, Smith's anti-materialistic aesthetic appealed to Stieglitz, who ridiculed the paintings of Henri and the Ashcan School as illustrational, colored photographs.

Like other fine-arts photographers of the late nineteenth and early twentieth centuries, Stieglitz had favored an atmospheric, soft-focus

7.12 Pamela Colman Smith
The Wave, 1903.
Watercolor,
10¼ x 17¾ in
(26 x 45.1cm).
Whitney Museum of
American Art,
New York. Gift of
Mrs Sidney N. Heller.

Pictorialist style (see fig. 7.16) that enabled photography to compete with the evocative, spiritual effects of paintings by Whistler (see fig. 6.64) and other Gilded Age artists. Pictorialist photographers evaded the realist, documentary qualities of photography with different techniques. Out-of-focus or gauze-covered lenses were often used to suppress detail and attain a hazy effect. During the development process, photographers could further blur the image, alter the tones, or introduce colors into the final, painterly print. The photographer Edward Steichen (1879–1973), Stieglitz's partner in organizing the Little Galleries of the Photo-Secession, even represented himself as a painter with brush and palette in a Pictorialist, darkly mysterious *Self-Portrait* (fig. 7.13).

For Stieglitz, secession was a code word that signified rebellion against the cultural status quo and conventional, illustrational art. Having first studied photography in Berlin, he borrowed the term from German and Austrian avant-garde artists, who formed secessionist groups during the 1890s in opposition to established academies and exhibition societies. Stieglitz's Little Galleries of the Photo-Secession was originally intended as a permanent exhibition space for those fine-arts photographers who wished to secede from large exhibitions that indiscriminately displayed amateur and journalistic photographs without regard for aesthetic quality or formal stylistic values.

7.13 Edward Steichen
Self-Portrait with Palette and Brush, 1902.
Gum-bichromate print, 10½ x 7⅞ in (26.7 x 20 cm). Art Institute of Chicago, Chicago, Illinois. Alfred Stieglitz Collection.

Steichen's atmospheric self-representation was strongly influenced by his deep admiration for the Symbolist paintings of the French artist Eugène Carrière (1849–1906). As an art of nuance and spiritual suggestion, Symbolism sought to transcend the materialism of everyday life.

During the late nineteenth century, George Eastman's invention of the Kodak hand-held camera, loaded with its small roll of film, had created a national mania for photography. This invention had been made possible by the new dry-plate process of the 1880s. Unlike the earlier, cumbersome wet-plate process, photographic dry plates could be prepared in advance with a more effective light-sensitive emulsion. Civil War photographers had been forced to transport

7.14 Lewis Hine
Breaker Boys Working in Ewen Breaker, South Pittston, Pennsylvania, 1911.
Records of the Children's Bureau, National Archives, Washington, D.C.

This group portrait is one of a series representing young boys who worked in breakers, the mechanical plants for breaking up coal. Probably the sons of immigrants, the stiffly posed children look toward the camera with somber, coal-smudged faces. Huddled within the rail tracks, they seem embarked upon, and trapped within, a journey through life without hope.

Through his friend Marius
de Zayas (a Mexican-born
caricaturist and critic for
Stieglitz's journal *Camera
Work*), he learned that
Pablo Picasso greatly
admired the photograph
and regarded its dynamic
grid of geometric patterns
as a creative act of self-
expression. Stieglitz later
developed a theory of
equivalents, in which he
argued that all of his
photographs, no matter
what the subject, were
symbolic equivalents or
representations of his own
individual self and unique
vision.

how the formal values of the subject, rather than
its specific social content, excited his interest:

> *A round straw hat, the funnel leaning left, the
> stairway leaning right, the white drawbridge with
> its railings made of circular chains, white
> suspenders crossing on the back of a man in the
> steerage below, round shapes of iron machinery, a
> mast cutting into the sky, making a triangular
> shape. . . . I saw a picture of shapes and
> underlying that the feeling I had about life (cited
> in Newhall, p. 111).*

Stieglitz later regarded *The Steerage* as the most
important photograph of his career. Its sharply
focused forms marked a break with the painterly, nuanced effects of the Pictorialist style as seen
in his earlier *Spring Showers*, an atmospheric
New York City street scene (fig. 7.16). By 1910,
Stieglitz was becoming an advocate of straight
photography. This style rejected the artificial
manipulation of photographic images in favor
of a sharper lens focus that underscored the
inherent formal values found within nature
or everyday modern life. Stieglitz eventually
believed that each medium should explore and
emphasize its own particular qualities and formal
characteristics. While the mechanical art of photography should not compete with painting or
sculpture for handmade effects, neither should
these more traditional media attempt to replicate
the realism of the camera. In a 1910 article published in *Camera Work*, his own fine-arts journal,
Stieglitz argued that photography's reproductive
accuracy had made realist painting and drawing
styles virtually obsolete.

After 1910, Stieglitz's refusal to promote Pictorialist photography alienated such fine-arts
photographers as Clarence White (1871–1925)
and Gertrude Kasebier (1852–1934). Instead, as
director of the 291 Gallery, Stieglitz exhibited
the straight photography of Paul Strand (1890–
1976) and, as editor of *Camera Work*, published
Strand's pictures in the last issues of the journal.
Strand's photograph, *The White Fence* (fig. 7.17),
focuses upon the abstract design of an American
vernacular form. For Stieglitz and his circle,
Modernist abstraction was not some alien force
but an expression of the democratic American
spirit. Nevertheless, prior to 1917, Stieglitz drew
inspiration from Europe, and devoted himself
to exhibitions of European and American

heavy wagons filled with chemicals and equipment onto battlefields. The wet-plate process
had required that glass plates, carefully hand-
coated with an emulsion just before shooting,
remain wet throughout the camera exposure
and darkroom development. The mechanical
simplification of photography allowed millions
of individual amateurs to take their own family
pictures. Influencing the paintings of the Ashcan
School and encouraging progressive social
reforms, a number of documentary photographers, led by Jacob Riis (see p. 295) and Lewis
Hine (1874–1940), utilized the new portability
of the camera to capture stark scenes of urban
blight, child labor, and immigrant and working-
class poverty (fig. 7.14).

Stieglitz's most famous photograph, *The
Steerage* (fig. 7.15), shares the same type of subject
matter as represented by Hine and the Ashcan
School of painters. Stieglitz took the picture on
the spur of the moment, while sailing to Europe
on a fashionable new German ocean liner. Having left his first-class accommodations, he
wandered toward the steerage, or lower levels of
the ship, where he saw the poorer passengers
crowded together. Stieglitz found himself energized by this scene of migratory European
workers, who were returning home after temporary employment in America. However,
unlike documentary photographers, he recalled

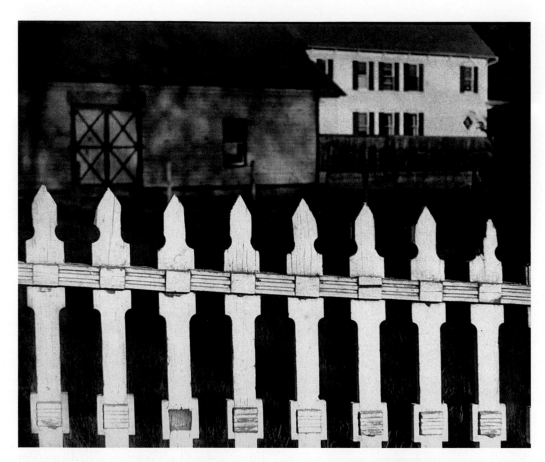

7.17 Paul Strand
The White Fence, 1917.
Photogravure in *Camera Work*, no. 49–50.
Museum of Modern Art,
New York.

7.18 Pablo Picasso
Drawing, 1910.
Photogravure,
19 1/16 x 12 5/16 in
(48.5 x 31.2 cm), from
Camera Work, no. 36,
October 1911.
Metropolitan Museum of
Art. Alfred Stieglitz
Collection, 1949.

Modernist painters and sculptors. Assisted by
Edward Steichen, who kept him abreast of artistic developments in Paris, Stieglitz did not
adhere to an exhibition schedule that favored
any single visual style. But in introducing to
American audiences the works of such major
French artists as Cézanne, Matisse, and Auguste
Rodin (1840–1917), the 291 Gallery became a
haven for anti-academic painters and sculptors
asserting their independence from the slavish
imitation of nature.

For Stieglitz, innovative avant-garde art was a
virtual religion, a spiritual alternative to Gilded
Age materialism and the Protestant, middle-class
repression of the senses. Thanks to his first wife's
income from a family brewery in Brooklyn,
Stieglitz had the luxury of operating the 291
Gallery as a high-minded aesthetic calling rather
than a crassly commercial enterprise. But his
cause was not the art for art's sake of an apolitical
aesthete. Although not associated with socialist
or communist political organizations, the gallery
director always regarded himself as a revolution-

ary, who broadly believed that radical, individualized artistic expression possessed the power to liberate society from the repressive, dead weight of economic utilitarianism and outmoded cultural conventions, traditions, and habits.

As his recollection of *The Steerage* suggests, Stieglitz did not reject twentieth-century technology and machinery, but rather sought to reconcile its rational structure and functionalism with the arbitrary, accidental movements and shifting, spontaneous perceptions of non-rational, immediate experience. Significantly, Stieglitz boasted that this photograph elicited words of praise from Pablo Picasso (1881–1973), the Spanish-born Parisian artist who promoted Cubism, the abstract geometric style that most vividly expressed the Modernist desire to integrate the diverse perspectives and fluctuating experiences of modern life. Beginning with his famous 1907 painting *Les Demoiselles d'Avignon*, Picasso launched the Cubist assault on Renaissance tradition by fracturing and merging the human figure with the flat, two-dimensional space of the picture plane. In fragmenting forms and destroying the Renaissance illusion of three-dimensional space, Picasso and other Cubist painters denied the existence of a fixed, objective reality. Influenced by developments in geometry, philosophy, and science, which demonstrated that truth was not absolute but relative and a matter of pragmatic usefulness, Cubists rebelled against the supposed objectivity and universality of academic rules and conventions.

Stieglitz played a major role in introducing Cubist art into the United States by giving Picasso his first American one-man show at the 291 Gallery in 1911 and by juxtaposing reproductions of the Spaniard's abstract drawings next to his own photographs in *Camera Work*. Picasso's drawing of a female nude (fig. 7.18) particularly pleased Stieglitz, who purchased the work and noted its formal resemblance to his photograph *Spring Showers* (see fig. 7.16), taken seven years before the beginning of the Cubist revolution. In 1913, Stieglitz also purchased five drawings by the Paris-based Russian sculptor Alexander Archipenko (1887–1964). With its geometric interplay of voids and convex-concave shapes, Archipenko's later Cubist sculpture, *Seated Woman* (fig. 7.19), employs empty spaces as

7.19 Alexander Archipenko
Seated Woman (Geometric Figure Seated), 1920. Painted plaster, 22½ in (57 cm) high. The Tel Aviv Museum, Israel.

After settling in the United States, Archipenko spent much of his time teaching art and art theory in schools throughout the nation. Building on his Cubist sculptures of interlocking positive-negative spaces and convex-concave forms, the Russian-born artist played a significant role in gaining public acceptance for sculpture as a non-narrative, abstract medium for studying tectonics, or formal structures.

7.20 Max Weber
Composition with Three Figures, 1910. Gouache and watercolor over black crayon on cardboard, 47 x 23 in (119.4 x 58.4 cm). Ackland Art Museum, University of North Carolina, Chapel Hill. Ackland Fund.

Weber's adoption of a Cubist figural style coincided with an article on "The Wild Men of Paris", published in the May 1910 issue of the *Architectural Record* and illustrated with reproductions of Picasso's Cubist paintings. Weber's figures possess sharply defined geometric features, borrowed from the simplified shapes of African masks and sculptures.

7.21 Alvin Langdon Coburn
The Octopus, New York, 1912.
International Museum of Photography and Film, George Eastman House, Rochester, New York.

Influenced by the art educator Arthur Wesley Dow (1857–1922), Coburn was attracted to the abstract, two-dimensional designs of Japanese art. Favoring an atmospheric, Pictorialist aesthetic, Coburn immersed himself in Symbolist, mystical thought and became involved in the occult, ritualistic lore of Freemasonry. This is one of a series of photographs that resulted from the camera lens being directed downward from the dizzying heights atop New York skyscrapers. The resulting images expressed the enigmatic, vitalistic spirit of modern life.

positive design elements. Just as Cubist painters merged abstract figures with the pictorial background, so did Archipenko (who moved to New York in 1923) integrate sculptural mass with ambient, activated space.

Stieglitz's education in Cubist aesthetics was facilitated by Max Weber (1881–1961), a Russian-born, Jewish immigrant whose devoutly religious family had settled in Brooklyn, New York, in 1891. At Brooklyn's Pratt Institute of Art from 1898 to 1900, Weber studied under Arthur Wesley Dow (1857–1922), a devotee of Oriental art, who taught students the radical principle that art developed from a consciousness of abstract formal relationships rather than any impulse or obligation to imitate nature. Dow's instruction prepared Weber for his eventual encounter with Matisse, Picasso, and other European Modernist artists, whom he met during his residence in Paris from 1906 to 1909. Together with other American expatriate painters such as Alfred Henry Maurer (1868–1932), John Marin (1870–1953), and Patrick Henry Bruce (1881–1936), Weber became a founding member of the New Society of American Artists in Paris, organized by Edward Steichen, Stieglitz's talent scout for the 291 Gallery.

Upon returning to New York in 1909, Weber had long conversations with Stieglitz about the meaning of the Cubist revolution, but it was not until 1910 that Weber began to assimilate the abstract new style into his own work. At first, he painted large female nudes (fig. 7.20), whose crystalline geometry and African, mask-like faces resembled early Cubist figurative works by

7.22 Max Weber
New York, 1913.
Oil on canvas,
40⅝ x 32½ in
(103.1 x 82.5 cm).
Thyssen-Bornemisza
Collection, Lugano,
Switzerland.

The English critic and art
theorist Roger Fry included
this Weber painting in an
exhibition of English
Modernist art in 1913. An
art review for *The London
Times*, entitled "Artist Cult of
the Horrible: Exhibition of
Wild Eccentricities,"
ridiculed Weber's picture by
comparing its forms to a
concertina or accordion that
had become fatally
ensnarled with the stars and
stripes of the American flag
and a serpent playing hide
and seek.

Picasso and Georges Braque (1882–1963), the French inventor of Cubism. However, like Stieglitz, Weber soon began to compare the fractured, interpenetrating planes of Cubism to the dynamic abstract geometry of the urban landscape captured by Modernist photography. The painter became a close friend of Alvin Langdon Coburn (1882–1966), who shared Stieglitz's interest in taking formalist photographs of New York City streets and skyscrapers. Coburn's most famous photograph, *The Octopus, New York* (fig. 7.21), was taken from the top of the Metropolitan Life Insurance Company Tower, a 700-foot, fifty-story structure that was for a brief time the tallest skyscraper in the world. Coburn aimed his camera downward at Madison Square, with its pattern of radiating paths resembling the multi-armed sea creature. In the photograph's left half,

the monumental tower casts its shadow over the snow-covered park and dwarfs the diminutive trees and street traffic below. For Coburn, the modern, mechanical art of photography was the medium most suited for recording skyscrapers and the new age of science and steel.

Max Weber, however, disagreed with his friend by arguing that the eye of the painter was more flexible and sensitive than the camera lens. Guided by the mind rather than a mechanical device, the painter's body is immersed more immediately and completely in the sensory experience of the moment, spiritually and physically stimulated by the city's kaleidoscopic sounds, motions, colors, lights, and forms. In *New York* (fig. 7.22), one of his first cityscapes, Weber attempts to induce in the beholder a dizzying reverie with a maze of tall architectural forms tilted at odd angles with one another. Disengaged from any firm ground or space below, the flat, light skyscraper forms seem to float toward the top of the canvas. Meanwhile, recalling Coburn's *Octopus*, Weber weaves a serpentine line throughout the picture. This urban boa constrictor represents New York's elevated trains and mass transportation system. Plunging into and emerging out of gaping earthen holes, the circulating, snakelike form also suggests the new subway system, which recently had been inaugurated in 1904.

The Influence of Futurism and the Vitalism of Nature

Stieglitz first exhibited Weber's paintings in 1910 in a group show of "Younger American Artists," which also included works by John Marin, Alfred Maurer, Arthur Dove (1880–1946), Marsden Hartley (1877–1943), and Arthur B. Carles (1882–1952), who were all adopting anti-realist painting styles. Like Weber, Marin had studied in Paris for several years, from 1905 to 1910, but he did not adopt an abstract style until after Picasso's one-man show at the 291 Gallery in 1911. In a series of watercolors representing the newly constructed Woolworth Building in Lower Manhattan, Marin abandoned his earlier more meditative and Whistlerian technique of paint application in favor of an explosive style that suggests not only the influence of Cubism, but also the paintings of the Italian Futurists (fig. 7.23). This group of artists, which included Giacomo Balla (1871–1958), Umberto Boccioni (1882–1916), Carlo Carrà (1881–1966), and Gino Severini (1883–1966), adopted Cubist fragmentation and interpenetration of forms to suggest lines of force, motion, and the dynamism of the machine age. Originating as a movement in Milan, the Italian Futurists opened their first group show in Paris in 1912 by dramatically proclaiming in their catalogue manifesto "we are young and our art is violently revolutionary" in its opposition to academicism and classical "traditionalism" (cited in Chipp, p. 294).

While the architect Cass Gilbert (1859–1934) designed the decorative details of the Woolworth Building in a historical-revival, Gothic style (fig. 7.24), Marin's spontaneous brushwork virtually obliterates all references to European medieval tradition. Marin's *Woolworth Building, No. 31* expresses a futuristic world in which the world's

7.23 John Marin
Woolworth Building, No.31, 1912.
Watercolor over graphite, 18½ x 15¹¹⁄₁₆ in (46.9 x 39.9 cm).
National Gallery of Art, Washington, D.C.
Gift of Eugene and Agnes E. Meyer.

tallest skyscraper appears to shudder with motion like a rocket ship preparing to take off from a collapsing launch pad. Despite the heavy masonry and steel structure of the actual building, Marin emphasizes its glassy transparency and anti-gravitational verticality as the architecture merges with the watery brushstrokes defining the luminous sky.

On the other hand, Stieglitz and his circle were wary of Futurist machine worship. Industrial technology was tainted by a base utilitarianism, or vulgar economic materialism, which seemed antithetical to the transcendent experience of the aesthetic emotion. As suggested by the animistic, serpentine forms of Weber and Coburn (see figs. 7.20–7.22), American modernists often reinterpreted cityscapes in organic, naturalistic terms to express more universal, essential feelings of growth and development. Marin's pulsating skyscrapers have also been compared with growing, juicy plants energized by the sun's light.

7.24 Cass Gilbert
Woolworth Building,
New York City,
1911–13.
New York Historical
Society, New York.

Though not a member of the Stieglitz circle, the Midwestern artist Charles Burchfield (1893–1967) painted in a manner equating organic and architectural, cathedral-like forms. His small watercolor of *The Luminous Tree* (fig. 7.25) is animated by a solar, radiating disc nestled within a womb of foliage. Pulsating white dots of paint and energetic, almost-airborne, leafy new growth cap tree and shrubbery with a protective arch, evocative of a Gothic cathedral. In its cosmic, luminous spirit, Burchfield's picture is reminiscent of Hannah Cohoon's Shaker visionary gift drawing, *Tree of Light or Blazing Tree* (see fig. 5.55).

Artists in the Stieglitz circle excelled in painting expressive, abstract landscapes, seascapes, and plant forms. Most famously, Stieglitz exhibited the work of Wisconsin-born artist Georgia O'Keeffe (1887–1986), who became known for her sensuous, sexually charged pictures of flowers. O'Keeffe's *Inside Red Canna* (fig. 7.26), invites beholders to imaginatively follow along the silken red tones of the flower petals, sliding inside and out of the blossom's vagina-like interior. The close-up, symmetrical view of the red canna lily accentuates the flower's abstract shape, which O'Keeffe exaggerates with overlapping, sharp petal edges that rhythmically and alternately penetrate inward and flow outward. The flower thus suggests the masculine as well as the feminine, an androgynous, vitalistic union of opposites at the heart of nature.

Stieglitz strongly promoted O'Keeffe's work as part of his campaign to liberate Americans from the sexually repressive legacy of Puritan tradition. But he also limited her identity and defined her strictly as a "female" artist, whose work was essentially biologically determined. In 1919, the same year O'Keeffe painted *Inside Red Canna*, Stieglitz wrote an essay on "Woman in Art," which made the following claim:

> *Woman feels the World differently than Man feels it. And one of the chief generating forces crystallizing into art is undoubtedly elemental feeling. The Woman receives the World through her Womb. That is the seat of her deepest feeling. Mind comes second (cited in Corn, p. 241).*

Though she married the much older Stieglitz in 1924, O'Keeffe resisted his gendered strictures on her creativity. Over her husband's opposition, she began painting a series of New York City skyscraper pictures. Stieglitz assumed the phallic, masculine skyscraper shapes were unsuitable subjects for a woman. However, in paintings such as *City Night* (fig. 7.27), O'Keeffe draws our gaze downward and inward as well as upward. The canyon-like space between the towering architectural forms successfully competes for our attention, thanks to the light of a full moon, a traditional feminine symbol. In reinterpreting the modern city, O'Keeffe brings it back down to nature and another androgynous marriage of male and female forms, signifying the hermetic, unifying harmonies of the creative act.

Outside the Stieglitz circle of painters, the Italian-American immigrant Joseph Stella (1877–1946) was more directly affected by the Italian Futurists, since he was in Paris for their widely publicized show. Having arrived in the United States from Naples in 1896, Stella identified closely with the immigrant community in New York and remained homesick for his native Italy, which he revisited in 1909 just as the Futurist movement was announced by the

7.25 Charles Burchfield
The Luminous Tree, 1917.
Watercolor on paper, 19⅞ x 14 in (50.5 x 35.5cm). Brauer Museum of Art, Valparaiso University, Valparaiso, Indiana. Gift of Charles E. Burchfield Foundation.

7.26 Georgia O'Keeffe
Inside Red Canna, 1919.
Oil on canvas, 22 x 17in (55.9 x 43.2cm). Scharf Family Collection.

7.27 Georgia O'Keeffe
City Night, 1926.
Oil on canvas, 48 x 30 in
(121.9 x 76.2 cm).
Minneapolis Institute of
Arts, Minnesota. Gift of
Regis Corporation, W.
John Driscoll, and the
Beim Foundation; the
Larsen Fund; and by
public subscription.

later recalled, the old-fashioned harmonies of Renaissance Old Master painters seemed remote or dead in contrast to the dazzling, conflicting riot of swirling forms and light rays which excited Coney Island crowds during the annual Mardi Gras celebration. Stella's *Battle of Lights, Coney Island, Mardi Gras* (fig. 7.28) represents the hedonistic, carnivalesque frenzy created by dizzying rides, popular games, side shows, colorful electric lights, and exotic, decorative architecture. Unlike the sedate, classical idealism of the White City at the World's Columbian Exposition in 1893 (see fig. 6.16), Coney Island's environment had no reformist, morally didactic purpose. Attempting to revitalize high art, Stella created a kaleidoscopic painting that implicitly endorsed commercialized mass culture's rejection of the refined, genteel tradition in favor of irrational, bodily pleasures.

Nevertheless, lower-class commercial amusements actually served to reinforce the social status quo by restricting bizarre, raucous behavior within a controlled environment for a brief period of leisure time. By contrast, leaders of the Modernist art movement in America hoped to radically transform society with forms and images that liberated the senses and human imagination from the stifling dictates of conventional morality and materialism. A few months before Stella's Coney Island conversion to anti-realist abstraction, the American public had responded with excitement and bewilderment to the International Exhibition of Modern Art held at the 69th Infantry Regiment Armory in New York City. The poster for this mammoth show of some 1,300 paintings, sculptures, and prints by both European and American artists featured a Revolutionary War pine-tree flag, thereby associating the Modernist rebellion against academic art with the American War for Independence. Ironically, the Association of American Painters and Sculptors, which sponsored the so-called Armory Show, had a membership that overlapped with that of the conservative National Academy of Design. But the organization's president, Arthur B. Davies, had earlier exhibited with the rebellious Robert Henri and The Eight. Davies's controversial conception of the Armory Show as a survey of modern art from its early-nineteenth-century European roots in the art of Eugène Delacroix (1798–1863) and

Milanese poet Filippo Tommaso Marinetti (1876–1944). Before his trip to Italy, Stella made numerous detailed drawings of hard-working laborers and impoverished immigrants, whose somber, anxious moods contrast starkly with the generally optimistic portraits of the poor by Ashcan School realists. However, a year after returning to New York, he underwent an enthusiastic, quasi-religious conversion to the Futuristic aesthetic when he visited the amusement parks of New York's Coney Island. As he

7.28 Joseph Stella
Battle of Lights, Coney Island, Mardi Gras, 1913–14.
Oil on canvas, 75¾ x 84 in (192.4 x 213.3 cm). Yale University Art Gallery, New Haven, Connecticut. Gift of Collection Société Anonyme.

American popular culture is celebrated in the cacophony of electric lights, honky-tonk signs, exotic dancers, confetti, and the radiating steel girders of amusement rides.

Jean-Auguste-Dominique Ingres (1780–1867) to its twentieth-century culmination in Picasso and the Cubist revolution inevitably alienated more tradition-bound artists.

Modernism and Political Radicalism

Although the Armory Show did not include works by the Italian Futurists, the participating Stella and other American artists were stirred by the generally hostile rhetoric of newspaper critics, which described Cubism as a distorted, futuristic style. Newspapers particularly lampooned the exhibition's most talked-about painting, *Nude Descending a Staircase No. 2* (fig. 7.29), by the French Cubist Marcel Duchamp (1887–1968). One cartoonist for the *New York Evening Sun* very wittily satirized Duchamp's canvas with a frenzied contemporary scene of *The Rude Descending the Staircase (Rush Hour at the Subway)* (fig. 7.30). Duchamp's painting may be compared to the visual multiplication of the human form as recorded in motion photography, a realist medium (see fig. 6.39). Like motion photography, his montage, or juxtaposition of diverse forms, parallels the pictorial flux of cinema, a new medium admired by Modernist artists.

7.29 Marcel Duchamp
Nude Descending a Staircase, No. 2, 1912.
Oil on canvas, 58 x 35 in (147.3 x 88.9 cm). Philadelphia Museum of Art, Philadelphia, Pennsylvania. Arensberg Collection.

Duchamp's painting was exhibited in the Cubist Room, which became popularly designated as the Chamber of Horrors. Nevertheless, the work attracted long lines of visitors. One critic suggested that the painting be renamed "Profit" for its role in attracting paying, if bemused, customers.

7.30 J. F. Griswold
The Rude Descending the Staircase (Rush Hour at the Subway).
Cartoon, New York Evening Sun, March 20, 1913.

The satirical cartoon of Duchamp's painting visually underscores the equation that academic artists and critics made between Cubism and anarchism. As the American Renaissance painter Kenyon Cox declared in the March 15th, 1913, issue of *Harper's Weekly*:

> . . . the real meaning of this Cubist movement is nothing else than the total destruction of the art of painting. . . . The important question is what it is proposed to substitute for this art of painting which the world has cherished since there were men definitely differentiated from beasts. They have abolished the representation of nature and all forms of recognized and traditional decoration; what will they give us instead?. . . In some strange way they [the French Cubists] have made their work revolting and defiling. To have looked at it is to have passed through a pathological museum where the layman has no right to go. One feels that one has not seen an exhibition, but an exposure.
>
> . . . The lack of discipline and the exaltation of the individual have been the destructive forces of modern art, and they began their work long ago. For a time the persistence of earlier ideals and the possession by the revolutionaries of the very training which they attacked as unnecessary saved the art from entire dissolution. Now all discipline has disappeared. . . (cited in McCoubrey, pp. 194–195).

When the Armory Show opened in February, 1913, its identification with the American revolutionary tradition was reinforced by a contemporaneous strike of textile workers led by the Industrial Workers of the World (see p. 305) in nearby Paterson, New Jersey. Big Bill Haywood, the union's leader, recruited the support of New York political activists as well as Modernist artists and writers, who lived and socialized primarily in Manhattan's Greenwich Village. Shortly after the Armory Show closed in March, Hutchins Hapsgood, a leftist critic for the *New York Globe*, likened Modernist art to the IWW and claimed that both Haywood and Stieglitz possessed a common revolutionary desire to "dynamite the baked and hardened earth so that fresh flowers can grow" (cited in Abrahams, p. 166). Hapsgood reviewed an exhibition by Arthur Dove at Stieglitz's 291 Gallery, in which he praised that painter's

7.31 Arthur Dove
Nature Symbolized
No.2, 1911.
Pastel on paper.
18 x 21 ⅝ in
(45.8 x 55cm).
Art Institute of Chicago,
Chicago, Illinois.
Alfred Strieglitz Collection.

One of a series of ten pastels that Dove exhibited in 1912, this composition was intended as a representation of the effect of wind blowing on a hillside. For the swirling forms, Dove chose earth colors, green for the trees and cyan-blue for the glimpses of sky.

simplification of nature to the rhythmic, harmonic essentials of color and form (fig. 7.31). He compared it with the labor movement's intense struggle to reject socioeconomic hierarchies and achieve independence and self-control. Hapsgood quoted Dove, who endorsed the notion that the contemporary artist could not "cut himself away from labor or other [social] movements" without sacrificing an essential vitality in art (cited in Antliff, p. 38). Contemporary cultural critics saw a connection between the Modernist revolt against academic art and the working class's rebellion against the capitalist system of wage labor and factory discipline. Both were opposed to the status quo and aspired to transcend the limitations of exploitative social relationships and deadening cultural habits. In their different spheres, both Modernist art and radical politics seemed to promise a future state of individual creative freedom and communal harmony.

On June 7, 1913, a manifestation of this alliance occurred when 1,200 textile workers from Paterson represented a history of their strike in a pageant organized by a group of radical Greenwich Village intellectuals and artists, who had earlier championed the Armory Show. Performing at New York's Madison Square Garden before an enormous crowd of 16,000 spectators, the striking workers and IWW members recreated dramatic scenes of their struggle against textile company owners. The Fifth Avenue socialite Mabel Dodge, who actively supported Modernist artists and wrote a favorable article on the Armory Show for *Camera Work*, assisted the radical political writer John Reed in rehearsing and directing the pageant. An exhibitor at the Armory Show, the Ashcan School realist John Sloan painted for the pageant a 200-foot theatrical backdrop representing a textile mill. A poster advertising the performance featured a youthful, virile worker boldly climbing upward and forward against a dark prison-house background of factory buildings and smokestacks (fig. 7.32). Despite this remarkable fusion of art and politics and an overflow

7.32 Robert Edmond Jones
Program cover for the Paterson Strike Pageant, 1913.
Poster. Tamiment Library, New York University, New York.

for the benefit of America's economic or corporate expansion abroad.

By contrast, the Modernist artist Marsden Hartley, who had exhibited at the 291 Gallery and the Armory Show, traveled to Berlin in 1913, where he painted a series of pictures celebrating the pageantry of German military parades, uniforms, flags, and medals. An avid reader of mystical occult texts and a participant in the German Expressionist art movement, Hartley associated Germany with its tradition of idealist philosophy and Romantic art, music, and poetry. While Cubist artists in Paris seemed preoccupied by technical, formal problems of pictorial representation, Berlin Expressionists appeared to Hartley more concerned with expressing an inner spiritual content by means of vivid colors and mysterious abstract signs. Led by the Russian painter Wassily Kandinsky (1866–1944), these artists had organized themselves into the Blaue Reiter (Blue Rider) group, a name that clearly conjured forth in Hartley's mind images of gallant, chivalrous knights or warriors willing to sacrifice themselves for a noble cause (fig. 7.33). Hartley's most famous military painting, *Portrait of a German Officer* (fig. 7.34), memorializes his friend and lover Karl von Freyburg, who was killed early in World War I. Rather than painting a traditional likeness, Hartley evokes his friend's spiritual presence with a funereal shroud of colorful flags, badges, and military paraphernalia, set against a melancholic black background. The initials K.V.F. in the lower-left corner identify the deceased, while a twisting letter E inscribed upon an epaulet refers to Hartley himself, whose original, given name was Edmund. During a period when homosexuality was not only illegal but still condemned by most doctors and intellectuals, Hartley declared his love for Freyburg in a private code of letters, numbers, and signs, and then only after his friend's death.

Despite his German sympathies, Hartley was forced to leave war-torn Berlin, where he found it impossible to find buyers for his paintings. The market in the United States for abstract, Modernist art was little better. While a number of new galleries displaying avant-garde art opened after 1913, the Armory Show had actually cast the works of young American artists in the shadows of leading European painters and sculptors.

audience of supporters, the pageant lost money and created divisions among the textile workers, who were soon forced to capitulate to the company's terms. In the process, thousands of strikers were arrested and replaced by strikebreakers, while the IWW declined as a force in the American labor movement.

Modernist Art and World War I

By the end of 1913, the optimistic spirit of collaboration between American artists and workers had suffered from the disillusioning failure to transform America's socioeconomic and cultural life. When World War I began in Europe in August of 1914, socialists at home and abroad were placed on the defensive as governments called upon workers to abandon class warfare in favor of an imperial war patriotically pursued for the advancement of national interests. When the United States entered the war against Germany in 1917, socialist and IWW leaders were arrested for arguing against the sacrifice of workers' lives

7.33 Marsden Hartley
Warriors, 1913.
Oil on canvas,
41¾ x 47⅓ in
(106 x 119.8 cm).
Curtis Galleries Inc.,
Minneapolis, Minnesota.

Hartley's painting
commemorates a military
parade in Berlin celebrating
the marriage of Kaiser
Wilhelm II's daughter. The
implicitly homoerotic
representation of the
equestrian guards' military
comradery centers upon a
tiered, phallic-shaped
mountain rising to the top
of the canvas as a symbol
of valorous, manly striving.

Typifying the contrast from a negative perspective, the conservative academic artist-critic Kenyon Cox had directed his bitter attack on the Armory Show at the wild, foreign productions of Picasso and the Parisian Cubists. At the same time, he dismissively referred to a pair of Hartley's drawings as "purely nugatory," or of no consequence.

Synchromism

In 1916, Hartley participated in the Forum Exhibition of Modern American Painters, which attempted to stimulate market demand by demonstrating the independent, consequential meaning of a national movement toward Modernist abstraction. Organized by the art critic and anti-war pacifist Willard Huntington Wright, the Forum Exhibition of sixteen artists' paintings at the Anderson Galleries in New York was publicized as an anti-commercial venture, representing a diversity of individual styles. Acknowledging that "many charlatans have allied themselves with the [modern art] movement," the Forum Exhibition Catalogue blamed "the commercial element" for confusing the American buying public, which had been, until

7.34 Marsden Hartley
Portrait of a German Officer, 1914.
Oil on canvas,
68¼ x 41⅜ in
(173.4 x 104.9 cm).
Metropolitan Museum of Art, New York. Alfred Stieglitz Collection, 1949.

7.35 Stanton Macdonald-Wright
Abstraction on Spectrum (Organization No. 5),
1914.
Oil on canvas,
30⅛ x 24³⁄₁₆ in
(76.5 x 61.5 cm).
Des Moines Art Center,
Des Moines, Iowa.
Purchased with funds
from the Coffin Fine Arts
Trust. Nathan Emory
Coffin Collection.

Macdonald-Wright did not
purport to represent any
recognizable object in this
work. Sharing much in
common with the French
Orphist paintings of Robert
Delaunay (1855–1941) and
Sonia Delaunay (1884–
1979), Macdonald-Wright's
color abstraction focused on
the expressive power of the
painting medium itself.

7.36 Morgan Russell
Cosmic Synchromy,
1913–14.
Oil on canvas,
16¼ x 13⅛ in
(41.2 x 33.3 cm).
Munson-Williams-Proctor
Institute, Museum of Art,
Utica, New York.

Although Synchromists
tended to reject traditional,
illustrative forms of
representation, they were
influenced by the formal
rhythms of figural works by
Michelangelo (1475–1564)
and Peter Paul Rubens
(1577–1640). Preparatory
drawings suggest that
Russell conceived these
spiraling, polychromatic
discs from the circular
motion of two nude figures,
interlocked in a yin-yang
configuration, an oriental
symbol signifying the cosmic
balance of opposing
principles such as male-
female and active-passive.
Russell's warm-cool,
advancing-receding colors
expressed a universal,
spiritual harmony.

now, "unable to differentiate between the sincere and insincere" (Anderson Galleries, p. 6). Nevertheless, Wright obviously designed the show to promote primarily the "Synchromist" paintings of his brother Stanton Macdonald-Wright (1890–1973) and his friend Morgan Russell (1886–1953). The two artists, working among the Cubists in Paris, had founded the Synchromist movement in 1913 to reassert the prominence of strong color contrasts as an integral, rhythmic dimension of abstract art. In explaining such works as *Abstraction on Spectrum (Organization No. 5)* (fig. 7.35), which was reproduced in the Forum Exhibition catalogue, Stanton Macdonald-Wright wrote that he strove to divest his colorfully pulsating art "of all anecdote and illustration, and to purify it to the point where the emotions of the spectator will be wholly aesthetic, as when listening to good music" (Anderson Galleries, p. 56). By stressing the aesthetic transcendence of daily existence, the artist

7.37 Man Ray
War (AD MCMXIV),
1914.
Oil on canvas,
36⅞ x 69¾ in
(92.7 x 177.2cm).
Philadelphia Museum
of Art, Philadelphia,
Pennsylvania.
A.E. Gallatin Collection.

Man Ray's flattened, blasted
landscape of robotic figures
includes a besieged mother
and her fallen child on the
right side of the
composition. The picture's
claustrophobic violence
expressed Man Ray's
opposition to the
oppressiveness of the
modern state and its
capitalistic, war-profiteering
supporters.

implicitly underscored the anti-commercial, quasi-religious emotional content of Modernist art. Similarly, Morgan Russell described his exhibition painting *Cosmic Synchromy* (fig. 7.36) as a modern-day version of medieval cathedral music.

These co-founders of Synchromism were necessarily motivated by financial self-interest. As Macdonald-Wright confided to Russell in a revealing letter about the Forum Exhibition dating from early 1916:

> Here goes to invite you to a big show . . . which will for once and all establish you as a selling factor in this country. Willard is getting it up in conjunction with Kennerley, the president of the Anderson Galleries (the biggest selling gallery in the world, and by the way, the most sumptuous and whose patrons are the Rockefellers, the Yerkes, Harrimans, the Morgans and the rest of the rich ones). . . . These galleries when they lend their name to a show are as good as cash. . . . You and I, because of our reputation will sell every thing (cited in Agee, p. 89).

Modernism for the Masses

Expressing political distance from the Modernist pre-war alliance with socialism, Macdonald-Wright unabashedly encouraged Russell to imagine the possible patronage of America's leading capitalist entrepreneurs. Ironically, John Weichsel (1870–1946), a Jewish socialist intellectual and advocate of introducing Modernist art to lower-class, immigrant communities, was on the organizing committee for the Forum Exhibition and wrote an exhibition catalogue statement criticizing American men of wealth for supporting reactionary classical art. Despite Macdonald-

Wright's hopes, the Forum Exhibition did not result in significant sales for the participating painters. Eight years earlier, at the Macbeth Gallery, the more conservative realist paintings of The Eight had garnered $4,000 in sales, which John Sloan regarded as a great success. However, the American art public was far less attracted to Modernist abstraction. By 1918, Macdonald-Wright's impoverished circumstances forced him to leave New York City for California. Similarly, Morgan Russell and Patrick Henry Bruce, the two other leading Synchromists in the Forum Exhibition, suffered financially from meager sales of their work. When Stieglitz suspended publication of *Camera Work* in 1917, this important Modernist art journal, which promoted avant-garde painting and sculpture, had a subscription list of only thirty-six names.

In contrast to Stieglitz, who refused to commercially advertise Modernist art exhibitions at the 291 Gallery, John Weichscl systematically attempted to popularize avant-garde art. He admired the work of Man Ray (1890–1977), the son of Russian Jewish immigrants whose first major abstract painting, *War (AD MCMXIV)* (fig. 7.37) visually critiqued the mechanistic inhumanity of the new war in Europe. The artist dedicated a sketch of *War* to Weichsel. During 1915–17, Weichsel established the People's Art Guild, which sponsored modern art exhibitions in the restaurants, theaters, schools, and immigrant settlement houses of poor New York neighborhoods. Although his socialistic goal of democratizing the audience for Modernist painting and sculpture was dismissed as naive by Stieglitz and Willard Wright, most of the artists who exhibited in Wright's Forum Exhibition, including Macdonald-Wright, later exhibited in 1917 at Weichsel's large, eighty-nine-person "Lower East Side Exhibition" at the Jewish Daily Forward Building on East Broadway, a down-market, downtown-Manhattan venue. The People's Art Guild's most popular exhibition, this event, known as the Forward Show, reportedly attracted numerous working-class visitors. They viewed not only familiar scenes of Lower East Side life by Ashcan School realists, but also the challenging abstract cityscapes of immigrant artists such as Joseph Stella (see fig. 7.28) and the Russian-born Abraham Walkowitz (1878–1965). Nevertheless, sales from the People's Art Guild exhibitions were negligible and, by 1919, Weichsel's organization had disappeared from the New York art scene.

Marcel Duchamp and New York Dada

The 1917 Forward Show was overshadowed by the far more glamorous and highly publicized first Exhibition of the Society of Independent Artists, the largest art show ever held in New York, comprising over 2,500 paintings and sculptures by more than 1,000 artists. Financially supported by a group of wealthy New York patrons, the independent exhibition was organized by realist artists but had no jury and was open to anyone who paid the Society's small initiation fee and modest annual dues. Joseph Stella

7.38 Marcel Duchamp
Fountain (original lost), 1917.
Gelatin silver print, 9¼ x 7 in (23.4 x 17.7 cm), by Alfred Stieglitz, reproduced in *The Blind Man*, No. 2 (May 1917). Philadelphia Museum of Art, Philadelphia, Pennsylvania. Louise and Walter Arensberg Archives.

and other Modernists from the Forward Show also participated in the independent exhibition. Despite its non-exclusionary policy, the Society's 1917 exhibition became famous for what its board of directors chose not to exhibit. Having already created a public sensation at the Armory Show (see fig. 7.29), Marcel Duchamp instigated yet another storm of controversy when he submitted a white porcelain urinal bearing the ironic title *Fountain* and signed with the pseudonym "R. Mutt." The name alluded to Mott Works, a plumbing manufacturer. But in altering the spelling, Duchamp also made a joking reference to a comic character from "Mutt and Jeff," a popular newspaper cartoon strip. Led by the Society's president, William Glackens, an Ashcan School realist, the board of directors quickly barred the work from the show and declared in a statement to the press that "*The Fountain* may be a very useful object in its place, but its place is not in an art exhibition and it is by no definition, a work of art" (cited in Naumann, p. 184). A few days later, however, *Fountain* was in the 291 Gallery under the care of Stieglitz, who took an evocative, mysteriously shadowed photograph of the nonfunctional urinal (fig. 7.38). Duchamp arranged to have Stieglitz's photograph reproduced in *The Blind Man*, a short-lived art journal that ran an article on "The Richard Mutt Case" or the "Buddha of the Bathroom." In the article, Duchamp defended *Fountain* against charges that it was not only vulgar and immoral, but also an act of plagiarism:

> Now Mr. Mutt's fountain is not immoral, that is absurd, no more than a bath tub is immoral. It is a fixture that you see every day in plumbers' show windows.
>
> Whether Mr. Mutt with his own hands made the fountain or not has no importance. He CHOSE it. He took an ordinary article of life, placed it so that its useful significance disappeared under the new title and point of view—created a new thought for that object (cited in Naumann, p. 185).

Escaping the war in Europe, Duchamp had arrived in New York in 1915. Together with the Parisian artist Francis Picabia (1879–1953), he helped to import an iconoclastic, anti-art movement into New York known as Dada. Named after a childish French term for a rocking horse,

Dada originated in war-torn Europe, as poets and artists in Zurich, Paris, Berlin, Hanover, and Cologne ridiculed patriotism, militarism, and all established political and cultural values. Blaming the cold rationalism of the modern state and the hypocrisy of middle-class morality for the senseless loss of millions of lives, Dadaists embraced the irrational by disrupting theatrical performances and concerts, engaging in street protests, and creating nonsensical, anti-art works. Two years prior to the appearance of *Fountain*, Picabia had drawn a playful emblematic portrait of Steiglitz, representing him as the mechanistic synthesis of a camera and automobile (fig. 7.39). The anti-aesthetic, engineering-style design of the drawing subverts the old-fashioned notion of the "IDEAL," as written nostalgically in German script at the top of the picture. Below the French inscription identifying this as an image of Stieglitz, the words "foi et amour," or faith and love, further parody the Romantic, transcendental tradition, which cast art in religious terms. The flaccid, phallic camera bellows signifies Stieglitz's and aesthetic idealism's loss of creative energy. Meanwhile, the camera-car is going nowhere: the brake is engaged and it's idling in neutral. Dadaists repeatedly attacked notions of aesthetic beauty and original genius for elevating art into a stultifying religion that only reinforced the status quo. Rejecting traditional fine-arts techniques and materials, Duchamp and other Dadaists sought to demolish the barrier between art and life, declaring that anyone could be an artist and anything could become a work of art. For Duchamp, art was more an act of finding than making or crafting, depending upon conceptual more than purely visual qualities.

Duchamp's *Fountain* was a "readymade," an object that he had found or purchased already made from a store or factory. In appropriating this utilitarian, manufactured object and then resituating it, signed and titled, within a gallery or exhibition space, the artist magically gave the object a new life and identity as a work of art. Significantly, given Dada's abhorrence of the war, Stieglitz chose to photograph *Fountain* against the backdrop of Marsden Hartley's *Warriors* (see fig. 7.33). The shape of the urinal echoed the painting's abstract mountain, ceremonially ascended by German cavalrymen. In its upside-down position on the pedestal, the urinal sports a projecting

7.39 Francis Picabia
Here, This Is Stieglitz (Ici, C'est Ici Stieglitz), 1915.
Pen and black ink on paper, 29⅞ x 20 in (75.9 x 50.8 cm). Metropolitan Museum of Art, New York. Alfred Stieglitz Collection, 1949.

black hole at its base. The circular projectile elicits sexual associations, but, given the wartime context of the photograph underscored by Hartley's militaristic painting, Stieglitz and his friends may have imagined themselves looking down the barrel of a gun. By 1917, as America was preparing to enter the war against Germany, Stieglitz gloomily viewed the prospect as a social and cultural catastrophe. Intentionally or not, Stieglitz's juxtaposition of Hartley's militaristic painting with Duchamp's scandalous Buddha or Madonna-shaped urinal seems itself a Dadaist critique of pre-war optimism and patriotic fervor.

Playing upon the concept of a changeable artistic identity, Duchamp's assumption of alternative personalities such as R. Mutt demonstrates that the former Cubist painter regarded art as a fluid process of self-transformation without any fixed rules or boundaries. His most notorious adopted persona was Rrose Sélavy, whose name became connected with a number of enigmatic readymades. The New York artist Man Ray, a convert to Dada, publicized the birth of this female alter ego by photographing Duchamp wearing fashionable women's clothing and make-up (fig. 7.40).

7.40 Man Ray
Marcel Duchamp Dressed as Rrose Sélavy, 1924.
Gelatin-silver print. Samuel S. White III and Vera White Collection. Philadelphia Museum of Art, Philadelphia, Pennsylvania.

7.41 (below)
Elsa von Freytag-Loringhoven and Morton Schamberg
God, c. 1917.
Gelatin silver print, 9½ x 7⁹⁄₁₆ in (24.1 x 19.2 cm). Metropolitan Museum of Art, New York. Elisha Whittelsey Collection and Fund, 1973.

Since Dada constituted an anti-art rebellion against traditional notions of authorship and originality, it is unsurprising that an iconoclastic woman like the German baroness made little apparent effort to claim this work as hers. On the other hand, Schamberg acted more conventionally by photographing *God* in front of one of his own signed machinist paintings. The plumbing trap appears here without a wooden miter box that the baroness used as an ironic, protective pedestal for the detumescent phallic form.

Contradicting Dada's anti-art subversion of formal beauty, Stieglitz's photograph of *Fountain* makes the urinal aesthetic, or visually interesting. By contrast, in apparent response to Duchamp's infamous work, Baroness Elsa von Freytag-Loringhoven (1874–1927), who most epitomized New York Dada's anarchistic ethos, chose an unaesthetic found object, a cast-iron plumbing trap, to create a sacrilegious, sexually suggestive readymade entitled *God* (fig. 7.41). The German baroness had arrived in New York in 1913, only to live in abject poverty after her aristocratic husband, Baron Leopold von Freytag-Loringhoven, returned to Germany and committed suicide during the war. While Duchamp enjoyed the hospitality and financial support of affluent patrons, the baroness scraped by in a cheap, two-room, Greenwich Village tenement, filled with pieces of junk that she found in the streets or shoplifted. Frequently arrested for petty theft, she sometimes earned money as an artist's model and published Dadaist poetry in avant-garde journals. More than a creator of readymades, the baroness dressed and lived Dada in a nearly continuous performance of shocking, outrageous behavior, such as parading half-naked through Greenwich Village in bizarre costumes that she had crafted from various pieces of cloth and decorative bric-a-brac. She once shaved her head bald and painted it with a bright red lacquer, explaining that the act of shaving one's head was like making love.

Emulating Duchamp's *Fountain*, the baroness's *God* treated American plumbing fixtures as ironic icons of divinity. In an essay that she later published in defense of James Joyce's Modernist novel *Ulysses* (1922), she sarcastically wrote that puritanical Americans were so preoccupied by the external machinery of sanitation facilities that they forgot about their own bodily functions or internal plumbing. For the baroness, iron plumbing was America's God.

Romancing the Machine in Art and Architecture

Traditionally, Morton Livingston Schamberg (1881–1918), a painter of sleek, abstract pictures of machines (fig. 7.42), has been credited with the creation of *God*. Certainly, he photographed the readymade and may have assisted in its assembly, but recent art historians have reattributed primary authorship to the irreverent baroness. The ironic, dark humor and crude, sexual appearance of *God* is not in character with Schamberg's elegant machine aesthetic. Though Schamberg admired the New York Dadaists, he did not share their anti-art tendencies. Originally trained as an architect, he employed a precise, linear drawing style to celebrate the machine's formal beauty and rational geometry.

Schamberg died prematurely, but many other painters also shed the Dadaist nihilism of the war years to portray with more optimism than skepticism the sublime power of the machine and the urban, industrialized American landscape. Working in Paris, the American expatriate painter Gerald Murphy (1888–1964) produced pictures inspired by American advertising, product design, and technology. In *Watch* (fig. 7.46), Murphy

7.42 Morton Schamberg
Mechanical Abstraction, 1916.
Oil on canvas, 30 x 20¼ in (76.2 x 51.4 cm). Philadelphia Museum of Art, Pennsylvania. Louise and Walter Arensberg Collection.

Inspired by both Duchamp and Francis Picabia, Schamberg began exhibiting machine paintings in 1916. But he did so without any apparent Dadaist irony or humor. Scholars have argued that this work, one of Schamberg's most refined images, was actually abstracted from a sewing machine or from an automated stitcher used in bookbinding. Painted with nuanced color harmonies, Schamberg's abstractions express an almost religious devotion to finely crafted mechanisms.

7.43 (right) **John Storrs**
New York, c.1925.
Brass and steel on black marble base, 25⅞ x 5½ x 3½ in (65.8 x 14 x 8.9 cm). Indianapolis Museum of Art, Indiana. Discretionary Fund.

7.44 Louis Lozowick
Pittsburgh, 1922–23.
Oil on canvas, 60 x 50 in
(152.4 x127cm). Whitney
Museum of American Art,
New York.

7.45 (below)
Alexander Calder
A Universe, 1934.
Motor-driven mobile.
Painted iron pipe, wire,
and wood with string,
40½ in (102.9 cm) high.
Museum of Modern Art,
New York. Gift of Abby
Aldrich Rockefeller.

Like other American
Modernists, Calder used
abstraction to express
spiritual ideas of cosmic
harmony and dynamism.
His sculpture of moving
spheres recalls the long-
popular orrery, or scientific
model of the solar system's
orbiting planets.
Accompanied by a
mechanical device placed
alongside it, Calder's
delicate construction
features just two spheres, a
small red one and larger
white orb, each
representing a star or
planet moving at different
speeds along separate
curved paths within the
wire construction's large
open sphere.

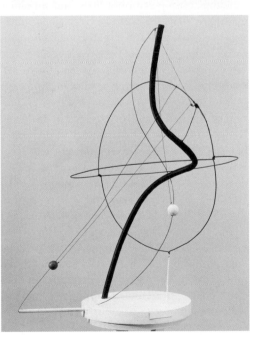

indirectly referred to American inventiveness and the importance of time, or being on time, in modern industrial life. However, Murphy's buoyant, swirling mechanical gears scarcely represent a critique of the tyranny of the clock. Historians and critics have employed the terms "immaculate" and "precisionist" to characterize the crisp, linear machine-age styles of Schamberg, Murphy and other American artists, including Charles Demuth (1883–1935) and Charles Sheeler (1883–1965).

The *Société Anonyme*

John Storrs (1885–1956), the son of a Chicago architect and real-estate developer, created a series of sleek, visionary skyscraper sculptures (fig. 7.43). He attributed religious meaning to the ancient human quest to control the elements of earth, water, air, and fire through art and architecture. An avid collector of American Indian artifacts, Storrs equated skyscrapers with Northwest Indian totem poles and houseposts, which symbolized unity between earth and sky. Looking beyond the purely functional, economic rationale for the construction of skyscrapers, he associated their verticality with an infinite spiritual growth toward the illumination of sun and sky. By contrast, for Storrs, horizontality signified all that was heavy, brutal, or purely materialistic. His simplified sculptures foreshadowed Modernist American skyscrapers, which eventually eliminated all decorative, historical details in favor of starkly cubical geometric towers and Precisionist slabs (see figs. 8.10–8.11). Cast with steel, the industrial metal of skyscraper construction, Storrs's *New York* was reproduced in 1926 for the cover of an exhibition catalogue of international art published by the Société Anonyme, the nation's first modern art museum.

Founded in 1920 by the New York painter and Dadaist art patron Katherine Dreier (1877–1952), the Société Anonyme was named after the French business term for an incorporated company. However, like Storrs, Dreier interpreted modern art forms in spiritualized terms. She admired Duchamp and other Dadaists for their apparent lack of concern for material gain in the production of anti-art readymades. But she also adhered to the religious

7.46 Gerald Murphy
Watch, 1924.
Oil on canvas,
78½ x 78⅞ in
(199.5 x 200.5 cm).
Dallas Museum of Art,
Dallas, Texas.

beliefs of Rudolf Steiner (1861–1925), founder of the Anthroposophical Society in Germany in 1912, who argued that artists, more than ordinary humans, were especially able to create visionary "thought-pictures," or colors and forms that communicated the ideas and feelings of a higher, spiritual world.

A determined social activist, Dreier especially favored the work of the Russian Constructivists, a group of artists led by Vladimir Tatlin (1885–1953), who allied themselves with the 1917 communist revolution in Russia and the establishment of the Soviet Union. As explained by Louis Lozowick (1892–1973) a Russian-born American painter who visited Constructivists in Moscow in 1922, construction was the "new Gospel" of art. Unlike the traditional aesthetic notion of composition, which Lozowick associated with illusion, art for art's sake, and mere decoration, Constructivisim was an activist art dedicated to life or the construction of a vigorous, new society through industry, machinery, and science. While in Europe, Lozowick painted

a series of diverse American urban-industrial landscapes (fig. 7.44) with monumental, soaring buildings, crisp precisionist lines, and simplified geometric shapes. Constructivists valued industrial machine forms and engineering technology for promising a higher new reality that would transcend the accidents of nature and the limitations of individual caprice or idiosyncratic creativity. The Société Anonyme held an exhibition of Russian Constructivist Art in 1924 and featured it again in an International Exhibition of Modern Art in 1926. Dreier's introduction of the Russian avant-garde to the American public encouraged the young Alexander Calder (1898–1976), whose metal and wire mobiles of the 1930s went much further than Alexander Archipenko in liberating sculpture from the tyranny of gravity and heavy, massive forms (fig. 7.45). Calder borrowed the term "mobile" for his motorized and wind-driven constructions from Duchamp, who assembled a kinetic, or moving, sculpture with his 1920 motorized *Rotary Glass Plates*, acquired by the Société Anonyme.

7.47 Charles Demuth
Incense of a New Church, 1921.
Oil on canvas,
26 x 20⅛ in.
(66 x 50.8 cm). Columbus
Museum of Art,
Columbus, Ohio. Gift of
Ferdinand Howald.

Demuth's painting
incorporates a large
chalice-shaped form amidst
the swirling incense of
industrial smoke. The
chalice equates the
alchemical, transformative
powers of industry with the
sacramental symbolism of
Holy Communion and the
transubstantiation of wine
into the blood of Christ.
During the pre-Depression
optimism of the 1920s,
numerous Americans, led
by President Calvin
Coolidge, equated factories
with temples or churches.

Charles Demuth

Charles Demuth, who wrote a poem defending "Richard Mutt" and his *Fountain*, employed Duchampian humor in comparing American factories, warehouses, and grain elevators to the sacred architectural forms of ancient and medieval history. A native and continuing resident of Lancaster, Pennsylvania, Demuth chose the ironic title *Incense of a New Church* to represent the stylized smokestacks and swirls of polluting smoke

7.48 Charles Demuth
The Figure 5 in Gold,
1928.
Oil on composition board,
36 x 29¾ in
(91.4 x 75.6 cm).
Metropolitan Museum of
Art, Washington D.C.
Alfred Stieglitz Collection.

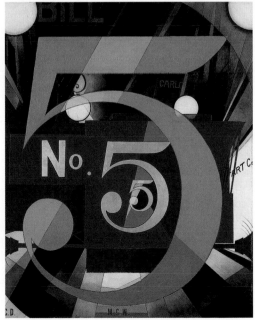

from a nearby industrial complex (fig. 7.47). Yet the somber humor of the title loses its critical punch, since Demuth's colorful suggestion of a precious, stained-glass church window clearly idealizes the subject. The artist encourages beholders to imagine the smokestacks as the pipes for a monumental organ, while the industrial plumes of smoke curve about in seductive serpentine lines that induce an otherworldly state of reverie. In contrast to the far more fragmented Cubist cityscapes of Max Weber (see fig. 7.22), Demuth's composition serenely harmonizes the cacophony and dislocations of economic modernization to create a relatively calm and stable order of industrial forms.

Later, from 1923 to 1929, Demuth devoted his energy to a series of portrait "posters" of friends and colleagues, among them the playwright Eugene O'Neill, the expatriate author and avant-garde art advocate Gertrude Stein, and members of the Stieglitz circle of artists. A close friend of Marsden Hartley, with whom he may have had a brief affair, Demuth conceived his portraits in a manner similar to Hartley's *Portrait of a German Officer* (see fig. 7.34). The portraits were not to be iconic likenesses of sitters, but highly personal, coded representations filled with significant letters, objects, and emblems evoking the subject's creative character or spiritual presence. The most famous work from the series, *The Figure 5 in Gold* (fig. 7.48) pays tribute to the American poet William Carlos Williams, one of Demuth's closest friends. The painting visually interprets Williams's minimalist poem "The Great Figure," published in 1921, which reads:

> *Among the rain*
> *and lights*
> *I saw the figure 5*
> *in gold*
> *on a red*
> *firetruck*
> *moving*
> *tense*
> *unheeded*
> *to gong clangs*
> *siren howls*
> *and wheels rumbling*
> *through the dark city*
> *(cited in Corn, p.204).*

Demuth captures the intensity and physical movement of this spare poetic expression of New York City street life by utilizing the fractured, rhythmic geometry of Cubism and Futurism, in conjunction with the two-dimensional, typographical precision of urban signs and numbers. Emanating from the flattened, hot-red forms of the firetruck, its advancing figure 5 is repeated four times, growing larger each time as it roars toward and then past us. To convey the impression that the truck has already sped by, the fourth gold 5 is only partially visible in the upper-right corner, cut off by the picture frame. The tail of this final large number also appears as a tiny streak of gold in the lower-left window.

Beyond imagery drawn from the poem, Demuth's portrait of New York at night includes graphic references to Williams's name. As Wanda Corn has observed, the cropped letters "BILL" at the top of the painting refer to Williams's nickname, but also punningly serves to remind us of all the city billboards competing for our attention. In addition, Williams's middle name "CARLOS" illuminates the dark night sky with Broadway-style theatrical lights. Demuth was a friend of the New York painter and socialite Florine Stettheimer (1871–1948), whose contemporaneous *Cathedrals of Broadway* (fig. 7.49) is filled with an electric, colorful array of Broadway theater signs, surrounding a black-and-white movie screen celebrating the invention of talking motion pictures. Much less cluttered than Stettheimer's carnivalesque composition, Demuth's entire painting was a kind of Broadway billboard inspired by the world of theater and commercial advertising. Recalling Katherine Dreier's Société Anonyme and its French language reference to a business company or corporation, Demuth spelled out the partially cropped letters "ART Co." on a brightly illuminated shop window at the far right of the picture. Meanwhile, the initials of both Demuth and Williams at the bottom of the picture plane, itself a kind of showroom window, appear mechanically reproduced. Demuth's portrait poster, painted on board rather than traditional canvas, visualized a personal friendship in the impersonal language of modern posters, billboards, and business signs, wittily marketing his own art and the art of his "company" of friends.

Art Deco and Modernity

America's romance with the machine was especially expressed in architecture and the decorative arts. In 1925, a major international exhibition on the decorative arts was held in Paris. The Exposition Internationale des Arts Décoratifs et Industriels Modernes spawned the Art Deco movement, which popularized a modern, machine-age style for buildings and everyday utilitarian objects. Art Deco designers also employed highly stylized, simplified natural forms to suggest energy, motion, and an efficient, sleek modernity. In New York City, the more than 6,000-seat Radio City Music Hall auditorium (fig. 7.50) mimics the cascading solar rays of a setting sun, telescoped toward the stage through a series of lofty arches. Though designed by the architect Wallace Harrison (1895–1981), the theatrical impresario Samuel L. "Roxy" Rothafel

7.49 Florine Stettheimer
Cathedrals of Broadway, 1929.
Oil on canvas,
60⅛ x 50⅛ in.
Metropolitan Museum of Art.
Gift of Ettie Stettheimer.

claimed credit for the setting-sun motif, which called attention to the Music Hall's sophisticated lighting system and its ability to suggest a variety of luminous effects, from sunsets and sunrises to the aurora borealis. Constructed as part of Rockefeller Center, a complex of buildings, anchored by the seventy-story RCA (Radio Corporation of America) Building, Radio City Music Hall was intended as a popular entertainment palace, offering primarily live, vaudeville-style stage productions, but also motion pictures. John D. Rockefeller, Jr., Rockefeller Center's originator and leading financier, professed himself "thrilled" by the "chic" modernity of the auditorium and the entire Art Deco style interior (cited in Alan Balfour, p. 202). Having violently suppressed striking miners of the Colorado Fuel and Iron Company in early 1914 (see fig. 7.10), Rockefeller was now devoting himself to philanthropic causes and a paternalistic style of real estate development that assumed "beautiful, soul satisfying and inspiring" architectural spaces would morally ennoble the people who experienced them (cited in Balfour, p. 202). When it first opened during the winter of 1932–33, with stage acts that ranged from comedians and acrobats to opera singers and the modern choreographer Martha Graham (1894–1991), the

Music Hall suffered substantial financial losses. But, during the Great Depression, three years after the October 1929 stock-market crash, the Music Hall's block-length marquee beckoned passersby, while its mirrored Grand Foyer and mural-decorated staircase ceremoniously guided patrons, as in a fashionable procession or communal ritual, into the gleaming auditorium, a seemingly trouble-free utopian space.

One of the most eye-catching examples of streamlined Art Deco design in the United States was the 185-foot-high spire of glistening stainless steel that capped the Chrysler Building in New York City (fig. 7.51). Commissioned by the car manufacturer Walter P. Chrysler, the architect William van Alen (1883–1954) ornamented the skyscraper with automotive decorative motifs. Like giant wheels or hubcaps, overlapping circles of silvery metal ascend toward the top of this commercial cathedral. Within each sleek parabolic curve of the spire, triangular windows create a radiant, sunburst pattern that equates industrial production with a godlike creative energy. As photographed by Margaret Bourke-White (1904–71) for *Fortune* magazine, the building's stainless-steel gargoyles, projecting from below the crowning spire, were modeled after the

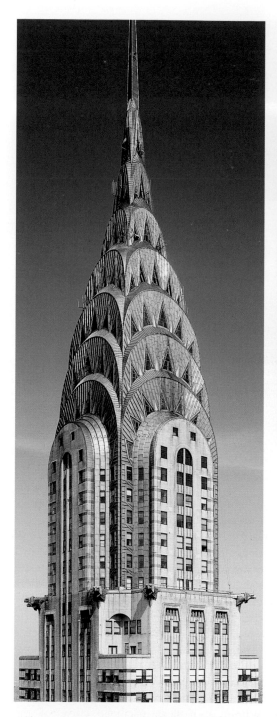

7.51 William van Alen
The Chrysler Building,
New York City,
1928–30.

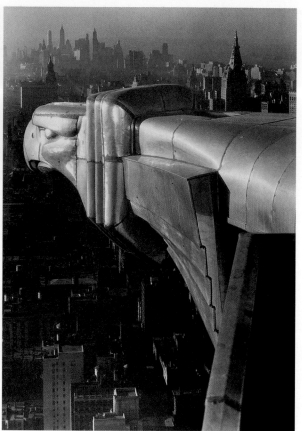

7.52 Margaret Bourke-White
Chrysler Building
Gargoyle, 1930.
Gelatin silver print.
George Eastman House,
Rochester, New York.

Chrysler automobile hood ornament (fig. 7.52). Bourke-White's dramatic, close-up view of a single gargoyle, overlooking the city below, expresses the aggressive energy of modern capitalist enterprises that *Fortune*, owned by publisher Henry Luce, was eager to encourage, following the 1929 stock-market crash. At the same time, these symbols of the market's predatory forces are also reminiscent of the ancient Egyptian, falcon-shaped god Horus, famed for his all-seeing eye.

Just as they stylized forms from nature, Art Deco designers also borrowed motifs and modern-appearing styles from ancient art and architecture. Thus, the elevator doors of the Chrysler Building were adorned with metal and wood veneers of Egyptian-Revival floral designs (fig. 7.53). For a few months, the Chrysler Building was the tallest in the world, but it was soon surpassed by the eighty-five-story Empire State Building further downtown. Like its competitor, the Empire State Building was crowned by a lofty spire, but its Art Deco design was less distinctive than Chrysler's automobile motifs.

7.53 William van Alen
*Elevator Doors for the
Chrysler Building,*
1927–30.

The Harlem Renaissance

Art Deco's expression of newness and modernity became associated in the minds of many artists and critics with the new urban rhythms of the Jazz Age and the development during the 1920s of a "Negro Renaissance" or "New Negro Movement," comprising the musical, visual, theatrical, and literary arts as a means of defining and expressing black culture and racial identity. More commonly, cultural historians today refer to this movement as the "Harlem Renaissance," since the Harlem section of northern Manhattan was claimed by contemporaries as the national center, or capital, of African-American life.

Prior to this period, Modernist American artists, like their European Cubist mentors, appropriated the dynamic, abstract geometry of African tribal masks and sculptures in their rebellion against academic tradition. However, as suggested by Max Weber's African nudes in *Composition with Three Figures* (see fig. 7.20), Africa was often personified by lethargic or sleeping figures, symbolizing the enervating sleep of slavery or, more broadly, an unenlightened, sleepy, primitive continent. In her sculpture *The Awakening of Ethiopia* (fig. 7.54), the Paris-educated African-American artist Meta Warrick Fuller (1877–1968) expressed the counter-notion of a regenerated Africa and a new day dawning for black culture and politics. Fuller had earlier met the African-American historian and sociologist W.E.B. DuBois, who was already using the term "new Negro" at the beginning of the century to encourage political, civil-rights activism. In 1909–10, he helped to found the National Association for the Advancement of Colored People (NAACP), which dedicated itself to fighting for racial equality, voting rights, and the repeal of segregationist laws. DuBois also encouraged Fuller and other black artists to create artworks that addressed black social, political, and cultural issues.

Fuller's personification of Ethiopia, executed in an Egyptian-Revival style, honored the one country in contemporary Africa that still remained independent of European colonialism, thanks to its defeat of Italian military forces at the battle of Adowa in 1896. Yet *The Awakening of Ethiopia* had wider political, cultural meaning, since the words "Ethiopia" and "Ethiopian" possessed popular currency for denoting all Africa and all Africans, including African-Americans. The sculpture reminded viewers of ancient Egypt as the great African birthplace of western civilization and, looking toward the future, offered hope that Ethiopia's anti-colonial struggle would fuel awakening political activism among African-Americans.

Fuller completed her sculpture in the midst of what became known as the Great Migration, when, during the first half of the century, millions of Southern blacks moved northward to the industrial cities of the Midwest and Northeast, seeking jobs and new economic, social opportunities. As we shall later see, the painter Jacob Lawrence (1917–2000) poignantly documented this epic migration in a series of narrative history paintings (see fig. 8.4). Just in the decade from 1910 to 1920, the population of African-Americans in Chicago more than doubled from 44,000 to 109,000. Meanwhile, in New York City, the proportion of blacks living in Manhattan jumped from one in seventy in 1890 to one in nine by 1930, with the greatest concentration of African-Americans living in Harlem.

In fleeing the South, African-Americans were hoping to escape segregationist laws and anti-black vigilante violence. But in the North, as well, they were often confronted by white mobs and were subjected to segregationist, racially discriminating practices in employment, housing, and public services. To cope with the problems of city life, African-Americans in New York founded the National Urban League in 1911, which merged several earlier organizations for the purpose of improving the social and economic conditions of African-American men and women in the expanding industrial cities of the United States. The Urban League also published an influential magazine, *Opportunity*, edited by the sociologist Charles S. Johnson, who, together with W.E.B. DuBois, Alain Locke, and other African-American intellectuals, sought to promote the work of emerging black writers and artists. Aaron Douglas (1898–1979), who became one of the leading painters of the Harlem Renaissance, was encouraged by Johnson to move from Kansas City to Harlem, where he met DuBois and Locke, editor of the seminal book *The New Negro: An Interpretation* (1925), an anthology of historical, political, and sociological articles celebrating Harlem as the mecca for New Negro culture and the blossoming of a black spirit or race consciousness. In the book, Locke strongly urged black writers and artists to draw inspiration from their African heritage and racial origins.

Aaron Douglas became closely identified with Locke's notion of a Negro Renaissance, since he provided illustrations for *The New Negro*. In magazine covers and book jackets designed for the African-American poet Langston Hughes and other major African-American authors, Douglas borrowed from the African-influenced style of Cubism and from the Egyptian-Revival manner of Art Deco, which evoked associations with ancient Africa.

Douglas's cover for the February 1926 issue of *Opportunity* represents the black contribution to American industrial life (fig. 7.55). Within an explosively dynamic, futuristic landscape, two black-silhouette figures are portrayed in the traditional guise of heroic blacksmiths, shaping hot metal with a sledge hammer and anvil. Factory smokestacks belch in the distance, while swirling forms, sharp bursts of fire and energy, similar to the sunburst motifs of the Chrysler Building spire, express the modernity of the machine age.

7.54 Meta Warrick Fuller
The Awakening of Ethiopia, 1914.
Painted plaster,
67 x 16 x 20 in
(170.3 x 40.7 x 50.8 cm).
Schomburg Center for Research in Black Culture, The New York Public Library, New York.

This sculpture is a later version of a lost original designed for the 1921 "America's Making Exposition" in New York City. Sponsored by the city and state governments, this large exhibition was intended as a celebratory showcase for the creative contributions of different immigrant and racial groups to the American cultural melting pot.

When he came to New York, Douglas was actually schooled by the white, German-born graphic artist and interior designer Winold Reiss (1886–1953), who was primarily responsible for the illustrations and graphic decoration of *The New Negro*. Combining his interest in issues of racial identity with the development of modern design, Reiss painted a pastel portrait of Langston Hughes, seated in front of an Art Deco background of musical notes, urban architecture, and interior spaces (fig. 7.56). With sheets of manuscript paper signifying his professional status as a writer, Hughes assumes the pose of poetic reverie, so that the kaleidoscopic, cloudy-blue forms behind him appear as projections of his fiercely inventive imagination.

Douglas went on to become a major New York muralist and continued to synthesize visual narratives of Negro life with an abstract, Modernist style (see fig. 7.78). Other African-American artists maintained a more traditional realist style, even when they followed Alain Locke's charge to explore their African identity. The Virginia-born, New York-based painter Palmer Hayden (1890–1973) won a prize for *Fétiche et Fleurs* (fig. 7.57) from the Harmon Foundation in New York City, an organization founded by William E. Harmon, an Iowa real estate developer, devoted to improving race relations through economic and cultural development, including sponsorship of juried, traveling exhibitions of African-American art. Within an otherwise conventional still-life format, comprising a vase of lilies and ashtray with cigarette, Hayden placed a Gabonese fetish, or reliquary sculpture, upon a cloth from Central Africa.

The flowers suggest, perhaps, the tropical lushness of an African rain forest environment, but otherwise the sculpture and textile appear out of place as imported art objects paying tribute to a distant cultural heritage. Any magical religious purpose that the fetish may have served in its original African context has been displaced by Hayden's professional goal of creating an expressionistic, aesthetically pleasing picture for a racially mixed American audience. While many white American art patrons stereotypically viewed African-Americans as modern primitives, closely tied to their African ancestors, Hayden was an academically trained artist working in a painterly, Post-Impressionist style. As suggested by the French title of his painting, he eagerly traveled to Paris in 1926 for a lengthy, six-year study of European art, before returning home to paint scenes of Harlem life in a self-consciously naive style.

The Chicago artist Archibald J. Motley, Jr. (1891–1981) lived at a distance from black neighborhoods and Harlem's intellectual and cultural debates. Born to a racially mixed family in New Orleans, Motley painted portraits of mulattos and scenes of interracial nightclubs. During, and even after, the Prohibition era, when, from 1920 to 1933, it was illegal to manufacture and sell alcoholic drinks, Motley was criticized by some African-American leaders for painting nightlife, drinking, gambling, and dancing scenes that seemed to fuel conventional racial stereotypes regarding black moral behavior. Like Hayden and other African-American artists, Motley traveled to Paris, where he found more tolerance for his own interracial marriage and where he painted *Blues* (fig. 7.58), an energetic portrait of the Jockey Club, an American-owned jazz nightclub. In this densely packed picture, black musicians play for a racially mixed crowd of dancing, smoking, drinking patrons. The lively parabolic forms

7.56 Winold Reiss
Portrait of Langston Hughes, 1925.
Pastel on artist board,
30¹⁄₁₆ x 21⅝ in
(76.3 x 54.9 cm).
National Portrait Gallery,
Washington D.C. Gift of
W. Tjark Reiss in memory
of his father, Winold Reiss.

Trained in Munich in both
art and industrial design,
Winold Reiss became a
friend of Alain Locke, who
invited him to contribute art
work to *The New Negro*.
After his arrival in the
United States in 1913, Reiss
had established his own
school of art and design in
New York City.

of the musical instruments, projecting into the colorful dance floor of overlapping, stylish figures, visually suggests the intense, pulsating rhythms of the new music. More than any other art form, the improvisational nature of jazz performances promoted the values of personal freedom and individual creativity. In that spirit, Motley generally began such complex pictorial arrangements by first experimenting with colorful, abstract shapes, only later arriving at his highly stylized manner of realism.

Many middle-class blacks exercised their economic freedom by fashioning new social and cultural identities through consumerism.

James Van Der Zee (1886-1983) spent his career photographing the citizenry and energetic street life of Harlem. Even during the Great Depression, Van Der Zee's documentary photographs tended to promote Harlem as a place of self-confident social mobility. In his famous portrait of *Couple Wearing Raccoon Coats with a Cadillac, taken on West 127th Street, Harlem, New York* (fig. 7.59), the fashionable figures pose with one of the most glamorous symbols of modern power and affluence, an elegant, elongated luxury sedan, its chrome metal and polished surfaces gleaming with machine-age optimism.

7.57 Palmer Hayden
Fétiche et Fleurs, 1926.
Oil on canvas,
23½ x 29 in
(59.6 x 73.6 cm).
Museum of African-
American Art, Los
Angeles, California.

**7.58 Archibald
Motley, Jr.**
Blues, 1929
Oil on canvas,
31½ x 39½ in
(80 x 100.3 cm).
Art Institute of Chicago,
Chicago, Illinois.
Archie Motley and Valerie
Gerard Browne Collection

7.59 James Van Der Zee
Couple Wearing Racoon Coats with a Cadillac, taken on West 127th Street, Harlem, New York, 1932.
Consolidated Freightways, Inc.

Fordism

During the 1920s, Fordism, or the scientifically managed production techniques of the automobile manufacturer Henry Ford, captured the imagination of European and American artists and architects, who believed that industrial technology was the best means for rebuilding a new world after the devastation of war. Before the war, Ford had hired the German-Jewish immigrant Albert Kahn (1869–1942) to design factory buildings in Highland Park, Michigan, a suburb of Detroit. Kahn's task was to accommodate the demands of assembly-line production: the continuous flow of raw materials and parts through the work space and their incorporation into the final, assembled automobile exiting at the opposite end of the factory. Hiring unskilled workers to fit into the separate steps of the assembly-line process, Ford followed Frederick Taylor's *Principles of Scientific Management* (1911), which recommended the division of labor into a seamless series of repetitive, routine motions timed to maximize productivity.

Though he designed the private, suburban homes of Detroit auto manufacturers in nostalgic historical-revival styles, Albert Kahn shaped his minimalist factory designs to the practical needs of factory management. At Highland Park and later, after the war, at Ford's River Rouge Plant in Dearborn, Michigan (fig. 7.60), he employed the modern industrial materials of steel and reinforced concrete to create vast, open

7.60 Albert Kahn
Ford Motor Company, Glass Plant, River Rouge Plant, Dearborn, Michigan, 1922.
Albert Kahn Associates, Inc., Architects and Engineers, Detroit, Michigan.

7.61 Charles Sheeler
Criss-Crossed Conveyors, Ford Plant, 1927.
Gelatin silver print,
10½ x 9⅜ in
(26.6 x 23.8 cm).
From the Collections of
Henry Ford Museum and
Greenfield Village,
Dearborn, Michigan.

When *Vanity Fair* reproduced
this photograph, the caption
not only quoted from
Matthew 7:20 but also
praised Henry Ford as a
virtually divine mastermind.
Ford's new River Rouge Plant
was an American Mecca or
holy site. Behind the criss-
crossing coke and cole
conveyers, eight enormous
smokestacks from one of the
plant's powerhouses loom
overhead. Sheeler's
composition, with its low
viewpoint, is meant to instill
feelings of reverential awe
before this sublime image of
godlike industrial power.

factory spaces uninterrupted by cumbersome
interior supports and brightly illuminated by
long ribbons of windows and skylights. Whereas
earlier American factories had been multi-story,
small-span buildings, Kahn's assembly-line factories were horizontal, single-story structures that
covered acres of land. Each structure in the self-
sufficient River Rouge complex was designed
for the production of a specific component, sub-
assembly, or auxiliary activity in transforming
raw materials into modestly priced automobiles.
The plant's buildings were connected by miles of
railroad tracks, conveyer belts, and roads to create
a giant assembly chain.

In 1927, the Ford Motor Company, working
through the N. W. Ayer advertising agency,
hired the American painter and photographer
Charles Sheeler to photograph its River Rouge
Plant. An admirer of Duchamp's detached,
unemotional, and mechanical images, Sheeler,
along with the photographer Paul Strand, in

7.62 Charles Sheeler
Classic Landscape,
1931.
Oil on canvas, 25 x 32¼
in (63.5 x 81.9 cm).
Collection Mr. and Mrs.
Barney A. Ebsworth
Foundation.

Sheeler synthesized
photographic realism with
classical order in this view
of a cement plant in Ford's
River Rouge complex.
Distant silos and
smokestacks evoke
associations with classical
columns. The sharply
receding railroad tracks
continue the rational,
spatial constructions of
Renaissance linear
perspective. The painting
possesses an eerie, airless
emptiness. The industrial
landscape seems strangely
inert and expressive of the
Depression, despite
billowing factory smoke
from the tall smokestack.

7.63 Charles Sheeler
Home, Sweet Home,
1931.
Oil on canvas,
7ft 7in x 6ft 1in
(232.2 x 187.2cm).
Detroit Institute of Arts,
Detroit, Michigan. Gift of
Robert H. Tannahill.

1920 had created *Manhatta*, a short, silent film of New York City architectural and engineering landmarks, which was shown at a Dada festival in Paris. However, Sheeler was more a devotee of Fordism than Dadaist nihilism. His most famous River Rouge photograph, *Criss-Crossed Conveyors* (fig. 7.61), was reproduced in *Vanity Fair* magazine with the biblically inspired caption "By Their Works Ye Shall Know Them." Indeed, Sheeler employed this dynamic shot of elevated conveyor belts for the centerpiece of a photographic triptych equivalent to a medieval or Renaissance altarpiece. Even after the stock-market crash of 1929 and the advent of the Great Depression, Sheeler paid homage to Ford's capitalist venture in a series of paintings that associated the industrial landscape with the rational grandeur of the classical past (fig. 7.62). At the same time, in pictures such as *Home, Sweet Home* (fig. 7.63), a partial interior view of his South Salem, New York, home, near the Connecticut state border,

Sheeler sought to demonstrate that stream-lined, machine-age froms were rooted in the anonymously crafted artifacts of the nation's pre-industrial material culture. With intense illumination, he focused upon the crisp, recti-linear forms of the room's antique American furnishings: a Delaware Valley, ladder-back chair from around 1800, rag rugs, and a nineteenth-century Shaker bench and table. All these handcrafted objects harmonize effortlessly with a modern, machine-manufactured gas heater, housed within a metal-gray rectangular casing at the far-right edge of this dynamic composi-tion of criss crossing lines and zig-zag patterns. Painting in a precise, quasi-photographic style, Sheeler, even more than his friend Demuth, abandoned the confusion of Cubist fragmenta-tion, while adopting the simplified, relatively abstract geometry of American machinery, functional architecture, and furniture.

The Ford Motor Company's River Rouge complex was represented in even more monu-mental, mythic terms by the internationally renowned Mexican muralist Diego Rivera (1886–1957). Commissioned by the Detroit Institute of Arts and Edsel Ford, Henry Ford's son, Rivera's multipaneled, epic history painting,

Detroit Industry, fills the art museum's garden, or central court (fig. 7.64). Unlike Sheeler's industri-al landscapes, which are devoid of human figures, *Detroit Industry* strongly suggests the productive, synergistic relationship between people and machine with factory, assembly-line scenes, pop-ulated by strong, dignified workers, adapted to the Frederick Taylor-inspired, time-motion sys-tem for the division of labor. The primary north and south walls feature personifications of the human race in a long, horizontal strip at the top of each wall: red and black figures on the north; white and yellow on the south. Otherwise, each of these main walls is dominated by a large panel, depicting the processes of automotive produc-tion: the manufacture of a Ford V-8 engine and transmission on the north and the production and final assembly of the automobile's exterior on the south. Portraits of Edsel Ford and Dr. William Valentiner, director of the Detroit Institute of Arts, appear in the lower-right corner of the south wall's large panel. A portrait of Henry Ford teaching workers in a trade-school engine class is found on a small panel just to the left of center, below the main scene.

Together with José Clemente Orozco (1883–1949) and David Alfaro Siqueiros (1896–1974),

Rivera was one of three major Mexican muralists to receive significant commissions in the United States. Beginning with the fall of the U.S.-supported dictator Porfirio Diaz in 1911 at the hands of a popular uprising, Mexico had experienced a tumultuous period of civil war and revolution, punctuated by the military and diplomatic intervention of the United States government. In 1921, after studying in Paris within the Cubist, avant-garde circle of artists, Rivera returned to Mexico to paint murals in public buildings for the new revolutionary government.

Ever since the Russian Revolution of 1917, which he also supported, the artist had abandoned Cubism for a popular, realist style, choosing subjects that both promoted revolutionary ideals and celebrated Mexico's pre-Columbian, indigenous culture. Though a change in government in 1924 led to a conservative, anti-communist political climate, Rivera maintained friendly ties to the new regime and continued to receive government commissions.

Given the Mexican government's continuing patronage of Rivera, Edsel Ford may have assumed that he and the Detroit Institute of Arts were not only hiring a superbly gifted muralist, but also an influential Latin American cultural leader, who could speak on behalf of Henry Ford's industrial vision to authorities in Mexico and elsewhere. United States corporate leaders were concerned to protect their investments south of the border, particularly their access to Mexican oil, a precious commodity for the automotive industry.

Arranged on four walls according to the four cardinal points of the compass, Rivera's *Detroit Industry* optimistically celebrates the modern technology of the Ford Corporation. For the Marxist painter, capitalism constituted an unjust exploitation of labor, but, at the same time, it could be viewed as a historically necessary stage of socioeconomic development on the inevitable path toward socialism. The technology and collective factory labor generated by capitalism was viewed by Rivera and other Marxists as a precondition for labor's ultimate revolutionary ascent in owning and controlling the means of production. Thus, on the right side of the south wall, the large panel depicting the River Rouge factory includes a large machine that resembles a well-known,

ancient Aztec sculpture of the serpent goddess Coatlicue, who was both a creator and a destroyer, symbolizing the womb as well as the tomb. Defined by large circular forms for its head and arms, the industrialized, robotic-appearing Coatlicue shares a close symbolic relationship with the ancient *uroboros*, or circular serpent biting its own tail, as detailed in earlier chapters (see figs. 1.11 and 4.29). Both Coatlicue and the *uroboros* signify the life-death, creation-destruction cycles of nature and, by extension, of revolutionary social and political change. As Francis V. O'Connor has argued, the entire wall arrangement of *Detroit Industry* is based upon the cyclical movement of the sun through the sky. On the east wall, Rivera painted the particularly significant image of a small infant, nestled within the bulb of a plant to express rebirth and the regenerative light of a new day. By identifying revolutionary socioeconomic changes as a natural, organic process, Rivera underscored its historical inevitability. But, at the same time, even as the Ford Motor Company was battling unions and demonstrating workers, Rivera's appropriation of ancient Aztec imagery and other mythic, cosmic forms defused the idea of immediate, revolutionary change in favor of a long, evolutionary view. Against those conservative critics who accused Rivera of incorporating communist content into *Detroit Industry*, both autoworkers and Edsel Ford strongly defended Rivera's long-term primordial vision of industry rising from the ancient geological composition of Michigan's soil.

Nature and the Machine Age in Domestic Architecture

The relationship between nature and machine also preoccupied architects of private homes. In Los Angeles, Vienna-born Richard Neutra (1892–1970) helped introduce International Style, modernist architecture into the United States. Invented by European architects, especially Walter Gropius (1883–1969) at Germany's Bauhaus school of design, the International Style rejected historical-revival, national traditions in favor of a more universal, functional machine aesthetic of steel, reinforced concrete, and glass, shaped into light and airy, crisply geometric, unornamented buildings.

Before emigrating to the United States in 1923, Neutra had worked with the Viennese

7.65 Richard J. Neutra
Philip Lovell House,
Hollywood Hills, Los
Angeles, 1927–9.

7.65 Richard J. Neutra
Philip Lovell House,
Hollywood Hills, Los
Angeles, 1927–9.

architect Adolf Loos (1870–1933), who argued in his book *Ornament and Crime* (1908) that a lack of ornamentation in architecture signified superior spiritual strength. As evident in his design for the "Health House," the multilevel home of Dr. Phillip M. Lovell in the Hollywood Hills section of Los Angeles, Neutra and his client also regarded the clean lines, asymmetrical openness, and light-flooded spaces of International Style architecture as an environment for physical well-being and hygiene (fig. 7.65). The author of a newspaper health column, Dr. Lovell strongly advocated exercise and outdoor activities. Neutra thus adapted the sprawling steel-skeleton residence to the configuration of the hilly landscape, creating a series of descending rectangular-shaped porches, balconies, and terraces, a pattern of light and shaded planar strips, overgrown by natural vegetation.

Neutra's integration of streamlined modernist architecture with the surrounding environment was strongly influenced by his admiration of Frank Lloyd Wright's prairie style of domestic architecture. Yet, unlike the Lovell house, which

7.66 Frank Lloyd Wright
Fallingwater, or The Kaufmann House, Bear Run, Pennsylvania, 1937.

seems to float over the earth like a sleek, white ocean liner, Wright's homes eschewed the machine aesthetic of the International Style and more firmly hugged the land to create organic, womb-like spaces. Already at the turn of the century, Wright had employed overhanging roofs and balconies that protected long ribbons of windows and established a dynamic interplay between interior and exterior spaces, while simultaneously creating a sheltered, cave-like sense of privacy (see fig. 6.19). Decades later, in Fallingwater, a country retreat designed for a Pittsburgh department-store owner, Wright fully realized his vision of creating a home that appears not only to imitate, but also to originate from, the earth's porous, underground network of caves, tunnels, and springs (fig. 7.66). Built over Bear Run and an actual waterfall, Fallingwater has deeply recessed interiors that mimic nature's cavernous spaces. Glass-wall openings or ribbon windows are shielded by roof overhangs and cantilevered or projecting reinforced concrete balconies. At the heart of this shaded refuge, an enormous fireplace offers the comfort of warmth and additional light in cold, damp weather.

Regionalism Versus Social Realism

Following World War I, as we have seen in Charles Sheeler's *Home, Sweet Home,* (see fig. 7.63) there was a strong trend toward cultural

7.67 Elie Nadelman
Tango, 1919.
Painted cherry wood and gesso, 3 units,
35⅞ x 26 x 13⅞ in
(91.1 x 66 x 35.2 cm).
Whitney Museum of American Art, New York.

These delicate, doll-like wooden figures are fashionably dressed and dancing the Argentine tango. Despite its Argentine folk origins, Nadelman's *Tango* expresses the sophistication of the modern hotel ballroom. The crisscrossed arms and interlocked gazes of the two figures sexually magnetize the "empty" space between them.

7.68 John Steuart Curry
Baptism in Kansas,
1928.
Oil on canvas, 40 x 50 in
(101.6 x 127 cm).
Whitney Museum of
American Art, New York.

This painting represents a
baptism conducted by the
Campbellites, a Christian
fundamentalist sect. The
scene is located on a farm
neighboring Curry's own
home. Standing in the
middle of a water tank, a
black-suited minister is
about to immerse a female
convert dressed in white.
Other white-robed figures
wait their turn for baptism.

7.69 Thomas Hart Benton
1927–New York Today,
1927.
Oil on canvas,
70 x 36 in
(177.8 x 91.5 cm).
Courtesy Hirschl-Adler
Galleries, New York.

nationalism in American Art. In 1919, in the wake of numerous anarchist bombings and the Soviet Union's establishment of the Communist Third International, which fostered revolutionary politics abroad, the United States government began rounding up thousands of working-class immigrants suspected of being communists. That same year, the Senate expressed support for an isolationist foreign policy by rejecting President Woodrow Wilson's proposal for an international League of Nations. During the 1920s and 1930s, the industrialists John D. Rockefeller, Jr. and Henry Ford collected American folk art and antiques and nostalgically re-created America's pre-modern past in the living museums of Colonial Williamsburg, Virginia, and Greenfield Village, Michigan.

By contrast, Modernist artists appropriated folk art for more radical ends: they employed the style's simplified forms to suggest that Americans possessed an instinctive taste for anti-academic art and abstraction. The Polish-American sculptor Elie Nadelman (1882–1946), who had a solo exhibition at Stieglitz's 291 Gallery in 1915 and was a member of John Weichsel's People's Art Guild, became an avid collector of American folk art and adapted its naive, self-taught appearance for many of his elegant, stylish sculptures (fig. 7.67). Meanwhile, American painters represented nationalist historical narratives, regional customs,

7.70 Grant Wood
American Gothic, 1930.
Oil on beaver board, 29⅞
x 24⅞ in (76 x 63.2 cm).
Art Institute of Chicago,
Chicago, Illinois.
Friends of American Art
Collection.

With its vertical board-and-
batten construction and
pointed arch window, Wood's
Iowa farmhouse echoes the
Gothic Revival architecture of
Alexander Jackson Davis (see
fig. 5.17). Although the couple
may be interpreted as
personifications of Midwestern
moral virtue, both figures have
frowning expressions. Perhaps
expressing a stereotypical
rural suspicion of strangers,
the couple's apparent lack of
hospitality is reinforced by the
pitchfork, held tightly by the
farmer as a possible weapon.

and folkways that had survived the forces of economic modernization. Indicative of the growth
of Protestant fundamentalism during the 1920s,
the Kansas painter John Steuart Curry (1897–
1946) first gained public recognition with his
painting *Baptism in Kansas* (fig.7.68) and a series
of other pictures representing rural American
religious piety. The wealthy railroad heiress and
art collector Gertrude Vanderbilt Whitney (1875–
1942) purchased Curry's *Baptism* and posed with
it for a publicity photograph, marking the 1931
opening of her Whitney Museum of American
Art. Unlike the Museum of Modern Art, which
opened two years earlier in New York, the
Whitney Museum dedicated itself to American
Art and the support of living American artists.
Herself a sculptor of the human figure, Whitney
collected a diverse array of modern American art,
but tended to favor realists, beginning with
members of the Ashcan School, whose gritty

street scenes she admired. Curry's *Baptism* represents the conflicted socioeconomic, cultural
landscape of the American heartland. Though
focused upon a traditional Midwestern religious
ritual, a line of Henry Ford's Model-T cars encir-
cles the ceremony, culminating in a vehicle that
presses toward us on the painting's left edge.
Meanwhile, with a touch of humor, the farmhouse in the background appears with
window-eyes to share our interest in this
exotic juxtaposition of local, regional customs
and modernizing consumerism.

Earlier, in 1919, Thomas Hart Benton
(1889–1975), great-nephew of a famed United
States Senator from Missouri (see p. 222), essentially launched the Regionalist painting
movement when he began a series of mural-size
pictures entitled *The American Historical Epic*.
In 1916, Benton had exhibited with the
Synchromists at the Forum Exhibition of

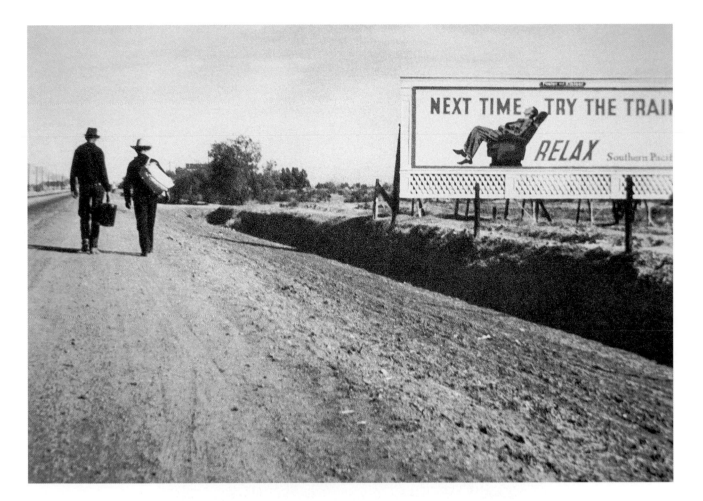

7.71 Dorothea Lange
Southern Pacific Railroad Billboard near Los Angeles, California, 1937.
Library of Congress, Washington, D.C.

Modern American Painters, but, unlike Stanton Macdonald-Wright and Morgan Russell, he was unwilling to give up recognizable subject matter. Far from being a reactionary anti-Modernist, Benton was attracted to John Weichsel's People's Art Guild and its attempt to make modern art more socially and politically connected to progressive, democratic reforms. Seeking to reach a broader audience, he synthesized the bold colors and rhythms of Synchromist compositional techniques with the modern medium of cinema to create a dynamic, popular visual history of the United States beginning with the Spanish discovery and conquest. Having worked as a set designer for numerous westerns and two-reel movies from 1913 to 1918, Benton appropriated the stereotypical cast of characters from cinema to create immediately recognizable, action-filled narrative paintings. Though Regionalist artists tended to focus upon rural themes of farming and small-town settlements, Benton did not hes-

itate to paint urban scenes. Following the western, pioneering picture *Over the Mountains,* his *1927—New York Today* (fig. 7.69) represented the futuristic culmination of *The American Historical Epic.*

This painting's verticality and towering skyscrapers recall the architectural forms of John Storrs and the machine aesthetic of the Precisionists. However, Benton preferred to focus upon people rather than buildings. Suggesting a political desire for humane, democratic control of the urban-industrial environment, Benton portrays a team of muscular construction workers, whose heroic, curvilinear forms dominate the picture space. During the 1920s, the Ku Klux Klan, the white supremacist terrorist organization, grew phenomenally to a nationwide membership of several million and dominated local and state politics, not only in the South, but also in many parts of the Midwest and West. Nevertheless, in *The American Historical Epic,* Benton

7.72 Walker Evans
Allie Mae Burroughs,
1936.
Gelatin silver print.
Library of Congress,
Washington, D.C.

represented the brutality of slavery and also depicted blacks and whites working harmoniously together to settle and build the nation. During the Depression of the 1930s, he painted numerous similar public murals that supported President Franklin Delano Roosevelt's "New Deal" social policies for stimulating the economy and providing welfare and work projects for millions who had lost jobs from bankrupt companies and closed factories. Opposed to the communist belief in class struggle, Benton shared the social viewpoint of the American commentator Lewis Mumford, who defined Regionalism as a progressive synthesis of industrial efficiency and pre-industrial communal values.

In 1930, a year after the stock-market crash, the Iowa painter Grant Wood (1892–1942) produced *American Gothic* (fig. 7.70), the most famous picture of Midwestern Regionalism.

Wood studied in Paris and Munich during the 1920s and attended Iowa State University, but he enjoyed posing for photographs dressed as a country farmer. Similarly, Wood's sister and the local Cedar Rapids dentist posed as the painting's fictive farming couple. While many critics and art historians have interpreted *American Gothic* as a humorous satire, the painting's representation of sturdy individualism, religious piety, and rural labor was also reassuring for a nation experiencing numerous farm foreclosures, bank failures, and a sharp decline in economic production.

Wood's portrait of Midwestern types is actually a history painting inspired by his discovery of a nineteenth-century farmhouse that had a distinctive Gothic-arch window, a form borrowed from church architecture and a symbol of religious piety. The painting nostalgically depicts 1880s Iowans, who may be imagined as the

7.73 Ben Shahn
Sheriff During Strike,
Morgantown, West
Virginia, 1935.
Gelatin silver print,
7⅛ x 9½ in
(18.4 x 24.1 cm).
Hallmark Photographic
Collection, Hallmark
Cards, Inc., Kansas City,
Missouri.

original occupants of the house. Wood studied nineteenth-century photographs and had his models stiffly pose with old-fashioned costumes and props. Wishing to demonstrate how the Midwestern rural environment was shaped by virtuous, hard-working settlers, he framed the Gothic window with human figures that reiterate the building's upright, vertical architecture. Symbolizing masculine work and strength, the pitchfork mimics the rectilinear patterns of the man's bib overalls and shirt as well as the house's wooden siding. By contrast, a circular pattern in the woman's dress, together with her oval, egg-shaped head and ivory cameo, accentuates the feminine gender and associates her with the domestic fertility of the potted plants resting upon the porch in the background.

During the 1930s, dust storms, floods, and other natural disasters aggravated the national economic crisis. The Farm Security Administration (FSA), an agency of Roosevelt's New Deal, hired a team of photographers to document the destitute living conditions of America's farmers.

In contrast to the prosperity and stability of Wood's Midwestern couple, Dorothea Lange's (1895–1965) photograph of a pair of migrant workers walking down the middle of a dusty California road underscores the rootless plight of contemporary agricultural labor (fig. 7.71). By juxtaposing the two men with the cruelly ironic message of a Southern Pacific Railroad billboard, Lange contradicts corporate advertising's images of upper- and middle-class affluence, which totally ignored the realities of the Depression. The billboard's representation of a comfortable, sleeping passenger particularly emphasizes this willful blindness toward the hardships of the unemployed and working poor.

Similarly FSA photographer Walker Evans (1903–1975) traveled the Deep South, where he poignantly documented the lives of impoverished sharecroppers or tenant farmers. Evans's dignified, yet unsettling, close-up portrait of the Alabama woman Allie Mae Burroughs (fig. 7.72) compresses the sitter's space and accentuates her vulnerability to our probing, privileged gaze. As opposed to the uplifting verticality of Grant Wood's *American Gothic* (see fig.7.70), here the emphatic horizontals of the clapboards seem confining, as the top of Burroughs's head presses against a restraining clapboard edge. Meanwhile, the sitter's planar forehead, straight, unarched eyebrows, and elongated, closed lips visually embed her within the horizontal grains of wood.

The painter Ben Shahn (1898–1969) also traveled the countryside working for the FSA, not only taking photographs, but also painting murals for small, working-class communities. Shahn used his photographs as material for many of his paintings. However, his snapshot of a Morgantown, West Virginia, sheriff during a coal miners' strike stands on its own as a powerful political statement against government repression of labor-union activities (fig. 7.73). By cropping the sheriff's head and concentrating upon his holstered gun and ample backside, Shahn creates the generic image of an authoritarian local policeman, serving the interests of

company owners and mine managers.

Photographers working outside of New Deal agencies also managed to capture the depressed national mood even if they did not direct their cameras toward the human figure. Primarily known for his sharply focused close-up shots of peppers, seashells, and other organic forms, Edward Weston (1886–1958) traveled throughout the western United States during the late 1930s. Published in a photographic travelogue, *California and the West* (1940), Weston's picture of *Dante's View, Death Valley* (fig. 7.74) represents a desolate California landscape that evokes an association with the *Inferno*, an epic vision of hell from the *Divine Comedy* (1313–14), by the Italian poet Dante Alighieri.

During the 1930s, the art market was also a casualty of the Depression. With most artists unable to sell their work, President Roosevelt in 1935 established the Works Progress Administration (WPA) and Federal Arts Project (FAP). Within a year the WPA-FAP was employing over

7.74 Edward Weston
Dante's View, Death Valley, 1938.
Gelatin silver print, 7⅝ x 9½ in (19 x 24 cm). Collection Center for Creative Photography, Arizona Board of Regents, University of Arizona, Tucson.

From Dante's View, 6,000 feet above sea level, Weston aimed his camera downward toward the salt beds of the valley floor, which continually changed, depending upon the amount of water that flowed into curving stream and lake shapes. Always shooting within inches of the same spot, he created photographs representing the different ghostly patterns of the valley's black, white, gray, and brown tones.

7.75 William Gropper
Construction of a Dam,
1938–9.
Mural, center panel 8 ft
11 in (2.69 m) high x 14
ft 6 in (4.41 m) wide; side
panels 8 ft 11 in (2.69 m)
high x 7 ft 9 in (2.36 m)
wide. Department of
Interior Museum,
Washington D.C.

5,000 artists and eventually sponsored the production of over 2,500 public murals, 108,000
easel paintings, and thousands of prints and
posters for post offices, public employment and
welfare agencies, and other government offices.
In addition, the U.S. Treasury Department created in 1934 the Section of Painting and Sculpture,
which commissioned over 1,100 murals and 300
sculptures for new federal buildings.

William Gropper (1897–1977), a cartoonist
for the left-wing journal *New Masses* and other
publications, was one among a number of politically active artists who painted large-scale
murals of American labor under the auspices
of the Treasury Section. Gropper's three-panel
wall painting, *Construction of a Dam* (Fig 7.75),
for the headquarters of the United States
Interior Department, was inspired by various

7.76 Moses Soyer
Artists on WPA, 1935.
National Museum of
American Art,
Washington, D.C.

Although no style of art was
proscribed by the WPA,
some government
administrators were hostile
to Modernist abstraction.
Furthermore, participating
artists sought to
communicate with a broad
public and, therefore,
tended to favor easily
recognizable subjects. As
Moses Soyer recalled,
Depression-era artists were
excited by the sense that
they had a social mission
and were needed by a
public hungry for visually
uplifting images such as
those being finished by this
workshop of painters.

7.77 Paul Cadmus
The Fleet's In! 1934.
Oil on canvas, 30 x 60 in
(76 x 152.5 cm).
United States Navy
Art Collection,
Washington, D.C.

dam projects sponsored by the government agency during the Great Depression, including the Grand Coulee Dam on the Columbia River in the Pacific Northwest. With strong masculine bodies dramatically silhouetted against a deep-perspective, mountainous landscape, Gropper celebrates the workers' daring gravity-defying bravery and collective solidarity.

Inevitably, artists experienced creative limitations in works they produced for government commissions. Rescued from unemployment by the Civil Works Administration (CWA), the aspiring New York artist Paul Cadmus (1904–83) was hired by the agency's Public Works of Art Project (PWAP) to paint easel pictures on American subjects of his choice. The paintings were to be exhibited by the PWAP at the Corcoran Gallery of Art in Washington, D.C. However, Cadmus's *The Fleet's In!* (Fig 7.77), a satirical, cartoonish representation of American sailors on leave, caused a public moral uproar, and it was removed from exhibition by the assistant secretary of the navy. Wearing skin-tight, revealing uniforms, the drunken sailors are in sexual negotiation with female prostitutes and, at the far left, an effeminate man. The dandy offers cigarettes to a sailor, whose buddy is sprawled out very suggestively between them. Though contemporaries did not employ the word "homosexual" to describe the content, the painting's homoerotic subtext was not limited to the dandy. With arms draped over each other, the sailors are all objects of the artist's own homosexual desire. Not openly acknowledging his homosexuality in the repressive atmosphere of the 193's, Cadmus claimed he was only painting a scene from real life and that he had frequently witnessed the spectacle of carousing sailors in Riverside Park near his home on Riverside Drive.

In his painting of *Artists on WPA* (fig. 7.76), the Russian-born, New York artist Moses Soyer (1899–1975) represents the collective nature of artistic production under the WPA's Portable Murals Project. From his chair in the lower-right corner, the portly, plainly dressed Soyer draws a sketch, while a female model casually sits in front of him smoking a cigarette. Soyer's assistants, two women and three men, are all absorbed by their work for *Children at Play*, a multi-panel mural for the children's ward of a New York hospital. Soyer, like Ben Shahn, was a Social Realist painter who was critical of the nostalgic provincialism and nationalism of the Regionalist or "American Scene" paintings that chauvinistically celebrated America. As suggested by the workmanlike, production-line character of Moses Soyer's studio, Social Realists personally

7.78 Aaron Douglas
Aspects of Negro Life: Song of the Towers, 1934.
Oil on canvas, 9 x 9 ft (2.74 x 2.74 m). Art and Artifacts Division, Schomburg Center for Research in Black Culture, New York Public Library, New York. Astor, Lenox, and Tilden Foundations.

Douglas's critical interpretation of American urbanism and industrialization expressed his socialist political views and strong support for labor unions. The plumes of smoke and towering urban-industrial forms create the demonic characteristics of a hellish underworld.

identified themselves with the working class.

The mural paintings of Aaron Douglas demonstrate that Social Realism also could encompass a more Modernist, abstract vocabulary of forms. His *Song of the Towers* (fig. 7.78) is one of a series of FAP murals on *Aspects of Negro Life* for a branch of the New York Public Library that serves Harlem. Painted after the optimistic height of the Harlem Renaissance during the 1920s, Douglas's Depression-era Public Library mural decoration expressed the new cultural pessimism caused by mass unemployment and poverty. His mural represents the silhouettes of several African-American men within a nightmarish urban-industrial landscape of mechanical wheel cogs, skyscrapers, and polluting smokestacks. At the center stands a jazz saxophonist, juxtaposed with New York harbor's Statue of Liberty in the far background. However, the distant promise of African-American freedom appears overwhelmed by an inhuman socio-economic environment. In the lower-left corner, an exhausted, muscular figure holds his head in despair, as serpentine and clawlike clouds of smoke threaten to imprison him, sapping his strength.

Modernism and the Defense of Democracy

In 1934, Douglas and many other artists formed the Artists' Union, a labor union that sought to create better working conditions and economic security for visual artists struggling against the decline in the private art market. A year later, most of these same artists joined the American Artists' Congress, which was supported by the American Communist Party as part of the larger Popular Front movement of labor unions, New Deal liberals, socialist political organizations, and leftist cultural groups, committed to defending democracy and freedom from the militaristic and totalitarian policies of Benito Mussolini's

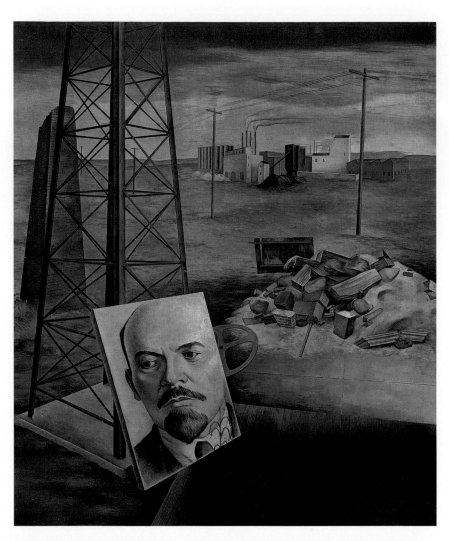

7.79
O. Louis Guglielmi
*Portrait and Background
(Phoenix)*, 1935.
Oil on canvas,
30 x 25 in
(76.2 x 63.5 cm).
Sheldon Memorial Art
Gallery and Sculpture
Garden, University of
Nebraska, Lincoln.

Guglielmi's painting is
indebted to the
hallucinatory, nightmarish
styles of the Italian artist
Giorgio de Chirico
(1888–1978) and the
Spanish Surrealist Salvador
Dalí (1904–1989).
However, unlike Dalí's
overtly sexual, Freudian
themes, Guglielmi's
bizarre juxtaposition of
motifs expressed his strong
social and political advocacy
for revolutionary, working-
class causes.

fascist dictatorship in Italy and Adolf Hitler's Nazi Party state in Germany.

The Egyptian-born O. Louis Guglielmi (1906–56) explicitly expressed his support for the Communist Party with *Portrait and Background (Phoenix)* (fig. 7.79), a strange, surreal dreamscape, juxtaposing a portrait of Vladimir Lenin, deceased Russian revolutionary and founder of the Soviet Union, against a desolate industrial landscape. Yet a slender corn stalk, an emblem of hope and regeneration, merges with Lenin's likeness to prophesy the ultimate, phoenix-like triumph of a Communist, working-class utopia upon the ruins of Depression-era capitalism. Contemporaneously, the New Deal FAP artist Alice Neel (1900–84), who later became identified with the feminist art movement of the 1970s, painted an impressive portrait of Pat

Whalen, an Irish-American labor organizer for the National Maritime Union (fig. 7.80). Though Whalen was a physically small man, Neel represented him in visionary, bigger-than-life terms. The sitter's rugged, determined gaze underscores an intensity of political commitment, while his enormous fists resting upon a copy of the Communist Party's *Daily Worker* suggests readiness to struggle for the rights of striking workers as proclaimed in the newspaper's banner headline.

The Depression had caused mass unemployment and unrest in Europe as well as in America. Appealing to the German capitalist and middle-class desire for order and promising revenge for Germany's defeat in World War I, Hitler gained power in 1933 by attacking Jews, communists, and the alleged decadence of

7.80 Alice Neel
Pat Whalen, 1935.
Oil on canvas,
27 x 33 in
(68.6 x 58.4 cm).
Whitney Museum of
American Art, New York.
Gift of Dr. Hartley Neel.

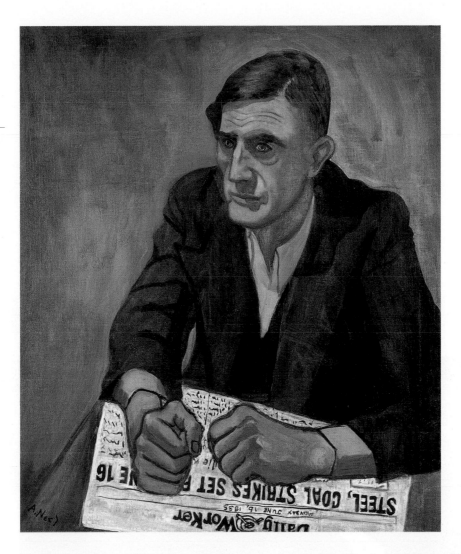

Modernist culture, while promoting Germans as a master race, descended from blond, blue-eyed Aryan peoples. Having begun his career as a minor painter, Hitler conservatively adopted academic neoclassicism as the official Nazi style in art and architecture and condemned as degenerate modern, abstract art, which he associated with communism, Judaism, and African primitivism.

Hitler's denunciation of Modernist art served to strengthen the perception that abstract painting and sculpture possessed a very strong, anti-fascist political content. Stuart Davis (1894–1964), the national chairman of the American Artists' Congress from 1936 to 1940, was a Cubist-inspired painter who believed that abstract, modern art was an antidote to fascism. It could stimulate positive and radical political changes in America and the world, because such art interpreted reality, not in terms of absolutes or static, unchanging truths, but rather as a material state of conflicting processes, dynamic individual relationships, and temporary negotiated solutions. Though he identified with socialist and working-class causes and had once worked in an Ashcan School style, Davis rejected Social Realist art as endorsed by the American Communist Party. Like Regionalist painting, which he despised as a reactionary form of nationalism, Davis regarded Social Realism as a backward, propagandistic style that failed to express the modern reality of change and motion. His *Hot Still-Scape for Six Colors—7th Avenue Style* (fig. 7.81) is, therefore, an implicitly political painting. As a "still-scape," completed in his Seventh Avenue studio, it combines forms

7.81 Stuart Davis
Hot Still-Scape for Six Colors —7th Avenue Style, 1940.
Oil on canvas, 36 x 44⅞ in (91.4 x 114 cm).
Museum of Fine Arts, Boston, Massachusetts. Gift of the William H. Lane Foundation and the Mr. and Mrs Karolik Collection, by exchange.

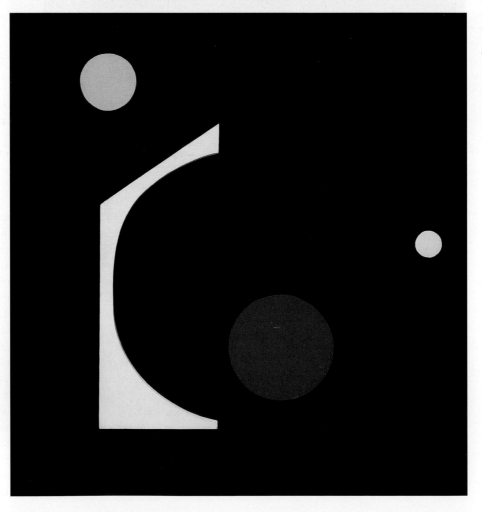

7.82 Burgoyne Diller
Construction, 1934.
Painted wood and fiberboard, 24 x 24 x 1 in (60.9 x 60.9 x 2.5 cm). Hirschhorn Museum and Sculpture Garden, Smithsonian Institution, New York. Gift of Joseph H. Hirschhorn, 1966.

from two different art traditions, still life and landscape painting. Davis draws upon the Cubist tradition of overlapping geometric forms to replicate in paint the colorful, "hot" rhythms and improvisational riffs of American jazz, which he frequently listened to in all-night jazz sessions at New York nightclubs. Jazz musicians who are "hot" are so thoroughly absorbed by their art that they freely experiment with melodies and rhythms, spontaneously expressing intense feelings. Within his jigsaw puzzle of hot- and cool-colored shapes, Davis creates doodling, twisting lines and shapes that suggest improvisational jazz techniques. These arbitrary doodles also recall European Surrealist painters such as Joan Miró (1893–1983), who developed relatively spontaneous, "automatic" drawing styles as a means for exploring the unconscious and releasing repressed feelings and desires. However, unlike the Surrealists and the Abstract Expressionists, whom we shall discuss in the next chapter, Davis created an abstract art that was primarily inspired by the urban-industrial environment of street signs, traffic, commercial advertising, cafés, clubs, radio, and other forms of mass communication.

Davis was one of a group of New York abstract artists who were hired to paint public murals under the New Deal's Federal Arts Project. Particularly influential was Burgoyne Diller (1906–1965), who was appointed director of the mural division of the FAP in New York City, despite his non-objective, anti realist style. Diller's own creative work was inspired, in part, by the geometric abstractions of Russian avant-garde artists exhibited at the Société Anonyme. A painted-wood *Construction* (fig. 7.82), assembled in 1934, also shares the buoyant cosmic energy and primal orbiting forms of Alexander Calder's mobiles (see fig. 7.45). Meanwhile, as an administrator, Diller recruited fellow abstract artists to execute murals for such sites as the Williamsburg Housing Project in Brooklyn, New York, a modern, low-income housing complex, designed by the International Style architect William Lescaze (1896–1969) for the FAP and New York Housing Authority. Though he eventually withdrew from the Williamsburg Project over a disagreement with Diller, Stuart Davis composed *Swing Landscape* (1938), a mural close in its jazz spirit to the later *Hot Still-scape*.

More successfully, the Russian-born painter Ilya Bolotowsky (1907–1981) persisted from sketch stage (fig. 7.83) to final installation for an abstract Williamsburg mural that harmonized

7.84 Morris Graves
Blind Bird, 1940.
Gouache and watercolor
on mulberry paper,
30 x 27 in
(76.2 x 68.5 cm).
Museum of Modern Art,
New York. Purchase.

with the modernist geometry of the architecture. Bolotowsky's installation sketch demonstrates how he attempted to adapt the horizontal shape of his mural and its interior directional lines to the surrounding architectural space designed by Lescaze. According to Diller, the Williamsburg murals were calculated to work with the functional architecture in creating relaxing, entertaining living spaces for residents. Bolotowsky, a political leftist, made no concessions to the populist Social Realist aesthetic. Instead, he sought a harmonizing balance of intense warm and cool colors, and of crisply rectilinear and vitalistic curvilinear shapes. Whether or not it was psychologically therapeutic for Williamsburg families, the mural's dynamic,

pulsating forms aesthetically suggest modernity, cultural progress, and an optimistic faith in human creativity.

By 1940, when he painted *Hot Still-scape*, Davis, like most other leftist American artists, had become disillusioned by the failure of the Popular Front. In August of 1939, Joseph Stalin, the communist dictator of the Soviet Union, had signed a non-aggression pact with Hitler, which enabled Nazi Germany to invade Poland the following month, marking the beginning of World War II. By April 1940, after the Soviet Union had invaded Finland, Davis quit the American Artists' Congress and condemned both communism and Nazism as totalitarian systems opposed to democracy. The United

States finally entered the war only after the Japanese, allies of Germany and Italy, bombed the Hawaiian U.S. naval base of Pearl Harbor on December 7, 1941.

In the next chapter, we shall see how World War II contributed to the international dominance of American art. Assisted by the arrival of numerous immigrants, American artists and architects would emerge from the war as leading, avant-garde inheritors of the European Modernist tradition.

On the other hand, American artists also became more open to influences from the East. Though his painting *Broadway* (see p.296) bears kinship with the cityscapes of Joseph Stella, Stuart Davis, and others, the Wisconsin-born artist Mark Tobey (1890–1976) invented his "white writing," or all-over drawing technique, after traveling to the Far East to study Zen Buddhism, Japanese calligraphy, and Chinese brushwork. Zen meditation techniques helped Tobey to lose himself in a receptive openness to universal spiritual forces, as expressed by his luminous, unifying web of linear energy.

Tobey shared his interest in Zen Buddhism and Asian art and philosophy with the Pacific Northwest painter Morris Graves (1910–2001). Graves adapted Tobey's white-writing method to create haunting symbolic images that often featured vulnerable, wounded, or dying birds in the tradition of Albert Pinkham Ryder's *The Dead Bird* (see fig. 6.61). In *Blind Bird* (fig. 7.84), Graves perched a black, meditative bird atop skeins of fine, white lines, encasing mounds of dark matter. Traditionally, physical blindness has been associated with a prophetic inner vision. Graves's dark, shrouded bird form ominously expressed the feeling of spiritual crisis gripping the world at the violent beginning of a new decade.

Chapter 8

Modernism, Postmodernism, and the Survival of a Critical Vision
1941–80

Willem de Kooning
Woman I, 1950–2.
Oil on canvas,
6 ft 3⅞ in x 4 ft 10 in
(1.92 x 1.47 m).
Museum of Modern Art,
New York.

Compared to a vampire as well as a modern, secular Madonna, this enthroned, fleshy *Woman*, like Leonardo da Vinci's *Mona Lisa* (1503–5), has elicited a number of conflicting interpretations regarding her oracular, sphinx-like presence. Exaggeratedly summarizing the entire history of female idolatry, de Kooning referred to the comic, hilarious nature of the *Woman* series, suggesting that he was lampooning traditional female stereotypes. Indeed, the figure's grin was inspired by a smiling model in a magazine advertisement for Camel cigarettes.

WHILE New Deal art patronage collapsed during World War II, the immigration of European artists into the United States made New York City the international refuge for avant-garde, Modernist art. The war's violent conclusion in 1945 did nothing to alleviate the sense of crisis experienced by most Americans, who were soon caught up in the Cold War rivalry with the Soviet Union and the frightening prospect that another world war could trigger a devastating nuclear holocaust.

Established in 1945 as an international forum for the resolution of world conflicts and human-rights issues, the United Nations also became embroiled in Cold War politics, as member nations were forced to choose sides in the struggle between the Soviet Union and the United States. John D. Rockefeller, Jr., donated $8.5 million toward the purchase of a New York City site for the organization's new headquarters. The United Nations' presence on Manhattan's East Side underscored the cultural and political preeminence of the United States in world affairs. Concurrently, during an international financial and monetary conference at Bretton Woods, New Hampshire, in 1944, the United States took the initiative in proposing to regulate the world economy by establishing the International Monetary Fund (IMF) and the International Bank for Reconstruction and Development, or the World Bank. These new international agencies, along with the General Agreement on Tariffs and Trade (GATT), established in 1947, were designed to promote the relatively free circulation of capital, free trade, and the openness of national markets and resources to capitalist investment. The fact that voting within the organizations would be proportional to the amount of capital contributed automatically guaranteed American supremacy in decision-making. Furthermore, the United States dollar, then backed by the nation's possession of about one third of the world's gold, became the dominant currency for the transactions of the new agencies. The Soviet Union and other socialist countries refused to cooperate with this postwar economic system, which benefited multinational corporations dependent upon a stable, international flow of capital and ready access to essential commodities, such as oil, natural rubber, coffee, manganese, aluminum, copper, and other resources. In Latin America alone, from 1950 to 1965, United States corporations invested $3.8 billion, while reaping $11.2 billion in profits.

While it financed the rebuilding of Japan and western Europe, the United States also established the secretive Central Intelligence Agency (1947). The spy organization operated covertly to overthrow left-leaning governments in Iran (1953), Guatemala (1954), and Chile (1973), or wherever there was a threat to expropriate or nationalize key industries owned by American corporations, their partners, and subsidiaries. The United States also intervened militarily on a far larger scale in the stalemated Korean War (1950–3) and the Vietnam War, which the American government entered in earnest during the early 1960s, only to withdraw in defeat by 1975. A few years later, in 1979, the United States suffered a further setback as Iranian revolutionaries, inspired by the Islamic religious leader Ayatollah Khomeini, overthrew the American-backed Shah and, in the process, held hostage for two years a group of Americans seized from the United States embassy in Tehran.

Spurred by rapid economic growth and the expansion of U.S. government and corporate interests, the American economy flourished until the late 1960s and 1970s, when a recovered Western Europe and Japan began competing more effectively for overseas markets. At the same time, the Vietnam War drained national resources, fueled inflation, and accelerated the decline of the dollar relative to the other currencies, thereby undermining the monetary equilibrium established under the Bretton Woods Agreements. Furthermore, an energy crisis erupted in 1973, when Middle Eastern Arab countries banned oil exports to the United States, Europe, and Japan in retaliation for their ongoing support for the Jewish state of Israel, founded in 1948 over violent Arab opposition.

The 1960s and 1970s were a period of intense political conflict, as college students throughout the United States and worldwide protested against American involvement in Vietnam. The anti-war protests were part of a larger, leftist political and counter-cultural movement that agitated for the rights of women, African-Americans, Native Americans, migrant Chicano farm laborers, and, more tentatively, gays and lesbians. Unlike the union and working-class radicalism of the 1920s and 1930s, 1960s activism drew heavily upon white, middle-class university youths, who rebelled against the military draft, government, corporate authority, patriarchal social institutions, and sexually, culturally repressive norms of moral behavior. Unable to achieve a significant working-class alliance, the student Left ultimately failed to foment a political revolution or indeed elect an anti-war President. Nevertheless, President Richard M. Nixon, having appealed to America's "Silent Majority" in pursuing the war, was forced to resign from office in 1974 over his participation in the Watergate Scandal, a Republican White House plot to bug the headquarters of the opposition Democratic National Committee during the 1972 presidential election.

Artists responded in a variety of ways to Cold War politics, race relations, Vietnam, women's rights, and the transformation of the American economy from industrial, blue-collar production to post-industrial, financial and information services, and mass-media communications. Artists and architects benefited directly from the intensified publicity generated by expanded media and communications opportunities in radio, television, popular glossy magazines, and new art journals. After World War II, dramatic growth in the art market and the number of working professional artists fueled a pluralism of styles and artistic techniques. From 1949 to 1977, New York City art galleries that handled twentieth-century American art increased over threefold, from ninety to 290. Nationwide, over one million individuals identified themselves as artists in the 1980 United States census, an increase of 67 percent over 1970. The broad professional category included designers, musicians, authors, dancers, actors, and art teachers, as well as painters, sculptors, photographers, and architects. Government and corporate funding stimulated the professional expansion. In 1965, the United States Congress passed legislation establishing the National Endowment for the Arts (NEA). During the late 1960s and early to mid-1970s, the NEA's Visual Arts Program played a significant role in funding alternative spaces for artists to work and exhibit outside of the commercial gallery system. The alternative space movement encouraged artistic experimentation and the production of works that opposed mainstream cultural conventions. P.S.1, one of the most famous alternative spaces in New York, opened in 1976 in a renovated school building, offering aspiring artists exhibition spaces and thirty-five low-rent working studios. Inspired by the example of the NEA, David and Nelson Rockefeller, grandsons of the Gilded Age oil baron John D. Rockefeller, founded the Business Committee for the Arts (BCA) in 1967–8. An exclusive, invitation-only club for the chief executive officers of the wealthiest corporations, the BCA encouraged large, blue-chip companies to support the arts as a means of promoting business and burnishing corporate America's public image.

By the late 1950s, as the new electronic medium of television invaded American homes and revolutionized the advertising, entertainment, and communications industries, artists and critics began to seriously question Modernism's elitist faith in an artistic avant-garde of original, lonely geniuses, standing in heroic opposition to the vulgarity of mass culture. As a result,

American art production expanded with a new pluralism of creative techniques, retrospectively labeled Postmodernist, a broad and imprecise term. Definitions of Postmodernism have varied, depending on the particular artistic medium in question and on differing definitions of Modernism. In fact, it can be argued that Postmodernism simply represented a continuation of Modernism's spirit of experimentation and rebellion.

But to the degree that Modernist critics stressed formal, compositional values and a socially disengaged aesthetic purity, artists identified with Postmodernism rejected that approach for a more eclectic appropriation of non-art materials and popular imagery from the mass media, advertising, and industry. They rejected the formalist notion of autonomous, self-contained art objects in favor of "real" non-art objects, theatrical happenings, installations, environments, performances, body art, video art, and conceptual art. The term Postmodernism became current, first in architectural and later in fine-arts criticism, by the 1970s and early 1980s, after French theorists and critics, led by Roland Barthes, Michel Foucault and Jacques Derrida, questioned the authoritarian power of artistic authorship to limit arbitrarily the fluctuating meanings of verbal and visual "texts," or the myriad readings that beholders produce during their encounters with artworks. However, Postmodernism also has been traced to the Pop Art movement of the 1960s and, earlier, to the revival of Dadaist readymades and other anti-formalist practices during the 1950s.

Subverting Modernist demands for originality, Postmodernist photographers have called attention to the immersion of "high" art into mass, consumer culture by imitating or reproducing the stereotypical imagery of advertising and the entertainment industry. Similarly, Postmodernist architects have derived inspiration from the garish, commercial-strip landscapes of Las Vegas, Nevada, and other hotel, motel, and leisure-resort sites. Breaking with the austere, functionalist aesthetic of Modernist architecture, Postmodernist architects have decorated buildings with historical-revival motifs and contemporary symbols of American consumerism and popular culture. With this pluralistic expansion of styles and creative tech-

niques, artists have struggled to maintain a critical vision amidst market demands for novelty and public celebrity.

Art and Propaganda During World War II

During the 1940s, as the United States battled the Japanese Empire in the Pacific and the German and Italian dictatorships in Europe, American corporations, working closely with government agencies, managed to rehabilitate their public image after industrial capitalism nearly collapsed during the Depression. In retooling factories for military production, American companies represented themselves as patriotic organizations dedicated to the defeat of Nazi tyranny. For example, the Chicago-based Container Corporation of America produced many public relations advertisements that identified the company with the Allied campaign to defeat Hitler (fig. 8.1). In fact, the company employed numerous artists who had formerly worked for the Bauhaus, an enormously influential German school of Modernist design closed by the Nazis in 1933. This nationalist renewal of corporate reputations occurred despite Henry Ford and other major American industrialists,

8.1 Jean Carlu
Gift Packages for Hitler,
1942.
Gouache and gelatin silver print collage on paper, 25 x 19 in (63.5 x 48.3 cm).
National Museum of American Art, Washington, D.C.

who had openly admired and supported the Nazi regime in its early years and initially resisted converting factories for the manufacture of armaments.

World War II brought the United States out of the Depression as the nation's one hundred largest corporations benefited from $117 billion in federal government contracts. Unemployment fell dramatically when able-bodied men joined the armed forces and women took over many jobs in factory assembly lines. During the war years, the democratic idealism, leftist politics, and labor activism of New Deal social programs were displaced by a far more conservative government alliance of business and military leaders. The Boston artist Jack Levine (b. 1915) later satirized this alliance in *Welcome Home* (fig 8.2), an expressionist social commentary, scathingly representing a lavish, triumphant banquet of profiteering businessmen and a smug, portly military officer, who evaded actual

combat, but now feasts upon the spoils of war.

During the war, while Congress passed anti-labor legislation to prevent strikes and to limit unions' financial contributions to political campaigns, the Roosevelt administration organized the Office of War Information (OWI) to galvanize working-class patriotism and discourage anti-nationalist radicalism. At the same time, New Deal programs for the arts were dismantled. By 1943 the Works Progress Administration (WPA), which had employed thousands of artists, was shut down, as were the art projects of the Treasury Department. Although disillusioned by Joseph Stalin's brutal Soviet dictatorship and its temporary alliance with Nazi Germany, leftist American artists, without official government support, founded Artists for Victory shortly after the German invasion of the Soviet Union in 1941. Uniting communists and non-communists, Artists for Victory was a nonprofit umbrella organization

8.2 Jack Levine
Welcome Home, 1946.
Oil on canvas, 40 x 60in
(101.6 x 152.4cm).
Brooklyn Museum of Art,
New York.
John B. Woodward
Memorial Fund.

Embittered by his experience of army life during the war, Levine exhibited this work at New York's Downtown Gallery, owned by Edith Halpert. Halpert strongly supported social, politically committed art. *Welcome Home* received considerable critical attention including coverage in *Time* magazine, where Levine was identified as an angry, alienated artist.

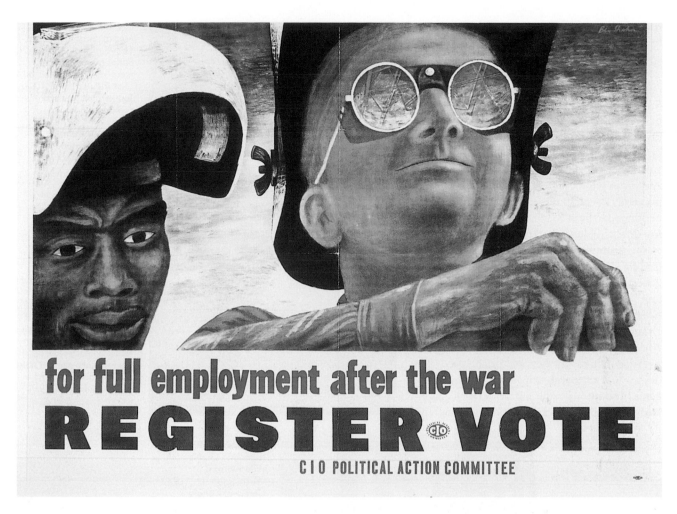

for full employment after the war
REGISTER·VOTE
C I O POLITICAL ACTION COMMITTEE

8.3 Ben Shahn
For Full Employment after the War: Register/Vote, 1944. Lithograph in colors, 29¾ x 39⅛ in (75.5 x 100 cm). New Jersey State Museum Collection, Trenton, New Jersey.

The white welder's large goggles, upward gaze, determined expression, and outstretched hand distinguish him from the secondary, relatively deferential African-American worker. The visionary appearance of the white figure seemed for many to suggest the leadership qualities of President Roosevelt, who, in 1944, was running for reelection to an unprecedented fourth term.

for nearly thirty smaller arts societies. Receiving commissions from various government and military agencies, its members designed propaganda posters, paintings, and advertisements for interest-bearing war bonds to finance the antifascist cause.

The government directly employed some artists to produce war posters. Nevertheless, these artists had little latitude for independent political expression since the government strictly controlled the posters' content. As head of the graphics division for OWI during 1942–3, the New Deal photographer and Social Realist painter Ben Shahn (see fig. 7.73) was frequently censored by his superiors over the imagery he chose. For example, they rejected his poster, originally entitled "A Need for All in Time of War, a Place for All in Time of Peace," which represented an African-American and a white welder. The poster was published later by the

Political Action Committee for the Congress of Industrial Organizations (CIO), the leading umbrella organization for activist labor unions demanding full employment (fig. 8.3). In addition to the controversial fact that the white welder bore too close a resemblance to President Franklin Delano Roosevelt, OWI officials apparently regarded the image of solidarity between black and white workers as too politically radical for a racially segregated nation. Influenced in part by earlier Shahn paintings, the African-American artist Jacob Lawrence (b.1917) vividly underscored the problem of race relations at the beginning of World War II. In a series of sixty paintings entitled *The Migration of the Negro*, the Harlem artist employed a Modernist synthesis of narrative realism and dynamic abstract design to represent the Great Migration of poor, rural Southern African-Americans to the industrial cities of the North (fig. 8.4).

Industrialists employed African-Americans as low-wage strikebreakers. This tactic contributed to white workers' resentments and triggered deadly anti-black race riots. Shahn's later poster optimistically suggests that unionization and full employment would foster racial harmony. Nevertheless, his white welder clearly is the dominant figure in the working-class brotherhood. Working in the nation's capital, for the Farm Security Administration, the African-American photographer Gordon Parks (b.1912) pointedly documented how racist hiring policies continued to limit socioeconomic opportunities for blacks, He reinterpreted Grant Wood's classic painting of white Midwestern virtue (see fig. 7.70), in his portrait of Ella Watson, a government-employed cleaning woman, standing with mop and broom in front of an oversized American flag (fig. 8.5). Like Walker Evans's *Allie Mae Burroughs* (see fig. 7.72), the African-American charwoman seems oppressively confined in her pictorial space. The descending stars and stripes, hanging against a blank, institutional wall, appear to mimic prison bars in this grim, black-and-white photograph.

8.4 Jacob Lawrence
Migration of the Negro, The Migration Series, Panel 50: Race Riots were very Numerous all over the North, 1940–1. Tempera on gesso on composition board, 18 x 12 in (45.7 x 30.5 cm). Museum of Modern Art, New York. Gift of Mrs. David M. Levy.

Lawrence's family had migrated from South Carolina to northern industrial cities. In this panel from the *Migration* series, Lawrence depicted several club and knife-wielding rioters in flattened, distorted patterns of violence directed against unseen victims beyond the picture frame. Although his abstract, simplified style recalls American folk art, Lawrence assimilated Cubist painting techniques and admired Aaron Douglas's fusion of realism and Modernist abstraction (see fig. 7.55).

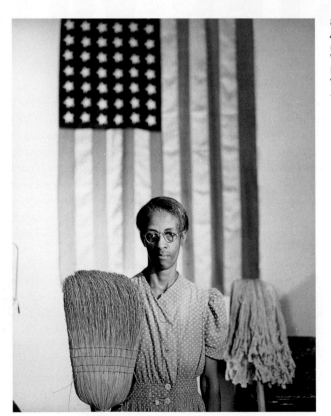

8.5 Gordon Parks
American Gothic (Ella Watson), Washington D.C., 1942. Library of Congress, Washington, D.C.

Modernism and Post-war Architecture

As African-American veterans learned after returning from the war against the racist Nazi dictatorship, American racism would persist in poor-quality segregated housing and public accommodations. Real-estate developer William J. Levitt (1907–94) marketed inexpensive suburban housing to the families of war veterans. Applying the assembly-line methods of Henry Ford, he used prefabricated materials and employed 15,000 non-unionized laborers to build the 17,447 standardized, single-family homes of Levittown, New York, on Long Island, twenty-five miles east of Manhattan (fig. 8.6). Levitt's company associated racial integration with communist, left-wing rabble-rousing. With official support from the Federal Housing Administration, the company legally barred African-Americans from buying property and living in Levittown until 1960. Well before that year, the development had sold out. Most post-war suburban developers were allowed to exclude black settlement. This first Levittown project met with such success that two more Levittowns were constructed during the 1950s and 1960s, one in Pennsylvania and the other in New Jersey.

Though suburban homes provided more space, privacy, and pride for new owners, the Levittown developments also became negative symbols of white, middle-class escapism and cultural uniformity. In 1962, Malvina Reynolds (1900–78), a leftist political activist and song-writer from San Francisco, composed "Little Boxes" after she witnessed a similar suburban development in nearby Daly City. As performed on college campuses and at Vietnam War protests during the 1960s and 1970s, the song's ridicule of "ticky-tacky" suburban tract housing led to other critical verses. These lyrics satirically attacked the social and cultural conformism represented by thoroughly insulated and homogeneous suburban lives.

To support the sprawling new suburban culture, car manufacturers successfully lobbied the United States government to redirect federal funds from public mass-transit projects to build new highways and roads. These thoroughfares would serve suburban families, who required at least one, often two, cars for commuting to work and shopping. Regional malls steadily displaced urban downtowns as active commercial hubs. Surrounded by parking lots, suburban shopping malls seemed to be constructed on the commercial theory that only people who could afford to travel by private car need be accommodated as desirable customers (fig. 8.7). More recently, with the aid of creative architects such as Frank Gehry (b.1929), corporate mall developers have managed to establish a highly sanitized substitute for the sense of community formerly offered by most downtown centers. Gehry's design for Santa Monica Place outside Los Angeles typifies mall design throughout the United States. In 1979–81, he recreated a pedestrian-friendly interior that nostalgically recalls busy city sidewalks and parks (fig. 8.8). Sky-lit trees visually unite tiered storefronts. Street benches, small vendor carts, and open food courts help to estab-

8.6 Levittown,
New York, 1954.

8.7 John Graham and Company
Northgate Regional Shopping Center, Seattle, 1947–50. DLR Group (formerly John Graham and Company), Seattle, Washington, D.C.

This aerial view shows two rows of stores situated along a pedestrian mall. Large department stores functioned as anchors or magnets for attracting mall customers, who could also then visit the smaller specialty shops. Located near main highway arteries, the complex is surrounded by acres of parking space.

lish a more intimate social space. Yet unlike public streets in city downtowns, privately owned malls can employ security forces to exclude commercially undesirable activities, including panhandling, political leafleting, and sidewalk speechmaking.

Emptied of shoppers by suburban malls, most American cities also were damaged by the construction of interstate freeways, which divided downtowns and destroyed established, mostly African-American and lower-class neighborhoods. Immediately after World War II, city governments confronted overcrowded housing, homelessness, and racial tension. With the return of war veterans and the continued Great Migration of African-Americans from the rural South, officials in Northern industrial cities tore down old, decaying neighborhoods. They relocated displaced, poor residents in high-rise public housing projects at sites distantly isolated from city centers and more desirable white enclaves (fig. 8.9)

A German émigré, Ludwig Mies van der Rohe (1886–1969), who settled in Chicago just before World War II, established the precedent for Modernist high-rise apartments in his luxurious, but starkly geometric twin towers along the city's prestigious and scenic North Lake Shore Drive overlooking Lake Michigan (fig.

8.10). Mies eliminated all architectural ornamentation and pared down the skyscraper design to a steel cage and an outer curtain wall of glass. The former director of the German Bauhaus school created an elegant, functionalist architecture that appealed to a machine-age corporate taste for rationality, homogeneity, and order. During the early 1930s, the American architect Philip Johnson (b.1906) and the architectural historian Henry-Russell Hitchcock coined the term "International Style." Their designation referred to the virtually styleless, pristine geometric forms of Mies and other European Modernists, whose functional building designs seemed essentially universal or transcendent of any particular national tradition. Once Mies had relocated to the United States, Johnson collaborated with him in designing New York City's Seagram Office Building (fig. 8.11), dominated by a clean, rectilinear skyscraper slab with a steel frame sheathed in dark amber glass that becomes luminously golden at night. Supported by a large service block in back, the tower is elevated by slender columns and set back from Park Avenue traffic. With a terrace plaza and fountain in front, the Seagram Building stands as a sleek icon of corporate power and sophistication.

American businessmen, real-estate developers, and public-housing authorities saw something

8.8 Frank Gehry
(architect) and **Rouse Corporation** (developer)
Santa Monica Place, Santa Monica, California, 1979–81.

8.9 Kleinweber, Yamasaki, & Hellmuth
Pruitt-Igoe Houses, St. Louis, Missouri, 1955.
Photograph by Ted McCrea, 1955.

8.10 Ludwig Mies van der Rohe
Apartment houses at 860–880 North Lake Shore Drive, Chicago, Illinois, 1951.
Chicago Historical Society.

Mies van der Rohe placed these two identical rectangular towers perpendicular to one another so that they would both fit within their trapezoidally shaped lot. Each stands on free standing columns with a recessed glass-enclosed entrance lobby on the ground floor. The glass towers thus seem to hover lightly in space, while each column leads upward to the thin piers that divide the building into regular four-window bays.

more than the sleek elegance of similar skyscrapers. They recognized that the austere functionalism of International Style architecture, which employed standardized, repeatable building elements, was a practical model for economic efficiency and construction cost reductions. Thus, for the low-income Pruitt-Igoe housing project in St. Louis, Missouri (see fig. 8.9), federal government officials rejected the architects' suggestion for low- and midsize apartment buildings in favor of thirty-three high-rise towers, constructed from substandard materials. Urban renewal projects such as the Pruitt-Igoe apartments effectively segregated African-Americans. Built on an inhuman scale without regard for parks, landscaping, or the surrounding environment, the projects housed residents within islands of inferior real estate and in monotonous structures that rapidly deteriorated, owing to negligible expenditure on maintenance.

8.11 Ludwig Mies van der Rohe and Philip Johnson
Seagram Building, New York City, 1954–8.

8.12 Edward Hopper
Nighthawks, 1942.
Oil on canvas,
33⅛ x 60 in
(84.1 x 152.4 cm).
Art Institute of Chicago,
Chicago, Illinois.
Friends of American
Art Collection.

Hopper had been a student
of Robert Henri from 1900
to 1906, but he did not
share his teacher's
optimistic view of modern
urban life. Paintings such as
this one were probably
informed, in part, by the
writings of Lewis Mumford,
a leading socio-cultural
critic of dehumanizing
urban spaces.

American Realism's Darker Visions

Already in the 1920s, the realist painter Edward Hopper (1882–1967) was producing disquieting images of the modern urban landscape that depicted isolated, lonely figures imprisoned within cold, comfortless architectural spaces. During World War II, Hopper's *Nighthawks* (fig. 8.12), representing a desolate city street corner, powerfully expressed the nation's darkened mood. This painting anticipates the ominous lighting, urban set designs, and predatory, fatalistic themes of many *film noir* motion pictures that Hollywood directors and writers produced after the war. Although the neighborhood in *Nighthawks* appears seedy and derelict, the large, plate-glass windows of the all-night diner signify the sleek geometry and transparency of modern architecture. Yet far from contributing to a liberating sense of spatial openness, Hopper's glass-encased, harshly lit diner merely exposes its lonely and hard-bitten nocturnal characters to our voyeuristic surveillance. The artist obscures our view of the darkened, apparently empty street around the corner of the diner, thereby

stimulating feelings of anxiety over city crime. Hopper's disturbing vision of an impersonal, alienated urban culture was shared by George Tooker and other realist painters. Tooker's later, nightmarish representation of the New York subway system (fig. 8.13) contrasts markedly with the optimistic dynamism of Modernists in the early twentieth century (see fig. 7.22).

In 1959, the Swiss-born photographer Robert Frank (b.1924) published *The Americans*, a book of photographs that undermined America's rose-colored image of affluence. Shot during a cross-country tour of the United States, his stark, black-and-white photographs contrasted images of cocktail parties, college commencements, and political rallies with disturbing pictures of urban blight, racial segregation, car accidents, and desolate parks and back roads. Frank's photograph *U.S. 285, New Mexico* (fig. 8.14) captures the lonely emptiness of an apparently endless highway to nowhere. In his introduction to *The Americans*, the novelist Jack Kerouac (1922–69) wrote poetically of Frank's "Long shot of night road arrowing forlorn into immensities and flat of impossible-to-believe America in New Mexico under the prisoner's moon—under the whang whang guitar star"

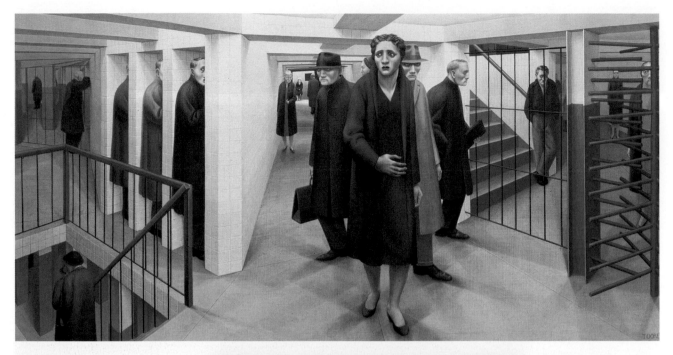

8.13 (above)
George Tooker
The Subway, 1950.
Egg tempera on
composition board,
18⅛ x 36⅛ in
(46 x 91.8 cm).
Whitney Museum of
American Art, New York.
Purchase, with funds from
the Juliana Force
Purchase Award.

8.14 (left)
Robert Frank
*U.S. 285, New Mexico,
from The Americans*,
1958.
Silver-gelatin print,
11½ x 7½ in
(29.1 x 19.2 cm).
Art Institute of Chicago,
Illinois. Restricted gift of
the Photography Gallery.

Prior to publication in New
York, Frank's *Les Américains*
was published in Paris in
1958. His photographs of
denim- and leather-clad
motorcyclists, gambling
tables, juke boxes, and
drive-in movies followed
upon Hollywood films such
as *Rebel Without a Cause*
(1955) starring James
Dean, who represented the
youthful, alienated, dark
side of American material
affluence.

8.15 William Klein
St Patrick's Day, 5th Avenue, 1955.
Gelatin silver print.
Howard Greenberg Gallery, New York.

Born and educated in New York, Klein has spent most of his career in Paris as a painter and filmmaker as well as photographer. This photograph is one of a series he did for a book on the chaotic, dynamic street life of New York City. He also later published photographic books on Rome, Moscow, and Tokyo.

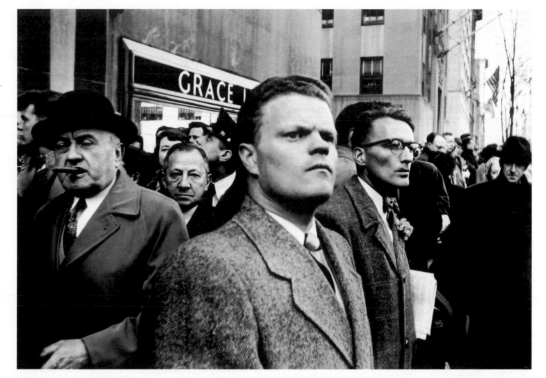

(p. 6). Kerouac's restless "Beat" movement novel *On the Road* (1957) portrayed, in part, a delinquent, alienated teenager just released from a New Mexico reform school. The youth dedicates his life to fast cars and the coast-to-coast search for a woman at the end of the road. Beat-generation authors of the late 1950s and early 1960s included Kerouac, Allen Ginsberg, William S. Burroughs, and Lawrence Ferlinghetti. These writers represented a bohemian counterculture, based primarily in San Francisco and New York's Greenwich Village, which rejected conventional, middle-class culture as materialistically crass and corrupt. The Beat authors helped develop an alternative culture of spontaneous, "hip" prose, free-form poetry, improvised jazz, and Buddhist philosophy, mixed with sexual experimentation and the use of mind-altering drugs.

Frank shot his photographs for *The Americans* before entering the Beat circles. Nevertheless, Kerouac clearly saw a kindred spirit in the photographer's highly personal, unidealized pictures of urban cowboys, factory workers, railroad station men's rooms, and coffee shops. Frank's photographs also share an emotional kinship with Edward Hopper's troubling paintings of modern loneliness and human despair (see fig. 8.12). Similarly, the photographer William Klein (b.1928) took spontaneous snapshots capturing the restless anxiety of city street traffic. His New York photograph of *St. Patrick's Day, 5th Avenue* (fig. 8.15) focuses not upon a community parade celebrating Irish-American ethnic pride, but rather a crowd of individual pedestrians and spectators, whose stern or impassive expressions belie the notion of a festive holiday. Diversely directed gazes underscore the enigma of an unpredictable urban environment, randomly populated by passing strangers.

Cultural Crisis and the Emergence of Abstract Expressionism

While many artists produced realist, narrative works during the 1940s and 1950s, an increasing number of painters and sculptors adopted abstract, spontaneous imagery to address universal themes on individual, creative freedom and the internal, psychic conflicts of the human condition. Shortly after the war, this loosely

8.16 Mark Rothko
Antigone, c. 1941.
Oil on canvas,
34 x 45¾ in
(86.4 x 116.2 cm).
National Gallery of Art,
Washington, D.C.
Gift of the Mark Rothko
Foundation.

connected group of artists was labeled Abstract Expressionist by a New York critic seeking to categorize their highly individualized styles. In contrast to Regionalist and Social Realist painters, who supported the American war effort with optimistic representations of nationalist myths and folk heroes, these rebellious artists alluded to the world crisis with raw, violent images inspired by primitive art and ancient myths and rituals. During the late 1930s, the New York painter Mark Rothko (1903–70), a Jewish-Russian immigrant, had been representing relatively serene pictures of the city's subway system. However, his *Antigone* (fig. 8.16) strongly diverges from the expressive realism of the subway series. Having turned toward classical Greek mythology for parallels to the contemporary traumatic events abroad, Rothko here refers to

the rebellious, tragic heroine Antigone. According to the ancient Greek playwright Sophocles, Antigone, the daughter of Oedipus, committed suicide after the Theban king Creon had imprisoned her for illegally performing funeral rites for her brother Polynices, a declared traitor to the Theban city-state.

Rothko does not conventionally illustrate Antigone's disobedience and violent death, but reinterprets it in purely visual terms with several layers of sketchily rendered dismembered heads and body parts spread across the picture surface in shallow, atmospheric space. The picture's mutilated bodies, male and female, are arranged schematically in registers similar to flattened, anti-illusionistic ancient Egyptian wall paintings.

American writers during the 1940s often made implicit analogies between World War II

8.17 Adolph Gottlieb
Hands of Oedipus,
1943.
Oil on linen,
40 x 35¹⁵⁄₁₆ in
(101.6 x 91.1 cm).
Adolph and Esther
Gottlieb Foundation, Inc.,
New York.

Eyes as well as hands play a prominent role in this compositional grid of pictographs. Pointed to by a large centrally located hand, two profile heads are joined at the back and face in opposite directions. The left face has an open eye in contrast to the closed eye of its opposing twin. These eyes may allude to the role of the artist, who remains open to the world and yet transforms sense impressions according to an inner vision.

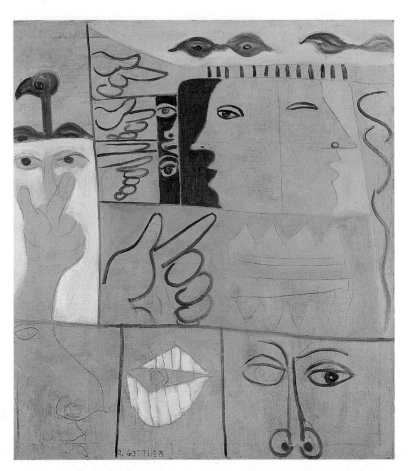

and the gruesome, seemingly universal, human tragedies of Greek myth. Rothko, a political leftist and self-declared anarchist, identified with Antigone's libertarian spirit and her willful disobedience of the inhuman King Creon, who personified for many American intellectuals the contemporary tyranny of Adolf Hitler. Conversely, the Greek heroine's suicide also suggested the fatalistic despair that had pervaded American intellectual circles. Other New York artists, such as Adolph Gottlieb (1903–74), shared Rothko's dark vision. Gottlieb's enigmatic *Hands of Oedipus* (fig. 8.17) refers to the violent mythic story of Antigone's father. Oedipus purposely blinded himself after learning that he had unwittingly both married his mother and killed his father. Dividing his canvas into a grid of animal and body parts, Gottlieb created what he called a "pictograph." The work features a primitive, hieroglyphic picture language of schematically drawn signs to evoke the myth's emotional, symbolic content. Believing

that these mysterious signs expressed more than mere words or narrative details, Gottlieb, like Rothko, emphasized the flat surface of the picture plane, the better to confront viewers with the psychological power of imaginative figures and abstract visual forms.

Sigmund Freud, the Viennese founder of psychoanalysis, had transformed the Oedipus myth into the psychological paradigm of what he called the Oedipus Complex. Freud's archetype symbolized in universal terms the sexual fixation or incestuous attachment male children have for their mothers. However, Gottlieb focuses on Oedipal guilt and self-mutilation rather than illicit desire. Throughout the painting, Oedipus's murderous hands, responsible for the death of his father, point ominously to floating eyes, foreshadowing the imminent act of self-blinding. In addition, the artist eerily contrasts opened eyes with closed or faded ocular forms. At the upper left, a dark, sharp-beaked bird menacingly sits above a pair of vulnerable, opened eyes.

Abstract Expressionism and the Surrealist Unconscious

Rothko, Gottlieb, and many other American artists rejected the technocratic, optimistic machine aesthetic of early Modernism. Instead, they were influenced by a group of European artists who had turned toward Freudian psychoanalytical theory and inward for revelations of unconscious thoughts and hidden, repressed desires. Emerging in 1924 from the Dadaist, anti-art movement of World War I, the Parisian poet and critic André Breton (1896–1966) announced the birth of Surrealism, a movement that sought to employ the visual and verbal arts to explore the subconscious mind and its profound, irrational contents. Breton linked the psychoanalytical interests of Surrealism with communist politics. He believed that bringing repressed thoughts and images to full conscious awareness could reform civilization to accommodate and more productively direct natural human desires and needs.

The self-taught New York sculptor Joseph Cornell (1903–73) had helped to introduce Surrealist art into the United States during the 1930s. Influenced by the Dadaist or Duchampian practice of appropriating found objects, Cornell specialized in assembling wooden and glass-encased boxes. These works were filled with small, ordinary objects, whose juxtaposition in the various compartments or spaces of the box could trigger private memories or emotional associations previously buried within the unconscious. Although the intimate, magical boxes tended to avoid explicit political content, his *Habitat Group for a Shooting Gallery* (fig. 8.18) clearly alludes to World War II. Behind a bullet-cracked pane of glass, found images of colorful, exotic birds are poised as targets amid splatters of paint and pasted pieces of paper carrying references to France, the birthplace of the Surrealist movement. Following the German conquest of France in 1940, Breton and other Parisian Surrealists had fled to New York. In 1942, the Pierre Matisse Gallery and Peggy Guggenheim's Art of the Century gallery held group exhibitions for exiled Surrealists and other European artists. Guggenheim, a wealthy American collector and niece of the copper tycoon Solomon Guggenheim, had married the German-born Surrealist Max Ernst (1891–1976), whose

8.18 Joseph Cornell *Habitat Group for a Shooting Gallery*, 1943. Wood, paper, glass, 15½ x 11⅛ x 4¼ in (39.4 x 28.3 x 10.8 cm). Des Moines Art Center, Illinois. Purchased with funds from the Coffin Fine Arts Trust. Nathan Emory Collection.

Cornell situated the mock bullet hole immediately over the bending central bird's head and splattered blood-red paint to mark the spot. This assemblage may have been Cornell's response to a particularly harsh review in *The New York Times*, which criticized the artist's work as escapist and irrelevant to the contemporary war-torn state of the world.

bizarre collages of found images had inspired Cornell's boxed assemblages. Guggenheim's gallery exhibited the works of European Surrealist exiles such as André Masson (1896–1987), Joan Miró, and Jean Arp (1887–1966). The gallery also became an important venue for Rothko, Gottlieb, and other American artists, who became identified with the Abstract Expressionist movement.

Abstract Expressionist artists borrowed ideas, techniques, and visual forms from the Surrealists, but rejected the hyper-illusionistic dreamscapes of Salvador Dalí (1904–89) and other Europeans. They also were skeptical of Surrealism's insistence on the primacy of the unconscious over conscious design, as evident in its relatively passive, anti-art technique of finding objects or accidental shapes that suddenly, unexpectedly aroused visionary thoughts. In his 1924 "Surrealist Manifesto," Breton particularly advocated automatism, or the technique of automatic drawing. Seated with a drawing instrument before a blank writing surface, practitioners of automatism were to place themselves in an entirely passive frame of mind. Within this receptive, trancelike state, beyond the repressive power of reason, unconscious desires would ideally surface and reveal themselves by spontaneously guiding the drawing hand and dictating the visual interplay of lines.

Dissenting from the apparent passivity of the Surrealists, Rothko, Gottlieb, and other Abstract Expressionists stressed the active, heroic making of art, originating from primitive man's confrontation with the infinite wonders and terrors of the cosmos. Barnett Newman (1905–70) painted simplified, abstract compositions that often alluded to ancient Greek myths and Judeo-Christian religious beliefs (see fig. 8.26). After the war, in a 1947 exhibition statement on "The Ideographic Picture," Newman expressed a masculine bias in comparing the profound spiritual content of Abstract Expressionist art with the ritualistic imagery of Native American hide painting:

The Kwakiutl artist painting on a hide did not concern himself with the inconsequentials that made up the opulent social rivalries of the Northwest Coast Indian scene, nor did he, in the name of a higher purity, renounce the living world for the meaningless materialism of design.

The abstract shape he used, his entire plastic language, was directed by a ritualistic will towards metaphysical understanding. The everyday realities he left to the toymakers; the pleasant play of non-objective pattern to the women basket weavers. To him a shape was a living thing, a vehicle for an abstract thought-complex, a carrier of the awesome feelings he felt before the terror of the unknowable (cited in Chipp, p. 550).

Newman's dismissal of women basket weavers and ordinary material objects might appear to marginalize Cornell's magical boxes, with their humble, found imagery. Nevertheless, Newman's insistence that an abstract shape could serve as a living, real vehicle for thoughts and feelings had been suggested by Surrealist painters and sculptors, who used biomorphic forms (*bio* meaning life and *morphe* meaning form).

Arshile Gorky (1904–48) bridged the gap between Surrealism and Abstract Expressionism. By the early 1940s, this Armenian-born painter abandoned the geometric abstraction of Cubism for abstract organic shapes expressing sexual desires and childhood memories. Foremost in

8.19 Arshile Gorky
The Liver Is the Cock's Comb, 1944.
Oil on canvas,
6 ft 1¼ in x 8 ft 2 in
(1.86 x 2.49 m).
Albright-Knox Art Gallery, Buffalo, New York. Gift of Seymour H. Knox, 1956.

his remembrance was his father's garden, named "the Garden of Wish Fulfillment," which grew in the family's small native village of Khorkom. As Gorky painted *The Liver is the Cock's Comb* (fig. 8.19), he wrote his sister that an ancient Armenian spirit seemed to guide his hand to re-create the lush, natural shapes of their garden and orchards. During World War I, Gorky's family had been forced to leave the country when Islamic Turks had pursued a genocidal campaign against Christian Armenians. The painting's bio-morphic Surrealist imagery evokes these deeply personal memories. The fecund shapes further suggest male and female genitalia and the key organ of the liver, which, in ancient and medieval legends, was the repository of all human passions.

Yet Gorky distrusted the automatic drawing and painting techniques favored by Surrealists. Automatism was a means of escaping the stric-tures of academic learning and conventional conscious thought. According to the theory espoused by Surrealist practitioners, the unpremeditated, spontaneous gestures of auto-matic drawing could generate dynamic new images of unconscious thoughts and desires through a psychic process of free association. However, Gorky rejected automatism's anti-art passivity and lack of conscious control. Meticu-lously detailed studies for *The Liver is the Cock's Comb* and his other paintings suggest that he carefully guided the spontaneous flow of line and juicy application of pigments.

While Surrealists praised the unconscious as the wellspring of a higher reality, Abstract Expressionist artists warned that the mind's darker recesses also harbored dangerous impuls-es, as evidenced by Nazi Germany's collective madness. The source of previously unthinkable possibilities, the unconscious had to be integrat-ed with conscious thought. Only then could it contribute to social and cultural progress by rec-onciling rational, civilized needs with the irrational pleasures of human sensuousness and emotions.

If Abstract Expressionist painters were skep-tical of André Breton's belief in the supremacy of the unconscious, they readily endorsed his conviction that artistic freedom was a critical weapon against totalitarian societies. In 1938, the *Partisan Review*, an influential New York

cultural journal, published a manifesto co-authored by Breton, the pro-communist Mexican muralist Diego Rivera (see pp. 343-344), and the anti-Stalinist Soviet communist Leon Trotsky, who lived in exile in Mexico. Filled with references to both Surrealist theory and the nineteenth-century, anti-capitalist writings of Karl Marx, founder of modern communism, this "Manifesto: Towards a Free Revolutionary Art" audaciously advo-cated an alliance between socialist political goals and an absolute freedom of artistic expression.

Abstract Expressionism and Cold War Politics

Some critics and art historians have characterized Abstract Expressionism as a retreat from social and political life. Others, however, led by the Marxist art historian Meyer Schapiro (1904–96), have claimed that this movement helped to maintain a radical critical spirit in America. After World War II, the Cold War between the United States and the Soviet Union began and grew. Meanwhile, Abstract Expressionist artists devel-oped innovative imagery that implicitly criticized both Stalinist communism and the nationalistic anti-communism of American liberals and right-wing conservatives. Responding to U.S. government policies that served corporate inter-ests but repressed union activism and leftist dissent, Schapiro, during the 1950s, praised Abstract Expressionism. He admired its aesthetic form of free, creative labor that opposed the dehumanized, mechanistic division of labor fos-tered by American capitalism.

Robert Motherwell (1915–91), a college-educated Abstract Expressionist painter, had taken Schapiro's art history courses at New York's Columbia University. According to Motherwell, modern artists should reaffirm the wholeness of individual life in a severely frag-mented world. Writing in 1944, he explained that his works attempted to synthesize the dual-ity between unconscious and conscious thought or between body and mind, senses and reason. Motherwell and other Abstract Expressionist painters strove to accomplish this synthesis by assimilating their automatic gestures and sponta-neous forms within flat, two-dimensional Cubist space, which they associated with aesthetic reality

8.20 Robert Motherwell
At Five in the Afternoon, 1949.
Casein on composition board, 15 x 20 in (38.1 x 50.8 cm).
Photograph by Peter. A. Juley & Son, Smithsonian Institution, New York.
Collection, Helen Frankenthaler, New York.

Lorca's poem about a fatally gored bullfighter symbolically contrasts the harsh white sunlight of the bullring with the shadows and blackness of death. Motherwell conceived his black-white elegy, or funeral lament, as a painted temple consecrated to the Spanish poet's unjust execution. The artist's gestural, dripping paint expressed the freedom of individual creativity and cultural resistance to political repression.

and anti-illusionistic honesty. Far from advocating an apolitical, socially escapist art for art's sake, Motherwell employed an abstract style that expressed opposition to many repressive political forces. His many targets included not only fascism and Stalinism, but also the subtler totalitarianism of modern capitalist consumerism, which subordinated human labor to the private interests of a property-owning elite. As World War II raged, Motherwell painted a sequence of somber works that referred to the tragic Spanish Civil War of 1936–9. The United States government and European democracies had stood idly by during the Spanish conflict, while the Nazi-supported military dictator Francisco Franco overthrew Spain's democratically elected socialist government. Several years after the war, Motherwell returned to the subject again in a mural-size painting entitled *At Five in the Afternoon* (fig. 8.20). The title refers to a poem by Federico García Lorca (1899–1936), a Spanish author executed by Franco's fascist regime, about the death of a great Spanish bullfighter (Ignacio Sánchez Mejías) in the bull ring. Motherwell's visual idea for the painting originated from an automatist, pen–and–ink drawing. He trans-

formed the image into a dramatic black-and-white open format of confining, oppressive bars or pillars and resisting, egg-shaped life forms. This was the first of many works in the *Spanish Elegy* series. During the 1950s, Motherwell returned to the series, even as John Foster Dulles, the U.S. Secretary of State under President Eisenhower, embraced the Franco regime as part of America's Cold War strategy.

From 1945 to the early 1950s, Abstract Expressionism emerged as a relatively cohesive and highly visible movement in New York galleries and in art journals, newspapers, and popular magazines. Writing for the *New Yorker* magazine in March 1946, the art critic Robert Coates formally coined the term Abstract Expressionist to refer to those painters who seemed uncompromising in their pursuit of spontaneous, abstract techniques. New York artist Jackson Pollock (1912–56), a former student of Thomas Hart Benton (see fig. 7.69), soon became the movement's leading figure. The fifth son of a farming family in Cody, Wyoming, Pollock was attracted to the democratic ethos and rhythmic forms of Benton's populist paintings. Yet the young artist's more radical, leftist politics led him away from the

8.21 Jackson Pollock
Guardians of the Secret,
1943.
Oil on canvas,
48⅜ x 75⅝ in
(122.9 x 191.5 cm).
San Francisco Museum
of Modern Art,
San Francisco, California.
Albert M. Bender
Collection and Bequest.

Regionalist imagery of his teacher. During the mid-1930s, he joined the New York workshop of the Mexican muralist David Alfaro Siqueiros, who was active in communist, working-class politics. Influenced by Surrealist automatism, Siqueiros taught Pollock to experiment with various spraying, splattering, and dripping techniques for applying non-traditional, industrial paints to figurative murals. Furthermore, the Mexican artist's belief in the revolutionary potential of Native American tribal art appealed to Pollock's western-frontier sensibility and psychoanalytical interests.

John Graham (1881–1961) was a Russian-born painter who befriended Pollock, Gorky, and other Abstract Expressionists. In a 1937 article on "Primitive Art and Picasso," he had argued that primitive peoples learned about the unconscious mind by creating images that visualized tribal taboos and sacred, totemic kinships with the animal world. This notion was borrowed from the mystical psychoanalytical theories of Carl Jung, a disciple of Freud. Jung claimed that artistic exploration of individual unconscious thoughts would give modern man contact with a collective unconscious, which appears in archetypal symbols that have existed since the human race began. He hoped that modern cul-

ture, by assimilating the psychic impulses and instinctual insights evoked by these universal symbols, could achieve a greater equilibrium between conscious thought and nature's realm of unconscious life forces. According to Jung, the centuries-old repression of unconscious desires in Western civilization had erupted in the volcanic, self-destructive madness of fascism. Ideally, humans would prevent future catastrophic outbursts of collective state violence by integrating emotional, irrational needs with reason, science, and technology.

Like other Abstract Expressionists, Jackson Pollock tended to equate the social problems of the world crisis with his own insecurity and alienation. Suffering from alcoholism and violent temper tantrums, he sought help from Jungian psychoanalysts. They encouraged him to explore archetypal symbols and the energetic, spontaneous release of unconscious impulses through drawing and painting. Works with animistic, ritualistic symbols such as *Guardians of the Secret* (fig. 8.21) possess a Cubist geometry overlaid with hieroglyphic scrawls and roughly painted, gestural forms. Apparently influenced by an 1894 photograph of Native American guardians of a secret knife society, the painting's mysterious figures include a bright red rooster sitting atop the guarded central rectangle, with a dog lying below. Convinced that his primitive imagery and spontaneous picture-writing surpassed words or realistic illusions, Pollock intended the painting's indecipherable energy as an expressive alternative to the technocratic rationalism of modern culture. Lee Krasner (1908–84), who married Pollock, also painted hieroglyphic paintings that seem written in an enigmatic, secretive code that defies facile, rational interpretation (fig. 8.22). However, Krasner's dense, linear calligraphy of pictorial signs appears far more orderly than Pollock's disparate hieroglyphs.

Three years after *Guardians of the Secret*, Pollock eliminated archetypal symbols and figurative imagery. Instead, he concentrated on painterly, physical traces that recorded a sponta-

neous, virtually continuous flow of psychic energy through the body. Pollock and Lee Krasner retreated to a ramshackle farmhouse on Long Island, where Pollock soon abandoned easel painting in favor of mural-size canvases laid on the studio floor. Moving his body around and inside the picture space, he employed sticks, hardened brushes, and paint cans to drip, fling, and pour pigments into dense, weblike energy fields. Pollock's drip painting technique obliterated the illusionistic, hierarchical distinction between figure and background. As we scan paintings such as *Number 1 (Lavender Mist)* (fig. 8.23), particular linear strokes temporarily appear to coalesce into figures only to dissolve back into the ground once our attention shifts to another area of the picture field. Many art

8.22 Lee Krasner
Composition, 1949.
Oil on canvas,
38$\frac{1}{16}$ x 27$\frac{13}{16}$ in
(96.6 x 70.5 cm).
Philadelphia Museum of
Art, Philadelphia,
Pennsylvania.
Gift of the Aaron E.
Norman Fund, Inc.

Krasner's pictorial language of abstract signs is densely packed and impossible to decode in verbal terms. Her hieroglyphs have been compared to the Hebraic script that she had once studied as a child. From this Jewish perspective, her mysterious signs may be interpreted as indirect, subliminal meditations upon World War II and the Holocaust.

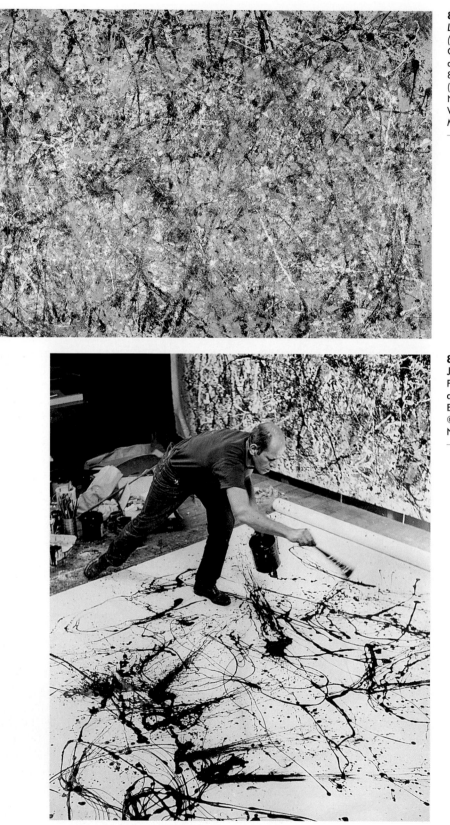

8.23 Jackson Pollock
*Lavender Mist
(Number 1),* 1950.
Oil, enamel, and
aluminum on canvas,
87 x 118 in
(221 x 299 cm).
National Gallery of Art,
Washington, D.C. Ailsa
Mellon Bruce Fund.

8.24 Hans Namuth
Jackson Pollock at work.
Pollock-Krasner House
and Study Center,
East Hampton, New York.
© 1990 Estate of Hans
Namuth.

historians have compared *Lavender Mist* and similar works to the waterlily paintings of Claude Monet. But Pollock went further than the French Impressionist in collapsing any objective distance from nature, and once declared that he *was* nature. Widely publicized photographs of Pollock crucially documented the manner in which the artist's entire body was present in the energetic interlacings of paint (fig. 8.24). In *Lavender Mist*, he impressed numerous handprints into the wet pigment toward the top edge of the painting. The artist's handprints graphically demonstrate an active participation or immersion in nature's rich flux of fluid, dynamic forces. These physical signs recall the pre-Columbian handprint designs that Native Americans spray-painted on rocks or sculpted from thin mica sheets and other materials as symbols of creative potency (see fig. 1.9). Pollock's drip paintings also echo the ancient technique of Native American sandpainting. As practiced for centuries by Navajo Indian wise men in the American southwest, sandpainting was a ritualistic healing process that drew on the earth's ancestral spiritual powers. The artist wise man designed elaborate patterns by pouring dry, granular pigments onto the ground. A sick patient could then sit or lie within the painting to absorb nature's healing, harmonizing forces. These temporary works, which were destroyed after the healing, suggested for Pollock the therapeutic importance of the artist's creative dialogue with paints and craft materials.

In 1952, the critic Harold Rosenberg (1906–78) coined the term "action painting" to characterize the work of Pollock and other Abstract Expressionists, who conceived the canvas as "an arena in which to act—rather than as a space in which to reproduce, re-design, analyze, or 'express' an object, actual or imagined" (cited in Chipp, p. 569). He argued that action painters had made the creative act inseparable from their own biographies or life experiences. Like many other postwar American intellectuals, this influential critic borrowed ideas from the contemporary French thinker Jean-Paul Sartre, whose Existentialist philosophy taught that human values and meanings do not derive from some preexisting deity or universal essence. Rather, meaning is created only through daily existence and the subjective choices and actions individuals take in a harsh, unsympathetic world.

Far from asserting an egoistic control over nature's forces, Pollock's performances in the drip technique seemed to open his body and mind to the new experiential possibilities offered by the canvas. However, his openness to nature did not mean that he lacked control or that his unconscious took over in an act of pure automatism. Insisting that there were no accidents in his work, Pollock composed paintings that possess linear delicacy as well as an overall unity of tone and color. In *Lavender Mist*, he did not create a shimmering, unitary color effect by using lavender pigment. Instead, he carefully interwove aluminum- and salmon-colored paints. Pollock suggested in a 1951 radio interview that his paintings were not simply private, individualistic expressions: they alluded to the modern age of airplanes, radio, and the atomic bomb. The art historian Serge Guibault contends that two of Pollock's earliest drip paintings from 1946 actually referred to the apocalyptic destructiveness of the atomic bomb, which the United States, in August of 1945, had twice devastatingly used in Hiroshima and Nagasaki, Japan.

During the same year as the bombing of Hiroshima and Nagasaki, the second-generation Japanese-American artist Isamu Noguchi (1904–88) created *Effigy (Gregory)*, a somber abstract sculpture (fig. 8.25) assembled from interlocking thin pieces of polished slate, a brittle, easily fractured material. Standing delicately on narrow, attenuated feet, the main body of the mournful work has been gouged with teardrop-shaped incisions. The tortured, fragile condition of the pierced torso is a visual elegy for the war's catastrophic toll in human life.

But the tragic figure also alludes to Noguchi's own struggle as the American-born son of a Japanese father and a mother of both Scottish and Native American ancestry. The sculpture's subtitle honors Gregor Samsa, the anti-hero in Franz Kafka's novel *Metamorphosis* (1915), who suddenly finds himself transformed into an enormous insect. Noguchi identified with the metamorphosed character's subsequent experience of social rejection, having earlier in his career been subjected to racist, anti-Japanese criticism. Following the Japanese attack upon Pearl Harbor, Noguchi had hoped to mitigate anti-Asian prejudice by voluntarily interning himself at the Colorado River Relocation Center, near Poston, Arizona, one of the notorious detainment camps created by the United States government for isolating and confining Americans of Japanese descent. However, even after he was allowed to leave the camp in 1942, Noguchi was placed under FBI surveillance and, later, in 1945, was barred from living on the West Coast and threatened with forcible relocation to another internment camp in east-central California. In evoking a character from Kafka, the besieged Noguchi was also paying tribute to the Austrian Jewish author, who had spent much of his life as part of an oppressed minority community in the Czech city of Prague. Though Kafka had already died in 1924, he had come to personify a European Jewish cultural heritage, decimated by deadly ethnic hatred.

Meanwhile, the haunting specter of nuclear annihilation had intensified by the late 1940s, as the United States and the Soviet Union began to wage a Cold War that soon divided the world into competing spheres of influence. The ideological and imperial rivalry between the two powers stopped just short of "hot," military conflict. Nonetheless, U.S. government officials ominously raised the possibility of again resorting to atomic weapons to prevent the spread of communism in Europe and Asia. The Soviet Union's first test explosion of an atomic bomb in 1949 particularly spurred President Harry Truman's decision to develop the even deadlier hydrogen bomb.

For most Abstract Expressionists, the catastrophic tragedy of contemporary history, especially the revelation of the Nazi concentration camps and the devastation of Hiroshima and Nagasaki, defied description or representation. Realistic narratives of these horrific events seemed unacceptably finite or limited. According to the painter Barnett Newman, modern painters and sculptors, like primitive artists, required abstract forms of thought and feeling to confront the chaos of existence. Rather than empathy for natural, organic forms, Newman came to believe that a hostile world environment demanded geometric abstraction. Rectilinear, geometric forms symbolized the human power to think and to spiritually transcend the terrifying, unconscious flux of nature. Nonetheless, Newman equally abhorred the celebratory machine aesthetic. A political anarchist, he developed an austere, elemental style that expressed his alienation from contemporary culture and his assertion of absolute artistic freedom against totalitarianism, capitalist greed, and consumerism. In 1948, Newman began his trademark series of "zip" paintings that equated straight, vertical stripes or zips with the original act of bringing order from chaos. Newman's *Onement I* (fig. 8.26) alludes to the book of Genesis and the primordial separation of light from darkness. With its russet colors, the painting further suggests the creation of the earth and of Adam, the first man, from mere clay. According to cabalistic or Jewish mystical thought, the concept of onement also encompassed Eve, the first woman. The perfection of creation was conceived as a unification of opposites, such as male-female and light-dark. In his later zip paintings, Newman increased their scale to mural size, so that viewers would feel themselves absorbed by the luminous, spiritualized color fields.

Closely associated with Newman's meditative, religious imagery, Mark Rothko, by the late 1940s, was also creating simplified color fields and abstract forms that appeared more universal in mythic, spiritual content than his earlier figurative paintings (see fig. 8.16). His mature paintings from the late 1940s and early 1950s were variations on a large, compositional format of vertically stacked, cloud-like, rectangular blocks and blurred, horizontal color bands. In *Green and Maroon* (fig. 8.27), the large areas of dark forest green and maroon seem to float over a blue ground to create a quiet space for meditation and reflection. Rothko wrote that he painted very large pictures not as grandiose statements, but as intimate environments into which beholders could enter for private contemplation. Although stylistically different from the energetic color fields of Pollock, Rothko's far more thinly painted canvases were also performances in which the fluid development of tone, color, and form could not be fully anticipated or plotted out in advance. The somber, irregularly toned colors and hazy forms of *Green and Maroon* create a mysterious atmosphere that expresses Rothko's obsession with mortality and the tragic fate of humanity.

Far from transcending the vulgarity of American commercialism or rejecting the figurative tradition in art, the Dutch-born New York action painter Willem de Kooning (1904–97)

8.25 Isamu Noguchi
Effigy (Gregory), 1945. Purple slate, 69 in (175.2cm) high. Isamu Noguchi Garden Museum, Long Island City, New York.

Noguchi admired the sleek abstract sculptures of the Romanian Modernist Constantin Brancusi (1876–1957) and the biomorphic, Surrealist works of Joan Miró and Jean Arp. During the early 1950s, Noguchi designed monumental cast-concrete bridges for Hiroshima's commemorative Peace Park. He soon became internationally celebrated for his sculpture gardens and public plaza designs.

8.26 Barnett Newman
Onement I, 1948.
Oil on canvas,
27¼ x 16¼ in
(69.2 x 41.2 cm).
Museum of Modern Art,
New York City. Gift of
Annalee Newman.

This painting's bilateral
symmetry signifies a
transcendent, spiritual
oneness with God.
Although Newman had
earlier experimented with
Surrealist automatism he
was more interested in
expressing cosmic themes
of creation than exploring
his individual psyche. Here,
the semitransparent,
elemental paint is divided
by a brown strip of adhesive
tape over which Newman
applied a thick, ragged
layer of reddish-orange
pigment.

created vigorous Abstract Expressionist works that were primarily inspired by the female figure. Yet, in a long series of *Woman* paintings, de Kooning expressed the Cold War mood of anxiety and crisis by violently attacking the fleshy, big-breasted figures with slashing, razor-sharp brushstrokes composed of strongly contrasting and clashing pigments (see p. 362). The artist employed brushes and a traditional easel rather than dripping or pouring paint onto the canvas-

covered studio floor. Yet, like Pollock, he also seemed to regard the picture space as an arena for action and perpetual self-expression. Rejecting the finished look of perfection, de Kooning created nervous, spontaneous compositions that appear unpremeditated or open to change and revision.

De Kooning's inspiration for *Woman* came from prehistoric sculptures of fertility goddesses and the toothy smiles of modern, commercial

8.27 (left)
Mark Rothko
Green and Maroon,
1953.
Oil on canvas,
91¼ x 54¾ in
(231.8 x 139.1 cm). The
Phillips Collection,
Washington, D.C.

8.28 (right)
Elaine de Kooning
Conrad, 1950.
Oil on canvas,
58 x 34 in
(147.3 x 86.4 cm).
Courtesy of the Elaine de
Kooning Estate.
Photograph courtesy
Salander-O'Reilly Gallery,
New York.

Elaine de Kooning
explained that even from a
distance, when faces cannot
be clearly seen, familiar
figures can still be identified
by the nature of their
physical build, movements,
and characteristic presence.
The bodily presence here is
made evident in the
painting's spontaneous,
gestural brushwork.

sex goddesses. His frightening women lack the natural beauty of traditional academic art. The figure in *Woman I* glares from the web of thick brushstrokes, embodying a nature that refuses to comfort or nurture beholders. At the same time, Elaine de Kooning (1918–89), Willem's fellow artist and spouse, was painting a parallel series of defaced or faceless portraits of men, fragmented and absorbed into the tense, gestural brushwork (fig. 8.28). While Willem's female figures seem aggressively threatening, Elaine's eyeless, vulnerable men lack identity or any power to return our gaze.

The Masculine Bias of Abstract Expressionism

Women artists had considerable difficulty in gaining recognition as Abstract Expressionists. The movement tended to be defined in heroic, hypermasculine terms. Harold Rosenberg compared these American avant-garde painters to the character of Ishmael in Herman Melville's

great American novel *Moby Dick* (1851). Like the young hero who joined the adventurous quest for a great white whale, Rosenberg's action painters daringly launched themselves on a vast sea of white canvas to prove their mettle in creating pioneering, original artworks. Rosenberg's conception of the dynamic action painter did not include Lee Krasner, Elaine de Kooning, or younger women artists, such as Joan Mitchell (1926–92), whose lush, gestural paintings shimmer with the sensations of nature: trees, flowers, light, rain, and air (fig. 8.29). More in keeping with the critic's gendered model for the ideal artist was Franz Kline (1910–62), whose rough, calligraphic works drew upon America's urban, industrial landscape. As a disciple of Willem de Kooning, Kline created large black-and-white action paintings from thick, rough slabs of pigment, applied with a house painter's broad brush (fig. 8.30). Later, the second-generation Abstract Expressionist Mark di Suvero (b.1933) adapted

8.29 Joan Mitchell
Hemlock, 1956.
Oil on canvas, 91 x 80 in
(231.1 x 203.2cm).
Whitney Museum of
American Art, New York.

By 1955, Mitchell had left
New York City for France,
residing first in Paris and
later in nearby Vétheuil on
the Seine River, where the
French Impressionist Claude
Monet had spent several
years painting landscapes.
Mitchell's nature-inspired
abstractions demonstrate a
kinship with the
Impressionist, painterly
tradition.

8.30 Franz Kline
Mahoning, 1956.
Oil and paper collage on
canvas, 80 x 100 in
(203.2 x 254cm).
Whitney Museum of
American Art, New York.

Kline's masculine, physical style to construct rugged, dynamic sculptures of found wooden beams and steel chains (fig. 8.31). With its manly title, thick lumber, and monumental forms suggesting heroic struggle, *Hankchampion* derives not only from di Suvero's earlier career as a carpenter; it also seems connected to his immigrant Italian father's labor in a San Francisco shipyard.

In contrast to di Suvero's early success, Louise Nevelson (1899–1988) had to wait until her sixties to receive recognition for her Surrealist-influenced assemblages. Like Joseph Cornell, the Russian-born Nevelson collected found objects in small wooden boxes. Working exclusively with pieces of wooden junk, she painted all the boxes and objects in black or some other unifying color such as gold or white. She then stacked the boxes together to create large, grid-like wall reliefs that enveloped beholders within a mysterious, spiritual space, as suggested by the title of a key work, *Sky Cathedral* (fig. 8.32).

Most Abstract Expressionist sculptors experimented with welding techniques, which associated their constructions with the gritty world of working-class men. During the same period as Elaine de Kooning's portraits of face-less men, the sculptor David Smith (1906–65), a former auto worker, represented himself as a blinded hero, who becomes the receptive object of the beholder's gaze (fig. 8.33). Steeped in the literature of ancient mythology and psychoanalytic theory, Smith believed that the modern artist was a heroic seer, who helped others to see and understand themselves. Yet in representing the image of himself as a blind, faceless man, he makes it clear that the material image doesn't dictate our vision. The artist represents himself as a mere object, which cannot lead or act as a moral guide for others. As the art historian Ann Gibson has argued, Smith's self-image ultimately deflects the power of sight and decision-making back toward the viewer. Adhering to libertarian, existentialist principles, Smith created oracular, enigmatic sculptures of welded steel that remain open to beholders' interpretations. In exercising their moral, critical faculties, viewers act heroically and help to create a world of free individuals opposed to totalitarianism and capitalist consumerism. For Smith, whose industrial welding knowledge was derived from working-class experience, individual freedom could only occur within a truly egalitarian socialist society.

8.32 (right)
Louise Nevelson
Sky Cathedral, 1958.
Wood, 135 in (342.9 cm)
high. Museum of Modern
Art, New York. Gift of Mr.
and Mrs. Ben Mildwoff.

Each modular unit is filled
with wooden bric-à-brac,
such as rolling pins, furniture
remnants, and even toilet
seats. By carefully painting,
housing, and stacking these
found pieces of debris, she
assembled modern
monuments that magically
transformed the ordinary
into an extraordinary
experience of personal
memory and meaning.

8.33 David Smith
The Hero, 1952.
Steel, 6 ft 1¹¹⁄₁₆ in x 2 ft
1½ in x 11¾ in
(1.87 x .64 x 2.98 m).
Brooklyn Museum of Art,
New York.
Dick S. Ramsay Fund.

Abstract Expressionism and Right-wing Attacks on Modernist Art

While Abstract Expressionist artists were gaining press notoriety, Midwestern Congressman George A. Dondero expressed the views of many American conservatives when he denounced Modernist art as a foreign conspiracy to support the communist overthrow of American capitalism. In an August 16, 1949, speech in the U.S. House of Representatives, Dondero listed Pablo Picasso, Marcel Duchamp, and several other European Modernists as dangerous subversives. He also named four American Abstract Expressionists as participants in the communist conspiracy, including Robert Motherwell and Jackson Pollock. The same year that Dondero delivered his public attack on Modernist art, the Paris-born American Surrealist Louise Bourgeois (b.1911) was called to testify before the House Un-American Activities Committee, which was investigating communist influence in the arts and Hollywood movie industry. In response, Bourgeois entitled a series of wooden sculptures *The Blind Leading the Blind* (fig. 8.34), after Christ's biblical characterization of his vain and blindly ignorant opponents (Matthew 15:14). The sculpture was originally constructed to represent her loneliness in America. But the artist's pointedly chosen title transformed the image of headless, regimented figures into a critical satire of right-wing American demagogues and inquisitors, who wished to suppress freedom of expression.

Dondero's 1949 speech established a pattern of conservative criticism that linked Modernist artists with any communist subversion. Anti-communist denunciations of Pollock and Motherwell were repeated by other congressmen during the 1950s, even after Dondero's retirement and Pollock's death in a car crash in 1956. Congressional attacks on Modernist art were quoted almost verbatim by agents for the

8.34 Louise Bourgeois
The Blind Leading the Blind, c. 1947–9. Painted wood, 70⅜ x 96⅞ x 17⅜ in (178.7 x 246.1 x 44.1 cm). Hirshhorn Museum and Sculpture Garden, Smithsonian Institution, Washington, D.C. Regents Collection Acquisition Program with Matching Funds from the Jerome L. Green, Agnes Gund, Sydney and Frances Lewis, and Leonard C. Yaseen Purchase Fund, 1989.

These two wooden rows of figures are without pedestals and appear actively to occupy the room in which they march or stand in place. Despite her work's implicit affirmation of individual creative freedom, Bourgeois's fragile, anti-heroic sculptures were often coolly received by a male-dominated New York avant-garde that favored the grand heroic gesture.

Federal Bureau of Investigation (FBI), who kept extensive files on numerous European and American artists suspected of communist or other left-wing affiliations. These suspicions of subversion were supported by the aesthetic judgments of politically conservative art critics. American liberals, meanwhile, ignored the socialist and radical libertarian views of Pollock, Rothko, Motherwell, and others and embraced Modernist, Abstract Expressionist art as a nationalist expression of American freedom in the face of Soviet communist totalitarianism. Working through the Museum of Modern Art and a Paris-based organization called the Congress for Cultural Freedom, the U.S. Central Intelligence Agency (CIA) adopted this liberal interpretation of Abstract Expressionism and avidly promoted New York art in international exhibitions as a symbol of individual liberty. Nevertheless, during the late 1940s and 1950s, right-wing conservatives succeeded in canceling several government-sponsored exhibitions of modern art scheduled to travel abroad.

Of all the painters associated with Abstract Expressionism, Ad Reinhardt (1913–67) was the most politically active. Next to Picasso and the Social Realist Ben Shahn (see fig. 8.3), Reinhardt had the largest FBI surveillance file (123 pages) of any modern artist. Having been a member of the American Communist Party and active in many causes to advance civil rights, peace, and labor unions, Reinhardt, nevertheless, rejected explicitly political artworks as compromising free expression. During the 1950s and 1960s, influenced by oriental Buddhist art, he painted a series of black-on-black, square paintings that asserted an absolute negation of the external world and of moralizing, propagandistic messages (fig. 8.35).

Though these black-square paintings bear similarity to Newman's and Rothko's more somber color field paintings, Reinhardt rejected the Abstract Expressionist tendency to attribute philosophical, spiritual content to the art object. He particularly ridiculed Newman for emphasizing the intellectual content of art over its

8.35 Ad Reinhardt
Abstract Painting No. 5,
1962.
Oil on canvas, 5 ft x 5 ft
(1.5 x 1.5 m).
Tate Gallery, London.

Despite his harsh criticism of Barnett Newman, Reinhardt himself couldn't resist philosophizing about his art and the relation of blackness to the mysterious, non-assertive mysticism of Chinese Taoism, as taught by the sixth-century-B.C.E. philosopher Lao-Tzu. Reinhardt's square, black paintings are never entirely blank or even black. Cross shapes often optically emerge from overlapping tonal bands, which reveal blue, red, green, or other blackened layers of colored underpainting.

physical presence. The cultural critic Susan Sontag later wrote in a 1964 essay:

> *In most modern instances, interpretation amounts to the philistine refusal to leave the work of art alone. Real art has the capacity to make us nervous. By reducing the work of art to its content and then interpreting* that, *one tames the work of art. Interpretation makes art manageable, conformable (p. 8).*

For Reinhardt and Sontag, interpretation also made art more marketable, more subject to the world of fashion and mass-media entertainment. Thus, popular magazines such as *Life* and *Time* quoted artists' statements and critics' explanations of Abstract Expressionism within articles that essentially trivialized the actual art works as faddish commodities and transformed artists into media celebrities. Called "Jack the Dripper" by a reporter for *Life,* Pollock especially was compared to movie stars such as Marlon Brando and James Dean, whose film roles portrayed existential social rebels against middle-class values and conventions. At the same time, corporate clients commissioned architects and designers to create more emotionally expressive commercial structures and spaces than the austere, rectilinear formalism of International-style buildings. The Finnish-American architect Eero Saarinen (1910–1961) employed vitalistic, biomorphic sculptural shapes in designing the Trans World Airlines (TWA) Terminal for New York's Idlewild (renamed John F. Kennedy) Airport (figs.8.36– 8.37). Soaring, cantilevered concrete shells sweep over glass walls and a buoyant interior space to excite passengers with the imminent prospect of flight.

Formalist Criticism and Abstract Art

Meanwhile, "high-brow" critics such as Clement Greenberg (1909–94) engaged in detailed formal analyses of Abstract Expressionist paintings and sculptures. These critiques interpreted the objects as art for art's sake, rather than as acts that merged art and life. Making the works palatable to wealthy American art patrons and museum directors, Greenberg's formalist interpretations examined how individual artists worked within the inherent logic of the flat, two-dimensional painting medium or, alternatively, the sculptural realm of three-dimensional space and mass. Greenberg opposed expressionist content, which he associated with the chaos of life. Instead, he praised those Abstract Expressionist painters who most distilled and disciplined anarchic life forces by rigorously subordinating them to the aesthetic unity of the

picture surface. He tended to ignore artists' philosophical intentions or the literary, mythological associations that many of them alluded to in their art. Instead, he wished to establish a set of rational, objective criteria for making aesthetic judgments. As an editor from 1945 to 1957 for *Commentary*, a New York journal of conservative thought, Greenberg defended congressional tactics in hunting down communists and communist sympathizers. Meanwhile, ignoring the leftist political sympathies of most Abstract Expressionists, he claimed that the images they produced were apolitical and free of subversive ideological content. As a critic, he normalized and aesthetically canonized their works by situating them within the stylistic, historical evolution of Modernist art. He argued that Abstract Expressionists were fulfilling the formalist goals of earlier Modernist painters such as Cézanne and Picasso, whose abstract pictures had dramatically furthered the inevitable progression toward the two-dimensionality of pure painting. For Greenberg, the flatness of paintings by Rothko, Pollock, and Newman seemed

8.36 Eero Saarinen
Trans World Airlines terminal, Idlewild (John F. Kennedy Airport), Queens, New York, 1956–62.

8.37 Eero Saarinen
Trans World Airlines
terminal, interior,
1956–62.

much newer or more stylistically advanced than the figurative imagery and expressionistic savagery of Willem de Kooning's *Woman* series.

Greenberg's formalist criticism greatly influenced the next generation of Abstract Expressionist painters. During the early 1950s, the critic befriended Helen Frankenthaler (b.1928), a recent graduate of Bennington College in Vermont and the daughter of a New York Supreme Court Justice. Greenberg introduced Frankenthaler to members of the Abstract Expressionist group and accompanied her to Pollock's studio in Long Island, where she became excited by the older artist's technique of dancing around and inside his drip paintings.

In 1952, Frankenthaler executed a large, nature-inspired work, *Mountains and Sea* (fig. 8.38), that complemented Greenberg's insistence that painters frankly acknowledge the two-dimensional nature of their medium. The artist's seminal picture affirmed an inherent flatness. Its diaphanous, transparent forms are non-sculptural. Virtually intangible washes of color appeal to purely optical sensations, rather than the sense of

touch or imagined grasp of three-dimensional objects. Frankenthaler created thin veils of lyrical colors by soaking or staining the unprimed canvas with highly diluted oil pigments. Her technique fused the gestural image with the two-dimensional canvas, leaving its weave entirely visible through the washes of paint. Despite Frankenthaler's adaptation of Pollock's spontaneous method, Harold Rosenberg refused to recognize her as an action painter. In contrast to Greenberg, his primary rival in the world of Modernist criticism, he emphasized energetic expressionist content and found it lacking in Frankenthaler's pictures. To Rosenberg, the artist's work seemed more passive than active, more content to allow the poured pigments to flow of their own accord. Yet Frankenthaler adopted Pollock's notion that the painted canvas is an expressive visual echo of nature's vitalistic processes or the artist's bodily experiences— and not a landscape representation of nature's objects.

Though Frankenthaler affirmed the gestural aesthetic of Abstract Expressionism, her staining

8.38 (above) **Helen Frankenthaler**
Mountains and Sea, 1952. Oil on canvas, 86⅝ x 117¼ in (2.2 x 2.98 m). Collection of the artist, on loan to the National Gallery of Art, Washington, D.C.

8.39 (left) **Morris Louis**
Ambi II, 1959. Acrylic on canvas, 98 x 142 in (248.9 x 360.7 cm). National Gallery of Art, Washington, D.C. The Nancy Lee and Perry Bass Fund.

Rather than employing a brush, Louis often used a stick to guide the gravitational flow of pigments or folded and pleated the canvas to create rivulets of paint.

8.40 Anne Truitt
A Wall for Apricots,
1968.
Acrylic on board,
72⅝ x 14 x 14 in
(184.6 x 35.5 x 35.5 cm).
Baltimore Museum
of Art, Maryland.

technique influenced a group of abstract, color field painters, who turned away from spontaneous, expressionist content toward a formalist preoccupation with the painting medium. In 1953, Greenberg brought Morris Louis (1912–62), a young Washington, D.C., painter, to Frankenthaler's New York studio. Louis's admiration for the unabashedly beautiful and harmonic optical forms of *Mountains and Sea* led him to adopt a staining or pouring technique. Employing liquid acrylics, a new, synthetic, water-based medium, Louis eliminated all brushwork and individualistic handwriting. He created large works that were more decorative than expressive. Louis's *Ambi II* (fig. 8.39) derives its optical illusion of deep space from the contrast between the lower foreground's flow of dark pigments and the more colorful red, orange, blue, and green tones that gush upward from a fountain of reds in the background. Yet the woven texture of the unprimed canvas is visible throughout and even fully exposed in areas to affirm the painting medium's essential flatness. Together with Kenneth Noland (b.1924) and other colorists, Louis directed abstract painting away from expressionism toward formalist experimentation with color's optical effects.

This interest in color and optics extended to sculpture, as another Washington, D.C., artist, Anne Truitt (b.1921), constructed and painted a series of simplified geometric "Primary Structures" that Clement Greenberg supportively compared to the reductive, luminous paintings of Barnett Newman. Though her earlier work displayed formal associations with white picket fences, colonial-era gravestones and other memories of the built environment near her childhood home on Maryland's eastern shore, Truitt's *A Wall for Apricots* (fig. 8.40) and similar, large columnar works more narrowly focused upon the optical vibrations of color. In this case, broad bands of orange, yellow, and light gray serve to dissolve the three-dimensional weight of the sculpture into bright, glowing surfaces that change color from side to side, depending upon differences in lighting. Truitt's fusion of painting and sculpture clearly violated the Modernist notion of purity, which dictated that each medium be true to its own respective two-dimensional or three-dimensional nature. Yet Greenberg praised the optical, pictorial quality of Truitt's painted constructions, since he was far more disturbed by the non-art look of Minimalist objects being produced by Donald Judd and other artists openly rebelling against traditional Modernist notions of formal, compositional relationships (see p. 407). For Greenberg, Truitt's reductive style represented a good, acceptable form of Minimalism, since the artist did not exhibit impersonal, mere objects, but rather seemed to express her own individual, feminine sensibility through the handcrafted manipulation of sculptural form and sanded coats of radiant paint.

Truitt's reductive, optically rich sculptures have been compared to the work of the older Canadian-born painter Agnes Martin (b.1912), who, by 1959, had abandoned a surrealist-influenced, abstract style. Shifting toward geometric abstraction, Martin meticulously began to hand draw finely meshed grids of horizontal and vertical lines over thinly painted, monochromatic surfaces (fig. 8.41). Martin's delicate, latticed lines affirmed the flatness of the picture plane, in accord with Greenbergian formalist criticism, and, at the same time, caused the surface of the painting to vibrate with optical energy. The empty, quiet, luminous qualities of her paintings subtly express a mystical, Zen-like loss of ego and lightness of being. As she later stated in a poetic essay, "The Untroubled Mind" (1972):

> If you can imagine that you're a rock
> all your troubles fall away
> It's consolation
> Sand is better
> you're so much smaller as a grain of sand
> We are so much less
> These paintings are about freedom from the cares
> of this world
> from worldliness
> not religion. You don't have to be religious to
> have inspirations
> Senility is looking back with nostalgia
> senility is lack of inspiration in life
> Art restimulates inspirations and awakens
> sensibilities
> that's the function of art
> (cited in Stiles and Selz, p. 132).

8.41 Agnes Martin
Night Sea, 1963.
Oil on canvas, with gold leaf, 72 x 72 in (182.9 x 182.9 cm). Pace Wildenstein, New York.

Although art historians often classify Martin as a Minimalist, she objects to the association of her allusive, pictorial works with that art movement's literalist aesthetic. Her shimmering canvases are informed by both Buddhism and the nineteenth-century Transcendentalist philosophy of Ralph Waldo Emerson.

Happenings, Performances, and Ready-made Assemblages

During the 1950s and 1960s, artists reacted against both the heroic individualism of Abstract Expressionism and Modernist formalism. The Texas-born artist Robert Rauschenberg (b.1925) particularly dissented from the psychological emotionalism and introspective philosophizing of the older generation. During the late 1940s, while a student at the experimental Black Mountain College near Asheville, North Carolina, he befriended the avant-garde composer John Cage (1912–92), who taught students a Zen Buddhist openness toward their immediate surroundings. Stemming from the Dadaist tradition, Cage's musical compositions incorporated accidental noises, long silences, and sounds not normally associated with music. In 1951, Rauschenberg finished *White Painting,* a series of plain white panels, which served as a stage backdrop for Cage's *Theater Piece #1* (1952), performed at Black Mountain College, a prototype of the "happenings" that became

8.42 Allan Kaprow
Chicken, 1962.
Photograph by Edwin
Sobol.

This photograph represents
the performance of
"Chicken man," who
displays a dead chicken
dangling from his neck and
crows like a rooster.
Suggesting a confusion of
gender roles, he
triumphantly stands over a
chicken egg. In an
anthology documenting his
happenings, Kaprow
offered no explanation for
the bizarre scene, but did
provide additional
photographs of *Chicken's*
anarchic scenario of events,
including a group of rioters
overturning a cage and a
policeman spraying a gas
canister.

popular during the late 1950s and 1960s. Lacking any fixed structure, Cage's "event" invited poets, dancers, musicians, and artists to engage in parallel but unrelated activities, thereby evading a rational sequence of cause-and-effect actions. Rauschenberg himself played phonograph records, while the musician David Tudor (1926–96) played a piano. Charles Olson (1910–70) recited poetry and the dancer Merce Cunningham (b.1919), chased by a barking dog, moved around members of the audience. Unlike Ad Reinhardt's non-referential black paintings (see fig. 8.35), the blank, visual silence of Rauschenberg's *White Painting* was equivalent to Cage's musical pieces, in which environmental, non-art noises and sounds constitute found music. The painting's white panels passively reflect randomly passing shadows of figures and objects moving in front of them. Cage described these panels as "airports" or runways for various lights, shadows, and particles.

As defined by the artist Allan Kaprow (b.1927), who was much influenced both by Cage and by Pollock's painting performances, happenings were an open-ended assemblage of theatrical events with no clear beginning, middle, or ending. Orchestrators of happenings rejected formalist art and the notion of art as a discrete object made by a lonely, creative genius. They purposely mingled art and life in transient, unpredictable fashion. Sometimes transforming viewers into participants, happenings were generally scripted but open to improvisational gestures and unplanned human interactions. The objective was to affirm the spontaneity of experience and to challenge conventional middle-class behavior and social inhibitions (fig. 8.42). Happenings emerged from an anti-conformist counterculture that included San Francisco and Greenwich Village Beat poets and writers such as Allen Ginsberg and Jack Kerouac. Beat poetry readings were relatively spontaneous vocal performances that paralleled the theatrical environments of Rauschenberg, Kaprow, and other visual artists. Happenings could be performed in the streets as well as in art galleries and studios. According to Kaprow, such events ought not be performed more than once, since repetition was boring and detrimental to originality and aesthetic immediacy. Nevertheless, photographs of these ephemeral occurrences became important for documenting the creativity of artist-directors and for preserving images of happenings as collectible art objects.

Happenings evolved into the more controlled and focused realm of performance art, in which the artist's own body became the medium. Whether directly performed before an audience or not, the action was generally recorded with film, video, or still photography. Inspired by a 1963 retrospective of Marcel Duchamp's paintings and readymades in Pasadena, California, Bruce Nauman (b.1941) paid homage to the French Dadaist's infamous *Fountain* (see fig. 7.37) by representing himself as a living fountain spitting a stream of water into the air (fig. 8.43). His *Self-portrait as a Fountain* was one of several works in which he used his own body as a readymade medium.

Earlier, in New York, the painter Carolee Schneemann (b. 1939) also had begun to use her own body as a medium. Reacting against traditional art history and the conventional representation of female nudes as mere objects for the male gaze, Schneemann performed *Eye Body*, a series of actions photographed in her loft

8.43 Bruce Nauman
Self-portrait as a Fountain, 1966.
Photograph,
20¹⁄₁₆ x 23¹⁵⁄₁₆ in
(51 x 60.8 cm). Whitney
Museum of American Art,
New York. Purchase.

Nauman's witty
performance actually
reverses the implied
ejaculatory content of
Duchamp's *Fountain*. The
French Dadaist's arid, inert
object was originally
fabricated as a passive
receptacle for urine. In
contrast, the youthful, bare-
chested Nauman spits forth
a sparkling, clear stream of
water, suggesting creative
energy rather than bodily
waste.

studio, where she ritualistically worked with her
nude body as part of an environmental continuum that incorporated a variety of found and
constructed objects and art materials (fig. 8.44).
Unlike documentary photographs of Jackson
Pollock at work (see fig. 8.24), showing a neat,
masterful distinction between painted image
and image-maker/performer, Schneemann was
photographed in a trance-like state, thoroughly
immersed in the material substance of her art-
making. Schneemann later identified her
actions with the "primal, archaic force" of an
earth goddess, and cast the meaning of *Eye Body*
in strongly feminist terms:

> Covered in paint, grease, chalk, ropes, plastic, I
> established my body as visual territory. Not only
> am I an image-maker, but I explore the image
> values of flesh as material I choose to work with.
> The body may remain erotic, sexual, desired,

*desiring, and yet still be votive—marked and
written over in a text of stroke and gesture
discovered by my creative female will.
(Schneemann, p. 55).*

Similarly feminist in content were the environments of Yayoi Kusama (b. 1929), a Japanese
artist who worked in New York during the
1960s. Influenced by Allan Kaprow, Claes
Oldenburg (see p.421), Jim Dine (b.1935) and
other creators of happenings and installation
spaces, Kusama's *The Infinity Mirror Room—Phalli's
Field (or Floor Show)* at New York's Castellane
Gallery (fig. 8.45) confronted visitors with a
dizzying maze of reflections from wall-size mirrors encircling the space. The mirrors explosively
multiplied reflected images of red, polka-dotted,
pillow-soft phalluses, scattered over the floor.
With considerable humor, but serious political
intent, Kusama had herself photographed luxu-

8.44 Carolee Schneemann
Eye Body:36 Transformative Actions for Camera, 1963. Photo by Erró.

In associating her sexuality with freedom of expression, Schneemann was influenced by the French feminist Simone de Beauvoir's book *The Second Sex* (1949) and by the writings of the Austrian-born Freudian psychologist, Wilhelm Reich (1897–1957). An advocate of birth control and sex education, Reich was censored and jailed by the U.S. government for his controversial experiments with a libidinous, healing form of cosmic energy he named "orgone."

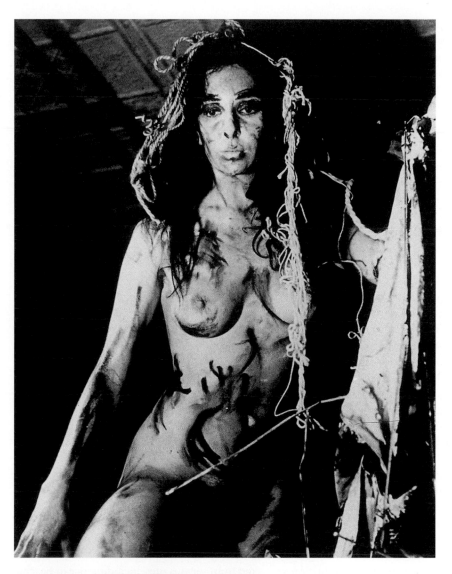

8.45 Yayoi Kusama
In *The Infinity Mirror Room—Phalli's Field (or Floor Show)* at Castellane Gallery, New York, 1965.

riating on top of the phallic field, a liberating act of feminist protest against the oppressive, patriarchal morals of her family upbringing in Japan. Later, Kusama also painted polka dots on the nude bodies of participants in numerous public happenings, staged not only inside Manhattan art studios, but also outdoors in Central Park and on New York City streets, in protest against the Vietnam War and corporate greed. As the "Priestess of Polka Dots," Kusama promoted their androgynous, humbling, yet unifying, cosmic symbolism:

> The polka dot has the form of the sun, signifying masculine energy, the source of life. The polka dot has the form of the moon, symbolizing the

feminine principle of reproduction and growth.
Polka dots suggest multiplication to infinity. Our
earth is only one polka dot among millions of
others....We must forget ourselves with polka dots!
We must lose ourselves in the ever-advancing
stream of eternity! (cited in Karia, p. 29).

Inspired by John Cage, the Korean-born artist Nam June Paik (b.1932) originally studied avant-garde music in Cologne, Germany, and participated in art festivals sponsored by Fluxus, an international movement of loosely associated artists engaged in various experimental, counter-cultural performance works and improvisational actions. Fluxus had been organized in the early 1960s by George Maciunas (1931–78), who promoted the anti-art spirit of Dada and embraced the idea of flux or the continuous flow of changes and successive actions, transgressing traditional boundaries between art and commerce, or artist and art audience. Paik's engagement with Fluxus led him toward video art, or the transformation of the popular, mass-audience television medium into an enigmatic, interactive art object. Having moved to New York, he created *Magnet TV* (fig. 8.46), one of a series of "prepared" television sets, in which he manipulated network broadcast transmissions by employing different image-altering techniques. In this case, a powerful magnet distorts the conventional mass-media image into a kaleidoscopic flux of abstract patterns. Normally an emblem of social and cultural conformity, the television is transformed into a kinetic sculpture, the screen's moving image subject to the individual viewer's manipulation of the magnet. Paik's work invites audience participation in a manner that parallels happening. Furthermore, the interactive experience of the work anticipates the popularity of the Internet and digital technology toward the end of the century.

Paik's assemblage of found objects and interest in kinetic art draws upon the legacy of Marcel Duchamp. But self-taught artists from outside the mainstream of modern-art production assembled works from unconventional, non-art materials, under the inspiration of their own popular, folk-art traditions. Most famously, in the Watts district of Los Angeles, the Italian-born construction worker and handyman Simon Rodia (1879–1954) finally completed

over three decades of obsessive labor in the fashioning of a series of monumental, steel-webbed, concrete-encased towers, rising nearly 100 feet high from their cement foundations (fig. 8.47). Rodia meticulously covered the latticework of Watts Towers with an assortment of colorful, glistening found objects and junk that he gathered from various sites, including ocean beaches and the railroad tracks near his ramshackle house. Seashells, rocks, pottery tiles, soft-drink and medicine bottles, different commercial brands of tableware, toy dolls, pots, and pans are some of the material treasures he recovered for decorating the towers in a mosaic of color. The aspiring towers were reminders of his native roots in southern Italian village life, where popular religious processions featured ceremonial towers that celebrated a local patron saint. During the 1950s, extensive press coverage brought Rodia's accomplishment national attention and encouraged the movement toward assemblage techniques among professional, Californian artists such as Edward Kienholz (see fig. 8.80) and Betye Saar (see fig. 8.84).

8.47 (above)
Simon Rodia
Watts Towers, Los
Angeles, California,
1925–54.
Photo by Julius Shulman

8.48 (below)
Robert Rauschenberg
Bed, 1955.
Combine painting: oil and
pencil on pillow, quilt, and
sheet on wood supports,
75¼ x 31½ x 8 in
(191.1 x 80 x 20.3 cm).
Museum of Modern Art,
New York.
Gift of Leo Castelli.

Rauschenberg's
spontaneous pairings of
objects lack programmatic
coherence or fixed
meanings. His combine
paintings compare with the
prose of William Burroughs,
whose *Naked Lunch* (1959)
captured the immediacy of
experience without a
continuous storyline.

Besides participating in happenings and performances, Robert Rauschenberg became an energetic assembler of found objects and materials. Calling his assemblages "combine" paintings, the artist parodied the art of Abstract Expressionism in *Bed* (fig. 8.48), which incorporated the pillow, quilt, and sheet from his own bed as support for Pollock-like drips of paint, striped toothpaste, and some fingernail polish. Rauschenberg's *Bed* humorously alludes to action painters' desire to get inside and move around within their canvases. Whereas Abstract Expressionists wished to plumb the depths of their unconscious being, Rauschenberg literalized their psychoanalytical, personal obsessions by using his own bedding materials, within which he had slept, dreamt, and presumably had sexual experiences. Indeed, the artist's messy rivulets of pigment conjure forth associations with semen spilled during erotic fantasies, thereby parodying the expressionist notion of art as a creative force that emerges volcanically from within the bodily self.

Readymade Signs, Minimalist Objects, and Real Space

Rauschenberg developed a close friendship with Jasper Johns (b.1930), who had arrived in New York in 1952 from South Carolina. After meeting Rauschenberg and Cage in 1954, Johns soon began creating collages and assemblages that also subverted the traditions of expressionist and formalist art. Inspired by Duchampian Dadaism, he chose to work with readymade signs that could be found in everyday material culture. These included targets, American flags, and printed maps of the United States. Being inherently flat, these signs ironically satisfied the strictures of Greenbergian formalism, which demanded that paintings affirm the flat picture plane. Yet Johns's series of flags and targets (see fig. 8.53) so closely imitated the real objects or signs that they made nonsensical any formal, stylistic analysis or psychological interpretation of the artist. Johns's target paintings particularly inspired the painters Kenneth Noland and Frank Stella (b.1936), whose starkly simplified canvases contributed to the Minimalist art movement of the 1960s. Minimalism emphasized art as a physical object and suppressed internal, formal relationships. By altering the shapes and eliminating the frames of paintings, Stella accentuated their identity as non-referential objects that do not mirror external reality or interior, psychological content. Thus, the internal pattern of symmetrical lines within his *Pagosa Springs* (fig. 8.49) repeats the H-shape of the canvas as a whole. A single horizontal axis between the copper bands of paint extends across the entire length of the picture, dividing it into two equal halves, each merely the mirror reflection of the other. Although the arbitrary title may suggest a landscape, Stella's painting does not provide an illusionistic window onto another, absent reality. By refusing to represent external, distant realities, Minimalist painters hoped to stimulate the beholder's immediate experience of the art object's physical presence.

Though scarcely minimal in its assemblage of diverse material and images, Johns's *Target with Plaster Casts* (fig. 8.53) invites beholders to focus on the essentially flat but relatively lumpy surface of the painting. Accentuating its material physicality, he employed encaustic paints, a thick, wax-based medium, which he laid over a collage of newspapers. Atop this mute, inexpressive sur-

face, he attached a row of small, lidded boxes. When opened, the boxes reveal painted plaster casts of such body parts as an eyeless face, a flat, nippled breast, and a penis luridly covered with green paint. Unlike Joseph Cornell's or Louise Nevelson's boxes (see figs. 8.18 and 8.32), which

8.49 Frank Stella
Pagosa Springs, 1960. Copper metallic enamel and pencil on canvas, 99 ⅜ x 99¼ in (252.4 x 252 cm). Hirshhorn Museum and Sculpture Garden, Smithsonian Institution, Washington, D.C. Gift of Joseph H. Hirshhorn, 1972.

8.50 Robert Morris
I-Box (open), 1962. Mixed media, approx. 12 x 18 in (30.4 x 45.7 cm). Leo Castelli Gallery, New York.

8.51
Tony Smith
Die, 1962.
Steel, edition of three,
6 x 6 x 6 ft
(1.83 x 1.83 x 1.83 m).
Whitney Museum of
American Art. Photograph
by Ivan Dalla Tana.

Though industrially made
without the intervention of
the artist's hand or personal
touch, this sculpture's dark
cube shape, human scale,
and poetic title were
designed to evoke private,
emotional feelings. Smith
appropriated Barnett
Newman's notion of a
holistic image or a form
seen at a glance as a
single, indivisible whole.

8.52 (below)
Donald Judd
Untitled, 1966.
Blue laquer on aluminum
and galvanized iron.
Norton Simon Museum of
Art, Pasadena, California.

In its exhibition "The Art of
the Real: USA 1948–1968,"
New York's Museum of
Modern Art promoted
Minimalism as a purely
"American" art. This
chauvinistic position was
supported by Judd, who
had rejected European
traditions of formal
composition and humanist
values. When the exhibition
traveled abroad, many
European critics attacked
Minimalist art as an
imperial, materialist
expression of American
capitalism and industrial
technology.

8.53 Jasper Johns
Target with Plaster Casts,
1955.
Collection David Geffen,
Courtesy of the Leo
Castelli Gallery, New
York.

The sexual, homoerotic imagery of this early Johns work was later repeated in *Painting with Two Balls* (1960), in which two small, sexually suggestive, plaster-cast balls insinuate themselves within a fissure dividing the lushly painted canvas. Unlike those of the Minimalists, Johns's paint surfaces possess a handcrafted sensual richness descended from Abstract Expressionism.

are filled with found objects that evoke personal associations, Johns's plaster body parts possess an emotionally cool, almost clinical impersonality, reinforced by the inert, banal surface of the target below. The bull's-eye image is a passive receptor for arrows, bullets, and darts. As a work of art, its traditionally feminine, circular forms invite the phallic, penetrating gaze of a beholder. Yet the newspaper print, legible just below the thick coat of paint, yields no intelligible meaning. The open boxes, with their otherwise hidden, private content, literalize and thus parody the psychic depth of Abstract Expressionist art. Considered from the perspective of Johns's homosexuality, *Target with Plaster Casts* may bear some comparison with Marsden Hartley's emblem- and sign-filled *Portrait of a German Officer*, which memorialized the painter's deceased lover (see fig. 7.34). However, Hartley's highly personal numbers, letters,

badges, and epaulets help to create an emotional, deeply contemplative space that differs markedly from Johns's unromantic, anti-expressionist assemblage of signs and anatomy. With its secretive placement of anonymous sexual organs and body parts, *Target with Plaster Casts* may be interpreted as an implicit, if unintentional, critique of the sexually repressive and conformist atmosphere of the 1950s, when homosexuals were routinely targeted or hounded out of jobs and positions of public trust. It would not be until the gay and lesbian liberation movement of the 1960s and 1970s that homosexuals would begin to emerge from closeted, hidden spaces.

Johns's restraint markedly contrasts with a later, rather ebullient parody of Abstract Expressionism by the sculptor Robert Morris (b.1931), whose small *I-Box*, when opened, revealed a photograph of the grinning hetero-

8.54 Carl Andre
Steel Magnesium Plain,
New York, 1969.
Steel and magnesium,
36 units, 12 x 12 in
(30.5 x 30.5 cm);
each unit 6 x 6 ft
(1.82 x 1.82 m) overall.
Private collection,
Switzerland.
Photograph courtesy
Paula Cooper Gallery.

Andre's art was influenced
by his sympathy with leftist
politics. He argued that
horizontal sculptures
running across the ground
signified a political
engagement with lived
space and the real world.

8.55 Dan Flavin
A Primary Picture, 1964.
Private collection.

Flavin's rectangular-shaped
A Primary Picture can be
seen in this installation
photograph. Although the
use of readymade
fluorescent light tubes
suggests ironic Dadaist
humor, Flavin's works were
more formalist than
allusively metaphorical. The
austere, but often colorful,
tubes of glowing light
created aesthetic, formally
beautiful environments.

sexual artist standing proudly naked behind a large I-shaped door (fig. 8.50). The first-person-singular pronoun directly connects with the heroic presence of the individual, male creator. Though far smaller than most Minimalist sculptures and more complex in its humorous, parodic content, Morris's *I-Box* expresses the Minimalists' aesthetic opposition to the dramatically gestural sculptures of Mark di Suvero and other Abstract Expressionists (see fig. 8.31). Nevertheless, some art historians have argued that in ridiculing the personal and expressive metaphorical qualities of art, Minimalism perpetuated a masculine bias in avant-garde-art

circles. Morris's own ironic pose of transcending autobiographical gesture itself constituted an act of self-assertion and self-promotion.

Minimalist sculptors such as Tony Smith (1912–81) and Donald Judd (1928–94) created large-scale, industrially crafted boxes that confronted viewers as literal, physical objects rather than referring to some fictive, illusionistic truth (figs. 8.51–8.52). Smith credited the styleless sameness and artificial, but non-artistic, geometry of the New Jersey Turnpike for eventually inspiring his Minimalist sculptures. Many Minimalists rejected the painting medium entirely. No matter how empty or minimal-appearing, paintings were too pictorial or composed and, therefore, no substitute for the direct, immediate experience of real, three-dimensional space.

Greenbergian formalist critics objected that Minimalist artists had gone too far in the anti-art eradication of internal formal relationships and the aesthetic distance between object and beholder. Meanwhile, defenders of the movement argued that it represented a new realism and artistic engagement with real space and materials. Sculptors like Judd stressed the literalness rather than the formal expressiveness of objects, which were not handcrafted but industrially manufactured according to the artist's specifications. Yet some Minimalists, more interested in space than mass, created sculptures that were virtually invisible. Carl Andre (b.1935) designed floor pieces from metallic square plates, which could be walked on by people who did not realize they were in the middle of an artwork (fig. 8.54). In their absolute flatness and inexpressiveness, Andre's "rugs" seem to squeeze out internal meanings or spiritual content. His floor pieces became aesthetically perceptible only for beholders who are actively looking for them. Their awareness of the artwork enlivens the surrounding space, creating an interactive, immediate experience between the viewer's body and an art environment that seems virtually continuous with the fabric of everyday life. Minimalism contributed to the notion of sculpture as installation art. Andre's floor pieces, composed of individual, modular units, could be altered or rearranged to adapt to different sites or exhibition spaces.

Artists working with lighting techniques created installations that explored perception as a complex interplay between visual fact and illusion. At New York's Green Gallery in 1964, the Minimalist artist Dan Flavin (1933-96) installed a series of works made entirely of industrially manufactured fluorescent light tubes (fig. 8.55). Flavin employed different standard sizes and colors to arrange tubes in elemental compositions that illuminated the gallery with a polychromatic glow. The artist's *A Primary Picture*, a simple, unadorned rectangular wall sculpture of fluorescent tubes in the primary colors of red, yellow, and blue, recalls Modernist paintings, such as the reductive, primary-colored abstractions of Dutch artist Piet Mondrian (1872-1944). Flavin was less interested in the literalness of objects than in the immediate, perceptual experience of light.

During the mid-1960s, the Los Angeles artist Robert Irwin (b.1928) fashioned mirage-like environments of light and shadow. A 1969 installation features a luminous white acrylic disk attached to, but floating in front of, a white wall (fig. 8.58). Illuminated by four spotlights, the translucent, convex circle casts four circular shadows that overlap within a square wall space. The disk's frosted glassiness, divided by a horizontal silver bar, seems to dematerialize into the insubstantial shadows through subtle tonal variations. From an apparently minimal, circular object, Irwin creates a perceptually complex arrangement of lights and shadows that challenges the eye's ability to distinguish visual reality from reflected, illusionistic forms.

By the late 1960s, many artists ignored formal concerns to focus on the fluid processes and materials of art. Working in a warehouse owned by New York's Castelli Gallery, the sculptor Richard Serra (b.1939) created *Casting* (fig. 8.56) by throwing molten lead into the angle between floor and wall. Once one lead piece had cooled and hardened, it was torn away from the wall and the process was repeated until a substantial portion of the floor was covered by roughly formed horizontal strips. Serra later professed unhappiness that the floor seemed to function in the pictorial manner of a painted canvas, thereby subverting his intention to emphasize real space and material, physical processes, rather than illusory space or a representational image. Documentary photographs showing Serra in the act of throwing the hot, molten lead (fig. 8.57) inevitably invited comparisons with the *Life* magazine snapshots of Jackson Pollock, dripping paint onto his canvas-covered studio floor (see fig. 8.24). Critic Rosiland Krauss has argued that the wearing of an industrial protective gas mask served to depersonalize Serra's action, in contrast to Pollock's expressive intention to explore interior states of mind. Yet the sculptor's dramatic action pose calls to mind a heroic, classical warrior from ancient or Renaissance art. Weapon-like instrument in hand, Serra stands in a metaphorical relationship to *Casting*, the material record of his Herculean actions.

More humorously, the New York sculptor Lynda Benglis (b.1941) responded to the rectilinear,

8.56 (above)
Richard Serra
Casting, 1969.
Cast lead, 4 x 25 x 15 in
(10.1 x 63.5 x 38.1cm).
Exhibition, Whitney
Museum of American Art,
New York, 1969.
Photo by Peter Moore.

8.57 (below)
Gianfranco Gorgoni
*Richard Serra throwing
lead,*1969.
Photograph.

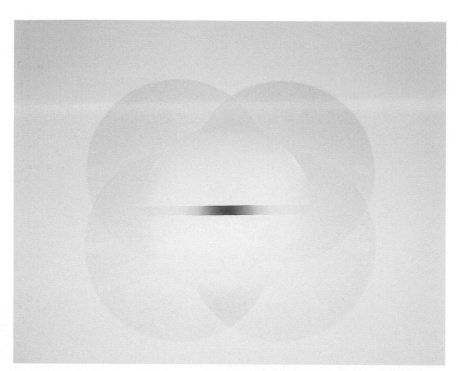

geometric floor pieces of Carl Andre by pouring onto the floor polyurethane foam that eventually congealed, yet retained the look of oozing layers, flowing downward and outward under the force of gravity (fig. 8.59). Despite the use of an industrial material, Benglis suggested organic, bodily processes and satirically critiqued the masculine bravado of grand, heroic gestures. Meanwhile, Eva Hesse (1936–1970), a German-born sculptor, exemplified Process art by rejecting the hard steel boxes of Donald Judd's industrial works to fabricate soft, malleable fiberglass, latex, and wire pieces that lack precise form (fig. 8.60). Hesse's rectangular or square wall panels appear to be a hybrid of painting and sculpture. Though blank and apparently non-representational, the luminous fiberglass and latex surfaces possess a malleable, translucency. Each box shape also has two long wire appendages that dangle on the floor. Unlike the gestural lines of an Abstract Expressionist sculpture, Hesse's loose wires have no fixed formal qualities that express an inner psychic center. She tended to regard the irregular, organic-appearing materials of her artworks as parallel to her own physical being, particularly after she became mortally ill with brain cancer in 1969.

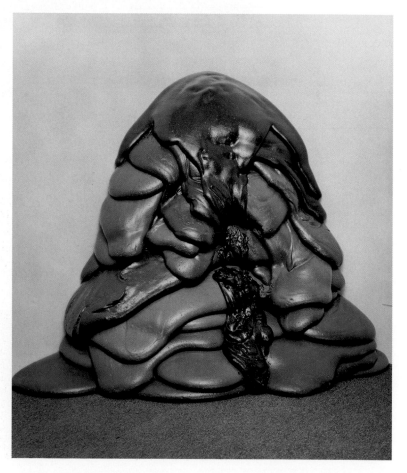

8.60 Eva Hesse
Untitled, 1970.
Fiberglass over wire
mesh, latex overcloth and
wire, 7 ft 6⅞ in x 12 ft 3⅝
in x 3 ft 6½ in
(2.31 x 3.75 x 1.08 m)
overall. Des Moines Art
Center, Iowa. Nathan
Emory Coffin Collection.
© Estate of Eve Hesse.

Process art or
Postminimalism was an
open, anti-formalist art that
rejected the rigid,
rectilinear forms of
Minimalism. It was often
characterized as feminine,
since softness and fluidity
are stereotypically female
attributes. Hesse's loose,
hanging appendages and
rubbery latex materials
typified Postminimalists'
irregular, scattered
installations of diverse
industrial and non-
industrial media.

Pop Art and the Culture of Mass Consumerism

If Minimalists and Process artists like Hesse stressed materials and real space, other artists reacted against Abstract Expressionism by returning to representational realist imagery appropriated from popular culture. The San Francisco artist Burgess Collins (b. 1923), who simply identified himself as "Jess," had been a student of the Abstract Expressionist painter Clyfford Still (1904–80). However, Jess reacted against his teacher's disdain for the everyday imagery of mass culture. He adopted the Dadaist technique of appropriating found images to create works with subversive, sometimes homoerotic, content. Together with his partner, the poet Robert Duncan (1919–88), Jess opened a short-

**8.61 Burgess Collins
("Jess")**
Tricky Cad—Case 1,
1954.
Collage, 9½ x 7½ x ½ in
(24.1 x 19 x 1.1 cm).
Odyssia Gallery,
New York.

In Jess's nonsensical,
reconfigured comic
collages, confusion reigns
as the legendary detective
futilely searches for rational
resolutions to life's chaotic,
anarchic forces. The *Tricky
Cad* series shares the
nonconformist, energetic
spirit of Beat poems such as
Allen Ginsberg's *Howl*
(1956).

8.62 Roy Lichtenstein
Drowning Girl, 1963.
Oil and synthetic polymer
paint on canvas,
67⅝ x 66¾ in
(171.6 x 169.5 cm).
Museum of Modern Art,
New York. Philip Johnson
Fund and gift of Mr. and
Mrs. Bagley Wright.

lived, non-commercial exhibition space in San Francisco that also became a venue for Beat poetry readings and other performances. In a series of collages from the 1950s, he took images from the popular newspaper comic strip *Dick Tracy*. He rearranged the hyper-masculine, detective-story narratives and the letters of the hero's name to create *Tricky Cad* (fig. 8.61), featuring unflattering variations on the Dick Tracy persona. Jess's chaotic reconfigurations subverted the conservatively moralizing, conformist messages normally pronounced by this all-American, crime-fighting hero. Jess began the eight *Tricky Cad* collages in 1954, shortly after the United States had first tested the hydrogen bomb. As a former nuclear scientist, the artist had worked on the secret Manhattan and Hanford projects, which had produced pluto-nium for the atomic bombs that had devastated Hiroshima and Nagasaki. By 1949, deeply disturbed by the terrible destructive force of nuclear technology, he had abandoned his science career. Jess's *Tricky Cad* series is an absurdist satire of America's Cold War faith in technology, rationalism, and absolute moral distinctions between good and evil. His attempt to confuse the law-and-order certitude of Dick Tracy as a symbol of American justice also probably alluded to Vice-President Richard Nixon. The future U.S. president had made his earlier congressional political career as an investigator and prosecutor of communist nuclear spies. However, in 1952, during his vice-presidential campaign, Nixon had become known as "Tricky Dick" after evading a scandal over misused political campaign funds.

8.63 Andy Warhol
Installation of Campbell's Soup Cans, Ferus Gallery, Los Angeles, 1962. Each painting synthetic polymer on canvas, 20 x 16 in (50.8 x 40.6 cm).

Jess's *Tricky Cad* collages preceded the commercial advent of the 1960s Pop Art movement in the United States, but the term had already been coined in Great Britain. During the early 1950s, several London artists transformed the artifacts and mass-media imagery of American popular culture into critical, satirical artworks. They were responding to a flood of American postwar exports of consumer goods, movies, magazines, comics, and advertising. British artists such as Richard Hamilton (b.1922) and Peter Blake (b.1932) contributed works to several highly publicized exhibitions, representing a materialist utopia of American media images and consumer goods.

The birth of Pop Art in the United States coincided with the maturation of mass-media advertising and the proliferation of television, a luxury that soon became a necessity for every American home. Exponentially multiplying the media and advertising images that barraged the public, television made Abstract Expressionist artists seem quaintly out of touch in their persistent evasion of mass culture's vulgar taint. In 1962, after New York's well-established Sidney Janis Gallery held a blockbuster exhibition of the "New Realists," which promoted the new Pop Art movement, several Abstract Expressionist artists abandoned their association with the gallery in protest. Roy Lichtenstein (1923–97), who exhibited in the New Realists show and became a leading Pop artist, retaliated by parodying Abstract Expressionist action painting in a series of works that impersonally imitated their supposedly individualized brushstrokes. Though painted by hand, he meticulously produced compositions that mimicked the regularized, mechanical appearance of a comic-strip cartoon. During the early 1960s, Lichtenstein became famous for his enlargements and croppings of single comic-strip panels. He rejected the mysterious, contemplative environments of Abstract Expressionism, arguing that the commercial terrain of media imagery now constituted the natural landscapes experienced by most Americans. As a manmade, industrial form of nature, commercial art represented a fertile source of subjects for painters and sculptors in the fine arts. In a 1963 interview, Lichtenstein commented that "The meaning of my work is that it's industrial, it's what all the world will soon become. Europe will be the same way soon, so it won't be American; it will be universal" (cited in Stiles and Selz, p. 339). The artist admired the way that popular cartoonists had created a vivid, pictorial vocabulary adapted to the processes of industrial or mechanical reproduction. He borrowed the visual shorthand of commercial art to compose pictures unified by bold, simplified shapes and flat planes of strongly contrasting colors. Lichtenstein purposely chose extremely violent or emotionally overwrought subjects from war comics or melodramatic romances (fig. 8.62). By presenting a single action frame, his pictures avoided the easy narrative resolutions and moral certitudes of the original comic sources, which generally affirmed the eventual triumph of good over evil or love over faithlessness.

In 1959, during his famous "kitchen debate" with the visiting Soviet leader Nikita Khrushchev, Vice-President Nixon argued capitalism's superiority over communism by pointing to the labor-saving, push-button conveniences of American household appliances. Shortly thereafter, Andy Warhol (1928–87) became the Pop Art personification for the consumerist world of mass-produced fast foods filling the cupboards and refrigerators of American kitchens. Though New York–based, Warhol, a former commercial artist, had his first major fine-art exhibition in 1962 in a Los Angeles art gallery. There he installed thirty-two paintings of individual Campbell's Soup cans (fig. 8.63). Ironically mimicking a grocery store shelf, the artist placed the paintings, each representing a different soup, on a narrow shelf encircling the gallery. Campbell's Soup, in business since 1897, had helped to pioneer the convenience-food industry with its simple cooking instruction to "just add water." Sporting a distinctive, bright red label, Campbell's Soup had become a familiar icon of American affluence. The company was a sponsor of family-oriented television shows, and its advertisements were designed to ensure that consumers would associate the eye-catching product label with moral as well as nutritional wholesomeness. Warhol flattened the three-dimensional cans to

subordinate their interior contents to the repetitive, uniform images of modern advertising and product design. Although he hand-painted the first series of *Soup Cans*, he soon switched to the silkscreen stencil process of comics and advertising. This process allowed him to reproduce *Soup Cans, Coca-Cola Bottles*, and other images hundreds of times, thereby imitating the assembly-line production techniques used in American factories. Explicitly rejecting the heroic individualism of Abstract Expressionism, Warhol called his own New York studio "The Factory," and here the artist and his assistants produced as many as eighty silkscreen paintings per day in addition to filming underground movies about New York's gay and drug subcultures. The Factory soon became a social and cultural mecca for drag queens, rock musicians, fashion designers, and radically chic socialites. Warhol became a celebrity and a performance artist, whose sphinxlike presence attracted admiring patrons. He even replicated himself by hiring a look-alike to deliver lectures in his stead. For about four months during 1967, the deception fooled college audiences.

In an early 1963 interview for *Art News*, Warhol blithely dismissed patriotic, Cold War rhetoric that championed the myth of American individualism over the social conformism of

8.64 Andy Warhol
Marilyn Monroe's Lips, 1962.
Synthetic polymer, enamel, and pencil on canvas,
panel A 82¾ x 80¾ in (210.1 x 205.1 cm),
panel B 82¾ x 82⅜ in (210.1 x 209.2 cm).
Hirshhorn Museum and Sculpture Garden, Smithsonian Institution, Washington, D.C. Gift of Joseph H. Hirshhorn, 1972.

Warhol originally appropriated these lips by cropping them from a film publicity photograph for Marilyn Monroe's role in *Niagara* (1953). The toothy smile of the movie star recalls Willem de Kooning's *Woman I* (see page 362), which had also been inspired by popular culture. Warhol's Monroe series foreshadowed the launching of his own career as a director of over fifty improvisational, underground films. Emulating Hollywood, he created stars out of New York drag queens, hustlers, and Greenwich Village eccentrics.

Soviet communism. Citing the German playwright Bertolt Brecht (1898–1956), he observed with ironic, deadpan seriousness:

> *Someone said that Brecht wanted everybody to think alike. I want everybody to think alike. But Brecht wanted to do it through Communism, in a way. Russia is doing it under government. It's happening here all by itself without being under a strict government: so if it's working without trying, why can't it work without being Communist? Everybody looks alike and acts alike, and we're getting more and more that way.*
>
> *I think everybody should be a machine (cited in Stich, pp. 91–2).*

As a gay man who had grown up in a Catholic, working-class family of Czech immigrants, Warhol knew that most Americans had little tolerance for individualistic behavior that deviated from established, heterosexual social norms. His appropriation of images from glossy movie and celebrity magazines underscored the mass media's transformation of film actors into marketable commodities. After the tragic suicide in 1962 of Hollywood's leading sex goddess, Marilyn Monroe, Warhol produced a series of often garishly colored silkscreen portraits taken from a glitzy publicity photograph. In *Marilyn Monroe's Lips* (fig. 8.64), the artist's fetishistic, assembly-line repetition of the star's toothy grin suggests the dehumanizing emptiness of American mass culture.

Though Warhol assumed a public persona of political naiveté and impassivity, his early 1960s *Disasters* series, which included sensational tabloid newspaper photographs of gruesome airplane and car crashes, graphically demonstrated the violence at the heart of American life. In one of the most critical images from the *Disaster* series, Warhol reproduced eerily colored, multiple images of a lone electric chair symbolizing the government-sanctioned technology of death (fig. 8.66).

Emerging from the realist, Pop Art aesthetic, the Minnesota artist Duane Hanson (1925–96) shared Warhol's dark vision of an affluent but violent American culture. Working with fiberglass cast molds taken from living human bodies, Hanson created uncannily realistic sculptures by painting the figures with convincing flesh tones and dressing them in appropriate clothing. He

8.65 Duane Hanson
Motorcycle Accident, 1969.
Fiberglass, polychromed in oil, lifesize figure with motorcycle. © 1999 Sotheby's, Inc., New York.

Hanson created this remarkably realistic sculpture by taking a fiberglass cast mold from a human body, painting it, and then dressing it in clothing suitable for a teenage motorcyclist. Like the photographer Robert Frank's unsettling representations of America's endless highways (see fig. 8.14), Hanson's violent assemblage of a mangled roadside victim and a wrecked motorcycle questions American prosperity and its restless culture of high-speed living.

8.66 Andy Warhol
Orange Disaster, 1963.
Acrylic and silkscreen
enamel on canvas,
106 x 81½ in
(269.2 x 207 cm).
Solomon R. Guggenheim
Museum, New York. Gift
of Harry N. Abrams
Family Collection, 1974.

The lifelessness of the death
chamber takes on an eerie
quality due to Warhol's
orange tinting of the grainy
black-and-white
photograph. A sign at the
upper right calls for
SILENCE. Presumably
directed at the witnesses to
executions, the message is
also directed at beholders
of this nightmarish series.

then installed the figures with accompanying props, so that they could mimic the banal, but sometimes horrific, incidents of everyday life. His grisly *Motorcycle Accident* (fig. 8.65) recalls Warhol's *Disasters* series and the photographs of car accidents that typically attract readers or viewers to the sensational tabloid media.

Hanson's assemblage can also be related to Allan D'Arcangelo's (1930–98) *Full Moon* (fig.8.68), one of a series of eerie, ominous highway paintings that this New York Pop artist produced during the early 1960s, following the advent of the national, interstate highway system. A reinterpretation of Robert Frank's *U.S. 285, New Mexico* (see fig.8.14), *Full Moon* multiplies the image of a lonely highway, while adding the orange advertising logo of the Gulf Oil Corporation in the ironic guise of a rising full moon. Painted in an impersonal, commercial art style, *Full Moon* transforms the American landscape into an artificial, synthetic space, dominated by motorists' endless thirst for gasoline. Hanson produced his later *Motorcycle Accident* (see fig.8.66) the same year that the popular, cult movie *Easy Rider* narrated the romance of rebel motorcyclists with life on the open road. Hanson became associated with the Super Realist movement, which included photo-realist painters such as Richard Estes (b.1936) and Chuck Close (b.1940). Like Hanson, John de Andrea (b.1941) used fiberglass and painted vinyl to create *trompe-l'oeil* figures that surpass the realism of Patience Wright (see fig. 4.8) and the early Anglo-American waxworks tradition.

Meanwhile, the painter Robert Bechtle (b.1932) joined Hanson and other Super Realists

8.67 Romare Bearden
Black Manhattan, 1969.
Collage. Schomburg
Center for Research in
Black Culture, The New
York Public Library.

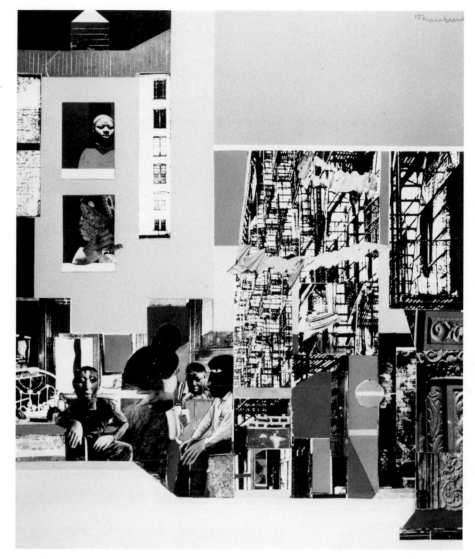

in exploring the commuter and motorized recreational culture of middle-class suburbia. With its photographic realism and portrayal of an affluent consumer standing next to a sleek luxury car, Bechtle's *'60 T-Bird* (fig. 8.69) bears comparison with James Van Der Zee's Depression-era photograph of a Harlem couple and their new Cadillac (see fig. 7.59). Yet Bechtle also captures the Californian, suburban ambience of hot, southwestern sun and white-stucco bungalow design that seamlessly frames the glistening streamlined car. The emphatic whiteness of Bechtle's color scheme implicitly underscores the white racial dominance of America's suburbs during a period when racial unrest in Newark, New Jersey, and Detroit, Michigan, among other places, was accelerating the exodus of white Americans from the nation's decaying cities. In contrast to Bechtle's Super Realist study of racially uniform suburbia, the African-American artist Romare Bearden (1912–88) employed real photographs, cut from popular magazines, to create unsettling abstract collages of urban ghetto life. Bearden's *Black Manhattan* (fig. 8.67) situates images of African-American residents within a fractured, painted, and pasted grid of prison-like tenements, defined by a labyrinth of fire escapes and run-down, claustrophobic spaces. The flat areas of bright-blue and orange paint enliven the composition, yet oppressively confine the three-dimensional inhabitants within the blighted architectural, urban maze.

8.68 Allan D'Arcangelo
Full Moon, 1962.
Acrylic on canvas, four panels, each 30 x 31⅞ in (76.2 x 80.96 cm) high. Virginia Museum of Fine Arts, Richmond, Virginia.

D'Arcangelo had his first one-person show in New York City in 1963, exhibiting paintings that focused upon the American highway system and the industrialized landscape. Later, during the 1970s, his pictures manifested a close affinity with the mechanistic, Precisionist style of Charles Sheeler.

8.69 Robert Bechtle
'60 T-Bird, 1967–8.
Oil on canvas, 72 x 98¾ in (182.8 x 250.8 cm). University Art Museum, University of California, Berkeley, California.

**8.70
Robert Venturi and
John Rauch**
Guild House,
Philadelphia,
Pennsylvania, 1960–3.

Venturi's Guild House
possesses an architectural
playfulness and
inventiveness that some
have compared to
sixteenth-century Italian
Mannerist architecture. Just
as Venturi willfully
contradicted the need for a
massive, granite entrance
column, so did Mannerist
architects such as Giulio
Romano (1492/9–1546)
purposely employ
architectural elements in
opposition to their original
purpose or meaning.

Pop Art and Postmodernist Architecture

Pop Art's transgression against the purity of abstract formalism inspired architects to design buildings that subverted the Modernist functionalism of the International Style. Countering Mies van der Rohe's anti-decorative maxim that "less is more," the architect Robert Venturi (b.1925) advocated a return of ornamental signs and historical references. Guided by the alternative notion that "less is a bore" (cited in Klotz, p. 142), Venturi's design for Philadelphia's Guild House, a Quaker retirement home, has been called the first significant example of Postmodern architecture (fig. 8.70). Although the term did not gain currency until the 1970s, Venturi's buildings and theoretical writings helped to define the Postmodern movement's rejection of the austere geometry of Modernist architecture. In his treatise *Complexity and Contradiction in Architecture* (1966), Venturi denounced the puritanical simplicity and functionalism of the International Style. Modernists such as Mies van der Rohe had tended to regard their box-like, steel-frame skeletons sheathed in glass (see figs. 8.10–8.11) as a universal, geometric vocabulary, adaptable to virtually any social or cultural function and building site. International Style architects often ignored the local, historic character of the urban neighborhoods or downtowns in which they constructed their sleek, skyscraper towers. Postmodernist architects have

8.71 (below) **Frank O. Gehry & Associates**
Chiat Day Mojo Offices,
Venice, California,
1985–91.

Flanking the giant
binoculars entranceway, the
advertising agency's
gleaming, white staff offices
on the left were designed to
evoke associations with a
yacht, further situating the
building within the area's
nearby beaches and
harbors. On the right side
of the building, Gehry
produced a canopy of tree
or branchlike forms for the
executive offices,
nostalgically recalling the
forests that once flourished
along the ocean shoreline.

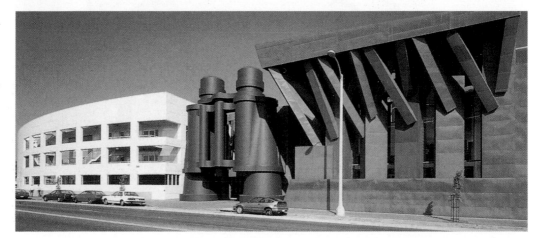

defined their movement, in part, by the principle of "contextualism" or the recognition that a building cannot be composed like a universal language of forms without any regard to the surrounding environment or to the vernacular, local building traditions of particular communities. Rejecting Modernist austerity for ornamental allusions, Postmodernists have playfully decorated buildings with historical-revival motifs and contemporary, popular signs to suggest various symbolic meanings and contextual associations. In his controversial book *Learning from Las Vegas* (1972), Venturi challenged the avant-garde elitism of Modernist art and architecture. He sided with Pop artists in praising the messy but eye-catching communicative power of the garish commercial "Strip" in Las Vegas, Nevada, lined by gaudy gambling casinos, resort hotels, billboards, and monumental electronic advertising signs.

Borrowing from the commercial-strip landscapes characterizing most American cities and suburbs, Venturi conceived the façade of the unpretentious, low-cost Guild House as a gigan-tic billboard with the name of the building emblazoned over a recessed entrance divided by a granite column. Contradicting the functional need for its massiveness, the column supports seemingly weightless forms: a flat sign, light balconies with perforated sheet-metal railings, and a crowning arched window. A top-floor window illuminates a communal TV lounge. Originally, Venturi had capped the building with a decorative golden television antenna to signify the residents' primary recreational activity. Though the architect had intended the symbol as a humorously ironic substitute for the Virgin Mary sculptures that often decorated Catholic retirement homes, critics accused him of being insensitive and demeaning to the elderly residents. The building's Quaker owners soon removed the offending, ornamental sign derived from Pop Art, leaving only the more inconspicuous functional antenna to project from the roof.

Later Postmodernist architects have continued to produce expressive designs in response to popular, consumerist culture. The California architect Frank Gehry (see fig. 8.8) even collabo-

8.72 Frank Lloyd Wright
Solomon R. Guggenheim Museum, New York, 1956–9. Robert E. Mates/Guggenheim Museum, New York.

rated with the sculptor Claes Oldenburg (b.1929) and Oldenburg's wife Coosje Van Bruggen (b.1942) to shape the façade of a Venice, California, advertising agency into a giant pair of binoculars (fig. 8.71). During the 1960s, Oldenburg had gained fame as a Pop artist, thanks to his large-scale sculptures of common consumer products, such as hamburgers, clothespins, and typewriters. Famous for its former nude beach and oceanside culture of beefy bodybuilders, the Los Angeles metropolitan community of Venice has long been a mecca for voyeurs, a cultural fact alluded to by this gigantic pair of binoculars.

Postmodernist architectural critics have claimed Frank Lloyd Wright as a forerunner of the movement. They have praised his synthesis of modern technology and building functions with traditional historical symbols and organic forms. Philip Johnson, spokesman for the International Style, had once sarcastically referred to Wright as the greatest architect of the nineteenth century. Yet, by the 1950s, the aging inventor of the Prairie house (see fig. 6.19) had become an even more powerful presence in American architecture. Among Wright's many commissions, none was more famous or spectacular than his design for the Solomon Guggenheim Museum on New York's Fifth Avenue. The circular building, a repository for the Guggenheim family's collection of non-representational Modern art, was modeled after a round, upside-down ziggurat. An ancient stepped tower or pyramid form dating from early civilization in the Middle East, the ziggurat is associated with the biblical tower of Babel (Genesis 11:1–9). In the Bible, this towering building form became a negative symbol of human pride. But Wright obviously interpreted the pyramidal ziggurat far more generously as a positive, hopeful form that signified humanity's godlike, progressive pursuit of knowledge and spiritual enlightenment. From this optimistic perspective, the ziggurat was symbolically suitable for an art museum. Since the eighteenth century, most architects had conceived art museums as public temples for celebrating human creativity and cultural refinement. For Wright, the ziggurat design was a means for creating a dynamic, spiraling space that suggested progress and human aspiration. The space of the

Guggenheim's interior (fig. 8.72) spirals upward and outward toward a brilliant, virtually circular glass dome. Constructed from reinforced concrete and painted entirely in cream white, the building's spiral has been compared to seashell forms. An elevator takes visitors to the top floor so that they may comfortably view exhibitions as they descend gradually along an inclined ramp. The vast, womb-like space at the interior's core facilitates a view of this human procession from all levels, thanks to the low rise of the sweeping ramp balconies. Understandably, many exhibiting painters and sculptors have complained that Wright's architecture overwhelms the art it is supposed to showcase.

Conceptual and Earth Art as Cultural Criticism

In 1971, the German-born artist Hans Haacke (b.1936) attempted to put on exhibit in the Guggenheim a photographic series documenting the Manhattan real-estate holdings of the museum's board of trustees (fig. 8.73). Rather than visually competing with the grandeur of Wright's architecture, Haacke's architectural record of derelict slum buildings would have been a subversive display of the trustees' hypocrisy in funding a temple of art, in part, from the rent and lease payments of low-income tenants living in substandard housing. When the museum's director discovered what Haacke intended to exhibit, he canceled the artist's show, which then moved to a less prestigious venue. In his combination of photographs and real estate records, Haacke was creating a work of conceptual art. Echoing the Dadaist tradition of Marcel Duchamp, the Conceptual Art movement of the late 1960s and early 1970s stressed artists' ideas rather than the making of material objects.

Following upon Pop Art, Conceptual artists responded to the growth of a consumerist, post-industrial economy of advertising, mass-media communications, and financial and information services. Joseph Kosuth (b.1945), one of the leading figures in the Conceptual art movement was not only an artist but also a critic-philosopher, gallery entrepreneur-curator, and art educator, who taught at New York's School of the Visual Arts. In his manifesto "Art after Philosophy"

(1969), Kosuth credited Marcel Duchamp's invention of the readymade for changing the focus of art from issues of form and aesthetic appearance to those of conception, idea, context, and function. Kosuth's *One and Three Hammers (English Version)* (fig. 8.74) is one of a series of conceptual works that the artist exhibited, which centered upon a readymade found object, flanked on the one hand by a photographic representation of the same object and on the other a photostat copy of the dictionary definition of the object. In choosing to situate an ordinary hammer within the context of art and mechanically reproduced visual and verbal languages, Kosuth calls attention to the transformation of the American economy from blue-collar labor to language or idea-based information, communication systems. The hammer here appears to be a relatively antiquated, ethnographic artifact, preserved from an earlier historical era.

In 1964, a year prior to Kosuth's conceptual piece, the Port Authority of New York and New Jersey announced plans to construct a pair of 110-story towers for the World Trade Center in lower Manhattan (fig. 8.75). For a brief period, these would be the tallest skyscrapers in the world. The Seattle-born, Japanese-American architect Minoru Yamasaki (1912–86) designed the buildings in the International Style tradition of unembellished steel-and-glass square shafts. The Twin Towers were dedicated on April 4, 1973, but not finally completed until 1977. Rising from a site that once housed small manufacturers and specialty electronic-parts stores, the Word Trade Center towers symbolized the deindustrialization of the New York City economy and, in fact, signified a national trend away from Fordism, or the industrial capitalism of Henry Ford, and toward

the post-industrial dominance of banking, financial services, global trade, and speculative investments in international money markets, stocks, and bonds. As multinational corporations increasingly shifted manufacturing overseas to poor, low-wage countries in the underdeveloped Third World, the American economy became less focused upon the production of real goods and values and more upon the international flow of money or investment capital from one global market, national stock exchange, and multinational bank to the next. Particularly after President Richard Nixon uncoupled the American dollar from the gold standard in 1971, the value of money itself seemed all the more abstract, conceptual, and ungrounded by anything real in the material world.

For many conceptual artists, the real seemed to lie far beyond New York City, the financial and cultural capital of the world, and, indeed, far from any overbuilt urban, suburban environment. Escaping the physical confines of art studios, galleries, and museums, several Conceptual artists launched the Earth Art movement during the late 1960s. Because their projects were often grandiose and impractical, many Earth Art works never went past the conceptual planning stages of maps, charts, sketches, and verbal instructions. Yet these documents were displayed and sold by galleries as art works. The New Jersey artist Robert Smithson (1938–73) became one of the most successful Earth artists before his career was cut short by an airplane crash near one of his projects in Amarillo, Texas. Critical of the quasi-religious aura of museum architecture, Smithson ridiculed the Guggenheim's organic, spiral design as an "inverse digestive tract" (cited in Shapiro, p. 168). Unlike later Postmodernist critics, he

8.73 Hans Haacke
Shapolosky et al. Manhattan Real Estate Holdings, a Real-Time Social System, as of May 1, 1971 (detail), 1971. Photograph 10 x 8 in (25.4 x 20.3 cm) and typewritten data sheet 10 x 8 in (25.4 x 20.3 cm).

Hammer (hæ·məɹ), *sb*. [Com. Teut.: OE. *hamor*, *-er*, *hƿmer* = ON. *hamarr*, etc. The Norse sense 'crag', and possible relationship to Slav. *kamy*, Russ. *kament* stone, point to an orig. meaning 'stone hammer'.] 1. An instrument having a hard solid head, usu. of metal, set transversely to the handle, used for beating, breaking, driving nails, etc. Hence, a machine in which a heavy block of metal is used for the same purpose (see STEAM-HAMMER, etc.). b. *fig.* A person or agency that smites, beats down, or crushes, as with blows of a hammer. Cf. L. *malleus*. ME.

8.74 Joseph Kosuth
One and Three Hammers (English Version), 1965. Hammer, photograph of a hammer, photostat of the definition of hammer, 24 x 53⅜ in (61 x 135.6 cm). Leo Castelli Gallery, New York.

situated Wright's Guggenheim entirely within Modernism's optimistic faith in historical progress and the artist's godlike genius. Smithson's most famous work, *Spiral Jetty* (fig. 8.76) was, in part, a response to Wright's transcendent, light-filled spiral.

Consisting of a coil of earth 1,500 feet long and fifteen feet wide, Smithson's flat, horizontal ramp spirals into the deadened western environment of Utah's inland sea, the Great Salt Lake. With financial support from the New York gallery owner Virginia Dwan and a Canadian art gallery in Vancouver, British Columbia, Smithson supervised the moving of some 6,650 tons of material into the relatively inaccessible desert lake site. Influenced by Minimalist sculpture, Smithson's spiral ramp could be entered and walked on by any adventurous person determined to make a long and difficult art pilgrimage. However, the ramp has been submerged by the lake's rising water level. Thus, as a work of art, *Spiral Jetty* is best known through aerial photographs, a film documenting the ramp's construction, and conceptual writings and sketches. Unlike the Guggenheim Museum's optimistic ascent skyward, Smithson's spiral leads nowhere. Moving in a counterclockwise direction, the visitor or beholder is directed to a point of entropy or dissipation of energy into disorder and chaotic nothingness. As Smithson explained, "Following the spiral steps we return to our origins, back to some pulpy protoplasm, a floating eye adrift in an antediluvian ocean" (cited in Shapiro, p. 137). The ramp's submersion beneath

8.76 (above)
Robert Smithson
Spiral Jetty, Great Salt Lake, Utah, 1969–70. Black basalt and limestone rocks and earth, 1,500 ft (457.2 m) long, 15 ft (4½ m) wide. Photograph Gianfranco Gorgoni.

Dependent upon meteorological conditions, *Spiral Jetty* has once again resurfaced into visibility with the recently receded water levels of the Great Salt Lake. Smithson began work on this monumental earthwork in 1969, the same year that the United States first landed astronauts on the moon. That event helped accelerate the environmental movement's campaign to increase public awareness of the earth and its fragile ecology, a theme forcefully addressed by Smithson's entropic work.

8.77 (left)
Michael Heizer
Double Negative, 1969–70. 240,000-ton displacement in rhyolite and sandstone, 1,500 x 50 x 30ft (457.2 x 15.24 x 9.14m). Mormon Mesa, Oveton, Nevada.

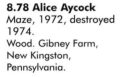

8.78 Alice Aycock
Maze, 1972, destroyed
1974.
Wood. Gibney Farm,
New Kingston,
Pennsylvania.

the lake's surface only underscored the principle of entropy and decay. Within a post-industrial wasteland of abandoned oil rigs and machinery, which the artist compared to dinosaurs, *Spiral Jetty* critiques America's environmentally destructive romance with technology and science. Significantly, Smithson began the *Spiral Jetty* project in 1969, the hundredth anniversary of the completion of the transcontinental railway. The artist's ramp to nowhere is, in fact, located near the Golden Spike national monument, which patriotically commemorates this transportation conquest of the American West. In contrast to the Spike Monument's celebration of national unity and economic modernization, *Spiral Jetty* may be interpreted as an allusion to the political chaos and disunity of the late 1960s, when violent anti-Vietnam War protests and urban riots in black ghettos shook confidence in the nation's future. Smithson's *Spiral Jetty* and his last work, *Amarillo Ramp*, both recall the ancient *uroboros*, or circular serpent biting its own tail. The *uroboros* was a popular symbol for cyclical regeneration during the American Revolution of the eighteenth century (see fig. 4.29). Even earlier, the *uroboros* had signified the dawn of the new age that followed the European discovery of America (see fig. 1.11). Smithson's fascination with entropy, decay, and dissolution implicitly contains the apocalyptic hope for future social renewal. Smithson and

other artists consciously drew parallels with Native American earthworks, which expressed the desire to harmonize with the vitalistic, cyclical forces of nature (see fig. 1.8).

Nevertheless, artists working on large-scale Earth Art projects have drawn criticism over environmental issues. In 1969, the California-born artist Michael Heizer (b.1944) supervised the removal of some 240,000 tons of sandstone and rhyolite from the relatively inaccessible Virgin River Mesa in the state of Nevada. Evoking associations with the earthworks of ancient primitive cultures, Heizer's *Double Negative* (fig. 8.77) comprises two deep cuts into the arid desert plateau that face each other across a steep canyon. Financed by the Virginia Dwan Gallery in New York, which exhibited and sold photographs of the spectacular site, *Double Negative* was sharply attacked by some critics for irresponsibly disturbing an ecologically sensitive environment. The desert topography surrounding the work also continues to be affected by the four-wheel-drive vehicles, employed to transport dedicated art tourists to the top of the mesa to experience the work directly.

Other artists have conceived temporary, less invasive projects for specific rural and urban sites. Shortly after graduating from Hunter College in New York, the sculptor Alice Aycock (b. 1946) constructed a twelve-sided wooden maze, thirty-two feet in diameter and six-feet-high on a farm near New Kingston, Pennsylvania (fig. 8.78). Aycock originally conceived the structure when she saw an encyclopedia reproduction of an ancient Egyptian plan for a circular labyrinth or prison. Yet the artist also drew parallels with Hopi Indian myths and their legendary tribal migrations, which spiraled inward in diminishing concentric circles toward permanent settlement at "the magnetic and spiritual center of the universe" in the American Southwest. (Aycock in Stiles and Selz, p. 560).

Christo Javacheff (b.1935), known simply as Christo, a Bulgarian-born artist, and the French-born artist Jeanne-Claude de Guillebon (b.1935) have created a series of particularly ambitious outdoor projects. Influenced by Dadaist and Surrealist readymades, Christo in 1958 began his art career by wrapping objects in fabric or plastic. In 1964 he created actual storefronts and wrapped buildings and landscapes, including, in 1969, 1 million square feet of the Australian coast

near Sydney. Christo and Jeanne-Claude have decorated various sites in the United States with, for example, a vast curtain, a fence, and objects made from synthetic fabric, steel, and aluminum. From 1970 to 1972, they planned and completed *Valley Curtain* (fig. 8.79) at Rifle Gap, Colorado. Composed of 200,000 square feet of translucent, bright orange, nylon fabric, the curtain, over 1,300 feet wide, was hung from 110,000 pounds of steel cable and anchored by 800 tons of concrete. Installed by a crew of workers, *Valley Curtain* lasted for only twenty-eight hours, since a powerful gale tore the work and forced its dismantling. From the artists' perspective, the physical realization of *Valley Curtain* constituted only one part of the artwork. Christo and Jeanne-Claude regard both the conceptual planning and the completion of projects as examples of artistic expression. They established a company, the Valley Curtain Corporation, which sold Christo's sketches and scale models to finance the construction of *Valley Curtain*. Even the legal

8.79 Christo and Jeanne-Claude
Valley Curtain, Grand Hogback, Rifle Gap, Colorado, 1970–72. Nylon polyamide and steel cables. Copyright © 1972 Christo.

Photographs of the fully-installed *Valley Curtain* evoke strong visual associations with the panoramic paintings of nineteenth-century Hudson River School artists. Particularly in this rugged Colorado site, the colorful, theatrical curtain continues the tradition of Americans' romance with the western frontier.

8.80 Edward Kienholz
*The Portable War
Memorial*, 1968.
Mixed-media installation,
9 ft 6 in x 32 ft x 8 ft
(2.89 x 9.75 x 2.43 m).
Museum Ludwig,
Cologne.

8.81 Leon Golub
Vietnam II, 1973.
Acrylic on canvas,
10 ft x 40 ft
(3.04 x 12.1 m).
Rhona Hoffman Gallery,
Chicago, Illinois.

Golub's brutal painting
technique was partially
inspired by the French artist
Jean Dubuffet (1901–85),
an advocate of *art brut* or
"raw art," encompassing
graffiti and the uncultivated
art of children and the
insane. Golub's wife, the
feminist artist Nancy Spero
(b.1926), has worked on a
smaller scale, employing a
graffiti-like technique.
During the Vietnam War
she, too, created numerous
political works protesting
American involvement.

petitions, government hearings, and local debates over the work's public authorization became part of the artistic process. To preserve the memory of the project, the artists engaged professional film crews to film the curtain's installation and established a photographic record of its dramatic, scenic realization. Forming a vivid contrast with the blue sky and ochre, muted colors of the rugged mountainous terrain, the artists' bright orange canvas temporarily drew together nature's elements to create a spacious, outdoor panorama of the western landscape.

Art and the Vietnam War: from Protest to Commemoration

While Abstract Expressionists had avoided explicit political content, many artists produced works critical of American intervention in the civil war between communist North Vietnam and the pro-Western government in South Vietnam. The California artist Edward Kienholz

(b.1927) paralleled Robert Rauschenberg as a prolific assemblage artist. However, unlike Rauschenberg, Kienholz created installations with a strong political and social content. In *The Portable War Memorial* (fig. 8.80), he produced a darkly ironic tableau that juxtaposed a copy of a World War II memorial celebrating America's victory over Japan with the image of a fast-food diner and other consumer or leisure-time furnishings. By recycling the war monument as a portable commodity, the artist deflates the heroic pretensions of the Southeast Asian war, which Kienholz thought served the imperial, economic interests of the United States.

The sculptural tableau also satirizes the jingoistic patriotism that the war generated on the home front. At the far left of the assemblage, Kienholz represents the portly singer Kate Smith, who became nationally renowned for her stirring rendition of "God Bless America." The obese figure, whose body resembles an upside-down garbage can, stands next to a World War I army recruiting poster with an image of Uncle Sam, the fabled personification of American

8.82 Maya Lin
Vietnam Veterans' War
Memorial, Washington,
D.C., 1981–4.
Black polished granite
wall; two wings, each
wing 246 ft (75 m).

nationalism, pointing outward to exclaim "I WANT YOU." Kienholz employed an audio recording of Smith's performance of the patriotic anthem to accentuate the eerie, ironic atmosphere of the work. Sandwiched between the war memorial sculpture and the image of oblivious fast-food consumers, a gigantic black-board looms like a tombstone, bearing the names of 475 nations extinguished by past wars.

The Chicago-born artist Leon Golub (b.1922) revived the art of politically charged history painting in works protesting American atrocities in Vietnam. In a 1969 series entitled *Napalm*, he had represented classical gladiator figures, whose bare flesh seems burned by some corrosive, acidic chemical such as napalm, the notorious anti-personnel weapon manufactured by the Dow Chemical Company and employed in Vietnam. Later, between 1972 and 1974, Golub produced *Vietnam*, a series of

mural-size paintings originally entitled *Assassins* that more specifically represents an American military massacre of Vietnamese civilians. The series alludes to the 1968 My Lai massacre and the 1971 U.S. military trial of several army officers held responsible for the killing at the village of some 500 Vietnamese, most of them defenseless women, children, and old men. In *Vietnam II* (fig. 8.81), frightened peasants rush toward us, away from a torched hut, while armed American soldiers and a tank take aim from the far left side of the composition. Golub accentuates the violence by tearing away sections of the canvas, which hangs unstretched on the wall like flayed skin. Employing an expressionistic technique, the artist roughly scraped the paint surface with a knife or cleaver to convey the raw, brutal nature of the subject. Golub's large work recalls the Spanish painter Francisco de Goya's famous *The Third of May*,

1808 (1814–1815), which represents occupying French Napoleonic troops mechanistically executing a group of pleading Spanish civilians outside the city of Madrid.

In 1975, the war terminated when North Vietnamese troops triumphantly marched into Saigon, South Vietnam. Since then, America's defeat in Vietnam has been a recurrent source of bitter political debate. No artist created more controversy over the meaning of the war than the Korean-American Maya Ying Lin (b.1959). Her quiet, abstract design for the Vietnam Veterans' War Memorial in Washington, D.C., stemmed from the 1960s Earth Art movement (fig. 8.82). The design contrasts dramatically with the nearby Iwo Jima monument of World War II soldiers triumphally raising the American Flag, the work mockingly copied by Edward Kienholz (see fig. 8.80). Instead of triumph, Maya Lin's funereal work memorializes military defeat and the tragic loss of over 58,000 American lives from 1959 to 1975. Situated within eyesight of the Washington Monument, a lofty Egyptian-style obelisk, the Vietnam Veterans' War Memorial emphasizes the horizontal and earthbound. Its two long, triangular wedges of polished black granite panels slope below the surface of the earth. Chronologically arranged, the names of those American men and women who died in the war have been inscribed on the mirror-like panels, which reflect the surrounding space of the site and the stream of visitors placing flowers and mementos before the memorial's embracing arms.

Lin's design aroused intense opposition from right-wing politicians, who complained that its intentionally anti-heroic profile constitutes an anti-war critique of U.S. intervention in Vietnam. Dissenters succeeded in placing a rival, more traditional sculpture of American soldiers in close proximity to Lin's strongly feminist memorial. As she recalled in 1983, a year after completing the project, her abstract design is not explicitly political, but it was meant to contrast with the vertical, phallic symbols of power that visually dominate the national capital's cultural landscape. Far from offending former participants in the war, Lin's memorial has become a pilgrimage site for friends and relatives of the deceased and for surviving war veterans.

Feminist Art and Politics

During the 1970s, a number of women collectively and individually challenged the dominance of male artists in gallery and museum exhibitions. In New York, Women Artists in Revolution (WAR) was founded to protest the Whitney Museum of American Art's 1969 annual exhibition of contemporary art, which included only eight women out of 143 participating artists. Over a decade later, a collective of women artists known as the Guerilla Girls organized to protest the sexual bias of major New York museums, which continued to favor exhibitions of male artists. To protect their anonymity, group members wore gorilla masks while picketing, leafleting, and plastering city streets with posters that sarcastically asked, among other things, "Do women have to be naked to get into the Metropolitan Museum?" Closely connected with the anti-war and black civil rights movements, women's liberation organizations had begun to proliferate with the founding of the National Organization for Women (NOW) in 1966. Local and national organizations of women artists were founded not only to combat the male monopoly in the art world, but also to focus on broader issues of social and political justice.

Yet feminists also struggled over internal divisions, as many heterosexual feminists in NOW and other organizations tended to distance themselves from lesbians and issues of gay civil rights. In 1969, riots against police harassment and arrests at the Stonewall Bar in New York's Greenwich Village marked the beginning of the Gay Liberation Movement. But it was not until a decade later, during the late 1970s, that the artist and feminist-lesbian activist Harmony Hammond (b.1950) curated the first significant exhibition of lesbian art in New York. As Hammond later recalled of this early pioneering period, "To exhibit as a lesbian took strength and courage and was a radical gesture not to be underestimated. It made one's personal life public, and artists risked aesthetic stereotyping or dismissal of their work" (cited in Robinson, p. 557). Hammond's own mixed-media sculptures cannot be categorized as distinctively lesbian. Her spiderlike wall sculpture *Kudzu* (fig. 8.83), fabricated from diverse materials, bears a certain kinship with the malleable wall panels of Eva Hesse (see fig. 8.60). More specifically, however, the piece refers to the kudzu plant, which was imported into the southeastern United States as a means to control soil erosion. With its rapid, rampant growth smothering pines and other diverse plant forms, kudzu is considered a major environmental disaster. Hammond thus regards her weed-like work, which threatens to grab hold of viewers, as a metaphor for racism, homophobia, xenophobia, and the fear of difference, or the other.

Meanwhile, other women addressed issues of race as well as gender. In Los Angeles, the African-American artist Betye Saar (b.1926) subversively reconfigured the popular racist imagery of American advertising and kitchenware in *The Liberation of Aunt Jemima* (fig. 8.84), a box construction that recalls the assemblage technique of Joseph Cornell (see fig. 8.18). Set against a background papered with the advertising logo for Aunt Jemima pancakes, a large Aunt Jemima note pad holder dominates the intimate space. Saar transforms the grossly caricatured figurine from a humble, happy servant into a proud, triumphant black militant, who holds a pencil-handled broom and a pistol in one hand and a rifle in the other. Furthermore, emerging from the bottom of the construction, between the rifle and broom, a large clenched fist symbolizes black power, apparently frightening a mulatto baby, held by another grinning Jemima figure. While the United States Congress had passed civil rights and voting rights laws during the 1960s, many African-American leaders noted their lax enforcement and called attention to the growing economic plight of impoverished blacks. Dissenting from the non-violent protests used by the Reverend Martin Luther King, Jr., the leading opponent of racial segregation, other black leaders employed the slogan "black power," with its image of a raised fist, to suggest the willingness to use more militant means to defend the interests of African-Americans. As a symbol of black power, Saar's armed Jemima liberates herself not only from a history of white oppression, but also from traditional gender roles that had once relegated her to the passive role of a happy domestic laborer or black mammy.

Substantially encouraged by feminist artists, Postmodernist ideas gained currency outside of

8.83 Harmony Hammond
Kudzu, 1981. Cloth, metal, gesso, acrylic, wax, glitter, charcoal, 90 x 90 in (228.6 x 228.6cm). Wadsworth Atheneum, Richmond, Virginia. Gift of Judith Daner.

architectural criticism. Following in the path of the Pop artists' appropriations from mass culture, Postmodern artists rebelled against the Modernist cult of original genius, which almost invariably had elevated men over women. Unlike the Abstract Expressionist painter Barnett Newman, who had belittled Native American basket weaving and the decorative arts, Postmodern, feminist artists and critics denounced Modernism's "high art" disdain for women's craft traditions. They also supported newer popular media such as video and performance to escape the arcane, formalist analysis that characterized the writings of Clement Greenberg and other Modernist critics. Reacting against Modernist formalism, feminist artists appropriated the decorative art tradition of women's crafts. They also returned to representational subject matter and historical narratives to make personal political statements.

Together with Judy Chicago (b. 1939), Miriam Schapiro (b.1923) educated a number of women artists, critics, and curators by establishing the short-lived Feminist Art Program at the California Institute of the Arts in Los Angeles, during the early 1970s. Wishing to celebrate the largely unheralded textile crafts of women, Schapiro also become a leading figure in the Pattern and Decoration movement. This movement to appropriate decorative motifs and patterns from quilts, samplers, and other traditional "low-art" domestic handicrafts gained

8.84 Betye Saar
The Liberation of Aunt Jemima, 1972.
Mixed media,
11¾ x 8 x 2¾ in
(29.8 x 20.3 x 7 cm).
Berkeley Art Museum,
University of California.
Purchased with the aid of
funds from the National
Endowment for the Arts.

In a contemporaneous
variation on the same
stereotype, *The Liberation of
Aunt Jemima: Measure for
Measure*, Saar comically but
pointedly supplied the
normally benevolent figure
of Jemima with two
measuring cups, one
carrying pancake mix, the
other explosives.

public attention during the mid-1970s and attracted men, as well as women artists, including Joyce Kozloff (b. 1942), Robert Zakanitch (b. 1935), Robert Kushner (b. 1949), and Kim MacConnel (b. 1946).

In 1976, Schapiro installed *Anatomy of a Kimono* at the Andre Emmerich Gallery in New York (fig. 8.85). Inspired by a book on traditional Japanese costume design, Schapiro created a

ten-panel, fifty-two-foot mural that combined painting with collaged fabrics, or what Schapiro called "femmage" in honor of the female tradition of quilting, needlework, and other textile arts. Though honoring women's work, *Anatomy of a Kimono* androgynously combined both rectilinear and curvilinear forms, conventionally gendered as male and female respectively. She later observed that, while the kimono was chosen as a power symbol for commemorating the "inner strength" of "the new woman," it was true that "men also wore kimonos, and so the piece eventually had an androgynous quality" (cited in Broude and Garrard, p. 216).

Judy Chicago, Schapiro's close colleague in the feminist art movement, created a major, room-size work in *The Dinner Party* (fig. 8.87), a triangular table composed of thirty-nine place settings for mythical and historical women throughout the ages, including a prehistoric goddess and the artist Georgia O'Keeffe. Each setting was composed of embroidered cloth placemats, napkins, painted and carved ceramic plates, utensils, and a porcelain chalice. With thirteen settings for each of its three sides, *The Dinner Party* purposely recalled the Last Supper of Christ and his twelve disciples, thereby suggesting the equivalent martyrdom of women heroes. But, according to Chicago, it also subversively referred to the thirteen members of a witches' coven, a traditional symbol of female occult powers. The triangular table was an act of "herstory," or historical resurrection for women swallowed up or ignored by the brotherhood of historians. An

8.85 Miriam Schapiro
Anatomy of a Kimono,
installation view, 1976.
Acrylic, collage,
7 x 50 ft (2.13 x 15.24m).
Galerie Bruno
Bischofberger, Zurich.

additional 999 names have been painted in gold on the white porcelain floor tiles below the table. Each of the glaze plates possesses a butterfly or an organic, vagina-like form as an emblem of feminine identity and women's liberation. *The Dinner Party* was a collaborative project that involved the anonymous labor of some 400 people over a five-year period. Chicago does not credit by name these individuals because the needlepoint workers, ceramicists, and other participants were not co-equal creators. The artist maintained control over the final design of every place setting. In contributing toward a more inclusive record of women's achievements in the face of Western civilization's repressive, patriarchal history, Chicago also challenged the masculine bias of art by reviving such traditional women's crafts as weaving, embroidery, and ceramics.

While *The Dinner Party* attracted thousands of enthusiastic visitors to exhibition spaces nationwide, Chicago's work also aroused considerable criticism from some feminists. They argued that the artist's sexual imagery and celebration of prehistoric goddess worship tended to make the differences between men and women essentially a function of biology. Influenced by French "deconstructionist" or "poststructuralist" literary theory, these feminists rejected nature-based "essentialism." In deconstructing the supposedly essential, objective nature of social relationships, they argued that gender roles are artificial, cultural constructs that have no necessary grounding in biological, sexual difference. Responding to the deconstructivist critique of fixed meanings and social identities, a number of feminist artists turned away from mythological fertility goddesses and biological symbols of femininity. Instead they explored the ways photography and the mass media have created cultural stereotypes that arbitrarily limit women and their relationships with men.

In *Carving: A Traditional Sculpture* (fig. 8.86), the feminist artist Eleanor Antin (b. 1935) combined photo-documentation with a conceptual, body-art critique of traditional high art and mass-media images of ideal beauty. Dieting over the course of thirty-six days, Antin documented her weight loss of some ten pounds by taking 144 photographs, side, rear, and frontal views, of her nude body. Antin poses as if she were in a police line-up and is being punished for not having a body that perfectly conforms to conventional standards of feminine beauty. Internalizing media-propagated conventions and seeking to win social approval, women have subjected themselves to grueling, often health-damaging diets.

In later performances, assuming various alter-egos for the camera, Antin and other artists also

8.86 Eleanor Antin
Carving: A Traditional Sculpture, 1972.
Each of 148 photographs
7 x 5 in (17.7 x 12.7cm).
Ronald Feldman Fine Arts,
New York. Collection
of The Art Institute of
Chicago.

8.87 Judy Chicago
The Dinner Party, 1979.
Mixed media,
48 x 42 x 3 ft
(17.6 x 12.8 x 0.9 m).
Courtesy Through the
Flower.

In 1990, when Judy
Chicago attempted to
donate *The Dinner Party* to
the University of the District
of Columbia, conservative
U.S. congressmen
denounced the work as a
pornographic sexual display
of female genitalia.
Congress even threatened
to punish the financially
strapped university for
daring to accept the gift as
a means of elevating the
school's academic and
cultural profile. Angrily and
regretfully, the artist
withdrew her donation.

began to question photography's documentary truthfulness. The photographer-performance artist Cindy Sherman (b.1954) has undermined the supposed journalistic objectivity of photography. By shooting pictures of herself in different disguises and in various melodramatic poses and narrative contexts, Sherman portrays a large cast of stereotypical female characters (fig. 8.88). The artist's "directorial" mode ironically mimics the craft of film directors. Sherman gives the illusion that her photographs are excerpted from a movie that she not only scripts and directs but also stars in, using exaggerated gestures and expressions. Each photograph appears to be a

8.88 Cindy Sherman
Untitled Film Still no. 3,
1977.
Black-and-white
photograph, 8 x 10 in
(20.3 x 25.4 cm).
Photograph courtesy of
Metro Pictures, New York.

Sherman stands over a
kitchen sink but does not
have her mind focused on
household duties. Wearing
tight-fitting clothing, she
looks seductively over her
shoulder away from the
dish rack and liquid soap
toward some unseen
presence beyond the
cropped image. In this
melodramatic tableau, a
dark, blurred pot handle in
the immediate foreground
also points in the direction
of Sherman's vixen-like
gaze. The photograph thus
parodies stereotypical soap-
opera imagery.

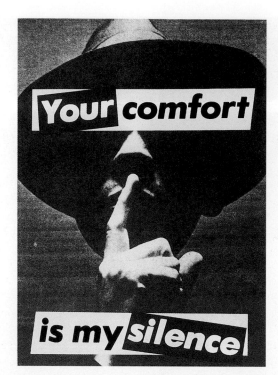

8.90 Barbara Kruger
Untitled (Your Comfort Is My Silence), 1981.
Photograph with added text,
4 ft 8 in x 3 ft 4 in
(1.4 x 1 m). Private collection.

Kruger's confrontational photomontages typically consist of rediscovered black-and-white photographs that are enlarged and overlaid by banners of accusatory words in bold type. Her poster-like style is partially indebted to the propaganda imagery and typography of politically engaged Russian Constructivists such as El Lissitzky (1890–1941), who were active during the early years of the Soviet Union.

still shot taken from a cinematic narrative of changing scenes and intriguing situations. Sherman's fictional images subvert the factual basis of the photographic medium and critically parody mass-media stereotypes. Her chameleon-like performances suggest that the individual self has no fixed identity but is an imaginative construct always in a state of flux, dependent on social interaction with others.

In work closely related to Sherman's critique of media imagery, the photographer Richard Prince (b.1949) has employed his camera to rephotograph and, thereby, appropriate ready-made pictures of female fashion models from chic advertisements (fig. 8.90). By isolating the heads of three women looking in the same direction and then displaying them in a series, he demonstrates how the supposedly meaningful expressions of each individual figure are mass-media poses or impersonal, conventional signs for creating consumer desires. Like other Postmodernist artists, Prince has questioned the Modernist premise that the individual artist-genius is the primary author of an art work. Arguing, instead, that "the audience has always been the author of an artist's work" (cited in Fineberg, p. 456), he conceived his acts of appropriation from the relatively passive perspective of

the consumer audience targeted by Madison Avenue advertisers. Fittingly or unsurprisingly, his rephotographed corporate images have been purchased, or reappropriated, by corporate art patrons. By Prince's own logic the circle becomes complete, in that these corporate patrons become not simply the audience but the very authors of the images attributed to the artist.

As opposed to Prince's subtle immersion into stereotypical advertising imagery, the feminist artist Barbara Kruger (b.1945) appropriates emotionally evocative photographic readymades and emblazons them with dramatic verbal headlines to virtually shout her opposition to male dominance (fig. 8.89). In *Your Comfort is My Silence*, the ominous, black-and-white cinematic image of a man gesturing for silence floats in an ambiguous dark space. Meanwhile, the words, attributable either to the aggressive man or his implicitly female antagonist, suggest a conventionalized sexual psychodrama akin to a pulp-fiction melodrama.

Kruger's billboard-like images never express comfort or endorse silence. For the artist, visual and verbal languages are the conflicted means through which individuals perpetually redefine themselves. Women must challenge or "deconstruct" the cultural stereotype of female passivity

8.89 Richard Prince
Untitled (Three Women Looking in the Same Direction), 1980.
Set of three Ektacolor prints, edition of ten, 3 ft 4 in x 5 ft (1.01 x 1.52 m) each. Collection of Chase Manhattan Bank, New York.

and obedience to liberate themselves from masculine control. Having worked as a commercial artist and graphic designer for *Mademoiselle, Vogue,* and other fashion magazines, Kruger unabashedly markets her confrontational images and messages through various consumer goods, including T-shirts, matchbooks, and tote bags.

Similarly, the conceptual artist Jenny Holzer (b.1950), who appropriated ideas from both corporate advertising and New York City street graffiti, created verbal art works that she disseminated outside restrictive gallery and museum spaces by using posters, leaflets, and T-shirts. More dramatically, Holzer's *Truisms,* a sequence of impersonal, broadly moral cultural messages, were flashed on an electrical sign overlooking Times Square in midtown Manhattan (fig. 8.91).

Such cautionary admonitions as "Abuse of power comes as no surprise" were designed to arrest the attention of busy pedestrians and motorists. The easily read *Truisms* temporarily altered the strictly commercial, functional character of the architectural site. Although employing an electronic advertising medium, the artist composed political, often feminist maxims more akin to graffiti than to corporate consumerist messages.

As we shall see in the next chapter, the last two decades of the twentieth century and beyond into the new millennium witnessed an accelerated corporate domination of American culture, as artists became ever more self-conscious regarding their relationship to the global, economic processes of cultural production and consumption.

8.91 Jenny Holzer
Truisms,1977–9: Abuse of Power Comes As No Surprise, 1982.
Spectacolor Board, 20 x 40 ft (6.1 x 12.2 m). Times Square, New York. Courtesy the artist and Cheim and Reid Gallery, New York.

Holzer's *Truisms* questioned power and authority with a series of messages advising passersby that "Private property created crime" and "Money creates taste." Flashed on a Spectacolor signboard overlooking Times Square in the world's financial capital, these maxims were intended as controversial challenges to conventional American capitalist thought.

Chapter 9
Globalization and the Culture Wars
1980–2003

THE last two decades of the twentieth century and the early years of the new millennium have witnessed dramatic change, as the Cold War has given way to a wide-ranging, indefinite "war on terrorism" and, concurrently, a social, political debate and struggle over the direction of economic globalization. In terms of the arts, media, and communications industries, the dominant free-market forces of globalization have further contributed to the private corporatization of cultural production and distribution. At the same time, on the national level, political conservatives declared a cultural war on government funding for the arts and on artworks they deemed immoral or irreligious. More recently, constitutional issues regarding freedom of expression and basic civil liberties have arisen since the U.S. Patriot Act granted the government new powers of law enforcement and intelligence-gathering following September 11, 2001. On that day, the nation was shocked by the first major foreign assault on the American mainland since the War of 1812, as a group of primarily Saudi Arabian Islamic extremists hijacked commercial airplanes in a suicidal mission that attacked the Pentagon in Arlington, Virginia, and destroyed the World Trade Center in New York City, killing some 3,000 people.

At the beginning of this period, in his prize-winning novel *Rabbit is Rich* (1981), John Updike described a bleak American landscape defined by the energy crisis of 1979, a crisis of inflated oil prices and supply shortages, exacerbated by the Iranian Revolution and the suspension of oil imports from Iran. Updike's antihero, Harry "Rabbit" Angstrom, owns a Toyota car dealership. As Rabbit cruises a Pennsylvania highway, past closed gas stations and Japanese and German car dealerships adver-

tising fuel-economy vehicles, he wryly observes that "gas pump shrouds," some "quite smartly tailored, in squared-off crimson canvas," are the newest signs of industry along the suburban strip (Updike, *Rabbit is Rich*, 1981, p. 20).

Updike's novel points toward a significant economic transformation in the United States, as Americans were now purchasing far more foreign-manufactured goods and resources than the nation was exporting. Furthermore, foreign investors from Japan, Europe, and Middle Eastern oil-producing countries took advantage of the declining dollar to buy American assets and invest in American markets. By the mid-1980s, the United States was no longer a creditor nation, as it had been since World War I. Becoming the world's largest debtor nation by the end of the 1980s, the United States continues today to owe more to foreigners than foreigners owe in return. Foreign capital investment sustains the American economy. Foreign countries lend the United States their surplus capital as a means of selling their exports, since America remains the world's largest consumer of goods imported from abroad.

In competing economically with Europe and Japan, the United States has joined them in continuing to support the free-trade, open-market policies of the International Monetary Fund (IMF), the World Bank, and the World Trade Organization (WTO), the successor, in 1995, to GATT (the General Agreement on Tariffs and Trade). As instruments of economic globalization dating from the end of World War II, these international financial, trade, and monetary agencies have served to restructure and monitor the diverse local, regional, and national economies of the world by integrating them into a global, capitalist market. With the collapse during the early 1990s of the corrupt, bureaucratic, totalitarian regimes in the Soviet Union and Eastern Europe,

Shahzia Sikander,
Perilous Order, 1994–7.
Vegetable color, dry pigment, watercolor and tea on hand-prepared Wash paper, 10½ x 8 in (26.6 x 20.3cm).
Whitney Museum of American Art, New York.

the United States government, led by President George H. W. Bush, envisioned the dawn of a "New World Order" marking the end of the Cold War. Yet this global vision of order and unity has been challenged by a series of worldwide, anti-corporate protests against the IMF, the World Bank, and the WTO. Anti-corporate activists argue that the impoverished masses in developing nations have been victimized by the financial and monetary policies of these global institutions. Indebted governments in Third World countries have been forced to cut social welfare, educational, and medical services, while selling or privatizing vital national, public resources as a means for paying back international loans.

Meanwhile, following a stock-market crash in 1987 and the savings-and-loan industry collapse in 1989, the United States economy of the 1990s temporarily recovered and, in fact, introduced a new and grander Gilded Age of expanded wealth and speculative investment, until the stock market fell again in 2001, amidst charges of improper corporate-accounting practices, illegal insider trading, and tax-evasion schemes. During the 1980s and 1990s, a new corporate elite arose from the digital technology, telecommunications, and media industries. Founded in 1977, Apple Computer, by 1982, became the first personal-computer company to reach $1 billion in annual sales, in competition with IBM (International Business Machines), which launched its first PC in 1981, using Microsoft software. While a host of smaller companies soon began cloning IBM PCs, Microsoft steadily garnered a virtual monopoly control on the manufacture of software and on the "Windows" operating systems necessary for computers to read software programs. By 1997, Microsoft, headquartered in Seattle, Washington, had become the world's most valuable company at $261 billion.

Meanwhile, in 1982, the term "Internet" was coined for a revolutionary technology that enabled users of personal computers to communicate with one another, creating a global information network. Having initially been established by the United States Department of Defense as a network that included universities and educational institutions, the Internet was opened for unrestricted commercial use in 1991 and grew rapidly as a tool for business sales, advertising, and communications. By the year 2000, there were 295 million Internet users and in 2002, just two years later, there were 530 million people "online." The Internet's World Wide Web enabled governments, businesses, and individual users to construct their own websites for the storage, retrieval, and exchange of information. Artists, art galleries, art museums, art publishers, arts funding and professional organizations, art historians, and critics worldwide now routinely employ the Internet as a means of promotion and information exchange in cyberspace. Through the use of digital photography, video, and scanning technology, artists, galleries, and museums have been able to create virtual exhibitions of their artwork and art collections. Digital artists have designed works to be experienced by Internet-users or "surfers," who log onto the artists' websites. But artists working in more traditional media also have learned to use computer software programs to conceptualize or modify their work. Architects and interior designers employ computer-aided design or 3-D modeling programs to conceive the shapes of buildings and their interior spaces. Digital printmaking, graphic design, and photography have challenged and transformed traditional studio practices and art school curricula.

Public Art and Arts Funding

The multicultural aesthetic of the Los Angeles Chicana artist Judith Baca (b. 1946) usefully reminds us that the processes of globalization are far from a recent phenomenon. America itself has, from pre-historical, pre-Columbian times, been a global crossroads for different migrating, transported peoples. Baca's almost half-mile long mural, *The Great Wall of Los Angeles* (fig. 9.1) visualizes a people's history of California. The work starts with the state's Native American origins, Spanish conquest, and years of Mexican rule. From there, Baca depicts the nineteenth-century Mexican-American War; the gold rush; European and Chinese immigration; and the twentieth-century aviation and movie industries. The artist looks at the Great Depression's impact on African-Americans, Native Americans, Mexican-Americans, and Japanese-Americans' in internment camps. The mural also focuses on the civil rights and gay liberation movements of the 1960s.

FAREWELL TO ROSIE RIVETER

DEVELOPMENT OF SUBURBIA

9.1 Judy Baca
Great Wall of Los Angeles, 1976–83. Overview of 762 meters (2,500 feet) long mural, Tujunga Wash Flood Control Channel, Van Nuys, California.

The U.S. Army Corps of Engineers, in the mid-1970s, originally commissioned the mural as a way to redevelop the Tujunga Wash Flood Control Channel in Van Nuys, California. The San Fernando Valley flood-channel grounds, with their concrete water-drainage canals, were to be transformed into recreational parks and bike paths. Baca, who grew up in a nearby Chicano neighborhood, worked with community activists, educators, and other professional artists and recruited over 200 teenage assistants to paint the mural over the course of five summers. The young "Mural Workers" were from various racial and ethnic backgrounds, and a number were juvenile delinquents on probation for drug or gang-related offenses. In painting a multicultural history, Baca purposely organized interracial painting crews, forcing teenagers to address issues of racial stereotyping and prejudice in their lives. During the course of working on the mural, the teenagers were taught history and drawing, painting and design skills. They also received job counseling, and, if necessary, drug therapy.

As a summer jobs program for underprivi-leged youths, the mural project was funded by government social service money, as well as by grants from the National Endowment for the Arts (NEA) and state and local cultural organizations. However, as art historian Erika Doss has observed, *The Great Wall of Los Angeles* was brought to a premature halt in 1983 by a conservative, "antipublic, antiethnic backlash" (*Spirit Poles*, p. 179). The election of former California governor Ronald Reagan in 1980 to become the fortieth President of the United States introduced a period of extreme political conservatism, resulting in larger military budgets and significant cuts in social programs. The conservative political climate adversely affected public-arts funding at all levels: local, state, and federal. Baca had hoped to include Los Angeles's most recent history and project a vision of the new millennium, but lack of funding and support from local businesses led her to suspend work on what was otherwise a successful, noncommercial community arts project, which gave creative work opportunities to hundreds of young people and provided San Fernando Valley residents with a dynamic, colorful narrative of

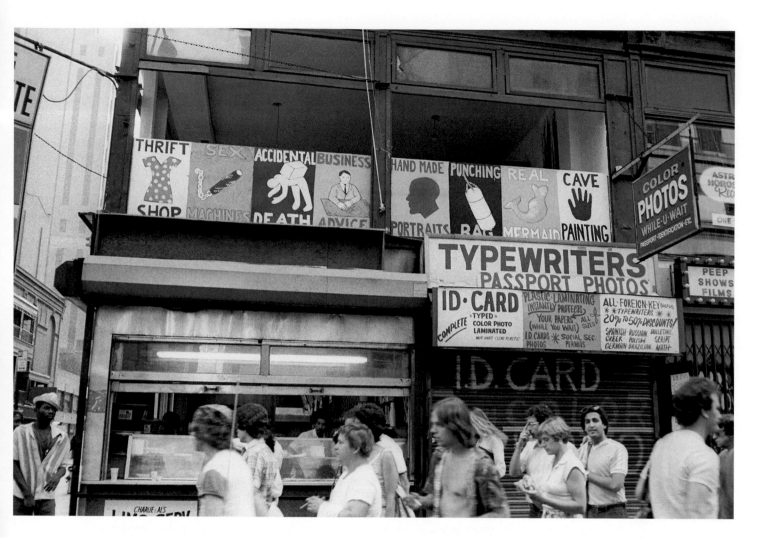

California's very diverse, collective history.

During the Reagan presidency, conservatives transformed the NEA from an arts-funding agency to a government fund-raiser, encouraging donations to the arts from private, corporate sponsors. Intentionally seeking to weaken the counter-cultural character of the alternative space movement of the late 1960s and 1970s, the Reagan NEA also encouraged the commercialization of alternative spaces for artists, defusing their potential for critical experimentation. As the art critic and editor Hilton Kramer argued in his politically conservative journal *The New Criterion*, unprofitable, government-funded alternative spaces were simply "licensed rebels at the taxpayers' expense" (cited in Wu, p. 74).

Certainly an atmosphere of rebellion pervaded the work of Collaborative Projects (COLAB), one of several artists' collectives in New York City that organized during the late 1970s in response to earlier alternative spaces becoming institutionalized and commercialized. Designed, in part, as a means to channel public, government grants to its individual artists, COLAB also focused on creating alternative spaces for art, thereby calling attention to the social problems of urban blight. Most famously, in 1980, COLAB temporarily occupied a dilapidated, abandoned massage parlor near Times Square and transformed it into an energetic exhibition of street art, performances, film, documentary photography, erotica, political statements and installations (fig. 9.2). Over 100 young artists appeared in the "Times Square Show," including Jenny Holzer (see fig. 8.91) and the photographer Nan Goldin (b. 1953), who presented a multimedia slide show of her spontaneous, highly personal snapshots of New York's Lower East Side punk rock, sex, and drug culture

9.2 Times Square Show
Second-floor window with paintings on masonite by Tom Otterness, June 1980. Photo © Lisa Kahane, New York.

As one of the show's organizers, Tom Otterness (b. 1952) displayed a series of painted signs playfully advertising the type of themes and inexpensive "hand made" art works available in the exhibition. The primitive signs mimic the commercial character of surrounding Times Square businesses. The simplified verbal and visual messages also possess an affinity with graffiti street art.

9.3 Nan Goldin
Cookie and Millie in the Girls' Room at the Mudd Club, New York, 1979.

In 1996, the Whitney Museum of American Art staged a retrospective exhibition of Nan Goldin's photographs focusing especially upon her pictures for *The Ballad of Sexual Dependency*. As exemplified by this early work in the series, Goldin's photography represents intimate, private moments in the lives of her friends who constitute a kind of extended family.

scene (fig. 9.3). Begun in 1976, Goldin's *The Ballad of Sexual Dependency* continued until 1992 and comprised hundreds of color slides, accompanied by a soundtrack. Goldin had first performed a slide show of photographs at the Mudd Clubb, one of several late-night, bohemian clubs that showcased new, street-wise art, music, film, and video. Goldin regards her work in terms of sexual politics, issues of gender, and the power struggles within relationships between autonomy and dependency.

Neo-Expressionism and the Revival of Representational Painting

Born to Haitian and Puerto Rican parents, the graffiti artist Jean-Michel Basquiat (1960–88) belonged to a band that played at the Mudd Clubb and CBGB, another East Village punk-rock venue. During the late 1970s, Basquiat had spray-painted poems on subway cars and city

streets, signing his "tag," or nickname, SAMO. He then exhibited at the Times Square Show, along with Keith Haring (1958-90), another graffiti artist. Basquiat's work quickly caught the attention of the New York gallery owner Annina Nosei, one of several major art dealers who were energetically promoting the careers of new German and Italian Neo-Expressionist painters, including Sandro Chia (b. 1946), Francesco Clemente (b. 1952), Anselm Kiefer (b. 1945), and Georg Baselitz (b. 1938).

Stimulated by international art exhibitions in London, Venice, and Berlin, this new movement in figurative and expressionist painting challenged those anti-pictorial practices of Minimalism and Conceptual art. Thanks to the expressionist revival, overdue critical attention focused upon the work of older American figurative painters, such as Leon Golub (see fig. 8.81), who was now producing brutal, mural-sized works, critical of United States support for anti-Communist dictatorships and mercenaries in Latin America and elsewhere.

9.4 Jean-Michel Basquiat
Charles The First, 1982. Acrylic and oilstick on canvas, triptych, 6ft 6in x 5ft 2¼ in (1.98 x 1.58 m). Robert Miller Gallery, New York. Estate of Jean-Michel Basquiat.

Basquiat entered the circle of Andy Warhol and became associated in the public mind with Julian Schnabel (b. 1951), the most commercially successful of the younger American group of Neo-Expressionist or figurative, representational painters, a group that also included David Salle (b. 1952), Eric Fischl (b. 1948), Susan Rothenberg (b. 1945), and Robert Longo (b. 1953). Beginning in 1984, Basquiat and Warhol formed a working, and sexual, relationship, collaborating on a series of jointly exhibited paintings.

However, in its use of comic-book imagery and the look of street graffiti, Basquiat's *Charles the First* (fig. 9.4) already demonstrates a lineage with Pop Art's practice of appropriating popular signs. At the same time, Basquiat's raw, vandalizing gestures are also rudely reminiscent of pictographic, Abstract Expressionist images. In particular, the painting's disembodied hands, signs of creativity, bear rough comparison with the pointing hands in Adolph Gottlieb's *Hands of*

Oedipus (see fig. 8.17). Basquiat's painting was one of several that paid homage to Charlie "Bird" Parker, an African-American jazz saxophonist who died prematurely following a life dedicated to music and an appetite for food, sex, and heroin. Basquiat memorializes Parker with a variety of heroic signs, including a crown over the name "Thor," god of thunder; the insignia for the comic-book hero Superman; a small crucifix in the top-center panel; and the words "most young Kings get thier [sic] heads cut off." Basquiat misspelled and partially crossed out or obscured words to force viewers to pay more attention to the work and the expressive act of communication or miscommunication. As Jonathan Weinberg has argued, by circling and crossing out the word "young," Basquiat calls attention to a life cut short. His misspelled "thier" also encourages us to pronounce a word that rhymes with "tear," generating associations with mournful crying.

In retrospect, it is very difficult to separate

9.5 Julian Schnabel
Portrait of Andy Warhol,
1982.
Oil on velvet,
107¾ x 120⅛ in
(273.6 x 305.1 cm).
Hirshhorn Museum and
Sculpture Garden,
Smithsonian Institution,
Washington, D.C. Joseph
H. Hirshhorn Purchase
Fund and Regents
Collections Acquisition
Program.

Basquiat's pictorial elegy for Charlie Parker from the young painter's own sudden death from a drug overdose in 1988. Though they were never personally close, Julian Schnabel later made a fictionalized, self-promoting film of Basquiat's meteoric rise and fall in the New York art world, essentially identifying himself with Basquiat, who is represented as the victim of an exploitative and commercial art system. Because the Basquiat estate refused to cooperate in the shooting of *Basquiat* (1996), Schnabel was forced to paint his own fake Basquiat paintings as movie props, an act of appropriation that actually contradicted his own expressionist aesthetic of individual authenticity and heroic, creative originality.

Throughout his career, Schnabel has been harshly attacked as a commercial opportunist for cynically recycling the masculine, action-painting persona of the heroic artist-genius. After selling out his first one-person show in New York before it even opened in 1979 at the Mary Boone Gallery, Schnabel also signed on with the prestigious Leo Castelli Gallery. Transformed into a media celebrity, Schnabel had himself photographed working directly on the studio floor, walking inside and around his canvases, just like a latter-day Jackson Pollock. Nevertheless, Schnabel's use of broken dishes, ceramic shards, antlers, and black velvet surfaces recalls the combine paintings of Robert Rauschenberg (see fig. 8.48) and the Dada and Pop Art traditions of employing vulgar or popular materials. In his large, somber *Portrait of Andy Warhol* (fig. 9.5), Schnabel painted on black velvet, a fabric widely used in garish, mass-produced paintings sold in souvenir stores. However, there is none of Pop Art's ironic humor in the artist's almost Christlike homage to that movement's most famous star. Warhol is represented bare-chested to show the bullet wounds and surgical scars that followed his attempted murder by a former admirer in 1968. Schnabel's gestural smearing and splattering of paint suggests the act of violence and the aging artist's nearness to death. Regarding the physical act of painting as a form of "displaced love" and a means for "transgressing death" (cited in Stiles and Selz, p. 268),

Schnabel chose black velvet as an expressive, meaningful support for the portrait. Warhol himself wore black velvet jackets and had sponsored the Velvet Underground rock band. Arguing that the artist's economic situation is a "separate issue" from any intention to know the unknowable and "transform the spirit" (cited in Stiles and Selz, pp. 267, 268) through art, Schnabel attempted to defend himself from charges of crass commercialism. Still, by romanticizing artists as unique individuals who feel more deeply and have a burning, inner need to communicate spiritual truths, he effectively promoted his heroically scaled paintings as valuable handmade objects. Schnabel's Pollock-like drip portrait of the Pop artist Andy Warhol implies an art-historical progression from past masters to a new generation of celebrity artists.

After earning a Fine Arts degree from State University College at Buffalo, New York, Robert Longo headed for New York City in 1977 and, like Jean-Michel Basquiat, performed in rock-and-roll bands in Lower East Side punk and New Wave music clubs. He also organized performance art programs at the Kitchen Center for Music, Video, and Dance, an NEA-funded alternative space. Longo's major art-world breakthrough came in 1981, when he had his first solo gallery show at Metro Pictures, exhibiting *Men in the Cities*, a series of large-scale charcoal drawings of young, urban professionals (men and women), posed in tortured, contorted positions. Influenced by the leftist German film-maker Rainer Werner Fassbinder, Longo's black-and-white drawings mimicked movie stills, particularly dark,

existential narratives of the film noir genre. The drawings were, in fact, based upon photographs that Longo took of his friends. Longo's willing subjects were forced to assume dramatic, violent poses when the artist threw tennis balls at them or pulled them back and forth with ropes as the camera shot them. The artist then projected the photographs onto large sheets of paper and traced over the images, altering or editing selected details. He also worked with a commercial illustrator to flesh out the final images. The series was a collaborative enterprise, involving actor-friends, professional technicians, and assistants. Longo's *National Trust* (fig. 9.6), a triptych comprising a cast aluminum relief of a New York City skyscraper flanked by two large panel drawings of a single male and a single female figure, finished, or "killed off," the *Men in the Cities* series (Longo, cited in Fox, p. 26). The isolated, dead figures appear to have been struck down by inhuman, urban surroundings, symbolized by the skyscraper, an icon of American corporate power. While admittedly bombastic and melodramatic, Longo intended his work as a major critique of what he regarded as a sick, corrupt American culture.

The Limits of Development

In a very different manner, the Hungarian-born artist Agnes Denes (b. 1938) also addressed the global, yet constricting, world of Wall Street stockbrokers, bankers, and corporate executives. Denes's *Wheatfield—A Confrontation* (fig. 9.7) was a two-acre, site-specific, environmental work, pur-

9.6 Robert Longo
National Trust, 1981. Two charcoal and graphite drawings on paper, one cast fibreglass and aluminum banded sculpture, three panels, overall 48 x 96in (121.9 x 243.8 cm). Art Center Acquisition Fund, 1981. Walker Art Center, Minneapolis, Minnesota.

9.7 Agnes Denes
Wheatfield A—Confrontation, 1982.
Two acres of wheat
planted and harvested.
Battery Park landfill,
downtown Manhattan,
New York.

Looming in the background
of this photograph are the
former Twin Towers of the
World Trade Center.
Standing in the midst of her
field of wheat, Denes, a
conceptual artist in the
Earth Art tradition (see pp.
422–427), obviously
intended her farming as a
critique of the skyscrapers,
which were much criticized
for their domineering
presence and impersonal
corporate style.

posely situated near Wall Street and the Twin
Towers of the World Trade Center. Denes and two
assistants worked with several volunteers to sow,
fertilize, water, and finally harvest almost one
thousand pounds of wheat. Denes intended
Wheatfield to resonate symbolically with global
issues: "It represented food, energy, commerce,
world trade, economics. It referred to mismanage-
ment and world hunger. It was an intrusion into
the Citadel, a confrontation of High Civilization.
Then again, it was also Shangri-la, a small paradise,
one's childhood, a hot summer afternoon in the
country, peace, forgotten values, simple pleasures"
(Denes in Stiles and Selz, p. 544). As Denes further
pointed out, the wheatfield redeemed an urban
landfill littered with garbage and debris, and created an amber, soothing space. The rural oasis stood
in contrast to the stressful congestion of a fortresslike city, dominated by the time clock and the
impersonal rule of money. In fact, the wheatfield
site was later transformed into a billion-dollar
real-estate development.

The African-American artist David Hammons
(b. 1943), a participant in the "Times Square
Show," also created a site-specific work on a
landfill in Lower Manhattan's southern tip.
Hammons's *Delta Spirit* or *Spirit House* (fig. 9.8),
a collaborative work, represents a southern shan-
ty or makeshift shack, fence, and clothesline,
constructed from scavenged wood and other
urban detritus, primarily found uptown in
Harlem. In contrast to the nearby Modernist
geometry and inhuman scale of the Twin
Towers, Hammons's humble assemblage evoked
associations with African-American folk traditions or the practice of creating something
aesthetic from leftovers, in the manner of a
patchwork quilt. Characterizing precise, pristine
geometric buildings as symbols of white, establishment culture, the Illinois-born Hammons
expressed his preference for vernacular African-
American architecture, found not only in the
South, but also in uptown Manhattan: "I really
love to watch the way black people make things,

**9.8 David Hammons,
Angela Valeria, Jerry
Barr**
Delta Spirit or *Spirit
House*, 1985.
Art on the Beach.

Hammons's use of found
objects recalls both the
tradition of Dadist anti-art
and the outsider,
assemblage art of the
carpenter handyman Simon
Rodia (see fig. 8.47). Yet
Hammons's constructions
and performances are most
often self-conscious
expressions of
contemporary racial issues.

houses or magazine stands in Harlem, for instance. Just the way we use carpentry. Nothing fits but everything works. The door closes, it keeps things from coming through. But it doesn't have that neatness about it, the way white people put things together" (cited in Finkelpearl, et al., p. 81).

The Yale-educated painter-critic Peter Halley (b. 1953) essentially corroborates Hammons's critique of functional Modernist architecture as a constricting, repressive manipulation of space. One of a group of Postmodernist painters identified with the "Neo-Geo" movement, Halley reinterpreted the Modernist tradition of geometric abstraction through the lens of critical theory adapted from the writings of French critics and philosophers such as Roland Barthes, Michel Foucault, and Jean Baudrillard. In bright, Day-Glo-colored pictures, such as *Two Cells with Conduit and Underground Chamber* (fig. 9.9), Halley parodies the mystical color-field paintings of Barnett Newman, Mark Rothko, and other Abstract Expressionists. Far from being transcen-

dental expressions of individual creative freedom, Halley's square, cellular forms signify prisons, hospital beds, school desks, or box-like apartment, office, and factory spaces that we voluntarily occupy, having internalized the disciplinary, regimenting conventions of modern, corporate society and its new consumer, cybernetic diversions. Questioning the values of Modernist geometric art and the Precisionist machine aesthetic, Halley laments that "Geometric art has sought to convince us, despite all the evidence to the contrary, that the progress of geometry is humanistic, that it is part of the 'march of civilization', that it embodies continuity with the past. In this, geometric art has succeeded completely." (Halley in Stiles and Selz, p. 166). According to Halley, we have thus become fascinated, enraptured by the geometric and its false, utopian promise. Geometric thinking has led us into the imprisoning enchantment of the hyperreal, the endless cellular network of cyberspace, a virtual, simulated community of

9.9 Peter Halley
*Two Cells with Conduit
and Underground
Chamber*, 1983.
Day-Glo, acrylic, and
Roll-a-tex on canvas,
70 x 80 in
(177.8 x 203.2 cm)
Gagosian Gallery, New
York.

individuals seated at isolated computer stations.

In 1986, a Neo-Geo group show at Sonnabend Gallery in New York generated enormous publicity and criticism. The work of Jeff Koons (b. 1955), a former Wall Street commodities broker, particularly aroused controversy. Koons did not share in Halley's Neo-Geo aesthetic, but did implicitly critique the high-art pretensions of the Modernist tradition. Inspired by Duchamp, Warhol, and Pop Art, Koons drew attention to the commodity status of art by appropriating mass-produced consumer goods. His earlier works included floating basketballs in fish tanks and the stacking of new deluxe vacuum cleaners and floor polishers in brilliantly illuminated plexiglass cases. Koons went on to create new sculptures replicating mass-produced plastic or inflatable children's toys. The artist's stainless-steel *Rabbit* (fig. 9.11), with a polished, mirror-like surface, retains the look of a light, airy, balloonlike toy. Koons intended his *Rabbit* to generate numerous meanings, but rabbits have traditionally served as symbols for sexual promiscuity. In John Updike's novel *Rabbit is Rich*, the character Harry "Rabbit" Angstrom is sexually prolific and always on the prowl. Updike's best-selling novel was the third in a series of four that he devoted

to "Rabbit" Angstrom, a literary personification of white, middle-class, male desire that parallels Koons's libidinous work.

Koons specifically cited as an inspiration for *Rabbit* the rabbit icon from *Playboy*, the popular men's magazine, featuring soft-core pornographic photo displays of nude women. The magazine's publisher, Hugh Hefner, also established resorts and restaurants served by Playboy "Bunnies," women dressed in skimpy rabbit costumes. Two decades earlier, the German artist Sigmar Polke (b.1941) had painted a Pop-inspired *Bunnies* (1966), mechanistically representing a group of Playboy Bunnies through a scrim of commercialized printer's dots, an analogue for the commodification of sex. Koons himself was married for a time to a European porn star and later promoted his art exhibitions through glossy art-magazine advertisements and commercial billboards, which depicted him having sex with his wife or in the company of other scantily-clad, voluptuous women. Critics from various positions on the political spectrum have condemned Koons's commercial hucksterism and use of sexual, playboy imagery. In terms of its squeaky clean polish, Koons's art also represents the white, consumerist culture rejected by self-consciously outsider artists like David Hammons.

9.10 Laurie Simmons
Walking House, 1989.
Photograph.

9.11 Jeff Koons
Rabbit, 1986.
Stainless steel,
41 x 19 x 12 in
(104.1 x 48.2 x 30.4 cm).
Private Collection.

Postmodernist Meditations on Death

Unlike Schnabel's reverent tribute to the Abstract Expressionist and Pop Art traditions, the Postmodernist painter Ross Bleckner (b.1949) has chosen to reexamine the history of modern art by exploring its failed or short-lived movements such as Op Art of the mid-1960s. Denounced by critics as a vulgarization of formalist geometric abstraction, paintings by Op artists created dizzying optical effects and vibrating retinal sensations. Their work used densely packed shapes, swirling stripes, wavy lines, and intense, contrasting colors. Quickly assimilated into product designs for rock album covers and the psychedelic posters of the anti-rationalist drug culture, Op Art came to signify the failure of Modernist abstraction. Unlike Pop Art's ironic ridicule of Abstract Expressionism, Bleckner's paintings seek to salvage something valuable from Modernism's historical devolution into hedonistic consumerism. As suggested by the metallic glow of *Architecture of the Sky III* (fig. 9.12), with its flickering lines of gold dots illuminating a dark, shiny surface, Bleckner admired and sought to preserve the faded memory of Op Art's intensely electric light effects. However, his shiny, spiritually evocative surface also evokes associations with Pictorialist photographs of the late nineteenth and early twentieth centuries. These works mimicked the atmospheric, hazy effects of tonalist pictures by Whistler (see fig. 6.64) and other Gilded Age painters. Pictorialism became a casualty of Modernist criticism, which insisted that each medium should define its own inherent nature. As seen in the contrast between Stieglitz's Pictorialist *Spring Showers* (see fig. 7.16) and his later *The Steerage* (see fig. 7.15), photography abandoned painterly effects for the clear realism and mechanical precision that only the camera could produce. The art historian Thomas Crow argues that Bleckner's morbid allusions to the "history of bypassed modernisms" ought to be interpreted within the context of the AIDS pandemic of the 1980s (p. 126). AIDS killed thousands of young and middle-aged gay men and devastated the artistic and cultural communities of American cities. Like Pictorialist photographers, whose pictures often conveyed

More critically than Koons, Laurie Simmons (b.1949) has playfully, but pointedly, photographed children's toys as a means of questioning gender roles culturally instilled from an early age. Her witty hybrid, *Walking House* (fig. 9.10), comprises a kind of doll house in which shapely, feminine legs support a model-size, suburban, middle-class home. Here, feminine identity becomes monstrously overwhelmed by an icon of domesticity and traditional, familial responsibilities. Like Barbara Kruger, Richard Prince, and Cindy Sherman, Simmons seeks to demonstrate the artifice or arbitrary nature of gender stereotypes and conventions. Its character defined by boxlike geometry, *Walking House* also reminds us of Malvina Reynolds's protest song "Little Boxes" (1962), which ridiculed the conformist environment of white suburbia (see p. 369). Simmons shares with Peter Halley a darker vision of confining, cellular spaces.

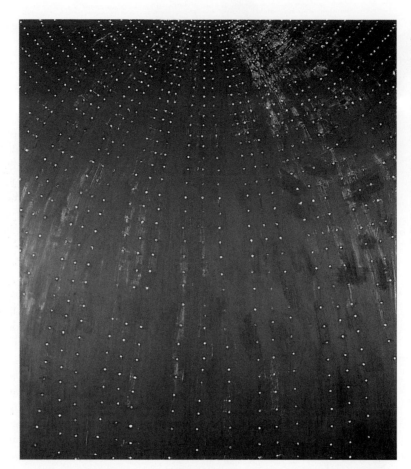

9.12 Ross Bleckner
Architecture of the Sky
III, 1988.
Oil on canvas,
8 ft 10 in x 7 ft 8 in
(2.7 x 2.3 m).
Collection Reinhard
Onnasch, Berlin.
Photograph courtesy of
the Mary Boone Gallery,
New York.

Bleckner's Whistler-like dots
of light against a dark,
nocturnal sky allude to the
interiors of church domes,
which traditionally
symbolized the sacred
dome of heaven.

spiritualist communications from beyond the grave, Bleckner characterized his luminous, glossy surfaces as meditations on death. He observed that "I think things shine with their maximum brilliance just at that point that they're about to die" (cited in Crow, p. 121). Unlike Schnabel's celebrity portrait of Warhol, Bleckner's *Architecture of the Sky III* expresses life's fragility by evoking memories of forgotten or reviled artists and art movements.

During the 1990s, the Connecticut-born sculptor Robert Gober (b.1954) also made works that indirectly allude to the AIDS crisis. Borrowing from the popular American tradition of wax figures, Gober created a series of eerily realistic sculptures of body fragments. The first in the series, a wax copy of his own left leg, replete with body hair, was dressed in trousers sock, and shoe (fig. 9.13). Placed directly against a wall, the leg fragment seems severed by the partition, suggesting an act of mutilation akin to Brook Watson's famous lost limb in John Singleton Copley's *Watson and the Shark* (see fig. 4.28). Gober recalled from childhood his mother's stories about working as a hospital nurse and holding amputated limbs after surgery. Yet, just as Copley's visual tale of Brook Watson evoked associations with Christ's martyrdom, so Gober's wax body fragments refer to his own Catholic upbringing and the church's cult of body relics honoring martyrs to the faith. Gober's own sense of fragmented being and martyrdom as a gay man arises in large measure from the Vatican's condemnation of homosexuality and established religion's tendency to interpret the AIDS plague as divine punishment for illicit sexual desire. However, as the critic Hal Foster has observed, Gober's amputated limbs and missing body parts also more broadly dissent from the technology of cybernetic space, which falsely promises a totally integrated system of digitalized images. Ironically, Gober uses wax sculpture, the popular medium that enraptured pre-industrial audiences, as an illusionist virtual reality.

9.13 Robert Gober
Untitled, 1990.
Wax, cotton, wood,
leather shoe, and human
hair, 10¾ x 20½ x 5⅝ in
(27.2 x 52 x 14.2 cm).
Hirshhorn Museum and
Sculpture Garden,
Smithsonian Institution,
Washington, D.C. Joseph
H. Hirshhorn Purchase
Fund, 1990.

The Cuban-born artist Felix Gonzalez-Torres (1957–1996) also addressed the personal tragedy of the AIDS crisis with understated works that invited audience participation and empathetic responses. Gonzalez-Torres had been a founding member of Group Material, an activist artists' collective headquartered in New York's Lower East Side. Group Material mounted exhibitions on a variety of social, cultural, and political issues, including United States interventionist policies in Central America and the nature of democracy in an advanced capitalist society. In 1989, the Collective organized "AIDS Timeline," an exhibition that traveled the country as an historical chronology of the crisis, documenting government inaction, media indifference, and community activism in combating prejudice, apathy, and misinformation.

Creating evocative public billboards and conceptual works, Gonzalez-Torres also became known for installations comprising replaceable piles of candy, individually wrapped in brightly colored cellophane (fig. 9.14). In contrast to the usual stern gallery or museum warnings against touching the art, the artist's *Untitled (Portrait of Ross in L.A.)* invited exhibition visitors to take and consume the pieces of candy. A "portrait" of his partner, who died of AIDS, the beautifully colored wrappings, the sweetness of the candy,

and the generous act of giving express personal qualities associated with the deceased and the nature of a loving relationship. Gonzalez-Torres's candy subtly resonates with humanistic, religious overtones. The consumption of candy recalls a sacramental communion or symbolic sharing in memory of a loved one. More broadly, the carefully wrapped candies may be viewed as metaphorical reminders for the practice of "safe sex" through the use of protective condoms. As every informed Halloween trick-or-treater knows, unwrapped, unprotected candy received from strangers carries potentially fatal risks.

The Culture Wars and the National Endowment for the Arts

Tragically, Gonzalez-Torres finally died of AIDS, as did a number of other talented artists, including the photographer Robert Mapplethorpe (1946–89) and the politically engaged mixed-media artist and writer David Wojnarowicz (1954–92). Not only did these artists struggle against the disease and its moral, social stigma, their artworks also faced political attack from right-wing Republicans in Congress, who were seeking to abolish the NEA and all government funding for the arts. In 1989, at the urging of the American Family Association, a Mississippi-based fundamentalist Christian organization, headed by the Reverend Donald Wildmon, the conservative Republicans in Congress pressured the Corcoran Gallery of Art in Washington, D.C., to cancel the opening of an NEA-funded retrospective exhibition of Robert Mapplethorpe's photographs. In addition to portraits of celebrities and still lifes of flowers, the exhibition also included parentally commissioned portraits of nude children and the homoerotic *X Portfolio*, a series from the late 1970s, featuring scenes of gay leather culture and sadomasochistic sex.

Mapplethorpe had died in March prior to the June opening, leading Republican Senator Jesse Helms of North Carolina and other right-wing critics to characterize the artist's death from AIDS as just punishment for a morally degenerate, homosexual lifestyle. The Corcoran director's cancellation of the show caused a storm of protest from the arts community. At a rally in front of the Corcoran on the eve of the cancelled opening, protestors projected slide reproductions

9.14 (left)
Felix Gonzalez-Torres
"Untitled" (Portrait of Ross in L.A.), 1991. Multicolored candies individually wrapped in cellophane; endless supply. © The Felix Gonzalez-Torres Foundation. Courtesy Andrea Rosen Gallery, New York.

Gonzalez-Torres had earlier exhibited works comprised of neatly stacked papers that parodied the look of Minimalist sculptures. There as here the artist invited visitors to take items from the stacks, thereby suggesting the essential importance of audience reception or consumption for completing the collaborative act of artistic communication.

9.15 (right) **Robert Mapplethorpe**
Self-Portrait, 1988. Gelatin silver print. Chase Manhattan Bank, New York. © Estate of Robert Mapplethorpe.

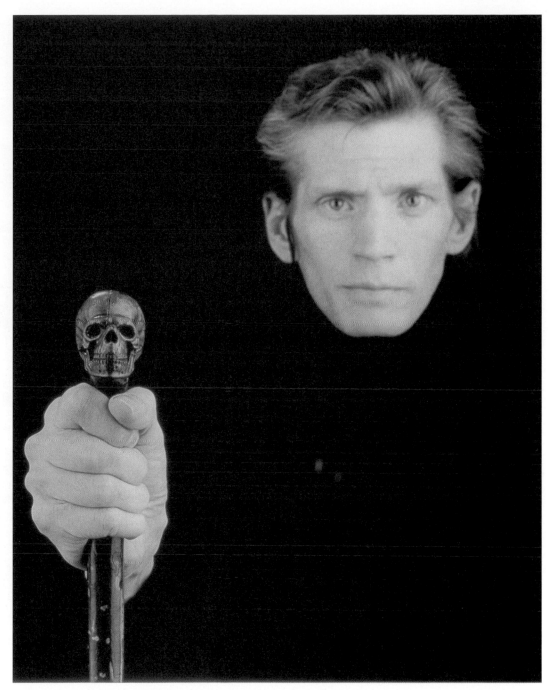

of the artist's work onto the museum's façade. The show's censorship generated intense publicity in the press, meaning that Mapplethorpe's photographs circulated in far more venues, including the floor of the United States Senate, than the artist might have expected.

Weeks after its cancellation at the Corcoran, Mapplethorpe's exhibition finally did open at

The Washington Project for the Arts, an alternative art space in Washington, D.C. However, when the show traveled to the Contemporary Art Center in Cincinnati, its director, Dennis Barrie, was arrested and put on trial for pandering obscenity and child pornography. Museum lawyers successfully argued against the charges, claiming that as works of art, the Mapplethorpe

**9.16 David
Wojnarowicz**
Untitled, from *Sex Series,*
1988–9.
Gelatin silver print.
Courtesy PPOW Gallery,
New York.

As a teenager, Wojnarowicz
ran away from home and
fled to New York City,
where he eked out a
precarious existence on the
streets before finding a
place in the East Village art
scene during the early
1980s. Wojnarowicz was
also a writer. He especially
gave expression to his
anger over the AIDS crisis
and homophobia following
the death of his lover Peter
Hujar (1934-87), a
photographer of New York
City's cultural underground.

photographs were also protected by the First Amendment's constitutional guarantee of freedom of expression.

One of the most frequently reproduced Mapplethorpe photographs in the popular press was a *Self-Portrait* (fig. 9.15), taken several months prior to the artist's death. Newspaper, magazine, and television commentators used this picture of the gaunt, black-costumed Mapplethorpe to moralize over the photographer's "sick" life and art. Yet, like Captain Thomas Smith's Puritan New England *Self-Portrait* (see fig. 2.32) from the late seventeenth century, Robert Mapplethorpe confronts death without fear. He refuses to play the helpless victim and, instead, projects a large, still powerful fist clutching a cane, crowned by a miniature human skull. Mapplethorpe's pale, determined face and hand hover in the inky darkness as symbolic metaphors of an unyielding creative, authorial presence. While the dying Mapplethorpe sought to maintain his artistic identity through one final act of self-representation, he also seems to speak to us prophetically. Like a ventriloquist's hand puppet, the small, grinning skull soberly reminds us that we all face the prospect of death. If there is also a hint of anger in Mapplethorpe's visionary expression, it is surely directed toward those who have used the AIDS pandemic as a political weapon to propagate cultural fear and hatred.

While the Mapplethorpe controversy continued to simmer, the art galleries of Illinois State University in Normal, Illinois, staged *Tongues of Flame*, a retrospective exhibition of the work of David Wojnarowicz, who had devoted his career to representing social, cultural outsiders or the "excluded, repressed, repulsive, despised, and phobically stigmatized" (cited in Stiles and Selz, p. 294). As a gay artist and activist diagnosed HIV positive, Wojnarowicz created posters and images attacking homophobia as a social, cultural disease that seriously exacerbated the AIDS crisis and endangered the lives of millions with legal, social sanctions and threats of anti-gay violence. Wojnarowicz's retrospective included his *Sex Series*, a suite of eight photomontages, in which negatively printed, black-and-white pornographic photographs from gay sex magazines were situated as floating bubbles within larger, negatively printed photographs of aerial, seascape or landscape views, in this case, a clapboard house and watertower (fig. 9.16). By printing negative images, distorting their clarity and cropping them from larger photographic sources, Wojnarowicz erased specific details, minimizing the particularities of the sexual acts and of the look and feel of human flesh. The sexual activity appears as a private thought bubble or clouded fantasy. Meanwhile, the peephole shape suggests a voyeuristic intrusion into a secretive, closeted space. Only a few years prior to *Sex Series*, the United States Supreme Court had upheld the constitutionality of state anti-sodomy laws, a position the Court only recently reversed in 2003. Thus, Wojnarowicz discussed the *Sex Series* as a challenge to the continued policing of private, sexual acts:

> *The spherical structures embedded in the series are about examination and/or surveillance. Looking through a microscope or looking through a telescope or the monitoring that takes place in looking through the lens of a set of binoculars. It's about oppression and suppression. Are you comfortable looking at these images of obvious sexual acts in a crowded room? Do you fear judgment if you pause for a long time before an image of sexual expression? Can you sense absurdity or embrace in the viewing of images?* (cited in Meyer, p. 254).

Moving from outward surveillance to inward self-examination, Wojnarowicz asks beholders to come to terms with their own feelings in the tension between sexual pleasure and repression. Yet the Reverend Donald Wildmon of the American Family Association wasted little time in attacking *Sex Series* and the retrospective exhibition as a whole, especially since its cata-

logue had been subsidized by an NEA grant. Wildmon's organization mailed nearly 200,000 flyers, condemning Wojnarowicz's work, to church leaders, Christian television, and radio celebrities, and members of Congress. The flyers were illustrated by selected sexual details from the artworks. In response, Wojnarowicz successfully sued Wildmon for libel and violation of copyright laws. He argued that Wildmon had mutilated and misrepresented his work by sensationally isolating for reproduction sexual particulars extracted from larger, far more nuanced compositions. In declaring in favor of Wojnarowicz, the U.S. District Court prohibited further distribution of the flyer and ordered the American Family Association to mail a communication correcting the organization's misrepresentations. Because the judge found that Wojnarowicz had not suffered financial loss from the flyer, the artist was awarded just one dollar in damages. Wojnarowicz insisted that the check be signed by Mr. Wildmon himself. Never cashed, the artist kept the check as a souvenir of his court victory.

Heterosexual artists have also triggered the wrath of Christian conservatives. A year prior to its attack on Wojnarowicz, the American Family Association mailed out one million letters condemning the provocatively titled *Piss Christ* (fig. 9.17), a color photograph by the Cuban-American artist Andres Serrano (b.1950). The photograph had won a $15,000 prize from the Southeastern Center for Contemporary Art in Winston Salem, North Carolina, an organization benefiting from NEA funding. But the photograph's representation of a plastic crucifix submerged in the artist's own golden urine enraged members of Congress, who responded to the AFA mailing by publicly tearing apart reproductions of Serrano's work and denouncing the NEA for supporting the exhibition of allegedly blasphemous art. Serrano responded to the public uproar in a letter to the acting chairman of the NEA. He denied any sacrilegious intention and criticized those who rushed to judgment against the photograph:

> *I am appalled by the claim of 'anti-Christian bigotry' that has been attributed to my picture, 'Piss Christ'. The photograph, and the title itself, are ambiguously provocative but certainly not*

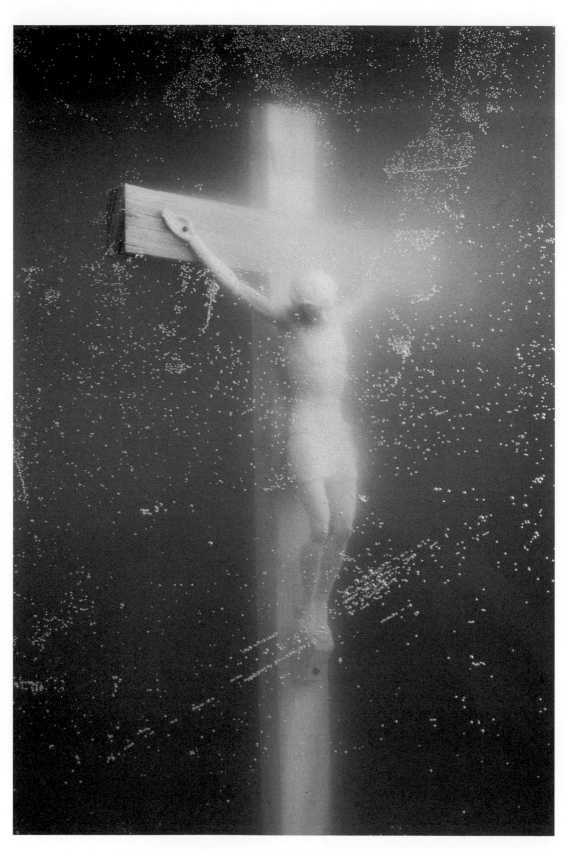

9.17 Andres Serrano
Piss Christ, 1987.
Cibachrome, silicone,
plexiglass, wood frame,
60 x 40 in
(152.4 x 101.6cm).
Edition of 4,
Paula Cooper Gallery.

This is one of a series of
works in which the artist
employed bodily fluids such
as blood and milk to
explore issues of personal
identity, sexuality, and
spirituality. He also created
photographic portrait
series focused on the
homeless and, more
strangely, members of
the Ku Klux Klan.

blasphemous. Over the years, I have addressed religion regularly in my art. My Catholic upbringing informs this work which helps me to redefine and personalize my relationship with God. My use of such bodily fluids as blood and urine in this context is parallel to Catholicism's obsession with 'the body and blood of Christ'. It is precisely in the exploration and juxtaposition of these symbols from which Christianity draws its strength. The photograph in question, like all my work, has multiple meanings and can be interpreted in various ways. So let us suppose that the picture is meant as a criticism of the billion dollar Christ-for-profit industry and the commercialization of spiritual values that permeates our society. That it is a condemnation of those who abuse the teachings of Christ for their own ignoble ends. Is the subject of religion so inviolate that it is not open to discussion? I think not (cited in Stiles and Selz, p. 280).

In 1990, the U.S. Congress passed a "decency clause" for NEA-funded projects. The clause stated that the NEA must guarantee that "artistic excellence and artistic merit are the criteria by which applications are judged, taking into consideration general standards of decency and respect for the diverse beliefs and values of the American public" (cited in Meyer, p. 278). But the question remained, who would decide these general standards of decency? How would they be defined? The problem of defining artistic worth is itself a political issue. Is it right that those in political power should set aesthetic standards?

Religious conservatives have frequently condemned performance artists, who use their own, often nude, bodies to address cultural issues, including misogyny, homophobia, and other psycho-social problems. Just prior to passage of the decency clause, a group of four, predominantly gay and lesbian, performance artists lost their peer-approved NEA grants when John Frohnmayer, the agency's politically appointed chairman, overturned the review panel's decision. Frohnmayer later admitted that he had been directly pressured to rescind the award by President George. W. Bush. The "NEA Four," Karen Finley (b. 1956), John Fleck (b. 1951), Holly Hughes (b. 1955), and Tim Miller (b. 1958), sued the NEA for violating their First Amendment, free-speech rights. They also claimed that the decency clause imposed on NEA funding decisions was in violation of the United States Constitution. In 1993, each of the NEA Four accepted out-of-court financial settlements from the government, compensating for their lost grants. But the artists continued to pursue the court battle against the decency clause. Defended by both Republican and Democratic presidential administrations, the decency clause was ultimately upheld in 1998 by the U.S. Supreme Court.

Representations of the Body: Issues of Identity, Power, and Control

Robert Gober's and Andres Serrano's interest in the human body as a locus of spiritual, personal meaning was shared by Kiki Smith (b. 1954), daughter of the sculptor Tony Smith (see fig. 8.51). Determined not to compete with her father's abstract, geometric aesthetic, Kiki Smith was already committing herself to exploring the human body, when, as a member of COLAB, she exhibited several anatomical paintings at the 1980 "Times Square Show". Later, in 1985, she and her sister studied to become emergency medical technicians. The course of study led her to focus on the internal, anatomical processes of the diseased, traumatized body. She began making sculptural objects based on the body's internal organs. In her democratic and nonhierarchical approach to the body, Smith created mixed-media sculptures that represented not only the heart and the brain, but also the stomach, bladder, and liver, or those organs associated with the more "base" digestive and excremental bodily functions. By the early 1990s, Kiki Smith had turned to crafting sculptures of the vulnerable, fleshy body as a whole. One of her most famous works, *Pee Body* (fig. 9.18), features a squatting, naked woman, composed of beeswax, who urinates golden, yellow streams of glass beads that flow behind her onto the floor. Rejecting the patriarchal tradition of the idealized female nude as an object of male desire, Smith chose to depict the female body in terms of its lived, physiological and psychological experience. Despite the humble, abject nature of *Pee Body*, the sculpture is not lacking in humor, as Smith applied nail polish to the figure's toes in an intentional, joking manner. The sculpture also has an emotionally evocative, quiet dignity. The figure's bowed head and closed, withdrawn form suggest psychic, spiritual introspection. Meanwhile, the golden, jewel-like beads allude to an alchemical transformation of excremental base matter into an aesthetic site of shimmering beauty. In its abject, biological presence, *Pee Body* confounds or deflects the erotic, voyeuristic gaze. Beholders experience a certain awkwardness in staring at this exposed, leaking body. In empathetic response, we become more self-conscious about our own mortal, permeable bodies.

Native American artists also have employed the body as a means of challenging the power of a dominant, controlling gaze. James Luna (b. 1950), a Luiseno Indian and a resident of southern California's La Jolla Indian Reservation, has created work that attempts to deconstruct cultural stereotypes of Native American identity. Beginning his career as a

painter, Luna eventually turned toward performance and multi-media video installations, which allowed him greater freedom in directly addressing museum and gallery audiences. Over the course of several years, from 1987 to 1990, Luna performed *The Artifact Piece* (fig. 9.19), in which the artist presented himself as an ethnographic exhibit. The performance/installation first appeared at the Museum of Man in San Diego, California, a museum largely devoted to anthropological displays of Native American cultures. Luna's *The Artifact Piece* was situated among other display cases representing the Kumeyaay Indians. Luna placed his semi-nude body on a bed of sand. Exhibition labels called attention to scars on the artist's body incurred from fighting or drunken incidents. Additional display cases included personal items documenting Luna's identity and Native American ritual objects from the artist's reservation community. Luna's performance as a living, ethnographic artifact intervenes politically in the cultural colonization

9.18 Kiki Smith
Pee Body, 1992.
Wax and glass beads,
27 x 28 x 28 in
(68.6 x 71.1 x 71.1 cm)
Installation dimensions
variable. Fogg Art
Museum. Harvard
University Art Museums,
Cambridge,
Massachusetts. Collection
of Barbara Lee, Emily
Pulitzer, and Harvard
University Art Museums.

9.19 James Luna
The Artifact Piece, 1987.
Installation and
performance.
Museum of Man,
San Diego, California.

of Native American history. As he lay upon the exhibition table, Luna asserted the active agency and subjecthood of Native American individuals and communities, who have a right to represent themselves and not be regarded as mere natural history objects for museum study and classification. During the 1980s and 1990s, Native American tribes campaigned for the return of Indian skeletal remains and other sacred grave objects. In Washington, D.C., the Smithsonian Institution's National Museum of the American Indian (NMAI) has responded by establishing a Repatriation Office for the purpose of consulting and assisting indigenous communities in the repatriation and care of particularly sensitive collections. Targeted to open in a new building on the National Mall in 2004, the NMAI has stated its commitment to work with Native communities in all aspects of the museum's educational, exhibition, and collections mission.

Luna's *The Artifact Piece* was finally installed/performed in "The Decade Show"

(1990) at the New Museum of Contemporary Art in New York. This large exhibition, subtitled "Frameworks of Identity in the 1980s," highlighted the multicultural diversity of contemporary art, particularly with respect to African-Americans, Latinos, Native Americans, Asian-Americans, women, and gays. Among the other, more than 100 exhibiting artists and art collectives was Lorna Simpson (b. 1960), an African-American woman, who abandoned a career in photojournalism to create photographic artworks from a feminist, Postmodern perspective. As in *You're Fine, You're Hired* (fig. 9.20), Simpson's works often juxtapose words and images and focus upon African-American women, whose backs face the viewer. Here, the words of the title appear at the top and the bottom of the four large, square photographs, together representing a reclining female figure. In addition, plastic plaques at the sides of the figure explain that the woman is applying for a "Secretarial Position." The plaque texts omi-

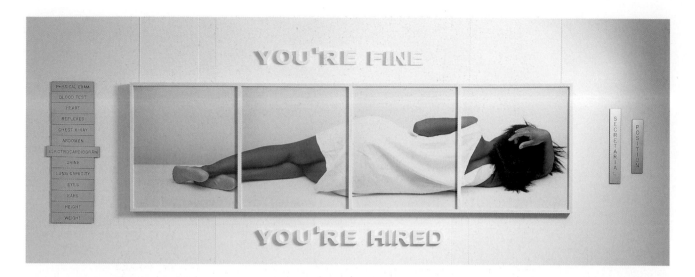

YOU'RE FINE

YOU'RE HIRED

nously suggest that the woman's physical characteristics are far more important than any clerical skills or work habits. Identifying a prone, recumbent position with the secretarial position further implies the potential for sexual harassment in the workplace. The fact that the woman is black also evokes historical associations with the slave trade and the physical examination of African slaves on the auction block. By turning her back away from the viewer, Simpson's subject quietly resists the objectifying male gaze and the prospect of sexual exploitation.

Similarly, Carrie Mae Weems (b.1953) has created a body of gender and race conscious works that create a dialogue between word and image. During the mid-1990s, she produced *From Here I Saw What Happened and I Cried*, a 32-piece photographic installation, inspired by an exhibition of early photographs of African-Americans from the mid-nineteenth century at the J. Paul Getty Museum just outside Los Angeles. In *You Became a Scientific Profile* (fig. 9.21) and other works in the series, Weems appropriated the historic photographs from the Getty show, enlarging and toning most of them in red. She then inscribed pointed textual commentary on the glass protecting the photographs. In this case, Weems calls attention to the dehumanizing, racist manner in which photography functioned as an instrument of white domination, subjecting powerless or enslaved women to the scrutiny of anthropological, physiological examination. By addressing the figure in the picture with the second-person,

singular pronoun "you," Weems suggests the woman's stolen identity and individuality. The words remind us that the anonymous woman was a real, unique person and not a mere racial type within a larger system of scientific classification. Weems's work parallels Luna's *The Artifact Piece* in its critique of the disciplines and discourses of the human sciences.

More controversially, the African-American artist Kara Walker (b. 1969) has appropriated the silhouette, a genteel, late-eighteenth- and early-nineteenth-century art form to unearth and recycle traditional, derogatory racial stereotypes that commonly circulated within the antebellum American South. Walker's flat, mural-sized black paper cutouts have also represented scenes of sexual assault, castration, murder, cannibalism, and bestiality. Walker likens the flat, two-dimensional silhouette to the reductive nature of stereotypes, in which complex individuals or personalities are reduced to simplified, caricatured forms. Like a comic book or cartoon artist, Walker exaggerates facial, physiognomic features and conjures forth fanciful animal-human hybrids. For instance, in the untitled work shown here (fig. 9 .22), a black woman, presumably a plantation house servant, is depicted holding by a pigtail a young African-American child, whose body assumes the shape of an alligator. The image alludes to popular racist expressions, current throughout antebellum America, which characterized black people as being of little more value than "gator bait" (Harris, p. 214). As we saw in paintings of the

9.20 Lorna Simpson
You're Fine, 1988.
Four-color Polaroid prints, fifteen engraved plastic plaques, ceramic letters, 40 x 103 in (101.8 x 261.6 cm). Courtesy Sean Kelly Gallery, New York.

Like Cindy Sherman and other feminists, Lorna Simpson questions photography's traditional claims to objective truth. Simpson's juxtaposition of verbal texts and visual images expresses the Postmodern premise that all representations are culturally constructed.

period, African-Americans were stereotypically identified with dark, reptilian creatures (see fig. 5.14). However, perhaps even more disturbing than the alligator caricature is the complicity of the black woman in treating the child as a pariah. Having apparently internalized or accepted the racial stereotype invented by the white slave-owning class, the adult servant acts as a kind of plantation enforcer of domestic decorum. Perhaps as a sarcastic, though still ambiguous, commentary on this acquiescence to the slave regime, Walker also depicts a small, black, liveried servant, who fawningly bows before the larger figures. Furthermore, barely visible on the white canvas ground, Walker lightly sketched erotic, scatological figures. She thereby situates the social regime of discipline and decorum within a larger, chaotic universe of uncontrollable bodily desires and functions.

Unlike Betye Saar, who unambiguously critiques stereotypical images by countering them with political signs of black power and resistance (see fig. 8.84), Walker has been criticized by Saar and other African-American artists and commentators for trivializing or identifying herself too closely with the demeaning racial stereotypes that she playfully, jokingly satirizes. Politically distant from the activist, black militancy of Saar's generation, Walker's ironic, Postmodern cartoon images employ vulgar bathroom humor and intentionally shocking sexual violence that may remind some of the often graphic, raw street language of contemporary hip-hop, or rap, music.

Shahzia Sikander (b.1969) also has adopted a traditional art medium to explore issues of personal identity and national heritage. Born in Lahore, Pakistan, Sikander, like Kara Walker,

9.22 Kara Walker
Untitled, 1996.
Cut paper, watercolor,
and graphite on canvas,
69½ x 66in
(176.5 x 167.6cm).
Courtesy the artist and
Brent Sikkema Gallery,
New York.

studied art at the Rhode Island School of Design, where she pursued her interest in learning the techniques of Asian miniature painting. Making her own paper, pigments, and squirrel-hair paint brushes, Sikander has studied the religious narratives and historical styles of Indian, Hindu, Muslim, and Persian miniatures from the fifteenth through eighteenth centuries. Pakistan, where Sikander was raised a Muslim, had been founded as an Islamic state in the Indian subcontinent, following World War II. Religious and military rivalry between Muslim Pakistan and predominantly Hindu India, long festering over the disputed territory of Kashmir, has now become a major global problem, since both countries successfully conducted tests of nuclear weapons in 1998. Through her paintings, Sikander symbolically strives to fuse opposing cultural identities: Hindu-Muslim, East-West, Asian-American.

In *Perilous Order* (see p. 436), she employed the Persian miniature tradition to portray a close gay friend in the historical guise of Aurangzeb, the late-seventeenth- and early-eighteenth-century Mughal emperor of India, who was a strict enforcer of the orthodox Islamic faith and yet, at the same time, a reputed homosexual. Before she could read the Koran in Arabic, Sikander, as a child, had studied Islam's holiest book for the abstract beauty of its calligraphic script. Muslims have generally prohibited figural representations in religious art, believing, instead, that calligraphic abstraction liberates the spirit from limiting, material distractions and conveys the spoken word of God. Transgressing Islam's ban on such imagery, Sikander surrounds the portrait image with voluptuous Hindu nymphs and the veiled, floating presence of a Hindu goddess, whose looped feet dangle below the square portrait frame. Sikander identifies herself with Hindu goddess imagery as an assertion of feminine, creative independence. Her modernizing miniature androgynously combines or synthesizes the binary opposition between masculine and feminine, while critiquing a religious orthodoxy intolerant of homosexuality and gender equality. The polka dots that are scattered over the image recall the work of Yayoi Kusama, the Japanese artist who proclaimed the polka dot as the androgynous symbol of the sun and the moon, male and female creative principles (see fig. 8.45).

Sikander's eclectic appropriation of various religious symbols, art forms, and ideas as a means of exploring personal identity and meaning loosely relates to so-called new-age religious practices, which became popular during the 1980s and 1990s. New-age religion is generally dissociated from organized, institutional, or denominational religion, and comprises a kind of individual, self-help search for spiritual meaning outside of traditional doctrines or orthodox dogmas. Environmentalism, vegetarianism, feminist goddess worship, and renewed interest in Native American and Eastern Asian mystical, meditative traditions have contributed to the wide-ranging interests of new-age seekers. New-age religion's global search for meaningful, therapeutic, spiritual truths also harkens back to the nineteenth-century's Transcendentalist movement, led by Henry David Thoreau and Ralph Waldo Emerson, who advocated a self-reliant, individual spiritual communication with the universal, vital energies of nature (see chapter 5). Electronic and digital media have facilitated the dissemination of new-age imagery, ideas, and values, promoting individual spiritual growth and physical well-being.

The video artist Bill Viola (b.1951) has employed modern technology to visualize transcendent spiritual states of being. Though raised an Episcopalian in New York, Viola began studying eastern religions and western esoteric traditions during the late 1960s and early 1970s, while attending Syracuse University. He has credited the writings of John Cage and the 1950s Beat poets, among other sources, for leading him toward Zen Buddhism and a more expansive view of eastern spirituality.

However, as Viola has stated, the thirteenth-century Persian poet Jalaluddin Rumi remains one of his favorite authors and a source of continuing inspiration. As a major figure in the mystical, Sufist strain of Islam, Rumi inspired the Mevlevi Order of Whirling Dervishes, a Sufi order, whose whirling movements were designed to achieve ecstatic union with God and the spinning state of the universe. Viola has credited Rumi for urging his followers to avoid scholarly theorizing and, instead, to plunge beneath the world's superficial appearances to experience its elemental, transformational energy.

Since the 1970s, Viola has been producing videos based on his religious conviction in art's power to transform the individual spirit or facilitate individual self-knowledge of one's place in the modern world. One of Viola's most famous video installations, *Stations* (fig. 9.23), comprises five laser discs, players, and projectors with five cloth projection screens, directly suspended over five matching slabs of polished, mirror-quality black granite. Each computer-controlled video screen features a single nude male figure, who plunges into water and remains submerged upside down until he gradually drifts off screen, only to plunge back in a whirling explosion of water turbulence. Viola intensely illuminates both the figures and the roiling water with strong cross lighting. The continuously playing video images and their shadowy, mirror reflections on the granite slabs starkly contrast with the darkened, open exhibition space, where viewers are free to wander and listen to underwater sounds, audible near each individual screen. In an erotic, dreamlike manner, the installation's primal, elemental, swirling imagery expresses Viola's mystical pursuit of spiritual transformation and Sufi-inspired immersion into the cyclical, dynamic processes of nature.

By employing new video-projection technology, introduced during the 1990s, Viola and other video artists have been able to create

9.23 Bill Viola
Stations, 1994.
Five-channel video/sound installation with 5 granite slabs, 5 projectors, and 5 projection screens.
Museum of Modern Art, New York.

theatrical video installations, liberated from the television-box format as used earlier by Nam June Paik. Beginning in 1993, the video artist Tony Oursler (b.1957) collaborated with the performance artist Tracy Leipold (b.1965) to create fifty video dolls. The dolls are small, stuffed cloth figures animated by video projections of Leipold's extremely plastic, expressive face and audio recordings of her wide-ranging voice (fig. 9.24). After recording Leipold's face in rehearsed performances of ten to fifteen minutes, Oursler projected her image onto the blank, oval faces of his dolls, creating uncanny, lifelike effects. As scripted by Oursler, most of Leipold's video-doll characters represent psychologically traumatized figures. These creations cry in pain, manically laugh, or make alienated pronouncements regarding their damaged lives. In *Let's Switch*, a relatively comic work, the chameleonlike Leipold plays feuding twins who eye each other suspiciously, trading insults and angry demands: "I'm going to close my eyes and wait for you to leave" (cited in Lawrence, n.p.). Through these childlike dolls and careful editing of Leipold's twin performances, Oursler crystallizes the image of an entirely dysfunctional family relationship. In doing so, he implicitly casts doubt on the conservative faith in traditional family values as a social panacea for America's moral and cultural ills.

9.24 Tony Oursler
Let's Switch, 1996.
Mixed media with video
projection, and
performance by Tracy
Leipold, 17 x 11 x 14 in
(43.2 x 27.9 x 35.6 cm).
The Broad Art
Foundation. Courtesy the
artist and Metro Pictures.

The technologically
sophisticated quality of this
work seems belied by the
childlike simplicity of the
soft, flannel-covered dolls,
one dressed in red, the
other in green. Here these
complementary colors
suggest conflict rather than
harmony. Elevated high on
a pedestal, the small figures
assume an eerie, larger-
than-life adult presence
when animated by the
video projection of Leipold's
expressive face.

Contemporary Art and Architecture and the Disney Vision

Toward the end of the twentieth century, video artists fostered a tendency to make the exhibition space an entertaining spectacle. For anyone who has visited America's leading amusement parks, Disneyland in Anaheim, California, and Walt Disney World Resort near Orlando, Florida, Oursler's video dolls may perversely recall the thematic boat ride "It's a Small World," which features a multinational army of singing "Audio-Animatronics dolls" dressed in native costumes.

However, Disney's smiling, mechanized dolls unflaggingly accentuate laughter and hopes, rather than Oursler's darkly disturbed world of tears and fears. As the creator of popular animated cartoons during the 1930s, Walt Disney (1901–66) became a major

force in American culture after 1945, when he created children's television programs and first opened Disneyland in 1955. An ardent anti-communist, hostile to unions and social welfare programs, Disney especially focused on the "imagineering" of Main Street, U.S.A. (fig. 9.25). As the arterial heart of Disneyland and the Magic Kingdom, Main Street, U.S.A. was conceived as the idealized, nostalgic re-creation of Disney's Midwestern hometown. Dominated by pedestrians and historical-revival architecture, the litter-free, tree-lined street incongruously leads to a soaring medieval castle and a host of other "Magic Kingdom" attractions. Disney amusements reinforce the guiding cultural themes of social harmony and historical, technological progress as culminating in the futuristic Tomorrowland.

Significantly, since 1984, when Michael Eisner became chairman of The Walt Disney Company's media and entertainment empire, several major architects have been hired for building projects. These ventures include hotels, restaurants, and a Team Disney corporate headquarters (1990) in Burbank, California. Most recently, Frank Gehry has completed the Walt Disney Concert Hall, the new home of the Los Angeles Philharmonic Orchestra, part of the Music Center complex on Bunker Hill in Downtown Los Angeles (fig. 9.26). Made possible by an initial $50 million donation from Lillian B. Disney, the philanthropic widow of Walt Disney, Gehry's building finally cost the enormous sum of $274 million. In fact, the architect's expensive design languished during much of the 1990s. Not until he received wide-spread international acclaim for a Guggenheim branch museum (1997) in Bilbao, Spain, was Gehry able to persuade leading Los Angeles art patrons to support the concert-hall project. Advanced computer-modeling technology has enabled Gehry to create wildly eccentric, curved forms that diverge radically from the austere, classical simplicity of International Style Modernism. The Walt Disney Concert Hall's exterior is clad in silvery stainless-steel metal, expressing the architect's vision of a grand music barge or sea galleon, with white, sun-reflecting, billowing sails visible from a distance. Intentionally or not, the building's nautical profile almost inevitably evokes associations with one of Disneyland's and Walt Disney World Resort's most popular attractions, "Pirates of the Caribbean," a theme ride that Walt Disney Pictures recently transformed into a major box-office movie. Critics have, in fact, compared the sweeping silver surfaces of the hall's exterior to panoramic movie screens, recalling such Disney fairytale cartoons as *Cinderella* (1950) or, perhaps, *Dumbo* (1941), the latter featuring a flying elephant with large, Gehrylike flapping ears. Prior to the Concert Hall, Gehry executed several projects directly for The Walt Disney Company, including the Entertainment Center (1989) for Disneyland Resort Paris and the Team Disneyland Administration Building (1987–96) in Anaheim, California. The interior of the latter building incorporates a large, colorful blow-up of

Goofy, one of Disney's most famous cartoon characters. Beyond having its name linked with the Los Angeles Philharmonic and a major civic, architectural monument in Los Angeles, The Walt Disney Company has more directly invested resources in urban development.

Architectural historians Vincent Scully and Beth Dunlop have praised Disney corporate executives for attempting to build Main Street, U.S.A., in real American towns and cities. While speculating that future Disney theme parks might help to revitalize otherwise depressed urban areas, these historians have especially praised Disney's development of Celebration, Florida, a new town south of Walt Disney World Resort. Designed by New York architect Robert A. M. Stern (b.1939), a former member of the company's board of directors, and

9.25 Main Street, U.S.A.
Walt Disney World Resort.
© Disney Enterprises, Inc.

Walt Disney World Resort in Florida, which opened in 1971, appealed to a number of architects and urban planners, since it featured a mass-transit monorail system, pedestrian malls, and the deployment of non-polluting motor vehicles. Furthermore, Disney World's Experimental Prototype Community of Tomorrow (EPCOT Center), opened in 1982, was intended as a venue for new design and building material ideas.

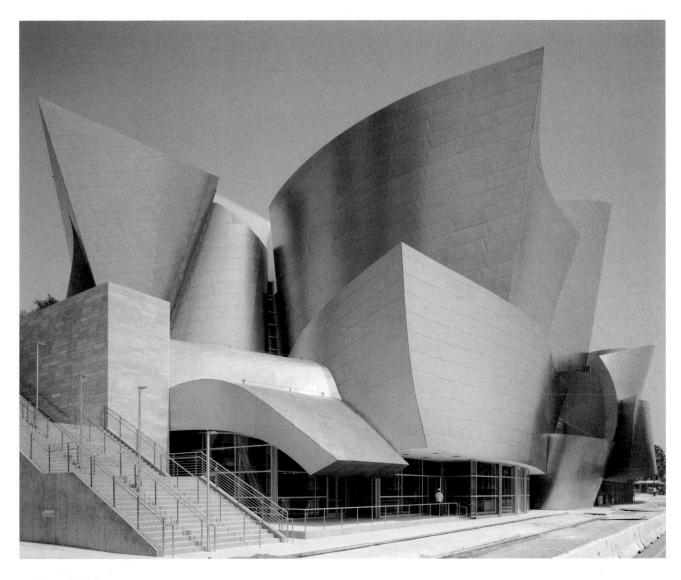

9.26 Frank Gehry
Walt Disney Concert
Hall (exterior view),
2003, Los Angeles,
California.
Photograph
© Walt Disney
Enterprises.

Jaquelin Robertson, Celebration opened in 1996 as a traditional, pedestrian-friendly town. Cohesively arranged streets and squares, as well as homes with spacious porches and verandas, in six different historical-revival styles, are intended to encourage old-fashioned neighborliness, says The Celebration Company. According to this Disney subsidiary, Celebration is now home to some 8,000 residents and is surrounded by a 4,700-acre greenbelt with walking paths and public golf course. Celebration is not a company town for Disney employees, since only a few can live in this carefully designed community, which now plans to expand to a maximum population of 12,000. With prices for residential homes presently starting near $200,000 it is dif-

ficult, in any case, to see how most Disney employees could afford to live in Celebration. Celebration is an Americana theme town and enclave for affluent citizens.

In the town's center MARKET STREET features theme restaurants and shops, such as the Lollipop Cottage, a children's clothing and gift boutique; and Sherlock's, an English tearoom and fine wine shop, themed around Sir Arthur Conan Doyle's detective Sherlock Holmes. Recently, Four Seasons Hotels and Resorts announced plans to build a new, 425-room luxury hotel and a number of exclusive, high-end, single-family homes. More disturbingly, Celebration's Town Hall (fig. 9.27), designed by Philip Johnson, appears reminiscent of Southern, antebellum plantation-house architecture. Having abandoned International Style Modernism for Postmodernist historical-revivalism, Johnson here adopts a conservative, classical style shared by such imposing, multicolumn plantation estates as Gaineswood, in Demopolis, Alabama (see fig. 5.16). The plantation-house theme is repeated at the Celebration Hotel on Bloom Street, which serves its Southern Cuisine in the "Plantation Room." In tourist-minded Celebration, Florida, cultural nostalgia for the genteel veneer of the Old South's plantation economy reassures prospective visitors, homebuyers, and real-estate developers that the town will remain predominantely white or socially privileged. A white clientele certainly responds far more comfortably to historical reminders of the Old South and southern plantation life than do blacks. African–Americans in the American Southern States continue to protest the flying of Confederate flags over state and local government buildings, as the flag still signifies a cultural heritage based upon plantation slavery.

Since the end of the Cold War, Disney's vision of "It's a Small World" seems to have been realized economically and technologically by the triumph of global capitalism and the computerized advent of the Internet. However, at the community level, the notion that the socially exclusive Celebration, Florida, can serve as a model for a new urbanism seems as naively optimistic as the town's corporately conceived name. Like the interiors of American shopping malls, this small real-estate development is a relatively controlled, sanitized island surrounded by a regional sea of car-clogged highways and commercial strips.

The Corporate Branding of Public Culture

The Walt Disney Concert Hall and Celebration, Florida, exemplify a general national and international trend toward the private corporatization of public culture. Increasingly, multinational corporations have used architecture and art patronage, and the sponsorship of cultural institutions and awards as a marketing, advertising, and public relations strategy for profitably disseminating their brand name and increasing market share, while also insulating themselves from public scrutiny and criticism. Oil and tobacco companies have been particularly active in arts sponsorship, as a means of neutralizing bad publicity over environmental and personal-health issues. For decades, the Philip Morris Companies, the largest national and international tobacco conglomerate, has financially supported virtually every major arts institution in America and the world, thereby garnering lavish praise from museum directors and art commentators. In 1983, the Whitney Museum of American Art opened a branch museum at the Philip Morris (recently renamed Altria Group Inc.) corporate headquarters on Park Avenue and 42nd Street, New York, the most successful among several Whitney corporate branch efforts. In 1994, when the City Council of New York was debating a smoking ban in public spaces, Philip Morris called upon arts organizations, the beneficiaries of its largesse, to oppose the proposal and even threatened to move its corporate headquarters outside New York City. Though the smoking ban was eventually passed into law, the Metropolitan Museum of Art allowed Philip Morris employees to hand out free cigarettes at the opening night for the 1994 *Origins of Impressionism* exhibition, a popular show the company had sponsored with a donation of $1 million.

Meanwhile, a few blocks further up Fifth Avenue, the Guggenheim Museum entered into a $5 million partnership with the German fashion designer Hugo Boss in the sponsorship of museum exhibitions and the establishment in 1996 of the $50,000 Hugo Boss Prize, awarded annually by an international jury of museum curators to innovative artists worldwide. With its corporate offices in Stuttgart, Germany, Hugo Boss had established itself as a fashion leader in men's clothes. Its association with the Guggenheim was intended to advertise its identification with cutting-edge styles and trend-setting movements in fashion and the arts. As part of the arrangement, the Guggenheim agreed to organize art workshops for Hugo Boss employees to stimulate their creative thinking. Hugo Boss also may have regarded the Guggenheim partnership as a good public-relations strategy, since the mid-1990s saw the beginning of organized protests on American university campuses against the apparel industry for its practice of selling clothes and shoes manufactured in unsanitary, low-wage sweatshops in the United States, as well as in impoverished Third World countries.

For the Guggenheim, the Hugo Boss partnership was itself part of a larger global strategy to market and exhibit its collections, while internationally disseminating the Guggenheim brand name to subsidiary branches or franchises, such as the new Frank Gehry-designed Guggenheim in Bilbao, Spain, or the Peggy Guggenheim Collection in Venice, Italy. By also creating a satellite branch in the reunited city of Berlin, the new capital of a reunified Germany following the end of the Cold War, the Guggenheim, with the encouragement of U.S. government officials, extended its global reach into formerly Communist, Soviet-bloc territory. Indeed, despite recent financial difficulties, the Guggenheim empire now includes the Guggenheim Hermitage Museum, an exhibition-space partnership with Russia's State Hermitage Museum, housed within the Venetian, a themed Las Vegas, Nevada, hotel and casino. Designed by the Dutch architect Rem Koolhaas, the Venetian Resort is replete with indoor canals and musical, Venetian-style gondola rides along a simulated Grand Canal, crossed by a simulated Rialto Bridge. The Venetian's "Jewel Box" room displays rotating artworks, drawn from both the Hermitage and the Guggenheim collections.

Thomas Krens, the current director of the Guggenheim and the person most responsible for its expansion, has, in fact, likened art museums to Disneyesque theme parks for tourists who have to be lured by sensational, blockbuster shows that blur, if not obliterate, the boundaries between art and entertainment, or art and commercial advertising. During the last five years, the Guggenheim has staged the "Art of the Motorcycle," a display of Giorgio Armani Italian fashion designs, and a retrospective of the folksy magazine illustrator Norman Rockwell (1894–1978), all popular box-office shows that have further distanced the museum from its original mission as a showcase for Modernist, non-objective, or non-representational, art.

In this distinctly Postmodernist vein, the Guggenheim's inaugural Hugo Boss Prize winner in 1996 was the athletic performance artist Matthew Barney (b. 1967), whose spectacular, ambitious, five-part film project, *The Cremaster Cycle* (1994–2002), was capped by a major Guggenheim retrospective of the artist's work in 2003. In its international, geographic breadth and its heroic but unrealized pursuit of oneness or unity, Barney's five feature-length *Cremaster* films seem perfectly congruent with the Guggenheim's entrepreneurial post-Cold War global vision. Schooled in the biology of the body and the self-disciplinary, competitive practices of body building and athletic training, Barney's performance art has stressed the form-building processes of repetitive, physical exercise. He has dreamt of the body becoming a virtually self-enclosed, self-sufficient organism in a manner akin to the *uroboros*, or circular serpent biting its own tail, a traditional, hermetic emblem for the endless cycles of nature (see figs. 4.13 and 4.29). However, given the necessary, failed nature of his pursuit, Barney prefers to think of a mythic satyr, a hybrid creature, who endlessly, futilely chases his own tail to complete a perfect circle, closing himself off from further development.

Barney named *The Cremaster Cycle* after a muscle in the male body, which monitors the temperature within the male reproductive organs, drawing the testicles upward when the body becomes too cold and lowering them to hang freely in the scrotal sac when the temperature is warm or normal. The upward or downward movement of the testicles assumes symbolic importance for Barney in relation to the embryonic development of the fetus, since gradual descent of the testes during fetal growth biologically differentiates the baby as a boy as opposed to a girl's ascended testicular state. Barney is interested in the fluidity and indeterminate nature of sexual identity during the early weeks of embryonic human development. His androgynous vision of sexually ambiguous, undifferentiated being suggests the goal of deconstructing the binary opposition between male and female. The *Cremaster* cycle is, to a certain extent, a vast, multipart allegory of embryonic life. The cycle proceeds in stages to imagine a prolongation of the moment of pure potential, undifferentiated being, prior to sexual definition, even as forces of development proceed inexorably toward division. But the cycle also traces Barney's own personal biography, connected to larger cultural, historical narratives comprising a dizzying phantasmagoria or sequence of bizarre, fantastic images, including scenes portraying organized American sports, Mormonism, Freemasonry, Irish myth, grand opera, scantily-clad Las Vegas-style showgirls, ritualistic murders, sadomasochistic dentistry, excremental body art, a punk-rock "mosh pit," and Barney's athletic scaling of the Guggenheim Museum.

In fact, Frank Lloyd Wright's architecture for the Guggenheim Museum (see fig. 8.72) with its five spiraling levels of ramps, represented a microcosmic symbol for the entire five-part *Cremaster* cycle. Filmed out of sequence, *Cremaster 3* was produced last and released just prior to Barney's Guggenheim retrospective, in which the entire museum was transformed into a kind of *Cremaster* theme park (fig 9.28). While a video installation suspended in the center of the museum's atrium continuously played the Guggenheim-staged scenes from *Cremaster 3*, all five *Cremaster* films were shown daily in the museum's theater. The spiraling spaces of the rotunda and additional galleries were filled with *Cremaster*-related objects or collectible spinoffs: sculptures, drawings, photographs, and videos of the film.

Barney interprets the organic shape of Wright's Guggenheim as a beehive. The beehive has long been an emblem of Freemasonry and the Masonic-inspired Mormon faith (see fig. 3.33). In *Cremaster 3*, Barney plays the role of a Depression-era Apprentice Freemason, who competes with an older Master Mason, played by fellow-artist Richard Serra, to complete the spire of the Chrysler Building (see fig. 7.51), Barney's analogue for the ancient Masonic quest to complete Solomon's Temple, the symbol of perfect architectural design (see figs. 3.9 and 3.10). However, the Guggenheim Museum itself, named after Solomon R. Guggenheim, also alludes to Solomon's Temple. The goal of finishing the Chrysler Building is metaphorically parodied by the sequence in which Barney laboriously climbs over the Guggenheim's ramps like a mountaineer, while also overcoming obstacles in his path, like a modern-day Hercules. In a still shot from *Cremaster 3*, a bloodied Barney poses in front of an Egyptian-revival, Art-Deco elevator door in the Chrysler Building (see fig. 9.28). Wearing a leather apron, he looks upward in heroic determination to achieve his goal.

Despite Barney's interest in a prenatal state prior to sexual differentiation, the overall Masonic, athletic symbolism of the *Cremaster* cycle gives it a strongly masculine bias. Even in *Cremaster 1*, which supposedly constitutes the most feminine installment in the series, the feminine is viewed through stereotypical male lenses. The film features two Goodyear Company blimps, both transporting a Hollywood starlet, and aerial views of a football field, with a troupe of smiling, dancing chorus girls. Their choreographic movements delineate embryonic cell formations and "a still-androgynous gonadal structure" (Spector, p. 34),

9.28 (right)
Matthew Barney
Cremaster 3, 2001.
Production still.
Courtesy Barbara
Gladstone Gallery.

echoing the shapes of the overhead blimps. More disturbingly, in *Cremaster 3*, Barney, the Apprentice Freemason, advances the inexorable process of sexual differentiation by killing off his own female alter ego, a hybrid female cheetah-like satyr, representing Barney's "lower self," in accordance with Masonic fraternal ritual (Spector, p. 57). Barney the Apprentice also murders the Master Mason and is himself killed when the base of the Chrysler Building spire crashes into his head, signifying the ever-elusive nature of divine secrets and perfected design.

Barney's *Cremaster Cycle* reinscribes in cinematic, epic terms the avant-garde, romantic myth of an essentially male artistic genius forever striving toward utopian perfection. In tracing the artist's genius, the cycle progresses geographically eastward from the American West, starting with Barney's boyhood home in Boise, Idaho, moving eventually toward New York (the artist's professional home), the Isle of Man in the Irish Sea (the site of the artist's Celtic ancestry), and finally to Budapest and the Hungarian State Opera House. Budapest was the birthplace of Barney's Masonic hero Harry Houdini (1874–1926), the athletic magician and performance artist who endured enormous physical and mental stress in escaping from padlocked trunks, handcuffs, and chains. As the Guggenheim curator Nancy Spector has observed, Houdini has been a model for Barney, given the legendary, escape artist's striving "for omnipotence through the exercise of sheer will" (Spector, p. 12). In following the source of his creative inspiration to Budapest, Hungary, Barney further replicates traditional Masonic lore, which teaches that all wisdom emanates, originates in the East, as further signified in the Masonic, alchemical emblems decorating the Hungarian State Opera House. But more importantly, from the perspective of the Guggenheim Museum, Barney's cinematic quintet culminates in a former Communist, Soviet-bloc nation. Through its patronage of the *Cremaster Cycle*, the Guggenheim thus celebrated the end of the Cold War and metaphorically alluded to its own corporate movement eastward in aggressive pursuit of new business partnerships and an expanded global audience for its collections, exhibitions, and museum-store sales.

Globalization and its Discontents

In December, 1999, some 50,000 anti-corporate activists gathered in Seattle, Washington, to protest global trade policies at a meeting of the World Trade Organization (WTO). Mobilized by e-mail communications over the Internet, the mostly young, college-age protesters argued that the corporate globalization fostered by the WTO, International Monetary Fund (IMF), and World Bank ignored labor and human-rights violations, and also overturned environmental laws protecting human health and endangered species. In their campaign to privatize, deregulate, or cut back basic public services worldwide, these international, corporate-supported, monetary, finance, and trade organizations have been accused of designing a market-oriented "template for one-size-fits-all government" (Klein, p. 78). The Seattle event was just one of a series of protests at annual meetings of the international agencies.

A number of artists have joined in this political critique of current globalization practices. For instance, the Houston-born conceptual artist and human-rights activist Mel Chin (b.1951) has organized an artists' collective known as the KNOWMAD Confederacy. Their *KNOWMAD/MAP: Motion + Action = Place* (fig. 9. 29) calls attention to nomadic societies in the Middle East, Africa, Central Asia, Turkey, and Afghanistan, threatened by repressive political regimes and the homogenizing economic and cultural policies of globalization. The installation project comprises an arcade video game station situated within a large nomadic tent space, the floor covered with elaborately woven rugs, designed in the diverse styles of traditional nomadic cultures. Visitors are invited to sit at the video station to navigate and examine the intricate rug designs in the virtual reality of a 3-D video game. Far from the simulated, competitive violence of most contemporary video games, KNOWMAD seeks to promote greater global awareness of different cultural, tribal art forms in a contemporary digital medium. Chin himself has observed that the kids who endlessly play video games are themselves practicing nomads, weaving their way through labyrinthine roads

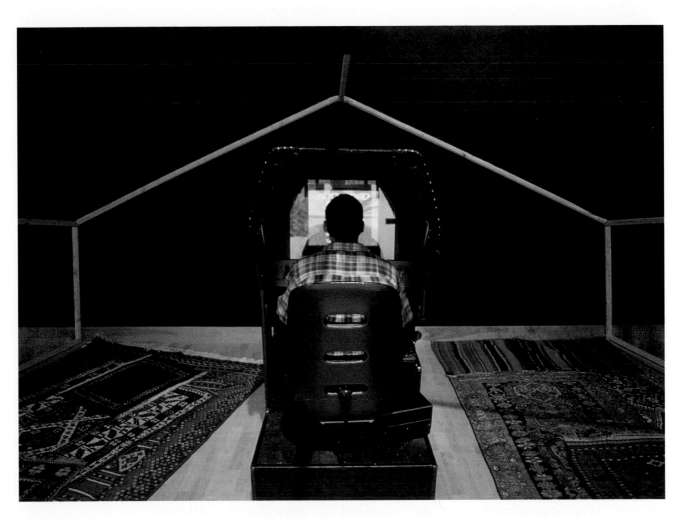

9.29 Mel Chin
Installation view of
KNOWMAD (detail),
1999.
Interactive video
installation with
Playstation, vintage
carpets, and fabric tent
for Weisman Art Museum
exhibition "World Views:
Maps & Art."

and passageways, without the benefit of a map or any real certainty of surviving the illusory journey or achieving a final, winning destination. As a Chinese-American who grew up in a primarily African-American and Latino neighborhood, Chin has long been interested in creating art projects that are politically engaged with community, environmental, and social issues.

September 11, 2001, and its Aftermath

In the aftermath of the horrific terrorist attack upon the Twin Towers of the World Trade Center and upon the Pentagon, a wave of nationalist, patriotic fervor and fear of more assaults cast a pall over political debate and dissent. The art world responded with shock, as images of the once-reviled towers now func-

tioned as funerary memorials. The ground upon which they had stood has been declared a sacred space in honor of the victims and the heroic rescue workers from police and fire departments, many of whom also died or were injured in the line of duty. According to the Polish-born architect Daniel Libeskind (b. 1946), master planner for rebuilding on the site, "The significance of the site of the World Trade Center has changed dramatically. This is no longer a fully commercial site because of the number of innocent people murdered there.... Whatever is built will have to acknowledge the permanent loss. The emptiness will remain and cannot be obliterated by any building" (cited in Protech, p. 85).

Inadvertently, the German, New York-based media artist Wolfgang Staehle (b. 1950) captured this sudden loss and emptiness in his 2001 exhibition at Postmasters gallery in New York. Opening in early September, Staehle's gallery installation comprised panoramic, live-feed video projections from three different sites: a hilltop monastery in Stuttgart, Germany (the artist's hometown); the television tower in Berlin's Alexanderplatz; and a distant view of lower Manhattan from across the East River in the south Williamsburg section of Brooklyn. Staehle had conceived the projections as essentially uneventful landscapes or cityscapes, equivalent in their relative tranquility to picturesque postcards or traditional nineteenth-century painted panoramas. The events of September 11, 2001, abruptly altered the work, as it became a historical narrative recording of the Twin Towers' attack and collapse, leaving only a smoking gaping void in the skyline (fig. 9.30). Stills from Staehle's video appeared in the centerfold of the November 2001 issue of *Artforum*. The New York City art journal's reviewer Alexi Worth observed that Staehle's now quasi-journalistic piece of archival footage seems problematic in its impersonal, emotional neutrality, given the tragic, catastrophic nature of the event. Yet as the video projection steadily returned to the recording of routine, boring movements and light changes in the skyline, the digital feed's evident indifference also reassuringly suggested the continuity of life beyond the deadly 9/11 rupture.

Two years prior to the World Trade Center attacks, the New York artist Stephen Vitiello (b. 1964) had a studio on the 91st floor of Tower One, as part of the Lower Manhattan Cultural Council's artist-in-residence program. The Twin Towers had long been criticized for their inhuman scale, for blotting out the sky at street level, where a featureless, windswept plaza offered little beauty or comfort to harried pedestrians. Vitiello became interested in the experiential disjuncture between the vital street life below and the eerie, hermetic silence of his lofty studio space. Attaching two contact microphones to the sealed windows of his studio interior, he increased their receptivity to the point that he

could hear through headphones sounds from the other side of the thick glass: church bells, street noise, wind currents, and a variety of other unidentifiable noises (fig. 9.31). In processing the sonic stream, Vitiello made only minimal adjustments with a soundboard filtering some frequencies, while accentuating others.

Following the collapse of the Twin Towers, Vitiello went back to his recording from Tower One to create a commemorative audio installation for the Whitney Museum of American Art's 2002 Biennial Exhibition of contemporary art. Vitiello chose to feature that portion of his project that had recorded the heavy, surging wind currents from Hurricane Floyd, a storm that had incurred considerable damage on the East Coast in 1999. Vitiello's installation conveyed the sounds of the swaying building, as it shifted back and forth from true center. The unsettling, rattling, crackling sounds implicitly suggested the skyscraper's human vulnerability to external forces and internal weaknesses.

The Whitney Biennial has traditionally functioned as a cultural barometer of the contemporary art world in the United States. Lawrence R. Rinder, the Whitney's contemporary art curator, observed in the 2002 show's catalogue that artists in the wake of 9/11/01 now seem keen "to reclaim the individual's expressive capacity from the corporate monolith of mass-media entertainment, from the market-dominated trends of the mainstream art world," and they seem more interested in issues of truth, however elusive, than in traditional beauty or Postmodernist irony and spectacle (p. 12). The show thus included the extremely simple and direct drawings of Conor McGrady (1970), an Irish-born Chicago artist, whose work has largely been based upon his life experiences in the sometimes violent, terror-plagued city of Belfast. Divided between working-class Catholics and the politically dominant Protestants of Northern Ireland, Belfast represents an urban armed camp, often rife with fear, insecurity, and paranoia.

9.30 Wolfgang Staehle
Untitled, (3 video stills of Twin Towers on 9/11), 2001. Postmasters Gallery, New York.

A media artist, Wolfgang Staehle is especially active on the Internet as founder and executive director of THE THING, an independent on-line meeting place for contemporary art sites, projects, video and audio programs, reviews, and information.

9.31 Stephen Vitiello
*Contact Microphones
Affixed to the Windows
of the 91st Floor of the
World Trade Center,*
1999.
Courtesy the artist and
The Project, New York/Los
Angeles.

McGrady's stark drawings evoke these disturbing emotions that now resonate with remarkable topicality in an American, post-9/11 political environment.

McGrady's *Inspection* (fig. 9.32) draws on the biblical story from John 20: 24–28 of Christ's disciple Thomas, who doubted the miracle of the Resurrection and stuck a finger in the wounded side of Christ's crucified and resurrected body to dispel disbelief and authenticate true identity. But more immediately, McGrady's drawing of youthful submission and vulnerability before a probing inspector expresses the sense of violated privacy rights in an era of both government and corporate surveillance. Even before the war on terrorism, surveillance cameras were monitoring schools, offices, factories, parks, shopping malls, highways, and airports. Under the October 2001 USA Patriot Act, FBI agents have far easier access to personal and business transactions, gleaned from corporate databases, ATMs, credit cards, Internet communications, telephones, cell phones, and public-library records. In November 2002, it was disclosed that the Pentagon had established a Total Information Awareness (TIA) program, initially with an all-seeing-eye logo appropriated from the Great Seal of the United States (see

9.32 Conor McGrady
Inspection, 2000.
Compressed charcoal
on paper, 20 x 28 in
(50.8 x 71.1cm).
Alberto Guevara
Collection.

fig. 4.18). This project centralizes the gathering of surveillance information and data records on both citizens and non-citizens. The probing finger in McGrady's *Inspection* seems an apt metaphor or parallel emblem for the Defense Department's employment of the all-seeing-eye's inspecting powers. Responding to adverse public criticism, the TIA has since removed the all-seeing-eye logo from its Internet website. It has also changed its name to Terrorism Information Awareness, obviously concerned that the dropped word "Total" inevitably elicited unwanted associations with the word "totalitarian."

More recently, during the summer and fall of 2003, the Whitney Museum, under the continued curatorship of Lawrence Rinder, staged *The American Effect: Global Perspectives on the United States, 1990–2003*, an exhibition of nearly fifty international artists from thirty countries in Africa, Europe, Australia, and the Americas.

The exhibition was a response to questions of how the rest of the world has perceived the United States during the post-Cold War era, now that its military and economic dominance has made it the lone global superpower. While most nations rallied to express sympathy and support for the United States in the immediate aftermath of the 9/11 attacks, President George W. Bush's inclination to follow a unilateral, extremely nationalist foreign policy has contributed to the decline of America's image abroad. Prior to the terrorist attack, the Bush administration already had backed out of a number of international treaties and agreements, including the Anti-Ballistic Missile Treaty, the Kyoto Protocol for Global-Warming Prevention, and the Treaty of Rome instituting an international criminal court. Since the war on terrorism, beginning with the American military invasion of Afghanistan, the United States has rapidly lost international support for

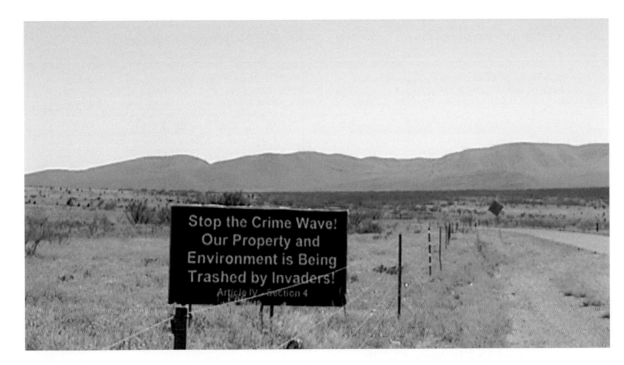

Stop the Crime Wave!
Our Property and
Environment is Being
Trashed by Invaders!
Article IV - Section 4

9.33 Chantal Akerman
Video still featuring border sign warning from *From the Other Side*, 2002.

Chantal Akerman began her prolific film career in the late 1960s and is probably best known for *Jean Dielman, 23 Quai du Commerce, 1080 Bruxelles* (1975), which focuses on the deteriorating lives of a Brussels widow and her son. Akerman has sometimes resided in New York City, where she developed relationships with Avant-Garde filmmakers, particularly the Canadian artist Michael Snow (b. 1929).

its aggressive policy of preemptive military strikes against foreign threats. In particular, the United States government's decision to invade Iraq in early 2003 without the authority of the United Nations Security Council has reinforced the negative image of America as an imperial monolith, whose power needs to be restrained by a renewed dedication to international, multilateral cooperation.

America's image abroad has also suffered from its treatment of prisoners, suspects, and illegal immigrants, seized in the war against terrorism. Many law-abiding Arab-Americans and Muslim Americans have been victimized by acts of vigilante violence and have been subjected to government detention. Meanwhile, plans to relax immigration policies with neighboring Mexico have confronted post-9/11 fears that the borders and ports of the United States are too porous, too vulnerable to foreign terrorist infiltration. The *American Effect* exhibition included *From the Other Side*, a film by the Belgian, Paris-based artist Chantal Akerman (b. 1950). Akerman's film focuses on the unofficial ground war against illegal immigrants along the Rio Grande, or the border between Mexico and the United States (fig. 9.33). She documents the fortress mentality of American ranchers, who have organized vigilante groups

to hunt down and detain illegal immigrants until the U.S. Border Patrol comes to take them back to Mexico. But what disturbed Akerman the most in her interviews with the ranchers was their use of the dehumanizing words "filth," "hordes," and "invaders" to describe these illegal Mexican immigrants, who would be all too willing to take menial, low-wage cleaning jobs as janitors, dishwashers, hotel maids and porters, and dry-cleaning assistants (cited in *Documenta 11*, p. 546).

With American troops occupying Iraq and suffering casualties from guerilla-style warfare, the United States has reached a pivotal moment in its history as a nation. Many of the foreign artists exhibiting in the *American Effect* show continue to view America in a decidedly positive light as a place that still inspires dreams of liberty and economic opportunity. Yet as the disparity in wealth between rich and poor countries grows, fueling anger and resentment, Chantal Akerman's unsettling image of a fortress-America, closed off to the rest of the world, suggests a major crisis in the corporate model of globalization institutionalized and supported by the United States. What role American artists will play or how American art will be redefined as the international crisis evolves are questions of enormous importance.

DATE	POLITICS AND RELIGION	SCIENCE AND CULTURE
PRE-1600	• Treaty of Tordesillas divides New World between Spain and Portugal, 1494 • Walter Raleigh founds colony of Virginia on Roanoke Island, 1584–87 • John White appointed governor of Roanoke Island colony, 1587	• Christopher Columbus's first landfall in Western Hemisphere, 1492 • John Cabot's voyages to North America, 1497–98 • Martin Waldseemüller coins the name "America" for map of the New World, 1507
1600	• Jamestown colony founded, 1607 • *Mayflower* pilgrims found Plymouth colony; John Carver first governor, 1620 • Maryland founded by Lord Baltimore, 1632 • Rhode Island founded by Roger Williams, 1636	• John Rolfe introduces tobacco cultivation in the colony of Virginia, 1612 • Harvard College founded, 1636 • Roger Williams's *A Key to the Languages of America*, 1643
1650	• Duke of York seizes New Amsterdam (renamed New York), 1664 • Pennsylvania founded by William Penn, 1681 • Salem witch trials, 1692	• First slave plantations established in the Carolinas, 1670 • Anne Bradstreet's *The Tenth Muse Lately Sprung up in America*, 1678
1700	• Queen Anne's War between Britain and France over control of North American territories, 1702–13 • New Orleans, LA, founded by French settlers, 1718 • Spanish mission established, San Antonio, TX, 1718	• Yale College founded, 1701 • The *Boston News-Letter*, first colonial weekly paper, established, 1704
1720	• North and South Carolina become Crown Colonies, 1729 • George Washington born, 1732 • Georgia becomes 13th colony, 1733 • Clergyman Jonathan Edwards preaches "The Great Awakening," fueling religious revivalism in New England, 1733 • First Moravian (United Brethren) community established at Savannah, GA, 1735 • William Byrd II founds the city of Richmond, VA, 1737	• William Byrd II's surveying expedition, 1728 • Boston physician Zabdiel Boylston becomes first American to inoculate patients against smallpox, 1721 • Benjamin Franklin founds Junto, a scientific, philosophical society and predecessor to the American Philosophical Society, Philadelphia, 1727 • New York newspaper publisher John Peter Zenger acquitted of seditious libel charges in a major victory for freedom of the press, 1735
1740	• King George's War between British and French colonies, 1744–48 • Ohio Company formed to extend English colonial settlements westward, 1747 • French construct Fort Duquesne (Pittsburgh) at the forks of the Ohio river, 1754 • French and Indian War, 1754–63	• Tuesday Club founded by Dr Alexander Hamilton in Annapolis, MD, 1745 • Benjamin Franklin invents lightning conductor, 1752 • First American Masonic Hall inaugurated in Philadelphia, 1755
1760	• British Parliament enacts Stamp Act, forcing anti-tax protests in colonies, 1765 • British Parliament repeals Stamp Act, passes Declaratory Act, asserting the right to legislate laws in the colonies, 1766 • British Parliament passes Townshend Acts requiring colonists to pay duties on tea and other imports, 1767 • Boston Massacre, 1770 • Boston Tea Party, 1773 • British Parliament passes "Intolerable Acts," closing Boston's port, forcing Bostonians to quarter British troops, 1774 • First Continental Congress meets, Philadelphia, 1774 • War of Independence, 1775–83 • Declaration of Independence, 1776	• Harvard professor John Winthrop leads Newfoundland expedition to observe the transit of Venus across the sun, 1761 • The St. Cecilia Society, the first musical society in America, founded in Charleston, SC, 1761 • First American medical school established at the College of Philadelphia, 1765 • Mastodon bones discovered at Big Bone Lick along the Ohio river, 1766 • Phillis Wheatley, an African-American from Boston, publishes *Poems on Various Subjects*, 1773 • "Yankee Doodle" becomes a popular revolutionary song for taunting British troops, 1775 • Tom Paine's *Common Sense*, 1776

FINE ART AND PHOTOGRAPHY	ARCHITECTURE AND EARTH ART
• Map Rock, Givens Hot Springs, Idaho, *c.* 1400 C.E.? (**1.1**) • Hand shape, Hopewell culture, Ohio, *c.* 200 B.C.E.–400 C.E. (**1.9**) • Gorget or neck pendant, Spiro Site, Oklahoma, *c.* 1200–1350 C.E. (**1.10**) • John White, *Indian Village of Secoton*, *c.* 1585 (**1.2**)	• Great Serpent Mound, Locust Grove, OH, *c.* 1070 C.E. (**1.8**) • Monk's Mound, Cahokia, IL, *c.* 900–1200 C.E. (**1.7**) • Pueblo, Taos, NM, pre-1400 (**1.3**) • Kiva, Chaco Canyon, pre-1400 (**1.5**) • Cliff Palace, Mesa Verde, pre-1400 (**1.6**)
• Anon., *La Conquistadora*, early 17th century (**2.10**) • Seal of the Massachusetts Bay Company, 1629 (**1.18**) • Boundary marker, Newbury, Massachusetts, 1636–50 (**2.5**) • Indian fort, from *News from America*, 1638 (**1.19**)	• San Estevan, Acoma, NM, 1629–42 (**2.7–2.9**)
• John Foster, *Richard Mather*, *c.* 1670 (**2.30**) • Anon., *John Freake, Elizabeth Freake, and Baby Mary*, *c.* 1671–4 (**2.28, 2.29**) • John Foster, "The Dominion of the Moon in Man's Body," 1678 (**2.6**) • City Hall, New Amsterdam (New York), 1679 (**3.16**) • Thomas Smith, *Self-Portrait*, *c.* 1680–90 (**2.32**) • Joseph Lamson (attrib.), Gravestone of Timothy Cutler, 1694 (**2.33**)	• St. Luke's, Smithfield, VA, *c.* 1680 (**2.16, 2.17**) • Old Ship Meetinghouse, Hingham, MA, 1681–1755 (**2.21, 2.22**) • Parson Capen House, Topsfield, MA, 1683 (**2.23, 2.24**) • Wren Building, Williamsburg, VA, 1695–8 (**3.8**)
• Justus Engelhardt Kühn, *Henry Darnall III*, *c.* 1710 (**3.4**) • John Simon after John Verelst, *Etow Oh Koam* and *Ho Nee Yeath Taw No Row*, 1710 (**1.21, 1.22**) • Mohawk Indian king's mural, Macpheadris–Warner House, *c.* 1716 (**1.23**)	• St. James's Church, Goose Creek, SC, 1708–19 (**2.19**)
• John Potwine, Silver flagon, *c.* 1720–30 (**2.20**) • William Burgis (attrib.), *A North East View of Boston*, *c.* 1723 (**2.26**) • John Senex, *A Front View of the Temple of Solomon*, 1725 (**3.9**) • John Smibert, *The Bermuda Group*, 1729 (**3.23**) • John Smibert, *Daniel, Peter, and Andrew Oliver*, 1732 (**3.26**) • John Smibert, *William Browne*, 1734 (**3.24**) • John Faber, *Governor Jonathan Belcher*, 1734 (**3.22**) • Peter Pelham, *The Reverend Benjamin Colman*, 1735 (**3.25**) • Gustavus Hesselius, *Tishcohan* and *Lapowinsa*, 1735 (**1.24, 1.25**) • Elizabeth Hudson, Sampler, 1737 (**2.15**)	• Dr. John Kearsley, Christ Church, PA, 1727–54 (**2.1**) • Robert Twelves, Old South Meetinghouse, Boston, MA, 1729–30 (**2.25**) • Westover, Charles City County, VA, 1730–4 (**3.12, 3.13**) • Isaac Royall House, Medford, MA, 1733–7 (**3.19, 3.20**) • Drayton Hall, Ashley River, SC, 1738–42 (**3.14, 3.15**)
• Robert Feke, *Isaac Royall and His Family*, 1741 (**3.21**) • Anon., *Belshazzar's Feast*, *c.* 1742 (**2.14**) • Robert Feke, *James Bowdoin II* and *Mrs James Bowdoin*, 1748 (**3.5, 3.6**) • Fray Andrés Garcia, *El Santo Entierro*, 18th century (**2.12**) • Alexander Hamilton, "Mr. Neilson's Anger," *c.* 1750 (**3.7**) • John Singleton Copley, *Mars, Venus, and Vulcan*, *c.* 1754 (**3.29**) • Benjamin Franklin, "Join or Die," 1754 (**4.25**) • John Greenwood, *Sea Captains Carousing in Surinam*, *c.* 1758 (**3.2**)	• Ursuline Convent, New Orleans, LO., 1745–53 (**2.4**) • Hexangular pulpit, 1750 (**2.18**) • Peter Harrison, Touro Synagogue, Newport, R.I., 1759–63 (**2.35**)
• John Valentine Haidt, *Lamentation over Christ's Body*, *c.* 1760 (**2.13**) • Benjamin West, *The Savage Chief (The Indian Family)*, *c.* 1761 (**1.27**) • John Singleton Copley, *Mrs. Samuel Quincy*, *c.* 1761 (**3.30**) • John Stevens II (attrib.), Gravestone of Rebecca Polock, *c.* 1764 (**2.34**) • John Singleton Copley, *Boy with a Squirrel*, 1765 (**3.31**) • Matthew Pratt, *The American School*, 1765 (**4.22**) • William Williams, *Deborah Hall*, 1766 (**3.27**) • Benjamin Franklin, *Magna Britannia*, *c.* 1766 (**4.2**) • John Singleton Copley, *Portrait of Paul Revere*, 1768 (**3.32**) • Paul Revere, Masonic Lodge 169, late 1760s (**3.33**) • Benjamin West, *The Departure of Regulus from Rome*, 1769 (**4.24**) • Benjamin West, *The Death of General Wolfe*, 1770 (**4.23**) • Paul Revere, *Bloody Massacre*, 1770 (**4.27**) • Samuel King, *Portrait of the Reverend Ezra Stiles*, 1771 (p. 38) • Paul Revere, *The Able Doctor*, 1774 (**4.3**) • John Singleton Copley, *Watson and the Shark*, 1778 (**4.28**)	• Quaker Meetinghouse, Stony Brook, NJ, 1760 (**2.2**) • William Buckland, Samuel Chase–Edward Lloyd House, Annapolis, MD, 1769–73 (**3.17, 3.18**) • Pedro Huizar, San José y San Miguel de Aguayo portal, San Antonio, TX, *c.* 1770–5 (**2.11**) • Thomas Jefferson, Monticello, Charlottesville, VA, 1770–1809 (**4.16**)

DATE	POLITICS AND RELIGION	SCIENCE AND CULTURE
1780	• Shays's Rebellion, a revolt by debt-ridden Massachusetts farmers, suppressed by government forces, 1786–87 • Constitution of the U.S. ratified, 1789 • George Washington 1st president of the U.S., 1789–97 • American Bill of Rights, 1791 • Fugitive Slave Act passed, making it illegal to aid runaway African-American slaves, 1793 • Washington declares neutrality in British war against French revolutionary government, 1793 • Naturalization Act passed requiring five-year residency for U.S. citizenship, 1795 • Washington's "Farewell Address" warns against U.S. entanglements in foreign affairs, 1796 • John Adams 2nd president of the U.S., 1797–1801 • Alien and Sedition Acts passed amid fears that radical French Revolutionary politics were threatening the U.S., 1798	• Great Seal of the United States adopted, 1782 • *Pennsylvania Evening Post*, first daily paper in the U.S., begins publication, 1783 • Thomas Jefferson's *Notes on the State of Virginia*, 1784–85 • Peale's Museum (later Philadelphia Museum) opened in Philadelphia, 1786 • John Fitch launches first American steamboat on Delaware river, 1787 • Federalist papers published in support of U.S. Constitution, 1788 • William Hill Brown publishes *The Power of Sympathy*, reputedly the first American novel, 1789 • Benjamin Franklin's *Autobiography*, posthumously published in Paris, 1791 • Organized by Charles Willson Peale, the short-lived Columbianum or American Academy of the Fine Arts, holds an art exhibition in Philadelphia's Philosophical Hall, 1795
1800	• Washington, DC, becomes the new national capital, as the government moves out of Philadelphia, 1800 • Thomas Jefferson 3rd president of the U.S., 1801–9 • Alien and Sedition Acts allowed to expire, 1802 • Louisiana Purchase, 1803 • War of 1812, 1812–15 • American Bible Society founded in New York City, 1816 • Spain cedes Florida to U.S., 1819	• Library of Congress founded, 1800 • American Academy of the Fine Arts founded, 1802 • Lewis and Clark's expedition, 1804–6 • Pennsylvania Academy of Fine Arts founded, 1805 • Noah Webster's *Compendious Dictionary of the English Language*, 1806 • Boston Athenaeum founded, 1807 • Henry Wadsworth Longfellow born, 1807 (d. 1882) • Francis C. Lowell opens first completely mechanized textile factory, Massachusetts, 1814
1820	• Missouri Compromise, 1820 • Slave rebellion suppressed in Charleston, SC, 1822 • Bureau of Indian Affairs established, 1824 • House of Representatives chooses John Quincy Adams as president, 1825 • John Adams and Thomas Jefferson both die July 4th, the 50th anniversary of the Declaration of Independence, 1826 • Anti-Masonic movement, 1826-40 • Democratic Party formed, Andrew Jackson elected first Democratic U.S. president, 1828 • Workingmen's Party formed in New York, 1829 • Joseph Smith founds first community of the Church of Jesus Christ of Latter-Day Saints (Mormons), 1830 • Indian Removal Act, 1830 • Nat Turner leads unsuccessful revolt of African-American slaves in Southampton County, VA, 1831 • Anti-Slavery Society founded, 1833 • Samuel F.B. Morse writes a series of nativist, anti-Catholic newspaper articles for the *New York Observer*, 1834 • Anti-abolition riots break out in New York City and Philadelphia, 1834 • Seminole Indian War, 1835–42 • Texas becomes an independent republic after defeating Mexican troops at San Jacinto, 1836 • U.S. troops force the removal of Cherokee Indians westward from Georgia, 1838 • Ralph Waldo Emerson gives Harvard Divinity School Address, 1838	• Washington Irving publishes *The Sketch Book*, a collection of stories featuring "Rip van Winkle" and "The Legend of Sleepy Hollow," 1820 • Emma Willard founds the Troy Female Seminary, the first women's college-level school, Troy, NY, 1821 • America's first school of science and engineering, later named the Rensselaer Polytechnic Institute, opens, 1824 • The Marquis de Lafayette's grand tour of the U.S., 1824–5 • Erie Canal opened, 1825 • National Academy of Design founded, 1825 • James Fenimore Cooper's *Last of the Mohicans*, 1826 • *Freedom's Journal*, the first African-American paper, begins publication in New York City, 1827 • John James Audubon's *Birds of America*, 1827–38 • Noah Webster's *An American Dictionary of the English Language*, 1828 • The Trumbull Gallery at Yale, the nation's first university art gallery, founded, 1831 • William Lloyd Garrison founds *The Liberator*, an abolitionist periodical, 1831 • Ralph Waldo Emerson's *Nature*, 1836 • Samuel Morse develops electric telegraph, 1837 • Nathaniel Hawthorne's *Twice-Told Tales*, 1837 • American Art-Union founded, 1839 • Retrospective exhibition of the paintings of Washington Allston at Chester Harding's Gallery in Boston, 1839

FINE ART AND PHOTOGRAPHY	ARCHITECTURE AND EARTH ART
• Anon., Master Mason's apron, *c.* 1780 (**3.10**) • John Singleton Copley, *Portrait of Elkanah Watson*, 1782 (**4.30**) • Benjamin West, *American Commissioners*, 1783–4 (**4.31**) • Mather Brown, *Portrait of Thomas Jefferson*, 1786 (**4.6**) • John Trumbull, *The Death of General Joseph Warren, 1775*, 1786 (**4.32**) • John Trumbull, *The Declaration of Independence*, 1787–1820 (**4.33**) • Jean-Antoine Houdon, *George Washington*, 1788 (**4.41**) • Charles Willson Peale, *William Smith and His Grandson*, 1788 (**4.42**) • Amos Doolittle, "View of the Federal Edifice in New York," 1789 (**4.19**) • Charles Willson Peale, *Benjamin Franklin*, 1789 (**4.43**) • Samuel Hill, *View of the Triumphal Arch and Colonnade*, 1790 (**4.12**) • Samuel Jennings, *Liberty Displaying the Arts and Sciences*, 1790–2 (**4.5**) • Anon., *Liberty*, *c.* 1790–1800 (p. 114) • John Trumbull, *General George Washington, Battle of Trenton*, 1792 (**4.34**) • Charles Willson Peale, *Staircase Group*, 1795 (**4.38**) • Gilbert Stuart, *George Washington*, 1795–6 (**4.39**) • Gilbert Stuart, *George Washington (Lansdowne portrait)*, 1796 (**4.40**)	• Thomas Jefferson, Virginia State Capitol, Richmond, VA, 1785–98 (**4.11**) • Pierre Charles L'Enfant, plan of the City of Washington, 1791 (**4.15**) • Charles Bulfinch, Massachusetts State House, Boston, MA, 1795–8 (**4.14**)
• Benjamin Henry Latrobe, Washington Mausoleum, *c.* 1800 (**4.36**) • John Vanderlyn, *The Death of Jane McCrea*, 1804 (**4.52**) • Washington Allston, *Self Portrait*, 1805 (**4.55**) • Charles Willson Peale, *The Exhumation of the Mastodon*, 1806–8 (**4.45**) • John Vanderlyn, *Marius amid the Ruins of Carthage*, 1807 (**4.53**) • John Trumbull, *View of the Falls of Niagara*, *c.* 1808 (**5.36**) • John Vanderlyn, *Ariadne Asleep on the Island of Naxos*, 1809–14 (**4.54**) • John L. Krimmel, *Fourth of July in Centre Square*, 1810–12 (**4.47**) • Rembrandt Peale, *The Roman Daughter*, 1811 (**4.48**) • Washington Allston, *Elijah in the Desert*, 1817–18 (**4.57**) • Washington Allston, *Belshazzar's Feast*, 1817–43 (**4.56**)	• Benjamin Henry Latrobe, Corn capital vestibule to the Supreme Court, 1808 (**4.20**) • Benjamin Henry Latrobe, Tobacco-leaf capital, *c.* 1815 (**4.21**)
• Rembrandt Peale, *The Court of Death*, 1820 (**4.49**) • Raphaelle Peale, *Venus Rising from the Sea*, *c.* 1822 (**4.49**) • Charles Willson Peale, *The Artist in His Museum*, 1822 (**4.44**) • Samuel Morse, *The Old House of Representatives*, 1822 (**4.58**) • Gilbert Stuart, *Portrait of Josiah Quincy*, 1824 (**5.5**) • William Rush, *Wisdom*, 1824 (**4.4**) • William Rush, *The Schuylkill Enchained* and *Freed*, 1825 (**5.9, 5.10**) • John Frazee, *Self-Portrait*, 1827 (**5.3**) • Thomas Cole, *Kaaterskill Falls*, 1826 (**5.38**) • Thomas Cole, *St. John in the Wilderness*, 1827 (**5.39**) • John Rubens Smith, *View of the West Front of the Capitol*, *c.* 1828 (**4.17**) • Charles Bird King, *The Anatomy of Art Appreciation*, 1830 (**5.29**) • Samuel Morse, *Chapel of the Virgin at Subiaco*, 1830 (**5.31**) • John Quidor, *Money Diggers*, 1832 (**5.14**) • George Catlin, *Buffalo Bull's Back Fat, Blood Tribe*, 1832 (**5.43**) • Thomas Doughty, *Mill Pond, Lowell, Massachusetts*, *c.* 1833 (**5.11**) • Thomas Cole, *The Course of Empire: The Savage State*, 1834 (**5.41**) • Thomas Cole, *The Course of Empire: Consummation*, 1835–6 (**5.42**) • Thomas Cole, *View from Mount Holyoke (The Oxbow)*, 1836 (**5.40**) • John Chapman, *Baptism of Pocahontas, 1613*, 1836–40 (**5.47**) • Hiram Powers, *Daniel Webster*, 1836–41 (**5.22**) • Robert W. Weir, *Embarkation of the Pilgrims, 1620*, 1836–43 (**5.46**) • Horatio Greenough, *Rescue*, 1837–53 (**5.49**) • Thomas Crawford, *Orpheus*, 1839–43 (**5.1**)	• John Haviland, Eastern State Penitentiary, Philadelphia, PA, 1821–37 (**5.6**) • Alexander Parris, Quincy Market, Boston, MA, 1825–6 (**5.4**) • Bunker Hill Monument, Charlestown, MA, 1825–43 (p. 162) • Thomas Jefferson, University of Virginia campus, Charlottesville, VA, 1826 (from an 1824 drawing) (**4.46**) • Jacob Bigelow, Gateway, Mount Auburn Cemetery, Cambridge, MA, 1831 (**5.25**) • Campbell–Whittlesey House, Rochester, N.Y., 1835–6 (**5.15**)

DATE	POLITICS AND RELIGION	SCIENCE AND CULTURE
1840	• Dorr's Rebellion in Rhode Island forces liberalization of voting requirements in the state, 1842 • Florida becomes 27th state, 1845 • Texas annexed by the U.S. and becomes 28th state, 1845 • Mexican War, 1846–48 • Mormons found Salt Lake City, UT, 1847 • Seneca Falls convention on universal suffrage, 1848 • Free Soil Party organized in opposition to slavery's territorial expansion, 1848 • Compromise of 1850 strengthens Fugitive Slave Act while admitting California as a free state and abolishing slave trade in the District of Columbia, 1850 • First American chapter of the Young Men's Christian Association (YMCA) opens in Boston, 1851 • Sioux Indians give up land in Iowa and Minnesota to U.S. government, 1851 • Commodore Matthew C. Perry leads U.S. fleet to Japan, seeking to open up trade, 1853 • Gadsden Purchase, 1853 • Kansas-Nebraska Act repeals Missouri Compromise of 1820 and allows all territories to permit or prohibit slavery, 1854	• Edgar Allen Poe's *Tales of the Grotesque and Arabesque,* 1840 • George Catlin's *Letters and Notes on the Manners, Customs, and Condition of the North American Indians,* 1841 • New York Philharmonic founded, 1842 • P.T. Barnum's American Museum opens in New York City, 1842 • Migration to Oregon Territory over Oregon Trail begins, 1843 • Smithsonian Institution established, 1846 • American Medical Association founded, 1847 • American Association for the Advancement of Science (AAAS) founded, 1848 • California Gold Rush, 1849 • Nathaniel Hawthorne's *The Scarlet Letter,* 1850 • Herman Melville's *Moby Dick,* 1851 • Harriet Beecher Stowe's *Uncle Tom's Cabin,* 1852 • Henry David Thoreau's *Walden,* 1854 • Walt Whitman's *Leaves of Grass,* 1855 • Frank Leslie's *Illustrated Newspaper* begins publication in New York City, 1855 • American Institute of Architects founded, 1857
1860	• U.S. Secret Service established, 1860 • Abraham Lincoln 16th president of the U.S., 1861–65 • Confederate States of America formed, 1861 • Seventh-Day Adventists founded, 1861 • American Civil War, 1861–65 • Homestead Act, 1862 • Emancipation Act, 1863 • Thirteenth Amendment to U.S. Constitution ratified abolishing slavery, 1865 • President Lincoln assassinated, 1865 • Ku Klux Klan formed, 1866 • First Young Women's Christian Association (YWCA) opens in Boston, 1866 • Reconstruction Acts, passed over President Andrew Johnson's vetoes, divide South into five military districts, 1867 • Purchase of Alaska from Russia, 1867 • Impeached by the House of Representatives, President Johnson is tried and acquitted by the Senate, 1868 • Susan B. Anthony and Elizabeth Cady Stanton organize the National American Woman Suffrage Association, 1869 • Reform Rabbi Isaac Meyer Wise organizes Union of Hebrew Congregations in Cincinnati, 1873 • National Women's Christian Temperance Union founded, 1874 • U.S.-Hawaii commercial treaty, 1875 • National Liberal League founded, 1876 • Battle of Little Bighorn ("Custer's Last Stand"), 1876 • Reconstruction ends as federal occupying troops leave the South, 1877 • U.S.-Samoa treaty establishes a coaling station for U.S. Navy, 1878 • Mary Baker Eddy founds First Church of Christ, Scientist, 1879	• Elisha Otis patents a steam-powered elevator, 1861 • Transcontinental telegraph service established between New York and San Francisco, 1861 • National Academy of Sciences founded, 1863 • New York engineer Alexander Holley acquires American rights to the Bessemer steelmaking process, 1863 • Abraham Lincoln's Gettysburg Address, 1863 • Massachusetts Institute of Technology (MIT) opens in Cambridge, MA, 1865 • First elevated railroad begins service in New York City, 1867 • Howard University chartered, 1867 • Horatio Alger's *Ragged Dick; or Street Life in New York,* 1867 • Christopher L. Sholes patents the first practical typewriter, 1868 • Louisa May Alcott's *Little Women,* 1868 • Union Pacific and Central Pacific railroads meet at Promontory Point, UT, 1869 • John D. Rockefeller forms the Standard Oil Company of Ohio, 1870 • Fire destroys large portions of Chicago, 1871 • Yellowstone National Park established, 1872 • Bethlehem Steel begins manufacturing in Pittsburgh, PA, 1873 • Louis Comfort Tiffany opens a factory for producing artistic glass household objects, 1874 • Mark Twain's *The Adventures of Tom Sawyer,* 1876 • Thomas Edison establishes the nation's first industrial research laboratory, Menlo Park, NJ, 1876 • Centennial Exposition, Philadelphia, 1876 • Alexander Graham Bell invents the telephone, 1876 • Society of American Artists founded, 1878 • Edison patents the phonograph, 1878

FINE ART AND PHOTOGRAPHY	ARCHITECTURE AND EARTH ART
• Horatio Greenough, *George Washington*, 1840 (**4.37**) • Thomas Cole, *The Voyage of Life: Youth*, 1840 (**5.44**) • Jeremiah Pearson Hardy, *Catherine Wheeler Hardy and Her Daughter*, 1842 (**5.32**) • Hiram Powers, *The Greek Slave*, 1843 (**5.65**) • Henry F. Darby, *Portrait of Reverend John Atwood and His Family*, 1845 (**5.33**) • William Sidney Mount, *Eel Spearing at Setauket*, 1845 (**5.2**) • Hannah Cohoon, *Gift Drawing: The Tree of Light or Blazing Tree*, 1845 (**5.55**) • George Caleb Bingham, *Jolly Flatboatmen*, 1846 (**5.51**) • Augustus Washington, *John Brown*, 1847 (**5.68**) • Asa Ames, *Phrenological Head*, 1847–50 (**5.20**) • Richard Caton Woodville, *War News from Mexico*, 1848 (**5.28**) • Thomas Chambers, *Mount Auburn Cemetery*, c. 1850 (**5.24**) • Rafael Aragón, *The Flight into Egypt*, c. 1850 (**5.30**) • Albert S. Southworth and Josiah J. Hawes, *Mount Auburn Cemetery*, c. 1850 (**5.27**) • Fitz Hugh Lane, *Boston Harbor at Sunset*, 1850–55 (**5.58**) • George Caleb Bingham, *Daniel Boone Escorting Settlers Through the Cumberland Gap*, 1851–2 (**5.50**) • Asher B. Durand, *God's Judgment upon Gog*, c. 1852 (**5.53**) • Asher B. Durand, *Progress (The Advance of Civilization)*, 1853 (**5.56**) • Robert Duncanson, *Uncle Tom and Little Eva*, 1853 (**5.63**) • Lilly Martin Spencer, *Shake Hands?*, 1854 (**5.34**) • Frederic Church, *Niagara Falls*, 1857 (**5.61**) • Harriet Hosmer, *Zenobia*, 1857–9 (**5.66**) • Frederic Church, *The Heart of the Andes*, 1859 (**5.62**)	• Gaineswood, Demopolis, AL, 1843–59 (**5.16**) • Sunstone Capital, Mormon Temple, Nauvo, IL, 1846 (**5.54**) • Alexander Jackson Davis, Gatehouse, Llewellyn Park, Orange, NJ, 1853 (**5.19**) • John Richards, Octagon House, Watertown, WI, 1854–6 (**5.21**) • Thomas Crawford, *Progress of Civilization*, Capitol, Washington, D.C., 1855–63 (**5.48**) • Thomas U. Walter, United States Capitol, Senate and House Wings, Washington, DC, 1855–65 (**5.45**) • Richard Morris Hunt, Studio Building, 15 West Tenth Street, New York City, 1857 (**6.10**) • Alexander Jackson Davis, Edward W. Nicholls House, Llewellyn Park, Orange, NJ, 1858–9 (**5.17**)
• Anon., Harriet Hosmer at work on her Statue of Senator Benton, c. 1861 (**5.67**) • Emanuel Leutze, *Westward the Course of Empire Takes Its Way*, 1861–2 (**5.71**) • Matthew B. Brady, *On the Antietam Battlefield*, 1862 (**5.70**) • Alexander Gardner and Timothy O'Sullivan, *A Harvest of Death, Gettysburg, Pennsylvania*, 1863 (**5.73**) • Jasper Francis Cropsey, *Starrucca Viaduct, Pennsylvania*, 1865 (**5.57**) • Winslow Homer, *The Veteran in a New Field*, 1865 (**6.24**) • Edmonia Lewis, *Forever Free*, 1867 (**6.22**) • Thomas Satterwhite Noble, *The Price of Blood*, 1868 (**6.23**) • William Henry Rinehart, *Sleeping Children*, 1869 (**5.26**) • John Rogers, *The Fugitive's Story*, 1869 (**6.21**) • Eastman Johnson, *The Brown Family*, 1869 (**6.25**) • James McNeill Whistler, *Arrangement in Gray and Black (Portrait of the Artist's Mother)*, 1871 (**6.63**) • John F. Kensett, *Eaton's Neck, Long Island*, 1872 (**5.60**) • Winslow Homer, *Snap the Whip*, 1872 (**6.26**) • Timothy O'Sullivan, *Ancient Ruins in the Canyon de Chelly, New Mexico*, 1873 (**1.4**) • Daniel Chester French, *Minute Man*, 1873–5 (**6.43**) • Thomas Eakins, *The Gross Clinic*, 1875 (p. 230) • James McNeill Whistler, *Nocturne in Black and Gold*, c. 1875 (**6.64**) • Margaret Foley, *Cleopatra*, 1876 (**5.12**) • William Wetmore Story, *Jerusalem*, 1876 (**6.32**) • James McNeill Whistler, *Harmony in Blue and Gold*, 1876–7 (**6.65**) • Thomas Eakins, *William Rush Carving his Allegorical Figure of the Schuylkill River*, 1876–7 (**6.33**) • Mary Cassatt, *Reading "Le Figaro,"* 1877–8 (**6.51**) • Mary Cassatt, *At the Opera (In the Loge)*, 1879 (**6.49**) • Albert Pinkham Ryder, *The Dead Bird*, c. late 1870s (**6.61**)	• Samuel Sloan, Longwood, Natchez, Mississippi, begun 1860 (**5.23**) • Peter B. Wight, National Academy of Design, New York City, 1862–5 (**6.11**) • John A. Roebling, Brooklyn Bridge, New York City, 1869–83 (**6.12**) • Frank Furness and George W. Hewitt, Pennsylvania Academy of Fine Arts, Philadelphia, PA, 1871–6 (**6.31**) • Richard Morris Hunt, Tribune Building, New York City, 1875 (**6.13**) • Henry Hobson Richardson with John La Farge, Trinity Church, Boston, MA, c. 1875 (**6.58**) • McKim, Mead, and White, Casino interior, Newport, R.I., 1879–80 (**6.5**)

DATE	POLITICS AND RELIGION	SCIENCE AND CULTURE
1880	• President James Garfield assassinated, 1881 • Chinese Exclusion Act, 1882 • American Federation of Labor launched, 1886 • Nationwide strike for eight-hour work day, 1886 • Pan-American Union formed, 1890 • Massacre of Wounded Knee, South Dakota, 1890 • National American Woman Suffrage Association founded, 1890 • Immigration center established on Ellis Island, New York City, 1892 • Hawaii becomes a U.S. Protectorate, 1893 • U.S. Supreme Court's Plessy v. Ferguson decision upholds "separate but equal" doctrine, racial segregation law, 1896 • Spanish-American War, 1898 • Brooklyn, Bronx, Queens, Staten Island, Manhattan boroughs unite to form Greater New York City, 1898	• American Red Cross founded, 1881 • Brooklyn Bridge opened, 1883 • Mark Twain's *Adventures of Huckleberry Finn*, 1884 • Statue of Liberty arrives in New York City from France, 1885 • Ezra Pound born, 1885 (d. 1972) • Coca-Cola invented 1886 • Charlie Chaplin born, 1889 (d. 1977) • Daughters of the American Revolution founded, 1890 • World Columbian Exposition, Chicago, 1893 • Klondike Gold Rush, 1896 • First motion picture shows, 1896 • Henry James's *The Turn of the Screw*, 1898 • Ernest Hemingway born, 1899 (d. 1961)
1900	• President William McKinley assassinated, 1901 • Theodore Roosevelt 26th president of the U.S., 1901–09 • International Workers of the World union founded, 1905 • U.S. military intervenes in Nicaraguan Civil War, 1912 • Paterson Strike Pageant, 1913 • Woodrow Wilson 28th president of the U.S., 1913–21 • World War I begins in Europe, 1914 • U.S. invades Haiti and Dominican Republic, 1915 • U.S. intervenes in Mexican Revolution, 1915 • U.S. intervenes militarily in Cuba, 1917 • U.S. enters World War I, 1917 • Russian Revolution, 1917 • U.S. acquires Virgin Islands from Denmark, 1917 • World War I ends, 1918 • Eighteenth Amendment to the Constitution (Prohibition), 1919 (repealed 1933) • U.S. Senate rejects Versailles Settlement and League of Nations, 1919	• Walt Disney born, 1901 (d. 1966) • Cadillac Automobile Company founded, 1901 • First radio broadcast, from Plymouth, Massachusetts, 1906 • Orville and Wilbur Wright achieve first powered flight, Kitty Hawk, N.C., 1908 • Exhibition of "The Eight," New York, 1908 • Ford Model T goes into production, 1908 • General Motors Corporation founded, 1908 • Leo Baekeland develops Bakelite, the first synthetic polymer, 1909 • First movie studio opens in Hollywood, 1911 • Armory Show, New York, 1913 • Henry Ford builds first moving assembly line, Detroit, 1913 • Panama Canal opened, 1914 • D.W. Griffith's *Birth of a Nation*, 1915 • World's first passenger air service begins in Florida, 1917 • H.L. Mencken's *The American Language*, 1919

FINE ART AND PHOTOGRAPHY	ARCHITECTURE AND EARTH ART
• William Merritt Chase, *In the Studio*, c. 1880 (**6.68**) • Thomas Pollock Anshutz, *The Ironworkers' Noontime*, 1880 (**6.40**) • Augustus Saint-Gaudens, *David Farragut Memorial*, New York, 1881 (**6.44**) • John Singer Sargent, *The Daughters of Edward Boit*, 1882–3 (**6.52**) • John Singer Sargent, *Madame X*, 1883–4 (**6.53**) • Augustus Saint-Gaudens, *Shaw Memorial*, Boston, 1884–97 (**6.45**) • Ralph A. Blakelock, *Moonlight and Indian Encampment*, 1885 (**6.57**) • Albert Pinkham Ryder, *Jonah*, c. 1885 (**6.62**) • Thomas Eakins, *The Swimming Hole*, c. 1885 (**6.36**) • Thomas Eakins, *Motion Study*, 1885 (**6.39**) • Winslow Homer, *The Fog Warning*, 1885 (**6.29**) • William Michael Harnett, *After the Hunt*, 1885 (**6.30**) • William Merritt Chase, *James A.M. Whistler*, 1885 (**6.67**) • John Twachtman, *Arques-la-Bataille*, 1885 (**6.69**) • Albert Bierstadt, *The Last of the Buffalo*, 1889 (**6.54**) • Childe Hassam, *Washington Arch, Spring*, 1890 (**6.70**) • Thomas Eakins, *The Concert Singer*, 1890–2 (**6.37**) • George Innes, *Sunset in the Woods*, 1891 (**6.60**) • Thomas Dewing, *After Sunset (Summer Evening)*, 1892 (**6.66**) • Henry Ossawa Tanner, *The Banjo Lesson*, 1893 (**6.47**) • Charles C. Curran, *World's Columbian Exposition of 1893*, 1893 (**6.18**) • Frederick MacMonnies, *Bacchante and Infant Faun*, 1893 (**6.34**) • Mary Cassatt, *The Boating Party*, 1893–4 (**6.50**) • Frederick Remington, *The Flight (A Sage-Brush Pioneer)*, 1895 (**6.55**) • Frederick Remington, *The Bronco Buster*, 1895 (**6.56**) • John La Farge, *The Entrance to the Tautira River, Tahiti*, c. 1895 (**6.59**) • Jacob Riis, *Street Arabs, Mulberry Street*, c. 1898 (**6.71**) • Henry Ossawa Tanner, *Christ Appearing to Nicodemus*, 1899 (**6.46**)	• Henry Hobson Richardson, Marshall Field Wholesale Store, Chicago, IL, 1885–7 (**6.15**) • McKim, Mead, & White, Boston Public Library, Boston, MA, 1887–95 (**6.1–6.2**) • Louis Sullivan, Wainwright Building, St. Louis, MO, 1890–1 (**6.14**) • Daniel H. Burnham, Masonic Temple, Chicago, IL, 1890–2 (**6.42**) • World's Columbian Exposition, Chicago, IL, 1893 (**6.16**) • Richard Morris Hunt, Biltmore, Asheville, NC, 1895 (**6.3**)
• Alfred Stieglitz, *Spring Showers—New York*, 1900 (**7.16**) • Cecilia Beaux, *Portrait of Mrs. Larz Anderson*, 1900–1 (**6.9**) • Edward Steichen, *Self-Portrait with Palette and Brush*, 1902 (**7.13**) • Pamela Colman Smith, *The Wave*, 1903 (**7.12**) • George Benjamin Luks, *The Spielers*, 1905 (**7.7**) • Robert Henri, *Eva Green*, 1907 (**7.6**) • Alfred Stieglitz, *The Steerage*, 1907 (**7.15**) • John Sloan, *Hairdresser's Window*, 1907 (**7.9**) • Maurice Prendergast, *St. Malo*, c. 1907 (**7.9**) • George Bellows, *Pennsylvania Excavation*, c. 1907–9 (**7.5**) • George Bellows, *Both Members of This Club*, 1909 (**7.8**) • Max Weber, *Composition with Three Figures*, 1910 (**7.20**) • Lewis Hine, *Breaker Boys*, 1911 (**7.14**) • Arthur Dove, *Nature Symbolized No. 2*, 1911 (**7.31**) • Alvin Langdon Coburn, *The Octopus*, 1912 (**7.21**) • John Marin, *Woolworth Building, No. 31*, 1912 (**7.23**) • Max Weber, *New York*, 1913 (**7.22**) • J.F. Griswold, *The Rude Descending the Staircase*, 1913 (**7.30**) • Robert Edmond Jones, Paterson Strike Pageant cover, 1913 (**7.32**) • Marsden Hartley, *Warriors*, 1913 (**7.33**) • Joseph Stella, *Battle of Lights, Coney Island, Mardi Gras*, 1913–14 (**7.28**) • Morgan Russell, *Cosmic Synchromy*, 1913–14 (**7.36**) • Marsden Hartley, *Portrait of a German Officer*, 1914 (**7.34**) • John Sloan, *Class War in Colorado*, 1914 (**7.10**) • Maurice Prendergast, *Central Park*, c. 1914 (**7.11**) • Man Ray, *War (AD MCMXIV)*, 1914 (**7.37**) • Kenyon Cox, *Tradition*, 1916 (**7.2**) • Morton Schamberg, *Mechanical Abstraction*, 1916 (**7.42**) • Paul Strand, *The White Fence*, 1917 (**7.17**) • Charles Burchfield, *The Luminous Tree*, 1917 (**7.25**) • Georgia O'Keeffe, *Inside Red Canna*, 1919 (**7.26**) • Elie Nadelman, *Tango*, 1919 (**7.67**)	• Frank Lloyd Wright, Ward W. Willitt's House, Highland Park, IL, 1900–2 (**6.19**) • McKim, Mead, & White, Pennsylvania Station, New York City, 1906–10 (**7.3, 7.4**) • Cass Gilbert, Woolworth Building, New York City, 1911–13 (**7.24**) • Henry Bacon, Lincoln Memorial, Washington, DC, 1911–22 (**7.1**)

DATE	POLITICS AND RELIGION	SCIENCE AND CULTURE
1920	• Nineteenth Amendment to the Constitution (women's suffrage), 1920 • Immigration controls introduced, 1921 • Calvin Coolidge 30th president of the U.S., 1923–29 • "Monkey Trial," Dayton, Tennessee, 1925 • Nicaragua occupied by U.S., 1926–33 • Herbert Hoover, 31st president of the U.S., 1929–33 • Wall Street Crash begins Great Depression, 1929 • Nation of Islam founded, 1930 • Franklin D. Roosevelt 32nd president of the U.S., 1933–45 • Roosevelt launches New Deal, 1933 • World War II begins in Europe, 1939	• First radio program broadcast, 1920 • Margaret Sanger founds American Birth Control League, 1921 • First portable radio, 1923 • George Gershwin, *Rhapsody in Blue*, 1924 • First talking picture, *The Jazz Singer*, 1927 • Charles Lindbergh's solo flight of the Atlantic, 1927 • First television broadcast in the U.S., 1928 • Technicolor introduces full color film, 1930 • Maiden flight of first modern airliner, the Boeing 247, 1933 • Artists' Union founded, 1934 • Works Progress Administration and Federal Arts Project established, 1935 • Wallace Carothers invents nylon, 1935 • First feature-length cartoon, *Snow White and the Seven Dwarfs*, 1937
1940	• Atlantic Charter issued by Roosevelt and Winston Churchill, 1941 • Japanese attack on Pearl Harbor brings U.S. into World War II, 1941 • American troops land in Normandy, 1944 • Conference between Roosevelt, Churchill, and Stalin, Yalta, 1945 • Harry Truman 33rd president of the U.S., 1945–53 • U.S. lands in Iwo Jima and Okinawa, 1945 • International Monetary Fund (IMF) founded, 1945 • U.S. drops atomic bombs on Hiroshima and Nagasaki, 1945 • World War II ends, 1945 • United Nations established, 1945 • CIA established, 1947 • NATO established, 1949 • Korean War, 1950–53 • Dwight D. Eisenhower 34th president of the U.S., 1953–61 • Heyday of McCarthyism, 1953–54 • Racial segregation in schools banned, 1954 • Bus boycott, Montgomery, Alabama, 1955 • U.S. military intervention in Iran, 1955	• Orson Welles's *Citizen Kane*, 1941 • First nuclear reactor built, Chicago, 1942 • Pan-Am begins round-the-world commercial flights, 1947 • Invention of transistor, 1947 • Sound barrier broken, 1947 • National network TV introduced, 1949 • William Faulkner receives Nobel Prize for Literature, 1949 • John Cage's *Theater Piece #2*, 1952 • Color television becomes available in the U.S., 1952 • Arthur Miller's *The Crucible*, 1953 • First credit card, the Diners' Club, launched, 1955 • First transatlantic telephone cable laid, 1956 • Jack Kerouac's *On the Road*, 1957 • First microchip developed, 1958

FINE ART AND PHOTOGRAPHY	ARCHITECTURE AND EARTH ART
• Charles Demuth, *Incense of a New Church*, 1921 (**7.47**) • Louis Lozowick, *Pittsburgh*, 1922–3 (**7.44**) • Gerald Murphy, *Watch*, 1924 (**7.46**) • Winold Reiss, *Portrait of Langston Hughes*, 1925 (**7.56**) • John Storrs, *New York*, c. 1925 (**7.43**) • Georgia O'Keeffe, *City Night*, 1926 (**7.27**) • Palmer Hayden, *Fétiche et Fleurs*, 1926 (**7.57**) • Thomas Hart Benton, *1927–New York Today*, 1927 (**7.69**) • Charles Sheeler, *Criss-Crossed Conveyors, Ford Plant*, 1927 (**7.61**) • John Steuart Curry, *Baptism in Kansas*, 1928 (**7.68**) • Charles Demuth, *The Figure 5 in Gold*, 1928 (**7.48**) • Florine Stettheimer, *Cathedrals of Broadway*, 1929 (**7.49**) • Archibald Motley, Jr., *Blues*, 1929 (**7.58**) • Grant Wood, *American Gothic*, 1930 (**7.70**) • Charles Sheeler, *Classic Landscape*, 1931 (**7.62**) • Charles Sheeler, *Home, Sweet Home*, 1931 (**7.63**) • Diego Rivera, *Detroit Industry*, 1932–3 (**7.64**) • Paul Cadmus, *The Fleet's In!*, 1934 (**7.77**) • Alexander Calder, *A Universe*, 1934 (**7.45**) • Aaron Douglas, *Aspects of Negro Life: Song of the Towers*, 1934 (**7.78**) • Moses Soyer, *Artists on WPA*, 1935 (**7.76**) • O. Louis Guglielmi, *Portrait and Background (Phoenix)*, 1935 (**7.79**) • Alice Neal, *Pat Whalen*, 1935 (**7.80**) • Mark Tobey, *Broadway*, 1935–6 (p. 296) • Dorothea Lange, *Southern Pacific Railroad Billboard*, 1937 (**7.71**) • Edward Weston, *Dante's View, Death Valley*, 1938 (**7.74**)	• Albert Kahn, Ford Motor Company, Glass Plant, Dearborn, MI, 1922 (**7.60**) • Simon Rodia, Watts Towers, Los Angeles, CA, 1925–54 (**8.47**) • Richard J. Neutra, Philip Lovell House, Hollywood Hills, Los Angeles, CA, 1927–9 (**7.65**) • William van Alen, Elevator Doors for the Chrysler Building, New York City, 1927–30 (**7.53**) • William van Alen, The Chrysler Building, New York City, 1928–30 (**7.51**) • Frank Lloyd Wright, Fallingwater, Bear Run, PA, 1937 (**7.66**)
• Morris Graves, *Blind Bird*, 1940 (**7.84**) • Stuart Davis, *Hot Still-scape for 6 Colors–7th Avenue Style*, 1940 (**7.81**) • Jacob Lawrence, *Migration of the Negro, Panel 50*, 1940–1 (**8.4**) • Mark Rothko, *Antigone*, 1941 (**8.16**) • Gordon Parks, *American Gothic (Ella Watson)*, 1942 (**8.5**) • Edward Hopper, *Nighthawks*, 1942 (**8.12**) • Jean Carlu, *Gift Packages for Hitler*, 1942 (**8.1**) • Joseph Cornell, *Habitat Group for a Shooting Gallery*, 1943 (**8.18**) • Adolph Gottlieb, *Hands of Oedipus*, 1943 (**8.17**) • Jackson Pollock, *Guardians of the Secret*, 1943 (**8.21**) • Arshile Gorky, *The Liver Is the Cock's Comb*, 1944 (**8.19**) • Ben Shahn, *For Full Employment after the War: Register/Vote*, 1944 (**8.3**) • Jack Levine, *Welcome Home*, 1946 (**8.2**) • Louise Bourgeois, *The Blind Leading the Blind*, c. 1947–9 (**8.34**) • Barnett Newman, *Onement I*, 1948 (**8.26**) • Robert Motherwell, *At Five in the Afternoon*, 1949 (**8.20**) • Lee Krasner, *Composition*, 1949 (**8.22**) • Jackson Pollock, *Lavender Mist, Number I*, 1950 (**8.23**) • Hans Namuth, *Jackson Pollock at work*, 1950 (**8.24**) • George Tooker, *The Subway*, 1950 (**8.13**) • Elaine de Kooning, *Conrad, Number 2*, 1950 (**8.28**) • Willem de Kooning, *Woman I*, 1950–2 (p. 362) • Helen Frankenthaler, *Mountains and Sea*, 1952 (**8.38**) • David Smith, *The Hero*, 1952 (**8.33**) • Mark Rothko, *Green and Maroon*, 1953 (**8.27**) • Burgess Collins ("Jess"), *Tricky Cad—Case I*, 1954 (**8.61**) • Robert Rauschenberg, *Bed*, 1955 (**8.48**) • Jasper Johns, *Target with Plaster Casts*, 1955 (**8.53**) • William Klein, *St Patrick's Day, 5th Avenue*, 1955 (**8.15**) • Joan Mitchell, *Hemlock*, 1956 (**8.29**) • Franz Kline, *Mahoning*, 1956 (**8.30**) • Louise Nevelson, *Sky Cathedral*, 1958 (**8.32**) • Robert Frank, *U.S. 285, New Mexico*, 1958 (**8.14**) • Morris Louis, *Ambi II*, 1959 (**8.39**)	• John Graham & Co., Northgate Regional Shopping Center, Seattle, WA, 1947–50 (**8.7**) • Ludwig Mies van der Rohe, Lake Shore Drive Apartments, Chicago, IL, 1951 (**8.10**) • Levittown, New York, 1954 (**8.6**) • Ludwig Mies van der Rohe and Philip Johnson, Seagram Building, New York City, 1954–8 (**8.11**) • Kleinweber, Yamasaki, & Hellmuth, Pruitt-Igoe Houses, St. Louis, MO, 1955 (**8.9**) • Frank Lloyd Wright, Solomon R. Guggenheim Museum, New York City, 1956–9 (**8.72**) • Eero Saarinen, Trans World Airlines Terminal, Idlewild (John F. Kennedy Airport), Queens, NY, 1956–62 (**8.36, 8.37**)

DATE	POLITICS AND RELIGION	SCIENCE AND CULTURE
1960	• John Kennedy 35th president of the U.S., 1961–63 • Berlin Wall erected, 1961 • Cuban Missile Crisis, 1962 • President Kennedy assassinated, 1963; Lyndon Johnson 36th president of the U.S., 1963–69 • Civil Rights Act, 1964 • Vietnam War, 1964–75 • Voting Rights Act, 1965 • Watts Race Riots, Los Angeles, 1965 • Student protests against Vietnam War, 1967 • Martin Luther King, Jr., assassinated, 1968 • Richard Nixon 37th president of the U.S., 1969–74 • Watergate scandal, 1972–74 • President Nixon resigns, 1974; Gerald Ford 38th president of the U.S., 1974–77 • Jimmy Carter 39th president of the U.S., 1977–81 • Camp David Accords between Israel and Egypt, negotiated by President Carter, 1978 • Moral Majority founded, 1979 • Iran Hostage Crisis, 1979–81	• Oral contraceptive pill goes on sale in the U.S., 1960 • Joseph Heller's *Catch-22*, 1961 • Rachel Carson's *The Silent Spring*, 1962 • First transatlantic TV transmission, 1962 • Martin Luther King, Jr., receives Nobel Peace Prize, 1964 • Peace Corps founded, 1966 • First moon landing, 1969 • Gilbert Hyatt invents microprocessor, 1970 • Boeing introduces first jumbo jet, 1970 • Fiber-optic telephone lines allow direct-dial transatlantic calls, 1970 • Bill Gates and Paul Allen form Microsoft company, 1975 • Apollo–Soyuz project, 1975 • Apple Computer founded, 1977
1980	• Ronald Reagan 40th president of the U.S., 1981–89 • George H. W. Bush 41st president of the U.S., 1989–93 • Destruction of Berlin Wall ends Cold War, 1989 • Gulf War, 1990–91 • Bill Clinton 42nd president of the U.S., 1993–2001 • Welfare Reform Act, 1996 • President Clinton acquitted by the U.S. Senate of impeachment charges, 1999 • U.S. turns over Panama Canal to Panama, 1999	• Space shuttle *Columbia* launched, 1981 • Apple launches first graphics-based Macintosh, 1984 • Hubble space telescope goes into orbit, 1990 • Toni Morrison, Nobel Prize for Literature, 1993 • New York Mayor Giuliani threatens to close Brooklyn Museum of Art over controversial British art exhibition, 1999 • Entire genetic code of a human chromosome is mapped, 1999
2000	• U.S. Supreme Court halts vote recount in Florida, effectively deciding the presidential election in favor of George W. Bush, who loses the popular vote but gains a narrow majority in the electoral college, 2000 • Suicidal Islamic fundamentalists crash four commercial airliners, destroying the Twin Towers of the World Trade Center in New York and damaging the Pentagon, September 11, 2001 • U.S. overthrows Islamic fundamentalist Taliban regime in Afghanistan and destroys Al Qaeda terrorist training camps, 2001 • Failing to win approval of the U.N. Security Council, the U.S. and U.K. invade and occupy Iraq, eventually capturing the Iraqi dictator Saddam Hussein, 2003	• President George W. Bush limits federal funding for embryonic stem cell research, 2001 • Enron Corporation, the Houston-based energy company, declares bankruptcy amidst charges of illegal accounting and business practices, 2001 • Architects Daniel Libeskind and David Childs unveil plans for "Freedom Tower" to rise 1,776 feet above Ground Zero at the World Trade Center site, New York, 2003 • U.S. Supreme Court declares anti-sodomy laws unconstitutional in a major victory for Gay civil rights, 2003 • Massachusetts Supreme Judicial Court legalizes gay marriages as religious conservatives campaign to pass an amendment to the U.S. Constitution that would ban gay marriages and civil unions, 2004

FINE ART AND PHOTOGRAPHY	ARCHITECTURE AND EARTH ART
• Mark di Suvero, *Hankchampion*, 1960 (**8.31**) • Frank Stella, *Pagosa Springs*, 1960 (**8.49**) • Allan Kaprow, *Chicken*, 1962 (**8.42**) • Ad Reinhardt, *Abstract Painting No. 5*, 1962 (**8.35**) • Andy Warhol, *Installation of Campbell's Soup Cans*, 1962 (**8.63**) • Tony Smith, *Die*, 1962 (**8.51**) • Carolee Schneemann, *Eye Body: 36 Transformative Actions for Camera*, 1963 (**8.44**) • Agnes Martin, *Night Sea*, 1963 (**8.41**) • Roy Lichtenstein, *Drowning Girl*, 1963 (**8.62**) • Yayoi Kusama, *In the Infinity Mirror Room—Phalli's Field*, 1965 (**8.45**) • Nam June Paik, *Magnet TV*, 1965 (**8.46**) • Bruce Nauman, *Self-Portrait as a Fountain*, 1966 (**8.43**) • Anne Truitt, *A Wall for Apricots*, 1968 (**8.40**) • Edward Kienholz, *The Portable War Memorial*, 1968 (**8.80**) • Donald Judd, *Untitled*, 1969 (**8.52**) • Carl Andre, *Steel Magnesium Plain*, 1969 (**8.54**) • Duane Hanson, *Motorcycle Accident*, 1969 (**8.65**) • Richard Serra, *Casting*, 1969 (**8.56**) • Romare Bearden, *Black Manhattan*, 1969 (**8.67**) • Eva Hesse, *Untitled*, 1970 (**8.60**) • Hans Haacke, *Shapolsky et al. Manhattan Real Estate Holdings*, 1971 (**8.73**) • Betye Saar, *The Liberation of Aunt Jemima*, 1972 (**8.84**) • Eleanor Antin, *Carving: A Traditional Sculpture*, 1972 (**8.86**) • Leon Golub, *Vietnam II*, 1973 (**8.81**) • Judy Baca, *Great Wall of Los Angeles*, 1976–83 (**9.1**) • Cindy Sherman, *Untitled Film Still No. 3*, 1977 (**8.88**) • Nan Goldin, *Cookie and Millie in the Girls' Room, Mudd Clubb*, 1979 (**9.3**) • Judy Chicago, *The Dinner Party*, 1979 (**8.87**)	• Robert Venturi and John Rauch, Guild House, Philadelphia, PA, 1960–3 (**8.70**) • Minoru Yamasaki, Twin Towers of the World Trade Center, New York City, 1964–77 (**8.75**) • Michael Heizer, *Double Negative*, Mormon Mesa, Oveton, NV, 1969–70 (**8.77**) • Robert Smithson, *Spiral Jetty*, Great Salt Lake, UT, 1969–70 (**8.76**) • Christo and Jeanne-Claude, Valley Curtain, Rifle Gap, CO, 1970–2 (**8.79**) • Alice Aycock, Maze, Gibney Farm, New Kingston, PA, 1972 (**8.78**) • Frank Gehry, Santa Monica Place, Santa Monica, CA, 1979–81 (**8.8**)
• Harmony Hammond, *Kudzu*, 1981 (**8.83**) • Robert Longo, *National Trust*, 1981 (**9.6**) • Maya Lin, Vietnam Memorial, Washington, D.C., 1981–4 (**8.82**) • Julian Schnabel, *Portrait of Andy Warhol*, 1982 (**9.5**) • Jean-Michel Basquiat, *Charles the First*, 1982 (**9.4**) • Peter Halley, *Two Cells with Conduit and Underground Chamber*, 1983 (**9.9**) • Jeff Koons, *Rabbit*, 1986 (**9.11**) • Andres Serrano, *Piss Christ*, 1987 (**9.17**) • Robert Mapplethorpe, *Self-Portrait*, 1988 (**9.15**) • Ross Bleckner, *Architecture of the Sky III*, 1988 (**9.12**) • David Wojnarowicz, *Untitled,* from *Sex Series*, 1988–9 (**9.16**) • Robert Gober, *Untitled*, 1990 (**9.13**) • Felix Gonzalez-Torres, *"Untitled" (Portrait of Ross in L.A.)*, 1991 (**9.14**) • Kiki Smith, *Pee Body*, 1992 (**9.18**) • Shahzia Sikander, *Perilous Order*, 1994–7 (p. 436) • Carrie Mae Weems, *You Became a Scientific Profile*, 1995 (**9.21**) • Tony Oursler, *Let's Switch*, 1996 (**9.24**) • Mel Chin, Installation view of *KNOWMAD*, 1999 (**9.29**)	• Agnes Denes, *Wheatfield A Confrontation*, 1982 (**9.7**) • David Hammons, Angela Valeria, Jerry Barr, *Delta Spirit* or *Spirit House*, 1985 (**9.8**) • Frank Gehry & Associates, Chiat Day Mojo Offices, Venice, CA, 1985–91 (**8.71**) • Philip Johnson, Celebration Town Hall, 1996 (**9.27**)
• Conor McGrady, *Inspection*, 2000 (**9.32**) • Matthew Barney, *Cremaster 3* (Production still), 2001 (**9.28**) • Wolfgang Staehle, *Untitled* (3 video stills of Twin Towers on 9/11), 2001 (**9.30**) • Chantal Akerman, *From the Other Side*, 2002 (**9.33**)	• Frank Gehry, Walt Disney Concert Hall, 2003 (**9.26**)

Bibliography

GENERAL WORKS, SURVEYS, ANTHOLOGIES

Baigell, Matthew. *A Concise History of American Painting and Sculpture*. Rev. edn. New York: HarperCollins; Icon Editions, 1996.

Baigell, Matthew. *Dictionary of American Art*. New York: Harper & Row; Icon Editions, 1979.

Bearden, Romare and Harry Henderson. *A History of African-American Artists from 1792 to the Present*. New York: Pantheon Books, 1993.

Brown, Milton W., et al. *American Art: Painting, Sculpture, Architecture, Decorative Arts, Photography*. Englewood Cliffs, NJ and New York: Prentice-Hall and Harry N. Abrams, 1979.

Burnham, Patricia M. and Lucretia Hoover Giese. *Redefining American History Painting*. Cambridge, MA and New York: Cambridge University Press, 1995.

Calo, Mary Ann, ed. *Critical Issues in American Art*. Boulder, CO: Westview Press, 1998.

Craven, Wayne. *Sculpture in America*. New York: Thomas Y. Crowell, 1968.

Doezema, Marianne and Elizabeth Milroy, eds. *Reading American Art*. New Haven, CT: Yale University Press, 1998.

Doss, Erika. *Twentieth-Century American Art*. Oxford and New York: Oxford University Press, 2002.

Gelernter, Mark A. *History of American Architecture: Buildings in their Cultural and Technological Context*. Hanover, NH: University Press of New England, 1999.

Gowans, Alan. *Images of American Living: Four Centuries of Architecture and Furniture as Cultural Expression*. New York: Harper & Row; Icon Editions, 1976.

Greenough, Sarah, et al. *On the Art of Fixing a Shadow: One Hundred and Fifty Years of Photography*. Washington, DC: National Gallery of Art, 1989.

Greenthal, Kathryn, et al. *American Figurative Sculpture in the Museum of Fine Arts, Boston*. Boston, MA: Museum of Fine Arts, 1986.

Groseclose, Barbara. *Nineteenth-Century American Art*. Oxford and New York: Oxford University Press, 2000.

Handlin, David P. *American Architecture*, rev. ed. London: Thames & Hudson, 2004.

Harris, Neil. *The Artist in American Society: The Formative Years, 1790–1860*. New York: G. Braziller, 1966.

Hills, Patricia. *Modern Art in the USA: Issues and Controversies of the Twentieth-Century*. Upper Saddle River, NJ: Prentice Hall, 2001.

Hughes, Robert. *American Visions: The Epic History of Art in America*. New York: Alfred A. Knopf, 1997.

James-Gadzinski, Susan and Mary Mullen Cunningham. *American Sculpture in the Museum of American Art of the Pennsylvania Academy of the Fine Arts*. Philadelphia, PA: Museum of American Art of the Pennsylvania Academy of the Fine Arts, 1997.

Kelly, Franklin. *American Paintings of the Nineteenth Century*, Part I. Washington, DC: National Gallery of Art, 1996.

McCoubrey, John W., ed. *American Art, 1700–1960: Sources and Documents*. Englewood Cliffs, NJ: Prentice-Hall, 1965.

Miller, David C., ed. *American Iconology: New Approaches to Nineteenth-Century Art and Literature*. New Haven, CT: Yale University Press, 1993.

Morgan, David and Sally M. Promey, eds. *The Visual Culture of American Religions*. Berkeley and Los Angeles: University of California Press, 2001.

Patton, Sharon F. *African American Art*. Oxford and New York: Oxford University Press, 1998.

Pohl, Frances K. *Framing America: A Social History of American Art*. New York: Thames & Hudson, 2002.

Powell, Richard J. *Black Art and Culture in the 20th Century*. London: Thames & Hudson, 2002.

Prieto, Laura R. *At Home in the Studio: The Professionalization of Women Artists in America*. Cambridge, MA: Harvard University Press, 2001.

Prown, Jules David. *Art as Evidence: Writings on Art and Material Culture*. New Haven, CT: Yale University Press, 2001.

Roth, Leland M. *American Architecture: A History*. Boulder, CO: Westview Press; Icon Editions, 2001.

Rubinstein, Charlotte Streifer. *American Women Artists from Early Indian Times to the Present*. New York: Avon Books, 1982.

Rubinstein, Charlotte Streifer. *American Women Sculptors: A History of Women Working in Three Dimensions*. Boston, MA: G.K. Hall, 1990.

Scully, Vincent, Jr. *American Architecture and Urbanism*. New York: Henry Holt, 1988.

Spencer, Harold, ed. *American Art: Readings from the Colonial Era to the Present*. New York: Charles Scribner's Sons, 1980.

Swinth, Kirsten. *Painting Professionals: Women Artists and the Development of Modern American Art, 1870–1930*. Chapel Hill, NC: University of North Carolina Press, 2001.

Taylor, Joshua C. *America as Art*. New York: Harper & Row; Icon Editions, 1976.

Taylor, Joshua C. *The Fine Arts in America*. Chicago, IL: University of Chicago Press, 1979.

Torchia, Robert Wilson. *American Paintings of the Nineteenth Century*, Part II. Washington, DC: National Gallery of Art, 1998.

Trachtenberg, Alan. *Reading American Photographs: Images as History, Matthew Brady to Walker Evans*. New York: Hill & Wang, 1989.

Turner, Jane, ed. *Encyclopedia of American Art before 1914*. New York: Grove's Dictionaries, 1999.

Upton, Dell. *Architecture in the United States*. Oxford and New York: Oxford University Press, 1998.

Wallach, Alan. *Exhibiting Contradiction: Essays on the Art Museum in the United States*. Amherst, MA: University of Massachusetts Press, 1998.

Whiffen, Marcus and Frederick Koeper. *American Architecture, 1607–1976*. Cambridge, MA: MIT Press, 1981.

Whitney Museum of American Art, New York. *200 Years of American Sculpture*. New York: David R. Godine in assoc. with Whitney Museum of American Art, 1976.

CHAPTER ONE

Works Cited

Alberts, Robert C. *Benjamin West: A Biography*. Boston, MA: Houghton Mifflin, 1978.

Bond, Richmond P. *Queen Anne's American Kings*. New York: Octagon Books, 1974.

Calloway, Colin G. *New Worlds for All: Indians, Europeans, and the Remaking of Early America*. Baltimore, MD: Johns Hopkins University Press, 1997.

Galt, John. *The Life and Studies of Benjamin West, Esq*. 2nd edn. London: T. Cadell & W. Davies and T. & G. Underwood, 1817.

Gunn, Giles, ed. *Early American Writing*. New York: Penguin Books, 1994.

Kibbey, Ann. *The Interpretation of Material Shapes in Puritanism: A Study of Rhetoric, Prejudice, and Violence*. Cambridge, England: Cambridge University Press, 1986.

Lorant, Stefan, ed. *The New World: The First Pictures of America Made by John White and Jacques Le Moyne and Engraved by Theodore de Bry with Contemporary Narratives of the Huguenot Settlement in Florida, 1562–1565, and the Virginia Colony, 1585–1590*. New York: Duell, Sloan & Pearce, 1946.

MacGregor, Arthur. "The Cabinet of Curiosities in Seventeenth-Century Britain," in *The Origins of Museums: The Cabinet of Curiosities in Sixteen- and Seventeen-Century Europe*, eds. Oliver Impey and Arthur MacGregor. Oxford: Clarendon Press, 1985, 147–58.

McCoubrey, John W., ed. *American Art, 1700–1960: Sources and Documents*. Englewood Cliffs, NJ: Prentice-Hall, 1965.

Middleton, Richard. *Colonial America: A History, 1585–1776*. 2nd edn. Oxford: Blackwell, 1996.

Myers, John Kenneth. "On the Cultural Construction of Landscape Experience: Contact to 1830," in *American Iconology*, ed. David C. Miller. New Haven, CT: Yale University Press, 1993, 58–79.

Nabakov, Peter and Robert Easton. *Native American Architecture*. Oxford and New York: Oxford University Press, 1989.

Sale, Kirkpatrick. *The Conquest of Paradise: Christopher Columbus and the Columbian Legacy*. New York: Alfred A. Knopf, 1991.

Sanders, Ronald. *Lost Tribes and Promised Lands: The Origins of American Racism*. 1978. Rprt. New York: HarperCollins; Harper Perennial, 1992.

Warhus, Mark. *Another America: Native American Maps and the History of Our Land*. New York: St. Martin's Press, 1997.

Works Consulted

Berlo, Janet C. and Ruth B. Phillips. *Native North American Art*. Oxford and New York: Oxford University Press, 1998.

Bunting, Bainbridge. *Early Architecture in New Mexico*. Albuquerque, NM: University of New Mexico Press, 1976.

Erffa, Helmut von and Allen Staley. *The Paintings of Benjamin West*. New Haven, CT: Yale University Press, 1986.

Fagan, Brian M. *Ancient North America: The Archaeology of a Continent*. Rev. edn. London: Thames & Hudson, 1995.

Fairbanks, Jonathan, Robert Trent, et al. *New England Begins: The Seventeenth Century*. 3 vols. Boston, MA: Museum of Fine Arts, 1982.

Feest, Christian F. *Native Arts of North America*. Rev. edn. London: Thames & Hudson, 1992.

Fleischer, Roland E. *Gustavus Hesselius: Face Painter to the Middle Colonies*. Trenton, NJ: New Jersey State Museum, 1988.

Grant, Campbell. *Canyon de Chelly: Its People and Rock Art*. Tuscon, AZ: University of Arizona Press, 1978.

Greene, Jack P. *The Intellectual Construction of America: Exceptionalism and Identity from 1492 to 1800*. Chapel Hill, NC: University of North Carolina Press, 1993.

Honour, Hugh. *The New Golden Land: European Images of America from the Discoveries to the Present Time*. New York: Pantheon Books, 1975.

Hulton, Paul. *America 1585: The Complete Drawings of John White*. Chapel Hill, NC: University of North Carolina Press, 1984.

King, Jonathan C. H. *First Peoples, First Contacts: Native Peoples of North America*. Cambridge, MA: Harvard University Press, 1999.

Lindsey, Jack L. *Worldly Goods: The Arts of Pennsylvania, 1680–1758*. Philadelphia, PA: Philadelphia Museum of Art, 1999.

Maurer, Evan M. *Visions of the People: A Pictorial History of Plains Indian Life*. Minneapolis, MN: Minneapolis Institute of Arts, 1992.

St. Louis Museum of Art. *Made in America: Ten Centuries of American Art*. New York: Hudson Hills Press, 1995.

Saunders, Richard H. and Ellen G. Miles. *American Colonial Portraits, 1700–1776*. Washington, DC: Smithsonian Institution Press for National Portrait Gallery, 1987.

Ulrich, Laurel Thatcher. *The Age of the Homespun: Objects and Stories in the Creation of an American Myth*. New York: Alfred A. Knopf, 2001.

Walthall, John A., ed. *French Colonial Archaeology: The Illinois Country and the Western Great Lakes.* Urbana, IL: University of Illinois Press, 1996.

CHAPTER TWO
Works Cited

Butler, John. *Awash in a Sea of Faith: Christianizing the American People.* Cambridge, MA: Harvard University Press, 1990.

Dillenberger, John. *The Visual Arts and Christianity in America: From the Colonial Period to the Present.* Rev. edn. New York: Crossroad Publishing, 1989.

Dominguez, Fray Francisco Atanasio. *The Missions of New Mexico, 1776.* Trans. and annot. Eleanor B. Adams and Fray Angelico Chavez. Albuquerque, NM: University of New Mexico Press, 1956.

Espinoza, José E. *Saints in the Valleys: Christian Sacred Images in the History, Life and Folk Art of Spanish New Mexico.* Rev. edn. Albuquerque, NM: University of New Mexico Press, 1967.

Hall, David D. *Worlds of Wonder; Days of Judgment: Popular Religious Belief in Early New England.* Cambridge, MA: Harvard University Press, 1990.

Horner, George F. and Robert A. Bain, eds. *Colonial and Federalist American Writing.* New York: Odyssey Press, 1966.

Jeffrey, David Lyle, ed. *A Dictionary of Biblical Tradition in English Literature.* Grand Rapids, MI: William B. Eerdmans, 1992.

Kubler, George. *The Religious Architecture of New Mexico: In the Colonial Period and Since the American Occupation.* 4th edn. Albuquerque, NM: University of New Mexico Press, 1972.

McCoubrey, John W., ed. *American Art, 1700–1960: Sources and Documents.* Englewood Cliffs, NJ: Prentice-Hall, 1965.

Philadelphia Museum of Art. *Philadelphia: Three Centuries of American Art.* Philadelphia, PA: Philadelphia Museum of Art, 1976.

Piwonka, Ruth and Roderic H. Blackburn. *A Remnant in the Wilderness: New York Dutch Scripture History Paintings of the Early Eighteenth Century.* Albany, NY: Albany Institute of History and Art, 1980.

Pointon, Marcia. "Quakerism and Visual Culture 1650–1800." *Art History*, vol.20 (Sept. 1997): 397–431.

Stein, Roger B. "Thomas Smith's Self-Portrait: Image/Text as Artifact." *Art Journal*, vol.44 (Winter 1984): 316–27

Touro Synagogue of Congregation Jeshuat Israel, Newport, Rhode Island. Newport, RI: Society of Friends of Touro Synagogue National Historic Shrine, 1948.

Upton, Dell. *Holy Things and Profane: Anglican Parish Churches in Colonial Virginia.* New Haven, CT: Yale University Press, 1997.

Weber, David J. *The Spanish Frontier in North America.* New Haven, CT: Yale University Press, 1992.

Works Consulted

Benes, Peter and Philip D. Zimmerman. *New England Meeting House and Church: 1630–1850.* Boston, MA, and Manchester, NH: Boston University Scholarly Publications and Currier Gallery of Art, 1979.

Boyd, E. *Popular Arts of Spanish New Mexico.* Santa Fe, NM: Museum of New Mexico Press, 1974.

Buhler, Kathryn C. and Graham Hood. *American Silver: Garvan and Other Collections in the Yale University Art Gallery,* Vol.1: *New England.* New Haven, CT: Yale University Press, 1970.

Dillenberger, Jane and Joshua C. Taylor. *The Hand and the Spirit: Religious Art in America, 1700–1900.* Berkeley, CA: University Art Museum, 1972.

Egbert, Donald Drew. "Religious Expression in American Architecture," in *Modern Perspectives in Western Art History: An Anthology of 20th Century Writings on the Visual Arts,* ed. W. Eugene Kleinbauer. New York: Holt, Rinehart & Winston, 1971, 312–38.

Fairbanks, Jonathan, Robert Trent, et. al. *New England Begins: The Seventeenth Century.* 3 vols. Boston, MA: Museum of Fine Arts, 1982.

Fowble, E. McSherry. *To Please Every Taste: Eighteenth-Century Prints from the Winterthur Museum.* Alexandria, VA: Art Services International, 1991.

Garfinkel, Susan. "Letting in 'The World': (Re)interpretive Tensions in the Quaker Meeting House," in *Gender, Class, and Shelter: Perspectives in Vernacular Architecture,* ed. Elizabeth Collins Cromley and Carter L. Hudgins. Knoxville, TN: University of Tennessee Press, 1995.

Jewish Museum [New York]. *The Jewish Heritage in American Folk Art.* New York: Universe Books, 1984.

Kennedy, Rick. "Thomas Brattle, Mathematician-Architect in the Transition of the New England Mind, 1690–1700." *Winterthur Portfolio,* vol.24 (Winter 1989), 231–45.

Morgan, David. *Visual Piety: A History and Theory of Popular Religious Images.* Berkeley and Los Angeles, CA: University of California Press, 1998.

Nelson, Vernon. *John Valentine Haidt.* Williamsburg, VA: Abby Aldrich Rockefeller Folk Art Collection, 1966.

Patton, Sharon F. *African-American Art.* Oxford History of Art. New York: Oxford University Press, 1998.

Poesch, Jessie and Barbara SoRelle Bacot, eds. *Louisiana Buildings, 1720–1940: The Historic American Buildings Survey.* Baton Rouge, LO: Louisiana State University Press, 1997.

Sweeney, Kevin M. "Meetinghouses, Town Houses, and Churches: Changing Perceptions of Sacred and Secular Space in Southern New England, 1720–1850." *Winterthur Portfolio,* vol.28, no.1 (1993), 59–94.

Tashjian, Dickran and Anne. *Memorials for Children: The Art of Early New England Stonecarving.* Middletown, CT: Wesleyan University Press, 1974.

Treib, Marc. *Sanctuaries of Spanish New Mexico.* Los Angeles, CA: University of California Press, 1993.

Ward, Barbara Mclean. "'In a Feasting Posture': Communion Vessels and Community Values in Seventeenth- and Eighteenth-Century New England." *Winterthur Portfolio,* vol.23 (Spring 1988), 1–24.

Williams, Peter W. *Houses of God: Region, Religion, and Architecture in the United States.* Urbana, IL: University of Illinois Press, 1997.

Wroth, William. *Images of Penance, Images of Mercy: Southwestern Santos in the Late Nineteenth Century.* Norman, OK: University of Oklahoma Press, 1991.

CHAPTER THREE
Works Cited

Bailyn, Bernard. *The Peopling of British North America: An Introduction.* New York: Vintage Books, 1988.

Bullock, Steven C. *Revolutionary Brotherhood: Freemasonry and the Transformation of the American Social Order, 1730–1840.* Chapel Hill, NC: University of North Carolina Press, 1996.

Fischer, David Hackett. *Albion's Seed: Four British Folkways in America.* New York: Oxford University Press, 1989.

Fleischer, Roland E. "Emblems and Colonial American Painting." *American Art Journal,* vol.20, no.3 (1988), 3–35.

Hamilton, Dr. Alexander. *The Tuesday Club: A Shorter Edition of 'The History of the Ancient and Honorable Tuesday Club',* ed. Robert Micklus. Baltimore, MD: Johns Hopkins University Press, 1995.

Horner, George F. and Robert A. Bain, eds. *Colonial and Federalist American Writing.* New York: Odyssey Press, 1966.

Kasson, John. *Rudeness and Civility: Manners in Nineteenth-Century America.* New York: Hill & Wang, 1990.

Lockridge, Kenneth A. *The Diary, and Life, of William Byrd II of Virginia, 1674–1744.* Chapel Hill, NC: University of North Carolina Press, 1987.

McCoubrey, John W., ed. *American Art, 1700–1960: Sources and Documents.* Englewood Cliffs, NJ: Prentice-Hall, 1965.

Pierson, William H., Jr. *American Buildings and their Architects: The Colonial and Neoclassical Styles.* Garden City, NY: Doubleday, 1970.

Sadik, Marvin S. *Colonial and Federal Portraits at Bowdoin College.* Brunswick, ME: Bowdoin College Museum of Art, 1966.

Sandoz, Ellis, ed. *Political Sermons of the American Founding Era: 1730–1805.* Indianapolis, IN: Liberty Press, 1991.

Saunders, Richard H. *John Smibert: Colonial America's First Portrait Painter.* New Haven, CT: Yale University Press, 1995.

Saunders, Richard H. and Ellen G. Miles. *American Colonial Portraits: 1700–1776.* Washington, DC: Smithsonian Institution Press, 1987.

Silverman, Kenneth. *A Cultural History of the American Revolution.* New York: Thomas Y. Crowell Company, 1976.

Works Consulted

Brand, Barbara Allston. "William Buckland, Architect in Annapolis," in *Palladian Studies in America: Building by the Book.* No.2, ed. Mario di Valmarana. Charlottesville, VA: University Press of Virginia, 1986, 65–85.

Breen, T. H. "The Meaning of 'Likeness': American Portrait Painting in an Eighteenth-Century Consumer Society." *Word & Image* 6 (Oct.–Dec. 1990), 325–50.

Brilliant, Richard. *Facing the New World: Jewish Portraits in Colonial and Federal America.* New York: Jewish Museum, 1997.

Bushman, Richard L. *The Refinement of America: Persons, Houses, Cities.* New York: Alfred A. Knopf, 1992.

Carson, Cary, Ronald Hoffman and Peter J. Albert. *Of Consuming Interests: The Style of Life in the Eighteenth Century.* Charlottesville, VA: University Press of Virginia, 1994.

Finney, Arthur, L. "The Royall House in Medford: A Re-Evaluation of the Structural and Documentary Evidence," in *Architecture in Colonial Massachusetts: A Conference Held by the Colonial Society of Massachusetts, September 19 and 20, 1974.* Boston, MA: Colonial Society of Massachusetts, 1979, 23–41.

Gowans, Alan. "Freemasonry and the Neoclassic Style in America." *Antiques* (Feb. 1960), 172–75.

Hamilton, John D. *Material Culture of the American Freemasons.* Lexington, MA: Museum of our National Heritage, 1994.

Lovell, Margaretta M. "Reading Eighteenth-Century American Family Portraits: Social Images and Self-Images," in *Critical Issues in American Art: A Book of Readings,* ed. Mary Ann Calo. Boulder, CO: Westview Press, 1998, 35–45.

Miles, Ellen G., ed. *The Portrait in Eighteenth-Century America.* Newark: University of Delaware Press, 1993.

Schimmelman, Janice G. *Architectural Treatises and Building Handbooks Available in American Libraries and Bookstores through 1800.* Worcester, MA: American Antiquarian Society, 1986.

CHAPTER FOUR
Works Cited

Alberts, Robert C. *Benjamin West: A Biography.* Boston, MA: Houghton Mifflin, 1978.

Berens, John F. *Providence and Patriotism in Early America, 1640–1815.* Charlottesville, VA: University Press of Virginia, 1978.

Bjelajac, David. *Millennial Desire and the Apocalyptic Vision of Washington Allston.* Washington, DC: Smithsonian Institution Press, 1988.

Bjelajac, David. *Washington Allston, Secret Societies and the Alchemy of Anglo-American Painting.* Cambridge, England, and New York: Cambridge University Press, 1997.

Cooper, Helen A., ed. *John Trumbull: The Hand and the Spirit of a Painter.* New Haven, CT: Yale University Press, 1982.

Dunlap, William. *A History of the Rise and Progress of the Arts of Design in the United States.* 2 vols. 1834. Rprt. New York: Dover Publications, 1969.

Fliegelman, Jay. *Declaring Independence: Jefferson, Natural Language and the Culture of Performance.* Stanford, CA: Stanford University Press, 1993.

Fortune, Brandon Brame. "A Delicate Balance: Raphaelle Peale's Still-Life Paintings and the Ideal of Temperance," in *The Peale Family: Creation of a Legacy, 1770–1870,* ed. Lillian B. Miller. New York: Abbeville Press, 1996, 135–49.

Fortune, Brandon Brame. "'From the World Escaped': Peale's Portrait of William Smith and His Grandson." *Eighteenth-Century Studies* 25 (Summer 1992), 587–615.

Kaplan, Sidney and Emma Nogrady Kaplan. *The Black Presence in the Era of the American Revolution.* Rev. edn. Amherst, MA: University of Massachusetts Press, 1989.

Lubin, David M. *Picturing a Nation: Art and Social Change in Nineteenth-Century America.* New Haven, CT: Yale University Press, 1994.

McCoubrey, John W., ed. *American Art, 1700–1960: Sources and Documents.* Englewood Cliffs, NJ: Prentice-Hall, 1965.

Miles, Ellen G. *American Paintings of the Eighteenth Century.* Collections of National Gallery of Art Systematic Catalogue. Washington, DC: National Gallery of Art, 1995.

Miller, Lillian B. *In Pursuit of Fame: Rembrandt Peale, 1778–1860.* Washington, DC: National Portrait Gallery, Smithsonian Institution, 1992.

Neff, Emily Ballew. *John Singleton Copley in England.* Houston, TX: Museum of Fine Arts, 1995.

Nemerov Alexander. *The Body of Raphaelle Peale: Still Life and Selfhood, 1812–1824.* Berkeley and Los Angeles, CA: University of California Press, 2001.

Prown, Jules David. *John Singleton Copley.* 2 vols. Cambridge, MA: Harvard University Press, 1996.

Prown, Jules David. "John Trumbull as History Painter," in *John Trumbull: The Hand and Spirit of a Painter,* ed. Helen A. Cooper. New Haven, CT: Yale University Art Gallery, 1982, 22–41.

Rigal, Laura. *The American Manufactory: Art, Labor, and the World of Things in the Early Republic.* Princeton, NJ: Princeton University Press, 1998.

Roth, Leland M. *A Concise History of American Architecture.* New York: Harper & Row; Icon Editions, 1979.

Scott, Pamela. *Temple of Liberty: Building the Capitol for a New Nation.* Oxford, England and New York: Oxford University Press, 1995.

Sellers, Charles Coleman. *Benjamin Franklin in Portraiture.* New Haven, CT: Yale University Press, 1962.

Sellers, Charles Colman. *Patience Wright: American Artist and Spy in George III's London.* Middletown, CT: Wesleyan University Press, 1976.

Simpson, Marc, Sally Mills, and Jennifer Saville, *The American Canvas: Paintings from the Collection of the Fine Arts Museums of San Francisco.* New York: Hudson Hill Press, 1989.

Trumbull, John. *The Autobiography of Colonel John Trumbull, Patriot-Artist, 1756–1843,* ed. Theodore Sizer. New Haven, CT: Yale University Press, 1953.

Works Consulted

Abrams, Ann Uhry. *The Valiant Hero: Benjamin West and Grand-Style History Painting.* Washington, DC: Smithsonian Institution Press, 1985.

Boston (Museum of Fine Arts). *Paul Revere's Boston: 1735–1818.* Boston, MA: Museum of Fine Arts, 1975.

Brigham, Clarence S. *Paul Revere's Engravings.* New York: Atheneum, 1969.

Brigham, David. *Public Culture in the Early Republic: Peale's Museum and Its Audience.* Washington, DC: Smithsonian Institution Press, 1995.

Burnham, Patricia M. "John Trumbull, Historian: The Case of the Battle of Bunker's Hill," in *Redefining American History Painting,* ed. Patricia M. Burnham and Lucretia Hoover Giese. Cambridge, England and New York: Cambridge University Press, 1995, 37–53.

Evans, Dorinda. *The Genius of Gilbert Stuart.* Princeton, NJ: Princeton University Press, 1999.

Evans, Dorinda. *Mather Brown: Early American Artist in England.* Middletown, CT: Wesleyan University Press, 1982.

Fortune, Brandon Brame and Deborah J. Warner. *Franklin & His Friends: Portraying the Man of Science in Eighteenth-Century America.* Washington, DC: National Portrait Gallery, Smithsonian Institution, 1999.

Fryd, Vivien Green. "Rereading the Indian in Benjamin West's *Death of General Wolfe.*" *American Art* 9 (Spring 1995), 73–85.

Hutson, James H. *Religion and the Founding of the American Republic.* Washington, DC: Library of Congress, 1998.

Johns, Elizabeth. *American Genre Painting: The Politics of Everyday Life,* New Haven, CT: Yale University Press, 1991.

Marks, Arthur S. "The Statue of King George III in New York and the Iconology of Regicide." *American Art Journal* 13 (Summer 1981), 61–82.

Maynard, W. Barksdale. *Architecture in the United States, 1800–1850.* New Haven, CT: Yale University Press, 2002.

Montgomery, Charles F. and Patricia E. Kane, eds. *American Art: 1750–1800, Towards Independence.* Boston, MA: New York Graphic Society for Yale University Art Gallery and Victoria and Albert Museum, 1976.

Olson, Lester C. *Emblems of American Community in the Revolutionary Era: A Study in Rhetorical Iconology.* Washington, DC: Smithsonian Institution Press, 1991.

Rebora, Carrie, Paul Staiti, Erika E. Hirshler, et al. *John Singleton Copley in America.* New York: Metropolitan Museum of Art, 1995.

Ring, Betty. *Girlhood Embroidery: American Samplers and Pictorial Needlework, 1650–1850,* Vol 1. New York: Alfred A. Knopf, 1993.

Savage, Kirk. "The Self-made Monument: George Washington and the Fight to Erect a National Memorial," in *Critical Issues in Public Art: Content, Context, and Controversy,* ed. Harriet F. Senie and Sally Webster. New York: HarperCollins; Icon Editions, 1992, 5–43.

Staiti, Paul. *Samuel F.B. Morse.* Cambridge: Cambridge University Press, 1989.

Stein, Roger B. "Charles Willson Peale's Expressive Design: *The Artist in His Museum.*" *Prospects,* 6 (1981), 139–85.

CHAPTER FIVE
Works Cited

Bjelajac, David. *Washington Allston, Secret Societies and the Alchemy of Anglo-American Painting.* Cambridge, England, and New York: Cambridge University Press, 1997.

Bjelajac, David. "William Sidney Mount and the Hermetic Tradition in American Art," in *The Visual Culture of American Religions,* eds. David Morgan and Sally M. Promey. Berkeley and Los Angeles, CA: University of California Press, 2001, 176–190.

Butler, Jon. *Awash in a Sea of Faith: Christianizing the American People.* Cambridge, MA: Harvard University Press, 1990.

Cayton, Andrew R.L. "The Fragmentation of 'A Great Family': The Panic of 1819 and the Rise of the Middling Interest in Boston, 1818–1822." *Journal of the Early Republic* 2 (Summer 1982), 143–67.

Colbert, Charles. *A Measure of Perfection: Phrenology and the Fine Arts in America.* Chapel Hill, NC: University of North Carolina Press, 1997.

Cole, Thomas. *The Collected Essays and Prose Sketches.* Ed. Marshall Tymn. St. Paul, MN: John Colet Press, 1980.

Cremin, Lawrence A. *American Education: The National Experience, 1783–1876.* New York: Harper & Row; Harper Torchbooks, 1980.

Davis, John. "Eastman Johnson's *Negro Life at the South* and Urban Slavery in Washington, DC." *The Art Bulletin,* Vol. 80 (March 1998), 67–92.

Davis, Keith F. "'A Terrible Distinctness': Photography of the Civil War Era," in *Photography in Nineteenth-Century America,* ed. Martha A. Sandweiss. Fort Worth, TX and New York: Amon Carter Museum and Harry N. Abrams, 1991, 131–79.

Dimmick, Lauretta. "Thomas Crawford's *Orpheus:* The American *Apollo Belvedere.*" *American Art Journal,* vol.19 (1987), 47–84.

Dunlap, William. *A History of the Rise and Progress of the Arts of Design in the United States.* 2 vols. 1834. Rprt. New York: Dover Publications, 1969.

Durand, John. *The Life and Times of A.B. Durand.* 1894. Rprt. New York: Kennedy Graphics and Da Capo Press, 1970.

Ellis, Elizabeth Garrity. "Fitz Hugh Lane and the American Union of Associationists." *American Art Journal* 17 (Spring 1985), 89.

Foresta, Merry A. and John Wood. *Secrets of the Dark Chamber: The Art of the American Daguerreotype.* Washington, DC: Smithsonian Institution Press, 1995.

Fowler, Orson S. *The Octagon House: A Home for All.* 1853. Rprt. with new intro. by Madeline B. Stern. New York: Dover Publications, 1973.

Fryd, Vivien Green. *Art and Empire: The Politics of Ethnicity in the United States Capitol, 1815–1860.* New Haven, CT: Yale University Press, 1992.

Greenough, Horatio. *Form and Function: Remarks on Art, Design, and Architecture,* ed. Harold A. Small. Berkeley and Los Angeles, CA: University of California Press, 1958.

Hawthorne, Nathaniel. *The House of the Seven Gables.* New York: Bantam Books; Bantam Classics, 1981.

Hills, Patricia. "The American Art-Union as Patron for Expansionist Ideology in the 1840s," in *Art in Bourgeois Society, 1790–1850,* eds. Andrew Hemingway and William Vaughan. Cambridge: Cambridge University Press, 1998, 314–39.

Howat, John K., ed. *American Paradise: The World of the Hudson River School.* New York: Metropolitan Museum of Art and Harry N. Abrams, 1987.

Husch, Gail E. *Something Coming: Apocalyptic Expectation and Mid-Nineteenth-Century American Painting.* Hanover, NH: University Press of New England, 2000.

Johns, Elizabeth. *American Genre Painting: The Politics of Everyday Life.* New Haven, CT: Yale University Press, 1991.

Josephson, Hannah. *The Golden Threads: New England's Mill Girls and Magnates.* New York: Duell, Sloan & Pearce, 1949.

Kasson, Joy. *Marble Queens and Captives: Women in Nineteenth-Century American Sculpture.* New Haven, CT: Yale University Press, 1990.

Kelly, Franklin. *Frederic Edwin Church.* Washington, DC: National Gallery of Art, 1989.

Kerr, Howard. *Mediums and Spirit-Rappers, and Roaring Radicals: Spiritualism in American Literature, 1850–1900.* Urbana, IL: University of Illinois Press, 1972.

Kloss, William. *Samuel F.B. Morse.* New York: Harry N. Abrams, 1988.

Lubin, David. *Picturing a Nation: Art and Social Change in Nineteenth-Century America.* New Haven, CT: Yale University Press, 1994.

Mabee, Carleton. *The American Leonardo: A Life of Samuel F.B. Morse.* New York: Alfred A. Knopf, 1944.

McCoubrey, John W., ed. *American Art, 1700–1960: Sources and Documents.* Englewood Cliffs, NJ: Prentice-Hall, 1965.

Miller, Angela. "Thomas Cole and Jacksonian America: *The Course of Empire* as Political Allegory." *Prospects: An Annual of American Cultural Studies* 14 (1989), 65–92.

Miller, Lillian B. *Patrons and Patriotism: The Encouragement of the Fine Arts in the United States, 1790–1860.* Chicago, IL: University of Chicago Press, 1966.

Oettermann, Stephan. *The Panorama: History of a Mass Medium.* Trans. Deborah Lucas Schneider. New York: Zone Books, 1997.

Parry, Ellwood C. III. *The Art of Thomas Cole: Ambition and Imagination.* Newark, NJ: University of Delaware Press, 1988.

Peabody, Elizabeth Palmer. *Reminiscences of Rev. Wm. Ellery Channing.* Boston, MA: Roberts Brothers, 1880.

Poesch, Jessie. *The Art of the Old South: Painting, Sculpture, Architecture and the Products of Craftsmen, 1560–1860.* New York: Harrison House, 1989.

Prime, Samuel Irenaeus. *The Life of Samuel F.B. Morse.* 1875. Rprt. New York: Arno Press, 1974.

Roque, Oswaldo Rodriguez. "The Last Summer's Work," in *John Frederick Kensett: An American Master,* ed. John Paul Driscoll and John K. Howat. New York: W.W. Norton, 1985, 137–61.

Schuyler, David. *Apostle of Taste: Andrew Jackson Downing, 1815–1852.* Baltimore, MD: Johns Hopkins University Press, 1996.

Shumard, Ann M. *A Durable Memento: Portraits by Augustus Washington. African-American Daguerreotypist.* Washington, DC: National Portrait Gallery, Smithsonian Institution, 2000.

Taylor, Alan. "The Early Republic's Supernatural Economy: Treasure Seeking in the American Northeast, 1780–1830." *American Quarterly* 38 (Spring 1986), 6–33.

Voorsanger, Catherine Hoover and John K Howat, eds. *Art and the Empire City: New York, 1825–1861.* New York: The Metropolitan Museum of Art, 2000.

Wallach, Alan. "Making a Picture of the View from Mount Holyoke," in *American Iconology: New Approaches to Nineteenth-Century Art and Literature,* ed. David C. Miller. New Haven, CT: Yale University Press, 1993.

Wallach, Alan. "Thomas Cole: Landscape and the Course of American Empire," in *Thomas Cole: Landscape into History,* ed. William H. Truettner and Alan Wallach. Washington, DC: National Museum of American Art, 1974, 23–111.

Wunder, Richard P. *Hiram Powers, Vermont Sculptor, 1805–1873.* 2 vols. Newark, NJ: University of Delaware Press, 1991.

Zinn, Howard. *A People's History of the United States, 1492–Present.* Rev. edn. New York: HarperCollins; Harper Perennial, 2003.

Works Consulted

Anderson, Nancy K. and Linda S. Ferber. *Albert Bierstadt: Art and Enterprise.* New York: The Brooklyn Museum, 1990.

Andrew, Laurel B. *The Early Temples of the Mormons: The Architecture of the Millennial Kingdom in the American West.* Albany, NY: State University of New York Press, 1978.

Burns, Sarah. *Pastoral Inventions: Rural Life in Nineteenth-Century American Art and Culture.* Philadelphia, PA: Temple University Press, 1989.

Davis, John. "Catholic Envy: The Visual Culture of Protestant Desire," in *The Visual Culture of American Religions,* eds. David Morgan and Sally M. Promey. Berkeley & L.A., CA: University of California Press, 2001, 105–28.

Davis, John. *The Landscape of Belief: Encountering the Holy Land in Nineteenth-Century American Art and Culture.* Princeton, NJ: Princeton University Press, 1996.

Hollander, Stacy C. *American Radiance: The Ralph Esmerian Gift to the American Folk Art Museum.* New York: American Folk Art Museum, 2001.

Jackson, Kenneth T. *Crabgrass Frontier: The Suburbanization of the United States.* Oxford, England and New York: Oxford University Press, 1985.

Ketner, Joseph D. *The Emergence of the African-American Artist: Robert S. Duncanson, 1821–1872.* Columbia, MO: University of Missouri Press, 1993.

Manthorne, Katherine Emma. *Tropical Renaissance: North American Artists Exploring Latin America, 1839–1879.* Washington, DC: Smithsonian Institution Press, 1989.

McLanathan, Richard. *Gilbert Stuart.* New York: Harry N. Abrams, 1986.

Miller, Angela. *The Empire of the Eye: Landscape Representation and American Cultural Politics, 1825–1875.* Ithaca, NY: Cornell University Press, 1993.

Novak, Barbara. *Nature and Culture: American Landscape Painting.* Rev. ed. Oxford, England and New York: Oxford University Press, 1995.

Nygren, Edward J. *Views and Visions: American Landscape before 1830.* Washington, DC: Corcoran Gallery of Art, 1986.

Pohl, Frances K. "Old World, New World: The Encounter of Cultures on the American Frontier," in *Nineteenth Century Art: A Critical History,* ed. Stephen F. Eisenman. London: Thames & Hudson, 1994, 144–62.

Promey, Sally. *Spiritual Spectacles: Vision and Image in Mid-Nineteenth-Century Shakerism.* Bloomington, IN: Indiana University Press, 1993.

Ramirez, Jan Seidler, ed. *Painting the Town: Cityscapes of New York.* New York: Museum of the City of New York, 2000.

Rothman, David J. *The Discovery of the Asylum: Social Order and Disorder in the New Republic.* Boston, MA: Little, Brown, 1971.

Stern, Madeline B. *Heads and Headlines: The Phrenological Fowlers.* Norman, OK: University of Oklahoma Press, 1971.

Sweeney, J. Gray. *The Columbus of the Woods: Daniel Boone and the Typology of Manifest Destiny.* St. Louis, MO: Washington University Gallery of Art, 1992.

Sweeney, J. Gray. "The Nude of Landscape Painting: Emblematic Personification in the Art of the Hudson River School." *Smithsonian Studies in American Art* 3 (Fall 1989), 43–65.

Trachtenberg, Alan. "Albums of War: On Reading Civil War Photographs," in *Critical Issues in American Art: A Book of Readings,* ed. Mary Ann Calo. Boulder, CO: Westview Press, 1998, 135–54.

Truettner, William H., ed. *The West as America: Reinterpreting Images of the Frontier, 1820–1920.* Washington, DC: Smithsonian Institution Press, 1991.

Voss, Frederick S. *John Frazee, Sculptor: 1790–1852.* Boston: Boston Athenaeum. 1986.

Weekley, Carolyn J. *The Kingdoms of Edward Hicks.* Williamsburg, VA: Colonial Williamsburg Foundation, 1999.

Wichita Art Museum. *John Quidor: Painter of American Legend.* Essay by David M. Sokol. Wichita, KS: Wichita Art Museum, 1973.

Wilton, Andrew and Tim Barringer. *American Sublime: Landscape Painting in the United States, 1820–1880.* Princeton, NJ: Princeton University Press, 2002.

Wolf, Bryan. "All the World's a Code: Art and Ideology in Nineteenth Century American Painting." *Art Journal 44* (Winter 1984), 328–37.

Wolf, Bryan Jay. *Romantic Re-Vision: Culture and Consciousness in Nineteenth-Century American Painting and Literature.* Chicago, IL: University of Chicago Press, 1982.

Wolff, Justin. *Richard Caton Woodville: American Painter, Artful Dodger.* Princeton, NJ: Princeton University Press, 2002.

Wroth, William. "New Mexican Santos and the Preservation of Religious Traditions," in *Critical Issues in American Art: A Book of Readings,* ed. Mary Ann Calo. Boulder, CO: Westview Press, 1998, 125–33.

CHAPTER SIX

Works Cited

Bearden, Romare and Harry Henderson. *A History of African-American Artists: From 1792 to the Present.* New York: Pantheon Books, 1993.

Bendix, Deanna Marohn. *Diabolical Designs: Paintings, Interiors, and Exhibitions of James McNeill Whistler.* Washington, DC: Smithsonian Institution Press, 1995.

Boime, Albert. *The Art of Exclusion: Representing Blacks in the Nineteenth Century.* London: Thames & Hudson, 1990.

Broun, Elizabeth. *Albert Pinkham Ryder.* Washington, DC: National Museum of American Art, Smithsonian Institution, 1989.

Buick, Kirsten P. "The Ideal Works of Edmonia Lewis: Invoking and Inverting Autobiography," in *Reading American Art,* ed. Marianne Doezema and Elizabeth Milroy. New Haven, CT: Yale University Press, 1998, 190–207.

Burns, Sarah. *Inventing the Modern Artist: Art & Culture in Gilded Age America.* New Haven, CT: Yale University Press, 1996.

Cikovsky, Nicolai, Jr. "The School of War," in *Winslow Homer,* ed. Nicolai Cikovsky, Jr. and Franklin Kelly. Washington, DC: National Gallery of Art, 1995, 17–37.

Edwards, Holly. *Noble Dreams, Wicked Pleasures: Orientalism in America, 1870–1930.* Princeton, NJ: Princeton University Press, 2000.

Griffin, Randall C. *Thomas Anshutz: Artist and Teacher.* Seattle, WA: Heckscher Museum in assoc. with University of Washington Press, 1994.

Jarves, James Jackson. *The Art-Idea.* 1864. Rprt. ed. Benjamin Rowland, Jr. Cambridge, MA: Harvard University Press, Belknap Press 1960.

Johns, Elizabeth. *Thomas Eakins: The Heroism of Modern Life.* Princeton, NJ: Princeton University Press, 1983.

Landau, Sarah Bradford and Carl W. Condit. *Rise of the New York Skyscraper: 1865–1913.* New Haven, CT: Yale University Press, 1996.

Lovell, Margaretta. "Picturing 'A City for a Single Summer': Paintings of the World's Columbian Exposition." *Art Bulletin,* vol.78 (March 1996), 40–55.

Lubin, David M. *Act of Portrayal: Eakins, Sargent, James.* New Haven, CT: Yale University Press, 1985.

McCoubrey, John W., ed. *American Art, 1700–1960: Sources and Documents.* Englewood Cliffs, NJ: Prentice-Hall, 1965.

McNamara, Brooks. *Day of Jubilee: The Great Age of Public Celebrations in New York, 1788–1909,* New Brunswick, NJ: Rutgers University Press, 1997.

Peck, Amelia and Carol Irish. *Candace Wheeler: The Art and Enterprise of American Design, 1875–1900.* New York: Metropolitan Museum of Art, 2001.

Pollock, Griselda. *Mary Cassatt: Painter of Modern Women.* London: Thames & Hudson, 1998.

Pyne, Kathleen. *Art and the Higher Life: Painting and Evolutionary Thought in Late Nineteenth-Century America.* Austin, TX: University of Texas Press, 1996.

Roth, Leland M. *American Architecture: A History.* Boulder, CO: Westview Press, Icon Editions, 2000.

Stein, Roger B. "Artifact as Ideology: The Aesthetic Movement in its American Cultural Context," in *In Pursuit of Beauty: Americans and the Aesthetic Movement,* by Doreen Bolger et al. New York: Rizzoli for Metropolitan Museum of New York, 1986, 23–51.

Tuckerman, Henry T. *Book of the Artists: American Artist Life Comprising Biographical and Critical Sketches of American Artists: Preceded by an Historical Account of the Rise and Progress of Art in America.* 1867. Rprt. New York: James F. Carr, 1967.

Upton, Dell. *Architecture in the United States.* Oxford History of Art. Oxford: Oxford University Press, 1998.

Wharton, Edith. *The House of Mirth.* Ed. Elizabeth Ammons. New York: W.W. Norton, 1990.

Works Consulted

Adams, Henry, et al. *John La Farge.* Pittsburgh, PA. Carnegie Museum of Art, 1987.

Baker, Paul R. *Richard Morris Hunt.* Cambridge, MA: MIT Press, 1980.

Berger, Martin A. *Man Made: Thomas Eakins and the Construction of Gilded Age Manhood.* Berkeley and Los Angeles CA: University of California Press, 2000.

Brooklyn Museum. *The American Renaissance, 1876–1917.* New York: Brooklyn Museum, 1979.

Cikovsky, J. Nicolai. *George Inness.* New York: Harry N. Abrahams, 1993.

Condit, Charles. *The Chicago School of Architecture: A History of Commercial and Public Building in the Chicago Area, 1875–1925.* Chicago, IL: University of Chicago Press, 1964.

Danly, Susan and Cheryl Leibold. *Eakins and the Photograph: Works by Thomas Eakins and His Circle in the Collection of the Pennsylvania Academy of the Fine Arts.* Washington, DC: Smithsonian Institution Press for Pennsylvania Academy of the Fine Arts, 1994.

Davidson, Abraham A. *Ralph Albert Blakelock.* University Park, PA: Pennsylvania State University Press, 1996.

Davis, John. "Children in the Parlor: Eastman Johnson's *Brown Family* and the Post-Civil War Interior." *American Art,* vol.10 (Summer 1996), 50–77.

Detroit Institute of Arts Founders Society, Detroit, MI. *American Paintings in the Detroit Institute of Arts.* Vol.2: *Works by Artists Born 1816–1847.* New York: Hudson Hills Press in assoc. with Detroit Institute of Arts Founders Society, 1997.

Fink, Lois Marie. *American Art at the Nineteenth-Century Paris Salons.* Washington, DC and Cambridge, England: Smithsonian Institution and Cambridge University Press, 1990.

Fisher, Irving D. "An Iconography of City Planning: The Chicago City Plan," in *Emanuel Swedenborg: A Continuing Vision,* ed. Robin Larsen et al. New York: Swedenborg Foundation, 1988, 245–62.

Fox, Sandi. *Wrapped in Glory: Figurative Quilts and Bedcovers.* Los Angeles, CA: Los Angeles County Museum of Art, 1990.

Harris, Neil. *Cultural Excursions: Marketing Appetites and Cultural Tastes in Modern America.* Chicago, IL: University of Chicago Press, 1990.

Lears, T.J. Jackson. *No Place of Grace: Antimodernism and the Transformation of American Culture, 1880–1920.* New York: Pantheon Books, 1981.

Makinson, Randall L. *Greene & Greene: Architecture as a Fine Art.* Salt Lake City, NV: Peregrine Smith, Inc., 1997.

Mosby, Dewey F. *Henry Ossawa Tanner.* New York: Rizzoli, 1991.

Neff, Emily Ballew. *Frederic Remington: The Hogg Brothers Collection of the Museum of Fine Arts, Houston.* Princeton, NJ: Princeton University Press, 2000.

Neff, Emily Ballew and George T.M. Shackelford. *American Painters in the Age of Impressionism.* Houston, TX: Museum of Fine Arts, 1994.

Prettejohn, Elizabeth. *Interpreting Sargent.* New York: Stewart, Tabori & Chang, 1999.

Promey, Sally M. *Painting Religion in Public: John Singer Sargent's "Triumph of Religion" at the Boston Public Library.* Princeton, NJ: Princeton University Press, 1999.

Riley, Terence, ed. *Frank Lloyd Wright, Architect.* New York: Museum of Modern Art, 1994.

Rosenbaum, Julia. "Displaying Civic Culture: The Controversy over Frederick MacMonnies' *Bacchante.*" *American Art* 14 (Fall 2000), 41–57.

Rosenberg, Eric M. "'… one of the most powerful, horrible, and yet fascinating pictures …': Thomas Eakins's *The Gross Clinic* as History Painting," in *Redefining American History Painting,* ed. Patricia M. Burnham and Lucretia Hoover Giese. New York and Cambridge: Cambridge University Press, 1995.

Sterngass, Jon. *First Resorts: Pursuing Pleasure at Saratoga Springs, Newport & Coney Island.* Baltimore, MD: The Johns Hopkins Press, 2001.

Tappert, Tara Leigh, *Cecilia Beaux and the Art of Portraiture.* Washington DC: National Portrait Gallery, Smithsonian Institution, 1995.

CHAPTER SEVEN
Works Cited

Abrahams, Edward. *The Lyrical Left: Randolph Bourne, Alfred Stieglitz and the Origins of Cultural Radicalism in America.* Charlotteville, VA: University Press of Virginia, 1986.

Agee, William C. "Willard Huntington Wright and the Synchromists: Notes on the Forum Exhibition." *Archives of American Art Journal,* vol.30, nos.1–4 (1990), 88–93.

Anderson Galleries [New York]. *The Forum Exhibition of Modern American Painters.* 1916. Rprt. New York: Arno Press, 1968.

Antliff, Allan. *Anarchist Modernism: Art, Politics, and the First Avant-Garde.* Chicago, IL: University of Chicago Press, 2001.

Balfour, Alan. *Rockefeller Center: Architecture as Theater.* New York: McGraw-Hill, Inc., 1978.

Chave, Anna C. "O'Keeffe and the Masculine Gaze," in *Reading American Art,* ed. Marianne Doezema and Elizabeth Milroy. New Haven, CT: Yale University Press, 1998, 350–70.

Corn, Wanda. *The Great American Thing: Modern Art and National Identity, 1915–1935.* Berkeley and Los Angeles, CA: University of California Press, 1999.

Doezema, Marianne. *George Bellows and Urban America.* New Haven, CT: Yale University Press, 1992.

Doss, Erika. *Benton, Pollock, and the Politics of Modernism: From Regionalism to Abstract Expressionism.* Chicago, IL: University of Chicago Press, 1991.

Henri, Robert. *The Art Spirit.* 1923. Rprt. Boulder, CO: Westview Press; Icon Editions, 1984.

Hills, Patricia. "John Sloan's Images of Working-Class Women: A Case Study of the Roles and Interrelationships of Politics, Personality, and Patrons in the Development of Sloan's Art, 1905–16," in *Reading American Art,* ed. Marianne Doezema and Elizabeth Milroy. New Haven, CT: Yale University Press, 1998, 311–49.

McCoubrey, John W., ed. *American Art, 1700–1960: Sources and Documents.* Englewood Cliffs, NJ: Prentice-Hall, 1965.

Naumann, Francis M. *New York Dada, 1915–23.* New York: Harry N. Abrams, 1994.

Newhall, Beaumont. *The History of Photography from 1839 to the Present Day.* Rev. and enlarged edn. New York: Museum of Modern Art, 1964.

O'Connor, Francis V. "An Iconographic Interpretation of Diego Rivera's *Detroit Industry* Murals in Terms of Their Orientation to the Cardinal Points of the Compass," in *Diego Rivera: A Retrospective,* ed. Cynthia Newman Helms. Detroit, MI: Founders Society Detroit Institute of Arts, 1986, 215–29.

Wattenmaker, Richard J. *Maurice Prendergast.* New York: Harry N. Abrams in assoc. with National Museum of American Art, Smithsonian Institution, 1994.

Works Consulted

Altshuler, Bruce. *The Avant-Garde in Exhibition: New Art in the 20th Century.* New York: Harry N. Abrams, 1994.

Ater, Renée. "Making History: Meta Warrick Fuller's *Ethiopia,*" *American Art* 17 (Fall 2003) 12–31.

Bloemink, Barbara J. *The Life and Art of Florine Stettheimer.* New Haven, CT: Yale University Press, 1995.

Brennan, Marcia. *Painting Gender, Constructing Theory: The Alfred Stieglitz Circle and American Formalist Aesthetics.* Cambridge, MA: MIT Press, 2001.

Conger, Amy. *Edward Weston: Photographs from the Collection of the Center for Creative Photography.* Tucson, AZ: Center for Creative Photography, University of Arizona, 1992.

Corn, Wanda. "The Birth of a National Icon: Grant Wood's *American Gothic,*" in *Reading American Art,* ed. Marianne Doezema and Elizabeth Milroy. New Haven, CT: Yale University Press, 1998, 387–408.

Davis, Keith F. *An American Century of Photography: The Hallmark Photographic Collection.* Kansas City, MO: Hallmark Cards, 1995.

Dennis, James M. *Grant Wood: A Study in American Art and Culture.* Columbia, MO: University of Missouri Press, 1986.

Dijkstra, Bram. *American Expressionism: Art and Social Change, 1920–1950.* New York: Harry N. Abrams, 2003.

Fine, Ruth E. *John Marin.* Washington, DC: National Gallery of Art, 1990.

Frackman, Noel. *John Storrs.* New York: Whitney Museum of Art, 1986.

Gambone, Robert L. *Art and Popular Religion in Evangelical America, 1915–1940.* Knoxville, TN: University of Tennessee Press, 1989.

Green, Martin. *New York 1913: The Armory Show and the Paterson Strike Pageant.* New York: Charles Scribner's Sons, 1988.

Guimond, James. *American Photography and the American Dream.* Chapel Hill, NC: University of North Carolina Press, 1991.

Haskell, Barbara. *The American Century: Art and Culture, 1900–1950.* New York: Whitney Museum of American Art, 1999.

Haskell, Barbara. *Burgoyne Diller.* New York: Whitney Museum of American Art, 1990.

Haskell, Barbara. *Charles Demuth.* New York: Whitney Museum of American Art in assoc. with Harry N. Abrams, 1987.

Haskell, Barbara. *Joseph Stella.* New York: Whitney Museum of American Art, 1994.

Hemingway, Andrew. *American Artists and the Communist Movement, 1926–1956.* New Haven, CT: Yale University Press, 2002.

Herzogenrath, Wulf and Andreas Kreul. *Sounds of the Inner Eye: John Cage, Mark Tobey, Morris Graves.* Tacoma, WA: Museum of Glass: International Center for Contemporary Art, 2002.

Hildebrand, Grant. *The Wright Space: Pattern and Meaning in Frank Lloyd Wright's Houses.* Seattle, WA: University of Washington Press, 1991.

Hills, Patricia. *Stuart Davis.* New York: Harry N. Abrams in assoc. with National Museum of American Art, Smithsonian Institution, 1996.

Hills, Patricia and Roberta K. Tarbell. *The Figurative Tradition and the Whitney Museum of American Art.* New York: Whitney Museum of American Art, 1980.

Junker, Patricia. *John Steuart Curry: Inventing the Middle West.* New York: Hudson Hills Press, 1998.

Kalaidjian, Walter. *American Culture Between the Wars: Revisionary Modernism and Postmodern Critique.* New York: Columbia University Press, 1993.

Kirstein, Lincoln. *Elie Nadelman.* New York: Eakins Press, 1973.

Kushner, Marilyn S. *Morgan Russell.* New York: Hudson Hills Press, 1990.

Levin, Gail. *Synchromism and American Color Abstraction, 1910–1925.* New York: G. Braziller, 1978.

Longwell, Dennis. *Steichen: The Master Prints, 1895–1914; The Symbolist Period.* New York: Museum of Modern Art, 1978.

Marter, Joan M. *Alexander Calder.* Cambridge: Cambridge University Press, 1991.

Meyer, Richard. *Outlaw Representation: Censorship and Homosexuality in Twentieth-Century American Art.* Oxford and New York: Oxford University Press, 2002.

Montclair Art Museum, Montclair, NJ. *Precisionism in America, 1915–1941: Reordering Reality.* New York: Harry N. Abrams in assoc. with Montclair Art Museum, 1994.

Morgan, David and Sally M. Promey. *Exhibiting the Visual Culture of American Religions.* Valparaiso, IN: Brauer Museum of Art, Valparaiso University, 2000.

North, Percy. *Max Weber: The Cubist Decade, 1910–1920.* Atlanta, GA: High Museum of Art, 1991.

Robertson, Bruce. *Marsden Hartley.* New York: Harry N. Abrams, 1995.

Sack, Manfred. *Richard Neutra.* Zurich: Verlag für Architectur; Studio Paperback, 1992.

Sawelson-Gorse, Naomi, ed. *Women in Dada: Essays on Sex, Gender, and Identity.* Cambridge, MA: MIT Press, 1998.

Singal, Daniel Joseph. "Toward a Definition of American Modernism." *American Quarterly* 39 (Spring 1987), 7–26.

Stavitsky, Gail. "John Weichsel and the People's Art Guild." *Archives of American Art Journal* 31, no.4 (1991), 12–19.

Weinberg, H. Barbara, Doreen Bolger, and David Park Curry. *American Impressionism and Realism: The Painting of Modern Life, 1885–1915.* New York: Metropolitan Museum of Art, 1994.

Weinberg, Jonathan. *Ambition & Love in Modern American Art.* New Haven, CT: Yale University Press, 2001.

Whiting, Cecile. *Antifascism in American Art.* New Haven, CT: Yale University Press, 1989.

CHAPTER EIGHT
Works Cited

Broude, Norma and Mary D. Garrard. *The Power of Feminist Art: The American Movement of the 1970s, History and Impact.* New York: Harry N. Abrams, 1994.

Chipp, Herschel B. ed. *Theories of Modern Art: A Sourcebook by Artists and Critics.* Berkeley and Los Angeles, CA: University of California Press, 1968.

Fineberg, Jonathan. *Art Since 1940: Strategies of Being,* rev. ed. New York: Harry N. Abrams, 2000.

Gibson, Ann Eden. *Abstract Expressionism: Other Politics.* New Haven, CT: Yale University Press, 1997.

Guibault, Serge. *How New York Stole the Idea of Modern Art: Abstract Expressionism, Freedom and the Cold War.* Trans. Arthur Goldhammer. Chicago, IL: University of Chicago Press, 1983.

Karia, Bhupendra, ed. *Yayoi Kusama.* New York: Center for International Contemporary Arts, 1989.

Kerouac, Jack. Introduction to *The Americans,* by Robert Frank. 1959. Rprt. New York: SCALO Publishers in assoc. with National Gallery of Art, Washington, DC, 1994.

Klotz, Heinrich. *The History of Postmodern Architecture.* Trans. Radka Donnell. Cambridge, MA: MIT Press, 1988.

Krauss, Rosiland, "Richard Serra: Sculpture," in *Richard Serra,* eds. Hal Foster and Gordon Hughes. Cambridge, MA: MIT Press, 2000, 99–145.

Robinson, Hilary, ed. *Feminism–Art–Theory: An Anthology, 1968–2000.* Oxford: Blackwell Publishers, 2001.

Schneemann, Carolee. *Imaging Her Erotics: Essays, Interviews, Projects.* Cambridge, MA: MIT Press, 2002.

Shapiro, Gary. *Earthwards: Robert Smithson and Art after Babel.* Berkeley and Los Angeles, CA: University of California Press, 1995.

Sontag, Susan. *Against Interpretation and Other Essays.* New York: Dell Publishing, 1961.

Stich, Sidra. *Made in U.S.A.: An Americanization in Modern Art, the '50s & '60s.* Berkeley and Los Angeles, CA: University of California Press, 1987.

Stiles, Kristine and Peter Selz. *Theories and Documents of Contemporary Art: A Sourcebook of Artists' Writings.* Berkeley and Los Angeles, CA: University of California Press, 1996.

Works Consulted

Alberro, Alexander. *Conceptual Art and the Politics of Publicity.* Cambridge, MA: MIT Press, 2003.

Alloway, Lawrence, et al. *The Pictographs of Adolph Gottlieb.* New York: Hudson Hills Press in assoc. with Adolph and Esther Gottlieb Foundation, 1994.

Anfam, David. *Abstract Expressionism.* London: Thames & Hudson, 1990.

Belgrad, Daniel. *The Culture of Spontaneity: Improvisation and the Arts in Postwar America.* Chicago, IL: University of Chicago Press, 1998.

Bertens, Hans. *The Idea of the Postmodern: A History.* London and New York: Routledge, 1995.

Bogart, Michele H. *Artists, Advertising, and the Borders of Art.* Chicago, IL: University of Chicago Press, 1995.

Chave, Anna C. "Minimalism and Biography." *The Art Bulletin,* Vol. 82 (March 2000), 149–63.

Cox, Anette. *Art-as-Politics: The Abstract Expressionist Avant-Garde and Society.* Ann Arbor, MI: UMI Research Press, 1982.

Crane, Diana. *The Transformation of the Avant-Garde: The New York Art World, 1940–1985.* Chicago, IL: University of Chicago Press, 1987.

Craven, David. *Abstract Expressionism as Cultural Critique: Dissent during the McCarthy Period.* Cambridge, England and New York: Cambridge University Press, 1999.

Crow, Thomas. *The Rise of the Sixties: American and European Art in the Era of Dissent.* New York: Harry N. Abrams, 1996.

Dijkstra, Bram. *American Expressionism: Art and Social Change, 1920–1950.* New York: Harry N. Abrams, 2003.

Doss, Erika. *Spirit Poles and Flying Pigs: Public Art and Cultural Democracy in American Communities.* Washington, DC: Smithsonian Institution Press, 1995.

Ellis, Diane C. and John C. Beresford. *Trends in Artist Occupations: 1970–1990.* Research Division Report #29. Washington, DC: National Endowment for the Arts, 1994.

Greenberg, Clement. *Art and Culture: Critical Essays.* Boston, MA: Beacon Press, 1961.

Hammond, Harmony. *Lesbian Art in America.* New York: Rizzoli, 2000.

Hemingway, Andrew. *American Artists and the Communist Movement, 1926–1956.* New Haven, CT: Yale University Press, 2002.

Hertz, Richard. *Theories of Contemporary Art.* Englewood Cliffs, NJ: Prentice-Hall, 1985.

Hobbs, Robert. *Lee Krasner.* New York: Abbeville Press, 1993.

Jencks, Charles. *Kings of Infinite Space: Frank Lloyd Wright & Michael Graves.* New York: St. Martin's Press, 1983.

Johnson, Ellen H. *American Artists on Art from 1940 to 1980.* New York: Harper & Row, 1982.

Kaprow, Allan. *Assemblage, Environments, and Happenings.* New York: Harry N. Abrams, 1966.

Kienholz, Edward and Nancy Reddin Kienholz. *Kienholz: A Retrospective.* New York: Whitney Museum of American Art, 1996.

Koenig, Gloria. *Iconic L.A: Stories of L.A.'s Most Memorable Buildings.* Glendale, CA: Balcony Press, 2000.

Krauss, Rosiland E. *The Originality of the Avant-Garde and Other Modernist Myths.* 1985. Rprt. Cambridge, MA: MIT Press, 1994.

Krauss, Rosiland E. *Passages in Modern Sculpture.* Cambridge, MA: MIT Press; pbk. edn., 1981.

Kuspit, Donald B. *Clement Greenberg.* Madison, WI: University of Wisconsin Press, 1979.

Kuspit, Donald B. *Leon Golub: Existentialist/Activist Painter.* New Brunswick, NJ: Rutgers University Press, 1985.

Lears, T.J. Jackson. *Fables of Abundance: A Cultural History of Advertising in America.* New York: Basic Books, 1994.

Leja, Michael. *Reframing Abstract Expressionism: Subjectivity and Painting in the 1940s.* New Haven, CT: Yale University Press. 1993.

Lippard, Lucy R. *Ad Reinhardt.* New York. Harry N. Abrams, 1981.

Lyford, Amy. "Noguchi, Sculptural Abstraction and the Politics of Japanese American Internment." *The Art Bulletin,* Vol. 84 (March 2003), 137–51.

Meyer, James. *Minimalism: Art and Polemics in the Sixties.* New Haven, CT: Yale University Press, 2001.

Moos, Stanislaus von. *Venturi, Rauch & Scott Brown.* New York: Rizzoli, 1987.

Owens, Craig. *Beyond Recognition: Representation, Power and Culture.* Berkeley and Los Angeles, CA: University of California Press, 1992.

Phillips, Lisa. *The American Century: Art and Culture, 1950–2000.* New York: Whitney Museum of American Art, 1999.

Pohl, Frances K. *Ben Shahn: New Deal Artist in a Cold War Climate, 1947–1954.* Austin, TX: University of Texas Press, 1989.

Rapaport, Brooke Kamin and Kevin L. Stayton. *Vital Forms: American Art and Design in the Atomic Age, 1940–1960.* New York: Brooklyn Museum of Art, 2001.

Robins, Corinne. *The Pluralist Era: American Art, 1968–1981.* New York: Harper & Row; Icon Editions, 1984.

Sandler, Irving. *Art of the Postmodern Era: From the Late 1960s to the Early 1990s.* New York: HarperCollins; Icon Editions, 1996.

Saunders, Frances Stonor. *Who Paid the Piper?: The CIA and the Cultural Cold War.* London: Granta, 1999.

Schellmann, Jörg and Joséphine Benecke, eds. *Christo and Jeanne-Claude: Prints and Objects 1963–95, A Catalogue Raisonné.* New York: Edition Schellmann, 1995.

Solomon, Deborah. *Utopia Parkway: The Life and Work of Joseph Cornell.* New York: Farrar, Straus & Giroux, 1997.

Steele, James. *Architecture Today.* London: Phaidon Press, 1997.

Taylor, Brandon. *Avant-Garde and After: Rethinking Art Now.* New York: Harry N. Abrams, 1995.

Varnedoe, Kirk. *Jackson Pollock.* New York: Museum of Modern Art, 1998.

Whitaker, Craig. *Architecture and the American Dream.* New York: Three Rivers Press, 1998.

Wood, Paul, et al. *Modernism in Dispute: Art Since the Forties.* New Haven, CT: Yale University Press in assoc. with Open University, 1993.

CHAPTER NINE

Works Cited

Crow, Thomas. *Modern Art in the Common Culture.* New Haven, CT: Yale University Press, 1996.

Documenta und Museum Fridericianum Veranstaltungs-GmbH, Kassel, Germany. *Documenta 11—Platform 5: Exhibition Catalogue.* Ostfildern-Ruit, Germany: Hatje Cantz, 2002

Doss, Erika. *Spirit Poles and Flying Pigs: Public Art and Cultural Democracy in American Communities.* Washington, D.C: Smithsonian Institution Press, 1995.

Dunlop, Beth. *Building a Dream: The Art of Disney Architecture.* Foreword by Vincent Scully. New York: Harry N. Abrams, 1996.

Finkelpearl, Tom. "On the Ideology of Dirt," in *David Hammons: Rousing the Rubble.* New York: The Institute for Contemporary Art, and Cambridge, MA: MIT Press, 1991, 61–89.

Fisher, Jean. "In Search of the 'Inauthentic': Disturbing Signs in Contemporary Native American Art," in *Race-ing Art History: Critical Readings in Race and Art History,* ed. Kymberly N. Pinder. London and New York: Routledge, 2002, 331–340.

Foster, Hal. "The Art of the Missing Part," in *Robert Gober,* ed. Paul Schimmel. Los Angeles, CA: Museum of Contemporary Art, 1997, 57–68.

Fox, Howard N. *Robert Longo.* Los Angeles, CA: Los Angeles County Museum of Art, 1989.

Harris, Michael D. *Colored Pictures: Race and Visual Representation.* Chapel Hill, NC: University of North Carolina Press, 2003.

Klein, Naomi. *Fences and Windows: Dispatches from the Front Lines of the Globalization Debate.* New York: St. Martin's Press; Picador USA, 2002.

Lawrence, Sidney. *Directions: Tony Oursler: Video Dolls with Tracy Leipold.* July 2–Sept. 7, 1998 exhibition. Washington, D.C.: Hirshhorn Museum and Sculpture Garden, 1998.

Meyer, Richard. *Outlaw Representation: Censorship and Homosexuality in Twentieth-Century American Art.* Oxford and New York: Oxford University Press, 2002.

Protetch, Max, ed. *A New World Trade Center: Design Proposals from Leading Architects Worldwide.* New York: HarperCollins; Regan Books, 2002.

Rinder, Lawrence. *The American Effect: Global Perspectives on the United States, 1990–2003.* New York: Whitney Museum of American Art, 2003.

Rinder, Lawrence R. *Whitney Biennial: 2002.* New York: Whitney Museum of American Art, 2002.

Spector, Nancy. *Matthew Barney: The Cremaster Cycle.* New York: The Guggenheim Museum, 2002.

Stiles, Kristine and Peter Selz. *Theories and Documents of Contemporary Art: A Sourcebook of Artists' Writings.* Berkeley and Los Angeles, CA: University of California Press, 1996.

Updike, John. *Rabbit Is Rich.* 1981, rpt. New York: Alfred A. Knopf; Borzoi Books, 1995.

Weinberg, Jonathan. *Ambition & Love in Modern Art.* New Haven, CT: Yale University Press, 2001.

Worth, Alexi. "Wolfgang Staehle, *Untitled, 2001."* *Artforum.* vol.40 (November 2001), 129.

Wu, Chin-tao. *Privatising Culture: Corporate Art Intervention Since the 1980s.* London and New York: Verso, 2002.

Works Consulted

Barron, Stephanie and Lynn Zelevansky. *Jasper Johns to Jeff Koons: Four Decades of Art from Broad Collections.* Los Angeles, CA: Los Angeles County Museum of Art, 2001.

Ferguson, Russell, ed. *Felix Gonzalez-Torres.* Los Angeles, CA: The Museum of Contemporary Art. 1994.

Friedman, Mildred, ed. *Architecture & Process: Gehry Talks.* New York: Rizzoli; Universe Publishing, 2002.

Goldin, Nan. "Nan Goldin Talks to Tom Holert." *Artforum,* vol. 51 (March 2003), 232–33, 274–75.

Hopkins, David. *After Modern Art, 1945–2000.* Oxford and New York: Oxford University Press, 2000.

Phillips, Lisa. *The American Century: Art and Culture, 1950–2000.* New York: Whitney Museum of American Art, 1999.

Posner, Helaine. *Kiki Smith.* Boston: Little, Brown and Company: A Bulfinch Press Book, 1998.

Rectanus, Mark W. *Culture Incorporated: Museums, Artists, and Corporate Sponsorships.* Minneapolis, MN: University of Minnesota Press, 2002.

Ross, David A. and Peter Sellars, eds. *Bill Viola.* New York: Whitney Museum of American Art, 1997.

Sorkin, Michael and Sharon Zukin, eds. *After the World Trade Center: Rethinking New York City.* New York and London: Routledge, 2002.

Steele, James. *Architecture Today.* London: Phaidon Press, 1997.

Storr, Robert, et al. *Art: 21: Art in the Twenty-First Century.* New York: Harry N. Abrams, 2001.

Varnedoe, Kirk. "Jeff Koons's *Rabbit."* *Artforum,* vol.51 (April 2003), 90.

Varnedoe, Kirk, Paola Antonelli and Joshua Siegel, eds. *Modern Contemporary Art at MOMA Since 1980.* New York: Museum of Modern Art, 2001.

Picture Credits

Page 12 Photo © Ashmolean Museum; 1.2, 1.4 © The British Museum; 1.5 National Park Service, Chaco Culture National Historical Park; 1.26 The Historical Society of Pennsylvania Collection, Atwater Kent Museum of Philadelphia; 1.27 Reproduced by kind permission of the President and Council of the Royal College of Surgeons of England; 2.4 Courtesy: Clarion Herald Photo Department; 2.11 Photo: G.E. Kidder-Smith, New York; 2.19 © Gibbes Museum of Art/Carolina Art Association 38. 36.59; 2.27 Museum Purchase. Courtesy, Winterthur Museum; page 77 American Jewish Historical Society, Newton Center, Massachussetts and New York, New York, 3.1 Gift of Mrs. Waldron Phoenix Belknap. Courtesy, Winterthur Museum; 3.14, 3.15 Courtesy of Drayton Hall, Charleston, South Carolina: A property of the National Trust for Historic Preservation; 3.25, 3.26, 3.28, 3.30, 3.31, 3.32, 3.34 Photograph © Museum of Fine Arts, Boston; page 114, 4.55, 4.57 Photograph © Museum of Fine Arts, Boston; 4.8 © Dean and Chapter of Westminster; 4.22 Photograph © 1992 The Metropolitan Museum of Art; 4.37, 4.48 Art Resource, New York; 4.46 University of Virginia Library; 4.47 Pennsylvania Academy purchase (from the estate of Paul Beck, Jr.); 4.50 Photo: Robert Newcombe (10/1994); 4.56 Photo: © 1977 The Detroit Institute of Arts; 5.1, 5.5, 5.55 Photograph © Museum of Fine Arts, Boston; 5.2 Photo: Richard Walker; 5.12, 5.26, 5.43 Art Resource, New York; 5.13 Promised Gift of Ralph Esmerian. Photo © 2000 John Bigelow Taylor, NYC; 5.15 Photo:Hans Padelt; 5.35 Photo: Colonial Williamsburg; 5.40, 5.60, 5.62 Photograph © The Metropolitan Museum of Art; 5.51 Photo: Jose A. Naranjo; 5.55 Promised Gift of Ralph Esmerian. Photo courtesy Sotheby's, New York; 5.59 Photograph © 1992 The Metropolitan Museum of Art; 5.68 Purchased with major acquisition funds and with funds donated by Betty Adler Schermer in honor of her great-grandfather, August M. Bondi; 5.69 Library of Congress; 5.72 Photograph © 1979 The Metropolitan Museum of Art; page 230 Bridgeman Art Library, London; 6.1 Wayne Andrews; 6.3 Used with permission from Biltmore Estate, Asheville, North Carolina; 6.6, 6.24, 6.28, 6.34, 6.67, 6.69 Photograph © The Metropolitan Museum of Art; 6.7 Courtesy Tiffany and Company; 6.8 Purchase, Sylvia and Leonard Marx Gift and Funds from various donors, 2002. Photograph © 2001 The Metropolitan Museum of Art; 6.14 Photo: Emil Boehl; 6.16 Chicago Historical Society; 6.19 © ARS, NY and DACS, London 2004. Photo: Esto Photographics, New York; 6.20 Photo: © Julius Shulman; 6.28 Photograph © 1995 The Metropolitan Museum of Art; 6.27, 6.29, 6.49, 6.52 Photograph © The Museum of Fine Arts, Boston; 6.37 Gift of Mrs. Thomas Eakins and Miss Mary Adeline Williams; 6.41 Peter Newark's American Pictures, Bath, England; 6.48 Library of Congress; 6.52 Gift of Mary Louisa Boit, Julia Overing Boit, Jane Hubbard Boit and Florence D. Boit in memory of their father, Edward Darley Boit. Photograph © Museum of Fine Arts, Boston; 6.53 Photograph © 1997 The

Metropolitan Museum of Art; 6.55, 6.56 The Hogg Brothers Collection, Gift of Miss Ima Hogg; 6.57 © 2004 Photo Smithsonian American Art Museum/Art Resource/Scala, Florence; 6.58 Photo: Paul Rocheleau, Richmond, MA; 6.63 RMN-Reversement Orsay; 6.71 The Jacob A. Riis Collection(#122); page 296 Arthur Hoppock Hearn Fund, 1942. Photograph © 1996 The Metropolitan Museum of Art; 7.1 Library of Congress; 7.11 Photograph © 1991 The Metropolitan Museum of Art; 7.12 Photo by Geoffrey Clements/Photograph Copyright © 1998 Whitney Museum of American Art, New York; 7.16, 7.34, 7.41 Photograph © The Metropolitan Museum of Art; 7.17 © 2004, Digital image, The Museum of Modern Art, New York/Scala, Florence; 7.18 © Succession Picasso/DACS 2004. Photograph © The Metropolitan Museum of Art; 7.19, 7.26, 7.27, 7.45 © ARS, New York and DACS, London 2004; 7.29, 7.38 © Succession Marcel Duchamp/ADAGP, Paris and DACS, London 2004; 7.31 Gift of Georgia O'Keeffe to the Alfred Stieglitz Collection. Reproduction, The Art Institute of Chicago, 7.37, 7.40 © Man Ray Trust/ADAGP, Paris and DACS, London 2004; 7.39 © ADAGP, Paris and DACS, London 2004. Photograph © The Metropolitan Museum of Art; 7.40 Photo: Lynn Rosenthal, 1993; 7.44 Gift of Louise and Joe Wissert. Photo by Geoffrey Clements/Photograph Copyright © Whitney Museum of American Art, New York; 7.45 © ARS, New York and DACS, London 2004; 7.46 Foundation for the Arts Collection, gift of the artist; 7.48 Photograph © 1986 The Metropolitan Museum of Art; 7.49 Photograph © 1980 The Metropolitan Museum of Art; 7.50 © Bo Parker Photo 1978; 7.51 Photo: Esto Photographics, New York, 7.53 Photo: Andrew Bordwin; 7.58 Reproduction, The Art Institute of Chicago; 7.57 Courtesy Consolidated Freightways, Inc.; 7.63 Photo: © 1987 The Detroit Institute of Arts; 7.62 Gift of Edsel B. Ford. Photo: © 2001 The Detroit Institute of Arts; 7.65 Photo: © Julius Shulman; 7.66 © ARS, NY and DACS, London 2004. Photo: Ralph Lieberman; 7.68 Gift of Gertrude Vanderbilt Whitney; 7.69 © T.H. Benton and R.P. Benton Testamentary Trusts / VAGA, New York/DACS, London 2004; 7.75 Photo: Michael Latil; 7.76, 7.82 © DACS, London/VAGA New York 2004; 7.77 Courtesy The Naval Historical Foundation; 7.79 Nelle Cochrane Woods Memorial Collection; 7.80 Photograph Copyright © 1997 Whitney Museum of American Art, New York; 7.81 © Estate of Stuart Davis/VAGA, New York/DACS, London 2004. Photograph © The Museum of Fine Arts, Boston; 7.83 50th Anniversary Gift of the Edward R. Downe, Jr., Purchase Fund, Mr. and Mrs. William A. Marsteller and the National Endowment for the Arts. © DACS, London/VAGA, New York 2004. Photo by Geoffrey Clements/Photograph Copyright © 1998 Whitney Museum of American Art, New York; 7.84 © 2004, Digital image, The Museum of Modern Art, New York/Scala, Florence; page 362 © Willem de Kooning Revocable Trust/ARS, NY and DACS, London 2004; 8.1 © ADAGP, Paris and DACS, London 2004. Photo: Art Resource, New York; 8.2 © DACS, London/VAGA, New York 2004-03-16; 8.3 © Estate of Ben Shahn/VAGA, New York/DACS, London 2004; 8.8, 8.70, 8.82 Esto Photographics, New York; 8.10, 8.11 © DACS 2004; 8.16, 8.27 © 1998 Kate Rothko Prizel & Christopher Rothko/DACS, 2004; 8.17 ©Adolph and Esther Gottlieb Foundation/VAGA, New York/DACS, London 2004; 8.18 © The Joseph and Robert Cornell Memorial Foundation/VAGA, New

York/DACS, London 2004; 8.19 © ADAGP, Paris and DACS, London 2004; 8.20 © Dedalus Foundation, Inc/VAGA, New York/DACS, London 2004; 8.21, 8.22, 8.23, 8.26, 8.30, 8.32, 8.35, 8.44, 8.49, 8.50, 8.51, 8.55, 8.56, 8.58, 8.72, 8.74, 8.76 8.91 © ARS, NY and DACS London 2004; 8.25 Photo: Shigeo Anzai; 8.29 Purchase, with funds from the Friends of the Whitney Museum of American Art. Photo by Geoffrey Clements/Photograph Copyright © 1989 Whitney Museum of American Art, New York; 8.30 Purchase, with funds from the Friends of the Whitney Museum of American Art. Photo by Steven Sloman/Photograph Copyright © 2001 Whitney Museum of American Art, New York; 8.33 © Estate of David Smith/VAGA, New York/DACS, London 2004; 8.34 © Louise Bourgeois/VAGA, New York/DACS, London 2004; 8.36 Courtesy TWA Archives; 8.37 J.William Rudd; 8.40 Gift of Helen B. Stern; 8.44 Courtesy the Artist; 8.45 Courtesy the Artist; 8.46 Purchase, with funds from Dieter Rosenkranz. Photo by Geoffrey Clements/Photograph Copyright © 1988 Whitney Museum of American Art, New York; 8.47 Photo: © Julius Shulman; 8.48 © Robert Rauschenberg/VAGA, New York/DACS, London 2004; 8.52 Gift of Mr. and Mrs. Robert A. Rowan, 1966. Art © Judd Foundation. Licensed by VAGA, New York/DACS, London 2004; 8.53 © Jasper Johns/VAGA, New York/DACS, London 2004; 8.54 © Carl Andre/VAGA, New York/DACS, London 2004; 8.59 © DACS, London/VAGA, New York 2004/Photo: David Wharton; 8.60 Photo: Lee Stalsworth; 8.62 © The Estate of Roy Lichtenstein/DACS 2004; 8.63 © The Andy Warhol Foundation for the Visual Arts, Inc./DACS, London, 2004. Trademarks Licensed by Campbell Soup Company. All Rights Reserved. Photo: Seymour Rosen–1991, Los Angeles; 8.64 © The Andy Warhol Foundation for the Visual Arts, Inc./DACS, London, 2004. Photo: Lee Stalsworth; 8.66 © The Andy Warhol Foundation for the Visual Arts, Inc./DACS, London, 2004. Photo: Robert E. Mates © The Solomon R.Guggenheim Foundation, New York; 8.67 © Romare Bearden Foundation/VAGA, New York/DACS, London 2004; 8.68 Collection of Sydney and Frances Lewis. © Virginia Museum of Fine Arts; 8.69 Photo: Colin McRae; 8.71 Photo: Grant Mudford; 8.73 © DACS 2004; 8.75 © Robert Harding Picture Library, London/Michael Newton; 8.77 Courtesy the Artist; 8.78 Courtesy the Artist; 8.85 Courtesy the Artist; 8.87 Collection: The Dinner Party Trust. Photo: © Donald Woodman; page 436 Purchase, with funds from the Drawing Committee. Photo by Geoffrey Clements/Photograph Copyright © 1997 Whitney Museum of American Art, New York; 9.1 Courtesy Judy Baca/Sparcmurals; 9.3 © Nan Goldin; 9.4 © ADAGP, Paris and DACS, London 2004; 9.5 Photo: Ricardo Blanc; 9.7 Photo: John McGrail; 9.8 Art on the Beach, a Creative Time Program; 9.11 Courtesy Jeff Koons Studio; 9.16 Courtesy of the Estate of David Wojnarowicz and P.P.O.W. Gallery, New York; 9.18 Promised gift in part of Barbara Lee, an Anonymous Donor and Purchase in part from the Joseph A. Baird, Jr., Francis H. Burr/Photo: Michael A. Nedzewski; 9.19 San Diego Museum of Man; 9.23 Courtesy Bill Viola Studio; 9.26 Photo: Tom Bonner; 9.28 © 2001 Matthew Barney. Photo: Chris Winget; 9.29 Courtesy Knowmad Confederacy; 9.31 Courtesy of Stephen Vitiello and The Project, NY and Los Angeles. Photo by Johnna MacArthur; 9.32 Collection of Alberto Guevara, Chicago. Photo: Steve Greiner; 9.33 Courtesy the Artist and Frith Street Gallery, London.

Index

Notes:
1. Page numbers for captions to illustrations are **emboldened**. In many cases there are also textual references on the same page
2. Sub-entries are arranged alphabetically except where *chronological* order is significant (*see* entry for chronology)